American Casebook Series
Hornbook Series and Basic Legal Texts
Nutshell Series

of

WEST PUBLISHING COMPANY
P.O. Box 64526
St. Paul, Minnesota 55164–0526

ACCOUNTING

Faris' Accounting and Law in a Nutshell, 377 pages, 1984 (Text)

Fiflis, Kripke and Foster's Teaching Materials on Accounting for Business Lawyers, 3rd Ed., 838 pages, 1984 (Casebook)

Siegel and Siegel's Accounting and Financial Disclosure: A Guide to Basic Concepts, 259 pages, 1983 (Text)

ADMINISTRATIVE LAW

Davis' Cases, Text and Problems on Administrative Law, 6th Ed., 683 pages, 1977 (Casebook)

Gellhorn and Boyer's Administrative Law and Process in a Nutshell, 2nd Ed., 445 pages, 1981 (Text)

Mashaw and Merrill's Cases and Materials on Administrative Law–The American Public Law System, 2nd Ed., 976 pages, 1985 (Casebook)

Robinson, Gellhorn and Bruff's The Administrative Process, 3rd Ed., 978 pages, 1986 (Casebook)

ADMIRALTY

Healy and Sharpe's Cases and Materials on Admiralty, 2nd Ed., 876 pages, 1986 (Casebook)

Maraist's Admiralty in a Nutshell, 2nd Ed., 379 pages, 1988 (Text)

Schoenbaum's Hornbook on Admiralty and Maritime Law, Student Ed., 692 pages, 1987 (Text)

Sohn and Gustafson's Law of the Sea in a Nutshell, 264 pages, 1984 (Text)

AGENCY—PARTNERSHIP

Fessler's Alternatives to Incorporation for Persons in Quest of Profit, 2nd Ed., 326 pages, 1986 (Casebook)

AGENCY—PARTNERSHIP—Cont'd

Henn's Cases and Materials on Agency, Partnership and Other Unincorporated Business Enterprises, 2nd Ed., 733 pages, 1985 (Casebook)

Reuschlein and Gregory's Hornbook on the Law of Agency and Partnership, 625 pages, 1979, with 1981 pocket part (Text)

Selected Corporation and Partnership Statutes, Rules and Forms, 621 pages, 1987

Steffen and Kerr's Cases and Materials on Agency-Partnership, 4th Ed., 859 pages, 1980 (Casebook)

Steffen's Agency-Partnership in a Nutshell, 364 pages, 1977 (Text)

AGRICULTURAL LAW

Meyer, Pedersen, Thorson and Davidson's Agricultural Law: Cases and Materials, 931 pages, 1985 (Casebook)

ALTERNATIVE DISPUTE RESOLUTION

Kanowitz' Cases and Materials on Alternative Dispute Resolution, 1024 pages, 1986 (Casebook)

Riskin and Westbrook's Dispute Resolution and Lawyers, 223 pages, 1987 (Coursebook)

Riskin and Westbrook's Dispute Resolution and Lawyers, Abridged Ed., 223 pages, 1987 (Coursebook)

Teple and Moberly's Arbitration and Conflict Resolution, (The Labor Law Group), 614 pages, 1979 (Casebook)

AMERICAN INDIAN LAW

Canby's American Indian Law in a Nutshell, 2nd Ed., about 319 pages, 1988 (Text)

Getches and Wilkinson's Cases on Federal Indian Law, 2nd Ed., 880 pages, 1986 (Casebook)

List current as of July, 1988

T7202—1g

I

LAW SCHOOL PUBLICATIONS—Continued

ANTITRUST LAW

Gellhorn's Antitrust Law and Economics in a Nutshell, 3rd Ed., 472 pages, 1986 (Text)

Gifford and Raskind's Cases and Materials on Antitrust, 694 pages, 1983 with 1985 Supplement (Casebook)

Hovenkamp's Hornbook on Economics and Federal Antitrust Law, Student Ed., 414 pages, 1985 (Text)

Oppenheim, Weston and McCarthy's Cases and Comments on Federal Antitrust Laws, 4th Ed., 1168 pages, 1981 with 1985 Supplement (Casebook)

Posner and Easterbrook's Cases and Economic Notes on Antitrust, 2nd Ed., 1077 pages, 1981, with 1984–85 Supplement (Casebook)

Sullivan's Hornbook of the Law of Antitrust, 886 pages, 1977 (Text)

See also Regulated Industries, Trade Regulation

ART LAW

DuBoff's Art Law in a Nutshell, 335 pages, 1984 (Text)

BANKING LAW

Lovett's Banking and Financial Institutions in a Nutshell, 2nd Ed., about 455 pages, 1988 (Text)

Symons and White's Teaching Materials on Banking Law, 2nd Ed., 993 pages, 1984, with 1987 Supplement (Casebook)

BUSINESS PLANNING

Painter's Problems and Materials in Business Planning, 2nd Ed., 1008 pages, 1984 with 1987 Supplement (Casebook)

Selected Securities and Business Planning Statutes, Rules and Forms, about 475 pages, 1987

CIVIL PROCEDURE

American Bar Association Section of Litigation—Reading on Adversarial Justice: The American Approach to Adjudication, edited by Landsman, 217 pages, 1988 (Coursebook)

Casad's Res Judicata in a Nutshell, 310 pages, 1976 (text)

Cound, Friedenthal, Miller and Sexton's Cases and Materials on Civil Procedure, 4th Ed., 1202 pages, 1985 with 1987 Supplement (Casebook)

Ehrenzweig, Louisell and Hazard's Jurisdiction in a Nutshell, 4th Ed., 232 pages, 1980 (Text)

Federal Rules of Civil-Appellate Procedure—West Law School Edition, about 600 pages, 1988

Friedenthal, Kane and Miller's Hornbook on Civil Procedure, 876 pages, 1985 (Text)

Kane's Civil Procedure in a Nutshell, 2nd Ed., 306 pages, 1986 (Text)

CIVIL PROCEDURE—Cont'd

Koffler and Reppy's Hornbook on Common Law Pleading, 663 pages, 1969 (Text)

Marcus and Sherman's Complex Litigation–Cases and Materials on Advanced Civil Procedure, 846 pages, 1985 (Casebook)

Park's Computer-Aided Exercises on Civil Procedure, 2nd Ed., 167 pages, 1983 (Coursebook)

Siegel's Hornbook on New York Practice, 1011 pages, 1978 with 1987 Pocket Part (Text)

See also Federal Jurisdiction and Procedure

CIVIL RIGHTS

Abernathy's Cases and Materials on Civil Rights, 660 pages, 1980 (Casebook)

Cohen's Cases on the Law of Deprivation of Liberty: A Study in Social Control, 755 pages, 1980 (Casebook)

Lockhart, Kamisar, Choper and Shiffrin's Cases on Constitutional Rights and Liberties, 6th Ed., 1266 pages, 1986 with 1988 Supplement (Casebook)—reprint from Lockhart, et al. Cases on Constitutional Law, 6th Ed., 1986

Vieira's Civil Rights in a Nutshell, 279 pages, 1978 (Text)

COMMERCIAL LAW

Bailey and Hagedorn's Secured Transactions in a Nutshell, 3rd Ed. about 390 pages, 1988 (Text)

Epstein, Martin, Henning and Nickles' Basic Uniform Commercial Code Teaching Materials, 3rd Ed., 704 pages, 1988 (Casebook)

Henson's Hornbook on Secured Transactions Under the U.C.C., 2nd Ed., 504 pages, 1979 with 1979 P.P. (Text)

Murray's Commercial Law, Problems and Materials, 366 pages, 1975 (Coursebook)

Nickles, Matheson and Dolan's Materials for Understanding Credit and Payment Systems, 923 pages, 1987 (Casebook)

Nordstrom, Murray and Clovis' Problems and Materials on Sales, 515 pages, 1982 (Casebook)

Nordstrom, Murray and Clovis' Problems and Materials on Secured Transactions, 594 pages, 1987 (Casebook)

Selected Commercial Statutes, about 1525 pages, 1988

Speidel, Summers and White's Teaching Materials on Commercial Law, 4th Ed., 1448 pages, 1987 (Casebook)

Speidel, Summers and White's Commercial Paper: Teaching Materials, 4th Ed., 578 pages, 1987 (Casebook)—reprint from Speidel, et al. Commercial Law, 4th Ed.

Speidel, Summers and White's Sales: Teaching Materials, 4th Ed., 804 pages, 1987 (Casebook)—reprint from Speidel, et al. Commercial Law, 4th Ed.

LAW SCHOOL PUBLICATIONS—Continued

COMMERCIAL LAW—Cont'd

Speidel, Summers and White's Secured Transactions—Teaching Materials, 4th Ed., 485 pages, 1987 (Casebook)—reprint from Speidel, et al. Commercial Law, 4th Ed.

Stockton's Sales in a Nutshell, 2nd Ed., 370 pages, 1981 (Text)

Stone's Uniform Commercial Code in a Nutshell, 2nd Ed., 516 pages, 1984 (Text)

Uniform Commercial Code, Official Text with Comments, 1155 pages, 1987

Weber and Speidel's Commercial Paper in a Nutshell, 3rd Ed., 404 pages, 1982 (Text)

White and Summers' Hornbook on the Uniform Commercial Code, 3rd Ed., Student Ed., about 1200 pages, 1988 (Text)

COMMUNITY PROPERTY

Mennell and Boykoff's Community Property in a Nutshell, 2nd Ed., 432 pages, 1988 (Text)

Verrall and Bird's Cases and Materials on California Community Property, 5th Ed., about 587 pages, 1988 (Casebook)

COMPARATIVE LAW

Barton, Gibbs, Li and Merryman's Law in Radically Different Cultures, 960 pages, 1983 (Casebook)

Glendon, Gordon and Osakive's Comparative Legal Traditions: Text, Materials and Cases on the Civil Law, Common Law, and Socialist Law Traditions, 1091 pages, 1985 (Casebook)

Glendon, Gordon, and Osakwe's Comparative Legal Traditions in a Nutshell, 402 pages, 1982 (Text)

Langbein's Comparative Criminal Procedure: Germany, 172 pages, 1977 (Casebook)

COMPUTERS AND LAW

Maggs and Sprowl's Computer Applications in the Law, 316 pages, 1987 (Coursebook)

Mason's Using Computers in the Law: An Introduction and Practical Guide, 2nd Ed., 288 pages, 1988 (Text)

CONFLICT OF LAWS

Cramton, Currie and Kay's Cases-Comments-Questions on Conflict of Laws, 4th Ed., 876 pages, 1987 (Casebook)

Scoles and Hay's Hornbook on Conflict of Laws, Student Ed., 1085 pages, 1982 with 1986 P.P. (Text)

Scoles and Weintraub's Cases and Materials on Conflict of Laws, 2nd Ed., 966 pages, 1972, with 1978 Supplement (Casebook)

Siegel's Conflicts in a Nutshell, 469 pages, 1982 (Text)

CONSTITUTIONAL LAW

Barron and Dienes' Constitutional Law in a Nutshell, 389 pages, 1986 (Text)

Engdahl's Constitutional Federalism in a Nutshell, 2nd Ed., 411 pages, 1987 (Text)

Lockhart, Kamisar, Choper and Shiffrin's Cases-Comments-Questions on Constitutional Law, 6th Ed., 1601 pages, 1986 with 1988 Supplement (Casebook)

Lockhart, Kamisar, Choper and Shiffrin's Cases-Comments-Questions on the American Constitution, 6th Ed., 1260 pages, 1986 with 1988 Supplement (Casebook)—abridgment of Lockhart, et al. Cases on Constitutional Law, 6th Ed., 1986

Manning's The Law of Church-State Relations in a Nutshell, 305 pages, 1981 (Text)

Marks and Cooper's State Constitutional Law in a Nutshell, about 300 pages, 1988 (Text)

Miller's Presidential Power in a Nutshell, 328 pages, 1977 (Text)

Nowak, Rotunda and Young's Hornbook on Constitutional Law, 3rd Ed., Student Ed., 1191 pages, 1986 with 1988 Pocket Part (Text)

Rotunda's Modern Constitutional Law: Cases and Notes, 2nd Ed., 1004 pages, 1985 with 1988 Supplement (Casebook)

Williams' Constitutional Analysis in a Nutshell, 388 pages, 1979 (Text)

See also Civil Rights, Foreign Relations and National Security Law

CONSUMER LAW

Epstein and Nickles' Consumer Law in a Nutshell, 2nd Ed., 418 pages, 1981 (Text)

Selected Commercial Statutes, about 1525 pages, 1988

Spanogle and Rohner's Cases and Materials on Consumer Law, 693 pages, 1979, with 1982 Supplement (Casebook)

See also Commercial Law

CONTRACTS

Calamari & Perillo's Cases and Problems on Contracts, 1061 pages, 1978 (Casebook)

Calamari and Perillo's Hornbook on Contracts, 3rd Ed., 904 pages, 1987 (Text)

Corbin's Text on Contracts, One Volume Student Edition, 1224 pages, 1952 (Text)

Fessler and Loiseaux's Cases and Materials on Contracts, 837 pages, 1982 (Casebook)

Friedman's Contract Remedies in a Nutshell, 323 pages, 1981 (Text)

Fuller and Eisenberg's Cases on Basic Contract Law, 4th Ed., 1203 pages, 1981 (Casebook)

Hamilton, Rau and Weintraub's Cases and Materials on Contracts, 830 pages, 1984 (Casebook)

LAW SCHOOL PUBLICATIONS—Continued

CONTRACTS—Cont'd

Jackson and Bollinger's Cases on Contract Law in Modern Society, 2nd Ed., 1329 pages, 1980 (Casebook)

Keyes' Government Contracts in a Nutshell, 423 pages, 1979 (Text)

Schaber and Rohwer's Contracts in a Nutshell, 2nd Ed., 425 pages, 1984 (Text)

Summers and Hillman's Contract and Related Obligation: Theory, Doctrine and Practice, 1074 pages, 1987 (Casebook)

COPYRIGHT

See Patent and Copyright Law

CORPORATE FINANCE

Hamilton's Cases and Materials on Corporate Finance, 895 pages, 1984 with 1986 Supplement (Casebook)

CORPORATIONS

Hamilton's Cases on Corporations—Including Partnerships and Limited Partnerships, 3rd Ed., 1213 pages, 1986 with 1986 Statutory Supplement (Casebook)

Hamilton's Law of Corporations in a Nutshell, 2nd Ed., 515 pages, 1987 (Text)

Henn's Teaching Materials on Corporations, 2nd Ed., 1204 pages, 1986 (Casebook)

Henn and Alexander's Hornbook on Corporations, 3rd Ed., Student Ed., 1371 pages, 1983 with 1986 P.P. (Text)

Jennings and Buxbaum's Cases and Materials on Corporations, 5th Ed., 1180 pages, 1979 (Casebook)

Selected Corporation and Partnership Statutes, Rules and Forms, 621 pages, 1987

Solomon, Schwartz' and Bauman's Materials and Problems on Corporations: Law and Policy, 2nd Ed., 1391 pages, 1988 (Casebook)

CORRECTIONS

Krantz's Cases and Materials on the Law of Corrections and Prisoners' Rights, 3rd Ed., 855 pages, 1986 with 1988 Supplement (Casebook)

Krantz's Law of Corrections and Prisoners' Rights in a Nutshell, 2nd Ed., 386 pages, 1983 (Text)

Popper's Post-Conviction Remedies in a Nutshell, 360 pages, 1978 (Text)

Robbins' Cases and Materials on Post Conviction Remedies, 506 pages, 1982 (Casebook)

CREDITOR'S RIGHTS

Bankruptcy Code, Rules and Forms, Law School Ed., 792 pages, 1988

Epstein's Debtor-Creditor Law in a Nutshell, 3rd Ed., 383 pages, 1986 (Text)

Epstein, Landers and Nickles' Debtors and Creditors: Cases and Materials, 3rd Ed., 1059 pages, 1987 (Casebook)

CREDITOR'S RIGHTS—Cont'd

LoPucki's Player's Manual for the Debtor-Creditor Game, 123 pages, 1985 (Coursebook)

Riesenfeld's Cases and Materials on Creditors' Remedies and Debtors' Protection, 4th Ed., 914 pages, 1987 (Casebook)

White's Bankruptcy and Creditor's Rights: Cases and Materials, 812 pages, 1985, with 1987 Supplement (Casebook)

CRIMINAL LAW AND CRIMINAL PROCEDURE

Abrams', Federal Criminal Law and its Enforcement, 882 pages, 1986 (Casebook)

Carlson's Adjudication of Criminal Justice, Problems and References, 130 pages, 1986 (Casebook)

Dix and Sharlot's Cases and Materials on Criminal Law, 3rd Ed., 846 pages, 1987 (Casebook)

Federal Rules of Criminal Procedure—West Law School Edition, about 500 pages, 1988

Grano's Problems in Criminal Procedure, 2nd Ed., 176 pages, 1981 (Problem book)

Israel and LaFave's Criminal Procedure in a Nutshell, 4th Ed., 461 pages, 1988 (Text)

Johnson's Cases, Materials and Text on Criminal Law, 3rd Ed., 783 pages, 1985 (Casebook)

Johnson's Cases on Criminal Procedure, 859 pages, 1987 with 1988 Supplement (Casebook)

Kamisar, LaFave and Israel's Cases, Comments and Questions on Modern Criminal Procedure, 6th Ed., 1558 pages, 1986 with 1988 Supplement (Casebook)

Kamisar, LaFave and Israel's Cases, Comments and Questions on Basic Criminal Procedure, 6th Ed., 860 pages, 1986 with 1988 Supplement (Casebook)—reprint from Kamisar, et al. Modern Criminal Procedure, 6th ed., 1986

LaFave's Modern Criminal Law: Cases, Comments and Questions, 2nd Ed., 903 pages, 1988 (Casebook)

LaFave and Israel's Hornbook on Criminal Procedure, Student Ed., 1142 pages, 1985 with 1987 P.P. (Text)

LaFave and Scott's Hornbook on Criminal Law, 2nd Ed., Student Ed., 918 pages, 1986 (Text)

Langbein's Comparative Criminal Procedure: Germany, 172 pages, 1977 (Casebook)

Loewy's Criminal Law in a Nutshell, 2nd Ed., 321 pages, 1987 (Text)

Saltzburg's American Criminal Procedure, Cases and Commentary, 3rd Ed., 1302 pages, 1988 with 1988 Supplement (Casebook)

CRIMINAL LAW AND CRIMINAL PROCEDURE—Cont'd

Uviller's The Processes of Criminal Justice: Investigation and Adjudication, 2nd Ed., 1384 pages, 1979 with 1979 Statutory Supplement and 1986 Update (Casebook)

Uviller's The Processes of Criminal Justice: Adjudication, 2nd Ed., 730 pages, 1979. Soft-cover reprint from Uviller's The Processes of Criminal Justice: Investigation and Adjudication, 2nd Ed. (Casebook)

Uviller's The Processes of Criminal Justice: Investigation, 2nd Ed., 655 pages, 1979. Soft-cover reprint from Uviller's The Processes of Criminal Justice: Investigation and Adjudication, 2nd Ed. (Casebook)

Vorenberg's Cases on Criminal Law and Procedure, 2nd Ed., 1088 pages, 1981 with 1987 Supplement (Casebook)

See also Corrections, Juvenile Justice

DECEDENTS ESTATES

See Trusts and Estates

DOMESTIC RELATIONS

Clark's Cases and Problems on Domestic Relations, 3rd Ed., 1153 pages, 1980 (Casebook)

Clark's Hornbook on Domestic Relations, 2nd Ed., Student Ed., 1050 pages, 1988 (Text)

Krause's Cases and Materials on Family Law, 2nd Ed., 1221 pages, 1983 with 1986 Supplement (Casebook)

Krause's Family Law in a Nutshell, 2nd Ed., 444 pages, 1986 (Text)

Krauskopf's Cases on Property Division at Marriage Dissolution, 250 pages, 1984 (Casebook)

ECONOMICS, LAW AND

Goetz' Cases and Materials on Law and Economics, 547 pages, 1984 (Casebook)

See also Antitrust, Regulated Industries

EDUCATION LAW

Alexander and Alexander's The Law of Schools, Students and Teachers in a Nutshell, 409 pages, 1984 (Text)

Morris' The Constitution and American Education, 2nd Ed., 992 pages, 1980 (Casebook)

EMPLOYMENT DISCRIMINATION

Jones, Murphy and Belton's Cases on Discrimination in Employment, 1116 pages, 1987 (Casebook)

Player's Cases and Materials on Employment Discrimination Law, 2nd Ed., 782 pages, 1984 (Casebook)

EMPLOYMENT DISCRIMINATION—Cont'd

Player's Federal Law of Employment Discrimination in a Nutshell, 2nd Ed., 402 pages, 1981 (Text)

Player's Hornbook on the Law of Employment Discrimination, Student Ed., 708 pages, 1988 (Text)

See also Women and the Law

ENERGY AND NATURAL RESOURCES LAW

Laitos' Cases and Materials on Natural Resources Law, 938 pages, 1985 (Casebook)

Rodgers' Cases and Materials on Energy and Natural Resources Law, 2nd Ed., 877 pages, 1983 (Casebook)

Selected Environmental Law Statutes, about 650 pages, 1988

Tomain's Energy Law in a Nutshell, 338 pages, 1981 (Text)

See also Environmental Law, Oil and Gas, Water Law

ENVIRONMENTAL LAW

Bonine and McGarity's Cases and Materials on the Law of Environment and Pollution, 1076 pages, 1984 (Casebook)

Findley and Farber's Cases and Materials on Environmental Law, 2nd Ed., 813 pages, 1985 with 1988 Supplement (Casebook)

Findley and Farber's Environmental Law in a Nutshell, 2nd Ed., about 348 pages, 1988 (Text)

Rodgers' Hornbook on Environmental Law, 956 pages, 1977 with 1984 pocket part (Text)

Selected Environmental Law Statutes, about 650 pages, 1988

See also Energy Law, Natural Resources Law, Water Law

EQUITY

See Remedies

ESTATES

See Trusts and Estates

ESTATE PLANNING

Lynn's Introduction to Estate Planning, in a Nutshell, 3rd Ed., 370 pages, 1983 (Text)

See also Taxation, Trusts and Estates

EVIDENCE

Broun, Meisenholder, Strong and Mosteller's Problems in Evidence, 3rd Ed., about 420 pages, 1988 (Problem book)

Cleary, Strong, Broun and Mosteller's Cases and Materials on Evidence, 4th Ed., about 1050 pages, 1988 (Casebook)

Federal Rules of Evidence for United States Courts and Magistrates, 370 pages, 1987

EVIDENCE—Cont'd

Graham's Federal Rules of Evidence in a Nutshell, 2nd Ed., 473 pages, 1987 (Text)

Kimball's Programmed Materials on Problems in Evidence, 380 pages, 1978 (Problem book)

Lempert and Saltzburg's A Modern Approach to Evidence: Text, Problems, Transcripts and Cases, 2nd Ed., 1232 pages, 1983 (Casebook)

Lilly's Introduction to the Law of Evidence, 2nd Ed., 585 pages, 1987 (Text)

McCormick, Sutton and Wellborn's Cases and Materials on Evidence, 6th Ed., 1067 pages, 1987 (Casebook)

McCormick's Hornbook on Evidence, 3rd Ed., Student Ed., 1156 pages, 1984 with 1987 P.P. (Text)

Rothstein's Evidence, State and Federal Rules in a Nutshell, 2nd Ed., 514 pages, 1981 (Text)

Saltzburg's Evidence Supplement: Rules, Statutes, Commentary, 245 pages, 1980 (Casebook Supplement)

FEDERAL JURISDICTION AND PROCEDURE

Currie's Cases and Materials on Federal Courts, 3rd Ed., 1042 pages, 1982 with 1985 Supplement (Casebook)

Currie's Federal Jurisdiction in a Nutshell, 2nd Ed., 258 pages, 1981 (Text)

Federal Rules of Civil-Appellate Procedure—West Law School Edition, about 600 pages, 1988

Forrester and Moye's Cases and Materials on Federal Jurisdiction and Procedure, 3rd Ed., 917 pages, 1977 with 1985 Supplement (Casebook)

Redish's Cases, Comments and Questions on Federal Courts, 878 pages, 1983 with 1988 Supplement (Casebook)

Vetri and Merrill's Federal Courts, Problems and Materials, 2nd Ed., 232 pages, 1984 (Problem Book)

Wright's Hornbook on Federal Courts, 4th Ed., Student Ed., 870 pages, 1983 (Text)

FOREIGN RELATIONS AND NATIONAL SECURITY LAW

Franck and Glennon's United States Foreign Relations Law: Cases, Materials and Simulations, 941 pages, 1987 (Casebook)

FUTURE INTERESTS

See Trusts and Estates

HEALTH LAW

See Medicine, Law and

IMMIGRATION LAW

Aleinikoff and Martin's Immigration Process and Policy, 1042 pages, 1985 with 1987 Supplement (Casebook)

IMMIGRATION LAW—Cont'd

Weissbrodt's Immigration Law and Procedure in a Nutshell, 345 pages, 1984 (Text)

INDIAN LAW

See American Indian Law

INSURANCE

Dobbyn's Insurance Law in a Nutshell, 281 pages, 1981 (Text)

Keeton's Cases on Basic Insurance Law, 2nd Ed., 1086 pages, 1977

Keeton and Wydiss' Insurance Law, Student Ed., about 1024 pages, 1988 (Text)

Wydiss and Keeton's Course Supplement to Keeton and Wydiss's Insurance Law, 425 pages, 1988 (Casebook)

York and Whelan's Cases, Materials and Problems on General Practice Insurance Law, 2nd Ed., about 811 pages, 1988 (Casebook)

INTERNATIONAL LAW

Buergenthal International Human Rights in a Nutshell, about 275 pages, 1988 (Text)

Buergenthal and Maier's Public International Law in a Nutshell, 262 pages, 1985 (Text)

Folsom, Gordon and Spanogle's International Business Transactions – a Problem-Oriented Coursebook, 1160 pages, 1986, with Documents Supplement (Casebook)

Folsom, Gordon and Spanogle's International Business Transactions in a Nutshell, 3rd Ed., about 484 pages, 1988 (Text)

Henkin, Pugh, Schachter and Smit's Cases and Materials on International Law, 2nd Ed., 1517 pages, 1987 with Documents Supplement (Casebook)

Jackson and Davey's Legal Problems of International Economic Relations, 2nd Ed., 1269 pages, 1986, with Documents Supplement (Casebook)

Kirgis' International Organizations in Their Legal Setting, 1016 pages, 1977, with 1981 Supplement (Casebook)

Weston, Falk and D'Amato's International Law and World Order—A Problem Oriented Coursebook, 1195 pages, 1980, with Documents Supplement (Casebook)

INTERVIEWING AND COUNSELING

Binder and Price's Interviewing and Counseling, 232 pages, 1977 (Text)

Shaffer and Elkins' Interviewing and Counseling in a Nutshell, 2nd Ed., 487 pages, 1987 (Text)

INTRODUCTION TO LAW STUDY

Dobbyn's So You Want to go to Law School, Revised First Edition, 206 pages, 1976 (Text)

LAW SCHOOL PUBLICATIONS—Continued

INTRODUCTION TO LAW STUDY—Cont'd

Hegland's Introduction to the Study and Practice of Law in a Nutshell, 418 pages, 1983 (Text)

Kinyon's Introduction to Law Study and Law Examinations in a Nutshell, 389 pages, 1971 (Text)

See also Legal Method and Legal System

JURISPRUDENCE

Christie's Text and Readings on Jurisprudence—The Philosophy of Law, 1056 pages, 1973 (Casebook)

JUVENILE JUSTICE

Fox's Cases and Materials on Modern Juvenile Justice, 2nd Ed., 960 pages, 1981 (Casebook)

Fox's Juvenile Courts in a Nutshell, 3rd Ed., 291 pages, 1984 (Text)

LABOR LAW

Gorman's Basic Text on Labor Law—Unionization and Collective Bargaining, 914 pages, 1976 (Text)

Grodin, Wollett and Alleyne's Collective Bargaining in Public Employment, 3rd Ed., (The Labor Law Group), 430 pages, 1979 (Casebook)

Leslie's Labor Law in a Nutshell, 2nd Ed., 397 pages, 1986 (Text)

Nolan's Labor Arbitration Law and Practice in a Nutshell, 358 pages, 1979 (Text)

Oberer, Hanslowe, Andersen and Heinsz' Cases and Materials on Labor Law—Collective Bargaining in a Free Society, 3rd Ed., 1163 pages, 1986 with Statutory Supplement (Casebook)

Rabin, Silverstein and Schatzki's Labor and Employment Law: Cases, Materials and Problems in the Law of Work, (The Labor Law Group), about 1000 pages, 1988 with Statutory Supplement (Casebook)

See also Employment Discrimination, Social Legislation

LAND FINANCE

See Real Estate Transactions

LAND USE

Callies and Freilich's Cases and Materials on Land Use, 1233 pages, 1986 (Casebook)

Hagman's Cases on Public Planning and Control of Urban and Land Development, 2nd Ed., 1301 pages, 1980 (Casebook)

Hagman and Juergensmeyer's Hornbook on Urban Planning and Land Development Control Law, 2nd Ed., Student Ed., 680 pages, 1986 (Text)

Wright and Gitelman's Cases and Materials on Land Use, 3rd Ed., 1300 pages, 1982, with 1987 Supplement (Casebook)

LAND USE—Cont'd

Wright and Wright's Land Use in a Nutshell, 2nd Ed., 356 pages, 1985 (Text)

LEGAL HISTORY

Presser and Zainaldin's Cases on Law and American History, 855 pages, 1980 (Casebook)

See also Legal Method and Legal System

LEGAL METHOD AND LEGAL SYSTEM

Aldisert's Readings, Materials and Cases in the Judicial Process, 948 pages, 1976 (Casebook)

Berch and Berch's Introduction to Legal Method and Process, 550 pages, 1985 (Casebook)

Bodenheimer, Oakley and Love's Readings and Cases on an Introduction to the Anglo-American Legal System, 2nd Ed., 166 pages, 1988 (Casebook)

Davies and Lawry's Institutions and Methods of the Law—Introductory Teaching Materials, 547 pages, 1982 (Casebook)

Dvorkin, Himmelstein and Lesnick's Becoming a Lawyer: A Humanistic Perspective on Legal Education and Professionalism, 211 pages, 1981 (Text)

Greenberg's Judicial Process and Social Change, 666 pages, 1977 (Casebook)

Kelso and Kelso's Studying Law: An Introduction, 587 pages, 1984 (Coursebook)

Kempin's Historical Introduction to Anglo-American Law in a Nutshell, 2nd Ed., 280 pages, 1973 (Text)

Murphy's Cases and Materials on Introduction to Law—Legal Process and Procedure, 772 pages, 1977 (Casebook)

Reynolds' Judicial Process in a Nutshell, 292 pages, 1980 (Text)

See also Legal Research and Writing

LEGAL PROFESSION

Aronson, Devine and Fisch's Problems, Cases and Materials on Professional Responsibility, 745 pages, 1985 (Casebook)

Aronson and Weckstein's Professional Responsibility in a Nutshell, 399 pages, 1980 (Text)

Mellinkoff's The Conscience of a Lawyer, 304 pages, 1973 (Text)

Pirsig and Kirwin's Cases and Materials on Professional Responsibility, 4th Ed., 603 pages, 1984 (Casebook)

Schwartz and Wydick's Problems in Legal Ethics, 2nd Ed., 341 pages, 1988 (Casebook)

Selected Statutes, Rules and Standards on the Legal Profession, 449 pages, 1987

Smith's Preventing Legal Malpractice, 142 pages, 1981 (Text)

Wolfram's Hornbook on Modern Legal Ethics, Student Edition, 1120 pages, 1986 (Text)

LAW SCHOOL PUBLICATIONS—Continued

LEGAL RESEARCH AND WRITING

Child's Materials and Problems on Drafting Legal Documents, 286 pages, 1988 (Text)

Cohen's Legal Research in a Nutshell, 4th Ed., 450 pages, 1985 (Text)

Cohen and Berring's How to Find the Law, 8th Ed., 790 pages, 1983. Problem book by Foster, Johnson and Kelly available (Casebook)

Cohen and Berring's Finding the Law, 8th Ed., Abridged Ed., 556 pages, 1984 (Casebook)

Dickerson's Materials on Legal Drafting, 425 pages, 1981 (Casebook)

Felsenfeld and Siegel's Writing Contracts in Plain English, 290 pages, 1981 (Text)

Gopen's Writing From a Legal Perspective, 225 pages, 1981 (Text)

Mellinkoff's Legal Writing—Sense and Non-sense, 242 pages, 1982 (Text)

Ray and Ramsfield's Legal Writing: Getting It Right and Getting It Written, 250 pages, 1987 (Text)

Rombauer's Legal Problem Solving—Analysis, Research and Writing, 4th Ed., 424 pages, 1983 (Coursebook)

Squires and Rombauer's Legal Writing in a Nutshell, 294 pages, 1982 (Text)

Statsky's Legal Research and Writing, 3rd Ed., 257 pages, 1986 (Coursebook)

Statsky and Wernet's Case Analysis and Fundamentals of Legal Writing, 3rd Ed., about 450 pages, 1988 (Text)

Teply's Programmed Materials on Legal Research and Citation, 2nd Ed., 358 pages, 1986. Student Library Exercises available (Coursebook)

Weihofen's Legal Writing Style, 2nd Ed., 332 pages, 1980 (Text)

LEGISLATION

Davies' Legislative Law and Process in a Nutshell, 2nd Ed., 346 pages, 1986 (Text)

Eskridge and Frickey's Cases on Legislation, 937 pages, 1987 (Casebook)

Nutting and Dickerson's Cases and Materials on Legislation, 5th Ed., 744 pages, 1978 (Casebook)

Statsky's Legislative Analysis and Drafting, 2nd Ed., 217 pages, 1984 (Text)

LOCAL GOVERNMENT

Frug's Cases and Materials on Local Government Law, about 1000 pages, 1988 (Casebook)

McCarthy's Local Government Law in a Nutshell, 2nd Ed., 404 pages, 1983 (Text)

Reynolds' Hornbook on Local Government Law, 860 pages, 1982, with 1987 pocket part (Text)

Valente's Cases and Materials on Local Government Law, 3rd Ed., 1010 pages, 1987 (Casebook)

MASS COMMUNICATION LAW

Gillmor and Barron's Cases and Comment on Mass Communication Law, 4th Ed., 1076 pages, 1984 (Casebook)

Ginsburg's Regulation of Broadcasting: Law and Policy Towards Radio, Television and Cable Communications, 741 pages, 1979 with 1983 Supplement (Casebook)

Zuckman, Gaynes, Carter and Dee's Mass Communications Law in a Nutshell, 3rd Ed., 538 pages, 1988 (Text)

MEDICINE, LAW AND

Furrow, Johnson, Jost and Schwartz' Health Law: Cases, Materials and Problems, 1005 pages, 1987 (Casebook)

King's The Law of Medical Malpractice in a Nutshell, 2nd Ed., 342 pages, 1986 (Text)

Shapiro and Spece's Problems, Cases and Materials on Bioethics and Law, 892 pages, 1981 (Casebook)

Sharpe, Fiscina and Head's Cases on Law and Medicine, 882 pages, 1978 (Casebook)

MILITARY LAW

Shanor and Terrell's Military Law in a Nutshell, 378 pages, 1980 (Text)

MORTGAGES

See Real Estate Transactions

NATURAL RESOURCES LAW

See Energy and Natural Resources Law

NEGOTIATION

Edwards and White's Problems, Readings and Materials on the Lawyer as a Negotiator, 484 pages, 1977 (Casebook)

Peck's Cases and Materials on Negotiation, 2nd Ed., (The Labor Law Group), 280 pages, 1980 (Casebook)

Williams' Legal Negotiation and Settlement, 207 pages, 1983 (Coursebook)

OFFICE PRACTICE

Hegland's Trial and Practice Skills in a Nutshell, 346 pages, 1978 (Text)

Strong and Clark's Law Office Management, 424 pages, 1974 (Casebook)

See also Computers and Law, Interviewing and Counseling, Negotiation

OIL AND GAS

Hemingway's Hornbook on Oil and Gas, 2nd Ed., Student Ed., 543 pages, 1983 with 1986 P.P. (Text)

Kuntz, Lowe, Anderson and Smith's Cases and Materials on Oil and Gas Law, 857 pages, 1986, with Forms Manual (Casebook)

Lowe's Oil and Gas Law in a Nutshell, 2nd Ed., about 402 pages, 1988 (Text)

See also Energy and Natural Resources Law

LAW SCHOOL PUBLICATIONS—Continued

PARTNERSHIP

See Agency—Partnership

PATENT AND COPYRIGHT LAW

Choate, Francis and Collins' Cases and Materials on Patent Law, 3rd Ed., 1009 pages, 1987 (Casebook)

Miller and Davis' Intellectual Property—Patents, Trademarks and Copyright in a Nutshell, 428 pages, 1983 (Text)

Nimmer's Cases on Copyright and Other Aspects of Entertainment Litigation, 3rd Ed., 1025 pages, 1985 (Casebook)

PRODUCTS LIABILITY

Fischer and Powers' Cases and Materials on Products Liability, 685 pages, 1988 (Casebook)

Noel and Phillips' Cases on Products Liability, 2nd Ed., 821 pages, 1982 (Casebook)

Phillips' Products Liability in a Nutshell, 3rd Ed., 307 pages, 1988 (Text)

PROPERTY

Bernhardt's Real Property in a Nutshell, 2nd Ed., 448 pages, 1981 (Text)

Boyer's Survey of the Law of Property, 766 pages, 1981 (Text)

Browder, Cunningham and Smith's Cases on Basic Property Law, 4th Ed., 1431 pages, 1984 (Casebook)

Bruce, Ely and Bostick's Cases and Materials on Modern Property Law, 1004 pages, 1984 (Casebook)

Burke's Personal Property in a Nutshell, 322 pages, 1983 (Text)

Cunningham, Stoebuck and Whitman's Hornbook on the Law of Property, Student Ed., 916 pages, 1984 with 1987 P.P. (Text)

Donahue, Kauper and Martin's Cases on Property, 2nd Ed., 1362 pages, 1983 (Casebook)

Hill's Landlord and Tenant Law in a Nutshell, 2nd Ed., 311 pages, 1986 (Text)

Kurtz and Hovenkamp's Cases and Materials on American Property Law, 1296 pages, 1987 with 1988 Supplement (Casebook)

Moynihan's Introduction to Real Property, 2nd Ed., 239 pages, 1988 (Text)

Uniform Land Transactions Act, Uniform Simplification of Land Transfers Act, Uniform Condominium Act, 1977 Official Text with Comments, 462 pages, 1978

See also Real Estate Transactions, Land Use

PSYCHIATRY, LAW AND

Reisner's Law and the Mental Health System, Civil and Criminal Aspects, 696 pages, 1985 with 1987 Supplement (Casebooks)

REAL ESTATE TRANSACTIONS

Bruce's Real Estate Finance in a Nutshell, 2nd Ed., 262 pages, 1985 (Text)

Maxwell, Riesenfeld, Hetland and Warren's Cases on California Security Transactions in Land, 3rd Ed., 728 pages, 1984 (Casebook)

Nelson and Whitman's Cases on Real Estate Transfer, Finance and Development, 3rd Ed., 1184 pages, 1987 (Casebook)

Nelson and Whitman's Hornbook on Real Estate Finance Law, 2nd Ed., Student Ed., 941 pages, 1985 (Text)

Osborne's Cases and Materials on Secured Transactions, 559 pages, 1967 (Casebook)

REGULATED INDUSTRIES

Gellhorn and Pierce's Regulated Industries in a Nutshell, 2nd Ed., 389 pages, 1987 (Text)

Morgan, Harrison and Verkuil's Cases and Materials on Economic Regulation of Business, 2nd Ed., 666 pages, 1985 (Casebook)

See also Mass Communication Law, Banking Law

REMEDIES

Dobbs' Hornbook on Remedies, 1067 pages, 1973 (Text)

Dobbs' Problems in Remedies, 137 pages, 1974 (Problem book)

Dobbyn's Injunctions in a Nutshell, 264 pages, 1974 (Text)

Friedman's Contract Remedies in a Nutshell, 323 pages, 1981 (Text)

Leavell, Love and Nelson's Cases and Materials on Equitable Remedies and Restitution, 4th Ed., 1111 pages, 1986 (Casebook)

McCormick's Hornbook on Damages, 811 pages, 1935 (Text)

O'Connell's Remedies in a Nutshell, 2nd Ed., 320 pages, 1985 (Text)

York, Bauman and Rendleman's Cases and Materials on Remedies, 4th Ed., 1029 pages, 1985 (Casebook)

REVIEW MATERIALS

Ballantine's Problems

Black Letter Series

SECURITIES REGULATION

Hazen's Hornbook on The Law of Securities Regulation, Student Ed., 739 pages, 1985, with 1988 P.P. (Text)

Ratner's Securities Regulation: Materials for a Basic Course, 3rd Ed., 1000 pages, 1986 (Casebook)

Ratner's Securities Regulation in a Nutshell, 3rd Ed., 316 pages, 1988 (Text)

LAW SCHOOL PUBLICATIONS—Continued

SECURITIES REGULATION—Cont'd

Selected Securities and Business Planning Statutes, Rules and Forms, 493 pages, 1987

SOCIAL LEGISLATION

Hood and Hardy's Workers' Compensation and Employee Protection Laws in a Nutshell, 274 pages, 1984 (Text)

LaFrance's Welfare Law: Structure and Entitlement in a Nutshell, 455 pages, 1979 (Text)

Malone, Plant and Little's Cases on Workers' Compensation and Employment Rights, 2nd Ed., 951 pages, 1980 (Casebook)

SPORTS LAW

Schubert, Smith and Trentadue's Sports Law, 395 pages, 1986 (Text)

TAXATION

Dodge's Cases and Materials on Federal Income Taxation, 820 pages, 1985 (Casebook)

Garbis, Struntz and Rubin's Cases and Materials on Tax Procedure and Tax Fraud, 2nd Ed., 687 pages, 1987 (Casebook)

Gelfand and Salsich's State and Local Taxation and Finance in a Nutshell, 309 pages, 1986 (Text)

Gunn and Ward's Cases and Materials on Federal Income Taxation, about 815 pages, 1988 (Casebook)

Hellerstein and Hellerstein's Cases on State and Local Taxation, 5th Ed., about 1060 pages, 1988 (Casebook)

Kahn and Gann's Corporate Taxation and Taxation of Partnerships and Partners, 2nd Ed., 1204 pages, 1985 (Casebook)

Kaplan's Federal Taxation of International Transactions: Principles, Planning and Policy, 635 pages, 1988 (Casebook)

Kragen and McNulty's Cases and Materials on Federal Income Taxation: Individuals, Corporations, Partnerships, 4th Ed., 1287 pages, 1985 (Casebook)

McNulty's Federal Estate and Gift Taxation in a Nutshell, 3rd Ed., 509 pages, 1983 (Text)

McNulty's Federal Income Taxation of Individuals in a Nutshell, 4th Ed., about 500 pages, 1988 (Text)

Pennell's Cases and Materials on Income Taxation of Trusts, Estates, Grantors and Beneficiaries, 460 pages, 1987 (Casebook)

Posin's Hornbook on Federal Income Taxation of Individuals, Student Ed., 491 pages, 1983 with 1987 pocket part (Text)

Rose and Chommie's Hornbook on Federal Income Taxation, 3rd Ed., 923 pages, 1988 (Text)

TAXATION—Cont'd

Selected Federal Taxation Statutes and Regulations, about 1400 pages, 1989

Solomon and Hesch's Cases on Federal Income Taxation of Individuals, 1068 pages, 1987 (Casebook)

TORTS

Christie's Cases and Materials on the Law of Torts, 1264 pages, 1983 (Casebook)

Dobbs' Torts and Compensation—Personal Accountability and Social Responsibility for Injury, 955 pages, 1985 (Casebook)

Keeton, Keeton, Sargentich and Steiner's Cases and Materials on Tort and Accident Law, 1360 pages, 1983 (Casebook)

Kionka's Torts in a Nutshell: Injuries to Persons and Property, 434 pages, 1977 (Text)

Malone's Torts in a Nutshell: Injuries to Family, Social and Trade Relations, 358 pages, 1979 (Text)

Prosser and Keeton's Hornbook on Torts, 5th Ed., Student Ed., 1286 pages, 1984, with 1988 pocket part (Text)

See also Products Liability

TRADE REGULATION

McManis' Unfair Trade Practices in a Nutshell, 2nd Ed., about 430 pages, 1988 (Text)

Oppenheim, Weston, Maggs and Schechter's Cases and Materials on Unfair Trade Practices and Consumer Protection, 4th Ed., 1038 pages, 1983 with 1986 Supplement (Casebook)

See also Antitrust, Regulated Industries

TRIAL AND APPELLATE ADVOCACY

Appellate Advocacy, Handbook of, 2nd Ed., 182 pages, 1986 (Text)

Bergman's Trial Advocacy in a Nutshell, 402 pages, 1979 (Text)

Binder and Bergman's Fact Investigation: From Hypothesis to Proof, 354 pages, 1984 (Coursebook)

Goldberg's The First Trial (Where Do I Sit?, What Do I Say?) in a Nutshell, 396 pages, 1982 (Text)

Haydock, Herr and Stempel's, Fundamentals of Pre-Trial Litigation, 768 pages, 1985 (Casebook)

Hegland's Trial and Practice Skills in a Nutshell, 346 pages, 1978 (Text)

Hornstein's Appellate Advocacy in a Nutshell, 325 pages, 1984 (Text)

Jeans' Handbook on Trial Advocacy, Student Ed., 473 pages, 1975 (Text)

Martineau's Cases and Materials on Appellate Practice and Procedure, 565 pages, 1987 (Casebook)

McElhaney's Effective Litigation, 457 pages, 1974 (Casebook)

Nolan's Cases and Materials on Trial Practice, 518 pages, 1981 (Casebook)

LAW SCHOOL PUBLICATIONS—Continued

TRIAL AND APPELLATE ADVOCACY—Cont'd

Sonsteng, Haydock and Boyd's The Trialbook: A Total System for Preparation and Presentation of a Case, Student Ed., 404 pages, 1984 (Coursebook)

See also Civil Procedure

TRUSTS AND ESTATES

Atkinson's Hornbook on Wills, 2nd Ed., 975 pages, 1953 (Text)

Averill's Uniform Probate Code in a Nutshell, 2nd Ed., 454 pages, 1987 (Text)

Bogert's Hornbook on Trusts, 6th Ed., Student Ed., 794 pages, 1987 (Text)

Clark, Lusky and Murphy's Cases and Materials on Gratuitous Transfers, 3rd Ed., 970 pages, 1985 (Casebook)

Dodge's Wills, Trusts and Estate Planning, Law and Taxation, Cases and Materials, 665 pages, 1988 (Casebook)

Kurtz' Cases, Materials and Problems on Family Estate Planning, 853 pages, 1983 (Casebook)

McGovern's Cases and Materials on Wills, Trusts and Future Interests: An Introduction to Estate Planning, 750 pages, 1983 (Casebook)

McGovern, Rein and Kurtz' Hornbook on Wills, Trusts and Estates including Taxation and Future Interests, about 924 pages, 1988 (Text)

Mennell's Wills and Trusts in a Nutshell, 392 pages, 1979 (Text)

Simes' Hornbook on Future Interests, 2nd Ed., 355 pages, 1966 (Text)

TRUSTS AND ESTATES—Cont'd

Turano and Radigan's Hornbook on New York Estate Administration, 676 pages, 1986 (Text)

Uniform Probate Code, Official Text With Comments, 578 pages, 1987

Waggoner's Future Interests in a Nutshell, 361 pages, 1981 (Text)

Waterbury's Materials on Trusts and Estates, 1039 pages, 1986 (Casebook)

WATER LAW

Getches' Water Law in a Nutshell, 439 pages, 1984 (Text)

Sax and Abram's Cases and Materials on Legal Control of Water Resources, 941 pages, 1986 (Casebook)

Trelease and Gould's Cases and Materials on Water Law, 4th Ed., 816 pages, 1986 (Casebook)

See also Energy and Natural Resources Law, Environmental Law

WILLS

See Trusts and Estates

WOMEN AND THE LAW

Kay's Text, Cases and Materials on Sex-Based Discrimination, 3rd Ed., about 979 pages, 1988 (Casebook)

Thomas' Sex Discrimination in a Nutshell, 399 pages, 1982 (Text)

See also Employment Discrimination

WORKERS' COMPENSATION

See Social Legislation

STATE AND LOCAL TAXATION

CASES AND MATERIALS

Fifth Edition

By

Jerome R. Hellerstein
*Adjunct Professor of Law, New York University
School of Law*

Walter Hellerstein
Professor of Law, University of Georgia

AMERICAN CASEBOOK SERIES

WEST PUBLISHING CO.
ST. PAUL, MINN., 1988

Library of Congress Cataloging-in-Publication Data

Hellerstein, Jerome R.
    State and local taxation: cases and materials / by Jerome R.
Hellerstein and Walter Hellerstein.—5th ed.
        p.   cm. — (American casebook series)
    Bibliography: p.
    Includes index.
    ISBN 0–314–39782–5
    1. Taxation, State—Law and legislation—Cases. 2. Local
taxation—Law and legislation—United States—Cases.
I. Hellerstein, Walter. II. Title. III. Series.
KF6730.A7H4 1988
343.7304'3—dc19
[347.30343]
                                                                    88–17196
                                                                       CIP

    ISBN 0–314–39782–5

    (H. & H.) State & Local Tax., 5th Ed. ACB

*To the memory of Pauline,
devoted wife and mother*

*

Preface

In the more than 35 years since the first edition of this work was published in 1952, the field of State and local taxation has undergone large, and, indeed, dramatic changes. Tax revenues collected by State and local governments from their own sources have increased nearly twenty-fold, rising from some $21 billion in 1952 to approximately $398 billion in 1987. Expenditures have bourgeoned at an even more rapid pace, mounting from some $28 billion in 1952 to $718 billion in 1986. To be sure, inflation has accounted for a substantial part of these astronomical expenditure rises, but the broadening of the nature and scope of the services regarded as a responsibility of State and local governments accounts for a good part of the rest. The gap between the revenues of State and local governments, including their non-tax resources, and their expenditures has to some extent been bridged by Federal grants-in-aid.

In expanding their tax collections, in order to meet the inflationary costs of welfare, education, police and fire protection, sewage, roads and other traditional services and to defray the costs of their widened role in providing medicaid, environmental protection, and other social services, State and local governments have been forced not only to increase tax rates under their traditional levies, but also to enact new taxes. Thirty-five years ago, there were 16 States which did not impose general retail sales or use taxes; at present there are only four States without such a tax. Sales and use tax rates have soared from the typical two percent to three percent during the 1950's to as high as five percent and six percent in some States; at the same time their scope has been expanded from their usual limitation in earlier decades essentially to the sale or use of tangible personal property to embrace more and more services. Corporate taxes measured by net income have been adopted during the intervening years by 11 of the 15 States which lacked them in 1952. Personal income taxes, which have had to overcome constitutional barriers in a number of States and have encountered stiff voter resistance to amendments authorizing the tax, have, nevertheless, been adopted by eight of the 17 States which had no general personal income taxes in 1952. A variety of new taxes, such as levies on admissions, occupancy, unincorporated businesses, and other persons or activities, have been added to the laws of a number of States. We have also witnessed a proliferation of new city and other local governmental sales and income taxes, as local governments have reached out, often desperately, for badly needed new sources of revenues to meet recurring fiscal crises. As a consequence, taxpayers in some States pay not only State sales, use, and income taxes, but also similar levies to literally thousands of cities and other local governmental subdivisions.

Congress, too, during the past 35 years, adopted legislation which significantly affects State and local taxation. For the first time in our history, Congress in 1959 enacted legislation restricting the power of the States to tax interstate manufacturing and mercantile companies (P.L. 86–272). Furthermore, since 1964, the year in which an extensive report on State taxation of interstate commerce was issued by the Congressional Willis Committee, there has been activity in virtually every session of Congress designed to impose further broad Federal limitations on State and local taxation—thus far without success. However, Congress has adopted legislation prohibiting specific State and local tax practices such as discriminatory taxation of railroads, motor carriers, and air carriers, gross receipts taxation of air transportation, and discriminatory taxation of electrical energy sales.

Collaboration among the States with respect to taxation has reached new dimensions since 1952. The most significant developments related to a major sore point in the taxation of multistate and multinational enterprises—the diverse and conflicting methods of apportionment and allocation of the net income measure of corporate taxes. More than half the 46 States (including the District of Columbia) which employ a net income measure enacted the Uniform Division of Income for Tax Purposes Act. Nineteen of those States have also entered into the Multistate Tax Compact, which not only incorporates the Uniform Act, but also provides for joint audits on behalf of various States by the Multistate Tax Commission. (There were 22 member States, but three States responded to strong attacks on the Compact led by large corporations by withdrawing.)

This mushroom-like growth of State and local taxation has, as was inevitable, resulted in a large volume of administrative proceedings and litigation. During the past 35 years, landmark decisions have been handed down in virtually every area of State and local taxation, including cases invalidating centuries of property tax assessment practices at fractional value under statutes and State constitutions calling for full value assessment; validating the application of progressive State income tax rates to non-residents; delineating the extent to which interstate vendors may be required to collect State sales or use taxes; and recharting the intergovernmental immunities doctrine in the property and sales tax areas and in the taxation of Indians. Far reaching changes took place in the views of the Supreme Court as to the limitations on State taxation imposed by the Import-Export and the Commerce Clauses of the Constitution. These developments, along with innumerable State court decisions filling in the interstices and lacunae of the taxing statutes, have greatly expanded the work of lawyers in State and local taxation, and underline the need for law school courses in the field. Lawyers have, of course, been involved not only in the day-by-day State and local tax problems of taxpayers, but also in the formulation of tax policies, the enactment of legislation, the drafting of the statutes and regulations, and the administration of the levies.

This work is planned for a course in which each student will study the taxing statutes and regulations of one State. The students will familiarize themselves with the State's laws and regulations relating to each tax studied, and the cases may be discussed in the light of the statutory and administrative treatment of the problems presented. In many law schools, presumably the entire class will study the statutes and regulations of the local State. However, in a national law school, the class work can be considerably enriched by allowing each student to study the materials of the State of his or her own choice. In this way, the class can become a laboratory in comparative State tax law, a teaching method that in practice has proved both instructive and stimulating to the students, and extremely useful to the students in the practice of law.

Most students taking the course will have had a course in constitutional law and will have at least a passing familiarity with the problems of the Commerce, Due Process and Equal Protection Clauses, although in many law schools little attention is paid in such courses to State tax problems. In order to focus the course primarily on statutory materials, and at the same time provide the students with the background needed for the important constitutional areas, we have prepared brief essays relating to these clauses, in the expectation that these materials will be assigned as background reading for the students. In these areas, only a few key recent Supreme Court decisions are printed as a basis for classroom discussion.

The law of taxation is, of course, closely interrelated with economics and public finance. An introduction to the economic and public finance problems which impinge on and underlie the legal issues is a sine qua non to the competent and intelligent practice of tax law, including State and local taxation, and in the preparation of lawyers for their important roles in designing tax policy and drafting tax laws. To help provide law students with such a background, we have included in this work some writings in economics and public finance; for those students and law teachers who may want to probe more deeply, we have made generous reference to other writings.

At a number of points in this work, there are excerpts from State Taxation I, Corporate Income and Franchise Taxes (1983) by Jerome R. Hellerstein or the Cumulative Supplement thereto by Jerome R. Hellerstein and Walter Hellerstein. At other points, the writing in this work is based on the Treatise or the Cumulative Supplement. Such uses are made with the consent of Jerome R. Hellerstein, the copyright owner, and Warren, Gorham & Lamont, the publisher.

We are grateful for the research assistance provided by Brian R. Balow, a student at the University of Georgia Law School, Class of

1988. We are also indebted to Doris Heimerle of New York City for her highly competent and cheerfully rendered secretarial services.

JEROME R. HELLERSTEIN,
New York, N.Y.
WALTER HELLERSTEIN,
Athens, Ga.

April 1988

Summary of Contents

Table of Contents

PART 6. DUE PROCESS CLAUSE RESTRICTIONS ON STATE TAXATION

Table of Cases

The principal cases are in bold type. Cases cited or discussed in the text are roman type. References are to pages. Cases cited in principal cases and within other quoted materials are not included.

Table of Abbreviations

ACIR	Advisory Commission on Intergovernmental Relations
CCH	Commerce Clearing House State Tax Service
IRC	Federal Internal Revenue Code
Mondale Comm. Hearings	Hearings Before the Subcommittee on State Taxation of Interstate Commerce of the Senate Finance Committee, 93rd Cong., 1st Sess. (1973)
MTC	Multistate Tax Commission
NTA	National Tax Association
P–H	Prentice-Hall State Tax Service
UDITPA	Uniform Division of Income for Tax Purposes Act
Willis Comm. Rep.	Report of the Special Subcommittee on State Taxation of Interstate Commerce, H.R. Rep. No. 1480, 88th Cong., 2d Sess. (1964), H.R. Rep. Nos. 565 and 952, 89th Cong., 1st Sess. (1965), 4 Volumes

EXPLANATORY NOTE REGARDING FOOTNOTES

Where we have retained footnotes in material quoted from cases, articles, books, and other materials, we have generally changed the footnote numbering so that it is integrated with our own footnotes, which are numbered consecutively for each chapter of the text.

*

STATE AND LOCAL TAXATION

CASES AND MATERIALS

Fifth Edition

Part 1

INTRODUCTION

Chapter 1

THE DEVELOPMENT OF THE AMERICAN STATE AND LOCAL TAX SYSTEM

SECTION 1. COLONIAL TAXATION

The colonial governments in their early days subsisted on voluntary payments, subsidies and allowances abroad, quit-rents, and occasional fees and fines of early justice. When compulsory levies developed, the tax systems followed the pattern of the local economies. In the democratic New England communities almost everyone owned land; and the distribution of property was fairly equal. Consequently, in New England, in addition to the poll tax, the colonies levied a tax on the gross produce of land, either actual or computed, according to the extent and quality of the land held. Gradually, this levy grew into a real property tax, which was soon expanded into a general property tax. The town artisans and other townsmen who subsisted on the fruit of their labor, instead of property, were not adequately taxed by the property levy. The "faculty tax" was added to reach these persons. The faculty tax was not an income tax, but instead a levy in a fixed amount, imposed rather arbitrarily, according to occupations and callings.[1]

An entirely different development took place in the Southern colonies, dominated by an aristocratic landed gentry with large holdings. There, the land tax played an insignificant role. After slavery was introduced, it became difficult to retain even the poll tax, which became in a sense a property tax on slaves. Consequently, the Southern colonies turned to excise taxes, particularly on imports and exports, which bore heavily on poorer consumers.

The middle colonies, particularly the New Netherlands, reflected the dominance of the moneyed interests and trading classes, who brought with them a Dutch tradition. Here, there was neither the

1. For the details of American faculty taxes, see E.R.A. Seligman, The Income Tax 367 (2d ed. 1914).

more or less equal distribution of wealth characteristic of New England, nor the preponderance of the landed interests typified by Virginia. Instead of a system of poll and property levies or of excises primarily on imports and exports, the fundamental characteristic of the tax structure was an excise system of taxation of trade, borrowed from Holland.

"Each section, therefore, had a fiscal system more or less in harmony with its economic conditions. It was not until these conditions changed during the eighteenth century that the fiscal systems began somewhat to approach each other; and it was not until much later that we find throughout the country a general property tax based not on the produce, but on the market value of property." [2]

SECTION 2. THE GROWTH OF STATE TAXATION

The outstanding development in State and local taxation during the nineteenth century was the rise of the property tax. As stated by Professor Ely, during the period from 1796 to the Civil War "the distinguishing feature of the system of state and local taxation in America may be described in one sentence. It is the taxation of all property, movable or immovable, visible or invisible, or real or personal * * * at one uniform rate." [3]

Nevertheless, the divergence of economic systems was reflected in the development of the State fiscal systems. In the Southern States, with imports and exports as a source of revenue cut off by the Federal Constitution, land had to bear a large part of the tax burden. As increased revenues were needed, these States, dominated by landed proprietors at least until the Civil War, turned primarily to license and privilege taxes on peddlers, auctioneers, saloon keepers, traders in slaves and horses, keepers of ferries, toll bridges and turnpikes, and indeed virtually all occupations carried on outside the farms.

In the Northern States, where business interests were dominant, the license or privilege tax system did not take hold. To supplement property tax yields, banks, insurance companies, canals, railroads, and other businesses were taxed; and as corporations came to play a more important role in the economy, general corporate franchise taxes were enacted. These levies were the precursors of the present day corporate taxes on or measured by net income. The newer States adopted the current tax philosophy of the older States, making the property tax the cornerstone of their tax structures.

The growth of State tax revenues has been rapid, particularly since 1927. State tax collections from all sources amounted to only $100 million in 1890. By 1915 they had reached $400 million. The billion dollar mark was reached in 1927. State tax collections doubled by 1935, reached $9 billion in 1950, totalled over $29 billion in 1965, soared to $89.3 billion in 1976, and mushroomed to $228 billion in 1986.

2. See E.R.A. Seligman, Essays in Taxation 16–17 (10th ed. 1931), on which this section is based.

3. R. Ely, Taxation in American States and Cities 131 (1888).

The increase in revenues has been brought about largely by a process of diversification of revenue sources, which has had the added advantage of bringing about a greater stability in State tax yields.

Table 1 reflects the rise in State tax collections from 1890 through 1986. Table 2 shows State tax collections by source from 1902 through 1986. Table 3 indicates the fiscal importance of specified types of State taxes by showing the percentage of specific tax collections to total State taxes from 1902 through 1986. Table 4 shows local revenue, including taxes, by source and percentage distribution from 1902 through 1985. Table 5 shows the yields of major State and local taxes by types for the 12 months ended June 30, 1987.

Some of the significant changes in revenues reflected are:

1. The gradual decline of the property tax as a major source of State tax revenue. In 1902 it produced over 50 percent of total State tax revenues. It declined sharply to 7.8 percent in 1940. The decline was accelerated until at present the property tax accounts for only 1.9 percent of State tax revenue. However, property taxes continue to bring in most of *local government's* tax revenue, approximately 74 percent in 1985.

2. The new sources of revenue in which the States have found fiscal support are income taxes, beginning with Wisconsin in 1911; motor vehicle taxes, starting in New York in 1901, and spreading rapidly so that by 1910 they had been adopted by most States; gasoline taxes, which were first introduced in 1919; tobacco and liquor taxes and general sales taxes, which became widespread in the 1930's; and corporate franchise and various types of business taxes.

3. The general sales tax is one of the major sources of current State revenues. This tax produced only $7 million in 1932 or 0.4 of 1 percent of total State tax revenues. In 1986, it was the second most fruitful source of State tax revenue with a yield of $74.8 billion, or 33 percent of the total.

4. Individual and corporate income taxes (including franchise taxes measured by net income) combined are currently the leading source of State tax revenue. They produced only $153 million or 8 percent of total State tax revenues in 1932, as compared with $85.8 billion or 37.7 percent of total State tax revenues in 1986.

5. Motor fuels taxes and motor vehicle taxes and licenses are still major sources of tax revenue, despite the fact that the percentage of total collections from these two taxes declined from 45 percent in 1932 to 14.2 percent in 1986. Dollar collections from these sources increased in the same period from $862 million to $32.5 billion. As additional revenues were needed, the States chose to tap new sources of revenue, such as soft drink and tobacco taxes and other excises, rather than rely on established taxes.

TABLE 1

State Tax Collections for Selected Years, 1890–1986 [4]

Year	Collections in Billions of Dollars [5]	Year	Collections in Billions of Dollars
1890	$ 0.1	1960	$ 20.2
1923	0.9	1965	29.1
1932	1.6	1970	48.0
1940	5.1	1975	80.1
1946	6.0	1980	136.9
1950	9.1	1985	214.9
1955	12.9	1986	228.1

4. Source: U.S. Bureau of the Census, "State Tax Collections," Series GF, through GF 86 No. 1 (Jan. 1987); in part compilation by Tax Foundation, Inc. Tables 1–5 are used with the consent of Tax Foundation, Inc.

5. The revenues reported in Table 1 are limited to State governments only.

TABLE 2
State Tax Collections by Source
Selected Fiscal Years 1902–1986 [a]
(Millions)

Year	Total [b]	General sales, use or gross receipts	Motor vehicle fuels sales	Tobacco products sales	Alcoholic beverage sales and licenses	Motor vehicle and operators' licenses	Income [c] Total	Income [c] Individual	Income [c] Corporation	Property	Death and gift	Severance	Other [d]	Year
1902	$ 156	—	—	—	e	$ 5	—	—	—	$ 82	e	e	$ 74	1902
1913	301	—	—	—	$ 2 [f]		—	—	—	140	e	e	154	1913
1922	947	—	$ 13	—	—	152	$ 101	$ 43	$ 58	348	$ 66	—	267	1922
1927	1,608	—	259	—	—	301	162	70	92	370	106	—	410	1927
1932	1,890	$ 7	527	$ 19	1	335	153	74	79	328	148	$ 19	353	1932
1936	2,618	364	687	44	166	360	266	153	113	228	117	34	354	1936
1940	3,313	499	839	97	255	387	361	206	155	260	113	53	449	1940
1945	4,349	776	696	145	368	414	810	357	453	276	136	83	643	1945
1950	7,930	1,670	1,544	414	497	755	1,310	724	586	307	168	211	1,053	1950
1955	11,597	2,637	2,353	459	550	1,184	1,831	1,094	737	412	249	306	1,616	1955
1960	18,036	4,302	3,335	923	734	1,573	3,389	2,209	1,180	607	420	420	2,333	1960
1965	26,126	6,711	4,300	1,284	1,050	2,021	5,586	3,657	1,929	766	731	503	3,171	1965
1970	47,905	14,127	6,277	2,308	1,540	2,955	12,921	9,183	3,738	1,090	996	686	5,005	1970
1975	80,141	24,780	8,256	3,286	2,106	3,937	25,461	18,819	6,642	1,451	1,418	1,741	7,705	1975
1980	136,913	43,167	9,721	3,737	2,656	5,324	50,410	37,089	13,321	2,892	2,035	4,167	12,804	1980
1985	214,874	69,207	13,352	4,247	3,262	7,636	81,281	63,644	17,637	3,984	2,327	7,211	22,367	1985
1986	228,054	74,821	14,087	4,449	3,302	8,374	85,832	67,469	18,363	4,354	2,534	6,125	24,176	1986

Source: See Note 4 supra.

[a] In 1945, and prior years, includes all local shares of State imposed taxes.

[b] Total does not include unemployment taxes.

[c] In several States, individual and corporation income taxes are not separable.

[d] Includes taxes on insurance, public utilities, parimutuels, corporation licenses, hunting and fishing licenses, documents and stock transfers, other, and unseparable.

[e] Unseparable, included in Other.

[f] Licenses included in Other.

TABLE 3
Percentage Distribution of State Tax Collections by Source
Selected Fiscal Years 1902–1986

Year	Total tax collections[a]	General sales, use, or gross receipts	Motor vehicle fuels sales	Tobacco products sales	Alcoholic beverage sales and licenses	Motor vehicle and operators' licenses	Income Total	Income Individual	Income Corporation	Property	Death and gift	Severance	Other
1902	100.0	—	—	—	[b]	—	—	—	—	52.6	[b]	—	47.4
1913	100.0	—	—	—	.7[c]	1.7	—	—	—	46.5	[b]	—	51.2
1922	100.0	—	1.4	—	—	16.0	10.7	4.5	6.1	36.7	7.0	—	28.2
1927	100.0	—	16.1	—	—	18.7	10.1	4.4	5.7	23.0	6.6	—	25.5
1932	100.0	.4	27.9	1.0	.1	17.7	8.1	3.9	4.2	17.4	7.8	1.0	18.7
1936	100.0	13.9	26.2	1.7	6.3	13.8	10.2	5.8	4.3	8.7	4.5	1.3	13.5
1940	100.0	15.1	25.3	2.9	7.7	11.7	10.9	6.2	4.7	7.8	3.4	1.6	13.6
1945	100.0	17.8	16.0	3.3	8.5	9.5	18.6	8.2	10.4	6.3	3.1	1.9	14.8
1950	100.0	21.1	19.5	5.2	6.3	9.5	16.5	9.1	7.4	3.9	2.1	2.7	13.3
1955	100.0	22.7	20.3	4.0	4.7	10.2	15.8	9.4	6.4	3.6	2.1	2.6	13.9
1960	100.0	23.8	18.5	5.1	4.1	8.7	18.8	12.2	6.5	3.4	2.3	2.3	12.9
1965	100.0	25.7	16.5	4.9	4.0	7.7	21.4	14.0	7.4	2.9	2.8	1.9	12.1
1970	100.0	29.5	13.1	4.8	3.2	6.2	27.0	19.2	7.8	2.3	2.1	1.4	10.4
1975	100.0	30.9	10.3	4.1	2.6	5.2	31.8	23.5	8.3	1.8	1.8	2.2	9.3
1980	100.0	31.5	7.1	1.9	2.7	3.9	36.8	27.1	9.7	2.1	1.5	3.0	9.3
1985	100.0	32.2	6.2	1.5	2.0	3.5	37.8	29.6	8.2	1.8	1.1	3.3	10.4
1986	100.0	32.8	6.2	1.4	1.9	3.7	37.6	29.6	8.0	1.9	1.1	2.7	10.6

[a] Total does not include unemployment taxes.
[b] Unallocable, included in Other.
[c] License taxes included in Other.

SECTION 3. THE DEVELOPMENT OF THE LOCAL TAX SYSTEM

The property tax has been the mainstay of local tax revenues throughout our history. The dominance of the property tax in the system of local revenue is attributable to a number of factors. Local units are small. The tax on real estate, which is the chief component of the tax, and in some States its exclusive base, does not readily escape the tax collector. The assessment and collection of the property tax lend themselves to local administration. It is a flexible tax, for its rate can easily be changed. And it is a dependable tax. Even in times of depression, the property tax will yield substantial revenues.

Nevertheless, in recent years and particularly since the depression of the 1930's, the property tax, despite its critical importance to local taxation, lagged far behind the mounting expenditure needs of cities and other local governmental units. Real estate values shrank during the 1930's while the needs of the unemployed skyrocketed relief expenditures. The Federal assumption of a large part of the burden of unemployment relief eased but did not cure the situation. World War II brought a decline in aggregate local governmental expenditures. Public works projects were postponed, interest payments reduced, and maintenance neglected. On the other hand, operating costs rose rapidly because of inflationary rises in salaries and in the costs of materials.

All this produced a crisis in the financial position of localities, particularly of cities. The post-World War II period has aggravated the situation, with the need to meet rising costs and provide schools and other facilities neglected during the war. The result has been a frantic search for new, untapped sources of local revenues.

SECTION 4.　TRENDS IN LOCAL REVENUE YIELDS

TABLE 4

Total Local Revenue by Source and Percentage Distribution
Selected Fiscal Years 1902–1985

AMOUNT (MILLIONS)

Year	Total[a]	Total own sources	General revenue — Total general	From own sources — Total (Taxes[c])	Property	Sales and gross receipts	Income[d]	License and other	Charges and miscellaneous	Utility	Liquor stores	Insurance trust[b]	Intergovernmental — From states	From Federal[e]
1902	$914	$858	$798	$704	$624	—	—	$80	$94	$60	—	—	$52	$4
1913	1,755	1,658	1,540	1,308	1,192	$3	—	113	232	116	—	$2	91	6
1922	4,148	3,827	3,545	3,069	2,973	20	—	76	476	266	—	16	312	9
1932	6,192	5,381	4,879	4,274	4,159	26	—	89	605	463	—	39	801	10
1940	7,724	5,792	5,007	4,497	4,170	130	$18	179	510	704	$13	68	1,654	278
1950	16,101	11,673	9,586	7,984	7,042	484	64	394	1,602	1,808	94	185	4,217	211
1954	22,402	16,468	13,629	10,978	9,577	703	122	576	2,651	2,403	119	317	5,635	298
1960	37,324	27,209	22,912	18,081	15,798	1,339	254	692	4,831	3,613	136	549	9,522	592
1965	53,815	38,583	32,703	25,451	22,152	2,059	433	807	7,251	4,908	177	795	14,077	1,155
1970	89,082	59,557	51,392	38,833	32,963	3,068	1,630	1,173	12,558	6,608	258	1,229	26,920	2,605
1975	159,731	97,757	84,357	61,310	50,040	6,468	2,635	2,166	23,047	10,867	338	2,194	51,068	10,906
1980	258,298	155,872	130,027	86,387	65,607	8,160	4,990	7,630	43,640	21,055	435	4,355	81,289	21,136
1985	402,544	264,461	216,103	134,473	99,772	14,663	7,974	12,063	81,630	38,630	482	9,246	116,359	21,724

PERCENTAGE DISTRIBUTION OF REVENUE FROM OWN SOURCES

| Year | Total [a] | From own sources | | Taxes[c] | | | | | Charges and miscellaneous | Utility | Liquor stores | Insurance trust[b] | Intergovernmental | |
		Total own sources	Total general	Total	Property	Sales and gross receipts	Income[d]	License and other					From states	From Federal[e]
1902	—	100.0	93.0	82.1	72.7	—	—	9.3	11.0	7.0	—	—	5.7[f]	.4[f]
1913	—	100.0	92.9	78.9	71.9	.2	—	6.8	14.0	7.0	—	.1	5.2	.3
1922	—	100.0	92.6	80.2	77.7	.5	—	2.0	12.4	7.0	—	.4	7.5	.2
1932	—	100.0	90.7	79.4	77.3	.5	—	1.7	11.2	8.6	—	.7	12.9	.2
1940	—	100.0	86.4	77.6	72.0	2.2	.3	3.1	8.8	12.2	.2	1.2	21.4	3.6
1950	—	100.0	82.1	68.4	60.3	4.1	.5	3.4	13.7	15.5	.8	1.6	26.2	1.3
1954	—	100.0	82.8	66.7	58.2	4.3	.7	3.5	16.1	14.6	.7	1.9	25.2	1.3
1960	—	100.0	84.2	66.5	58.1	4.9	.9	2.5	17.8	13.3	.5	2.0	25.5	1.6
1965	—	100.0	84.8	66.0	57.4	5.3	1.1	2.1	18.8	12.7	.5	2.1	26.2	2.1
1970	—	100.0	86.3	65.2	55.3	5.2	2.7	2.0	21.1	11.1	.4	2.1	30.2	2.9
1975	—	100.0	86.3	62.7	51.2	6.6	2.7	2.2	23.5	11.1	.3	2.2	32.0	6.8
1980	—	100.0	83.4	55.4	42.1	5.2	3.2	4.9	28.0	13.5	.3	2.8	31.4	8.2
1985	—	100.0	81.7	50.8	37.7	5.5	3.0	4.6	30.9	14.6	.2	3.5	28.9	5.4

Source: U.S. Bureau of the Census, Governmental Finances in 1974–1985 and prior years; Historical Statistics on Government Finance and Employment (Census of Governments 1962, Vol. VI); compiled in part by Tax Foundation, Inc.

[a] Duplicative transactions between levels of government are excluded in arriving at aggregates.

[b] Collections from employees for financing locally administered employee retirement systems and from employers for unemployment compensation taxes in District of Columbia.

[c] Excludes unemployment tax collections.

[d] Principally individual income.

[e] Amounts received directly from Federal Government not transfers of Federal funds initially received by States.

[f] Intergovernmental revenue as a percent of total revenue.

SECTION 5. THE GROWTH OF LOCAL NON–PROPERTY TAXES

Since 1940 the most significant trend in State and local fiscal relations has been the grant to localities of authority to enact non-property taxes on an unprecedented scale.

Table 4 discloses that although the property tax still dominates local tax collections and accounted for $99.8 out of $134.5 billion or 74 percent of all local *tax revenues* in 1985, in recent years there has been a growth in permissive or non-property tax collections.

The rapid growth of metropolitan areas in recent decades, which has exacerbated some of the most troublesome social and economic problems facing the country, has resulted in the predominance of the urban centers in local finance. To meet their pressing needs for public services, local governments in the 51 largest cities (all with populations of 300,000 or more), collected over half of all city government revenues in the country in 1984–85.[6]

Non-property taxes are sometimes referred to as "permissive" local taxes and include levies on incomes, sales, hotel room occupancy, restaurant meals, taxi rides, amusements, occupations, realty transfers, trailers, utility bills, cigarettes, cigars, gasoline, gross receipts of business, per capita taxes, licenses, fees and the like imposed by local authorities such as cities, counties, townships, school districts and special districts. Some of these permissive local taxes are as old as the localities themselves; many of them, however, are new levies for local governments. They have become relatively important because of their revenue yields, their diversity, their economic impact, and their place in the State-local tax structure. Prior to 1940 only a few localities made practical use of such measures and the revenues from them were quite insignificant.[7]

New York and New Orleans pioneered in the adoption of sales taxes in 1934 and 1941, respectively, and Philadelphia's enactment of an income-payroll tax was an innovation in local finance. Gasoline and cigarette taxes were virtually unknown among the larger cities. Factors such as the ever-increasing public demand for new and improved local governmental services, the increasing preemption by the State and Federal Governments of tax sources, coupled with a breakdown of the property tax during the depression of the 1930's, all caused local governmental officials to look for new and more productive sources of revenue.[8] In the immediate postwar years the localities were plagued with fiscal problems created by rising expenditures and the tendency of assessed values to lag behind price changes. Proposals for expanding local taxing powers became increasingly frequent, and in the space of a

6. U.S. Bureau of the Census, "City Government Finances in 1984–85," GF No. 4, Table 2, p. 4 (1986).

7. Stout & Myers, "The Development of Permissive Local Taxation since 1945," 13

Current Economic Comment 20, Bureau of Business and Economic Research (University of Illinois, 1951).

8. R. Sigafoos, The Municipal Income Tax 1 (1955).

few years the status of non-property taxes in municipal finance changed from virtual nonexistence to an important source of revenue. After 1946, net income taxes came into greater use in Ohio and Pennsylvania. In 1947 New York and Pennsylvania pioneered with legislation making broad grants of taxing powers to local governments. By 1949 more than 100 cities in California were using retail sales levies. Authorizations of a more limited character were enacted by Missouri (St. Louis income tax); by Kentucky in the use of license and income taxes; by New Jersey in the use of commodity taxes; by Florida in the use of cigarette taxes; and by Maryland in granting Baltimore broad taxing powers.

Local Income Taxes. Major cities in ten States have adopted income taxes to supplement their revenue needs. Today, cities in Alabama, California, Delaware, Kentucky, Maryland, Michigan, Missouri, New York, Ohio and Pennsylvania are resorting to net income taxes. Four of the fourteen cities in the country with populations of over 700,000 have adopted income taxes.[9] Income tax levies accounted for 13.9 percent of municipal tax collections in 1984–85, generating $6.6 billion in revenue.[10] In 1966, New York City became the first city (other than Washington, D.C.) to impose a graduated city income tax.

Local Sales Taxes. Although many cities attempted to adopt the sales tax, at the outbreak of World War II there were but two municipal sales taxes in the United States—in New York City and New Orleans. Toward the end of the war, the pent-up demand for greater local spending made itself felt, and the pressure for new sources of revenue was on once again. The number of local governments imposing sales taxes during the next several years burgeoned. This development was attributable in part to the adoption by California, Illinois, Mississippi, and Utah of systems for State collection of locally imposed taxes. Compared with the mere handful of a little more than forty years ago, by 1973 the overall total of sales tax localities had risen to 4,300 composed of 3,780 municipalities, 614 counties, and 47 school districts, as well as a number of parishes, boroughs, and rapid transit districts. They were located in 26 States; Illinois led the way with 1,345 taxing units; California had 439 sales tax jurisdictions.[11]

References. R. Ely, Taxation in American States and Cities (1888); Myers, "Permissive Local Taxes; A Review and a Forecast," 1960 Nat. Tax.Ass'n Procs. 428; Advisory Commission on Intergovernmental Relations ("ACIR"), Local Nonproperty Taxes and the Coordinating Role of the State (1962); ACIR, State Constitutional and Statutory Restrictions on Local Taxing Powers (1962); Frieden, Metropolitan America: Challenge to Federalism, submitted to the House Committee on Government Operations (89th Cong.2d Sess.), ACIR Rep. M–31, (1967); J.

9. U.S. Bureau of the Census, "City Government Finances in 1984–85," GF 85, No. 4, Table 7, pp. 94–105 (1986).

10. Id. at p. v.

11. Advisory Commission on Intergovernmental Relations, Local Revenue Diversification: Income, Sales Taxes, and User Charges 51–54 (1974).

Maxwell & J. Aronson, Financing State and Local Governments (3d ed. 1977); Diamond, "Emerging Fiscal Patterns in Metropolitan Areas," 1966 Nat.Tax Ass'n Procs. 5; Zubrow, "Fiscal Profile and Problems of the City of Denver," 1966 Nat.Tax Ass'n Procs. 32; ACIR, Local Revenue Diversification: Income, Sales Taxes, and User Charges (1974). For a discussion of the types of net income tax patterns used by the various municipalities, as well as the legal road-blocks in the path of the tax, see Hartman, "Municipal Income Taxation," 31 Rocky Mtn.L. Rev. 123 (1959).

SECTION 6.　CURRENT STATE AND LOCAL TAXES[12]

(a) The Mounting Costs of State and Local Services

During the decade 1975 to 1985, State and local general expenditures increased nearly 150 percent from $266.2 billion to $658.1 billion.[13] True, part of the rising State and local costs was met by Federal grants-in-aid, but the State and local governments in 1985 provided over 83 percent of the funds needed to meet their costs from their own resources; $106 billion came from Federal sources.[14]

To a considerable extent the sharp rise in the costs of providing State and local governmental services involves merely the need to run faster to stay at the same place, due to the rapidly increasing costs of goods and services and the growth in population. Such additional costs accounted for about two-thirds of the rise in costs over the decade from 1955–65,[15] and, with the inflation we experienced over the 1965–75 decade, they probably accounted for at least that proportion of the rise in costs during that period.

Education is by far the largest factor in State and local governmental expenditures. In 1985, 29.3 percent of the outlay of these governments went for schooling, including higher education; public welfare accounted for 10.9 percent, highways for 6.8 percent, hospitals and health for 7.5 percent, and police and fire protection for 3.2 percent. Education costs of State and local governments rose between 1975 and 1985 from $87.9 billion to $192.7, and highway expenditures from $22.5 billion to $45.0 billion.[16]

(b) The Rise of State and Local Revenues

The responsiveness of State and local revenues to increasing expenditure pressures has been a source of considerable surprise to a good

---

12. This section is based in part on J. Hellerstein, "Current Issues in Fiscal Federalism: Federal Grants-in-Aid," 20 U.Fla. L.Rev. 505 (1968). This material and part of Section 8 infra, are used by permission. Copyright 1968 by the University of Florida Law Review.

13. U.S. Bureau of the Census, "Governmental Finances in 1974–75," GF 75, No. 5, Table 3, p. 16 (1976); U.S. Bureau of

the Census, "Governmental Finances in 1984–85," GF 85, No. 5, Table 5, p. 6 (1986).

14. U.S. Bureau of the Census, "Governmental Finances in 1984–85," GF 85, No. 5, Table 5, p. 6 (1986).

15. See Committee for Economic Development, A Fiscal Program for a Balanced Federalism 19 n.15 (1967).

16. See note 13 supra.

many observers. In the past decade State and local tax collections more than doubled. Thus, in 1975, State and local governments collected $141.5 billion in taxes; [17] ten years later, this figure had risen to $349.7 billion.[18] The property tax alone rose by nearly $52 billion during the decade and accounted in 1985 for 30 percent of State and local tax total revenues.[19] Indeed, the property tax whose "demise * * * has long been predicted," [20] produced more revenues in 1986 than any tax levied in this country other than the Federal income tax. See Table 5. The sales and use tax and related gross-receipts taxes (the general sales and use tax, as distinguished from specific levies on motor fuels, tobacco, alcohol and other "luxury" or "evil" goods, made its appearance in the 1930's) have continued to grow rapidly. In 1985, they brought State and local treasuries $126.3 billion, as compared with $49.8 billion a decade earlier.[21] Sales and use taxes now bring in about one-third of all State and local taxes; they are in force in 46 States and in many local governments.[22]

TABLE 5

State and Local Taxes 12 Months Ended June 30, 1987

Level of Government	Amount (billions of $)	Percent
All State and local taxes	398.4	100.00
State	246.6	61.9
Local	151.9	38.1
By type of tax		
Property	119.9	30.1
Other than property	278.6	69.9
General sales and gross receipts	95.0	23.8
Motor fuel sales	15.8	4.0
Individual income	85.0	21.3
Motor vehicle and operators' licenses	9.3	2.3
Corporate income	20.7	5.2
Other	52.7	13.2

Source: U.S. Bureau of the Census, "Quarterly Summary of Federal, State, and Local Tax Revenue, April–June 1987, GT8702, Table 3, p. 5 (Nov. 1987).

17. U.S. Bureau of the Census, "Governmental Finances in 1974–75," GF 75 No. 5, Table 3, p. 16 (1976).

18. U.S. Bureau of the Census, "Governmental Finances in 1984–85," GF 85, No. 5, Table 5, p. 6 (1986).

19. U.S. Bureau of the Census, note 17 supra; U.S. Bureau of the Census, note 18 supra. Property tax collections rose from $51.5 billion to $103.7 billion in the 10-year span.

20. See Committee for Economic Development, A Fiscal Program for a Balanced Federalism 18 (1967).

21. U.S. Bureau of the Census, note 17 supra; U.S. Bureau of the Census, note 18 supra.

22. U.S. Bureau of the Census, note 18 supra and Table 6 infra.

The other "growth" taxes have been the personal and corporate income taxes. Forty-three States at this writing have general, broad-based personal income taxes, and 46 States impose corporate taxes using income as one of the measures.[23] But the other side of the coin is that seven States have no broad-based personal income tax. And, given the low rates of tax—the individual rates seldom exceed ten percent and the corporate rates generally are somewhat lower—the revenues produced by income taxes are not of the magnitude of property taxes or of sales and related gross receipts taxes.[24] In 1985, State individual income and corporate income based taxes produced $89 billion, more than tripling the $28 billion figure for 1975.[25] Unlike the Federal Government, which obtains about two-thirds of its revenues from taxes on personal and business incomes, the State and local tax system relies much more heavily on regressive levies, sales and use taxes, and property taxes.[26] See Table 6.

23. See Table 6 infra.

24. See Table 5 supra.

25. U.S. Bureau of the Census, note 18 supra.

26. See Council on Economic Advisers, "Federal State and Local Fiscal Relations," Revenue Sharing Compendium 688–689; Advisory Commission on Intergovernmental Relations, Federal–State Coordination of Personal Income Taxes, ch. 2 (1965). Dr. W. Irvin Gillespie has made an interesting study "Effect of Distribution of Public Expenditures on the Distribution of Income," which concludes that when expenditure benefits are taken into account, the net pattern favors low income groups. See R. Musgrave, Essays in Federalism, ch. 3 (Brookings Inst. 1965).

TABLE 6

Chart of State Taxes *

State	Taxes	Cap. Values Franchise	Corp. Income	Individual Income	Sales	Use	Tangible Personalty	Intangibles	Stock Transfer	Recording Documents
Alabama	*	*	*	*	*	*	*	*		*
Alaska			*	(27)			*			
Arizona			*	*	*	*	*	*(5)		*
Arkansas	*	*	*	*	*	*	*			*
California			*	*	*	*	*			*
Colorado			*	*	*	*	*			*
Connecticut		*(10)	*	*(26)	*	*	*			*
Delaware	*	*	*	*	(4)	(4)				*
Dist. Columbia	*	*	*	*(8)	*	*	*			*(35)
Florida			*		*	*	*	*(12)	*	*
Georgia	*	*	*	*	*	*	*	*(12)		*
Hawaii			*	*	*	*				*
Idaho			*	*	*	*	*			
Illinois	*		*	*	*(6)	*				*
Indiana			*	*	*	*	*	*(18)		
Iowa	*	*	*	*	*	*	(30)	*(12,30)		*
Kansas	*	*	*	*	*	*	*	*(12)		*(17)
Kentucky	*	*	*	*	*	*	*	*(12)		*
Louisiana	*	*	*	*	*	*	*(34)	*		
Maine			*	*	*	*	*			*
Maryland			*	*	*	*	*	*(20)		*(24)
Massachusetts	*	*	*	*	*(3)	*(3)	*			*
Michigan			*(7)	*(7)	*	*	*	*(12,31)		*
Minnesota			*	*	*	*	*			*
Mississippi	*		*	*	*	*	*	*(20)		
Missouri	*		*	*	*	*	*			
Montana			*	*			*	*(12)		
Nebraska	*		*	*	*	*	*			*
Nevada					*	*	*	*(20)		*
New Hampshire	*		*(13)	*(9)	(1)		*			*
New Jersey		*(16)	*	*(16)	*	*	*			*
New Mexico			*	*	*	*	*			
New York		*(10)	*	*	*	*			*(32)	*(2)
North Carolina	*		*	*	*	*	*	*(12)		*
North Dakota			*	*	*	*	*(36)	*(20)		
Ohio	*	*	*	*	*	*	*			*
Oklahoma	*	*	*	*	*	*	*			*(25)
Oregon			*	*			*			
Pennsylvania	*	*	*	*	*	*	*	*(12)		*
Rhode Island	*	*	*	*	*	*	*	*(11)		
South Carolina	*	*	*	*	*	*	*	*(5)	*(22)	*
South Dakota		*(23)			*	*	*(19)	*(19)		*
Tennessee	*	*		*(9)	*	*	*	*(20)		*
Texas	*				*	*	*	*(20)		
Utah			*	*	*	*	*			
Vermont			*	*	*(3)	*(3)	*			*
Virginia			*	*	*	*	*			*
Washington					*(21)	*(21)	*			*
West Virginia	*		*	*	*(21)	*	*	*(12)		*
Wisconsin			*	*	*	*	*			*
Wyoming	*				*	*	*			*

* From Prentice–Hall, All States Guide ¶ 210 (Oct. 27, 1987) used with the consent of Prentice–Hall, Inc., the copyright owner.

State Taxes	Estate	Gift	Inheritance	Motor Fuel	Admissions & Amusement	Chain Store	Tobacco	Minerals	Timber
Alabama	*			*	*(15)	*	*	*	*
Alaska	*			*			*	*	
Arizona	*			*	*(15)		*	*	
Arkansas	*			*	*(15)		*	*	*
California	*			*			*	*	
Colorado	*			*		*	*	*	
Connecticut	*		*	*	*		*		*
Delaware	*	*	*	*	*		*		
Dist. Columbia	*			*	*(15)		*		
Florida	*			*	*(15)		*	*	*
Georgia	*			*	*(15)		*		
Hawaii	*			*	*(15)		*		
Idaho	*		*	*	*(15)		*	*	*
Illinois	*			*			*		
Indiana	*		*	*	*(15)		*	*	
Iowa	*		*	*	*(15)		*		
Kansas	*		*	*	*(15)		*	*	
Kentucky	*		*	*	*(15)		*	*	
Louisiana	*	*	*	*	*(15)	*	*		*
Maine	*			*			*		
Maryland	*		*	*	*	*	*	*(33)	
Massachusetts	*			*			*		*
Michigan	*		*	*			*	*	*
Minnesota	*			*	*(15)		*	*	*
Mississippi	*			*	*		*	*	*
Missouri	*			*	*(15)		*		*
Montana	*		*	*		*	*	*	
Nebraska	*		*	*	*(15)		*	*	
Nevada	*			*			*	*	
New Hampshire	*		*	*			*		
New Jersey	*		*(16)	*	*(15)		*		
New Mexico	*			*	*(15)		*	*	*
New York	*	*		*	*(15)		*		*
North Carolina	*	*	*	*	*	*	*	*	*
North Dakota	*			*	*(15)		*	*	
Ohio	*			*			*		
Oklahoma	*			*	*(15)		*	*	
Oregon	*	(28)	(28)	*			*	*	*
Pennsylvania	*		*	*(10)			*		
Rhode Island	*			*	*		*		
South Carolina	*	*(14)		*	*		*		
South Dakota	*		*	*	*(15)		*	*	
Tennessee	*	*	*	*	*		*	*	
Texas	*		*	*	*(15)		*	*	
Utah	*			*	*(15)		*	*	
Vermont	*			*	*(15)		*		
Virginia	*			*	*(15)		*		*
Washington	*			*	*(15)		*		*
West Virginia	*			*	*(15)	*(29)	*		
Wisconsin	*	*	*(34)	*	*(15)		*	*	*
Wyoming	*			*	*(15)		*	*	

FOOTNOTES to chart ¶ 210 (corresponding to parenthetical numbers in chart):

(1) N.H.—Meals and rooms tax.

(2) N.Y.—Mortgage tax. Realty transfer tax.

(3) Mass. & Vt.—Sales-use plus meals and rooms tax.

(4) Del.—Tax based on gross receipts (retailing, wholesaling, services and other businesses). Use tax on leasing tangible personalty also levied.

(5) Ariz., & S.C.—Law on books apparently unenforced.

(6) Ill.—Tax is on retailers, servicemen and specified professionals—based on gross receipts.

(7) Mich.—"Single Business Tax" applies to corporations and individuals.

(8) D.C.—Net income tax imposed on unincorporated business also.

(9) N.H. & Tenn.—Tax is on income from intangibles only.

(10) Added tax on oil cos.

(11) R.I.—Only bank deposits are taxed.

(12) Intangibles taxable at lower value or lower rate than other property. In Kans., intangibles tax imposed at local level; no state tax.

(13) N.H.—Business profits tax on corporations, partnerships, individuals and other organizations operated for profit.

(14) S.C.—Gift tax repealed 7–1–91.

(15) Amusements taxable under gross income, gross receipts or sales tax laws.

(16) N.J.—Net worth base of corporation business tax is phased out eff. for tax periods after 6–30–86. Gross (personal) income tax is paid by residents and non-residents. Inheritance tax is being phased out.

(17) Kan.—Mortgages—instruments creating liens.

(18) Ind.—Intangibles tax ends after 1995.

(19) S.Dak.—Tax on personalty is repealed eff. 1–1–79 except for centrally assessed property.

(20) Md., Miss., Nev., N.D., Tex.—Nearly all intangibles exempt by law.

(21) Wash. & W.Va.—Business & occupation tax also levied. W.Va. tax is repealed eff. 7–1–87 except for tax on utilities.

(22) S.C.—Tax ends after 1986–87 fiscal year.

(23) S.D.—Only banks pay tax.

(24) Md.—State realty transfer tax is added to document recording tax (rates vary locally).

(25) Okla.—Mortgage and realty transfer taxes.

(26) Conn.—Tax on capital gains, dividends, interest—and estate income.

(27) Alaska—Local sales taxes; no state tax.

(28) Ore.—Inheritance and gift taxes are repealed after 1986.

(29) W. Va.—Business franchise registration tax based on number of locations.

(30) Iowa—Intangibles tax applies only to loan agencies. Tangible personalty not assessed starting 1–1–86; tax repealed 7–1–87.

(31) Mich.—Intangibles of those paying "Single Business Tax" are exempt.

(32) N.Y.—100% rebate of stock transfer taxes.

(33) Md.—Taxes collected in some counties.

(34) Wis.—Inheritance tax repealed 1–1–92.

(35) D.C.—Added excise tax on transfers of residential realty.

(36) N.D.—Nearly all tangible personalty exempt.

The result of these developments was to produce State and local tax collections for fiscal 1985 of $349.8 billion.[27] California led the way in tax revenues collecting approximately $43.4 billion from State and local taxes. Other leading tax collectors were: New York, $41.5 billion; Texas, $20.7 billion; Illinois, $17.0 billion; Pennsylvania, $16.4 billion; and Michigan, $14.6 billion.[28] During fiscal 1985, per capita State and local taxes rose in every State, ranging from a high of $4,585 in Alaska to a low of $918 in Mississippi.[29]

References. There is an illuminating survey of the development of taxation in Europe and this country in E.R.A. Seligman, Essays in Taxation (10th ed. 1931). M. Kendrick, Public Finance, ch. 7 (1951), provides a workable student history of State and local taxation. The details of the current tax structures of the States and local governments may be found in CCH State Tax Reporters and P–H State & Local Taxes, with summaries in the respective All States Guides. For broad changes, see Advisory Commission on Intergovernmental Relations ("ACIR"), Measures of State and Local Fiscal Capacity and Tax Effort (1962); "State and Local Taxes on Business," Symposium (Tax Institute of America 1965); ACIR, State–Local Finances: Significant Features and Suggested Legislation (1972); ACIR, Significant Features of Fiscal Federalism (1984). There are also available useful in-depth studies of the tax systems of individual States, with recommendations for changes. See Report of New Jersey Tax Policy Committee (N.J. State Library, Trenton 1972); Report of the New York Temporary State Tax Commission on State and Local Finances (Albany 1975). The New York Legislative Tax Study Commission issued a number of useful studies of various aspects of the State's tax system during the mid-1980's. Other relatively recent State-specific studies include: Final Report of the Connecticut Bipartisan Commission on State Tax Revenue and Related Fiscal Policy (1983); Georgia Tax Commission Combined Report (1981); Final Report of the Minnesota Tax Study Commission (1986); Final Report of the Pennsylvania State Tax Commission (1981); and A Tax Study for West Virginia in the 1980's (1984).

SECTION 7. THE REVOLT AGAINST RISING PROPERTY AND OTHER TAXES AND INCREASING STATE AND LOCAL GOVERNMENT EXPENDITURES

In 1978 State and local governments throughout the country received a severe jolt from the overwhelming approval of Proposition 13 by the California electorate.[30] The proposition amended the State constitution by limiting property taxes to 1% of the 1975–1976 valuations and prohibiting any increase of more than 2% in the valuation of

---

27. U.S. Bureau of the Census, "Governmental Finances in 1984–85," GF 85, No. 5, Table 17, p. 20 (1986).

28. Id.

29. Id., Table 30, p. 98.

30. See Cal. Const., Art. XIII–A; ACIR, "The Taxpayers Speak: Proposition 13 and Intergovernmental Relations," 4 Intergovernmental Perspective, No. 4, p. 8 (Summer 1978); N.Y. Times, June 11, 1978.

property, unless it is sold.[31]   The amendments also forbade the enactment of any additional *State* tax unless it is approved by at least two-thirds of all the members of both houses of the legislature, or any additional *local* tax unless it is approved by at least two-thirds of the qualified voters.[32]

Although there was widespread taxpayer dissatisfaction throughout the country during the 1970's with constantly mounting taxing and spending by State and local governments—14 States imposed limits during the 1970's on the power of local officials to raise taxes [33]—none of the legislative or constitutional restrictions adopted had the sweep of Proposition 13.   Once the California voters approved Proposition 13, the property tax rebellion spread rapidly over the country.   Amendments virtually identical to Proposition 13 were approved in the year of its adoption, 1978, in Idaho and Nevada,[34] and less drastic restrictions were enacted in Alabama, Massachusetts, Michigan, North Dakota (restrictions on income taxation) and Wisconsin.[35]

At the time the California voters approved Proposition 13, the State had a large surplus—$5.5 billion—to cushion the effects of the limitations on taxation through increased State aid to finance local public services.[36]   As that reserve was used up and Californians began to suffer the consequences of severe reductions in local services resulting from the lowering of property taxes by some $6 billion, more sober second thoughts began to set in, and the head-long rush to emulate Proposition 13 subsided.[37]   As a consequence, in 1980, "[a]lthough over 35 percent of the states considered tax-cutting proposals (by far the most states to do so in a single year) most of the measures were defeated, including all five Proposition 13 look-alikes." [38]   And in California the chastening effects of the experience of living with limitations of Proposition 13, once the 1978 surplus was depleted, were reflected in the "overwhelming defeat" by the California voters in 1981 of Jarvis II, a counterpart to Proposition 13 proposed by one of its principal authors, under which the State income taxes would have been cut in half.[39]

Missouri and Massachusetts were the exceptions to the backlash of Proposition 13.[40]   The aftermath of the adoption of Proposition 2½ in

31. The California voters approved the initiative by a 2 to 1 vote. N.Y. Times, June 11, 1978. The limitation imposed is 1% of "full cash value", which is defined as meaning the county assessor's evaluation * * * as shown on the 1975–1976 tax bill, or thereafter, the appraised value of property when purchased, newly constructed or a change in ownership has occurred after the 1975 assessment. Cal. Const., Art. XIII-A. The amendment was attacked, inter alia, as working unconstitutional discrimination against persons who purchase or build properties after the 1975 assessment date. The amendment was upheld in Amador Valley v. State Board of Equalization, 22 Cal.2d 318, 149 Cal.Rptr. 239, 583 P.2d 1281 (1981).

32. See Cal. Const. note 30 supra.

33. See ACIR, note 30 supra, at 9.

34. See N.Y. Times, Nov. 9, 1978.

35. Id.

36. See ACIR, note 30 supra at 8.

37. See Wall St. J., Feb. 16, 1979.

38. See ACIR, "Fiscal Issues Dominate As States Meet the Eighties", 7 Intergovernmental Perspective No. 1, pp. 19, 20 (Winter 1981).

39. Id. at 20.

40. Id.

Massachusetts (thus named because it limited the property tax rate of every taxing jurisdiction in the State to 2½ percent of 1979 market value) is instructive.[41]   The property tax rate in the City of Boston was approximately 10.4 percent of the market value of property at the time Proposition 2½ was approved.   Under the constitutional amendment each taxing jurisdiction whose rate exceeded 2½ percent of property values was permitted to phase in the limitation by reducing its tax rate 15 percent a year until the 2½ percent level is reached.   Once that has been accomplished, property taxes may not be increased in the local jurisdiction by more than 2½ percent in any one year, regardless of what happens to property values.   Consequently, Boston is required by the constitutional amendments to reduce its tax rate over the years by about 75 percent.[42]   The Statewide average tax rate at the time the amendment was adopted was reported to be 3.5 percent of market value;   the new mandated 2½ percent ceiling was reported as being exceeded in 351 jurisdictions in the State.[43]

The consequences of this type of bulldozer approach to local finance problems were not long in making themselves felt.   By the spring of 1981, the City of Boston was faced with possible insolvency.[44]   The Boston school system ran out of funds and was threatened with closing. The schools were kept open only by court order, while city and State officials searched for and quarreled over new revenue sources.[45]   The Boston Public Library, founded in 1852 and the world's oldest free public city library supported by taxes, was also faced with the need to close its neighborhood branches that had first been opened to the public in 1891, and a freeze was put on the purchase of new books.[46]   Thirteen fire companies and the city's seven neighborhood police substations in Boston were closed, as 200 policemen were dismissed and virtually all foot patrols were ended.[47]   In Cambridge, it was expected that with a loss of one-third of local revenues during the next two years, the city would have to lay off one-third of its teachers, firemen, policemen, public workers and other employees.[48]   The ACIR reported predictions that Proposition 2½ will provoke "the most severe fiscal crisis in the State's history," and that it is expected that efforts would be made to modify the amendments.[49]   In fact, the major finding of one of the early studies of the impact of Proposition 2½ was that "municipalities were not forced to make devastating budget cuts."[50]   Property revaluation permitted higher than expected levy limits.   State aid yielded a second unexpected source of revenue.   Finally, local officials imposed hiring

41. Id.

42. Id.

43. Id.

44. N.Y. Times, April 17, 1981.

45. See N.Y. Times, May 5–6, 1981.

46. See N.Y. Times, April 5, 1981.

47. Id.

48. See ACIR, note 9 supra, at 20.

49. Id.

The Massachusetts Municipal Association estimated at the end of 1981 that Proposition 2½ had thus far cost cities and towns of Massachusetts $550 million to $600 million in revenues.   See N.Y. Times, Dec. 13, 1981, Review of the Week.

50. Susskind and Horan, "Proposition 2½: The Response to Tax Restrictions in Massachusetts," in C.L. Harriss, ed., The Property Tax and Local Finance 158 (1983).

freezes soon after Proposition 2½ was passed thus preventing some scheduled budget cuts. The long-term impact of Proposition 2½ and similar measures remains to be seen.

For the first time since World War II, this rash of State constitutional limitations on taxation and legislation cutting taxes reversed the tendency of State and local taxes to grow more rapidly than the gross national product.[51]

SECTION 8. FEDERAL GRANTS–IN–AID TO STATE AND LOCAL GOVERNMENTS *

Federal grants in aid to State and local governments have had a long and checkered history in American public finance, reflecting the changing dominant political philosophies.[52] At the beginning of the 1930's, Federal grants amounted to only about $200 million a year and accounted for about three percent of State and local general revenues.[53] Depression programs and Social Security legislation raised them above the $1 billion level. While there was a decline before and during World War II, beginning in the mid–1960's grants-in-aid became one of the principal tools for Federal attempts to cope with a wide range of domestic problems. Although many grants-in-aid are related to welfare programs, transfers from the Federal government to the States far transcend the welfare area. They have been used across virtually the entire gamut of State activity, from environmental protection to education to law enforcement, financing, at least in part, such diverse State activities as highway beautification, disaster relief, preservation of historic properties, health services, and school lunches.[54]

Categorical and Block Grants. Until the introduction of general revenue sharing in 1972 (see General Revenue Sharing infra), Federal grants in aid took the form of categorical or block grants. Traditionally, the Federal Government favored categorical grants over more broadly focused block grants.[55] Categorical grants may be used by the recipient State or local government for only a single purpose. In addition, such grants often have conditions attached prescribing the precise circumstances under which the funds may be spent. Many

51. See Manvel, "State–Local Tax Trends," 9 Taxation With Representation Newsletter, No. 10, Oct. 10, 1980, pp. 2–3.

* This Section is based in part on excerpts from Dam, "The American Fiscal Constitution," 44 U.Chi.L.Rev. 271 (1977), reprinted with the permission of the University of Chicago Law Review, the copyright owner. The Section also draws on J. Hellerstein, "Current Issues in Fiscal Federalism: Federal Grants-in-Aid," 20 U.Fla. L.Rev. 505 (1968).

52. The history of Federal grants-in-aid is detailed in Elazar, "Federal–State Collaboration in the Nineteenth Century," 79 Pol.Sci.Q. No. 2 (June, 1964); Elazar, "The Shaping of Intergovernmental Relations in the Twentieth Century," 359 Annals of Am.Acad. of Pol. and Social Science 10 (1965).

53. Schaller, "Federal Grants-in-Aid: A Review," 1965 Nat. Tax Ass'n Procs. 96; J. Maxwell, Financing State and Local Governments, ch. 3 (1965).

54. Office of Management & Budget, Special Analyses, Budget of the United States Government, Fiscal Year 1978, at 288–89 (Table 0–9) (1977) [hereinafter cited as Special Analyses 1978].

55. See notes 52 and 53 supra.

categorical grants also require recipient governments to match the Federal funds out of their own revenue. The Federal Government is thereby enabled to control the expenditure of grants-in-aid so as to accomplish a particular administration's objectives.[56]

A block grant consolidates a number of related specific-purpose grants into a single grant with a more general purpose. Block grants permit State and local governments considerable autonomy in their expenditures of the funds. Not surprisingly, State and local officials, whose treasuries were augmented and whose discretionary powers of expenditure were enhanced, welcomed the growth of block grants at the expense of categorical grants.[57] Others, however, were critical of the shift. Labor leaders, liberals and black leaders were concerned at the way in which the Federal block grants would be likely to be used by State and local governments.[58] Indeed, many were aghast at the thought of turning over Federal funds, without effective strings, to some Southern States for schools or hospitals, or to local governments that have made a "national disgrace" of their welfare systems.[59] They believed that the crucial problems of the great urban centers could not be solved by distributing funds to rural dominated State administrations, for reallocation within the State; and that only imaginative, bold, nationally developed programs could even begin to cope with the conditions faced by the metropolitan centers.[60]

The Nixon administration, coming to power in 1969, with its philosophical and political bent in favor of vesting greater powers in State and local governments in designing and administering programs, embraced block grants.[61]

General Revenue Sharing. In 1972 a new development of signal importance in Federal–State fiscal relations took place with the introduction of general revenue sharing by the Federal government. The name is something of a misnomer because revenues are not shared. The general revenue sharing program was an expenditure program in which Federal grants were made each year to the States without the extensive restrictions and conditions that are the hallmark of conventional grants-in-aid. Although general revenue sharing is often referred to as a "no strings" program, nevertheless, a number of conditions were in fact imposed on the recipient State and local governments. Not only were they, for example, prohibited from discriminating on the basis of race, color, national origin, sex, age, or

---

56. See Advisory Commission on Intergovernmental Relations (ACIR) "Categorical Grants and Role and Design" A–52 (1978).

57. Wall Street Journal, March 27, 1975; see statements of Mayor Moon Landrieu of New Orleans and Mayor Joseph Alioto of San Francisco.

58. See Keyserling, The New Republic, March 25, 1967; Committee for Economic Development, A Fiscal Program for a Balanced Federalism (1967); Frieden, "Metropolitan America: Challenge to Federalism," ACIR Report to House Committee on Governmental Operations (89th Cong. 2d Sess.), ACIR Rep. M–31 (1967).

59. Id.

60. Id.

61. See note 56 supra.

religion in the expenditure of the funds,[62] but, in addition, only prevailing wage rates could be paid on projects financed with general revenue sharing funds.[63]

The conflicts between liberals and conservatives, and Federalists and States' righters were exacerbated by general revenue sharing. Credence was soon given to the fears of the proponents of categorical grants that the block grants, and particularly revenue sharing, would be diverted by the States and local governments from social welfare programs. A 1974 study disclosed that:

> only 1.6 percent of the revenue sharing funds went for social services and only 1.15 percent went for health care.
>
> The bulk of the money, [as] * * * found in a canvass of 212 cities with populations greater than 50,000, was used for law enforcement, fire protection, street and road repair and environmental protection.[64]

Moreover, there was criticism that the provisions of the revenue sharing legislation barring discrimination against minorities were inadequately enforced.[65] A spokesman for a major organization of blacks summarized this view of the matter by saying that "few" State or local governments "have used the federal revenue-sharing money for the benefit of the poor"; if revenue-sharing "doesn't benefit the people who need it most," the money ought to be "used for federal aid aimed at specific social problems." [66]

Growth of Grants-in-Aid, Including Revenue Sharing (1972–1986). The first revenue sharing act enacted in 1972 provided for the distribution of about $6 billion a year by 1975 to State and local governments (about 14 percent of the then Federal expenditures).[67] By 1986, when the general revenue sharing program was repealed during the Reagan Administration, it had already fallen to an annual figure of $4.4 billion.[68]

The overall grant-in-aid programs—categorical and block grants and revenue sharing—had grown rapidly and continued to grow even after the introduction of revenue sharing. Not surprisingly, under the Reagan Administration, block grants grew from 11 percent of total

62. 15 U.S.C. § 1242, as amended by State and Local Financial Assistance Amendments of 1976, Pub.L. No. 94–488, § 8, 90 Stat. 2341. In United States v. City of Chicago, 395 F.Supp. 329 (N.D.Ill.1975), a federal judge enjoined payment of revenue sharing funds to the City of Chicago because of discrimination in hiring in the police department. Cf. Lau v. Nichols, 414 U.S. 563, 569, 94 S.Ct. 786 (1974) (sustaining § 601 of the Civil Rights Act of 1964, 42 U.S.C. § 2000d (1970), which forbids discrimination by a program or activity receiving Federal financial assistance).

63. 31 U.S.C. § 1243(a)(6) (Supp. II 1972).

64. N.Y. Times, March 8, 1976. The reference is to a study by the Tax Foundation.

65. See Wall Street Journal, March 15, 1976.

66. See Wall Street Journal, March 27, 1975. Statement by Vernon Jordan, Executive Director of the National Urban League.

67. Office of Management & Budget, Special Analyses: Budget of the United States Government, Fiscal Year 1987, Section H, p. H–23 (1986) [hereinafter cited as Special Analyses 1987].

68. Id.

Federal aid in 1980 to more than 13 percent of such aid in 1986.[69] Federal grants-in-aid of various types to State and local governments had burgeoned from $10.4 billion in 1964 (1.6 percent of GNP and 19.5 percent of Federal domestic expenditure) to $43 billion in 1974 (3.1 percent of GNP and 22.3 percent of Federal domestic expenditure)[70] to $105 billion in 1985.[71]

Reduction in Federal Grants-in-Aid and the Abandonment of General Revenue Sharing During the Reagan Administration. The ascendancy of Ronald Reagan to the White House witnessed a radical alteration and sharp reduction in the grants-in-aid program. Reaganist political philosophy shifted the focus of the programs from the earlier search for the most desirable and efficacious methods of distributing Federal funds to State and local governments to the replacement or elimination of grant-in-aid programs altogether. The impact of the reductions was felt throughout the grant-in-programs, not sparing even such high priority programs as Medicaid and mass transit.[72] While the rhetoric of the new administration emphasized the Reaganists' objective as being the "creation of a fiscal environment that forces State and local officials to become more self-reliant",[73] the translation of that objective into fiscal terms meant that "Federal aid as a percentage of total state-local outlays * * * dropped from 25% in 1981 to an estimated 19% for FY 1987."[74]

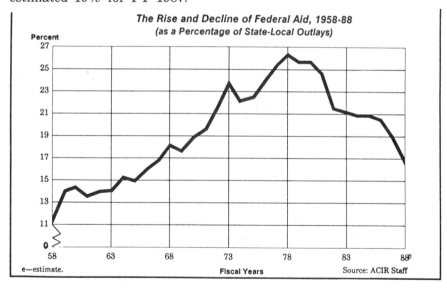

The Rise and Decline of Federal Aid, 1958-88
(as a Percentage of State-Local Outlays)

e—estimate.   Fiscal Years   Source: ACIR Staff

[E5032]

Source: Shannon, note 73 supra.

69. Id.

70. Dam, note * supra, at 305.

71. Special Analyses 1987, note 67 supra, at H–22.

72. Id. at H–2.

73. Shannon, "The Return to Fend-for-Yourself Federalism: The Reagan Mark," 13 Intergovernmental Perspective 34, 36 (Summer/Fall 1987).

74. Id.

SECTION 9. BIBLIOGRAPHICAL NOTE

Most students of the law of taxation have a nodding acquaintance with the Tax Law Review, Taxes—The Tax Magazine, The Journal of Taxation, and Tax Notes which publish some papers dealing with State and local taxes. There are also the Multistate Tax Commission Review, published by the Multistate Tax Commission, and the Tax Lawyer, published by the Section of the Taxation of the American Bar Association, which contains useful materials in the field. The Tax Lawyer publishes an annual survey of recent Supreme Court decisions in State and local taxation, and from time to time substantial, scholarly papers on particular topics in the area. In recent years, there has been an outcropping of new publications in the field, in view of the greatly increased interest of lawyers in State taxation. These include the Journal of State Taxation, which is largely expository and weak on critical analysis, the Multistate Tax Analyst and the Interstate Tax Report, both of which generally publish quickie, brief summaries of recent cases and legislation, and are short on critical analysis. There is a real need for a scholarly periodical publishing extensive studies of top-notch law review quality with respect to State taxation and local non-property taxation.

Few students, however, appear to be aware of the highly useful materials available in the publications of economists, tax administrators and others. The National Tax Journal (formerly the Bulletin of the National Tax Association) and the annual Proceedings of the National Tax Association are probably the most useful distinctly "non-legal" publications for the lawyer. The extensive studies made by the State tax and legislative commissions, research reports prepared in the universities, and the publications and proceedings of organizations, such as the National Association of Tax Administrators, the National Association of Assessing Officers, the Municipal Finance Officers Association, the National Industrial Conference Board, and others interested in public finance, are useful in providing history, data, and analyses in many branches of the field. Periodic compilations of fiscal statistical data of States, cities and other local governments are published by the Governments Division, Bureau of the Census, United States Department of Commerce.

Lawyers can often broaden their knowledge of State and local taxation, and otherwise profit from the studies of economists in this field. Economists have long devoted serious study to State and local taxation. The contributions of Professor Seligman in this field have made his Essays in Taxation (10th ed. 1931) and The Income Tax (2d ed. 1914) classics. Lawyers have suffered in their understanding of the field because of insufficient contact with the economics and history of State and local levies. The law student who has not had a good course in public finance will profit from a reading of a first rate college text in that field. Among the leading standard texts are R. Musgrave & P. Musgrave, Public Finance in Theory and Practice (4th ed. 1984); J.

Buchanan & M. Flowers, The Public Finances (1975); B. Herber, Modern Public Finance (1975). See also R. Musgrave & C. Shoup, Readings in the Economics of Taxation (1959); J. Pechman, Federal Tax Policy (1966); J. Maxwell & J. Aronson, Financing State and Local Governments (3d ed. 1977).

Chapter 2

PRELIMINARY MATERIALS

SECTION 1. BASIC ELEMENTS IN THE ANALYSIS OF TAXES

In the approach to problems in State and local taxation, three basic elements of each levy should be analyzed.

(1) What is the nature of the tax, i.e., how is the tax to be classified?

(2) What is the subject of the tax?

(3) What is the measure of the tax?

An income tax may be invalid under a State's constitutional provision requiring uniformity of taxation if it is classified as a property tax, whereas it may be sustained if it is deemed to be an excise tax. Likewise, a State tax on the sale of goods across State lines may violate the Interstate Commerce Clause of the Federal Constitution because the subject of the tax is the interstate sale, whereas a tax measured by the same gross receipts will be upheld if the subject of the tax is the local use of such goods. A State property or capital stock tax levied on securities issued by an instrumentality of the Federal Government may infringe on Federal immunity from State taxation, because the subject of the tax is Federal securities, whereas a State estate tax measured by the value of the same securities will be upheld, because the subject of the tax is the privilege of transmitting property at death.

Although the courts often have attributed far greater importance to the classification of taxes and to the distinction between subject and measure than many commentators feel is warranted by the differences (which often are formal and without substantial economic significance), nevertheless, the opinions in this field abound with lines drawn by reference to classification, subject, and measure. As will be seen later in the course, the mechanical statutory "subject-measure" ritual in which the taxing statute is cast has, at times, been crucial in determining the constitutionality of the tax.

It is important, therefore, that at the outset of the course the student should develop the habit, in reading each case, of analyzing the three basic elements of the tax—its classification, subject, and measure.

There are two other elements of taxes which should be noted for purposes of completing the analysis—rate of tax and the taxpayer. In some situations these elements of the tax present interesting problems (see Chapter 10, dealing with sales and use taxes), but by and large no great difficulty is presented by these features of levies.

A. *The Classification of Taxes.* The classification of taxes, like most classifications, depends largely on the purposes of the classifier. See, e.g., the classifications in Encyclopedia Britannica, "Taxation." Thus, under the Federal Constitution, direct taxes are generally required to be apportioned in accordance with the population, whereas indirect taxes need not be apportioned. Art. I, § 9, Cl. 4. Hence, the classification of taxes as "direct" and "indirect" has been developed in the Federal tax cases. See Pollock v. Farmers' Loan & Trust Co., 157 U.S. 429, 15 S.Ct. 673 (1895). A typical judicial statement of the direct and indirect tax classification of taxes is set forth in Foster & Creighton Co. v. Graham, 154 Tenn. 412, 285 S.W. 570 (1926):

> A direct tax is one that is imposed directly on property according to its value. It is generally spoken of as a property tax, or an ad valorem tax. An indirect tax is a tax upon some right or privilege, and it is also called an excise or occupation tax.

See Bullock, "The Origin, Purpose and Effect of the Direct Tax Clause in the Constitution," 15 Pol.Sci.Q. 217, 452 (1900). The classification of taxes as "direct" and "indirect" is, generally speaking, not significant for State and local tax purposes.[1]

John Stuart Mill, looking to the problems of incidence and the shifting of tax burdens, classified taxes as follows:

> Taxes are either direct or indirect. A direct tax is one which is demanded from the very persons who it is intended or desired should pay it. Indirect taxes are those which are demanded from one person in the expectation and intention that he shall indemnify himself at the expense of another; such as the excise or customs. [Principles of Political Economy 823 (Ashley, ed., 1936).]

In Judge Cooley's classic treatise on taxation, taxes are classified as (1) capitation or poll taxes, (2) taxes on property, and (3) excise taxes. T. Cooley, The Law of Taxation § 38 (4th ed. 1924). An alternative classification is made by categorizing taxes as (1) specific, or (2) ad valorem. Id.[2]

The classification which appears to be most useful in State and local taxation, in the light of the issues which arise, is the following:

1. Property taxes.

---

1. However there is an important area of State taxation in which the distinction between "direct" and "indirect" taxes was historically significant, namely, in the Commerce Clause restrictions on State taxation. See Chapter 6 infra. The issues there arising relate to the directness or indirectness of the taxation of interstate commerce.

2. For a more detailed statement of the classification of taxes for various purposes, see, N. Jacoby, Retail Sales Taxation 3 et seq. (1938).

2. Excise taxes.

3. Income taxes.

4. Capitation or poll taxes.

Capitation or poll taxes are levies of a fixed amount on all persons, or a selected group of persons, within the taxing area. They are imposed without reference to property, income or activities. 51 Am. Jur. § 38.

Property taxes may be regarded as levies on the entire bundle of rights of ownership, as distinguished from a levy on the exercise of a special power of ownership, such as, e.g., sale or transfer or gift. Property taxes are typically levied on all or selected property in accordance with its value on a stated day—tax day.

Excise taxes are levies on an activity or event, or the exercise of a specific right in property, or on a privilege granted. Thus, a tax on a gift or sale, or a tax on bequeathing or inheriting property at death, or a tax on doing business—these are all excise taxes. Likewise, a tax on the privilege granted by a State to carry on business within its borders, or to exist as a domestic corporation is an excise tax.

Judge Cooley defined excises in an oft quoted definition as "taxes levied upon the manufacture, sale, or consumption of commodities within the country, upon licenses to pursue certain occupations, and upon corporate privileges." 2 T. Cooley, Constitutional Limitations § 988 (8th ed. 1927). This definition was given in the context of the term "excises," as used in the Federal constitutional grant of power to Congress to levy taxes. In his work on taxation, Cooley adopted a broader use of the term: "An excise tax, using the term in its broad meaning as opposed to a property tax, includes taxes sometimes designated by statute or referred to as privilege taxes, license taxes, occupation taxes and business taxes." T. Cooley, The Law of Taxation § 45 (4th ed. 1924).

Income taxes and other levies have presented troublesome classification problems, as the cases set out in Chapter 3 show, under State uniformity and equality constitutional provisions.[3] The income tax, whether gross income, gross receipts, or net income, appears to deserve its own separate classification. The economic differences between a tax levied on wealth or property as of a particular day and the net income from property or labor during a stated period of one year appear to warrant the separate classification of the income tax.

For cases turning on the proper classification of a tax, see Johnson v. City and County of Denver, 186 Colo. 398, 527 P.2d 883 (1974), in which the Denver Employee Occupational Privilege Tax (known as the "head tax") was invalidated, as applied to employees of the United States Air Force Finance Center located on a Federal enclave in

---

3. For other illustrations of the importance of the classification of a tax see the cases in Chapter 6 infra arising under the Commerce Clause and the cases in Chapter 15 infra dealing with the immunity of Federal instrumentalities from State taxation.

Denver, on the ground that the tax was not a sales, use, or income tax. Those are the only levies permitted by the Buck Act to be imposed on persons working on Federal property. In Schwinden v. Burlington Northern, Inc., ___ Mont. ___, 691 P.2d 1351 (1984), it was held that interest income from United States Treasury notes is includible in the measure of the Montana corporate levy, because the tax was properly classified as a franchise tax, not a direct income tax. See also Reuben L. Anderson–Cherne, Inc. v. Commissioner, 303 Minn. 124, 226 N.W.2d 611 (1975), appeal dismissed 423 U.S. 886, 96 S.Ct. 181 (1975). The question of classification has also arisen in connection with provisions that do not permit taxpayers to deduct "income" taxes from the State corporate income tax base. Thus in King v. Procter & Gamble Distributing Co., 671 S.W.2d 784 (Mo.1984), the court held that franchise taxes measured by net income did not constitute income taxes and were therefore deductible from Missouri's income tax base. The New Jersey Supreme Court has ruled, on the other hand, that the Federal Windfall Profit tax constitutes a tax "measured by profits or income" under New Jersey law and is therefore not deductible from the State income tax base. Amerada Hess Corp. v. Director, Division of Taxation, 107 N.J. 307, 526 A.2d 1029 (1987).

B. *The Distinction Between the Subject and the Measure of a Tax.* A workable definition of the *subject* of a tax is (1) the property taxed in the case of a property tax; (2) the activity, event, privilege, or specific property right taxed in the case of an excise tax; and (3) the income received or accrued in the case of an income tax.

The *measure* of a tax is the yardstick or base to which the tax rate is applied.

Thus, in the typical real property tax the subject of the tax is the real property. The measure is the value of the property; and the basic rate in Athens, Georgia, for example, for 1987 was $58.60 per $1,000 of the assessed value. In sales taxes, which are excise taxes, the subject of the tax is the making of a sale. The measure usually is the sales price of the goods; and the rate, often three percent to five percent, is applied to the sales price. With income taxes, whether net income or gross income, the subject of the tax and the measure of the tax are the same, or very close to being the same. Thus, the receipt or accrual of $10,000 of net or gross income is the subject of the tax. The same net income (reduced for personal exemptions and allowances for dependents) is the measure of the tax to which the rate is applied.

Measures of taxes vary widely. The following is a list of the more prevalent measures of taxes in use in this country:

(1) *The Value of Property:*

Property taxes

Death taxes (estate and inheritance)

Capital stock taxes

(2) *Income or Receipts:*

Gross receipts taxes

Gross income taxes

Net income taxes

(3) *Selling Price:*

Sales and use taxes

(4) *Fixed or Flat Sums:*

Four or five cents a package on cigarettes, six cents per gallon of gasoline, etc.

License taxes

Stock issue and transfer taxes

(5) *Miscellaneous Measures:*

Weight of car in auto license tax

Face amount of bond in bond issue tax

Amount of authorized capital in corporate organization tax

C. The importance of the analysis of a tax according to its three basic elements—its classification, subject, and measure—is demonstrated in a case decided by the Court of Appeals of New York. New York City's commercial rent or occupancy tax, levied on tenants renting commercial property and computed by a percentage of rent paid, was challenged by a tenant. The court first held that this was not a real property tax, which it was asserted violated the State constitutional limitations on real property taxes. The court held that the tax was imposed neither on real estate nor owners but on lessees of real estate, measured by the base rent paid. In New York a leasehold for years is deemed personalty, not real estate. The court also held that the tax was not an ad valorem tax on "intangible" property, which is prohibited by the New York Constitution. Ad valorem taxes are imposed on property according to its value, and are payable whether or not the property is used; moreover, a leasehold is not "intangible" personal property but is regarded in New York as tangible property. Ampco Printing–Advertisers' Offset Corp. v. City of New York, 14 N.Y.2d 11, 247 N.Y.S.2d 865, 197 N.E.2d 285 (1964). The Supreme Court of the United States, however, rejected the New York Court of Appeals' classification for purposes of a Federal statute that excepted taxes on tangible personal property from a prohibition on State taxation of national banks: "Whether the tax at issue is a tax on tangible personal property within the meaning of [the Federal statute] is a question of federal law; and for the purposes of that statute, it appears to us that Congress did not consider real estate occupancy taxes to be taxes on personal property." Chase Manhattan Bank, N.A. v. Finance Administration, 440 U.S. 447, 449, 99 S.Ct. 1201 (1979).

ASSIGNMENT

Analyze the following types of taxes, setting forth as to each levy: (1) the nature of the tax, (2) the subject, (3) the measure, (4) the type of rate normally employed, and (5) the taxpayer.

Property	Use	Employment
Franchise	Storage and withdrawal	Stock issue
Capital stock	Estate	Stock transfer
Net income	Inheritance	Severance
Gross receipts	Gift	Motor vehicle
Excess profits	Poll	Mortgage recording
Sales	Capitation	Admissions

In working out the assignment consult the statutes and regulations of your State and localities for the details of these levies, to the extent that they are imposed in your jurisdiction.

SECTION 2. PURPOSES OF TAXATION

There is a body of State cases holding that the taxing power may not be exercised for private purposes; it may be exercised solely to serve public purposes. Thus, in Opinion of the Justices to the Senate and the House of Representatives, 341 Mass. 738, 167 N.E.2d 745 (1960), the court rendered an advisory opinion on the validity of proposed legislation authorizing the Massachusetts Turnpike Authority to construct a truck terminal and public garage in Boston. This was part of an urban redevelopment plan in which Prudential Insurance Company undertook to rehabilitate a blighted area of the city. The legislation provided tax exemption for the properties to be built. Although the court recognized that the redevelopment of a blighted part of Boston did constitute a public purpose, it ruled that the private aspects of the legislation were predominant, and that the provisions for protecting the public interest were inadequate, and accordingly, it held that the proposed legislation was unconstitutional.[4]

Notes and Problems

A. *The Constitutional Basis for Restricting Taxing Power to Raising Revenue for Public Purposes.* The restriction of the taxing powers of the States to the raising of revenues for public purposes has at times been rested on the Due Process Clause. In some States, however, there are specific constitutional provisions limiting taxation to public purposes. Union Ice & Coal Co. v. Ruston, 135 La. 898, 66 So. 262 (1914). In other States, it has been held that the exercise of the taxing power for private purposes collides with the eminent domain provisions. Opinion of the Justices (Re Municipal Fuel Plants), 182 Mass. 605, 66 N.E. 25 (1903). Still others have regarded the imposition of levies for non-public purposes as an

---

4. Following the decision in this case, the Massachusetts legislature amended the statute so as to meet the court's objections. In a subsequent advisory opinion the stat- ute was upheld. Opinion of the Justices, 341 Mass. 760, 168 N.E.2d 858 (1960); compare Wayland v. Snapp, 232 Ark. 57, 334 S.W.2d 633 (1960).

inherent limitation on the taxing power. Beach v. Bradstreet, 85 Conn. 344, 82 A. 1030 (1912).

B. *Furnishing of Utilities as a Public Purpose.* Jones v. City of Portland, 245 U.S. 217, 38 S.Ct. 112 (1917), was one of the milestones in the judicial broadening of the conception of acceptable public purpose. The Supreme Court of Maine had upheld the power of the City of Portland to raise taxes in order to maintain a municipal fuel yard, at which coal, wood, and other fuel would be sold to local inhabitants at cost. Laughlin v. City of Portland, 111 Me. 486, 90 A. 318 (1914). The State court regarded the venture not as embarking on a commercial enterprise for profit but instead as a venture designed "to enable the citizens to be supplied with something which is a necessity in its absolute sense to the enjoyment of life and health, which would otherwise be obtained with great difficulty and at times perhaps not at all and whose absence would endanger the community as a whole." 111 Me. at 500, 90 A. at 324. The Supreme Court of the United States refused to disturb this holding as a violation of the Fourteenth Amendment.

The States or municipalities may levy taxes to acquire or operate public utilities. Petition of Board of Directors of Tillamook People's Utility District, 160 Or. 530, 86 P.2d 460 (1939); Jones v. City of Portland, supra. However, in Opinion of the Justices, 88 N.H. 484, 190 A. 425 (1937), the court, relying on a constitutional provision that government is "instituted for the common benefit * * * of the whole community, and not for the private interest or emolument of any one man, family or class of men" (Const., Pt. I, Art. 10), invalidated a bounty to aid the development of a utility company because the court concluded that existing power facilities were adequate for the State's own needs.

C. *State Bank, Grain Elevator, and Housing Aid.* In Green v. Frazier, 253 U.S. 233, 40 S.Ct. 499 (1920), a taxpayer's suit was brought to enjoin the enforcement of a North Dakota statute which authorized the creation of a State bank and grain elevator and a building and loan association to provide funds to residents for private housing. The State court had held that public purposes were being served; that private marketing of grain in this predominantly agricultural State prevented farmers from realizing just prices on their crops and that the grain elevator and banking facilities were required to carry out these purposes; and that the provision of homes for the people would promote the general welfare of the State. The Supreme Court refused to disturb this judgment of the State court that the public purpose would be served by the legislation.

D. *Unemployment Relief.* Because the expenditure of public funds for unemployment relief is a public purpose, a State unemployment compensation act was upheld against attack as a use of the taxing power for private purposes. Carmichael v. Southern Coal & Coke Co., 301 U.S. 495, 57 S.Ct. 868 (1937). The constitutionality of the Pennsylvania Unemployment Compensation Law was assailed, *inter alia,* on the ground that raising and appropriating revenues for unemployment compensation violated the provision of the State constitution that "no appropriations, except for pensions or gratuities for military services, shall be made for charitable, educational, or benevolent purposes to any person or community." Commonwealth v.

Perkins, 342 Pa. 529, 21 A.2d 45 (1941), affirmed 314 U.S. 586, 62 S.Ct. 484 (1942). The Court held that the use of State funds to deal with unemployment is not a "charitable" or "benevolent" expenditure but instead the performance of a proper function of the State. It quoted the concurring opinion of Justice Maxey in Commonwealth v. Liveright, 308 Pa. 35, 90, 161 A. 697 (1932), as follows:

> I hold that an appropriation of state money to combat widespread poverty arising from unemployment, can no more justly be characterized as "charity" [or] "benevolence" than could an appropriation of state money with which to combat a plague sweeping over Pennsylvania.

E. *Tax Exemption to Attract Manufacturers.* The granting of property tax exemption for a limited period as an incentive for a manufacturer to locate its plant in the county has been held in some cases to constitute a proper local governmental purpose. State ex rel. Tomasic v. Kansas City, 237 Kan. 572, 701 P.2d 1314 (1985); Byrd v. Lawrimore, 212 S.C. 281, 47 S.E.2d 728 (1948); Duke Power Co. v. Bell, 156 S.C. 299, 152 S.E. 865 (1930).

In Citizen's Sav. & Loan Association v. Topeka, 87 U.S. (20 Wall.) 655 (1874), on the other hand, the Court held that a municipality could not issue bonds payable out of taxes in order to give a bounty to a manufacturer to encourage its location in the city. It said:

> It is undoubtedly the duty of the legislature which imposes or authorizes municipalities to impose a tax to see that it is not to be used for purposes of private interest instead of a public use, and the courts can only be justified in interposing when a violation of this principle is clear and the reason for the interference cogent. And in deciding whether in the given case, the object for which the taxes are assessed falls upon the one side or the other of this line, they must be governed mainly by the course and usage of the government, the objects for which taxes have been customarily and by long course of legislation levied, what objects or purposes have been considered necessary to the support and for the proper use of the government, whether State or municipal. [87 U.S. at 664–65.]

Other cases have held that a public bounty or transfer of property in return for an agreement to establish an industrial enterprise in the locality is an invalid gift and is not for a public purpose. Clee v. Sanders, 74 Mich. 692, 42 N.W. 154 (1899); Village of Suring v. Suring State Bank, 189 Wis. 400, 207 N.W. 944 (1926).

Tax exemption as a means of promoting industrial activity has been utilized at least since the eighteenth century in this country. These exemptions have generally been sustained as satisfying the public purpose requirement even where not specifically authorized by constitutional provisions. Note, "Legal Limitations on Public Inducements to Industrial Location," 59 Colum.L.Rev. 618 (1959). In the valuable discussion of this problem in the note cited, the apparent anomaly between the bounty and tax exemption cases is explained on two grounds. First, the power to grant exemptions is implicit in the grant of the taxing power; second, because the public purpose limitations were developed primarily to prevent the creation of public financial liability for the benefit of private industry, they are more properly applicable to an outlay of funds in the form of a gift than to tax exemption. See also Note, "Municipal Inducements to Private Industry," 40 Minn.L.Rev. 681 (1956); Gray, "Industrial Development Subsidies and Efficiency in Resource Allocation," 17 Nat.Tax J. 164 (1964); Gray, "Economic View of Municipal Subsidies to Industry," 36 Munic.Finance 153 (1964).

We have seen a growing wave of tax incentives designed to attract business to one State rather than another, and to the suburbs instead of a central city—marked by the burgeoning of industrial parks with the use of State borrowed funds, the lending of State credit at low rates of interest to finance the construction of industrial facilities, and an accelerating offering of tax exemptions and concessions. Becker, "Urban Development and Federal Grants," 1965 Nat.Tax Ass'n Procs. 112, 121; Committee for Economic Development, A Fiscal Program for a Balanced Federalism 44 (1967). The report last cited concludes that the "competition for industrial firms is so intense between municipalities that they tend to provide industrial services below cost and require little, if any, compensation from industry for social costs." Id. By 1967, issues by the States of industrial aid bonds reached the $1 billion mark leading Congress in 1968 to impose restrictions on the size of the issues, unless the proceeds of the bonds were used for specified exempt activities. I.R.C. § 103(c). Despite these limitations, "small issue" sales of industrial revenue bonds increased from $1.3 billion in 1975 to $8.4 billion in 1980, and were employed by 48 of the 50 States. Recent Trends in the Use of Tax-Exempt Bonds for Private Purposes, Hearings on the Administration's Fiscal Year 1983 Budget Proposal Before the Senate Comm. on Finance, 97th Cong., 2d Sess., pt. 3 at 65 (1982). In 1984 and 1986, Congress imposed substantial additional limitations on the use of tax-exempt financing for private purposes. I.R.C. §§ 141–50. These limitations are described in Chapter 15, § 3 infra.

The revenue lost by the States through tax exemptions tends to be financed by taxes that are unobjectionable to businesses. And as a result of this interstate tax competition, virtually every piece of tax legislation offered is watered down by the rates and exclusions from the tax base in other States. The result is, as one leading student of the area, Dr. George F. Break, has stated:

> Active tax competition, in short, tends to produce either a generally low level of tax effort or State local tax structures with strong regressive features. Paradoxically, the more widespread it is, the more likely it is to produce these debilitating fiscal effects without creating the stimulating economic effects sought by the tax competitors. [Intergovernmental Fiscal Relations in the United States 121 (Brookings Inst. 1967).]

See Jackson, "Interlocal Tax Conflicts," 39 Munic.Finance 12 (1966).

A report prepared by a New York tax study commission concludes, after a review of over 30 years of research and after conducting computer simulations, that State business tax incentives generally play an insignificant role in business location. New York Legislative Commission on the Modernization and Simplification of Tax Administration and the Tax Law, "Interstate Business Locational Decisions and the Effect of the State's Tax

Structure on After–Tax Rate of Return of Manufacturing Firms" (Preliminary Report, 1984). The report points out that innumerable factors such as site availability, access to transportation, the quality of labor, proximity to markets and supplies, access to utilities, the regulatory environment, the quality of education, the availability of housing, and the State's ambience are important to business location decisions and may easily swamp interstate differences in State taxes. The report recommends the de-emphasis of tax incentives as a tool for attracting business. See also Pomp, "A New York Perspective on Tax Incentives: The Role of State Tax Incentives in Attracting and Retaining Business," 1985 Multistate Tax Comm.Rev. 1.

F. *Soldiers' Bonuses.* A striking illustration of the fluid character of the conception of public purpose is to be found in a series of Connecticut cases dealing with soldiers' bonuses. In Beach v. Bradstreet, 85 Conn. 344, 82 A. 1030 (1912), the court enjoined enforcement of an act providing for a bonus of $30 a year for soldiers and sailors of the Civil War, or their dependents, who resided in Connecticut. The legislation included residents of Connecticut who volunteered or were drafted while residing in other States; but it excluded veterans who filled the Connecticut quotas, as draftees or volunteers, but who no longer resided in that State. The court held that the grant of a bounty to a veteran who was not a resident of Connecticut when he enlisted or was drafted served no Connecticut public purpose and therefore was beyond the State's taxing power. Because the court regarded the grant to Connecticut's own veterans as inseparable from the grant to veterans of other States, then residing in Connecticut, the entire act was invalidated.

In Lyman v. Adorno, 133 Conn. 511, 52 A.2d 702 (1947), the court sustained a soldiers' bonus granted to veterans of World War II who had been domiciled in the State for at least one year.

In Walsh v. Jenks, 135 Conn. 210, 62 A.2d 773 (1948), the court upheld an exemption from property taxes of $1,000 in property owned by veterans of any United States war, as applied to persons who did not serve as part of the Connecticut quota, since they were not residents of the State at the time of draft or enlistment. After discussing the *Beach* case, supra, the court said:

> * * * No reasonable person, considering the recent history of this country can doubt that the principle there enunciated expresses too narrow a view of the services rendered to promote the welfare of this state by persons in the armed forces of the United States who became a part of them when residents of other states, or in fulfillment of quotas assigned to those states. [135 Conn. at 219, 220, 67 A.2d at 778, 779 (1948).]

G. *Benefit to Taxpayer From Utilization of Levy.* Despite a State constitutional provision that "government is instituted for their equal protection and benefit," it does not follow that a tax may be assailed on the ground that the taxpayer derives no benefit from a particular levy. In Capitol Novelty Co. v. Evatt, 145 Ohio St. 205, 61 N.E.2d 211 (1945), certiorari denied 326 U.S. 738, 66 S.Ct. 48 (1945), the owner of slot machines attacked a personal property tax on the machines on the ground that, since his ownership or use of these gambling devices was illegal, he got no benefit from a tax on the machines. In rejecting the contention, the court quoted from Carmichael v. Southern Coal & Coke Co., supra, as follows:

> A tax is not an assessment of benefits. It is, as we have said, a means of distributing the burden of the cost of government. The only benefit to which the taxpayer is constitutionally entitled is that derived from his enjoyment of the privileges of living in an organized society established and safeguarded by the devotion of taxes to public purposes. * * * A corporation cannot object to the use of the taxes which it pays for the maintenance of schools because it has no children. Thomas v. Gay, 169 U.S. 264, 18 S.Ct. 340, 42 L.Ed. 740. This Court has repudiated the suggestion, wherever made, that the Constitution requires the benefits derived from the expenditure of public moneys to be apportioned to the burdens of the taxpayer or that he can resist the payment of the tax because it is not expended for purposes which are peculiarly beneficial to him. [301 U.S. 495 at 522, 57 S.Ct. 868 at 878 (1937).]

In Nashville, C. & St. L. Ry. v. Wallace, 288 U.S. 249, 53 S.Ct. 345 (1933), the Court sustained a storage tax on the taxpaying railroad over the objection that it was repugnant to the Fourteenth Amendment because the tax was levied for the use of highways which the taxpayer did not use. In rejecting the contention, the Court declared that "constitutional power to levy taxes does not depend upon the enjoyment by the taxpayer of any special benefit from the use of the funds raised by taxation." 288 U.S. at 267, 53 S.Ct. at 350.

H. *Tax Purpose and Regulation.* Is a tax enacted in order to regulate or prohibit a business a valid exercise of the taxing power? In Magnano Co. v. Hamilton, 292 U.S. 40, 54 S.Ct. 599 (1934), a State of Washington excise tax of 15 cents a pound on butter substitutes was assailed by a vendor of oleomargarine. In sustaining the tax, the Court disposed of the taxpayer's contention that "the tax is not levied for a public purpose, but for the sole purpose, of burdening or prohibiting the manufacture, importation and sale of oleomargarine, in aid of the dairy industry" (292 U.S. at 42) by saying:

> That the tax is for a public purpose is equally clear, since that requirement has regard to the use which is to be made of the revenue derived from the tax, and not to any ulterior motive or purpose which may have influenced the legislature in passing the act. And a tax designed to be expended for a public purpose does not cease to be one levied for a public purpose because it has the effect of imposing a burden on one class of business enterprise in such a way as to benefit another class. [Id. at 43.]

More recently the Court, quoting the *Magnano* case, had occasion to observe: "The premise that a tax is invalid if so excessive as to bring about the destruction of a particular business * * * [has] been 'uniformly rejected as furnishing no juridical ground for striking down a taxing act.'" City of Pittsburgh v. Alco Parking Co., 417 U.S. 369, 374, 94 S.Ct. 2291 (1974).

Compare United States v. Butler, 297 U.S. 1, 56 S.Ct. 312 (1936), in which the processing taxes levied *by Congress* under the Agricultural Adjustment Act of 1933 were held invalid as a regulation of agricultural production and hence an infringement of State power. Justices Stone, Brandeis, and Cardozo dissented. The case was the subject of extensive discussion in the law reviews. See Hart, "Processing Taxes and Protective Tariffs," 49 Harv.L.Rev. 610 (1936); Holmes, "The Federal Spending Power and State Rights," 34 Mich.L.Rev. 637 (1936).

I. *References.* There is an excellent discussion of the tax purpose problem in McAllister, "Public Purpose in Taxation," 18 Calif.L.Rev. 137, 241 (1929); see also Kneier, "Municipal Functions and the Law of Public Purpose," 76 U.Pa.L.Rev. 824 (1928); Note, 41 Harv.L.Rev. 755 (1928); 51 Am.Jur. § 321 et seq.; Note, "Financing Industrial Development in the South," 14 Vand.L.Rev. 621 (1961); Floyd, "State and Local Financing for Industrial Development," 1963 Nat. Tax Ass'n Procs. 187; Tilden, "Public Inducements for Industrial Locations: Lesson from Massachusetts," 18 Maine L.Rev. 1 (1966).

THE CANONS OF TAXATION

Adam Smith's canons of taxation, published in his Wealth of Nations in 1776, are the classic statement of the goals of taxation:

> The tax which each individual is bound to pay, ought to be certain, and not arbitrary. The time of payment, the manner of payment, the quantity to be paid, ought all to be clear and plain to the contributor, and to every other person. * * *

> Every tax ought to be levied at the time, or in the manner, in which it is most likely to be convenient for the contributor to pay it. * * *

> Every tax ought to be so contrived as both to take out and to keep out of the pockets of the people as little as possible, over and above what it brings into the public treasury * * * though vexation is not, strictly speaking, expence, it is certainly equivalent to the expence at which every man would be willing to redeem himself from it.

See "The Goals of Taxation," 16 Tax Policy (Jan. 1949).

SECTION 3. NOTE ON STATUTORY CONSTRUCTION

Perhaps the most striking development in the law in recent times has been the tremendous growth of statutory law. The field of State and local taxation is a branch of statutory and constitutional law. Inevitably, a large part of the task of lawyers and judges dealing with problems in this field is that of interpreting taxing statutes. The importance of statutory interpretation is reflected in John Chipman Gray's quotation from a sermon by Bishop Hoadly that "Whoever hath an *absolute authority to interpret* any written or spoken laws, it is *he* who is truly the Lawgiver to all intents and purposes, and not the person who first wrote or spoke them." J. Gray, Nature and Sources of the Law 102 (2d ed. 1921).

Lord Coke's classic formulation of the rules of statutory construction remains one of the gems in the literature of the field. Lord Coke held that four factors must be considered:

> 1st. What was the common law before the making of the act? 2nd. What was the mischief and defect for which the common law did not provide? 3rd. What remedy the parliament hath resolved and appointed to cure the disease of the commonwealth? And 4th. The true reason of the remedy. And then the office of all the judges is always to make such construction as shall suppress the mischief, advance the remedy, and to suppress subtle inventions and evasions for continuance of the mischief, and *pro privato commodo,* and to add force and life to the cure and remedy, according to the true intent of the makers of the act, *pro publico bono.* [Heydon's Case, 3 Co.Rep. 72, 76 Eng.Rep. 637 (1584).]

The modern literature in the field of statutory interpretation has elaborated upon Coke's insight, but does not add to his acute perception of the essential problem of statutory interpretation.

Justice Holmes' views as to the search for the open sesame of legislative intention were expressed in a letter written by him:

> Only a day or two ago—when counsel talked of the intention of a legislature, I was indiscreet enough to say I don't care what their intention was. I only want to know what the words mean. Of course the phrase is often used to express a conviction not exactly thought out—that you construe a particular clause or expression by considering the whole instrument and any dominant purpose that it may express. In fact, intention is a residuary clause intended to gather up whatever other aids there may be to interpretation beside the particular words and the dictionary. [See Frankfurter, "Some Reflections on the Reading of Statutes," 47 Colum.L.Rev. 527 (1947).]

Judge Learned Hand, whose wisdom has enriched most branches of jurisprudence, has said of statutory interpretation:

> * * * It does not follow that Congress meant to cover such a transaction, not even though the facts answer the dictionary definitions * * * the meaning may be more than that of the separate words as a melody is more than the notes, and no degree of particularity can ever obviate recourse to the setting in which all appear and which all collectively create. [Helvering v. Gregory, 69 F.2d 809, at 810, 811 (2d Cir.1934).]

> It is one of the surest indexes of a mature and developed jurisprudence not to make a fortress out of the dictionary, but to remember that statutes always have some purpose or object to accomplish whose sympathetic and imaginative discovery is the surest guide to their meaning. [Cabell v. Markham, 148 F.2d 737, at 739 (2d Cir.1945), affirmed 326 U.S. 404, 66 S.Ct. 193 (1945).]

The cases in State and local taxation abound with elaborate statements of canons of construction. The most frequently cited canon in the field is that taxing statutes must be construed most strongly against the taxing authority. Many courts elaborate by adding that if there are doubts or ambiguities, they must be resolved in favor of the taxpayer, or that if the statute is susceptible of more than one interpretation, the construction most favorable to the taxpayer must be given. This rule was stated early in American judicial history. See, e.g., Story, J., in United States v. Wigglesworth, Fed.Cas. No. 16,690, 2 Story 369 (C.C.Mass.1842); United States v. Isham, 84 U.S. (17 Wall.) 496 (1873). The reasons given for strict construction of taxing statutes suggest that the courts regarded taxation as a kind of confiscation; for the State to deprive a person of his property required the clearest kind of showing that the legislative act covered the taking. Thus, in the Wigglesworth case, Justice Story said:

> In the first place, it is as I conceive, a general rule in the interpretation of all Statutes levying taxes or duties upon subjects or citizens, not to extend their provisions, by implication beyond the clear import of the language used, or to enlarge their operation so as to embrace matters, not specifically pointed out, although standing upon a close analogy. In every case, therefore, of doubt, such Statutes are construed most strongly against the Government, and in favor of the subjects or citizens because burthens are not to be imposed, nor presumed to be imposed beyond what the Statutes expressly and clearly impart. Revenue Statutes are in no just sense either remedial laws, or laws founded upon any permanent public policy, and, therefore, are not to be liberally construed. [2 Story 369 at 371–374; Fed. Cas. No. 16,690 at 596, 597.]

When the issue arose as to whether a particular taxpayer or property was exempt from a tax, the opposite rule developed. Exemption provisions are most strongly construed against the person claiming an exemption. The claimant must clearly fall within the exemption, the argument being that the courts will not lightly grant special preferences.

Is the rule of strict construction of taxing statutes consonant with the modern American political economy? Is it a relic of nineteenth century hostility toward taxation which should not survive Justice Holmes' dictum that "taxes are what we pay for civilized society." Compañia General de Tabacos v. Collector, 275 U.S. 87, at 100, 48 S.Ct. 100 at 105 (1927), Holmes, J., dissenting.[5] Instead of the rule of strict

---

5. In F. Frankfurter, Mr. Justice Holmes and the Supreme Court 42 (1938), it is reported that a secretary to Justice Holmes, upon exclaiming "Don't you hate to pay taxes!" was met by Holmes' response, "No, young feller. I like to pay taxes; with them I buy civilization."

It is interesting to note that in the field of property taxation, which in the early development of this country was the major source of our revenues, the rule of strict construction appears to have little or no force. On the contrary, valuations of the assessing officers administering an ad valorem tax are highly respected. Indeed, in a number of States the valuation cannot be overturned without proof of "intentional or constructive fraud." (See Chapter 4 infra.) The valuation issue, of course, may be distinguished from other problems in the property tax field, e.g., the determination whether a taxpayer is exempt from tax, as to which the tax collector's determination is treated much more lightly; but it is significant that side by side with a rule of strict construction of taxing statutes,

construction, why shouldn't taxing statutes be sensibly construed in the light of all the relevant facts? And why shouldn't exemption issues be disposed of by a similar process, instead of with a sharp judicial eye out to deny exemption, if it is at all possible?

In "Remarks on the Theory of Appellate Decision and the Rules on Canons about How Statutes Are to Be Construed," 3 Vand.L.Rev. 395 (1950), and expanded in The Common Law Tradition: Deciding Appeals (1960), Professor Karl Llewellyn brought together a devastating collection of rules of construction. For his work shows that for virtually every rule of statutory construction, there is a counter and conflicting rule. Llewellyn held that:

> Plainly, to make any canon take hold in a particular instance, the construction contended for must be sold, essentially, by means other than the use of the canon: The good sense of the situation and a *simple* construction of available language to achieve that sense, *by tenable means, out of the statutory language.*

There has been a significant development in administrative law which has served to undermine the rule of strict construction. The rule has taken hold in administrative law that the determinations of an expert administrative body established by the legislature are to be given great weight in construing the statute. In the field of Federal taxation, while the rule that taxing statutes are to be construed strictly against the taxing authority is still sometimes stated (see 1 Mertens, Law of Federal Income Taxation § 3.05 [(1981)]), the Federal courts have increasingly, in recent years, placed emphasis on the doctrine that the determination by the Commissioner of Internal Revenue should prevail in the absence of a clear showing of error. And where the Commissioner has promulgated regulations which have remained in force for a substantial period, without disturbance by Congress, which has in the meantime reenacted the revenue acts, the regulations have often been held to have the force of law. See United States v. Correll, 389 U.S. 299, 88 S.Ct. 445 (1967); Brown, "Regulations, Reenactment and the Revenue Acts," 54 Harv.L.Rev. 376 (1941); Griswold, "A Summary of the Regulations Problem," 54 Harv.L.Rev. 398 (1941). See, however, on this issue and on the extent to which legislative committee reports and other extrinsic aids may be relied on in construing a statute, Commissioner v. Acker, 361 U.S. 87, 80 S.Ct. 144 (1959), commented on in Lyon, "1959 Survey of Federal Income Taxation," 35 N.Y.U.L.Rev. 697, 712–715 (1960). Some State courts now give at least lip service to this rule of administrative law in the field of taxation. Others disregard or repudiate it altogether as applied to taxes. Can the rule of strict construction of taxing statutes be squared with this development in administrative law?

there developed in many States a recognition of the need to leave the valuation job to the assessing officer and to disturb his findings only in a clear case of striking error.

A reading of cases in the field of State and local taxation reveals a bewildering welter of other canons of construction, often conflicting with each other, which are stated and restated by the courts at length. Some courts state the rules and then proceed to ignore them. Others painstakingly make their selection of an appropriate rule to follow. The canons and their exceptions and qualifications have become so numerous and so difficult to apply that the question may be properly asked whether the canons have not become worthless as judicial guides. Their principal virtue has been that they may constitute a distillation of judicial experience for the guidance of other justices. Query, however, whether the canons of construction have not become so serious an impediment to judicial statesmanship, imposing a kind of mental straight jacket on judges who might otherwise approach problems of construction with greater freedom to reach an overall result, as to require their being discarded altogether. Does the use of canons of interpretation assist in finding the legislative purpose or policy?

References. Frankfurter, "Some Reflections on the Reading of Statutes," 47 Colum.L.Rev. 527 (1947); Frank, "Words and Music: Some Remarks on Statutory Construction," 47 Colum.L.Rev. 1259 (1947); Cox, "Judge Learned Hand and the Interpretation of Statutes," 60 Harv.L.Rev. 370 (1947); Eisenstein, "Some Iconoclastic Reflections on Tax Administration," 58 Harv.L.Rev. 477 (1945); S. Thorne, A Discourse Upon the Exposition & Understanding of Statutes (1942); E. Crawford, Statutory Construction (1940); Radin, "Statutory Interpretation," 43 Harv.L.Rev. 863 (1930); Radin, "Realism in Statutory Interpretation," 23 Calif.L.Rev. 156 (1935). See also Page, "Statutes in Derogation of Common Law," 1956 Wisc.L.Rev. 78; Witherspoon, "Administrative Discretion to Determine Statutory Meaning," 35 Tex.L. Rev. 63 (1956); Note, "The Effect of the Statutory Construction Act in Pennsylvania," 12 U.Pitt.L.Rev. 283 (1951); Blum, "Knetsch v. United States: A Pronouncement on Tax Avoidance," 1961 Sup.Ct.Rev. 135; J. Hellerstein, "Judicial Approaches to Tax Avoidance," Procs. 1964 Conf., Canadian Tax Foundation 62.

*

Part 2

UNIFORMITY AND EQUALITY REQUIREMENTS OF STATE AND FEDERAL CONSTITUTIONS, AND THE PRIVILEGES AND IMMUNITIES PROTECTION FOR CITIZENS OF OTHER STATES

Chapter 3

UNIFORMITY AND EQUALITY REQUIREMENTS OF STATE AND FEDERAL CONSTITUTIONS; PRIVILEGES AND IMMUNITIES

A. STATE UNIFORMITY AND EQUALITY REQUIREMENTS

Almost all the State constitutions embody some provisions for uniform or equal taxes. The constitutions of Connecticut and New York, however, contain no guaranties of equality or uniformity. Typical uniformity provisions are the following:

> All taxes upon real and personal estate, assessed by authority of this State, shall be apportioned and assessed equally, according to the just value thereof. [Me. Const., Art. IX, § 8.]

> [A]ll taxation shall be uniform upon the same class of subjects within the territorial limits of the authority levying the tax. [Ga. Const., Art. VII, § 1.]

The rate of taxation or assessment is expressly required to be equal and uniform in some States:

> The General Assembly shall provide, by law, for a uniform and equal rate of property assessment and taxation and shall prescribe regulations to secure a just valuation for taxation of all property, both real and personal. [Ind. Const., Art. X, § 1.]

Other States have a similar requirement for the "rule of taxation."

> Property shall be assessed for taxation under general laws and by uniform rules. All real property assessed and taxed locally or by the State for allotment and payment to taxing districts shall be assessed according to the same standard of value except as otherwise permitted herein; and such real property shall be taxed at the general tax rate of the taxing district in which the property is situated for the use of such taxing district. [N.J. Const., Art. VIII, § 1.]

Several State constitutions require taxes to be both "equal" and "uniform," or "proportional" and "uniform," while others require only "uniformity." A considerable number of States require "uniformity" only within the classes of persons or property taxed. Thus, Section 1, Article VIII of the Delaware Constitution requires that taxes "be uniform upon the same class of subjects within the territorial limits of the authority levying the tax," while the West Virginia Constitution provides that "taxation shall be * * * uniform throughout the State." W.Va.Const., Art. X, § 1.

The question sometimes arises whether a particular levy is a "tax" within the meaning of uniformity and equality provisions. In Holmes v. Cheney, 234 Ark. 503, 352 S.W.2d 943 (1962), the court held that a charge for a motor vehicle certificate of title was a "fee" rather than a "tax" and was therefore not subject to the State's constitutional uniformity and equality requirements. Nor are special assessments for local improvements accruing to the benefit of particular property generally considered to be "taxes" for the purposes of such provisions. Newman v. City of Indianola, 232 N.W.2d 568 (Iowa 1975); Heavens v. King County Rural Library District, 66 Wash.2d 558, 404 P.2d 453 (1965). A volume-based charge imposed on commercial and industrial municipal haulers qualified as a "fee" as opposed to a "tax" for purposes of North Carolina's constitutional prohibition against nonuniformity of taxation. Barnhill Sanitation Service, Inc. v. Gaston County, 362 S.E.2d 161 (N.C.App.1987). But a "fire service fee" was held to be an ad valorem property tax subject to State uniformity and equality strictures because it was levied at a fixed amount per hundred dollars of assessed value of property in the city. City of Fairmont v. Pitrolo Pontiac–Cadillac Co., 308 S.E.2d 527 (W.Va.1983).

As the movement has grown in the United States for the adoption of a classified property tax system, i.e., the taxation of real property differently from personalty—either by rate or fractional value differentials or by exemption of certain types of personalty—the major obstacle has been the State constitutional uniformity and equality provisions. In re Assessment of Kanawha Valley Bank, 144 W.Va. 346, 109 S.E.2d 649 (1959), considered a case in which a bank's capital stock was assessed for ad valorem tax purposes at 100 percent of its actual value, whereas other types of real and personal property were assessed at only fractions of their value. The constitutional provision, adopted over 100 years ago, reads:

> Subject to the exceptions in this section contained, taxation shall be equal and uniform throughout the State, and all property, both real and personal, shall be taxed in proportion to its value to be ascertained as directed by law. No one species of property from which a tax may be collected shall be taxed higher than any other species of property of equal value * * *.

The taxing authority cited a long line of West Virginia cases interpreting the constitution as permitting classification of property and requiring uniformity only within that class—a construction which would have supported the assessment in the instant case. The court conceded that under this construction of the constitution, the assessment was unassailable, but refused to follow the earlier decisions. It held that the cases had failed to give sufficient weight to the requirement that "no one species of property * * * shall be taxed higher than any other species of property of equal value." This language, said the court, relying on cases decided in Tennessee and Arkansas [1] which have similar restrictions, and on the debates in the West Virginia Constitutional Convention, prohibits variation in valuation fractions for different classes of property; all property must be taxed on the same valuation basis. Hormond, J., dissented. See also Schladweiler v. Board of Equalization, 131 Mont. 13, 306 P.2d 673 (1957) (uniformity and equality provision violated by the exemption of personal property); Idaho Telephone Co. v. Baird, 91 Idaho 425, 423 P.2d 337 (1967) (statutory provision calling for assessment of utility operating properties at 40 percent of full cash value, whereas property generally was taxed at 20 percent of full cash value, repugnant to State constitutional requirement of uniformity). The *Baird* case contains an extensive review of the cases construing the application of the traditional uniformity and equality clause.

Railroads have long complained that they are discriminated against through unequal assessments, despite constitutional and statutory equality and uniformity requirements, and they have been in constant litigation with State and local authorities. Congressional studies give credence to these complaints. See "National Transportation Policy," Committee on Commerce, U.S. Senate (87th Cong., 1st Sess.), Report of Special Study Group on Transportation Policies in the U.S., Rep. No. 445 (1965). Congressional legislation designed to prevent such discrimination has often been proposed. See, e.g., H.R. 4972 (89th Cong., 1st Sess.), and Hearings before the Committee on Interstate and Foreign Commerce on "Tax Assessments on Common Carrier Property," March 1 and 2, 1966; and H.R. 6547 and S. 927 (90th Cong.), on which hearings were held on Aug. 7 and 8, 1967 before the Senate Committee on Commerce, Surface Transportation Committee. See also "Railroad Property Assessment Process," 1967 Nat.Tax Ass'n Procs. 512 et seq.; Udall, "Equalization," id. at 522; Cohen, "Recent Railroad Tax Litigation and the Valuation of Railroads," 1965 Nat.Tax Ass'n Procs. 179. In 1976, Congress finally enacted legislation prohibiting the States and their subdivisions from assessing property taxes upon railroad property "at a value which bears a higher ratio to the true market value of such * * * property than the ratio which the assessed value of all other commercial and industrial property in the same assessment jurisdiction bears to the true market value of all such other commercial and industrial property." P.L. 94–210, § 306 (94th

---

1. Taylor v. Louisville & N. Ry. Co., 88 Fed. 350 (6th Cir.1898), dealing with the Tennessee Constitution; White River Lumber Co. v. State, 175 Ark. 956, 2 S.W.2d 25 (1928), dealing with the Arkansas Constitution.

Cong., 2nd Sess.), 90 Stat. 54, codified at 49 U.S.C. § 11503. In 1980, Congress extended to motor carriers protection against discriminatory State property taxes that is similar to protection it had enacted for the railroads. 49 U.S.C. § 11503a. In 1982, it extended the protection to air carriers. 49 U.S.C. § 1513(d).

References. The classic work regarding State uniformity and equality provisions is Professor Newhouse's Constitutional Uniformity and Equality in State Taxation (2d ed., 1984). See also Morrow, "State Constitutional Limitations on Taxing Authority of State Legislatures," 9 Nat.Tax J. 126 (1956); Mathews, "Function of Constitutional Provisions Requiring Uniformity of Taxation," 38 Ky.L.J. 31, 181, 377, 503 (1949–1950); Note, "Florida Constitution and Legislative Classification for Tax Assessment Purposes," 17 U.Fla.L.Rev. 609 (1965); 51 Am.Jur. 150.

SECTION 1. CLASSIFICATION PROBLEMS ARISING UNDER UNIFORMITY AND EQUALITY PROVISIONS

In many States the uniformity provisions apply only to property taxes. A graduated income tax by its very nature lacks the uniformity of taxation typically required by the State constitutional restrictions. A controversy which raged throughout the country, as State income tax laws were enacted, was whether the income tax constituted a property tax that violated the uniformity provisions. Other cases arise in which the validity of a State tax under the uniformity provisions depends on its classification, e.g., where a particular type of property already subjected to an ad valorem tax is specially selected for an additional tax.[2]

DOUGLAS AIRCRAFT CO., INC. v. JOHNSON

Supreme Court of California, 1939.
13 Cal.2d 545, 90 P.2d 572.

PER CURIAM. * * * From the complaints, which are substantially identical, it appears that the plaintiffs Kettleman North Dome Association and Chanslor–Canfield Midway Oil Company are each engaged in this state in the business of drilling for and producing oil, gas and other petroleum substances; that plaintiff Douglas Aircraft Company, Inc., is engaged in the business of designing, manufacturing and fabricating airplanes and airplane parts; that since the effective date of the Use Tax Act all of the plaintiffs have purchased and are still purchasing supplies, equipment and machinery used by them in their respective businesses; that these purchases were made outside the State of California and from dealers not maintaining a place of business in this state; that, as required by the terms of the Use Tax Act, plaintiffs filed

2. The uniformity and equality provisions, of course, play an important role in the decisions of many State courts dealing with the assessment and valuation of property under ad valorem taxes. Those problems are dealt with in Chapter 4. In addition, other uniformity and equality problems are treated in the chapters devoted to sales and use taxes, personal income taxes and other levies.

with the state board of equalization returns disclosing the above purchases, and paid the amount of the tax imposed by the act; that with said returns plaintiffs filed written protests in which the unconstitutionality of the act was alleged. The plaintiff Douglas Aircraft Company, Inc., alleged, in addition, that much of the tangible personal property purchased by it outside the state consists of special tools, machinery, materials and supplies which cannot be purchased in this state, and can be acquired only from sellers not maintaining places of business within this state. It is conceded that in all of the cases the property was purchased by the plaintiffs outside the state for their own use, and not for resale, and was shipped direct to them in interstate transactions.

Appellants urge that the Use Tax Act is unconstitutional for two main reasons:

1. That the tax imposed by the act, in operation and effect, is a property tax, and is therefore unconstitutional because not levied in proportion to the value of the property and because it imposes double taxation, in violation of article XIII, sections 1 and 14 of the state Constitution; further, if the tax imposed is an excise tax, then it violates article I, section 1, of the state Constitution, in that it is a tax on the right of ownership as such, which is a nontaxable privilege; and

2. The tax constitutes a direct burden upon and discriminates against interstate commerce in violation of the commerce and due process clauses of the Constitution of the United States.

This last contention has been exhaustively briefed and vigorously argued by appellants. After the filing of all of the briefs, the United States Supreme Court passed upon this identical question. It held, in cases where the interstate nature of the transactions was much closer than in the instant cases, that the Use Tax Act of California does not violate either the commerce clause of or the Fourteenth Amendment to the federal Constitution. (Southern Pac. Co. v. Gallagher, (Jan. 30, 1939) 306 U.S. 167 [59 S.Ct. 389, 83 L.Ed. 586]; Pacific Tel. & Tel. Co. v. Gallagher, (Jan. 30, 1939) 306 U.S. 182 [59 S.Ct. 396, 83 L.Ed. 595]; see, also, Felt & Tarrant Mfg. Co. v. Gallagher, (Jan. 30, 1939), 306 U.S. 62 [59 S.Ct. 376, 83 L.Ed. 488].) These decisions are conclusive on this court on these issues. On the authority of the above cases it must be held that appellants' second point is without merit.

Equally untenable is the first contention of appellants. The argument on this point is that if the tax is a property tax it violates the provisions of article XIII of the Constitution. Section 1 of that article provides that "all property in the state except as otherwise in this Constitution provided * * * shall be taxed in proportion to its value". Section 9a provides that taxes levied on personal property where not secured by real estate, shall be based on the tax levied on real property for the preceding year. Section 14, as amended in 1933, however, confers upon the legislature wide discretion in classifying or exempting from taxation any and all kinds of personal property. One of respondents' contentions is that even if the tax is a property tax it would be valid under section 14. Appellants contend that any special tax on personal property violates section 1, that section, according to their contention, requiring uniformity and equality in taxation and prohibiting double taxation. We do not find it necessary to pass upon this point for the reason that we are of the opinion that the tax is an excise tax, and therefore the provisions of article XIII have no application. (Kaiser Land & Fruit Co. v. Curry, 155 Cal. 638 [103 P. 341]; Ingels v. Riley, 5 Cal.2d 154 [53 P.2d 939, 103 A.L.R. 1].)

Before directly discussing the contention of appellants that the statute in question imposes a property tax, some brief reference must be made to the provisions of the statute. The title of the act provides in part as follows: "An act imposing an excise tax on the storage, use or other consumption in this State of tangible personal property." Section 2(a) defines "storage" as "any keeping or retention in this State for any purpose except sale in the regular course of business of tangible personal property purchased from a retailer." The term "use" is defined in section 2(b) as "the exercise of any right or power over tangible personal property incident to the ownership of that property, except that it shall not include the sale of that property in the regular course of business." Section 3 provides that "An excise tax is hereby imposed on the storage, use or other consumption in this State of tangible personal property purchased from a retailer on or after July 1, 1935, for storage, use or other consumption in this State at the rate of three per cent of the sales price of such property." Section 4 exempts from the operation of the tax, among other things, the storage, use or other consumption of property the gross receipts from the sale of which are taxed under the sales tax; motor vehicle fuel, the gross receipts from the sale or distribution of which are taxed under the Motor Vehicle Fuel License Tax Act; and food products purchased for human consumption which are exempted from the sales tax.

Appellants concede that the sales tax and the motor vehicle license tax are excise and not property taxes. It will be noted that when the use tax is considered in connection with the other two taxes mentioned, the legislature has provided a comprehensive taxing system applicable to the sale, use, storage or consumption of personal property. The three taxes are mutually exclusive, each taxing privileges not taxed by the other two. * * *

The determination of whether a particular tax is a property or excise tax is not always an easy matter. In discussing this problem in Ingels v. Riley, supra, 5 Cal.2d page 159, 53 P.2d page 941, 103 A.L.R. 1, it is stated:

> "The distinction between a tax on a privilege and a property tax is many times a close one. Generally speaking, the function of a property tax is to raise revenue. Such a tax does not impose any condition nor does it place any restriction upon the use of the property taxed. A privilege tax, although also passed to raise revenue, and as such is to

be distinguished from the license tax or regulatory charge imposed under the state's police powers, is imposed upon the right to exercise a privilege, and its payment is invariably made a condition precedent to the exercise of the privilege involved. 37 Cor.Jur., p. 171, § 9, and cases cited. * * *"

Applying this test to the statute here under consideration we have no hesitancy in holding that the tax imposed is an excise tax, for revenue purposes, levied on the privilege of use, storage, or consumption. In the first place, as indicated by the quotations from the statute, supra, the legislature has denominated the levy an excise tax. Although not conclusive this is entitled to considerable weight in ascertaining the nature of the tax. * * *

In the second place it is obvious, from a reading of the act, that the tax here levied is not imposed on the ownership of property as such. It does not apply to the use of property to be resold. It does not recur annually, but falls due only once. It is not imposed on a fixed day, although it is collectible quarterly—in short, it does not fall upon the owner because he is the owner, regardless of the use or disposition he may make of the property. It is imposed on certain of the privileges of ownership, but not on all of them.

The contention made by the appellants that a use tax, such as is here involved, is in fact a tax on ownership of property and is not a tax on the privilege of use, storage or consumption, is not a new one. It has been made in one form or another in attacking nearly every use tax statute that has been enacted. There is a long line of authorities most of them of recent date, holding that use taxes, including taxes imposed on the privilege of use, or storage, or withdrawal from storage, are excise taxes and not property taxes. In Gregg Dyeing Co. v. Query, supra, the United States Supreme Court upheld as imposing an excise tax a South Carolina statute levying a tax on the storage of foreign gasoline when stored for future use. When the same cause was before the South Carolina court the tax was designated by it (166 S.C. 117, 164 S.E. 588, 594) as "an excise tax and not a property tax." The same court in Nashville, C. & St. L. Ry. v. Wallace, 288 U.S. 249, 53 S.Ct. 345, 77 L.Ed. 730, 87 A.L.R. 1191, upheld a Tennessee statute imposing a tax on the privilege of selling, storing or distributing gasoline, the tax being payable on the withdrawal from storage. In Bowman v. Continental Oil Co., 256 U.S. 642, 41 S.Ct. 606, 65 L.Ed. 1139, the court, in answering the contention that a New Mexico statute levying a tax on the sale or use of gasoline was in fact a property tax and therefore void under the state constitution, stated (256 U.S. page 649, 41 S.Ct. page 608, 65 L.Ed. 1139): "The tax imposed by the act under consideration upon the 'sale or use of all gasoline sold or used in this state' is not property taxation, but in effect, as in name, an excise tax." In West India Oil Co. v. Gallardo, 1 Cir., 6 F.2d 523, the court upheld a 10 per cent tax levied by Porto Rico on all automobiles produced, manufactured, sold or used in Porto Rico. The court stated (6 F.2d page 525):

"We think it plain that this is an excise tax on sale or use, and not an import tax. * * * Equally untenable is the contention that this is a tax on property and void for lack of uniformity. The tax is upon automobiles 'manufactured, sold or used in Porto Rico.' It is not a tax upon ownership as distinguished from the production, sale or use." In American Airways v. Wallace, D.C., 57 F.2d 877, the court had under consideration the validity of a Tennessee statute imposing a tax on persons engaged in the business of selling, storing or distributing gasoline. In discussing the nature of the tax the court stated (57 F.2d page 880): "The statute in question does not impose a property tax upon the gasoline, but it imposes an 'excise' or 'privilege' tax upon the business of storing and withdrawing the gasoline and the amount is computed upon withdrawals." In Central Vermont Ry. v. Campbell, 108 Vt. 510, 192 A. 197, 198, 199, 111 A.L.R. 175, the supreme court of Vermont, in upholding that state's tax upon the "use, distribution or sale" of gasoline, declared: "It is an excise tax upon the domestic sale or use of the gasoline, measured by gallonage." Many of the use tax cases are reviewed in this opinion. In Commonwealth v. Dixie Greyhound Lines, 255 Ky. 111, 72 S.W.2d 1032, 1033, the court described the Kentucky gasoline use tax as "an excise tax on distribution, consumption, or use". It is also worth noting that the United States Supreme Court in Southern Pac. Co. v. Gallagher, supra, in analyzing the nature of the very tax here challenged, refers to it as one that (59 S.Ct. page 391) "imposes an excise on the consumer * * * for the storage, use or other consumption in the state of such property." There is an excellent discussion of the problem in Henneford v. Silas Mason Co., supra—the case which upheld as an excise tax the use or "compensating" tax of the state of Washington, a tax substantially similar to the one here under attack. * * *

The cases of Dawson v. Kentucky Distilleries & Warehouse Co., 255 U.S. 288, 41 S.Ct. 272, 65 L.Ed. 638, and City of Los Angeles v. Lankershim, 160 Cal. 800, 118 P. 215, 216, cited and relied upon by appellants are not in point. In the Dawson case the court held that a Kentucky statute imposing a gallonage tax on persons engaged in the business of owning and storing whisky in bonded warehouses, such tax being payable when the whisky was either withdrawn from bond or transferred in bond from Kentucky to a point outside the state, was in fact a property tax upon ownership as such, and was not a license tax. This conclusion was predicated upon the peculiar terms of that statute, and upon the fact that the emergency clause of the statute indicated that the legislature of Kentucky considered that it was taxing the whisky and not a privilege. This case is not contrary nor inconsistent with the later Supreme Court cases cited, supra, holding that use taxes are excise taxes. In the Lankershim case this court expressly refused to determine whether a so-called license tax, payable yearly by persons engaged in "maintaining, managing or conducting a building for the purpose of letting office rooms," the tax being measured by the size of the building, was a property or an excise tax.

The appellants' last contention (urged in their closing briefs) is that under the declaration of rights of the California Constitution (art. I, § 1) every person possesses "certain inalienable rights, among which are those of * * * acquiring, possessing, or protecting property"; that under this section an excise tax upon the privilege of ownership and use may not be levied by the state, although concededly the section does not prohibit property taxes. The contention is obviously unsound. As already held, the tax is not upon ownership as such, but upon the privilege of use, storage or consumption. The cited provision no more prohibits a tax on the privilege of use than it does a tax on the property itself.

For the foregoing reasons the judgments appealed from should be and each is hereby affirmed.

Notes and Problems

A. In Dawson v. Kentucky Distilleries, 255 U.S. 288, 41 S.Ct. 272 (1921), a license tax of 50 cents a gallon was imposed on all whiskey withdrawn from bond or transferred in bond from Kentucky to a point outside the State. At the time the levy was enacted, the plaintiff had a large amount of whiskey in bond in Kentucky and sought to enjoin the enforcement of the tax as a violation of the State constitutional provision requiring that all taxes be "uniform upon all property of the same class subject to taxation." It was conceded by the State that if the tax was a property tax, the constitutional provision had been infringed, since whiskey was also subjected to the general property tax. The Court rejected the State's contention that the tax was an excise upon the business of owning and storing whiskey in bonded warehouses, and instead held it to be a property tax violating the uniformity clause, saying:

> But as stated by the lower Court, "the thing really taxed is the act of the owner in taking his property out of storage into his own possession (absolute or qualified) for the purpose of making some one of the only uses of which it is capable, i.e., consumption, sale or keeping for future consumption or sale. * * * The whole value of the whiskey depends upon the owner's right to get it from the place where the law has compelled him to put it and to tax the right is to tax the value." To levy a tax by reason of the ownership of property is to tax the property. [255 U.S. at 294.]

How does this point of view square with the holding in the principal case that a tax on "use," defined to include "the exercise of any right or power over tangible personal property incident to the ownership of property," except a sale in the regular course of business, is an excise tax?

See also Eastler v. State Tax Assessor, 499 A.2d 921 (Me.1985) (per acre levy imposed on specified forest lands to raise money for forest fire protection and denominated an "excise tax" is a property tax); Cherry Hills Farm v. City of Cherry Hills, 670 P.2d 779 (Colo.1983) (charge to defray expansion of city services measured by square footage is excise not property tax); City of Huntington Beach v. Superior Court, 78 Cal.App.3d 333, 144 Cal.Rptr. 236 (1978) (real property transfer fee is excise not property tax, since it is levied on only one of the incidents of ownership); Weaver v. Prince George's County, 34 Md.App. 189, 366 A.2d 1048 (1976) (tax on rentals from multifamily dwellings is an excise, not a property tax); Apartment Operators Ass'n of Seattle, Inc. v. Schumacher, 56 Wash.2d 46, 351 P.2d 124 (1960) (tax on rental of real property is property tax).

B. *Severance Tax As Property Tax.* A Mississippi privilege or occupation tax on persons pursuing the business of extracting turpentine from standing trees was held, under a State uniformity provision, to be a property tax as applied to an individual who extracted turpentine from land owned or leased by him, on the ground that the property rights in the turpentine were meaningless without the ability to extract it. Thompson v. McLeod, 112 Miss. 383, 73 So. 193 (1916). In Apache Gas Products Corp. v. Oklahoma Tax Comm'n, 509 P.2d 109 (Okl.1973), on the other hand, the court held that Oklahoma's gross production tax on natural gas imposed "in lieu of" property taxes was an excise tax and not a property tax subject to the State's uniformity and equality requirements. Most courts that have considered this issue have concluded that severance taxes are excise taxes that fall outside the scope of State constitutional provisions requiring uniformity and equality in the taxation of property. See W. Hellerstein, State and Local Taxation of Natural Resources in the Federal System: Legal, Economic, and Political Perspectives 76–77 (1986).

(a) The Constitutionality of State Income Taxes Under Uniformity and Equality Provisions

AMIDON v. KANE

Supreme Court of Pennsylvania, 1971.
444 Pa. 38, 279 A.2d 53.

ROBERTS, JUSTICE.*

In this consolidated appeal, we are asked to review a May 20, 1971 decree of the Commonwealth Court dismissing three separate complaints in equity challenging the constitutionality of the recently enacted Personal Income Tax provided by Article III of the Tax Reform Code of 1971, adopted March 4, 1971, Act No. 2, 72 P.S. § 7101 et seq.

* * *

The Personal Income Tax contained in Article III of the Tax Reform Code of 1971 operates as follows:

Section 305 of the Code purports to impose a tax "[f]or the privilege of receiving, earning or otherwise acquiring income from any source whatsoever * * *." However, the annual tax of $3\frac{1}{2}\%$ is levied not upon all income "from any source whatsoever" but rather only upon "the taxable income of the taxpayer." "Taxable income" is defined in Section 302(q) to mean with a few specific variations "the same as 'taxable income' as defined in the Internal Revenue Code * * *."

---

* [The footnotes to the opinions in this case have been omitted.]

The concept of taxable income in the Internal Revenue Code is of course an artificial construct, in many ways far removed from the common and ordinary meaning of the term income. For example, income derived from gifts and inheritances, interest on the obligations of a state or political subdivision, contributions by employers to employee health and accident plans, and the first one hundred dollars received by a taxpayer as dividends from domestic corporations is all specifically excludable from taxable income. In addition, the Internal Revenue Code permits the deduction of myriad items from actual or gross income in order to compute taxable income. Some of the more common and well known examples of such deductions are real estate taxes, interest on real estate mortgages and other personal financing, alimony payments and various other state and local taxes.

* * *

After defining taxable income in terms of the federal tax base, the Tax Reform Code of 1971 provides four types of tax credits. Section 316 allows a credit for income taxes imposed by another state, Section 317 provides a similar credit for 30% of certain local taxes, and Section 318 deals with a credit for taxes paid by a trust on accumulated income. Finally, Section 319 sets out a variable schedule of "vanishing tax credits" for the benefit of individuals whose state taxable income does not exceed $9,900.

Does then the foregoing scheme of taxation conform to the requirements of the Uniformity Clause?

The constitutional imperative of uniformity in the imposition of taxes has remained unchanged since its first adoption in the Pennsylvania Constitution of 1874. Article IX, Section 1 of that constitution directed without qualification that:

> "All taxes shall be uniform, upon the same class of subjects, within the territorial limits of the authority levying the tax, and shall be levied and collected under general laws."

Legislative proposals to amend the Uniformity Clause were rejected by the electorate in 1913 and 1928, and the May, 1967 referendum submitted to the people of Pennsylvania concerning whether a constitutional convention would be called specifically provided that the convention would *not* revise that portion of the constitution. Likewise, the constitutional convention enabling act stated in no uncertain terms that " * * * nor shall that part of Article IX, Section 1 of the Constitution providing that: 'All taxes shall be uniform * * *' be *modified, altered or changed in any respect whatsoever.*" Act of March 16, 1967, P.L. 2, § 7 [1967] Pa.Laws 7. (Emphasis added.)

In addition to its unbroken historical continuity, the constitutional standard of uniformity also possesses widespread and far reaching application. While some other jurisdictions adhere to the view that uniformity applies only to property taxes, our particular constitutional mandate that "[a]ll taxes shall be uniform * * *" is quite clear, and it is settled that this mandate applies to all species of taxes. As was stated in Saulsbury v. Bethlehem Steel Co., 413 Pa. 316, 196 A.2d 664 (1964):

> "The question of whether or not the constitutional requirement of uniformity applies to a particular kind of tax depends upon the peculiar wording of the requirement itself. The Pennsylvania Constitution specifically states that '*All taxes* shall be uniform, upon the same class of subjects.' (Emphasis supplied). This language is as broad and comprehensive as it could possibly be and must necessarily be construed to include all kinds of taxes, be they in the nature of property or excise levies. The Pennsylvania constitutional provision is all inclusive and is clearly not limited to requiring uniformity on property taxes alone. * * * Kelley v. Kalodner, supra [320 Pa. 180, 181 A. 598 (1935)] * * * It is thus quite clear that the instant tax must satisfy the requirement of uniformity.

The substantive content of the Uniformity Clause is of course less susceptible to precise definition than is the scope of its application. However, certain general principles are well established. As this Court declared in the Allentown School District Mercantile Tax Case, 370 Pa. 161, 87 A.2d 480 (1952):

> "[The Uniformity Clause] means that the classification by the legislative body must be reasonable and the tax must be applied with uniformity upon similar kinds of business or property and with substantial equality of the tax burden to all members of the same class: Commonwealth v. Girard Life Ins. Co., 305 Pa. 558, 158 A. 262 * * *.

> * * *

> "Uniformity requires substantial equality of tax burden: Com. v. Overholt & Co., Inc., 331 Pa. 182, 200 A. 849; Com. v. Repplier Coal Co., 348 Pa. 372, 35 A.2d 319; Moore v. Pittsburgh School District, 338 Pa. 466, 13 A.2d 29. While taxation is not a matter of exact science and perfect uniformity and absolute equality in taxation can rarely ever be attained, Wilson v. Philadelphia, 330 Pa. 350, 352, 198 A. 893, the imposition of taxes which are to a substantial degree unequal in their operation or effect upon similar kinds of business or property, or upon persons in the same classification, is prohibited: Cf. Com. v. Overholt & Co., Inc., 331 Pa. 182, 190–191, 200 A. 849; Pollock v. Farmers' Loan and Trust Co., 157 U.S. 429, 599, 15 S.Ct. 673, 39 L.Ed. 759. Moreover while reasonable and practical classifications are justifiable where a formula or method of computing a tax will, in its operation or effect, produce arbitrary or unjust or unreasonably discriminatory results, the constitutional provision relating to uniformity is violated. Turco Paint & Varnish Co. v. Kalodner, 320 Pa. 421, 184 A. 37; Hans Rees' Sons v. State of North Carolina, 283 U.S. 123, 51 S.Ct. 385, 75 L.Ed. 879."

> * * *

In addition to these general principles, two prior decisions of this Court are particularly pertinent to our disposition of this appeal.

The first of these, Kelley v. Kalodner, 320 Pa. 180, 181 A. 598 (1935), involved a 1935 Pennsylvania statute imposing an annual tax upon the entire net income of Pennsylvania residents and upon net income received by non-residents from property owned or from any business or occupation carried on in the Commonwealth. That act authorized many exemptions for purposes of calculating "gross income" and numerous deductions for the computation of "net income". It likewise sought to enact a standard deduction for living expenses ($1,000 in the case of single persons and $1,500 in the case of married persons and heads of households), and an additional $400 deduction for each dependent under the age of eighteen. The tax was then imposed upon net income at a graduated rate: incomes under five thousand dollars were taxed at 2%; incomes between five and ten thousand dollars at 2½%; incomes between ten and twenty-five thousand dollars at 3%; etc.

Reasoning as follows, this Court declared the tax invalid:

"The question then arises, does the act fulfill the rule of uniformity prescribed by the Constitution. Plaintiffs contend it does not, and for several reasons. The first is that the provision exempting from taxation those persons whose incomes fall below $1,000 or $1,500, depending upon whether they are single or married, shows upon its face a lack of uniformity. There can be no doubt that these exemptions were inserted for the purpose of putting the burden of the tax upon those most able to bear it, *but it results in taxing those whose incomes arise above a stated figure merely because the Legislature believes their incomes are sufficiently great to be taxed. It is obvious that the application of the tax is not uniform * * *.*

"Moreover, the tax is in violation of the uniformity clause in its application to the persons whose incomes fall within the various brackets designated in the act. * * *"

320 Pa. at 188–89, 181 A. at 602 (emphasis added). The *Kelley* decision, in other words, clearly involved an alternative holding: the tax was deemed constitutionally deficient both because of the personal exemptions and because of the graduated rate.

The second of the two decisions most significant to the instant case is Saulsbury v. Bethlehem Steel Company, supra, decided in 1964. In that case we ruled that an "occupation and occupational privilege tax" which exempted individuals with an annual income of less than $600 transgressed the limits of uniformity. In so holding this Court reaffirmed the rule of Kelley v. Kalodner and largely on the basis of that decision concluded that:

"If a tax is levied on an occupational privilege, it must apply to *all* who share the privilege. Part of the class may not be excused, regardless of the motive behind the action."

413 Pa. at 320, 196 A.2d at 666 (emphasis added).

It is true that the challengers of the constitutionality of state or local taxation bear a heavy burden in their efforts to overturn such legislation. See, e.g., Commonwealth v. Life Assurance Company of Pennsylvania, supra, 419 Pa. at 376–77, 214 A.2d at 214. Nevertheless, in comparing the taxing schemes in *Kelley* and *Saulsbury* with that involved in the instant case, the conclusion is unescapable that the personal income tax presently challenged violates uniformity. Although the Tax Reform Code of 1971 purports to impose a flat 3½% tax upon "taxable income", the concept of "taxable income" already reflects the federal personal exemptions for the taxpayer and his qualified dependents. * * * Thus, built-in to the Tax Reform Code of 1971 are *exactly the same elements of nonuniformity* as were condemned in both *Kelley* and *Saulsbury.*

A further noteworthy feature of inequality is the instant tax's exclusion from taxable income of all interest received on the obligations of the Commonwealth or any of its political subdivisions. The Tax Reform Code of 1971 imposes in its own terms a tax "[f]or the privilege of receiving, earning or otherwise acquiring income from any source whatsoever * * *." The holder of tax exempt Pennsylvania securities certainly enjoys this privilege of receiving income yet is not taxed for the privilege but instead is given a tax preference. This situation is manifestly contrary to our holding in *Saulsbury* that a tax upon a privilege " * * * must apply to all who share the privilege." In addition, despite the existence of a legislative policy favoring this type of tax preference for state and local obligations of this Commonwealth, such a legislative policy cannot prevail over a clear constitutional mandate of uniformity.

We need not, however, limit our present analysis to these particular inequalities, for the Personal Income Tax is replete with other commonly occurring instances of nonuniformity. * * *

[The court proceeds to demonstrate, by comparing the effective tax rates paid by hypothetical taxpayers earning the same dollar amount of annual income but having different deductions, that the effect of the Personal Income Tax in these situations is nonuniform in that it imposes different tax burdens upon persons enjoying the same privilege of "receiving, earning, or otherwise acquiring" the same dollar amount of annual income "from any source whatsoever."]

These inequalities result, of course, from the manifold tax preferences afforded taxpayers depending among other things upon whether a particular taxpayer is a wage earner or self-employed, renter or home owner, etc. * * *

Whether or not these or any or all of the myriad other tax preferences implicit in Article III of the Tax Reform Code of 1971 might be thought to serve some useful social policy, the fact remains that unequal burdens are being imposed upon similar privileges in violation of the Uniformity Clause. These pervasive and impermissible discriminations between similarly situated taxpayers render Article III invalid.

We cannot agree with the Commonwealth's contention that since the Pennsylvania Corporate Net Income Tax Act, Act of May 16, 1935, P.L. 208, as amended, 72 P.S. § 3420a et seq., has been held constitutional, see Turco Paint & Varnish Co. v. Kalodner, 320 Pa. 421, 184 A.

37 (1936), the Personal Income Tax imposed by the Tax Reform Code of 1971 is likewise permissible.

In passing upon the validity of the corporate net income tax, this Court emphasized that it was " * * * *not* considering an income tax, but an excise tax for the privilege of doing business in the Commonwealth * * *." Commonwealth v. Warner Bros. Theatres, Inc., 345 Pa. 270, 271, 27 A.2d 62, 63 (1942) (emphasis added), and any attempted analogy between the instant tax and the corporate net income tax is unpersuasive. Corporations are artificial legal entities created with the permission of the state for the purpose of maximizing profits for shareholders, and the corporate net income tax is imposed upon a tax base which " * * * is the net income attributable to this state." *Turco Paint,* supra 320 Pa. at 426, 184 A. at 40.

Natural persons, on the other hand, cannot be likened to profit-maximizing entities. Individuals spend their resources for an infinite variety of reasons unrelated to the making of a "profit". Thus, unlike the corporate context, it would be exceedingly difficult, if not impossible to create a personal income tax designed to take into account the "cost" of producing individual income. Certainly the instant tax does not even attempt to do so, and the corporate net income taxes are accordingly inapposite.

In light of our decision that Article III of the Tax Reform Code of 1971 creates widespread tax preferences and thus is in direct conflict with the mandate of the Uniformity Clause, we need not pass upon the other issues presented in this appeal, namely, the validity of the vanishing tax credit provision, the validity of the thirty percent local tax credit, or whether the tax is invalid because the Governor failed to submit a balanced operating budget prior to recommending additional sources of revenue.

For the foregoing reasons, the decree of the Commonwealth Court is reversed. Each party to pay own costs.

[The concurring opinion of Chief Justice Bell has been omitted.]

POMEROY, JUSTICE (concurring).

* * *

Were we writing on a clean slate, I might agree that the built-in inequalities in the federal tax base serve to render the same tax base, when adopted by Pennsylvania, impermissibly non-uniform under our Constitution. But the slate is not clean. Unlike the majority, I think the decisions of this Court approving the Corporate Net Income Tax, Act of May 16, 1935, P.L. 208, as amended, 72 P.S. § 3420a, et seq. (C.N.I.), compel an approval of the taxable income definition in Article III of the Tax Reform Code of 1971 *insofar as the Internal Revenue Code provisions relating to corporate taxable income are substantially parallel to the provisions of the same Code relating to individual taxable income.* The C.N.I., from its beginning in 1935, has defined "net income" (which is there the measure of the tax) as meaning "net income as returned to and ascertained by the Federal Government." 72 P.S. § 3420b. This figure is in general gross receipts, less cost of goods sold and/or of operations, plus other income items, less allowable deductions. The federal tax structure is thus basically the same whether the taxpayer be an individual or a corporation.

In Turco Paint & Varnish Co. v. Kalodner, 320 Pa. 421, 184 A. 37 (1936), one of the contentions of the taxpayer in a broad assault upon the constitutionality of the C.N.I. was that although the tax was at a flat 6% rate of net income (the present rate is 12%), it was in effect a graded tax because of the process by which net income was determined. This Court held explicitly to the contrary. The C.N.I. was again challenged in Commonwealth v. Warner Bros., 345 Pa. 270, 27 A.2d 62 (1942). The Court there held that the incorporation by reference of the net income definition applicable to corporations as used in the Internal Revenue Code did not involve a delegation of legislative power in violation of Article IX, Section 1 of the Constitution of 1874. The Pennsylvania Act, said the Court, "does not delegate the power to tax to the Federal Tribunal, it only takes the net income fixed by it, as the base for the excise privilege tax levied by the Commonwealth." (345 Pa. at 272) The Court also, following Turco Paint & Varnish Co., supra, again rejected the charge that the C.N.I. violated the uniformity clause. See also Commonwealth v. Budd, 379 Pa. 159, 108 A.2d 563 (1954).

The majority would distinguish these cases principally on the ground that corporations are "artificial legal entities" engaged in business for profit, whereas natural persons spend their resources for a number of reasons unrelated to profit-making, some of which give rise to income tax deductions not applicable to corporations. This seems to me unimportant as far as the power of the state to adopt a federally determined tax base is concerned.

But although the *Turco Paint & Varnish* authority goes far to validate the present tax, as far as the legality of the federal base is concerned, it does not, in my view, go the whole way. The reason is that, in addition to certain deductions allowed to individuals which have no similarity to those allowed to corporations (notably deductions for medical expenses and alimony payments), there is no parallel in the federal income tax on corporations with the exemptions which are an integral part of the federal income tax on individuals. The federal income tax on individuals, as is well known, allows a personal exemption of $625 for each taxpayer and for each of his dependents as defined, allows an additional exemption if the taxpayer is 65 years of age or older, and an additional exemption if the taxpayer is blind. I agree with Judge Bowman that these exemptions, "while meritorious in terms of ability to pay, bear no rational relationship to a tax on net income." * * *

EAGEN, JUSTICE (dissenting).

Neither from my understanding of the Uniformity Clause, nor from past decisions by our Court in this area of law nor indeed from the reasoning of the majority am I inexorably led to conclude that the general features of the Personal Income Tax (Article III, Tax Reform Code of 1971, adopted March 4, 1971, Act No. 2, 72 P.S. § 7107 et seq.) violate Article VIII, Section 1 of the Pennsylvania Constitution and for this reason I am compelled to dissent.

In 1935 this Court answered with a resounding NO the question of whether Pennsylvania could enact a *graduated* personal income tax which would comport with the Uniformity Clause of the Taxation and Finance Article of the Constitution. Kelley v. Kalodner, 320 Pa. 180, 181 A. 598 (1935). But just as importantly we did not say that the Legislature could never enact any form of income tax. The injunction was simply that the constitutional mandate of uniformity must be observed.

My review of the decisions of this Court encourages me in the conclusion that the Legislature in framing Article III of the Tax Reform Code has remained faithful to the constitutional guidelines and nice distinctions of the concept of uniformity as set down by this Court.

At the outset it might be helpful for purposes of clarity and comparison to review briefly the majority's position. It is their contention that although the Tax Reform Code of 1971 purports to impose a flat 3½ per cent tax on 'taxable income', the concept of 'taxable income' already reflects the federal personal exemptions for the taxpayer and his qualified dependents and hence embodies exactly the same elements of nonuniformity as were condemned in Kelley v. Kalodner, supra, and Saulsbury v. Bethlehem Steel Company, 413 Pa. 316, 196 A.2d 664 (1964). "The effect of the Personal Income Tax * * * is entirely nonuniform by imposing differing tax burdens upon persons enjoying identical privileges." [Opinion of the Majority, page 62]

The rejoinder to this position is that the Legislature in resorting to the federal system for its tax base in the present instance acted in no wise differently than it did in imposing the Corporate Net Income Tax Act of 1935, 72 P.S. 3420a et seq., a taxing statute which was upheld by this Court in Turco Paint & Varnish Company v. Kalodner, 320 Pa. 421, 184 A. 37 (1936) and again in Commonwealth v. Warner Bros. Theatres, Inc., 345 Pa. 270, 27 A.2d 62 (1942).

The contention in the *Turco Paint & Varnish Company* case was that the corporate net income tax could not be uniform *because of the process by which net income was determined.*

Despite the fact that permitted deductions from gross income might vary drastically with respect to corporations having the same gross income and therefore result in widely varying taxable net income, our Court *did not* find this use of net income returned to and ascertained by the Federal Government as a Pennsylvania tax base to be violative of the Uniformity Clause. As Mr. Chief Justice Kephart wrote:

"Plaintiff has not pointed to a single provision of the act which would demonstrate a legislative intent to impose a graded income tax. The rate used, 6 per cent, is the same for all corporations. The tax base to which this rate is to be applied is also identical. It is the net income attributable to this state. It certainly should be axiomatic that the same impost, when applied to the same subject-matter, does not make the tax graded simply because of the fact that one association, owning more of the particular taxable subject-matter than another, pays, on this account, a greater sum total of tax." 320 Pa. at 426, 184 A. at 40.

A compelling question now arises: If a federally determined base (and one freighted with exemptions and deductions) is held to meet the constitutional test of uniformity in the instance of the corporate net income tax, why does not the same hold true for the personal income tax; how does it come to pass that the base of the latter tax is so fatally defective?

The majority's answer is that it is inapposite to refer to this Court's approval of the corporate net income tax since what was being considered there was an excise tax on the privilege of doing business in the Commonwealth, not an income tax; the implication being that while the former is an excise levy, the latter is a property tax and never the twain shall meet.

Such a contention cannot square with what Mr. Justice, now Chief Justice Bell, so pellucidly wrote in Commonwealth v. Eastern Motor Express, Inc., 398 Pa. 279, 298, 157 A.2d 79, 89 (1959):

> "The constitutionality of the Corporate Net Income Tax Act of May 16, 1935, as reenacted and amended, was sustained on the ground that it was a *property* tax on net income, in spite of the declaration in the Act that it was an excise tax: Blauner's Inc. v. City of Philadelphia, 330 Pa. 342, 345, 198 A. 889; National Biscuit Co. v. Philadelphia, 374 Pa. 604, 612, 98 A.2d 182; Murray v. Philadelphia, 364 Pa. 157, 169, 71 A.2d 280; Philadelphia v. Samuels, 338 Pa. 321, 326, 12 A.2d 79 * * *." [Emphasis not ours] [footnote omitted]

But even granting for the sake of argument that the corporate net income tax is an excise tax, the import of the majority's distinction (and its conclusion of inappositeness) continues to elude me.

In Saulsbury v. Bethlehem Steel Co., 413 Pa. 316, 319, 196 A.2d 664, 666 (1964), we restated what has so often been repeated, that:

> "The Pennsylvania Constitution specifically states that 'All taxes shall be uniform, upon the same class of subjects.' This language is as broad and comprehensive as it could possibly be and must necessarily be construed to include all kinds of taxes, be they in the nature of property or excise levies. The Pennsylvania constitutional provision is all inclusive and is clearly not limited to requiring uniformity in property taxes alone." [citations omitted]

Hence it is fair to again ask that if it is constitutionally permissible for the measure of the corporate net income tax to be the income upon which tax is paid to the Federal Government, why cannot the same be true for a personal income tax? An apple is not an orange and an excise tax is not a property tax, but when the Uniformity Clause applies to both, as we have seen that it does, how can the latter tax be determined to be defective for using the federally determined base in conjunction with a flat 3.5 per cent rate? The genetics of these two types of taxation are of little moment when analyzed for purposes of uniformity.

My conclusion is and must be that such denial of an analogy between the instant tax and the corporate net income tax does not withstand analysis unless we are willing to turn the clock back thirty-five years and retroactively brand the *Turco Paint & Varnish Company* case and its progeny as aberrations.

* * *

Mindful that this Court has written that "Absolute equality is of course unattainable; a mere approximate equality is all that can reasonably be expected", Commonwealth v. Delaware Div. Canal Company, 123 Pa. 594, 620, 16 A. 584, 588 (1889), and also that there is a presumption of constitutionality attending legislative enactments, see Hadley's Case, 336 Pa. 100, 6 A.2d 874 (1939), I would hold that Article III of the Tax Code, with the exceptions of Sections 317 and 319, meets the constitutional standards of uniformity.

* * *

Notes and Problems

A. After the decision in *Amidon,* the Pennsylvania Legislature repealed Article III of the Tax Reform Code of 1971 and replaced it by a so-called schedular tax levied at a flat rate upon specified classes of income including compensation, net profits from business, and capital gains. P.L. 362, No. 93 (Aug. 31, 1971), Pa.Stat.Ann., tit. 72, §§ 7301 et seq., CCH ¶ 100–410 et seq., P–H ¶ 57,005 et seq. The revised statute was challenged under Pennsylvania's uniformity and equality provision on the ground that it excluded *reimbursed* expenses from the definition of taxable compensation, but did not allow a deduction for *unreimbursed* expenses. In order to avoid the constitutional problem, the Pennsylvania Supreme Court construed the statute as permitting a deduction for unreimbursed expenses. Commonwealth v. Staley, 476 Pa. 171, 381 A.2d 1280 (1978); see also Ritz v. Commonwealth, 50 Pa.Cmwlth. 155, 412 A.2d 1114 (1980) (holding *Staley* inapplicable to taxpayer's claim for a deduction of union dues and home office expenses). A tax similar to Pennsylvania's is used in Massachusetts as a result, there too, of the decisions of the highest court of the State invalidating under the State's equality and uniformity clause a proportional income tax which applies to the resident taxpayer's global income. See Mass.Ann.Laws, ch. 62, CCH ¶ 90–991, P–H ¶ 57,020–A, and Note B infra.

B. *Other State Income Taxes Under the Uniformity and Equality Provisions.* Featherstone v. Norman, 170 Ga. 370, 153 S.E. 58 (1930), is a leading authority for the proposition that an income tax is not a property tax within the meaning of State uniformity and equality provisions. In holding that Georgia's income tax was not limited by the constitutional provision that "all taxation shall be * * * ad valorem on all property subject to be taxed," the court relied upon the frequently quoted passage from Cooley on Taxation § 1751 (4th ed.):

> Constitutional prohibitions and limitations applicable to property taxes are generally held not applicable to an income tax, unless the income tax is held to be a property tax.   And even where an income tax is held to be a tax on property, the courts sometimes have failed to apply such constitutional limitations to them.   The better rule seems to be that an income tax is not a tax on property within a constitutional requirement that taxation on property shall be in proportion to value.

Accord: Thorpe v. Mahin, 43 Ill.2d 36, 250 N.E.2d 633 (1969), which overruled the earlier decision in Bachrach v. Nelson, 349 Ill. 579, 182 N.E. 909 (1932), that had reached the opposite conclusion.

Many of the cases holding that an income tax is subject to the State's equality and uniformity provisions have their roots in Pollock v. Farmers' Loan & Trust Co., 157 U.S. 429, 15 S.Ct. 673 (1895), which these courts have construed as holding that an income tax is to be classified as a property tax.   See, e.g., Eliasberg Bros. Mercantile Co. v. Grimes, 204 Ala. 492, 86 So. 56 (1920).

Other courts, however, have rejected this interpretation of the *Pollock* case and have sustained graduated income taxes.   In Miles v. Dep't of Treasury, 193 N.E. 855 (Ind.1935), affirmed, 209 Ind. 172, 199 N.E. 372, appeal dismissed 298 U.S. 640, 56 S.Ct. 750 (1936), the court said:

> When it is considered that, until the Pollock case, general income taxes were generally accepted as an excise and not a tax upon property because of ownership, the force of the Pollock case in affecting decisions to the contrary must have been considerable. * * * Currently, as in the period preceding the Pollock case, recognized text writers generally express the view that a general income tax is not a property tax, but an excise. [193 N.E. at 859.]

The history of this controversy is dealt with extensively in W. Newhouse, Constitutional Uniformity and Equality in State Taxation (2d ed. 1984).   The author points out that an early landmark decision was the 1915 Advisory Opinion of the Massachusetts Supreme Court which held, in reliance on the Pollock case, that a tax on income from property would constitute a property tax, that it would be subject to the uniformity and equality clause, and if graduated would be unconstitutional.[3]   Three years later the Supreme Court of Missouri rejected this holding and concluded

---

3. In re Opinion of the Justices, 220 Mass. 613, 108 N.E. 570 (1915).   As a result of this decision Massachusetts does not have a graduated income tax.   A constitutional amendment was adopted in 1915 to limit the impact of the court's decision, but the court held that the new provision merely permits specific and varying rates on differing types of income but does not permit a general graduated income tax. In re Opinion of the Justices, 266 Mass. 583, 165 N.E. 900 (1929).   In 1981, the court reaffirmed that a graduated State income tax would be unconstitutional. Opinion of the Justices, 383 Mass. 940, 423 N.E.2d 751 (1981).   And in 1986, the court struck down legislation providing a graduated series of personal exemptions from the personal income tax because it violated the State's uniformity requirement.   Massachusetts Taxpayers Foundation, Inc. v. Secretary of Administration, 398 Mass. 40, 494 N.E.2d 1311 (1986).   This discussion of the income tax cases is taken largely from J. Hellerstein's review of the first edition of Professor Newhouse's book. 9 Buf.L. Rev. 402 (1960).

that an income tax is not a property tax and was not within the scope of the State's uniformity and equality clause.[4] These two decisions spearheaded the struggle in the courts over the State income tax, a struggle which swept the country as the movement spread for the enactment of the levy. Holdings that a graduated income tax violated the State constitutional restrictions have had their repercussions to this day and have thwarted the efforts of legislators in Illinois, New Hampshire, Massachusetts, Pennsylvania, Washington and other States, to adopt this modern, progressive levy.[5] In some States the problem was dealt with by constitutional amendments explicitly authorizing the enactment of graduated net income taxes.[6] Certainly, the clear trend in recent years, as Professor Newhouse points out, has been to exclude the income tax from the restrictive clauses.[7] As a result of these developments some 45 States now impose income taxes.[8]

C. *References.* For collections of cases and analyses of the conflicting views as to the validity of graduated income taxes in the light of uniformity provisions, see 11 A.L.R. 313; 70 A.L.R. 468; 71 A.L.R. 256; 97 A.L.R. 1488; CCH All States Guide ¶ 10–040, P–H All States Guide ¶ 3343. The Kentucky authorities are analyzed in Trimble, "Excise Taxes and the Uniformity Clause of the Constitution of Kentucky," 25 Ky.L.J. 342 (1937), and the Washington cases are treated in O'Connor & Schillberg, "A Study of State Income Taxation in Washington," 33 Wash.L.Rev. 398 (1958). See also Cohn, "Constitutional Limitations on Income Taxation in Illinois," 1961 U. of Ill.L.F. 586 (1961).

SECTION 2. DIFFERENCES IN TREATMENT OF TAXPAYERS OR PROPERTY UNDER UNIFORMITY AND EQUALITY CLAUSES

Notes and Problems

A. *Occupational Privilege Tax With Minimum Dollar Exemption and Varying Rates.* In Pharr Road Investment Co. v. City of Atlanta, 224 Ga. 403, 162 S.E.2d 333 (1968), the court invalidated a city ordinance imposing varying license fees on occupations, measured by gross revenues, as in conflict with the uniformity provision of the Georgia Constitution. The court found "palpable ∗ ∗ ∗ discrimination" in the provisions that (a) exempted from the license fees businesses with gross revenues of $8,000 or less; (b) levied differing rates depending on the number of employees, so

---

4. Ludlow–Saylor Wire Co. v. Wollbrinck, 275 Mo. 339, 205 S.W. 196 (1918).

5. Bachrach v. Nelson, 349 Ill. 579, 182 N.E. 909 (1932), overruled in Thorpe v. Mahin, 43 Ill.2d 36, 250 N.E.2d 633 (1969); Kelley v. Kalodner, 320 Pa. 180, 181 A. 598 (1935); Culliton v. Chase, 174 Wash. 363, 25 P.2d 81 (1933); Opinion of the Justices, 99 N.H. 525, 113 A.2d 547 (1955).

6. See, e.g., Alabama, Kentucky and Wisconsin.

7. Miles v. Department of Treasury, 209 Ind. 172, 199 N.E. 372 (1935), appeal dismissed 298 U.S. 640, 56 S.Ct. 750 (1936);

Sims v. Ahrens, 167 Ark. 557, 271 S.W. 720 (1925); Reynolds Metal Co. v. Martin, 269 Ky. 378, 107 S.W.2d 251, appeal dismissed 302 U.S. 646, 58 S.Ct. 146 (1937); Reed v. Bjornson, 191 Minn. 254, 253 N.W. 102 (1934); Hattiesburg Grocery Co. v. Robertson, 126 Miss. 34, 88 So. 4 (1921), error dismissed 260 U.S. 710, 43 S.Ct. 249 (1923).

8. P–H All States Guide ¶ 210 et seq. For a consideration of differences in treatment between residents and non-residents under state income tax laws, see Chapter 13.

that businesses with given gross revenues but fewer than 1,600 employees were subject to a fee of $12,000, whereas those with the same gross revenues but having more than 1,600 employees were subject to a fee of $18,000. Conceding that the classification and graduation schedule "manifest a desire to gear the amounts to ability to pay and the expenses to protect and serve," the court nevertheless was "convinced that uniformity as demanded by the Constitution is lacking." 162 S.E.2d at 335. Accord: Saulsbury v. Bethlehem Steel Co., 413 Pa. 316, 196 A.2d 664 (1964), noted in Amidon v. Kane, p. 58 supra.

B. *Challenges to Tax Rate Structures Under Uniformity and Equality Provisions.* New Hampshire's business profits tax is imposed at the rate of 9.08 percent (8 percent plus 13.5 percent surcharge) on taxable business profits. In addition, a minimum tax of $250 was imposed on all businesses with gross business income in excess of $12,000 but with business profits of less that $2,753. (At the latter amount, the regular business profits tax applied, because it exceeded the minimum). The court held that the minimum tax violated the State's uniformity requirement because it imposed a regressive graduated tax—i.e., the tax was imposed at a higher effective rate on business profits when business profits were less than $2,753 and gross income exceeded $12,000 than when business profits were more than $2,753 and gross income exceeded $12,000. 'Such a tax, held the court, was neither uniform nor proportional. Johnson & Porter Realty Co., Inc. v. Commissioner of Revenue Administration, 122 N.H. 696, 448 A.2d 435 (1982).

Both the *Johnson* case and the *Pharr* case, Note A supra, present essentially the same problem, namely, the constitutionality of applying different effective tax rates under business excise taxes to taxpayers whose businesses have differing characteristics. The critical question in the cases is whether the differing characteristics—the amount of gross revenues, the number of employees, or the amount of net profits, and the like—justify the separate classification for purposes of the levies' effective tax rate. In both the *Johnson* and *Pharr* cases the courts applied a standard of strict scrutiny in invalidating the nonuniform rate under the State's uniformity and equality provision. Query whether the courts in these cases would have evinced the same hostility to rate differentials found in most personal income taxes? See Section 1(a) supra.

C. *Tax on Rentals Under Uniformity and Equality Clause.* A Washington tax "on every person engaging within this state in the business of * * * the renting or leasing of real property" at the rate of one-quarter of one percent of gross rentals was held a property tax, not an excise tax, and hence subject to the State's uniformity clause. The levy was invalidated because gross income under $300 was excluded and because a double tax—the property tax and the levy at issue—was thereby imposed on rented property, whereas only a single tax was imposed on non-rental property. Apartment Operators Ass'n of Seattle v. Schumacher, 56 Wash.2d 46, 351 P.2d 124 (1960). Contra: Weaver v. Prince George's County, 34 Md.App. 189, 366 A.2d 1048 (1976) (tax on rentals from multifamily dwellings is an excise, not a property tax).

D. *Exemptions Under the Uniformity and Equality Provisions.* The constitutional provisions typically permit exemptions for property owned by charitable, religious, and educational organizations and other specified groups. Questions have arisen as to exemption of other taxpayers. In State v. Armstrong, 17 Utah 166, 53 P. 981 (1898), the court invalidated a provision allowing the Board of Equalization to "remit or abate the taxes of any insane, idiotic, infirm or indigent person to an amount not exceeding ten dollars for the current year"; the uniformity provision was violated because this was an exemption from tax not specified in the constitution.

The Utah constitution was amended in 1900 to provide explicitly that "the taxes of the indigent poor may be remitted or abated at such times and in such manner as may be provided by law." Utah Const. art. XIII, § 2. In 1982, the provision was amended again to delete the word indigent.

The line between proper classification under a constitutional provision permitting classification and unwarranted exemption is often difficult to draw. Thus, in Victor Chemical Works v. Silver Bow County, 130 Mont. 308, 301 P.2d 730 (1956), the statute classified property in various categories and provided for assessment at differing percentages of value. The taxpayer's industrial plant was placed in class 4, which covered land, manufacturing and mining machinery, and equipment; class 4 was assessed at 30 percent of value. However, the statute excepted from class 4, and placed in class 5 for assessment at 7 percent of value, industrial property that had been included in class 4 for a period of 3 years; the taxpayer sought the benefit of this provision. The county contended, and the court held, that class 5 could not be justified as a reasonable classification but instead constituted an unauthorized legislative attempt to grant partial exemption. The court's view was that reclassification must bear some relation "to the productivity or the use of the property"; and that the length of time property had been assessed could not meet the test of reclassification.

Would such a decision prevent the legislature from granting tax exemption of a reduced percentage of assessment for an initial 5 or 10 year period in order to lure new industries into the State?

By way of contrast, the New Hampshire uniformity and equality provisions have been held to permit either reasonable classification or exemption. In an advisory opinion the State court regarded as reasonable the exemption from ad valorem taxation of merchandise, feed, tools and supplies consigned to a warehouse for storage or assembly, but ultimately destined for shipment outside the State. Opinion of the Justices, 101 N.H. 539, 134 A.2d 278 (1957). The court rested its holding that the classification was reasonable on the widespread practice in the country of exempting from tax goods in transit in interstate commerce.

More recently, that same tribunal struck down the State's homeowner's exemption law as violative of the constitutional uniformity requirement. The law provided that resident homeowners were entitled "to an exemption of five thousand dollars of equalized assessed valuation * * *; providing, however, that in no case shall the remaining equalized assessed valuation be less than eight thousand dollars on any homestead." N.H. Rev.Stat.Ann. § 72:45 (Supp.1973). Although the court noted that the legislature may legitimately provide relief to homeowners as a class, it held that to make such relief contingent on property being valued in excess of a minimum figure favored richer over poorer property owners, causing an unconstitutional nonuniformity. Felder v. City of Portsmouth, 114 N.H. 573, 324 A.2d 708 (1974).

A Pennsylvania court held that a Philadelphia city wage tax imposed on Federal employees and exempting members of the armed forces who are residents of the city did not violate the uniformity provision of the State constitution, which requires that taxes shall be uniform upon the same class of subjects. The basis for classification was regarded as reasonable. Service in the armed forces, said the court, represents a sacrifice which should be entitled to exemption. City of Philadelphia v. Farrell, 205 Pa. Super. 263, 209 A.2d 867 (1965).

An Indiana statute imposes a tax of two percent on the value of motor vehicles and mobile homes, in lieu of the ad valorem property tax; the levy is designated as an excise tax by the statute. Without deciding whether this was an excise or a property tax, the court held that it violated the Indiana Constitution. If the levy is considered a property tax, the court declared that it violated the uniformity and equality of rate requirement of the Indiana Constitution. Since motor vehicles were taxed at two percent of their value, this was neither uniform nor equal with the general tax rate established annually on all property. Treating the exaction as an excise tax, the court decided that it ran afoul the constitutional provision which prohibits exemption from ad valorem property taxes, except for property used for municipal, educational, literary, scientific, religious or charitable purposes. Wright v. Steers, 242 Ind. 582, 179 N.E.2d 721 (1962).

E. *Distinctions Based on Ownership of Property and State of Incorporation of Owner.* In Topeka Cemetery Ass'n v. Schnellbacker, 218 Kan. 39, 542 P.2d 278 (1975), the court held that failure to provide an exemption from ad valorem property taxation for cemetery lands owned by corporations while doing so for such lands owned by individuals violated the State uniformity and equality provision: "We have consistently held that where public property is not involved, a tax exemption must be based upon the use of property and not on the basis of ownership alone * * * We find no rational basis for treating differently land owned by individuals and that owned by the corporation, except ownership, which is not a permissible basis of classification." 542 P.2d at 281, 283. But see Lehnhausen v. Lake Shore Auto Parts Co., 410 U.S. 356, 93 S.Ct. 1001 (1973) at pp. 72–75 infra.

While different tax treatment based on the distinction between domestic and foreign corporations frequently raises equal protection problems, see pp. 88–105 infra, it may raise parallel problems under State uniformity and equality provisions. In Columbia Gas Transmission Corp. v. State, 468 Pa. 145, 360 A.2d 592 (1976), the court struck down an excise tax levied upon foreign corporations at a rate higher than upon domestic corporations. The court held that the tax violated Pennsylvania's uniformity clause, see Amidon v. Kane, 444 Pa. 38, 279 A.2d 53 (1971), pp. 55–64 supra, and did not reach the question whether it also violated the Federal Equal Protection Clause. In another case involving a distinction between domestic and foreign corporations, the same court struck down a provision of

Pennsylvania's capital stock tax that granted to domestic but not foreign corporations an election to use an alternative to the regularly prescribed statutory apportionment formula. Gilbert Assocs., Inc. v. Commonwealth, 498 Pa. 514, 447 A.2d 944 (1982). In this instance, the preference was held violative of both the State uniformity and equality provision as well as the Federal Equal Protection Clause.

F. *Classification of Property.* Most State uniformity and equality provisions permit classification of property. W. Newhouse, Constitutional Uniformity and Equality in State Taxation 1903 (2d ed. 1984). The leeway that legislatures have in classifying property, however, varies widely from State to State. Id. *passim.* Some State constitutions specify the permissible classes of property. For example, the Georgia Constitution, which provides generally that "taxation shall be uniform upon the same class of subjects within the territorial limits of the authority levying the tax," Ga. Const. art. VII, § 1, specifies that "classes of subjects of taxation of property shall consist of tangible property and one or more classes of intangible personal property including money." Id. The Constitution was amended in 1983 to provide for special treatment of certain agricultural land. Id.

Minnesota's uniformity clause, on the other hand, has been construed to permit extensive classification of property. In Hegenes v. State, 328 N.W.2d 719 (Minn.1983), for example, the court sustained a distinction between residential real estate containing four or more units, which was assessed at 40 percent of market value, and residential real estate containing three or less units, which was assessed at 32 percent of market value. While conceding that "this is a close case," the court concluded that "the line drawn by the legislature between apartment buildings of four or more and three or less units is not 'wide of any reasonable mark' and is based on distinctions which are genuine and have a rational basis." 328 N.W.2d at 722. The uniformity and equality issues bearing on classification of property are considered further in Chapter 4, § 2 infra.

The Chicago Transaction Tax Ordinance, which imposed a levy on transactions consummated in the City of Chicago involving the lease or rental of specified categories of personal property, was at issue in Williams v. City of Chicago, 66 Ill.2d 423, 362 N.E.2d 1030 (1977). The court sustained the tax over the objection that it violated both the State uniformity and equality provisions and the Federal Equal Protection Clause because it allegedly singled out, on an arbitrary basis, particular types of personal property which were subject to the levy. The court referred to the fact that "[i]t is well established that legislative bodies have very broad powers in establishing classification defining the object of taxation which will withstand constitutional attack so long as the classifications are reasonable." 362 N.E.2d at 1035. It is worth noting that in the past the Illinois courts have viewed the Legislature's power to classify more narrowly. See, e.g., Lake Shore Auto Parts Co. v. Korzen, 49 Ill.2d 137, 273 N.E.2d 592 (1971), reversed 410 U.S. 356, 93 S.Ct. 1001 (1973), p. 72 infra.

G. *Differentiation in Taxation Based on Geography or Population.* A geographical differentiation in taxation was invalidated under the Georgia Constitution. Counties imposing sales taxes were granted the option by the legislature of reducing the county property tax in unincorporated areas outside municipalities, but not on property in municipalities. This differentiation was invalidated under the constitutional provision quoted in Note F supra. Martin v. Ellis, 242 Ga. 340, 249 S.E.2d 23 (1978). Legislatures often draw geographical lines in State taxing statutes under the pretext that they are drawing lines based on population. For example, legislation in Illinois provides rules for "counties with more than 3,000,000 inhabitants," Ill.Rev.Stat. § 501(e)—an unmistakable reference to Cook County, where Chicago is located. These population-based distinctions have generally withstood constitutional scrutiny under the State uniformity and equality provisions. See Annot., 98 A.L.R.3d 1083.

H. *Classification of Taxpayers by Marital Status.* The Oklahoma Supreme Court has held that the State's uniformity clause (as well as the Federal Equal Protection Clause) were no bar to the separate classification of single and married taxpayers for State income tax purposes. Sowders v. Oklahoma Tax Comm'n, 552 P.2d 698 (Okl.1976). A bachelor was therefore denied a refund of the difference between the amount of income tax he actually paid and the amount he would have paid had he been married and filed a joint return.

I. *References.* Professor Newhouse's two-volume treatise, Constitutional Uniformity and Equality in State Taxation (2d ed. 1984) is a valuable reference tool in this area. There is an extensive annotation on "classification and problems arising under uniformity and equality provisions" in 103 A.L.R. 18. See also Myers, "Open Space Taxation and State Constitutions," 33 Vand.L.Rev. 837 (1980); Comment, "Classification of Real Property for Tax Purposes in Illinois," 28 De Paul L.Rev. 849 (1979); Matthews, "The Function of Constitutional Provisions Requiring Uniformity in Taxation," 30 Ky.L.J. 31 (1949); Matthews, "Constitutional Uniformity as a Rule for the Validity of License Taxes in Kentucky," 36 Ky.L.J. 357 (1948); Garden, "Uniformity of Taxation in Missouri," 20 Wash.U.L.Q. 242 (1939).

B.   EQUAL PROTECTION OF THE LAWS

    * * * nor [shall any State] deny to any person within its jurisdiction the equal protection of the laws. * * * [U.S. Const., Amend. XIV, § 1.]

In 1886, the Supreme Court settled the law that the term "person," as used in the Equal Protection Clause (as well as in the Due Process Clause) of the Fourteenth Amendment, applies to corporations. Santa Clara County v. Southern Pacific R.R. Co., 118 U.S. 394, 6 S.Ct. 1132 (1886). Mr. Justice Black revived the issue in Connecticut General Life Insurance Co. v. Johnson, 303 U.S. 77, 58 S.Ct. 436 (1938), and in his dissent concluded that the clauses apply only to natural persons. Mr. Justice Douglas joined in this position in the dissent in Wheeling Steel Corporation v. Glander, 337 U.S. 562, 69 S.Ct. 1291 (1949). See Sholley, "Corporate Taxpayers and the 'Equal Protection' Clause," 31 Ill.L.Rev. 463, 567 (1936–1937); McLaughlin, "The Court, the Corporation and Conkling," 46 Am.Hist.Rev. 45 (1940). It is, however, well settled that corporations are not "citizens" and therefore are not protected by the

Privileges and Immunities Clause of the Fourteenth Amendment. See Western Turf Ass'n v. Greenberg, 204 U.S. 359, 27 S.Ct. 384 (1907).

SECTION 1. CLASSIFICATION OF PROPERTY AND TAX-PAYERS

LEHNHAUSEN v. LAKE SHORE AUTO PARTS CO.

Supreme Court of the United States, 1973.
410 U.S. 356, 93 S.Ct. 1001.

MR. JUSTICE DOUGLAS delivered the opinion of the Court.*

In 1970 the people of Illinois amended its constitution adding Art. IX–A to become effective January 1, 1971, S.H.A., and reading:

> "Notwithstanding any other provision of this Constitution, the taxation of personal property by valuation is prohibited as to individuals."

There apparently appeared on the ballot when Art. IX–A was approved the following:

> "The amendment would abolish the personal property tax by valuation levied against individuals. It would not affect the same tax levied against corporations and other entities not considered in law to be individuals. The amendment would achieve this result by adding a new article to the Constitution of 1870, Article IX–A, thus setting aside existing provisions of Article IX, Section 1 that require the taxation by valuation of all forms of property, real and personal or other, owned by individuals and corporations."

Respondent Lake Shore Auto Parts Co., a corporation, brought an action against Illinois officials on its behalf and on behalf of all other corporations and "non-individuals" subject to the personal property tax, claiming that the tax violated the Equal Protection Clause of the Fourteenth Amendment since it exempts from personal property taxes all personal property owned by individuals but retains such taxes as to personal property owned by corporations and other "non-individuals." The Circuit Court held the Revenue Act of Illinois, as amended by Art. IX–A, unconstitutional as respects corporations by reason of the Equal Protection Clause of the Fourteenth Amendment.

Shapiro and other individuals also brought suit alleging they are natural persons who own personal property, one for himself and his family, one as a sole proprietor of a business, and one as a partnership. A different trial judge entered an order in these cases dismissing the complaints except as to Shapiro and members of his class. The trial judge held that all other provisions of Illinois law imposing personal property taxes on property owned by corporations and other "non-individuals" were unaffected by Art. IX–A, in line with the statement on the ballot, quoted above.

* [Some of the Court's footnotes have been omitted.]

All respondents in both cases appealed to the Illinois Supreme Court, which held that Art. IX–A did not affect all forms of real and personal property taxes but only personal property taxes on individuals, which it construed to mean "ad valorem taxation of personal property owned by a natural person or by two or more natural persons as joint tenants or tenants in common." 49 Ill.2d 137, 148, 273 N.E.2d 592, 597. As so construed, the Illinois Supreme Court held that the tax violated the Equal Protection Clause of the Fourteenth Amendment. Id., at 151, 273 N.E.2d, at 599, one Justice dissenting. The cases are here on writs of certiorari which we granted. 405 U.S. 1039, 92 S.Ct. 1307, 31 L.Ed.2d 579.

The Equal Protection Clause does not mean that a State may not draw lines that treat one class of individuals or entities differently from the others. The test is whether the difference in treatment is an invidious discrimination. Harper v. Virginia Board of Elections, 383 U.S. 663, 666, 86 S.Ct. 1079, 1081, 16 L.Ed.2d 169. Where taxation is concerned and no specific federal right, apart from equal protection, is imperiled,[3] the States have large leeway in making classifications and drawing lines which in their judgment produce reasonable systems of taxation. * * *

[In Allied Stores of Ohio v. Bowers, 358 U.S. 522, 79 S.Ct. 437 (1959),] we used the phrase "palpably arbitrary" or "invidious" as defining the limits placed by the Equal Protection Clause on state power. Id., at 530, 79 S.Ct., at 442. State taxes which have the collateral effect of restricting or even destroying an occupation or a business have been sustained, so long as the regulatory power asserted is properly within the limits of the federal-state regime created by the Constitution. Magnano Co. v. Hamilton, 292 U.S. 40, 44–47, 54 S.Ct. 599, 601–602, 78 L.Ed. 1109. When it comes to taxes on corporations and taxes on individuals, great leeway is permissible so far as equal protection is concerned. They may be classified differently with respect to their right to receive or earn income. In Lawrence v. State Tax Comm'n, 286 U.S. 276, 283, 52 S.Ct. 556, 558, 76 L.Ed. 1102, a state statute relieved domestic corporations of an income tax derived from activities carried on outside the State, but imposed the tax on individuals obtaining such income. We upheld the tax against the claim that it violated the Equal Protection Clause, saying:

> "We cannot say that investigation in these fields would not disclose a basis for the legislation which would lead reasonable men to conclude that there is just ground for the difference here made. The existence, unchallenged, of differences between the taxation of incomes of individuals and of corporations in every federal revenue act since the adoption

3. Classic examples are the taxes that discriminated against newspapers, struck down under the First Amendment (Grosjean v. American Press Co., 297 U.S. 233, 56 S.Ct. 444, 80 L.Ed. 660) or that discriminated against interstate commerce (see Michigan–Wisconsin Pipe Line Co. v. Calvert, 347 U.S. 157, 74 S.Ct. 396, 98 L.Ed. 583) or required licenses to engage in interstate commerce.

of the Sixteenth Amendment, demonstrates that there may be." Id., at 283–284, 52 S.Ct., at 558.

It is true that in Quaker City Cab Co. v. Pennsylvania, 277 U.S. 389, 48 S.Ct. 553, 72 L.Ed. 927, the Court held that a gross receipts tax levied on corporations doing a taxi business violated the Equal Protection Clause of the Fourteenth Amendment, when no such tax was levied on individuals and partnerships operating taxicabs in competition with the corporate taxpayers. * * *

* * * [C]ases following *Quaker City Cab* have somewhat undermined it. White River Co. v. Arkansas, 279 U.S. 692, 49 S.Ct. 457, 73 L.Ed. 903, involved a state statute for collection of back taxes on lands owned by corporations but not individuals. The Court sustained the statute. Mr. Justice Butler, Mr. Chief Justice Taft, and Mr. Justice Van Devanter dissented, asserting that *Quaker City Cab* was not distinguishable. The majority made no effort to distinguish *Quaker City Cab* beyond saying that it did not involve, as did *White River,* back taxes. Id., at 696, 49 S.Ct., at 459.

In Rapid Transit Co. v. New York, 303 U.S. 573, 58 S.Ct. 721, 82 L.Ed. 1024, an excise tax was levied on every utility but not on other business units. In sustaining the tax against the claim of lack of equal protection, the Court said:

> "Since carriers or other utilities with the right of eminent domain, the use of public property, special franchises, or public contracts, have many points of distinction from other businesses, including relative freedom from competition, especially significant with increasing density of population and municipal expansion, these public service organizations have no valid ground by virtue of the equal protection clause to object to separate treatment related to such distinctions." Id., at 579, 58 S.Ct., at 724.

* * *[5]

Approval of the treatment "with that separateness" which distinguishes public service corporations from others, ibid., leads us to conclude in the present cases that making corporations and like entities, but not individuals, liable for ad valorem taxes on personal property does not transcend the requirements of equal protection.

5. In Atlantic & Pacific Tea Co. v. Grosjean, 301 U.S. 412, 57 S.Ct. 772, 81 L.Ed. 1193, a State classified chain stores for purposes of a chain store tax according to the number of stores—inside and outside the State. The Court sustained the tax, saying: "The statute bears equally upon all who fall into the same class, and this satisfies the guaranty of equal protection." Id., at 424, 57 S.Ct., at 776. In Carmichael v. Southern Coal Co., 301 U.S. 495, 57 S.Ct. 868, 81 L.Ed. 1245, a State laid an unemployment tax on employers, excluding, *inter alia,* agriculture, domestic service, crews of vessels on navigable waters, and eleemosynary institutions. The Court sustained the tax, saying: "This Court has repeatedly held that inequalities which result from a singling out of one particular class for taxation or exemption, infringe no constitutional limitation." Id., at 509, 57 S.Ct., at 872. And it added: "A legislature is not bound to tax every member of a class or none. It may make distinctions of degree having a rational basis, and when subjected to judicial scrutiny they must be presumed to rest on that basis if there is any conceivable state of facts which would support it." Id.

In Madden v. Kentucky, 309 U.S. 83, 60 S.Ct. 406, 84 L.Ed. 590, a State laid an ad valorem tax of 50 cents per $100 on deposits in banks outside the State and only 10 cents per $1,000 on deposits within the State. The classification was sustained against the charge of invidious discrimination, the Court noting that "in taxation, even more than in other fields, legislatures possess the greatest freedom in classification." Id., at 88, 60 S.Ct., at 408. There is a presumption of constitutionality which can be overcome "only by the most explicit demonstration that a classification is a hostile and oppressive discrimination against particular persons and classes." Id. And the Court added, "The burden is on the one attacking the legislative arrangement to negative every conceivable basis which might support it." Id. That idea has been elaborated. Thus, in Carmichael v. Southern Coal Co., 301 U.S. 495, 57 S.Ct. 868, 81 L.Ed. 1245, the Court, in sustaining an unemployment tax on employers,[6] said:

> A state legislature, in the enactment of laws, has the widest possible latitude within the limits of the Constitution. In the nature of the case it cannot record a complete catalogue of the considerations which move its members to enact laws. In the absence of such a record courts cannot assume that its action is capricious, or that, with its informed acquaintance with local conditions to which the legislation is to be applied, it was not aware of facts which afford reasonable basis for its action. Only by faithful adherence to this guiding principle of judicial review of legislation is it possible to preserve the legislative branch its rightful independence and its ability to function. [301 U.S. at 510.]

Illinois tells us that the individual personal property tax was discriminatory, unfair, almost impossible to administer, and economically unsound. Assessment practices varied from district to district. About a third of the individuals paid no personal property taxes at all, while the rest paid on their bank accounts, automobiles, household furniture, and other resources, and in rural areas they paid on their livestock, grain, and farm implements as well. As respects corporations, the State says, the tax is uniformly enforceable. Illinois says, moreover that Art. IX–A is only the first step in totally eliminating the ad valorem personal property tax by 1979 but for fiscal reasons it was impossible to abolish the tax all at once.

We could strike down this tax as discriminatory only if we substituted our judgment on facts of which we can be only dimly aware for a legislative judgment that reflects a vivid reaction to pressing fiscal problems. Quaker City Cab Co. v. Pennsylvania is only a relic of a bygone era. We cannot follow it and stay within the narrow confines of judicial review, which is an important part of our constitutional tradition.

Reversed.*

6. Note 5 supra.

* [This case is considered in Blackmon, "Implications of Lehnhausen v. Lake Shore Auto Parts—Weakening Equal Protection for Corporations," 16 Ariz.L.Rev. 41 (1974).]

Notes and Problems

A. *The Supreme Court's General Approach to the Equal Protection Clause.* As the Court observed in the principal case, "[w]here taxation is concerned and no specific federal right, apart from equal protection is concerned, the States have large leeway in making classifications and drawing lines which in their judgment produce reasonable systems of taxation." In Ohio Oil Co. v. Conway, 281 U.S. 146, 159, 50 S.Ct. 310, 314 (1929), the Court said:

> The States, in the exercise of their taxing power, as with respect to the exertion of other powers, are subject to the requirements of the due process and the equal protection clauses of the Fourteenth Amendment, but that Amendment imposes no iron rule of equality, prohibiting the flexibility and variety that are appropriate to schemes of taxation. The State may tax real and personal property in a different manner. It may grant exemptions. The State is not limited to ad valorem taxation. It may impose different specific taxes upon different trades and professions and may vary the rates of excise upon various products. In levying such taxes, the State is not required to resort to close distinctions or to maintain a precise, scientific uniformity with reference to composition, use, or value. To hold otherwise would be to subject the essential taxing power of the State to an intolerable supervision hostile to the basic principles of our Government and wholly beyond the protection which the general clause of the Fourteenth Amendment was intended to assure.

In Exxon Corp. v. Eagerton, 462 U.S. 176, 103 S.Ct. 2296 (1983), the Court reiterated its view of the broad leeway the States are accorded in drawing lines for tax purposes under the Equal Protection Clause. The taxpayers had attacked an Alabama statute that exempted royalty owners from an increase in the State's severance tax and that prohibited producers from passing the tax increase on to their purchasers. In addressing the equal protection challenge to these provisions, the Court observed:

> Because neither of the challenged provisions adversely affects a fundamental interest or contains a classification based upon a suspect criterion, they need only be tested under the lenient standard of rationality that this Court has traditionally applied in considering equal protection challenges to regulation of economic and commercial matters. Under that standard, a statute will be sustained if the legislature could have reasonably concluded that the challenged classification would promote a legitimate state purpose.

462 U.S. at 195–196, 103 S.Ct. at 2308 (citations omitted). The Court went on to conclude that the classifications passed muster under this standard. The pass-through prohibition "plainly bore a rational relationship to the State's legitimate purpose of protecting consumers from excessive prices." 462 U.S. at 196, 103 S.Ct. at 2308. As for the royalty-owner exemption, the Court declared that "the Alabama Legislature could have reasonably determined that * * * [the exemption] would encourage investment in oil or gas production." Id. In reaching its conclusion, the Court repeated its view that "[l]egislatures have especially broad latitude in creating classifi-

cations and distinctions in tax statutes." Id. (quoting Regan v. Taxation with Representation of Washington, 461 U.S. 540, 103 S.Ct. 1997 (1983)).

B. *Classification by Sex.* In Kahn v. Shevin, 416 U.S. 351, 94 S.Ct. 1734 (1974), the Supreme Court held that a Florida statute that provided an annual $500 property tax exemption for widows without providing any comparable exemption for widowers did not offend the Equal Protection Clause. The Court found that the gender-based classification had a rational basis and thus lay well within permissible limits as established by such cases as *Lehnhausen.* The dissenters would have struck down the exemption on the grounds that a gender-based classification, like classifications based on race and national origin, cannot be sustained simply because it rationally promotes legitimate governmental interests, and that the State had failed to show that its interest could not be achieved by a more precisely tailored statute or by the use of less drastic means.

C. *The Equal Protection Clause and the Classified Property Tax.* The Equal Protection Clause does not preclude the separate classification and taxation of different types of property. In Charlestown Federal Savings & Loan Association v. Alderson, 324 U.S. 182, 65 S.Ct. 624 (1945), the Court said:

> It is plain that the Fourteenth Amendment does not preclude a state from placing notes and receivables in a different class from personal property used in agriculture and the products of agriculture, including livestock, and taxing the two classes differently, even though the state places them in a single class for other purposes of taxation.
>
> * * *
>
> * * * Nor does the equal protection clause prohibit inequality in taxation which results from mere mistake or error in judgment of tax officials. * * * or which is not shown to be the result of intentional or systematic undervaluation of some but not all of the taxed property in a single class. * * * [321 U.S. at 191.]

After the New York Court of Appeals invalidated the State's long standing practice of assessing real property at fractional value as contrary to the statutory mandate requiring assessment at full value, Hellerstein v. Assessor of the Town of Islip, 37 N.Y.2d 1, 371 N.Y.S.2d 388, 332 N.E.2d 279 (1975), the legislature modified the statute by authorizing fractional assessment. Except in New York City and the adjoining Nassau County, the fraction to be applied uniformly is to be determined by the local taxing jurisdiction (N.Y.Real Prop.Tax § 305, CCH ¶ 91–990, P–H ¶ 32,105–D). In New York City and Nassau, a prescribed classified property tax system was established. See Chapter 4, § 3, Note E infra. At the same time, the legislature enacted provisions that permitted cities or towns, other than local taxing jurisdictions that had revalued their property in compliance with standards established by the State Board of Equalization and Assessment (SBEA), to adopt a classified dual rate structure. N.Y.Real Prop.Tax § 1901 et seq.

In accordance with the statute, the City of Rochester, which had undergone revaluation of its property in accordance with SBEA standards, classified all property into two classes: homestead property, defined as property housing three or fewer families, and all other property, and taxed

them at different rates. See Foss v. City of Rochester, 65 N.Y.2d 247, 491
N.Y.S.2d 128 (1985). The dual rate system was designed to preserve for one
to three family homeowners the preferential tax treatment they had
traditionally received under the assessment practices in vogue before the
Town of Islip decision came down. That was done by "allocating the share
of government costs * * * in the same manner as the owners of the two
classes historically had paid." 491 N.Y.S.2d at 132. The result was that
homestead property, which comprised 45.5 percent of the total assessed
value of the property in the city, paid only 34.5 percent of the property tax.

In discussing the challenges to this dual method of valuation, the Court
of Appeals stated:

> The Federal and State Constitutions do not prohibit dual tax rates
> or require that all taxpayers be treated the same. They require only
> that those similarly situated be treated uniformly. Thus, the creation
> of different classes for purposes of taxation is permissible as long as the
> classification is reasonable and the taxes imposed are uniform within
> the class (see, Shapiro v. City of New York, 32 N.Y.2d 96, 103–107, 343
> N.Y.S.2d 323, 296 N.E.2d 230, appeal dismissed 414 U.S. 804, 94 S.Ct.
> 68, 38 L.Ed.2d 40; New York Steam Corp. v. City of New York, 268
> N.Y. 137, 197 N.E. 172; People ex rel. Hatch v. Reardon, 184 N.Y. 431,
> 77 N.E. 970, supra; Matter of McPherson, 104 N.Y. 306, 10 N.E. 685;
> see, Lehnhausen v. Lake Shore Auto Parts Co., 410 U.S. 356, 93 S.Ct.
> 1001, 35 L.Ed.2d 351). "[S]ubject to constitutional inhibitions, the
> Legislature has very nearly unconstrained authority in the design of
> taxing impositions" (Matter of Long Is. Light. Co. v. State Tax Commn.,
> 45 N.Y.2d 529, 535, 410 N.Y.S.2d 561, 382 N.E.2d 1337; see also,
> Trump v. Chu, 65 N.Y.2d 20, 25, 489 N.Y.S.2d 455, 478 N.E.2d 971).
> [491 N.Y.S.2d at 133.]

The court, nevertheless, held that the assessment violated the Equal
Protection Clause, because of the effect the Rochester classified tax system
had on Monroe County taxes, of which Rochester is a part:

> Though such geographic classifications are not per se prohibited (Mat-
> ter of Colt Indus. v. Finance Administrator, 54 N.Y.2d 533, 446 N.Y.S.
> 2d 237, 430 N.E.2d 1290, appeal dismissed sub nom. Equitable Life
> Assur. Socy. v. Finance Admin., 459 U.S. 983, 103 S.Ct. 335, 74 L.Ed.2d
> 379, and cases cited at p. 544; Hess v. Mullaney, 213 F.2d 635, 639;
> Weissinger v. Boswell, 330 F.Supp. 615, 623), when article 19 is applied
> in this case the taxes levied result in invidious discrimination between
> owners of similar properties in different assessing units.

> Monroe County is taxing non-homestead property in Rochester at a
> higher rate than similar non-homestead properties outside of the City
> of Rochester simply because, under the provisions of article 19, Roches-
> ter imposes a higher share of the tax levy on non-homestead properties
> than do the other towns in the county. It does so by establishing rates
> which are artificial constructs based upon the statutory formulae. The
> resulting disparity in taxes imposed on Rochester and town properties
> cannot be equalized because the Rochester rate is not related to the full
> or assessed value of the property or to any other county-wide norm. It
> is based upon the proportionate share of the tax burden borne by

properties within the city in the past and not upon the relative assessed values of properties in the two assessing units. The effective rate cannot be equalized after determining the shares of the levy to be raised in the various assessing units, as in the past, because the shares of the levy are apportioned to two classes of property in Rochester, each with a different rate, and to one class of property in the towns, taxed at a single rate wholly unrelated to the assessments or rates in Rochester. Moreover, uniform rates for homestead and non-homestead properties in the city and the towns could not be determined or "equalized", even if a system for equalizing them existed, until and unless these various assessing units elect to adopt article 19 because the measuring assessment roll is not determined until after that election is made (Real Property Tax Law § 1901[*l*]). Inevitably then, as plaintiff contends, non-homestead property in the city will pay a higher county tax than similar property in other assessing units of Monroe County because the City of Rochester has elected to impose a higher tax rate on such properties whereas the other assessing units have not. [491 N.Y.S.2d at 134.]

After the *Foss* case was decided, the legislature adopted mandatory legislation which shifted the responsibilities for calculating the tax or tax rates and levying the tax on individual properties from the counties to the cities and towns. That provision was, likewise, held unconstitutional on the ground that the "imposition of demonstrably different county tax burdens, solely by geographic location, continues unabated". Foss v. City of Rochester, 66 N.Y.2d 872, 498 N.Y.S.2d 758 (1985).

D. *Illustrations of Distinctions Between Taxpayers Sustained Under the Equal Protection Clause.* In Independent Warehouses, Inc. v. Scheele, 331 U.S. 70, 67 S.Ct. 1062 (1947), the Court sustained a tax which applied only to commercial warehouses and not to private warehouses. The taxpayer contended that this was a discriminatory levy which infringed the Equal Protection Clause. In rejecting this contention, it was stated that the "Court has repeatedly held that inequalities which result from a singling out of one particular class for taxation or exemption, infringe no constitutional limitation."

In Dixie Ohio Express Co. v. State Revenue Commission, 306 U.S. 72, 59 S.Ct. 435 (1938), the taxpayer contended the Georgia tax on its trucks violated the Equal Protection Clause, since truckers for hire paid higher taxes than trucks operated to carry the owner's freight or goods. The Court said (306 U.S. at 78, 59 S.Ct. at 438):

Is the act repugnant to the Equal Protection Clause? Appellant insists that it is because of the higher taxes imposed on those who haul for hire. But it fails to show lack of facts sufficient to justify the discrimination. In the absence of proof to the contrary, it is to be assumed that the use of the roads by one hauling not for hire is generally limited to transportation of his own property as an incident to his occupation or business and that it is substantially less than that of one who is engaged in the business of common carrier thereon for hire. As hauling not for hire is likely to be occasional and accessory and as hauling for hire is a business the success of which depends on the loading of the vehicles used and mileage made by them, the classification complained of may not be held arbitrary or without reasonable foundation.

New York City's commercial rent or occupancy tax, levied on tenants renting commercial property and computed by a percentage of rent paid, was challenged, *inter alia,* on the ground that the taxing of tenant occupants of real estate, while owner occupants are not taxed violated the Equal Protection Clause of the Federal and State Constitutions. The Court sustained the classification as a reasonable one. Ampco Printing–Advertisers' Offset Corp. v. City of New York, 14 N.Y.2d 11, 197 N.E.2d 285 (1964).

E. *Illustrations of Other Distinctions Sustained Under the Equal Protection Clause.* The Florida Supreme Court has held that the legislature may constitutionally tax a leasehold of public property as realty rather than personalty, and that it was neither arbitrary nor unreasonable to treat such a lease for a term of 99 years or more as ownership for valuation purposes. Williams v. Jones, 326 So.2d 425 (Fla.1975), appeal dismissed 429 U.S. 803, 97 S.Ct. 34 (1976). The Mississippi Supreme Court has held that a State tax on diesel fuel did not violate the Equal Protection Clause although other fuels such as propane gas were not taxed. Sharpe v. Standard Oil Co., 322 So.2d 457 (Miss.1975), appeal dismissed 425 U.S. 947, 96 S.Ct. 1720 (1976).

F. *Illustrations of Taxes Held Violative of the Equal Protection Clause.* In Matter of Merchants Refrigerating Co. v. Taylor, 275 N.Y. 113, 9 N.E.2d 799 (1937), the court declared that it would constitute an unreasonable classification to tax refrigerated warehouses at the higher rate applicable to public utilities, while businesses generally, including non-refrigerated warehouses, were subjected to the lower rates applicable to business generally.

A classification issue arose in a Nebraska case in connection with a reporting requirement imposed on public warehouses. The statute required the warehousemen to report all tangible personal property stored with them on March 1st of each year, except used household articles. The court held that the statute violated the Federal Equal Protection Clause in arbitrarily discriminating between warehouses of used household goods and of all other goods. United States Cold Storage Corp. v. Stolinski, 168 Neb. 513, 96 N.W.2d 408 (1959). While recognizing the legislature's wide discretion in classifying businesses or persons, the court held that it "may not arbitrarily divide a natural class of persons in two fractions and then enact different rules for the government of each" (168 Neb. at 525, 96 N.W.2d at 417.) In view of the purpose of the statute to uncover untaxed articles, the court found no reasonable basis for excluding used household goods.

G. *Separate Taxation of Wage and Salary Earners as Compared with Business Income.* A challenge to the St. Louis municipal income tax by wage and salary earners, whose gross earnings are taxed, on the ground that only the net profits of self-employed persons, corporations and other business enterprises are taxed, was rejected as premature in Walters v. City of St. Louis, 347 U.S. 231, 74 S.Ct. 505 (1954), commented on in 40 Am. Bar Ass'n J. 517 (1954). Because the regulations had not been passed upon in the State court, the Supreme Court held that it did not know that, as claimed by the complainants, "corporations and self-employed persons would be allowed to deduct such items as taxes and charitable contributions, whereas such deductions would not be allowed to employees." Would the statute, if thus implemented, violate the Equal Protection Clause? The Court did declare that "[c]lassification of earned income as against profits is not uncommon," pointing to social security taxes and the separate treatment of earned income and capital gains in the Federal Internal Revenue Code. "We cannot say that a difference in treatment of the taxpayers deriving income from these different sources is *per se* a prohibited discrimination." (347 U.S. at 236, 74 S.Ct. at 509). Justices Douglas and Black in concurring stated that they were "saving for a future day the serious and substantial question under the Equal Protection Clause raised by the regulations which grant employers deductions for taxes paid the Federal Government, yet do not allow employees a deduction for the same tax." (347 U.S. at 238, 74 S.Ct. at 510.) Cf. Estes v. City of Gadsden, 266 Ala. 166, 94 So.2d 744 (1957).

In Barhorst v. City of St. Louis, 423 S.W.2d 843 (Mo.1967), the St. Louis gross earnings tax came before the Supreme Court of Missouri which upheld the propriety of the separate classification for tax purposes of "salaries, wages, commissions and other compensation earned" which were taxed, while "rents, dividends, interest and the like" were not taxed. In rejecting attacks on the levy both under the State uniformity clause and the Federal Equal Protection Clause, the court found the classification reasonable in part because, "[r]ents, dividends, and interest are derived primarily from property already subject to city tax if within the jurisdiction, and a classification to avoid double taxation has been recognized as constitutionally sound * * *." (423 S.W.2d at 846.) The court also denied that the levy was "arbitrary" in that it "unreasonably discriminates between resident individual taxpayers and corporate taxpayers," because it taxes the "entire earned income of the individual, but only that earned in the City by the corporation." Here, the court relied largely on the existing widespread practice of limiting corporate franchise and net income taxation to income from sources within the States, whereas resident individuals are typically taxed on income from all sources.

In Shapiro v. City of New York, 32 N.Y.2d 96, 343 N.Y.S.2d 323, 296 N.E.2d 230, appeal dismissed 414 U.S. 804, 94 S.Ct. 68 (1973), the Court of Appeals, per Fuld, J., upheld the extension of New York City's unincorporated business income tax to previously exempted self-employed professionals. The taxpayer, a lawyer, had argued that the levy violated the Equal Protection Clause on the grounds that it imposed a heavier burden on self-employed individuals than on corporations and salaried wage earners, and that it impermissibly classified self-employed professionals as unincorporated businesses. Cf. O'Connor v. State Tax Comm'n, 50 A.D.2d 675, 375 N.Y.S.2d 425 (1975), appeal dismissed 38 N.Y.2d 937, certiorari denied 429 U.S. 923, 97 S.Ct. 321 (1976).

H. *Chain Store Taxes.* The chain store tax cases have produced a number of key equal protection decisions. In State Board of Tax Commissioners of Indiana v. Jackson, 283 U.S. 527, 51 S.Ct. 540 (1931), the Court upheld one of the most direct methods of reaching chain organizations—

that of a license tax on each store, graduated according to the number of stores under unified ownership or control. There, an Indiana statute imposed on persons maintaining stores in the State an annual fee, with a sliding scale based on the number of stores under the same management, running from $3 for one store to a maximum rate of $25 for each store in excess of 20. The taxpayer operated 225 small grocery stores, paying a fee of $5,443. Many other single unit stores had a larger volume of business, but paid a fee of only $3. Owners of chain stores having only one store in Indiana paid only the $3 fee. Four justices dissented from the decision sustaining the tax. The case is noted in 7 Ind.L.J. 179 (1931).

In Fox v. Standard Oil Co. of N.J., 294 U.S. 87, 55 S.Ct. 333 (1935), the Court upheld a West Virginia graduated license tax, running from $2 for one store to $250 for each store in excess of 75, as not involving a denial of equal protection to the operator of a large chain of gasoline filling stations. It held that the levy of heavier tax burdens on filling station chains than on chains selling other commodities was not unreasonable in view of the large number of units in the gasoline business.

The vice of the Florida license tax on chain stores invalidated in Louis K. Liggett Co. v. Lee, 288 U.S. 517, 53 S.Ct. 481, 85 A.L.R. 699 (1933), noted in 17 Marq.L.Rev. 296 (1933), was that the rate of tax on each store increased if the chain operated in more than one county. The Court followed the Jackson case, supra, and upheld the Florida tax in all respects, except the distinction between intra- and intercounty chains, in which it found no material differences in the two classes as to number of stores operated, buying power or size of the chains, the number of customers served, or the privileges enjoyed. If, as the Court said, a tax based merely on the number of stores operated in a chain is fair and reasonable, why should a tax be invalidated which is increased by reference to the number of counties in which the chain operates?

In Great Atlantic & Pacific Tea Co. v. Grosjean, 301 U.S. 412, 57 S.Ct. 772 (1937), the Court upheld a license tax graduated by reference to the total number of stores under the same management or ownership, including stores located outside the State. The A & P chain was subjected to a rate of $550 per store located in Louisiana, because its total chain consisted of more than 500 stores; competitors with 10 or fewer stores paid only $10 per store. The Court held that the overall size of the chain contributed to its economic power, purchasing power, and so forth, and could be considered in fixing the rate of tax.

I. *Graduation of Rate by Reference to Gross Receipts.* In Stewart Dry Goods Co. v. Lewis, 294 U.S. 550, 55 S.Ct. 525 (1935), noted in 13 Texas L.Rev. 469 (1935), 21 Iowa L.Rev. 93 (1935), a Kentucky license tax on retail merchants was graduated according to gross sales. The rate began at one-twentieth of one percent of the first $400,000 of gross sales and rose to one percent of gross sales in excess of $1,000,000. In invalidating the tax as repugnant to the Equal Protection Clause, the Court (per Roberts, J.) characterized the levy as "unequal, whimsical and arbitrary, as much so as would be a tax on tangible personal property, say cattle, stepped up in rate on each additional animal owned by the taxpayer, or a tax on land similarly graduated according to the number of parcels owned." If an income tax may be graduated by reference to the amount of the taxpayer's net income, why may a tax not be graduated by reference to gross sales?

J. *Validity of Tax on National Bank Shares at Higher Rate Than Tax on State Savings and Loan Associations Under Federal Statute.* The Court, in a divided opinion, has upheld the validity of a Michigan tax on owners of shares of a national bank at a higher stated rate than that applied to savings and loan associations. Michigan National Bank v. State of Michigan, 365 U.S. 467, 81 S.Ct. 659 (1961). The controversy grew out of a 1953 amendment to the Michigan tax on intangibles, which imposed a tax of 5½ mills "on the privilege of ownership of each share of stock" of national or State banks, measured in substance by the value of the shares. A national bank contested the validity of the tax on the ground that it exceeded the limits of Congressional authorization of State taxation of shares of national banks (U.S.Rev.Stat. § 5219, as amended 12 U.S.C. § 548) because the shares of competitors, savings and loan associations, are taxed only at ⅖ of a mill or ¼ of a mill. The Federal statute authorizes the States to tax such shares but "not at a greater rate than is assessed upon other moneyed capital in the hands of individual citizens of such state coming into competition with the business of national banks." Analyzing the Michigan tax structure, a majority of the Court found that no discrimination was effected, in part because a dollar invested in national bank shares controls a larger amount of moneyed capital than a dollar invested in shares of a savings and loan association. But see United States v. State Tax Comm'n, 481 F.2d 963 (1st Cir.1973), holding under a similar nondiscrimination provision that limiting deductions under Massachusetts taxing statutes to losses from unpaid loans secured by out-of-state realty within a 50-mile radius of the home office effectively placed a higher tax on Federal than on non-Federal savings and loan associations because the Federal associations were permitted to make loans within a 100–mile radius of such office whereas the making of such loans by State associations was limited to a 50-mile radius. For the mass of litigation that has ensued over the Federal statute at issue in these cases and the refinements, complications, obscurities, and difficulties it has engendered, see the extensive study by Professor Simeon E. Leland, "The History and Impact of Section 5219 on the Taxation of National Banks," App. 6, in Report of Study Under P.L. 91–156 and 92–213, Board of Governors, Federal Reserve System, for the Senate Banking, Housing, and Urban Affairs Committee (92d Cong., 2d Sess.1972).

K. *Discrimination Between Domestic Corporations.* In F.S. Royster Guano Co. v. Virginia, 253 U.S. 412, 40 S.Ct. 560 (1920), a domestic corporation engaged in manufacturing both in Virginia and other States was taxed on its net income derived from all sources. The statutes exempted from the net income tax domestic corporations which conducted no business within the State. The Court invalidated the inclusion of income derived from out-of-state business operations in the measure of the plaintiff's tax under the Equal Protection Clause. It declared that "no ground is suggested, nor can we conceive of any, sustaining this exemption which does not apply with equal or greater force as a ground for exempting from taxation the income of Virginia corporations derived from sources without the State where they also transact income-producing business within the State." 253 U.S. at 416, 40 S.Ct. at 562. Justices Brandeis and

Holmes dissented, rejecting the view that the classification "is illusory and the State's action arbitrary." The dissent suggested that with the widespread practice of incorporating businesses in certain States and the consequent loss of incorporation and registration fees, Virginia had adequate basis for discouraging its citizens from resorting to such out-of-state incorporation, where no business was to be done in the State. The advantages of incorporating elsewhere would not be present where a part of the business was to be done in the State. It is interesting to note that the justification given by the dissent was based on conjecture, not on any facts as to the reason for the exemption offered by the State. For a case following the decision in the *Royster Guano* case, see Cheney v. Stephens, Inc., 231 Ark. 541, 330 S.W.2d 949 (1960); see also 122 A.L.R. 983. It has been held that an individual may complain of discrimination in favor of a corporation. Frost v. Corporation Commission of Oklahoma, 278 U.S. 515, 49 S.Ct. 235 (1929).

L. *The Poll Tax as a Requirement to Vote in State Elections.* In a historic decision growing out of the civil rights revolution, the Supreme Court struck down, as offensive to the Equal Protection Clause, a Virginia statute authorizing a poll tax, which had to be paid in order to vote in State elections. Harper v. Virginia Board of Elections, 383 U.S. 663, 86 S.Ct. 1079 (1966). The Court concluded that a "State violates the Equal Protection Clause of the Fourteenth Amendment whenever it makes the affluence of the voter or payment of any fee an election standard. Voter qualifications have no relation to wealth nor to paying or not paying this or any other tax." 383 U.S. at 666, 86 S.Ct. at 1081. Justices Black, Harlan and Stewart dissented. The case is noted in 80 Harv.L.Rev. 124 (1966); 8 Wm. & Mary L.Rev. 161 (1966); 16 Am.U.L.Rev. 128 (1966).

M. *State Court Decisions Under the Equal Protection Clause.* State courts are, of course, bound by the Supreme Court's precedents when they construe the *federal* Equal Protection Clause. When construing equal protection clauses of State constitutions, however, the States are free to depart from the Supreme Court's views of equal protection. The most far-reaching State court decisions that have varied from the Supreme Court's equal protection doctrine are the school financing cases, in which some State courts have struck down, under their equal protection clauses, property taxes that would have been sustained by the Supreme Court. See Note N infra. Other State court decisions that may run counter to the Supreme Court's relaxed interpretation of the Federal Equal Protection Clause include the invalidation of a tax on gummed cigarette papers because ungummed papers were not taxed, Robert Burton Associates, Ltd. v. Eagerton, 432 So.2d 1267 (Ala.1983), the invalidation of a tax on tangible personal property stored in public warehouses because household goods were not taxed, United States Cold Storage Corp. v. Stolinski, 168 Neb. 513, 96 N.W.2d 408 (1959), and the invalidation of a public utilities gross receipts tax imposed upon a nonregulated refrigerated warehouse because the tax was not imposed on other warehouses or on businesses generally. Merchants Refrigerating Co. v. Taylor, 275 N.Y. 113, 9 N.E.2d 799 (1937). The New York Court of Appeals' current approach to equal protection analysis appears to be more in line with the Supreme Court's views. In Trump v. Chu, 65 N.Y.2d 20, 478 N.E.2d 971, 489 N.Y.S.2d 455 (1985), appeal dismissed 474 U.S. 915, 106 S.Ct. 285 (1985), the court sustained over equal protection objections New York's 10 percent tax on transfers of realty where the consideration is $1,000,000 or more. The court was unmoved by the fact that a taxpayer who sells his property for $999,999 and has a gain of $500,000 pays no tax whereas a taxpayer who sells his property for $1,000,001 and has a similar $500,000 gain must pay a tax of $50,000.

N. *Uniformity and Equality Provisions as Compared to Equal Protection Clause.* In Reed v. Bjornson, 191 Minn. 254, 253 N.W. 102 (1934), a graduated income tax was held not to contravene the Minnesota constitutional provision that "taxes shall be uniform upon the same class of subjects." The court compared the State constitutional requirements with the Equal Protection Clause of the Fourteenth Amendment and concluded that the State uniformity clause imposed no broader restrictions on the legislative power of the State in respect to classification for purposes of taxation than did the Equal Protection Clause. Accord, National Tea Co. v. State, 205 Minn. 443, 286 N.W. 360, 362 (1939), remanded 309 U.S. 551, 60 S.Ct. 676 (1940), reaffirmed 208 Minn. 607, 294 N.W. 230 (1940).

A two percent gross receipts tax applicable only to merchants who have their trading stamps redeemed by some person other than the merchant who gives the stamps was held to be an unreasonable classification, violating the Tennessee constitutional equivalent of the Equal Protection Clause of the Federal Constitution. Logan's Supermarkets, Inc. v. Atkins, 202 Tenn. 438, 304 S.W.2d 628 (1957); see Note, 11 Vand.L.Rev. 1397 (1958); 25 Tenn.L.Rev. 397 (1958).

A Florida statute provides that all agricultural lands being used as such should be assessed on an acreage basis, even though they are part of a subdivision plot, commercially zoned. This was held not to violate the uniformity requirement of the Florida Constitution, which applies only to rates of taxation and does not prohibit classification of property to achieve a just valuation of different property. Moreover, the separate classification of agricultural lands was not regarded as unreasonable, arbitrary or unjustly discriminatory, so as to violate State and Federal Equal Protection Clause provisions. Lanier v. Overstreet, 175 So.2d 521 (Fla.1965).

Some State courts have declared that "the equal protection clause of the federal constitution and state constitutional provisions pertaining to equality and uniformity of taxation are substantially similar and that, in general, what violates one will contravene the other, and vice versa." Associated Railway Equipment Owners v. Wilson, 167 Kan. 608, 617, 208 P.2d 604, 612 (1949); Recanzone v. State Tax Comm'n, 92 Nev. 302, 550 P.2d 401 (1976). In many States this statement would be untrue, for the State uniformity and equality provisions have frequently been construed to prevent classifications of property, graduated income taxes, and other differences in tax treatment held permissible under the Equal Protection Clause. Thus in State ex rel. La Follette v. Torphy, 85 Wis.2d 94, 270 N.W.2d 187 (1978), the Wisconsin Supreme Court ruled that the property tax credit granted to owners of certain homes and rental units who make improvements to the home or rental unit violated the State's uniformity clause even though it passed muster under the Federal and State Equal Protection Clauses.

O. *School Financing, the Equal Protection Clause, and Related State Requirements.* In its landmark ruling in San Antonio Independent School Dist. v. Rodriguez, 411 U.S. 1, 93 S.Ct. 1278 (1973), the Supreme Court rejected the argument that a system of public school financing which relies on local property taxation denies equal protection because of substantial interdistrict disparities in per pupil expenditures resulting primarily from differences in the value of assessable property and the comparative densities of school populations among the districts. While the Court's opinion has undermined other decisions to the extent that they had reached a contrary conclusion on *Federal* constitutional grounds, e.g., Van Dusartz v. Hatfield, 334 F.Supp. 870 (D.Minn.1971); cf. Serrano v. Priest, 5 Cal.3d 584, 96 Cal.Rptr. 601, 487 P.2d 1241 (1971), school financing systems which rely on local property taxation have been and continue to be assailed on State grounds.[9]

Relying on equal protection and similar clauses of State constitutions, courts in Arkansas, Michigan, and Wyoming have struck down their States' systems of school financing that were based on local property taxation. Dupree v. Alma School District No. 30, 279 Ark. 340, 651 S.W.2d 90 (1983); Milliken v. Green, 389 Mich. 1, 203 N.W.2d 457 (1972);[10] Washakie County School District Number One v. Herschler, 606 P.2d 310 (Wyo.1980), cert. denied 449 U.S. 824, 101 S.Ct. 86 (1980). In Connecticut, New Jersey, Washington, and West Virginia, the school financing systems have also been struck down on the ground that they conflicted with constitutional provisions requiring the furnishing of a "thorough and efficient" or a "free" or an "ample" public education system for all children. Horton v. Meskill, 172 Conn. 615, 376 A.2d 359 (1977); Robinson v. Cahill, 62 N.J. 473, 303 A.2d 273 (1973), cert. denied 414 U.S. 976, 94 S.Ct. 292 (1973); Seattle School District No. 1 v. State, 90 Wash.2d 476, 585 P.2d 71 (1978); Pauley v. Kelly, 162 W.Va. 672, 255 S.E.2d 859 (1979). However, similar State constitutional challenges to school financing by property taxation were rejected in Arizona, Colorado, Idaho, Maryland, New York, Ohio, Oregon, and Virginia. Shofstall v. Hollins, 110 Ariz. 88, 515 P.2d 590 (1973); Lujan v. Colorado State Board of Education, 649 P.2d 1005 (Colo.1982); Thompson v. Engelking, 96 Idaho 793, 537 P.2d 635 (1975); Hornbeck v. Somerset County Board of Education, 295 Md. 597, 458 A.2d 758 (1983); Board of Education, Levittown Union Free School District v. Nyquist, 57 N.Y.2d 27, 453 N.Y.S.2d 643, 439 N.E.2d 359 (1982) appeal dismissed 459 U.S. 1138, 103 S.Ct. 775 (1983); Board of Education of City School District of Cincinnati v. Walter, 58 Ohio St.2d 368, 390 N.E.2d 813 (1979), cert. denied 444 U.S. 1015, 100 S.Ct. 665 (1980); Olsen v. State, 276 Or. 9, 554 P.2d 139

9. The *Serrano* case, which was the first decision of the highest court of any State holding the school financing system unconstitutional, was decided under both the Federal and State Equal Protection Clauses, which the court regarded as subject to the same interpretation. This is the leading opinion in the field; it deals extensively with the issues and has been followed by other States. No petition for certiorari was made to the Supreme Court from the *Serrano* decision. Instead the California system for school financing was revised to satisfy the requirements of *Serrano*.

10. Following the Supreme Court's decision in *Rodriguez*, the Michigan court vacated its earlier decision, even though it rested on State law grounds, and upheld the constitutionality of Michigan's school financing system. Milliken v. Green, 390 Mich. 389, 212 N.W.2d 711 (1973).

(1976); Burruss v. Wilkerson, 310 F.Supp. 572 (W.D.Va.1969), affirmed memorandum 397 U.S. 44, 90 S.Ct. 812 (1970).

The New Jersey experience with the legality of school financing is a fascinating illustration of the interaction between the legal and political processes. In Robinson v. Cahill, 62 N.J. 473, 303 A.2d 273, certiorari denied 414 U.S. 976, 94 S.Ct. 292 (1973) (*Robinson I*), the New Jersey Supreme Court ruled that New Jersey's system of financing public education by local property taxation violated the State's obligation to furnish a thorough and efficient system of free public schools. However, in *Robinson II* (Robinson v. Cahill, 63 N.J. 196, 306 A.2d 65, certiorari denied 414 U.S. 976, 94 S.Ct. 292 (1973)), the court decided to take no action if the State legislature acted by December 31, 1974 to enact a comprehensive constitutional plan for State public education. When the legislature refused to change the system of school financing from one based on local property taxation to one funded by some other means, the court first delayed action and then ordered the disbursement of funds to finance the schools in accordance with specific criteria approved by the court. Robinson v. Cahill, 67 N.J. 35, 335 A.2d 6 (1975) (*Robinson III*); Robinson v. Cahill, 67 N.J. 333, 339 A.2d 193 (1975), republished at 69 N.J. 133, 351 A.2d 713 (1975) (*Robinson IV*). In response to this judicial action, the State legislature passed the Public School Education Act of 1975, which was designed to equalize payments among schools; the legislature, however, did not specifically provide for funding of the Act. The Act was held to be constitutional on its face, on the assumption that it would be fully funded. Robinson v. Cahill, 69 N.J. 449, 355 A.2d 129 (1976) (*Robinson V*). When the State legislature refused to enact an income tax to fund the Act, the court enjoined State public officials from operating the schools under existing financing schemes. Robinson v. Cahill, 70 N.J. 155, 358 A.2d 457 (1976) (*Robinson VI*). Resistance to a State income tax was very strong in New Jersey, but when the State's public schools closed and a Federal court refused to lift the State court's injunction, the legislature adopted a modified type of income tax to fund the Public School Education Act. The New Jersey Supreme Court then lifted its own injunction. Robinson v. Cahill, 70 N.J. 464, 360 A.2d 400 (1976) (*Robinson VII*).

State constitutional restrictions have also been held to limit the power of State legislatures to equalize educational opportunity through property tax reform. In Buse v. Smith, 74 Wis.2d 550, 247 N.W.2d 141 (1976), the court held that those parts of the Wisconsin School Finance Act which required property-rich districts to transfer a portion of their local tax revenues to the State for redistribution to districts with relatively lower valuations violated the State's uniformity provision. The case is noted in 90 Harv.L.Rev. 1528 (1977).

There is an extensive literature on the school finance issue. See Coons, Clune & Sugarman, "Educational Opportunity: A Workable Constitutional Test for State Financial Structures," 57 Calif.L.Rev. 305 (1969); Benson, "State Assumption of Educational Costs," and other papers on "Financing Elementary and Secondary Education," 1971 Nat. Tax Ass'n Procs. 750 et seq.; Carrington, "Financing the American Dream: Equality and School Taxes," 73 Colum.L.Rev. 1227 (1973); ACIR, "Financing Schools and Property Tax Relief: A State Responsibility" (A–40 1973); "Future Directions for School Finance Reform: A Symposium," 38 Law & Contemp. Prob. 293 (1974); Dugan, "Constitutionality of School Finance Systems under State Law: New York's Turn," 27 Syracuse L.Rev. 573 (1976); Zelinsky, "Educational Equalization and Suburban Sprawl: Subsidizing the Suburbs through School Finance Reform," 71 Nw.U.L.Rev. 161 (1976); Andersen, "School Finance Litigation—The Styles of Judicial Intervention," 55 Wash.L.Rev. 137 (1979); Note, "School Finance Reforms for Ohio," 12 Akron L.Rev. 771 (1979).

SECTION 2. SEPARATE CLASSIFICATION OF FOREIGN AND DOMESTIC CORPORATIONS

(a) The Insurance Company Cases

Historical Background. Taxes levied on foreign insurance companies for the privilege of doing business in the State have played a large role in the development of equal protection principles under the Fourteenth Amendment. Foreign corporations are, of course, protected by the Commerce Clause from more onerous taxes on the conduct of interstate business than those levied on the same type of intrastate business. See Chapter 6, Subd. B, § 8 infra. That constitutional protection does not, however, extend to a foreign corporation which seeks to enter a State to conduct an *intrastate* business. Atlantic Refining Co. v. Virginia, 302 U.S. 22, 58 S.Ct. 75 (1937). Consequently, the only Federal constitutional barrier against discriminatory taxation of foreign corporations seeking licenses to carry on intrastate business within the State is the Equal Protection Clause. Southern Ry. v. Greene, 216 U.S. 400, 30 S.Ct. 287 (1910). The Supreme Court, however, had given that clause a rigidly restrictive interpretation, which excluded from its scope a foreign corporation that had not yet entered the State to do business, on the theory that until that had occurred, the corporation is not "a person within its [the State's] jurisdiction" and is not, therefore, entitled to the equal protection of its laws. Philadelphia Fire Ass'n v. New York, 119 U.S. 110, 7 S.Ct. 108 (1886); Lincoln Nat. Life Ins. Co. v. Read, 325 U.S. 673, 65 S.Ct. 1220 (1945).

This reading of the Equal Protection Clause had a bizarre development in the taxation of out-of-state insurance companies. Shortly after the end of the Civil War, the Court held that "insurance is not commerce." As a consequence, fees imposed as a condition of obtaining licenses to operate in a State were upheld, even though no comparable taxes were levied on domestic insurers. Paul v. Virginia, 75 U.S. (8 Wall.) 168 (1868), and cases cited above. However, once the foreign corporation has been licensed and has entered the State, it becomes entitled to equal protection of the laws as a person within the State's jurisdiction. Southern Ry. v. Greene, supra. A number of discriminatory, and at times retaliatory, levies based on the laws of the insurer's State of incorporation have been struck down by the Court under the Equal Protection Clause. See Concordia Fire Ins. Co. v. Illinois, 292 U.S. 535; 54 S.Ct. 830 (1934); Hanover Fire Ins. Co. v. Carr, 272 U.S.

494, 47 S.Ct. 179 (1926). See 91 A.L.R. at 798 as to retaliatory insurance tax cases. In State v. Firemen's Fund Ins. Co., 223 Ala. 134, 134 So. 858 (1931), noted in 16 Minn.L.Rev. 433 (1932), an Alabama statute imposed a license tax on foreign fire insurance companies doing business within that State. A California insurance company, duly authorized to do business in Alabama, was sought to be taxed at a higher rate on the ground that California taxed foreign fire insurance companies at such higher rate. The court held such a retaliatory tax invalid as a violation of the Equal Protection Clause. See Hale, "Unconstitutional Conditions and Constitutional Rights," 35 Colum.L. Rev. 321 (1935).

Except for the insurance and liquor businesses, the States have not generally sought to impose discriminatory taxes, as a condition of the granting of a license to do business, on foreign corporations deemed not to be engaged in interstate commerce. See J. Hellerstein, "State Tax Discrimination Against Out-of-Staters," 21 Nat.Tax J. 113 (1977).

METROPOLITAN LIFE INSURANCE COMPANY v. WARD

Supreme Court of the United States, 1985.
470 U.S. 869, 105 S.Ct. 1676.

JUSTICE POWELL delivered the opinion of the Court.*

This case presents the question whether Alabama's domestic preference tax statute, Ala.Code §§ 27–4–4 and 27–4–5 (1975), that taxes out-of-state insurance companies at a higher rate than domestic insurance companies, violates the Equal Protection Clause.

I

Since 1955, the State of Alabama has granted a preference to its domestic insurance companies by imposing a substantially lower gross premiums tax rate on them than on out-of-state (foreign) companies.[2] Under the current statutory provisions, foreign life insurance companies pay a tax on their gross premiums received from business conducted in Alabama at a rate of 3 percent, and foreign companies selling other types of insurance pay at a rate of 4 percent. Ala.Code § 27–4–4(a) (1975). All domestic insurance companies, in contrast, pay at a rate of only 1 percent on all types of insurance premiums. § 27–4–5(a). As a result, a foreign insurance company doing the same type and volume of business in Alabama as a domestic company generally will pay three to four times as much in gross premiums taxes as its domestic competitor.

---

* [Some of the Court's footnotes have been omitted.]

2. For domestic preference tax purposes, Alabama defines a domestic insurer as a company that both is incorporated in Alabama and has its principal office and chief place of business within the State. Ala.Code § 27–4–1(3) (1975). A corporation that does not meet both of these criteria is characterized as a foreign insurer. § 27–4–1(2).

Alabama's domestic preference tax statute does provide that foreign companies may reduce the differential in gross premiums taxes by investing prescribed percentages of their worldwide assets in specified Alabama assets and securities. § 27–4–4(b). By investing 10 percent or more of its total assets in Alabama investments, for example, a foreign life insurer may reduce its gross premiums tax rate from 3 to 2 percent. Similarly, a foreign property and casualty insurer may reduce its tax rate from 4 to 3 percent. Smaller tax reductions are available based on investment of smaller percentages of a company's assets. Ibid. Regardless of how much of its total assets a foreign company places in Alabama investments, it can never reduce its gross premiums tax rate to the same level paid by comparable domestic companies. These are entitled to the 1 percent tax rate even if they have no investments in the State. Thus, the investment provision permits foreign insurance companies to reduce, but never to eliminate, the discrimination inherent in the domestic preference tax statute.

II

Appellants, a group of insurance companies incorporated outside of the State of Alabama, filed claims with the Alabama Department of Insurance in 1981, contending that the domestic preference tax statute, as applied to them, violated the Equal Protection Clause. They sought refunds of taxes paid for the tax years 1977 through 1980. The Commissioner of Insurance denied all of their claims on July 8, 1981.

Appellants appealed to the Circuit Court for Montgomery County, seeking a judgment declaring the statute to be unconstitutional and requiring the Commissioner to make the appropriate refunds. Several domestic companies intervened, and the court consolidated all of the appeals, selecting two claims as lead cases to be tried and binding on all claimants. On cross-motions for summary judgment, the court ruled on May 17, 1982, that the statute was constitutional. Relying on this Court's opinion in Western & Southern Life Ins. Co. v. State Board of Equalization of California, 451 U.S. 648, 101 S.Ct. 2070, 68 L.Ed.2d 514 (1981), the court ruled that the Alabama statute did not violate the Equal Protection Clause because it served "at least two purposes, in addition to raising revenue: (1) encouraging the formation of new insurance companies in Alabama, and (2) encouraging capital investment by foreign insurance companies in the Alabama assets and governmental securities set forth in the statute." App. to Juris. Statement 20a–21a. The court also found that the distinction the statute created between foreign and domestic companies was rationally related to those two purposes and that the Alabama Legislature reasonably could have believed that the classification would have promoted those purposes. Id., at 21a.

After their motion for a new trial was denied, appellants appealed to the Court of Civil Appeals. It affirmed the Circuit Court's rulings as to the existence of the two legitimate state purposes, but remanded for an evidentiary hearing on the issue of rational relationship, concluding that summary judgment was inappropriate on that question because the evidence was in conflict. 437 So.2d 535 (1983). Appellants petition-ed the Supreme Court of Alabama for certiorari on the affirmance of the legitimate state purpose issue, and the State and the intervenors petitioned for review of the remand order. Appellants then waived their right to an evidentiary hearing on the issue whether the statute's classification bore a rational relationship to the two purposes found by the Circuit Court to be legitimate, and they requested a final determi-nation of the legal issues with respect to their equal protection chal-lenge to the statute. The Supreme Court denied certiorari on all claims. Appellants again waived their rights to an evidentiary hearing on the rational relationship issue and filed a joint motion with the other parties seeking rehearing and entry of a final judgment. The motion was granted, and judgment was entered for the State and the intervenors. This appeal followed, and we noted probable jurisdiction. 466 U.S. ——, 104 S.Ct. 1905, 80 L.Ed.2d 455 (1984). We now reverse.

III

Prior to our decision in Western & Southern Life Ins. Co. v. State Board of Equalization of California, supra, the jurisprudence of the applicability of the Equal Protection Clause to discriminatory tax statutes had a somewhat checkered history. Lincoln National Life Ins. Co. v. Read, 325 U.S. 673, 65 S.Ct. 1220, 89 L.Ed. 1861 (1945), held that so-called "privilege" taxes, required to be paid by a foreign corporation before it would be permitted to do business within a State, were immune from equal protection challenge. That case stood in stark contrast, however, to the Court's prior decisions in Southern R. Co. v. Greene, 216 U.S. 400, 30 S.Ct. 287, 54 L.Ed. 536 (1910), and Hanover Fire Ins. Co. v. Harding, 272 U.S. 494, 47 S.Ct. 179, 71 L.Ed. 372 (1926), as well as to later decisions, in which the Court had recognized that the Equal Protection Clause placed limits on other forms of discriminatory taxation imposed on out-of-state corporations solely because of their residence. See, e.g., WHYY, Inc. v. Glassboro, 393 U.S. 117, 89 S.Ct. 286, 21 L.Ed.2d 242 (1968); Allied Stores of Ohio, Inc. v. Bowers, 358 U.S. 522, 79 S.Ct. 437, 3 L.Ed.2d 480 (1959); Wheeling Steel Corp. v. Glander, 337 U.S. 562, 69 S.Ct. 1291, 93 L.Ed. 1544 (1949).

In Western & Southern, supra, we reviewed all of these cases for the purpose of deciding whether to permit an equal protection chal-lenge to a California statute imposing a retaliatory tax on foreign insurance companies doing business within the State, when the home States of those companies imposed a similar tax on California insurers entering their borders. We concluded that Lincoln was no more than "a surprising throwback" to the days before enactment of the Four-teenth Amendment and in which incorporation of a domestic corpora-tion or entry of a foreign one had been granted only as a matter of privilege by the State in its unfettered discretion. 451 U.S., at 665, 101 S.Ct., at 2081. We therefore rejected the longstanding but "anachronis[tic]" rule of Lincoln and explicitly held that the Equal

Protection Clause imposes limits upon a State's power to condition the right of a foreign corporation to do business within its borders. Id., at 667, 101 S.Ct., at 2082. We held that "[w]e consider it now established that, whatever the extent of a State's authority to exclude foreign corporations from doing business within its boundaries, that authority does not justify imposition of more onerous taxes or other burdens on foreign corporations than those imposed on domestic corporations, unless the discrimination between foreign and domestic corporations bears a rational relation to a legitimate state purpose." Id., at 667–668, 101 S.Ct., at 2082–2083.

Because appellants waived their right to an evidentiary hearing on the issue whether the classification in the Alabama domestic preference tax statute bears a rational relation to the two purposes upheld by the Circuit Court, the only question before us is whether those purposes are legitimate.[5]

A

(1)

The first of the purposes found by the trial court to be a legitimate reason for the statute's classification between foreign and domestic corporations is that it encourages the formation of new domestic insurance companies in Alabama. The State, agreeing with the Court of Civil Appeals, contends that this Court has long held that the promotion of domestic industry, in and of itself, is a legitimate state purpose that will survive equal protection scrutiny. In so contending, it relies on a series of cases, including *Western & Southern,* that are said to have upheld discriminatory taxes. See Bacchus Imports, Ltd. v. Dias, 468 U.S. ——, 104 S.Ct. 3049, 82 L.Ed.2d 200 (1984); Pike v. Bruce Church, Inc., 397 U.S. 137, 90 S.Ct. 844, 25 L.Ed.2d 174 (1970); Allied Stores of Ohio, Inc. v. Bowers, supra; Parker v. Brown, 317 U.S. 341, 63 S.Ct. 307, 87 L.Ed. 315 (1943); Carmichael v. Southern Coal & Coke Co., 301 U.S. 495, 57 S.Ct. 868, 81 L.Ed. 1245 (1937); Board of Education v. Illinois, 203 U.S. 553, 27 S.Ct. 171, 51 L.Ed. 314 (1906).

The cases cited lend little or no support to the State's contention. In *Western & Southern,* the case principally relied upon, we did not hold as a general rule that promotion of domestic industry is a legitimate state purpose under equal protection analysis. Rather, we held that California's purpose in enacting the retaliatory tax—to promote the *interstate* business of domestic insurers by deterring *other States* from enacting discriminatory or excessive taxes—was a legitimate one. 451 U.S., at 668, 101 S.Ct., at 2083. In contrast, Alabama asks us to approve its purpose of promoting the business of its domestic insurers *in Alabama* by penalizing foreign insurers who also want to do business

---

5. The State and the intervenors advanced some 15 additional purposes in support of the Alabama statute. As neither the Circuit Court nor the Court of Civil Appeals ruled on the legitimacy of those purposes, that question is not before us, and we express no view as to it. On remand, the State will be free to advance again its arguments relating to the legitimacy of those purposes.

in the State. Alabama has made no attempt, as California did, to influence the policies of other States in order to enhance its domestic companies' ability to operate interstate; rather, it has erected barriers to foreign companies who wish to do interstate business in order to improve its domestic insurers' ability to compete at home.

The crucial distinction between the two cases lies in the fact that Alabama's aim to promote domestic industry is purely and completely discriminatory, designed only to favor domestic industry within the State, no matter what the cost to foreign corporations also seeking to do business there. Alabama's purpose, contrary to California's, constitutes the very sort of parochial discrimination that the Equal Protection Clause was intended to prevent. As Justice Brennan, joined by Justice Harlan, observed in his concurrence in Allied Stores of Ohio, Inc. v. Bowers, 358 U.S. 522, 79 S.Ct. 437, 3 L.Ed.2d 480 (1959), this Court always has held that the Equal Protection Clause forbids a State to discriminate in favor of its own residents solely by burdening "the residents of other state members of our federation." Id., at 533, 79 S.Ct., at 444. Unlike the retaliatory tax involved in *Western & Southern*, which only burdens residents of a State that imposes its own discriminatory tax on outsiders, the domestic preference tax gives the "home team" an advantage by burdening *all* foreign corporations seeking to do business within the State, no matter what they or their States do.

The validity of the view that a State may not constitutionally favor its own residents by taxing foreign corporations at a higher rate solely because of their residence is confirmed by a long line of this Court's cases so holding. WHYY, Inc. v. Glassboro, 393 U.S., at 119–120, 89 S.Ct., at 287; Wheeling Steel Corp. v. Glander, 337 U.S., at 571, 69 S.Ct., at 1296; Hanover Fire Ins. Co. v. Harding, 272 U.S., at 511, 47 S.Ct., at 183; Southern R. Co. v. Greene, 216 U.S., at 417, 30 S.Ct., at 291. See Reserve Life Ins. Co. v. Bowers, 380 U.S. 258, 85 S.Ct. 951 (1965) (per curiam). As the Court stated in *Hanover Fire Ins. Co.*, with respect to general tax burdens on business, "the foreign corporation stands equal, and is to be classified with domestic corporations of the same kind." 272 U.S., at 511, 47 S.Ct., at 183. In all of these cases, the discriminatory tax was imposed by the State on foreign corporations doing business within the State solely because of their residence, presumably to promote domestic industry within the State.[7] In relying on these cases and rejecting *Lincoln* in *Western & Southern*, we reaffirmed the continuing viability of the Equal Protection Clause as a means of challenging a statute that seeks to benefit domestic industry within the State only by grossly discriminating against foreign competitors.

The State contends that Allied Stores of Ohio, Inc. v. Bowers, supra, shows that this principle has not always held true. In that case,

---

7. Although the promotion of domestic business was not a purpose advanced by the States in support of their taxes in these cases, such promotion is logically the primary reason for enacting discriminatory taxes such as those at issue here.

a domestic merchandiser challenged on equal protection grounds an Ohio statute that exempted foreign corporations from a tax on the value of merchandise held for storage within the State. The Court upheld the tax, finding that the purpose of encouraging foreign companies to build warehouses within Ohio was a legitimate state purpose. The State contends that this case shows that promotion of domestic business *is* a legitimate state purpose under equal protection analysis.

We disagree with the State's interpretation of *Allied Stores* and find that the case is not inconsistent with the other cases on which we rely. We agree with the holding of *Allied Stores* that a State's goal of bringing in new business is legitimate and often admirable. *Allied Stores* does not, however, hold that promotion of domestic business by *discriminating* against foreign corporations is legitimate. The case involves instead a statute that *encourages non-residents*—who are not competitors of residents—to build warehouses within the State. The discriminatory tax involved did not favor residents by burdening outsiders; rather, it granted the non-resident business an exemption that residents did not share. Since the foreign and domestic companies involved were not competing to provide warehousing services, granting the former an exemption did not even directly affect adversely the domestic companies subject to the tax. On its facts, then, *Allied Stores* is not inconsistent with our holding here that promotion of domestic business within a State, by discriminating against foreign corporations that wish to compete by doing business there, is not a legitimate state purpose. See 358 U.S., at 532–533, 79 S.Ct., at 443–444 (BRENNAN, J., concurring).

(2)

The State argues nonetheless that it is impermissible to view a discriminatory tax such as the one at issue here as violative of the Equal Protection Clause. This approach, it contends, amounts to no more than "Commerce Clause rhetoric in equal protection clothing." Brief for Appellee Ward 22. The State maintains that because Congress, in enacting the McCarran–Ferguson Act, 15 U.S.C. §§ 1011–1015, intended to authorize States to impose taxes that burden interstate commerce in the insurance field, the tax at issue here must stand. Our concerns are much more fundamental than as characterized by the State. Although the McCarran–Ferguson Act exempts the insurance industry from Commerce Clause restrictions, it does not purport to limit in any way the applicability of the Equal Protection Clause. As noted above, our opinion in *Western & Southern* expressly reaffirmed the viability of equal protection restraints on discriminatory taxes in the insurance context.[8]

---

8. In fact, as we noted in *Western & Southern,* the legislative history of the McCarran–Ferguson Act reveals that the Act was Congress's response only to United States v. South–Eastern Underwriters Assn., 322 U.S. 533, 64 S.Ct. 1162, 88 L.Ed. 1440 (1944), and that Congress did not intend thereby to give the States any power to tax or regulate the insurance industry other than what they had previously possessed. Thus Congress expressly left undisturbed this Court's decisions holding

* * *

In whatever light the State's position is cast, acceptance of its contention that promotion of domestic industry is always a legitimate state purpose under equal protection analysis would eviscerate the Equal Protection Clause in this context. A State's natural inclination frequently would be to prefer domestic business over foreign. If we accept the State's view here, then any discriminatory tax would be valid if the State could show it reasonably was intended to benefit domestic business.[10] A discriminatory tax would stand or fall depending primarily on how a State framed its purpose—as benefiting one group or as harming another. This is a distinction without a difference, and one that we rejected last term in an analogous context arising under the Commerce Clause. Bacchus Imports, Ltd. v. Dias, 468 U.S., at ——, 104 S.Ct., at ——. See n. 6, supra. We hold that under the circumstances of this case, promotion of domestic business by discriminating against non-resident competitors is not a legitimate state purpose.

B

The second purpose found by the courts below to be legitimate was the encouragement of capital investment in the Alabama assets and governmental securities specified in the statute. We do not agree that this is a legitimate state purpose when furthered by discrimination. Domestic insurers remain entitled to the more favorable rate of tax regardless of whether they invest in Alabama assets. Moreover, the investment incentive provision of the Alabama statute does not enable foreign insurance companies to eliminate the discriminatory effect of the statute. No matter how much of their assets they invest in Alabama, foreign insurance companies are still required to pay a higher gross premiums tax than domestic companies. The State's investment incentive provision therefore does not cure, but reaffirms, the statute's impermissible classification based solely on residence. We hold that encouraging investment in Alabama assets and securities in this plainly discriminatory manner serves no legitimate state purpose.

IV

We conclude that neither of the two purposes furthered by the Alabama domestic preference tax statute and addressed by the Circuit Court for Montgomery County, see supra, at 1679, is legitimate under the Equal Protection Clause to justify the imposition of the discriminatory tax at issue here. The judgment of the Alabama Supreme Court

that the Equal Protection Clause places limits on a State's ability to tax out-of-state corporations. See 451 U.S., at 655, n. 6, 101 S.Ct., at 2076, n. 6.

10. Indeed, under the State's analysis, *any* discrimination subject to the rational relation level of scrutiny could be justified simply on the ground that it favored one group at the expense of another. This case

does not involve or question, as the dissent suggests, post, at 1693, the broad authority of a State to promote and regulate its own economy. We hold only that such regulation may not be accomplished by imposing discriminatorily higher taxes on non-resident corporations solely because they are non-residents.

accordingly is reversed, and the case is remanded for further proceedings not inconsistent with this opinion.

It is so ordered.

JUSTICE O'CONNOR, with whom JUSTICE BRENNAN, JUSTICE MARSHALL and JUSTICE REHNQUIST join, dissenting.

This case presents a simple question: Is it legitimate for a state to use its taxing power to promote a domestic insurance industry and to encourage capital investment within its borders? In a holding that can only be characterized as astonishing, the Court determines that these purposes are illegitimate. This holding is unsupported by precedent and subtly distorts the constitutional balance, threatening the freedom of both state and federal legislative bodies to fashion appropriate classifications in economic legislation. Because I disagree with both the Court's method of analysis and its conclusion, I respectfully dissent.

I

* * * As the Court emphatically noted in *Allied Stores of Ohio, Inc. v. Bowers:*

> "[I]t has repeatedly been held and appears to be entirely settled that a statute which encourages the location within the State of needed and useful industries by exempting them, though not also others, from its taxes is not arbitrary and does not violate the Equal Protection Clause of the Fourteenth Amendment. Similarly, it has long been settled that a classification, though discriminatory, is not arbitrary or violative of the Equal Protection Clause of the Fourteenth Amendment if any state of facts reasonably can be conceived that would sustain it." 358 U.S. 522, 528, 79 S.Ct., at 441 (1959) (citations omitted).

* * *

Alabama claims that its insurance tax, in addition to raising revenue and promoting investment, promotes the formation of new domestic insurance companies and enables them to compete with the many large multistate insurers that currently occupy some 75% to 85% of the Alabama insurance market. App. 80. Economic studies submitted by the State document differences between the two classes of insurers that are directly relevant to the well-being of Alabama's citizens. See id., at 46–129. Foreign insurers typically concentrate on affluent, high volume, urban markets and offer standardized national policies. In contrast, domestic insurers such as intervenors American Educators Life Insurance Company and Booker T. Washington Life Insurance Company are more likely to serve Alabama's rural areas, and to write low-cost industrial and burial policies not offered by the larger national companies.[1] Additionally, Alabama argues persuasive-

---

1. "Industrial insurance" is the trade term for a low face-value policy typically sold door-to-door and maintained through home collection of monthly or weekly premiums. Alabama currently has more industrial insurance in force than any other State. Burial insurance is another form of insurance popular in rural Alabama that is offered exclusively by local insurers. By contrast, Metropolitan Life, like many multistate insurers, has discontinued writing even whole-life policies with face values below $15,000. App. 173–176.

ly that it can more readily regulate domestic insurers and more effectively safeguard their solvency than that of insurers domiciled and having their principal places of business in other states.

Ignoring these policy considerations, the Court insists that Alabama seeks only to benefit local business, a purpose the Court labels invidious. Yet if the classification chosen by the State can be shown *actually* to promote the public welfare, this is strong evidence of a legitimate State purpose. See Note, Taxing Out-of-State Corporations After *Western & Southern:* An Equal Protection Analysis, 34 Stan.L. Rev. 877, 896 (1982). In this regard, Justice Frankfurter wisely observed that:

> "[T]he great divide in the [equal protection] decisions lies in the difference between emphasizing the actualities or the abstractions of legislation.

> "To recognize marked differences that exist in fact is living law; to disregard practical differences and concentrate on some abstract identities is lifeless logic." Morey v. Doud, 354 U.S. 457, 472, 77 S.Ct. 1344, 1353, 1 L.Ed.2d 1485 (1957) (Frankfurter, J., dissenting).

A thoughtful look at the "actualities of [this] legislation" compels the conclusion that the State's goals are legitimate by any test.

* * *

[Justice O'Connor's opinion proceeds to argue that Congressional intent underlying the McCarran–Ferguson Act favored local concerns in State regulation and taxation of insurance and encompassed taxes that discriminated in favor of local insurers. She observed that the Court in Prudential Insurance Co. v. Benjamin, 328 U.S. 408, 66 S.Ct. 1142 (1946), involving a Commerce Clause challenge to a discriminatory insurance tax, had declared that the McCarran Ferguson Act's effect was "clearly to sustain the exaction and that this can be done without violating *any* constitutional provision." She observed that the Court had often upheld regulatory and tax classifications that distinguished between domestic and foreign corporations. She further noted that the cases cited by the majority in which such classifications had been invalidated on equal protection grounds were inapposite because in none of those cases had the "tax statutes at issue rested on relevant difference between domestic and foreign corporations or had purposes other than raising of revenue at the out-of-state corporation's expense." By contrast, in her view, "Alabama does *not* tax at a higher rate solely on the basis of residence; it taxes insurers, domestic as well as foreign, who do not maintain a principal place of business or substantial assets in Alabama, based on conceded distinctions in the contributions of these insurers *as a class* to the State's insurance objectives." (Emphasis in original.)]

IV

* * *

Western & Southern established that a state may validly tax out-of-state corporations at a higher rate if its goal is to promote the ability of its domestic businesses to compete in *interstate* markets. Nevertheless, the Court today concludes that the converse policy is forbidden, striking down legislation whose purpose is to encourage the *intrastate* activities of local business concerns by permitting them to compete effectively on their home turf. In essence, the Court declares "We will excuse an unequal burden on foreign insurers if the State's purpose is to foster its domestic insurers activities in *other* States, but the same unequal burden will be unconstitutional when employed to further a policy that places a higher social value on the domestic insurer's *homestate* than interstate activities." This conclusion is not drawn from the Commerce Clause, the textual source of constitutional restrictions on State interference with interstate competition. Reliance on the Commerce Clause would, of course, be unavailing here in view of the McCarran–Ferguson Act. Instead the Court engrafts its own economic values on the Equal Protection Clause. Beyond guarding against arbitrary or irrational discrimination, as interpreted by the Court today this Clause now prohibits the effectuation of economic policies, even where sanctioned by Congress, that elevate local concerns over interstate competition. Ante, at 1681. "But a constitution is not intended to embody a particular economic theory. * * * It is made for people of fundamentally differing views." Lochner v. New York, 198 U.S. 45, 75–76, 25 S.Ct. 539, 546–547, 49 L.Ed. 937 (1905) (Holmes, J., dissenting). In the heyday of economic due process, Justice Holmes warned:

> "Courts should be careful not to extend [the express] prohibitions [of the Constitution] beyond their obvious meaning by reading into them conceptions of public policy that the particular Court may happen to entertain." Tyson & Brother v. Banton, 273 U.S. 418, 445–446, 47 S.Ct. 426, 433, 71 L.Ed. 718 (1927) (Holmes, J., dissenting, joined by Brandeis, J.) (emphasis added).

Ignoring the wisdom of this observation, the Court fashions its own brand of economic equal protection. In so doing, it supplants a legislative policy endorsed by both Congress and the individual States that explicitly sanctioned the very parochialism in regulation and taxation of insurance that the Court's decision holds illegitimate. This newly unveiled power of the Equal Protection Clause would come as a surprise to the Congress that passed the McCarran–Ferguson Act and the Court that sustained the Act against constitutional attack. In the McCarran–Ferguson Act, Congress expressly sanctioned such economic parochialism in the context of state regulation and taxation of insurance.

The doctrine adopted by the majority threatens the freedom not only of the States but also of the Federal Government to formulate economic policy. The dangers in discerning in the Equal Protection Clause a prohibition against barriers to interstate business irrespective of the Commerce Clause should be self-evident. The Commerce Clause is a flexible tool of economic policy that Congress may use as it sees fit, letting it lie dormant or invoking it to limit as well as promote the free flow of commerce. Doctrines of equal protection are constitutional limits that constrain the acts of federal and state legislatures alike.

See, e.g., Califano v. Webster, 430 U.S. 313, 97 S.Ct. 1192, 51 L.Ed.2d 360 (1977); Cohen, Congressional Power to Validate Unconstitutional State Laws: A Forgotten Solution to an Old Enigma, 35 Stan.L.Rev. 387, 400–413 (1983). The Court's analysis casts a shadow over numerous congressional enactments that adopted as federal policy "the type of parochial favoritism" the Court today finds unconstitutional. White v. Massachusetts Council of Construction Employers, 460 U.S., at 213, 103 S.Ct., at 1047. Contrary to the reasoning in *Benjamin,* the Court today indicates the Equal Protection Clause stands as an independent barrier if courts should determine that either Congress or a State has ventured the "wrong" direction down what has become, by judicial fiat, the one-way street of the Commerce Clause. Nothing in the Constitution or our past decisions supports forcing such an economic straightjacket on the federal system.

V

Today's opinion charts an ominous course. I can only hope this unfortunate adventure away from the safety of our precedents will be an isolated episode. I had thought the Court had finally accepted that

> "the judiciary may not sit as a superlegislature to judge the wisdom or desirability of legislative policy determinations made in areas that neither affect fundamental rights nor proceed along suspect lines; in the local economic sphere, it is only the invidious discrimination, the wholly arbitrary act, which cannot stand consistently with the Fourteenth Amendment. New Orleans v. Dukes, 427 U.S., at 303–304, 96 S.Ct., at 2516–2517 (citations omitted).

Because I believe that the Alabama law at issue here serves legitimate State purposes through concededly rational means, and thus is neither invidious nor arbitrary, I would affirm the court below. I respectfully dissent.

Notes and Problems

A. In Western and Southern Life Insurance Co. v. State Board of Equalization of California, 451 U.S. 648, 101 S.Ct. 2070 (1981), which is considered in the principal case, the Court sustained a retaliatory insurance tax that discriminated against out-of-state insurers. Applying its "rational basis" equal protection standard—that a tax be "rationally related to a legitimate state purpose"—the Court held that the California Legislature rationally could have believed that a discriminatory tax could promote the legitimate State purpose of promoting domestic insurers in interstate commerce by deterring other States from enacting discriminatory or excessive taxes.

The Court's decision in *Western & Southern* was significant for two reasons. First, it discarded the Court's earlier doctrine approving discriminatory taxes predicated upon the States' power to condition an insurance company's entry into the State to do business. Second, it sanctioned discriminatory taxation of foreign corporations under the Equal Protection Clause if that discrimination was rationally related to a legitimate State purpose. The Court's earlier decisions had established a much broader requirement of equality in taxation than that enunciated in *Western & Southern*. In *Metropolitan Life*, the Court appears to have returned to the sound principle of constitutional adjudication supported by its pre–*Western & Southern* precedents that the Equal Protection Clause forbids the States from "imposing discriminatorily higher taxes on non-residents solely because they are non-residents."

Was the Court's distinction of *Western & Southern* in *Metropolitan Life* persuasive? Could not Alabama's purpose in the principal case have been characterized as promoting the domestic insurance industry by inducing insurers to incorporate and maintain their principal place of business in Alabama in order to serve the needs of local residents that were inadequately served by out-of-state insurers? If thus characterized, would such a purpose be any less legitimate than the purpose of California's retaliatory tax?

The *Metropolitan Life* and *Western & Southern* cases are critically analyzed in the authors' State Taxation I, Corporate Income and Franchise Taxes, Cum.Supp. ¶ 3.7[3]; Cohen, "Federalism in Equality Clothing: A Comment on *Metropolitan Life Insurance Company v. Ward*," 38 Stan.L. Rev. 1 (1985); W. Hellerstein & Leegstra, "Supreme Court in *Metropolitan Life* Strikes Down Discriminatory State Insurance Tax," 63 J.Tax. 108 (1985); W. Hellerstein, "Supreme Court Bars Louisiana's First Use Tax, Upholds California's Retaliatory Insurance Tax," 55 J.Tax. 106 (1981); Note, "Taxing Out-of-State Corporations After *Western & Southern:* An Equal Protection Analysis," 34 Stan.L.Rev. (1982).

B. *Discriminatory Taxation of Domestic Corporations as Compared to Foreign Corporations.* In Allied Stores of Ohio, Inc. v. Bowers, 358 U.S. 522, 79 S.Ct. 437 (1959), which is discussed in the principal case, the Court sustained over equal protection objections an ad valorem property tax that exempted foreign corporations that stored merchandise in a storage warehouse in the State, but taxed domestic corporations. The Court found that the discrimination was not arbitrary because it was based on factors other than the residency of the corporation—namely encouraging the location of industry in the State. It distinguished an earlier case, Wheeling Steel Corp. v. Glander, 337 U.S. 562, 69 S.Ct. 1291 (1949), which had struck down a tax exemption for accounts receivable owned by residents on the grounds that it arbitrarily discriminated against non-residents, even though the State argued that it was designed to create a scheme of reciprocal exemptions with other States. Justice Brennan, joined by Justice Harlan, wrote the following concurring opinion:

> We hold today that Ohio's ad valorem tax law does not violate the Equal Protection Clause in subjecting the property of Ohio corporations to a tax not applied to identical property of non-Ohio corporations.* Yet in Wheeling Steel Corp. v. Glander, 337 U.S. 562, 69 S.Ct. 1291, 93 L.Ed. 1544, the Court struck down, as violating the Equal Protection Clause, another provision of Ohio's ad valorem tax law

* [Some of the footnotes in the concurring opinion have been deleted.]

which subjected the property of non-Ohio corporations to a tax not applied to identical property of Ohio corporations.

The question presented in the two cases, if stated generally, and as I shall show, somewhat superficially, is: Measured by the demands of the Equal Protection Clause, is a State constitutionally permitted separately to classify domestic and foreign corporations for the purposes of payment of or exemption from an ad valorem tax? In both cases the distinction complained of as denying equal protection of the laws is that the incidence of the tax in fact turns on "the different residence of the owner." With due respect to my Brethren's view, I think that if this were all that the matter was, Wheeling and this case would be indistinguishable.[3] Therefore, while I agree with my Brethren that the classification is valid in this case, I cannot reach that conclusion without developing the ground on which *Wheeling* is distinguishable.

Why is the "different residence of the owner" a constitutionally valid basis for Ohio's freeing the property of the foreign corporation from the tax in this case and an invalid basis for its freeing the property of the domestic corporation from the tax involved in the *Wheeling* case?

I think that the answer lies in remembering that our Constitution is an instrument of federalism. The Constitution furnishes the structure for the operation of the States with respect to the National Government and with respect to each other. The maintenance of the principles of federalism is a foremost consideration in interpreting any of the pertinent constitutional provisions under which this Court examines state action. Because there are 49 States and much of the Nation's commercial activity is carried on by enterprises having contacts with more States than one, a common and continuing problem of constitutional interpretation has been that of adjusting the demands of individual States to regulate and tax these enterprises in light of the multistate nature of our federation. While the most ready examples of the Court's function in this field are furnished by the innumerable cases in which the Court has examined state taxation and regulation under the Commerce and Due Process Clauses, still the Equal Protection Clause, among its other roles, operates to maintain this principle of federalism.

Viewing the Equal Protection Clause as an instrument of federalism, the distinction between *Wheeling* and this case seems to me to be apparent. My Brethren's opinion today demonstrates that in dealing with as practical and complex a matter as taxation, the utmost latitude, under the Equal Protection Clause, must be afforded a State in defining categories of classification. But in the case of an ad valorem

---

3. The statute in *Wheeling* "discriminated" against non-residents in the same way that the present statute "discriminates" against residents. What my Brethren describe as the forbidden purpose of the distinction in *Wheeling* seems to me clearly to be only a rejected argument made by the State to show that there was no discrimination in fact. 337 U.S. at pages 572–574, 69 S.Ct. at pages 1296–1297. I see no indication in *Wheeling* that the Court's condemnation of the tax was based solely on its rejection of the "reciprocity" argument.

property tax, *Wheeling* teaches that a distinction which burdens the property of non-residents but not like property of residents is outside the constitutional pale. But this is not because no rational ground can be conceived for a classification which discriminates against non-residents solely because they are non-residents: could not such a ground be found in the State's benign and beneficent desire to favor its own residents, to increase their prosperity at the expense of outlanders, to protect them from, and give them an advantage over, "foreign" competition? These bases of legislative distinction are adopted in the national policies of too many countries, including from time to time our own, to say that, absolutely considered, they are arbitrary or irrational. The proper analysis, it seems to me, is that *Wheeling* applied the Equal Protection Clause to give effect to its role to protect our federalism by denying Ohio the power constitutionally to discriminate in favor of its own residents against the residents of other state members of our federation. On the other hand, in the present case, Ohio's classification based on residence operates *against* Ohio residents and clearly presents no state action disruptive of the federal pattern. There is, therefore, no reason to judge the State action mechanically by the same principles as state efforts to favor residents. As my Brethren's opinion makes clear, a rational basis can be found for this exercise by Ohio of the latitude permitted it to define classifications under the Equal Protection Clause. One could, in fact, be found in the concept that it is proper that those who are bound to a State by the tie of residence and accordingly the more permanently receive its benefits are proper persons to bear the primary share of its costs. Accordingly, in this context, it is proper to say that any relief forthcoming must be obtained from the State Legislature. [358 U.S. at 530–33.]

Compare Kay v. Pacific Telephone & Telegraph Co., 83 Cal.App.3d 814, 148 Cal.Rptr. 213 (1978), in which the court sustained a telephone user tax on intrastate but not interstate calls. The court found that the classification "had a rational relationship to a reasonable municipal purpose" in view of the administrative burden of taxing interstate calls and the "substantial possibility" that a tax on interstate calls would violate the Commerce Clause unless apportioned.

C. *Discriminatory Taxation of Foreign Corporations as Compared to Domestic Corporations.*

1. *Tax Exemption.* Some State tax laws have granted to domestic corporations exemptions not allowed to foreign corporations. Thus, New Jersey denied a property tax exemption to a foreign corporation, which was engaged in non-commercial educational television, and owned and maintained a station and transmittal tower in the State. Thirty percent of the television station's audience was in that State. Admittedly, a New Jersey corporation would have been exempt from all State real and personal property taxes, if it had conducted the same activities in the State. The State court upheld the denial of exemption on the ground that it was permissible for the legislature to "decide that the State should not be burdened with the administrative problem of checking the status of foreign corporations under foreign laws and evaluating them with our require-

ments." WHYY, Inc. v. Borough of Glassboro, 50 N.J. 6, 231 A.2d 608 (1967). The Supreme Court reversed, per curiam, on the ground that once foreign corporations are admitted to the State,

> the adopted corporations are entitled to equal protection with the state's own corporate progeny, at least to the extent that their property is entitled to an equally favorable ad valorem tax basis. [WHYY, Inc. v. Borough of Glassboro, 393 U.S. 117, 89 S.Ct. 286 (1968).]

Accord, Mary C. Wheeler School, Inc. v. Board of Assessors of Seekonk, 368 Mass. 344, 331 N.E.2d 888 (1975).

There are decisions indicating that a State may deny tax exemption to out-of-state charitable, educational, and other organizations which do not conduct their operations within the State, without running afoul of the Equal Protection Clause. See Board of Educ. v. Illinois, 203 U.S. 553, 27 S.Ct. 171 (1906). Although the opinion in that case, which sustained a denial of an inheritance tax exemption for a gift to a foreign organized and operating educational organization, was largely based on "the greater control and direction the State had over domestic than over foreign corporations" (203 U.S. at 562), the *WHYY* case put the earlier holding on a different footing, one which was mentioned briefly at the end of the Illinois case:

> This is not a case in which the exemption was withheld by reason of the foreign corporation's failure or inability to benefit the State in the same measure as do domestic nonprofit corporations. Compare Board of Educ. v. Illinois ∗ ∗ ∗ [393 U.S. at 120.]

The rationale behind such decisions is that the out-of-state organizations do not meet the condition underlying the grant of tax exemption to charities, namely, that they relieve the State of the costs and burdens of public functions it would otherwise have to perform and that they perform other services benefiting the people of the State. See Killough, "Exemptions to Educational, Philanthropic and Religous Organizations," in Symposium on Tax Exemptions 23 (Tax Policy League, 1938). That policy ought to suffice as a justification under the Equal Protection Clause for the denial to out-of-state charities of the benefits of exemption or deductions for death and income tax purposes allowed to in-state charities. In any event, this matter is largely academic under estate and inheritance tax laws, since virtually all, if not all, States either grant exemption for bequests to out-of-state charitable and similar organizations, or do so on a reciprocal basis, i.e., conditioned on the allowance by the State in which the charity is organized of similar exemption for bequests made to the taxing State's charities. See 1 P–H Inheritance & Transfer Tax Serv. ¶ 854. Such reciprocal provisions should present no serious equal protection controversy.

2. *Other Types of Discrimination Against Foreign Corporations.* The Supreme Court followed the *Wheeling Steel* case in reversing, per curiam, the decision of the Ohio Supreme Court in Reserve Life Insurance Co. v. Bowers, 175 Ohio St. 468, 196 N.E.2d 87 (1964). 380 U.S. 258, 85 S.Ct. 951 (1965). The Ohio ad valorem tax applies to all the tangible personal property located in the State owned by foreign insurers. Domestic insurance companies, however, are not taxed as such on their tangible personal

property. Instead they are subjected to the lesser of two levies: (a) a tax on their capital stock and surplus, which includes their tangible personal property, or (b) a tax on gross premiums originating in Ohio. However, foreign insurers also pay the gross premiums tax. The Ohio court had sustained the tax under both the State's uniformity and equality provision and the Federal Equal Protection Clause, stating:

> The net result is that the question of whether or not this particular tax is discriminatory against this particular taxpayer is not the controlling factor, the applicable principle being whether or not a specific tax is discriminatory between permissible classifications of taxpayers. Whether or not this particular tax system results in tax discrimination in the very narrow sense of one taxpayer paying more than another individual taxpayer, becomes a matter of mathematical calculation individual by individual,—a calculation in which courts are not constitutionally required or even permitted to indulge. The problems existing between foreign and domestic insurance companies in respect of methods and rates of taxation, are recognized by Section 5729.06 of the Revised Code relative to retaliatory tax rates. Here again it would seem that whether or not a particular tax discriminates as between foreign and domestic taxpayers would involve, in addition, a consideration of the tax structure of the state of which the foreign corporation is a resident. [196 N.E.2d at 117–118.]

Under the tests utilized by the Ohio court, it would appear virtually impossible for any taxpayer to demonstrate that the requisite lack of uniformity or unreasonableness of classification exists.

3. *State Court Decisions.* State courts, especially in recent years, have invalidated a number of provisions that discriminated against foreign corporations when the States were unable to advance any persuasive justifications for the unequal treatment of the foreign corporation. Thus the Pennsylvania Supreme Court struck down a provision of the State's capital stock tax that granted an election to domestic corporations to apportion their income by either of two alternative methods but limited foreign corporations to a single method of apportionment. Gilbert Associates, Inc. v. Commonwealth, 498 Pa. 514, 447 A.2d 944 (1982). The Florida Supreme Court struck down a provision of the State's intangible tax that limited the privilege of filing consolidated returns to affiliated groups of corporations whose parent company is either incorporated or maintains its commercial domicile in the State. Department of Revenue v. Amrep Corp., 358 So.2d 1343 (Fla.1978). The Florida Court of Appeals invalidated a tax exemption for homes for the aged limited to such homes owned by Florida nonprofit corporations. Miller v. Board of Pensions, 431 So.2d 350 (Fla. App.1983). See also Missouri Pacific R.R. v. Kirkpatrick, 652 S.W.2d 128 (Mo.1983).

A license tax imposed on a Delaware corporation resulting from a merger of a Missouri corporation and seven other operating railroads was invalidated under the Equal Protection Clause as discriminatory against foreign corporations. If the merged corporation had been a Missouri corporation an organization tax of only $50 would have been payable, but the license tax on the foreign merged company amounted to $96,600.

Missouri Pacific R.R. v. Kirkpatrick, 652 S.W.2d 128 (Mo.1983). The New York courts have, likewise, held unconstitutional a license tax on foreign corporations imposed at higher rates than the organization tax on domestic corporations, even though the disparity had existed for more than half a century. In re Aurora Corp. of Ill. v. Tully, 60 N.Y.2d 338, 469 N.Y.S.2d 630, 457 N.E.2d 735 (1983). The cases are discussed in the authors' State Taxation I, Corporate Income and Franchise Taxes, Cum.Supp. ¶ 3.7[2][e].

An equal protection issue was raised in connection with the interpretation of Wisconsin's statutory analog to § 337 of the Internal Revenue Code (Wis.Stat.Ann. § 71.337(1), CCH ¶ 91–748, P–H ¶ 12,670), which permits a corporation under specified conditions, to avoid recognition of any gain or loss in the course of a liquidation. These provisions are designed to avoid double taxation of the liquidating corporation and its shareholders, the theory being that the shareholders will be taxed upon receipt of their share of the corporate assets. The Wisconsin modification of § 337 denied nonrecognition treatment to liquidating corporations to the extent that its shareholders were non-residents. Over the complaint of the corporation that this amounted to a discriminatory classification for tax purposes based solely on the proportion of its non-resident shareholders in violation of the Equal Protection Clause, the court sustained the provision. It reasoned that the classification was rationally related to the statute's purpose, since non-resident shareholders would not ordinarily be subject to personal income taxation by Wisconsin and without the provision at issue, gain from a corporate liquidation might escape taxation altogether. Simanco, Inc. v. Department of Revenue, 57 Wis.2d 47, 203 N.W.2d 648, appeal dismissed 414 U.S. 804, 94 S.Ct. 151 (1973); see also WKBH Television, Inc. v. Department of Revenue, 75 Wis.2d 557, 250 N.W.2d 290 (1977) (following *Simanco* and rejecting additional arguments based on the Commerce and Privileges and Immunities Clauses). Interpreting a substantially similar statute, the Oregon Tax Court concluded that it violated the Equal Protection Clause. Columbia Motor Hotels, Inc. v. State Tax Comm'n, 3 O.T.R. 48 (1967).

D. *Discrimination Against Non-residents.*

1. *Denial of Use Tax Credit for Sales Taxes Paid by Non-residents.* Vermont imposes a use tax on cars purchased elsewhere and subsequently registered in Vermont. Although Vermont, like most States, generally grants a credit against the use tax for sales taxes paid to other States, Vermont did not grant a credit for sales taxes paid on cars purchased in other States if the taxpayer was not a resident of Vermont when he purchased the car. In Williams v. Vermont, 472 U.S. 14, 105 S.Ct. 2465 (1985), the Supreme Court held that the discrimination against non-residents in Vermont's taxing scheme violated the Equal Protection Clause. The Court found that the discrimination was not justified by the only plausible legitimate State purpose advanced in its defense—that those using the roads should pay for them. Residents purchasing cars elsewhere likewise used Vermont roads yet they were permitted a credit against their out-of-state sales tax. The Court dismissed the other allegedly legitimate State purposes, such as encouraging out-of-staters to purchase in Vermont

and enabling Vermont residents to shop without penalty, as fanciful. The Court concluded that

> we can see no relevant difference between motor vehicle registrants who purchased their cars out-of-state while they were Vermont residents and those who only came to Vermont after buying a car elsewhere. To free one group and not the other from the otherwise applicable tax burden violates the Equal Protection Clause. [472 U.S. at 27, 105 S.Ct. at 2474.]

2. *Other Differences in Tax Treatment of Residents and Non-residents.* A number of equal protection issues have arisen as a result of the differences in treatment of residents and non-residents. In General American Tank Car Corp. v. Day, 270 U.S. 367, 46 S.Ct. 234 (1926), a tax imposed on non-residents in lieu of local property taxes was upheld. In a New Mexico case a claim was made that residents were being discriminated against by reason of the operation of a vendor's retail sales tax and a use tax. A resident retailer of chemicals and reagents used in processing ores was subjected to the vendor's two percent tax on his gross receipts. This levy is generally integrated with the compensating use tax, under which articles purchased at retail outside the State in transactions which would not be subject to the vendor's tax are subject to the two percent use tax when brought into the State and there used. However, the vendor's tax covers sales of chemicals and reagents used in processing ores but such items are exempt from the compensating use tax. In Edmunds v. Bureau of Revenue, 64 N.M. 454, 330 P.2d 131 (1958), the taxpayer contended that an unconstitutional discrimination was thus effected as between in-state vendors and out-of-state vendors and their customers; a two percent advantage was thereby given to the out-of-state vendor, and the taxpayer sought a refund of the vendor's tax paid on the sales. In upholding the classifications used in the acts, the court found reasonable: (1) the taxation of vendors for the privilege of doing business in the State, a privilege not exercised by the out-of-state vendor and (2) the taxation of the purchaser on the use of property in the State. It found no constitutional requirement that the legislature protect local vendors "against the unfair competition of importations into New Mexico." The court does not, however, consider the exemption issue underlying the entire case, namely, whether the exemption from use tax of chemicals and reagents used in ore processing was arbitrary and unreasonable, when such items were not exempt from the vendor's tax. Query, could the court properly consider that issue, since the question in the case was whether the taxpayer was entitled to a refund of the vendor's sales tax, not the use tax, which granted the exemption? What procedure could the taxpayer have employed to accomplish the desired equality?

A curious discrimination against non-resident decedents was held offensive to the Equal Protection Clause in Burge v. Marcum, 394 S.W.2d 908 (Ky.1965). A former resident of Kentucky was domiciled in Guatemala when he died, but he was still a United States citizen. The State's estate tax called for taxing all shares of stock in Kentucky corporations owned by persons domiciled outside the United States, but not if the decedent was domiciled outside Kentucky but within the United States. The court found no constitutionally acceptable basis for classifying separately citizens of the United States who are non-residents of Kentucky, as between those domiciled within and those domiciled without the United States.

3. *Limiting Tax Exemption to Long-term State Residents.* Closely allied to the question of discrimination against non-residents is the question of discrimination against short-term in favor of long-term residents. In Zobel v. Williams, 457 U.S. 55, 102 S.Ct. 2309 (1982), the Court held that the Equal Protection Clause forbids a State from making cash distributions to its residents, when such distributions are graduated according to the number of years that the individual has been a resident of the State. In Hooper v. Bernalillo County Assessor, 472 U.S. 612, 105 S.Ct. 2862 (1985), the Court considered the constitutionality of a New Mexico property tax exemption for Vietnam War veterans who were residents of the State before May 8, 1976. Vietnam veterans who became residents of the State after that date were ineligible for the exemption. The Court held that the distinction between the two classes of resident veterans was not rationally related to the purposes New Mexico offered to support the classification, and it struck the classification down under the Equal Protection Clause. New Mexico sought to justify the classification as an incentive to encourage Vietnam veterans to move to New Mexico. But the Court observed that the legislature established the eligibility date long after the triggering date occurred and that "[t]he legislature cannot plausibly encourage veterans to move to the State by passing such retroactive legislation." 472 U.S. at 619, 105 S.Ct. at 2867. The State also sought to defend the statute on the ground that it was designed to reward veterans who resided in the State before May 8, 1976. But the Court again found that the distinction drawn was not rationally related to the asserted purpose:

Even assuming that the State may legitimately grant benefits on the basis of a coincidence between military service and past residence, the New Mexico statute's distinction between resident veterans is not rationally related to the State's asserted legislative goal. The statute is not written to require any connection between the veteran's prior residence and military service. Indeed, the veteran who resided in New Mexico as an infant long ago would immediately qualify for the exemption upon settling in the State at any time in the future regardless of where he resided before, during, or after military service. [472 U.S. at 621–22, 105 S.Ct. at 2868.]

G. *References.* Sholley, "Equal Protection in Tax Legislation," 24 Va. L.Rev. 229, 388 (1938); 51 Am.Jur., "Taxation," § 167 et seq.; Berman, "The Chain Store Tax: A Study of its Nature and Effects," 25 Taxes 627 (1947); Note, 9 Geo.Wash.L.Rev. 489 (1941); Note, 29 Geo.L.J. 373 (1940); J. Hellerstein, "State Tax Discrimination Against Out-of-Staters," 21 Nat.Tax J. 113 (1977).

C. PRIVILEGES AND IMMUNITIES

There are two clauses in the Federal Constitution dealing with privileges and immunities. Article IV, Section 2 is the "interstate privileges clause," which provides that:

The Citizens of each State shall be entitled to all Privileges and Immunities of Citizens in the several States.

This clause prevents a State from denying to citizens of other States privileges and immunities conferred on its own citizens. Paul v. Virginia, 75 U.S. (8 Wall.) 168 (1868); Blake v. McClung, 172 U.S. 239, 19 S.Ct. 165 (1898). Article IV, Section 2 does not, however, confer any benefits or protection on a citizen of a State.

The second privileges and immunities provision, which is in the Fourteenth Amendment, provides that:

No State shall make or enforce any law which shall abridge the privileges or immunities of citizens of the United States.

The Slaughter House Cases, 83 U.S. (16 Wall.) 36 (1873), established the principle that the Privileges and Immunities Clause of the Fourteenth Amendment created no new rights of national citizenship, but merely furnished an additional guaranty of rights which citizens of the United States already possessed. Although some 50 cases had come before the Supreme Court in which State statutes were challenged as violating the Privileges and Immunities Clause of the Fourteenth Amendment, no State statute had been held to violate that clause until the 1935 decision in Colgate v. Harvey, 296 U.S. 404, 56 S.Ct. 252 (1935). In that case a Vermont statute imposed an income tax on interest from notes and mortgages but allowed a deduction for such interest income where the obligations involved loans within the State. Colgate, a Vermont resident, successfully attacked this discrimination against out-of-state interest under the Privileges and Immunities Clause of the Fourteenth Amendment. The basis for the decision was the Court's holding (over the dissent of Justices Stone, Brandeis and Cardozo) that "the right of a citizen of the United States to engage in business, to transact any lawful business, or to make a lawful loan of money in any state other than that in which he resides" (296 U.S. at 430, 56 S.Ct. at 259) is a privilege of a citizen of the United States protected by the Fourteenth Amendment.

Five years later in Madden v. Kentucky, 309 U.S. 83, 60 S.Ct. 406 (1940), the Court considered a Kentucky statute which imposed an ad valorem tax on bank deposits of its citizens at 10 cents per $100 for deposits within the State and 50 cents per $100 on deposits outside the State. Madden, a resident of Kentucky, had substantial deposits in New York banks; in a suit involving the validity of the higher tax on such deposits during Madden's lifetime, his executors challenged the levy. The Supreme Court, after sustaining the classification as reasonable under the Equal Protection Clause on the ground that collection of tax on out-of-state deposits is more difficult and more expensive than on local deposits, held that the Privileges and Immunities Clause was not violated (with two Justices dissenting). *Colgate v. Harvey* was explicitly overruled and the Court repudiated the view that "the right to carry out an incident to a trade, business or calling such as a deposit of money" is a privilege of national citizenship.

The consequence of this decision is that the Fourteenth Amendment is held to have created no new privileges or immunities for citizens of the United States; it protects only those rights otherwise granted by the Constitution. Accordingly, this clause does not prevent a State from exempting from inheritance tax bequests and devises made by a resident to religious and educational institutions within a State, while denying exemption for such transfers to similar out-of-state organizations. Board of Education v. Illinois, 203 U.S. 553, 27 S.Ct. 171 (1906). For a discussion of this clause and its scope, see Note, "Privileges and Immunities of Citizens of the United States—Colgate v. Harvey Overruled," 9 Geo.Wash.L.Rev. 106 (1940).

In the State taxation field, therefore, it is Article IV, Section 2, the so-called "interstate privileges" clause, which has been the principal basis for a claim of denial of privileges and immunities since 1940. This privileges and immunities provision of the Constitution does confer rights on citizens of the States; as stated by the Supreme Court in the early case of Ward v. Maryland (79 U.S. (12 Wall.) 418, 430 (1870)):

> Beyond doubt those words are words of very comprehensive meaning, but it will be sufficient to say that the clause plainly and unmistakably secures and protects the right of a citizen of one State to pass into any other State of the Union for the purpose of engaging in lawful commerce, trade, or business without molestation; to acquire personal property; to take and hold real estate; to maintain actions in the courts of the State; and to be exempt from any higher taxes or excises than are imposed by the State upon its own citizens.

Corporations are not "citizens," and therefore (unlike the Due Process and Equal Protection Clauses which protect all "person[s]"), the Privileges and Immunities Clause provides no protection for corporations. See Western Turf Ass'n v. Greenberg, 204 U.S. 359, 27 S.Ct. 384 (1907). The Privileges and Immunities Clause is also limited by the fact that it embraces only "fundamental" rights. "Only with respect to those 'privileges and immunities' bearing upon the vitality of the Nation as a single entity must the State treat all citizens, resident and non-resident, equally." Baldwin v. Montana Fish and Game Commission, 436 U.S. 371, 383, 98 S.Ct. 1852 (1978). The Court therefore upheld an elk-hunting license scheme that imposed substantially higher fees on non-residents than on residents because access by non-residents to recreational big game hunting in Montana did not fall within the category of rights protected by the Privileges and Immunities Clause. Id.

In Austin v. New Hampshire, 420 U.S. 656, 95 S.Ct. 1191 (1975), the Supreme Court struck down under Article IV, Section 2 of the Constitution a New Hampshire income tax that effectively taxed only the incomes of non-resident taxpayers. Since the amount of the tax was equal to the maximum credit permitted by the law of the non-residents' State of residence, the taxpayers themselves paid no additional taxes as a result of the scheme. But this did not save the levy when considered against the "background establishing a rule of substantial equality of treatment for the citizens of the taxing State and non-resident taxpayers." 420 U.S. at 665. The *Austin* case and its aftermath are examined in more detail in connection with the consideration of State individual income taxes at pp. 953–956 infra.

In Toomer v. Witsell, 334 U.S. 385, 68 S.Ct. 1156 (1948), South Carolina imposed a license fee on shrimp fishing boats in its coastal waters at the rate of $25 for each resident-owned boat and $2,500 for each boat owned by a non-resident. The Court invalidated the levy under the Privileges and Immunities Clause of Article IV, concluding that the purpose and effect of the fee were not to conserve shrimp but to exclude non-residents and thereby create a commercial shrimp monopoly for South Carolina residents. In that case, the Court said (334 U.S. at 395, 68 S.Ct. at 1162):

> The primary purpose of this clause, like the clauses between which it is located—those relating to full faith and credit and to interstate extradition of fugitives from justice—was to help fuse into one Nation a collection of independent, sovereign States. It was designed to insure to a citizen of State A who ventures into State B the same privileges which the citizens of State B enjoy. For protection of such equality the citizen of State A was not to be restricted to the uncertain remedies afforded by diplomatic processes and official retaliation. "Indeed, without some provision of the kind removing from the citizens of each State the disabilities of alienage in the other States, and giving the equality of privilege with citizens of those States, the Republic would have constituted little more than a league of States; it would not have constituted the Union which now exists." Paul v. Virginia, 8 Wall. 168, 180 (1868).
>
> In line with this underlying purpose, it was long ago decided that one of the privileges which the clause guarantees to citizens of State A is that of doing business in State B on terms of substantial equality with the citizens of that State.
>
> Like many other constitutional provisions, the privileges and immunities clause is not an absolute. It does bar discrimination against citizens of other States where there is no substantial reason for the discrimination beyond the mere fact that they are citizens of other States. But it does not preclude disparity of treatment in the many situations where there are perfectly valid independent reasons for it. Thus the inquiry in each case must be concerned with whether such reasons do exist and whether the degree of discrimination bears a close relation to them. The inquiry must also, of course, be conducted with due regard for the principle that the States should have considerable leeway in analyzing local evils and in prescribing appropriate cures.*

* The case is noted in 46 Mich.L.Rev. 559 (1948). Cf. also, Mullaney v. Anderson, 342 U.S. 415, 72 S.Ct. 428 (1952), noted in 28 Wash.L.Rev. and State B.J. 55, in which an Alaskan license fee which discriminated against non-resident fishermen was invalidated.

Contrast with the *Toomer* case, State v. Reefer King Co. Inc., 559 P.2d 56 (Alaska 1976), modified on rehearing 562 P.2d 702 (Alaska 1977), in which the court upheld over Commerce Clause and Equal Protection Clause objections Alaska's fishery license tax imposed at the rate of four percent of the value of raw fish taken by floating processors, but only at one percent of such value for "shore-based" processors. Query, would the result have been any different if the plaintiff had not been a corporation and thus had been able to invoke the Privileges and Immunities Clause?

In Maxwell v. Bugbee, 250 U.S. 525, 40 S.Ct. 2 (1919), the Supreme Court passed on the validity of an attack on a New Jersey inheritance tax as applied to the estate of a non-resident. In that case, a non-resident of New Jersey owned shares of stock in Standard Oil Company of New Jersey, valued at approximately $1,000,000; these assets were shares in a New Jersey corporation, which were admittedly includible in the measure of the State's tax. The remainder of the assets in the $4,000,000 estate were not, however, subject to death tax by New Jersey. In order to subject the estate to New Jersey's graduated inheritance tax rates, the tax was first computed by taking into account the value of the decedent's entire estate, wherever located, just as if he had been a resident of the State. The tax as thus computed was then reduced to the ratio of in-state assets to the value of the entire estate. The Supreme Court upheld the State's power thus to apply its progressive inheritance rate schedule to a non-resident, against attack under the Privileges and Immunities Clause, the Equal Protection Clause and the Due Process Clause.

The Court, however, disposed of the privileges and immunities contention on a ground that it has since repudiated. The New Jersey inheritance tax statute was drawn in terms of taxation of estates of "non-residents," not in terms of decedents who were not "citizens" of the State. In passing on this issue, the Court declared:

> The alleged discrimination, here complained of, so far as privileges and immunities of citizenship are concerned, is not strictly applicable to this statute because the difference in the method of taxation rests upon residence and not citizenship. [250 U.S. at 538–539.]

Later Supreme Court decisions involving State taxation have held that, although the Privileges and Immunities Clause speaks of "citizens" and not "residents," a "general taxing scheme * * * if it discriminates against all non-residents has the necessary effect of including in the discrimination those who are citizens of other States." Travis v. Yale & Towne Manufacturing Co., 252 U.S. 60, 79, 40 S.Ct. 228, 231 (1920). Accord: Toomer v. Witsell, supra. Although the ground on which *Maxwell v. Bugbee* rejected the privileges and immunities contention is no longer tenable, New Jersey's technique for taxing non-residents has long been employed by a number of States over the country.[11]

11. Ala.Code tit. 40, § 40–15–7 (1985);   Stat.Ann. §§ 198.03–.04 (1980); Ga.Code
Ark.Stat.Ann. § 63–104 (Supp.1986); Fla.   Ann. § 48–12–3 (1982); Hawaii Rev.Stat.

Mr. Justice Holmes wrote a dissenting opinion in the case, concurred in by three other Justices, that relies essentially on the Due Process Clause; the dissent regarded the use of a tax rate determined by out-of-state property not taxable by a State, nor includible within the measure of the State's tax, as extraterritorial taxation.

Does the New Jersey method of taxing non-resident estates meet the constitutional test, under the Privileges and Immunities Clause, of a "disparity of treatment" of non-resident, as compared with resident, estates that is justified by "valid independent reasons"? See Lowndes, "Rate and Measure in Jurisdiction to Tax—Aftermath of *Maxwell v. Bugbee*," 49 Harv.L.Rev. 756 (1936). For a consideration of the related problem of State income taxes on non-residents, which take into account out-of-state income not taxable to a non-resident in order to apply the State's progressive rates in the light of the non-resident's income from all sources, see Chapter 13 infra.

In Smith v. Loughman, 245 N.Y. 486, 157 N.E. 753 (1927), certiorari denied 275 U.S. 560, 48 S.Ct. 119 (1927), a New York estate tax that provided different exemptions and rates for non-residents, as compared with residents, was held to constitute an unconstitutional discrimination under the Privileges and Immunities Clause. See also Luman v. Resor, 406 P.2d 527 (Wyo.1965). But a State death tax that restricts exemption for contributions to charities to in-state charitable organizations was not offensive to the constitutional provision. Board of Education v. Illinois, 203 U.S. 553, 27 S.Ct. 171 (1906).

New Jersey's Homestead Rebate Act provides a property tax rebate for "every citizen and resident" of the State for the dwelling and land "which constitutes the place of his domicile and which is owned and used by him as his principal residence." Two Pennsylvania residents, who owned a vacation home in New Jersey, challenged the Act on the grounds that the limitation of the rebate solely to the house and land which serve as a principal residence violates the Privileges and Immunities Clause. In Rubin v. Glaser, 83 N.J. 299, 416 A.2d 382 (1980), the court denied the claim. From its review of the Privileges and Immunities Clause decisions of the Supreme Court and other State tribunals, the New Jersey court derived the following principle: "[S]tate taxing statutes, conferring a benefit or advantage only on residents, do not run afoul of the Privileges and Immunities Clause, provided they bear a 'close' or 'substantial relationship' to a legitimate purpose independent of discrimination against non-residents." Applying this principle, the court found that the Act's application solely to principal places of residence was closely related to the beneficent purpose of alleviating

tit. 14, § 236–4 (1976); Iowa Code Ann. § 451.2 (1971); Mont.Code Ann. § 72–16–905 (1987); N.J.Stat.Ann. § 54:34–3 (1960); N.M.Stat.Ann. § 7–7–4 (1983); N.Y.Tax Law § 960 (McKinney Supp.1986); N.C. Gen.Stat. § 105–21 (1985); Ohio Rev.Code § 5731.19 (1985); Okla.Stat.Ann. tit. 68, § 818 (1966); Utah Code Ann. § 59–12A–4 (Supp.1987); Va.Code § 58.1–903 (1984). See also CCH Inheritance, Estate & Gift Tax Reporter; P–H State Inheritance Taxes.

the heavy realty tax burden. It also observed that the statutory purpose was not directed against non-residents.

> New Jersey residents who do not own a principal residence in the State are on the same footing as non-residents. For example, a New Jersey resident whose principal place of residence is a rented apartment would not receive a rebate on a home he owned at the New Jersey shore. Moreover no one is entitled to a rebate of taxes paid on a second home. Thus, plaintiffs are treated the same as New Jersey residents who own a second home for summer vacations in New Jersey with respect to rebates on that second home. [83 N.J. at 307, 416 A.2d at 386].

References. Varat, "State 'Citizenship' and Interstate Equality," 48 U.Chi.L.Rev. 487 (1981); Simson, "Discrimination Against Nonresidents and the Privileges and Immunities Clause of Article IV," 128 U.Pa.L. Rev. 379 (1979); Howard, "The Privileges and Immunities of Federal Citizenship and Colgate v. Harvey," 87 U. of Pa.L.Rev. 262 (1939); Comment, 9 Geo.Wash.L.Rev. 106 (1940); Lowen, "Privileges and Immunities under the Fourteenth Amendment," 18 Wash.L.Rev. 120 (1943). For a broader discussion of the Privileges and Immunities Clause, see W. Lockhart, Y. Kamisar, J. Choper & S. Shiffrin, Constitutional Law: Cases, Comments, Questions 299–306 (1986). See also 122 A.L.R. 983; 67 A.L.R.2d 1322, 1328.

*

Part 3

AD VALOREM PROPERTY TAXES

INTRODUCTORY NOTE

Early Property Taxation. Although property taxes were regarded as an extraordinary source of revenue in early history, they nevertheless have ancient origins. In Athens, the land tax was originally levied on gross produce, but it gradually developed into a property tax imposed not only on land and houses but also on slaves, cattle, furniture, and money. Rome taxed many forms of personalty as well as realty. In Europe, the early property taxes were levied on land but were gradually extended to buildings and cattle, until they became general property taxes. As new types of movable and intangible property developed, evasion became prevalent and assessment difficult. The principle of the general property tax broke down and personal property taxes were gradually abandoned. By 1800, the base of European property taxes had largely dwindled down to land alone or land and buildings.

The Development of the General Property Tax in the United States. As is indicated in the historical survey of the American State and local tax system (Chapter 1), the general property tax became formally established in this country for the States and localities during the nineteenth century.

At first the property tax was really a tax on land at a fixed sum per acre of different types of land—cleared and uncleared, cultivated and cleared, and so forth. It soon was expanded to include livestock, buildings, and personal property. Each item of taxable property was listed and taxed at a fixed sum for each cow, each barn, and so on. The increasing complexity of this taxable list led finally to (1) the general property tax—general taxation of all properties, instead of the growing lists of specified taxable properties; (2) appraisal of property—the tax rates were imposed as percentages or per millage of the property valuation, rather than as a fixed sum of money per unit of property; (3) the adoption of the principle of uniformity—whereas earlier laws provided for varying rates for different classes of property, the uniformity concept adopted by State constitutions required real and personal property to be taxed at a uniform proportion of value.

Professor Seligman lists five practical defects in the general property tax in his Essays in Taxation, ch. 2 (10th ed. 1931).*

1. *Lack of uniformity or inequality of assessment.* Most taxing statutes require property to be assessed at "full value" or "fair cash value" or by equivalent standards of value. Yet, it is notorious that in scarcely two contiguous counties is even the same real estate appraised in the same manner or at the same rate. Assessors follow local usage or decide by mere caprice. Seligman found that the establishment of equalization boards has not succeeded in dealing effectively with the inequality problem.

2. *Lack of universality or failure to reach personal property.* Personal property such as jewelry, stocks, bonds, and other intangibles were not reported by their owners and escaped the notice of assessors. Thus, a large and increasing part of the wealth of the community escaped taxation altogether.

3. *Incentive to dishonesty.* The shifting of personal property on the eve of tax day to United States bonds, notes, and saving bank deposits, the transfer of goods to another State on consignment, and the failure to report taxable property caused one report to conclude that "instead of being a tax on personal property, it has in effect become a tax upon ignorance and honesty * * * its imposition is restricted to those who are not informed of the means of evasion, or knowing the means, are restricted by a nice sense of honor from resorting to them." Report of the Commissioners of Taxes and Assessments in the City of New York 9 (1872).

4. *Regressivity.* "Taxes are progressive when their increase is more than proportional to the increases of the property or income taxed, i.e., when the rate itself increases with the increase of the property. Taxes are regressive when the rate increases as the property or income decreases." Seligman, supra, at 28. Seligman held that the general property tax is regressive because it taxes only the visible, readily ferreted out property which cannot be converted into non-taxable property. He quoted Walpole's saying that it is safer to tax real than personal estate because "landed gentlemen are like the flocks upon their plains, who suffer themselves to be shorn without resistance; whereas the trader part of the nation resemble the boar, who will not suffer a bristle to be pluckt from his back without making the whole parish to echo with his complaints." From 3 J. Sinclair, History of the Public Revenue, App. p. 79.

5. *Double taxation.* The treatment of indebtedness under property taxes was regarded by Seligman as the greatest weakness of the general property levy. If real estate on which there is a mortgage is taxed to the owner at its full value, the taxpayer is being taxed on what he owes, not on what he owns. Seligman argued that if the holder of the mortgage debt is taxed on the intangible, there is double taxation. On the other hand, the exemption of indebtedness "is

* The quotations from this work are reprinted with the permission of the Estate of E.R.A. Seligman.

thoroughly pernicious in its operation. It is the universal testimony that no portion of the tax laws offers more temptation to fraud and perjury than this system of offsets. The creation of fictitious debts is a paying investment. In the states where such deductions are permitted, attempts to obtain immunity from taxation in this way are widespread and generally successful." E.R.A. Seligman, supra, at 30.

Professor Groves considers the question as to why the property tax has survived the devastating criticisms which have been made of it: (1) The tax is being improved by administrative reform and classification; (2) property has been bought and sold on the assumption that the tax will be levied and to eliminate the levy now would produce a large windfall for property owners; (3) the alternatives (the principal alternative is the sales tax) are even less palatable than the property tax; (4) with all its faults, the property tax has the great fiscal virtues of being a large dependable source of revenue, with the added feature of elasticity; (5) it is particularly well suited to the local needs of a nation imbued with the spirit of home rule; and (6) there is a widespread belief that the ownership of property affords a proper basis for taxation, particularly in view of the local services rendered to the property owner. H. Groves, Financing Government 73–74 (1945).

In his Economics of the Property Tax (1966), Professor Dick Netzer states:

> The American property tax abounds in anomalies. During the past century, no major fiscal institution, here or abroad, has been criticized at such length and with such vigor; yet no major fiscal institution has changed so little in modern times. There is a vast literature on the property tax; yet less is known about its overall impact, incidence, and effects than is known about any major tax. The demise of the property tax as a major factor in the American fiscal scene has long been heralded; yet it continues to finance more than one-fifth of the civilian general expenditures of federal, state, and local governments. The United States is the citadel of capitalism; yet this tax on wealth is more important in the fiscal system and relative to national income than are comparable taxes in any other advanced country in the world except Canada.

> By and large, the keys to the paradoxes lie in the venerability and diversity of the property tax. It is an old institution and it is actually not a single national tax but an incredibly complex collection of taxes with literally thousands of local variations.

> Property taxation has been the major fiscal resource of American local governments since seventeenth century colonial days. During the first two centuries of its existence, the property tax gradually became a general tax measured by the value of all types of privately owned assets, with all assets taxed at a uniform rate. However, in the last hundred years, it has become less general in coverage, in large part because of the difficulty of administering so universal a tax uniformly in an increasingly complex society. In most of the States the tax is now one chiefly on real estate and business equipment and

inventories. Although the property tax is no longer virtually the sole support of state-local government in the United States as it was at the turn of the twentieth century, it remains the single most important factor in state-local finance, by a wide margin.*

See Chapter 1 for a discussion of the role of the property tax in State and local finance.

The Development of the Classified Property Tax. The movement to reform property taxes found one of its expressions in the classified property tax. Instead of a tax on all property at the same rate, various types of property are classified and taxed at varying rates or at different percentages of full value. The adoption of "the principle that property is heterogeneous rather than homogeneous and that all kinds of tangible and intangible property cannot be taxed uniformly" is "designed to preserve the practicable elements of property taxation and save an important source of revenue." A. Buehler, Public Finance 367 (3d ed. 1948).

Although the laws of most States contemplate assessment at full value, some States have adopted classified property taxes under which various classes of property are assessed at specified percentages of full value. State laws requiring assessors to classify property according to its use proliferated during the 1970's and early 1980's. See Roemer, "Classification of Property," in C.L. Harriss, ed., The Property Tax and Local Finance 108 (1983). Arthur Roemer, Commissioner of Revenue of Minnesota—a State with an elaborate classified property tax system, has observed:

> The purpose of a property-classification system is not necessarily to raise revenue; rather, it is a social policy tool used to determine who should pay what share of the total amount of revenue to be collected. State legislators use the system to shift the burden of tax among the various groups of property owners to accomplish social goals, such as reducing taxes on homes and family-operated farms and stimulating the growth of new or expanding businesses. In addition, classification systems are used as a social-policy tool to make taxes progressive for a group of property owners in the same class—often for family-owned farms and residences. [Id.]

The major form of classification in the United States is the separation of intangibles from general property for taxation at especially low rates. In 1986, twenty-four States had some type of tax on intangibles on their statute books. CCH All States Guide ¶ 20–200 et seq., P–H All States Guide ¶ 210 (chart). In most cases, these were low-rate taxes or were taxes limited to only specified types of intangibles. Id. Other States have gone further and have adopted the proposal made in the Model Plan of State and Local Taxation proposed in 1933 by a committee of the National Tax Association that intangibles should be exempted from ad valorem tax, substituting instead a tax on the income from

---

* This material is used with the consent of the Brookings Institution. Footnotes and a chart of revenue collections have been omitted.

such property. See 1933 Nat. Tax Ass'n Procs. 381; CCH All States Guide ¶ 20–200 et seq., P–H All States Guide ¶ 210 (chart).

Professor Leland concluded from his studies that the chief contributions of the classified property tax have not been the increased revenues which were expected to result, but instead, a greater equity in the tax burden and more flexibility in the taxation of property. S. Leland, "Some Observations Concerning the Classified Property Tax," Property Taxes, ch. 7 (1940). The development of the graduated State income tax has tended to equalize the burden of taxation of the owner of intangibles with the tax load carried by the owner of real property and readily visible tangible personal property. For further consideration of the classified property tax, see pp. 148–49 infra.

Alternative Methods of Taxing Real Property. The movement to modify the taxation of real property in the United States has taken a number of forms. Administrative reforms, beginning with the establishment of local boards of equalization to review and equalize assessments, later the establishment of State equalization boards, and more recently the setting up of State tax commissions with broad supervisory powers, have been instituted by many States, and have served to strengthen and improve property tax assessments.

A number of schools of thought which advocate more basic changes in the ad valorem tax have emerged. One group advocates low rate taxation of improvements on land (the so-called graded tax) in order to shift a greater portion of the real estate tax burden to land values— particularly to the increment or windfalls in land values created by the community's growth and development—and to stimulate building and the rehabilitation of blighted and slum areas. This method of taxation has been employed widely in New Zealand and Australia. There has been experimentation with the graded tax in Pittsburgh and Scranton and in some California irrigation districts. See Cord, "Taxing Land More than Buildings: The Record in Pennsylvania," in C.L. Harriss, ed., The Property Tax and Local Finance 172 (1983).

Others have urged that the taxation of real estate on the basis of its capital value be abandoned in favor of assessments based on rental income. This method, which is in vogue in local governments in England and Wales, results in the imposition of a tax on occupiers of real estate, whether owners or tenants, at a uniform rate applied to a hypothetical net rent. The major administrative problem is that of converting reported gross annual rentals into hypothetical net rents which enter into the tax base. See generally Woolery, "Alternative Methods of Taxing Property," in C.L. Harriss, ed., The Property Tax and Local Finance 180 (1983).

References. E.R.A. Seligman, Essays in Taxation (10th ed. 1931), contains the classic critique of the general property tax and an excellent history of the levy. S. Leland, The Classified Property Tax (1928), is the outstanding study of that levy in this country. The authoritative complete work devoted to American ad valorem taxation is J. Jensen,

Property Taxation in the United States (1931). The Tax Policy League's Symposium on Property Taxes (1939) contains a number of excellent papers dealing with various aspects of property taxation. See also Cornick, "Evaluation of Alternative Bases for Property Tax," 1952 Nat. Tax Ass'n Procs. 60 (1952); Advisory Commission on Intergovernmental Relations, The Role of the States in Strengthening the Property Tax (1963); D. Netzer, Economics of the Property Tax (1966); Property Taxation: U.S.A. (Procs. Symposium, Committee on Taxation, Resources and Economic Development, U. of Wisc.1967); Hearings on the Property Tax Relief and Reform Act of 1973 Before the Subcomm. on Intergovernmental Relations of the Senate Comm. on Government Operations, 93rd Cong., 1st Sess. (1973); Advisory Commission on Intergovernmental Relations, The Property Tax in a Changing Environment, (1974); D. Halstead, Tax Wealth in Fifty States (1978); C.L. Harriss, ed., The Property Tax and Local Finance (1983). For the continuing debate as to the incidence of the property tax, see Mieszkowski, "The Property Tax: An Excise or Profits Tax?," 1 J. of Public Economics 73 (1972); Netzer, "The Incidence of the Property Tax Revisited," 26 Nat.Tax J. 515 (1973); H. Aaron, Who Pays the Property Tax: A New View (1975); McLure, "The 'New View' of the Property Tax: A Caveat," 30 Nat.Tax J. 69 (1977); Heilbrun, "Who Bears the Burden of the Property Tax," in C.L. Harriss, ed., supra, at 57. Compare H. George, Progress and Poverty (1926 repr.), for Henry George's disquisition in support of the single tax.

Chapter 4

REAL PROPERTY TAXES

SECTION 1. TAXABLE REAL PROPERTY

Notes and Problems

A. *Separation of Interests in Realty in General.* Although some States provide for the separate taxation of leasehold interests, real estate is generally taxed as a unit to the owner of the fee interest without separate listing or taxation of leasehold or other interests in the property. See, e.g., Hamilton Manufacturing Co. v. Lowell, 185 Mass. 114, 69 N.E. 1080 (1904); Town of Brattleboro v. Smith, 117 Vt. 425, 94 A.2d 407 (1953) (holding that the remainderman, not the life tenant, is the "owner" of real estate and hence liable for real estate taxes); 71 Am.Jur.2d § 201 et seq.; 84 C.J.S. § 95. There are two important exceptions to this generalization. First, leasehold interests in tax-exempt property are taxable in many States. See Note C and Section (a) infra. Second, separate interests in natural resource property are generally required to be separately listed on the property tax roll and separately taxed to the owner of the interest. See generally W. Hellerstein, State and Local Taxation of Natural Resources in the Federal System: Legal, Economic, and Political Perspectives 48–49 (1986); Note D infra. Furthermore, in some jurisdictions, the parties to a real estate lease may determine by private agreement the ownership of their respective interests in the realty for tax purposes. See Note B infra. Even if separate interests in realty are otherwise taxable, however, the particular interest in question may not be taxable if it amounts to a mere license to use—a usufruct—rather than a discrete property interest. See, e.g., Richmond County Board of Tax Assessors v. Richmond Bonded Warehouse Corporation, 173 Ga.App. 278, 325 S.E.2d 891 (1985).

B. *Separation of Interests in Realty: The Effect of Private Agreements.* A lessor (Portland Terminal Company) owned land on which there were 41 buildings owned and occupied by lessees. As to all but one of the buildings, the lease of the land occupied by the buildings was revocable by the lessor, and the buildings were removable by the lessee at the termination of the lease. One particular building was to remain the property of the lessee during the term of the lease and, at its expiration, to become the property of the lessor. All 41 buildings were assessed to the lessor for real estate tax purposes. The statute provided that real estate, for purposes of taxation, includes all lands and all buildings erected on or affixed to land, and taxed property to the owner, or the party in possession. The buildings were assessed to the lessor under the so-called Massachusetts rule, which holds that an agreement between the landowner and the building owner as to the status of the building owner's interest as a separate estate is operative only as between the parties to the agreement. The court in setting aside the assessment refused to follow the Massachusetts view, and instead followed the New York rule, which holds that it is competent for parties by contract to so regulate their respective interests that one may be the owner of the buildings and another the land. Nor was the lessor liable for property taxes on the single building which, by the terms of the lease, became the property of the lessor at the termination of the lease. During the term of the lease, the lessee was the owner of the building, which should be taxed to him. Portland Terminal Co. v. Hinds, 141 Me. 68, 39 A.2d 5 (1944), annotated in 154 A.L.R. 1302.

C. *The Taxation of Separate Interests in Tax–Exempt Realty.* The separation of various interests in property and their taxation to their respective owners has become the linchpin on which immunity from ad valorem taxation may depend, where property is owned by the United States and it is leased to, or made available for, use by a contractor with the Federal government. The immunity problem is considered in Chapter 15 infra. Similar issues arise in connection with the taxation of interests in State-owned lands. See, e.g., Williams v. Jones, 326 So.2d 425 (Fla.1975), appeal dismissed, 429 U.S. 803, 97 S.Ct. 34 (1976).

The underlying problem of State law in determining whether separate leasehold or possessory interests are taxable is illustrated by Matter of Fort Hamilton Manor v. Boyland, 4 N.Y.2d 192, 149 N.E.2d 856 (1958), in which the issue was the legality of a local real estate tax assessment of a private housing project built by the taxpayer on land leased from the United States for a term of 75 years in a military reservation in Brooklyn. The houses were rented by the taxpayer to military and civilian personnel located at the Fort Hamilton military reservation. Title to the houses remained in the taxpayer and will revert to the United States only if they are not removed by the end of the lease term. The United States had consented by statute to taxation of the property to the lessee. The Court said in part:

> Under a long line of New York decisions, the interest of a tenant of realty under a real estate lease is not realty but is a chattel real which is personal property. * * * The most recent expression of this court upon the point is in Grumman Aircraft Eng. Corp. v. Board of Assessors, 2 N.Y.2d 500, 507, 161 N.Y.S.2d 393, 397, 141 N.E.2d 794, 797; where it was said: "It is significant to note that nowhere in the Tax Law has the Legislature characterized a leasehold as taxable real property. Such omission is understandable, as a lease for years is deemed personalty. * * * Restatement, Property, § 8; 1949 Op. Atty.Gen. 90, 91. We do not read subdivision 17 of section 4 of the Tax Law as changing this basic concept." Yet, although the interest of appellant in this housing project is thus personal property, there is no New York State tax against personal property. It was repealed by an amendment to section 3 of the Tax Law in 1933 (L.1933, ch. 470).

The New York State tax upon real property is the sole basis for this assessment. A tax on real property does not touch the leasehold interest of petitioner-appellant since that is personal property. If the fee were privately owned, the real property tax would attach to the combined interests of all parties interested in this land. That is impossible here inasmuch as this fee is vested in the Government. Only the lessee's interest is permitted to be taxed by Federal law, even though under the Borg–Warner case, 355 U.S. 466, 78 S.Ct. 474, supra, the value of the lessee's interest may be measured by the value of the fee. Inasmuch as the lessee's interest in the land is personal property, it escapes taxation in the absence of authorization to the city to levy taxes on personal property. The circumstance that our Legislature would be at liberty to tax this leasehold interest does not establish that it has done so. Consequently, so much of the assessment in question is invalid as attaches to the land where this housing development is situated. The land cannot be taxed since it belongs to the United States. The leasehold interest of appellant *has not been taxed,* since it is personal property and the New York State personal property tax has been repealed, and, unlike Michigan, we have no special tax against leaseholds of exempt real estate.

It is different, however, for a special reason, with respect to the buildings and improvements erected on this leased land. The Legislature may classify property for tax purposes in any reasonable manner which it chooses, and the statute imposing our real property tax is phrased so as to reach buildings and other structures even though constructed upon leased land where the fee is nontaxable (Tax Law, § 2, subd. 6; § 3; People ex rel. Hudson River Day Line v. Franck, 257 N.Y. 69, 177 N.E. 312). The cited case holds that where land is nontaxable, being owned by the State, buildings thereon are assessable to the lessee if they are removable from the property under the terms of the lease.

Consequently the order appealed from should be reversed, the assessment which has been imposed annulled insofar as it is against the land, and this proceeding should be remanded to the Tax Commission of the City of New York to assess the buildings and improvements only. [4 N.Y.2d at 197–98, 149 N.E.2d at 858–59.]

D. *The Taxation of Separate Interests in Natural Resource Property.* * Separate interests are frequently created in natural resource property when the owner of the fee interest in the property conveys part of the interest to others while reserving part for himself. Indeed, natural resources are not usually extracted by the owner of the surface land. The separate interest conveyed or reserved by the landowner may consist of the rights to all the minerals in the property, rights to a portion of those minerals, rights to specific types of minerals, or interests such as royalties, overriding royalties, and payments-in-kind. Most jurisdictions require that these interests be separately listed on the property tax roll and separately

---

* This Note is taken substantially from W. Hellerstein, State and Local Taxation of Natural Resources in the Federal System: Legal, Economic, and Political Per- spectives 48–49 (1986) and is used with the permission of the copyright owner, the American Bar Association.

taxed to the person who is determined to be the owner of the interest. See, e.g., Straughn v. Sun Oil Co., 345 So.2d 1062 (Fla.1977) (leasehold interest in subsurface minerals taxable as interest in real property); Contos v. Herbst, 278 N.W.2d 732 (Minn.1979) (severed mineral interests taxable as real property). This generalization should be read with several cautionary notes in mind, however. First, there is a bewildering maze of variations among the States, often rooted in arcane concepts of traditional property law, in the classification of these separate interests as real or personal property. These variations may have implications as to where and, in some cases, as to whether the property may be taxed. Second, there are striking differences among the States in their determination whether particular mineral interests are taxable to the surface landowner or to the person to whom the interest has been conveyed or by whom it has been reserved. Finally, insofar as these separate interests represent interests in nonproducing property, they frequently will not be taxed at all. See Wade "Recent Oil and Gas Cases," 18 Miss.L.J. 243 (1947); Tippit, "Property Taxation of Oil and Gas Interests," 24 Rocky Mtn.L.Rev. 170 (1952); Note, "Ad Valorem Taxation of Mineral Property," 21 Baylor L.Rev. 46 (1969); Kearns, "Property Taxation of the Mining Industry in Arizona," 12 Ariz.L. Rev. 763 (1970); Paschall, "A Comparison of Minerals Tax Systems," 12 Assessors J. 221 (1977).

E. *T,* owner of Blackacre, leased the property to *X,* a utility company. The State levies a tax measured by gross earnings of such companies in lieu of all ad valorem taxes upon its property. *X* paid the "in lieu taxes." Is *T* liable for ad valorem property taxes on the leased property? See State v. Fawkes, 210 Minn. 587, 299 N.W. 666 (1941), noted in 42 Col.L.Rev. 159 (1942) and 26 Minn.L.Rev. 413 (1942).

F. *Taxation of Time–Share Property.* One of the more innovative forms of real property interests is time-sharing. Time-sharing generally encompasses all forms of recurring, fractionalized usage of real property. Note "Ad Valorem Taxation of Time–Share Properties: Should Time–Share Estates Be Separately Assessed and Taxed?," 37 U.Fla.L.Rev. 421 (1985). Individual owners acquire an exclusive right periodically to occupy or use a building or other structure. Twenty-five States have statutes that expressly recognize time-sharing as a form of real property ownership. Id. at 423. They differ, however, as to how to treat these interests for ad valorem tax purposes. Some States, including Arkansas, Georgia, Nebraska, Tennessee, Virginia, and West Virginia, specify that time-share arrangements constitute separate interests in real property but are to be assessed as if a single taxpayer owned the unit. Id. at 428. Other States, including Hawaii, California, Colorado, Louisiana, Maine, and Vermont, provide that time-share interests are to be separately assessed and taxed to their individual owners. Id. at 429.

G. *Realty vs. Personalty: Fixtures.* The question whether machinery or equipment affixed to buildings or other realty constitutes real property presents ad valorem tax issues because personal property may be exempt from taxation or may be taxed in a different manner from real property. In Roseville Pottery, Inc. v. County Board of Revision, 149 Ohio St. 89, 77

N.E.2d 608 (1948),[1] the issue was whether kilns used in the manufacture of pottery and tile constituted real or personal property. Under the Ohio law, personal property may be classified separately from real property and is taxable at a lower percentage of true value than real property. The court found that the "primary distinction between a fixture and a chattel * * * is that a fixture is accessory to the use of the real estate as such [e.g., a heating plant in a factory building], whereas a chattel is accessory to the particular business conducted on the real estate." It held that the kilns were chattels, because they are designed specially for the ceramics business, are removable and hence are an incident to the manufacturing operation, not the building.

In Abex Corp. v. Commissioner, 295 Minn. 445, 207 N.W.2d 37 (1973), the Minnesota Supreme Court, addressing the issue of the definition of fixtures for tax purposes as a matter of first impression, held that machinery used by a foundry was taxable as real property. In an exhaustive opinion, the court declined to follow the Ohio rule and concluded that "[p]roperty which (a) is ponderous and therefore annexed to real estate, whether or not actually attached and (b) has been annexed with the intent to make a nontemporary accession to the freehold is a fixture * * * " 295 Minn. at 466, 207 N.W.2d at 49.

California imposes a tax on fixtures, but not on other personal property of national banks. The issue arose as to the taxability of electronic computer systems installed by a bank for accounting purposes. The court held the computer equipment to be a taxable fixture, although not permanently attached to the land or improvements. Most of the buildings in which the computer systems were installed were special purpose buildings, designed as accounting centers requiring computer systems. The computers of each system were interconnected by many signal and power cables; air conditioning and humidity controls were established for optimum operating efficiency of the computers; and the buildings were specially constructed to accommodate the systems. Each system weighed eleven tons, and it would have been difficult and expensive to move the computers. Bank of America National Trust and Savings Ass'n v. County of Los Angeles, 224 Cal.App.2d 108, 36 Cal.Rptr. 413 (1964).

H. Are house trailers taxable as realty? May they be made taxable to the owners of the land? Litigation has developed under a New York statute taxing such trailers as realty to the owner of the land, where the trailer has been on the land for at least 60 days. Barnes v. Gorham, 12 Misc.2d 285, 175 N.Y.S.2d 376 (Sup.Ct.1957) held the tax invalid but the Court of Appeals sustained the levy in New York Mobile Homes Ass'n v. Steckel, 9 N.Y.2d 533, 215 N.Y.S.2d 487, 175 N.E.2d 151 (1961). At the outset, the court held that the legislature has the power to classify trailers as real property for purposes of taxation. The trailers were used as residences and were attached to the freehold, through the water supply system, sewage system and utilities. In sustaining the assessment of trailers as an improvement on the land, the court pointed to the analogy of

1. Noted in 17 U.Cin.L.Rev. 297 (1948). See Zangerle, "Fixtures—What Are Fixtures in Ohio?," 33 Ohio Op. 142 (1946); Note, "Defining Real Estate for the Tax Gatherer," 12 U.Pitt.L.Rev. 604 (1951).

a lessee who erects a building or other improvement on the realty of his landlord. See also Koester v. Hunterdon County Board of Taxation, 79 N.J. 381, 399 A.2d 656 (1979) (mobile homes taxable as realty); 7 A.L.R. 4th 1016.

I. Is a barge moored to a bulkhead and utilized as a restaurant assessable as real property? A New York court held that it was. Despite the fact that the barge could have been moved without injury to the upland, the court relied on the facts that it had been in place for eleven years and was served by electric, telephone, and water lines on the adjacent dock as proving that the barge was "affixed" to the land within the meaning of the real property tax statute. Capri Marina & Pool Club v. Board of Assessors, 84 Misc.2d 1096, 379 N.Y.S.2d 341 (Sup.Ct.1976); accord, Consolidated Edison Co. v. City of New York, 44 N.Y.2d 536, 406 N.Y.S.2d 727, 378 N.E.2d 91 (1978) (barge-mounted power plant).

J. Is airspace superjacent to real property taxable as real estate? See Chicago Union Station Co. v. Korzen, 96 Ill.App.3d 780, 52 Ill.Dec. 381, 422 N.E.2d 62 (1981); Macht v. Department of Assessments, 266 Md. 602, 296 A.2d 162 (1972).

(a) Leaseholds

Notes and Problems

A. After the decisions of the Supreme Court holding that a possessory interest in property owned by the United States and its instrumentalities could be subjected to property tax without running afoul of the intergovernmental immunities doctrine (see Chapter 15, § 5 infra), many States changed their property tax laws to tax such possessory interests. Because the Supreme Court had found no Federal constitutional objection to valuing leaseholds at what appeared to be the full value of the fee (id.), the controversy shifted to the construction and administration of the State statutes in determining assessed values. The valuation issue arises under leases on properties owned by States and local governments, as well as the Federal government.

B. *Conflicting Approaches to Valuation of Leaseholds.* In People ex rel. Korzen v. American Airlines, Inc., 39 Ill.2d 11, 233 N.E.2d 568 (1967), the Illinois Supreme Court considered the appropriate approach to valuing a taxable leasehold in tax-exempt property—American Airlines' leasehold interest in a hangar and a hangar site owned by the City of Chicago. The Illinois statute calls for valuing a leasehold at its "fair cash value," which the Illinois courts have construed as synonymous with fair market value. The taxpayer contended that the value of the leasehold should be ascertained by capitalizing the amount, if any, by which the present market rental value of the leasehold exceeded the rent called for by the lease (the contract rent). The court disagreed, holding that the value of the right to use and occupy the leased property—not merely the equity of the lessee in the lease—was the interest being valued. The court declared that "the fair cash value of a leasehold is its rental value in the market—the amount a willing lessee will pay a willing lessor, in a voluntary transaction for the right to use and occupy the premises." According to the court, the appropriate method for valuing such an interest "is to calculate the lump sum that represents the present economic equivalent of a periodic market rental to be paid through the unexpired term of the lease." The Washington Supreme Court has taken essentially the same view of the valuation of leases as the Illinois Supreme Court. Pier 67, Inc. v. King County, 78 Wash.2d 48, 469 P.2d 902 (1970), certiorari denied 401 U.S. 911, 91 S.Ct. 876 (1971).

In another case involving a property tax of a lessee of a hangar and other buildings at the St. Louis airport, the court accepted the testimony of the airline's expert that the value of a leasehold interest is "the present worth of the rental saving where the contractual rent is less than the fair market value of the leased premises," and held that the lease had a "zero or no value." St. Louis County v. State Tax Comm'n, 406 S.W.2d 644 (Mo. 1966). Cf., however, Iron County v. State Tax Comm'n, 437 S.W.2d 665 (Mo.1968), which appears to reflect a departure from the rule of the *St. Louis County* case. In West Virginia, where the statute provides that the assessment of leasehold estates must be deducted from the value of the freehold estate, the court has held that a leasehold is taxable only if it has a separate and independent value from the freehold, i.e., only if the fee interest is burdened by an unfavorable lease. Great A & P Tea Co., Inc. v. Davis, 167 W.Va. 53, 278 S.E.2d 352 (1981).

C. The Supreme Court of California dealt with the valuation of property leased from the United States Government in DeLuz Homes Inc. v. County of San Diego, 45 Cal.2d 546, 290 P.2d 544 (1955). DeLuz Homes was a 562–unit housing project located on land owned by the United States Government at Camp Pendleton, a military installation in San Diego County. The project provided housing for military and civilian personnel stationed at the camp, which the taxpayer rented to the occupants. The buildings and other improvements erected by the lessee became the property of the United States, as they were completed.

The California statute provides that all taxable property should be assessed at its full cash value. The leases in question were taxable possessory estates under the California law. They should be assessed, said the court, in accordance with the standard of valuation applicable to all other property, namely, the price the leasehold would bring on an open market.

In valuing the leasehold by an income capitalization method, the court rejected the lessee's contentions that the rent it paid and the amortization of the improvements it made to the property were properly deductible. The *DeLuz* decision is criticized in Hicks, "Possessory Interests in Publicly Owned Property: Improperly Assessed," 20 Nat. Tax J. 347 (1967), but it was followed in Host Int'l, Inc. v. County of San Mateo, 35 Cal.App.3d 286, 110 Cal.Rptr. 652 (1973).[2]

2. The *DeLuz* case is also discussed in Keesling, "Property Taxation of Leases and Other Limited Interests," 47 Calif.L. Rev. 470 (1959). Keesling notes that following the decision in the *DeLuz* case, the California legislature added Section 107.1 to the State's Revenue and Taxation Code, which provides that the rule of the *DeLuz* case should be inapplicable to leases created prior to the date of the decision. This provision was sustained in Forster Shipbuilding Co. v. Los Angeles County, 54 Cal. 2d 450, 6 Cal.Rptr. 24, 353 P.2d 736 (1960).

D.   In dealing with long term leases, there may be an alternative basis for assessing the lease at the full value of the fee. This type of case is illustrated by the facts of the *Iron County* case, Note B supra. There the City of Annapolis leased to a manufacturer, Ruberoid, property the city had built with the proceeds of tax exempt industrial revenue bonds. Ruberoid had an option to acquire the fee for $1 after paying off the bonds; it had a basic 20 year lease (covering the term of the revenue bonds), with renewal rights for another 75 years, at the nominal rental of $1,000 a year. The arrangement made with the city was simply a technique for financing the building with the use of the city's credit—a deplorable, growing practice alluded to elsewhere in this work (see p. 36 supra). Could not the court have taxed Ruberoid as the owner of the land and buildings—which it was, as an economic matter? In these circumstances, treating the company as the owner would have facilitated reaching what appears to be the proper result—an assessment based on the full value of the property. Compare Williams v. Jones, 326 So.2d 425 (Fla.1975), appeal dismissed 429 U.S. 803, 97 S.Ct. 34 (1976), in which the taxpayers contended unsuccessfully that they were denied equal protection through the operation of a statutory provision making lessees of property leased for 99 years or more "owners" for property tax purposes.

E. *References.* Brothers, "Appraisal of Possessory Interests," Calif. State Bd. of Equalization (1955); Annot., 154 A.L.R. 1309; Dale, "Possessory Interests: A Tax Without a Test?," 25 Santa Clara L.Rev. 65 (1985); Skoppek & Wolfram, "Taxation of Leasehold Interests in Michigan: The Lessons from the CAF Investment Case," 3 Cooley L.Rev. 491 (1985).

SECTION 2. UNIFORMITY AND EQUALITY IN ASSESSMENT

PEOPLE EX REL. SCHLAEGER v. ALLYN

Supreme Court of Illinois, 1946.
393 Ill. 154, 65 N.E.2d 392.

FULTON, JUSTICE. This matter comes to us on appeal from the judgment of the county court of Cook county overruling the objections of C.B. Allyn, hereafter referred to as the taxpayer, to the application of the ex officio county collector of Cook county, hereafter referred to as the collector, for judgment and order of sale on property belonging to the taxpayer for certain 1943 taxes paid under protest.

The taxpayer's property lies within the corporate limits of the village of Barrington, which municipality, while mainly located in Lake county, extends over into Cook county. Property in this village is subject to taxes for different counties, townships, and road and bridge districts, but the village of Barrington, Barrington park district and school district No. 4 are common taxing bodies. The objections herein are concerned only with the latter three tax levies. The levy is objected to as being discriminatory and constituting constructive fraud in violation of section 1 of article IX and section 2 of article II of the constitution of the State of Illinois, Smith–Hurd Stats., and of the due-process and equal-protection clauses of the fourteenth amendment to the constitution of the United States.

* * * By the stipulation it was agreed that for the year 1943 the tax rate for $100 of assessed valuation for the village of Barrington was $.65, for the Barrington park district, $.29 and for school district No. 4, $1.82; that the property of the taxpayer here was assessed by the Cook county assessor for the year 1943 at its fair cash value as of April 1, 1943, and the assessed value of the property was the amount determined by the assessor of Cook county as the fair cash value as of April 1, 1943; that the Department of Revenue determined the assessed value of all property throughout Cook county and throughout Lake county for the year 1943, and determined the ratio of assessed value to full cash valuation for each of said counties; that the ratio of assessed valuation to full valuation in Lake county as determined by the Department of Revenue was 21 per cent and that the ratio of assessed valuation to full valuation in Cook county for the year 1943 was 75 per cent; that the county clerk of Cook county and the county clerk of Lake county caused to be filed in the Department of Revenue an abstract of the assessed valuation of all the taxable property in their respective counties for the year 1943. The only oral testimony produced at the hearing was by C.B. Allyn, the objecting taxpayer. It appears that Allyn, at the time of the hearing, was, and had been since 1943, head of the tax department of a large Chicago merchandising corporation. Prior to 1943, he had spent nineteen years with the Jewel Tea Company, the last nine years of which he was engaged as chief accountant and assistant comptroller in charge of accounting and taxes at the headquarters of the Jewel Tea Company in Barrington, Illinois; that, as a part of his duties in connection with the analysis of taxes for the Jewel Tea Company, he was familiar with the valuation methods used in Cuba township, Lake county, wherein the greater portion of the municipality of Barrington lies; that he was familiar with the report of the Department of Revenue disclosing the ratios of assessed valuation to full cash valuation for the year 1943, and that the figure of 21 per cent was a fair statement of the average as it existed in Cuba township in 1943; that he had made a study of assessment values from the records. He also testified that except for minor variations in the ratio of assessed value to full cash value, the ratio in Cuba township had been the same since 1930. Allyn further testified that the figure of 75 per cent of full value by the Department of Revenue as to Cook county was approximately correct as to the property in Barrington township, Cook county, and that this latter ratio has existed only starting in 1943. Prior thereto, an equalizing figure of 37 per cent had been applied to the previous 75 per cent of full value, which equalizing figure brought the assessed value down to 28 per cent.

Much of the testimony of Allyn was objected to by counsel for the collector on the ground of lack of qualification in Allyn to testify as to the assessment ratio used and that the testimony of Allyn was opinion evidence and conclusions. Over objection there was admitted in evidence taxpayer's exhibit 5, which was a computation of taxes as extended for the three taxing districts in question here on a sample piece of property worth $10,000 located in Cook county and in Lake county. For the three districts it appears that the $10,000 property in Cook county had been taxed at $207 and for Lake county, $57.96. The taxpayer also introduced as exhibit 6, over objection, his computation showing that the tax extended against his own property was $141.45 and that the tax extended against similar property in Lake county was $39.61.

Allyn further testified that in connection with exhibit 6, mentioned above, the property used as a comparison was a house built by a business associate of Allyn's the same year that Allyn built his house, that the same contractor and subcontractor were used and that the cost of the business associate's house exceeded Allyn's by 10 per cent. This same property, however, for the same municipal services paid a total tax of $39.61, whereas, Allyn's property was subject to a tax of $141.45. It further appears that a complaint was filed on the property here involved before the Board of Appeals based upon the grounds of lack of uniformity and the complainant asked for a hearing. No hearing was granted and on December 10, 1944, an order was entered by the Board of Appeals as follows: "No reduction."

* * *

While considerable emphasis is placed by counsel for the collector in his reply brief upon the fact that the proof and evidence in this case were not sufficient to overcome the stipulated prima facie case made by the collector, we are of the opinion from a reading of the whole record, including the stipulations entered into, that for the year 1943 the average assessed value of real property in the county of Cook was 75 per cent of the full, fair, cash, market value of said property, and that for the year 1943, the average assessed valuation of real property in Lake county was 21 per cent of the full, fair, cash, market value of said property. We are further of the opinion that on the average the above percentage figures applied to Barrington township in Cook county and to Cuba township in Lake county. We are called upon, therefore, to decide this question, Does a subsidiary corporate tax levy where the boundaries of the taxing unit extend into two or more counties violate the constitutional mandate of uniformity in taxation where the assessed valuation in one county is disproportionate to the assessed valuation in the other county?

The three common taxing bodies, Barrington village, Barrington park district, and school district No. 4, are each separate taxing bodies with statutory authority to levy taxes for their separate corporate purposes. These corporate purposes are separate and distinct from those for which counties are authorized to levy taxes and bear no relationship to corporate purposes of counties. The authorities of the three taxing bodies, however, have no power to assess and fix values of properties in their respective districts.

In support of his contention that a lack of uniformity exists in the above-mentioned taxing districts as required by section 1 of article IX of the constitution of 1870, the appellant has cited and quoted from a large number of Illinois cases where inequalities in taxation have been held improper and invalid. These cases have been so many times cited and analyzed that a detailed discussion of them is not necessary to this opinion. They all hold that courts will grant relief against inequality in taxation resulting from favoritism, fraud or intentional misconduct on the part of assessing bodies or officers. Most of them are cases where a given equalization factor has been applied to one class of property, or to property of one owner, and a different factor to another.

*   *   *

They further hold that the great central and dominant idea of the constitution is uniformity of taxation. But it also can be said of those cases that the question arose over the misconduct of the assessor or the assessing bodies where the properties were State-wide or located in the same county and the factor adopted by the assessor was not applied equally to all property within the State or county. The rule of uniformity applies to property of like kind and character and similarly situated. *   *   * Section 1 of article IX of the constitution provides:

> "The general assembly shall provide such revenue as may be needful by levying a tax, by valuation, so that every person and corporation shall pay a tax in proportion to the value of his, her or its property—such value to be ascertained by some person or persons, to be elected or appointed in such manner as the general assembly shall direct, and not otherwise."

None of the cases relied upon by appellant presents a similar situation to that in the instant case. Here the values were fixed by the assessor or the assessing officers of the counties of Cook and Lake, respectively. The assessor is the officer who has been provided by the legislature for fixing the valuation of property for the purpose of taxation. In this record there is no suggestion of fraud made against the assessing bodies, nor any claim that the assessment was made on a wrong basis or an excessively high valuation placed thereon.

The appellant merely says he is paying a greater burden of the taxation for the three subsidiary corporations than like property similarly situated over in Lake county. In First National Bank v. Holmes, 246 Ill. 362, at page 367, 92 N.E. 893, at page 895, we said: "While the Constitution declares the rule of equality, it also provides that the value of property shall be ascertained by some person or persons to be elected or appointed in such manner as the General Assembly shall direct, and not otherwise. No system has ever been devised which has produced perfect equality and uniformity of taxation as between persons or corporations or different classes of property, and such a result cannot reasonably be expected. *   *   * Under the statute, the valuation is to be made by the assessor or board of review, and the judgments of such officers, when honestly exercised, will naturally differ. If their judgment is so exercised, the Constitution forbids a valuation by any other authority."

There is nothing in the briefs to indicate or suggest how uniformity might be maintained as between properties located in different counties but included within one park or school district. If he be correct in his position, it would necessitate all the property throughout the State being valued alike before absolute uniformity in overlapping districts, located partially in two or more counties, could be accomplished. In such situations, as long as the assessment and levy of taxes is based upon the judgment of the assessing officers in each separate county, absolute uniformity cannot be achieved. This matter is one exclusively for the legislature, and the relief, if any, in the several counties must come from the legislature and not from the courts. People ex rel. Hempen v. Baltimore & Ohio R. Co., 379 Ill. 543, at page 546, 42 N.E.2d 69.

In the case of People ex rel. Toman v. Olympia Fields Country Club, 374 Ill. 101, 28 N.E.2d 109, it was stated by this court that, concerning a taxpayer's claim of constructive fraud, the rule is that fraud in the valuation of property for purposes of taxation must be proved by clear and sufficient evidence. The presumption is that the tax is just and that the tax levying officers have performed their duties. The objector must establish by clear and convincing evidence that fraud has been committed.

In the present case there is nothing to show that the assessment was not made in the exercise of honest judgment, or that the assessor committed any act of discrimination against the appellant. There is no appearance of fraud or inequality between properties in either Lake or Cook counties.

"It is the law that the assessed value of property for taxation purposes cannot be impeached merely because of the difference of opinion as to values between the assessing bodies and the court," People ex rel. Wangelin v. Wiggins Ferry Co., 357 Ill. 173, 191 N.E. 296, 299. There is no claim, in the present case, that the valuation placed upon the property of the taxpayer was willful or arbitrary or at a valuation grossly in excess of its market value.

We do not feel that the taxpayer here has sustained the burden of proof imposed upon him by establishing by such clear and convincing evidence either actual or constructive fraud on the part of the taxing authorities such as would warrant a reversal of the judgment of the county court. The judgment of the county court of Cook county, is, therefore, affirmed.

Judgment affirmed.[*]

Notes and Problems

A. Any expectation that the Illinois standard of review in property tax assessment cases would be broadened as a result of the adoption of a

---

* [Discussed in Troupis, "Full Fair Value Assessment in Illinois," 44 Ill.L.Rev. 160 (1949); see, also, Weil, "Property Tax Equalization in Illinois," 6 Nat.Tax J. 157 (1953).]

new revenue article in the 1970 Constitution was dashed in LaSalle Nat. Bank v. County of Cook, 57 Ill.2d 318, 312 N.E.2d 252 (1974). See Gardner, "Judicial Developments in the Taxation of Real Property Since the Adoption of the Illinois Constitution of 1970," 9 John Marshall J. of Prac. & Proc. 233 (1975–76); Gore & Emmerman, "Real Estate Tax Assessments—A Study of Illinois Taxpayers' Judicial Remedies," 24 DePaul L.Rev. 465 (1975); see also the Iowa cases which have adhered to a restrictive rule of judicial review despite the broadening of the scope of review by statute, including a provision for hearing appeals de novo. Tiffany v. County Bd. of Review, 188 N.W.2d 343 (Iowa 1971); Maytag Co. v. Partridge, 210 N.W.2d 584 (Iowa 1973). In Florida, as in Illinois, the courts have held that there is no constitutional requirement of intercounty assessment uniformity. Straughn v. GAC Properties, Inc., 360 So.2d 385 (Fla.1978). But see McCarthy v. Jones, 449 F.Supp. 480 (S.D.Ala.1978), where the court held that different assessment ratios in different counties violated the Federal Equal Protection Clause.

B. *Application of Uniformity and Equality Provisions to Different Assessment Methods.* In R. Cross, Inc. v. City of Newport News, 228 S.E.2d 113 (Va.1976), the court rejected the taxpayer's claim that the assessment of his tangible personal property by a method different from the assessment of other tangible personal property resulted in a higher effective rate of taxation on his property in violation of Article X, § 1 of the Virginia Constitution, which provides: "All taxes * * * shall be uniform upon the same class of subjects within the territorial limits of the authority levying the tax." The court held that nothing in the relevant statute prescribes "the procedure to be followed by commissioners of the revenue in determining taxable values or prohibits the use of multiple methods" and that "there is no constitutional requirement that such methods be identical." 228 S.E.2d at 116. Contra: State ex rel. Stephan v. Martin, 230 Kan. 759, 641 P.2d 1020 (1982) (assessing value of farm machinery by reference to "average loan value," while assessing other property by willing buyer/ willing seller standard, violates uniformity and equality requirement).

C. *Uniformity Provision as Applied to Valuation of Condominiums.* The Pennsylvania uniformity clause, considered at p. 55 supra, provided the basis for an attack on the valuation of condominium units for real estate tax purposes. The unit owners argued that the assessed values of their individual apartments should be based on values which could be assigned as a proportion of the total value of the entire building, which would be assessed as a whole in a manner similar to the assessment of non-condominium rental apartment buildings. The county assessment board, however, had assessed the apartment units on the basis of the separate market value of each unit alone. While the assessed value of each unit closely compared with the assessed value of other types of condominium property under this method of assessment, the total assessed value of all the units together exceeded the assessed value of similar rental apartment buildings. Rejecting the taxpayers' argument that this disparity amounted to a violation of the constitutional uniformity provision, the court stated:

> [T]here is no lack of uniformity involved in taxing a property owner only on the market value of the property he owns, for it is real estate

generally which is entitled to uniform treatment, and the condominium apartments here are separate parcels of real estate which as such have been treated uniformly with other separate parcels of real estate. The condominium building as a whole is simply not the parcel of real estate here subject to assessment, even though its physical attributes may compare to those of a rental apartment building which would, of course, be subject to assessment as a single parcel of real estate. [In re Summit House Real Property Assessment Appeals, 22 Pa.Cmwlth.Ct. 462, 466, 349 A.2d 505, 507 (1975).]

Does the court's opinion amount to a holding that the whole is less than the sum of its parts or is there an economic justification for the difference in treatment of condominiums and rental apartments? See also Rothman v. Pelcher, 89 Misc.2d 560, 392 N.Y.S.2d 536 (Sup.Ct.1977); Annot., 71 A.L.R.3d 952.

D. *Uniformity Provision as Applied to Multiple Dwellings as Compared with Single Family Dwellings.* In McClelland v. Board of Supervisors, 30 Cal.2d 124, 180 P.2d 676 (1947), the assessors had systematically increased the 1946 values of multiple dwellings by substantial amounts but had, with minor exceptions, left the values of private dwellings at the 1945 rates. The explanation offered by the assessors was that the sales prices of private dwellings did not reflect market values, but included "a bonus for occupancy" because of the housing shortage. In the case of multiple units purchased for rental, however, the sales did evidence market because "this was not capital buying shelter but rather * * * capital soundly seeking safe investment at the highest rate of interest available with safety." The court upheld the levies on the multiple dwellings, finding no arbitrary discrimination.

E. *Proof of Inequality.* * In a proceeding based on a claim of inequality, the taxpayer's burden of proving inequality can often be an undertaking of considerable magnitude and expense.[3] Inequality is not established merely by proving that one's neighbor's house or a few isolated houses are assessed at a lower value; their properties may not be typical or representative of assessment levels in the taxing district generally, which is the test of inequality.[4] Nor may a taxpayer, at least in some States, utilize State equalization ratios to show inequality, because the ratios are designed in many States to reflect inter-district inequalities and not to achieve intra-district equality, and suffer from other defects which make them unsuitable as an individual taxpayer equalization device. What, then, is there left to the taxpayer who seeks to show the level at which comparable properties are assessed generally in the taxing district? He may be able in a court

* The ensuing discussion is based on J. Hellerstein, "Judicial Review of Property Tax Assessments," 14 Tax L.Rev. 327 (1959) and 1958 Nat. Tax Ass'n Procs. 429.

3. See the description of the problem as set forth in the dissenting opinion of Chief Justice Vanderbilt in Baldwin Constr. Co. v. Essex County Bd. of Taxation, 16 N.J. 329, 108 A.2d 598 (1954), discussed at p. 139 infra. As one court has said consolingly in denying relief to a taxpayer: "The

problem of determining relative values in a situation of this kind is one of the most difficult with which the courts have to contend." Butler v. City of Des Moines, 219 Iowa 956, 961, 258 N.W. 755, 758 (1935), as quoted in Corn Belt Theatre Corp. v. Board of Review, 234 Iowa 355, 12 N.W.2d 820 (1944).

4. See Wolf v. Assessors of the Town of Hanover, 308 N.Y. 416, 126 N.E.2d 537 (1955).

proceeding or otherwise to obtain from the assessor or other official agencies their statements as to assessment percentages used. If not, unless the State has adopted a short-cut method of proving inequality, he may be faced with the necessity of offering proof of the value of a large number of other properties.

If the taxpayer is prepared to present proof of the value of other properties in the taxing district and their lower percentage assessments, he may also be faced in some States with difficult and, at times, insurmountable obstacles in finding comparable properties to be valued. To make out a case of inequality, the taxpayer must show that his assessment is "inequitable as compared to the valuation of similar and comparable properties in the same district," [5] and if there be no such comparable property in the district, the taxpayer may be unable to obtain relief.[6] Consequently, at least partly on this score, a farm machinery company which owned and operated a small arms plant was denied relief from an asserted inequality in the valuation of its machinery because "there is no property in Polk County or in Iowa similar or comparable to plaintiff's." [7] A taxpayer, complaining that his farm was assessed at a greater proportion of value than comparable farm property, was rebuffed because of lack of comparability between low lands and high lands and the differences in their comparative rates of rainfall.[8] These are doubtless relevant factors in differentiating property, but such nice delineations emphasize the extremely difficult task imposed in some States on a taxpayer seeking to prove inequality in assessment and tend to contribute to the perpetuation of inequalities.

Many courts, however, do not interpose such formidable obstacles to an attack on inequality in assessment. In an Idaho case 165 merchants of Kootenai County complained that their stocks of merchandise had been assessed at 20 percent of actual cash value, whereas other property in the county generally was assessed at ten percent. The Board of Equalization having denied relief, appeal to the courts followed, where the county defended its position by urging burden of proof and the presumption of correctness of the action of the Board of Equalization. The county also argued that in valuing merchandise at 20 percent of cash value, it is to be

5. Clark v. Lucas County Board of Review, 242 Iowa 80, 44 N.W.2d 748 (1950). For similar taxpayer difficulties with comparable problems in Illinois, see Cushman, "The Judicial Review of Valuation in Illinois Property Tax Cases," 35 Ill.L.Rev. 689 (1941); Young, "Taxpayers' Remedies, Illinois Property Tax Cases," 1932 Ill.L.F. 248; Gardner, "Judicial Developments in the Taxation of Real Property Since Adoption of the Illinois Constitution of 1970," 9 John Marshall J. of Prac. & Proc. 333 (1975–76); Gore & Emmerman, "Real Estate Tax Assessments—A Study of Illinois Taxpayers' Judicial Remedies," 24 DePaul L.Rev. 465 (1975).

6. Deere Manufacturing Co. v. Zeiner, 247 Iowa 1364, 78 N.W.2d 527 (1956).

7. Id. Although the *Deere* case has not been overruled, subsequent Iowa decisions make it clear that sales need not be in the taxing district to be treated as comparables. Thus in Farmers Grain Dealers Ass'n v. Sather, 267 N.W.2d 58, 62 (Iowa 1978), the court declared that "[t]he fact that some of the sales were some distance from Polk County and most of them were outside the State of Iowa did not render the appraisal testimony based on such sales incompetent."

8. Daniels v. Board of Review of Monona County, 243 Iowa 405, 52 N.W.2d 1 (1952).

presumed that the assessor considered the "superior earning power" of merchandise as compared with other property. The court agreed that this consideration would be relevant if the assessor had considered the matter, but pointed out that there was no evidence that it had been done.[9] It declared: [10]

> * * * Without explanation the assessments were fixed at 20% of this value, while according to the testimony of those who qualified as experts other property was assessed at 10% of current market values. If this disparity is not reasonably justified, the constitutional requirement of uniformity has been violated.

Likewise, a New Hampshire court was satisfied that inequality was established by proof that the taxpayer's stock in trade was assessed at 100 percent of value, whereas land in the city was assessed at 80 percent, buildings at 65 percent, and machinery at 60 percent.[11]

F. *Proof of Injury to Taxpayer.* In a real sense the problem of uniformity and equality among taxpayers is the major problem in the ad valorem property tax field, for if all taxpayers properly within a particular classification are treated alike, it can be argued that none has a legitimate grievance. The courts have given credence to this principle by adopting the view that "uniformity and equality * * * is * * * the just and ultimate purpose of the law." [12] Starting from this premise, some courts have taken the next step by ruling that so long as there is equality among taxpayers, no legal injury has been suffered by an individual taxpayer, even though the assessors have violated their duty to assess all property at full value.[13] As a result of this doctrine, taxpayers in some States have been denied relief *from overvaluation* in the absence of proof by them that taxpayers generally in the taxing district have not been similarly overassessed.[14] And where taxpayers have complained in cases of *inequality*

9. Anderson's Red & White Store v. Kootenai County, 70 Idaho 260, 215 P.2d 815 (1950).

10. 215 P.2d at 818. The case was remanded to the trial court to determine whether there was systematic overvaluation and, if so, to reduce taxpayers' assessments so as to achieve an equalization.

11. Bemis Bros. Co. v. Claremont, 98 N.H. 446, 102 A.2d 512 (1954). See also Sears, Roebuck & Co. v. State Tax Commission, 214 Md. 550, 136 A.2d 567 (1957). But compare Wadhams Co. v. State Tax Commission, 202 Or. 132, 273 P.2d 440 (1954), in which it was held that under a statute authorizing judicial review to determine whether property is overvalued and whether the assessment is reasonably proportionate to the "assessed valuation of similar property in the county," the court had no jurisdiction to set aside an assessment of merchandise inventory valued at 60 percent of its true cash value while the buildings were valued at only 25 percent of such valuation. The properties were found to be dissimilar. In effect, the Oregon stat-

ute was held to authorize a classified property tax which, of course, admits a varying fractional percentage of full value. The classified property tax is unauthorized and, indeed, prohibited in many States.

12. In Cumberland Coal Co. v. Board of Revision of Tax Assessments, 284 U.S. 23, 29, 52 S.Ct. 48, 50 (1931), the Court declared, quoting from Sioux City Bridge Co. v. Dakota County, 260 U.S. 441, 446, 43 S.Ct. 190, 192 (1923): " * * * 'where it is impossible to secure both the standard of the true value, and the uniformity and equality required by law, the latter requirement is to be preferred as the just and ultimate purpose of the law.' "

13. Lindahl v. State, 244 Minn. 506, 70 N.W.2d 866 (1955); Whelan v. Texas, 155 Tex. 14, 282 S.W.2d 378 (1955); see Hodges v. Town of Kensington, 102 N.H. 649, 157 A.2d 649 (1960).

14. People ex rel. Ruchty v. Saad, 411 Ill. 390, 104 N.E.2d 273 (1952); see cases cited in notes 5–13 supra. In Wisconsin the statutory provision for judicial review

without overassessment, many courts have denied relief because the taxpayer had established no "legal injury" merely by showing inequality. He is required to show "substantial injury" by proof that he has borne more than his just share of the "tax burden." [15] This "inequity exists when the assessment placed on plaintiff's property as a whole is disproportionately higher in relation to its true value than is the case as to other property in general in the taxing district." [16]

The Hawaii statutory provisions governing appeals of real property tax assessments actually incorporated such a rule by providing that "no taxpayer * * * shall be deemed aggrieved by an assessment * * * unless there is shown: (1) Assessment of the property in excess of its one hundred percent fair market value." The provision was sustained against a challenge under the Due Process and Equal Protection Clauses. In re Hawaiian Land Co., 53 Hawaii 45, 487 P.2d 1070 (1971), appeal dismissed 405 U.S. 907, 92 S.Ct. 938 (1972). It has since been amended so as to provide that no taxpayer shall be deemed aggrieved unless the "[a]ssessment of the property exceeds by more than twenty percent the ratio of assessment to market value used by the director of taxation as the real property tax base." Hawaii Rev.Stat. § 232–3, CCH ¶ 92–003, P–H ¶ 65,573–B. But see State ex rel. Poulos v. State Bd. of Equalization, 552 P.2d 1134 (Okl.1976) (variance of between 8 and 17.91 percent in valuation of realty and personalty violates constitutional and statutory requirements).

Again and again taxpayers with grievances of unequal tax assessment, which at least from the opinions appear to be highly compelling, have been denied relief in the courts because they could not show "injury." [17] To illustrate, a Texas court reviewed an assessment of producing oil wells assessed at one-third their value, when non-producing wells leased at $5 to $200 per acre were assessed at a flat basis of $1 per acre, cattle selling at $40 to $1,000 per head was assessed at $15 per head, and bank deposits were entirely omitted from assessment rolls. The court held the bank deposit omission to be error; but insofar as the facts as to oil properties and

of assessments contains the following provisions: " * * * no action shall be maintained under this section unless it appears that the plaintiff has paid more than his equitable share of such taxes." Wis.Stat. § 74.73(2m) (Supp.1986). "A showing of mere overvaluation, without showing that the valuation imposed an inequitable burden upon the taxpayer, is not enough on which to base an action. * * * " Highlander Co. v. City of Dodgeville, 249 Wis. 502, 506, 25 N.W.2d 76, 78–79 (1946). The taxpayer must show that "the assessment is so out of line with the valuation of other property in the same locality as to impose an inequitable burden upon the taxpayer." Id. at 509, 25 N.W.2d at 80. Consequently, where the taxpayer alleged that the property had been purchased at a judicial sale for $19,500 on August 22, 1944, and that it was assessed for 1944 at $53,500 and for

1945 at $47,500, this was insufficient "to charge that the property was so assessed as to put an inequitable burden of taxation upon plaintiff." Id. Cf. the Oregon court's doctrine of "relative uniformity," which it holds is all that is required to satisfy constitutional mandates. Robinson v. Stewart, 216 Or. 532, 339 P.2d 432 (1959).

15. Whelan v. Texas, note 13 supra, and Bemis Bros. Co. v. Claremont, note 11 supra; see also State v. Federal Land Bank of Houston, 160 Tex. 282, 329 S.W.2d 847 (1959).

16. See Bemis Bros. Co. v. Claremont, note 11 supra.

17. Poland v. City of Pahokee, 157 Fla. 179, 25 So.2d 271 (1946); People ex rel. Callahan v. Gulf, Mobile and Ohio Railroad Co., 8 Ill.2d 66, 132 N.E.2d 544 (1956).

cattle were concerned, the taxpayer could get no relief without meeting the heavy burden of showing "substantial injury." [18]

Some courts have rejected this doctrine,[19] and others have accepted shortcuts as proof of injury from inequality. In a New Hampshire case, a taxpayer's stock in trade was assessed at 100 percent of value, whereas land in the city was assessed at 80 percent, buildings at 65 percent, and machinery at 60 percent. Over the city's objection, the court accepted proof of a weighted average of all property in the city, derived from the percentages applied by the assessor to various types of properties, and granted a reduction to the taxpayer.[20] The court recognized that this method is not precise but apparently felt that it achieved rough justice. The difficulty of ascertaining and proving these facts in many taxing jurisdictions would frequently make this shortcut method prohibitive as a practical matter.

G. *Remedies Open to Taxpayer Complaining of Inequality in Assessment; Full Value Assessments.* The notion that a taxpayer is not aggrieved so long as equality is achieved has led some courts down another road, which has also served to obstruct judicial relief to taxpayers. These are the holdings that the taxpayer's remedy is not to obtain a reduction of his own assessment but, instead, to take steps to obtain an increase in the assessments of all other taxpayers.

In cases arising out of the depression of the 1930's, this principle was used by some courts to deny taxpayers relief where assessment in excess of actual value was unmistakably clear. Thus, a Michigan court, in dismissing the complaint of a taxpayer seeking to set aside his 1931 assessment, said: [21]

> * * * it is not shown that plaintiff has been injured in fact as all property has been overassessed upon the same basis. Consequently, the proportion of each parcel to the tax levy is the same as though proper assessment had been made.

The court relegated the taxpayer to a proceeding to obtain a reassessment of all property in the city.[22]

The operation of this rule may be illustrated by the complaint of a group of railroads heard by the Tennessee courts in 1948 that the State constitutional uniformity and equality clause, as well as the taxing statutes, had been violated by a reassessment of railroad properties by the State commission at 100 percent of "actual cash value," whereas property

---

18. Whelan v. Texas, note 13 supra.

19. Harleigh Realty Co.'s Case, 299 Pa. 385, 149 A. 653 (1930); People ex rel. Amalgamated Properties, Inc. v. Sutton, 274 N.Y. 309, 8 N.E.2d 871 (1937); In re Brooks Building, 391 Pa. 94, 137 A.2d 273 (1958); for the treatment of a claim of inequality by the Ohio court, see Benedict v. Hamilton, 170 Ohio St. 62, 162 N.E.2d 479 (1959), certiorari denied 362 U.S. 962, 80 S.Ct. 877 (1960).

20. Bemis Bros. Co. v. Claremont, note 11, supra; Hodges v. Town of Kensington, 102 N.H. 649, 157 A.2d 649 (1960).

21. Sloman–Polk Co. v. City of Detroit, 261 Mich. 689, 692, 247 N.W. 95, 96 (1933).

22. A taxpayer and resident of a county may file a petition in Maryland demanding a hearing in respect to the undervaluation of other properties in the county and the county commissioners are required to grant the hearing. Board of County Commissioners v. Buch, 190 Md. 394, 58 A.2d 672 (1949).

of non-utilities assessed by county authorities ranged from 40 percent to 80 percent of actual values, with an average of perhaps 60 percent.[23] The court denied relief, *inter alia,* on the ground that since at least 1898 a taxpayer whose property is not assessed in excess of its cash value but complains of inequality cannot obtain a reduction, but can only seek to have the Board of Equalization increase the assessments of other property owners.[24]

This view virtually nullified inequality grievances and largely emasculated the uniformity and equality provisions of the State constitution. It is apparent that as a practical matter the remedy of seeking a revision of all properties in the taxing district is, at least to the typical taxpayer, no remedy at all. Only a large or wealthy property owner or a group of holders of valuable properties can undertake the expense of such a proceeding. Yet the courts of a number of States have been satisfied to allow this condition to prevail.

The Supreme Court of the United States, however, has held that this procedure constitutes a denial of an effective remedy and hence violates the Equal Protection Clause of the Fourteenth Amendment.[25] It was the Supreme Court's decision in Doris Duke Cromwell's case—a flagrant case of inequality without adequate remedy—that started the recent series of cases that revolutionized New Jersey assessments.[26] See Section 3, Note A infra. The Supreme Court held that where discrimination is shown and the State neither grants the taxpayer a reduction in his assessment nor provides machinery whereby the taxing authority must itself raise other taxpayers' assessments, the imposition of the burden on the taxpayer to commence proceedings to equalize other assessments violates his constitutional right to equality of treatment. It is paradoxical to note that this was not new law; the principle had been enunciated by the Supreme Court in the famous *Sioux City Bridge Company* case [27] as far back as 1923, but in the interim the doctrine had been widely ignored by State courts.[28]

SECTION 3. THE JUDICIAL SHAKEUP OF ASSESSMENT PRACTICES

A. *The New Jersey Judicial Revolution in Ad Valorem Taxation.* *
When a group of taxpayers in Essex County indignantly challenged an

23. McCord v. Southern Ry. Co., 187 Tenn. 247, 213 S.W.2d 184 (1948); McCord v. Nashville, Chattanooga & St. L. Ry., 187 Tenn. 277, 213 S.W.2d 196 (1948); McCord v. Alabama Great Southern R. Co., 187 Tenn. 302, 213 S.W.2d 207 (1948). Compare People ex rel. Callahan v. Gulf, Mobile and Ohio Railroad Co., note 17 supra; People ex rel. Ruchty v. Saad, 411 Ill. 390, 104 N.E.2d 273 (1952).

24. The court relied on the more than half century old case of Taylor v. Louisville & N.R. Co., 88 F. 350 (6th Cir.1898).

25. It is interesting to note that State court judges, operating under the broader uniformity and equality clause, found no constitutional defect in this procedure.

26. Township of Hillsborough v. Cromwell, 326 U.S. 620, 66 S.Ct. 445 (1946).

27. Sioux City Bridge Co. v. Dakota County, 260 U.S. 441, 43 S.Ct. 190 (1923).

28. The rule enunciated in Royal Mfg. Co. v. Board of Equalization of Taxes, 76 N.J.L. 402, 70 A. 978 (1908), affirmed 78 N.J.L. 337, 74 A. 525 (1909), continued unaffected by the *Sioux City Bridge* case until the recent development discussed in the text.

* The ensuing discussion is based on J. Hellerstein, "Judicial Review of Property Tax Assessments," 14 Tax L.Rev. 327 (1959) and 1958 Nat. Tax Ass'n Procs. 429.

upward reassessment of selected groups of properties while property in the county generally remained at the old level, the New Jersey Supreme Court repudiated the pre-existing New Jersey law and held that in view of constitutional requirements the taxpayers were entitled to a reduction of their assessments to the basis used generally. Baldwin Constr. Co. v. Essex County Bd. of Taxation, 16 N.J. 329, 108 A.2d 598 (1954).[29] But the most far-reaching aspect of the case was the taxpayers' contention that because the assessments were admittedly not made, as required by the statute, at full value but instead at varying percentages, they were a nullity and should be set aside—a position approved in the dissenting opinion of Chief Justice Vanderbilt and concurred in by Justice Brennan (who is now a Justice of the United States Supreme Court).

Taking the hint thrown out in the *Baldwin* case that mandamus was the proper procedure to force full value assessments, a group of taxpayers brought a proceeding against the assessors of the Township of Middletown seeking an order directing them to assess all property at its full value. In one of the most momentous decisions in the property tax field in modern times, a majority of the New Jersey Supreme Court, writing a virtual treatise on both the law of mandamus and the evils of departing from the statutory mandate that properties be assessed at full value, held that the mandamus order should issue.[30] The court, however, granted two years for compliance, to enable the legislature to act, in order to avoid chaos in the New Jersey property tax system. In 1960 the New Jersey legislature enacted a new statute permitting each county to select its own assessment percentage of true value.[31] The statute also provides for business personal property tax assessments at book value determined by the "common level" at which real estate is actually assessed within each municipality.[32] Fearing possible havoc resulting from substantial shifts in tax burdens, in 1964 the New Jersey legislature adopted a transitional measure to assure municipalities that the ratio of tax dollar yield from tangible personal property used in business to the total tax yield from all property would be at least as great in 1965 and in 1966 as it was in 1963.[33]

New Jersey has thus made a highly persuasive and clear-cut judicial challenge to the deeply rooted practice of ignoring statutory provisions calling for full value assessments.

29. See Lasser, "Assessment of Real Property in New Jersey: An Appraisal of the Baldwin Case," 9 Rutgers L.Rev. 497 (1955).

30. Switz v. Township of Middletown, 23 N.J. 580, 130 A.2d 15 (1957); see, also, Village of Ridgefield Park v. Bergen County Board of Taxation, 31 N.J. 420, 157 A.2d 829 (1960).

31. N.J.S.A. 54:4-2.25 (1960). See the study by Arnold, "New Jersey Property Taxes and Tax Classification," prepared for the N.J. Committee on Taxation of the Constitutional Convention Ass'n (Aug. 1960).

32. N.J.S.A. 54:4-2.25 (1960).

33. For a description of the purpose of Chapter 141, see Thomas v. Kingsley, 43 N.J. 524, 206 A.2d 161 (1965), which upheld the validity of the legislation over Equal Protection Clause and uniformity clause objections.

Unless there is either full valuation or an explicit statutory mandate for a stated percentage of valuation, such as Georgia's 40 percent or Illinois' 33⅓ percent, and these standards are followed by the assessors, no real assurance of fairness of treatment among taxpayers can be furnished. The actions of the assessors where full value assessments (or reduced statutory percentages) are not used are beclouded in mystery and uncertainty. The taxpayer does not know the standards which have been used or which he must consider in order to evaluate his own assessment. The problems of establishing the actual percentages used have proved overwhelming. Only through publicly established standards can inequalities and improprieties in assessment be kept at a minimum, and incompetence, favoritism, and corruption at least be subject to exposure to the public. Such standards would greatly simplify the role of the courts, as well as of taxpayers and their counsel, in reviewing the action of assessors and would eliminate a considerable source of taxpayer dissatisfaction with the vaguenesses, uncertainties, and mysteries of property tax assessments. Moreover, from the assessor's point of view, a fixed, established standard of assessment should simplify and standardize his own work.

B. *Repercussions of the New Jersey Decisions in Other States.* The New Jersey decisions have resulted in a wave of judicial and legislative reaction throughout the country that is severely shaking up traditional assessment practices. While some courts were reluctant, particularly in the first year or two after the *Baldwin* decision, to upset long standing practices in local communities,[34] in more recent years the courts have increasingly exercised their full judicial powers to try to put an end to open, widespread, flagrant discriminatory assessment practices.[35]

The developments in Massachusetts are a striking case in point. In 1959, the Massachusetts Supreme Judicial Court had gone to great lengths to deny taxpayers a hearing on the issue of inequality of assessment, by finding that the pleadings did not allege with sufficient specificity that there had been intentional assessment of all real estate in the taxing area at widely different percentages and by holding that no relief could be granted affecting the overall assessment for the year because time had made the issues moot.[36] Moreover, the court refused to enjoin a continuation of the alleged discriminatory practices for future years.

Two years later, however, in Bettigole v. Assessors of Springfield, 343 Mass. 223, 178 N.E.2d 10 (1961), the court viewed the situation from

34. The Ingraham Co. v. Town and City of Bristol, 144 Conn. 374, 132 A.2d 563 (1957); Stembler & Ford, Inc. v. Mayor and Common Council of Capitol Heights, 221 Md. 113, 156 A.2d 430 (1959); and Southern Pacific Co. v. Cochise County, 92 Ariz. 395, 377 P.2d 770 (1963).

35. See Note, "Inequality in Property Tax Assessments: New Cures for an Old Ill," 75 Harv.L.Rev. 1374 (1962).

36. Carr v. Assessors of Springfield, 339 Mass. 89, 157 N.E.2d 880 (1959); Stone v. City of Springfield, 341 Mass. 246, 168 N.E.2d 76 (1960).

a different perspective.[37] Reviewing assessment practices in the City of Springfield, the court found that "43 percent of the total fair cash value of taxable property in Springfield is paying over 33 percent of the total property taxes; whereas 28 percent of the total is paying 37 percent of the property taxes" (178 N.E.2d at 13) and that the use of assessment ratios ranging from 50 percent to 85 percent of fair cash value was "deliberate and intentional," and it granted the petitions of a group of taxpayers for drastic relief. It set aside the entire assessment for the year 1961 as illegal—the timing of the proceeding permitted this step—and enjoined the assessors and the collector from taking any action to collect the taxes thus assessed.

Similar actions have been taken by the courts of other States. In Kentucky, the court rejected as an inadequate remedy the lowering of the assessments for taxpayers who suffered from inequality practices; it nullified the assessment roll and directed the Commissioner of Revenue to take steps to end unequal assessment practices.[38] A writ of mandamus was granted by the Ohio court requiring the correction of the inequality in assessment from which commercial property suffered in Cuyahoga County, as compared with other real estate.[39] The Ohio court adopted the salutary procedure of directing the Board of Tax Appeals to review the county assessments in question and to require that discrepancies be corrected by equalization procedures. Similar results have been reached in Florida, Maryland, Minnesota and Washington.[40]

In Tennessee, a Federal district court granted a railroad an injunction against the enforcement of property tax assessments in 54 counties, on the ground that its property was systematically and intentionally assessed at substantially higher ratios to actual value than the average assessment ratios for other properties.[41] Federal jurisdiction was grounded in the absence of an adequate remedy under State law to correct the unequal assessment, in view of the fact that the property was admittedly not assessed at a value in excess of its actual cash value. The Tennessee courts in 1948 had denied a railroad relief from discriminatory assessment, taking the position that the only available remedy was to seek an increase in the assessed values of other proper-

---

37. For the astonishment among taxing officials caused by this case, see Note, "Inequality in Property Tax Assessments: New Cures for an Old Ill," 75 Harv.L.Rev. 1374 (1962); for additional comment, see 42 B.U.L.Rev. 246 (1962).

38. Russman v. Luckett, 391 S.W.2d 694 (Ky.1965), noted in 12 Wayne L.Rev. 527 (1966).

39. State ex rel. Park Investment Co. v. Board of Tax Appeals, 175 Ohio St. 410, 195 N.E.2d 908, certiorari denied 379 U.S. 818, 85 S.Ct. 35 (1964). See Note, "Real Property Assessment in Ohio," 30 Ohio St. L.J. 840 (1969).

40. State v. Atkisson, 170 So.2d 455 (Fla.App. 2nd Dist.1965); McNayr v. State ex rel. Dupont Plaza Center, Inc., 166 So.2d 142 (Fla.1964); Walter v. Schuler, 176 So. 2d 81 (Fla.1965); Hamm v. State, 225 Minn. 64, 95 N.W.2d 649 (1959), overruling State v. Cudahy Packing Co., 103 Minn. 419, 115 N.W. 645 (1908); Union Pacific Railroad Co. v. Hoefke, 232 Or. 521, 376 P.2d 80 (1962); Barlow v. Kinnear, 70 Wash.2d 482, 423 P.2d 937 (1967).

41. Louisville & N.R.R. v. Public Service Comm'n, 249 F.Supp. 894 (M.D.Tenn. 1966), affirmed 389 F.2d 247 (6th Cir.1968). The case is noted in 33 Tenn.L.Rev. 522 (1966).

ties.[42] In a more recent decision the State court has granted the petition of a railroad to have other properties raised to its assessment ratio,[43] but such relief does not satisfy the Supreme Court's test as to what constitutes an adequate remedy to satisfy the Equal Protection Clause.

The West Virginia Supreme Court has construed the State's constitutional mandate that property must be taxed equally and uniformly throughout the State and "in proportion to its value" (W.Va. Const. art. 10, § 1) as requiring full-value assessment. Killen v. Logan County Commission, 295 S.E.2d 689 (W.Va.1982). The court concluded that "[v]alue means the market value of property" and that "[e]qual and uniform taxation cannot result when each county assessor can vary assessments up to 50 percent of the appraised value * * * of property." Id. at 705. An illuminating survey and analysis of these developments appear in Note, "The Road to Uniformity in Real Estate Taxation: Valuation and Appeal," 124 U.Pa.L.Rev. 1418 (1976); see also Janata, "Effect of the Trend Toward Requiring Assessment at Market Value," 48 J.Tax. 36 (1978); Baldinger, "Property Tax Assessment Review: A Reassessment," 45 Albany L.Rev. 958 (1981); Annot., 42 A.L.R. 4th 676.

C. *Fractional Versus Full Value Assessment.* The assumption that it makes no difference whether assessors use fractional or full value as their standard of valuation of property, so long as the same ratio is applied to all property, appears to be contrary to experience. James E. Luckett, the Kentucky Commissioner of Revenue who had unsuccessfully opposed the action of that State's highest court holding illegal the long standing practice of assessing properties at a fraction of full value and directing reassessment at full value, in reporting on the Kentucky experience, concluded that "The most impressive result * * * was * * * the undeniable gain in assessment equity among individuals and classes of property. * * * The closer the level is to full value, the greater the potential equity." [44]

The explanations given for the tendency of fractional assessment to increase inequalities are the following:

> (1) Fractional assessment obscures the magnitude of inequalities. A taxpayer whose house is assessed at $50,000, which he regards as its value, will readily understand that he is being overassessed and may protest on grievance day, if he finds that his neighbor's house, which the taxpayer regards as worth at least as

---

42. McCord v. Nashville, Chattanooga & St. Louis Ry., 187 Tenn. 277, 213 S.W.2d 196 (1948); Mayor and Aldermen of Town of Morristown v. Burke, 207 Tenn. 180, 338 S.W.2d 593 (1960); Biltmore Hotel Court v. City of Berry Hill, 216 Tenn. 62, 390 S.W.2d 223 (1965).

43. Southern Ry. v. Clement, 57 Tenn. App. 54, 415 S.W.2d 146 (1966).

44. Luckett, "The Administrator's Response to Full Value Assessment," 1966 Nat.Tax.Ass'n Procs. 190, 196, 198. See, in accord, Johnson, "Fractional Ratios and Their Effect on Achievement of Uniform Assessment," in Symposium of the Tax Institute of America, The Property Tax: Problems and Potentials 209 (1967).

much as his own, is assessed at only $40,000. But if a 25 percent ratio is used by the assessor, so that the taxpayer's house is assessed at $12,500 and the neighbor's at $10,000, the taxpayer may regard the inequality as insufficient to warrant his filing a protest and incurring the costs of litigation, if need be. Yet, the taxpayer will be suffering the same 20 percent inequality in both cases in the tax he will pay.[45]

(2) Once the taxpayer has gone to the trouble of ascertaining the percentage of full value used by the assessors (and current ratios are often difficult to ferret out), he must translate his assessment and those of his neighbors into full values, a task which many laymen find formidable.

(3) The taxpayer may also refrain from protesting what he believes to be inequality in assessment because he may suffer from what Professor Maxwell has termed "an undervaluation illusion. Since the assessed value of his property is below market value, he may fondly believe that he is especially favored and therefore be silent." [46]

(4) Assessors also tend to be beguiled by the comparatively small dollar differentials involved in assessments made on a fractional basis, which, at full values, would be regarded as substantial. It is for that reason that one experienced State tax assessor has reported that "it is not unusual to find that, while a $15,000 property is valued at $5,000, a $45,000 property will be valued only at $10,000. And in such cases one is likely to find that the $2,500 property is valued at $1,000. I do not believe there is any question but that fractional valuations constitute a very real hindrance to true equalization of assessments." [47]

D. *Hellerstein v. Town of Islip.* In 1975 the New York Court of Appeals, in a four to three decision, ruled that the statutory mandate that "All real property in each assessing unit shall be assessed at the full value thereof" prohibited fractional value assessments. Hellerstein v. Assessor of Town of Islip, 37 N.Y.2d 1, 371 N.Y.S.2d 388, 332 N.E.2d 279 (1975). This decision was handed down despite the fact that "for nearly 200 years our statutes have required assessments to be made at full value and for nearly 200 years assessments have been made on a percentage basis throughout the State." 371 N.Y.S.2d at 398. Recognizing that the invalidation of the entire assessment roll for the year at issue and other years still open to contest would "bring fiscal chaos to the Town of Islip," the court, as requested by the petitioner in the case, exercised its equity powers by postponing the required date for full value assessment approximately 18 months. The Town of Islip, working in collaboration with the State Board of Equalization and Assessment (SBEA), which was sympathetic to full value assessment, em-

---

45. See J. Maxwell, Financing State and Local Governments 141 (1965); Johnson, note 44 supra, at 211–12.

46. J. Maxwell, note 45 supra, at 141.

47. Johnson, note 44 supra, at 212.

barked on a program of reassessment at full value of the approximately 100,000 parcels of real property in the town. It adopted modules developed by the SBEA for keeping assessed values up to date by feeding current data as to sales, construction costs, and other information into a computer. See Motion to Amend Remittitur, filed May, 1976, in Hellerstein v. Town of Islip. The Town Board authorized a capital improvement project of approximately $3,000,000 for the reassessment project, and with the consent of the plaintiff in the case, the town's time within which to comply with the order was extended by the court.[48]

For comments on the case, see Beebe & Sinott, "In the Wake of *Hellerstein* : Whither New York," 43 Albany L.Rev. 203 (Part I), 411 (Part II), and 777 (Part III) (1979); and Note, "Hellerstein v. Assessor of the Town of Islip: A Response to Inequities in Real Property Assessment in New York," 27 Syracuse L.Rev. 1045 (1976).

E. *Aftermath of the Case.* The immediate reaction to the decision in the *Town of Islip* case of some State legislators, representing districts having a concentration of one- and two-family owner-occupied homes, was one of alarm and bitter denunciation, but others welcomed the decision.[49]

By the end of 1981, substantial progress had been made by many taxing subdivisions in the State of New York in reassessing their properties on a full-value basis, without awaiting a court order so directing. As of the end of 1980, 276 of the approximately 1,000 towns and cities in New York, more than a fourth of the total, were assessing on a full value basis, using the computer assisted process developed by the State Board of Equalization and Assessment (SBEA). See SBEA, "1980 Revaluation: Property Tax Shift Analysis" (Dec.1980); and SBEA News Release, Oct. 22, 1981. No large city in the State, however, had reassessed on a full value basis.

The shift to the full value standard brought a marked improvement in equality of assessments. As the SBEA found in its study of the revaluations at full value that had been completed in 1978, "intra-class

---

48. Motion to Amend Remittitur, filed May, 1976, in Hellerstein v. Town of Islip. The SBEA computerized system of assessment record keeping was installed in a number of taxing jurisdictions in the State. See Lesnick, "Does Full Value Mean Full Value? Prospects for Assessment Reform in New York in Light of the Experience of Other States with *Hellerstein's* Progenitors," 5 Hofstra L.Rev. 235, 273 n. 210 (1977). For a description of the SBEA's modules, see State Board of Equalization and Assessment, "The New York State Real Property Information System: A Non-technical Description for Local Officials" (1975).

49. " 'The Hellerstein decision has thrown into complete chaos the entire ba-

sis on which New York City and New York State always raised tax revenue,' said Assemblyman Brian Sharoff * * * 'It has threatened directly the middle-class taxpayer with the possibility of increases two or three times in taxes. There would be substantial dislocations in urban areas.' " N.Y. Times, March 11, 1976. However, "an adviser to the Republican majority in the State Senate 'has recommended that legislators avoid any action on the situation until counties, towns and villages have completed revaluations.' 'Some people will have to pay more taxes, but they have been subsidized for many years,' a Senate G.O.P. spokesman said." Reporter Dispatch, White Plains, Oct. 14, 1975.

changes far outweigh the overall shift in tax burdens between the residential and other classes of property." SBEA, 1978 Revaluations, Intra–Class Tax Shift Analysis p. 4, March, 1979. The Executive Director of the SBEA reported that the study showed that "the primary reason for tax shifts in the residential class is the elimination of relative assessment inequities *among homeowners* and not a result of reductions in the tax burdens of other classes." Letter of SBEA Executive Director accompanying March, 1979 report, supra.

Despite the salutary results of full value assessments, the decision in the *Town of Islip* case was jettisoned by the State Legislature in December, 1981, and the full value requirement of the statute was eliminated. This was done notwithstanding the strong support for the full value standard by a Temporary Commission on the Real Property Tax (see Report to the Governor and the State Legislature, March 27, 1979), by the SBEA and civic groups. All this was swept aside by the political pressure from homeowners. Some of the homeowners, as long-time owners of one- or two-family residences that had greatly appreciated in value, were protecting their vested interests in preferentially low assessments, but others, including some homeowners who would actually benefit from full value reassessments, acted out of ignorance or fear that reassessment at full value would mean higher taxes for them. Although Governor Hugh Carey vetoed the bill, his veto was overridden by the Legislature. S.B. 7182, effective Dec. 31, 1981.

The new legislation, in addition to repealing the statutory requirement that property be assessed at "full value," authorizes fractional value assessment. Ch. 1057, N.Y.Laws of 1981, amending § 305, Real Property Tax Law. It classifies property in New York City and Nassau County (which adjoins New York City on Long Island) into four classes: (1) one-, two- and three-family residential real property, (2) other residential property, (3) utility real property, and (4) all other real property. In the assessment of property outside New York City and Nassau County, classification into two classes is authorized: (1) one-, two- and three-family residential real property, and (2) all other real property, if the city, town, or other local taxing jurisdiction has revalued its property in compliance with standards established by the State Board of Equalization and Assessment. N.Y.Real Prop.Tax § 1901, CCH ¶ 93–520, P–H ¶ 32,469–U. There are elaborate provisions in the amendments that are designed to protect one-, two-, and three-family homes from bearing a larger proportion of the property tax load than formerly. Whatever may be said of the legislation on the merits, the problems it has created appear to be formidable.

F. *The Use of State Equalization Ratios to Establish Inequality of Administration.* Most States have established equalization boards, which are charged with the duty of determining the ratios at which property is assessed in various taxing districts, and equalizing them. The equalization rates were not designed to enable taxpayers to establish *intradistrict* inequality and thereby obtain relief from unequal assessments. Instead, they were designed to equalize *interdistrict* inequality, so as to lay a foundation for distribution of State aid to local governments, since the wealth of a local district, as measured by the value of its taxable real estate, is used in many States as a factor in determining how State aid is distributed.[50] Equalization rates are also relevant to State constitutional limitations on the indebtedness that local governments may incur, and the level of property taxes that may be imposed.[51] They may also have a bearing on exemptions and other provisions of property tax laws.[52]

State-wide equalization rates are typically based on selected samplings of various classes of property, such as one- and two-family dwellings, apartment houses, commercial, industrial, farm, forest, utility, and other classifications. Averages of *each class* of property are then translated into a single district-wide average. Because of the asserted defects in such an overall average rate in establishing inequality of taxation of a particular parcel of property, courts have rejected the rates as evidence in suits by taxpayers seeking to establish inequality.[53] Inequality had to be established instead by sales prices of comparable properties, where such evidence existed, and by expert appraisals of other properties. These methods of proof frequently foreclosed all practicable remedy for taxpayers claiming inequality, because of the "discouraging and enormous expense for the taxpayer."[54] As a consequence, in a number of States the statutes have been amended so as to allow the use of the State equalization rate established for the taxing district in proving intradistrict inequality.[55] The New York courts have construed a 1969 amendment to the State's Real Property Tax

50. See Welch, "A New Multiple–Purpose Equalization Program," 1949 Nat.Tax Ass'n Procs. 260, 261–62; New York State Finance Law, Art. 4–A.

51. See, e.g., N.Y. Const., Art. 8, §§ 4 and 10.

52. See the veterans' exemption and the provisions for assessment by the State of the property taxes of railroads and special franchises of other public utilities. N.Y.Real Prop.Tax Law §§ 458, 489*l*, and 600 et seq., CCH ¶¶ 92–096, 92–301, 92–613 et seq., P–H ¶¶ 32,138, 32,153–*o*, and 32,195 et seq.

53. Koeppel, "Inequality in Real Property Tax Review," 19 Buffalo L.Rev. 565 (1970); Note, "Inequality in Property Tax Assessments: New Cures for an Old Ill," 75 Harv.L.Rev. 1374 (1962). "∗ ∗ ∗ [T]he range in values as established from the list of sales used by SBEA in the 1968 survey for the Town of Oyster Bay [N.Y.] reflect a range in ratio from 8.02% to 142.84% of true value ∗ ∗ ∗" 860 Executive Towers v. Board of Assessors of the

County of Nassau, 84 Misc.2d 525, 528, 377 N.Y.S.2d 863, 866 (1975).

54. Ed Guth Realty, Inc. v. Gingold, 34 N.Y.2d 440, 449, 358 N.Y.S.2d 367, 372, 315 N.E.2d 441, 445 (1974).

55. Id. See also Welch, "Use of State Ratio Findings in the Local Equalization Process," 1975 Nat.Tax Ass'n—Tax Inst. of Amer.Procs. 139. Welch lists California, New Jersey, New York, and Ohio as States in which the use of equalization rates is required or authorized by statute, and Illinois and Michigan as those in which they are used at the State level without specific statutory directive. Kansas, Minnesota, and Pennsylvania are stated as prohibiting the use of the rates. Welch also concludes from his questionnaire sent to the various States that "There are about 20 states in which the [equalization ratios] are infrequently or never used by assessment appeal agencies. These 20 states, plus the 14 states in which there are no ratio findings account for about 58% of the Nation's population." Id. at 142.

Law as permitting reliance on the State equalization rate as the sole evidence of the prevailing level of assessment.[56]

G. *The Classified Property Tax as a Substitute for Fractional Valuation.* As is illustrated by the New York experience (see Note D supra), the response of some legislators to decisions holding fractional valuation illegal, in an effort to preserve the lower ratios at which some classes of property have been traditionally assessed, notably one- and two-family houses, has been to advocate the use of a classified property tax embodying varying ratios of assessed to full values for different classes of property.

Prior to the 1960's, only three States—Minnesota (1913), Montana (1917), and West Virginia (1921)—had adopted classified property tax systems. Minnesota's system utilized different ratios of assessed to full values. In Montana and West Virginia, the same result was achieved by employing varing tax rates for different classes of property.[57] In the 1960's, two additional States adopted classified property tax systems, during the 1970's nine more States and the District of Columbia put property-tax classification schemes into effect.[58]

Illinois permits counties with populations over 200,000 to classify property for taxation. Cook County, where Chicago is located, divides property into seven classes for tax purposes. Unimproved realty is taxed at 22 percent of fair market value; residential property including farms is taxed at 16 percent; residential property consisting of more than six units is taxed at 33 percent; realty used in furtherance of charter purposes of non-profit corporations is assessed at 30 percent; industrial and commercial property located in areas in need of industri-

---

56. Ed Guth Realty, Inc. v. Gingold, note 54 supra. The Court of Appeals, however, did not hold that the rate is an "absolute." Instead, it ruled that "[t]he party who seeks to use the rate will be put to his proof that such use is justified in that case." 37 N.Y.2d at 450. The Assessor of Nassau County relied on that qualification in opposing the taxpayer's reliance on the State rate in the *860 Executive Towers* case, note 53 supra. An extensive litigation ensued which consumed many months, and produced over 7,000 pages of testimony and 293 exhibits. Appraisals of 33 separate parcels were reviewed by the court, which also heard the SBEA and the plaintiff's experts defend, and the county's experts attack, the SBEA's methods. Three "distinguished" statisticians from academia and a "recognized" real estate appraiser analyzed the SBEA's techniques. Justice Howard Hogan, long the dean of the New York's judiciary in the trial of property tax cases, upheld the use of the SBEA rates, saying:

From the totality of the evidence, I find the State rates statistically ade-

quate, legally operative and fairly representative when weighed against any other known method. A most redeeming feature of their use is that these permit a petitioner to seek relief in the courts without prohibitive expense. [377 N.Y.S.2d at 877.]

Justice Hogan's decision was affirmed by an intermediate appellate court. 860 Executive Towers, Inc. v. Board of Assessors of the County of Nassau, 53 A.D.2d 463, 385 N.Y.S.2d 604 (2d Dep't 1976). For the use of average assessment ratios in proving inequality in New Jersey, see Appeals of Kents 2124 Atlantic Ave., Inc., 33 N.J. 21, 166 A.2d 763 (1961); Borough of Matawan v. Tree Haven Apartments, Inc., 108 N.J. Super. 111, 260 A.2d 235 (App.Div.1969); Continental Paper Co. v. Village of Ridgefield Park, 122 N.J.Super. 446, 300 A.2d 850 (App.Div.) certification denied 63 N.J. 328, 307 A.2d 101 (1973).

57. See Roemer, "Classification of Property," in C.L. Harriss, ed., The Property Tax and Local Finance 108 (1983).

58. Id.

al and commercial development is taxed at 16 percent; and all realty outside a designated class is taxed at 40 percent.[59]

Minnesota, the first State to utilize the classified system, started with four classes of property, once had 20 classes, and now has six classes.[60] Former Commissioner Roland F. Hatfield of Minnesota, who had sought to do away with his State's classified tax, has declared that it is "a tribute to the legislature that there are [only] twenty classes" and that if the legislature had

> yielded to all the pressures involved we could easily have had over two hundred * * * I do not recall that anyone has proposed and gotten passed a higher percentage than was then existing on a certain class. * * * The result is that the tax base becomes constantly eroded and the tax rates skyrocketed.[61]

H. *Circuit Breakers.* Circuit breakers are designed to cut off or reduce a qualified taxpayer's tax load when the property tax reaches too high a proportion of the family's household income.[62] They made their first appearance in State legislation during the 1940's; only five States had enacted circuit breakers by 1970; then they began to spread and by the end of the 1970's they were in force in 31 States.[63] The first phase of the circuit breaker legislation limited the benefits to elderly householders with low household income ("household income" typically includes social security, welfare payments and strike benefits) and usually to owner-occupiers. More recently, however, the States have begun to broaden the legislation so as to extend circuit breaker relief to broader classes of property owners, such as veterans or farmers; and several States have extended the relief to residential tenants, by treating fixed percentages of their rent as having been paid on account of the landlord's property tax.[64] Qualified owners or occupiers receive either a credit against the State income tax or a cash refund. The amount of the credit or refund depends on the percentage of the property tax to the household income; it increases as the percentage rises; and there is usually a fixed dollar maximum credit.[65] It has been suggested that the heavy tax burden which might otherwise be imposed on some homeowners of modest means who have owned and occupied

---

59. P–H ¶ 31,520.

60. Hatfield, "Minnesota's Experience with Classification," in Symposium of the Tax Institute of America, The Property Tax: Problems and Potentials 239, 242 (1967); Minn.Stat § 273.13, CCH ¶ 91–765h–2 et seq.

61. Hatfield, note 60 supra, at 242, 243.

62. See Shannon, "Property Tax Relief and Reform Act of 1973," Hearings on S. 1255 Before the Subcomm. on Intergovernmental Relations (Muskie Committee) of the Senate Comm. on Government Operations 191 et seq. (93rd Cong., 1st Sess.1973): N.Y. Temporary Commission on State and Local Finance, Report on State and Local

Finances, "The Real Property Tax," Vol. 2, 154 et seq. (1975).

63. Gold, "Circuit-breakers and Other Relief Measures," in C.L. Harriss, The Property Tax and Local Finance 148, 150 (1983).

64. Cf. Kee and Moan, "The Property Tax and Tenant Equality," 89 Harv.L.Rev. 531 (1976), which recommends that the tenant of rented property be made the real property "taxpayer," in order (hopefully) to enable him to claim the Federal income tax deduction allowed for property taxes.

65. See note 62 supra and Bendick, "Designing Circuit Breaker Property Tax Relief," 27 Nat.Tax J. 19 (1974).

their property for a considerable number of years, as a result of the reassessment of property at full value, can be alleviated by the enactment or broadening of a circuit breaker.[66]

I. *Reappraisal Program Spread Over a Period of Years.* When a property reappraisal program is undertaken in a county or a large city, utilizing new valuation methods or designed to effect a more equitable equalization, the program ordinarily takes a number of years. Suppose a five-year program is projected, may the new assessed values be made effective on one-fifth of the properties each year as the reappraisal progresses, or must the new assessed values be held in abeyance and made applicable to all properties in the same year? This problem has arisen in a number of States. New Jersey sidestepped this facet of the problem by postponing the effective date of its tax reforms and by enacting a transitional tax measure to prevent interim havoc resulting from substantial shifts in tax burdens.[67] In Skinner v. New Mexico State Tax Commission,[68] a newly elected appraiser sought, beginning with 1957, to equalize real property assessments in the county on the basis of 16 percent of actual market value. Because of staff and fund limitations, only about 20 percent of the 120,000 properties were reappraised in 1957. He assessed those properties at the new basis for that year and used the 1956 assessment for all other property. The record showed that the latter ranged from 1 percent to 160 percent of actual market. The plaintiffs, whose properties had been reappraised, attacked the assessment as violating the State's uniformity and equality provisions. The court upheld the assessment on the ground that:

> In New Mexico it has long been the rule that a taxpayer who is not assessed more than the law provides has no cause for complaint in the courts in the absence of some well-defined and established scheme of discrimination or some fraudulent action.[69]

For other cases sustaining the validity of staggered assessments, see Hamilton v. Adkins, 250 Ala. 557, 35 So.2d 183 (1948), certiorari denied 335 U.S. 861, 69 S.Ct. 133 (1948); May Dept. Stores Co. v. State Tax Comm'n, 308 S.W.2d 748 (Mo.1958); Apex Motor Fuel Co. v. Barrett, 20 Ill.2d 395, 169 N.E.2d 769 (1960); Carkonen v. Williams, 76 Wash.2d 617, 458 P.2d 280 (1969); Recanzone v. Nevada Tax Comm'n, 92 Nev. 302, 550 P.2d 401 (1976); Hamer v. Kirk, 64 Ill.2d 434, 357 N.E.2d 506 (1976); Parker v. Board of Trustees of Odessa Junior College, 584 S.W.2d 569 (Tex.Civ.App.1979); Justus v. Board of Equalization, 101 Idaho 743, 620 P.2d 777 (1980); Rogan v. County Comm'r of Calvert Co., 194 Md. 299, 71 A.2d 47 (1950), in which the court sustained the validity of a statute authorizing the reassessment of one-fifth of the

---

66. See Lesnick, note 48 supra, at 275–76.

67. See textual material Note A supra. For a history of the New Jersey developments, see Thomas v. Kingsley, 43 N.J. 524, 206 A.2d 161 (1965), which narrates the action taken in connection with the

postponement and upholds the validity of the transitional legislative enactment.

68. 66 N.M. 221, 345 P.2d 750, 76 A.L.R.2d 1071 (1959).

69. 66 N.M. at 223, 345 P.2d at 752.

property in each county in a year, with the result that over a five-year period all properties in the district would be reassessed. The Supreme Court denied certiorari in several cases upholding the staggered reassessment of commercial property in the New Orleans central business district. Probst v. City of New Orleans and Walgreen Louisiana Co. v. City of New Orleans, 337 So.2d 1081 (La.1976), certiorari denied 430 U.S. 916, 97 S.Ct. 1329 (1977).

The Virginia Supreme Court was not as tolerant of the disparities resulting from a county reappraisal program spread over a period of years. In holding that the program violated the constitutional provision that "all taxes * * * shall be uniform upon the same class of subjects within the territorial limits of the authority levying the tax," the court in Perkins v. County of Albemarle, 214 Va. 240, 198 S.E.2d 626 (1973), noted:

> Defendant acknowledges * * * disparity but insists that it constitutes only a "technical lack of uniformity" which is constitutionally "tolerable" as unavoidable "start-up pains" in the transition from the old to the new system. For how many years it could remain constitutionally untainted defendant does not say. While absolute and constant uniformity may be an unattainable ideal, we do not agree that the lack of uniformity which exists here is merely technical or constitutionally tolerable, because we do not agree that it was unavoidable.

> Neither the Constitution nor the statute requires that before the new system becomes operative *appraisals* must be completed county-wide within a 12–month frame. What is required is uniformity in *assessments* upon which tax liability is uniformly levied. The "start-up pains" experienced here could have been avoided had defendant taken whatever period of years proved necessary to complete county-wide appraisals, postponed assessments county-wide until the appraisals first made had been arithmetically adjusted by the intervening growth factor to comport with the appraisals last made, and then levied tax liability on assessments based on appraisals up-dated county-wide. Such a process would have delayed receipt of the additional revenue defendant sought, but such was the price of constitutional uniformity. And if the price was too dear, and if defendant was unable or unwilling to hire the additional appraisers necessary to minimize the delay, defendant could have acquired additional revenue during the period of delay by increasing tax rates county-wide, a politically sensitive but fiscally viable alternative. [196 S.E.2d at 628–29.]

See also Xerox Corp. v. Karnes, 217 Neb. 728, 350 N.W.2d 566 (1984), which invalidated a statutory provision requiring valuation of property in odd-numbered years because it failed to recognize depreciation to personal property in even-numbered years. In Sparks v. McCluskey, 84 Ariz. 283, 327 P.2d 295 (1958), commercial properties on a few streets in the county were selected for reappraisal under a new assessment method and it was contemplated that at some indefinite future time other properties would be reassessed. Relief was granted to an owner of commercial property that had been reassessed. The cases involving staggered reassessment, and the problems they raise, are thoughtfully considered in Oldman & Youngman, "Current Issues of Assessment Equity," 13 Assessors J. 31 (1978).

J. *Discriminatory Assessments Against Railroads.* The railroads, whose property has historically been assessed at a different and substantially higher percentage of value for ad valorem tax purposes than is true of the great bulk of property owners subject to the same tax, turned to Congress for relief. Congressional legislation now forbids States from taxing railroad property more heavily than other commercial and industrial property. 49 U.S.C.A. § 11503. See p. 48 supra. There has been a considerable amount of litigation over the construction of this statute, as well as Congress' authority to enact it. The constitutional challenges have uniformly been rebuffed, but the constructional issues are a source of continuing controversy. See, e.g., Burlington Northern Railroad Co. v. Oklahoma Tax Commission, ___ U.S. ___, 107 S.Ct. 1855 (1987); Atchison, T. & S.F. Ry. Co. v. Lennen, 732 F.2d 1495 (10th Cir.1984); Clinchfield R. Co. v. Lynch, 700 F.2d 126 (4th Cir.1983); General American Transportation Corp. v. Louisiana Tax Commission, 680 F.2d 400 (5th Cir.1982); see generally Gossett, "Assessment Law Notes: The Continuing Battle Over the 4–R Act and Its Progeny," 1 Prop.Tax J. 245 (1982); Note, "Discriminatory Demands and Divided Decisions: State and Local Taxation of Rail, Motor, and Air Carrier Property," 39 Vand.L.Rev. 1107 (1986).

K. *References.* Aaron, "Some Observations on Property Tax Valuation and the Significance of Full Value Assessment," in A. Lynn, The Property Tax and Its Administration 193 (1969); Lesnick, "Does Full Value Mean Full Value? Prospects for Assessment Reform in New York in Light of the Experience of Other States with *Hellerstein's* Progenitors," 5 Hofstra L.Rev. 235 (1977); Wheaton, "The Statewide Impact of Full Property Revaluation in Massachusetts" (Fed.Res.Bank of Boston, 1975); Advisory Comm. on Intergovernmental Relations, The Property Tax in a Changing Environment; Selected State Tax Studies 88 (1974); Note, "100% Assessment in Kentucky," 54 Ky.L.J. 98 (1965); Beebe & Sinott, In the Wake of Hellerstein: Whither New York (N.Y. State Board of Equalization and Assessment, 1977), substantially reprinted in 43 Albany L.Rev. 203 (Part I), 411 (Part II), and 777 (Part III) (1979); Note, "Alabama's Property Tax: Ineffective, Inefficient, and Inequitable," 36 Ala.L.Rev. 147 (1984); Wershow & Schwartz, "Ad Valorem Assessments in Florida—Recent Developments," 36 U. Miami L.Rev. 67 (1982); Handy, "Valuation and Taxation of Residential Real Property in Arizona," 1984 Ariz.St.L.J. 145; Note, "The Kansas Property Tax: Mischievous, Misunderstood, and Mishandled," 22 Washburn L.J. 318 (1983); Hudson, "Florida's Property Appraisers," 7 Nova L.J. 477 (1983).

SECTION 4. OVERVALUATION

(a) *The Scope of Judicial Review in Overvaluation Cases*

HELIN v. GROSSE POINTE TOWNSHIP

Supreme Court of Michigan, 1951.
329 Mich. 396, 45 N.W.2d 338.

BUSHNELL, JUSTICE. Plaintiffs Charles Helin and Lempi Helin, his wife, reside in the village of Grosse Pointe Park and are the owners of lots 23 and 24, Windmill Pointe subdivision of private claim 696, and part of private claims 126 and 127, 379 and 570. The Helins purchased this property on land contract from the State land office board in 1945 for $40,000. It is adjacent to that involved in Moran v. Grosse Pointe Township, 317 Mich. 248, 26 N.W.2d 763, and has a 200–foot frontage on Lake St. Clair and a depth of 400 feet. A 55 × 105 foot mansion-type stone dwelling and a four-car garage with five rooms on its second floor are located on the property. The house has seven rooms and two lavatories on the first floor; eight bedrooms and six bathrooms on second floor; and five rooms and two bathrooms on third floor. It was built in 1924 at a cost of $250,000. The original owner paid about $50,000 for the land.

In 1943 when it was assessed at about $135,000 the then owner permitted his title to revert to the State for the nonpayment of approximately $15,000 accumulated taxes. There were no bids at the public auction, held under § 7 of the State land office board act, Act No. 155, P.A.1937, as amended, 1948 C.L. § 211.351 et seq., Stat.Ann. § 7.951 et seq.

The property was appraised at $60,000 on November 6, 1944, under the authority of § 8 of the act, C.L.1948, § 211.359, Stat.Ann. § 7.958. No offers were received, although it was advertised and listed with brokers. On April 23, 1945, Helin made an offer of $35,000, which was not accepted. The property was thereafter reappraised at $40,000, and again offered for sale. On May 16th the State accepted Helin's offer in this amount.

The proceeds, less commissions, were distributed, 23.58 per cent of which went to the treasurer of defendant township. Thereafter, defendant township placed the property on the tax rolls at an assessed valuation of $133,270. Helin made timely protest, was accorded a hearing before the board of review and, upon receiving no relief, appealed to the State tax commission. On November 4, 1947, the commission reduced the assessed valuation to $123,770. The adjusted tax of $2,894.98 was paid under protest and suit was brought to recover claimed excess taxes.

Trial by jury was waived. The trial judge held that the fair cash value of the property, as of the date of assessment, was not more than $50,000, and that plaintiff was entitled to recover payments on the assessed value in excess of $50,000.

Defendant township appealed from a judgment in the sum of $1,879.34. Plaintiffs took a cross-appeal on the ground that the court erred in failing to render judgment for the entire amount of the 1947 taxes paid under protest.

*   *   *

Plaintiffs and cross-appellants claim discrimination because other property in the taxing district was assessed at less than 50 per cent of its cash value. They argued that a valuation of their property, based entirely upon cost of reproduction less depreciation and obsolescence, resulted in this instance in an assessment so excessive and constructively fraudulent as to make it illegal. They also urge that they are entitled to judicial remedy after exhausting all administrative remedies, that there was no error in the admission of testimony, and that the judgment, if not proper, should be increased to include the full amount of the taxes paid. The county of Wayne and city of Detroit were granted leave to file a brief amici curiae.

The testimony indicates that the area in which the property is located is the most highly restricted in the community, and that homes of this type, although at one time quite desirable, are no longer being built and are generally considered to be presently unsalable. Helin testified that, because of the expense of upkeep, he is only able to use eight or ten rooms, and that these cost $250 per month to heat.

The former owner, Herbert V. Book, testified that he was unable to obtain any tax relief and made every effort to sell his property. He let it go to tax sale in 1943 because he could not obtain anything for his equity, although the property was free and clear of encumbrances, except the unpaid taxes.

The record contains exhibits in tabulated and chart form, prepared by a broker who sold 184 parcels in the area between July 1944 and May 1946. They show the relationship between sale prices and assessed valuations of these parcels. These exhibits indicate that in the four municipalities in Grosse Pointe township, i.e., Grosse Pointe Park, Grosse Pointe Farms, Grosse Pointe Shores, and Grosse Pointe Woods, the assessed valuations of improved property averaged only 52 per cent of their sales prices. The testimony of another broker, who sold 26 parcels in 1947, indicates that the assessed valuations of those parcels averaged 38.6 per cent of sales prices.

An appraiser for the State land office board testified that on November 6, 1944, when he appraised the property at $60,000, he had in mind the statute relating to tax scavenger sales, which required such appraisal to be at the highest price obtainable. When he learned that neither the board nor its agents were able to sell the property at this price, he subsequently appraised it at $40,000, believing that to be the highest price then obtainable.

In support of its assessed valuation, defendant township produced the testimony of Albert E. Champney, director of the Wayne county bureau of taxation. Champney testified that all of the townships in the county of Wayne employ the basic method of assessment that the bureau had established and recommended, with some variations in its application in various areas. These are adjusted through an equalization process by the county board of supervisors.

The system employed is based upon a land value map for each district. The assessing officer arrives at his judgment of the unit values of land for each area, with allowances for depth and variations in size. Champney stated that the assessment level in Grosse Pointe township is at present 20 per cent below the equalization level applied in the county of Wayne.

The system provides for division of structures into various classes, with a separate class for mansion-type houses. Various factors are used for differences in area, number of stories, and type of construction. The schedule developed in the years 1936 to 1939, as applied to mansion-type homes, includes a substantial allowance for obsolescence. It reflects about 50 per cent of the reproduction cost from 1936 to 1939. In addition, an obsolescence formula, devised by the Michigan state tax commission, is applied to residential luxury-type homes. This, he explained, is a formula which contemplates an increased rate of obsolescence, depending upon total value, and ranges from 10 to 50 per cent. Based upon the original construction cost of $250,000 in 1924 and 1925, this formula produced a total reproduction cost of $113,814 for the buildings before depreciation. Champney added that the assessment made by the township supervisor was exactly the amount that the bureau recommended in 1947.

James McMahon, an examiner for the State tax commission, testified that, in reassessing this property, he recommended a land value of $51,330 and a building value of $72,440, which totaled $9,500 less than the township valuation. This reduction in building value was the result of an increase in the obsolescence factor. He stated that the formula used for mansion-type buildings is uniformly applied by the commission to all appeals of this type from Wayne county. He admitted that the problem is difficult because "sales of so-called mansion-type property do not always reflect the true cash value of those properties." McMahon estimated that construction costs in 1949 were double those of 1924 to 1925, and, if applied to the Helin property, this would result in a reproduction cost of $600,000 to $650,000.

As stated in Moran v. Grosse Pointe Township, 317 Mich. 248, 254, 26 N.W.2d 763, the words "cash value" as defined by 1 C.L.1929, § 3415, Stat.Ann. § 7.27, C.L.1948, § 211.27, is the usual selling price that could be obtained at the time of assessment, but not the price that could be obtained at a forced or auction sale. See, also, Twenty–Two Charlotte, Inc., v. City of Detroit, 294 Mich. 275, 283, 293 N.W. 647.

* * *

Appellees argue that the State land office board acts as the agent of the taxing units for the purpose of obtaining the highest price out of which such taxing units could recover the delinquent taxes in whole or in part. The conclusion is drawn that, since the township did not object to the price at which the board proposed to sell the property, the board's determination that $40,000 was the true cash value of the property thus became binding upon the township.

No authority is cited in support of this proposition. * * * in Baker v. State Land Office Board, 294 Mich. 587, 293 N.W. 763, this Court held that the State became the absolute owner. * * *

This accepted rule requires the conclusion that when the State land office board appraised and sold the property in question for $40,000, it was, as required by statute, sold "to the best advantage." § 8, State land office board act. The State land office board thus acted as an agent for the township to the extent of 23.58 per cent of the purchase price. The township cannot be heard to deny the fact that this was a fair cash value.

All of the circumstances leading up to this sale indicate that there was no demand for this type of property. It was a drug on the market, and more or less unsalable.

* * *

"A valuation is necessarily fraudulent where it is so unreasonable that the assessor must have known that it was wrong. If the valuation is purposely made too high through prejudice or a reckless disregard of duty in opposition to what must necessarily be the judgment of all competent persons, or through the adoption of a rule which is designed to operate unequally upon a class and to violate the constitutional rule of uniformity, the case is a plain one for the equitable remedy by injunction." IV Cooley on Taxation, 4th ed., § 1645.

Intentional over-assessment is fraud. Sloman–Polk Co. v. City of Detroit, 261 Mich. 689, 247 N.W. 95, 87 A.L.R. 1294. In the eyes of the law an assessment at variance with undisputed facts is a fraud upon the rights of the taxpayer. S.S. Kresge Co. v. City of Detroit, 276 Mich. 565, 571, 268 N.W. 740, 107 A.L.R. 1258.

The use of a method of valuation which does not determine true cash values is fraud in law. Newport Mining Co. v. City of Ironwood, 185 Mich. 668, 152 N.W. 1088.

An examination of the testimony and the exhibits in support thereof requires the conclusion that plaintiffs' property was not assessed at its true cash value.

An assessment against lands for taxation may be assailed in court if it can be shown that the supervisor or board of review acted fraudulently. City of Birmingham v. Board of Oakland County Supervisors, 276 Mich. 1, 268 N.W. 409.

Courts have jurisdiction to relieve the burden of such oppression. Twenty–Two Charlotte, Inc., v. City of Detroit, 294 Mich. 275, 282, 293 N.W. 647.

The property in question is restricted to use for a single residence. It may not be used for an apartment house, multiple residence, or institutional purposes. Taxes, heating, repairs and upkeep, and the large amount of help required to properly maintain it, make the cost of living in such a home prohibitive except possibly for a very limited number of people. As the record shows, some of the owners of similar homes in the subdivision have either torn down the houses or permitted them to be sold for taxes, or sold them for but a small fraction of their original cost. The restrictions mentioned are largely responsible for the destruction of the larger part of the value of the property and should result in a very material reduction in assessments if they are to be made in a legal manner. The present action, however, is based on what amounts in law to a fraudulent assessment.

The trial judge substituted his judgment for that of the taxing authorities in arriving at a valuation of $50,000.

"Courts cannot substitute their judgment as to the valuation of property for the judgment of the duly constituted tax authorities." S.S. Kresge Co. v. City of Detroit, 276 Mich. 565, 572, 268 N.W. 740, 743, 1107 A.L.R. 1258.

In the light of the factual recitals in this opinion and the law applicable thereto, as herein stated, the trial judge did not err in denying defendants' motions to dismiss. Nor did he err in overruling the objections to the admissibility of evidence relating to the purchase price of the property and its appraisal by the State land office board, the adoption of a claimed wrong principle of assessment, and that tending to show discrimination or fraud.

The judgment entered for the difference between the tax paid and the rate computed on a valuation of $50,000 must be vacated and one entered for the entire amount of the protested tax paid, without prejudice to a proper reassessment.

The judgment is vacated and the cause is remanded for the entry of a judgment in accordance with this opinion. Costs to appellees.

ROSBROC ASSOCIATES v. ASSESSOR AND BD. OF REVIEW OF THE CITY OF NEW ROCHELLE

New York Supreme Court, Westchester County.
New York Law Journal, November 3, 1976. pp. 16–17.

SLIFKIN, JUSTICE. These are proceedings to review real property assessments to the City of New Rochelle pursuant to article 7 of the Real Property Tax Law. The property known as the Sheraton Motor Inn and Office Building is located at 1 Sheraton Plaza and is designated on the Tax and Assessment Map as section 1, Block 247, Lot 1. The assessments under review are those for 1975 and 1976. By virtue of a motion by petitioner at trial, the proceedings were consolidated.

The subject property is improved with a 10 story building which consists of a hotel and related facilities on the first 6 floors and offices on the top four floors. It is located in the major central business district of the City. Further, it is located in the heart of the urban renewal area of the City near the newly constructed "Mall" and near the recently completed Longines Wittnauer building.

During the years under review, the property was assessed as follows:

1975—Land $297,350; Improvement $1,630,000;
Total $1,927,350.

1976—Land $300,000; Improvement $1,720,000;
Total $2,020,000.

The petitioner's protests and petitions with respect to each year are based on claimed over-valuation and inequality.

With respect to the issue of inequality, a Notice to Admit pursuant to Real Property Tax Law section 716 served on respondents and not denied, established an admission from respondents that for purposes of these proceedings, the following percentages represent the percentages at which other real property in the assessing district were assessed: 1975—45%; 1976—45%.

By reason of the applicable percentages thus established for each of the assessment years under review and the stipulation by the parties as to their use by the court, the issue of inequality will be decided merely by a mathematical computation involved in applying the appropriate percentage to the full market value of the subject property to be found by the court upon the evidence introduced with respect to the issue of valuation.

Petitioner's expert appraiser appraised the fair market value of the property as follows:

1975—Land $523,400; Improvement $1,940,110;
Total $2,463,510.

1976—Land $523,400; Improvement $1,976,093;
Total $2,499,493.

Respondent's expert appraiser appraised the fair market value of the property as follows:

1975—Land $714,000; Improvement $4,586,000;
Total, $5,300,000.

[Figures for 1976 are not given. Ed.]

The market value of a piece of real estate is not ordinarily the subject of ready computation. Market value is largely a theoretical construct. Among the factors to be considered are:

    1. Physical conditions of premises;

    2. Description of the physical characteristics of the property and its situation in relation to points of importance in the area;

    3. A consideration of the uses for which the land is adopted and which it is available;

    4. The value of the improvements if they are such as to increase the value of the land.

As the court has indicated, the valuation of property is not an exact science. The experts for the respective parties, both of whom are well qualified, considered all the factors enumerated but utilized different approaches in reaching the value attributed to the property.

LAND

The court first turns to a discussion of the value to be attributed to the land. The land consists of 118,956 square feet and covers one square city block.

In appraising the land, petitioner's appraiser considered a number of land sales, some of which grew out of the Urban Renewal project in the City. He noted that two large parcels of this project remain unsold. One of these consists of 51,000 square feet and is directly opposite the subject. The other is nearby and contains 108,000 square feet. Petitioner's expert, Mr. William G. Scott, notes that both of these parcels are being offered at less than his conclusion that the subject be valued at $4 a square foot. To this $4 a square foot, he adds a 10 percent factor by reason of frontage on four streets to reach a total value of $523,400.

Petitioner's expert relies on 6 sales. They date from 1967 to 1973 and represent sales prices of $3 to $6 per square foot. Five of the six parcels represent sales by the City and are part of the Urban Renewal project. The parcels range in size from 10,900 square feet to 139,880 square feet. The court notes that no grid or adjustment sheet has been furnished by petitioner's appraiser adjusting the sales to the subject parcel.

Respondent's expert, Mr. Robert W. Jones, relied on 4 sales, including the land sale of the subject in 1972. He notes that urban renewal sales are generally below market value to attract buyers and he adjusts these sales upward. The first sale relied on by respondent was the 1972 sale of the subject parcel and indicated a purchase price of $3 a square foot. The other three sales occurred between 1972 and 1974 and represent unadjusted sales prices of $3.90 to $7 a square foot.

Respondent's expert also fails to include a grid, but indicates adjustments upward of 3 of the sales by reason of their urban renewal character, time of sale, type of property, and plot size. He concludes that the land be valued at $6 per square foot for a total of $714,000. Thus, he finds a 100 percent increase in value of the subject between October, 1972, and the 1975 valuation date.

Based on the foregoing, the court finds that a value of $4.75 per square foot represents the fair market value on the valuation dates in question. Thus, the court concludes that the total fair market value of the land was $565,000.

The court approves of the use of urban renewal sales as comparables (In re Presidential Plaza v. Srogi, 50 A.D.2d 717). Yet, the court agrees that the presence of substantial tracts of unsold urban renewal land tends to depress the land value of the parcels in the area including the subject. In reviewing the testimony, the court notes that there is a ground lease of the premises at $80,000 per year. There was limited testimony with respect thereto as an "in-house" transaction, but were the court to capitalize this lease at 14 percent representing the equalized tax rate and a return of approximately 9 percent, the value obtained would be $571,000, a figure which is extremely close to the value found on a per square foot basis and supports the findings of this court.

IMPROVEMENT

The court now turns to a discussion of the improvement and its value.

Construction of the subject took place in 1974. As represented by both the description furnished by the appraisers, as well as by the pictures supplied to this court, it is an impressive structure on one square block of land in the heart of the business district of New Rochelle.

In reaching his conclusion as to value, petitioner's expert, Mr. Scott, relied upon an income approach known as the building residual method. His appraisal includes statements of income and expenses for the years in question. Mr. Scott concedes that since the hotel opened in March, 1975, the 1975 year was an incomplete experience. Accordingly, he concludes that the statements of income and expense for the first 6 months of 1976 represent a more realistic financial picture. He has therefore doubled most of these figures to project a full year's operation. It is the income produced by these figures that he utilized in the building residual method for the two years under review.

Petitioner's expert recognizes that hotel income is produced by the combination of real estate together with furnishings, working capital and good will and business ability of the operator. His consideration of the hotel income included a deduction from income of sufficient moneys for a return to and a depreciation of the actual investment in the furnishings. All remaining income was then treated as though developed by the land improvement. This approach would then negate any claim that an income method may not be used to value a hotel property (People ex rel. Hotel Paramount Corp. v. Chambers, 298 N.Y. 375, Matter of Hilton Inns v. Board of Assessors of the Village of Tarrytown, 39 Misc.2d 792, 794). By making no deduction for the business ability or entrepreneurial skills of the operator, petitioner's expert is able to utilize the income method and further to attempt to establish that the structural improvements are not suitable to the site and constitutes, in effect, an overimprovement.

Mr. Scott notes that the office space on the top 4 floors is 75 percent rented, far above the rate of occupancy for the surrounding area, and the hotel rooms are 62.5 percent rented. He points out that the surrounding areas contain a great deal of unrented office space, vacant commercial and retail space, as well as unused vacant land.

This leads him to conclude that the Urban Renewal project in New Rochelle has not been a total success and that the subject is an overimprovement albeit the highest and best use.

In view of the above, petitioner's expert concludes that the net annual income before taxes to be capitalized under the building residual method is $462,671. Against this, he applies a capitalization rate of 10 percent on the land, 12 percent on the improvement, together with the equalized tax rate and a recapture rate of 2.5 percent.

Petitioner's expert also deals with the reproduction cost of the building, less economic depreciation and functional obsolescence. Through references to the Dodge Building Cost Calculator, he concludes that the reproduction cost would be $6,351,458. However, he finds a very high degree of functional obsolescence because of his conclusion that the structure is an overimprovement.

Petitioner's expert concludes that because of the high degree of functional obsolescence and the general pattern of prevailing economic conditions in the urban renewal area, the proper means of valuing this improvement is the income method and not the reconstruction cost less the depreciation or summation method.

Respondent's expert notes that for a new building such as the subject, the cost approach is used to assist the appraiser in arriving at a reliable indication of value. He utilizes the Marshall Valuation Service to arrive at a total replacement cost of $6,481,600. He finds a physical and functional depreciation of 5 percent for nominal obsolescence of fixtures and minor design deficiencies. He also points out that the recent economic downturn which he labels "recession/depression" substantially reduced the anticipated return expected from the improvement although properties such as the subject equally suffer a loss of economic rentability for the first several years of operation. The respondent's expert concludes that the normal loss in income due to the nature of this property and the general economic condition was a significant factor in the decline in value of the subject and that the property has not yet reached its economic potential. Therefore, he estimates an economic depreciation of 25 percent.

The total 30 percent depreciation is then applied to obtain a depreciated improvement value by the cost approach of $4,536,800, to which the land value is added and a total value of $5,250,800 is reached by respondent's expert.

As will be discussed at a later point, the key factor in the cost approach is the respondent's recognition of a substantial economic depreciation of the subject.

Respondent's expert also uses an income approach through the imputation of a market rental value for the office space and by estimating the annual hotel revenue. For his purposes, this expert has created and used an economic rent or income rather than the actual income and has applied economic rather than actual costs and expenses. The result reached by respondent's appraiser is a net income before taxes of $764,387. In so doing, he applied estimated expense figures far below the actual experience of the subject. Further, in estimating income, he assumed a 95 percent occupancy rate of the office portion of the building.

Against the net income before taxes, respondent's expert applies a 7.5 percent return to land and improvements, a 1.66 percent recapture rate and the two year equalized tax rate. He then arrives at an improvement value of $4,653,000, which is coincidentally within $100,000 of his depreciated improvements value. Upon the addition of the land value, he found a total value of $5,367,000 through the income method utilizing the building residual method.

Respondent's ultimate conclusion as to value is the sum of $5,300,000 which is a figure lower than that figure which he obtains through the income method and higher than the figure reached through the cost method. Although the mathematical difference is not significant, the ultimate conclusion of a value greater than that obtained under the cost method violates one of the prime rules of valuation for certiorari purposes, to wit, that structural value based on reproduction cost less depreciation fixes the maximum value, even if the capitalized income would indicate a higher valuation (see People ex rel. Manhattan Square Beresford Inc. v. Sexton, 284 N.Y. 145, 149; People ex rel. Parklin Operating Corp. v. Miller, 287 N.Y. 126, 131). However, since it is clear that respondent relies chiefly on the cost approach, the court will treat his finding of a value of $5,251,000 under the cost method as his ultimate conclusion as to the value of the subject.

Having discussed in detail the approaches set forth in the respective appraisals, the court will now turn to certain legal principles and their application to the case at bar.

While petitioner relies upon an income approach herein, the case law generally indicates that during the early years of income producing property, such a method is not reliable because of the start up time needed to establish the property as a viable income producer. Thus, the cost method should be utilized (see Suburbia Apts. v. Board of Assessors, 66 Misc.2d 918, 922, 923). On the other hand, unless a building is a specialty or a prestige structure, the income method usually provides the surest guide to value (see People ex rel. N.Y. Stock Exchange v. Cantor, 221 App.Div. 193, aff'd 248 N.Y. 533; Matter of Seagram & Sons v. Tax Comm'n, 18 A.D.2d 109; People ex rel. Gale v. Tax Comm'n, 17 A.D.2d 225, 230).

While construction and reproduction costs set the maximum value for which property may lawfully be assessed (Matter of J.W. Mays, Inc. v. Tax Comm'n, 21 A.D.2d 801, aff'd 16 N.Y.2d 529), the theory on which the cost less depreciation method rests is that no investor will pay more for a building than the cost of reproducing it (see People ex rel. Parklin Operating Corp. v. Miller, 287 N.Y.2d 126). Moreover, and most significant herein, reproduction cost less depreciation is not relevant to a particular case where the building would normally not be reproduced at the time in question and is not well suited to the site (Matter of 860 5th Avenue v. Tax Comm'n, 8 N.Y.2d 29, 32; Chiloway Charcoal v. State of N.Y., 33 A.D.2d 712, 713, aff'd 28 N.Y.2d 914). Where the property is shown to be unable to achieve a stabilized income commensurate with its cost due to overbuilding, the reproduction cost less depreciation must be offset by this factor and reliance placed on use of the income method (Matter of Roosevelt Field v. Podeyn, 47 Misc.2d 677, 692).

Finally, in the absence of proof that the building is a specialty reliance solely on cost less depreciation is erroneous absent unusual circumstances (Matter of Pepsi–Cola Co. v. Tax Comm'n, 19 A.D.2d 56, 59–60; Matter of Elmhurst Towers, Inc. v. Tax Comm'n, 34 A.D.2d 570).

In the case at bar, petitioner's expert reliance upon the income method is based on his view that the income level utilized represents a realistic one and therefore, in his opinion, is not subject to a successful claim that the subject has not been operated long enough to give a true picture of income. This claim is based on and supported by the rather poor economic picture existing in the urban renewal area of New Rochelle. Thus, while the percentage of room occupancy of the hotel space is lower than that of similar facilities in other areas in the county, it must be considered as having stabilized sufficiently to be relied upon. Further, since the percentage of rental of office space is higher than some of the surrounding properties and since there is a great deal of available office space in the area, it too must be considered to have reached a sufficiently stable use.

In addition, there is no claim that the * * * specialty * * * would have to be reproduced elsewhere if destroyed requiring reproduction cost less depreciation as the test (People ex rel. N.Y. Stock Exchange, supra).

While respondent relies on the reproduction cost less depreciation, the fact that their expert finds a 30 percent economic obsolescence is indicative that as claimed by petitioner, the subject is an overimprovement, not well suited to the site and thus, would not be reproduced and therefore, the cost approach may not be used (Matter of 860, 5th Avenue, supra; Chiloway Charcoal v. State, supra).

Economic or functional obsolescence has been defined as that reduction in the value of an improvement which results from the inability to fully utilize the improvement, not because of the improvement itself, but because of outside factors (see Onondaga Water District v. Board of Assessors, 44 A.D.2d 258, 262, rev'd on other grounds, 39 N.Y.2d 601, 604). Here, because of the downturn in business in general and the lack of success of the New Rochelle Urban Renewal project, the appraisers have agreed that substantial economic or functional obsolescence exists. From this it follows that the building is an overimprovement and would not be reproduced. This requires a conclusion that the holding of Matter of 860 5th Ave., supra, must apply and the cost test may not be relied upon and is not relevant in this case.

The court also notes that the sole proof as to reproduction and replacement cost less depreciation was adduced by reference to certain manuals and not through the testimony of a builder or professional engineer. Such an approach has often been criticized (see Matter of Long Beach Urban Renewal Agency, 67 Misc.2d 259, 263; U.S. v. 5.77 Acres of Land, 52 F.Supp. 68; Matter of White Plains Properties Corp. v. Tax Assessor, City of White Plains, Supreme Court, White Plains, Westchester County, Index No. 3016/69, June 10, 1976 (Slifkin, J.)).

Based on the foregoing, the court concludes that the responsible reliance on reproduction cost less depreciation is unwarranted in this case and it finds that the improvement herein is an overimprovement not suited to the site and that it would not be reproduced (Matter of 860 Fifth Avenue, supra). Accordingly, the court will deal with the income method and value the property pursuant thereto.

As previously noted, the petitioner's expert relies on actual income and expenses for the first six months of 1976 and doubles these figures to achieve his income and expense figure. Respondent, on the other hand, utilizes economic or projected income and expenses. Where the property is producing its maximum income, the actual income and expenses is extremely relevant. If it is less than the fair rental income, then fair rental income should be considered on the gross rent. However, the alleged fair rental income must be firmly and equivocally established by comparable market data. If not, it becomes pure speculation (Saks & Company v. Board of Assessors, Supreme Court, Nassau County, April 26, 1974 [Hogan, J.]; aff'd 52 A.D.2d 585).

Further the actual rent received is in ordinary cases an important factor in determining what the fair market rental value is (People ex rel. Gale v. Tax Commission, 17 A.D.2d 225, 230).

In the case at bar, the court finds the use of the actual experience of this property to be a surer guide to the fair market income and expenses than the speculative approach of respondent.

In concluding that the actual experience of the property is a surer guide to fair market income and expenses, the court does not adopt in toto the figures used by petitioner, but finds that the net income before taxes to be capitalized is $500,000. To this the court has applied a basic capitalization rate and an equalized tax rate of 14.3 percent and a recapture rate of 2 percent to obtain an improvement value of $2,571,000 for each of the two years in question. To this is added the land value of $565,000 to obtain a total fair market value of $3,136,000. Thus, the court finds the fair market value of the parcel as follows:

Year	Land	Improvement	Total
1975	$565,000	$2,571,000	$3,136,000
1976	565,000	2,571,000	3,136,000

Accordingly, the court upon the application of the equalization rate of the remaining years, finds the assessed valuation of the subject property to be as follows:

Year	Land	Improvement	Total
1975	$254,250	$1,156,950	$1,411,200
1976	254,250	1,156,950	1,411,200

Notes and Problems

A. *Functional Obsolescence or Depreciation.* In Onondaga County Water Dist. v. Board of Assessors of the Town of Minetto, 39 N.Y.2d 601, 385 N.Y.S.2d 13, 350 N.E.2d 390 (1976), referred to in the *Rosbroc* case, Judge Breitel stated:

> Functional depreciation has been defined as "obsolescence" or as "the loss of operating efficiency" (see, e.g., 1 Bonbright, Valuation of Property, at pp. 187–188; 2 Orgel, Valuation Under Eminent Domain, §§ 211, 213, at pp. 97–98, 105–106). More sophisticated analysis has recognized various subclasses, based upon causal distinctions, of the class "functional depreciation". Thus, for example, the writers have distinguished among "physical obsolescence", the out of datedness of an asset; "inadequacy", the failure of the asset to meet present or projected needs; and "superfluity", "duplication of facilities", or "overbuilding", the opposite of "inadequacy", where the capacity of the asset exceeds reasonable anticipated demands (1 Bonbright, Valuation of Property, at p. 188; 2 Orgel, Valuation Under Eminent Domain, at p. 107).

> The common thread running through each subclass of functional depreciation is that each is an "undesirable feature", an "adverse influence", or a "deterioration"; in short, a disutility diminishing in some way the value of the property (see Piazza v. Town Assessor of Town of Porter, 16 A.D.2d 863, 228 N.Y.S.2d 397; Matter of Putnam Theat. Corp. v. Gingold, 16 A.D.2d 413, 417, 228 N.Y.S.2d 93, 97; 1 Bonbright, Valuation of Property, at pp. 187–188). Thus, true "superfluity" is present where there is "duplication of facilities or overbuilding * * * where the capacity or the existing plant is beyond the reasonable limit of possible demand" (2 Orgel, Valuation Under Eminent Domain, at p. 107). Put another way, functional obsolescence in the form of superfluity occurs when there is a capacity for service in excess of reasonably anticipated needs and thus is functionally useless, now and in the future. [350 N.E.2d at 392.]

The court rejected the taxpayer's contention that its newly constructed water system was entitled to a 75 percent reduction from an assessment based on actual cost for functional depreciation since the system was operating at only 25 percent of capacity. The court noted:

> This type of functional depreciation, termed "superfluity", is properly deductible from cost as a factor diminishing the value of the property. Where, however, as in this case, the excess capacity for production was planned and constructed in reasonable anticipation of future needs, that is, with deferred utility, there is no functional depreciation. This

is because the excess capacity does not diminish the value of the property but instead constitutes a real element of value. [Id. at 391.]

A building had been erected as a vaudeville theatre, with elaborate facilities for dressing rooms, stage equipment, scenery, and so on; but it was now used as a motion picture house. The taxpayer argued that one-third of the building was obsolete and of no value and sought a reduction based on the value of the property as a motion picture house. See B.F. Keith Columbus Co. v. Board of Revision Franklin County, 148 Ohio St. 253, 74 N.E.2d 359 (1947), noted in "Functional Obsolescence as a Factor in Valuation," 17 U. of Cin.L.Rev. 165 (1948); cf. State v. Petrick, 172 Wis. 82, 178 N.W. 251 (1920). Would it affect the result if the building is usable as a stage theatre or vaudeville house? For further discussion of functional and economic obsolescence, see Teledyne Continental Motors v. Muskegon Township, 145 Mich.App. 749, 378 N.W.2d 590 (1985); Kansas City So. Ry. Co. v. Arkansas Commerce Comm., 230 Ark. 392, 323 S.W.2d 193 (1959).

B. *Trial De Novo in Overvaluation Cases.* In contrast to the *Helin* case, consider Sheraton–Midcontinent Corp. v. County of Pennington, 77 S.D. 554, 95 N.W.2d 892 (1959), which illustrates the practice in some jurisdictions of conducting de novo trials in overvaluation cases. In the *Pennington* case, the court noted that the traditional presumption of the correctness of the assessor's valuation disappears when some evidence of error is introduced at trial. See also Board of Supervisors of Fairfax County v. Donatelli & Klein, Inc., 228 Va. 620, 325 S.E.2d 342 (1985); Gradoville v. Board of Equalization of Cass County, 207 Neb. 615, 301 N.W.2d 62 (1981); Yadco, Inc. v. Yankton County, 89 S.D. 651, 237 N.W.2d 665 (1975); Tiffany v. County Bd. of Review, 188 N.W.2d 343 (Iowa 1971).

References. 4 Cooley on Taxation §§ 1610 et seq. (4th ed. 1924); Stason, "Judicial Review of Tax Errors—Effect of Failure to Resort to Administrative Remedies," 28 Mich.L.Rev. 637 (1930); Throckmorton, "Judicial Review of Tax Assessments in Iowa," 26 Iowa L.Rev. 723 (1941); Cushman, "The Judicial Review of Valuation in Illinois Property Tax Cases," 35 Ill.L.Rev. 689 (1941); Young, "Taxpayers' Remedies, Illinois Property Tax Problems," 1952 U.Ill.L.F. 248; McKay, "Remedies for Defects in General Property Tax Assessments in Wyoming, The General Property Tax in Wyoming—A Symposium," 4 Wyo.L.J. 226, 240 (1950); Slomowitz, "Property Tax Administration in Florida and the Scope of Judicial Review," 24 Fla.L.J. 223 (1950); Morgan, "Remedies of Taxpayers to Correct Assessments of Real Estate Taxes," 14 J.Bar Ass'n of D.C. 476 (1947); Holbrook, "Judicial Review of Determinations by County Boards of Equalization," 14 So.Cal.L.Rev. 276 (1941); Faught, "Procedure for the Assessment of Real Estate for Taxation Purposes and the Review of Such Assessments," 6 U.Pitt.L.Rev. 231 (1940); Means, "Assessment Standards and Property Tax Equity in Florida," 17 U. of Fla.L.Rev. 83 (1964); Institute for Studies in Federalism and Lincoln School of Public Finance, American Property Tax: Its History and Administration, and Economic Impact (Claremont College 1965); Harriss, "Property Tax Reform: Is This Where We Came In?" Tax Policy (July–Aug.1966); "Report of the Committee on Model Property Tax Assessment and Equalization Methods on Property Tax Policy," 1964 Nat.Tax Ass'n Procs. 157; Schoettle, "Review of

Real Property Valuations in the Courts," 4 Int.Prop.Assess.Admin. 161 (1972).

ASSIGNMENT

Examine the statutes and decisions of your State or locality dealing with the scope of judicial review in ad valorem tax assessments. Where does your State fit *vis-a-vis* the scope of review, as compared with the cases discussed above, both as to overassessment and inequality cases?

(b) Valuation Methods and Problems

Notes and Problems

A. *Approaches to Valuation for Ad Valorem Tax Purposes.* There are several widely-accepted methods for determining the value of real property under the ad valorem tax. The "market data" method determines values by reference to "the price at which a willing seller would sell and a willing buyer would buy, neither being under abnormal pressure." See O. Oldman & F. Schoettle, State and Local Taxes and Finance 141 (1974). The "cost" method determines value by reference to the current cost of reproducing the property, less depreciation from physical deterioration and economic obsolescence, or by replacement cost. Replacement cost is the cost of replacing the structure with a similar one that has an equivalent utility. Id. at 146. In some States, reproduction cost is used merely as a ceiling on value. See p. 171 infra. The "income" method determines value by capitalizing the income produced by the property into a corresponding value for the underlying property producing the income.

Although the foregoing are the standard tests of valuation, in actual practice in tax certiorari proceedings it is common to introduce in evidence other facts that may have a bearing on value, such as the historical cost of the property less depreciation, or the historical cost factored for changes in the price of construction of the buildings since they were built, and the amount of the mortgage on the property, and the amount of fire and other casualty insurance, as evidence of the views of bankers and insurers as to the value of the property.

B. *Sales Price and Valuation.* A more or less recent sales price of the property, or comparable property, which is the touchstone of valuation under the market data method, is universally recognized as significant evidence in determining value for tax assessment purposes, and in some States is regarded as the best evidence. The key controversies over the use of sales price in determining value concern the weight that should be given to sales price and to the reliability of the market data that is relied on. In some jurisdictions, the rule prevails that the price paid in a fair sale is conclusive evidence of a property's value. See, e.g., State ex rel. Geipel v. Milwaukee, 68 Wis.2d 726, 229 N.W.2d 585 (1975). In other States, however, the rule is that the sales price is not necessarily conclusive of value.

The assessed valuation of a group of parcels of land in New Haven, part of which bordered on a stream, on which were buildings used for manufacturing and warehousing and an office building, was reduced by a committee appointed by the trial court (the procedure in vogue in Connecticut); the committee's report was accepted by the trial court. On appeal the City of New Haven argued that "prices realized from sales of comparable property in a normal market furnish the primary test of fair market value and this test is exclusive when it is applicable, as it was in the instant case." National Folding Box Co., Inc. v. City of New Haven, 146 Conn. 579, at 584, 153 A.2d 420, at 425 (1959). The court rejected this contention, holding that no one method of valuation is controlling and that the testimony of experts, reproduction cost less depreciation, capitalization of earnings, and the other evidence must also be considered. The committee had reached its valuation by determining that the best use of the plaintiff's property would be "as separate buildings or spaces in buildings by manufacturers who required relatively small areas," and it determined these values by the sales prices of other industrial properties in the area and by the net income an investor would expect to obtain on his investment in the property. The court upheld this method of valuation as a "justifiable one" for the trier of the facts. Is this an acceptable basis for valuation? Does it lead to excessive speculation and to the necessity of presenting evidence far afield from the property as it exists? See generally Annot., 89 A.L.R.3d 1126. In some jurisdictions, there is an expressed preference for the market data method, with recourse to the income or cost method permitted only when there is no reliable market data. See, e.g., Great Atlantic & Pacific Tea Co., Inc. v. Kiernan, 42 N.Y.2d 236, 397 N.Y.S.2d 718, 366 N.E.2d 808 (1977); Guild Wineries & Distilleries v. Fresno County, 51 Cal. App.3d 182, 124 Cal.Rptr. 96 (1975).

In a number of cases, a taxpayer who purchased property within a few weeks or months prior to tax day in an arm's-length deal has found himself obliged to pay real estate tax on a valuation considerably higher than the purchase price. See, e.g., Thaw v. Town of Fairfield, 132 Conn. 173, 43 A.2d 65 (1945); Des Moines Building, Loan & Savings Ass'n v. Bomer, 240 Iowa 1192, 36 N.W.2d 366 (1949); State ex rel. Hein v. City of Barron, 3 Wis.2d 127, 87 N.W.2d 785 (1958). If there is any evidence indicating that the market price was not paid for the property, there can be no quarrel with the result. Where, however, there is no such evidence, how can such a result be justified? Some courts take refuge in a slavish deference to the assessor's valuation. Is this an abandonment of the proper function of the courts? The difficulty with ascertaining market value (whether the statutory term used is "fair value" or "true value" or "actual value," in ordinary circumstances the terms all come down to market value) is that ordinarily there is no current market quotation for the particular property or a similar close-by property. In addition, real estate taxes have to be assessed and paid when there is no market for the property. For these reasons, a variety of techniques has been developed to work out values. Earnings, location, building costs, cubic foot value of improvements, original cost less depreciation, reproduction cost—all are considered. But if there is a current bona fide arm's-length sale of the very property being assessed between a willing buyer and a willing seller, unadulterated by special circumstances, query whether this elaborate facade of guessing at values should be resorted to.

An Oregon statute provides that property shall be assessed at a percentage of its true cash value, which "means market value." The State

Tax Commission's regulations call for using sales prices of comparable properties, where they exist, in order to determine "market value" and if none exist, other standard methods are employed. Finding no readily available data as to sales of canning machinery and equipment, the Commission assessed a canning plant's personal property by reference to replacement cost, less depreciation. The court set aside the assessment on the ground that there "was a market for the majority of the canning equipment," although it was "a highly specialized market, with which only a limited number of persons, who dealt in the business, were familiar." Portland Canning Co. v. State Tax Comm'n, 241 Or. 109, 404 P.2d 236 (1965). The absence of published price lists was not enough, in the court's view, to justify the use of other valuation methods. The court concluded that the State must either educate the appraisers regarding the market, or employ someone who is already familiar with it. The case is noted in 45 Or.L.Rev. 149 (1966).

C. *Valuation of Real Property During a Depression or Period of Inflation.* In Tremont & Suffolk Mills v. City of Lowell, 271 Mass. 1, 170 N.E. 819 (1930), the court considered the valuation of a cotton textile mill in 1926 several months before it was sold for $500,000. The taxpayer contended that the sale price should govern the value of the property for tax purposes. The taxing authority defended the higher valuation found by the trial commissioner based essentially on the ground that the depression conditions in the New England cotton mills during the period deprived the sales price of probative significance. The commissioner had declared that in depression conditions "there are no measures of value which ordinarily obtain under normal conditions," and it concluded that "in April, 1926 there was no real market for a cotton textile mill of the size and kind of the petitioner's plant." The Massachusetts Supreme Court, while disavowing the commissioner's extreme position, nevertheless sustained the valuation because it satisfied the statutory requirement that property be assessed at its "fair cash value." The court stated:

> It is the duty of the assessors within reasonable limits to seek light from every available source bearing on the "fair cash value" of all property to be assessed by them for purposes of taxation. Taxable value does not rest finally upon commercial disaster or prosperity attaching to a particular manufacturing plant as distinguished from other property of the same general nature. On the other hand, periods of great general business depression actually affecting the cash which in exchange for the property a willing buyer would give and a willing seller take, not as a matter of fleeting fluctuation but of matured financial judgment covering a measurably substantial time, must be regarded by the assessors and reflected in the assessed valuation. Times of panic sufficiently long in duration to affect fair cash value when sales occur must be reflected in assessed valuation. [170 N.E.2d at 826.]

Does your State statute contain any provision for the valuation of property during a depression, a recession? See N.Y. City Adm.Code § E17–8.b, under which real property is to be assessed at the value at which it would sell "under ordinary circumstances". (P–H ¶ 34,480–B, CCH ¶ 190–

577). If the existence of a depression must be taken into account by increasing values reached by the usual methods, should values be decreased during a period of inflation? If the issue arises during a period then regarded as inflationary, how can one determine what are "ordinary circumstances"? Some economists regard inflation as a more or less permanent characteristic of the current United States economy, even during periods of economic stagnation.

D. *"Creative Financing," Sales Price, and Property Tax Valuations.* During the late 1970's and early 1980's, high mortgage rates made it difficult for many prospective home buyers to purchase homes with conventional long-term, fixed rate mortgages. As a consequence, some real estate buyers and sellers employed different forms of so-called "creative financing" to finance their property sales. Under such arrangements, a seller might agree to accept a note with a lower interest rate, with a longer term, or with a different payment schedule than would be found in a conventional loan from a bank. Under such circumstances, the buyer might be expected to pay more for the property than he would have if the property were purchased for cash. The question has arisen whether assessors must make a downward adjustment in the sales price of property sold pursuant to creative financing when determining the value of such property for ad valorem tax purposes. The courts that have thus far addressed the question have generally answered it in the affirmative. See State ex rel. Flint Building Co. v. Kenosha County Board of Review, 126 Wis.2d 152, 376 N.W.2d 364 (1985); County of Washtenaw v. State Tax Commission, 126 Mich.App. 535, 337 N.W.2d 565 (1983). Indeed, the Michigan court declared that to do otherwise would violate constitutional strictures:

> [A] tax assessment system which does not consider creative financing is in fact unconstitutional. Two people owning identical pieces of real property, both worth precisely the same amount and both bought simultaneously, should not be taxed at different rates merely because they purchased their properties under different financing arrangements. As such, the Legislature has no power not to allow appropriate adjustments for * * * "creative financing" sales. [337 N.W.2d at 568.]

The Ohio Supreme Court, however, relying on the rule in the State that appraisals based upon factors other than sales price are appropriate for use in determining value only when no arm's-length sales has taken place, has declared that the fact that a taxpayer "obtained favorable financing does not render the sales price unrepresentative of true value." Columbus Board of Education v. Fountain Square Associates, Ltd., 9 Ohio St.3d 218, 459 N.E.2d 894 (1984).

E. *Comparative or Rating Chart Method of Valuation.* A Colorado statute provides that in determining the true value of taxable property, the market value shall be the guide. In assessing the taxpayer's property, located in a shopping center, the assessor selected a Sears Roebuck store in another shopping center, about five miles away from the taxpayer's property, as the optimum or model shopping center and assigned it a 100 percent value in seven categories, viz.: trade area, competition, drawing power, access, shape, parking, and main street frontage, and compared the taxpayer's shopping center with it. In selecting the Sears store as the model, the assessor relied primarily on the fact that there had been a greater number of realty sales in the vicinity of that store than around other shopping centers. The assessor disregarded possible sales in the immediate vicinity of the taxpayer's property in assessing the taxpayer. The court held this comparative approach or rating chart method of assessing the taxpayer's property was not valid. It was regarded as an unreliable guide for the ascertainment of the market value of the property. There was a dissent. May Stores Shopping Centers, Inc. v. Shoemaker, 151 Colo. 100, 376 P.2d 679 (1962).

F. *Reproduction Cost Less Depreciation as a Factor in Valuation.* In People ex rel. Parklin Operating Corp. v. Miller, 287 N.Y. 126, 38 N.E.2d 465 (1941), the Court of Appeals said:

> Evidence of income derived, or which can be derived, from real property may at times constitute more persuasive evidence of the price at which the income-producing property can be sold in ordinary circumstances than evidence of actual sales of more or less similar property under more or less similar conditions, for we know that in ordinary circumstances investors will pay for income-producing property a price measured in large part by the amount and certainty of the income which can be obtained from such property. On the other hand, we also know that an investor will not pay more for an income-producing property than the amount for which he could acquire at less cost property which would with equal certainty produce an equal income, either by purchase in the open market or by purchasing unimproved property and erecting upon it a similar improvement.

> For these reasons we have recently said in People ex rel. Manhattan Square Beresford, Inc. v. Sexton (284 N.Y. 145, 29 N.E.2d 654 [opinion by Conway, J.]): "The value of the improvement arrived at by capitalization of potential or actual income may well be weighed and considered but if it be more than reconstruction cost less depreciation, at least in the absence of extraordinary circumstances not present here, the latter still remains the maximum value which may be assessed upon the property." That case was decided after the order of Special Term in the proceedings we are now reviewing was entered. The rule stated in that case applies with equal force here. [287 N.Y. at 129, 38 N.E.2d at 467.]

Cf. Rosbroc Associates v. Assessor and Bd. of Review of the City of New Rochelle, pp. 157–65 supra; contrast Bornstein v. State Tax Comm'r, 227 Md. 331, 176 A.2d 859 (1962). See Gifford, "Should Replacement Cost Impose a Ceiling on Real Property Tax Assessments?," 26 J. Taxation 314 (1967).

G. *Computerized Mass Appraisals.* A computerized mass appraisal system, which developed different multiplication factors for different subclasses of property based on an analysis of the relationship between building characteristics and market price and between cash value and sales data, was held not to violate the State constitutional uniformity requirement or the Equal Protection Clause. State v. Rella Verde Apartments, Inc., 25 Ariz.App. 458, 544 P.2d 675, certiorari denied 429 U.S. 831, 97 S.Ct.

92 (1976). The use of computer-generated assessments in court is considered in Oldman & Youngman, "Current Legal Issues of Assessment Equity," 13 Assessors J. 31, 43–45 (1978); see also the New York modules developed after the decision in Hellerstein v. Town of Islip, Section 2, Note E, p. 145 supra.

H. *"Development Cost" or "Anticipated Use" Method of Land Valuation.* In the absence of satisfactory evidence of comparable sales of undeveloped realty, taxpayers and assessors have occasionally sought to establish the value of the *undeveloped* land by comparing it with another *developed* parcel for which individual lot sale prices are known. As one court has stated, "the question is the admissibility of evidence designed to prove the fair market value of raw land by 'backing into' that value, i.e., by deducting the estimated costs of developing that land to particular use from the income expected from the sale or lease of that land when finished for such use." Fruit Growers Express Co. v. City of Alexandria, 216 Va. 602, 221 S.E.2d 157 (1976). The court proceeded to uphold the exclusion of such evidence on the ground that it was "conjectural and speculative." 221 S.E.2d at 162. Compare West Hills, Inc. v. State Tax Comm'r, 255 Or. 172, 465 P.2d 233 (1970) (per agreement of parties, "development method" of appraisal proper if there is insufficient evidence of comparable sales). See American Institute of Real Estate Appraisers, The Appraisal of Real Estate 142–44 (1973).

References. J. Bonbright, 1 Valuation of Property, ch. 17 (1937), contains one of the best studies of the legal materials relating to property tax valuations; Advisory Commission on Intergovernmental Relations, Role of the States in Strengthening Property Tax (1963); Kress, "Suggested Legislation to Implement Advisory Commission's Property Tax Recommendations," 1964 Nat'l Tax Ass'n Procs. 103, 157; Doerr & Sullivan, "Taxation of Property in California," Report of Interim Committee on Revenues and Taxation to California State Assembly (1964); Tax Institute of America Symposium, The Property Tax: Problems and Potentials (1967) and The Property Tax (A. Lynn., Jr., ed. 1969) contain valuable collections of papers by leading scholars and tax administrators examining the major aspects of property tax policy and administration.

An extensive Note on "Tax Assessments of Real Property: A Proposal for Legislative Reform," in 68 Yale L.J. 335 (1958), is one of the best briefer studies of the cases, problems and methods of valuation employed; this note is particularly commended for students' use. See also Note, "Conveyance and Taxation of Air Rights," 64 Colum.L.Rev. 338 (1964).

The proceedings of the Annual Conferences of the National Tax Association, the National Association of Tax Administrators and the International Association of Assessing Officers typically contain papers dealing with current aspects of property taxation and afford a wealth of relevant materials with which lawyers are, unfortunately, frequently unfamiliar.

AETNA LIFE INSURANCE CO. v. CITY OF NEWARK

Supreme Court of New Jersey, 1952.
10 N.J. 99, 89 A.2d 385.

BURLING, J. Aetna Life Insurance Co., a corporation (hereinafter called the plaintiff) has appealed under Rule 3:81–8 from two judgments of the Division of Tax Appeals affirming assessments made by the taxing authorities of the City of Newark (hereinafter called the defendant) in this State, on real property situate in the City of Newark. The appeals were addressed to the Superior Court, Appellate Division, but prior to hearing there we allowed certification upon our own motion.

The appeals in this case concern assessments made for the tax years 1949 and 1950 upon what is commonly known as the Bamberger Department Store, consisting of land and improvements lying in the rectangular area formed by Market, Halsey, Washington and Bank Streets in the City of Newark, exclusive of that portion of the entire store area located at the northwest corner of Market and Halsey Streets, known locally as the Weiler property—the store area includes both the property subject to the assessments from which these appeals stem and the Weiler property. Plaintiff acquired the entire property exclusive of the Weiler portion from the store operating concern, L. Bamberger & Co. (hereinafter called Bamberger) in December 1945, and immediately thereafter leased to Bamberger the same premises for a term of 22 years with renewal options for subsequent periods which if invoked will extend the period of occupancy by Bamberger thereunder to the year 2034. The lease gave to Bamberger many of the rights and laid upon it many of the duties incidental ordinarily to ownership for the period of its leasehold. The physical structures constituting the improvements were erected in three parts, the first in 1912–13, the second in 1923–24 and the final portion in 1928–29. Subsequently modernization and reconstruction of the premises has occurred in several respects, and the lessee conducts therein an extensive merchandising business.

The plaintiff's property which constitutes a considerable portion of the above described Bamberger store premises was assessed for the tax year 1949 at a valuation of $3,018,800 for land and $5,549,700 for improvements, and for the tax year 1950 at the identical figures. The plaintiff appealed from both assessments to the Essex County Board of Taxation. The county board dismissed the appeals and the plaintiff thereupon pursued its statutory right of appeal to the Division of Tax Appeals, Department of the Treasury, State of New Jersey. The appeals were consolidated and hearings were had on the consolidated appeals before the Division of Tax Appeals. On November 23, 1951, the Division of Tax Appeals entered judgments on both appeals, affirming the assessments at the amount levied by the defendant and dismissing the appeals. The plaintiff then appealed both said judgments to the Superior Court, Appellate Division, which on January 7, 1952 ordered the appeals consolidated. Prior to hearing there we allowed certification of the consolidated appeals upon our own motion, as hereinbefore stated.

* * *

On the merits in this case the first question involved is whether the Division of Tax Appeals correctly applied the principles of law relating to the presumption of correctness of an assessment for tax purposes and the burden of proof in reviewing the assessments. The settled rule is that there is a presumption that an assessment made by the proper authority is correct and the burden of proof is on the taxpayer to show otherwise. L. Bamberger & Co. v. Division of Tax Appeals, supra (1 N.J., at page 159, 62 A.2d 389). And the taxpayer has not met this burden unless he has presented the appellate tribunal with sufficient competent evidence to overcome the presumption, that is, to establish a true valuation of the property at variance with the assessment. Riverview Gardens v. North Arlington Borough, 9 N.J. 167, 175, 87 A.2d 425 (1952). In other words, it is not sufficient for the taxpayer merely to introduce evidence: the presumption stands until sufficient competent evidence is adduced to prove a true valuation different from the assessment. Such evidence must be definite, positive and certain in quality and quantity to overcome the presumption. Central R.R. Co. of N.J. v. State Tax Dept., 112 N.J.L. 5, 8, 169 A. 489 (E. & A.1933).

The next questions involved include those relating to the determination of the Division of Tax Appeals as to the true value of the plaintiff's property, including the sufficiency and competency, or probative value, of the plaintiff's proofs.

Of the formulae for determination of "fair value" upon which evidence was adduced or proffered by the plaintiff in the proceedings before the Division of Tax Appeals was one relating to computation of value of the improvements on the land by a method of capitalization of actual current and prospective rental income under the lease between Aetna (owner) and L. Bamberger & Co. (lessee). Another formula was designed to prove "fair value" of the subject property by a method of capitalization of income based upon a percentage of gross sales, computed by application in part of a real estate expense factor derived from statistical analyses known as the "Harvard Studies." The plaintiff contends that the Division of Tax Appeals erred in holding that plaintiff failed to carry the burden of proof, arguing that the Division improperly disregarded the plaintiff's "uncontroverted" evidence of true value asserted on these two bases.

While it is necessary to treat these two classifications of evidence separately in determining their probative value, which in this case we find to be inconsequential, in general we recognize and reaffirm the law of this State that rental income may be a relevant factor in reaching true value of real estate for tax assessment purposes. * * *

But mathematical calculations in appraisals, though made in the best of faith, can lead to divergent results and should be closely scrutinized. * * *

Upon the actual rental basis, the plaintiff introduced experts' appraisals and supporting testimony based upon the existing long term lease between the plaintiff and its lessee, Bamberger. Under the circumstances of this case, the lease in question is a net rental lease. In other words, the lessee, Bamberger, has practically all the duties and responsibilities of an owner, by paying in addition to a graduated net rental over the 22 year term of the lease, and as additional rental real estate taxes, assessments, water rates, meter and other governmental charges which occur during the term of the lease; [it] also has the duty to keep the improvements in good and substantial order and repair. See L. Bamberger & Co. v. Division of Tax Appeals, supra (1 N.J., at page 154, 62 A.2d 389).

The plaintiff's experts reached their valuations by a capitalization formula including only the net rental to the owner. When it is recalled that under the statute the full and fair value of the property must be based upon such price as in the opinion of the assessor "it would sell for at a fair and bona fide sale by private contract," Riverview Gardens v. North Arlington Borough, supra (9 N.J., at page 175, 87 A.2d at page 429), it must be seen that this basis as asserted by the plaintiff under the circumstances of this case is not reliable. A purchaser of real property ordinarily understands that he will pay real estate taxes thereon and of course will expect to receive in addition a fair income (if he purchases to hold the property as an investment for rental to others). * * *

When the actual taxes on this property (which are "additional rentals" to Aetna under the lease and would be included in an investor's study of gross rentals) are considered, it results approximately in a doubling of the rental basis for capitalization purposes. On this basis the value would exceed the highest appraisals introduced in evidence. Such a gross income multiplier formula, of course, is unreliable under the circumstances of this case, for here the gross income includes a variable factor, the existing tax, which is in turn the end result sought to be determined in these proceedings. The theory might be applicable under other circumstances, for instance where a property has a gross rental history which does not *rest* on the taxes actually paid. However, even in this case the theory does indicate a weakness in the plaintiff's appraisals for it demonstrates that a purchaser might be well pleased to acquire the property for investment purposes and it indicates the discrepancy between the net rental capitalization formula asserted under the lease in this case and the probable value of the property on a properly applied income capitalization formula.

Upon the basis of gross sales percentage other evidence was submitted by the plaintiff. The foundation for this evidence was the introduction of evidence of Bamberger's net sales, which over the period (1947–

1950) on which plaintiff's appraisal was based ranged from $52,946,000 (1949) to $57,011,000 (1948) averaged by plaintiff's witnesses to $55,308,000 per year, and calculation by application of a multiplier factor derived from the "Harvard Studies." The latter consist of a survey undertaken by the Harvard Bureau of Business Research with the financial cooperation and assistance of the National Retail Dry Goods Association. As related to this case the studies introduced concerned a real estate operating cost comparison representing rents, real estate taxes, insurance, depreciation and other rents (such as warehouse rents, taxes and insurance), and derivation of a percentage of owned department sales. The application of this formula was designed to show the rental value of the subject property for capitalization purposes to determine full and fair value. The plaintiff's exhibits, the product of the appraisers who testified in its behalf, include deductions from the real estate operating cost computation derived from application of the "Harvard Studies" percentage factor, of various items of real estate expense, including rental of the Weiler portion of the principal store property, other store properties used by Bamberger, two specific warehouses and other warehousing expenses and insurance. There was no endeavor, however, to show the relative proportions of the value of these items and of the subject (Aetna) property in the production of the sales upon which the computations were grounded. In the absence of such proof little consideration should be given to this formula, for in the event that the proportions of value to the business are not equal it is evident that the balance of the cost factor remaining after deduction of the real estate cost of other properties may well be unrelated to the true value of the Aetna property. Further there is no proof that the real estate costs of these other properties are reasonable. If not, if they should be the result of factors unrelated to the value of the properties, then full deduction thereof from the basic cost study figure would be unjustified in the effort to evaluate the Aetna property on this basis.

Further there is judicial authority to support a complete rejection of this type of evidence as a test for full and fair value of property for assessment purposes. For instance, in Somers v. Meriden, 119 Conn. 5, 174 A. 184, 95 A.L.R. 434, 435, 442 (Sup.Ct.Err.1934), it was held that evidence of financial results of the business conducted by the lessees was properly excluded inasmuch as profits or losses of a business are so commonly dependent upon causes other than the value of the premises in which it is conducted that, except in some instances as to public utilities, they are not evidence of that value. In Assessors of Quincy v. Boston Consol. Gas Co., 309 Mass. 60, 34 N.E.2d 623, 626 (Sup.Jud.Ct. 1941), it was held that "the general rule is that the profits from a business located upon the land are not a fair measure of the value of the land because the financial returns from a commercial undertaking are dependent upon so many material factors having no real relation to the land itself that the profits cannot be said to be derived from the land." The rule in New York State is to the same effect. People ex rel.

Hotel Paramount Corp. v. Chambers, 298 N.Y. 372, 83 N.E.2d 839, 840 (Ct.App.1949). In this State this rule has not been defined in detail, but examples of its application in general have occurred. See Hurd v. Cook, 60 N.J.L. 70, 36 A. 892 (Sup.Ct.1897); Griffith v. Newark, 125 N.J.L. 57, 13 A.2d 860 (Sup.Ct.1940). In the present case the theory asserted is a formula based on sales volume and therefore is subject to the variables of goodwill and management practices which are factors entirely foreign to the true value of the real estate as such. For this reason the evidence adduced in this category was neither competent nor sufficient to establish the fair and full value of the property.

* * *

The further point under this question involved is whether the lease in this case was of evidential value as a "condition" in which the owner holds the land. It is settled that property to be assessed is to be taken and valued in the actual condition in which the owner holds it, State v. State Board of Tax Appeals, 134 N.J.L. 34, 43, 45 A.2d 599 (Sup.Ct. 1946), and we may assume for the purpose of argument that a long term lease may be a "condition" in which an owner holds land. However, application of the theory in this case works to the support of the assessment, for the *gross* rental value of the property as subject to the lease as above discussed is indicative of a considerably higher value of the property than the plaintiff asserts, plaintiff relying on the net rental. Further the arbitrary figure set by the terms of the lease for valuation of the land and improvements as between vendor and vendee in the event of the occurrence of a contingency of condemnation in itself indicates (as it provides for the payment to the lessee of the balance of any condemnation award *over* those arbitrary values) that the plaintiff and Bamberger did not intend those values to represent the fair and full value of the premises. In addition, the values expressed in the lease represent a repayment of principal to the owner, i.e., they represent the sales price less depreciation and obsolescence percentage agreed upon between the parties, and do not include the rental value of the property. This has been covered *ante*. We are of the opinion that the Division of Tax Appeals did not err in its determination as to the probative value of the lease as a "condition" in which the owner holds the property under the circumstances of this case.

* * *

The plaintiff also asserts that the Division of Tax Appeals failed to give probative value to the plaintiff's book value of the property. Under all the facts of this case, we find no merit in the plaintiff's contention. It is also to be noted that the tax history of this property, while not conclusive, is evidential and lends support to the judgments of the Division of Tax Appeals. Cf. L. Bamberger & Co. v. Division of Tax Appeals, supra (1 N.J., at page 147, 62 A.2d 389).

* * *

CONCLUSION

The evidence in these cases supports the determination of the Division of Tax Appeals, although in some instances as hereinbefore indicated its conclusions are supportable upon reasons other than those advanced by it.

For the reasons stated in this opinion the judgments of the Division of Tax Appeals, consolidated for argument on these appeals, are affirmed.

JOSEPH E. SEAGRAM & SONS, INC. v. TAX COMMISSION OF THE CITY OF NEW YORK

Supreme Court of New York, Appellate Division, First Department, 1963.
18 A.D.2d 109, 238 N.Y.S.2d 228.

STEUER, JUSTICE.

The appeal is from an order confirming the assessments for tax purposes for the tax years 1956–57 to 1961–62, inclusive, on the real estate located at 375 Park Avenue. * * *

The building in question is an unusual one in its nature, though not unique. It has these distinctive features which are the hallmarks of its class: It is generally known by its name (having relationship to the owner) instead of a street address; it is constructed of unusual and striking materials; its architecture is noteworthy; and it is well set back from the streets on which it fronts, the space involved being employed in distinctive decorative effects. The net effect is that this building, and the limited number that resemble it, gives up a substantial fraction of the land that might be built upon, with a consequent diminution of the rentable space, and its construction involves a cost materially in excess of utilitarian standards.

These buildings serve their owners in a fourfold way: 1. They house their activities. 2. They provide income from the rental of the space not used by the owner. 3. They advertise the owner's business. 4. They contribute to the owner's prestige.[1]

Just how a building whose construction is designed to serve these particular purposes is to be appraised, presents certain difficulties. The enhancement of the owner's ego is not a factor that can have a market value. In this city at present buildings in this special category, though few, are not unique. The time may come when they are so numerous that they become subject to sale, rent and the other transac-

---

1. In this connection they exemplify a well known economic theory (see T. Veblen, *The Theory of the Leisure Class*). Though the author did not foresee this particular manifestation of his "Doctrine of Conspicuous Waste", it comes well within the specifications he provides for its successful application:

"In order to impress these transient observers * * * the signature of one's pecuniary strength should be written in characters which he who runs may read. It is evident, therefore, that the present trend of the development is in the direction of heightening the utility of conspicuous consumption as compared with leisure." Modern Library Edition, p. 87.

tions of commerce, so that by trading a market price which reflects the extra-commercial aspect can be ascertained. Meanwhile in this proceeding it must first be determined whether a valuation based on the special character is necessary. It would not be necessary if the building, as a conventional office building, is of a value at least equal to the assessments.

The assessments for the last three years are the only ones in question. There is little material difference in the relevant figures, so a calculation for a single year will suffice to make the determination based on capitalization of net income. For the year ending July 31, 1960, the actual income was $3,005,510. This does not include any income for the space occupied by the owner. Petitioner's expert appraised this space as having a rental value of $927,850, giving a total income of $3,933,360. Petitioner further claims a vacancy allowance of 5%, which would not be unreasonable. The net estimated return would therefore be $3,735,692. Expenses would vary somewhat. Petitioner's average for the three years is $1,401,000. This includes an item of $288,000 in each year for tenant changes. The city has taken the position that this item is not allowable because the improvements are personalty and not a part of the realty, relying on Matter of 666 Fifth Corporation v. Tax Commission, 11 N.Y.2d 915, 228 N.Y.S.2d 670, 183 N.E.2d 76. We find the argument inappropriate. The figure represents a maintenance charge. Whether it has to do with realty or personalty is immaterial. We question the figure on a different ground. Petitioner, having the burden of proof, must justify its calculations. The record is not clear as to how the expert estimated this figure, nor what it includes. It may be gathered that the figure is the total expenditure on behalf of tenants amortized over a period of years—just what period is by no means certain. But the record does show that it includes expenditures of sums which might be considered so far beyond the range of ordinary tenant accommodation in a commercial venture as to be considered fantastic. Expenditures in excess of a million dollars went into the fitting of a restaurant. Some explanation would be required to show that these amounts were proper business charges and that there was a reasonable expectation that rents would be enhanced or made possible through them. In the absence of any attempt at justification, they must be rejected. This reduces the expenses to $1,113,000 annually, with a net income of $2,623,000 (figure rounded out). Using petitioner's capitalization figures for the land and the taxes thereon there is a residual income for the building of $2,186,000. Petitioner claims the proper capitalization rate is 8% (made up of 6% for income and 2% for depreciation) plus taxes. Aside from the claim, this rate is not supported, and the city offered no proof on the subject. These figures represent the conservative view of an investor's expectations and, while they might be subject to revision in the special circumstances here presented, the record is barren of any proof upon which any lesser rate might be adopted. Using these figures, the value of the building would be $17,802,000.

While this exceeds the petitioner's estimate by almost $4,000,000, it is still $3,200,000 under the assessment, and only about half the actual cost of construction.

It would seem to follow beyond the hope of successful contradiction that the traditional method of ascertaining value by capitalization is not applicable in this situation. Nowhere in the record is it explained how just two years before the period under review an experienced owner employing a reliable contractor and having the services of outstanding architects put $36,000,000 into a structure that was only worth $17,800,000. Such a startling result requires more than speculation before it can be accepted as fact.

The conclusion, therefore, is that petitioner proceeded upon an untenable theory and failed to show error in the assessments which calls for affirmance of the confirmation by the referee. It would, however, be unfair to leave the impression that a building of this sort presents an insoluble problem and that the owner is never in a position to contest the assessment of the city's appraisers. Nor is it necessary to await the day when the number of buildings of this kind reaches a point where they can be determined to have a market or rental value in consonance with their special features. Naturally, determination will have to await a proper presentation of the issue, but it will not be idle to indicate the lines along which presentation might be made.

Two possible theories occur. The first, and perhaps more obvious, is that advanced by the city here, namely, replacement value—the reasonable cost of construction less depreciation. To date this method of appraisal has been limited to two situations, in both of which the logic of its use is impregnable. The first is where the building is unique and would, if destroyed, have to be replaced (People ex rel. New York Stock Exchange Building Co. v. Cantor, 221 App.Div. 193, 223 N.Y.S. 64, aff'd, 248 N.Y. 533, 162 N.E. 514). The second situation is where the owner claims it as the highest value which can be put on the building (Matter of 860 Fifth Ave. Corp. v. Tax Comm., 8 N.Y.2d 29, 200 N.Y.S.2d 817, 167 N.E.2d 455). Neither of these categories embraces the issue here. But an approach to that method of valuation may be found through them. Buildings that are unique through their design for a special purpose which not only serves that purpose but renders them unsuitable for any other use are unsalable if the owner is the only one engaged in that enterprise or the number of persons is so few that the practical effect is the same. Likewise, the owner cannot replace the building by purchase. Consequently its value to him is the cost of replacement. Buildings so specialized as to have a restricted use, that is, a use by a limited number of people, are appraised similarly where there is an absence of proof of what such buildings sell or rent for (Matter of City of N.Y. (Kramer Realty), 16 A.D.2d 148, 226 N.Y.S.2d 288). While here the special features do not restrict the use, they do affect the value and the absence of proof of that effect could well lead to a valuation on replacement value as a last resort.

Another approach would be through the rental value of the space occupied by the owner. We have seen that the peculiar feature of this building, and the few that resemble it, is the identification in the public mind of the magnificent structure, and the consequent effect it has on the aesthetic improvement of the neighborhood with the owner. The public does not know or care about the actual ownership of the fee. The same effect could be produced if the building were identified in the public mind by the name of a tenant. In calculating the income of the building the additional increment that a tenant who could afford and would be willing to pay for such a privilege should be included. This increment could be added to the estimated rental of the owner-occupied space. Having determined this figure, capitalization of the result should produce a scientific appraisal.

The order should be affirmed, with costs.

* * *

VALENTE and EAGER, JJ., concur in concurring opinion by BREITEL, J.P.

BREITEL, JUSTICE PRESIDING (concurring).

* * *

Taxpayer has argued cogently that the value of the building should be determined in the usual way by capitalization of the net income, using 6% as the rate of capitalization and 2% as the rate of depreciation. The 6% rate of income capitalization, the only rate proven in the case, is a modest, presumptively proper, return in the absence of any proof that financial and real estate market conditions justify a lower rate. A commercial building is an investment that is being amortized and it is unlikely that a prudent investor would regard anything more than 50 years as a conservative basis on which to gamble physical depreciation, technological obsolescence, area deterioration, or other physical devaluation (Am.Inst. of Real Est.App., The Appraisal of Real Estate [3rd ed.] ch. 14, esp. at pp. 204–205; 1 Bonbright, Valuation of Property, ch. X). Hence, the 2% rate, in the absence of proof to the contrary, would seem reasonable. * * *

The recent cost of construction of this building stands out, however, as a seeming contradiction of the result derived by capitalization of net income. It is because of this that the City has attempted to resolve the problem by the concept of a limited specialty—and to base value on replacement cost less depreciation. At this point it is not necessary to reach that hurdle.

It has been held with respect to new buildings that the cost of construction is a highly significant indicator of value (Mtr. of 860 Fifth Avenue Corp. v. Tax Comm., 8 N.Y.2d 29, 32, 200 N.Y.S.2d 817, 819, 167 N.E.2d 455, 456 * * *

* * *

Given a profit-minded owner with available experience and resources, and a competent builder, the cost of construction is likely to represent the value of the newly finished product. Consequently, in the absence of credible qualifying explanation, for a new building the cost of construction is, *prima facie,* the true value. Indeed, because it would escape this fact, the taxpayer is in the anomalous position of urging that vast corporate funds were used to construct a building of much less value. This, if so, is never satisfactorily explained and does not do much credit to the sagacity of the corporate managers.

The maximum assessment for the building for the years in question was $21 million. The building, according to the City's examination of the taxpayer's books, cost $36 million to complete. Even if one were to eliminate the cost of all tenant improvements at taxpayer's figure of $9.5 million, contrary to what has already been concluded with respect to tenant-changes, there would be a residue of $26.5 million. Taxpayer's expert, without knowledge of the actual costs, gave $19 million as the reproduction cost of the building before depreciation, excluding all tenant installations. Adding only a part of the cost of the tenant installations it would match the assessment; adding all the tenant installations the cost would exceed the building assessment generously. * * * Consequently, in the absence of any satisfactory explanation to show excessive costs, the construction cost establishes value, *prima facie* —a value substantially in excess of the building assessment.

But the discrepancy here between capitalized rental income and cost of construction merits further analysis. The capitalized rental income as computed by taxpayer, using 6% as the rate of capitalization and 2% as the rate of depreciation, but including as an amortized expense the rejected tenant-changes, is $14.5 million. Excluding adjustments for tenant-changes the result would be $17 million—$4 million short of the building assessment, and up to $19 million short of the construction cost. Given a new building, prudently constructed for commercial purposes, the answer must be that the rental value assigned to the owner-tenant is too low, and, perhaps too, that the building as a whole bearing the name of its owner includes a real property value not reflected in commercial rental income. Of course, this would mean that, to begin with, the owner did not build for commercial rental-income purposes alone, and, as a consequence, capitalization of such income without adjustments produces a false result. * * *

It is self-evident that an owner who builds, as did this taxpayer, a prestige (monumental) building for itself, requires the leasing to other commercial tenants simply as an important way of bearing the heavy costs involved. The prestige building has a rental value not based alone on commercially rented space, but on the building's value in promoting the economic interests of an owner. Thus, such an owner is not wasting assets. Rather, it is investing in a real estate project that will contribute to the production of income in its principal enterprise. Since this practice is becoming a common feature of urban areas, such investment has ceased to be idiosyncratic and is undoubtedly translatable into market value terms. Typically, such value would be related to owner-occupancy of principal or prestige offices with choice space, the continued power to control its choice of space, and most often, identification by name of the building with that of the owner.[1]

On this view the rental value assigned to the taxpayer's space is understated, if there is merely charged to that space the prorated value assigned to other tenants. And, undoubtedly too, there is value to be assigned to the building as a whole, independent of commercial rental income, since the building, qua building, is also held for business purposes, unrelated to the receipt of commercial rental income.

At this time, it is not necessary to work out the values last discussed, so long as, the building being new, the cost of construction, otherwise unexplained, suffices to justify the building assessment. With the passage of time both the taxpayer and the City will have, with respect to future assessments, the burden of providing proof and market values, that may do. If not, reproduction cost less appropriate adjustments may have to be utilized to find the value of so much of the property as definably is not held for commercial rental income purposes—perhaps with the present ratio between adjusted original cost and capitalized commercial rental income as a starting point. In this connection it would be likely, although not necessarily so, that the prestige or monumental value of the building would depreciate economically at a much greater rate than the value attributed to the rental income potential.

It is unlikely, however, that a formulation based upon the physical ratio of owner-occupied space to commercially rented space would be valid. The reason is simply that an owner's quantitative need for space may be wholly unrelated to the economic value to it of the building as a whole, either as a prestige monument or as the seat of power to control the choice and use of space.

Worth discarding, although urged, is the argument that because a building does not occupy all of the assembled land, there is an inadequate improvement. This does not follow. The improvement is inadequate to the land only if that is not a sound economic way to construct a building. Indeed, a discernible trend in modern prestige building, for at least a quarter of a century, may make construction to the building line an inadequate improvement—economically. Exclusively utilitarian construction may produce more "rentable" space, but not more valuable space.

VALENTE and EAGER, JJ., concur.

---

1. Where, as sometimes happens, a major tenant's name is borne by the building, presumably, the rental paid reflects the name-bearing value. Or, in another situation, it may be that the tenant's name is used to enhance the prestige of the building; but in that case the rental income of the other tenants will reflect that value. The permutations are many, and whether the increased value attaches to the real estate or to business good-will may well, in some cases, present problems difficult of solution.

JOSEPH E. SEAGRAM & SONS, INC. v. TAX COMMISSION OF THE CITY OF NEW YORK

New York Court of Appeals, 1964.
14 N.Y.2d 314, 251 N.Y.S.2d 460, 200 N.E.2d 447.

CHIEF JUDGE DESMOND. * * *

Although we do not concur in everything said in the two Appellate Division opinions, we agree that for an office building like this, well suited to its site, the actual building construction cost of $36,000,000 is some evidence of value, at least as to the tax years soon after construction * * *. Petitioner urges, however, that for a building built to rent and be rentable, capitalization of net income is the only basis for valuation and that the building assessment here can be justified only by assigning an inflated value to the office space occupied by petitioner itself. This, says petitioner, really means that petitioner, having for its own reasons constructed an unusually costly and beautiful building, is being taxed ostensibly for building value but really for the prestige and advertising value accruing to petitioner because the "Seagram Building" has become world-renowned for its striking and imposing beauty. We do not agree with this interpretation of the opinions and order of the Appellate Division.

Usually, the assumed rent for the space occupied by a building owner would for purposes of capitalization of net rent income be computed at about the same rate as the rents actually paid by other tenants. But there can be many reasons why, as both of the Appellate Division opinions state, "the building as a whole bearing the name of its owner includes a real property value not reflected in commercial rental income" since "the owner did not build for commercial rental-income purposes alone, and, as a consequence, capitalization of such income without adjustments produces a false result" and, therefore, "one must not confuse investment for commercial rental income with investment for some other form of rental value unrelated to the receipt of commercial rental income". In other words, the hypothetical rental for owner-occupied space need not be fixed at the same rate as paid by tenants. This does not mean that advertising or prestige or publicity value is erroneously taxed as realty value. It certainly does not mean that a corporate sponsor of esthetics is being penalized for contributing to the metropolis a monumental and magnificent structure.

The order should be affirmed, with costs.

BURKE, J. (dissenting). We do not suggest that cost of construction is not relevant, that it may not be taken into consideration as bearing on value. That it may be so considered is an old rule recognized in many cases * * *. We do criticize as erroneous in law the holding of the Appellate Division—and also the holding of this court insofar as it refuses to meet the issue—that cost of construction is prima facie evidence of value in the case of "a newly-erected structure built especially for prestige and advertising value as well as for the headquarters use of its owner." (Matter of Pepsi–Cola Co. v. Tax Comm. of City of N.Y., 19 A.D.2d 56, 59.)

While the well-settled rule is that capitalized net income is the best measure of the value of commercial rental property[†] * * * it has now been decided that this measure must be displaced as "false" where the building is of such renown that the court feels that its owner must benefit economically thereby, over and above the rental commanded by the building. In such a case, it is said, the rental value of the space occupied by the owner-tenant, Seagram, must be valued not in proportion to the value of space occupied by the other tenants but at some higher value that reflects the business advantage accruing to one whose name is associated with such an outstanding and well-known building. Since the petitioner failed to so value its space it is held to have failed to carry the burden of showing excessive assessment.

* * *

The narrow and highly technical character of the rule applied by the Appellate Division may be highlighted by comparison with Matter of Pepsi–Cola Co. v. Tax Comm. of City of N.Y. (19 A.D.2d 56, supra) decided by the same court three months after the instant case. There, the court was confronted with a brand new structure quite similar in novelty to the Seagram Building in that it "is unusually distinctive and individualistic in appearance, [and] is set back approximately 14 feet on Park Avenue and 34 feet on 59th Street to provide on said sides a promenade and plaza ornamented with plants and shrubbery." (19 A.D.2d p. 57.) Yet the court held that it is not "in the same category as the Seagram Building, that is, a newly-erected structure built especially for prestige and advertising value as well as for the headquarters use of its owner." (19 A.D.2d p. 59.) Since both are new, held for business rental, and used as headquarters for the owner, the only difference is the presumed benefit accruing to the Seagram Company from having its name associated with an architecturally superior and well-known building.

"Value" under section 306 of the Real Property Tax Law is market value given willing sellers and buyers. (Administrative Code of City of New York, § 158–1.0). * * * In our view, this approach to value necessarily excludes any element that is unique to the present owner of a building. Any increment in Seagram's outside business enterprises deriving from public appreciation of the Seagram Building will not pass to a buyer of the building in a sale. Such an element would disappear if the building were sold to another investor, engaged in another business or in no business at all, other than real estate investment. The good will follows Seagram and cannot be regarded as real property value inherent in the building itself.

[†] The city offered no testimony as to economic value, i.e., capitalization of net income.

Of course, the prestige of the Seagram Building undoubtedly enhances the value of the building in any hands. This is undoubtedly real estate value—value which is transferable in a sale, and for which a buyer will pay. Such value also affects the rental commanded by the building. But, if tenants are willing to pay more for space in the Seagram Building than for similar space elsewhere, that is fully reflected in the capitalization of earnings. In turn, it would seem to follow that such capitalization adequately comprehends any increase in value that the building would bring in a sale—without resorting to concepts foreign to real estate value.

By the consideration of a so-called value element without regard to its place in light of the ultimate statutory norm of market value, and thereby displacing income capitalization as an acceptable measure of value and giving undue prima facie effect to cost, the Appellate Division has committed legal error for which the order appealed from should be reversed and the case remitted for reconsideration without regard to any supposed theory that the building is a specially built structure representing more of a real estate investment in its owner-occupant's business than a commercial office building.

JUDGES DYE, FULD and BERGAN concur with CHIEF JUDGE DESMOND; JUDGE BURKE dissents in a separate opinion in which JUDGES VAN VOORHIS and SCILEPPI concur.*

Notes and Problems

A. In 1976, the owners of the Seagram Building asked New York City to declare the building an official landmark. The request was unusual since landlords normally oppose having their properties designated as landmarks with the consequent restrictions it generally imposes upon their alteration. The New York Times reported that the request surprised Mayor Beame who told an aide that "it's the first time I've ever heard of anyone wanting their building to become a landmark." N.Y. Times, November 8, 1976. The Times also reported:

> Even at the current low point of the New York City office market, the 34 floors that Seagram rents to other tenants are 98–percent occupied at rents substantially higher than those charged at neighboring buildings. A spokesman for the company said yesterday that "we have turned away several tenants because we simply didn't have room for them." [Id.]

Youngman, "Defining and Valuing the Base of the Property Tax," 58 Wash.L.Rev. 713 (1983), characterizes the dilemma which arose in *Seagram* as the divergence between cost and income data not explicable as the result of mistaken planning. Id. at 762. The most serious problem apparent in *Seagram* is the potential inclusion of nonproperty values in the tax base. "If association of its name with an acclaimed landmark increased Seagram's sales but could not be expected to do the same for a prospective

* [The principal case is commented on in "Cost Method Proposed for Future Assessment of Distinctive Buildings Having Prestige Value," 39 N.Y.U.L.Rev. 528 (1964); 77 Harv.L.Rev. 1161 (1964); and 63 Colum. L.Rev. 1528 (1963).]

purchaser, should this effect enhance value for property tax purposes?" Id. at 763.

B. *Income as a Factor in Valuation.* For some years the trend in valuing properties for investment, rate making, and estate and inheritance tax purposes, and in bankruptcy and Securities and Exchange Commission Utility Holding Company Act proceedings, has been to give increasing weight to earnings. That earnings are a significant tool in measuring real property values is attested by the experience of every investor in real property. As the court points out in the *Aetna* case, a part of the earnings of a hotel enterprise must be attributed to the furnishings, to management, to good will, and to other factors. Is management a significant factor in the operation of office buildings and apartment houses? Does the technique of valuing the land and of adding a separate value for the buildings, in order to obtain a total assessment, ignore the integrated character of a piece of property, the whole of which may have a greater value than the sum of its parts? Capitalization of earnings is being used increasingly as a weighty factor in real estate tax valuations of apartments and office buildings.

In People ex rel. 379 Madison Ave., Inc. v. Boyland, 281 App.Div. 588, 121 N.Y.S.2d 238 (1st Dep't 1953), the court said:

> Assessments cannot be made to trail behind every turn in the fortunes of real property. There are times when property must bear a share of taxation proportionate to value even though it may then have no income, or an income inadequately focused to true value. There are times when the full measure of ephemeral surges of increased income should not be reflected in assessments in fairness to the owner.

> But income is one factor which a court must weigh into consideration in undertaking to review, and to revise, the judgment which assessing officers have applied to their tasks. When a general trend of increases in values for an area is shown; when there is proof both of actual physical improvements to the structures and marked increases in depreciated reconstruction costs; and, finally, when there are dramatic increases in net income which appear sustained rather than spasmodic, the changes reflected in the decision of the assessors should be reflected also in the order of the court. [281 A.D. at 590, 121 N.Y.S.2d at 241.]

What should be the proper method for determining the market value of a shopping center consisting of 50 acres of land on which 70 commercial stores, located in three building units, are erected? In deciding the proper assessment process for such property, the Pennsylvania court rejected reproduction cost less depreciation as a factor, declaring that it had no probative value for any purpose in fixing the fair market value of such improved real estate for tax purposes. The court was of the opinion that the capitalization of net income is, overall, the most scientific and accurate method of finding the fair market value of a purely commercial property, such as a shopping center. Appeal of Pennsylvania's Northern Lights Shoppers City, Inc., 419 Pa. 31, 213 A.2d 268 (1965). But see G.R.F., Inc. v. Board of Assessors of Nassau County, 41 N.Y.2d 512, 393 N.Y.S.2d 965, 362 N.E.2d 597 (1977), in which the court held that a department store's presence in a shopping center had value apart from income that use of the store would have brought, so that income capitalization did not adequately reflect the property's total value; the court sustained an assessment based both on income capitalization and on reproduction cost less depreciation. See generally, Gossett, "The Myriad Problems of Shopping Center Assessment," 4 J. State Tax. 113 (1985).

C. *"Contract" Versus "Fair Market" or "Economic" Rent Under the Income Method.* A North Carolina statute, in fixing guidelines which assessors must use in valuing property for taxes, includes as a factor "the past income therefrom, its probable future income." The taxpayer had entered into a long-term lease, yielding income substantially less than that of comparable income-producing properties in the vicinity. In rejecting the taxpayer's contention that his property was overvalued, since the value was not based on current rent from the long-term lease, the court held that the statute was flexible enough to include income which could be obtained by the proper and efficient use of the property. If income actually received is less than fair earning capacity of the property, said the court, earning capacity should be substituted as a factor rather than actual earnings. In re Property of Pine Raleigh Corp., 258 N.C. 398, 128 S.E.2d 855 (1963). In a later case, this reasoning worked in favor of the taxpayer. The actual rent being paid under a long-term lease was shown to have been "improvident from the point of view of the tenant," and the court upheld a valuation based in part on an income capitalization of a "fair rental" that was less than what was actually being received. In re F.W. Woolworth Co., 282 N.C. 71, 191 S.E.2d 692 (1972). Compare the cases on the valuation of leaseholds, pp. 126–27 supra.

The North Carolina decisions reflect the majority rule—that "fair market" or "economic" rent should be capitalized in determining the value of property burdened by an unfavorable (or blessed with a favorable) lease. The attraction of a rule of valuation based upon actual, realizable sale price, however, has produced some contrary decisions. For example, the Michigan Supreme Court has declared:

> [T]rue cash value must equal the fair market value of the property to the owner * * * [T]o equate economic income with hypothetical income in every situation where actual rent under a long-term lease is less than the prevailing market rental would be to ignore the effect of the lease on a prospective investor's judgment regarding the fair market value of the property. [C.A.F. Investment Co. v. Township of Saginaw, 410 Mich. 428, 302 N.W.2d 164, 171 (1981).]

The unfavorable lease cases and the questions they raise are thoughtfully considered in Youngman, "Defining and Valuing the Base of the Property Tax," 58 Wash.L.Rev. 713, 718–45 (1983); see also Koeppel, "Where Were You When the Contract Rent Fell Below Market," 5 J.State Tax. 69 (1986).

D. *Valuation of Subsidized Housing.* A problem similar to the "improvident lease" cases has arisen in connection with the valuation of subsidized housing. In Royal Gardens Co. v. City of Concord, 114 N.H. 668, 328 A.2d 123 (1974), the taxpayer owned a Federally subsidized housing project for low and middle income families. In exchange for the financing subsidy, the taxpayer was required to charge rentals below market rates and was limited as to the rate and amount of return it could realize. The trial court had approved a valuation based in part on an estimation of the rentals the project would earn in the open market. The taxpayer appealed contending that the valuation should have taken into account the lower rentals it in fact earned under HUD regulations. The New Hampshire Supreme Court held that the factor of Federal regulation should have been considered and it remanded the case. Two dissenting Justices argued that the result was inconsistent with the cases involving long-term leases which prove to yield below market returns under prevailing economic conditions. "In such cases, the taxpayer owner may not require the taxing authority to abate its taxes because the owner's bargain proves to be improvident." 328 A.2d at 126. Is the analogy to the improvident lease cases a persuasive one? The Rhode Island Supreme Court initially answered this question in the affirmative, but later disavowed its suggestion that the example of the long-term lease cases should produce a valuation of limited-income housing based upon full market rent. Compare Kargman v. Jacobs, 113 R.I. 696, 325 A.2d 543 (1974) with Kargman v. Jacobs, 122 R.I. 720, 411 A.2d 1326 (1980); see Youngman, Note C supra, at 793–95.

E. *Public Utility Property.* The capitalization of earnings method of valuation is widely used in assessing public utilities. For a discussion of some of the problems arising in the use of this method, see "Appraising Public Utilities: Choosing a Capitalization," papers presented by Kennedy, Martin and Gronuski in 1953 Nat.Tax Ass'n Procs. 417 et seq.; Chapman et al., "Appraisal of Railroad and other Public Utility Property for Ad Valorem Tax Purposes" (Nat. Ass'n of Tax Administrators 1953); McSpadden, "Appraisal of Public Utilities for Ad Valorem Assessment," 9 Assessors J. 66 (1974). Utility property is often valued by adjusting the actual cost of construction by the increase in construction costs during the intervening period, less depreciation on the adjusted cost. This method is designed to approximate reproduction cost less depreciation.

A company providing steam heat had suffered losses for a number of years; efforts to sell the plant had failed. Eventually the property was acquired by a corporation organized by the consumers being served at a price substantially below the depreciated book value of the plant. The assessors valued the property at historical cost, disregarding the acquisition cost as being a forced sale price. The circuit court set aside the assessment as excessive, but the Oregon Supreme Court reinstated it. State Tax Commission v. Consumers' Heating Company, 207 Or. 93, 294 P.2d 887 (1956). The court indicated that in dealing with a utility company, it is difficult to ascertain the price at which the property would sell under ordinary circumstances. Moreover, the court refused to follow the values fixed by the Public Utility Commission to be used for rate making purposes where different standards of valuation are involved. Cf. Staten Island Edison Corp. v. State Board of Equalization, 6 A.D.2d 369, 177 N.Y.S.2d 129 (3rd Dep't 1958).

F. *Valuation of Property Adapted to a Special Purpose.* In Kennecott Copper Corp. v. Salt Lake County, 122 Utah 431, 250 P.2d 938 (1952), the State Tax Commission had valued the taxpayer's 980–acre millsite and tailings dump at $45.73 per acre. Unimproved land in the same area used for grazing and similar to the millsite was assessed at $5.44 to $6.86 per acre and land similar to the tailings dump at $4.14 to $20.27 per acre. There was also a 632–acre tract of land similar to the tailings dump, used in harvesting salt, which was assessed at $66.16 per acre. After observing that under the Utah statute property is assessed at 40% of its "reasonable fair cash value" and that this term means "the price which would be agreed upon at a voluntary sale between an owner willing to sell and a purchaser willing to buy," the court recognized that the property had become valueless for grazing purposes and that there is no market for the property as a millsite and tailings dump. "But that does not mean that it is worthless or has only a nominal value. Plaintiff does make a profitable use of these lands * * * The Commission properly considered these elements in determining the assessed valuation." (122 Utah at 435, 250 P.2d at 940.)

In People ex rel. New York Stock Exchange Building Company v. Cantor, 221 A.D. 193, 223 N.Y.S. 64 (1st Dep't 1927), aff'd 248 N.Y. 533, 162 N.E. 514 (1928), the taxpayer contended that its Wall Street building housing the stock exchange had no value for no other taxpayer could adapt the building to its own use; and that "as a teardown proposition" the building is an "encumbrance which diminishes the value of the land," because the demolition costs would exceed salvage. The court rejected the notion that "simply because the property cannot be sold under ordinary circumstances" or because it has no "market value" that it has no value for ad valorem tax purposes. "Full value," "fair cash value," "fair value" and the other standards used in property tax statutes are not synonymous with "market value." It held that the building should be assessed at its reproduction cost, less depreciation.

The New York Court of Appeals, which has been called upon with some frequency to determine whether a particular property is a "specialty" to be valued by the reproduction-cost-new-less-adopted the following definition of that elusive classification:

> In Matter of County of Suffolk (C.J. Van Bourgondien, Inc.), 47 N.Y.2d 507, 512, 419 N.Y.S.2d 52, 392 N.E.2d 1236, we reaffirmed that a property is a "specialty" when it meets the four criteria enunciated by the Appellate Division in Matter of County of Nassau (Colony Beach Club), 43 A.D.2d 45, 349 N.Y.S.2d 422, affd. 39 N.Y.2d 958, 386 N.Y.S. 2d 886, 353 N.E.2d 849: "(a) [t]he improvement must be *unique* and must be specially built for the specific purpose for which it is designed; (b) [t]here must be a *special use* for which the improvement is designed and the improvement must be so specially used; (c) [t]here must be *no market* for the type of property * * * and no sales of property for such use; and (d) [t]he improvement must be an appropriate improvement at the time of the taking and its use must be *economically feasible and reasonably expected to be replaced*" (43 A.D.2d, at p. 49, 349 N.Y.S.2d 422 [emphasis in original]). [Brooklyn Union Gas Co. v. State Board of Equalization and Assessment, 65 N.Y.2d 472, 486, 492 N.Y.S.2d 598, 482 N.E.2d 77 (1985).]

In Tuckahoe Woman's Club v. City of Richmond, 199 Va. 734, 101 S.E. 2d 571 (1958), the assessment dealt with a clubhouse building which was restricted by covenant to use as a women's club. The assessor conceded that if the property were offered on the market, it would not bring more than $75,000 to $85,000 but he assessed it at $105,000 on the theory that it was worth that to the present owners. He reached that figure by relying solely on reproduction cost less depreciation, which he regarded as proper where no market value exists for property. The court set aside the assessment on the basis of testimony of the taxpayer's expert witnesses, real estate men and building contractors, as to what the property would sell for on the market. The court said (199 Va. at 740, 101 S.E.2d at 575):

> Depreciated reproduction cost may be an element for consideration in ascertaining fair market value, but cannot of itself be the standard used for assessment.

The Supreme Court of Washington held that a golf course which was built at considerable expense had no "fair market value" for real estate tax purposes. The court noted that the golf course, which was constructed and operated as an integral part of a residential community, was encumbered with restrictive covenants, subject to recreational zoning limitations, and had been and would continue to be operated at a loss. The court concluded that "[w]hen the use of land is so restricted that its ownership is of no benefit or value, the assessment for tax purposes should be nothing." Twin Lakes Golf and Country Club v. King County, 87 Wash.2d 1, 548 P.2d 538, 540 (1976). Accord: Tualatin Development Co. v. Department of Revenue, 256 Or. 323, 473 P.2d 660 (1970); cf. State v. Petrick, 172 Wis. 82, 178 N.W. 251 (1920), in which a golf course was assessed by reference to the value of farm land on the ground that "there is no sale for a golf course in or adjacent to a city the size of Oshkosh. Should the club disband or abandon the undertaking, the property would have to be sold for farming purposes." 172 Wis. at 84, 178 N.W. at 252. The valuation of specialty property is critically analyzed in Youngman, Note C supra, at 746–74.

G. *Zoning Restrictions and Valuation.* Suppose that property is restricted in its uses by present zoning ordinances, but that it might be put to more profitable use if the restrictions were lifted. Is such possible future use a proper consideration to be taken into account in valuing the property? Addressing this issue as a matter of first impression, the Supreme Court of Ohio concluded:

> Since the proper method of valuation in Ohio is based on the fair market value that the assessed real property would bring if sold on the open market, evidence of potential uses of the land under future zoning laws cannot be *completely* proscribed from the valuation process in *all* cases. Because the proper test of fair market value is what a willing buyer will pay to a willing seller, the record may show in a proper case that a willing buyer will pay more for property than its current zoning classification would justify. However, before the taxing authority may increase a taxpayer's assessment to reflect this willingness of buyers to speculate, the record must support such conclusion. [Porter v. Cuyahoga County Board of Revision, 50 Ohio St.2d 307, 364 N.E.2d 261, 265 (1977) (footnote omitted, emphasis in original).]

G. *References.* Youngman, "Defining and Valuing the Base of the Property Tax," 58 Wash.L.Rev. 713 (1983); Oldman & Aaron, "Assessment—Sales Ratio under the Boston Property Tax," 18 Nat.Tax J. 36 (1965); Annot., 96 A.L.R.2d 666; Proc.Third Ann.Inst. for Assessing Officers (Rutgers U.1957); Allen et al., "Use of Income Data in Determination of Real Estate Assessments," Thirteenth Nat.Conf.Nat. Ass'n of Assessing Officers 26 (1948); Lenox, "Use of Sales Data," id. at 90; Zangerle, "Historical Development of Scientific Assessment Systems," id. at 17; Rice, "Primary Problems in Property Tax Valuation," 17 U.Cin.L.Rev. 217 (1948), reprinted in 27 Taxes 135 (1949); Note, "Capitalized Income as a Factor in Valuing Realty for Taxation," 48 Colum.L.Rev. 638 (1948). For a consideration of the valuation of special purpose structures, see Nichols, "Two Problems in Tax Valuation," 24 B.U.L.Rev. 1 (1944).

AN EVALUATION OF THE PROPER ROLE OF THE COURTS IN REVIEWING PROPERTY TAX ASSESSMENTS *

The preceding materials indicate the wide disparities existing in the various states as to the role of the courts in reviewing the action of assessing officials or review boards. In this highly sensitive and controversial area of administrative law, there are fervent advocates of the view that the action of the administrative body to which functions have been delegated by the legislature should be subject only to the narrowest type of review and that the courts should not interfere with the actions of the administrative officer unless there has been impropriety in procedure or violation of substantive rules of law. Others, with equal conviction, argue that the protection of the individual in his dealings with government requires full-fledged review by the courts, trials de novo, and the setting aside of determinations that are not reasonably supported by the evidence. Between these two poles are varying shades of opinion, including the school that favors judicial intervention only for errors of procedure or law or the lack of substantial evidence to support the determination.

The proper relationship between the courts, assessing officials, and review boards cannot be charted in vacuo. The nature and scope of judicial review ought to depend on the character of the review provided in the administrative process. If the taxpayer is given a fair hearing to review the action of the assessor before a competent, impartial, and independent review board, where he is given adequate opportunity to present his evidence and make his arguments, then it is hard to see why the courts should do more than consider what are typically regarded as problems of law, errors of method, and impropriety in procedure. On the other hand, if the review offered in the administrative proceeding is a perfunctory, rubber-stamp type of hearing, conducted by the taxing agency itself, or by other departments or persons in the executive branch of government with responsibilities for budgets or tax collections, or other persons who, because of the nature of their

* Reprinted from J. Hellerstein, "Judicial Review of Property Tax Assessments," 14 Tax L.Rev. 327 (1959) and 1958 Nat.Tax Ass'n Procs. 429, as supplemented by later materials.

duties, are likely to tend to favor the administration, then there is considerable justification for a broad scope of judicial review.

In most states the administrative machinery does not meet acceptable standards of independence and impartiality. Typically, the action of the local assessors is subject to review by county boards of review made up of officials who are responsible for local budgets, or state tax commissions which function in the collection of taxes or the meeting of budgets, or appeal boards which consist of representatives of various executive departments. These boards are by their very nature partisan and cannot provide fair and impartial review. A survey of state administrative tax review procedures [70] disclosed that while there were 11 states that have set up boards of tax appeal which formally operate independently of the state revenue department, in three of these states, Michigan, North Carolina, and Pennsylvania, the members of the tax appeal board consist of the attorney general, the state treasurer or auditor, the secretary of revenue, or persons holding similar office. It appeared that there are only four states and the District of Columbia in which there were administrative review boards dealing substantially with property tax assessments that meet the elementary requirements of independence and impartiality—Massachusetts, New Jersey, Ohio, and the most recent addition, Kansas.[71] The published reports of the operation of these tax boards of appeal indicate that they have contributed significantly to providing adequate and independent administrative review of action of the assessors.[72]

70. Federation of Tax Administrators, "State Administrative Tax Review: Organization and Practices," Research Rep. No. 44 (May, 1958).

71. Id.

72. For a study of the Massachusetts Appellate Tax Board, see Dane, "Are State Tax Courts Necessary? The Massachusetts Experience," address before National Association of Tax Administrators, Coronado, Cal., June 11, 1958. Mr. Dane reports: "Despite some dissatisfaction on the part of officials of some municipalities whose assessments have been reduced upon litigation, it can be categorically stated without fear of contradiction that the Appellate Tax Board has served and continues to serve a highly useful purpose in the economy of the Commonwealth. Congestion of crowded court dockets by a flood of real estate tax abatement cases has been eliminated and the decision of tax controversies has been centralized in a single, tax-sophisticated body. Its existence has proved to be a definite economic asset to the Commonwealth. Businessmen have been found to be more willing to commence new or enlarge existing activities in Massachusetts when it has been pointed out to them that effective safeguards exist against arbitrary actions of taxing officials."

The study by the Federation of Tax Administrators, note 70 supra, at 11–12, and 14, disclosed salutary results as to the relationships of the number of appeals filed with tax appeal boards and the courts: "Among the agencies which have jurisdiction over property assessments, the Massachusetts Appellate Tax Board in fiscal 1957 had filed with it 6,328 appeals against local assessors involving both formal and informal procedures and 53 appeals against the state tax commission. The Ohio Board of Tax Appeals, in calendar 1956, had approximately 3,480 appeals filed with it, including 125 appeals from the state tax commissioner's assessments. The workload in New Jersey in 1956 totaled about 2,000 appeals, of which 1,857 were from county tax boards and most of the others from equalization rulings. * * * During fiscal 1957, when the Massachusetts Appellate Tax Board disposed of 4,339 appeals, of which 60 were appeals against the state tax commission, only seven decisions of the board were appealed to the supreme judicial court. Six appeals were decided by the court during the year, in four of which the board was sustained and in two, it was

Given such a tax appeal board, it would appear that the role of the courts should be limited, as is the case in Massachusetts and Ohio, to testing out the validity of assessing methods and procedures and to considering whether there is reasonable evidence to support the assessment. In such circumstances, there should not be trials or hearings de novo before the courts, for the entire record should be made before the tax appeal board and should be heard on appeal by a state appellate court on the record made before the board. And no appeal to the courts should be authorized, at least in the absence of extraordinary circumstances, until the administrative remedy before the tax appeal board has been exhausted.[73] Such a procedure seems to be most appropriate to provide adequately for the interests of taxpayers as well as the state, while at the same time establishing a proper allocation of functions as between the administrative agency and the courts. In recent years increased interest in the establishment of adequate tax review boards has been shown by the American Bar Association and the National Conference of Commissioners on Uniform State Laws. This has resulted in the preparation of a Model State Tax Court Act, which moves in the direction here suggested. It goes without saying that such institutional changes—setting up the structure of independence and impartiality—cannot of themselves ameliorate the difficulties; the key to the operation of boards of tax appeal will, in the final analysis, depend on the calibre, integrity, and independence of the personnel of the boards.

Given, however, the type of administrative review which exists in most states, in which there is either essentially a rubber-stamp approval by appeal boards of the action of assessors (except where there are obvious or extreme errors), or in which impartiality and independence of the executive arm are lacking, the courts should, and many courts will, find ways of granting broad relief to taxpayers. The solution to the problem of scope of judicial review of property tax assessments requires a solution to the problem of administrative review.

Finally, it should be observed that the establishment of an independent state board of tax appeals and the realignment of the interrelations of the assessor and the courts will not meet the needs of the average small taxpayer who feels aggrieved by his assessment. He shies away from a formal proceeding before boards of tax appeal or the

reversed. In calendar 1956, when almost 3,500 appeals were made to the Ohio Board of Tax Appeals (including property tax appeals), 30 decisions of the board were appealed to the state supreme court."

It is illuminating to contrast these results with the plethora of court proceedings in states such as New York. In New York City alone an average of about 10,000 new property tax review proceedings per year were filed for the years 1953–1956. See Annual Reports, 1954–55 to 1957–58, N.Y.C. Tax Commission. For the year

1975–76, 19,311 petitions were filed; for the year 1976–77, 19,201 petitions were filed, based on information furnished the authors by the New York City Tax Commission.

73. For studies of the problem of exhaustion of administrative remedies, see Stason, "Timing of Judicial Redress from Erroneous Administrative Action," 25 Minn.L.Rev. 560 (1941); Comment, "Exhaustion of Administrative Remedies," 39 Cornell L.Q. 273 (1954).

courts because of the need and expense of hiring a lawyer and his general distaste for the formalities and delays of such proceedings. In some respects, the single most important problem in the entire property tax system, in terms of equality among taxpayers and the dissatisfaction of the citizenry with the tax system, is that of providing an informal, inexpensive, and impartial forum where the ordinary citizen can have his day in court without lawyers, delay, or the paraphernalia of a judicial proceeding.

For that reason, a program for the establishment of adequate tax appeal machinery should include the institution of a small claims branch of the appeal board, which would be fashioned to meet the needs of the smaller taxpayer. Lawyers and formal records and appeals to the courts would thus be dispensed with. Some states have already developed procedures along these lines,[74] and we can learn from the broad experience these states and localities have had with their general small claims courts. A fair hearing before an impartial reviewer is indispensable if the citizenry are to feel, whether they agree or disagree with the decision, that they have had a fair hearing and that the property tax system, too, effectively operates as government by law and not merely by the caprice or favoritism of the local assessor.

References. Freedman, "Some Personal Reflections on the Establishment of the Philadelphia Tax Review Boards," 109 U. of Pa.L.Rev. 663 (1961); Shmukler, "The Philadelphia Tax Review Board: An Experiment in Municipal Administrative Law," 109 U. of Pa.L.Rev. 670 (1961); Krawood, "Michigan's Need for Tax Court and Inadequacy of Appeal Procedures Provided by General Property Tax Law," 11 Wayne L.Rev. 508 (1965).

SECTION 5. PROPERTY TAX EQUALIZATION

Equalization boards have been established in many States. The major function of such boards is to bring assessments made in separate taxing subdivisions of the State into line with each other for a variety of purposes. The problem of equalization has been beset with a great many difficulties. As the secretary of one equalization board has said, "inter-county equalization is like a mule—no hope of progeny and no pride in ancestry." Welch, "A New Multiple–Purpose Equalization Program," 1949 Nat.Tax Ass'n Procs. 260.

References. Maynard, "The Illinois Program of Equalization," 1949 Nat.Tax Ass'n Procs. 267; Note, "Constitutionality of State Equalization of Property Assessments in Illinois," 17 U.Chi.L.Rev. 93 (1949); Kress, "Operations of the State Equalization Board in Pennsylvania," 1949 Nat.Tax Ass'n Procs. 255; Myers & Stout, "Recent Trends in Property Tax Equalization," 3 Nat.Tax J. 179 (1950); Lee, "State Equalization of Local Assessments," 6 Nat.Tax J. 176 (1953); Welch "Inter-county Equalization in California," 10 Nat.Tax J. 57 (1957);

---

74. See provision in Ala.Code, Tit. 51, § 110(1) (1940), as amended, for "Expedi-tious and Economical Tax Appeals"; M.G. L.A. 58A, §§ 7, 7A.

Carr, "Property Assessments," 39 Cal.Bar J. 877 (1964); Smith, "Equalization of the Property Tax and Equity," 1963 Nat.Tax Ass'n Procs. 611; Lynn, "Report of the Committee on Model Property Tax Assessment and Equalization Methods on Property Tax Policy," 1964 Nat.Tax Ass'n Procs. 157.

SECTION 6. TAX RATE LIMITS

State constitutions are replete with a variety of provisions limiting the powers, of States and local governments, to borrow money and to impose taxes. The "careless use of state credit in the public works era of the 1830's and early 1840's, with its waste, extravagance, and thievery, led to greatly increased tax burdens and the demand for constitutional safeguards." As a result of the deep public distrust of State legislators and local governmental officials of the last century, there were adopted a whole crop of constitutional restrictions on the taxing powers entrusted to legislators. Perhaps the most common limitation, now in the charters of about one third of the States, is a ceiling on tax rates, typically limited to the ad valorem tax and utilizing an overall limitation.

Likewise, county boards, cities, towns and school districts are not free to increase their property tax rates at will. Limitations are placed on local levies both by State constitutional and statutory provisions.

The most common type of local tax rate restriction is the fixed limitation, varying usually between 10 and 20 mills for each class of government—counties, first class cities, second class cities, school districts, and so forth. Such a millage limitation is frequently graduated according to the assessed valuation or the population of the governmental units affected. This regular millage limitation may be exceeded upon referendum or, under recent legislation, upon review by the State tax commission or other central control body. In some States, instead of placing fixed millage limitations upon local levies, it is provided that any one year's levy must not exceed the levy of the preceding year by more than a fixed amount or stated proportion. Occasional instances occur of limitations of the total levy that may be made, or of limitations which fix a ratio between a local property tax levy and revenue received from other sources. Finally, many States limit particular levies for specific governmental purposes, as well as the total levy for each class of government.

The most recent development in property tax rate restriction is the blanket or overall limitation, applying not merely to the tax levies of particular classes of governmental units, but to the combined levies imposed upon property anywhere in the State. Beginning with West Virginia in 1932, a number of States incorporated such overall limitations in their constitutions or tax laws. Some students of the subject regard the tax rate limitations as a financial strait jacket for local governments and as an infringement on the home rule principle.

References. J. Jensen, Property Taxation in the United States, 45 (1931); Morrow, "State Constitutional Limitations on the Taxing Authority of State Legislatures," 9 Nat.Tax J. 126 (1956); Landers, "Taxation and Finance," in W. Graves, Major Problems in State Constitutional Revision, 228 et seq. (1960); Advisory Commission on Intergovernmental Relations, "State Constitutional and Statutory Restrictions on Local Taxing Powers," (1962); Remmlein, Tax Limitation Laws (Nat.Ed.Ass'n 1965); Advisory Commission on Intergovernmental Relations, Measuring the Fiscal Capacity of State and Local Areas (1971).

Chapter 5

PERSONAL PROPERTY TAX

Many of the problems considered in the chapter on the Real Property Tax, Chapter 4, are equally applicable to the personal property tax. The material here presented deals with problems peculiar to the personal property tax. Due Process of Law issues presented in the personal property tax field are considered in Chapter 11 infra.

INTRODUCTORY NOTE

Tax avoidance and evasion have since ancient times undermined the effectiveness of a general personal property tax. A. Buehler, "Personal Property Taxation," Property Taxes ch. 7 (1939). Intangibles, jewelry, silver, and other personal household furnishings are hidden from the tax collector, taxpayers grossly understate values in their returns, merchants shift inventories on the eve of tax day, and transfers are temporarily made into exempt securities.

The escape from personal property tax is not indigenous to America alone. Professor Seligman found the same weakness in the Athenian, Roman and medieval European tax systems. E.R.A. Seligman, Essays on Taxation ch. 2 (10th ed. 1931). And by the end of the sixteenth century in England, not five men in London were assessed at as much as £200 on their goods. Id. at 46. The English courts added to the escape of personalty from tax by sharply restricting taxes on intangibles. Id. at 53–54; see J. Bonbright, Valuation of Property 504 et seq. (1937).

"Modern nations have as a result almost universally shunned general property taxation and have contented themselves with applying property taxes to real property only." A. Buehler, supra, at 117. In this country exemptions have sharply reduced the taxable base. In many States, household furnishings and personal effects have long enjoyed substantial exemption. Intangibles have been exempted from the levy in a number of States, particularly as State income taxes have developed. Indeed, two States, New York and Delaware, have eliminated the personal property tax altogether from their taxing systems.

References. J. Jensen, Property Taxation in the United States chs. 7 and 11 (1931); Connolly, "The Effects of Personal Property Taxes on Business," 1949 Nat.Tax Ass'n Procs. 205; "Interim Report of Committee on Personal Property Taxation on the Taxation of Tangible Personal Property Used in Business," 1952 Nat.Tax Ass'n Procs. 76; Lynn, "Trends in Personal Property Taxation," in Symposium, The Property Tax: Problems and Potentials 321 (Tax.Inst. of America, 1966); Sanders, "A Defense of Personal Property Taxation," id. at 331; Miller "The Case Against Personal Property Taxation," id. at 342; Gwinn, "Taxation of Business Personalty," Report of Connecticut Tax Study Commission (1967.) The proceedings of the International Association of Assessing Officers are replete with reports and papers relating to personal property taxation.

SECTION 1. THE PLACE OF TAXATION OF TANGIBLE PERSONAL PROPERTY

Notes and Problems

A. *The Temporary Shifting of Property on the Eve of Tax Day.* In Brock & Co. v. Board of Supervisors of Los Angeles County, 8 Cal.2d 286, 65 P.2d 791 (1937), the taxpayer, which was engaged in the jewelry business in Los Angeles, shipped about half of its stock of jewelry to Hawaii shortly before tax day. The stock was returned to Los Angeles shortly after tax day, except for one bracelet that was left in Hawaii. The taxpayer's intention in taking the stock to Hawaii was two-fold: (1) to exhibit the stock to potential customers; (2) to reduce its personal property taxes in Los Angeles County. The California statute provided that property was taxable in the district "in which it is situated." The taxpayer contended that Los Angeles could not tax its jewelry because it was not situated in Los Angeles on tax day. The court disagreed. It acknowledged that "[t]he doctrine *mobilia sequuntur personam* [movables follow the person] is no longer a conclusive guide as to the situs for tax purposes of tangible personalty and that such property now, by statute or otherwise, is taxable in the locality where it has an established permanent situs, irrespective of the owner's domicile." The court nevertheless rejected the taxpayer's narrow reading of the term "situated" and construed the phrase as connoting "a more or less permanent location or situs." The court held that the temporary removal of the jewelry to Hawaii did not interrupt the permanency of its situs in Los Angeles, where it remained taxable.

The States have sought to cope with the temporary shifting of taxable personal property on the eve of tax day in a variety of ways. A Nebraska statute provided that personal property brought into the State after April 1, assessment day, and before July 1, should be taxed for the year unless the owner established that the property or the price paid for it had been taxed. This levy was upheld in Courtright v. Dodge, 94 Neb. 669, 144 N.W. 241 (1913).

A West Virginia statute dealing with the assessment of tangible personal property was amended to provide that all property should be assessed annually as of the first day of July, rather than December 31st. All of the taxpayer's property, which had been used as heavy equipment on a construction job in West Virginia, was removed from the State in December, 1961. In January, 1962, the taxpayer was assessed for the equipment located in the State on July 1, 1961. In sustaining the tax, the court held that the statutory assessment date (July 1, 1961), rather than the date the actual assessment was made (January, 1962), determined the taxability of property. The court decided that the legislature had the power to fix the time when property within its jurisdiction would be assessed. George F. Hazelwood Co. v. Pitsenbarger, 149 W.Va. 485, 141 S.E.2d 314, appeal dismissed 382 U.S. 201, 86 S.Ct. 392 (1965). See also Appeal of Plushbottom and Peabody, Ltd., 51 N.C.App. 285, 276 S.E.2d 505 (1981) (clothing manufacturer's inventory retained tax situs in State despite temporary absence outside the State for stitching and laundering).

B. *Taxation of Property in County Where "Situated" or "Located."* Controversies arise as to the particular town or village in a State in which movables are taxable. Thus, in City of Dallas v. Texas Prudential Insurance Co., 156 Tex. 36, 291 S.W.2d 693 (1956), an insurance company maintained its principal office in Galveston County and a branch office in the City of Dallas. The State constitution provides for the taxation of personalty in the county "where situated." The Texas insurance code provides that the situs of property of insurance companies is, for State and local tax purposes, its home office. The City of Dallas assessed the tangible personal property there located, contending that the statute applied only to intangibles and that to apply it to tangibles would be unconstitutional. The court set aside the levy, holding that the constitutional provision does not fix the situs of property; that this is left to the discretion of the legislature, which had acted within its power in fixing the situs at the principal place of business. Cf. Claborn Corp. v. Waxahachie Independent School Dist., 540 S.W.2d 544 (Tex.Civ.App.1976); Nacogdoches Independent School Dist. v. McKinney, 504 S.W.2d 832 (Tex.1974). A motor vehicle owner who had residences in two different Virginia counties was taxable in the county in which the vehicle was normally garaged or parked. County Bd. of Arlington Cty. v. Stull, 217 Va. 238, 227 S.E.2d 698 (1976).

In Assessors of Sheffield v. J.F. White Contracting Co., 333 Mass. 306, 130 N.E.2d 696 (1955), a domestic construction company with its principal office in Cambridge sought abatement of a property tax by the Township of Sheffield on equipment in the township on tax day. The equipment had been brought in for use in a local construction job with the intention of removing it as soon as the job was completed. The Massachusetts law provides for taxation of machinery by the township where it is "situated." The court abated the tax, declaring that personal property is taxable at the domicile of the owner unless it acquires a permanent situs elsewhere and that temporary lodgement or a migratory presence is insufficient to establish such a situs. A North Carolina court, on the other hand, upheld the assessment of an airplane owned by a foreign corporation on the ground that it satisfied the statutory requirement that it have "a more or less permanent location for the time being" in the State. Appeal of Bassett

Furniture Industries, Inc., 79 N.C.App. 258, 339 S.E.2d 16 (1986). Although the corporation's headquarters were located across the border in Virginia, the plane was hangared for approximately a year in North Carolina under a month-to-month lease.

A Wisconsin statute provides that personal property shall be assessed in the assessment district where it is located or customarily kept. The court held that this statute did not permit local taxation of steel, purchased for use in constructing public highways and temporarily unloaded along the railroad right-of-way for about three weeks before the tax assessment day, with removal of the property commencing four days thereafter. The property was said to have no fixed location within the purview of the statute. F.F. Mengel Co. v. Village of North Fond du Lac, 25 Wis.2d 611, 131 N.W.2d 283 (1964).

Under Florida law, the taxable site of road building equipment, temporarily in Sumter County, Florida, remained in Broward County, which was the owner's domicile. The Court was of the opinion that actual physical location of the personal property is not necessarily the same as its tax situs under the relevant Florida statute. Curcie Bros., Inc. v. Caruthers, 183 So. 2d 594 (Fla.Dist.Ct.App.1966).

For cases holding that a State may fix the place of taxation of tangible and intangible personal property within its borders without violating the Due Process or Equal Protection Clauses, see Columbus Southern Ry. v. Wright, 151 U.S. 470, 14 S.Ct. 396 (1894); General American Tank Car Corp. v. Day, 270 U.S. 367, 46 S.Ct. 234 (1926); General Motors Acceptance Corp. v. Hulbert, 317 U.S. 590, 63 S.Ct. 56 (1942).

C. In Capitol Construction Co. v. City of Des Moines, 211 Iowa 1228, 235 N.W. 476 (1931), an Iowa corporation maintaining its principal office in Des Moines, and carrying on a construction business, objected to a 1929 ad valorem assessment by the City of Des Moines of its cement mixers, graders, and other equipment. During the year 1928 the taxpayer had been engaged in concrete pavement jobs in Iowa, and about July 1, 1928, it shipped the construction equipment in issue to Illinois to complete a concrete pavement job in that State. On January 1, 1929, tax day, the machinery was in Illinois, but in July 1929, when the job in that State was completed, the machinery was again returned to Iowa for use on a contract in that State. The evidence showed that the taxpayer customarily moved its machinery from job to job in this same manner. The court upheld the Des Moines tax on the machinery because the absence from Iowa was only temporary. See also, Packard Contracting Co. v. Roberts, 70 Ariz. 411, 222 P.2d 791 (1950). Cf. Chapter 10, subd. C infra, where the issue is considered as to whether construction machinery more or less similarly employed may be subjected to use tax by a State into which it is brought for work on a particular job.

D. *Property Held under Conditional Sales and Similar Contracts.* In State v. White Furniture Co., 206 Ala. 575, 90 So. 896 (1921), the court held that when property is sold under a conditional sales agreement with reservation of legal title in the vendor until the full price is paid and there is an option in the vendor on default either to repossess the property or enforce payment of the debt, the property tax is to be assessed to the beneficial owner, not to the holder of a security title. The same conclusion was reached in General Electric Co. v. Andreen, 74 Nev. 199, 326 P.2d 731 (1958).

In some States property held under a conditional sales contract may be taxed to either the vendor or the vendee. Weber Showcase & Fixture Co. v. Kaufman, 45 Ariz. 397, 44 P.2d 158 (1935). Some courts have held, unlike the court in the Alabama case, that the technical legal title of the vendor is deemed sufficient to require the levy to be made on the vendor alone. Remington Cash Register Co. v. State Board of Taxes and Assessments, 8 N.J.Misc. 875, 152 A. 330 (1930), aff'd 108 N.J.L. 418, 159 A. 93 (1932).

A conditional seller of personal property was not subject to the Ohio personal property tax, since he was not the owner for tax purposes. He held legal title only as a security for payment, and he was required to transfer title to the vendee after a specified sum had been paid. Since the vendee had an obligation to accept and pay for the property in the future, with no option to return it, he was regarded as the owner for the purpose of the tax. Even though the sales contract designated the vendee as a lessee, this did not change the operative fact that he was a purchaser. Alzfan v. Bowers, 175 Ohio St. 349, 194 N.E.2d 852 (1963).

E. *Property Leased With Option to Buy.* In Alban Tractor Co. v. State Tax Commission, 219 Md. 593, 150 A.2d 456 (1956), the taxpayer entered into leases of construction equipment, granting to the lessee an option to purchase the equipment. The tax had been assessed to the lessor as the "owner" of the property. The court set aside the levy; the disproportionately large rental and the option to purchase indicated that the lessor's title was merely a security interest; the case was analogized to the vendor under a conditional sale, who is not taxed in Maryland. But see RCA Corp. v. State Tax Comm'r, 513 S.W.2d 313 (Mo.1974), in which the court held RCA taxable on data processing equipment leased to the Missouri Department of Revenue under a statute making "[e]very person owning or holding tangible personal property * * * liable for taxes thereon." The court rejected RCA's argument that its formal retention of title was merely a security interest.

F. *Merchandise on Consignment.* The California statutes subject to tax all "real and personal property * * * owned by such person, or in his possession, or under his control" on tax day. May the taxing authority collect the tax on goods held by a merchant on consignment from the owner or the merchant, as it chooses? See S. & G. Gump Co. v. San Francisco, 18 Cal.2d 129, 114 P.2d 346, 135 A.L.R. 595 (1941).

A District of Columbia tax is levied on "all general merchandise or stock in trade owned or held in trust or otherwise." The taxpayer, a retail jeweler, held most of his merchandise under "memorandum agreement" permitting display and sale. The court sustained a property tax, holding that consigned merchandise when dealt in freely by the consignee falls within the statutory definition. District of Columbia v. King, 243 F.2d 248 (D.C.Cir.1957); cf. S. & G. Gump Co. v. San Francisco, supra.

G. One method which has been used to induce taxpayers to disclose unassessed property is illustrated in a Florida case. A taxpayer complained of a personal property tax assessment and obtained a $10,000 reduction in valuation from the Board of County Commissioners. The County Tax Assessor, however, was upheld in his refusal to honor this reduction because the taxpayer in protesting the assessment had failed to comply with the statutory requirement that he file "a complete list of his tangible personal property under oath with the full cash value of the same." Sanders v. State ex rel. Shamrock Properties, Inc., 46 So.2d 491 (Fla.1950).

H. *References.* Annot., 2 A.L.R.4th 432; Liniger, "Exemption of Inventories from Ad Valorem Taxation," 1966 Nat.Tax Ass'n Procs. 499; Shapiro, "Assessment and Taxation of Tangible Personal Property on Farms," 18 Nat.Tax J. 25 (1965); Tarrant, "Taxation of Manufacturers' Inventories," in Symposium, State and Local Taxes on Business 165 (Tax. Inst. of America, 1964); Carter, "Problems in Regulation and Taxation of Mobile Homes," 48 Iowa L.Rev. 16 (1962).

SECTION 2. TEMPORARY CONVERSION TO EXEMPT PROP-ERTY ON THE EVE OF TAX DAY

Notes and Problems

A. In State ex rel. St. Louis Union Trust Co. v. Hoehn, 351 Mo. 382, 173 S.W.2d 393 (1943), the taxpayer had purchased on May 26, 1941, five days before tax day, $378,000 of United States Treasury bills which matured on June 4, 1941. Federal obligations are generally exempt from State and local property taxes. See Chapter 15 infra. The court declared:

> We think that our own Court en banc (State ex rel. Orr v. Buder, 308 Mo. 237, 271 S.W. 508, 512, 39 A.L.R. 1199) has properly stated the question and correctly ruled the matter as follows: "Is there any fraud, actual or constructive, in holding property which is nontaxable in a way to avoid taxation? * * * There is no fraud in doing a lawful act. A man may change his residence to avoid taxation. He may change the form of his property by putting his money in nontaxable securities, or in the form of property which would be taxed less, and is not guilty of fraud. * * * One cannot be guilty of fraud by doing what he has a legal right to do. A court does not inquire into one's motives for doing a lawful act." We think this is the only sound answer and that it is the rule that must be followed in this case. * * * In other words, the rightful ownership of nontaxable property may avoid taxes but such an ownership does not evade taxes.

Does the Missouri court sanction a form of tax avoidance that is unwarranted by the statute, which provided that "every person owning or holding property on the first day of June" is liable for property taxes? Not all courts have tolerated this practice. See, e.g., Mitchell v. Leavenworth County Commissioners, 9 Kan. 344 (1875), affirmed 91 U.S. 206, 23 L.Ed. 302 (1875); Holly Springs Sav. & Ins. Co. v. Board of Supervisors of Marshall County, 52 Miss. 281 (1876). In Shotwell v. Moore, 129 U.S. 590, 9 S.Ct. 362 (1889), the Supreme Court characterized this practice as "an evasion, and a discreditable one, of the tax laws of the state, if it could be made successful." Compare the cases considered in Section 1, Note A, supra.

B. A headline in the New York Times for March 3, 1966 reads, "Crews in Hollywood Racing to Beat Tax Deadline." The article declares:

Blue Monday, a bizarre phenomenon in the movie business, disrupts filmmakers' lives, plays hob with their digestion and, some charge, often hurts the quality of motion pictures.

The frantic race is to avoid an unusual personal property tax assessed on the first Monday of every March. When applied to motion pictures, the tax is based on the value of films held at the Hollywood studios on that date. Hence, if a studio has an $8–million picture in the final stages of editing the tax may run to about $200,000.

The movie studios go to considerable lengths to minimize this tax. Production schedules are normally planned so that films are sure to be completed and shipped out of the State before Blue Monday.

As a result, relatively few pictures are started in the early months of the year. Employment in the movie business plummets in January and February and many actors, extras and technicians assume they will be unemployed in this period. Once the tax deadline is passed all the studios come to life again and employment soars.

* * *

The motion picture industry has tried several times to get legislation passed that would eliminate Blue Monday. The industry is now worried by talk that the Blue Monday deadline will be erased and the tax will be assessed quarterly, thus giving the studios four deadlines to meet.

According to industry officials, the March date was set because it suited the purposes of the farmers, and legislators from agricultural areas who dominated the State legislature. Farm inventories are relatively low at this time of year.

The Los Angeles County tax assessors compute the tax on a sliding scale so that the tax keeps rising as the film nears completion. The worst predicament is for a film to be complete or in the final stages of editing since, at that point, the tax reaches its peak.

SECTION 3. THE TAXATION OF INTANGIBLES

A property tax on intangibles frequently results in substance in a second layer tax on underlying real and tangible personal property, which is itself subject to the same levy. This is most strikingly illustrated in the case of corporate securities. Conceivably, there may be sound reasons for this type of double taxation in view of differences in ownership of the securities and the underlying property, the advantages of incorporation, and the concentration of wealth in corporations and their security holders.[1] The taxation of mortgages on real and personal property likewise involves double taxation in the same sense.

The virtually insuperable difficulties in ferreting out intangibles by the tax collector, the double taxation problem, and other considerations

---

1. A similar problem is presented by an income tax on corporate income and the taxation of dividends to stockholders. See the discussion of this problem in Symposium, How Should Corporations Be Taxed? (Tax Inst. of America, 1946).

have caused many fiscal authorities to urge that intangibles be withdrawn from ad valorem taxation altogether, a recommendation which more than a third of the States have adopted. In other States specific intangibles such as bank deposits, mortgages secured by taxed domestic property, and securities of corporations which are otherwise taxed by the State have been exempted from the property tax.

Since intangibles are not subject to taxation in many States, the issue arises whether property should be characterized as tangible (and therefore taxable) or intangible (and therefore exempt). In District of Columbia v. Universal Computer Associates, Inc., 465 F.2d 615 (D.C.Cir. 1972), the taxpayer successfully contended that its computer "software" (programs consisting of punched cards) was an intangible, exempt from the District of Columbia's personal property tax. The taxpayer was also able to persuade the court that the software constituted 50 percent of the value of the entire package of hardware and software and that the assessment should, therefore, be based on one-half the purchase price of the entire package. Although the court was somewhat skeptical as to the accuracy of the allocation of values, it concluded: "[w]ith a different set of facts, King Solomon did no better in making a similar choice." Id. at 620. See Matter of Protest of Strayer, 239 Kan. 136, 716 P.2d 588 (1986), Chapter 10, p. 696 infra, for a consideration as to whether a computer software operational program is tangible property for ad valorem tax purposes.

Some States tax intangibles. Thus, to illustrate the extent of coverage, in Pennsylvania stocks, all moneys owing by solvent debtors (including debt evidenced by notes, bonds, or mortgages), and interest bearing accounts are taxed. Pa.Stat.Ann. § 3244, CCH ¶ 95–885. Kentucky taxes

> (a) Accounts receivable, notes, bonds, credits, non-domestic bank deposits, and any other intangible property rights arising out of or created in the course of regular and continuing business transactions substantially performed outside this state. (b) Patents, trade-marks, copyrights and licensing or royalty agreements, relating thereto. (c) Shares of capital stock of any affiliated company * * * and notes, bonds, accounts receivable and all other intercompany intangible personal property due from such company.

Ky.Rev.Stat. § 132.020, CCH ¶ 92–401b, P–H ¶ 33,458.

Notes and Problems

A. *The Situs of Intangibles.* In Kroger Grocery & Baking Co. v. Evatt, 149 Ohio St. 448, 79 N.E.2d 228 (1948), the question was whether minimum bank balances maintained by an Ohio-domiciled corporation in accounts outside the State had a situs in Ohio for property tax purposes. While intangibles are generally held to have a tax situs at the domicile of their owner, the Ohio statute excludes from its tax deposits "used in and arising out of business transacted outside of this state." Ohio law further provided that this exception applied only if the deposits were "withdrawable in the course of such business by an officer or agent having an office in such other state." Funds in excess of the minimum balances were withdrawn regularly from the accounts by employees outside the State and were sent to the main office. The majority read the statute as requiring the entire out-of-state account, not merely the minimum balance, be used for out-of-state purposes, and therefore held that the regular transfer of the excesses over the minimum balances to the main office took the accounts out of the statutory exception. Three judges dissented on the ground that the statute did not require that the full amount of the deposits be used "exclusively" in business in a State other than Ohio in order to acquire an out-of-state situs. They read the statute as requiring only that the minimum balances be so used.

B. A Kansas corporation with its principal office in that State was taxed in Oklahoma on the value of notes receivable arising principally from its purchases of installment notes from Oklahoma retail dealers in automobiles and appliances. The notes were secured by chattel mortgages. The taxpayer maintained an office in Tulsa to carry on this finance business but direction and control of the operations were lodged in the Kansas main office. The taxpayer maintained a revolving fund in a Tulsa bank on which the Tulsa office manager drew in buying installment paper and in which collections were deposited. The Oklahoma statute taxes "all intangible personal property" which is "deemed to have a taxable situs in this State"; included among such taxable items are intangibles owned by:

> A non-resident * * * foreign corporation * * * where such property has acquired a business situs in Oklahoma.

Holding that the notes were an "integral part of, indeed the essence" of the "continuing business activity conducted in this State," the court sustained the tax. Thompson v. Bankers Investment Co., 288 P.2d 364 (Okl.1955).

In an earlier case arising under the same statute, a securities brokerage company maintained offices in the State through which it solicited and handled purchases and sales for its Oklahoma customers; its principal office was outside the State. The court set aside an intangibles tax on the debit balances of local customers, finding that the principal business activities of the taxpayer were not conducted in the State, that the balances owing by local customers were merely incidents to the buying and selling of securities, and that the debts had not, therefore, acquired a taxable situs in the State. In re Harris, Upham & Co., 194 Okl. 155, 148 P.2d 191 (1944).

C. Where a foreign corporation conducted a life insurance business in Georgia and made loans through a local agent, who was employed on a salary basis and who maintained his own office in the State but was reimbursed for the office expenses, the loans were not subject to property taxation as a part of the insurance business, since the loan business was conducted without reference to policyholder relationships. However, the loans were taxable because a loan business was being conducted in Georgia by the taxpayer; the credits had become an integral part of the loan business carried on within the State. Suttles v. Northwestern Mutual Life Ins. Co., 193 Ga. 495, 21 S.E.2d 695 (1942). The court declared that this result could not be grounded merely on the fact that the debtors resided in the State; the State's jurisdiction to tax was not altered by the fact that the notes evidencing the loans were at all times kept outside the State.

D. Is a liquor license an intangible which is subject to property tax? See Roehm v. County of Orange, 32 Cal.2d 280, 196 P.2d 550 (1948), noted in 1 Stan.L.Rev. 370 (1949).

E. In connection with a government contract for war goods, a special bank deposit was established by a Federal agency on which drawings were to be made by the contractor as the job progressed. Is this an account receivable or solvent credit which is subject to personal property tax? See Timm Aircraft Corp. v. Byram, 34 Cal. 632, 213 P.2d 715 (1950). For materials dealing with the problem of intergovernmental immunities, as applied to taxation of claims against the Federal government, see Chapter 15 infra.

F. *References.* Ford & Wood, "Taxation of Intangibles in Michigan," Staff Studies of the Michigan Tax Study Commission 347 (1939); Roesken, "Trends in Ad Valorem Taxation of Intangibles," 26 Taxes 639 (1948); Blackburn, "Intangibles Taxes: A Neglected Revenue Source for States," 18 Nat.Tax J. 214 (1965); Aronson, "Intangibles Taxes: A Wisely Neglected Revenue Source for States," 19 Nat.Tax J. 184 (1966); Nielson, "Intangibles Tax Avoidance: An Empirical Study of Six Midwestern States," 34 Tax Policy Nos. 2–3 (Feb.–March 1967); Snyder, "Taxing the Unlanded Gentry: A New Trend in Taxation of Intangible Property," 4 Conn.L.Rev. 310 (1971). There are extensive annotations on "business situs for purpose of property taxation of intangibles in state other than domicil of owner" in 76 A.L.R. 806 and 143 A.L.R. 361.

SECTION 4. VALUATION OF PERSONAL PROPERTY

Notes and Problems

A. *Valuation of Inventories at Retail Sales Value or Cost of Purchases by the Retailer.* A number of personal property taxes calling for valuation at "cash value" or "full cash value" or "true cash value" have been construed, as applied to inventories, as calling for valuation at cost or market, whichever is lower. County of Hillsborough v. Knight & Wall Co., 153 Fla. 346, 14 So.2d 703 (1943); Appeal of Sears, Roebuck & Co., 74 Idaho 39, 256 P.2d 526 (1953). Cf. In re AMP, Inc., 287 N.C. 547, 215 S.E.2d 752 (1975). A series of Louisiana cases rejected this view and held that "actual cash value" means the price at which the goods would be sold by the retailer-taxpayer in the ordinary course of trade. Baker–Lawhorn & Ford, Inc. v. La. Tax Comm., 15 La.App. 189, 130 So. 642 (1930); Lee–Baker Dry Goods Co. v. La. Tax Comm., 15 La.App. 237, 130 So. 877 (1930); Peavy–Wilson Lumber Co. v. Jackson, 161 La. 669, 109 So. 351 (1926). This holding was, however, overruled by the Louisiana legislature, La. Act 1932, No. 78; La.Rev.Stat. § 47:1961 (1950), substituting the rule that inventories are to be assessed at an average value for a year at cost or purchase price plus carrying charges.

The average overall value method of assessing inventories over the entire tax year has been increasingly used by the States. Of the eighteen States that tax business inventories, nine assess them on the basis of average value. 2 CCH All States Guide p. 2022 (Chart); P–H All States Guide ¶ 1360. Thirty-two States, however, either exempt business inventories from property taxation or do not tax personal property at all. Id.

B. *LIFO and FIFO Methods of Valuing Inventory.* The New Jersey franchise tax act, applicable to both domestic and foreign corporations transacting business in the State, is computed upon that portion of the entire net worth of the corporation as is allocable to the State. This tax was enacted in lieu of an ad valorem tax on intangible personalty and the capital stock tax. In valuing the inventories of a corporation for determining corporate net worth for tax purposes, the New Jersey tax administrator substituted the FIFO (first in first out) method of valuing corporate inventory for the LIFO (last in first out) method, which had been used by taxpayer in determining its net worth. The FIFO method assumes that the first merchandise purchased is that which is first sold, while the LIFO method assumes the last merchandise purchased is the first sold. The court held that the taxing authority had not abused its discretion in making the change. The taxpayer's decision to operate on a LIFO basis for general accounting purposes did not compel the taxing authorities to accept the LIFO inventory costs as conclusive of fair value in assessing the tax. The standard of fair value for the assets was satisfied by the FIFO method of values, since it provides a reasonable reflection of the taxpayer's net worth with respect to inventories. R.H. Macy & Co., Inc. v. Director, Division of Taxation, 77 N.J.Super. 155, 185 A.2d 682 (1962). The Ohio Supreme Court likewise sustained the Tax Commissioner's use of FIFO rather than LIFO to value the taxpayer's inventories, despite the fact that the taxpayer carried its inventories on its books under LIFO, because FIFO produced a result more representative of the company's actual inventory practices. Champion Spark Plug Co. v. Lindley, 6 Ohio St.3d 56, 451 N.E.2d 514 (1983). See also Note C infra, with regard to inventory valuation in Ohio.

A Maryland court, however, rejected a taxpayer's use of FIFO, sustaining the State Tax Commission in its view that FIFO tends to distort current values by keeping in inventory the cost of goods based on earlier years' prices. The Commission was held to be justified in using the traditional LIFO method. May Department Stores Co. v. State Tax Commission, 213 Md. 570, 132 A.2d 593 (1957).

C. *Retail Inventory Method of Valuation.* Under the Ohio personal property tax, in the case of personal property used in business, the book value less depreciation is required to be listed; this book value is treated as the true value, unless the assessor determines otherwise. R.H. Macy & Co. used the LIFO method to determine the valuation of the inventory of its retail stores in Ohio. The assessor rejected this valuation, and, instead, used the retail inventory method, which employs a technique of using retail markup by departments. In upholding the method used by the assessor, over the taxpayer's objections, the court decided that the retail inventory method was more realistic and consonant with ordinary business practices than the LIFO method. It concluded that the retail inventory method tends to value merchandise on hand at current values. R.H. Macy Co. v. Schneider, 176 Ohio St. 94, 197 N.E.2d 807 (1964).

D. In assessing the value of a stock of liquor of a wholesaler, the Maryland authorities included in "the full cash value thereof" Federal tax stamps on distilled spirits. The stamps had been affixed by the distiller from whom the taxpayer had purchased the liquor. The court upheld the assessment, finding that the tax was payable by the distiller on producing the liquor and that the affixation of the stamps enhanced the value of the liquor. Pierce & Hebner v. State Tax Commission, 194 Md. 254, 71 A.2d 6 (1950). It rejected the contrary holding of the Louisiana court that the stamp tax was "in effect an imposition of a purchase or use tax on liquor, with the burden of paying it being placed solely on the ultimate consumer," which did not enhance the value of the liquor. F. Strauss & Son v. Coverdale, 205 La. 903, 18 So.2d 496 (1944). See also Dade County v. Atlantic Liquor Co., 245 So.2d 229 (Fla.1970) (agreeing with the *Pierce & Hebner* case, which it found to be "in accord with the weight of authority").

E. Obsolescence of machinery must be taken into account in determining its assessed value. J.I. Case Co. v. Chambers, 210 Or. 680, 314 P.2d 256 (1957).

F. Suppose stock is purchased on margin from a stock broker. Is the full value of stock taxed to the purchaser, or only his equity in the stock? See Putnam v. Ford, 155 Va. 625, 155 S.E. 823 (1930).

G. *Valuation of Leased Equipment.* The increasing practice of leasing special equipment manufactured by the taxpayer has raised difficult valuation problems, for often there are no sales on the basis of which value can be established. In State ex rel. International Business Machines Corporation v. Board of Review of City of Fond du Lac, 231 Wis. 303, 285 N.W. 784 (1939), IBM calculators leased to businesses in the City were assessed at $42,000 under a statute requiring assessment at "true cash value." The lessees paid some $10,000 a year for the use of the machines and the taxpayer's services in their use and operation. The assessed value was determined by taking the gross rental, subtracting an amount equal to the estimated value of the services, and capitalizing the remainder at 20 percent. There were no sales of the type of machine in question by the taxpayer or by any other manufacturer. The court, after reviewing the evidence, cited Wisconsin cases holding that while income is a relevant factor in determining value, it is not conclusive. It held that the value of the machines should be determined by the cost of manufacture to the taxpayer plus a profit to the taxpayer (determined by reference to the ratio of selling price to cost for the taxpayer's electric typewriters, which are sold), reduced by an allowance for depreciation. Does this holding in effect reject the view expressed in the merchants' inventory cases that stock in trade is to be valued at cost to the taxpayer and not its sales value to the vendor? That issue, as raised by the *International Business Machines* case, is discussed in Note, "Taxation—Inconsistent Assessment of Merchant Inventories in Wisconsin," 1956 Wis.L.Rev. 171. Compare State ex rel. National Dairy Products Corp. v. Peasecki, 2 Wis.2d 421, 86 N.W.2d 402 (1957).

The Xerox Corporation, most of whose equipment was leased rather than sold during the 1970's, has generally attacked assessments of its equipment based on sales price less depreciation, and has argued that the appropriate approach to valuation of its income producing equipment is to capitalize its rentals. Although Xerox has occasionally been successful in making such arguments, see Xerox Corp. v. King County, 94 Wash.2d 284, 617 P.2d 412 (1980); cf. Xerox Corp. v. County of Hennepin, 309 Minn. 239, 244 N.W.2d 135 (1976), more often than not its arguments have been greeted with the response offered by the Iowa Supreme Court:

> [Xerox] devoted almost its entire case to demonstrating that there were better methods of determining actual value than the sales price formula. Even if we accept that premise arguendo, it would avail Xerox nothing. Good or bad, the sales price principle must be resorted to if possible. We have found it was correctly used here, and therefore the formidable testimony concerning other methods never becomes relevant. [Xerox Corp. v. Board of Review, 298 N.W.2d 416, 419 (Iowa 1980).]

See also Xerox Corp. v. Department of Revenue, 114 Wis.2d 522, 339 N.W.2d 357 (App.1983), review denied 115 Wis.2d 704, 343 N.W.2d 811 (1983); Xerox Corp. v. Board of Tax Review, 175 Conn. 301, 397 A.2d 1367 (1978); Xerox Corp. v. City of Jackson, 328 So.2d 330 (Miss.1976). Compare City of St. Louis v. State Tax Comm'n, 505 S.W.2d 75 (Mo.1974) (affirming State Tax Commission's valuation of leased IBM equipment as a multiple of monthly rentals).

H. There are extensive discussions of personal property tax valuation issues, raising questions essentially similar to issues considered in connection with real property tax valuation in Chapter 4 supra, in Maytag Co. v. Partridge, 210 N.W.2d 584 (Iowa 1973) and Xerox Corp. v. City of Jackson, 328 So.2d 330 (Miss.1976).

SECTION 5. EXEMPTIONS FROM PERSONAL PROPERTY TAX

For a consideration of exemptions generally, see Chapter 14 infra.

Exemptions from personal property tax have gone hand in hand with the development of other forms of taxation. The development of State income taxes has accelerated the movement to exempt intangibles from personal property tax. In many States motor vehicles have been exempted from the property tax because they are subjected to special license taxes. Gross receipts taxes have long been imposed on railroads and other public utilities in a large number of States in lieu of property taxes on both realty and personalty.

The influence of special economic situations is also reflected in the taxes on personal property. Thus, Ohio, North Dakota, and Wisconsin exempt grain elevators from tax and impose, in lieu, bushel taxes. Several States on the Atlantic Coast and on the Great Lakes have withdrawn vessels from property taxation and have substituted tonnage taxes. Severance taxes on cut trees have been adopted in a number of States as a substitute for property taxes.

Notes and Problems

A. *Exemption of Machinery of "Manufacturing Corporations."* Massachusetts exempts from local taxation machinery used by "manufacturing corporations," and instead imposes a franchise tax of $5 per $1000 of value of such machinery. The Massachusetts courts have, in consequence, become the fountainhead for a stream of decisions defining "manufacturing." In Board of Assessors of Boston v. Commissioner of Corp. & Taxation, 323 Mass. 730, 84 N.E.2d 129 (1949), and Commissioner of Corp. & Taxation v. Board of Assessors of Boston, 324 Mass. 32, 84 N.E.2d 531 (1949), the court included among "manufacturing corporations" companies which are engaged in the importation of green coffee beans and their preparation for market by roasting and grinding; the preparation of soft drinks from syrup and carbonated water; the extraction of fruit juices from oranges and lemons; the making of butter, cheese, and ice cream; the cutting and edging of sheets of glass manufactured for use in windows, store fronts, table tops, and mirrors; the cutting and gluing of paper for use in printing candy wrappers, wedding invitations, and envelopes; the folding, cutting, stapling, and binding of pamphlets, books, and briefs; the scouring of wool; the cutting of mahogany logs and the processing of them into veneer and lumber; and the cutting, blending, and bagging of tea leaves. In holding that all these operations constitute manufacturing, the court quoted an earlier opinion as follows:

> Involved in the conception of manufacture is the implication of change wrought through the application of forces directed by the human mind, which results in the transformation of some pre-existing substance or element into something different, with a new name, nature or use. [84 N.E.2d at 136.]

The court held, however, that the pasteurization and homogenization of milk are not "manufacturing."

The justification for this all-embracing conception of "manufacturing" is the "legislative intent and purpose to promote the general welfare of the Commonwealth by inducing new industries to locate here and to foster the expansion and development of our own industries, so that the production of goods shall be stimulated, steady employment afforded to our citizens, and a large measure of prosperity obtained." Id. at 137. See also the exhaustive opinion by the Maryland Court of Appeals in Perdue Foods, Inc. v. State Dept. of Assessments and Taxation, 264 Md. 672, 288 A.2d 170 (1972), holding that a chicken processing plant was within the scope of the Maryland manufacturing exemption. The court reviews cases involving vegetable canning, butchering, fish processing, and flour milling.

B. *Exemption of Pollution Control Facilities.* During the 1960's, a majority of the States adopted tax incentives for the installation of pollution control facilities. The most common incentive has been the exemption of qualifying facilities from State real and personal property taxation. Facilities typically qualify for such an exemption if they are "primarily" for or for the "primary purpose" of controlling, reducing, or eliminating air or water pollution.

Taxpayers and State tax authorities have clashed over the interpretation of the "primary purpose" standard. Some courts have narrowly construed the exemption as applicable only to facilities whose primary function is pollution control without regard to the taxpayer's reason for installing the device. Thus in Illinois Cereal Mills, Inc. v. Department of Revenue, 37 Ill.App.3d 379, 346 N.E.2d 69 (1976), the court held that although the taxpayer had installed gas fired boilers to reduce the pollution previously caused by coal fired boilers, the tax exemption was not available since the primary purpose of the boilers was to produce heat, not control pollution. The dissent equated "primary purpose" with the taxpayer's "reason" for installing the facilities. This interpretation has found favor in other States. See Statler Industries, Inc. v. Board of Environmental Protection, 333 A.2d 703 (Me.1975) (whether a paper repulper which serves a manufacturing function qualifies for the tax exemption is a factual issue as to the taxpayer's reason for installing the device); Meijer, Inc. v. State Tax Comm'r, 66 Mich.App. 280, 238 N.W.2d 582 (1975) (taxpayer's reason for installing the facility determinative of tax exemption).

The nature of the pollution control facility has also determined the availability of the exemption. In Ohio Ferro–Alloys Corp. v. Donahue, 7 Ohio St.2d 29, 218 N.E.2d 452 (1966), the court held that a property tax exemption was unavailable for a smokestack which dispersed but did not eliminate any pollutants. See generally McNulty, "State Tax Incentives to Combat Pollution," 56 A.B.A.J. 747 (1970); Note, "Tax Incentives to Combat Pollution," 50 J. Urban Law 273 (1972).

C. *State "Free Port" Laws.* More than 35 States have enacted "free port" laws designed to encourage the shipment or storage of goods in the State. See CCH, All States Guide p. 2021, P–H All States Guide ¶ 265. Chart of State Free Port Law Requirements. These laws generally permit the temporary storage of goods in the State tax-free under specified conditions, including some or all of the following: the goods must have an out-of-state origin and/or destination; they must be stored in a public or other facility not owned by the consignee or consignor; they must remain in their original packages. But see Michelin Tire Corp. v. Wages, 423 U.S. 276, 96 S.Ct. 535 (1976), Chapter 7, § 1 infra, with respect to the diminished significance of the "original package" doctrine in connection with the *constitutional* immunity enjoyed by imports.

D. *References.* Jacobs, "Exemption of Tangible Personalty," Tax Exemptions 141 (Tax Policy League, 1939); Welch, "The Exemption of Intangibles from Property Tax," id. at 155; Feldman, "Exemption of House Furnishings from Property Taxation," 2 Nat.Tax J. 334 (1949); Browne, "Leased Machinery in Massachusetts—A General Property Tax Exemption Problem," 30 B.U.L.Rev. 191 (1950); Beck, "Exemption of Business Tangibles from Property Taxation: A Survey of Current Practices and an Evaluation of Their Influence on Industrial Location Decisions," 1959 Nat. Tax Ass'n Procs. 150.

Part 4

COMMERCE AND IMPORT–EXPORT CLAUSE RESTRICTIONS ON STATE TAXATION

Chapter 6

INTERSTATE COMMERCE CLAUSE RESTRICTIONS ON STATE AND LOCAL TAXATION

INTRODUCTORY NOTE

The Congress shall have Power * * * To regulate Commerce with foreign Nations and among the several States and with the Indian Tribes * * * [U.S. Const., Art. 1, § 8, Cl. 3.]

Conflict between the taxing powers and revenue needs of the States and the requirements of a unified, national economy is inherent in the Federal system. This clash emerged unmistakably in the last quarter of the nineteenth century, when the accelerated industrial transformation of the country gave new impetus to the expansion of trade, industry, and finance on a national scale. With the rapid growth of large-scale industry and the foreshortening of distances through modern transportation and communication, State lines lost much of their economic importance. At the same time the constantly increasing demands upon the States for schools, roads, relief, and other social services forced them to seek out every available source of revenue.

"As prices have spiraled under the increasing pressure of meeting our domestic and foreign civilian and military commitments, the revenue problem grows more acute.[1] It is costing the States and local governments more money to do their existing jobs, to say nothing of shouldering additional responsibilities.

* * *

"The States have understandably persisted in their efforts to get some return for the benefits they have conferred upon all business transacted within their borders, whether it be local business or interstate operations.

1. The excerpt is from Hartman, "State Taxation of Corporate Income from a Multistate Business," 13 Vand.L.Rev. 21 (1959); it is reprinted with the consent of the Vanderbilt Law Review.

214

"On the other side of the coin, the Federal Government is saddled with staggering military and civilian expenditure obligations both at home and abroad. The maintenance of a high rate of economic activity with resultant tremendous revenue yields remains a grim necessity. It is of vital importance, therefore, that our national economy not be strangled with tax barriers that will prevent optimum employment and production. The economic well-being of our nation, from which our gigantic amounts of revenue must come, furnishes urgent and impelling reason for insistence against action by one State to gain fiscal advancement at a cost that is too great for the economic health of sister States and the Federal Government. A wise reconciliation of these conflicting and competing demands of the state and national interests is imperative.

"Moreover, if one State in order to supply her fiscal needs or promote the commercial and economic well-being of her citizens may shield them from competition from sister States by the taxing process, we have opened a Pandora's box of troubles in the nature of reprisals and trade wars that were meant to be averted by subjecting commerce among the States to the power of the Federal Government.[2]

"Each new means of production and transportation has generated Commerce and Due Process Clause controversy relative to the taxing power of the States."

Consequently, "there is little wonder that there has been no end of cases testing out State tax levies," with the Supreme Court of the United States having "handed down some three hundred full-dress opinions" dealing with the constitutionality of tax measures challenged on Commerce Clause grounds, producing what the Court itself has described as a "quagmire" of decisions that have been "not always clear * * * consistent or reconcilable."[3]

A. A SURVEY OF THE COURT'S CHANGING APPROACHES TO STATE TAXATION OF INTERSTATE BUSINESS UNDER THE COMMERCE CLAUSE

SECTION 1. THE FREE TRADE APPROACH TO THE COMMERCE CLAUSE

The invalidation of State taxes on the ground that they conflict with the grant to Congress of the power to regulate interstate commerce is of comparatively recent origin. Case of the State Freight Tax, 82 U.S. (15 Wall.) 232 (1872) was the first decision invalidating a State

2. The Federalist, Nos. 7, 11, 22 (Hamilton); The Federalist, No. 42 (Madison); Madison, Debates in the Federal Convention of 1787, 10, 11 (1920); 1 Elliot, Debates on the Federal Constitution 106–18 (2d ed. 1888); 2 Farrand, Records of the Federal Convention of 1787, 308 (rev. ed. 1937); id. at 487, 547–48.

3. Northwestern States Portland Cement Co. v. Minnesota, 358 U.S. 450, 457–458, 79 S.Ct. 357, 361–362 (1959).

tax as a violation of the unexercised power of Congress to regulate the commerce.[4] This decision was the result of a protracted struggle within the Court [5] whereby the view was developed that State legislation may constitute a burden upon or regulation of commerce, in derogation of the power granted to Congress to regulate the commerce. Accordingly, State taxes may be struck down as violative of the unexercised power of Congress, as a negation of the Congressional power even while Congress remains silent. Of course, when Congress acts under its power over interstate commerce, State legislation in conflict with the Congressional action must yield. See p. 326 infra. Likewise, Congress may remove the barrier of the Interstate Commerce Clause by authorizing the States to act. Id. The great issues that have raged since *Case of the State Freight Tax* in the field of State taxation of interstate commerce have revolved about the extent to which the States may tax transactions, events, and subjects in interstate commerce in the absence of Congressional action.

Before the Commerce Clause was fully utilized for invalidation of State taxes, the Court used several other provisions of the Constitution.[6]

During the half century following *Case of the State Freight Tax* in which the Court held unconstitutional a State tax on freight levied at rates varying from two to five cents per ton, as applied to an interstate carrier, it invalidated State tax barriers to interstate businesses in a series of decisions which curtailed the taxing powers of the States. The rationale for the holdings was that:

4. Earlier cases either upheld the tax against attack under the Interstate Commerce Clause, [Nathan v. Louisiana, 49 U.S. (8 How.) 73 (1850); Woodruff v. Parham, 75 U.S. (8 Wall.) 123 (1868); Hinson v. Lott, 75 U.S. (8 Wall.) 148 (1868)], or relied on other clauses in the Constitution to invalidate. Hays v. Pacific Mail Steamship Co., 58 U.S. (17 How.) 596 (1854), which involved ships engaged in interstate commerce, invalidated a tax on grounds of extraterritoriality, the use of the Commerce Clause not having been suggested by the Court. As to Brown v. Maryland, 25 U.S. (12 Wheat.) 419 (1827), see note 6 infra.

5. Gibbons v. Ogden, 22 U.S. (9 Wheat.) 1 (1824); Cooley v. Board of Wardens, 53 U.S. (12 How.) 299 (1851). For studies of this controversy in the Court, see F. Frankfurter, The Commerce Clause (1937); F. Ribble, State and National Power Over Commerce (1937); P. Hartman, State Taxation of Interstate Commerce (1953). For the view that no State tax should be struck down as an infringement on the unexercised power of Congress to regulate commerce, see J. Hellerstein & Hennefeld, "State Taxation in a National Economy,"

54 Harv.L.Rev. 949 (1941). In preparing the discussion in the text, the authors have drawn heavily from the article cited immediately above (this material is used with the consent of the copyright owner, Harvard Law Review Association, copyright 1940, 1941), and from J. Hellerstein, "State Franchise Taxation of Interstate Businesses," 4 Tax.L.Rev. 95 (1948).

6. The Imports Clause, Art. I, § 10, cl. 2; Brown v. Maryland, 25 U.S. (12 Wheat.) 419 (1827), and Low v. Austin, 80 U.S. (13 Wall.) 29 (1871), both decided also under the Foreign Commerce Clause, Art. I, § 8, cl. 3. The Exports Clause, Art. I, § 10, cl. 2; Almy v. California, 65 U.S. (24 How.) 169 (1860) (water shipment between California and New York). The Privileges and Immunities Clause, Art. IV, § 2, cl. 1; Crandall v. Nevada, 73 U.S. (6 Wall.) 35 (1867); Ward v. Maryland, 79 U.S. (12 Wall.) 418 (1870). The Contracts Clause, Art. I, § 10, cl. 1; Wilmington Railroad v. Reid, 80 U.S. (13 Wall.) 264 (1871). The Tonnage Clause, Art. I, § 10, cl. 3; State Tonnage Tax Cases, 79 U.S. (12 Wall.) 204 (1870), and Cannon v. New Orleans, 87 U.S. (20 Wall.) 577 (1874).

* * * no state has the right to lay a tax on interstate commerce in any form, * * * and the reason is that such taxation is a burden on that commerce, and amounts to a regulation of it, which belongs solely to Congress. [Leloup v. Port of Mobile, 127 U.S. 640, 648, 8 S.Ct. 1380, 1384 (1888).]

> Interstate commerce cannot be taxed at all, even though the same amount of tax should be laid on domestic commerce, or that which is carried on solely within the state. [Robbins v. Shelby County Taxing District, 120 U.S. 489, 497, 7 S.Ct. 592, 596 (1887).]

Applying this approach to the Commerce Clause restrictions on State taxation, the Court set aside license, franchise, and privilege taxes on foreign corporations or individuals doing an exclusively interstate business within a State. Robbins v. Shelby County Taxing District, 120 U.S. 489, 7 S.Ct. 592 (1887); Leloup v. Port of Mobile, 127 U.S. 640, 8 S.Ct. 1380 (1888); Western Union Telegraph Co. v. Kansas, 216 U.S. 1, 30 S.Ct. 190 (1910); Atlantic & Pacific Telegraph Co. v. Philadelphia, 190 U.S. 160, 23 S.Ct. 817 (1903). The States, it was said, have no power to tax the "privilege of doing interstate commerce" because it is a privilege granted by the Federal Government. This holding had its origin in the doctrine that a State may not keep a foreign corporation engaged solely in interstate commerce out of its territory. Crutcher v. Kentucky, 141 U.S. 47, 11 S.Ct. 851 (1891); International Textbook Co. v. Pigg, 217 U.S. 91, 30 S.Ct. 481 (1910). To do so would impede the free movement of goods between the States which the Commerce Clause was designed to safeguard. From this premise, it is an easy, although not a necessary, step to conclude that a State may not exact a tax as a condition precedent to entering a State to do business. Therefore, in the silence of Congress, it was held that no State may exact a levy as a condition to commencing business. See, e.g., Leloup v. Port of Mobile, supra; Western Union Telegraph Co. v. Kansas, supra. When the issue arose as to whether a State, without exacting a tax or license fee as a condition to commencing business, could impose a general franchise tax—applicable to foreign and domestic corporations and to interstate and intrastate business alike—upon a foreign corporation doing exclusively interstate business, the Court held that such a levy likewise violated the Commerce Clause. Cheney Brothers Co. v. Massachusetts, 246 U.S. 147, 38 S.Ct. 295 (1918); Alpha Portland Cement Co. v. Massachusetts, 268 U.S. 203, 45 S.Ct. 477 (1925).[7]

(a) The Direct–Indirect Test of Validity of Taxes Affecting Interstate Commerce

While these decisions established an area of trade for the interstate business free of State and local license, franchise, and privilege taxes,

---

7. For a consideration of the early cases in this field, see Powell, "Indirect Encroachment on Federal Authority by the Taxing Powers of the States," 31 Harv.L. Rev. 572, 721 (1918), and "State Income Taxes and the Commerce Clause," 31 Yale L.J. 799 (1922); and see J. Hellerstein, "State Franchise Taxation of Interstate Businesses," 4 Tax L.Rev. 95 (1948).

the Court recognized at the outset that the Commerce Clause did not serve to invalidate all State taxation affecting interstate business. In seeking to draw a line between the prohibited and permissible areas of State taxation of interstate business and transactions and property employed in interstate commerce, the Court developed the distinction between "direct" and "indirect" taxes; only the former constituted "undue burdens" on or "regulations" of the commerce and therefore were held to run afoul of the unexercised power of Congress to regulate interstate commerce. Thus in sustaining property taxes on property of instrumentalities of interstate commerce—telegraph companies, railroads, express companies, and others—the Court declared:

> The tax imposed by the act in question affects commerce among the States and impedes the transit of persons and property from one State to another just in the same way, and in no other, that taxation of any kind necessarily increases the expenses attendant upon the use or possession of the thing taxed. That taxation produces this result of itself constitutes no objection to its constitutionality. As was very justly observed by this court in a recent case, "Every tax upon personal property, or upon occupations, business, or franchises, affects more or less the subjects, and the operations of commerce. Yet it is not everything that affects commerce that amounts to a regulation of it, within the meaning of the Constitution." [The Delaware Railroad Tax, 85 U.S. (18 Wall.) 206, 232 (1873), quoting from State Tax on Railway Gross Receipts, 82 U.S. (15 Wall.) 284, 293 (1872).]

In implementing this view of the Commerce Clause, the Court invalidated not only license, franchise, and other levies on the conduct of an interstate business (see cases cited above), but also taxes on the gross receipts from interstate commerce, Crew Levick Co. v. Pennsylvania, 245 U.S. 292, 38 S.Ct. 126 (1917); Sonneborn Bros. v. Cureton, 262 U.S. 506, 43 S.Ct. 643 (1923), and levies on transportation and communication companies and other instrumentalities of interstate commerce. Fargo v. Michigan, 121 U.S. 230, 7 S.Ct. 857 (1887); Philadelphia & Southern Steamship Co. v. Pennsylvania, 122 U.S. 326, 7 S.Ct. 1118 (1887); Western Union Telegraph Co. v. Pennsylvania, 128 U.S. 39, 9 S.Ct. 6 (1888); Galveston, H. & S.A. Ry. Co. v. Texas, 210 U.S. 217, 28 S.Ct. 638 (1908); Fisher's Blend Station, Inc. v. State Tax Commission, 297 U.S. 650, 56 S.Ct. 608 (1936). Levies that discriminated against interstate commerce were likewise condemned under the Commerce Clause. Welton v. Missouri, 91 U.S. 275 (1875); Robbins v. Shelby County Taxing District, 120 U.S. 489, 7 S.Ct. 592 (1887); Caldwell v. North Carolina, 187 U.S. 622, 23 S.Ct. 229 (1903); Rearick v. Pennsylvania, 203 U.S. 507, 27 S.Ct. 159 (1906); Real Silk Hosiery Mills v. Portland, 268 U.S. 325, 45 S.Ct. 525 (1925); Nippert v. City of Richmond, 327 U.S. 416, 66 S.Ct. 586 (1946).

Property taxes and taxes in lieu of property taxes were, however, upheld as indirect levies as applied to all businesses, including instrumentalities of the commerce. Cleveland, Cincinnati, Chicago & St. Louis Railway Co. v. Backus, 154 U.S. 439, 14 S.Ct. 1122 (1894); Postal

Telegraph Cable Co. v. Adams, 155 U.S. 688, 15 S.Ct. 268 (1895); Pullman's Palace Car Co. v. Pennsylvania, 141 U.S. 18, 11 S.Ct. 876 (1891); Sanford v. Poe, 165 U.S. 194, 17 S.Ct. 305 (1897).

SECTION 2. THE DEVELOPMENT OF THE MULTIPLE TAXA- TION DOCTRINE

The Great Depression and the wave of political liberalism which swept the country from the first Roosevelt administration to World War II had a powerful impact on the Supreme Court. In the field of State taxation, it was inevitable that the new realpolitik, the re-evaluation of the roles of big and small businesses in our economy, and the increasing reluctance of the Court to thwart the States in meeting modern economic conditions should result in a broadening of the power of the States to tax businesses carried on across State lines. A new cycle in the history of the taxing power of the States under the Commerce Clause was opened.

The chief architect of the new juridical structure was Justice Stone. He swept away the traditional view that under the Commerce Clause "interstate commerce may not be taxed at all" and that the Commerce Clause created an area of trade free of State taxation. In its place, he erected the multiple taxation doctrine, under which interstate business-es were no longer immune from tax merely because the levy was imposed on interstate commerce or on the receipts from the commerce. Instead, such levies would be invalidated only if the Court thought that they subjected interstate commerce to a risk of multiple taxation not borne by local commerce. Western Live Stock v. Bureau of Revenue, 303 U.S. 250, 58 S.Ct. 546 (1938); McGoldrick v. Berwind–White Coal Mining Co., 309 U.S. 33, 60 S.Ct. 388 (1940); International Harvester Co. v. Department of Treasury, 322 U.S. 340, 64 S.Ct. 1019 (1944); International Harvester Co. v. Evatt, 329 U.S. 416, 67 S.Ct. 444 (1947).

As a result of the multiple taxation doctrine, the permissible area of State taxation was broadened, so as to sanction levies which were apportioned by methods which the Court thought were reasonably designed to measure the State's nexus with the receipts, income, or property taxed. Apportionment thus became one of the keys to the validation of State taxes. At the same time, the Court narrowed the area of what constitutes an interstate business or transaction. This was a natural result of measuring the interstate or local character of the business or activities taxed by the yardstick of multiple taxation. Unapportioned levies which the Court found did not subject interstate commerce to the prohibited risks of multiple taxation were increasingly determined to be taxes on local incidents; only those levies which were found to run afoul of the test of multiple taxation tended to be proscribed as taxes on interstate transactions. See J.D. Adams Manu-facturing Co. v. Storen, 304 U.S. 307, 58 S.Ct. 913 (1938). It was left to Mr. Justice Rutledge in his opinions to amplify and expound the multiple taxation doctrine.

In developing the multiple taxation doctrine, Justice Stone did not repudiate the doctrine that taxes may not be imposed on the privilege of engaging in an exclusively interstate business. Thus, in McGoldrick v. Berwind–White Coal Mining Co., 309 U.S. 33, 48, 60 S.Ct. 388, 393 (1940), Justice Stone enumerated among the levies which "may, if permitted at all, so readily be made the instrument of impeding or destroying interstate commerce as plainly to call for their condemnation as forbidden regulations" those which "impose a levy for the privilege of doing it [interstate commerce]." Justice Douglas, who also embraced the doctrine, repeated the same view. See Joseph v. Carter & Weekes Stevedoring Co., 330 U.S. 422, 442, 67 S.Ct. 815 (1947). Justice Rutledge, however, who, in a series of notable opinions, greatly refined and improved the doctrine as advanced by Justice Stone, did not repeat this statement (although he did concur in Justice Douglas' dissent in Joseph v. Carter & Weekes Stevedoring Co., supra). Thus, in his opinion written to voice his concurrence in International Harvester Co. v. Department of Treasury, supra, and General Trading Co. v. State Tax Commission, 322 U.S. 335, 64 S.Ct. 1028 (1944), and his dissent from McLeod v. J.E. Dilworth Co., 322 U.S. 327, at 349, 64 S.Ct. 1023, at 1030 (1944)—an opinion which takes its place alongside Justice Stone's opinion in the *Western Live Stock* case and Justice Black's dissent in the *J.D. Adams Manufacturing Co.* case as the outstanding contributions in modern times to the judicial thinking in the Commerce Clause State tax cases—Justice Rutledge abstained from embodying in his formulation any reference to the invalidity of taxes on the privilege of doing an exclusively interstate business. Instead, he stated his views as follows:

> * * * The long history of this problem boils down in general statement to the formula that the states, by virtue of the force of the commerce clause, may not unduly burden interstate commerce. This resolves itself into various corollary formulations. One is that a state may not single out interstate commerce for special tax burden. Mc-Goldrick v. Berwind–White Coal Mining Co., 309 U.S. 33, 55–56, 60 S.Ct. 388. Nor may it discriminate against interstate commerce and in favor of its local trade. Welton v. Missouri, 91 U.S. at 275; Guy v. Baltimore, 100 U.S. 434; Voight v. Wright, 141 U.S. 62, 11 S.Ct. 855. Again, the State may not impose cumulative burdens upon interstate trade or commerce. Gwin, White & Prince v. Henneford, 305 U.S. 434, 59 S.Ct. 325; Adams Mfg. Co. v. Storen, 304 U.S. 307, 58 S.Ct. 913. Thus, the State may not impose certain taxes on interstate commerce, its incidents or instrumentalities, which are no more in amount or burden than it places on its local business, not because this of itself is discriminatory, cumulative or special or would violate due process, but because other States also may have the right constitutionally, apart from the commerce clause, to tax the same thing and either the actuality or the risk of their doing so makes the total burden cumulative, discriminatory or special. [322 U.S. at 358.]

Again in his carefully considered concurring opinion in *Freeman v. Hewit,* Justice Rutledge made no reference to the invalidity of a tax on the privilege of engaging in an exclusively interstate business. Finally, Justice Rutledge's concurring opinion in the *Memphis Natural Gas* case, discussed infra, appears to adopt the view that a tax on the privilege of carrying on an exclusively interstate business is valid, provided it is properly apportioned to the events taking place or the property located within the taxing State. See Memphis Natural Gas Co. v. Stone, 335 U.S. at pp. 96–98, 68 S.Ct. at 1483–1484 (1948).[8]

SECTION 3. THE TEMPORARY REVERSION TO EARLIER DOCTRINE

Within eight years after the full-blown enunciation of the multiple taxation doctrine by the majority opinion in the *Western Live Stock* case, the doctrine was repudiated by a new majority led by Mr. Justice Frankfurter. In Freeman v. Hewit, 329 U.S. 249, 67 S.Ct. 274 (1946), the Court held that the Indiana gross income tax could not be applied to the proceeds of a sale of securities made by a resident of Indiana through a local broker on the New York Stock Exchange. In so holding the Court went out of its way to repudiate the multiple taxation doctrine and to reassert the direct-indirect test of taxation of interstate commerce. Mr. Justice Frankfurter declared that the Commerce Clause by its own force created an area of trade free from interference by the States; that a State cannot "justify what amounts to a levy on the very process of commerce across States lines by pointing to a similar hobble on its local trade"; that "a tax on gross receipts" is a "direct imposition on that very freedom of commercial flow which for more than a hundred and fifty years has been the ward of the Commerce Clause." 329 U.S. at 254, 256, 67 S.Ct. at 277, 278.

The partial restoration of the *ancien régime* reached its high water mark in Spector Motor Service, Inc. v. O'Connor, 340 U.S. 602, 71 S.Ct. 508 (1951). There, Connecticut had levied a tax on the privilege of doing business measured by net income allocated to the State. The taxpayer, a foreign corporation, operated an interstate trucking business with terminals and pick-up trucks and over-the-road trucks operated in Connecticut. A strong opinion by the Court of Appeals for the Second Circuit had taken the position that the States have the power to

8. For a statement of Justice Rutledge's philosophy of the Commerce Clause, see W. Rutledge, A Declaration of Legal Faith, 72, 73 (1947), in which Justice Rutledge referred to the Commerce Clause as "a chapter in democratic living." He wrote:

"The commerce clause has been by no means perfect in its application and administration. Some large blunders there have been; others no doubt will be. But on the whole the clause has accomplished its great objective. From the disunited states of 1786, which interstate trade barriers had created, has grown the United States of 1946. No small part of that growth has been due to the effects of the commerce clause and its administration. Perhaps no other constitutional provision has played a greater part.

"That part must continue if the nation would remain great and democratic. A balkanized America today would be vulnerable to attack from without and would be unequal to maintaining our people within. Our dream comprehends something more than a subsistence level of living. For tomorrow as for yesterday, it can be realized only by giving the commerce clause its originally intended application."

impose a tax on the privilege of doing business measured by net income, where the measure of the tax is properly apportioned. 181 F.2d 150 (2d Cir.1950). The Supreme Court held otherwise, determining that the States are precluded from taxing the privilege of doing an exclusively interstate business, despite a fairly apportioned net income measure.

SECTION 4. THE NEW ASCENDANCY OF STATE TAXING POWERS: THE REPUDIATION OF TRADITIONAL RESTRICTIVE COMMERCE CLAUSE DOCTRINE

(a) The Validation of Direct Net Income Taxes on Exclusively Interstate Business: Northwestern–Stockham Valves

The reversion to the tax-free haven philosophy of Commerce Clause limitations on the taxing powers of the States was short-lived. In 1959 the Court for the first time explicitly held that there is no Commerce Clause barrier to the imposition of a fairly apportioned direct corporate income tax on a foreign corporation carrying on an exclusively interstate business within the taxing State.[9] This levy has been the center of the controversy in recent years between interstate business and the States; the decision put the States in the position, in the absence of Congressional action, to exact apportioned net income taxes from most businesses touching the State.

In upholding the net income tax on interstate commerce, the Court built on the established doctrine that the Commerce Clause prohibits "direct," but not "indirect," State taxation of exclusively interstate business.

The majority distinguished the *Spector* case as involving a tax on the privilege of doing business, albeit measured by net income, and cited that decision without disapproval. The practical consequences of the decision in *Northwestern–Stockham Valves* were far reaching. The corporation net income tax, whether as a measure of a franchise tax or as a direct corporate income tax, is the most widely used State corporation business tax in the country. A number of States promptly took steps to avoid the barrier of the *Spector* doctrine by substituting for their franchise taxes on doing business direct net income taxes, or by adding to the franchise taxes a supplementary so-called second tier direct net income tax applicable only to corporations not subject to the franchise tax.[10] The same rates, methods of apportionment, and essen-

9. See p. 229 infra. The majority of the Court disavowed the notion that it was making new law, and cited, inter alia, the *West Publishing* case (discussed in the opinion at p. 234 infra) in support of its position. On its face that case may be fairly regarded as having sustained a net income tax, as applied to an out-of-state vendor engaged solely in interstate commerce, but the Court's brief per curiam opinion failed to announce this momentous development to the bench or the bar, and three dissenting Justices read the *West Publishing* case more narrowly. See p. 242 infra.

10. See chart of State taxes, p. 16 supra. California and some other States employed the second tier supplementary net income tax before the *Northwestern–Stockham Valves* cases were decided. See West

tially the same tax base are used under the franchise and direct net income taxes.[11]

(b) The Overruling of Spector Motor Service, Inc. v. O'Connor

The force of the doctrine that the Commerce Clause condemns taxes levied on the privilege of conducting an exclusively interstate business was also substantially weakened by a series of decisions of the high Court narrowing the scope of an exclusively interstate business. Thus, in Memphis Natural Gas Co. v. Stone, 335 U.S. 80, 68 S.Ct. 1475 (1948), a case involving a tax on an interstate pipeline, the Court accepted the "construction" given by the Mississippi Supreme Court to a tax which, in the words of the statute, was imposed on "doing business," as being a tax on the "local activities" in maintaining and keeping in repair and otherwise maintaining the pipeline. On that dubious construction, the Supreme Court of the United States sustained the tax on the theory that it was not levied on the conduct of an interstate pipeline but was a tax on local activities not barred by the Commerce Clause. In two cases, Railway Express Agency challenged Virginia tax assessments, measured by gross receipts from operations within the State. In the first case, the Supreme Court struck down the levy, which was an "annual license tax" "for the privilege of doing business in this State," as a prohibited franchise tax on the conduct of an exclusively interstate business. Railway Express Agency v. Virginia, 347 U.S. 359, 74 S.Ct. 558 (1954). Virginia thereupon revised the wording of its statute so as to impose a "franchise tax" on "intangible property," in the form of "going concern" value as measured by gross receipts. This levy was sustained in an opinion in which the Court recognized that under its decision "the use of magic words or labels" can be decisive as to the constitutionality of a tax. Railway Express Agency v. Virginia, 358 U.S. 434, 441, 79 S.Ct. 411, 416 (1959).

During the same period the Court was also broadening the State taxing powers by narrowly circumscribing the area of exclusively interstate selling. In several cases arising under the State of Washington's excise tax, the Court seized on activities traditionally treated as an integral part of interstate sales solicitation to hold that the taxpayer was engaged in intrastate commerce subject to privilege taxes. See General Motors Corp. v. Washington, 377 U.S. 436, 84 S.Ct. 1564 (1964) and Standard Pressed Steel Co. v. Department of Revenue, 419 U.S. 560, 95 S.Ct. 706 (1975). Surprisingly, in the light of the then apparent

Publishing Co. v. McColgan, 328 U.S. 823, 66 S.Ct. 1378 (1946).

11. There is one principal difference between the permissible measures of the two levies, which grew out of the intergovernmental immunity doctrine. As that doctrine was developed, the States are prohibited, in the absence of the consent of Congress, from imposing direct net income taxes on interest from securities issued by the United States Government or its agencies or instrumentalities, but there is no prohibition on the inclusion of such interest in the measure of a franchise tax. See Chapter 15 infra. This difference in the allowable tax base has been a major reason for the retention of franchise taxes and the use of the second tier direct net income levy.

continued vitality under the Commerce Clause of the direct-indirect tax distinction, the Washington privilege taxes upheld were measured by the unapportioned gross receipts from sales of goods delivered across State lines to in-state customers.[12] A new peak in judicial casuistry in the Commerce Clause area was reached in 1975, when the Court sustained a Louisiana tax on an exclusively interstate pipeline. Colonial Pipeline Co. v. Traigle, 421 U.S. 100, 95 S.Ct. 1538 (1975). There, as in the Virginia cases, the original statute, which imposed a tax on the privilege of carrying on or doing business in the State, had been invalidated. Colonial Pipeline Co. v. Mouton, 228 So.2d 718 (La.App. 1969), affirmed 255 La. 474, 231 So.2d 393 (1970). Thereupon, the statute was rephrased as a levy on "the qualification to carry on or do business in this state or the actual doing of business within this state in a *corporate* form." (Our emphasis.) This time, a tax on the interstate pipeline was upheld by both the State court and by the United States Supreme Court in an opinion which whittled the *Spector* doctrine down to the *reductio ad absurdum* that a tax on foreign corporations for the privilege of doing an exclusively interstate business in the State is repugnant to the Commerce Clause, whereas a tax on foreign corporations for the privilege of doing such a business in the State *in corporate form*—the only form in which corporations can do business—is permissible.[13] Two years later the Court took the direct and wholesome step of explicitly overruling the by then impaired *Spector* doctrine. Complete Auto Transit, Inc. v. Brady, 430 U.S. 274, 97 S.Ct. 1076 (1977).

The Court concluded:

> Simply put, the *Spector* rule does not address the problems with which the Commerce Clause is concerned. Accordingly, we now reject the rule of Spector Motor Service, Inc. v. O'Connor, supra, that a state tax on the "privilege of doing business" is *per se* unconstitutional when it is applied to interstate commerce, and that case is overruled. [97 S.Ct. at 1084.]

SECTION 5. MR. JUSTICE BLACK'S COMMERCE CLAUSE APPROACH

Mr. Justice Black espoused a view of the Commerce Clause that apparently is not shared by any members of the present Court except for Justice Scalia [14]—that in the silence of Congress only discriminatory taxation of interstate commerce by the States or local governments is forbidden by the Commerce Clause. In a series of vigorous and provoc-

---

12. The Washington cases have been criticized for lack of apportionment. For an analysis of the decisions, see W. Hellerstein, "State Taxation of Interstate Business and the Supreme Court, 1974 Term: Standard Pressed Steel and Colonial Pipeline," 62 Va.L.Rev. 149 (1976).

13. Colonial Pipeline Co. v. Traigle, 421 U.S. 100, 95 S.Ct. 1538 (1975). For a critical view of the *Colonial* case, see W. Hellerstein, note 12 supra.

14. In his dissenting opinions in Tyler Pipe Industries, Inc. v. Washington State Department of Revenue, ___ U.S. ___, 107 S.Ct. 2810 (1987) and American Trucking Associations, Inc. v. Scheiner, ___ U.S. ___, 107 S.Ct. 2829 (1987), considered at pp. 266, 293, and 309 infra, Justice Scalia expressed considerable skepticism over the theoretical justification for the Court's negative Commerce Clause doctrine.

ative dissents soon after being placed on the Court in 1937, he made clear his opposition to judicial limitation on State action in the tax area. In the absence of actual discrimination against interstate commerce, Mr. Justice Black was of the view that the Commerce Clause (unassisted by Congressional action) did not warrant the invalidation of State taxes. In his 1937 dissent in Adams Manufacturing Co. v. Storen, 304 U.S. 307, 316, 58 S.Ct. 913, 918 (1938), he voiced the opinion that the "interests of interstate commerce will best be fostered, preserved and protected—in the absence of direct regulation by Congress—by leaving those engaged in it in the various states subject to the ordinary and non-discriminating taxes of the states from which they receive governmental protection." To him a "century and a half of constitutional history and government admonishes this Court to leave the choice to the elected legislative representatives of the people themselves * * *." Southern Pacific Co. v. Arizona ex rel. Sullivan, 325 U.S. 761, 65 S.Ct. 1515 (1945). He was also of the opinion that overall policies, comprehensive and fair to the State and nation alike, cannot be devised within the framework of the judicial process. In a dissent in McCarroll v. Dixie Greyhound Lines he articulated the view that:

> Judicial control of national commerce—unlike legislative regulations—must from inherent limitations of the judicial process treat the subject by the hit-and-miss method of deciding single local controversies upon evidence and information limited by the narrow rules of litigation. Spasmodic and unrelated instances of litigation cannot afford an adequate basis for the creation of integrated national rules which alone can afford that full protection for interstate commerce intended· by the Constitution. [McCarroll v. Dixie Greyhound Lines, Inc., 309 U.S. 176, 188, 60 S.Ct. 504, 510 (1939).] [15]

In some respects, Mr. Justice Black's views were a reversion to Chief Justice Taney's. However, Taney apparently would not, with Mr. Justice Black, have made an exception for discriminatory State legislation. License Cases, 46 U.S. (5 How.) 578 (1847).

References. Powell, "New Light on Gross Receipts Taxes," 53 Harv.L.Rev. 909 (1940); Brown, "State Taxation of Interstate Commerce—What Now?," 48 Mich.L.Rev. 899 (1950); Barrett, "Substance v. Form in the Application of the Commerce Clause to State Taxation," 101 U.Pa.L.Rev. 740 (1953); Dowling, "Introduction—State Taxation of Multistate Business," 18 Ohio St.L.J. 3 (1957); Hartman, "State Taxation of Interstate Commerce: A Survey and Appraisal," 46 Va.L.Rev. 1051 (1960). The October 1960 issue of the Virginia Law Review (Vol. 46, No. 6, pp. 1051–1326) contains a number of other useful articles in

---

15. Mr. Justice Black's failure to dissent from the invalidation in Michigan–Wisconsin Pipe Line Co. v. Calvert, 347 U.S. 157, 74 S.Ct. 396 (1954), of an apparently non-discriminatory Texas tax on the "gathering" of natural gas, was puzzling. The Justice's silent vote with the majority was particularly surprising in view of the fact that the unanimous opinion in the case explicitly rejected the view that "the wisest course would be for this Court to uphold all state taxes not patently discriminatory, and wait for Congress to adjust conflicts when and as it wished." 347 U.S. at 166, 74 S.Ct. at 401.

"A Symposium on State Taxation of Interstate Commerce" as does the March 1976 issue of the Vanderbilt Law Review (Vol. 29, No. 2, pp. 335–495) in "Symposium on State Taxation of Interstate Business." See also J. Hellerstein, "State Taxation of Interstate Business: The Time Has Come for Uniformity," 16 J.Tax. 246 (1962); Britton, "Multistate Taxation: Representation Without Taxation," 49 A.B.A.J. 62 (1963); Cox, "The Constitutional Power and Limitations of States to Tax Interstate Commerce," 42 Taxes 195 (1964); Del Duca & Wagner, "Uniformity or Preferential Immunity for Multi–State Firms—Tax Equity and Federal State Relations," 70 Dick.L.Rev. 283 (1966); W. Hellerstein, "State Taxation and the Supreme Court: Toward a More Unified Approach to Constitutional Adjudication?," 75 Mich.L.Rev. 1426 (1977); Lockhart, "A Revolution in State Taxation of Commerce?," 65 Minn.L.Rev. 1025 (1981); W. Hellerstein, "Commerce Clause Restraints on State Taxation: Purposeful Economic Protectionism and Beyond," 85 Mich.L.Rev. 758 (1987); W. Hellerstein, "State Taxation of Interstate Business: Perspectives on Two Centuries of Constitutional Adjudication," 41 Tax.Law. 37 (1987).

B. THE IMPLEMENTATION OF THE COMMERCE CLAUSE RESTRICTIONS IN THE DECIDED CASES

The protection which the Commerce Clause affords against State and local taxation has not been limited to actual movement of commodities, as such, in interstate channels, but extends to the vehicles and instrumentalities used for carrying on that commerce; to the attribution of the tax base to the taxing State; and to taxes that discriminate against interstate commerce.

SECTION 1. THE STREAM OF COMMERCE

The determination as to whether interstate commerce has commenced, or having begun, whether it has terminated, before the point at which the questioned tax was imposed, has given rise to extensive litigation. In the leading property tax case of Minnesota v. Blasius, 290 U.S. 1, 54 S.Ct. 34 (1933), the Court said:

> * * * the States may not tax property in transit in interstate commerce. But, by reason of a break in the transit, the property may come to a rest within a State and become subject to the power of the State to impose a nondiscriminatory property tax. Such an exertion of state power belongs to that class of cases in which, by virtue of the nature and importance of local concerns, the State may act until Congress, if it has paramount authority over the subject, substitutes its own regulations. The "crucial question," in determining whether the State's taxing power may thus be exerted, is that of "continuity of transit." Carson Petroleum Co. v. Vial, 279 U.S. 95, 101, 49 S.Ct. 292.

If the interstate movement has not begun, the mere fact that such a movement is contemplated does not withdraw the property from the

State's power to tax it. ∗ ∗ ∗ If the interstate movement has begun, it may be regarded as continuing, so as to maintain the immunity of the property from state taxation, despite temporary interruptions due to the necessities of the journey or for the purpose of safety and convenience in the course of the movement. ∗ ∗ ∗ Formalities, such as the forms of billing, and mere changes in the method of transportation do not affect the continuity of the transit. The question is always one of substance, and in each case it is necessary to consider the particular occasion or purpose of the interruption during which the tax is sought to be levied. ∗ ∗ ∗

Where property has come to rest within a State, being held there at the pleasure of the owner, for disposal or use, so that he may dispose of it either within the State, or for shipment elsewhere, as his interest dictates, it is deemed to be a part of the general mass of property within the State and is thus subject to its taxing power. [290 U.S. at 9–10.]

The Court has not given very useful guidance in deciding the validity of a tax where the interstate transportation has been interrupted after it has begun, but before reaching its final destination. The purpose of the cessation of the transit has been regarded as the benchmark for determining tax validity during a transportation break. If the journey comes to a halt because of the "owner's business reasons" (to secure some "independent local advantage"), the Commerce Clause does not insulate the commerce from taxation. Minnesota v. Blasius, supra. If, however, the break in the interstate journey is for a "transit reason," then the Commerce Clause bars taxation. Carson Petroleum Co. v. Vial, 279 U.S. 95, 49 S.Ct. 292 (1929); Kelley v. Rhoads, 188 U.S. 1, 23 S.Ct. 259 (1903). This test of taxability is much easier to state than to apply to a particular situation, since there may be an intermingling of both "owner's business reasons" and "transit reasons." The owner's "business reasons" for stoppage may be dictated in whole or in part by "transit reasons." This intermingling of purposes was so realistically demonstrated in General Oil Co. v. Crain, 209 U.S. 211, 28 S.Ct. 475 (1908), that the Court sharply divided on the purpose of stoppage and, consequently, on the question of taxability of the oil, which was stored and later shipped to customers who were out of State. See also Independent Warehouses, Inc. v. Scheele, 331 U.S. 70, 67 S.Ct. 1062 (1947).

It should be noted that most of the cases discussed in the preceding paragraphs arose during the period when the Supreme Court generally viewed direct taxes on interstate commerce as violating the Commerce Clause. A corollary to that principle was that the States may not tax goods in interstate transit. See Coe v. Errol, 116 U.S. 517, 525, 29 L.Ed. 715 (1886). As noted above, in the 1970's the Supreme Court repudiated the view that direct taxes on interstate commerce are per se violations of the Commerce Clause. In considering the current viability of cases such as *Coe v. Errol*, it has been pointed out that "a tax on goods in transit that is fairly apportioned to the mileage or ton-miles of freight in the States would not be vulnerable under the multiple taxation doctrine." J. Hellerstein, State Taxation I, Corporate Income and Franchise Taxation ¶ 4.11 (1983). See also Lockhart, "A Revolution in State Taxation of Commerce?," 65 Minn.L.Rev. 1025, 1045–47 (1981).

(a) The Cases Dealing With the Congressional Regulatory Power

In addressing the question as to whether a tax was a direct levy "on" interstate commerce prohibited by the negative implications of the Commerce Clause, the Court has distinguished cases dealing with Congressional regulation of interstate commerce. Such holdings appeared to be based on the view that Congressional regulation of interstate business presents different problems from the State tax cases under the Commerce Clause and are, therefore, not authority for similar tax results. In Minnesota v. Blasius, 290 U.S. 1, 54 S.Ct. 34 (1933), the Court upheld a property tax on cattle shipped into the St. Paul stockyards from outside the State and there bought and held on assessment day by a stockyards dealer for sale and shipment, usually outside the State. The Court held that the cattle had come to rest and were commingled with the general mass of local property and therefore subject to tax. In Swift & Co. v. United States, 196 U.S. 375, 25 S.Ct. 276 (1905) and Stafford v. Wallace, 258 U.S. 495, 42 S.Ct. 397 (1922), the Court had upheld the power of the Congress to regulate stockyards, stockyards dealers, and commission agents under the Commerce Clause. In the latter case the stockyards had been described by the Court as "the throat of the commerce."

In *Minnesota v. Blasius* the Court distinguished the two regulatory cases by saying:

> But because there is a flow of interstate commerce which is subject to the regulating power of the Congress, it does not necessarily follow that, in the absence of a conflict with the exercise of that power, a State may not lay a nondiscriminatory tax upon property which, although connected with that flow as a general course of business, has come to rest and has acquired a situs within the State. [290 U.S. at 8.]

Cf. also United States v. South–Eastern Underwriters Association, 322 U.S. 533, 64 S.Ct. 1162 (1944), which upheld the application of the Sherman Anti–Trust Act to insurance companies, and Prudential Insurance Company v. Benjamin, 328 U.S. 408, 66 S.Ct. 1142 (1946), in which a State tax on a foreign insurance company was sustained against attack under the Commerce Clause.

In several more recent cases, the Court has expressed the view that "the same interstate attributes that establish Congress' power to regulate commerce also support constitutional limitations on the powers of the States." Lewis v. BT Investment Managers, Inc., 447 U.S. 27, 39, 100 S.Ct. 2009 (1980); see also Philadelphia v. New Jersey, 437 U.S. 617, 622–23, 98 S.Ct. 2531 (1978); Commonwealth Edison Co. v. Montana, 453 U.S. 609, 101 S.Ct. 2946 (1981), which is set out at p. 296 infra. This dictum may not, however, be intended as meaning that the powers of Congress to regulate interstate commerce is coterminous with the limitations imposed by the Commerce Clause on the powers of the States to tax interstate commerce.

SECTION 2. TAXES IMPOSED ON NET INCOME DERIVED FROM INTERSTATE BUSINESS

NORTHWESTERN STATES PORTLAND CEMENT COMPANY v. STATE OF MINNESOTA

T.V. WILLIAMS, as State Revenue Commissioner v. STOCKHAM VALVES AND FITTINGS, INC.

Supreme Court of the United States, 1959.
358 U.S. 450, 79 S.Ct. 357, 67 A.L.R.2d 1292.

MR. JUSTICE CLARK delivered the opinion of the Court.

These cases concern the constitutionality of state net income tax laws levying taxes on that portion of a foreign corporation's net income earned from and fairly apportioned to business activities within the taxing State when those activities are exclusively in furtherance of interstate commerce. No question is raised in either case as to the reasonableness of the apportionment of net income under the State's formulas nor to the amount of the final assessment made. The Minnesota tax was upheld by its Supreme Court, 250 Minn. 32, 84 N.W.2d 373, while the Supreme Court of Georgia invalidated its statute as being violative of "both the commerce and due-process clauses of the Federal Constitution * * *." 213 Ga. 713, 101 S.E.2d 197, 202. The importance of the question in the field of state taxation is indicated by the fact that thirty-five States impose direct net income taxes on corporations. Therefore, we noted jurisdiction of the appeal in the Minnesota case, 1958, 355 U.S. 911, 78 S.Ct. 341, 2 L.Ed.2d 272, and granted certiorari in the other, 1958, 356 U.S. 911, 78 S.Ct. 670, 2 L.Ed. 2d 585. * * * It is contended that each of the State statutes, as applied, violates both the Due Process and the Commerce Clauses of the United States Constitution. Article 1, § 8, cl. 3; Amend. 14. We conclude that net income from the interstate operations of a foreign corporation may be subjected to state taxation provided the levy is not discriminatory and is properly apportioned to local activities within the taxing State forming sufficient nexus to support the same.

No. 12.—*Northwestern States Portland Cement Co. v. State of Minnesota.*

This is an appeal from judgments of Minnesota's courts upholding the assessment by the State of income taxes for the years 1933 through 1948 against appellant, an Iowa corporation engaged in the manufacture and sale of cement at its plant in Mason City, Iowa, some forty miles from the Minnesota border. The tax was levied under § 290.03 [1] of the Minnesota statutes, which imposes an annual tax upon the taxable net income of residents and non-residents alike. One of four classes taxed by the statute is that of "domestic and foreign corporations * * * whose business within this State during the taxable year consists exclusively of foreign commerce, interstate commerce, or both." Minnesota has utilized three ratios in determining the portion of net income taxable under its law. [2] The first is that of the taxpayer's sales assignable to Minnesota during the year to its total sales during that period made everywhere; the second, that of the taxpayer's total tangible property in Minnesota for the year to its total tangible property used in the business that year wherever situated. The third is the taxpayer's total payroll in Minnesota for the year to its total payroll for its entire business in the like period. As we have noted, appellant takes no issue with the fairness of this formula nor of the accuracy of its application here.

Appellant's activities in Minnesota consisted of a regular and systematic course of solicitation of orders for the sale of its products, each order being subject to acceptance, filling and delivery by it from its plant at Mason City. It sold only to eligible dealers, who were lumber and building material supply houses, contractors and ready-mix companies. A list of these eligible dealers was maintained and sales would not be made to those not included thereon. Forty-eight percent of appellant's entire sales were made in this manner to such dealers in Minnesota. For efficient handling of its activity in that State, appellant maintained in Minneapolis a leased sales office equipped with its own furniture and fixtures and under the supervision of an employee-salesman known as "district manager." Two salesmen, including this district manager, and a secretary occupied this three-room office. Two additional salesmen used it as a clearing house. Each employee was paid a straight salary by the appellant direct from Mason City and two cars were furnished by it for the salesmen. Appellant maintained no bank account in Minnesota, owned no real estate there, and warehoused no merchandise in the State. All sales were made on a delivered price basis fixed by the appellant in Mason City and no "pick ups" were permitted at its plant there. The salesmen, however, were authorized to quote Minnesota customers a delivered price. Orders received by the salesmen or at the Minneapolis office were transmitted

---

1. § 290.03:

"Classes of taxpayers. An annual tax for each taxable year, computed in the manner and at the rates hereinafter provided, is hereby imposed upon the taxable net income for such year of the following classes of taxpayers:

"(1) Domestic and foreign corporations not taxable under section 290.02 which own property within this State or whose business within this State during the taxable year consists exclusively of for-

eign commerce, interstate commerce, or both;

"Business within the State shall not be deemed to include transportation in interstate or foreign commerce, or both, by means of ships navigating within or through waters which are made international for navigation purposes by any treaty or agreement to which the United States is a party; * * *." Minn.Stat. 1945, § 290.03, M.S.A.

2. Minn.Stat. (1945) § 290.19, M.S.A.

daily to appellant in Mason City, were approved there, and acknowledged directly to the purchaser with copies to the salesman.

In addition to the solicitation of approved dealers, appellant's salesmen also contacted potential customers and users of cement products, such as builders, contractors, architects, and state, as well as local government purchasing agents. Orders were solicited and received from them, on special forms furnished by appellant, directed to an approved local dealer who in turn would fill them by placing a like order with appellant. Through this system appellant's salesmen would in effect secure orders for local dealers which in turn were filled by appellant in the usual manner. Salesmen would also receive and transmit claims against appellant for loss or damage in any shipments made by it, informing the company of the nature thereof and requesting instructions concerning the same.

No income tax returns were filed with the State by the appellant. The assessments sued upon, aggregating some $102,000, with penalties and interest, were made by the Commissioner of Taxation on the basis of information available to him.

No. 33—*T. V. Williams, Commissioner v. Stockham Valves & Fittings, Inc.*

The respondent here is a Delaware Corporation with its principal office and plant in Birmingham, Alabama. It manufactures and sells valves and pipe fittings through established local wholesalers and jobbers who handle products other than respondent's. These dealers were encouraged by respondent to carry a local inventory of its products by granting to those who did so a special price concession. However, the corporation maintained no warehouse or storage facilities in Georgia. It did maintain a sales-service office in Atlanta, which served five States. This office was headquarters for one salesman who devoted about one-third of his time to solicitation of orders in Georgia. He was paid on a salary-plus-commission basis while a full-time woman secretary employed there received a regular salary only. She was "a source of information" for respondent's products, performed stenographic and clerical services and "facilitated communications between the * * * home office in Birmingham, * * * [the] sales representative * * * and customers, prospective customers, contractors and users of [its] products." Respondent's salesman carried on the usual sales activities, including regular solicitation, receipt and forwarding of orders to the Birmingham office and the promotion of business and good will for respondent. Orders were taken by him, as well as the sales-service office, subject to approval of the home office and were shipped from Birmingham direct to the customer on an "f.o.b. warehouse" basis. Other than office equipment, supplies, advertising literature and the like, respondent had no property in Georgia, deposited no funds there and stored no merchandise in the State.

Georgia levies a tax [3] on net incomes "received by every corporation, foreign or domestic, owning property or doing business in this State." [4] The Act defines the latter as including "any activities or transactions" carried on within the State "for the purpose of financial profit or gain" regardless of its connection with interstate commerce. To apportion net income, the Act applies a three-factor ratio based on inventory, wages and gross receipts. Under the Act the State Revenue Commissioner assessed and collected a total of $1,478.31 from respondent for the taxable years 1952, 1954 and 1955, and after claims for refund were denied the respondent filed this suit to recover such payments. It bases its right to recover squarely upon the constitutionality of Georgia's Act under the Commerce and the Due Process Clauses of the Constitution of the United States.

That there is a "need for clearing up the tangled underbrush of past cases" with reference to the taxing power of the States is a concomitant to the negative approach resulting from a case-by-case resolution of "the extremely limited restrictions that the Constitution places upon the states. * * *" State of Wisconsin v. J.C. Penney Co., 1940, 311 U.S. 435, 445, 61 S.Ct. 246, 250, 85 L.Ed. 267. Commerce between the States having grown up like Topsy, the Congress meanwhile not having undertaken to regulate taxation of it, and the States having understandably persisted in their efforts to get some return for the substantial benefits they have afforded it, there is little wonder that there has been no end of cases testing out state tax levies. The resulting judicial application of constitutional principles to specific state statutes leaves much room for controversy and confusion and little in the way of precise guides to the States in the exercise of their indispensable power of taxation. This Court alone has handed down some three hundred full-dress opinions spread through slightly more than that number of our reports. As was said in Miller Bros. Co. v. State of Maryland, 1954, 347 U.S. 340, 344, 74 S.Ct. 535, 538, 98 L.Ed. 744, the decisions have been "not always clear * * * consistent or reconcilable. A few have been specifically overruled, while others no longer fully represent the present state of the law." From the quag-

3. Ga.Code Ann. (1937), § 92–3102. "Rate of taxation of corporations.—Every domestic corporation and every foreign corporation shall pay annually an income tax equivalent to five and one-half per cent. of the net income from property owned or from business done in Georgia, as is defined in section 92–3113: * * *"

Ga.Code Ann. (1937), § 92–3113. "Corporations, allocation and apportionment of income.—The tax imposed by this law shall apply to the entire net income, as herein defined, received by every corporation, foreign or domestic, owning property or doing business in this State. Every such corporation shall be deemed to be doing business within this State if it engages within this State in any activities or transactions for the purpose of financial profit or gain, whether or not such corporation qualifies to do business in this State, and whether or not it maintains an office or place of doing business within this State, and whether or not any such activity or transaction is connected with interstate or foreign commerce. * * *"

4. The tax on corporations is part of a general scheme of income taxation which Georgia imposes on individuals (§ 92–3101), corporations (§ 92–3102), and fiduciaries (§ 92–3103).

mire there emerge, however, some firm peaks of decision which remain unquestioned.

It has long been established doctrine that the Commerce Clause gives exclusive power to the Congress to regulate interstate commerce, and its failure to act on the subject in the area of taxation nevertheless requires that interstate commerce shall be free from any direct restrictions or impositions by the States. Gibbons v. Ogden, 1824, 9 Wheat. 1, 6 L.Ed. 23. In keeping therewith a State "cannot impose taxes upon persons passing through the state, or coming into it merely for a temporary purpose" such as itinerant drummers. Robbins v. Taxing District, 1887, 120 U.S. 489, 493–494, 7 S.Ct. 592, 594, 30 L.Ed. 694. Moreover, it is beyond dispute that a State may not lay a tax on the "privilege" of engaging in interstate commerce. Spector Motor Service v. O'Connor, 1951, 340 U.S. 602, 71 S.Ct. 508, 95 L.Ed. 573. Nor may a State impose a tax which discriminates against interstate commerce either by providing a direct commercial advantage to local business, Memphis Steam Laundry Cleaner v. Stone, 1952, 342 U.S. 389, 72 S.Ct. 424, 96 L.Ed. 436; Nippert v. City of Richmond, 1946, 327 U.S. 416, 66 S.Ct. 586, 90 L.Ed. 760, or by subjecting interstate commerce to the burden of "multiple taxation," Michigan–Wisconsin Pipe Line Co. v. Calvert, 1954, 347 U.S. 157, 74 S.Ct. 396, 98 L.Ed. 583; Adams Mfg. Co. v. Storen, 1938, 304 U.S. 307, 58 S.Ct. 913, 82 L.Ed. 1365. Such impositions have been stricken because the States, under the Commerce Clause, are not allowed "one single taxworth of direct interference with the free flow of commerce." Freeman v. Hewit, 1946, 329 U.S. 249, 256, 67 S.Ct. 274, 279, 91 L.Ed. 265.

On the other hand, it has been established since 1918 that a net income tax on revenues derived from interstate commerce does not offend constitutional limitations upon State interference with such commerce. The decision of Peck & Co. v. Lowe, 247 U.S. 165, 38 S.Ct. 432, 62 L.Ed. 1049, pointed the way. There the Court held that though true it was that the Constitution provided "No Tax or Duty shall be laid on Articles exported from any State," Art. I, § 9, still a net income tax on the profits derived from such commerce was not "laid on articles in course of exportation or on anything which inherently or by the usages of commerce is embraced in exportation or any of its processes * * *. At most, exportation is affected only indirectly and remotely." Id., 247 U.S. at pages 174–175, 38 S.Ct. at page 434. The first case in this Court applying the doctrine to interstate commerce was that of United States Glue Co. v. Town of Oak Creek, 1918, 247 U.S. 321, 38 S.Ct. 499, 62 L.Ed. 1135. There the Court distinguished between an invalid direct levy which placed a burden on interstate commerce and a charge by way of net income derived from profits from interstate commerce. This landmark case and those usually cited as upholding the doctrine there announced, i.e., Underwood Typewriter Co. v. Chamberlain, 1920, 254 U.S. 113, 41 S.Ct. 45, 65 L.Ed. 165, and Memphis Natural Gas Co. v. Beeler, 1942, 315 U.S. 649, 62 S.Ct. 857, 858, 86 L.Ed. 1090, dealt with corporations which were domestic to the taxing State (United States

Glue Co. v. Town of Oak Creek, supra), or which had "established a 'commercial domicile'" there, Underwood Typewriter Co. v. Chamberlain, supra; Memphis Natural Gas Co. v. Beeler, supra.

But that the presence of such a circumstance is not controlling is shown by the cases of Bass, Ratcliff & Gretton, Ltd. v. State Tax Commission, 1924, 266 U.S. 271, 45 S.Ct. 82, 69 L.Ed. 282, and Norfolk & W.R. Co. v. State of North Carolina, 1936, 297 U.S. 682, 56 S.Ct. 625, 80 L.Ed. 977. In neither of these cases was the taxpayer a domiciliary of the taxing State, incorporated or with its principal place of business there, though each carried on substantial local activities. Permitting the assessment of New York's franchise tax measured on a proportional formula against a British corporation selling ale in New York State, the Court held in Bass, Ratcliff & Gretton, Ltd., supra, that "the Company carried on the unitary business of manufacturing and selling ale, in which its profits were earned by a series of transactions beginning with the manufacture in England and ending in sales in New York and other places—the process of manufacturing resulting in no profits until it ends in sales—the State was justified in attributing to New York a just proportion of the profits earned by the Company from such unitary business." Id., 266 U.S. at page 282, 45 S.Ct. at page 84. Likewise in Norfolk & W.R. Co., supra, North Carolina was permitted to tax a Virginia corporation on net income apportioned to North Carolina on the basis of mileage within the State. These cases stand for the doctrine that the entire net income of a corporation, generated by interstate as well as intrastate activities, may be fairly apportioned among the States for tax purposes by formulas utilizing in-state aspects of interstate affairs. In fact, in Bass, Ratcliff & Gretton the operations in the taxing State were conducted at a loss, and still the Court allowed part of the over-all net profit of the corporation to be attributed to the State. A reading of the statute in Norfolk & W.R. Co. reveals further that one facet of the apportionment formula was specifically designed to attribute a portion of the interstate hauls to the taxing State.

Any doubt as to the validity of our position here was entirely dispelled four years after Beeler, in a unanimous *per curiam* in West Publishing Co. v. McColgan, 328 U.S. 823, 66 S.Ct. 1378, 90 L.Ed. 1603, citing the four cases of Beeler, United States Glue Co., both supra, Interstate Busses Corp. v. Blodgett, 1928, 276 U.S. 245, 48 S.Ct. 230, 72 L.Ed. 551, and International Shoe Co. v. State of Washington, 1945, 326 U.S. 310, 66 S.Ct. 154, 90 L.Ed. 95. The case involved the validity of California's tax on the apportioned net income of West Publishing Company, whose business was exclusively interstate. See 27 Cal.2d 705, 166 P.2d 861, 862. While the statement of the facts in that opinion recites that "The employees were given space in the offices of attorneys in return for the use of plaintiff's books stored in such offices," it is significant to note that West had not qualified to do business in California and the State's statute itself declared that the tax was levied on income derived from interstate commerce within the State, as well as any arising intrastate. The opinion was not grounded on the triviality that office space was given West's solicitors by attorneys in exchange for the chanceful use of what books they may have had on hand for their sales activities. Rather, it recognized that the income taxed arose from a purely interstate operation.

"In relying on the foregoing cases for the proposition that a foreign corporation engaged within a State solely in interstate commerce is immune from net income taxation by that State, plaintiff [West Publishing Co.] overlooks the distinction made by the United States Supreme Court between a tax whose subject is the privilege of engaging in interstate commerce and a tax whose subject is the net income from such commerce. It is settled by decisions of the United States Supreme Court that a tax on net income from interstate commerce, as distinguished from a tax on the privilege of engaging in interstate commerce, does not conflict with the commerce clause." 27 Cal.2d 705, 708–709, 166 P.2d 861, 863. (Citations omitted.)

We believe that the rationale of these cases, involving income levies by States, controls the issues here. The taxes are not regulations in any sense of that term. Admittedly they do not discriminate against nor subject either corporation to an undue burden. While it is true that a State may not erect a wall around its borders preventing commerce an entry, it is axiomatic that the founders did not intend to immunize such commerce from carrying its fair share of the costs of the state government in return for the benefits it derives from within the State. The levies are not privilege taxes based on the right to carry on business in the taxing State. The States are left to collect only through ordinary means. The tax, therefore, is "not open to the objection that it compels the company to pay for the privilege of engaging in interstate commerce." Underwood Typewriter Co. v. Chamberlain, supra, 254 U.S. at page 119, 41 S.Ct. at page 46. As was said in State of Wisconsin v. Minnesota Mining & Mfg. Co., 1940, 311 U.S. 452, 453, 61 S.Ct. 253, 254, 85 L.Ed. 274, "it is too late in the day to find offense to that [commerce] clause because a state tax is imposed on corporate net income of an interstate enterprise which is attributable to earnings within the taxing State * * *."

While the economic wisdom of state net income taxes is one of state policy not for our decision, one of the "realities" raised by the parties is the possibility of a multiple burden resulting from the exactions in question. The answer is that none is shown to exist here. This is not an unapportioned tax which by its very nature makes interstate commerce bear more than its fair share. As was said in Central Greyhound Lines of New York v. Mealey, 1948, 334 U.S. 653, 661, 68 S.Ct. 1260, 1265, 92 L.Ed. 1633, "it is interstate commerce which the State is seeking to reach and * * * the real question [is] whether what the State is exacting is a constitutionally fair demand by the State for that aspect of the interstate commerce to which the State bears a special relation." The apportioned tax is designed to meet this very requirement and "to prevent the levying of such taxes as will discriminate against or prohibit the interstate activities or will place the interstate commerce at a disadvantage relative to local commerce." Id., 334 U.S. at page 670, 68 S.Ct. at page 1270. Logically it is impossible, when the tax is fairly apportioned, to have the same income taxed twice. In practical operation, however, apportionment formulas being what they are, the possibility of the contrary is not foreclosed, especially by levies in domiciliary States.[5] But that question is not before us. It was argued in Northwest Airlines v. State of Minnesota, 1944, 322 U.S. 292, 64 S.Ct. 950, 952, 88 L.Ed. 1283, that the taxation of the entire fleet of its airplanes in that State would result in multiple taxation since other States levied taxes on some proportion of the full value thereof. The Court rejected this contention as being "not now before us" even though other States actually collected property taxes for the same year from Northwest upon "some proportion" of the full value of its fleet.[6] Here the records are all to the contrary. There is nothing to show that multiple taxation is present. We cannot deal in abstractions. In this type of case the taxpayers must show that the formula places a burden upon interstate commerce in a constitutional sense. This they have failed to do.

It is also contended that Spector Motor Service v. O'Connor, 1951, 340 U.S. 602, 71 S.Ct. 508, 509, 95 L.Ed. 573, requires a contrary result. But there it was repeatedly emphasized that the tax was "imposed upon the franchise of a foreign corporation for the privilege of doing business within the State * * *." Thus, it was invalid under a long line of precedents, some of which we have mentioned.[7] It was not a levy on net income but an excise or tax placed on the franchise of a foreign corporation engaged "exclusively" in interstate operations. Therefore, with the exception of Beeler, heretofore mentioned, the Court made no reference to the net-income-tax cases which control here. We do not construe that reference as intended to impair the validity of the Beeler opinion. Nor does it reach our problem. The taxes here, like that in West Publishing Co. v. McColgan, supra, are based only upon the net

5. In Standard Oil Co. v. Peck, 1952, 342 U.S. 382, 72 S.Ct. 309, 96 L.Ed. 427, we struck down Ohio's ad valorem property tax on vessels domiciled there but plying in interstate trade because it was not apportioned.

6. The Court nevertheless pointed out that such payments did "not abridge the power of taxation of * * * the home State." 322 U.S. at page 295, 64 S.Ct. at page 952.

7. See also Alpha Portland Cement Co. v. Commonwealth of Massachusetts, 1925, 268 U.S. 203, 216, 45 S.Ct. 477, 480, 69 L.Ed. 916, where this Court, striking down a Massachusetts excise tax on a foreign corporation engaged exclusively in interstate commerce, noted that "[t]he right to lay taxes on tangible property or on income is not involved; * * *"

Furthermore, none of the cases which the dissent relies on for the proposition that "[N]o State has the right to lay a tax on interstate commerce in any form * * *" was a net income tax case. In fact, all involved taxes levied upon corporations for the privilege of engaging in interstate commerce. This Court has consistently held that the "privilege" of engaging in interstate commerce cannot be granted or withheld by a State, and that the assertion of state power to tax the "privilege" is, therefore, a forbidden attempt to "regulate" interstate commerce. Cf. Murdock v. Commonwealth of Pennsylvania, 1943, 319 U.S. 105, 112–113, 63 S.Ct. 870, 874–875, 87 L.Ed. 1292.

profits earned in the taxing State. That incidence of the tax affords a valid "constitutional channel" which the States have utilized to "make interstate commerce pay its way." In Spector the incidence was the privilege of doing business, and that avenue of approach had long been declared unavailable under the Commerce Clause. As was said in Spector, "taxes may be imposed although their payment may come out of the funds derived from petitioner's interstate business, provided the taxes are so imposed that their burden will be reasonably related to the powers of the State and [are] nondiscriminatory." 340 U.S. at page 609, 71 S.Ct. at page 512. We find that the statutes here meet these tests.

Nor will the argument that the exactions contravene the Due Process Clause bear scrutiny. The taxes imposed are levied only on that portion of the taxpayer's net income which arises from its activities within the taxing State. These activities form a sufficient "nexus between such a tax and transactions within a state for which the tax is an exaction." State of Wisconsin v. J.C. Penney Co., supra, 311 U.S. at page 445, 61 S.Ct. at page 250. It strains reality to say, in terms of our decisions, that each of the corporations here was not sufficiently involved in local events to forge "some definite link, some minimum connection" sufficient to satisfy due process requirements. Miller Bros. Co. v. State of Maryland, 1954, 347 U.S. 340, 344–345, 74 S.Ct. 535, 539, 98 L.Ed. 744. See also Ott v. Miss. Valley Barge Line Co., 1949, 336 U.S. 169, 69 S.Ct. 432, 93 L.Ed. 585; International Shoe Co. v. State of Washington, 1945, 326 U.S. 310, 66 S.Ct. 154, 90 L.Ed. 95, and West Publishing Co. v. McColgan, supra. The record is without conflict that both corporations engage in substantial income-producing activity in the taxing States. In fact in No. 12 almost half of the corporation's income is derived from the taxing State's sales which are shown to be promoted by vigorous and continuous sales campaigns run through a central office located in the State. While in No. 33 the percent of sales is not available, the course of conduct was largely identical. As was said in State of Wisconsin v. J.C. Penney Co., supra, the "controlling question is whether the State has given anything for which it can ask return." Since by "the practical operation of [the] tax the State has exerted its power in relation to opportunities which it has given, to protection which it has afforded, to benefits which it has conferred * * *" it "is free to pursue its own fiscal policies, unembarrassed by the Constitution * * *." Id., 311 U.S. at page 444, 61 S.Ct. at page 250.

No. 12—Affirmed.

No. 33—Reversed.

Mr. Justice Harlan, concurring.

In joining the opinion of the Court, I deem it appropriate to make some further comments as to the issues in these cases because of the strongly held contrary views manifested in the dissenting opinions of Mr. Justice Frankfurter and Mr. Justice Whittaker. I preface what follows by saying that in my view the past decisions of this Court clearly point to, if indeed they do not compel, the sustaining of these two state taxing measures.

Since United States Glue Co. v. Town of Oak Creek, 247 U.S. 321, 38 S.Ct. 499, 62 L.Ed. 1135, decided in 1918, this Court has uniformly held that a State, in applying a net income tax of general impact to a corporation doing business within its borders, may reach income derived from interstate commerce to the extent that such income is fairly related to corporate activities within the State. See, e.g., Shaffer v. Carter, 252 U.S. 37, 57, 40 S.Ct. 221, 227, 64 L.Ed. 445; Atlantic Coast Line R. Co. v. Daughton, 262 U.S. 413, 416, 43 S.Ct. 620, 621, 67 L.Ed. 1051. See also Underwood Typewriter Co. v. Chamberlain, 254 U.S. 113, 119–120, 41 S.Ct. 45, 46, 65 L.Ed. 165; Bass, Ratcliff & Gretton, Ltd. v. State Tax Commission, 266 U.S. 271, 45 S.Ct. 82, 69 L.Ed. 282; Norfolk & W.R. Co. v. State of North Carolina, 297 U.S. 682, 56 S.Ct. 625, 80 L.Ed. 977.

As I read the cases the existence of some income from *intrastate* business on the part of the taxed corporation, while sometimes adverted to, has never been considered essential to the valid taxation of such "interstate" income. The cases upholding taxes of this kind cannot, in my opinion, properly be said to rest on the theory that the income earned from the carrying on of interstate commerce was not in fact being taxed, but rather was being utilized simply to measure the income derived from some separate, but unidentified, intrastate commerce, which income was in truth the subject of the tax. That this is so seems to me apparent from United States Glue itself. There the Court explicitly recognized that the question before it was whether net income from exclusively interstate commerce could be taxed by a State on an apportioned basis together with other income of a corporation. The careful distinction, drawn more than once in the course of the opinion, between gross receipts from interstate commerce, assumed to be immune from state taxation, and net income therefrom, 247 U.S. at pages 324, 326, 327, 328, 329, 38 S.Ct. at pages 500, 501, would be altogether meaningless if the case is to be explained on the basis suggested by my dissenting brethren, for if all that was in fact being taxed was income from intrastate commerce there is no reason why gross receipts as well as net income could not have been reached by the State.[1]

1. As early as 1919 such a discriminating commentator as the late Thomas Reed Powell had this to say, in commenting on the decisions of this Court in Peck & Co. v. Lowe, 247 U.S. 165, 38 S.Ct. 432, 62 L.Ed. 1049, and United States Glue Co. v. Town of Oak Creek, supra: "We may take it for granted, then, that the legal character of the recipient and the nature of the business in which the recipient is engaged are immaterial elements in considering the constitutionality of a statewide, all-inclusive general tax on net income from business done within the state. The recipient may be an individual, a partnership, a domestic or a foreign corporation. The business may be exclusively interstate." Indirect Encroachment on Federal Authority by the Taxing Powers of the States. VII, 32 Harv.L.Rev. 634, 639. That nothing in United States Glue turned on the fact that the taxpayer there happened to be a domestic corporation is shown by the line of cases following it where the taxpayers were foreign corporations doing an in-

Surely any possible doubt on this score is removed by West Publishing Co. v. McColgan, 328 U.S. 823, 66 S.Ct. 1378, 90 L.Ed. 1603, where this Court unanimously affirmed, without oral argument, a decision of the California Supreme Court upholding the validity of a statute taxing "income from any activities carried on in this State, regardless of whether carried on in intrastate, interstate or foreign commerce" as applied to reach a portion of the net income of a Minnesota corporation not qualified to do intrastate business in California and assumed by the California court to be deriving income in California *entirely* "from activities in furtherance of a purely interstate business * * *." 27 Cal.2d 705, 712, 166 P.2d 861, 865.

It is suggested that the Court's summary affirmance in the West case went on the ground that the taxpayer there was found by the state court to have been engaged in intrastate commerce in California, and that it was only the income earned from such commerce that had in truth been taxed by the State. In my view, this explanation of West is unacceptable. Apart from the fact that the California Supreme Court did not proceed on any such basis (see especially the quotation from the state court's opinion set forth at page 364 of 79 S.Ct.), the only facts elucidated in support of this view of the West case are that employees of the taxpayer solicited business in California, that they were authorized to receive payments on orders taken by them, to collect delinquent accounts, and to adjust complaints, and that they were given space in California lawyers' offices in return for the use of the taxpayer's books there stored, which locations were also advertised as the taxpayer's local offices. It is said that these are "the usual criteria which this Court has consistently held to constitute the doing of intrastate commerce" and that "California determined and taxed only the amount of that intrastate commerce." With deference, this seems to me to be both novel doctrine and unreal analysis; novel doctrine because this Court has never held that activities of this kind, performed solely in aid of interstate sales, are intrastate commerce; unreal analysis, because it is surely stretching things too far to say that California was seeking to measure and tax office renting and complaint adjusting rather than part of the income from concededly interstate sales transactions.

I think that West squarely governs the two cases now before us.[2]

terstate business. See cases cited on page 366 of 79 S.Ct.

2. Apart from the considerations discussed in the text of this opinion, it is noteworthy that the Court in West, in relying on Memphis Natural Gas Co. v. Beeler, 315 U.S. 649, cited directly to page 656 of the Beeler opinion, 62 S.Ct. 857, 862, 86 L.Ed. 1090, where it was said: "In any case even if taxpayer's business were *wholly interstate commerce* [italics supplied], a nondiscriminatory tax by Tennessee upon the net income of a foreign corporation having a commercial domicile there [citation], or upon net income derived from within the State [citations], is not prohibited by the commerce clause on which the taxpayer alone relies [citing among other cases United States Glue Co. v. Town of Oak Creek, supra]. There is no contention or showing here that the tax assessed is not upon net earnings justly attributable to Tennessee [citations]."

It is said that the taxes presently at issue were "paid on income from [interstate commerce] because of its source." If this were so I should of course vote to strike down their application here as unconstitutionally discriminatory against interstate commerce. But this seems to me plainly not such a case. As the opinion of the Court demonstrates, the Minnesota and Georgia taxes are each part of a general scheme of state income taxation, reaching all individual, corporate, and other net income. The taxing statutes are not sought to be applied to portions of the net income of Northwestern and Stockham *because* of the source of that income—interstate commerce—but rather *despite* that source. The thrust of these statutes is not hostile discrimination against interstate commerce, but rather a seeking of some compensation for facilities and benefits afforded by the taxing States to income-producing activities therein, whether those activities be altogether local or in furtherance of interstate commerce. The past decisions of this Court establish that such compensation may be had by the States consistent with the Commerce Clause.

I think it no more a "regulation of," "burden on," or "interference with" interstate commerce to permit a State within whose borders a foreign corporation engages *solely* in activities in aid of that commerce to tax the net income derived therefrom on a properly apportioned basis than to permit the same State to impose a nondiscriminatory net income tax of general application on a corporation engaging in *both* interstate and intrastate commerce therein and to take into account income from both categories. Cf. Peck & Co. v. Lowe, 247 U.S. 165, 38 S.Ct. 432, 62 L.Ed. 1049. In each case the amount of the tax will increase as the profitability of the interstate business done increases. This Court has consistently upheld state net income taxes of general application so applied as to reach that portion of the profits of interstate business enterprises fairly allocable to activities within the State's borders. We do no more today.

MR. JUSTICE WHITTAKER, with whom MR. JUSTICE FRANKFURTER and MR. JUSTICE STEWART join, dissenting.

I respectfully dissent. My disagreement with the Court is over what I think are constitutional fundamentals. I think that the Commerce Clause of the Constitution, Art. I, § 8, cl. 3, as consistently interpreted by this Court until today, precludes the States from laying taxes directly on, and thereby regulating, "exclusively interstate commerce." But the Court's decision today holds that the States may do so.

[MR. JUSTICE WHITTAKER's statement of the facts and his analysis of the statutes have been omitted.]

I submit that these simple recitals clearly show (1) that the Minnesota and Georgia statutes, in plain terms, purport to tax income derived "exclusively [from] interstate commerce," (2) that the Minnesota and Georgia courts have found that the income involved was derived "exclusively [from] interstate commerce," and (3) that the taxes were laid directly on that interstate commerce.

[The dissent proceeds with a detailed analysis of the cases relied on by the majority opinion, which has been omitted.]

With this demonstration of the holdings in the commerce cases relied upon by the Court, surely we can repeat, with the conviction of demonstrated truth, our statement that none of the cases relied on by the Court supports its holding "that net income from the interstate operations of a foreign corporation may be subjected to state taxation provided the levy is not discriminatory and is properly apportioned to local activities within the taxing State * * *." The fact that such taxes may be fairly or "properly apportioned" is without legal consequence, for "The constitutional infirmity of such a tax persists no matter how fairly it is apportioned to business done within the state." Spector Motor Service v. O'Connor, supra, 340 U.S. at page 609, 71 S.Ct. at page 512. That this Court has always sustained state taxes on fairly determined amounts of intrastate income should be evidence enough from the shown fact that it has struck them down only when there was none.

The Court says "We believe that the rationale of these cases, involving income levies by States, controls the issues here." I agree that the rationale of those cases controls the issues here. But I cannot agree that those cases involved *like* "income levies by States." They involved levies of income taxes on intrastate commerce, not on "exclusively interstate commerce." Whereas, here both the Minnesota and Georgia courts have found that the income taxed by those States had derived "exclusively [from] interstate commerce," and that the tax was not levied upon any intrastate commerce for there was none.

In these circumstances, I submit it is idle to say that the taxes were not laid "on" interstate commerce, but on the taxpayer's general income after all commerce had ended, and, therefore, did not burden, nor hence regulate, interstate commerce. For in addition to the plainness of the fact, the courts of Minnesota and Georgia have explicitly held in these cases that the income involved was derived "exclusively [from] interstate commerce," and that the taxes were laid on that income. The taxes do not purport to have been, and could not have been, laid on any income derived from intrastate commerce in those States for there was none. It necessarily follows that the taxes were "laid on income from [interstate commerce] because of its source," Peck & Co. v. Lowe, supra, 247 U.S. at page 174, 38 S.Ct. at page 434, just as in Spector Motor Service v. O'Connor, supra.

The Commerce Clause denies state power to regulate interstate commerce. It vests that power exclusively in Congress. Direct taxation of "exclusively interstate commerce" is a substantial regulation of it and, therefore, in the absence of congressional consent, the States may not directly tax it. This Court has so held every time the question has been presented here until today. Without congressional consent, the States of Minnesota and Georgia have laid taxes directly on what they admit was "exclusively interstate commerce." Hence, in my view, those levies plainly violated the Commerce Clause of the Constitution and cannot stand consistently therewith and with our prior cases. I would, therefore, reverse the judgment of the Supreme Court of Minnesota in No. 12 and affirm the judgment of the Supreme Court of Georgia in No. 33.

Mr. Justice Frankfurter, dissenting.

By way of emphasizing my agreement with my brother Whittaker, I add a few observations.

The Court sustains the taxing power of the States in these two cases essentially on the basis of precedents. For me, the result of today's decisions is to break new ground. I say this because, among all the hundreds of cases dealing with the power of the States to tax commerce, there is not a single decision adjudicating the precise situation now before us. Concretely, we have never decided that a State may tax a corporation when that tax is on income related to the State by virtue of activities within it when such activities are exclusively part of the process of doing interstate commerce. That is the precise situation which the state courts found here, to wit:

> "[Northwestern's] activities in this State were an integral part of its interstate activities, and all revenue received by it from customers in Minnesota resulted from its operations in interstate commerce."

and,

> "[W]ithout dispute [Stockham] was engaged exclusively in interstate commerce insofar as its activities in Georgia are concerned." 213 Ga. 713, 719, 101 S.E.2d 197, 201.

It is vital to realize that in no case prior to this decision in which the taxing power of a State has been upheld when applied to corporations engaged in interstate commerce, was there a total absence of activities pursued or advantages conferred within the States severable from the very process which constitutes interstate commerce.

The case that argumentatively comes the closest to the situation now before the Court is West Publishing Co. v. McColgan, 328 U.S. 823, 66 S.Ct. 1378, 90 L.Ed. 1603.[1] But in that case too, as the opinion of the

---

1. The West case was a *per curiam* affirmance without opinion. The Court cited four cases in support: United States Glue Co. v. Town of Oak Creek, 247 U.S. 321, 38 S.Ct. 499, 62 L.Ed. 1135; Interstate Busses Corp. v. Blodgett, 276 U.S. 245, 48 S.Ct. 230, 72 L.Ed. 551; Memphis Natural Gas Co. v. Beeler, 315 U.S. 649, 656, 62 S.Ct. 857, 862, 86 L.Ed. 1090; International Shoe Co. v. State of Washington, 326 U.S. 310, 66 S.Ct. 154, 90 L.Ed. 95. Not one of these cases presented the issue now here; in none had the Court to sustain a state net income tax on a business whose revenue derived solely from interstate commerce.

In United States Glue Co. v. Town of Oak Creek, supra, this Court upheld an apportioned net income tax levied by the State of Wisconsin on a Wisconsin corporation having its principal office and manufacturing establishment in that State. A substantial part of the corporation's business was intrastate. The only issue before the Court was the power of the State to include interstate income in its apportionment computation.

Interstate Busses Corp. v. Blodgett, supra, decided that appellant had not sustained the burden of showing that an excise tax of one cent per mile levied by Connecticut on motor vehicles using its highways in interstate commerce fell with discriminating weight on interstate commerce when the tax was viewed as part of

California Supreme Court which we there summarily sustained clearly set forth, 27 Cal.2d 705, 166 P.2d 861, the West Publishing Company did not merely complete in California the business which began in Minnesota. It employed permanent workers who engaged in business activities localized in California, activities which were apart from and in addition to the purely interstate sale of law books. These activities were more than an essential part of the process of interstate commerce; they were, in legal shorthand, local California activities constituting intrastate business. In dealing with those purely local activities the State could properly exert its taxing power in relation to opportunities and advantages which it had given and which it could have withheld by simply not allowing a foreign corporation to do local business, whereas no State may withhold from a foreign corporation within its borders the right to exercise what is part of a process of exclusively interstate commerce. The State gives to a corporation so engaged nothing which it can withhold and therefore nothing for which it can charge a price, whether the price be the cost of a license to do interstate business or a tax on the profits accruing from that business.

I venture to say that every other decision—I say decision, not talk or dicta—on which reliance is placed, presented a situation where conjoined with the interstate commerce was severable local state business on the basis of which the state taxing power became constitutionally operative. The difference between those situations and this, as a matter of economics, involves the distinction between taking into account the total activity of the enterprise as a going business in determining a fairly apportioned tax based on locally derived revenues, and taxing a portion of revenue concededly produced by exclusively interstate commerce. To be sure, such a distinction is a nice one, but the last word on the necessity of nice distinctions in this area was said by Mr. Justice Holmes in Galveston, H. & S.A.R. Co. v. State of Texas, 210

the State's entire taxing scheme. Aside from this issue of discrimination, the case was merely another instance of a State charging for the use of its highways.

The Court in Memphis Natural Gas Co. v. Beeler, supra, upheld a net income tax imposed by the State of Tennessee on revenues earned by the Memphis Gas Company from shipping gas into the State and selling it, together with another company, to retail consumers in that State. The decision was explicitly based on a determination that the revenue was, in fact, derived from intrastate rather than interstate commerce. In addition the Memphis Company was licensed to do business in Tennessee, maintained its principal place of business there, and sold much of its gas in that State. It is true that on the page cited in Beeler the opinion indulged in a dictum that net income from interstate commerce was taxable. But this was an almost by-the-way observation, itself relying on cita-

tions which do not support it, by a writer prone to uttering dicta.

International Shoe Co. v. State of Washington, supra, decided that the Due Process Clause of the Fourteenth Amendment did not prohibit the State of Washington from exercising jurisdiction over the International Shoe Co., in the light of the frequency and extent of the company's business contacts within the State. There was no doubt that the unemployment compensation contributions exacted by Washington were entirely consistent with the Commerce Clause, since Congress had explicitly authorized such levies.

Thus none of the cases cited in West support an interpretation of that decision which goes beyond the actual situation of severable local activities presented in that case. Nor do they support the present taxes levied on exclusively interstate business.

U.S. 217, 225, 28 S.Ct. 638, 639, 52 L.Ed. 1031: "It being once admitted, as of course it must be, that not every law that affects commerce * * * is a regulation of it in a constitutional sense, nice distinctions are to be expected."

Accordingly, today's decision cannot rest on the basis of adjudicated precedents. This does not bar the making of a new precedent. The history of the Commerce Clause is the history of judicial evolution. It is one thing, however, to recognize the taxing power of the States in relation to purely interstate activities and quite another thing to say that that power has already been established by the decisions of this Court. If new ground is to be broken, the ground must be justified and not treated as though it were old ground.

I do not think we should take this new step. My objection is the policy that underlies the Commerce Clause, namely, whatever disadvantages may accrue to the separate States from making of the United States a free-trade territory are far outweighed by the advantages not only to the United States as a Nation, but to the component States. I am assuming, of course, that today's decision will stimulate, if indeed it does not compel, every State of the Union, which has not already done so, to devise a formula of apportionment to tax the income of enterprises carrying on exclusively interstate commerce. As a result, interstate commerce will be burdened not hypothetically but practically, and we have been admonished again and again that taxation is a practical matter.

I think that interstate commerce will be not merely argumentatively but actively burdened for two reasons:

> *First.* It will not, I believe, be gainsaid that there are thousands of relatively small or moderate size corporations doing exclusively interstate business spread over several States. To subject these corporations to a separate income tax in each of these States means that they will have to keep books, make returns, store records, and engage legal counsel, all to meet the divers and variegated tax laws of forty-nine States, with their different times for filing returns, different tax structures, different modes for determining "net income," and different, often conflicting, formulas of apportionment. This will involve large increases in bookkeeping, accounting, and legal paraphernalia to meet these new demands. The cost of such a far-flung scheme for complying with the taxing requirements of the different States may well exceed the burden of the taxes themselves, especially in the case of small companies doing a small volume of business in several States.[2]

> *Second.* The extensive litigation in this Court which has challenged formulas of apportionment in the case of railroads and express companies [3]—challenges addressed to the natural temptation of the

---

2. For a detailed exposition of the manifold difficulties in complying with the diverse and complex taxing systems of the States, see Cohen, State Tax Allocations and Formulas which Affect Management

Operating Decisions, 1 Jour.Taxation, No. 2 (July 1954), p. 2.

3. See, e.g., Wallace v. Hines, 253 U.S. 66, 67, 40 S.Ct. 435, 436, 64 L.Ed. 782; Pullman's Palace Car Co. v. Common-

States to absorb more than their fair share of interstate revenue—will be multiplied many times when such formulas are applied to the infinitely larger number of other businesses which are engaged in exclusively interstate commerce. The division in this Court on these railroad apportionment cases is a good index of what might reasonably be expected when cases involving the more numerous non-transportation industries come before the Court. This is not a suggestion that the convenience of the Court should determine our construction of the Commerce Clause, although it is important in balancing the considerations relevant to the Commerce Clause against the claims of state power that this Court should be mindful of the kind of questions it will be called upon to adjudicate and its special competence for adjudicating them. Wholly apart from that, the necessity for litigation based on these elusive and essentially non-legal questions cast a burden on businesses, and consequently on interstate commerce itself, which should not be imposed.

These considerations do not at all lead to the conclusion that the vast amount of business carried on throughout all the States as part of what is exclusively interstate commerce should not be made to contribute to the cost of maintaining state governments which, as a practical matter, necessarily contribute to the conduct of that commerce by the mere fact of their existence as governments. The question is not whether a fair share of the profits derived from the carrying on of exclusively interstate commerce should contribute to the cost of the state governments. The question is whether the answer to this problem rests with this Court or with Congress.

I am not unmindful of the extent to which federal taxes absorb the taxable resources of the Nation, while at the same time the fiscal demands of the States are on the increase. These conditions present far-reaching problems of accommodating federal-state fiscal policy. But a determination of who is to get how much out of the common fund can hardly be made wisely and smoothly through the adjudicatory process. In fact, relying on the courts to solve these problems only aggravates the difficulties and retards proper legislative solution.

At best, this Court can only act negatively; it can determine whether a specific state tax is imposed in violation of the Commerce Clause. Such decisions must necessarily depend on the application of rough and ready legal concepts. We cannot make a detailed inquiry into the incidence of diverse economic burdens in order to determine the extent to which such burdens conflict with the necessities of national economic life. Neither can we devise appropriate standards for dividing up national revenue on the basis of more or less abstract principles of constitutional law, which cannot be responsive to the subtleties of the interrelated economies of Nation and State.

wealth of Pennsylvania, 141 U.S. 18, 11 S.Ct. 876, 35 L.Ed. 613; Adams Express Co. v. Ohio State Auditor, 165 U.S. 194, 17 S.Ct. 305, 41 L.Ed. 683; Id., 166 U.S. 185, 17 S.Ct. 604, 41 L.Ed. 965 (opinion denying rehearing).

The problem calls for solution by devising a congressional policy. Congress alone can provide for a full and thorough canvassing of the multitudinous and intricate factors which compose the problem of the taxing freedom of the States and the needed limits on such state taxing power.[4] Congressional committees can make studies and give the claims of the individual States adequate hearing before the ultimate legislative formulation of policy is made by the representatives of all the States. The solution to these problems ought not to rest on the self-serving determination of the States of what they are entitled to out of the Nation's resources. Congress alone can formulate policies founded upon economic realities, perhaps to be applied to the myriad situations involved by a properly constituted and duly informed administrative agency.* †

Notes and Problems

A. *Multiple Taxation: Actual or Potential Multiple Taxation as the Test.* In enunciating the multiple taxation doctrine, Justices Stone and Rutledge referred to the "risk" that other States might tax interstate commerce. See p. 219 supra. In the *Northwestern States–Stockham Valves* case, the Court appeared to regard the doctrine as requiring proof of actual multiple taxation. See p. 235 supra. In Mobil Oil Corp. v. Commissioner of Taxes of Vermont (p. 610 infra), the Court stated:

4. See Northwest Airlines, Inc., v. State of Minnesota, 322 U.S. 292, 64 S.Ct. 950, 88 L.Ed. 1283. In Northwest we pointed to the desirability of congressional action to formulate uniform standards for state taxation of the rapidly expanding airline industry. Following our decision Congress directed the Civil Aeronautics Board to study and report to Congress methods of eliminating burdensome, multiple state taxation of airlines. See H.R.Doc. No. 141, 79th Cong., 1st Sess. This report of the Board was a 158–page document whose length and complex economic content in dealing with only a single subject of state taxation, illustrate the difficulties and non-judicial nature of the problem. Following the presentation of this extensive report, several bills were introduced into Congress providing for a single uniform apportionment formula to be used by the States in taxing airlines. H.R. 1241, 80th Cong., 1st Sess.; S. 2453, 80th Cong., 2d Sess.; S. 420, 81st Cong., 1st Sess. None of these bills was enacted.

Australia has resolved the problem of conflicting and burdensome state taxation of commerce by a national arrangement whereby taxes are collected by the Commonwealth and from these revenues appropriate allocations are made annually to the States through the mechanism of a Premiers' Conference—the Prime Minister of the Commonwealth and the Premiers of the several States.

* [For references to the protest which the principal cases evoked among business groups and the resulting enactment of Congressional legislation restricting the power of the States to tax net income of interstate businesses, see Congressional Committee Reports, p. 388 n. 12 infra. For a development of the "nexus" issue, which is essentially a Due Process problem, see Chapter 11, § 4(d) infra. Cf. also, the "minimum activities" protected by P.L. 86–272, p. 387 infra.]

† [The drawing of the line between direct and indirect taxes was a major preoccupation of legislators, lawyers, and courts prior to the *Complete Auto Transit* case, which is set out at p. 247 infra. The determination as to whether a tax was levied on net income instead of gross income or gross receipts was one of the lines of demarcation drawn. See Atlantic Coast Line v. Doughton, 262 U.S. 413, 43 S.Ct. 620 (1922); Armco Steel Corp. v. Commissioner of Revenue, 359 Mich. 430, 102 N.W.2d 552 (1960), appeal dismissed 364 U.S. 337, 81 S.Ct. 124 (1960); see generally Dunham, "Gross Receipts Taxes on Interstate Transactions," 47 Colum.L.Rev. 211 (1947); Powell, "More Ado About Gross Receipts Taxes," 60 Harv.L.Rev. 501 (1947).]

Inasmuch as New York does not presently tax the dividends in question, actual multiple taxation is not demonstrated on this record. The Vermont courts placed some reliance on this fact, see, e.g., 136 Vt., at 548, 394 A.2d, at 1149, and much of the debate in this Court has aired the question whether an actual burden need be shown. Compare Standard Pressed Steel Co. v. Department of Revenue, 419 U.S. 560, 563–564, 95 S.Ct. 706, 709, 42 L.Ed.2d 719 (1975), and Freeman v. Hewit, 329 U.S. 249, 256, 67 S.Ct. 274, 278, 91 L.Ed. 265 (1946), with Northwestern States Portland Cement Co. v. Minnesota, 358 U.S., at 462–463, 79 S.Ct., at 364, and Northwest Airlines, Inc. v. Minnesota, 322 U.S. 292, 64 S.Ct. 950, 88 L.Ed. 1283 (1944). See also Japan Line, Ltd. v. County of Los Angeles, 441 U.S. 434, 452, n. 17, 99 S.Ct. 1813, 1823, n. 17, 60 L.Ed.2d 336 (1979). We agree with Mobil that the constitutionality of a Vermont tax should not depend on the vagaries of New York tax policy. But the absence of any existing duplicative tax does alter the nature of appellant's claim. Instead of seeking relief from a present tax burden, appellant seeks to establish a theoretical constitutional preference for one method of taxation over another. In appellant's view, the Commerce Clause requires allocation of dividend income to a single situs rather than apportionment among the States. [445 U.S. at 444, 100 S.Ct. at 1235].

What do you regard the present law to be: must the taxpayer show proof of actual duplicative taxation if the tax at issue should be sustained, or is the risk that another State would also be able to tax sufficient to invalidate the tax under the multiple taxation doctrine? What should the rule be?

SECTION 3. DOING BUSINESS TAXES

COMPLETE AUTO TRANSIT, INC. v. BRADY

Supreme Court of the United States, 1977.
430 U.S. 274, 97 S.Ct. 1076.

MR. JUSTICE BLACKMUN delivered the opinion of the Court.

Once again we are presented with " 'the perennial problem of the validity of a state tax for the privilege of carrying on within a state, certain activities' relating to a corporation's operation of an interstate business." Colonial Pipeline Co. v. Traigle, 421 U.S. 100, 101, 95 S.Ct. 1538, 1539, 44 L.Ed.2d 1 (1975), quoting Memphis Gas Co. v. Stone, 335 U.S. 80, 85, 68 S.Ct. 1475, 1477, 92 L.Ed. 1832 (1948). The issue in this case is whether Mississippi runs afoul of the Commerce Clause, Const., Art. I, § 8, cl. 3, when it applies the tax it imposes on "the privilege of * * * doing business" within the State to appellant's activity in interstate commerce. The Supreme Court of Mississippi unanimously sustained the tax against appellant's constitutional challenge. 330 So. 2d 268 (1976). We noted probable jurisdiction in order to consider anew the applicable principles in this troublesome area. 429 U.S. 813, 97 S.Ct. 52, 50 L.Ed.2d 72 (1976).

I

The taxes in question are sales taxes assessed by the Mississippi State Tax Commission against the appellant, Complete Auto Transit, Inc., for the period from August 1, 1968, through July 31, 1972. The assessments were made pursuant to the following Mississippi statutes:

"There is hereby levied and assessed and shall be collected privilege taxes for the privilege of engaging or continuing in business or doing business within this state to be determined by the application of rates against gross proceeds of sales or gross income or values, as the case may be, as provided in the following sections." Miss.Code Ann. § 10105 (1942), as amended.[1]

"Upon every person operating a pipeline, railroad, airplane, bus, truck, or any other transportation business for the transportation of persons or property for compensation or hire between points within this State, there is hereby levied, assessed, and shall be collected, a tax equal to five per cent (5%) of the gross income of such business * * *." Id., § 10109(2), as amended.[2]

Any person liable for the tax is required to add it to the gross sales price and, "insofar as practicable," to collect it at the time the sale price is collected. Section 10117, as amended.[3]

Appellant is a Michigan corporation engaged in the business of transporting motor vehicles by motor carrier for General Motors Corporation. General Motors assembles outside Mississippi vehicles that are destined for dealers within the State. The vehicles are then shipped by rail to Jackson, Miss., where, usually within 48 hours, they are loaded onto appellant's trucks and transported by appellant to the Mississippi dealers. App. 47–48, 78–79, 86–87. Appellant is paid on a contract basis for the transportation from the railhead to the dealers.[4] Id., at 50–51, 68.

1. The statute is now § 27–65–13 of the State's 1972 Code.

2. This statute is now § 27–65–19(2) of the 1972 Code. It was amended, effective August 1, 1972, to exclude the transportation of property. Laws 1972, c. 506, § 2.

Section 10109, as codified in 1942, imposed a tax on gross income from all transportation, with gross income defined to exclude "so much thereof as is derived from the business conducted in commerce between this state and other states of the United States * * * which the state of Mississippi is prohibited from taxing under the constitution of the United States of America." In 1955, this exclusionary language was eliminated and the statute was amended to cover only transportation "between points within this state." Laws 1955, c. 109, § 10. The amendment gave the statute essentially the form it possessed during the period relevant here.

It might be argued that the statute as so amended evinces an intent to reach only intrastate commerce, and that it should be so construed. Appellant, however, does not make that argument, and the Supreme Court of Mississippi clearly viewed that statute as applying to both intrastate commerce and interstate commerce.

We are advised by the appellee that the tax has been applied only to commercial transactions in which a distinct service is performed and payment made for transportation from one point within the State to another point within the State. Tr. of Oral Arg. 34–35, 38.

3. This statute is now § 27–65–31 of the 1972 Code. Violation of the requirements of the section is a misdemeanor. Ibid.

4. The parties understandably go to great pains to describe the details of the bills of lading, and the responsibility of various entities for the vehicles as they

By letter dated October 5, 1971, the Mississippi Tax Commission informed appellant that it was being assessed taxes and interest totalling $122,160.59 for the sales of transportation services during the three-year period from August 1, 1968, through July 31, 1971.[5] Remittance within 10 days was requested. App. 9–10. By similar letter dated December 28, 1972, the Commission advised appellant of an assessment of $42,990.89 for the period from August 1, 1971, through July 31, 1972. Id., at 11–12. Appellant paid the assessments under protest and, in April 1973, pursuant to § 10121.1, as amended, of the 1942 Code (now § 27–65–47 of the 1972 Code), instituted the present refund action in the Chancery Court of the First Judicial District of Hinds County.

Appellant claimed that its transportation was but one part of an interstate movement, and that the taxes assessed and paid were unconstitutional as applied to operations in interstate commerce. App. 4, 6–7. The Chancery Court, in an unreported opinion, sustained the assessments. App. 99–102.

The Mississippi Supreme Court affirmed. It concluded:

> "It will be noted that Taxpayer has a large operation in this State. It is dependent upon the State for police protection and other State services the same as other citizens. It should pay its fair share of taxes so long, but only so long, as the tax does not discriminate against interstate commerce, and there is no danger of interstate commerce being smothered by cumulative taxes of several states. There is no possibility of any other state duplicating the tax involved in this case." 330 So.2d, at 272.

Appellant, in its complaint in Chancery Court did not allege that its activity which Mississippi taxes does not have a sufficient nexus with the State; or that the tax discriminates against interstate commerce; or that the tax is unfairly apportioned; or that it is unrelated to services provided by the State.[6] No such claims were made before the Mississippi Supreme Court, and although appellant argues here that a tax on "the privilege of doing interstate commerce" creates an unac-

---

travel from the assembly plant to the dealers. Appellant seeks to demonstrate that the transportation it provides from the railhead to the dealers is part of a movement in interstate commerce. Appellee argues that appellant's transportation is intrastate business, but further argues that even if the activity is part of interstate commerce, the tax is not unconstitutional. Brief for Appellant 11–14; Brief for Appellee 12–24; Reply Brief for Appellant 14–16. The Mississippi courts, in upholding the tax, assumed that the transportation is in interstate commerce. For present purposes, we make the same assumption.

5. Although appellant had been operating in Mississippi since 1960, App. 77, the state audit and assessment covered only the period beginning August 1, 1968. Id., at 37–38. No effort had been made to apply the tax to appellant for any period prior to that date.

6. See Boston Stock Exchange v. State Tax Comm'n, 429 U.S. 318, 97 S.Ct. 599, 50 L.Ed.2d 514 (1977); General Motors Corp. v. Washington, 377 U.S. 436, 84 S.Ct. 1564, 12 L.Ed.2d 430 (1964); Illinois Cent. R. Co. v. Minnesota, 309 U.S. 157, 60 S.Ct. 419, 84 L.Ed. 670 (1940); Ingles v. Morf, 300 U.S. 290, 57 S.Ct. 439, 81 L.Ed. 653 (1937). See also Standard Pressed Steel Co. v. Department of Revenue, 419 U.S. 560, 95 S.Ct. 706, 42 L.Ed.2d 719 (1975), and Clark v. Paul Gray, Inc., 306 U.S. 583, 59 S.Ct. 744, 83 L.Ed. 1001 (1936).

ceptable risk of discrimination and undue burdens, Brief for Appellant 20–27, it does not claim that discrimination or undue burdens exist in fact.

Appellant's attack is based solely on decisions of this Court holding that a tax on the "privilege" of engaging in an activity in the State may not be applied to an activity that is part of interstate commerce. See, e.g., Spector Motor Service v. O'Connor, 340 U.S. 602, 71 S.Ct. 508, 95 L.Ed. 573 (1951); Freeman v. Hewit, 329 U.S. 249, 67 S.Ct. 274, 91 L.Ed. 265 (1946). This rule looks only to the fact that the incidence of the tax is the "privilege of doing business"; it deems irrelevant any consideration of the practical effect of the tax. The rule reflects an underlying philosophy that interstate commerce should enjoy a sort of "free trade" immunity from state taxation.[7]

Appellee, in its turn, relies on decisions of this Court stating that "[i]t was not the purpose of the commerce clause to relieve those engaged in interstate commerce from their just share of state tax burden even though it increases the cost of doing the business," Western Live Stock v. Bureau of Revenue, 303 U.S. 250, 254, 58 S.Ct. 546, 548, 82 L.Ed. 823 (1938). These decisions [8] have considered not the formal language of the tax statute, but rather its practical effect, and have sustained a tax against Commerce Clause challenge when the tax is applied to an activity with a substantial nexus with the taxing State, is fairly apportioned, does not discriminate against interstate commerce, and is fairly related to the services provided by the State.

Over the years, the Court has applied this practical analysis in approving many types of tax that avoided running afoul of the prohibition against taxing the "privilege of doing business," but in each instance it has refused to overrule the prohibition. Under the present state of the law, the *Spector* rule, as it has come to be known, has no relationship to economic realities. Rather it stands only as a trap for the unwary draftsman.

7. The Court summarized the "free trade" view in Freeman v. Hewit, 329 U.S., at 252, 67 S.Ct. at 276:

"[T]he Commerce Clause was not merely an authorization to Congress to enact laws for the protection and encouragement of commerce among the States, but by its own force created an area of trade free from interference by the States. In short, the Commerce Clause even without implementing legislation by Congress is a limitation upon the power of the States. * * * This limitation on State power * * * does not merely forbid a State to single out interstate commerce for hostile action. A State is also precluded from taking any action which may fairly be deemed to have the effect of impeding the free flow of trade between States. It is immaterial that local commerce is subjected to a similar encumbrance."

8. See, e.g., General Motors Corp. v. Washington, supra; Northwestern Cement Co. v. Minnesota, 358 U.S. 450, 79 S.Ct. 357, 3 L.Ed.2d 421 (1959); Memphis Gas Co. v. Stone, 335 U.S. 80, 68 S.Ct. 1475, 92 L.Ed. 1832 (1948); Wisconsin v. J.C. Penney Co., 311 U.S. 435, 444, 61 S.Ct. 246, 249, 85 L.Ed. 267 (1940).

II

The modern origin of the *Spector* rule may be found in Freeman v. Hewit, supra.[9] At issue in *Freeman* was the application of an Indiana tax upon "the receipt of the entire gross income" of residents and domiciliaries. 329 U.S., at 250, 67 S.Ct., at 275. Indiana sought to impose this tax on income generated when a trustee of an Indiana estate instructed his local stockbroker to sell certain securities. The broker arranged with correspondents in New York to sell the securities on the New York Stock Exchange. The securities were sold, and the New York brokers, after deducting expense and commission, transmitted the proceeds to the Indiana broker who in turn delivered them, less his commission, to the trustee. The Indiana Supreme Court sustained the tax, but this Court reversed.

Mr. Justice Frankfurter, speaking for five Members of the Court, announced a blanket prohibition against any state taxation imposed directly on an interstate transaction. He explicitly deemed unnecessary to the decision of the case any showing of discrimination against interstate commerce or error in apportionment of the tax. Id., at 254, 256–257, 67 S.Ct., at 277, 278–79. He recognized that a State could constitutionally tax local manufacture, impose license taxes on corporations doing business in the State, tax property within the State, and tax the privilege of residence in the State and measure the privilege by net income, including that derived from interstate commerce. Id., at 255, 67 S.Ct., at 278. Nevertheless, a direct tax on interstate sales, even if fairly apportioned and nondiscriminatory, was held to be unconstitutional *per se.*

Mr. Justice Rutledge, in a lengthy concurring opinion, argued that the tax should be judged by its economic effects rather than by its formal phrasing. After reviewing the Court's prior decisions, he concluded: "The fact is that 'direct incidence' of a state tax or regulation * * * has long since been discarded as being itself sufficient to outlaw state legislation." Id., at 265–266, 67 S.Ct., at 283–284. In his view, a state tax is unconstitutional only if the activity lacks the necessary connection with the taxing State to give "jurisdiction to tax," id., at 271, 67 S.Ct., at 286, or if the tax discriminates against interstate commerce, or if the activity is subject to multiple taxation. Id., at 276–277, 67 S.Ct., at 289.[10]

9. Although we mention *Freeman* as the starting point, elements of the views expressed therein, and the positions that underlie that debate, were evident in prior opinions. Compare State Tax on Railway Gross Receipts, 15 Wall. (82 U.S.) 284, 21 L.Ed. 164 (1872), with Fargo v. Michigan, 121 U.S. 230, 7 S.Ct. 857, 30 L.Ed. 888 (1887); and compare Di Santo v. Pennsylvania, 273 U.S. 34, 47 S.Ct. 267, 71 L.Ed. 524 (1927), and Cooney v. Mountain States Tel. Co., 294 U.S. 384, 55 S.Ct. 477, 79 L.Ed. 934 (1935), with Western Live Stock v. Bureau of Revenue, 303 U.S. 250, 58 S.Ct. 546, 82 L.Ed. 823 (1938). See generally, P. Hartman, State Taxation of Interstate Commerce (1953); Barrett, "State Taxation of Interstate Commerce—'Direct Burdens,' 'Multiple Burdens,' or What Have You?," 4 Vand.L.Rev. 496 (1951), and writings cited therein at 496 n. 1; Dunham, "Gross Receipts Taxes on Interstate Transactions," 47 Col.L.Rev. 211 (1947).

10. Mr. Justice Rutledge agreed with the result the Court reached in *Freeman*

The rule announced in *Freeman* was viewed in the commentary as a triumph of formalism over substance, providing little guidance even as to formal requirements. See P. Hartman, State Taxation of Interstate Commerce 200–204 (1953); Dunham, "Gross Receipts Taxes on Interstate Transactions," 47 Col.L.Rev. 211 (1947). Although the rule might have been utilized as the keystone of a movement toward absolute immunity of interstate commerce from state taxation,[11] the Court consistently has indicated that "interstate commerce may be made to pay its way," and has moved toward a standard of permissibility of state taxation based upon its actual effect rather than its legal terminology.

The narrowing of the rule to one of draftsmanship and phraseology began with another Mississippi case, Memphis Gas Co. v. Stone, 335 U.S. 80, 68 S.Ct. 1475, 92 L.Ed. 1832 (1948). Memphis Natural Gas Company owned and operated a pipeline running from Louisiana to Memphis. Approximately 135 miles of the line were in Mississippi. Mississippi imposed a "franchise or excise" tax measured by "the value of the capital used, invested or employed in the exercise of any power, privilege or right enjoyed by [a corporation] within this state." Miss. Code Ann. § 9313 (1942). The Mississippi Supreme Court upheld the tax, and this Court affirmed.

In an opinion for himself and two others, Mr. Justice Reed noted that the tax was not discriminatory, that there was no possibility of multiple taxation, that the amount of the tax was reasonable, and that the tax was properly apportioned to the investment in Mississippi. 335 U.S., at 87–88, 68 S.Ct., at 1478–79. He then went on to consider whether the tax was "upon the privilege of doing interstate business within the state." Id., at 88, 68 S.Ct., at 1479. He drew a distinction between a tax on "the privilege of doing business" and a tax on "the privilege of exercising corporate functions within the State," and held that while the former is unconstitutional, the latter is not barred by the Commerce Clause. Id., at 88–93, 68 S.Ct., at 1481. He then approved the tax there at issue because:

> "[T]here is no attempt to tax the privilege of doing an interstate business or to secure anything from the corporation by this statute except compensation for the protection of the enumerated local activities of 'maintaining, keeping in repair, and otherwise in manning the facilities.'" Id., at 93, 68 S.Ct., at 1482.

Mr. Justice Black concurred in the judgment without opinion. Id., at 96, 68 S.Ct., at 1483. Mr. Justice Rutledge provided the fifth vote, stating in his concurrence:

because of his belief that the apportionment problem was best solved if States other than the market State were forbidden to impose unapportioned gross receipts taxes of the kind Indiana sought to exact.

of course, would have necessitated overruling the cases approved by the *Freeman* Court that upheld taxes whose burden, although indirect, fell on interstate commerce.

11. A consistent application of the doctrine of immunity for interstate commerce,

"[I]t is enough for me to sustain the tax imposed in this case that it is one clearly within the state's power to lay insofar as any limitation of due process or 'jurisdiction to tax' in that sense is concerned; it is nondiscriminatory, that is, places no greater burden upon interstate commerce than the state places upon competing intrastate commerce of like character; is duly apportioned, that is, does not undertake to tax any interstate activities carried on outside the state's borders; and cannot be repeated by any other state." Id., at 96–97, 68 S.Ct., at 1483–1484. (footnotes omitted).

Four Justices dissented, id., at 99, 68 S.Ct., at 1485, on the grounds that it had not been shown that the State afforded any protection in return for the tax,[12] and that, therefore, the tax must be viewed as one on the "privilege" of engaging in interstate commerce. The dissenters recognized that an identical effect could be achieved by an increase in the ad valorem property tax, id., at 104, 68 S.Ct., at 1487 but would have held, notwithstanding, that a tax on the "privilege" is unconstitutional.

The prohibition against state taxation of the "privilege" of engaging in commerce that is interstate was reaffirmed in Spector Motor Service v. O'Connor, 340 U.S. 602, 71 S.Ct. 508, 95 L.Ed. 573 (1951), a case similar on its facts to the instant case. The taxpayer there was a Missouri corporation engaged exclusively in interstate trucking. Some of its shipments originated or terminated in Connecticut. Connecticut imposed on a corporation a "tax or excise upon its franchise for the privilege of carrying on or doing business within the state," measured by apportioned net income. 340 U.S., at 603–604, n. 1, 71 S.Ct. at 509. Spector brought suit in federal court to enjoin collection of the tax as applied to its activities. The District Court issued the injunction. The Second Circuit reversed. This Court, with three Justices in dissent, in turn reversed the Court of Appeals and held the tax unconstitutional as applied.

The Court recognized that "where a taxpayer is engaged both in intrastate and interstate commerce, a state may tax the privilege of carrying on intrastate business and, within reasonable limits, may compute the amount of the charge by applying the tax rate to a fair proportion of the taxpayer's business done within the state, including both interstate and intrastate." Id., at 609–610, 71 S.Ct., at 512 (footnote omitted). It held, nevertheless, that a tax on the "privilege" of doing business is unconstitutional if applied against what is exclusively interstate commerce. The dissenters argued, on the other hand, id., at 610, 71 S.Ct., at 512, that there is no constitutional difference

---

12. In arriving at this conclusion, the dissent relied upon a construction of a stipulation entered into by the parties, 335 U.S. at 100–101, 68 S.Ct., at 1485–86, and upon an independent review of the record. The plurality rejected the dissent's reading of the stipulation and noted, in addition, that the question presented in the petition for certiorari did not raise a claim that the State was providing no service for which it could ask recompense. Id., at 83–84, 68 S.Ct., at 1476–77. The plurality then relied on the Supreme Court of Mississippi's holding that the State did provide protection that could properly be the subject of a tax.

between an "exclusively interstate" business and a "mixed" business, and that a fairly apportioned and nondiscriminatory tax on either type is not prohibited by the Commerce Clause.

The *Spector* rule was applied in Railway Express Agency v. Virginia, 347 U.S. 359, 74 S.Ct. 558, 98 L.Ed. 337 (1954) (*Railway Express I*), to declare unconstitutional a State's "annual license tax" levied on gross receipts for the "privilege of doing business in this State." The Court, by a 5 to 4 vote, held that the tax on gross receipts was a tax on the privilege of doing business rather than a tax on property in the State, as Virginia contended.

Virginia thereupon revised the wording of its statute to impose a "franchise tax" on "intangible property" in the form of "going concern" value as measured by gross receipts. The tax was again asserted against the Agency which in Virginia was engaged exclusively in interstate commerce. This Court's opinion, buttressed by two concurring opinions and one concurrence in the result, upheld the reworded statute as not violative of the *Spector* rule. Railway Express Agency v. Virginia, 358 U.S. 434, 79 S.Ct. 411, 3 L.Ed.2d 450 (1959) (*Railway Express II*). In upholding the statute, the Court's opinion recognized that the rule against taxing the "privilege" of doing interstate business had created a situation where "the use of magic words or labels" could "disable an otherwise constitutional levy." Id., at 441, 79 S.Ct., at 416.

There was no real economic difference between the statutes in *Railway Express I* and *Railway Express II*. The Court long since had recognized that interstate commerce may be made to pay its way. Yet under the *Spector* rule, the economic realities in *Railway Express I* became irrelevant. The *Spector* rule had come to operate only as a rule of draftsmanship, and served only to distract the courts and parties from their inquiry into whether the challenged tax produced results forbidden by the Commerce Clause.

On the day it announced *Railway Express II*, the Court further confirmed that a State, with proper drafting, may tax exclusively interstate commerce so long as the tax does not create any effect forbidden by the Commerce Clause. In Northwestern Cement Co. v. Minnesota, 358 U.S. 450, 79 S.Ct. 357, 3 L.Ed.2d 421 (1959), the Court held that net income from the interstate operations of a foreign corporation may be subjected to state taxation, provided the levy is not discriminatory and is properly apportioned to local activities within the taxing State forming sufficient nexus to support the tax. Limited in that way, the tax could be levied even though the income was generated exclusively by interstate sales. *Spector* was distinguished, briefly and in passing, as a case in which "the incidence" of the tax "was the privilege of doing business." Id., 358 U.S. at 464, 79 S.Ct., at 365.

Thus, applying the rule of *Northwestern Cement* to the facts of *Spector*, it is clear that Connecticut could have taxed the apportioned net income derived from the exclusively interstate commerce. It could not, however, tax the "privilege" of doing business as measured by the apportioned net income. The reason for attaching constitutional significance to a semantic difference is difficult to discern.

The unsatisfactory operation of the *Spector* rule is well demonstrated by our recent case of Colonial Pipeline Co. v. Traigle, 421 U.S. 100, 95 S.Ct. 1538, 44 L.Ed.2d 1 (1975). Colonial was a Delaware corporation with an interstate pipeline running through Louisiana for approximately 258 miles. It maintained a work force and pumping stations in Louisiana to keep the pipeline flowing, but it did no intrastate business in that State. Id., at 101–102, 95 S.Ct., at 1539–40. In 1962, Louisiana imposed on Colonial a franchise tax for "the privilege of carrying on or doing business" in the State. The Louisiana Court of Appeal invalidated the tax as violative of the rule of *Spector.* 228 So.2d 718 (La.App. 1969). The Supreme Court of Louisiana refused review. 255 La. 474, 231 So.2d 393 (1970). The Louisiana Legislature, perhaps recognizing that it had run afoul of a rule of words rather than a rule of substance, then redrafted the statute to levy the tax, as an alternative incident, on the "qualification to carry on or do business in this state or the actual doing of business within this state in a corporate form." Again, the Court of Appeal held the tax unconstitutional as applied to the appellant. 275 So.2d 834 (La.App.1973). But this time the Louisiana Supreme Court upheld the new tax. 289 So.2d 93 (La.1974).

By a 7 to 1 vote, this Court affirmed. No question had been raised as to the propriety of the apportionment of the tax, and no claim was made that the tax was discriminatory. 421 U.S., at 101, 95 S.Ct., at 1539. The Court noted that the tax was imposed on that aspect of interstate commerce to which the State bore a special relation, and that the State bestowed powers, privileges, and benefits sufficient to support a tax on doing business in the corporate form in Louisiana. Id., at 109, 95 S.Ct., at 1543. Accordingly, on the authority of *Memphis Gas,* the tax was held to be constitutional. The Court distinguished *Spector* on the familiar ground that it involved a tax on the privilege of carrying on interstate commerce, while the Louisiana Legislature, in contrast, had worded the statute at issue "narrowly to confine the impost to one related to appellant's activities within the State in the corporate form." Id., at 113–114, 95 S.Ct., at 1546.[13]

> While refraining from overruling *Spector,* the Court noted that
>
> "decisions of this Court, particularly during recent decades, have sustained nondiscriminatory, properly apportioned state corporate taxes upon foreign corporations doing an exclusively interstate business when the tax is related to a corporation's local activities and the State has provided benefits and protections for those activities for which it is justified in asking a fair and reasonable return." Id., at 108, 95 S.Ct., at 1543.

13. Five Members of the Court joined in the opinion distinguishing *Spector.* Two concurred in the judgment, but viewed *Spector* as indistinguishable and would have overruled it. 421 U.S., at 114–116, 95 S.Ct., at 1546–47. One also viewed *Spector* as indistinguishable, but felt that it was an established precedent until forthrightly overruled. Id., at 116, 95 S.Ct., at 1547. Mr. Justice Douglas took no part.

One commentator concluded: "After reading *Colonial,* only the most sanguine taxpayer would conclude that the Court maintains a serious belief in the doctrine that the privilege of doing interstate business is immune from state taxation." W. Hellerstein, "State Taxation of Interstate Business and the Supreme Court, 1974 Term: *Standard Pressed Steel* and *Colonial Pipeline,*" 62 Va.L.Rev. 149, 188 (1976).[14]

III

In this case, of course, we are confronted with a situation like that presented in *Spector.* The tax is labeled a privilege tax "for the privilege of * * * doing business" in Mississippi, § 10105 of the State's 1942 Code, as amended, and the activity taxed is, or has been assumed to be, interstate commerce. We note again that no claim is made that the activity is not sufficiently connected to the State to justify a tax, or that the tax is not fairly related to benefits provided the taxpayer, or that the tax discriminates against interstate commerce, or that the tax is not fairly apportioned.

The view of the Commerce Clause that gave rise to the rule of *Spector* perhaps was not without some substance. Nonetheless, the possibility of defending it in the abstract does not alter the fact that the Court has rejected the proposition that interstate commerce is immune from state taxation:

> "It is a truism that the mere act of carrying on business in interstate commerce does not exempt a corporation from state taxation. 'It was not the purpose of the commerce clause to relieve those engaged in interstate commerce from their just share of state tax burden even though it increases the cost of doing business.' Western Live Stock v. Bureau of Revenue, 303 U.S. 250, 254, 58 S.Ct. 546, 548, 82 L.Ed. 823 (1938)." Colonial Pipeline Co. v. Traigle, 421 U.S., at 108, 95 S.Ct., at 1543.

Not only has the philosophy underlying the rule been rejected, but the rule itself has been stripped of any practical significance. If Mississippi had called its tax one on "net income" or on the "going concern value" of appellant's business, the *Spector* rule could not invalidate it. There is no economic consequence that follows necessarily from the use of the particular words, "privilege of doing business," and a focus on that formalism merely obscures the question whether the tax produces a forbidden effect. Simply put, the *Spector* rule does not address the problems with which the Commerce Clause is concerned.[15] Accordingly, we now reject the rule of Spector Motor Service,

14. Less charitably put: "In light of the expanding scope of the state taxing power over interstate commerce, *Spector* is an anachronism. * * * Continued adherence to *Spector,* especially after *Northwestern States Portland Cement,* cannot be justified." Comment, "Pipelines, Privileges and Labels: Colonial Pipeline Co. v. Traigle," 70 Nw.U.L.Rev. 835, 854 (1975).

15. It might be argued that "privilege" taxes, by focusing on the doing of business, are easily tailored to single out interstate businesses and subject them to effects forbidden by the Commerce Clause, and that, therefore, "privilege" taxes should be subjected to a *per se* rule against their imposition on interstate business. Yet property taxes also may be tailored to differentiate

Inc. v. O'Connor, supra, that a state tax on the "privilege of doing business" is *per se* unconstitutional when it is applied to interstate commerce, and that case is overruled.

There being no objection to Mississippi's tax on appellant except that it was imposed on nothing other than the "privilege of doing business" that is interstate, the judgment of the Supreme Court of Mississippi is affirmed.

It is so ordered.

Notes and Problems

A. Although the tax at issue in the principal case is designated a "sales tax," the statutory provisions involved are not those imposing a retail sales tax. Instead, like the Washington business activities tax, the Mississippi levy is imposed for "the privilege of doing business in the State," and it applies to transportation, manufacturing, wholesaling, and various other types of businesses. The tax is measured by "the gross proceeds of sales or gross income or values." Miss.Code § 27–65–13 et seq., CCH ¶ 97–154, P–H ¶ 22,005. The same statute also imposes a retail sales and use tax which is patterned after those in force in most States, and is required to be collected as such by the vendor from the purchaser. Miss. Code §§ 27–65–17, 25–65–31, CCH ¶¶ 97–154 and 97–241, P–H ¶¶ 22,020 and 22,065.

There was no apportionment controversy in the case, even though the tax was imposed on the full amounts paid by General Motors to the taxpayer, because the entire transportation service was rendered between points in Mississippi. Under the usual methods of dividing the measures of taxes on transportation companies, receipts or income are apportioned or allocated to the State to the extent the transportation takes place within its borders. See Chapter 9 infra.

B. The principal case has implications far beyond the overruling of the *Spector* case doctrine. The Connecticut tax on the privilege of doing business at issue in *Spector* was measured by net income. The rationale of the Second Circuit in sustaining the constitutionality of the tax was that because it was measured by net income as distinguished from gross income

between property used in transportation and other types of property, see *Railway Express II*, supra; an income tax could use different rates for different types of business; and a tax on the "privilege of doing business in corporate form" could be made to change with the nature of the corporate activity involved. Any tailored tax of this sort creates an increased danger of error in apportionment, of discrimination against interstate commerce, and of a lack of relationship to the services provided by the State. See Freeman v. Hewit, 329 U.S., at 265–266, n. 13, 67 S.Ct., at 283 (concurring opinion). A tailored tax however accomplished, must receive the careful scrutiny of the courts to determine whether it pro-

duces a forbidden effect on interstate commerce. We perceive no reason, however, why a tax on the "privilege of doing business" should be viewed as creating a qualitatively different danger so as to require a *per se* rule of unconstitutionality.

It might also be argued that adoption of a rule of absolute immunity for interstate commerce (a rule that would, of course, go beyond *Spector*) would relieve this Court of difficult judgments that on occasion will have to be made. We believe, however, that administrative convenience, in this instance, is insufficient justification for abandoning the principle that "interstate commerce may be made to pay its way."

or gross receipts, it imposed only an indirect burden on interstate commerce. Spector Motor Service, Inc. v. O'Connor, 181 F.2d 150 (2d Cir.1950). The Supreme Court reversed on the ground that the Commerce Clause precludes State taxation of the privilege of conducting an exclusively interstate business, regardless of the measure of the tax.

In the principal case the Court not only overruled that holding of *Spector,* but in addition embraced a view of the taxing powers of the States, under the Commerce Clause, which appears to make irrelevant the classification of a tax as a direct, as distinguished from an indirect, levy on interstate commerce. The Court repudiated the tax-free haven for interstate commerce approach to the Commerce Clause, whose most ardent advocate during the 1940's and 1950's had been Justice Frankfurter. It rejected the "blanket prohibition against any state taxation directly on an interstate transaction" "announced by" Justice Frankfurter for the Court in *Freeman v. Hewit,* and instead approved the Commerce Clause philosophy that had been enunciated by Justice Rutledge in that case:

> "The fact is that 'direct incidence' of a state tax or regulation * * * has long since been discarded as being itself sufficient to outlaw state legislation." In [Justice Rutledge's] view, a state tax is unconstitutional only if the activity lacks the necessary connection with the taxing state to give "jurisdiction to tax," or if the tax discriminates against interstate commerce, or if the activity is subject to multiple taxation. [97 S.Ct. at 1080.]

In the principal case, the Court articulated the guiding principles in the following terms: "[Our] decisions * * * have sustained a tax against Commerce Clause challenge when the tax is applied to an activity with a substantial nexus with the taxing State, is fairly apportioned, does not discriminate against interstate commerce, and is fairly related to the services provided by the State." The Court has consistently repeated this four-part test in its Commerce Clause decisions following *Complete Auto Transit* (see, e.g., Japan Line, Ltd. v. County of Los Angeles, p. 313 infra; Commonwealth Edison Co. v. Montana, p. 296 infra), and it has emerged as the starting point for much of modern Commerce Clause analysis of State taxes.

In the third edition of this work, published in 1969, we stated:

> The present posture of the Court is characteristic of its entire history in dealing with Commerce Clause tax issues—the great issues involved reflect sharp differences in approach among the Justices, the leading cases are decided by slim majorities over strong dissent, and both the rationale and holdings are fluid and dynamic, with one decade's minority becoming the next decade's majority, only to be displaced in another decade by a new majority. * * * [I]n two decisions which are among the most significant in the history of the Commerce Clause—the 1959 decisions in the *Northwestern Portland Cement* and the *Stockham Valves* case—the Court validated the direct net income tax as applied to exclusively interstate businesses. [P. 169.]

Justice Clark wrote the opinion for the majority in those cases, and his opinion was joined by Chief Justice Warren and Justices Black, Douglas, and Brennan. Justice Harlan concurred in a separate opinion, Justices Frankfurter, Whittaker and Stewart dissented.

By way of contrast, *Complete Auto Transit* was a unanimous decision. However, three Justices dissented in the subsequent *Commonwealth Edison* case, p. 296 infra, and one Justice dissented in *Japan Line*, p. 313 infra. See generally W. Hellerstein, "State Taxation and the Supreme Court: Toward a More Unified Approach to Constitutional Adjudication?," 75 Mich.L.Rev. 1426 (1977).

C. *Comparison of the Requirements of the Commerce and Due Process Clauses.* Of the four criteria that the Court identified as controlling Commerce Clause adjudication over State taxes, see Note B supra, two of them—nexus and apportionment—have likewise been held to be required under the Due Process Clause. See Chapters 8 and 9 infra. Indeed, the Court itself has declared that the substance of the nexus and apportionment requirements embodied in the two clauses is essentially the same. See National Bellas Hess, Inc. v. Department of Revenue, 386 U.S. 753, 756, 87 S.Ct. 1389 (1967) (nexus), p. 812 infra; Container Corp. of America v. Franchise Tax Bd., 463 U.S. 159, 169, 103 S.Ct. 2933 (1983) (apportionment), p. 578 infra. Since the impact of the fourth prong of the Commerce Clause test was severely limited by Commonwealth Edison Co. v. Montana, 453 U.S. 609, 101 S.Ct. 2946 (1981), which is set out at p. 296 infra, it may well be that what is left of the Commerce Clause as an independent restraint on State taxation is the prohibition against discrimination and the related restraint against multiple taxation.

SECTION 4. GROSS RECEIPTS TAXES

INTRODUCTORY NOTE

(a) Gross Receipts Taxes on Instrumentalities of Interstate Commerce

The tax at issue in *Complete Auto Transit* was applied to a transportation company, it was measured by gross receipts, and the opinion proceeded on the premise that, like Spector Motor Service, the taxpayer was engaged in "exclusively interstate commerce." The decision upholding such a tax may be read as the Court's coup de grace to sixty years of decisions, beginning in 1887, in which non-discriminatory gross receipts taxes on the instrumentalities of interstate commerce had been invalidated. In more recent cases, including the two *Railway Express* cases discussed in the opinion in *Complete Auto Transit*, the Court had begun to whittle away at its former zealous safeguarding of interstate communication and transportation from State gross receipts taxes.

From 1887 to 1937 the Supreme Court expressly invalidated nine non-discriminatory State taxes on or measured by gross receipts from interstate commerce. All of these involved receipts from transportation or communication. Lockhart, "Gross Receipts Taxes on Interstate Transportation or Communication," 57 Harv.L.Rev. 40 (1943).

The foundation for these holdings was the oft repeated dictum in Leloup v. Port of Mobile, 127 U.S. 640, 648, 8 S.Ct. 1380 (1888) that:

no state has the right to lay a tax on interstate commerce in any form, whether by way of duties laid on the transportation of the subject of that commerce, or on the receipts derived from that transportation, or on the occupation or business of carrying it on, and the reason is that such taxation is a burden on that commerce, and amounts to a regulation of it, which belongs solely to Congress.

As pointed out by Professor Lockhart, this rule was applied to condemn gross receipts taxes on railway, steamship, telegraph and telephone companies and to both apportioned and unapportioned levies alike. And it was applied to stevedoring companies, all of whose receipts were derived from loading and unloading vessels engaged in interstate or foreign commerce but where the stevedores' activities took place in a single State. Puget Sound Stevedoring Co. v. State Tax Commission, 302 U.S. 90, 58 S.Ct. 72 (1937); Joseph v. Carter & Weekes Stevedoring Co., 330 U.S. 422, 67 S.Ct. 815 (1947). In those cases the taxes were levied on the privilege of doing business, measured by gross receipts, and the Court held that the stevedores were engaged in interstate or foreign commerce.

In Department of Revenue of the State of Washington v. Association of Washington Stevedoring Co., 435 U.S. 734, 98 S.Ct. 1388 (1978), however, the Court overruled the stevedoring cases on the basis of its opinion in *Complete Auto Transit.* The Court stated that the earlier cases were based on two premises:

(1) Taxes on the privilege of doing business conflict with the power of Congress to regulate commerce, when they are applied to a business conducted exclusively in interstate or foreign commerce.

(2) Direct taxes on interstate commerce constitute undue burdens on the commerce; taxes measured by gross receipts from the commerce are direct taxes and, therefore, violate the Commerce Clause.

Since both the foregoing premises had been repudiated in *Complete Auto Transit,* the State of Washington's business and occupation tax on the privilege of doing business, although measured by gross receipts, could be applied to stevedores engaged in loading and unloading vessels operating exclusively in interstate and foreign commerce.

[The Court's treatment of the Import–Export Clause issues is considered in Chapter 7.]

Two cases involving interstate transportation did not neatly fit into the rationale of the Court's earlier decisions dealing with gross receipts taxes on instrumentalities of interstate commerce. In Central Greyhound Lines, Inc. v. Mealey, 334 U.S. 653, 68 S.Ct. 1260 (1948), the Court invalidated a New York State tax levied on gross receipts derived from bus transportation between points within New York State but over routes that utilized highways in New Jersey and Pennsylvania. The Court held that the bus operation constituted interstate commerce and that the vice of the tax under the Commerce Clause lay in the fact that it was unapportioned, that New York sought to tax receipts from the roughly 40 percent of the routes in the neighboring States, as well as the receipts from the 60 percent traveled in New York. Mr. Justice Frankfurter stated that although the tax was construed by the New York courts as levying an unapportioned gross receipts tax "the entire tax need not fail. The tax may be 'fairly apportioned' to the 'business done within the State by a fair method of apportionment' * * * [and] the tax may constitutionally be sustained on the receipts from the transportation apportioned as to the mileage within the State." 334 U.S. at 663, 68 S.Ct. at 1266. The rationale of the *Central Greyhound* case was followed in Canton R. v. Rogan, 340 U.S. 511, 71 S.Ct. 447 (1951), in sustaining a Maryland franchise tax as applied to a railroad engaged in interstate commerce; the levy was apportioned according to mileage within the State.

In Cooney v. Mountain States Telephone & Telegraph Co., 294 U.S. 384, 55 S.Ct. 477 (1935), the Court invalidated a tax on an instrumentality of interstate commerce which carried on a combined intrastate and interstate business, on the ground that the two aspects of the business were so "inextricably intermingled" that, as a practical matter, the intrastate business could not be given up without also abandoning the interstate business. See also City of Chicago v. Willet Co., 344 U.S. 574, 73 S.Ct. 460 (1953); but cf. Pacific Telephone & Telegraph Co. v. Tax Comm'n of Washington, 297 U.S. 403, 56 S.Ct. 522 (1936). Cases involving interstate broadcasting and telecasting present the intermingled intrastate-interstate business problem, which has presumably lost any importance after the decision in *Complete Auto Transit*. For the cases dealing with the taxation of radio and television stations, see Section 7(b) infra. The intermingled intrastate-interstate business cases are discussed in the third edition of this work at page 244.

(b) Taxes in Lieu of Property Taxes

The Court had sustained a number of gross receipts taxes aimed expressly at railroads and other instrumentalities of interstate commerce as taxes in lieu of property levies. Maine v. Grand Trunk Railway Co., 142 U.S. 217, 12 S.Ct. 121 (1891); Postal Telegraph Cable Co. v. Adams, 155 U.S. 688, 15 S.Ct. 268 (1895); United States Express Co. v. Minnesota, 223 U.S. 335, 32 S.Ct. 211 (1912). The rationale of these holdings was that the levies are not imposed on interstate commerce or receipts from the commerce, but that the gross receipts apportioned to the State are used as a measure of the value of the corporation's property, including its franchises, measures which the Court found not unreasonable. Where, however, the levies on interstate transportation or communication companies were found by the Court to have been imposed on "gross receipts" or on "the interstate business" and not in truth "a just equivalent" for the "ordinary property tax," they had been condemned. Galveston, H. & S.A. Ry. Co. v. Texas, 210 U.S. 217, 28 S.Ct. 638 (1908) (here the levy was imposed in addition to the usual ad valorem property tax); Meyer v. Wells, Fargo & Co., 223 U.S. 298, 32 S.Ct. 218 (1912); New Jersey Bell Telephone Co. v. State Board of Taxes, 280 U.S. 338, 50 S.Ct. 111 (1930). The distinctions between the levies sustained and those invalidated were frequently based on formal language differences, with the nature and effects of apportionment given insufficient consideration. Indeed, the Court declared that "we will not inquire into the exactitudes of the formula where appellant has not shown it to be so baseless as to violate due process." Railway Express Agency, Inc. v. Virginia, 358 U.S. 434, 436, 79 S.Ct. 411, 413 (1959).

Notes and Problems

A. *Broad-based Gross Receipts Taxes.* The States have long employed gross receipts taxes directed specifically at interstate transportation and communication (and at other public utilities.) A few States have employed an excise tax on most business activity in the State. The taxes are measured by the gross receipts, gross income, gross proceeds, or gross values derived from the activity in question. The States of Washington and West Virginia have employed such levies (denominated Business and Occupation (B & O) Taxes) for many years, although West Virginia replaced its B & O tax with a net income tax as of July 1, 1987. Hawaii and New Mexico also employ broad-based taxes measured by gross receipts as do many municipalities.

B. In Field Enterprises, Inc. v. State, 47 Wash.2d 852, 289 P.2d 1010 (1955), affirmed 352 U.S. 806, 77 S.Ct. 55 (1956), a publisher of encyclopedias sold throughout the country challenged the application to it of the State of Washington's excise tax on the privilege or act of doing business in the State; the tax is measured by the gross proceeds of sales. The taxpayer, a Delaware corporation with its principal office in Chicago, maintained a divisional office in Seattle, which supervised sales in the State of Washington, two neighboring States and Alaska. The Seattle divisional office and the three district offices in Washington supervised the work of 410 salesmen, 175 of whom resided in the State of Washington. In addition, the Seattle divisional office conducted classes for new salesmen, held sales promotion meetings and issued periodic promotional newsletters to the salesmen in its territory.

When the salesmen took orders for the encyclopedias, they typically received a down-payment, and in some cases payment in full; the order and the payments were turned over to the Seattle office, which forwarded them to Chicago for acceptance. On occasion, the Chicago office requested a credit investigation. If the order was not accepted, the down-payment was returned directly to the purchaser by the Chicago office. Shipments of the books were made directly to the customer from outside the State of Washington. No stocks of books were kept in the State, except sample and display sets. All payments other than the initial payments to the salesmen were made by the customer directly to the Chicago office.

The Washington Supreme Court upheld the tax, measured by the Washington sales, on the ground that "the services rendered by the taxpayer's Seattle office are decisive factors in establishing and holding the market in this state for its publications." 47 Wash.2d at 856, 289 P.2d at 1012. This decision was affirmed on appeal by the United States Supreme Court in a brief opinion, which cited as authority Norton Co. v. Department of Revenue, 340 U.S. 534, 71 S.Ct. 377 (1951). That case is treated in Chapter 10, Subd. G, p. 810 infra.

Unlike Norton, however, Field Enterprises maintained no local branch store making admittedly taxable sales; all the activities carried on by Field Enterprises in Washington were an adjunct to solicitation by salesmen and resulted in the acceptance of orders outside the State and deliveries directly to the customers across State lines. Did Field Enterprises lose its interstate status in Washington because it did more than solicitation in the State, because it maintained regional and divisional offices which recruited, trained, and directed activities of salesmen operating both within and without the State? Or was the sheer magnitude of its selling operations in Washington—175 local salesmen and their offices and attendant supervisory and clerical staffs—the factor which transformed the activities from those of an itinerant drummer to the status of a local merchant? If so, we may now be faced with a quantitative test of what constitutes a local business.

C. In General Motors Corp. v. Washington, 377 U.S. 436, 84 S.Ct. 1564 (1964), the Supreme Court considered the application of Washington's business and occupation tax to an out-of-state wholesaler, General Motors. The tax was measured by the unapportioned gross receipts from the company's sales of motor vehicles, parts, and accessories delivered in the State. General Motors' activities in Washington were extensive: it engaged in promotional and supervisory work through its local employees to foster sales and preserve the quality of its dealer organization, it maintained a warehouse from which some parts and accessories were sold to local dealers, and it had a local branch office which assisted Washington dealers in getting better service on their orders. [The company conceded the taxability of receipts from sales made by its local warehouse but contested the State's power to tax receipts from sales of items shipped from its out-of-state offices to in-state dealers in response to orders sent by the dealers to these offices] The Court had little difficulty in holding General Motors taxable on the disputed receipts: "In the bundle of corporate activity, which is the test here, we see General Motors' activity so enmeshed in local connections that * * * we cannot say that the Supreme Court of Washington erred in holding that these local incidents were sufficient to form the basis for the levy of a tax that would not run contrary to the Constitution." 377 U.S. at 447.

With respect to the taxpayer's claim that the gross receipts tax was unconstitutional because it was unapportioned, the Court declared:

> The tax that Washington levied is measured by the wholesale sales of the respective General Motors divisions in the State. It is unapportioned and, as we have pointed out, is, therefore, suspect. We must determine whether it is so closely related to the local activities of the

corporation as to form "some definite link, some minimum connection, between a state and the person, property or transaction it seeks to tax." Miller Bros. Co. v. Maryland, 347 U.S. 340, 344–345, 74 S.Ct. 535, 539, 98 L.Ed. 744 (1954). On the basis of the facts found by the state court we are not prepared to say that its conclusion was constitutionally impermissible. Norton Co. v. Department of Revenue, supra, 340 U.S. at 538, 71 S.Ct. at 380. Here, just as in *Norton*, the corporation so mingled its taxable business with that which it claims nontaxable that we can only "conclude that, in the light of all the evidence, the judgment attributing ∗ ∗ ∗ [the corporation's Washington sales to its local activity] was within the realm of permissible judgment. Petitioner has not established that such services as were rendered ∗ ∗ ∗ [through in-state activity] were not decisive factors in establishing and holding this market." [377 U.S. at 448.]

Justice Brennan dissented, taking particular issue with the Court's treatment of the apportionment question:

This case presents once again the thorny problem of the power of a State to tax the gross receipts from interstate sales arising from activities occurring only partly within its borders. In upholding the Washington gross receipts tax the Court has, in my judgment, confused two quite different issues raised by the case, and in doing so has ignored a fatal defect in the Washington statute.

In order to tax any transaction, the Due Process Clause requires that a State show a sufficient "nexus between such a tax and transactions within a state for which the tax is an exaction." Northwestern States Portland Cement Co. v. Minnesota, 358 U.S. 450, 464, 79 S.Ct. 357, 366, 3 L.Ed.2d 421. This question, which we considered in McLeod v. J.E. Dilworth Co., 322 U.S. 327, 64 S.Ct. 1023, 88 L.Ed. 1304, and Norton Co. v. Department of Revenue, 340 U.S. 534, 71 S.Ct. 377, 95 L.Ed. 517, is the most fundamental precondition on state power to tax. But the strictures of the Constitution on this power do not stop there. For in the case of a gross receipts tax imposed upon an interstate transaction, even though the taxing State can show "some minimum connection," Northwestern States Portland Cement Co., supra, 358 U.S. at 465, 79 S.Ct. at 366, the Commerce Clause requires that "[t]axation measured by gross receipts from interstate commerce ∗ ∗ ∗ [be] fairly apportioned to the commerce carried on within the taxing state." Western Live Stock v. Bureau of Revenue, 303 U.S. 250, 256, 58 S.Ct. 546, 549, 82 L.Ed. 823. See J.D. Adams Mfg. Co. v. Storen, 304 U.S. 307, 58 S.Ct. 913, 82 L.Ed. 1365.

The Court recognizes that "taxation measured by gross receipts is constitutionally proper if it is fairly apportioned," ante, p. 1568. In concluding that the tax in this case includes a fair apportionment, however, the Court relies upon the fact that Washington has sufficient contacts with the sale to satisfy the *Norton* standard, which was formulated to meet the quite different problem of defining the requirements of the Due Process Clause. See Part IV, ante. Our prior decisions clearly indicate that a quite different scheme of apportionment is required. Of course, when a sale may be localized completely in one State, there is no danger of multiple taxation, and, as in the case of a retail sales tax, the State may use as its tax base the total gross receipts arising within its borders. See McGoldrick v. Berwind–White Coal Mining Co., 309 U.S. 33, 60 S.Ct. 388, 84 L.Ed. 565. But far more common in our complex economy is the kind of sale presented in this case, which exhibits significant contacts with more than one State. In such a situation, it is the commercial activity within the State, and not the sales volume, which determines the State's power to tax, and by which the tax must be apportioned. While the ratio of in-state to out-of-state sales is often taken into account as one factor among others in apportioning a firm's total net income, see, e.g., the description of the "Massachusetts Formula" in Note, 75 Harv.L.Rev. 953, 1011 (1962), it nevertheless remains true that if commercial activity in more than one State results in a sale in one of them, that State may not claim as all its own the gross receipts to which the activity within its borders has contributed only a part. Such a tax must be apportioned to reflect the business activity within the taxing State. Cf. my concurring opinion in Railway Express Agency v. Virginia, 358 U.S. 434, 446, 79 S.Ct. 411, 3 L.Ed.2d 450. Since the Washington tax on wholesales is, by its very terms, applied to the "gross proceeds of sales" of those "engaging within this State in the business of making sales at wholesale," Rev. Code Wash. 82.04.270, it cannot be sustained under the standards required by the Commerce Clause. [377 U.S. at 449–51.]

For comments on the *General Motors* case, see 49 Minn.L.Rev. 571 (1965); 18 Vand.L.Rev. 796 (1965); 78 Harv.L.Rev. 241 (1964). For an extended discussion of gross receipts taxes, including the Commerce Clause problems, see Subcommittee on State Taxation of Interstate Commerce of the House Committee on the Judiciary, "State Taxation of Interstate Commerce," H.R.Rep. No. 565, 89th Cong. 1st Sess., Vol. 3, p. 1005 (June 30, 1965), here referred to as "Willis Committee Report."

D. The Supreme Court once again considered Washington's gross receipts tax in Standard Pressed Steel Co. v. Department of Revenue, 419 U.S. 560, 95 S.Ct. 706 (1975). Standard produced industrial aerospace fasteners and made substantial sales to its principal Washington customer, the Boeing Company. Standard's only activities in the State were those carried on by the company's single resident employee and by its non-resident engineers who visited the State for three days every six weeks. The resident employee was an engineer whose primary responsibility was to consult with Boeing personnel regarding the company's needs for fasteners, to qualify Standard Pressed Steel as an approved source of various items, and to follow up any difficulties in the use of the products. Standard maintained no inventory in the State, and its sales dealings and negotiations were carried on directly between its in-state customers and its out-of-state offices, which received orders from the customers and filled them by shipments to the customers by common carrier.

The Court upheld the levy, disposing of the due process challenge by saying

[T]he question in the context of the present case verges on the frivolous for appellant's employee * * * with a full-time job within the State made possible the realization and continuance of valuable contractual relations between appellant and Boeing. [419 U.S. at 562, 95 S.Ct. at 708.]

The Court also reiterated the position taken in the *General Motors* case that the engineer's activities carried on from his home served the taxpayer "as effectively * * * as from 'offices.'" Id.

In meeting the Commerce Clause challenge to the tax for lack of apportionment and hence as violative of the multiple taxation doctrine, the Court said:

> In the instant case, as in Ficklen v. Shelby County Taxing District,[2] 145 U.S. 1, 12 S.Ct. 810, 36 L.Ed. 601 (1892), the tax is on the gross receipts from sales made to a local consumer, which may have some impact on commerce. Yet as we said in *Gwin, White,* 305 U.S. at 440, 59 S.Ct. at 328, in describing the tax in *Ficklen,* it is "apportioned exactly to the activities taxed," all of which are intrastate. [419 U.S. at 564, 95 S.Ct. at 709.]

For a detailed discussion of the *Standard Pressed Steel* case and its implications, see W. Hellerstein, "State Taxation of Interstate Business and the Supreme Court, 1974 Term: Standard Pressed Steel and Colonial Pipeline," 62 Va.L.Rev. 149 (1976).

E. The Court again considered a challenge to Washington's gross receipts tax in Tyler Pipe Industries, Inc. v. Washington Department of Revenue, ___ U.S. ___, 107 S.Ct. 2810 (1987). Tyler sold a large volume of pipe and drainage products in Washington. Tyler's marketing activities in Washington, however, were carried on by an independent contractor located in the State. Tyler itself maintained no office, owned no property, and had no employees in Washington. Its solicitation of business was directed by executives who maintained their offices out-of-state and by the in-state independent contractor. The independent contractor called on Tyler's customers, maintained Tyler's sales relationships with its customers, and provided Tyler with virtually all its information regarding the Washington market.

Tyler claimed that the Commerce Clause barred Washington from imposing its B & O tax on Tyler's wholesale sales to its Washington customers because it lacked sufficient nexus with the State. The Supreme Court rejected the claim. It agreed with the State court's conclusion that a "showing of sufficient nexus could not be defeated by the argument that the taxpayer's representative was properly characterized as an independent contractor instead of as an agent." 107 S.Ct. at 2821. Relying on its decision in Scripto, Inc. v. Carson, 362 U.S. 207, 80 S.Ct. 619 (1960), considered in Chapter 10, Subd. G, p. 815 infra, in which it had rebuffed a similar argument, the Court declared that the distinction between salesmen who were employees and salesmen who were independent contractors

---

2. In that case the taxpayers did business as brokers in Tennessee. They solicited local customers and sent their orders to out-of-state vendors who shipped directly to the purchaser. Tennessee levied a tax on their gross commissions. The Court, in distinguishing the "drummer" cases illustrated by Robbins v. Shelby County Taxing Dist., 120 U.S. 489, 7 S.Ct. 592, 30 L.Ed. 694 (1887), stated that in *Ficklen* Tennessee did not tax more than its own internal commerce. [Footnote is the Court's. Ed.]

was, for purposes of establishing nexus, a " 'distinction * * * without constitutional significance.' " 107 S.Ct. at 2821 (quoting *Scripto*, 362 U.S. at 621).   In addition, the Court quoted with approval the Washington Supreme Court's statement that " 'the crucial factor governing nexus is whether the activities performed in this State on behalf of the taxpayer are significantly associated with the taxpayer's ability to establish and maintain a market in this State for sales.' " Id.

Tyler also challenged the application of Washington's B & O tax to its sales in the State on the ground that it was unapportioned. The Court rejected this argument.

> Washington taxes the full value of receipts from in-state wholesaling or manufacturing; thus, an out-of-state manufacturer selling in Washington is subject to an unapportioned wholesale tax even though the value of the wholesale transaction is partly attributable to manufacturing activity carried on in another State that plainly has jurisdiction to tax that activity. This apportionment argument rests on the erroneous assumption that through the B & O tax, Washington is taxing the unitary activity of manufacturing and wholesaling. We have already determined, however, that the manufacturing tax and wholesaling tax are not compensating taxes for substantially equivalent events in invalidating the multiple activities exemption. Thus, the activity of wholesaling—whether by an in-state or an out-of-state manufacturer—must be viewed as a separate activity conducted wholly within Washington that no other State has jurisdiction to tax. See * * * Standard Pressed Steel Co. v. Washington Revenue Dept., 419 U.S., at 564, 95 S.Ct., at 709 (selling tax measured by gross proceeds of sales is "apportioned exactly to the activities taxed"). [107 S.Ct. at 2822.]

The portion of the Court's opinion in *Tyler Pipe* addressed to the claim that Washington's B & O tax discriminated against interstate commerce is considered in Section 8 infra.

F. *Lack of Apportionment.* Does the Court give an acceptable answer to Justice Brennan's dissent in *General Motors* that the tax should have been invalidated because of a lack of apportionment of the receipts from Washington sales? The States from which the orders were filled in the *General Motors, Field Enterprises, Standard Pressed Steel,* and *Tyler Pipe* cases should be able to include in the measure of an excise, through apportionment, at least part of the proceeds of the same sales. Yet the Court permitted the State of destination to include the full sales price in the measure of a doing business tax. Compare National Liberty Life Ins. Co. v. State, 62 Wis.2d 347, 215 N.W.2d 26 (1974), appeal dismissed and certiorari denied 421 U.S. 940, 946, 95 S.Ct. 1668 (1975), in which it was held that Wisconsin's gross premiums tax was unconstitutional as applied to an out-of-state insurance company due to lack of apportionment; State Dept. of Revenue v. P.F. Goodrich Corp., 260 Ind. 41, 292 N.E.2d 247 (1973), in which the court held that Indiana's gross income tax could not constitutionally be applied to the proceeds of a liquidation dividend received from an out-of-state corporation, unless it was properly apportioned. See Chapter 9 infra.

At first blush,* these decisions [*Field Enterprises, General Motors* and *Standard Pressed Steel*] appear incomprehensible, since they dealt with out-of-state manufacturers selling to Washington customers products produced by them outside the State. Indeed, one of the cases involved General Motors, on whose challenge the Court had struck down the District of Columbia's single factor sales formula, because it resulted in the taxation of income

> "* * * not fairly attributable to * * * income * * * from sources within the District [quoted from the District statute]," because "The inescapable and determinative fact * * * is that the company carries on business both inside and outside the District with respect to the income" which is taxed.[16]

The explanation for the Washington cases lies in the Court's treating the State's business activities tax as if it were a general retail sales tax. Apportionment is not used by the States under their retail sales and use taxes on interstate sales. Instead, a sale or use is either taxable or nontaxable by a State, and if it is taxable, the entire sales price is taxed. This method of taxation springs from the nature of retail sales and use taxes, which are imposed on, and are designed to be collected as such from, the customer; and in many States the tax is required to be stated separately from the sales price.[17] In essence, the seller is not the taxpayer, but an involuntary tax collector for the State. Consequently, taxable sales must be separated, transaction by transaction, from nontaxable sales, such as sales for resale, sales of goods for use as a component part of other articles manufactured or processed for sale, and exempt sales of machinery, airplane fuel, and the like.[18] It is because of these characteristics of the tax that the Supreme Court has made the pragmatic judgment, in sustaining the constitutionality of retail sales and use taxes on interstate sales, that the entire tax may be imposed by the market State on the purchaser-user, and that the vendor may ordinarily be required to collect the tax.[19] Else, interstate sales would largely escape taxation altogether, since virtually no State taxes sales of goods shipped by the seller to customers in other States.

* This paragraph and the one that follows it are taken from J. Hellerstein, "State Tax Discrimination Against Out-of-Staters," 30 Nat.Tax J. 113, 122–23 (1977). The excerpt is used with the permission of the copyright owner, National Tax Association—Tax Institute of America.

16. General Motors Corp. v. District of Columbia, 380 U.S. [553, 85 S.Ct. 1156 (1965)] at 554 and 559.

17. See "Sales and Use Taxes," Vol. 3, H.Rep. No. 565, 89th Cong. 1st Sess. (1965), the Willis Committee Report.

18. Id.

19. See [Henneford v. Silas Mason Co., 300 U.S. 577, 57 S.Ct. 524 (1937); International Harvester Co. v. Department of Treasury of Indiana, 322 U.S. 340, 64 S.Ct. 1019 (1944); Utah Tax Comm'n v. Pacific States Cast Iron Pipe Co., 372 U.S. 605, 83

S.Ct. 925 (1963). See Chapter 10 infra dealing with sales and use taxes, at p. 802 et seq.] The view here expressed as to the rationale back of the Court's action in upholding retail sales and use taxes on interstate sales is supported by the opinion of Justice Rutledge in those cases. In his concurring opinion in Freeman v. Hewit, 329 U.S. 249 (1961), Justice Rutledge held that the Indiana tax there at issue, which was imposed on the entire receipts derived from trades, business, or commerce, should have been invalidated with respect to the proceeds of an interstate sale, because it was unapportioned, which lends support to the views here taken concerning the Washington business activities tax. See, also, the reference to Justice Rutledge's opinion in *Freeman v. Hewit* in Complete Auto Transit v. Brady, 430 U.S. 274, 281 n. 10, 97 S.Ct. 1076, 1080 n. 10 (1977).

And double taxation of interstate sales is largely avoided through the credit the States allow for sales or use taxes paid to other States.[20]

This eminently sensible and practicable resolution of the treatment of retail sales and use taxes was misapplied by the Supreme Court in sustaining Washington's business activities tax on the entire proceeds of the in-state sales.[21] While tax classification has it own esoteric refinements, proper classification is largely governed by the purposes of the classification.[22] The Washington levy is, as the statute declares, a tax on "every person for the privilege of engaging in business activities," including manufacturers, wholesalers, and retailers.[23] The tax is not collectible as such from the customer, or required to be separately stated. Moreover, Washington also imposes a sales-use tax on sales for consumption, which has the usual characteristics of retail sales levies.[24] Consequently, for purposes of applying the Due Process and Commerce Clause limitations on the State taxing powers, the Washington business activities tax ought to have been treated, not in the way retail sales tax cases have been decided, but as an excise on the privilege of doing business. Mr. Justice Brennan, therefore, was on impeccable ground in concluding in his dissent from the Washington *General Motors* case that the tax was unconstitutional for lack of apportionment.[25]

SECTION 5. DELINEATION OF WHAT CONSTITUTES INTERSTATE COMMERCE

Notes and Problems

A. The solicitation within a State of orders for the sale of goods in cases in which the orders are accepted and shipments are made to the in-state customers from other States was traditionally treated as an integral part of interstate commerce. Consequently, such activities did not support the imposition of doing business or other franchise taxes before the decision in the *Complete Auto Transit* case. Cheney Brothers v. Massachusetts, 246

20. "Sales and use taxes are imposed in 45 states and the District of Columbia. In all but one of these states, a credit is allowed for a sales or use tax paid to another state. However, in two of these states, the credit is limited to contractors' equipment, tools and machinery and in another the credit is allowed only if the purchase was made in a state which had enacted the Multistate Tax Compact." Testimony of Kenneth Back, President, National Ass'n of Tax Administrators, Hearings, Subcommittee on State Taxation of Interstate Commerce (Mondale Committee), Senate Finance Committee, at 107, 108, 93rd Cong. 1st Sess. (Sept. 18, 1973).

21. See the principal case and *Standard Pressed Steel* supra, and the analysis of the cases in the writings cited in note 25 infra.

22. See [J. Hellerstein, State and Local Taxation, Cases and Materials (3d ed. 1969)] at 24 et seq.

23. Wash.Rev.Code, § 82.04.220, .240–270, P–H Wash.Tax Service. ¶ 22,525 et seq.

24. Wash.Rev.Code, § 82.04.500 and § 82.08.050, P–H Wash.Tax Serv. ¶ 22,670 and ¶ 22,820. The statute provides that the "taxes herein levied on persons engaging in business" [the business activities tax] "shall be levied upon and collectible from, the persons engaged in the business activities" taxed, whereas the retail sales tax is "imposed" upon and "shall be payable by the buyer to the seller * * *" Id.

25. For critical comments on the Court's decisions in the Washington cases, see J. Hellerstein, note 22 supra, at 184 et seq., and W. Hellerstein, "State Taxation of Interstate Business and the Supreme Court: 1974 Term: Standard Pressed Steel and Colonial Pipeline," 62 Va.L.Rev. 149 (1976).

U.S. 147, 38 S.Ct. 295 (1918); Memphis Steam Laundry Cleaner, Inc. v. Stone, 342 U.S. 389, 72 S.Ct. 424 (1952). Such taxes are still debarred to the States by P.L. 86–272, which prohibits the States from imposing franchise, doing business, or other excise taxes measured by net income (as well as direct net income taxes) on interstate sellers of goods who confine their operations in a State to the type of activities described above. See Chapter 8, § 2 infra.

B. The Court has long sustained unapportioned doing business taxes on total gross receipts derived from activities carried on wholly within a State, in cases in which the Court treated the activities as taking place before the stream of commerce begins. American Manufacturing Co. v. St. Louis, 250 U.S. 459, 39 S.Ct. 522 (1919) (manufacturing); Hope Natural Gas Co. v. Hall, 274 U.S. 284, 47 S.Ct. 639 (1927) (production of natural gas); Oliver Iron Mining Co. v. Lord, 262 U.S. 172, 43 S.Ct. 526 (1923) (mining); but see Commonwealth Edison Co. v. Montana, 453 U.S. 609, 101 S.Ct. 2946 (1981), p. 296 infra, in which the Court disapproved cases like *Hope Natural Gas* and *Oliver Iron Mining* insofar as they held that a tax is "immunized from Commerce Clause scrutiny by a claim that the tax is imposed on goods prior to their entry into the stream of commerce." 453 U.S. at 617. If an out-of-state purchaser enters a State and there takes delivery of the goods, the total gross proceeds from the sale are taxable by the State of origin, even though the goods are immediately taken out of the State, with the ultimate out-of-state destination having been contemplated by the parties when the sale was negotiated. International Harvester Co. v. Dep't of Revenue, 322 U.S. 340, 64 S.Ct. 1091 (1944). Apart from these exceptions the State of origin has had great difficulty in taxing gross receipts from the sale of goods shipped out of State. Prior to the decision in the *Complete Auto Transit* case, the Commerce Clause was held to bar gross receipts taxes imposed by the State of origin on such outshipments. J.D. Adams Mfg. Co. v. Storen, 304 U.S. 307, 58 S.Ct. 913 (1938); Gwin, White & Prince, Inc. v. Henneford, 305 U.S. 434, 59 S.Ct. 325 (1939); Freeman v. Hewit, 329 U.S. 249, 67 S.Ct. 274 (1946). In the light of *Complete Auto Transit,* however, the States would now appear to be free to impose the taxes invalidated in the cases cited if the levies are properly apportioned.

C. In businesses other than local selling, the process of drawing the line between the interstate and the local business has been tortuous and uncertain. Manufacturing or producing goods for interstate shipment is a local activity preceding the commerce. American Manufacturing Co. v. St. Louis, 250 U.S. 459, 39 S.Ct. 522 (1919); Western Live Stock v. Bureau of Revenue, 303 U.S. 250, 58 S.Ct. 546 (1938); but see Commonwealth Edison Co. v. Montana, 453 U.S. 609, 101 S.Ct. 2946 (1981), noted in Note B above and set out at p. 296 infra. A marketing agent selling interstate the produce of domestic fruit growers, Gwin, White & Prince, Inc. v. Henneford, 305 U.S. 434, 59 S.Ct. 325 (1939), and stevedores loading and unloading ships plying in interstate waters are engaged in interstate commerce. Joseph v. Carter & Weekes Stevedoring Co., 330 U.S. 422, 67 S.Ct. 815 (1947). *Carter & Weekes* was overruled, however, in Department of Revenue v. Association of Washington Stevedoring Cos., 435 U.S. 734, 98 S.Ct. 1388 (1978), insofar as it held that a tax imposed on the privilege of engaging in the interstate business of stevedoring was per se unconstitutional. Cf. Ramsay Travel, Inc. v. Kondo, 53 Hawaii 419, 495 P.2d 1172 (1972), appeal dismissed 410 U.S. 949, 93 S.Ct. 1418 (1973), in which it was held that unapportioned commissions received by travel agents from sales and services relating to interstate travel are taxable.

Nice distinctions in the physics of the generation and transmission of gas and electricity have produced incomprehensible constitutional differences in the taxing powers of the States. A tax on the generation of electricity transmitted for sale to an out-of-state consumer has been held to impose no burden on commerce, because the generation is analogous to manufacturing, as a local activity preceding the commerce. Utah Power & Light Co. v. Pfost, 286 U.S. 165, 52 S.Ct. 548 (1932); Virginia Electric and Power Co. v. Haden, 200 S.E.2d 848 (W.Va.1973), certiorari denied 416 U.S. 916, 94 S.Ct. 1624 (1974). An interstate pipeline was held to be engaged in an intrastate business, on the ground that its generation of electricity used in compressing the gas into the lines was a local activity separate from the interstate pipeline. Coverdale v. Arkansas–Louisiana Pipe Line Co., 303 U.S. 604, 58 S.Ct. 736 (1938). Likewise, whereas the movement of natural gas in high pressure lines from the gas wells across State lines is an interstate business, the movement of the gas into local supply mains at reduced pressure was held to constitute a local business. East Ohio Gas Co. v. Tax Commission, 283 U.S. 465, 51 S.Ct. 499 (1931). Yet in State Tax Commission v. Interstate Natural Gas Co., 284 U.S. 41, 52 S.Ct. 62 (1931), the Court ruled that the State has no taxable grip on the sale of gas in the State, if it is made to a distributing company which, in turn, resells the gas, even though the taxpayer reduces the pressure of the gas and meters it before delivery into the purchaser's pipes. The activity was regarded as merely in furtherance of additional interstate transportation operations and not as a taxable, local privilege.

In Michigan–Wisconsin Pipe Line Co. v. Calvert, 347 U.S. 157, 74 S.Ct. 396 (1954), the Court struck down a Texas tax imposed on the occupation of gathering gas as applied to a pipeline company. The tax was measured by a percentage of the value of the gas. The gas went from the well through a refining plant of a petroleum company, where it was cleaned. It was then sent through pipes under 200 pounds of pressure to the taxpayer's premises. There the gas was compressed by increasing the pressure to 925 pounds and sent through the pipeline to its destination, i.e., Michigan and Wisconsin distributors. The State court in sustaining the tax had held that the tax was on "the taking or retaining of the gas at the gasoline plant outlet which the court concluded is just as local in nature as the production itself." 347 U.S. at 164, 74 S.Ct. at 400. Mr. Justice Clark, in an opinion written for a unanimous Court, characterized the tax instead as a levy on the "taking off" of the gas in interstate commerce and therefore a tax imposed after interstate commerce had begun, a levy on "a part of interstate commerce itself." The Court stated the rule as follows:

> It is now well settled that a tax imposed on a local activity related to interstate commerce is valid if, and only if, the local activity is not such an integral part of the interstate process, the flow of commerce, that it cannot realistically be separated from it. Memphis Natural Gas Co. v. Stone, 335 U.S. 80, 87 (1948); Western Live Stock v. Bureau of

Revenue, supra, at 258. And if a genuine separation of the taxed local activity from the interstate process is impossible, it is more likely that other States through which the commerce passes or into which it flows can with equal right impose a similar levy on the goods, with the net effect of prejudicing or unduly burdening commerce. [347 U.S. at 166, 74 S.Ct. at 401.]

The Court also pointed out:

> Here it is perhaps sufficient that the privilege taxed, * * * is not so separate and distinct from interstate transportation as to support the tax. But additional objection is present if the tax be upheld. It would "permit a multiple burden upon that commerce," Joseph v. Carter & Weekes Stevedoring Co., supra, at 429, for if Texas may impose this "first taking" tax measured by the total volume of gas so taken, then Michigan and the other recipient States have at least equal right to tax the first taking or "unloading" from the pipeline of the same gas when it arrives for distribution. Oklahoma might then seek to tax the first taking of the gas as it crossed into that State. The net effect would be substantially to resurrect the customs barriers which the Commerce Clause was designed to eliminate. [347 U.S. at 170, 74 S.Ct. at 403.]

How could any State other than Texas impose a tax on the "first taking" of the gas at the gasoline plant so as to impose a multiple tax burden not borne by local commerce on the same taxed event? Isn't the multiple burdens doctrine as here announced an *additional* hurdle for a tax to cross in order to satisfy the Commerce Clause requirement, instead of the method evolved by Justice Stone to permit States to tax a segment of interstate commerce, so long as the tax did not subject that commerce to a risk of multiple tax burdens not borne by local commerce? Insofar as the holdings of the cases considered in this section rested on the ground that the taxpayer was engaged in exclusively interstate commerce that was immune from State taxation under the Commerce Clause, or, alternatively, on the ground that the tax was not subject to Commerce Clause scrutiny because it was imposed on an activity that preceded interstate commerce, they must be reevaluated in light of *Complete Auto Transit, Association of Washington Stevedoring,* and *Commonwealth Edison.*

D. *References.* Strecker, " 'Local Incidents' of Interstate Business," 18 Ohio St.L.J. 69 (1957). The *Michigan–Wisconsin Pipe Line* case is discussed in Hartman, "The Commerce Clause and the States' Power to Tax the Oil and Gas Industry," 1955 Procs. Seventh Annual Institute 387; 68 Harv.L.Rev. 124 (1954); and 32 Tex.L.Rev. 760 (1954).

SECTION 6. THE TAXATION OF INTERSTATE SALES AND THE VENDOR'S DUTY TO COLLECT SALES AND USE TAXES

The cases and materials dealing with the constitutional issues raised in connection with the taxation of interstate sales and the interstate vendor's duty to collect sales and use taxes appear in the Sales Taxation chapter, Chapter 10, p. 802 et seq. infra.

SECTION 7.   TAXATION OF INSTRUMENTALITIES OF INTER-STATE COMMERCE

(a) Property Taxes

Notes

A. *Property Taxes on Land Carriers.* The instrumentalities of interstate commerce have long been subjected to property taxes by the States. Thus, property taxes have been upheld as applied to property lying wholly within the State even though used in interstate commerce. Cleveland Railway Co. v. Backus, 154 U.S. 439, 14 S.Ct. 1122 (1894); Postal Telegraph Cable Co. v. Adams, 155 U.S. 688, 15 S.Ct. 268 (1895); Western Union Telegraph Co. v. Gottlieb, 190 U.S. 412, 23 S.Ct. 730 (1903); Old Dominion Steamship Co. v. Virginia, 198 U.S. 299, 25 S.Ct. 686 (1905). Where the instrumentality was used both within and without the State in interstate transportation, property taxes have been sustained, where apportioned on a mileage or other acceptable basis. Pullman's Palace Car Co. v. Pennsylvania, 141 U.S. 18, 11 S.Ct. 876 (1891); Sanford v. Poe, 165 U.S. 194, 17 S.Ct. 305 (1897); American Refrigerator Transit Co. v. Hall, 174 U.S. 70, 19 S.Ct. 599 (1899); Union Refrigerator Transit Co. v. Lynch, 177 U.S. 149, 20 S.Ct. 631 (1900).

Unless so apportioned, taxes on instrumentalities of interstate commerce have been invalidated as a violation of either the Commerce Clause (Fargo v. Hart, 193 U.S. 490, 24 S.Ct. 498 [1904]), the Due Process Clause (Union Refrigerator Transit Co. v. Kentucky, 199 U.S. 194, 26 S.Ct. 36 [1905]; Johnson Oil Co. v. Oklahoma, 290 U.S. 158, 54 S.Ct. 152 [1933]; Union Tank Line Co. v. Wright, 249 U.S. 275, 39 S.Ct. 276 [1919]), or both (Fargo v. Hart, supra). But see Billings Transfer Corp. v. County of Davidson, 276 N.C. 19, 170 S.E.2d 873 (1969), in which the court considered the above cases and concluded that an unapportioned ad valorem property tax imposed by the domiciliary State of an interstate common carrier engaged in extensive out-of-state activities was valid because, inter alia, "[n]o other state has attempted to levy an ad valorem tax on any portion of plaintiff's property." 276 N.C. at 35, 170 S.E.2d at 885. Can this view be reconciled with the Supreme Court's statement that "the domiciliary State is precluded from imposing an ad valorem tax on any property to the extent that it *could* be taxed by another State, not merely on such property as *is* subjected to tax elsewhere," Central Railroad Co. v. Pennsylvania, 370 U.S. 607, 614, 82 S.Ct. 1297 (1962) (emphasis in original)?

B. *Property Taxation of Airplanes.* In Northwest Airlines, Inc. v. Minnesota, 322 U.S. 292, 64 S.Ct. 950 (1944), the majority of the Court refused to extend the principles developed in the land transportation cases to air transport equipment. Mr. Justice Frankfurter, who was not sympathetic to the apportionment principle as a device for dealing with interstate commerce taxation problems, in writing the plurality opinion for a sharply divided Court, refused to apply "the rule of apportionment ＊ ＊ ＊ beset with friction, waste and difficulties ＊ ＊ ＊ and established ＊ ＊ ＊ in regard to, land commerce" to air commerce. Instead, the decision permitted Minnesota, the State of Northwest's incorporation, the locus of its principal place of business and its major repair and overhaul base, to tax the entire value of the planes, without apportionment. Justice Frankfurter strongly implied that no other State in which Northwest operated its planes and maintained terminals and repair bases could tax any part of the value of the planes on an apportionment basis. Justice Jackson, who adverted to the apportionment theory as "a mongrel one," reached a similar conclusion, but grounded his holding on the analogy to vessels moving in interstate commerce, which had been held subject to property tax only at the "home port"; he analogized the point of registration of the planes with the Civilian Aeronautics Authority—here St. Paul—to the home port of a vessel. Justice Black in concurring made it clear that he would not foreclose States other than Minnesota from taxing on an apportioned basis. Chief Justice Stone dissented in an opinion joined in by Justices Roberts, Reed, and Rutledge, holding that the traditional railroad apportionment cases should be applied to property taxation of airlines.

The authority of the *Northwest Airlines* case as permitting a single State and no other to tax the full value of airplanes was short-lived. In Braniff Airways, Inc. v. Nebraska State Board of Equalization, 347 U.S. 590, 74 S.Ct. 757 (1954), the issue was whether Nebraska, which was not the State of incorporation or principal office or major overhaul and repair station or C.A.A. registration State, could impose an apportioned property tax on planes of an airline whose planes regularly flew over, landed at, and departed from airports in the State. Mr. Justice Reed, who had dissented in the *Northwest Airlines* case, wrote the majority opinion sustaining Nebraska's tax; Justices Frankfurter and Jackson dissented. The *Braniff* decision appears to reestablish the full application of the land transport cases to airlines, although it did not explicitly face the issue as to whether Minnesota would now be precluded from taxing Northwest Airlines on an unapportioned basis. For a later case dealing with the problems presented by the *Northwest Airlines* and the *Braniff* decisions, see Flying Tiger Line v. County of Los Angeles, 51 Cal.2d 314, 333 P.2d 323 (1959), cert. denied 359 U.S. 1001, 79 S.Ct. 1140 (1959).

The county of San Bernardino, California imposed an apportioned ad valorem property tax on the flight equipment of a foreign corporation engaged in interstate air transportation of cargo and passengers under government contracts. The taxpayer owned a fleet of 24 planes, which it operated on regularly scheduled flights. The planes were assessed on the basis of their average physical presence, which included the ground time in the county and the flight time within California. The taxpayer had contended that the inclusion of flight time in the apportionment formula violated the Due Process Clause, on the ground that the tax on flight time had no relation to the opportunities, benefits, or protection afforded the taxpayer by the State or county. In sustaining the assessment, the court pointed out that the protection of State law extends to air space; and that State and local agencies must contend with numerous problems stemming from the use of air space for interstate air commerce, particularly as such use affects the use of subjacent land. These include problems of noise, air crashes, and regulation of land under take-off and approach patterns. It was unrealistic, concluded the court, to suggest that the owner of aircraft does not begin to enjoy the benefits, opportunities, and protection afforded by the State until the moment the plane touches down and ceases to enjoy them the instant the plane is again air-borne. Zantop Air Transport v. County of San Bernardino, 246 Cal.App.2d 433, 54 Cal.Rptr. 813 (1966).

    C. *Property Taxes on Instrumentalities of Water Transportation.* In Ott v. Mississippi Valley Barge Line Co., 336 U.S. 169, 69 S.Ct. 432 (1949), a group of barge lines sought to utilize the *Northwest Airlines* case to set aside Louisiana and New Orleans property taxes on tugboats and barges used up and down the Mississippi and Ohio rivers. The taxpayers were foreign corporations with out-of-state ports of registry of their vessels. The facts showed that the vessels of one taxpayer spent 10 percent to 17 percent of their time in Louisiana during the tax years before the Court, with smaller percentages for the other barge lines. The district court and the court of appeals, following the *Northwest Airlines* case, determined that the vessels had found a "permanent home" and a "tax situs" outside Louisiana, and allowed a refund of the taxes. The Supreme Court (with Justice Jackson dissenting) upheld the tax, which had been apportioned to activities in Louisiana, determining that the principle of the *Pullman's Palace Car* case should apply to the case. It said, "[w]e can see no reason which should put water transportation on a different constitutional footing than other interstate enterprises." This case is noted in 97 U.Pa.L.Rev. 913 (1949); 9 La.L.Rev. 545 (1949); 48 Mich.L.Rev. 116 (1949).

    In Standard Oil Co. v. Peck, 342 U.S. 382, 72 S.Ct. 309 (1952), there is a corollary of the rationale of the *Ott* decision. The domiciliary State of Standard Oil was not permitted to tax the whole value of its craft used in interstate river transportation of oil, since they were subject to taxation on an apportioned basis in several other States where they operated. The taxation of all of Standard Oil's boats and barges by the State of domicile was prevented by the Due Process Clause because it resulted in multiple taxation of interstate operations. This reflects an interesting interplay of the Commerce Clause multiple taxation doctrine and the Due Process Clause.

    In Japan Line, Ltd. v. County of Los Angeles, 441 U.S. 434, 99 S.Ct. 1813 (1979), which held that the Commerce Clause imposes more exacting limitations on the States when they seek to tax foreign (as distinguished from interstate) commerce (see p. 313 infra), the Court also repudiated the home port doctrine as a tool of constitutional analysis. The case presented the question whether Los Angeles could impose an apportioned property tax on foreign-owned and foreign-based shipping containers used exclusively in international commerce. The first issue the Court addressed was whether the home port doctrine retained any viability as a criterion of Commerce Clause analysis. The Court recognized that the home port doctrine had been sapped of much of its vitality over the years. It observed that the doctrine of *mobilia sequuntur personam* (movables follow the person) in which the home port doctrine is rooted "has fallen into desuetude" and that the doctrine had "yielded to a rule of fair apportionment among the States." 441 U.S. at 442. The Court noted that it had "held that various instrumentalities of commerce may be taxed on a properly apportioned basis by the nondomiciliary States through which they travel." Id. Nevertheless, even in "discarding the 'home port' theory of apportionment, * * * the Court has consistently distinguished the case of ocean-going vessels." Id. Faced with the question whether to rehabilitate the home port doctrine for purposes of the Commerce Clause or to reject it completely, the Court chose the latter course. Unable to identify any constitutional source for the doctrine, the Court characterized it as "anachronistic" and declared that its underpinnings had been "abandoned." Id. at 443. The Court therefore proceeded to analyze the question before it under the substantive criteria for determining the validity of a tax on foreign commerce that it articulated in the *Japan Line* case. See p. 313 infra. For a comprehensive treatment of the development of the home port doctrine prior to the Court's decision in *Japan Line,* see Note, "Limitations on State Taxation of Foreign Commerce: The Contemporary Vitality of the Home Port Doctrine," 127 U.Pa.L.Rev. 817 (1979).

D. *Gross Receipts Taxes on Instrumentalities of Interstate Commerce.* The cases involving gross receipts taxes on the instrumentalities of interstate commerce are considered in the Introductory Note to Section 4, supra, which deals generally with gross receipts taxes. See pp. 259–61 supra.

E. *References.* Powell, "Northwest Airlines v. Minnesota: State Taxation of Airplanes," 57 Harv.L.Rev. 1097 (1944); Sutherland, Jr. & Vinciguerra, "The Octroi and the Airplane," 32 Cornell L.Q. 161 (1946); Snell, "Northwest Airlines Revisited," 33 Taxes 659 (1955); Brabson, "Multistate Taxation of the Transportation Industry," 18 Ohio St.L.J. 22 (1957); "Application of 'Home Port Doctrine' and Due Process Clause to State Taxation of Aircraft," 35 S.Cal.L.Rev. 316 (1962); "State Taxation of International Air Carriers," 57 Nw.U.L.Rev. 92 (1962); Kronenberg, "State Taxation of Moving Equipment Engaged in Interstate Commerce," 15 Ala. L.Rev. 186 (1962); O'Reilly, "Constitutional Law—Ability of Domicile State to Tax Railway Rolling Stock," 4 B.C.Ind. and Comm.L.Rev. 185 (1962). For an extended discussion of the impact of the Commerce and Due Process Clauses on property taxation in a multistate business, see P. Hartman, Federal Limitations on State and Local Taxation 381 (1981).

(b) Taxation of Interstate Broadcasting

In Fisher's Blend Station, Inc. v. State Tax Commission, 297 U.S. 650, 56 S.Ct. 608 (1936), a privilege tax measured by apportioned gross receipts was applied to a radio broadcasting station whose programs were heard by all the States. The levy was struck down under the Commerce Clause because the conduct of an interstate business was being taxed. Actually, both intrastate and interstate commerce were carried on simultaneously. Query: Does this holding retain its validity after *Complete Auto Transit* ?

In the Western Live Stock v. Bureau of Revenue, 303 U.S. 250, 260, 58 S.Ct. 546, 551 (1938), Stone, J., said, "[i]f broadcasting could be taxed, so also could reception." Is this statement consistent with the multiple taxation doctrine? Would not a possible tax on the loading of the coal in Pennsylvania in McGoldrick v. Berwind–White Coal Mining Co., 309 U.S. 33, 60 S.Ct. 388 (1940), have presented a similar danger of multiple taxation?

In Albuquerque Broadcasting Co. v. Bureau of Revenue, 51 N.M. 332, 184 P.2d 416, 11 A.L.R.2d 966 (1947), the court considered a New Mexico "privilege tax," measured "by the amount or volume of business done, on account of * * * business activities * * * within the state," levied at the rate of two percent of the gross receipts of various businesses, including "radio broadcasting stations." The facts as described by the court were as follows:

The appellant is engaged in three classes of broadcasting, two of which are described in the findings of the Court, as follows:

1. "Network programs supplied by national network broadcasting companies through the State of New Mexico on the interstate wires of the American Telephone and Telegraph Company, which wires are tapped by KOB at Albuquerque. These chain broadcasting companies programs so transmitted and taped originate in studios maintained in other states and countries. * * *

"The program is thereupon delivered by a voice into the microphone of NBC in its studio in New York, Hollywood, or elsewhere outside the state of New Mexico. KOB receives the voice's message over interstate telephone wires from the studio outside the state, and by the turning of a switch, connects the interstate telephone wire with the mechanical facilities of KOB. The program, including the advertisers' message, goes out on the ether and is relayed and amplified and broadcast by the broadcasting facilities of KOB.

2. "National spot advertising which is a program supplied by national advertisers and reaches the studio of the plaintiff for broadcast by means of transcription from outside of New Mexico, or by phonograph records or transcriptions transmitted in interstate commerce from other states to the KOB studio for broadcasting." [184 P.2d at 430.]

The court said:

These programs are thus broadcast over sixteen states and parts of Canada and Mexico. They are communications directed to all persons listening to the broadcasts wherever they may be. This business is strictly interstate and we can discover no incident in connection therewith that could be classed as a "taxable event." The idea that there are means by which the state can lay a tax on these activities so that appellant will be required to pay "its just share of state taxation" in return for the protection it receives, is either a delusion, or else we are unable to discover the means through which it may be required to respond, in view of *Freeman v. Hewit*. We are of the opinion that the tax so laid and collected on the gross receipts from these broadcasts must be returned to appellant.

The third class of broadcasts is described in the findings as "Local advertising broadcasts which originate locally in the studio of KOB at Albuquerque but are heard in all sixteen States." It is a matter of common knowledge that most, if not all of such broadcasts are local advertising of merchandise or other businesses that are of interest only to local people, notwithstanding that such broadcasts may be heard by people in other states not interested in the advertising. Such also are broadcasts of local political parties and candidates, addressed to the state's electorate. It is only the fact that the range of radio, unlike communications by telegraph or telephone, is limited only by the power employed in broadcasting, that it may be heard by people to whom the message is of no interest. As a practical matter this business is intrastate.

We are aware that there are authorities holding otherwise, U.S. v. American Bond & Mtg. Co., 31 F.2d 448; Atlanta v. Atlanta Journal Co., 186 Ga. 734, 190 S.E. 788; Whitehurst v. Grimes, 21 F.2d 787. But if they are correct, then radio broadcasting, though the receipts and business are all intrastate, cannot be taxed, whether or not it transcends state lines. After all, it is the business that is the subject of taxation, and if the receipts of local broadcasting are from local people and the business obtained from such advertising is local; then the business is intrastate. Telegraph and telephone companies may be taxed on their intrastate business (Ratherman v. Western Union Tel. Co., supra) and radio should not be an exception. * * *

We are of the opinion that local advertising by radio for local business is subject to the tax, (1) because it is intrastate business, and (2) in any event the advertising of local business to secure local patronage is a "taxable event" open to the states. Western Live Stock v. Bureau of Revenue, supra. The appellee should be permitted to retain the receipts collected from taxes laid on appellant's intrastate business, the amount of which can be determined at another trial. Ratherman v. Western Union Tel. Co., supra. [184 P.2d at 430–31.] *

Should cable television operators be treated like local or interstate broadcasters when the television signals they retransmit originate outside the State? In Rhoden v. Goodling Enterprises, Inc., 295 So.2d 433 (Miss.1974), a cable television operator received television signals emanating from both within and without the State and retransmitted these signals to local subscribers to the cable system. The individual housing units of the subscribers were connected to the system and they paid a monthly charge of $4.75 for the service which permitted them to receive television signals which otherwise would be inaccessible due to the distance between the residences of the subscribers and the broadcasting stations. The State Tax Commission had assessed a doing business tax measured by gross income upon the CATV operator but the lower court had held this improper under the *Fisher's Blend* case on the ground that part of the signals emanated from out-of-state broadcasting stations. The Mississippi Supreme Court reversed, noting that "all of the income upon which the tax could be imposed is derived within this state. The character of appellee's business is such that it is not subject to the danger of burdensome cumulative taxation by other states." 295 So.2d at 436.

* [On a second appeal to the New Mexico
Supreme Court, after remand, a similar
result was reached. 216 P.2d 698 (1950).]

References. The *Albuquerque Broadcasting Company* case is noted in 17 U.Cin.L.Rev. 195 (1948); 2 Wyo.L.J. 135 (1948). See Ruehlmann, "State Taxation of Radio and Television," 20 U.Cin.L.Rev. 19 (1951); Note, "Gross Receipts Tax on Radio Stations," 1 Stan.L.Rev. 740 (1949); Katz, "State and Local Taxation of Radio and Television Broadcasting," 12 Fed.Communications Bar J. 49 (1952).

SECTION 8. LEVIES DISCRIMINATING AGAINST INTER-STATE COMMERCE

INTRODUCTORY NOTE

A Brief Historical Survey. Beginning shortly after the Civil War, the Court was faced with a large crop of drummers' and merchants' license taxes imposed on vendors of goods from other States. They were enacted chiefly by the Southern and Western States and were aimed at an army of Northern drummers descending upon rural sections with order blanks for the products of industrial centers. Many of these enactments required the payment of license fees in flat amounts, bearing no relation to the volume of the business done. It has been estimated that almost 800 municipal ordinances directed at drummers were enacted for the purpose of embarrassing this competition with local merchants. See Hemphill, "The House to House Canvasser in Interstate Commerce," 60 Am.L.Rev. 641 (1926); McGoldrick v. Berwind–White Coal Mining Co., 309 U.S. 33, 60 S.Ct. 388 (1940). The drummer was prohibited, under the pain of criminal penalties, from seeking to sell his wares. These taxes invariably were invalidated as to drummers who obtained shipment of the goods into the State. Welton v. Missouri, 91 U.S. 275 (1876), is the first case in which such a tax was invalidated under the Commerce Clause. A similar tax had been invalidated in Ward v. Maryland, 79 U.S. (12 Wall.) 418 (1870), but under the Privileges and Immunities Clause of Article IV, § 2, although Justice Bradley's concurring opinion stated that the tax violated the Commerce Clause as well. The leading case in this line of vendor's license tax cases is Robbins v. Shelby County Taxing District, 120 U.S. 489, 7 S.Ct. 592 (1887). Vendors' license taxes were, however, sustained as to peddlers who brought their goods into the State for sale directly from their wagons. Howe Machine Co. v. Gage, 100 U.S. 676 (1879); Emert v. Missouri, 156 U.S. 296, 15 S.Ct. 367 (1895); American Steel & Wire Co. v. Speed, 192 U.S. 500, 24 S.Ct. 365 (1904); Kehrer v. Stewart, 197 U.S. 60, 25 S.Ct. 403 (1905); Baccus v. Louisiana, 232 U.S. 334, 34 S.Ct. 439 (1914); Wagner v. City of Covington, 251 U.S. 95, 40 S.Ct. 93 (1919).

Some of the taxes invalidated were unmistakably discriminatory against interstate business since they were expressly limited to the merchants or products of other States. Welton v. Missouri, supra; Cook v. Pennsylvania, 97 U.S. 566 (1878); Webber v. Virginia, 103 U.S.

344 (1880); Walling v. Michigan, 116 U.S. 446, 6 S.Ct. 454 (1886). In others, the discrimination was less clear. They involved taxes limited either to persons not having an established place of business in the taxing jurisdiction, or to selected articles not produced in the State. Robbins v. Shelby County Taxing District, supra; Norfolk & West. Ry. Co. v. Sims, 191 U.S. 441, 24 S.Ct. 151 (1903); Caldwell v. North Carolina, 187 U.S. 622, 23 S.Ct. 229 (1903); Dozier v. Alabama, 218 U.S. 124, 30 S.Ct. 649 (1910); Stewart v. Michigan, 232 U.S. 665, 34 S.Ct. 476 (1914); cf. West Point Wholesale Grocery Co. v. City of Opelika, 354 U.S. 390, 77 S.Ct. 1096 (1957). Another equally offensive form of discrimination that has called for Commerce Clause condemnation is that of subjecting non-resident businesses to higher tax rates than local business. E.g., Memphis Steam Laundry Cleaners, Inc. v. Stone, 342 U.S. 389, 72 S.Ct. 424 (1952).

In still other cases the problem was a nicer one, for there were fixed sum license fees payable by local as well as out-of-state solicitors as conditions to negotiating or making sales. Nevertheless, many of these taxes have been found to be invalid discriminations. Asher v. Texas, 128 U.S. 129, 9 S.Ct. 1 (1888); Stoutenburgh v. Hennick, 129 U.S. 141, 9 S.Ct. 256 (1889); Brennan v. Titusville, 153 U.S. 289, 14 S.Ct. 829 (1894); Stockard v. Morgan, 185 U.S. 27, 22 S.Ct. 576 (1902); Rearick v. Pennsylvania, 203 U.S. 507, 27 S.Ct. 159 (1906); Crenshaw v. Arkansas, 227 U.S. 389, 33 S.Ct. 294 (1913); Rogers v. Arkansas, 227 U.S. 401, 33 S.Ct. 298 (1913); Davis v. Virginia, 236 U.S. 697, 35 S.Ct. 479 (1915); Western Oil Refining Co. v. Lipscomb, 244 U.S. 346, 37 S.Ct. 623 (1917); Real Silk Hosiery Mills v. Portland, 268 U.S. 325, 45 S.Ct. 525 (1925).

The Modern Precedents. In Nippert v. City of Richmond, 327 U.S. 416, 66 S.Ct. 586 (1946), the Court set aside under the Commerce Clause a license tax laid by the City of Richmond, Virginia on engaging "in business as solicitors." The tax was at the rate of $50 plus one-half percent of gross earnings for the preceding year in excess of $1,000. The defendant, who was convicted below for failing to obtain the required license, solicited orders for an out-of-state garment company. Mr. Justice Rutledge, who wrote the majority opinion, emphasized the risks to the out-of-state vendor of the fixed-fee license tax required to be paid before any business is done and the burdens such a levy imposes on "the small operator particularly and more especially the casual or occasional one." The *Nippert* case is noted in 44 Mich.L.Rev. 1135 (1946); 20 Temp.L.Q. 586 (1947); 9 Detroit L.Rev. 214 (1946).

In Dunbar–Stanley Studios, Inc. v. Alabama, 393 U.S. 537, 89 S.Ct. 757 (1969), a foreign corporation that sent photographers into Alabama to take children's photographs and return them to the taxpayer's studios in North Carolina, where the negatives were developed and the finished photographs were sent back to Alabama for delivery to the customer, was held subject to the State's license tax of $5 per week on "each transient or traveling photographer." The business was conducted under a contractual arrangement made by the taxpayer with the

J.C. Penney stores located in Alabama. The Penney stores advertised the services and recruited customers. When the photos were completed, they were sent by the taxpayer to the Penney stores for delivery to the customers. The Penney stores took all the orders for the photographs, which were sent to the taxpayer's offices in North Carolina for acceptance.

In sustaining the tax, the Supreme Court held that the taking of photographs in the State was a locally taxable event, separable from the interstate aspects of the operations, and that the taxpayer was carrying on a local business at the Penney stores. The Court also rejected the contention that the tax operated to discriminate against interstate commerce:

> Alabama's tax is levied equally upon all transient or traveling photographers whether their travel is interstate or entirely within the State. On the record before us, there is no basis for concluding that the $5 per week tax on transient out-of-state photographers is so disproportionate to the tax imposed on photographers with a fixed location [which generally amounted to $25 per year] as to bear unfairly on the former. [393 U.S. at 542, 89 S.Ct. at 761.]

HALLIBURTON OIL WELL CEMENTING CO. v. REILY

Supreme Court of the United States, 1963.
373 U.S. 64, 83 S.Ct. 1201.

MR. CHIEF JUSTICE WARREN delivered the opinion of the Court.

The sole issue before us is whether the Louisiana use tax, as applied to the appellant, discriminates against interstate commerce in violation of the Commerce Clause of the Constitution.

The Louisiana sales and use taxes follow the basic pattern approved by this Court in Henneford v. Silas Mason Co., 300 U.S. 577, 57 S.Ct. 524, 81 L.Ed. 814. Louisiana Revised Statutes, Tit. 47, § 302, LSA, provides for the imposition of a tax "[a]t the rate of two per centum (2%) of the sales price of each item or article of tangible personal property *when sold at retail in this State * * *.*" [1] It imposes another tax "[a]t the rate of two per centum (2%) of the cost prices of each item or article of tangible personal property *when the same is not sold but is used * * * in this State * * *.*" [2] This latter tax, commonly known as a use tax, is to be reduced by the amount of any similar sales or use tax paid on the item in a different State. La. Rev.Stat.Ann. § 47:305. As noted by the Louisiana Supreme Court below and approved in Silas Mason, the purpose of such a sales-use tax scheme is to make all tangible property used or consumed in the State subject to a uniform tax burden irrespective of whether it is acquired within the State, making it subject to the sales tax, or from without the State, making it subject to a use tax at the same rate. The appellant

---

1. Emphasis added.   2. Emphasis added.

admits the validity of such a scheme. It contends, however, that in this case Louisiana has departed from the norm of tax equality and imposes on the appellant a greater tax burden solely because the property it uses in Louisiana is brought from out-of-state. The difference in tax burden is admitted by the appellee.

The facts were stipulated by the parties. The appellant is engaged in the business of servicing oil wells in a number of oil producing States, including Louisiana. Its business requires the use of specialized equipment including oil well cementing trucks and electrical well logging trucks. These trucks and their equipment are not generally available on the retail market, but are manufactured by the appellant at its principal place of business in Duncan, Oklahoma. The raw materials and semifinished and finished articles necessary for the manufacture of these units are acquired on the open market by the appellant and assembled by its employees. The completed units are tested at Duncan and then assigned to specific field camps maintained by the appellant. The assignment is permanent unless better use of the unit can be made at another camp. None of these units is manufactured or held for sale to third parties.

Between January 1, 1952, and May 31, 1955, the appellant shipped new and used units of its specialized equipment to field camps in Louisiana. In its Louisiana tax returns filed for these years, the appellant calculated and paid use taxes upon the value of the raw materials and semifinished and finished articles used in manufacturing the units. The appellant did not include in its calculations the value of labor and shop overhead attributable to assembling the units. It is admitted that this cost factor would not have been taxed had the appellant assembled its units in Louisiana rather than in Oklahoma. The stipulation of facts stated:

> "If Halliburton had purchased its materials, operated its shops, and incurred its Labor and Shop Overhead expenses at a location within the State of Louisiana, there would have been a sales tax due to the State of Louisiana upon the cost of materials purchased in Louisiana and a Use Tax on materials purchased outside of Louisiana; but there would have been no Louisiana sales tax or use tax due upon the Labor and Shop Overhead."

Nevertheless, in September 1955, the Louisiana Collector of Revenue, the appellee, assessed a deficiency of $36,238.43 in taxes, including interest, on the labor and shop overhead cost of assembling the units. The Collector held that this was required by the language of the use tax section of the statute which levies the 2% use tax on the "cost price" of the item, "cost price" being defined in an earlier section as the actual cost without deductions on account of "labor or service cost, * * * or any other expenses whatsoever." La.Rev.Stat.Ann. § 47.301(3).

Also during this period, the appellant purchased 14 oil well cementing service units from the Sparton Tool and Service Company of Houston, Texas. Spartan was not regularly engaged in the sale of such equipment and made the sale after deciding to liquidate its oil well servicing business. The appellant transferred these units to Louisiana. On one other occasion, the appellant purchased an airplane from the Western Newspaper Union of New York, a company not regularly engaged in the business of selling airplanes. The appellant acquired the plane for use in Louisiana. No Louisiana use tax was declared or paid subsequent to the transfer of these items to Louisiana. It is admitted in the stipulation of facts that had these acquisitions been made within Louisiana, they would have not been taxed. This is occasioned by the fact that the sales tax section of the statute applies only to sales made at retail and not to isolated sales by those not regularly engaged in the business of selling the item involved. Nevertheless, the Collector assessed a deficiency of $4,404.22 on the value of these items since the use tax on goods imported from out-of-state contains no equivalent distinction between isolated and retail sales.

The appellant paid the deficiency under protest and brought an action in the Louisiana District Court for the Nineteenth District for a refund pursuant to La.Rev.Stat.Ann. § 47:1576, alleging that this unequal tax burden is a discrimination against interstate commerce. The District Court found the assessment discriminatory. On appeal, the Louisiana Supreme Court reversed, holding that since no unreasonable distinctions or classifications had been drawn in the Louisiana sales and use tax statute, the incidental discrepancy in tax burden did not amount to a discrimination against interstate commerce. 241 La. 67, 127 So.2d 502. On appeal to this Court, we noted probable jurisdiction. 368 U.S. 809, 82 S.Ct. 60, 7 L.Ed.2d 19. The case was first argued during the October Term 1961. We subsequently ordered it reargued. 369 U.S. 835, 82 S.Ct. 865, 7 L.Ed.2d 841.

I.

This is another in a long line of cases attacking state taxation as unduly burdening interstate commerce. As this Court stated in Best & Co. v. Maxwell, 311 U.S. 454, 455–456, 61 S.Ct. 334, 335, 85 L.Ed. 275: "In each case it is our duty to determine whether the statute under attack, whatever its name may be, will in its practical operation work discrimination against interstate commerce." This concern with the actuality of operation, a dominant theme running through all state taxation cases, extends to every aspect of the tax operations. Thus, in Nippert v. Richmond, 327 U.S. 416, 66 S.Ct. 586, 90 L.Ed. 760, the City of Richmond placed a fixed fee and earnings tax on itinerant solicitors of sales within the city. On its face, the ordinance applied to in-state as well as out-of-state distributors doing business by means of itinerant solicitors. The Court noted, however, the very fact that a distributor is out-of-state makes his use of, and dependence on, solicitors more likely. Thus, "the very difference between interstate and local trade, taken in conjunction with the inherent character of the tax, makes equality of application as between those two classes of commerce, generally speaking, impossible." 327 U.S. at 432, 66 S.Ct. at 594. The Court concluded that the tax was "discriminatory in favor of the local merchant as against the out-of-state one." 327 U.S. at 431, 66 S.Ct. at 593. Considered in isolation, the Louisiana use tax is discriminatory; it was intended to apply primarily to goods acquired out-of-state and used in Louisiana.[3] If it stood alone, it would be invalid. However, a proper analysis must take "the whole scheme of taxation into account."

* * *

The conclusion is inescapable: equal treatment for in-state and out-of-state taxpayers similarly situated is the condition precedent for a valid use tax on goods imported from out-of-state.

The inequality of the Louisiana tax burden between in-state and out-of-state manufacturer-users is admitted. Although the rate is the same, the appellant's tax base is increased through the inclusion of its product's labor and shop overhead. The Louisiana Supreme Court characterized this discrepancy as incidental. However, equality for the purposes of competition and the flow of commerce is measured in dollars and cents, not legal abstractions.[4] In this case the "incidental discrepancy"—the labor and shop overhead for the units in dispute— amounts to $1,547,109.70. The use tax rate in Louisiana is 2% and has risen in some States to 4%.[5] The resulting tax inequality is clearly substantial.

But even accepting this, the Louisiana Supreme Court concluded that the comparison between in-state and out-of-state manufacturer-users is not the proper way to frame the issue of equality. It stated: "The proper comparison would be between the use tax on the assembled equipment and a sales tax on the same equipment if it were sold." On the basis of such a comparison, the out-of-state manufacturer-user is on the same tax footing with respect to the item used as the retailer of a similar item, or the competitor who buys from the retailer rather than manufacture his own. However, such a comparison excludes from consideration, without any explanation, the very in-state taxpayer who is most similarly situated to the appellant, the local manufacturer-user. If the Louisiana Legislature were in fact concerned over any tax break the manufacturer-user obtains, it would surely have made special arrangements to take care of the in-state as well as out-of-state loophole—unless, of course, it intended to discriminate. We can only conclude, therefore, that the proper comparison on the basis of this

---

3. In fact, it was just such isolated consideration that led the trial court in Silas Mason Co. v. Henneford, D.C., 15 F.Supp. 958, 962, rev'd 300 U.S. 577, 57 S.Ct. 524, 81 L.Ed. 814, to strike down the State of Washington use tax.

4. Thus in Memphis Steam Laundry Cleaner, Inc., v. Stone, supra, and Best & Co. v. Maxwell, supra, the Court compared the actual tax bills of the local and out-of-state taxpayers. In the former, the Court found discriminatory a $50 license tax on each truck used by an out-of-state laundry business soliciting and picking up laundry in Mississippi because resident laundries were required to pay only $8 per truck. In the latter, the Court found determinative a similar discrepancy between the $1 tax paid by local merchants and the $250 tax paid by the itinerant solicitor.

5. Michigan, Pennsylvania, and Washington each has 4% sales and use taxes. 2 P–H 1963 Fed.Tax Serv. ¶ 13,299.

record is between in-state and out-of-state manufacturer-users. And if this comparison discloses discriminatory effects, it could be ignored only after a showing of adequate justification.

While the inequality in question may have been an accident of statutory drafting, it does in fact strike at a significant segment of economic activity and carries economic effects of a type proscribed by many previous cases. The appellant manufactures equipment specially adapted to its oil servicing business. The equipment is expensive; because of its limited and custom production, the labor and shop overhead is necessarily a significant cost factor. Activity of this character is often on the forefront of economic development where equipment and methods have yet to reach the standardization and acceptance necessary for mass production. If Louisiana were the only State to impose an additional tax burden for such out-of-state operations, the disparate treatment would be an incentive to locate within Louisiana; it would tend "to neutralize advantages belonging to the place of origin." Baldwin v. G.A.F. Seelig, Inc., 294 U.S. 511, 527, 55 S.Ct. 497, 502, 79 L.Ed. 1032. Disapproval of such a result is implicit in all cases dealing with tax discrimination since a tax which is "discriminatory in favor of the local merchant," Nippert v. Richmond, supra, also encourages an out-of-state operator to become a resident in order to compete on equal terms.[6] If similar unequal tax structures were adopted in other States, a not unlikely result of affirming here, the effects would be more widespread. The economic advantages of a single assembly plant for the appellant's multistate activities would be decreased for units sent to every State other than the State of residence. At best, this would encourage the appellant to locate his assembly operations in the State of largest use for the units. At worst, it would encourage their actual fractionalization or discontinuance. Clearly, approval of the Louisiana use tax in this case would "invite a multiplication of preferential trade areas destructive of the very purpose of the Commerce Clause." Dean Milk Co. v. Madison, 340 U.S. 349, 356, 71 S.Ct. 295, 299, 95 L.Ed. 329.*

In light of these considerations we see no reason to depart from the strict rule of equality adopted in Silas Mason, and we conclude that the Louisiana use tax as applied to the appellant's specialized equipment discriminates against interstate commerce.

A similar disposition of the tax on the isolated sales follows as a matter of course. The disparate treatment is baldly admitted by the Louisiana Supreme Court: "The exemption of an isolated sale from the provisions of the sales tax applies strictly to sales within the State of Louisiana; it has no effect whatsoever on any transaction without the state." The out-of-state isolated sale, it concludes, must therefore be treated "as if" it were a sale at retail. As the facts of this case indicate,

6. See cases collected in Memphis Steam Laundry Cleaner, Inc., v. Stone, supra, p. 392, n. 7, 72 S.Ct. p. 426.

* [Footnote omitted].

isolated sales involve primarily the acquisition of second-hand equipment from previous users. The effect of the tax is to favor local users who wish to dispose of equipment over out-of-state users similarly situated. Whatever the Louisiana Legislature's reasons for granting such an exemption to this segment of the local second-hand market,[8] no attempt has been made to justify it or to show how its purpose would be defeated by extending the same exemption to similar out-of-state transactions.[9] We therefore conclude that the use tax on isolated sales in this case departs from the equality required by Silas Mason and discriminates against interstate commerce.

Thirty-five States other than Louisiana have sales and use tax statutes. At this juncture, Louisiana, according to the parties, is the only State to adopt the constructions presented for decision in this case. Those few States which have considered these issues at all appear to have rejected the Louisiana position for reasons in accord with our opinion here. Both Ohio and North Dakota have by administrative regulations excluded labor and shop overhead from the tax base of the out-of-state manufacturer-user on the ground that its inclusion might violate the Commerce Clause.[10] In Chicago Bridge & Iron Co. v. Johnson, 19 Cal.2d 162, 119 P.2d 945, the California Supreme Court upheld the application of its use tax to an out-of-state manufacturer-user, expressly pointing out that because labor and shop overhead had been excluded from its tax base, the taxpayer was in no different position from its in-state competitor. The parties have been able to find only one state case passing directly on either question. In State v.

---

8. The appellee argues that the reason for the exemption is that any item sold in a local isolated sale has already been subjected to either a sales tax if it was originally acquired in Louisiana or a use tax if it was imported, whereas there is no assurance that an item acquired in an out-of-state isolated sale has ever sustained such a tax burden. The appellee further maintains that the taxes here in question could have been reduced by any such previous taxation. If the record supported the appellee's position, it would be carefully considered. However, the appellee has shown us no regulations providing for the deduction of sales or use taxes paid on the item prior to the out-of-state isolated sale; the appellee stated in the stipulation of facts that all evidence showing an isolated sale was irrelevant; and the above-quoted statement of the Louisiana Supreme Court leaves little room for such modification.

9. Although no evidence was presented on the issue, one reason for not taxing local isolated sales and the labor and shop overhead of the local manufacturer-user may be the difficult administrative burden in either calculating or enforcing the tax. However, such a local administrative prob-

lem would not justify a different treatment of the similar out-of-state transaction, since the mere extension of the special treatment to the out-of-state transaction would satisfy both the local problem and the Commerce Clause.

We fail to see a similar administrative problem in calculating the appellant's labor and shop overhead, since the tax base under either approach is calculated on the basis of the cost factors recorded in the appellant's books.

10. CCH Ohio State Rep., Cir. No. 18, Mar. 1, 1954, ¶ 60371.70; North Dakota Tax Commission, Rules Nos. 55 and 113.

Moreover, as this Court noted in Henneford v. Silas Mason Co., 300 U.S. 577, 581, 57 S.Ct. 524, 526, the State of Washington, recognizing the latent inequality, made special arrangements for the manufacturer-user:

"The tax presupposes everywhere a retail purchase by the user before the time of use. If he has manufactured the chattel for himself, * * * he is exempt from the use tax, whether title was acquired in Washington or elsewhere."

Bay Towing & Dredging Co., Inc., 265 Ala. 282, 90 So.2d 743, the Alabama Supreme Court held that the in-state exemption for isolated sales had to be extended to out-of-state isolated sales to avoid discrimination against interstate commerce.

The judgment of the Supreme Court of Louisiana is reversed and the case remanded for further proceedings not inconsistent with this opinion.

Reversed and remanded.

MR. JUSTICE BRENNAN, concurring.

I fully concur in the opinion of the Court insofar as it treats of isolated sales. It seems clear that Louisiana exempts from sales taxation within the State the purchase of items which, if bought outside the State and brought in, would eventually incur a Louisiana use tax. The equality of treatment which my Brother CLARK finds assured by the credit for taxes already paid to other States seems to me wholly fortuitous. The credit for prior sales or use taxes will avert discrimination in the taxation of casual sales only if the out-of-state purchaser has already paid a sales or use tax equal to or greater than Louisiana's use tax, so that the credit is fully effective. If the purchaser abroad has paid no prior tax, or one of smaller amount, then upon his first use of the article in Louisiana he incurs a tax liability which he would clearly have escaped had he made the identical purchase at an exempted casual sale within the State. No justification for such discrimination has been suggested, and I can think of none beyond a mere possibility of administrative convenience.

I also agree that, under the circumstances of this case, the application of Louisiana's use tax statute to appellant is constitutionally impermissible. This result does not, I think, flow from any duty upon the States to ensure absolute equality of economic burden as between sales and use taxpayers. For we have sustained the constitutionality of the sales and compensating use tax system, Henneford v. Silas Mason Co., 300 U.S. 577, 57 S.Ct. 524, 81 L.Ed. 814, even though as a matter of economic fact the out-of-state use taxpayer is likely ultimately to incur a heavier burden than his in-state counterpart, the sales taxpayer. Such a disparity may result, though the rate of taxation upon the two is identical, because the in-state seller is somewhat likelier to absorb some part of the sales-tax burden than is the out-of-state seller to absorb the burden of the use tax which his customer eventually must pay. Warren and Schlesinger, Sales and Use Taxes: Interstate Commerce Pays Its Way, 38 Col.L.Rev. 49, 70–74 (1938). And we have also intimated, 300 U.S., at 587, that a State may not be constitutionally obliged to credit the amount of sales taxes paid in other States against the use tax it imposes. See Note, 51 Harv.L.Rev. 130, 132–133 (1937). Nevertheless, if the Constitution does not mandate absolute equality of treatment as between in-state and out-of-state sales, it assuredly does forbid discriminatory treatment by the States. Discrimination would result if different rates of taxation were imposed by the State on use and sale, and it is the result here because Louisiana, while it taxes the full value of property assembled without and used but not sold within the State, does not tax the full value of property assembled within the State and used but not sold there.

It does not follow, however, nor do I read the Court's opinion as so holding, that as a result of today's decision Louisiana has no option but to adopt the practice of Ohio, North Dakota, and California, see pp. 1206–1207, supra, and exclude labor and shop overhead from the tax base of the out-of-state manufacturer-user. That might be the case if the sole justification for the use tax were to offset the effect of sales taxes imposed on in-state purchasers, and thereby to deter domestic consumers from seeking to evade the sales tax by purchasing out of state. But we have recognized an alternative justification for the use tax as a levy upon "the privilege of use after commerce is at an end." 300 U.S., at 582, 57 S.Ct. at 526; see Hartman, State Taxation of Interstate Commerce (1953), 162–163. Thus Louisiana surely may if it chooses tax appellant's trucks and equipment, when they come to rest in the State, at their full value. Since this alternative is available to Louisiana and any other use-tax State, I fail to see the inevitability of my Brother CLARK's prediction that "this decision will deprive Louisiana of millions of dollars under its sales tax." The Court holds no more than that if Louisiana chooses to levy such a use tax it cannot constitutionally exempt in-state manufacturer-users as it now does; it must tax "the privilege of use" within the State of the property of such users at full value and at the same rates. Nothing in the Court's opinion nor in my view of the case prescribes the particular manner in which Louisiana must obey the Constitution.*

Notes and Problems

A. For an examination of the issues relating to the inclusion of transportation charges, trade-ins, and the like in the measure of sales and use taxes, which frequently raise problems of the type considered in the principal case, see Chapter 10, p. 793 infra.

B. *Discriminatory Transfer Taxation of Stock Sold on Out-of-State Exchanges.* The Supreme Court demonstrated its continuing sensitivity to the importance of preventing discrimination against out-of-state businesses by striking down provisions of the New York stock transfer tax statute on the ground that they disadvantaged trading on regional stock exchanges in favor of New York exchanges. Boston Stock Exchange v. State Tax Comm'n, 429 U.S. 318, 97 S.Ct. 599 (1977).† * * * Before 1968, the New York stock transfer tax, which has long been a source of substantial

---

* [The dissenting opinion of Justices Clark and Black has been omitted. The case is the subject of an extensive comment in Taylor, "Burdening Interstate Commerce via the Sales and Use Tax—The Halliburton Case," 1962 Nat.Tax Ass'n Procs. 528.]

† The ensuing discussion in this Note is taken from J. Hellerstein, "State Tax Discrimination Against Out-of-Staters," 30 Nat.Tax J. 113, 119–20 (1977). The excerpt is used with the consent of the copyright owner, National Tax Association—Tax Institute of America.

revenue for the State, "was neutral as to in-state and out-of-state sales." [26] The tax was broadly drawn, so as to cover any aspect of a stock transfer that takes place in New York, a sale, an agreement of sale, a memorandum of sale, a delivery or transfer of shares or certificates of stock.[27]

In recent years, the New York stock exchanges have been experiencing increasing competition from regional exchanges located in other parts of the country. To provide "long term relief from some of the competitive pressures outside the State," and to keep in New York City the New York Stock Exchange, which had threatened to move if the stock transfer tax were not repealed,[28] the statute was amended in 1968 in two respects:

(1) A non-resident of New York who makes a "sale" of stock in New York was taxed at only half the regular rates.

(2) If the sale is made in New York, the tax was limited to $350 on a single transaction, no matter how many shares are sold, whether the sales were made by a resident or non-resident, but if not sold in New York, the regular per share tax rate would apply.

Sales made in New York, as the statute has been construed in the typical transaction, means sales in regular course through New York stock exchanges; and those made outside the State refer typically to sales made on the regional stock exchanges located in other parts of the country. A large part of the sales made on the regional exchanges have been taxed by New York, because the stock transfer agents of many large corporations are located within the State, with the result that stock certificates are issued or delivered or other aspects of the transactions frequently occur in New York.[29]

Six regional stock exchanges, spread across the country from Boston to San Francisco, filed suit in the New York courts, seeking a declaratory judgment determining that the 1968 amendments were invalid, on the ground that they discriminated against interstate commerce, by imposing a greater tax burden on out-of-state transactions than on similar in-state transactions. Predictably, the New York courts found no constitutional

26. [Boston Stock Exchange v. State Tax Comm.] 429 U.S. at 330, 97 S.Ct. at 607.

27. § 270.1, N.Y. Tax Law. Despite the interstate character of a great many purchases and sales of stock made through the out-of-State brokers on the New York stock exchanges, the imposition of New York's stock transfer tax has survived attack under the Commerce Clause. See Hatch v. Reardon, 204 U.S. 152, 161–162 (1907); O'Kane v. New York, 283 N.Y. 439, 28 N.E.2d 905 (1940). See, however, note 29 infra.

28. See memorandum by Governor Nelson Rockefeller supporting the proposed amendments. 429 U.S. at 327, 97 S.Ct. at 605.

29. Following the decision of the New York Court of Appeals in the *Boston Stock Exchange* case, note 30 infra, the Federal Securities Act was amended so as to prohibit the imposition of a stock transfer tax where the sole event taking place in the State is the delivery, or transfer to, or by, a registered clearing agency or registered transfer agent, as defined by the Securities Act of 1934. The effectiveness of the Federal legislation in accomplishing that result has been recognized in an opinion of counsel to the N.Y. State Tax Commission. See CCH N.Y. Tax Serv., ¶ 57–101.605. These developments may have resulted in a substantial diminution of New York stock transfer taxes collectible on sales on the regional exchanges, without reference to the decision in the case.

discrimination in the amendments.[30] The Supreme Court, however, found that the amendments had upset the "equilibrium" of tax neutrality that had previously existed between in-state and out-of-state sales: [31]

> * * * The obvious effect of the tax is to extend a financial advantage to sales on the New York exchanges at the expense of the regional exchanges. Rather than "compensating" New York for a supposed competitive disadvantage resulting from § 270, the amendment forecloses tax-neutral decisions and creates both an advantage for the exchanges in New York and a discriminatory burden on commerce to her sister States.[32]

The case confronted the Court with an aspect of discriminatory taxation that it had not previously passed on, that the discrimination in rates and in the maximum tax distinguished between *two types of non-residents,* those who made in-state sales and those who made out-of-state sales. The Court disposed of the argument that only discrimination *against non-residents in favor of residents* is proscribed by the Commerce Clause by first observing that "non-resident, in-state sales * * * may also be considered as interstate commerce," and concluded:

> A State may no more use discriminatory taxes to assure that non-residents direct their commerce to businesses within the State than to assure that residents trade only in intrastate commerce. As we stated at the outset, the fundamental purpose of the Clause is to assure that there be free trade among the several States. This free trade purpose is not confined to the freedom to trade with only one State; it is a freedom to trade with any State, to engage in commerce across all State boundaries.[33]

C. *Discrimination Against Out-of-State Users by First Use Tax on Off-Shore Natural Gas.* In an original action filed in the Supreme Court by the State of Maryland and several other States and supported by the United States and the Federal Energy Regulatory Commission, the Court invalidated a Louisiana First-Use Tax on natural gas that had been produced principally in the Outer Continental Shelf (OCS), on the ground, *inter alia,* that the tax discriminated against interstate commerce. Maryland v. Louisiana, 451 U.S. 725, 101 S.Ct. 2114 (1981). (Chief Justice Burger filed a concurring opinion and Justice Rehnquist dissented; both opinions were concerned entirely with the question whether the case was an appropriate one for exercise of the Court's original jurisdiction). Most of the gas extracted from the lands underlying the Gulf of Mexico is piped to refining plants in Louisiana where it is "dryed"—the liquefiable hydrocarbons gathered and removed—on its way to ultimate distribution to consumers in over 30 States. Ninety percent of the OCS gas processed in Louisiana is

30. Boston Stock Exchange v. State Tax Comm., 37 N.Y.2d 535, 337 N.E.2d 758 (1975).

31. Boston Stock Exchange v. State Tax Comm., 429 U.S. 318, 331, 97 S.Ct. 599, 607–608 (1977).

32. In reversing the State court, the Supreme Court rejected New York's "argu-ment that the tax should be sustained be-cause it is imposed on a local event at the end of interstate commerce." 429 U.S. at 332 n. 12, 97 S.Ct. at 608 n. 12.

33. 429 U.S. at 334–35, 97 S.Ct. at 609.

eventually sold to out-of-state consumers, with the 2 percent remainder consumed within Louisiana.

In discussing the Commerce Clause, the Court first rejected Louisiana's contention that the taxable "uses" within the State break the flow of commerce and are, therefore, wholly local taxable events. Even though the Louisiana uses may possess a sufficient local nexus to support otherwise valid taxes (451 U.S. at 755 n. 27, 101 S.Ct. at 2133, n. 27, and see, Michigan–Wisconsin Pipeline Co. v. Calvert, 347 U.S. 157, 74 S.Ct. 396 [1954]), the Court was of the view that the flow of gas from the wellhead to the consumer is, nevertheless, a continual flow of gas in interstate commerce.

In considering the claimed discrimination against interstate commerce, the Court analyzed the exemptions and credits allowed for the use of the gas in Louisiana. Thus, OCS gas consumed in Louisiana for (1) producing oil, natural gas, or sulphur; (2) processing natural gas for the extraction of liquefiable hydrocarbons; or (3) manufacturing fertilizer and anhydrous ammonia, is exempt from the First–Use Tax. Moreover, the credit provisions of the Louisiana tax statutes favored local interests. Under the Louisiana severance tax an owner paying the First–Use Tax on OCS gas receives an equivalent tax credit on any State severance tax that is owed in connection with production in Louisiana. The Court concluded that the economic effect of the severance tax credit is to encourage natural gas owners producing OCS gas to invest in mineral exploration and development within Louisiana, rather than in further OCS development or in production in other States. In addition, any utility producing electricity with OCS gas, any natural gas distributor dealing in OCS gas, or any direct purchaser of OCS gas for consumption by the purchaser within the State was permitted to recoup any increase in the cost of gas attributable to the First–Use Tax through credits against various taxes owed the State. Given these preferences for Louisianians, as compared with out-of-staters, the Court had no difficulty in concluding that "the Louisiana First–Use Tax unquestionably discriminates against interstate commerce in favor of local interests as the necessary result of various tax credits and exclusions." 451 U.S. at 756, 101 S.Ct. at 2134.

The Court also held that certain features of the First–Use Tax were in conflict with Federal legislation regulating natural gas and, accordingly, violated the Supremacy Clause of the Constitution. These are considered in Subd. C, Section 2. For review of the case, see W. Hellerstein, "State Taxation in the Federal System: Perspectives on Louisiana's First Use Tax on Natural Gas," 55 Tulane L.Rev. 601 (1981).

D. *Credit Allowed DISC Only for Goods Exported From the Taxing State.* In an effort to provide tax incentives for American corporations to increase their exports and to help solve the nation's balance of payments problems, Congress in 1971 accorded preferred treatment to Domestic International Sales Corporations (DISCs). New York's corporate franchise tax included DISC income in the tax base by combining the income of the DISC and its parent. At the same time, in order to encourage DISC activity in New York, the State provided a credit against the corporate franchise tax for the portion of the tax attributable to the Federally exempt

DISC income included in the New York tax base. The credit was limited, however, to the percentage of DISC receipts from export shipments from New York.

In Westinghouse Electric Corp. v. Tully, 466 U.S. 388, 104 S.Ct. 1856 (1984), the Supreme Court held that the credit discriminated against interstate commerce in violation of the Commerce Clause. The credit transgressed the fundamental principle that "[n]o State, consistent with the Commerce Clause, may 'impose a tax which discriminates against interstate commerce * * * by providing a direct commercial advantage to local business.'" 466 U.S. at 403 (quoting Boston Stock Exchange v. State Tax Comm., Note B supra). Furthermore, by encouraging the diversion of DISC-related activity from the State, New York had "'foreclose[d] tax-neutral decisions and * * * created * * * an advantage' for firms operating in New York by placing 'a discriminatory burden on commerce to its sister States.'" 466 U.S. at 406 (quoting Boston Stock Exchange v. State Tax Comm., Note B supra).

Westinghouse raises the question as to the constitutional status of various tax incentives designed to induce in-state location. Are investment tax credits and similar credits limited to in-state expenditures under a constitutional cloud after *Westinghouse*? See Michael, "The Constitutionality of Minnesota's Business Tax Credits After *Westinghouse Electric Corp.*," 4 J. State Tax'n 163 (1985), who concludes that they are. What about the practice of limiting favorable methods of depreciation, such as ACRS, to investments in in-state property?

E. *Discriminatory "Multiple Activities" Exemption in Business and Occupation Tax.* In Armco, Inc. v. Hardesty, 467 U.S. 638, 104 S.Ct. 2620 (1984), the Court considered a claim of State tax discrimination under West Virginia's broad-based Business and Occupation (B & O) Tax. See Section 4, Note A supra, for a description of such levies. The B & O tax was levied upon both manufacturers and wholesalers, but it exempted manufacturers who were subject to the manufacturing tax from liability for the wholesaling tax. The manufacturing tax was imposed at a higher rate than the wholesaling tax.

The Supreme Court agreed that the tax discriminated on its face against interstate commerce. The existence of a higher B & O tax on in-state manufacturers did not cure the discrimination because the manufacturing tax could not be viewed as substantially equivalent to the wholesaling tax. Furthermore, the Court did not saddle the taxpayer with the burden of demonstrating actual discrimination, i.e., that it was disadvantaged in comparison to an intrastate West Virginia manufacturer-wholesaler because it was required to pay both a wholesaling tax to West Virginia as well as a manufacturing tax elsewhere. The Court, drawing on its analysis in Container Corp. of America v. Franchise Tax Bd., 463 U.S. 159, 103 S.Ct. 2933 (1983), see p. 578 infra, held that the tax would violate the Commerce Clause's bar against State tax discrimination so long as it lacked "internal consistency":

> [A] tax must have "what might be called internal consistency—that is the [tax] must be such that, if applied by every jurisdiction," there would be no impermissible interference with free trade. In that case,

the Court was discussing the requirement that a tax be fairly apportioned to reflect the business conducted in the State. A similar rule applies where the allegation is that a tax on its face discriminates against interstate commerce. A tax that unfairly apportions income from other States is a form of discrimination against interstate commerce. * * * Any other rule would mean that the constitutionality of West Virginia's tax laws would depend on the shifting complexities of the tax codes of 49 other States, and that the validity of the taxes imposed on each taxpayer would depend on the particular other States in which it operated. [467 U.S. at 644–45.]

In Tyler Pipe Industries, Inc. v. Washington Department of Revenue, ___ U.S. ___, 107 S.Ct. 2810 (1987),* the Court applied the internal consistency doctrine to invalidate a provision of the Washington B & O tax. The tax was applied to the gross receipts from various business activities carried on in the State, including manufacturing and wholesaling. Like West Virginia in the *Armco* case, Washington had a "multiple activities" exemption that limited to one tax the levy on taxpayers engaged in both manufacturing and wholesaling in the State. However, instead of exempting local manufacturer-wholesalers from the wholesaling tax, as West Virginia had done, Washington exempted local manufacturer-wholesalers from the manufacturing tax. Thereby the Washington tax was no longer facially discriminatory. Out-of-state manufacturers that made wholesale sales in Washington would pay the same tax on their wholesaling activities as would their Washington-based competitors who manufactured and wholesaled their products in the State.

Nevertheless, the Court struck down the tax as discriminatory against out-of-state wholesalers under the "internal consistency" doctrine. It was found that if every State adopted Washington's taxing scheme, the interstate manufacturer-wholesaler would be put at a competitive disadvantage in relation to the intrastate manufacturer-wholesaler. The interstate manufacturer-wholesaler would pay both a manufacturing tax to the State of manufacture and a wholesaling tax to the State of sale, whereas the intrastate manufacturer would pay but one tax—a manufacturing tax.

After concluding that "Washington's multiple activities exemption discriminates against interstate commerce," the Court suggested two alternatives by which the State could make the statute constitutionally acceptable by "eliminating exposure to the burden of a multiple tax on manufacturing and wholesaling." Either it could repeal the tax on manufacturing or it could allow a credit against Washington manufacturing tax liability for wholesale taxes paid by Washington manufacturers to any State and a credit against Washington wholesale tax liability for manufacturing taxes paid by out-of-state manufacturers to other States. 107 S.Ct. 2819–2821.

Justice Scalia dissented, attacking the Court's imposing

on state taxes a requirement of "internal consistency," demanding that they " 'be such that, if applied by every jurisdiction,' there would be no impermissible interference with free trade." * * * It is equally clear

---

* The balance of the discussion in this note is based on J. Hellerstein & W. Hellerstein, "Highlights of Recent Developments," 1987 Cumulative Supplement to J. Hellerstein, State Taxation I, Corporate Income and Franchise Taxes (1983).

to me, however, that this internal consistency principle is nowhere to be found in the Constitution. Nor is it plainly required by our prior decisions. Indeed, in order to apply the internal consistency rule in this case, the Court is compelled to overrule a rather lengthy list of prior decisions. [107 S.Ct. at 2823–24.]

As pointed out by Justice Scalia, the "internal consistency" requirement appears to have had its origin in a statement of Justice Brennan in the unitary apportionment case of Container Corp. of America v. Franchise Tax Bd., 463 U.S. 159, 103 S.Ct. 2933 (1983), set out in Chapter 9, pp. 578–606 infra:

> The first, and again obvious, component of fairness in an apportionment formula is what might be called internal consistency—that is the formula must be such that, if applied by every jurisdiction, it would result in no more than all of the unitary business's income being taxed. [463 U.S. at 169.]

There was no suggestion by Justice Brennan that he was advancing a new general test of validity of taxes under the Commerce Clause. On the contrary, the "internal consistency" requirement was discussed solely in the context of fair apportionment. Nor did Justice Brennan present the "internal consistency" as a new requirement in apportionment cases, but only as an "obvious component of fairness in any apportionment formula." Id. For a detailed consideration of the "internal consistency" doctrine, see W. Hellerstein, "Is 'Internal Consistency' Foolish?: Reflections on an Emerging Commerce Clause Restraint on State Taxation", 87 Mich.L.Rev. ___ (Oct.1988).

F. *Flat Highway Taxes, Discrimination Against Interstate Commerce, and the "Internal Consistency" Requirement.* In American Trucking Associations, Inc. v. Scheiner, ___ U.S. ___, 107 S.Ct. 2829 (1987), the Court was faced with the question whether Pennsylvania's flat taxes on trucks discriminated against interstate commerce. Relying on the "internal consistency" test, see Note E supra, the Court concluded that the taxes were discriminatory. The "inevitable effect" of the "unapportioned flat taxes" is

> to threaten the free movement of commerce by placing a financial barrier around the State of Pennsylvania. To pass the internal consistency test, a state tax must be of a kind that, "if applied by every jurisdiction, there would be no impermissible interference with free trade." Armco Inc. v. Hardesty, 467 U.S., at 644, 104 S.Ct., at 2623 (1984). If each State imposed flat taxes for the privilege of making commercial entrances into its territory, there is no conceivable doubt that commerce among the States would be deterred. [107 S.Ct. at 2840.]

The State contended that the axle tax did not discriminate against interstate commerce, because it was only part of an overall scheme of taxes designed to finance the State's highway system; and that such taxes, considered in the aggregate, imposed a greater tax burden on Pennsylvania-based trucks than on trucks registered in other States. This argument was rejected on the ground that "the Commerce Clause does not permit compensatory measures for the disparities that result from each State's choice of tax levels." 107 S.Ct. at 2843. As the Court observed:

"[i]mplementation of a rule of law that a tax is nondiscriminatory because other taxes of at least the same magnitude are imposed by the taxing State on other transactions would plunge the Court into the morass of weighing comparative tax burdens." [107 S.Ct. at 2843 (quoting J. Hellerstein, State Taxation I, Corporate Income and Franchise Taxes ¶ 4.12[5], p. 150 (1983)).]

The *American Trucking Associations* case is considered further in Section 10 infra in connection with State highway use taxes.

G. *Tax Exemption Favoring Local Alcoholic Beverages.* In Bacchus Imports, Ltd. v. Dias, 468 U.S. 263, 104 S.Ct. 3049 (1984), the Supreme Court struck down an exemption for locally produced alcoholic beverages from an excise tax on the wholesale sale of liquors. The State sought to avoid the force of the Court's precedents prohibiting such local favoritism by arguing that the locally produced beverages did not compete with other products sold by the wholesalers and that this in substance mooted the Commerce Clause issue. The Court rejected this argument on the ground that some competition existed between the exempted and the nonexempted liquors and that the extent of the competition was irrelevant under Commerce Clause analysis. The State also claimed the exemption was designed to promote a struggling industry, but the Court found that fact unacceptable as a justification for the discriminatory tax under the Commerce Clause. The *Bacchus* case also marked an important change in the Court's reading of the Twenty-first Amendment. See Section 11 infra.

H. *Complementary Taxes as a Defense to State Tax Discrimination Under the Commerce Clause.* The Court has sometimes held that a State tax which appears to discriminate against interstate commerce is nevertheless constitutionally permissible because of a complementary exaction that offsets the apparent discrimination. See, e.g., Henneford v. Silas Mason Co., 300 U.S. 577, 57 S.Ct. 524 (1937) (use tax imposed on goods purchased out-of-state complemented by sales tax on in-state purchases); Hinson v. Lott, 75 U.S. (8 Wall.) 148 (1868) (tax on importation of liquor into State complemented by tax on in-state distillers). In several recent cases, however, the Court has rejected the States' attempts to cure the apparent discrimination in their taxing statutes by reference to allegedly complementary taxes. See Maryland v. Louisana, note C supra (First–Use Tax on natural gas not complemented by local severance tax); Armco, Inc. v. Hardesty, Note E supra (tax on wholesaling not complemented by tax on manufacturing). The complementary tax doctrine is explored in detail in W. Hellerstein, "Complementary Taxes as a Defense to Unconstitutional State Tax Discrimination," 39 Tax Law. 405 (1986).

SECTION 9. SEVERANCE TAXES

COMMONWEALTH EDISON CO. v. MONTANA

Supreme Court of the United States, 1981.
453 U.S. 609, 101 S.Ct. 2946.

JUSTICE MARSHALL delivered the opinion of the Court.[*]

Montana, like many other States, imposes a severance tax on mineral production in the State. In this appeal, we consider whether the tax Montana levies on each ton of coal mined in the State, Mont. Code § 15–35–101 et seq. (1979), violates the Commerce and Supremacy Clauses of the United States Constitution.

I

Buried beneath Montana are large deposits of low sulfur coal, most of it on federal land. Since 1921, Montana has imposed a severance tax on the output of Montana coal mines, including coal mined on federal land. After commissioning a study of coal production taxes in 1974, see House Resolution Nos. 45 and 63, Senate Resolution No. 83, Laws of Montana, 1619–1620, 1653–1654, 1683–1684 (March 14 & 16, 1974); Montana Legislative Council, Fossil Fuel Taxation (1974), in 1975, the Montana Legislature enacted the tax schedule at issue in this case. Mont.Code § 15–35–103 (1979). The tax is levied at varying rates depending on the value, energy content, and method of extraction of the coal, and may equal at a maximum, 30% of the "contract sales price."[1] Under the terms of a 1976 amendment to the Montana Constitution, after Dec. 31, 1979, at least 50% of the revenues generated by the tax must be paid into a permanent trust fund, the principal of which may be appropriated only by a vote of three-fourths of the members of each house of the legislature. Montana Const. Art. IX, § 5.

Appellants, 4 Montana coal producers and 11 of their out-of-state utility company customers, filed these suits in Montana state court in 1978. They sought refunds of over $5.4 million in severance taxes paid under protest, a declaration that the tax is invalid under the Supremacy and Commerce Clauses, and an injunction against further collection of the tax. Without receiving any evidence the court upheld the tax and dismissed the complaints.

On appeal, the Montana Supreme Court affirmed the judgment of the trial court. Mont., 615 P.2d 847 (1980). The supreme court held that the tax is not subject to scrutiny under the Commerce Clause because it is imposed on the severance of coal, which the court characterized as an intrastate activity preceding entry of the coal into inter-

---

[*] Some footnotes have been omitted.

1. Under Mont.Code § 15–35–103 (1979), the value of the coal is determined by the "contract sales price" which is defined as "the price of coal extracted and prepared for shipment f.o.b. mine, excluding the amount charged by the seller to pay taxes paid on production * * *." § 15–35–102(1) (1979). Taxes paid on production are defined in § 15–35–102(6) (1979). Because production taxes are excluded from the computation of the value of the coal, the effective rate of the tax is lower than the statutory rate.

state commerce. In this regard, the Montana court relied on this Court's decisions in Heisler v. Thomas Colliery Co., 260 U.S. 245, 43 S.Ct. 83, 67 L.Ed. 237 (1922), Oliver Iron Mining Co. v. Lord, 262 U.S. 172, 43 S.Ct. 526, 67 L.Ed. 929 (1923), and Hope Natural Gas Co. v. Hall, 274 U.S. 284, 47 S.Ct. 639, 71 L.Ed. 1049 (1927), which employed similar reasoning in upholding state severance taxes against Commerce Clause challenges. As an alternative basis for its resolution of the Commerce Clause issue, the Montana court held, as a matter of law, that the tax survives scrutiny under the four-part test articulated by this Court in Complete Auto Transit, Inc. v. Brady, 430 U.S. 274, 97 S.Ct. 1076, 51 L.Ed.2d 326 (1977). The Montana court also rejected appellants' Supremacy Clause challenge, concluding that appellants had failed to show that the Montana tax conflicts with any federal statute.

We noted probable jurisdiction, 449 U.S. 1033, 101 S.Ct. 607, 66 L.Ed.2d 494 (1980), to consider the important issues raised. We now affirm.

II

A

As an initial matter, appellants assert that the Montana Supreme Court erred in concluding that the Montana tax is not subject to the strictures of the Commerce Clause. In appellants' view, *Heisler's* "mechanical" approach, which looks to whether a state tax is levied on goods prior to their entry into interstate commerce, no longer accurately reflects the law. Appellants contend that the correct analysis focuses on whether the challenged tax substantially affects interstate commerce, in which case it must be scrutinized under the *Complete Auto Transit* test.

We agree that *Heisler's* reasoning has been undermined by more recent cases. The *Heisler* analysis evolved at a time when the Commerce Clause was thought to prohibit the States from imposing any direct taxes on interstate commerce. See, e.g., Helson & Randolph v. Kentucky, 279 U.S. 245, 250–252, 49 S.Ct. 279, 280–81, 73 L.Ed. 683 (1929); Ozark Pipe Line Corp. v. Monier, 266 U.S. 555, 562, 45 S.Ct. 184, 185, 69 L.Ed. 439 (1925). Consequently, the distinction between intrastate activities and interstate commerce was crucial to protecting the States' taxing power.

The Court has, however, long since rejected any suggestion that a state tax or regulation affecting interstate commerce is immune from Commerce Clause scrutiny because it attaches only to a "local" or intrastate activity. See Hunt v. Washington Apple Advertising Comm'n, 432 U.S. 333, 350, 97 S.Ct. 2434, 2445, 53 L.Ed.2d 383 (1977); Pike v. Bruce Church, Inc., 397 U.S. 137, 141–142, 90 S.Ct. 844, 847, 25 L.Ed.2d 174 (1970); Nippert v. City of Richmond, 327 U.S. 416, 423–424, 66 S.Ct. 586, 589–90, 90 L.Ed. 760 (1946). Correspondingly, the Court has rejected the notion that state taxes levied on interstate commerce are *per se* invalid. See, e.g., Washington Revenue Dept. v. Association of Wash. Stevedoring Cos., 435 U.S. 734, 98 S.Ct. 1388, 55 L.Ed.2d 682 (1978); Complete Auto Transit, Inc. v. Brady, supra. In reviewing Commerce Clause challenges to state taxes, our goal has instead been to "establish a consistent and rational method of inquiry" focusing on "the practical effect of a challenged tax." * * * We conclude that the same "practical" analysis should apply in reviewing Commerce Clause challenges to state severance taxes.

In the first place, there is no real distinction—in terms of economic effects—between severance taxes and other types of state taxes that have been subjected to Commerce Clause scrutiny. See, e.g. Michigan–Wisconsin Pipe Line Co. v. Calvert, 347 U.S. 157, 74 S.Ct. 396, 98 L.Ed. 583 (1954); Joseph v. Carter & Weekes Stevedoring Co., 330 U.S. 422, 67 S.Ct. 815, 91 L.Ed. 993 (1947); Puget Sound Stevedoring Co. v. State Tax Comm'n, 302 U.S. 90, 58 S.Ct. 72, 82 L.Ed. 68 (1937), both overruled in Washington Revenue Dept. v. Association of Wash. Stevedoring Cos., supra. State taxes levied on a "local" activity preceding entry of the goods into interstate commerce may substantially affect interstate commerce, and this effect is the proper focus of Commerce Clause inquiry. * * * Second, this Court has acknowledged that "a State has a significant interest in exacting from interstate commerce its fair share of the cost of state government," Washington Revenue Dept. v. Association of Wash. Stevedoring Cos., supra, 435 U.S., at 748, 98 S.Ct., at 1398. As the Court has stated, " '[e]ven interstate business must pay its way.' " * * * Consequently, the *Heisler* Court's concern that a loss of state taxing authority would be an inevitable result of subjecting taxes on "local" activities to Commerce Clause scrutiny is no longer tenable.

We therefore hold that a state severance tax is not immunized from Commerce Clause scrutiny by a claim that the tax is imposed on goods prior to their entry into the stream of interstate commerce. Any contrary statements in *Heisler* and its progeny are disapproved. We agree with appellants that the Montana tax must be evaluated under *Complete Auto Transit's* four-part test. Under that test, a state tax does not offend the Commerce Clause if it "is applied to an activity with a substantial nexus with the taxing State, is fairly apportioned, does not discriminate against interstate commerce, and is fairly related to services provided by the State." 430 U.S., at 279, 97 S.Ct. at 1079.

B

* * * Appellants do contend, * * *, that the Montana tax is invalid under the third and fourth prongs of the *Complete Auto Transit* test.

Appellants assert that the Montana tax "discriminate[s] against interstate commerce" because 90% of Montana coal is shipped to other States under contracts that shift the tax burden primarily to non-Montana utility companies and thus to citizens of other States. But the Montana tax is computed at the same rate regardless of the final destination of the coal, and there is no suggestion here that the tax is administered in a manner that departs from this evenhanded formula. We are not, therefore, confronted here with the type of differential tax treatment of interstate and intrastate commerce that the Court has found in other "discrimination" cases. See, e.g., Maryland v. Louisiana, 451 U.S. 725, 101 S.Ct. 2114, 68 L.Ed.2d 576 (1981); Boston Stock Exchange v. State Tax Comm'n, 429 U.S. 318, 97 S.Ct. 599, 50 L.Ed.2d 514 (1977). * * *

Instead, the gravamen of appellants' claim is that a state tax must be considered discriminatory for purposes of the Commerce Clause if the tax burden is borne primarily by out-of-state consumers. Appellants do not suggest that this assertion is based on any of this Court's prior discriminatory tax cases. In fact, a similar claim was considered and rejected in *Heisler*. There, it was argued that Pennsylvania had a virtual monopoly of anthracite coal and that, because 80% of the coal was shipped out of State, the tax discriminated against and impermissibly burdened interstate commerce. 260 U.S. 251–253, 43 S.Ct., at 84. The Court, however, dismissed these factors as "adventitious considerations." 260 U.S., at 259, 43 S.Ct., at 86. We share the *Heisler* Court's misgivings about judging the validity of a state tax by assessing the State's "monopoly" position or its "exportation" of the tax burden out of State.

The premise of our discrimination cases is that "[t]he very purpose of the Commerce Clause was to create an area of free trade among the several States." McLeod v. J.E. Dilworth Co., 322 U.S. 327, 330, 64 S.Ct. 1023, 1025, 88 L.Ed. 1304 (1944). * * * Under such a regime, the borders between the States are essentially irrelevant. As the Court stated in West v. Kansas Natural Gas Co., 221 U.S. 229, 255, 31 S.Ct. 564, 571, 55 L.Ed. 716 (1911), "in matters of foreign and interstate commerce there are no state lines." See Boston Stock Exchange v. State Tax Comm'n, supra, 429 U.S., at 331–332, 97 S.Ct., at 607–08. Consequently, to accept appellants' theory and invalidate the Montana tax solely because most of Montana's coal is shipped across the very state borders that ordinarily are to be considered irrelevant would require a significant and, in our view, unwarranted departure from the rationale of our prior discrimination cases.

Furthermore, appellants' assertion that Montana may not "exploit" its "monopoly" position by exporting tax burdens to other States, cannot rest on a claim that there is need to protect the out-of-state consumers of Montana coal from discriminatory tax treatment. As previously noted, there is no real discrimination in this case; the tax burden is borne according to the amount of coal consumed and not according to any distinction between in-state and out-of-state consumers. Rather, appellants assume that the Commerce Clause gives residents of one State a right of access at "reasonable" prices to resources located in another State that is richly endowed with such resources, without regard to whether and on what terms residents of the resource-rich State have access to the resources. We are not convinced that the

Commerce Clause, of its own force, gives the residents of one State the right to control in this fashion the terms of resource development and depletion in a sister State. Cf. Philadelphia v. New Jersey, supra, 437 U.S., at 626, 98 S.Ct., at 2536.

In any event, appellants' discrimination theory ultimately collapses into their claim that the Montana tax is invalid under the fourth prong of the *Complete Auto Transit* test: that the tax is not "fairly related to the services provided by the State." 430 U.S., at 279, 97 S.Ct., at 1079. Because appellants concede that Montana may impose *some* severance tax on coal mined in the State, the only remaining foundation for their discrimination theory is a claim that the tax burden borne by the out-of-state consumers of Montana coal is excessive. This is, of course, merely a variant of appellants' assertion that the Montana tax does not satisfy the "fairly related" prong of the *Complete Auto Transit* test, and it is to this contention that we now turn.

Appellants argue that they are entitled to an opportunity to prove that the amount collected under the Montana tax is not fairly related to the additional costs the State incurs because of coal mining. Thus, appellants' objection is to the *rate* of the Montana tax, and even then, their only complaint is that the *amount* the State receives in taxes far exceeds the *value* of the services provided to the coal mining industry. In objecting to the tax on this ground, appellants may be assuming that the Montana tax is, in fact, intended to reimburse the State for the cost of specific services furnished to the coal mining industry. Alternatively, appellants could be arguing that a State's power to tax an activity connected to interstate commerce cannot exceed the value of the services specifically provided to the activity. Either way, the premise of appellants' argument is invalid. Furthermore, appellants have completely misunderstood the nature of the inquiry under the fourth prong of the *Complete Auto Transit* test.

The Montana Supreme Court held that the coal severance tax is "imposed for the general support of the government." Mont., 615 P.2d, at 856, and we have no reason to question this characterization of the Montana tax as a general revenue tax. Consequently, in reviewing appellant's contentions, we put to one side those cases in which the Court reviewed challenges to "user" fees or "taxes" that were designed and defended as a specific charge imposed by the State for the use of state-owned or state-provided transportation or other facilities and services. * * *

This Court has indicated that States have considerable latitude in imposing general revenue taxes. The Court has, for example, consistently rejected claims that the Due Process Clause of the Fourteenth Amendment stands as a barrier against taxes that are "unreasonable" or "unduly burdensome." * * * Moreover, there is no requirement under the Due Process Clause that the amount of general revenue taxes collected from a particular activity must be reasonably related to the value of the services provided to the activity. Instead, our consistent rule has been:

"Nothing is more familiar in taxation than the imposition of a tax upon a class or upon individuals who enjoy no direct benefit from its expenditure, and who are not responsible for the condition to be remedied.

"A tax is not an assessment of benefits. It is, as we have said, a means of distributing the burden of the cost of government. The only benefit to which the taxpayer is constitutionally entitled is that derived from his enjoyment of the privileges of living in an organized society, established and safeguarded by the devotion of taxes to public purposes. Any other view would preclude the levying of taxes except as they are used to compensate for the burden on those who pay them, and would involve abandonment of the most fundamental principle of government—that it exists primarily to provide for the common good." Carmichael v. Southern Coal & Coke Co., 301 U.S. 495, 521–522, [57 S.Ct. 868, 878–79, 81 L.Ed. 1245 (1937) (citations omitted).

* * *

There is no reason to suppose that this latitude afforded the States under the Due Process Clause is somehow divested by the Commerce Clause merely because the taxed activity has some connection to interstate commerce; particularly when the tax is levied on an activity conducted within the State. "The exploitation by foreign corporations [or consumers] of intrastate opportunities under the protection and encouragement of local government offers a basis for taxation as unrestricted as that for domestic corporations." Ford Motor Co. v. Beauchamp, 308 U.S. 331, 334–335, 60 S.Ct. 273, 275, 84 L.Ed. 304 (1939); see also Ott v. Mississippi Valley Barge Line Co., 336 U.S. 169, 69 S.Ct. 432, 93 L.Ed. 585 (1949). To accept appellants' apparent suggestion that the Commerce Clause prohibits the States from requiring an activity connected to interstate commerce to contribute to the general cost of providing governmental services, as distinct from those costs attributable to the taxed activity, would place such commerce in a privileged position. * * * The "just share of state tax burden" includes sharing in the cost of providing "police and fire protection, the benefit of a trained work force, and 'the advantages of a civilized society.'" Exxon Corp. v. Wisconsin Dept. of Revenue, 447 U.S. 207, 228, 100 S.Ct. 2109, 2123, 65 L.Ed.2d 66, quoting Japan Line, Ltd. v. County of Los Angeles, 441 U.S., at 445, 99 S.Ct. 1813, 1819–20.

* * *

Furthermore, there can be no question that Montana may constitutionally raise general revenue by imposing a severance tax on coal mined in the State. The entire value of the coal, before transportation, originates in the State, and mining of the coal depletes the resource base and wealth of the State, thereby diminishing a future source of taxes and economic activity.[13] Cf. Maryland v. Louisiana, 451 U.S., at

13. Most of the States raise revenue by levying a severance tax on mineral production. The first such tax was imposed by Michigan in 1846. See United States De-

____, 101 S.Ct., at 2135–36. In many respects, a severance tax is like a real property tax, which has never been doubted as a legitimate means of raising revenue by the situs State (quite apart from the right of that or any other State to tax income derived from use of the property). * * * When, as here, a general revenue tax does not discriminate against interstate commerce and is apportioned to activities occurring within the State, the State "is free to pursue its own fiscal policies, unembarrassed by the Constitution, if by the practical operation of a tax the state has exerted its power in relation to opportunities which it has given, to protection which it has afforded, to benefits which it has conferred by the fact of being an orderly civilized society." Wisconsin v. J.C. Penney Co., 311 U.S. 435, 444, 61 S.Ct. 246, 249, 85 L.Ed. 267 (1940). * * *

The relevant inquiry under the fourth prong of the *Complete Auto Transit* test is not as appellants suggest, the *amount* of the tax of the *value* of the benefits allegedly bestowed as measured by the costs the State incurs on account of the taxpayer's activities. Rather, the test is closely connected to the first prong of the *Complete Auto Transit* test. Under this threshold test, the interstate business must have a substantial nexus with the State before *any* tax may be levied on it. See National Bellas Hess, Inc. v. Illinois Revenue Dept., 386 U.S. 753, 87 S.Ct. 1389, 18 L.Ed.2d 505 (1967). Beyond that threshold requirement, the fourth prong of the *Complete Auto Transit* test imposes the additional limitation that the *measure* of the tax must be reasonably related to the extent of the contact, since it is the activities or presence of the taxpayer in the State that may properly be made to bear a "just share of state tax burden," Western Live Stock Bureau v. Bureau of Revenue, 303 U.S., at 254, 58 S.Ct., at 548. * * * As the Court explained in Wisconsin v. J.C. Penney Co., supra, 311 U.S., at 446, 61 S.Ct., at 250 (emphasis added), "the incidence of the tax *as well as its measure* [must be] tied to the earnings which the State * * * has made possible, insofar as government is the prerequisite for the fruits of civilization for which, as Mr. Justice Holmes was fond of saying, we pay taxes."

Against this background, we have little difficulty concluding that the Montana tax satisfies the fourth prong of the *Complete Auto Transit* test. The "operating incidence" of the tax, see General Motors Corp. v. Washington, supra, 377 U.S., at 440–441, 84 S.Ct., at 1567–68, is on the mining of coal within Montana. Because it is measured as a percentage of the value of the coal taken, the Montana tax is in "proper proportion" to appellants' activities within the State and, therefore, to their "consequent enjoyment of the opportunities and protections which the State has afforded" in connection to those activities. *Id.,* at 441, 84 S.Ct., at 1568. Compare Nippert v. City of Richmond, 327 U.S., at 427, 66 S.Ct., at 591. When a tax is assessed in proportion to a taxpayer's activities or presence in a State, the taxpayer is shouldering its fair

partment of Agriculture, State Taxation of Mineral Deposits and Production (1978). By 1979, 33 States had adopted some type of severance tax. See Bureau of Census, State Government Tax Collections in 1979, Table 3 (1980).

share of supporting the State's provision of "police and fire protection, the benefit of a trained work force, and 'the advantages of a civilized society.'" Exxon Corp. v. Wisconsin Dept. of Revenue, 447 U.S., at 228, 100 S.Ct., at 2123, quoting Japan Line, Ltd. v. County of Los Angeles, 441 U.S., at 445, 99 S.Ct., at 1819–20.

Appellants argue, however, that the fourth prong of the *Complete Auto Transit* test must be construed as requiring a factual inquiry into the relationship between the revenues generated by a tax and costs incurred on account of the taxed activity, in order to provide a mechanism for judicial disapproval under the Commerce Clause of state taxes that are excessive. This assertion reveals that appellants labor under a misconception about a court's role in cases such as this. The simple fact is that the appropriate level or rate of taxation is essentially a matter for legislative, and not judicial, resolution. See Halson & Randolph v. Kentucky, 279 U.S. 245, 252, 49 S.Ct. 279, 281, 73 L.Ed. 683 (1929) * * *. In essence, appellants ask this Court to prescribe a test for the validity of state taxes that would require state and federal courts, as a matter of federal constitutional law, to calculate acceptable rates or levels of taxation of activities that are conceded to be legitimate subjects of taxation. This we decline to do.

In the first place, it is doubtful whether any legal test could adequately reflect the numerous and competing economic, geographic, demographic, social, and political considerations that must inform a decision about an acceptable rate or level of state taxation, and yet be reasonably capable of application in a wide variety of individual cases. But even apart from the difficulty of the judicial undertaking, the nature of the factfinding and judgment that would be required of the courts merely reinforces the conclusion that questions about the appropriate level of state taxes must be resolved through the political process. Under our federal system, the determination is to be made by state legislatures in the first instance and, if necessary, by Congress, when particular state taxes are thought to be contrary to federal interests. Cf. Mobil Oil Corp. v. Commissioner of Taxes, 445 U.S., at 448–449, 100 S.Ct., at 1237–38; Moorman Manufacturing Co. v. Bair, 437 U.S., at 280, 98 S.Ct. at 2348.

Furthermore, the reference in the cases to police and fire protection and other advantages of civilized society is not, as appellants suggest, a disingenuous incantation designed to avoid a more searching inquiry into the relationship between the *value* of the benefits conferred on the taxpayer and the *amount* of taxes it pays. Rather, when the measure of a tax is reasonably related to the taxpayer's activities or presence in the State—from which it derives some benefit such as the substantial privilege of mining coal—the taxpayer will realize, in proper proportion to the taxes it pays, "[t]he only benefit to which it is constitutionally entitled * * * that derived from his enjoyment of the privileges of living in an organized society, established and safeguarded by the devotion of taxes to public purposes." Carmichael v. Southern

Coal & Coke Co., 301 U.S., at 522, 57 S.Ct., at 878. Correspondingly, when the measure of a tax bears no relationship to the taxpayer's presence or activities in a State, a court may properly conclude under the fourth prong of the *Complete Auto Transit* test that the State is imposing an undue burden on interstate commerce. See Nippert v. City of Richmond, 327 U.S., at 427, 66 S.Ct., at 591; cf. Michigan–Wisconsin Pipe Line Co. v. Calvert, 347 U.S. 157, 74 S.Ct. 396, 98 L.Ed. 583 (1954). We are satisfied that the Montana tax, assessed under a formula that relates the tax liability to the value of appellant coal producers' activities within the State, comports with the requirements of the *Complete Auto Transit* test. We therefore turn to appellants' contention that the tax is invalid under the Supremacy Clause.

* * *

[The Court rejected the taxpayer's contention that the Montana tax, as applied to mining of Federally-owned coal, is invalid under the Supremacy Clause, because it substantially frustrates the purposes of the Mineral Land Leasing Act of 1920, as amended by the Federal Coal Leasing Amendments Act of 1975. Similarly, the Court found no merit in the taxpayer's claim that the Montana tax substantially frustrates national energy policies as embodied in several statutes encouraging the production and use of coal, particularly low-sulphur coal, such as that found in Montana.]

IV

In sum, we conclude that appellants have failed to demonstrate either that the Montana tax suffers from any of the constitutional defects alleged in their complaints, or that a trial is necessary to resolve the issue of the constitutionality of the tax. Consequently, the judgment of the Supreme Court of Montana is affirmed.

So ordered.

JUSTICE WHITE, concurring.

This is a very troublesome case for me, and I join the Court's opinion with considerable doubt and with the realization that Montana's levy on consumers in other States may in the long run prove to be an intolerable and unacceptable burden on commerce. Indeed, there is particular force in the argument that the tax is here and now unconstitutional. Montana collects most of its tax from coal lands owned by the Federal Government and hence by all of the people of this country, while at the same time sharing equally and directly with the Federal Government all of the royalties reserved under the leases the United States has negotiated on its land in the State of Montana. This share is intended to compensate the State for the burdens that coal mining may impose upon it. Also, as JUSTICE BLACKMUN cogently points out * * * another 40% of the federal revenue from mineral leases is indirectly returned to the States through a reclamation fund. In addition, there is statutory provision for federal grants to areas affected by increased coal production.

But this very fact gives me pause and counsels withholding our hand, at least for now. Congress has the power to protect interstate commerce from intolerable or even undesirable burdens. It is also very much aware of the Nation's energy needs, of the Montana tax and of the trend in the energy-rich States to aggrandize their position and perhaps lessen the tax burdens on their own citizens by imposing unusually high taxes on mineral extraction. Yet, Congress is so far content to let the matter rest, and we are counseled by the Executive Branch through the Solicitor General not to overturn the Montana tax as inconsistent with either the Commerce Clause or federal statutory policy in the field of energy or otherwise. The constitutional authority and the machinery to thwart efforts such as those of Montana, if thought unacceptable, are available to Congress, and surely Montana and other similarly situated States do not have the political power to impose their will on the rest of the country. As I presently see it, therefore, the better part of both wisdom and valor is to respect the judgment of the other branches of the Government. I join the opinion and the judgment of the Court.

JUSTICE BLACKMUN, with whom JUSTICE POWELL and JUSTICE STEVENS join, dissenting.

In Complete Auto Transit, Inc. v. Brady, 430 U.S. 274, 97 S.Ct. 1076, 51 L.Ed.2d 326 (1977), a unanimous Court observed: "A tailored tax, however, accomplished, must receive the careful scrutiny of the courts to determine whether it produces a forbidden effect upon interstate commerce." Id., at 288–289, n. 15, 97 S.Ct., at 1084, n. 15. In this case, appellants have alleged that Montana's severance tax on coal is tailored to single out interstate commerce, and that it produces a forbidden effect on that commerce because the tax bears no "relationship to the services provided by the State." Ibid. The Court today concludes that appellants are not entitled to a *trial* on this claim. Because I believe that the "careful scrutiny" due a tailored tax makes a trial here necessary, I respectfully dissent.

*   *   *

II

This Court's Commerce Clause cases have been marked by tension between two competing concepts: the view that interstate commerce should enjoy a "free trade" immunity from state taxation, see, e.g., Freeman v. Hewit, 329 U.S. 249, 252, 67 S.Ct. 274, 276, 91 L.Ed. 265 (1946), and the view that interstate commerce may be required to " 'pay its way,' " see, e.g., Western Live Stock v. Bureau of Revenue, 303 U.S. 250, 254, 58 S.Ct. 546, 548, 82 L.Ed. 823 (1938). See generally Complete Auto Transit, Inc. v. Brady, 430 U.S., at 278–281, 288–289, n. 15, 97 S.Ct., at 1078–80, 1083–84, n. 15; Simet & Lynn, Interstate Commerce Must Pay Its Way: The Demise of Spector, 31 Nat.Tax J. 53 (1978); Hellerstein, Foreword, State Taxation Under the Commerce Clause: An Historical Perspective, 29 Vand.L.Rev. 335, 335–339 (1976). In *Complete Auto Transit,* the Court resolved that tension by unanimously reaffirming that interstate commerce is not immune from state taxation. 430 U.S., at 288, 97 S.Ct., at 1083. But at the same time the Court made clear that not all state taxation of interstate commerce is valid; a state tax will be sustained against Commerce Clause challenge *only* if "the tax is applied to an activity with a substantial nexus with the taxing State, is fairly apportioned, does not discriminate against interstate commerce, and is fairly related to the services provided by the State." Id., at 279, 97 S.Ct., at 1079. See Maryland v. Louisiana, 451 U.S. 725, ——, 101 S.Ct. 2114, 2133, 68 L.Ed.2d 576 (1981).

* * * The Court also correctly observes that Montana's severance tax is facially neutral. It does not automatically follow, however, that the Montana severance tax does not unduly burden or interfere with interstate commerce. The gravamen of appellants' complaint is that the severance tax does not satisfy the fourth prong of the *Complete Auto Transit* test because it is tailored to, and does, force interstate commerce to pay *more* than its way. Under our established precedents, appellants are entitled to a trial on this claim.

The Court's conclusion to the contrary rests on the premise that the relevant inquiry under the fourth prong of the *Complete Auto Transit* test is simply whether the *measure* of the tax is fixed as a percentage of the value of the coal taken. Ante at 2958. This interpretation emasculates the fourth prong. No trial will ever be necessary on the issue of fair relationship so long as a State is careful to impose a proportional rather than a flat tax rate; thus, the Court's rule is no less "mechanical" than the approach entertained in Heisler v. Thomas Colliery Co., 260 U.S. 245, 43 S.Ct. 83, 67 L.Ed. 237 (1922), disapproved today * * *. Under the Court's reasoning any ad valorem tax will satisfy the fourth prong; indeed, the Court implicitly ratifies Montana's contention that it is free to tax this coal at 100% or even 1000% of value should it choose to do so. Tr. of Oral Arg. 21. Likewise, the Court's analysis indicates that Montana's severance tax would not run afoul of the Commerce Clause even if it raised sufficient revenue to allow Montana to eliminate all other taxes upon its citizens.

The Court's prior cases neither require nor support such a startling result. * * *

[T]he Court has been particularly vigilant to review taxes that "single out interstate business," since "[a]ny tailored tax of this sort creates an increased danger of error in apportionment, of discrimination against interstate commerce, and of a lack of relationship to the services provided by the State." *Complete Auto Transit*, 430 U.S., at 288–289, n. 15, 97 S.Ct., at 1084, n. 15. Moreover, the Court's vigilance has not been limited to taxes that discriminate upon their face: "Not the tax in a vacuum of words, but its practical consequences for the doing of interstate commerce in applications to concrete facts are our concern." *Nippert,* 327 U.S., at 431, 66 S.Ct., at 593. See Maryland v. Louisiana, 451 U.S., at ——, 101 S.Ct., at 2134. This is particularly true when the challenged tax, while facially neutral, falls so heavily upon interstate commerce that its burden "is not likely to be alleviated by those political restraints which are normally exerted on legislation where it affects adversely interests within the state." McGoldrick v. Berwind–White Co., 309 U.S. 33, 46, n. 2, 60 S.Ct. 388, 392, n. 2, 84 L.Ed. 565 (1940). Cf. Raymond Motor Transportation, Inc. v. Rice, 434 U.S. 429, 446–447, 98 S.Ct. 787, 797, 54 L.Ed.2d 664 (1978). In sum, then, when a tax has been "tailored" to reach interstate commerce, the Court's cases suggest that we require a closer "fit" under the fourth prong of the *Complete Auto Transit* test than when interstate commerce has not been singled out by the challenged tax.

As a number of commentators have noted, state severance taxes upon minerals are particularly susceptible to "tailoring." "Like a tollgate lying athwart a trade route, a severance or processing tax conditions access to natural resources." Developments in the Law, Federal Limitations on State Taxation of Interstate Business, 75 Harv. L.Rev. 953, 970 (1962) (Harvard Developments). Thus, to the extent that the taxing jurisdiction approaches a monopoly position in the mineral, and consumption is largely outside the State, such taxes are "[e]conomically and politically analogous to transportation taxes exploiting geographical position." Brown, The Open Economy: Justice Frankfurter and the Position of the Judiciary, 67 Yale L.J. 219, 232 (1957). See also Hellerstein, Constitutional Constraints on State and Local Taxation of Energy Resources, 31 Nat.Tax J. 245, 249–250 (1978); R. Posner, Economic Analysis of Law 510–514 (2d ed. 1977). But just as a port State may require that imports pay their own way even though the tax levied increases the cost of goods purchased by inland customers, see Michelin Tire Corp. v. Wages, 423 U.S. 276, 288, 96 S.Ct. 535, 542, 46 L.Ed.2d 495 (1976), so also may a mineral-rich State require that those who consume its sources pay a fair share of the general costs of government, as well as the specific costs attributable to the commerce itself. Thus, the mere fact that the burden of a severance tax is largely shifted forward to out-of-state consumers does not, standing alone, make out a Commerce Clause violation. See Hellerstein, supra, at 249. But the Clause *is* violated when, as appellants allege is the case here, the State effectively selects "a class of out-of-state taxpayers to shoulder a tax burden grossly in excess of any costs imposed directly or indirectly by such taxpayers on the State." Ibid.

III

It is true that a trial in this case would require "complex factual inquiries" into whether economic conditions are such that Montana is in fact able to export the burden of its severance tax * * *. I do not believe, however, that this threshold inquiry is beyond judicial competence. If the trial court were to determine that the tax is exported, it would then have to determine whether the tax is "fairly related," within the meaning of *Complete Auto Transit*. The Court to the contrary, this would not require the trial court "to second-guess legislative decisions about the amount or disposition of tax revenues."

* * *. If the tax is in fact a legitimate general revenue measure identical or roughly comparable to taxes imposed upon similar industries, a court's inquiry is at an end; on the other hand, if the tax singles out this particular interstate activity and charges it with a grossly disproportionate share of the general costs of government, the court must determine whether there is some reasonable basis for the legislative judgment that the tax is necessary to compensate the State for the particular costs imposed by the activity.

To be sure, the task is likely to prove to be a formidable one; but its difficulty does not excuse our failure to undertake it. This case poses extremely grave issues that threaten both to "polarize the Nation," see H.R.Rep. No. 96–1527, pt. 1, p. 2 (1980), and to reawaken "the tendencies toward economic Balkanization" that the Commerce Clause was designed to remedy. See Hughes v. Oklahoma, 441 U.S. 322, 325–326, 99 S.Ct. 1727, 1731, 60 L.Ed.2d 250 (1979). It is no answer to say that the matter is better left to Congress[:] * * *

I would not lightly abandon that role. Because I believe that appellants are entitled to an opportunity to prove that, in Holmes' words, Montana's severance tax "embodies what the Commerce Clause was meant to end," I dissent.

Notes and Problems

A. The *Commonwealth Edison* case is analyzed in W. Hellerstein, "Constitutional Limitations on State Tax Exportation," 1982 A.B.F.Res.J. 1; "The Supreme Court, 1980 Term," 95 Harv.L.Rev. 93, 102 (1981).

B. *Indian Severance Taxes.* In Merrion v. Jicarilla Apache Tribe, 455 U.S. 130, 102 S.Ct. 894 (1982), the Supreme Court sustained the power of an Indian Tribe to impose severance taxes on extraction by non-Indians of oil and gas from tribal lands. The Court held that Indian Tribes had inherent power to impose severance taxes and that Congress had not, by establishing national energy policies or by enacting statutes governing leasing of oil and gas interests on tribal land, preempted the Tribes' right to tax. The Court also held that the Tribes' enactment of a severance tax pursuant to a scheme established by Congress precluded judicial review of the Tribes' taxing power under the negative implications of the Commerce Clause.

The Court went on to observe that "[t]he tax challenged here would survive judicial scrutiny under the Interstate Commerce Clause, even if such scrutiny were necessary," 455 U.S. at 156, because the tax met the standards of *Complete Auto Transit*. The Court did remark in a footnote, however, that:

> Petitioners contend that because New Mexico may tax the same mining activity at full value, the Indian tax imposes a multiple tax burden on interstate commerce in violation of the Commerce Clause. The multiple taxation issue arises where two or more taxing jurisdictions point to some contact with an enterprise to support a tax on the entire value of its multi-state activities, which is more than the contact would justify. E.g., Standard Oil Co. v. Peck, 342 U.S. 382, 384–385

(1952). This Court has required an apportionment of the tax based on the portion of the activity properly viewed as occurring within each relevant State. See, e.g., Exxon Corp. v. Wisconsin Dept. of Revenue, 447 U.S. 207, 219 (1980); Washington Revenue Dept. v. Association of Washington Stevedoring Cos., 435 U.S. 734, 746, and n. 16 (1978).

This rule has no bearing here, however, for there can be no claim that the Tribe seeks to tax any more of petitioners' mining activity than the portion occurring within Tribal jurisdiction. Indeed, petitioners do not even argue that the Tribe is seeking to seize more tax revenues than would be fairly related to the services provided by the Tribe. * * *. In the absence of such an assertion, and when the activity taxed by the Tribe occurs entirely on tribal lands, the multiple taxation issue would arise only if a *State* attempted to levy a tax on the same activity, which is more than the *State's* contact with the activity would justify. In such a circumstance, any challenge asserting that tribal and state taxes create a multiple burden on interstate commerce should be directed at the state tax, which, in the absence of congressional ratification, might be invalidated under the Commerce Clause. These cases, of course, do not involve a challenge to state taxation, and we intimate no opinion on the possibility of such a challenge. [455 U.S. at 158–59 n. 26.]

SECTION 10. HIGHWAY USE TAXES AND OTHER USER CHARGES

The States have long imposed levies on interstate truck and bus operators as compensation for the use of their highways or for the cost of administering State traffic regulations. See generally Clark v. Paul Gray, Inc., 306 U.S. 583, 59 S.Ct. 744 (1939); Mid–States Freight Lines, Inc. v. Bates, 304 N.Y. 700, 107 N.E.2d 603 (1952), cert. denied 345 U.S. 908, 73 S.Ct. 648 (1953); Kauper, "State Taxation of Interstate Motor Carriers," 32 Mich.L.Rev. 171 (1933).

In a series of cases decided between 1935 and 1950, the Supreme Court upheld highway user charges of fixed amounts over the objection that they violated the Commerce Clause because they were not proportioned to the vehicle's use of the roads in the State. See, e.g., Aero Mayflower Transit Co. v. Georgia Public Service Commission, 295 U.S. 285, 55 S.Ct. 709 (1935); Aero Mayflower Transit Co. v. Board of Railroad Commissioners, 332 U.S. 495, 68 S.Ct. 167 (1947); Capitol Greyhound Lines v. Brice, 339 U.S. 542, 70 S.Ct. 806 (1950). In 1987, the Supreme Court overruled these cases in holding that flat highway taxes on trucks discriminated against interstate commerce. American Trucking Associations, Inc. v. Scheiner, ___ U.S. ___, 107 S.Ct. 2829 (1987).* The Court observed that many of the earlier cases had turned on the fact that the taxes were exacted in consideration for the "privilege" of using the State's highways, a taxable "local" subject,

---

* The discussion of *American Trucking Associations* is based on J. Hellerstein & W. Hellerstein, "Highlights of Recent Developments," 1987 Cumulative Supplement to J. Hellerstein, State Taxation I, Corporate Income and Franchise Taxes (1983).

rather than the privilege of doing interstate business. In recent years, however, the Court had taken considerable pains to discredit the privilege doctrine and to eliminate it from its Commerce Clause analysis. Consequently, the Court declared that:

> the precedents upholding flat taxes can no longer support the broad proposition * * * that every flat tax for the privilege of using a State's highways must be upheld even if it has a clearly discriminatory effect on commerce by reason of that commerce's interstate character. Although out-of-state carriers obtain a privilege to use Pennsylvania's highways that is nominally equivalent to that which local carriers receive, imposition of the flat taxes for a privilege that is several times more valuable to a local business than to its out-of-state competitors is unquestionably discriminatory and thus offends the Commerce Clause. [107 S.Ct. at 2847.]

The Court did not, however, completely jettison its precedents upholding flat highway taxes. It reaffirmed the principle that the Commerce Clause does not prevent the States from employing flat taxes if they are the only practicable means of collecting revenue from highway users and if more refined methods of taxation would impose genuine administrative burdens. There was no basis for such a disposition of the case at hand. Pennsylvania routinely uses mileage figures to determine motor carriers' fuel taxes and their registration fees (when such fees are figures on an apportioned basis). It likewise apportions its corporate net income tax imposed on interstate carriers on a mileage basis. Hence, administrative necessity did not save Pennsylvania's marker fee and axle tax, given the availability of administrative machinery "capable of taking into account at least the gross variations in cost per unit of highway usage between Pennsylvania-based and out-of-state carriers." 107 S.Ct. at 2847.

The Court also rejected the State's effort to justify flat highway taxes as analogous to user charges that had been upheld in other cases. See Evansville–Vanderburgh Airport Auth. Dist. v. Delta Airlines, Inc., 405 U.S. 707, 92 S.Ct. 1349 (1972), considered infra in this Section. Unlike the airport passenger fee sustained in that case, the Pennsylvania flat highway taxes were found to "discriminate against out-of-State vehicles by subjecting them to a much higher charge per mile traveled in the State." 107 S.Ct. at 2841. They "imposed a cost per mile on appellant's trucks that is approximately five times as heavy as the cost per mile borne by local trucks." Id. And "they do not even purport to approximate fairly the cost or value of the use of Pennsylvania's roads." Id. at 2844. The Court's treatment of the claim that the tax discriminated against interstate commerce under the "internal consistency" doctrine is considered in Section 8, Note F, supra.

In Safeway Trails, Inc. v. Furman, 76 N.J.Super. 90, 183 A.2d 788 (1962), reversed 41 N.J. 467, 197 A.2d 366, appeal dismissed 379 U.S. 14, 85 S.Ct. 144 (1964), the issue arose as to whether New Jersey could impose an excise tax of one-half cent per mile on interstate buses operated over the New Jersey Turnpike and Garden State Parkway, both of which are toll roads, for the use of which the buses separately paid the regular tolls. In upholding the levy, the court held that the mileage tax was intended to compensate the State for providing a complete network of highways throughout the State, and not as a charge for the use of these particular two highways. The saving of time and money, plus the additional convenience resulting from the use of the toll roads, rather than the alternative highways, opined the court, provided the users with benefits equivalent to the tolls charged. The mileage tax, said the court, was for the cost of building and maintaining the general highways in the State. There was no showing that the total taxes paid by taxpayers, plus turnpike tolls, exceeded fair compensation for the use of State highways. This rather far-fetched rationalization indicates that Commerce Clause objections to commercial highway use levies seldom survive the growing heavy costs of maintaining highways; the courts go far to conjure up benefits commensurate with special levies on trucks and buses. See Zettel, "Whither Highway User Charges," 1961 Nat. Tax Ass'n Procs. 675; Boot, "Problems of Transportation Tax Confronting the Interstate Motor Carrier." 1964 Nat. Tax Ass'n Procs. 464; Annot., 17 A.L.R.2d 421.

In 1972,* the Supreme Court upheld airport user taxes in two cases that may fairly be regarded as overruling the century-old decision in Crandall v. Nevada, 73 U.S. (6 Wall.) 35 (1867).[34] In *Crandall,* the Court had held that Nevada's one-dollar tax on every person leaving the State by railroad, stagecoach, or other vehicle employed in the business of transporting passengers for hire violated the Constitution because it "may totally prevent or seriously burden all transportation of passengers from one part of the country to the other." Id. at 46. Coincidentally, the tax rates imposed in the two airport levies challenged in the recent cases were likewise one dollar per passenger emplaning at the Indiana airports on a commercial plane, and 50 cents to one dollar per passenger in the New Hampshire case (depending on the gross weight of the plane), although the tax burden in the *Crandall* case was, of course, much heavier in view of 100 years of inflation of the dollar. Relying on a line of cases upholding taxes drawn as levies compensating the State for the use of interstate and intrastate transportation facilities, which the Court found reasonable in amount and fixed according to uniform, fair, and practical standards, the Court upheld both airport taxes as reasonable amounts charged to defray the

---

* This paragraph is taken from J. Hellerstein, "State Taxation Under the Commerce Clause: An Historical Perspective," 29 Vand.L.Rev. 335 (1976), and is reprinted with the consent of the Vanderbilt Law Review, the copyright owner.

34. See Evansville–Vanderburgh Airport Auth. Dist. v. Delta Airlines, Inc., 255 Ind. 436, 265 N.E.2d 27 (1970) (charge constitutes unreasonable burden on interstate commerce); Northeast Airlines, Inc. v. New Hampshire Aeronautics Comm'n, 111 N.H. 5, 273 A.2d 676 (1971) (charge constitutional). On a consolidated appeal, the Supreme Court reversed the Indiana decision and affirmed the New Hampshire decision. Evansville–Vanderburgh Airport Auth. Dist. v. Delta Airlines, Inc., 405 U.S. 707, 92 S.Ct. 1349 (1972).

costs of building or maintaining the airport facilities used by the passenger. Evansville–Vanderburgh Airport Auth. Dist. v. Delta Airlines, Inc., 405 U.S. 707, 92 S.Ct. 1349 (1972). Hence, one may regard the interment of *Crandall v. Nevada* as foreshadowed by decades of cases upholding highway and other tolls for the use of the State's transportation facilities in interstate traffic. In any event, this victory for the States in airport taxation was shortlived. In 1973, the year after the decisions came down, Congress, acting under its Commerce Clause powers, prohibited such levies. 49 U.S.C. § 1513(a).

SECTION 11. TAXATION OF INTOXICATING LIQUORS

It was settled early that the States may prohibit and regulate sales of liquor brought within their territorial limits, as a proper exercise of their police power. The License Cases, 46 U.S. (5 How.) 504 (1847); Bartemeyer v. Iowa, 85 U.S. (18 Wall.) 129 (1873); Beer Co. v. Mass., 97 U.S. 25 (1877). However, a State fee as a condition to the transportation of liquor into the State was held to be an invalid regulation of interstate commerce. Bowman v. Chicago, etc., Ry. Co., 125 U.S. 465, 8 S.Ct. 689 (1888). Subsequently, Leisy v. Hardin, 135 U.S. 100, 10 S.Ct. 681 (1890), held that the Commerce Clause prevented a State from regulating the sale of liquor still in the original package. The Wilson Act, 25 Stat. 313 (1890), sought to alleviate this situation by eliminating the Interstate Commerce Clause barrier to the State's police power over goods in the original package. See Wilkerson v. Rahrer, 140 U.S. 545, 11 S.Ct. 865 (1891). A divided Court, however, in Rhodes v. Iowa, 170 U.S. 412, 18 S.Ct. 664 (1898), decided that the State's authority did not extend to the liquors until delivered to the consignee. Fifteen years later Congress passed the Webb–Kenyon Act, 37 Stat. 699 (1913), 49 Stat. 877, which prohibits transportation of liquor into any State in violation of its laws. This Act is still in force. See McCormick & Co. v. Brown, 286 U.S. 131, 52 S.Ct. 522 (1932).

Over the past half-century, the States' power to tax intoxicating liquor has been shaped in important part by the Court's interpretation of the Twenty-first Amendment to the Constitution, which brought an end to prohibition. The amendment provides that "[t]he transportation or importation into any State, Territory, or possession of the United States for delivery or use therein of intoxicating liquors, in violation of the laws thereof, is hereby prohibited." The Court adopted the view during the early years following adoption of the amendment that "by virtue of [the Twenty-first Amendment's] provisions a State is totally unconfined by traditional Commerce Clause limitations when it restricts the importation of intoxicants destined for use, distribution, or consumption within its borders." Hostetter v. Idlewild Bon Voyage Liquor Corp., 377 U.S. 324, 330, 84 S.Ct. 1293 (1964); see also State Board of Equalization v. Young's Market Co., 299 U.S. 59, 57 S.Ct. 77 (1936) (sustaining license fee on the privilege of importing beer into California). In Bacchus Imports, Ltd. v. Dias, 468 U.S. 263, 104 S.Ct. 3049 (1984), however, the Court enunciated a more limited view of the

Twenty-first Amendment's impact on the Commerce Clause. (See Section 8, Note G supra for a discussion of the Commerce Clause aspects of the case.) In rejecting the State's contention that a tax discriminating against out-of-state liquor was insulated from Commerce Clause attack by the Twenty-first Amendment, the Court referred to the obscurity of the legislative history underlying the pertinent language of the amendment. The Hawaii exemption for local wine was held vulnerable to Commerce Clause objections despite the amendment:

> Doubts about the scope of the Amendment's authorization notwithstanding, one thing is certain: The central purpose of the provision was not to empower States to favor local industries by erecting barriers to competition. It is also beyond doubt that the Commerce Clause itself furthers strong federal interests in preventing economic Balkanization. * * * [T]he State does not seek to justify its tax on the ground that it was designed to promote temperance or to carry out any other purpose of the Twenty-first Amendment, but instead acknowledges that the purpose was to "promote a local industry." * * * Consequently, because the tax violates a central tenet of the Commerce Clause but is not supported by any clear concern of the Twenty-first Amendment, we reject the State's belated claim based on the Amendment. [468 U.S. at 276.]

SECTION 12. TAXATION OF FOREIGN COMMERCE

JAPAN LINE, LIMITED v. COUNTY OF LOS ANGELES

Supreme Court of the United States, 1979.
441 U.S. 434, 99 S.Ct. 1813.

MR. JUSTICE BLACKMUN delivered the opinion of the Court.*

This case presents the question whether a State, consistently with the Commerce Clause of the Constitution, may impose a nondiscriminatory ad valorem property tax on foreign-owned instrumentalities (cargo containers) of international commerce.

I

The facts were "stipulated on appeal," App. 29, and were found by the trial court, id., at 33–36, as follows:

Appellants are six Japanese shipping companies; they are incorporated under the laws of Japan, and they have their principal places of business and commercial domiciles in that country. Id., at 34. Appellants operate vessels used exclusively in foreign commerce; these vessels are registered in Japan and have their home ports there. Ibid. The vessels are specifically designed and constructed to accommodate large cargo shipping containers. The containers, like the ships, are owned by appellants, have their home ports in Japan, and are used exclusively for hire in the transportation of cargo in foreign commerce. Id., at 35. Each container is in constant transit save for time spent

---

* Some footnotes have been omitted.

undergoing repair or awaiting loading and unloading of cargo. All appellants' containers are subject to property tax in Japan and, in fact, are taxed there.

Appellees are political subdivisions of the State of California. Appellants' containers, in the course of their international journeys, pass through appellees' jurisdictions intermittently. Although none of appellants' containers stays permanently in California, some are there at any given time; a container's average stay in the State is less than three weeks. Ibid. The containers engage in no intrastate or interstate transportation of cargo except as continuations of international voyages. Id., at 30. Any movements or periods of nonmovement of containers in appellees' jurisdictions are essential to, and inseparable from, the containers' efficient use as instrumentalities of foreign commerce. Id., at 35–36.

Property present in California on March 1 (the "lien date" under California law) of any year is subject to ad valorem property tax. Cal. Rev. & Tax.Code Ann. §§ 117, 405, 2192 (West 1970 & Supp.1978). A number of appellants' containers were physically present in appellees' jurisdictions on the lien dates in 1970, 1971, and 1972; this number was fairly representative of the containers' "average presence" during each year. App. 35. Appellees levied property taxes in excess of $550,000 on the assessed value of the containers present on March 1 of the three years in question. Id., at 36. During the same period, similar containers owned or controlled by steamship companies domiciled in the United States, that appeared from time to time in Japan during the course of international commerce, were not subject to property taxation in Japan, and therefore were not, in fact, taxed in that country. Id., at 35.

Appellants paid the taxes, so levied, under protest and sued for their refund in the Superior Court for the County of Los Angeles. * * *

[The California Supreme Court rejected the "home port" doctrine, under which the vessels had been held taxable by the trial court only in Japan, and sustained the Los Angeles tax. 20 Cal.3d 180, 141 Cal.Rptr. 905, 571 P.2d 254 (1977).]

The California Supreme Court concluded that "the threat of double taxation from foreign taxing authorities has no role in commerce clause considerations of multiple burdens, since burdens in international commerce are not attributable to discrimination by the taxing state and are matters for international agreement." Id., at 185, 141 Cal. Rptr., at 908, 571 P.2d, at 257. Deeming the containers' foreign ownership and use irrelevant for purposes of constitutional analysis, id., at 186, 141 Cal.Rptr., at 908, 571 P.2d, at 257–258, the court rejected appellants' Commerce Clause challenge and sustained the validity of the tax as applied. [99 S.Ct., at 1816.]

[The U.S. Supreme Court first disposed of a jurisdictional objection and then considered the challenge to the tax under the home port doctrine. It reviewed the cases and concluded that the home port doctrine "has fallen into desuetude, and * * * has yielded to a rule" that "various instrumentalities of commerce may be taxed, on a properly apportioned basis, by the nondomiciliary States through which they travel." Id. 441 U.S. 442. Nevertheless, it was recognized that "In discarding the 'home port' theory for the theory of apportionment * * * the Court consistently has distinguished the case of ocean-going vessels." (Ibid.,), but it found even that exception "anachronistic", and stated that "it may indeed be said to have been 'abandoned'. Northwest Airlines v. Minnesota, 322 U.S. 292, 320 (1944) (Stone, C.J. dissenting)." Id. at 443. The court, accordingly, declined to rest its decision on the home port doctrine,[7] and turned to the general Commerce Clause issues presented.].

B

The Constitution provides that "Congress shall have Power * * * To regulate Commerce with foreign Nations, and among the several States, and with the Indian Tribes." Art. I, § 8, cl. 3. In construing Congress' power to "regulate Commerce * * * among the several States," the Court recently has affirmed that the Constitution confers no immunity from state taxation, and that "interstate commerce must bear its fair share of the state tax burden." Washington Revenue Dept. v. Association of Wash. Stevedoring Cos., 435 U.S. 734, 750, 98 S.Ct. 1388, 1399, 55 L.Ed.2d 682 (1978). Instrumentalities of interstate commerce are no exception to this rule, and the Court regularly has sustained property taxes as applied to various forms of transportation equipment. See *Pullman's Palace,* supra (railroad rolling stock); *Ott,* supra (barges on inland waterways); *Braniff,* supra (domestic aircraft). Cf. Central Greyhound Lines v. Mealey, 334 U.S. 653, 663, 68 S.Ct. 1260, 1266, 92 L.Ed. 1633 (1948) (motor vehicles). If the state tax "is applied to an activity with a substantial nexus with the taxing State, is fairly apportioned, does not discriminate against interstate commerce, and is fairly related to the services provided by the State," no impermissible burden on interstate commerce will be found. Complete Auto Transit, Inc. v. Brady, 430 U.S. 274, 279, 97 S.Ct. 1076, 1079, 51 L.Ed.2d 326 (1977); Washington Revenue Dept., 435 U.S., at 750, 98 S.Ct. at 1399.

Appellees contend that cargo shipping containers, like other vehicles of commercial transport, are subject to property taxation, and that the taxes imposed here meet *Complete Auto's* four-fold requirements. The containers, they argue, have a "substantial nexus" with California because some of them are present in that State at all times; jurisdic-

---

7. Accordingly, we do not reach questions as to the taxability of foreign-owned instrumentalities engaged in interstate commerce, or of domestically-owned instrumentalities engaged in foreign commerce. Cf. Sea–Land Service, Inc. v. County of Alameda, 12 Cal.3d 772, 117 Cal.Rptr. 448, 528 P.2d 56 (1974) (domestically-owned containers used in intercoastal and foreign commerce held subject to apportioned property tax); Flying Tiger Line, Inc. v. County of Los Angeles, 51 Cal.2d 314, 333 P. 323 (1958) (domestically-owned aircraft used in foreign commerce held subject to apportioned property tax).

tion to tax is based on "the habitual employment of the property within the State," *Braniff,* 347 U.S., at 601, 74 S.Ct. at 764, and appellants' containers habitually are so employed. The tax, moreover, is "fairly apportioned," since it is levied only on the containers' "average presence" in California.[8] The tax "does not discriminate," thirdly, since it falls evenhandedly on all personal property in the State; indeed, as an ad valorem tax of general application, it is of necessity nondiscriminatory. The tax, finally, is "fairly related to the services provided by" California, services that include not only police and fire protection, but the benefits of a trained work force and the advantages of a civilized society.

These observations are not without force. We may assume that, if the containers at issue here were instrumentalities of purely interstate commerce, *Complete Auto* would apply and be satisfied, and our Commerce Clause inquiry would be at an end. Appellants' containers, however, are instrumentalities of foreign commerce, both as a matter of fact and as a matter of law.[10] The premise of appellees' argument is that the Commerce Clause analysis is identical, regardless of whether interstate or foreign commerce is involved. This premise, we have concluded, must be rejected. When construing Congress' power to "regulate Commerce with foreign Nations," a more extensive constitutional inquiry is required.

When a State seeks to tax the instrumentalities of foreign commerce, two additional considerations, beyond those articulated in *Complete Auto,* come into play. The first is the enhanced risk of multiple taxation. It is a commonplace of constitutional jurisprudence that multiple taxation may well be offensive to the Commerce Clause. * * * In order to prevent multiple taxation of interstate commerce, this Court has required that taxes be apportioned among taxing jurisdictions, so that no instrumentality of commerce is subjected to more

8. By taxing property present on the "lien date," California roughly apportions its property tax for mobile goods like containers. For example, if each of appellants' containers is in California for three weeks a year, the number present on any arbitrarily selected date would be roughly $\frac{3}{52}$ of the total entering the State that year. Taxing $\frac{3}{52}$ of the containers at full value, however, is the same as taxing all the containers at $\frac{3}{52}$ value. Thus, California effectively apportions its tax to reflect the containers' "average presence," i.e., the time each container spends in the State per year.

10. Appellants' containers entered the United States pursuant to the Customs Convention on Containers, * * * which grants containers "temporary admission free of import duties and import taxes and free of import prohibitions and restrictions," provided they are used solely in foreign commerce and are subject to re-exportation. 20 U.S.T., at 304. Similarly, 19 CFR § 10.41a(a)(3) (1978) designates containers "instruments of international traffic," with the result that they "may be released without entry or the payment of duty" under 19 U.S.C. § 1322(a). See 19 CFR § 10.41a(a)(1) (1978). A bilateral tax Convention between Japan and the United States associates containers with the vehicles that carry them, and provides that income "derived by a resident of a Contracting State * * * from the use, maintenance, and lease of containers and related equipment * * * in connection with the operation in international traffic of ships or aircraft * * * is exempt from tax in the other Contracting State." Convention Between the United States of America and Japan for the Avoidance of Double Taxation, Mar. 8, 1971, [1972] 23 U.S.T. 967, 1084–1085, T.I.A.S. No. 7365.

than one tax on its full value. The corollary of the apportionment principle, of course, is that no jurisdiction may tax the instrumentality in full. "The rule which permits taxation by two or more states on an apportionment basis precludes taxation of all of the property by the state of the domicile. * * * Otherwise there would be multiple taxation of interstate operations." Standard Oil Co. v. Peck, 342 U.S., at 384–385, 72 S.Ct. at 310; *Braniff*, 347 U.S., at 601, 74 S.Ct. at 764. The basis for this Court's approval of apportioned property taxation, in other words, has been its ability to enforce full apportionment by all potential taxing bodies.

Yet neither this Court nor this Nation can ensure full apportionment when one of the taxing entities is a foreign sovereign. If an instrumentality of commerce is domiciled abroad, the country of domicile may have the right, consistently with the custom of nations, to impose a tax on its full value.[11] If a State should seek to tax the same instrumentality on an apportioned basis, multiple taxation inevitably results. Hence, whereas the fact of apportionment in interstate commerce means that "multiple burdens logically cannot occur," *Washington Revenue Dept.*, 435 U.S., at 746–747, 98 S.Ct. at 1397–98, the same conclusion, as to foreign commerce, logically cannot be drawn. Due to the absence of an authoritative tribunal capable of ensuring that the aggregation of taxes is computed on no more than one full value, a state tax, even though "fairly apportioned" to reflect an instrumentality's presence within the State, may subject foreign commerce " 'to the risk of a double tax burden to which [domestic] commerce is not exposed, and which the commerce clause forbids.' " Evco v. Jones, 409 U.S., at 94, 93 S.Ct. at 351, quoting *J.D. Adams Mfg. Co.*, 304 U.S., at 311, 58 S.Ct. at 915.

Second, a state tax on the instrumentalities of foreign commerce may impair federal uniformity in an area where federal uniformity is essential. Foreign commerce is pre-eminently a matter of national concern. "In international relations and with respect to foreign intercourse and trade the people of the United States act through a single government with unified and adequate national power." Board of Trustees v. United States, 289 U.S. 48, 59, 53 S.Ct. 509, 510, 77 L.Ed. 1025 (1933). Although the Constitution, Art. I, § 8, cl. 3, grants Congress power to regulate commerce "with foreign Nations" and "among the several States" in parallel phrases, there is evidence that the Founders intended the scope of the foreign commerce power to be the greater. Cases of this Court, stressing the need for uniformity in treating with other nations, echo this distinction. In approving state

11. Ocean-going vessels, for example, are generally taxed only in their nation of registry; this fact in part explains the phenomenon of "flags of convenience" (a term deemed derogatory in some quarters), whereby vessels are registered under the flags of countries that permit the operation of ships "at a nominal level of taxation." See B. Boczek, Flags of Convenience 5, 56–57 (1962). Aircraft engaged in international traffic, apparently, are likewise "subject to taxation on an unapportioned basis by their country of origin." Note, 11 Stan.L. Rev., at 519, and n. 11. See, e.g., *SAS*, 56 Cal.3d, at 17, and n. 3, 14 Cal.Rptr., at 28, 363 P.2d, at 28, and n. 3.

taxes on the instrumentalities of interstate commerce, the Court consistently has distinguished ocean-going traffic * * * these cases reflect an awareness that the taxation of foreign commerce may necessitate a uniform national rule. Indeed, in *Pullman's Palace,* supra, the Court wrote that the " 'vehicles of commerce by water being instruments of intercommunication with other nations, the regulation of them is assumed by the national legislature.' " 141 U.S., at 24, 11 S.Ct. at 878, quoting Railroad Co. v. Maryland, 21 Wall. 456, 470, 22 L.Ed. 678 (1874). Finally, in discussing the Import–Export Clause, this Court, in Michelin Tire Corp. v. Wages, 423 U.S. 276, 285, 96 S.Ct. 535, 540, 46 L.Ed.2d 495 (1976), spoke of the Framers' overriding concern that "the Federal Government must speak with one voice when regulating commercial relations with foreign governments." The need for federal uniformity is no less paramount in ascertaining the negative implications of Congress' power to "regulate Commerce with foreign Nations" under the Commerce Clause.

A state tax on instrumentalities of foreign commerce may frustrate the achievement of federal uniformity in several ways. If the State imposes an apportioned tax, international disputes over reconciling apportionment formulae may arise. If a novel state tax creates an asymmetry in the international tax structure, foreign nations disadvantaged by the levy may retaliate against American-owned instrumentalities present in their jurisdictions. Such retaliation of necessity would be directed at American transportation equipment in general, not just that of the taxing State, so that the Nation as a whole would suffer. If other States followed the taxing State's example, various instrumentalities of commerce could be subjected to varying degrees of multiple taxation, a result that would plainly prevent this Nation from "speaking with one voice" in regulating foreign commerce.

For these reasons, we believe that an inquiry more elaborate than that mandated by *Complete Auto* is necessary when a State seeks to tax the instrumentalities of foreign, rather than of interstate, commerce. In addition to answering the nexus, apportionment, and non-discrimination questions posed in *Complete Auto,* a court must also inquire, first, whether the tax, notwithstanding apportionment, creates a substantial risk of international multiple taxation, and, second, whether the tax prevents the Federal Government from "speaking with one voice when regulating commercial relations with foreign governments." If a state tax contravenes either of these precepts, it is unconstitutional under the Commerce Clause.

C

Analysis of California's tax under these principles dictates that the tax, as applied to appellants' containers is impermissible. Assuming, *arguendo,* that the tax passes muster under *Complete Auto,* it cannot withstand scrutiny under either of the additional tests that a tax on foreign commerce must satisfy.

First, California's tax results in multiple taxation of the instrumentalities of foreign commerce. By stipulation, appellants' containers are owned, based, and registered in Japan; they are used exclusively in international commerce; and they remain outside Japan only so long as needed to complete their international missions. Under these circumstances, Japan has the right and the power to tax the containers in full. California's tax, however, creates more than the *risk* of multiple taxation; it produces multiple taxation in fact. Appellants' containers not only "are subject to property tax * * * in Japan," App. 32, but, as the trial court found, they "are, in fact, taxed in Japan." Id., at 35. Thus, if appellees' levies were sustained, appellants "would be paying a double tax." Id., at 23.[17]

Second, California's tax prevents this Nation from "speaking with one voice" in regulating foreign trade. The desirability of uniform treatment of containers used exclusively in foreign commerce is evidenced by the Customs Convention on Containers, which the United States and Japan have signed. See n. 10, supra. Under this Convention, containers temporarily imported are admitted free of "all duties and taxes whatsoever chargeable by reason of importation," 20 U.S.T., at 304. The Convention reflects a national policy to remove impediments to the use of containers as "instruments of international traffic." 19 U.S.C. § 1322(a). California's tax, however, will frustrate attainment of federal uniformity. It is stipulated that American-owned containers are not taxed in Japan. App. 35. California's tax thus creates an asymmetry in international maritime taxation operating to Japan's disadvantage. The risk of retaliation by Japan, under these circumstances, is acute, and such retaliation of necessity would be felt by the Nation as a whole.[18] If other States follow California's example

17. The stipulation of facts, App. 32, like the trial court's finding, id., at 35, states that "[a]ll containers of [appellants] are subject to property tax and are, in fact, taxed in Japan." The record does not further elaborate on the nature of Japan's property tax. Appellants have uniformly insisted, Brief 9, Tr. of Oral Arg. 3, that Japan's property tax is unapportioned, i.e., that it is imposed on the containers' full value, and we so understand the trial court's finding. Although appellees do not seriously challenge this understanding, Brief 10–11, and n. 2, *amicus curiae* Multistate Tax Commission suggests that the record is inadequate to establish double taxation in fact: Japan, *amicus* says, may offer "credits * * * for taxes paid elsewhere." Brief 8. *Amicus* provides no evidence to support this theory. Both the Solicitor General, Brief for United States as *Amicus Curiae* 19 n. 9, and the Department of State, id., at 17a, assure us that Japan taxes appellants' containers at their "full value," and we accept this interpretation of the trial court's factual finding.

Because California's tax in this case creates multiple taxation in fact, we have no occasion here to decide under what circumstances the mere *risk* of multiple taxation would invalidate a state tax, or whether this risk would be evaluated differently in foreign, as opposed to interstate, commerce. Compare *Moorman Mfg. Co. v. Bair*, 437 U.S. 267, 276–277, 98 S.Ct. 2340, 2346, 57 L.Ed.2d 197 (1978), and *Washington Revenue Dept.*, 435 U.S., at 746, 98 S.Ct. at 1397, with e.g., *Central R. Co.*, 370 U.S., at 615, 82 S.Ct. at 1303; *Ott*, 336 U.S., at 175, 69 S.Ct., at 435; and *Northwest Airlines*, 322 U.S., at 326, 64 S.Ct. at 967 (Stone, C.J., dissenting).

18. Retaliation by some nations could be automatic. West Germany's wealth tax statute, for example, provides an exemption for foreign-owned instrumentalities of commerce, but only if the owner's country grants a reciprocal exemption for German-owned instrumentalities. Vermögensteuergesetz (VStG) § 2, ¶ 3, reprinted in I Bundesgesetzblatt (BGB1) 949 (Apr. 23,

(Oregon already has done so), foreign-owned containers will be subjected to various degrees of multiple taxation, depending on which American ports they enter. This result, obviously, would make "speaking with one voice" impossible. California, by its unilateral act, cannot be permitted to place these impediments before this Nation's conduct of its foreign relations and its foreign trade.

Because California's ad valorem tax, as applied to appellants' containers, results in multiple taxation of the instrumentalities of foreign commerce, and because it prevents the Federal Government from "speaking with one voice" in international trade, the tax is inconsistent with Congress' power to "regulate Commerce with foreign Nations." We hold the tax, as applied, unconstitutional under the Commerce Clause.

D

Appellees proffer several objections to this holding. They contend, first, that any multiple taxation in this case is attributable, not to California, but to Japan. California, they say, is just trying to take its share; it should not be foreclosed by Japan's election to tax the containers in full. California's tax, however, must be evaluated in the realistic framework of the custom of nations. Japan has the right and the power to tax appellants' containers at their full value; nothing could prevent it from doing so. Appellees' argument may have force in the interstate commerce context. Cf. Moorman Mfg. Co. v. Bair, 437 U.S. 267, 277, and n. 12, 98 S.Ct. 2340, 2346, 57 L.Ed.2d 197 (1978). In interstate commerce, if the domiciliary State is "to blame" for exacting an excessive tax, this Court is able to insist upon rationalization of the apportionment. As noted above, however, this Court is powerless to correct malapportionment of taxes imposed from abroad in foreign commerce.

Appellees contend, secondly, that any multiple taxation created by California's tax can be cured by congressional action or by international agreement. We find no merit in this contention. The premise of appellees' argument is that a State is free to impose demonstrable burdens on commerce, so long as Congress has not preempted the field by affirmative regulation. But it long has been "accepted constitutional doctrine that the commerce clause, without the aid of Congressional legislation * * * affords some protection from state legislation inimical to the national commerce, and that in such cases, where Congress has not acted, this Court, and not the state legislature, is under the commerce clause the final arbiter of the competing demands of state and national interests." Southern Pacific Co. v. Arizona, 325 U.S. 761, 769, 65 S.Ct. 1515, 1520, 89 L.Ed. 1915 (1945). Accord, Hughes v. Oklahoma, 441 U.S. 322, 326, and n. 2, 99 S.Ct. 1727, 1731, 60 L.Ed.2d

1974). The European Economic Community (EEC), when apprised of California's tax on foreign-owned containers, apparently determined to consider "suitable counter- measures." Press Release, 521st Council Meeting—Transport (Luxembourg, June 12, 1978), p. 21.

250 (1979); Boston Stock Exchange v. State Tax Comm'n, 429 U.S. 318, 328, 97 S.Ct. 599, 606, 50 L.Ed.2d 514 (1977). Appellees' argument, moreover, defeats, rather than supports, the cause it aims to promote. For to say that California has created a problem susceptible only of congressional—indeed, only of international—solution is to concede that the taxation of foreign-owned containers is an area where a uniform federal rule is essential. California may not tell this Nation or Japan how to run their foreign policies.

Third, appellees argue that, even if California's tax results in multiple taxation, that fact, after *Moorman* is insufficient to condemn a state tax under the Commerce Clause. In *Moorman,* the Court refused to invalidate Iowa's single-factor income tax apportionment formula, even though it posed a credible threat of overlapping taxation because of the use of three-factor formulae by other States. See also the several opinions in *Moorman* in dissent. 437 U.S., at 281, 282, and 283, 98 S.Ct. at 2348–2349. That case, however, is quite different from this one. In *Moorman,* the existence of multiple taxation, on the record then before the Court, was "speculative," id., at 276, 98 S.Ct. at 2346; on the record of the present case, multiple taxation is a fact. In *Moorman,* the problem arose, not from lack of apportionment, but from mathematical imprecision in apportionment formulae. Yet, this Court consistently had held that the Commerce Clause "does not call for mathematical exactness nor for the rigid application of a particular formula; only if the resulting valuation is palpably excessive will it be set aside." Northwest Airlines v. Minnesota, 322 U.S., at 325, 64 S.Ct. at 967 (Stone, C.J., dissenting). Accord, *Moorman,* 437 U.S., at 274, 98 S.Ct. at 2345 (citing cases). See Hellerstein, State Taxation Under the Commerce Clause: An Historical Perspective, 29 Vand.L.Rev. 335, 347 (1976). This case, by contrast, involves no mere mathematical imprecision in apportionment; it involves a situation where true apportionment does not exist and cannot be policed by this Court at all. *Moorman,* finally, concerned interstate commerce. This case concerns foreign commerce. Even a slight overlapping of tax—a problem that might be deemed *de minimis* in a domestic context—assumes importance when sensitive matters of foreign relations and national sovereignty are concerned.

Finally, appellees present policy arguments. If California cannot tax appellants' containers, they complain, the State will lose revenue, even though the containers plainly have a nexus with California; the State will go uncompensated for the services it undeniably renders the containers; and, by exempting appellants' containers from tax, the State in effect will be forced to discriminate against domestic, in favor of foreign, commerce. These arguments are not without weight, and, to the extent appellees cannot recoup the value of their services through user fees, they may indeed be disadvantaged by our decision today. These arguments, however, are directed to the wrong forum. "Whatever subjects of this [the commercial] power are in their nature national, or admit only of one uniform system, or plan of regulation, may justly be said to be of such a nature as to require exclusive legislation by Congress." Cooley v. Board of Wardens, 12 How. 299, 319, 53 U.S. 299, 13 L.Ed. 996 (1851). The problems to which appellees refer are problems that admit only of a federal remedy. They do not admit of a unilateral solution by a State.

The judgment of the Supreme Court of California is reversed.

It is so ordered.

Substantially for the reasons set forth by Justice Manuel in his opinion for the unanimous Supreme Court of California, MR. JUSTICE REHNQUIST is of the opinion that the judgment of that court should be affirmed.*

Notes and Problems

A. *"The Multiple Taxation Doctrine Applied to Foreign Commerce.*** It was the additional 'considerations' referred to by the Court, that foreign commerce must be safeguarded against risks of multiple State taxation to an extent not required with respect to interstate commerce, that may give the *Japan Line* case seminal importance as enunciating a new constitutional doctrine. Although there had been a few scattered dicta before *Japan Line* suggesting that foreign commerce was entitled to greater constitutional protection from State action than interstate commerce, no prior decision of the Supreme Court had so held. The essential difference between State taxation of foreign and interstate commerce was stated in *Japan Line* at p. 313 supra.

"The dicta in the earlier cases were the following:

It may be argued, however, that, aside from such regulations as these, which are purely local, the inference to be drawn from the absence of legislation by Congress on the subject excludes state legislation affecting commerce with foreign nations more strongly than that affecting commerce among the States.

Bowman v. Chicago & Nw. Ry., 125 U.S. 465, 482, 8 S.Ct. 689 (1888).

'[D]ecisions of this court dealing with the subject of the power of Congress to regulate interstate commerce' do not govern questions arising under the Foreign Commerce Clause, because of 'the broad distinction which exists between the two powers.'

Chief Justice White, in Brolan v. United States, 236 U.S. 216, 222, 35 S.Ct. 285 (1915).

* For extensive critical reviews of the home port doctrine published prior to the Supreme Court's decision in Japan Lines, see Clark, "Property Taxation of Foreign Goods and Enterprises—A Study in Inconsistency," 4 Pepperdine L.Rev. 39 (1976); Note, "Limitations on State Taxation of Foreign Commerce: The Contemporary Vitality of the Home–Port Doctrine," 127 U. of Pa.L.Rev. 817 (1979). For analyses and comments on the Japan Line case, see W. Hellerstein "State's Power to Tax Foreign Commerce Dominates Supreme Court's 1978 Agenda", 51 J.Tax. 106 (1979); P. Hartman, Federal Limitations on State and Local Taxation § 2.17 (1981).

** This note is taken from J. Hellerstein, State Taxation I, Corporate Income and Franchise Taxes ¶ 4.14[2] (1983), which comments generally on the *Japan Line* case. Used with the consent of the copyright owner and publisher.

"A three-judge District Court had stated that 'when foreign commerce is involved the national interest is even more clearly paramount' than when State action affecting interstate commerce is involved. Epstein v. Lordi, 261 F.Supp. 921, 931 (D.N.J.1966), aff'd, 389 U.S. 29 (1967).

"See also the 1976 opinion in Michelin Tire Corp. v. Wages, p. 335 infra which dealt with State taxation under the Imports Clause." J. Hellerstein, State Taxation I, Corporate Income and Franchise Taxes ¶ 4.14[2], pp. 168–69 (1983).

B. What are the implications of *Japan Line* for other taxes affecting foreign commerce? In the context of State taxation of income from foreign commerce, the Court has limited the force of *Japan Line*. See Container Corp. of America v. Franchise Tax Bd., 463 U.S. 159, 103 S.Ct. 2933 (1983), p. 578 infra, in which the Court upheld worldwide combined apportionment of corporate income despite evidence of multiple taxation; see also Mobil Oil Corp. v. Commissioner of Taxes, 445 U.S. 425, 100 S.Ct. 1223 (1980), p. 610 infra, in which the Court upheld State taxation of foreign source dividends. [In the *Container* case, the Court distinguished *Japan Line* on the grounds, inter alia, that it involved a property tax, instrumentalities of foreign commerce, and actual—not merely possible—multiple taxation that it found could be remedied only by an allocation approach.] In both *Container* and *Mobil Oil,* the taxpayers also challenged the assessments as frustrating Federal income tax policy, but the Court found no such conflict. In other cases that potentially raised the question whether the State tax at issue was barred by the negative implications of the Foreign Commerce Clause, the Court either found that Congress had consented to the tax at issue, see Wardair Canada, Inc. v. Department of Revenue, 477 U.S. 1, 106 S.Ct. 2369 (1986), or that Congress had preempted it. See Xerox Corp. v. County of Harris, 459 U.S. 145, 103 S.Ct. 523 (1982).

C. *Preferential Treatment of Foreign Vis a Vis Interstate Commerce.* Do the States discriminate against interstate commerce in violation of the Commerce Clause by providing preferential treatment to foreign as compared to interstate commerce? The California Court of Appeal held that the grant of a property tax exemption for goods imported from abroad but not for goods shipped from other States violated the Commerce Clause because it gave goods of foreign origin a competitive advantage over goods manufactured in other States. Sears Roebuck & Co. v. County of Los Angeles and Zee Toys, Inc. v. County of Los Angeles (consolidated cases), 85 Cal.App.3d 763, 149 Cal.Rptr. 750 (2d Dist.1978). The court declared that the levy violated the Commerce Clause because "state taxes which discriminate between classes of interstate and foreign goods on the basis of their origin are not permitted." 85 Cal.App.3d at 774. On appeal to the U.S. Supreme Court, where the Solicitor General of the United States filed a brief amicus supporting the constitutionality of the exemption, the California court's decision was affirmed without opinion by an equally divided Court. Sears, Roebuck & Co. v. County of Los Angeles, 449 U.S. 1119, 101 S.Ct. 933 (1981). The California Supreme Court has subsequently reaffirmed the view that the exemption for foreign but not for interstate imports is unconstitutional. Star–Kist Foods, Inc. v. County of Los Angeles, 42 Cal.3d 1, 227 Cal.Rptr. 391, 719 P.2d 987 (1986), cert. denied ____ U.S. ____, 107 S.Ct. 1565 (1987).

C. THE ROLE OF CONGRESS IN DEALING WITH STATE TAXATION OF INTERSTATE AND FOREIGN COMMERCE

In 1959 Congress for the first time in our history enacted legislation restricting the powers of the States to tax interstate businesses. For more than one hundred years the great Commerce Clause controversies had been fought out largely in the courts, with little aid from Congress. Although Congress possessed the constitutional power and legislative resources adequate to cope with the major conflicts, it failed to take the required action. The role which Congress neglected to perform was assumed by the Supreme Court, employing as its principal instruments the Commerce Clause and the Due Process Clause.

The Inadequacy of the Judicial Solutions of the Interstate Commerce Tax Problem. Because the Court has only the restricted function of invalidating State action by fixing the "outside limits of decency" (Powell, "Indirect Encroachment on Federal Authority by the Taxing Powers of the States," 32 Harv.L.Rev. 634, 670 [1919]), it is argued that the Court is incapable of reconciling the competing interests involved in a satisfactory manner. More refined and flexible methods are required. Thus, in McCarroll v. Dixie Greyhound Lines, Inc., 309 U.S. 176, 60 S.Ct. 504 (1939), Justices Black, Frankfurter, and Douglas wrote a dissenting opinion in which they said:

> Judicial control of national commerce—unlike legislative regulations—must from inherent limitations of the judicial process treat the subject by the hit-and-miss method of deciding single local controversies upon evidence and information limited by the narrow rules of litigation. Spasmodic and unrelated instances of litigation cannot afford an adequate basis for the creation of integrated national rules which alone can afford that full protection for interstate commerce intended by the Constitution. We would, therefore, leave the questions raised by the Arkansas tax for consideration of Congress in a nationwide survey of the constantly increasing barriers to trade among the States. Unconfined by "the narrow scope of judicial proceedings" Congress alone can, in the exercise of its plenary constitutional control over interstate commerce, not only consider whether such a tax as now under scrutiny is consistent with the best interests of our national economy, but can also on the basis of full exploration of the many aspects of a complicated problem devise a national policy fair alike to the States and our Union. [309 U.S. at 188, 189.]

In the *Stockham Valves* and *Northwestern Portland Cement* cases, Mr. Justice Frankfurter, dissenting, said:

> Congress alone can provide for a full and thorough canvassing of the multitudinous and intricate factors which compose the problem of

the taxing freedom of the States and the needed limits on such state taxing power. [358 U.S. at 476.]

The Court expressed similar sentiments in Commonwealth Edison Co. v. Montana, 453 U.S. 609, 101 S.Ct. 2946 (1981), p. 296 supra, and in Moorman Manufacturing Co. v. Bair, 437 U.S. 267, 98 S.Ct. 2340 (1978), p. 452 infra.

For other comments as to the inadequacy of a judicial solution of Commerce Clause taxing issues, see Hartman, "State Taxation of Corporate Income from a Multistate Business," 13 Vand.L.Rev. 21 (1959); Kust, "State Taxation of Interstate Income: New Developments of an Old Problem," 11 Tax Exec. 45 (1959); Studenski, "The Need for Federal Curbs on State Taxes on Interstate Commerce: An Economist's Point of View," 46 Va.L.Rev. 1121 (1960); J. Hellerstein, "State Taxation Under the Commerce Clause: An Historical Perspective," 29 Vand. L.Rev. 335 (1976). For the views of State tax administrators opposing Congressional intervention in State taxation of interstate commerce, see Mondale Committee Hearings, *passim.*

Cooperation Among the States. Cooperative action among the States affords another means of alleviating some of the problems in the field of taxation of national businesses. Through the work of tax administrators, the Interstate Commission on Conflicting Taxation, and the National Tax Association, considerable progress has been made in improving apportionment formulas. In 1957 the American Bar Association approved a uniform apportionment act which has the blessings of the National Conference of Commissioners on Uniform State Laws. But the efforts to achieve uniformity were painfully slow [35] until Congress enacted Public Law 86–272 in 1959; and a Congressional Committee in 1965 recommended further action by Congress requiring uniformity of apportionment.[36] To stave off further Federal intervention, the States moved with surprising speed to adopt the NCCUSL Uniform Division of Income for Tax Purposes Act.[37] By 1987, 25 States and the District of Columbia had enacted in haec verba, or substantially, the Uniform Act,[38] and 18 States and the District of Columbia had adopted the Multistate Tax Compact, which embraces the NCCUSL Act.[39] For further consideration of the Multistate Tax Compact and the attack on its validity by major multistate corporations, see Chapter 9, subd. C, § 14 infra.

35. See Progress Report of the Interstate Commission on Conflicting Taxation (1933); Long, "Interstate Reciprocity," in Tax Relations Among Governmental Units 72 (Tax Policy League, 1938); Ostertag, "General Possibilities of Interstate Cooperation," id. at 50.

36. The Report of this Congressional Committee is discussed at p. 419 infra.

37. The Model Uniform Division of Income for Tax Purposes Act is printed at p. 500 infra.

38. See CCH All States Guide, p. 1043 (Oct. 1987).

39. P–H All States Guide ¶ 564 (Oct. 1987). In addition to the States which are party to the Compact, 10 States hold associate memberships. Id. ¶ 565. For a list of States that have adopted the Compact, see CCH All States Guide, p. 1043 P–H All States Guide ¶ 564. See also Battle, "Fiscal Responsibility v. Tax Compliance Simplicity for Interstate Business," 34 Tax Policy, Nos. 11–12 (Nov.–Dec. 1967).

SECTION 1. THE POWER OF CONGRESS TO BROADEN AND RESTRICT STATE TAXATION UNDER THE COMMERCE CLAUSE

If Congress is to take serious hold of the field of State taxation of interstate business and achieve the objectives of uniformity of apportionment and a satisfactory reconciliation of the competing interests, many believe that Congress must both *restrict* and *broaden* the State taxing powers. Congress might in effect give the following mandate to the States, with respect to taxes on or measured by net income, gross receipts, capital stock, and any other levies to be covered:

> You may tax all interstate businesses which touch your borders or which derive income from your State, whether or not the Commerce Clause up to now prevented such taxation, provided you tax local businesses on the same basis and utilize Congressionally approved uniform apportionment and allocation formulas or methods. Likewise, you are prohibited from taxing any business that engages in interstate commerce to any extent, even though it is now clearly subject to your taxing power, unless you apply the Congressionally approved uniform formulas or methods.

The broadening of the State taxing powers is also required to sweep away whatever other Commerce Clause immunities are possessed by interstate businesses—whether radio stations reaching into several States, or mail order houses, or otherwise.

The power of Congress to lift the Commerce Clause barriers to State taxation is unquestioned and, indeed, that power is well established by decisions of the Supreme Court.

In the field of unemployment insurance taxes, Congress has removed any Commerce Clause objection to State taxation by providing that "no person required under any State law to make payments to an unemployment fund, shall be relieved from compliance therewith on the ground that he engaged in interstate commerce." See International Shoe Co. v. Washington, 326 U.S. 310, 66 S.Ct. 154 (1945).

In Prudential Insurance Co. v. Benjamin, 328 U.S. 408, 66 S.Ct. 1142 (1946), the Court held that an annual State tax on a foreign insurance company imposed as a condition of receiving a certificate of authority to carry on the business of insurance within the State did not violate the Commerce Clause. In 1944, United States v. South–Eastern Underwriters Association, 322 U.S. 533, 64 S.Ct. 1162 (1944), overturned 75 years of contrary decision by holding that the business of insurance was within the Federal regulatory power under the Commerce Clause. In 1945, Congress responded to the possible threat of this decision to the validity of State regulation of insurance by passing the Ferguson–McCarran Act, 59 Stat. 33 (1945), 15 U.S.C.A. § 1011, which set aside any Commerce Clause barrier to State regulation of insurance. Then followed the *Prudential* case, which upheld the constitutionality of the above Act as applied to taxes. See Powell, "Insurance

As Commerce," 57 Harv.L.Rev. 937 (1944); 4 Wash. & Lee L.Rev. 157 (1947).

In State Board of Insurance v. Todd Shipyards Corp., 370 U.S. 451, 82 S.Ct. 1380 (1962), the Supreme Court held that the Due Process Clause prevented a State from taxing premiums on an out-of-state insurance contract, when the only contacts between the taxing State and the insurance transactions were the presence of the insured property in the State and the fact that the insured was doing business in the State. The Court was unable to find sufficient contacts between the out-of-state insurer and the State to justify the tax. Justice Black dissented. For comments on this case, some critical, see 76 Harv.L.Rev. 152 (1962); 61 Mich.L.Rev. 1171 (1963); 16 Vand.L.Rev. 226 (1962).[40]

A. *The Constitutionality of Public Law 86–272.* The power of Congress to restrict State taxation of interstate commerce, as distinguished from broadening the powers of the States to tax the commerce, was challenged by some tax administrators in connection with Public Law 86–272, codified at 15 U.S.C. § 381 et seq. That statute limited the States' power to tax income from interstate commerce. (The substantive provisions of Public Law 86–272 are considered in Chapter 8, which deals generally with questions of jurisdiction to tax.) These tax administrators attacked P.L. 86–272 on the ground that "the imposition of a tax measured by net income from sources within a state does not constitute a regulation of interstate commerce, and hence, Congress is without power to forbid it." International Shoe Co. v. Cocreham, 246 La. 244, 255, 164 So.2d 314, 318 (1964). The leading spokesman for this view was Robert L. Roland, formerly Collector of Revenue of Louisiana; see his "Public Law 86–272: Regulation or Raid," 46 Va.L.Rev. 1172 (1960). This position was based on a misconception of the cases sustaining a State net income tax on an exclusively interstate business, whose rationale was that because a fairly apportioned net income tax does not impose an undue burden on the commerce, it is within the taxing powers of the States, in the silence of Congress. See the *Northwestern Portland Cement–Stockham Valves* cases, p. 229 supra.

In the *International Shoe* case supra, the Louisiana court, in upholding P.L. 86–272, said:

> What these cases stand for, as we shall hereinafter demonstrate, is that, while income taxes levied on net profits derived from interstate activities are indirect burdens, as distinguished from tax levies mea-

---

40. In United National Life Ins. Co. v. California, 58 Cal.Rptr. 599, 427 P.2d 199, appeal dismissed 389 U.S. 330, 88 S.Ct. 506 (1967), the State of California obtained an injunction against United National and other companies, enjoining them from carrying on an insurance business within the State until such time as they register and obtain licenses to conduct the business in the State. All the insurers conduct their California business by mail order. As a result of the *United National* case, a number of States have contended that mail-order insurers are subject to premium taxes imposed on receipts from policies issued to residents of the State, and have begun steps to enforce such levies. The insurance industry is apparently girding for a legal battle to contest such levies. See Shoemaker, "State Taxation of Mail Order Insurers," 24 Drake L.Rev. 825 (1975).

sured on gross receipts (see Spector Motor Service Inc. v. O'Connor, 340 U.S. 602, 71 S.Ct. 508, 95 L.Ed. 573, for example) which are direct burdens on such commerce, income taxes are not to be regarded, in the absence of action by Congress, either as a regulation of commerce or as burdening the free flow of commerce to such an extent as to be violative of the commerce clause of the Constitution or to deprive the taxpayers of due process under the Fourteenth Amendment, in instances where the activities of the taxpayers are deemed to have sufficient nexus with the taxing State.

Of the many matters presented to the Supreme Court concerning the unconstitutionality of State taxation of activities in interstate commerce, there is none in which the Court has ever suggested that Congress has not retained plenary power to regulate the activity by prohibiting the imposition of a State tax when it determines such tax to unduly burden the free flow of such commerce. Indeed, these cases are authority for holding that the Supreme Court has been able to act negatively only because Congress has not heretofore spoken. [164 So. 2d at 319.]

The Supreme Court denied certiorari in the *International Shoe* case, sub nomine Mouton v. International Shoe Co., 379 U.S. 902, 85 S.Ct. 193 (1964).[41] The Supreme Courts of Oregon and Missouri have likewise rejected State tax administrators' challenges to the constitutionality of P.L. 86–272. Smith, Kline & French Laboratories, Inc. v. State Tax Comm'n, 241 Or. 50, 403 P.2d 375 (1965); State ex rel. Ciba Pharmaceutical Products, Inc. v. State Tax Comm'n, 382 S.W.2d 645 (Mo.1964). State taxing authorities appear to have bowed to these decisions as establishing the validity of the Congressional act.

For analyses which reach the conclusion that the Congressional action taken under P.L. 86–272 is valid and that Congress has ample power to restrict State taxation of businesses engaged to any extent in interstate commerce, including local manufacturing which is followed by sale and shipment of goods across State lines, see J. Hellerstein "The Power of Congress to Restrict State Taxation of Interstate Income," 11 J.Tax. 302 (1960) and "An Academician's View of State Taxation of Interstate Commerce," 1960 Nat'l Tax Ass'n Procs. 201, reprinted in 16 Tax L.Rev. 159 (1961); Mickey & Mickum, "Congressional Regulation of State Taxation of Interstate Income," 38 N.C.L.Rev. 119 (1960). For general background materials, see Hartman & Sanders, "The Power of Congress To Prohibit Discrimination in the Assessment of Property of Interstate Carriers for State Ad Valorem Taxes," 33 I.C.C. Practitioners J. 654 (1966); J. Hellerstein & Hennefeld, "State Taxation in a National Economy," 54 Harv.L.Rev. 949 (1941); Ribble, "National and State Cooperation Under the Commerce Clause," 37 Colum.L.Rev. 43 (1937); Rodell, "A Primer on Interstate Taxation," 44 Yale L.J. 1166, 1182–84 (1935).

41. The case is discussed in 14 Am.U.L. Rev. 88 (1964); 14 De Paul L.Rev. 195 (1964); 39 N.Y.U.L.Rev. 1130 (1964); 18 Vand.L.Rev. 313 (1964).

Notes and Problems

A. *Possible Limitations on the Congressional Power to Restrict State Taxation of Interstate Commerce.* Although the power of Congress to restrict State taxation under the Commerce and Supremacy Clauses of the Constitution appeared to be plenary and all-pervasive, and unrestricted by competing State interests, a 1976 decision of the Supreme Court put the matter in controversy. In National League of Cities v. Usery, 426 U.S. 833, 96 S.Ct. 2465 (1976), the Court held that Congress had exceeded its power under the Commerce Clause by amending the Fair Labor Standards Act so as to extend to almost all public employees of the States and local governments the minimum wage and maximum hour requirements of the Act.

Justice Rehnquist wrote the majority opinion in which four other Justices joined. Although Justice Blackmun joined the Court's opinion, he wrote a separate concurring opinion expressing his own views. Four Justices dissented.[42]

Justice Rehnquist declared that the "Court has never doubted that there are limits upon the power of Congress to override state sovereignty, even when exercising its otherwise plenary powers to tax or regulate commerce * * *." 426 U.S. at 833. The basis for this view was the Tenth Amendment to the Constitution, as to which Justice Rehnquist stated:

> The Amendment expressly declares the constitutional policy that Congress may not exercise power in a fashion that impairs the State's integrity or their ability to function effectively in a federal system.[43]

The opinion found that under the amendments to the Fair Labor Standards Act, the minimum wage and maximum hours provisions "will impermissibly interfere with the integral governmental functions" of the States and their political subdivisions, and accordingly, the amendments were held unconstitutional. Id. at 851.

In concurring, Justice Blackmun declared that he had not "read" Justice Rehnquist's "opinion so despairingly as does my Brother Brennan," one of the dissenters who wrote the principal dissenting opinion. 426 U.S. at 856. Instead, in Mr. Justice Blackmun's view, that opinion "adopts a balancing approach, and does not outlaw federal power in areas such as environmental protection, where the federal interest is demonstrably greater and where state facility compliance with imposed federal standards would be essential." Id.

Justice Brennan viewed the decision as repudiating:

> principles governing judicial interpretation of our Constitution settled since the time of Mr. Chief Justice John Marshall, discarding his postulate that the Constitution contemplates that restraints upon

---

42. Brennan, White, Marshall and Stevens, JJ.

43. The Tenth Amendment contains no such explicit statement; it provides:

The powers not delegated to the United States by the Constitution, nor prohibited by it to the States, are reserved to the States respectively, or to the people.

exercise by Congress of its plenary commerce power lie in the political process and not in the judicial process.[44]

The *Usery* case has evoked considerable debate as to whether, and the extent to which, the conventional wisdom that "the power confided to Congress to regulate commerce among the States" is "complete and paramount" and "at all times adequate to meet the varying exigencies that arise" (see Houston East & West Texas Railway Co. v. United States, 234 U.S. 342, 350, 34 S.Ct. 833, 835 [1914]; and J. Hellerstein, "The Power of Congress to Restrict State Taxation of Interstate Commerce," 12 J.Tax. 302 [1960]), must now be qualified or restricted with respect to the power of Congress to regulate State action, including taxation. For discussions of the *Usery* case, see P. Hartman, Federal Limitations on State and Local Taxation § 13:2 (1981); L. Tribe, American Constitutional Law §§ 5–20 to 5–23 (2d ed. 1988); the testimony of W. Hellerstein, "The Commerce Clause and State Severance Taxes," in Fiscal Disparities, Pt. 2, Hearings before the Subcommittee on Intergovernmental Relations of the Senate Committee on Governmental Affairs, 97th Cong., 1st Sess. 19 (July 15, 1981); Parnell, "Constitutional Considerations of Federal Control over the Sovereign Taxing Authority of the States," 28 Cath.U.L.Rev. 227 (1979); Blumstein, "Some Intersections of the Negative Commerce Clause and the New Federalism: The Case of Discriminatory State Income Tax Treatment of Out-of-State Tax–Exempt Bonds," 31 Vand.L.Rev. 473, 527 (1978).

The reign of *National League of Cities* was short-lived. In 1985, the Court overruled the decision in Garcia v. San Antonio Metropolitan Transit Authority, 469 U.S. 528, 105 S.Ct. 1005 (1985). Justice Blackmun, speaking for the Court's five-to-four majority, repudiated the earlier case on both doctrinal and practical grounds, and sustained the application of the Fair Labor Standards Act to employees of San Antonio's public transportation system. Largely adopting the views of the dissenters in *National League of Cities,* the Court concluded that the States' continued role in the Federal system is primarily guaranteed not by any externally imposed limits on the commerce power, but by "the structure of the Federal Government itself." 469 U.S. at 556. It is through their control over and representation in the Federal Government that the States are protected from overreaching by Congress. Moreover, the Court found it "difficult, if not impossible" to draw the boundaries of State immunity by reference to "integral operations of areas of traditional governmental functions" described by *National League of Cities.* Id. at 539. The Court therefore rejected "as unsound in principle and unworkable in practice, a rule of state immunity from federal regulation that turns on a judicial appraisal of whether a particular governmental function is 'integral' or 'traditional.'" Id. at 546–47.

---

44. 426 U.S. at 859. Justice Brennan also observed that "It must * * * be surprising that my Brethren should choose this bicentennial year of our independence to repudiate" Chief Justice Marshall's view of the Constitution. Id. He also said:

It is unacceptable that the judicial process should be thought superior to the political process in this area. Under the Constitution the Judiciary has no role to play beyond finding that Congress has not made an unreasonable legislative judgment respecting what is "commerce." Id. at 876.

In their dissenting opinions, Chief Justice Burger and Justices Powell, Rehnquist, and O'Connor reiterated their commitment to the doctrine and holding of *National League of Cities*. Thus, Justice Rehnquist in his brief dissent found it unnecessary "to spell out further the fine points of a principle that will, I am confident, in time again command the support of a majority of this Court." Id. at 580. And Justice O'Connor, speaking for herself and Justices Rehnquist and Powell, "share[d] Justice Rehnquist's belief that this Court will in time again assume its constitutional responsibility." Id. at 589. These remarks take on greater significance when one recognizes that the Court's reversal of *National League of Cities* may be attributed entirely to the fact that Justice Blackmun revised his views about the correctness of the Court's decision in that case. In light of the elevation of Justice Rehnquist to Chief Justice and the likelihood of additional changes in the personnel of the Court in the near future, the controversy over the doctrine of *National League of Cities* may be far from over.

SECTION 2. STATE TAXES THAT CONFLICT WITH OR FRUSTRATE ESTABLISHED FEDERAL POLICY

Under the Supremacy Clause of the Constitution, State action that conflicts with a valid exercise of Congressional power must give way. U.S. Const. art. VI. Consequently, State taxes on interstate or foreign commerce that conflict with Federal legislation, enacted pursuant to the grant to Congress of the power to regulate commerce, are invalid. Thus in Aloha Airlines, Inc. v. Director of Taxation, 464 U.S. 7, 104 S.Ct. 291 (1983), the Supreme Court struck down a Hawaii tax on the gross income of airlines because it conflicted with Congressional legislation prohibiting any State taxes on air commerce "or the gross receipts derived therefrom." 49 U.S.C. § 1513. See also Exxon Corp. v. Hunt, 475 U.S. 355, 106 S.Ct. 1103 (1986) (express language of Federal "Superfund" legislation designed to provide relief for specified environmental costs preempted in part a New Jersey tax designed to fund the State's Spill Compensation and Control Act).

The Supremacy Clause extends beyond taxes that are expressly prohibited by Congress or are in direct conflict with Congressional legislation. State action that frustrates the purposes and objectives of Federal legislation likewise violates the Supremacy Clause. In McGoldrick v. Gulf Oil Corp., 309 U.S. 414, 60 S.Ct. 664 (1940), the taxpayer attacked a New York City sales tax imposed on sales of fuel oil made by the company to the owners of vessels engaged in foreign commerce. Gulf imported crude oil from Venezuela, and entered it with the U.S. Custom Service under bond. The Federal statute authorized the importation of crude oil duty free, if the oil was placed under bond in the importer's warehouse for export, or for manufacture of fuel oil by the importer and the sale as ships' stores to vessels engaged in foreign commerce. The fuel oil in controversy had been manufactured in New York City by Gulf; no Federal duty was payable because the statutory exemption procedures had been complied with. Gulf challenged the

New York City sales tax on sales of fuel oil to oceangoing vessels as conflicting with that policy. The Court agreed, and invalidated the tax, saying:

> As we have seen, the exemption and drawback provisions were designed, among other purposes, to relieve the importer of the import tax so that he might meet foreign competition in the sale of fuel as ships' stores. * * * It is evident that the purpose of the Congressional regulation of the commerce would fail if the state were free at any stage of the transaction to impose a tax which would lessen the competitive advantage conferred on the importer by Congress, and which might equal or exceed the remitted import duty. * * * The Congressional regulation, read in the light of its purpose, is tantamount to a declaration that in order to accomplish constitutionally permissible ends, the imported merchandise shall not become a part of the common mass of taxable property within the state, pending its disposition as ships' stores and shall not become subject to the state taxing power. * * * The state tax in the circumstances must fail as an infringement of the Congressional regulation of the commerce. [309 U.S. at 428–29.]

See also Xerox Corp. v. County of Harris, 459 U.S. 145, 103 S.Ct. 523 (1982) in which the Supreme Court applied the Gulf Oil case to invalidate a property tax on copying machines held in a bonded warehouse in Texas.

The Court has also held that Congressional legislation preempted State taxes that sought to control the manner in which the economic burden of a tax on natural gas was distributed. In Maryland v. Louisiana, 451 U.S. 725, 101 S.Ct. 2114 (1981), considered at p. 290 supra, the Louisiana Legislature had sought to ensure that the economic burden of the State's First–Use Tax on natural gas would fall on the owners of natural gas, or their customers, by providing that the "tax shall be deemed a cost associated with uses made by the owner in preparation of marketing of the natural gas." La.Rev.Stat.Ann. § 47:1303(C), CCH ¶ 94–747. Agreements to the contrary were declared to be against public policy. In substance, the legislation prohibited the statutory "owners" of natural gas, who were generally pipeline companies, from passing back the burden of the First–Use Tax to producers, and compelled the pipelines either to absorb the burden of the tax themselves or to pass it on to their customers, who would ordinarily be out-of-state consumers.

The Supreme Court held that these provisions of the Louisiana statute were preempted by the Federal Natural Gas Act. That act was designed "to assure that consumers of natural gas receive a fair price and also to protect against the economic power of the interstate pipelines." 451 U.S. at 747–48. The Court concluded:

> The effect of [these provisions] is to interfere with the FERC's authority to regulate the determination of the proper allocation of costs associated with the sale of natural gas to consumers. * * * By specifying that the First–Use Tax is a processing cost to be either borne

by the pipeline or other owner without compensation, an unlikely event in light of the large sums involved, or passed on to purchasers, Louisiana has attempted a substantial usurpation of the authority of the FERC by dictating to the pipelines the allocation of processing costs for the interstate shipment of natural gas. [451 U.S. at 749–50.]

See also Exxon Corp. v. Eagerton, 462 U.S. 176, 103 S.Ct. 2296 (1983), where the Court, relying on Maryland v. Louisiana, struck down a provision of Alabama's oil and gas severance tax that forbade producers from passing the tax on to consumers.

The cases in which the Court has invalidated State taxes that were not explicitly prohibited by Congress nor in direct conflict with congressional action are relatively rare. The Court has generally rebuffed arguments by taxpayers that taxes are preempted because they frustrate the policy or objectives of Congressional legislation. See, e.g., Commonwealth Edison Co. v. Montana, 453 U.S. 609, 101 S.Ct. 2946 (1981), p. 296 supra (coal severance tax not preempted by Federal policy intended to encourage the use of coal); Mobil Oil Corp. v. Commissioner of Taxes, 445 U.S. 425, 100 S.Ct. 1223 (1980), p. 610 infra (taxation of foreign source dividends by States not preempted by Federal policy not to tax such income); Container Corp. of America v. Franchise Tax Bd., 463 U.S. 159, 103 S.Ct. 2933 (1983), p. 578 infra (use of worldwide apportionment on a combined basis not preempted by Federal income tax policy that employs separate accounting for foreign subsidiaries). Most recently, the Court rejected the claim that Congress had occupied the field of international aviation and preempted a Florida tax on the sale of airline fuel to foreign carriers. Wardair Canada, Inc. v. Florida Department of Revenue, 477 U.S. 1, 106 S.Ct. 2369 (1986). The Court relied in part on a statute that explicitly permitted such taxes. 106 S.Ct. at 2372, citing 49 U.S.C. § 1513(b).

SECTION 3. CONGRESSIONAL LEGISLATION RESTRICTING STATE TAXING POWERS UNDER THE COMMERCE CLAUSE

Although P.L. 86–272 is the most significant piece of Federal legislation restricting the taxing powers of the States under the Commerce Clause, see Section 1 supra and Chapter 8, Section 2 infra, Congressional limitations affecting particular industries have also been enacted in recent years. In adopting the Railroad Revitalization and Regulatory Reform Act of 1975, P.L. 94–210, 90 Stat. 54, 49 U.S.C. § 11503, Congress prohibited the States from taxing railroad property more heavily than other commercial and industrial property. This legislation is discussed at pp. 48–49 supra. Congress subsequently extended similar protection to motor carriers, 49 U.S.C. § 11503a, and to air carriers. 49 U.S.C. § 1513(d). In amending the securities acts in 1975, Congress imposed limitations on the power of States to levy stock transfer taxes. See P.L. 94–29, 89 Stat. 97 and 15 U.S.C.A. § 78bb(d). Federal legislation also prohibits the States from imposing user charges in connection with the carriage of persons in air commerce. 49 U.S.C.

§ 1513. See p. 312 supra. For a consideration of Congressional legislation relating to State taxation of Federal instrumentalities, see pp. 1004–14 infra.

Congress has forbidden the states from imposing electrical energy taxes discriminating against out-of-state purchasers. 15 U.S.C. § 391. The Supreme Court held that the statute rendered New Mexico's tax on electrical energy invalid because the tax, although imposed on the generation of all electricity in the State, could be credited against a taxpayer's gross receipts tax on local sales of electricity. Since the credit was unavailable to taxpayers that sell electricity out-of-state, the Court held that the statutory scheme was prohibited by the Federal nondiscrimination provision. Arizona Public Service Co. v. Snead, 441 U.S. 141, 99 S.Ct. 1629 (1979); cf. Maryland v. Louisiana, p. 290 supra, in which the Court invalidated a similar crediting device on constitutional grounds.

Chapter 7

IMPORTS AND EXPORTS

No State shall, without the Consent of the Congress, lay any Imposts or Duties on Imports or Exports, except what may be absolutely necessary for executing its Inspection Laws: and the net Produce of all Duties and Imposts, laid by any State on Imports or Exports, shall be for the Use of the Treasury of the United States; and all such Laws shall be subject to the Revision and Control of the Congress. [U.S. Const. Art. I, § 10, Cl. 2.]

SECTION 1. IMPORTS

MICHELIN TIRE CORP. v. WAGES

Supreme Court of the United States, 1976.
423 U.S. 276, 96 S.Ct. 535.

Mr. Justice Brennan delivered the opinion of the Court.*

Respondents, the Tax Commissioner and Tax Assessors of Gwinnett County, Ga., assessed ad valorem property taxes against tires and tubes imported by petitioner from France and Nova Scotia that were included on the assessment dates in an inventory maintained at its wholesale distribution warehouse in the county. Petitioner brought this action for declaratory and injunctive relief in the Superior Court of Gwinnett County, alleging that with the exception of certain passenger tubes that had been removed from the original shipping cartons,[1] the ad valorem property taxes assessed against its inventory of imported tires and tubes were prohibited by Art. I, § 10, cl. 2, of the Constitution, which provides in pertinent part that "No State shall, without the Consent of the Congress, lay any Imposts or Duties on Imports or Exports, except what may be absolutely necessary for executing its Inspection Laws * * *." After trial, the Superior Court granted the requested declaratory and injunctive relief. On Appeal, the Supreme Court of Georgia

---

* [Some of the Court's footnotes have been omitted.]

1. Petitioner's complaint conceded the taxability of certain passenger tubes that had been removed from the original shipping cartons. These had a value of $633.92 on the assessment date January 1, 1972, and of $664.22 on the assessment date January 1, 1973. The tax for 1972 on the tubes was $8.03 and for 1973 was $8.73.

affirmed in part and reversed in part, agreeing that the tubes in the corrugated shipping cartons were immune from ad valorem taxation, but holding that the tires had lost their status as imports and become subject to such taxation because they had been mingled with other tires imported in bulk, sorted, and arranged for sale. Wages v. Michelin Tire Corp., 233 Ga. 712, 214 S.E.2d 349 (1975). We granted petitioner's petition for certiorari, 422 U.S. 1040, 95 S.Ct. 2652, 45 L.Ed.2d 692 (1975). The only question presented is whether the Georgia Supreme Court was correct in holding that the tires were subject to the ad valorem property tax.[2] We affirm without addressing the question whether the Georgia Supreme Court was correct in holding that the tires had lost their status as imports. We hold that, in any event, Georgia's assessment of a nondiscriminatory ad valorem property tax against the imported tires is not within the constitutional prohibition against laying "any Imposts or Duties on Imports * * *" and that insofar as Low v. Austin, 13 Wall. 29, 20 L.Ed. 517 (1871) is to the contrary, that decision is overruled.

I

Petitioner, a New York corporation qualified to do business in Georgia, operates as an importer and wholesale distributor in the United States of automobile and truck tires and tubes manufactured in France and Nova Scotia by Michelin Tires Ltd. The business is operated from distribution warehouses in various parts of the country. Distribution and sale of tires and tubes from the Gwinnett County warehouse is limited to the 250–300 franchised dealers with whom petitioner does all of its business in six southeastern States. Some 25% of the tires and tubes are manufactured in and imported from Nova Scotia and are brought to the United States in tractor-driven over-the-road trailers packed and sealed at the Nova Scotia factory. The remaining 75% of the imported tires and tubes are brought to the United States by sea from France and Nova Scotia in sea vans packed and sealed at the foreign factories. Sea vans are essentially over-the-road trailers from which the wheels are removed before being loaded aboard ship. Upon arrival of the ship at the United States port of entry, the vans are unloaded, the wheels are replaced, and the vans are tractor-hauled to petitioner's distribution warehouse after clearing customs upon payment of a 4% import duty.

The imported tires, each of which has its own serial number, are packed in bulk into the trailers and vans, without otherwise being packaged or bundled. They lose their identity as a unit, however, when unloaded from the trailers and vans at the distribution warehouse. When unloaded they are sorted by size and style, without segregation by place of manufacture, stacked on wooden pallets each bearing four stacks of five tires of the same size and style, and stored in pallet stacks

---

2. The respondents did not cross-petition from the affirmance of the holding of the Superior Court that the tubes in the corrugated shipping cartons were immune from the tax, and that holding is therefore not before us for review.

of three pallets each. This is the only processing required or performed to ready the tires for sale and delivery to the franchised dealers.

Sales of tires and tubes from the Gwinnett County distribution warehouse to the franchised dealers average 4,000–5,000 pounds per sale. Orders are filled without regard to the shipments in which the tires and tubes arrived in the United States or the place of their manufacture. Delivery to the franchised dealers is by common carrier or customer pickup.

II

Both Georgia courts addressed the question whether, without regard to whether the imported tires had lost their character as imports, Georgia's nondiscriminatory ad valorem tax fell within the constitutional prohibition against the laying by States of "any Imposts or Duties on Imports * * *." The Superior Court expressed strong doubts that the ad valorem tax fell within the prohibition but concluded that it was bound by this Court's decisions to the contrary. * * *

[The Georgia Supreme Court likewise rested the decision on the cases.]

Low v. Austin, supra [80 U.S. (13 Wall.) 29 (1872)], is the leading decision of this Court holding that the States are prohibited by the Import–Export Clause from imposing a nondiscriminatory ad valorem property tax on imported goods until they lose their character as imports and become incorporated into the mass of property in the State. The Court there reviewed a decision of the California Supreme Court that had sustained the constitutionality of California's nondiscriminatory ad valorem tax on the ground that the Import–Export Clause only prohibited taxes upon the character of the goods as imports and therefore did not prohibit nondiscriminatory taxes upon the goods as property. See 13 Wall., at 30–31. This Court reversed on its reading of the seminal opinion construing the Import–Export Clause, Brown v. Maryland, 12 Wheat. 419, 6 L.Ed. 678 (1827), as holding that "Whilst retaining their character as imports, a tax upon them, in any shape, is within the constitutional prohibition." 13 Wall., at 34.

Scholarly analysis has been uniformly critical of Low v. Austin. It is true that Chief Justice Marshall, speaking for the Court in Brown v. Maryland, 12 Wheat., at 442, said that " * * * while [the thing imported remains] the property of the importer, in his warehouse, in the original form or package in which it was imported, a tax upon it is too plainly a duty on imports to escape the prohibition in the constitution." Commentators have uniformly agreed that Low v. Austin misread this dictum in holding that the Court in *Brown* included nondiscriminatory ad valorem property taxes among prohibited "imposts" or "duties," for the contrary conclusion is plainly to be inferred from consideration of the specific abuses which led the Framers to include the Import–Export Clause in the Constitution. See, e.g., Powell, State Taxation of Imports—When Does an Import Cease to Be an Import?, 58

Harv.L.Rev. 858 (1945); The Supreme Court, 1958 Term, 73 Harv.L. Rev. 126, 176 (1959); Early & Weitzman, A Century of Dissent: The Immunity of Goods Imported for Resale From Nondiscriminatory State Personal Property Taxes, 7 S.W.U.L.Rev. 247 (1975); Dakin, The Protective Cloak of the Export–Import Clause: Immunity for the Goods or Immunity for the Process?, 19 La.L.Rev. 747 (1959).

Our independent study persuades us that a nondiscriminatory ad valorem property tax is not the type of state exaction which the Framers of the Constitution or the Court in *Brown* had in mind as being an "impost" or "duty" and that Low v. Austin's reliance upon the *Brown* dictum to reach the contrary conclusion was misplaced.

III

One of the major defects of the Articles of Confederation, and a compelling reason for the calling of the Constitutional Convention of 1787, was the fact that the Articles essentially left the individual States free to burden commerce both among themselves and with foreign countries very much as they pleased. Before 1787 it was commonplace for seaboard States to derive revenue to defray the costs of state and local governments by imposing taxes on imported goods destined for customers in inland States. At the same time, there was no secure source of revenue for the central government. James Madison, in his Preface to Debates in the Convention of 1787, 3 M. Farrand, The Records of the Federal Convention of 1787, at 542 (1911), provides a graphic description of the situation:

> "The other source of dissatisfaction was the peculiar situation of some of the States, which having no convenient ports for foreign commerce, were subject to be taxed by their neighbors, thro whose ports, their commerce was carried on. New Jersey, placed between Phila. & N. York, was likened to a Cask tapped at both ends: and N. Carolina between Virga. & S. Carolina to a patient bleeding at both Arms. The Articles of Confederation provided no remedy for the complaint: which produced a strong protest on the part of N. Jersey; and never ceased to be a source of dissatisfaction & discord, until the new Constitution, superseded the old."

And further, id., at 546–547:

> "Rh. I. was the only exception to a compliance with the recommendation from Annapolis [to have a Const. Convention], well known to have been swayed by an obdurate adherence to an advantage which her position gave her of taxing her neighbors thro' their consumption of imported supplies, an advantage which it was foreseen would be taken from her by a revisal of the Articles of Confederation. The same want of a general power over Commerce led to an exercise of this power separately, by the States, which not only proved abortive, but engendered rival, conflicting and angry regulations. Besides the vain attempts to supply their respective treasuries by imposts, which turned their commerce into the neighbouring ports, and to co-erce a relaxation of the British monopoly of the W. Indn. navigation, which was at-

tempted by Virga. the States having ports for foreign commerce, taxed & irritated the adjoining States, trading thro' them, as N.Y. Pena. Virga. & S–Carolina."

The Framers of the Constitution thus sought to alleviate three main concerns by committing sole power to lay imposts and duties on imports in the Federal Government, with no concurrent state power: the Federal Government must speak with one voice when regulating commercial relations with foreign governments, and tariffs, which might affect foreign relations, could not be implemented by the States consistently with that exclusive power;[4] import revenues were to be the major source of revenue of the Federal Government and should not be diverted to the States;[5] and harmony among the States might be disturbed unless seaboard States, with their crucial ports of entry, were prohibited from levying taxes on citizens of other States by taxing goods merely flowing through their ports to the inland States not situated as favorably geographically.[6]

Nothing in the history of the Import–Export Clause even remotely suggests that a nondiscriminatory ad valorem property tax which is also imposed on imported goods that are no longer in import transit was the type of exaction that was regarded as objectionable by the Framers of the Constitution. For such an exaction, unlike discriminatory state taxation against imported goods as imports, was not regarded as an impediment that severely hampered commerce or constituted a form of tribute by seaboard States to the disadvantage of the interior States.

It is obvious that such nondiscriminatory property taxation can have no impact whatsoever on the Federal Government's exclusive regulation of foreign commerce, probably the most important purpose of the clause's prohibition. By definition, such a tax does not fall on imports as such because of their place of origin. It cannot be used to create special protective tariffs or particular preferences for certain domestic goods, and it cannot be applied selectively to encourage or discourage any importation in a manner inconsistent with federal regulation.

4. See, e.g., Brown v. Maryland, 12 Wheat. 419, 439 (1827); Cook v. Pennsylvania, 7 Otto 566, 574 (1878); Youngstown Sheet & Tube Co. v. Bowers, 358 U.S. 534, 555–556, 79 S.Ct. 383, 3 L.Ed.2d 490 (1959) (Frankfurter, J., dissenting); Federalist Nos. 11 (Hamilton), 12 (Hamilton), 42 (Madison), 44 (Madison); 2 M. Farrand, The Records of the Constitutional Convention of 1787, at 135, 157–158, 169 (1911) (notes of Committee of Detail); id., at 441; 3 id., at 520–521 (letter of James Madison to Professor Davis); 3 id., at 547–548.

5. See, e.g., Brown v. Maryland, 12 Wheat. 419, 439 (1827); Youngstown Sheet & Tube Co. v. Bowers, 358 U.S. 534, 556, 79 S.Ct. 383, 3 L.Ed.2d 490 (1959) (Frankfurter, J., dissenting); Federalist No. 12.

6. See, e.g., Brown v. Maryland, 12 Wheat. 419, 440 (1827); Cook v. Pennsylvania, 7 Otto 566, 574 (1878); Youngstown Sheet & Tube Co. v. Bowers, 358 U.S. 534, 545, 79 S.Ct. 383, 3 L.Ed.2d 490 (1959); id., at 556–557, 79 S.Ct. 383 (Frankfurter, J., dissenting); 2 M. Farrand, The Records of the Constitutional Convention of 1787, at 441–442, 589 (1911); 3 id., at 519 (letter of James Madison to Professor Davis).

Nor will such taxation deprive the Federal Government of the exclusive right to all revenues from imposts and duties on imports and exports, since that right by definition only extends to revenues from exactions of a particular category; if nondiscriminatory ad valorem taxation is not in that category, it deprives the Federal Government of nothing to which it is entitled. Unlike imposts and duties, which are essentially taxes on the commercial privilege of bringing goods into a country, such property taxes are taxes by which a State apportions the cost of such services as police and fire protection among the beneficiaries according to their respective wealth; there is no reason why an importer should not bear his share of these costs along with his competitors handling only domestic goods. The Import–Export Clause clearly prohibits state taxation based on the foreign origin of the imported goods, but it cannot be read to accord imported goods preferential treatment that permits escape from uniform taxes imposed without regard to foreign origin for services which the State supplies. See, e.g., May v. New Orleans, 178 U.S. 496, 20 S.Ct. 976, 44 L.Ed. 1165, 502–504, 507–509 (1900). It may be that such taxation could diminish federal impost revenues to the extent its economic burden may discourage purchase or importation of foreign goods. The prevention or avoidance of this incidental effect was not, however, even remotely an objective of the Framers in enacting the prohibition. Certainly the Court in *Brown* did not think so. See 12 Wheat., at 443–444. Taxes imposed after an initial sale, after the breakup of the shipping packages, or the moment goods imported for use are committed to current operational needs are also all likely to have an incidental effect on the volume of goods imported; yet all are permissible. See, e.g., Waring v. The Mayor, 8 Wall. 110, 19 L.Ed. 342 (1868) (taxation after initial sale); May v. New Orleans, 178 U.S. 496, 20 S.Ct. 976, 44 L.Ed. 1165 (1900) (taxation after breakup of shipping packages); Youngstown Sheet & Tube Co. v. Bowers, 358 U.S. 534, 79 S.Ct. 383, 3 L.Ed.2d 490 (1959) (taxation of goods committed to current operational needs by manufacturer). What those taxes and nondiscriminatory ad valorem property taxes share, it should be emphasized, is the characteristic that they cannot be selectively imposed and increased so as substantially to impair or prohibit importation.[7]

Finally, nondiscriminatory ad valorem property taxes do not interfere with the free flow of imported goods among the States, as did the

---

7. Of course, discriminatory taxation in such circumstances is not inconceivable. For example, a State could pass a law which only taxed the retail sale of imported goods, while the retail sale of domestic goods was not taxed. Such a tax, even though operating after an "initial sale" of the imports would, of course, be invalidated as a discriminatory imposition that was, in practical effect, an impost. Nothing in the opinion in Brown v. Maryland should suggest otherwise. The Court in *Brown* merely presumed that at these later stages of commercial activity, state impositions would not be discriminatory. But merely because *Brown* would have authorized a nondiscriminatory charge on even an importer's use of the services of a public auctioneer, see 12 Wheat., at 443, does not mean that it would have disapproved the holding of Cook v. Pennsylvania, 7 Otto 566 (1878), which invalidated a tax on the sale of goods by auction that discriminated against foreign goods.

exactions by States under the Articles of Confederation directed solely at imported goods. Indeed, importers of goods destined for inland States can easily avoid even those taxes in today's world. Modern transportation methods such as air freight and containerized packaging, and the development of railroads and the Nation's internal waterways, enable importation directly into the inland States. Petitioner, for example, operates other distribution centers from wholesale warehouses in inland States. Actually, a quarter of the tires distributed from petitioner's Georgia warehouse are imported interstate directly from Canada. To be sure, allowance of nondiscriminatory ad valorem property taxation may increase the cost of goods purchased by "inland" consumers.[8] But as already noted, such taxation is the *quid pro quo* for benefits actually conferred by the taxing State. There is no reason why local taxpayers should subsidize the services used by the importer; ultimate consumers should pay for such services as police and fire protection accorded the goods just as much as they should pay transportation costs associated with those goods. An evil to be prevented by the Import–Export Clause was the levying of taxes which could only be imposed because of the peculiar geographical situation of certain States that enabled them to single out goods destined for other States. In effect, the clause was fashioned to prevent the imposition of exactions which were no more than transit fees on the privilege of moving through a State.[10] A nondiscriminatory ad valorem property tax obviously stands on a different footing, and to the extent there is any conflict whatsoever with this purpose of the clause, it may be secured merely by prohibiting the assessment of even nondiscriminatory property taxes on goods which are merely in transit through the State when the tax is assessed.[11]

Admittedly, the wording of the prohibition of the Import–Export Clause does not in terms except nondiscriminatory taxes with some impact on imports or exports. But just as clearly, the clause is not written in terms of a broad prohibition of every "tax." The prohibition is only against States laying "imposts or duties" on "imports." By contrast, Congress is empowered to "lay and collect Taxes, Duties, Imposts, and Excises" which plainly lends support to a reading of the Import–Export Clause as not prohibiting every exaction or "tax" which falls in some measure on imported goods. Indeed, Professor Crosskey makes a persuasive demonstration that the words "imposts" and "duties" as used in 1787 had meanings well understood to be exactions upon imported goods as imports. "Imposts" were like customs duties, that is charges levied on imports at the time and place of importation. "Duties" was a broader term embracing excises as well as customs duties, and probably only capitation, land, and general property exac-

---

8. Of course, depending on the relevant competition from domestic goods, an importer may be forced to absorb some of these ad valorem property assessments rather than passing them on to consumers.

10. See, e.g., *License Cases,* 5 How. 504, 575–576 (1847).

11. Such an assessment would also be invalid under traditional Commerce Clause analysis.

tions were known by the term "tax" rather than the term "duty." 1 W. Crosskey, Politics and the Constitution in the History of the United States, at 296–297 (1953). The characteristic common to both "imposts" and "duties" was that they were exactions directed at imports or commercial activity as such and, as imposed by the seaboard States under the Articles of Confederation, were purposefully employed to regulate interstate and foreign commerce and tax States situated less favorably geographically.

In any event, since prohibition of nondiscriminatory ad valorem property taxation would not further the objectives of the Import–Export Clause, only the clearest constitutional mandate should lead us to condemn such taxation. The terminology employed in the clause— "Imposts or Duties"—is sufficiently ambiguous that we decline to presume it was intended to embrace taxation that does not create the evils the clause was specifically intended to eliminate.

IV

The Court in Low v. Austin nevertheless expanded the prohibition of the clause to include nondiscriminatory ad valorem property taxes, and did so with no analysis, but with only the statement that Brown v. Maryland had marked the line "where the power of Congress over the goods imported ends, and that of the State begins, with as much precision as the subject admits." 13 Wall., at 32. But the opinion in Brown v. Maryland cannot properly be read to propose such a broad definition of "imposts" or "duties." The tax there held to be prohibited by the Import–Export Clause was imposed under a Maryland statute that required importers of foreign goods, and wholesalers selling the same by bale or package, to obtain a license and pay a $50 fee therefor, subject to certain forfeitures and penalties for noncompliance. The importers contested the validity of the statute, arguing that the license was a "palpable invasion" of the Import–Export Clause because it was essentially equivalent to a duty on imports. They contended that asserted differences between the license fee and a tax directly imposed on imports were more formal than substantial: the privilege of bringing the goods into the country could not realistically be divorced from the privilege of selling the goods, since the power to prohibit sale would be the power to prohibit importation, 12 Wheat., at 422; the payment of the tax at the time of sale rather than at the time of importation would be irrelevant since it would still be a tax on the same privilege at either time, id., at 423; and the fact that a license operates on the person of the importer while the duty operates on the goods themselves is irrelevant in that either levy would directly increase the cost of the goods, ibid. Since the power to impose a license on importers would also entail a power to price them out of the market or prohibit them entirely, the importers concluded that such a power must be repugnant to the exclusive federal power to regulate foreign commerce, id., at 423–425.

The Attorney General of Maryland, Roger Taney, later Chief Justice Taney, defended the constitutionality of Maryland's law. He argued that the fee was not a prohibited "impost" or "duty" because the license fee was not a tax upon the imported goods, but on the importers, a tax upon the occupation and nothing more, and the Import–Export Clause prohibited only exactions on the right of importation and not an exaction upon the occupation of importers. He contended that, in any event, the clause, if not read as prohibiting only exactions on the right of importation, but more broadly as also prohibiting exactions on goods imported, would necessarily immunize imports from all state taxation at any time. Moreover, if the privilege of selling is a concomitant of the privilege of importing, the argument proved too much; the importer could sell free of regulation by the States in any place and in any manner, even importing free of regulations concerning the bringing of noxious goods into the city, or auctioning the goods in public warehouses, or selling at retail or as a traveling peddler, activities that had traditionally been subject to state regulation and taxation.

The Court in *Brown* refused to define "imposts" or "duties" comprehensively, since the Maryland statute presented only the question "whether the legislature of a State can constitutionally require the importer of foreign articles to take out a license from the State, before he shall be permitted to sell a bale or package so imported." 12 Wheat., at 436. However, in holding that the Maryland license fee was within prohibited "imposts, or duties on imports ＊ ＊ ＊" the Court significantly characterized an impost or duty as "a custom or a tax levied on articles brought into a country," id., at 437, although also holding that, while normally levied before the articles are permitted to enter, the exactions are no less within the prohibition if levied upon the goods as imports after entry; since "imports" are the goods imported, the prohibition of imposts or duties on "imports" was more than a prohibition of a tax on the act of importation; it "extends to a duty levied after [the thing imported] has entered the country," id., at 438. And since the power to prohibit sale of an article is the power to prohibit its introduction into the country, the privilege of sale must be a concomitant of the privilege of importation, and licenses on the right to sell must therefore also fall within the constitutional prohibition. Id., at 439.

Taney's argument was persuasive, however, to the extent that the Court was prompted to declare that "＊ ＊ ＊ the words of the prohibition ought not to be pressed to their utmost extent; ＊ ＊ ＊ in our complex system, the object of the powers conferred on the government of the Union, and the nature of the often conflicting powers which remain in the States, must always be taken into view ＊ ＊ ＊." Id., at 441. "＊ ＊ ＊ there must be a point of time when the prohibition ceases, and the power of the State to tax commences ＊ ＊ ＊." Ibid.

The Court stated that there were two situations in which the prohibition would not apply. One was the case of a state tax levied after the imported goods had lost their status as imports. The Court devised an evidentiary tool, the "original package" test, for use in making that determination. The formula was: "It is sufficient for the present to say, generally, that when the importer has so acted upon the thing imported, that it has become incorporated and mixed up with the mass of property in the country, it has, perhaps, lost its distinctive character as an import, and has become subject to the taxing power of the State; but while remaining the property of the importer, in his warehouse, in the original form or package in which it was imported, a tax upon it is too plainly a duty on imports to escape the prohibition in the constitution." 12 Wheat., at 441–442. "It is a matter of hornbook knowledge that the original package statement of Justice Marshall was an illustration, rather than a formula, and that its application is evidentiary, and not substantive ∗ ∗ ∗." Galveston v. Mexican Petroleum Corp., 15 F.2d 208 (SD Tex.1926).

The other was the situation of particular significance to our decision of this case, that is, when the particular state exaction is not a prohibited "impost" or "duty." The Court first stated its view of the characteristics of prohibited state levies. It said that the obvious clue was the express exception of the Import–Export Clause authorizing "imposts or duties" that "may be absolutely necessary for executing [the state's] Inspection Laws." "[T]his exception," said the Court, "in favour of duties for the support of inspection laws, goes far in proving that the framers of the constitution classed taxes of a *similar character* with those imposed for the purposes of inspection, with duties on imports and exports, and supposed them to be prohibited." Id., at 438 (emphasis supplied). The characteristic of the prohibited levy, the Court said later in the opinion—illustrated by the Maryland license tax—was that " ∗ ∗ ∗ the tax intercepts the import, *as an import*, in its way to become incorporated with the general mass of property, and denies it the privilege of becoming so incorporated until it shall have contributed to the revenue of the State." Id., at 443 (emphasis supplied). The Court illustrated the kinds of state exactions that in its view fell without the prohibition as examples of neutral and nondiscriminatory taxation: a tax on itinerant peddlers, a service charge for the use of a public auctioneer, a property tax on plate or furniture personally used by the importer. These could not be considered within the constitutional prohibition because they were imposed without regard to the origin of the goods taxed. Id., at 443, 444. In contrast, the Maryland exaction in question was a license fee which singled out imports, and therefore was prohibited because "the tax intercepts the import, *as an import*, in its way to become incorporated with the general mass of property." Id., at 443. (Emphasis supplied.)

Thus, it is clear that the Court's view in *Brown* was that merely because certain actions taken by the importer on his imported goods would so mingle them with the common property within the State so as to "lose their distinctive character as imports" and render them subject to the taxing power of the State, did not mean that in the absence of such action, no exaction could be imposed on the goods. Rather, the Court clearly implied that the prohibition would not apply to a state tax that treated imported goods in their original packages no differently from the "common mass of property in the country"; that is, treated it in a manner that did not depend on the foreign origins of the goods.

Despite the language and objectives of the Import–Export Clause, and despite the limited nature of the holding in Brown v. Maryland, the Court in Low v. Austin, ignored the warning that the boundary between the power of States to tax persons and property within their jurisdictions and the limitations on the power of the States to impose imposts or duties with respect to "imports" was a subtle and difficult line which must be drawn as the cases arise. Low v. Austin also ignored the cautionary remark that, for those reasons, it "might be premature to state any rule as being universal in its application." 12 Wheat., at 441. Although it was "sufficient" in the context of Maryland's license tax on the right to sell imported goods to note that a tax imposed directly on imported goods which have not been acted upon in any way would clearly fall within the constitutional prohibition, that observation did not apply, as the foregoing analysis indicates, to a state tax which treated those same goods without regard to the fact of their foreign origin.

* * *

It follows from the foregoing that Low v. Austin was wrongly decided. That decision therefore must be, and is, overruled.[13]

V

Petitioner's tires in this case were no longer in transit. They were stored in a distribution warehouse from which petitioner operated a wholesale operation, taking orders from franchised dealers and filling

13. In another context, this Court said that "[i]n view of the fact that the Constitution gives Congress authority to consent to state taxation of imports and hence to lay down its own test for determining when the immunity ends, we see no convincing practical reason for abandoning the test which has been applied for more than a century * * *." Hooven & Allison Co. v. Evatt, 324 U.S. 652, 668, 65 S.Ct. 870, 878, 89 L.Ed. 1252 (1945). However, this overlooked the fact that the Import–Export Clause contains a provision that "the Net Produce of all Duties and Imposts, laid by any State on Imports or Exports, shall be for the Use of the Treasury of the United States * * *." Although the Constitutional Convention had refused to make the Import–Export Clause's prohibition of state exactions absolute, it immediately added this proviso, which Mr. Madison supported "as preventing all State imposts." 2 M. Farrand, at 441–442. See also, e.g., 3 id., at 215–216 (Luther Martin's "General Information").

Of course, Congress presumably could enact other legislation transferring the funds back to the States after they were put to "the Use of the Treasury of the United States." But may Congress consent to state exactions if they are not uniform throughout the United States, since any congressional taxation must conform to the mandate of Art. I, § 8, cl. 1, that "all Duties, Imposts and Excises shall be uniform throughout the United States?" If Congress may authorize, under the Import–Export Clause, an exaction that it could not directly impose under the Tax Clause, would that not permit Congress to undermine the policies which both clauses were fashioned to secure? Since, however, we hold that Low v. Austin was not properly decided, there is no occasion to address the question whether Congress could have constitutionally consented to state nondiscriminatory ad valorem property taxes if they had been within the prohibition of the Import–Export Clause.

them from a constantly replenished inventory. The warehouse was operated no differently than would be a distribution warehouse utilized by a wholesaler dealing solely in domestic goods, and we therefore hold that the nondiscriminatory property tax levied on petitioner's inventory of imported tires was not interdicted by the Import–Export Clause of the Constitution. The judgment of the Supreme Court of Georgia is accordingly

Affirmed.

MR. JUSTICE STEVENS took no part in the consideration or decision of this case.

MR. JUSTICE WHITE, concurring in the judgment.

Being of the view that the goods involved here had lost their character as imports and that subjecting them to ad valorem taxation was consistent with the Constitution as interpreted by prior cases, including Low v. Austin, 13 Wall. 29 (1871), I would affirm the judgment. There is little reason and no necessity at this time to overrule Low v. Austin. None of the parties has challenged that case here, and the issue of its overruling has not been briefed or argued.

Notes and Problems *

A. *Michelin and the "Original Package" Doctrine.* The Supreme Court's opinion in *Michelin* marks a fundamental reexamination of the purpose and scope of the Import–Export Clause's prohibition against State taxation of imports. The Court's prior opinions in this area were often characterized by a mechanistic application of the "original package" doctrine to determine whether the goods under consideration had ceased to be imports. Thus, French champagne stored by the importer in a San Francisco warehouse, "whilst remaining in the original cases, unbroken and unsold," enjoyed immunity from State taxation. Low v. Austin, 80 U.S. (13 Wall.) 29 (1872) (ad valorem property tax). European dry goods packed in separate parcels or bundles but exposed or offered for sale in opened shipping boxes did not. May v. New Orleans, 178 U.S. 496, 20 S.Ct. 976 (1900) (ad valorem property tax). An importer of hundred-pound bags of Chilean nitrate stored in an Alabama warehouse and kept in the original packages until sold enjoyed immunity from State taxation. Anglo–Chilean Nitrate Sales Corp. v. Alabama, 288 U.S. 218, 53 S.Ct. 373 (1933) (franchise tax). A wholesaler of fish caught in the Gulf of Mexico who is assessed by their weight after washing and re-icing did not. Gulf Fisheries Co. v. MacInerney, 276 U.S. 124, 48 S.Ct. 227 (1928) (license tax). Bales of Philippine hemp stored in an Ohio warehouse awaiting use in the manufacture of cordage and similar products enjoyed immunity from State taxation. Hooven & Allison Co. v. Evatt, 324 U.S. 652, 65 S.Ct. 870 (1945) (ad valorem property tax). Piles of foreign ore and plywood awaiting use in manufacturing processes did not. Youngstown Sheet and Tube Co. v. Bowers and

* [The following discussion is based on W. Hellerstein, "*Michelin Tire Corp. v. Wages*: Enhanced State Power to Tax Imports," 1976 Sup.Ct.Rev. 99 (1977), and is used with the consent of the copyright holder, The University of Chicago Press.]

United States Plywood Corp. v. City of Algoma, 358 U.S. 534, 79 S.Ct. 383 (1959) (ad valorem property taxes).

Moreover, the application of the original package doctrine often raised a host of theoretical questions. Are sea vans and trailers considered to be the "original packages"? Compare Volkswagen Pacific, Inc. v. City of Los Angeles, 7 Cal.3d 48, 101 Cal.Rptr. 869, 496 P.2d 1237 (1972) (sea van constitutes "original package") with Garment Corp. of America v. State Tax Comm'n, 32 Mich.App. 715, 189 N.W.2d 72 (1971) (sea van does not constitute "original package"). Do unpackaged imports enjoy an immunity different in scope from packaged imports, and, in any event, how does one apply the doctrine to an unpackaged import that never changes its "original form"? And is there a distinction between the application of the doctrine to goods imported for use and goods imported for sale? See, e.g., E.J. Stanton & Sons v. Los Angeles County, 78 Cal.App.2d 181, 177 P.2d 804 (1947).

In contrast to the factual and theoretical inquiries that lay at the heart of the opinions applying the original package doctrine, the Court's opinion in *Michelin* focused on the nature of the exaction at issue to ascertain whether it constituted a forbidden "impost" or "duty." Although the determination whether an exaction is an "impost" or "duty" will not necessarily render academic the question whether it has been imposed upon an "import," the Court's approach to the former issue appears substantially to reduce the need for inquiring into that question.

B. *State Taxation of Imports After Michelin.* In the wake of *Michelin,* probably the two most critical questions confronting courts which are faced with a contention that a State tax constitutes an "impost" or "duty" on "imports" will be (1) whether the levy in question is an "impost" or "duty" and (2) if not, whether the goods are still "in transit." The Court's opinion gives adequate guidance on how to approach the first question. With respect to the second, although the Court does not deal with it in detail, there is abundant case law on essentially the same question as it arises under the Commerce Clause. See, e.g., Minnesota v. Blasius, 290 U.S. 1, 54 S.Ct. 34 (1933) and pp. 28–226 supra. For a sampling of the post-*Michelin* cases that have dealt with these problems, see Sears, Roebuck & Co. v. County of Kings, 59 Cal.App.3d 446, 130 Cal.Rptr. 694 (1976); Ralston Purina Co. v. County of Los Angeles, 56 Cal.App.3d 547, 128 Cal.Rptr. 556 (1976); Japan Food Corp. v. County of Sacramento, 56 Cal.App.3d 442, 128 Cal.Rptr. 550 (1976); New England Petroleum Corp. v. State, 111 Misc.2d 471, 444 N.Y.S.2d 532 (Sup.Ct., Albany Cty.1981).

C. *The Overruling of Limbach v. Hooven & Allison.* In Hooven & Allison Co. v. Evatt, 324 U.S. 652, 65 S.Ct. 870 (1945) (*Hooven I*), cited in Note A supra, the Court held that the Import–Export Clause barred a State ad valorem property tax on bales of Philippine hemp stored in an Ohio warehouse awaiting use in the manufacture of cordage and similar products. In Limbach v. Hooven & Allison Co., 466 U.S. 353, 104 S.Ct. 1837 (1984) (*Hooven II*), involving the same parties and the same issues as *Hooven I,* the Court overruled *Hooven I* on the grounds that, under the analytical framework established in *Michelin,* the Ohio tax was not an "Impost or Duty." The Court also rejected the claim that Ohio was collaterally estopped from relitigating the issue that had been decided in *Hooven I.* The doctrine was held inapplicable in cases in which intervening decisions make manifest the error of the earlier decision. See Commissioner v. Sunnen, 333 U.S. 591, 68 S.Ct. 715 (1948).

D. *The Tonnage Duty Prohibition.* For the rejection of the contention that a use tax imposed on a barge built in the State and there sold for use in the State was a "duty of tonnage" violating Article I, § 10, cl. 3 of the Federal Constitution, see In re Los Angeles Lumber Products Co., 45 F.Supp. 77 (S.D.Cal.1942). Cf. Japan Lines, Ltd. v. County of Los Angeles, 61 Cal.App.3d 562, 132 Cal.Rptr. 531 (1976), reversed on other grounds, 441 U.S. 434, 99 S.Ct. 1813 (1979) (fairly apportioned ad valorem property tax on foreign-owned cargo shipping containers not a prohibited tonnage duty).

E. *The Impact of the Twenty-first Amendment on the Import–Export Clause.* The impact of the Twenty-first Amendment on the Import–Export Clause was the pivotal point in Department of Revenue v. James B. Beam Distilling Co., 377 U.S. 341, 84 S.Ct. 1247 (1964). A Kentucky statute provided: "No person shall ship or transport or cause to be shipped or transported into the state any distilled spirits from points without the state without first obtaining a permit from the department and paying a tax of ten cents on each proof gallon contained in the shipment." The distiller imported whiskey into the United States from Scotland, storing it in its warehouses in Kentucky. The tax was imposed while the whiskey remained in the original package in the taxpayer's bonded warehouse, from which it was sold to customers throughout the United States. The Court held that the tax violated the Import–Export Clause. The Twenty-first Amendment did not remove the import-export restrictions on State taxation of liquor as it had once been thought to remove equivalent Commerce Clause restrictions. See p. 312 supra. There was a dissent. This case is noted in 65 Colum.L.Rev. 153 (1965); 33 Fordham L.Rev. 306 (1964); 78 Harv.L.Rev. 237 (1964); 17 Vand.L.Rev. 1524 (1964). Query: in light of the reliance by the Court in the *James Beam* case on the "original package" doctrine in striking down the levy there at issue, is that case still good law after *Michelin?*

SECTION 2. EXPORTS

Notes and Problems

A. *State Taxation of Exports Prior to Washington Stevedoring: Richfield Oil Corp. v. State Board of Equalization.* Just as the limitations of the Import–Export Clause on the power of the States to tax imports was delineated during most of our constitutional history by reference to the status of the goods as an "import," so the parallel limitation on the taxation of goods as exports has for most of our constitutional history been delineated by reference to the status of goods as an "export." Whether goods were an "export" depended on whether exportation had commenced. Thus in Richfield Oil Corp. v. State Board of Equalization, 329 U.S. 69, 67 S.Ct. 156 (1946), the taxpayer sold oil to the New Zealand government f.o.b. Los Angeles. The oil was transported by pipeline from the taxpayer's California refinery to storage tanks at the harbor where the oil was pumped into a New Zealand navy vessel. California sought to impose a sales tax on the transaction, but the Court held the levy was an invalid exaction on exports, because when the tax was imposed "the oil had started upon its export journey." 329 U.S. at 83.

In Kosydar v. National Cash Register Co., 417 U.S. 62, 94 S.Ct. 2108 (1974), on the other hand, the Court upheld an ad valorem personal property tax on the taxpayer's "international inventory" of business machines which were stored in a warehouse awaiting shipment abroad. In support of its contention that the inventory in question was made up of exports, the taxpayer offered evidence to show that because of their unique construction and special adaptation for foreign use, the machines in question were not salable domestically; that none of the machines built for its international division had ever gone anywhere but into that division; that there was no recorded instance of a machine sold to a foreign purchaser being returned; and that no exported item ever found its way back into the United States market. In sustaining the tax, the Court reaffirmed the "settled doctrine" that the "essential question" in such cases is the "narrow one: is the property upon which a tax has been sought to be imposed an 'export'"; that it therefore had to "decide whether a sufficient commencement of the process of exportation has occurred so as to immunize the article at issue from state taxation"; and that this depends on the factual inquiry whether the article has begun "its physical entry into the stream of exportation." 417 U.S. at 66–71. See also Empresa Siderurgica, S.A. v. County of Merced, 337 U.S. 154, 69 S.Ct. 995 (1949) (tax on portion of manufacturing plant committed for export, 12 percent of which had already been shipped abroad, sustained because portion of plant still in country had not yet entered the "export stream" by delivery to common carrier). See generally Abramson, "State Taxation of Exports: The Stream of Constitutionality," 54 N.C.L.Rev. 59 (1975).

B. *The Application of the Michelin Policy Analysis to State Taxation of Exports: the Washington Stevedoring Case.* In Department of Revenue v. Association of Washington Stevedoring Cos., 435 U.S. 734, 98 S.Ct. 1388 (1978), the Court extended to the Exports Clause the principles it had enunciated in the *Michelin* case with respect to the Imports Clause. See p. 335.[1] It sustained the application of Washington's business activities tax, measured by gross receipts, to stevedoring that included the handling of goods destined for foreign countries. The Court reasoned that despite "formal differences" in the treatment of taxation of imports and of exports under prior law:

> * * * the *Michelin* approach should apply to taxation involving exports as well as imports. The prohibition on the taxation of exports is contained in the same Clause as that regarding imports. The export-tax ban vindicates two of the three policies identified in *Michelin*. It precludes state disruption of the United States foreign policy. It does not serve to protect federal revenues, however, because the Constitution forbids federal taxation of exports. U.S. Const., Art. I, § 9, cl. 5; see United States v. Hvoslef, 237 U.S. 1, 35 S.Ct. 459, 59 L.Ed. 813

1. The Court's disposition of the Commerce Clause issue in this case is noted in Chapter 6, p. 260 supra.

(1915). But it does avoid friction and trade barriers among the States. * * * If the constitutional interests are not disturbed, the tax should not be considered an "Impost or Duty" any more than should a tax related to imports. This approach is consistent with *Canton R. Co.,* which permitted taxation of income from services connected to both imports and exports. The respondents' gross receipts from loading exports, therefore, are as subject to the Washington business and occupation tax as are the receipts from unloading imports. [435 U.S. at 758].

In *Michelin,* the court indicated that nondiscriminatory taxes on imported goods while still in transit are proscribed by the Imports Clause, but it did not pass on that question, because the tires taxed in *Michelin* were found to be "no longer in transit" (423 U.S. at 302). The *Washington Stevedoring* case appeared to bring the court closer to the necessity of deciding the "in-transit" issue, because the activity taxed was the loading and unloading of goods onto or from ships at a time that the court found the goods "to be imports and exports * * * in transit." (435 U.S. at 755). Once more, however, the Court avoided a decision as to the validity of a duty or impost on imports or exports in transit.

In Canton Railroad Co. v. Rogan, 340 U.S. 511, 71 S.Ct. 447 (1951), the Court had upheld a gross receipts tax on a steam railroad operating exclusively in the Port of Baltimore. The receipts taxed were derived from switching and hauling cars, storing imports and parts pending transportation, and related activities. The taxpayer's contention that the income was immune from tax under the Import–Export Clause had been rejected:

> * * * primarily on the ground that immunity of services incidental to importing and exporting was not so broad as the immunity of the goods themselves:

> > "The difference is that in the present case [*Canton Railroad*] the tax is not on the *goods,* but on the *handling* of them at the port. An article may be an export and immune from a tax long before or long after it reaches the port. But when the tax is on activities connected with the export or import the range of immunity cannot be so wide. * * *" [435 U.S. at 736].

In the *Washington Stevedoring* case, the Court concluded that there was no reason to distinguish the port railroad services held taxable in *Canton Railroad* from the stevedoring in the ports in Washington:

> * * * the only distinction between stevedoring and the railroad services was that the loading and unloading of ships crossed the waterline. This is a distinction without economic significance in the present context. The transportation services in both settings are necessary to the import-export process. Taxation in neither setting relates to the value of the goods, and therefore in neither can it be considered taxation upon the goods themselves. The force of *Canton R. Co.* therefore prompts the conclusion that the *Michelin* policy analysis should not be discarded merely because the goods are in transit, at least where the taxation falls upon a service distinct from the goods and their value. [435 U.S. at 758].

Justice Powell, who concurred in the holding, had a different view of the goods in transit question. He found "rather artificial" the majority's distinction between taxes on the handling of goods and taxes on the goods themselves, which he averred "harks" back to the arid " 'direct indirect' distinction that we rejected in Complete Auto Transit v. Brady * * * in favor of analysis framed in light of economic reality" (435 U.S. at 762). Instead, he justified the holding on the following grounds:

> In my view, this issue can be resolved only with reference to the analysis adopted in *Michelin*. * * * In questioning the validity of "transit fees," the *Michelin* Court was concerned with exactions that bore no relation to services and benefits conferred by the State. Thus, the transit-fee inquiry cannot be answered by determining whether or not the tax relates to the value of the goods; instead, it must be answered by inquiring whether the State is simply making the imported goods pay their own way, as opposed to exacting a fee merely for "the privilege of moving through a State." Id.

> The Court already has answered that question in this case. In Part II–C, the Court observes that "nothing in the record suggests that the tax is not fairly related to services and protection provided by the State." Ante, at 1399. Since the stevedoring companies undoubtedly avail themselves of police and fire protection, as well as other benefits Washington offers its local businesses, this statement cannot be questioned. For that reason, I agree with the Court's conclusion that the business tax at issue here is not a "transit fee" within the prohibition of the Import–Export Clause. [435 U.S. at 764–765].

C. *"State Taxation of Goods in Import or Export Transit.** The distinction drawn by Justice Powell in the *Washington Stevedoring* case between 'making the imported goods pay their own way,' as opposed to exacting a fee for the 'privilege of moving through a state' is not as simple as the Justice assumes. To be sure, Justice Powell's statement that 'the stevedores undoubtedly avail themselves of police and fire protection, as well as other benefits Washington offers its local businesses' was correct. But the same can also be said of the police, fire, and other benefits and protection the imports and exports themselves receive from the State as they are being loaded or unloaded onto or from the vessels (in both cases without benefit of any evidence in the record on the point). Consequently, Justice Powell's preferred distinction does little to advance the determination as to whether a tax is a prohibited 'transit fee.'

"The position of the majority, in contrast, offers a workable delineation of what is taxable and nontaxable with respect to at least two major types of situations involving imports or exports in transit:

    (1) Taxes on receipts from services performed on, or in handling, imports or exports. Such receipts are taxable.

    (2) Property taxes on the imports or exports. Despite the Court's reluctance to decide the issue in the *Washington Stevedoring* case, such a tax is clearly repugnant to the Import–Export Clause.

* This note is taken from J. Hellerstein, State Taxation I, Corporate Income and Franchise Taxes ¶ 5.4 (1983). Used with the consent of the copyright owner and publisher.

"Such lines between taxability and nontaxability would respond to the language and history of the Import–Export Clause. There is nothing in the language or purposes of the clause that would warrant the view that non-discriminatory taxes on persons servicing or handling imports or exports were intended to be prohibited. Per contra, both the language and the expressed purpose of the clause as being designed to prohibit the seaboard States 'from * * * taxing goods merely flowing through their ports to other States,' indicate that property taxes imposed on exports awaiting shipment abroad or imports awaiting delivery to other States were intend-ed to be proscribed. See *Michelin* supra at p. 339. The pre-*Michelin* cases, of course, so held.

Turning to other types of cases involving taxes relating to goods in transit, the *Richfield* case, Note A supra, raises questions under the Court's current approach to the Import–Export Clause. In that case, the Court struck down a general nondiscriminatory California sales tax, assessed on sales of oil to a New Zealand purchaser. The oil was delivered to the purchaser by delivery to a vessel in a California port for shipment to New Zealand.

"The tax at issue was construed by the State court as being not a levy on the purchaser (even though the seller was permitted to collect the tax from the purchaser), but as an excise on the privilege of conducting a retail business. The measure of the tax was the gross receipts from sales. The Court held that the incident that gave rise to the tax, namely, the delivery of the oil which resulted in the passing of title and the conclusion of the sale, 'was a step in the export process.' 329 U.S. at 84. Since the oil was regarded as an export at the point at which the sale was taxed, under the then reigning doctrine the tax was found to contravene the Import–Export Clause.

"Our question is whether that decision would be followed today. In comparing the tax invalidated in *Richfield* with the tax sustained in *Washington Stevedoring*, we start with the fact that in both cases the goods had entered the export stream and, therefore, constituted exports in transit. Similarly, in both cases, the taxes were imposed on the conduct of business by the taxpayers, although the businesses were different, selling oil in *Richfield* and loading and unloading goods from vessels in *Washington Stevedoring*.

"By way of distinguishing the two cases, one can argue that the tax in *Richfield*, unlike the tax in *Washington Stevedoring*, fell on the goods themselves, because selling goods involves the essence of the goods, whereas handling or servicing goods is merely an incidental activity. Moreover, the Court in *Washington Stevedoring* appeared to regard a tax measured by the value of goods as tantamount to a tax on the goods themselves. 435 U.S. at 756 n. 21.

"Hence, the Court could distinguish the cases on such grounds, but such niceties and refinements as to direct and incidental taxes do not commend themselves as the proper basis for delineating the constitutional taxing powers of the States. A more acceptable basis for deciding the in-transit tax cases under the new Import–Export Clause jurisprudence may be found in the purpose of the clause to prevent the seaboard States from exacting a sale on 'goods merely flowing through their ports.' See *Michelin*, p. 339 supra, 423 U.S. at 285–86. A sales tax on goods being exported that is imposed at the point of delivery of title and possession of the goods to the purchaser or his shipper for transport to the purchaser can be fairly regarded as such an exaction and, therefore, as a 'transit fee' that is repugnant to the Import–Export Clause." J. Hellerstein, State Taxation I, Corporate Income and Franchise Taxes ¶ 5.4, pp. 187–90 (1983).

D. *State Income Tax on Income from Exportation.* In Peck & Co. v. Lowe, 247 U.S. 165, 38 S.Ct. 432 (1918), the net income of a corporation derived from exporting goods from the United States and selling them abroad was held subject to the Federal income tax. The Court stated,

> If articles manufactured and intended for export are subject to taxation under general laws up to the time they are put in course of exportation, as we have seen they are, the conclusion is unavoidable that the net income from the venture when completed, that is to say, after the exportation and sale are fully consummated, is likewise subject to taxation under general laws. In that respect, the status of the income is not different from that of the exported articles prior to the exportation. [247 U.S. at 175, 38 S.Ct. at 434.]

E. *State Sales Taxes on Sales of Vessels for Use in Foreign Shipping and Under Foreign Registry.* For an extension of the *Richfield Oil* case, Note A supra, under the pre-*Washington Stevedoring* analysis, see the series of Washington cases testing the validity of the State's sales tax as applied to sales of vessels to a foreign corporation, registered under a foreign flag, for use in foreign shipping. That foreign registry was intended from the outset was established by the applications filed with the United States Maritime Commission, whose approval of the sales was required. The court invalidated the tax on the ground that the vessels were "exports" at the time of their transfer to the purchaser because the ship had been committed to exportation at the date of sale. Alaska S.S. Co. v. State, 31 Wash.2d 445, 196 P.2d 1001 (1948). In another case, the vessel sailed from Seattle to San Francisco, where it picked up a cargo before getting under way for the Philippine Islands. This fact did not alter the result. The vessel was still an export, though self-transported abroad. Manila S.S. Co. v. State, 31 Wash.2d 1052, 198 P.2d 1015 (1948).

F. *Tax on Fuel Used by Vessel Engaged in Export Trade.* The California sales tax was imposed on purchases of fuel oil used as fuel by vessels engaged exclusively in interstate and foreign commerce. The court rejected the Exports Clause objection on the ground that only the goods transported, not the fuels, were an export. In the case of oil sold and delivered to ships of foreign registry, the court held that the ships could not be deemed to be "foreign territory," so as to treat the oil as being exported on delivery. Nor was the sales tax found to impose an unconstitutional burden on interstate commerce, since it was levied before the commerce began; the oil was delivered to the vessels in port in California. The court also rejected taxpayer's contention that Congress by a statute had occupied the field so as to invalidate the tax. Shell Oil Co. v. State Board of Equalization, 64 Cal.2d 713, 51 Cal.Rptr. 524, 414 P.2d 820 (1966), noted in 51 Minn.L.Rev. 151 (1966) and 55 Calif.L.Rev. 559 (1967). Compare the cases holding that the sale of gasoline used by planes exclusively in interstate commerce is subject to a sales tax. Eastern Air Transport, Inc. v. South Carolina Tax Commissioner, 285 U.S. 147, 52 S.Ct. 340 (1932).

The facts of business life, however, have precluded some States from exercising the taxing power upheld in the Shell Oil Company case. Because of the interstate competition for sales of fuel oil, some States exempt from sales and use tax oil and gasoline sold to airlines, and to commercial vessels engaged primarily in interstate and foreign commerce, for use as fuel for the planes or vessels. See, e.g., N.Y.Tax Law, §§ 1115(a)(8) and (9). The New York provision also exempts all provisions and supplies purchased for use by such vessels. Id.

Part 5

BUSINESS TAXES

INTRODUCTORY NOTE

The Development of State Corporate Taxes. Most States impose annual franchise or privilege taxes on corporations. The right to exist as a domestic corporation, or the license to do business in the State as a foreign corporation, or the actual conduct or carrying on of business by a corporation in a State is made the subject of the franchise taxes of most States.

The development of the existing structure of State corporate franchise taxation has its roots in the property tax. The earliest form of general corporation tax in this country, the corporate excess tax, was not a special tax but a modification of the general property tax. It was a levy on the value of a corporate business in excess of the appraised value of its assets including good will, going-business value, and other factors that are reflected in the market value of the corporation's stock. At first this intangible "corporate excess" value was assessed and taxed to the shareholders. Subsequently, it was levied on the corporations themselves. This form of corporate taxation has largely given way to the capital stock tax.[1]

The capital stock tax has a long history in State taxation; its development paralleled the growth of the American corporation. Such levies developed in the early nineteenth century, when incorporation was a special privilege or franchise for which a tax exaction was regarded as appropriate.[2] Around the turn of the century, capital stock taxes grew rapidly; in 1902 they were imposed by 13 States, by 1912 the number had reached 25, and by 1929 there were 33 States imposing such tax levies. That is approximately the current level, with 27 States and the District of Columbia levying capital stock taxes.[3]

1. For a historical account of the development of State corporate taxation in this country, see E.R.A. Seligman, Essays in Taxation 137 et seq. (1st ed. 1895).

2. Id.

3. P–H All States Guide ¶ 210. For a brief history of State capital stock taxation, see Report of Subcommittee on State Taxation of Interstate Commerce of the House Committee on the Judiciary, "State Taxation of Interstate Commerce," H.R. Rep. No. 565, 88th Cong., 1st Sess., Vol. 3, at 903 (1965). This report is hereafter referred to as the Willis Committee Report, and it will be cited as __ Willis Comm.Rep. __, with the volume number preceding and the page number succeeding the citation.

The capital stock tax is typically an annual franchise tax, imposed on domestic corporations for the privilege of existing as a corporation, and on foreign corporations for the privilege of doing business, or the actual conduct of business, within the taxing State. The measures employed fall into two general classifications:

> In one category are narrow bases taken from the corporation's statement of capital, either authorized shares or outstanding (or issued) shares, generally valued at par in the case of par-value shares and at various arbitrary amounts, such as $100 a share, in the case of no-par shares. Tax bases of this type will be classified under the term "capital-account" bases. In the other category are broader bases reflecting in a variety of ways historical earning capacity or value as a continuing business enterprise. These bases are generally defined in terms of balance sheet items with some adjustments for more realistic valuation. They may be measured by corporate net worth (i.e., the excess of assets over liabilities); or by the market value of the corporation's shares. All of these bases will be classified under the term "capital-value" bases.[4]

The most widely used of the corporate State tax measures is the latest arrival in the family of corporate tax measures—net income attributed to the State.[5] Some States tax corporate net incomes directly, without interposing the holding of a franchise or the doing of business as the subject of the tax. The States taxed corporate incomes occasionally during the nineteenth century. Virginia imposed an income tax on corporations in 1844 and Georgia in 1863. Most of the States, however, did not enter this area of taxation until the twentieth century. In 1911, Wisconsin taxed corporate incomes and thereafter other States followed suit.

There are 27 States and the District of Columbia which use the value of capital stock as a measure of their corporate taxes. In a number of States capital stock is one of the tax measures—net income being utilized as an alternative or additional tax measure.[6]

In 1987, 46 States and the District of Columbia had either direct corporate net-income taxes, or franchise taxes measured by net income. Of these, California, Idaho, Montana, New Jersey, Oregon, Pennsylvania, Utah, and Wisconsin utilize so-called "double-barreled" taxes—i.e., they impose both a direct tax and a franchise tax measured by net income.[7] The direct net income tax was developed as a statutory technique for taxing corporations engaged in exclusively interstate business that could not, under Supreme Court decisions prior to 1977, be subjected to a franchise tax measured by net income. Compare the *Spector* with *Northwestern–Stockham Valves* cases, Chapter 6, subd. A, §§ 4(a), and 4(b) supra. Minnesota, in 1933, was the first State to adopt

---

4. 3 Willis Comm.Rep. 903–04.

5. C. Penniman and W. Heller, State Income Tax Administration 2–5 (1959).

6. 3 Willis Comm.Rep. 903.

7. P–H All States Guide ¶ 220.

the "double-barreled" system.[8] The total tax yield for corporate income taxes for 1986 was $18.36 billion, which was 8.0 percent of total State tax collections for that year.[9]

Special Taxes on Selected Businesses. Public utilities have been traditionally singled out for special levies. Difficulties were experienced in applying simple property tax assessment techniques to a railroad or a power company, whose special franchises and properties are spread over the State or country. This, coupled with political considerations and other factors, led to the wide imposition on public utilities of gross income taxes apportioned to the State, often in lieu of property, franchise, and income taxes. Likewise, severance taxes, which are levies to be paid by the extractors of natural resources, frequently utilize the gross receipts from, or gross value of, the product as the measure of the tax. Taxes on premiums apportioned to the State are widely applied to insurance companies as a substitute for the more general franchise or other business tax levied on corporations generally, and special levies are applied to banks.

Organization and Entrance Taxes. The gap between a fee for the State's filing and other costs incurred in the incorporation of a business and a tax on the privilege of incorporation has been bridged by the States. During the nineteenth century, it was customary for the States to collect flat fees to cover the costs of incorporation. After the Civil War, these fees were gradually increased and evolved into taxes. These levies are based on the par value of authorized stock and a flat rate on each share of authorized no-par value stock. They are collected at the time the incorporation papers are filed; and upon the subsequent filing of a certificate increasing the corporation's authorized capital, an additional fee is collected.

In 1894, Ohio extended this principle to foreign corporations by imposing a tax on the grant of a license to do business in the State, measured by the amount of capital stock to be employed in the State. This type of entrance tax spread throughout the country. In some States, there is a flat amount, which may more nearly resemble a fee than a tax. Many States, however, measure the tax by the amount of authorized or issued capital stock apportioned to the State. Unlike the corporate franchise tax, these entrance taxes are not annually recurring levies. They come into play after the initial entrance only if the amount of authorized or issued capital is increased, or if the amount of property or volume of business in the State, or other apportionment factor, increases.

8. There is a summary of the development of State corporate taxes in this country in the Willis Committee Report, Vol. 1, pp. 100–103.

9. See Chapter 1, Tables 2 and 3 supra.

Chapter 8

JURISDICTION TO TAX

SECTION 1. DUE PROCESS LIMITATIONS ON STATE CORPORATE INCOME AND FRANCHISE TAXES *

INTRODUCTORY NOTE

A. *"Principles Governing Due Process Limitations on State Franchise and Income Taxes."** The seminal cases sustaining the power of the States to tax non-residents on income derived from sources within the State were decided on the same day in 1920. In *Shaffer* v. *Carter,* the Court sustained an Oklahoma income tax on income derived by a non-resident individual from the ownership and operation of oil and gas producing properties and oil and gas leases located in the State.[1] Emphasizing the nature of the tax as a levy on income and not property, the taxpayer had contended that because he conducted the business at his office in Illinois, Oklahoma could not tax him on his income. The Court's reply to this position was as follows:

> [W]e deem it clear, upon principle as well as authority, that just as a State may impose general income taxes upon its own citizens and residents whose persons are subject to its control, it may, as a necessary consequence, levy a duty of like character, and not more onerous in its effect, upon incomes accruing to non-residents from their property or business within the State, or their occupations carried on therein. * * *[2]

"The argument that a State is without jurisdiction to tax the income of non-residents from business or occupations conducted within its borders, as distinguished from taxing income derived from property

---

* This section deals primarily with Due Process Clause restrictions on State power to impose business income and franchise taxes. Due Process Clause restrictions on sales and use taxes are treated in Chapter 10; and Due Process Clause restrictions on property, death, and personal income taxes are treated in Chapter 11.

** The first part of this note is taken from J. Hellerstein, State Taxation I, Corporate Income and Franchise Taxes ¶ 6.3 (1983). Used with the consent of the copyright owner and publisher.

1. 252 U.S. 37, 40 S.Ct. 221 (1920).

2. Id. 252 U.S. at 52, 40 S.Ct. at 225.

located in the State, whose taxability was conceded, had been emphasized in the companion case of *Travis* v. *Yale & Towne Manufacturing
Co.*[3] In that case, the issue was the power of the State to tax the wages
and salaries of non-resident employees working in New York. In
Shaffer v. *Carter,* the Court put the contentions made in *Yale & Towne*
as follows:

> [I]t was contended, in substance, that while a State may tax the
> property of a non-resident situate within its borders, or may tax the
> incomes of its own citizens and residents because of the privileges they
> enjoy under its constitution and laws and the protection they receive
> from the State, yet a non-resident, although conducting a business or
> carrying on an occupation there, cannot be required through income
> taxation to contribute to the governmental expenses of the State
> whence his income is derived; that an income tax, as against non-
> residents, is not only not a property tax but is not an excise or privilege
> tax, since no privilege is granted; the right of the non-citizen to carry
> on his business or occupation in the taxing State being derived, it is
> said, from the provisions of the Federal Constitution.[4]

"This view of the State taxing power was summarily rejected by
the Court, which said:

> This radical contention is easily answered by reference to funda-
> mental principles. In our system of government the States have
> general dominion, and, saving as restricted by particular provisions of
> the Federal Constitution, complete dominion over all persons, property,
> and business transactions within their borders; they assume and
> perform the duty of preserving and protecting all such persons, proper-
> ty, and business, and, in consequence, have the power normally per-
> taining to governments to resort to all reasonable forms of taxation in
> order to defray the governmental expenses. Certainly they are not
> restricted to property taxation, nor to any particular form of excises.
> In well-ordered society, property has value chiefly for what it is
> capable of producing, and the activities of mankind are devoted largely
> to making recurrent gains from the use and development of property,
> from tillage, mining, manufacture, from the employment of human
> skill and labor, or from a combination of some of these; gains capable
> of being devoted to their own support, and the surplus accumulated as
> an increase of capital. That the State, from whose laws property and
> business and industry derive the protection and security without which
> production and gainful occupation would be impossible, is debarred
> from exacting a share of those gains in the form of income taxes for the
> support of the government, is a proposition so wholly inconsistent with
> fundamental principles as to be refuted by its mere statement.[5]

3. 252 U.S. 60, 40 S.Ct. 228 (1920).

4. Shaffer v. Carter, note 1 supra, 252
U.S. at 49–50.

5. These views were elaborated in the
opinion in Shaffer v. Carter, id. 252 U.S. at
50–52, by the following observations:

In McCulloch v. Maryland, 4 Wheat. 316,
while denying their power to impose a
tax upon any of the operations of the
Federal Government, Mr. Chief Justice
Marshall, speaking for the court, conceded (pp. 428–429) that the States have full
power to tax their own people and their

"In a later case that dealt with the power of a State to impose a tax on a foreign corporation for the privilege of declaring and paying dividends out of income derived from property located and business transacted in the State, Justice Frankfurter stated:

> A state is free to pursue its own fiscal policies, unembarrassed by the Constitution, if by the practical operation of a tax the state has exerted its power in relation to opportunities which it has given, to protection which it has afforded, to benefits which it has conferred by the fact of being an orderly, civilized society.[6]

"These factors—the State's power or dominion over the objects taxed, the benefits and protection afforded by the State, along with the costs to the State of the business or activities taxed—have all been used one way or another as the judicial tests of the jurisdiction of the States to tax.[7] In a sweeping oversimplification of the matter, Justice Frankfurter made an assertion that has been repeated in later cases: 'The simple but controlling question is whether the State has given anything for which it can ask return.'[8] Such generalizations do not, of course, resolve concrete cases, but they indicate the framework in which the Supreme Court decides jurisdictional cases." J. Hellerstein, State Taxation I, Corporate Income and Franchise Taxes ¶ 6.3 (1983). For other cases, see id.

The Court has also made the statement in a vendor's use tax collection case, which it has repeated in corporate income and franchise tax cases, that "due process requires some definite link, some minimum connection between a state and the person, property, or transaction it seeks to tax." Miller Bros. v. Maryland, 347 U.S. 340, 344–45, 74 S.Ct. 535, 538–39 (1954); see Exxon Corporation v. Wisconsin Dep't of Revenue, p. 528 infra. More recently the Court has stated: "For a State to tax income generated in interstate commerce, the Due Process Clause of the Fourteenth Amendment imposes two requirements: a 'minimal connection' between the interstate activities and the taxing State, and a rational relationship between the income attributed to the State and the intrastate values of the enterprise." Mobil Oil Corp. v.

own property, and also that the power is not confined to the people and property of a State, but may be exercised upon every object brought within its jurisdiction; saying: "It is obvious, that it is an incident of sovereignty, and is co-extensive with that to which it is an incident. All subjects over which the sovereign power of a State extends, are objects of taxation," etc. * * * "The power of taxation, however vast in its character and searching in its extent, is necessarily limited to subjects within the jurisdiction of the State. These subjects are persons, property, and business. * * * It [taxation] may touch business in the almost infinite forms in which it is conducted, in professions, in commerce, in manufactures, and in transportation. * * *" State Tax on Foreign–Held Bonds, 15 Wall. 300, 319.

6. Wisconsin v. J.C. Penney Co., 311 U.S. 435, 444, 61 S.Ct. 246 (1940).

7. In Curry v. McCanless, 307 U.S. 357, 367–368, 59 S.Ct. 900, 906 (1939), a death tax case, Justice Stone observed that Chief Justice Marshall regarded the right of a State to tax as being "founded on power over the object taxed," whereas other Justices relied "on the benefit and protection conferred by the taxing sovereignty."

8. Wisconsin v. J.C. Penney Co., note 6 supra, 311 U.S. at 444.

Commissioner of Taxes, 445 U.S. 425, 436–37, 100 S.Ct. 1223, 1231 (1980).

B. *Interrelation of Due Process and Commerce Clauses.* Before the "revolution" in Commerce Clause jurisprudence that took place from the middle 1930's to 1977 (see Chapter 6 supra), the Commerce Clause was at least widely believed to prohibit direct net income taxes on the conduct of an exclusively interstate business within a State. And there was no doubt that franchise taxes on the conduct of an exclusively interstate business were invalid. Consequently, franchise taxes on the conduct of manufacturing or mercantile corporations were invalidated under the Commerce Clause, even though the corporation had employees in the State who were stationed there at offices maintained by the taxpayer. See, e.g., Cheney Bros. Co. v. Massachusetts, 246 U.S. 147, 38 S.Ct. 295 (1918); Alpha Portland Cement Co. v. Massachusetts, 268 U.S. 203, 45 S.Ct. 477 (1925). When the Court reinterpreted the Commerce Clause and determined explicitly that the States are not debarred from taxing income derived from interstate commerce or the privilege of conducting an exclusively interstate business in the State, the jurisdictional issue came to depend solely on the Due Process Clause. The Commerce Clause continued to preclude discriminatory taxes against the commerce, supplemented by the corollary that States may not impose on interstate commerce a risk of multiple taxation to which intrastate commerce is not subjected. See Chapter 6, subd. A, § 2 supra.

Once jurisdiction to impose a net income or franchise tax on a foreign corporation is established, the Due Process Clause also imposes restrictions on the measure of the tax. See Chapter 9 infra.

C. *Fiscal Policy Justification for States Franchise or Income Taxation of Foreign Corporations.* Although a State's power or dominion over a foreign corporation operating within its borders may justify, as a political matter, the application by a State of its franchise or income tax to the corporation, in interpreting Due Process limitations on State taxation, the Supreme Court has relied on other factors of fiscal policy to justify such taxation. Three factors have been recognized by the court, the presence of any of which justifies such taxes:

(1) The benefits and protection afforded the business and its employees and agents by the State;

(2) The costs to the State of furnishing public services and facilities to the business and its employees and agents; and

(3) The extent of the source of the income in the State.

Historically, the source principle does appear to have been the basis on which the States regarded their jurisdiction to tax income as depending, but as State corporate income taxation developed, there was a growing recognition that the benefits and protection afforded a multistate or multinational business and the public costs incurred in furnishing public service facilities and resources to the business ought also be given weight in the apportionment, both for purposes of determining the State's taxing jurisdiction under the U.S. Constitution[70] and as a matter of fiscal policy.[71]

70. Curry v. McCanless, 307 U.S. 357, 367–368, 59 S.Ct. 900 (1939); Wisconsin v. J.C. Penney Co., 311 U.S. 435, 444, 61 S.Ct. 246 (1940); Shaffer v. Carter, 252 U.S. 37, 49, 53, 40 S.Ct. 221 (1920). In General Motors Corp. v. District of Columbia, 380 U.S. 553, 561, 85 S.Ct. 1156 (1965), the court said:

> The standard three-factor formula can be justified as a rough, practical approximation of the distribution of either a corporation's sources of income or the social costs which it generates.

71. The Willis Committee stated:

* * * a company's net income should be viewed only as a measure of the company's ability to contribute to governmental costs, and that once this ability is established the contribution should be divided among the States without regard to how this ability was obtained. Instead of locating income by its geographical source, the division-of-income rules should measure the relative extent to which the company has caused the various States to incur governmental costs. [1 Willis Comm.Rep., note 69 supra at p. 159.]

See, also, W. Beaman, Paying Taxes to Other States 7.1 (1963); Wilkie, "A Basis for Taxing Corporate Net Income," 36 Taxes 807, 815 (1958).

The preceding quotation, including the footnotes, is taken from J. Hellerstein, "Allocation and Apportionment of Dividends and the Delineation of the Unitary Business" Tax Notes, Jan. 25, 1982, pp. 163–164.

    D. *Physical Presence in a State as an Essential Requirement of State Income or Franchise Taxation of a Foreign Corporation.* Nexus of a foreign corporation with a State sufficient to justify the imposition of an income or franchise tax has been traditionally regarded as requiring a physical presence of the corporation. Such physical presence usually depended on the existence of one or more of the following in the State.

1. The corporation maintains an office or other business establishment in the State. Northwestern States Portland Cement Co. v. Minnesota, p. 229 supra.

2. The corporation maintains employees or agents in the State who conducts its activities. International Shoe Co. v. Washington, 326 U.S. 310, 66 S.Ct. 154 (1945); Standard Pressed Steel Co. v. Dep't of Revenue, p. 265 supra.

3. The corporation maintains property in the State. Cheney Brothers Co. v. Massachusetts, 246 U.S. 147, 38 S.Ct. 295 (1918) (the Lanston Monotype Co); see Norfolk & Western Railway Co. v. Missouri State Tax Comm'n, p. 425 infra.

The physical presence requirement has been challenged in recent cases.

AVCO FINANCIAL SERVICES CONSUMER DISCOUNT COMPANY ONE, INC., Plaintiff–Appellant v. DIRECTOR, DIVISION OF TAXATION, Defendant–Respondent

Supreme Court of New Jersey, 1985.
100 N.J. 27, 494 A.2d 788.

The opinion of the Court was delivered by

O'HERN, J.

* * *

In this case, a Pennsylvania financial services company, linked through its national parent with New Jersey affiliated offices, protests the payment to New Jersey of a corporate income tax upon an apportioned share of the interest and service income it received from New Jersey borrowers. The amounts at stake are modest—$1308 for 1974 and $2123 for 1975, in comparison to the $150,000 in revenues derived from doing business in New Jersey during each of those years—but the issues are important. We agree with the Director of the Division of Taxation and the Appellate Division that the taxpayer had the "minimal connection" with New Jersey sufficient to sustain a tax that bears a "rational relationship between the income attributed to the State and the intrastate values of the enterprise." Silent Hoist & Crane, supra, 100 *N.J.* at 8, 494 A.2d at 778 (quoting Mobil Oil Corp. v. Commissioner of Taxes, 445 U.S. 425, 436–37, 100 S.Ct. 1223, 1231–32, 63 L.Ed.2d 510, 520 (1980)).

The differing considerations in this case are that (1) we do not deal with a contention by the Division that the taxpayer's income can be reached as part of a "unitary business," and (2) the tax involved is a corporate income tax rather than a corporate franchise tax. As we have seen, since Complete Auto Transit, Inc. v. Brady, 430 U.S. 274, 97 S.Ct. 1076, 51 L.Ed.2d 326 (1977), the constitutional analysis of state taxation of interstate commerce depends not on the label given the tax but on the economic effects of the tax. There being no charge that the tax discriminates against interstate commerce, analysis will focus again on the nexus or minimal connection of the activity taxed to the State, and the rational relationship of the fairly apportioned tax to the services provided by the State.

I.

THE STATE TAX

The Corporation Income Tax Act (N.J.S.A. 54:10E–1 to –24), commonly referred to as a second tier tax (L.1973, c. 170), imposes a direct corporate income tax (CIT) on corporations deriving income from sources within this state that are not subject to the tax imposed under the Corporation Business Tax Act (N.J.S.A. 54:10A–1 to –40).* * * *

* [Ed. note. The Corporation Business Tax is a franchise tax measured by both apportioned net income and apportioned net worth.]

[T]he CIT is a tax on the corporation's "entire net income," measured in the first instance by its federal taxable income. See N.J.S.A. 54:10E–4. That "entire net income" is apportioned to New Jersey by the application of the three-part formula based on receipts, property and payroll within and without the State. N.J.S.A. 54:10E–6. To this allocated income is applied the tax rate of 7¼%. N.J.S.A. 54:10E–5.

In connection with the Corporation Income Tax Act, the Legislature passed the Corporation Business Activities Reporting Act, N.J.S.A. 14A:13–14 to –23. That act's purpose

> is to enable the Division of Taxation to obtain pertinent data from any foreign corporation which carries on an activity or owns or maintains property in this State but which has not obtained a certificate of authority to do business in New Jersey, to the end that a proper determination may be made as to whether such corporation is subject to any State tax.

[Associates Consumer Discount Co. v. Bozzarello, 149 N.J.Super. 358, 362, 373 A.2d 1016 (App.Div.1977).]

See also American Bank & Trust Co. of Pennsylvania v. Lott, 99 N.J. 32, 490 A. 308 (1985) (N.J.S.A. 14A:13–20, requiring all foreign corporations to file a Notice of Business Activities Report, was not intended to apply to foreign banks).

N.J.S.A. 14A:13–15 requires a foreign corporation that, among other things, receives payments from persons residing in this state, or businesses located in this state, aggregating more than $25,000 (as plaintiff did here), to file a Notice of Business Activities Report. The Legislature viewed the receipt of such payments as at least a preliminary indication that a foreign corporation derived income from sources within New Jersey and was subject to the corporation income tax. By filing its report, Avco became subject to the Division's scrutiny.

II.

The Taxpayer and Its Activities

The taxpayer, Avco Financial Services Consumer Discount Company One, Inc. (Avco Pa.), is one of many subsidiaries of Avco Financial Services, Inc. (Avco) linked through Avco Financial Services Management Company (the Management Company) with over 900 branch offices nationwide. Avco Pa. is a Pennsylvania corporation. Among its branch offices are several on the New Jersey border, including Philadelphia, Levittown, Morrisville, and Easton. New Jersey residents have taken out consumer loans or purchased credit life, accident and health and credit property insurance through the Pennsylvania offices. Avco Pa. also purchased installment contracts from a New Jersey retailer. Avco, through its affiliates, also operates and maintains similar branch offices in New Jersey. The record does not disclose whether the borrower would have any conscious understanding that the Pennsylvania and New Jersey branch offices were of different subsidiaries since Avco has a policy that permits payments to be made on the loans made by the Pennsylvania branches at the New Jersey branches. The loan agreement is between a New Jersey borrower and Avco Pa. "and/ or its Parent, Affiliates or Subsidiaries." A sample promissory note in the stipulated exhibits was made payable to Avco Financial Services, Inc. [the parent], "and/or * * * its affiliates or subsidiaries." Mailings from the parent or the management company to existing New Jersey customers invited the customer to refinance or extend existing credit lines. The mailings are warm and encourage the reader to resolve gift, tax and vacation problems, referring in generic terms to "Avco Financial Services," the lender that "believes in you." In addition, the Management Company also provides general radio advertising in New Jersey for the benefit of the parent and its affiliates.

Avco Pa. sends its own personnel into New Jersey to service accounts. Some customers were afforded "once or twice monthly visits" to remind borrowers of their obligations. Avco Pa. estimates that its branch managers spend "three to five percent" of their working hours in New Jersey. When loans are in default, Avco Pa. uses the New Jersey court system to enforce collections (about $3,000 per year), including wage garnishment and repossession of a few New Jersey automobiles. As a result of these activities, Avco Pa. estimates that its interest and other income for each of the years 1974 and 1975 was approximately $150,000.

* * *

The Director issued a final tax deficiency assessment against Avco Pa. with respect to each of the taxable years in question. Based upon Avco Pa.'s estimates regarding receipts from New Jersey residents, the Director assessed taxes of $1308.99 plus interest for 1974 and $2,123.46 plus interest for 1975.

On Avco Pa.'s appeal, the Tax Court ruled that the Director's imposition of the Income Tax Act in this matter violates both the Due Process Clause and the Commerce Clause of the United States Constitution, and granted Avco Pa.'s refund claim. 4 N.J.Tax 349 (1982). The Appellate Division reversed the Tax Court finding that there was

> a rational relationship between plaintiff's income attributed to New Jersey and the benefits conferred by New Jersey to justify the imposition of the tax levied here. The internal regulation of the credit market which enables plaintiff's parent to accept payments and process loans; the administration of the Retail Installment Sales Act which regulates the issuance and transfer of the installment paper that plaintiff buys from Dean's Appliance; the maintenance of the courts and the general regulation of collection processes that permit plaintiff to realize on loans which are in default, are all elements of such a foundation.

[193 N.J.Super. 503, 512, 475 A.2d 66 (1984).]

We granted the taxpayer's petition for certification. 97 N.J. 624, 483 A.2d 155 (1984).

III.

A.

Does the Statute Apply to Income from Intangibles Without a Situs in New Jersey?

The taxpayer has contended that it earned no income in New Jersey and is therefore not subject to the tax. It contends that its loans, promissory notes and the interest and proceeds thereon are all intangible personal property and that the taxable situs of such an intangible is the domicile of the creditor. This is the sort of theoretical distinction that has historically encumbered analysis of state taxation. The underpinning of the argument rests on the maxim *mobilia sequuntur personam* (movables follow the person). Like other maxims, this has been questioned for "stat[ing] a rule without disclosing the reasons for it." Mobil, supra, 445 U.S. at 445, 100 S.Ct. at 1235, 63 L.Ed.2d at 526 (quoting First Bank Stock Corp. v. Minnesota, 301 U.S. 234, 241, 57 S.Ct. 677, 680, 81 L.Ed. 1061, 1065 (1937)). The Court equated the taxation of income from intangibles, not with situs, but with the relation the income bears "to benefits and privileges conferred by several States." Mobil, supra, 445 U.S. at 446, 100 S.Ct. at 1236, 63 L.Ed.2d at 526. We believe that the CIT is related to benefits conferred by the State. It is direct in its reach, speaking, with certain exceptions, of a tax on income "derived from sources" in New Jersey. N.J.S.A. 54:10E–2. Putting aside traditional concepts relating to intangibles, the real source of Avco Pa.'s income is not a piece of paper, but New Jersey borrowers. In Chemical Realty Corp. v. Taxation Div. Director, 5 N.J.Tax 581, 593–94 (1983), the Tax Court reviewed the history of the CIT and concluded that the Legislature's intent was not to restrict the taxation of intangibles to the place of commercial domicile. In that case, the subsidiary of a New York bank contested application of the CIT to income it derived from real estate financing activities in New Jersey. In the absence of a legislative intent that the mobilia maxim be construed as part of the CIT, interest income received from New Jersey borrowers is "derived from sources within New Jersey" under the act, and thus is subject to the constitutional reach of the State. Chemical Realty Corp., supra, 5 N.J.Tax at 605;[2] see also CIT Fin. Services, etc. v. Director, Div. of Taxation, 4 N.J.Tax 568, 578 (1982) (surrogate activities of New Jersey affiliates sustain conclusion that a Pennsylvania lender's interest income from New Jersey residents is amenable to New Jersey taxation).

2. In *Chemical,* the Court found an insufficient level of minimal connection to satisfy due process.

B.

Is There a Minimal Connection?

We agree with the Director and the Appellate Division that a sufficient showing has been made to satisfy this requirement. Concededly, there is no litmus test that will resolve the issue for all cases. We can best look to available precedent.

The taxpayer relies primarily on National Bellas Hess Inc. v. Illinois Rev. Dep't, 386 U.S. 753, 87 S.Ct. 1389, 18 L.Ed.2d 505 (1967), and Miller Bros. Co. v. Maryland, 347 U.S. 340, 74 S.Ct. 535, 98 L.Ed. 744 (1954). Both of those cases, involving sales taxes, were seen as involving "the almost total lack of contacts" between the seller and the state of delivery. National Geographic Soc. v. California Bd. of Equalization, 430 U.S. 551, 559, 97 S.Ct. 1386, 1391, 51 L.Ed.2d 631, 639 (1977). But where there is "some definite link, some minimum connection, between [the State and] the person ＊ ＊ ＊ it seeks to tax," the nexus will be met. Id. at 561, 97 S.Ct. at 1393, 51 L.Ed.2d at 640 (quoting Miller Bros., supra, 347 U.S. at 344–45, 74 S.Ct. at 538–39, 98 L.Ed. at 748). Thus, in Scripto, Inc. v. Carson, 362 U.S. 207, 80 S.Ct. 619, 4 L.Ed.2d 660 (1960), local solicitation by commission salesmen sufficed to provide the nexus.

In terms of constitutional analysis, the question turns on how the taxpayer has come into the state to work the market. We think here, at a minimum, that:

(1) the presence of Avco Pa.'s employees in the State to collect their overdue accounts evidenced a vigorous, systematic and persistent effort, aided by a substantial physical presence, to exploit the New Jersey market. See Clairol, Inc. v. Kingsley, 109 N.J.Super. 22, 262 A.2d 213 (App.Div.), aff'd, 57 N.J. 199, 270 A.2d 702 (1970), dismissed for want of a substantial federal question, 402 U.S. 902, 91 S.Ct. 1377, 28 L.Ed.2d 643 (1971); Tuition Plan of New Hampshire v. Taxation Div. Director, 4 N.J.Tax 470 (1982); and

(2) the use by the taxpayer of its affiliate offices in New Jersey to receive payments "made possible the realization and continuance of valuable contractual relations" between Avco Pa. and its New Jersey borrowers. Standard Pressed Steel Co. v. Washington Dep't of Revenue, 419 U.S. 560, 562, 95 S.Ct. 706, 708, 42 L.Ed.2d 719, 722 (1975);

(3) the ongoing use of New Jersey's courts and process to enforce its obligations demonstrates that the taxpayer's activities enjoyed the protection and services for which the State is entitled to something in return. See National Geographic, supra, 430 U.S. at 561, 97 S.Ct. at 1392, 51 L.Ed.2d at 640.[3]

---

3. Of course, we recognize that activities reasonably related to the foreclosure of a mortgage on New Jersey realty do not subject a foreign bank to the New Jersey Corporation Business Tax Act because of such activities. American Bank & Trust Co. v. Lott, 99 N.J. 32, 36, 490 A.2d 308, 310 (citing Op.Atty.Gen. No. 5 (April 18, 1961) at 110). But when a foreign corporation "has access to [state] courts to enforce any rights growing out of its transactions" in the state, that access may be considered

The taxpayer chooses to emphasize, as does the dissent, that the taxpayer does not maintain an office in New Jersey, nor own or lease property here, or have resident representatives. Had any of those factors been present, it would be paying the higher rates due under the Corporation Business Tax Act " * * * for the privilege of having or exercising its corporate franchise in this State, or for the privilege of doing business, employing or owning capital or property, or maintaining an office, in this State." N.J.S.A. 54:10A–2.

It is precisely the absence of these factors that requires us to explore the constitutional reach of the CIT, for their absence has not always been dispositive of the issue.

> The requisite nexus was held to be shown when the out-of-state sales were arranged by the seller's local agents working in the taxing State, Felt & Tarrant Co. v. Gallagher, 306 U.S. 62, 59 S.Ct. 376, 83 L.Ed. 488 (1939); General Trading Co. v. Tax Comm'n, 322 U.S. 335, 64 S.Ct. 1028, 88 L.Ed. 1309 (1944), and in cases of maintenance in the State of local retail store outlets by out-of-state mail-order sellers. Nelson v. Sears, Roebuck & Co., supra [312 U.S. 359, 61 S.Ct. 586, 85 L.Ed. 888 (1941)]; Nelson v. Montgomery Ward, 312 U.S. 373, 61 S.Ct. 593, 85 L.Ed. 897 (1941). In Scripto, Inc. v. Carson, 362 U.S. 207, 80 S.Ct. 619, 4 L.Ed.2d 660 (1960), the necessary basis was found in the case of a Georgia-based company that had "10 wholesalers, jobbers, or 'salesman' conducting continuous local solicitation in Florida and forwarding the resulting orders from that State to Atlanta for shipment of the ordered goods," id., at 211, 80 S.Ct. 619, 4 L.Ed.2d 660, *although maintaining no office or place of business in Florida, and having no property or regular full-time employees there.*
>
> [National Geographic, supra, 430 U.S. at 556–57, 97 S.Ct. at 1390, 51 L.Ed.2d at 637 (emphasis added).]

The dissent chides us for recalling these words of *Scripto,* which are reaffirmed in *National Geographic.* It calls attention to the number of wholesalers, salesmen, and jobbers who were active in Florida. However, the significance of *Scripto* lies not in the number of those persons, but in the fact that *none* was an employee of Scripto. They devoted only a part of their time to Scripto sales. Scripto, supra, 362 U.S. at 211, 80 S.Ct. at 621, 4 L.Ed.2d at 664. Even then, without in-state offices, without full-time resident employees, the Court found the "minimum connections" to be more than sufficient.

In considering then not what is absent, but what is present, we find distinctive contacts with the State of New Jersey not found in the

as part of the minimal contacts sustaining the state's jurisdiction over the foreign corporation. *Carl F. W. Borgward G.M.B.H. v. Superior Court,* 51 *Cal.*2d 72, 78, 330 *P.*2d 789, 793 (1958); *see also Pope v. National Aero Finance Co.,* 220 *Cal.App.*2d 709, 33 *Cal.Rptr.* 889 (1963) (systematic financing program enhanced by physical entrance to repossess aircraft and resort to aid of state courts demonstrate minimum contacts with state); *Staley v. Homeland, Inc.,* 368 *F.Supp.* 1344 (E.D.N.C.1974) (that foreign seller could "freely use North Carolina law to enforce its obligations" related to mobile home purchases is a factor to be considered in sustaining jurisdiction over foreign-state seller).

precedent the taxpayer invokes. Unlike the mail order house in *National Bellas Hess,* or the department store in *Miller Brothers,* this seller of financial services has entered the taxing state to dun its customers, has used affiliated in-state offices for customers to drop payments, has used New Jersey credit service agencies, and has invoked the State's process to enforce its contracts. Surely the New Jersey borrowers did not consider themselves visited with only the "slightest presence" when Avco Pa. knocked on their doors to collect its money. Surely the New Jersey taxpayers are entitled to something in return for the benefits that the State conferred upon the foreign lender.[4]

We therefore believe that, applying the principles that the Supreme Court has laid down, it is well within the "realm of permissible judgment" to conclude that there are sufficient minimum contacts between the taxpayer and the State to justify the imposition of the tax.

C.

Is There a Rational Relationship Between the Tax and the Instate Values?

The rationality of relationship almost springs forth from the arithmetic in this case. The test is whether the tax liability is "out of all appropriate proportion to the business transacted." Hans Rees' Sons, Inc. v. State of North Carolina ex rel. Maxwell, 283 U.S. 123, 135, 51 S.Ct. 385, 389, 75 L.Ed. 879, 908 (1931), cited in Silent Hoist, supra, 100 N.J. at 10, 494 A.2d at 780.

In this case, as a result of application of the three-part formula, only a distinct appropriate portion of Avco Pa.'s income was subject to tax. Its entire net income was in excess of $5,000,000 for each of the taxable years. As a result of the formula, less than $20,000 of that was attributed to New Jersey, although approximately $150,000 per year was derived from New Jersey borrowers. The taxes assessed for 1974 and 1975 on the entire net incomes of $5,225,745 and $5,867,326, respectively, were $1308 and $2123. The formula appears to have done "the job it was developed to do." Silent Hoist, supra, 100 N.J. at 10, 494 A.2d at 780. In context, that amounts to a levy of less than 1% on the 1974 New Jersey gross, not a disproportionate factor considering the fact that branch managers spend 3 to 5% of their time in New Jersey. In light of the activities of the taxpayer in New Jersey to

---

4. We note in addition that certain of Avco Pa.'s loan activities are subject to regulation in New Jersey. Turner v. Aldens, Inc., 179 N.J.Super. 596, 433 A.2d 439 (App.Div.1981) (state consumers have protection of Retail Installment Sales Act no matter from where seller deals). When foreign state business activities are conducted under a state regulatory scheme, the state confers a benefit for which it may ask something in return. Evanston Ins. Co., Inc. v. Merin, 598 F.Supp. 1290, 1309 (D.N.J.1984) ("Notwithstanding [*National Bellas Hess* holding that the minimal link is not present when a taxpayer's only connection with customers is by common carrier or mail] a state does have the power to impose tax liability on a seller if it has virtually any other contact with the state." Sarokin, J., id. at 1306, citing Scripto and National Geographic).

realize and continue these contractual relations, we cannot conclude that these figures are out of all appropriate proportion.

Nor is the Constitution offended because the taxpayer may have included some or all of the allocated $20,000 in income in its Pennsylvania returns. Each of the states cannot police the activities of the others to guarantee that some overlap may not occur. "Taxation in one state is not an immunization against taxation in other states." West Publishing Co. v. McColgan, 27 Cal.2d 705, 710, 166 P.2d 861, 864, aff'd, 328 U.S. 823, 66 S.Ct. 1378, 90 L.Ed. 1603 (1946) (citations omitted); see Moorman Mfg. Co. v. Bair, 437 U.S. 267, 276–79, 98 S.Ct. 2340, 2346–47, 57 L.Ed.2d 197, 206–09 (1978); State Tax Comm'n of Utah v. Aldrich, 316 U.S. 174, 181, 62 S.Ct. 1008, 1011, 86 L.Ed. 1358, 1370 (1942). Many states have joined the Multistate Tax Compact to eliminate or minimize that potential.

In the last analysis, a wise commentator has put the limits of state taxing power in the simple context of whether the State "has exceeded the bounds of decency" in asserting its taxing power. Professor Thomas Reed Powell, quoted in Hellerstein, "State Taxation Under the Commerce Clause: An Historical Perspective," 29 Vand.L.Rev. 335, 350 (1976).

We are satisfied that given the homogeneous identity of Avco Pa. with its parent and management company, its own direct penetration of the New Jersey consumer finance market through its follow-up customer work, the employment of its New Jersey affiliates as collection offices, and its recurrent recourse to the protection that New Jersey's courts afford it as creditor, its activities establish a connection with the State which far exceeds the "slightest presence" suggested by the dissent. Given the fair allocation of income that New Jersey has sought, these bounds of constitutional decency have been met and disclose the required "minimum contacts" and "rational relationship" necessary to sustain the tax.

The judgment of the Appellate Division is affirmed.

CLIFFORD, J., dissenting.

Today the Court holds that a foreign corporation that does not maintain an office in New Jersey; does not employ officers, employees, agents, or representatives with offices here; does not own or lease any real or tangible personal property in this state; and does not list itself in any New Jersey telephone directory is nonetheless subject to state taxation. So different from the majority's is my understanding of the stipulated record, my reading of the pertinent authorities, and my sense of justification for imposition of the corporate income tax that I register a dissent. On the facts before us there is not a sufficient nexus on which to support the tax.

Avco argues that in every instance in which a tax has been constitutionally imposed, the Supreme Court has found some physical presence, *i.e.,* some purposeful and deliberate resort by the nondomiciliary corporation to the taxing state's laws and services. Although not always written precisely in those terms, the pertinent decisions plainly favor Avco's position that a sustained, definite presence on the part of the taxpayer—not to be found in the instant case—is required.

In Northwestern States Portland Cement Co. v. Minnesota, 358 U.S. 450, 79 S.Ct. 357, 3 L.Ed.2d 421 (1959), a foreign corporation whose plant was located in Mason City, Iowa, made nearly 50 percent of its entire sales in Minnesota, the taxing jurisdiction. The corporation also maintained in Minnesota an office consisting of a secretary, three salesmen, and a district director. Id. at 454, 79 S.Ct. at 360, 3 L.Ed.2d at 425. Not surprisingly, the Court upheld the tax liability of the corporation, stating:

> The taxes imposed are levied only on that portion of the taxpayer's net income which arises from its activities within the taxing State. These activities form a sufficient nexus between such a tax and transactions within a state for which the tax is an exaction. *It strains reality to say, in terms of our decisions, that * * * the corporation[ ] here was not sufficiently involved in local events* to forge some definite link, some minimum connection sufficient to satisfy due process requirements.
>
> [Id. at 464, 79 S.Ct. at 365, 3 L.Ed.2d at 431 (emphasis added).]

Likewise, in Standard Pressed Steel Co. v. Washington Revenue Dep't, 419 U.S. 560, 95 S.Ct. 706, 42 L.Ed.2d 719 (1975), the Court sustained a tax against a non-domiciliary corporation that had some physical presence within the taxing jurisdiction. In *Standard Pressed Steel,* a Pennsylvania manufacturer sold fasteners and other parts to the Boeing Company in Seattle, Washington. In order to facilitate consultation with Boeing regarding its anticipated needs and requirements, the manufacturer stationed in Washington an employee who was paid a salary and who operated out of his home. The employee was assisted by a group of the manufacturer's engineers who visited Seattle about three days every six weeks, or at least 24 days a year. Id. at 561, 95 S.Ct. at 708, 42 L.Ed.2d at 722. In upholding tax liability, the Court stressed that the manufacturer's employee, with a full-time position within the state, "made possible the realization and continuance of valuable contractual relations between [the manufacturer] and Boeing." Id. at 562, 95 S.Ct. at 708, 42 L.Ed.2d at 722.

In Scripto, Inc. v. Carson, 362 U.S. 207, 80 S.Ct. 619, 4 L.Ed.2d 660 (1960), the Court was faced with a somewhat different problem, namely, the application of a so-called "use" tax. Briefly stated, this form of levy imposes on a corporation responsibility for the collection of a tax on certain goods or products. Not as direct as the income tax, a tax on use is nonetheless governed by the same constitutional standards that apply to a tax on income, requiring some minimal connection between the taxpayer's activity and the taxing state. In *Scripto,* a foreign corporation maintained ten brokers within the taxing jurisdiction for the purpose of soliciting sales. Each of the wholesalers was under the contractual employ of the corporation, and each was a resident of the taxing state. In upholding the tax against the corporation, the Court stressed that the brokers or salesmen were conducting "continuous local solicitation" in the taxing jurisdiction. That circumstance, coupled with the nondiscriminatory nature of the tax, was sufficient to sustain it. Id. at 211, 80 S.Ct. at 621, 4 L.Ed.2d at 663, 664.

The majority somehow concludes that Avco's overall affairs in New Jersey amount to a "substantial physical presence," and, more specifically, that its collection activity evidences a "vigorous, systematic and persistent effort" to exploit the New Jersey market. Ante at 794. No such thing. Recall that the record before us amounts to a Rule 8:8–1(b) stipulation of facts—no room for creative interpretation here, no margin for massaging. Return with me, then, to the lamp, and re-read the stipulation. It takes little study to uncover that which is plainly so: there is no continuous solicitation by Avco in New Jersey, nor are there any physical plants or offices here. Quite to the contrary, Avco operates offices exclusively in Pennsylvania and is not authorized to do business in any other state. It has no offices in New Jersey nor does it have officers, employees, agents, or representatives whose offices are located here. Avco neither owns nor leases any real or tangible personal property in New Jersey, nor is it listed in any New Jersey telephone directories.

The Court emphasizes Avco's so-called "distinctive contacts" with New Jersey, which appear by the majority's own analysis to be little more than random visits by collectors to New Jersey borrowers and the occasional use of in-state offices and of our courts to facilitate payments. Ante at 795. The Tax Court considered each of these factors and found it to be clearly *de minimis* and therefore an insufficient basis on which to sustain a tax. 4 N.J.Tax at 357. I agree. The record indicates that somewhere around one-half percent of Avco's total outstanding loans to New Jersey borrowers were collected through the use of our courts, and that Avco's managers spent about three to five percent of their working time in the state. These contacts, as "distinctive" as they might be, do not amount to a "substantial physical presence" by any reasonable definition of that term.

The situation before us is a far cry from the legitimate example of a "substantial physical presence" found in Roadway Express, Inc. v. Director, Div. of Taxation, 50 N.J. 471, 236 A.2d 577 (1967). There, a Delaware trucking corporation maintained two terminals in New Jersey, one in Kearny and the other in Bound Brook. The terminals were part of the company's interstate network, servicing an estimated 100 trucks a week. Additionally, more than 60 vehicles were regularly parked in Kearny and registered, licensed, and inspected in the state. Id. at 478, 236 A.2d 577. In sustaining a franchise tax against the corporation, this Court emphasized the "physical nature" of the Kearny terminal and the company's "very substantial" activities in New Jersey. Id. at 479, 236 A.2d 577. It is important to note, however, that the Kearny facility was comprised of a two-story office building, a one-story loading dock, and a one-story service garage. Employed in this facility were three management representatives, six dispatchers, three supervisors, 55 dock employees, an office manager, a claim supervisor, 48 clerical workers, six garage employees, and a sales manager in charge of five salesmen. Id. at 479–80, 236 A.2d 577. With respect to other activities, the Court found that the company's vehicles used over two and a half million miles of New Jersey roadway, and the corporation itself derived over $5,000,000 from operations in this State. Id. at 479, 236 A.2d 577. The activities of the taxpayer in the instant case do not approach the activities demonstrated in *Roadway Express*.

Another illustration of a "vigorous, systematic and persistent effort" to exploit the New Jersey market is found in Tuition Plan of New Hampshire v. Taxation Div., Director, 4 N.J.Tax 470 (Tax Ct.1982). There, a foreign corporation was in the business of making educational loans and derived its income wholly from the interest that it charged to its borrowers. Significantly, although it did not maintain an office here, the company made use of its district managers from other areas whose respective districts included New Jersey. It was the job of these district managers to drum up business in New Jersey on behalf of the plaintiff corporation. As the court concluded:

> Plaintiff, through its district managers, engaged in a systematic, regular program of on-site solicitation and exploitation of the New Jersey market. Plaintiff's representatives paid regular visits to New Jersey educational institutions; they were physically present in this State at least 54 times during each of the years 1974 and 1975 and at least 59 times during each of the years 1976 and 1977. One of plaintiff's district managers assigned to New Jersey estimated that he spent as much as 20% of his time in this State. The recurring visits of two district managers to New Jersey "made possible the realization and continuance of valuable contractual relations" between plaintiff and the targeted New Jersey schools. Standard Pressed Steel Co. v. Washington Dep't. of Revenue, 419 U.S. 560, 95 S.Ct. 706, 42 L.Ed.2d 719 (1975).

> 　　　[Id. at 479.]

By contrast, no one in the employ of Avco is charged with carrying out such a program of solicitation in New Jersey.

Indeed, Avco's activities in New Jersey differ only slightly in degree from the level of the taxpayer's activity in Miller Bros. Co. v. Maryland, 347 U.S. 340, 74 S.Ct. 535, 98 L.Ed. 744 (1954). There, the State of Maryland sought to levy a use tax against a merchandising corporation that sold products directly to customers at its store in Wilmington, Delaware. Nearby residents of Maryland would travel to the store and buy items, some of which were delivered to their homes by the corporation's own truck. In addition to making these deliveries, the corporation mailed circulars to former customers, including customers in Maryland, and it also did some general advertising that reached into the taxing state. Id. at 342–43, 74 S.Ct. at 537–38, 98 L.Ed.2d at

747. Despite the foregoing activities the Supreme Court concluded that there was an insufficient nexus on which to sustain a tax.

Finally, in National Bellas Hess Inc. v. Department of Revenue of Illinois, 386 U.S. 753, 87 S.Ct. 1389, 18 L.Ed.2d 505 (1967), the State of Illinois sought to levy a use tax against a mail order house that had its principal place of business in North Kansas City, Missouri. The corporation did not maintain any office in Illinois, did not have any agent or salesman in the state, did not own any tangible property in the taxing jurisdiction, and did not advertise its merchandise in newspapers or by radio or television. The company's only contacts with its Illinois customers were via the mail or common carrier. Id. at 754–55, 87 S.Ct. at 1389–90, 18 L.Ed.2d at 507. Relying in part on *Miller,* the Court had little difficulty in invalidating the tax.

In holding in favor of the Director, the Appellate Division, whose decision the majority now affirms, stated that the trial court, although using the correct standards, had "failed to appreciate the minimum showing that a taxing district such as New Jersey would have to make as to the activities that would provide a basis for income taxation." 193 N.J.Super. at 507, 475 A.2d 66. The court emphasized that the internal regulation of the credit market and the regulation of certain commercial items, such as installment paper, could all be used as a basis for taxation. Id. at 512, 475 A.2d 66.

In underscoring the adequacy, for taxing purposes, of a "minimum" showing, the Appellate Division apparently overlooked the Supreme Court's decision in National Geographic v. California Bd. of Equalization, 430 U.S. 551, 97 S.Ct. 1386, 51 L.Ed.2d 631 (1977). Although the majority does not ignore the case, it does maul it a bit by applying its principle to the facts before us. In *National Geographic* the State of California sought to levy a use tax on a non-domiciliary corporation that maintained two offices within the taxing jurisdiction. In sustaining the tax, the California Supreme Court suggested that "the slightest presence within such taxing state" could form the basis of taxation. Id. at 556, 97 S.Ct. at 1390, 51 L.Ed.2d at 637. Although the United States Supreme Court affirmed the taxpayer's liability, the Court was careful to state:

> Our affirmance of the California Supreme Court is not to be understood as implying agreement with that court's "slightest presence" standard of constitutional nexus. [The taxpayer's] maintenance of two offices in the State and solicitation by employees assigned to those offices of advertising copy in the range of $1 million annually * * * establish a much more substantial presence that the expression "slightest presence" connotes.
>
> [Id.]

Thus, the Court relied on the physical location of the taxpayers' two offices as a basis for sustaining the tax.

The majority's labored reference to *National Geographic* and Scripto, Inc. v. Carson, supra, 362 U.S. 207, 80 S.Ct. 619, 4 L.Ed.2d 660, attests to the difficult position in which those cases put the Court—sort of *a fronte praecipitium a tergo lupi* (roughly, between a rock and a hard place). Surely they lend no support for the majority's astonishing position that in the absence of such factors as an in-state office, in-state representatives, in-state property holdings, or, at the very least, in-state solicitation, a taxpayer may nevertheless be subject to taxation. The Supreme Court's reliance, in *National Geographic,* on *Scripto,* makes the point, unmistakably: *even though* the taxpayer in *Scripto* had no office or place of business or property or regular full-time employees in Florida, it nevertheless was subject to Florida tax because of its other activities there, namely, (1) maintenance of ten wholesalers, jobbers, or salesmen (2) continuously soliciting orders in Florida and (3) forwarding those orders from Florida to the taxpayer's home base in Georgia for (4) shipment back to Florida—quite a different picture from that painted by this Court. Focusing on Scripto's ten "wholesalers, salesmen, and jobbers who were active in Florida," *ante* at 795, the majority dismisses their numbers as unimportant but attaches surpassing significance to the fact that even though "*none* was an employee" of the taxpayer, the foreign corporation was nevertheless subject to tax.

Come now. The contractual relationship between Scripto and its salesmen in Florida is a matter of complete indifference to the holding of the case. It is what that horde of salesmen did that counts. The critical point, again, is that Scripto maintained in Florida its resident brokers who descended, much as a swarm of locusts, on prospective customers for the purpose of actively engaging in "attracting, soliciting and obtaining" business. 362 U.S. at 209, 80 S.Ct. at 621, 4 L.Ed.2d at 663. The test, as the Supreme Court sensibly observed, is "simply the nature and extent of the activities of the [taxpayer]" in the taxing state, id. at 211–12, 80 S.Ct. at 622, 4 L.Ed.2d at 664, rather than who performed those activities on behalf of the taxpayer. And Scripto's activities, as I have endeavored to demonstrate, bear little resemblance to Avco's. The two cases illustrate the difference between a "substantial presence" and "the slightest presence"—a difference significant enough to call for the tax in one instance and not the other.

Contrary to the majority's suggestion, I have drawn attention to *Scripto* again not in the spirit of chiding, see ante at 795 so much as of depression, even sheer, miserable frustration, that the Court and I can ascribe to the simple language of that case such diametrically different meanings. Clearly, the five in the majority are wrong, or I am. The numbers favor them, so I must leave it with the careful reader of these opinions and of the authorities on which we rely.

It is my view that the tax against Avco ought to be invalidated. At best, the taxpayer maintains only the "slightest presence" in New Jersey, a standard of constitutional nexus specifically and emphatically rejected by the Supreme Court but nevertheless adopted today by this Court. I would therefore reverse the judgment of the Appellate Division and reinstate the judgment of the trial court.

For affirmance—CHIEF JUSTICE WILENTZ, and JUSTICES HANDLER, POLLOCK and O'HERN—4.

For reversal—JUSTICE CLIFFORD—1.

AMERICAN REFRIGERATOR TRANSIT CO. v. STATE TAX COMMISSION

Supreme Court of Oregon, 1964.
238 Or. 340, 395 P.2d 127.

O'CONNELL, JUSTICE. This is an appeal from a decree of the Oregon Tax Court setting aside defendant's order requiring plaintiff to pay the Oregon corporate income tax for the calendar years 1955 through 1960. The following statement of facts is adopted from the opinion of the Oregon Tax Court.

Plaintiff (hereafter referred to as "ART") owns refrigerator cars which it leases to operating railroads. "It is not a public carrier, it issues no bills of lading, it has no dealings with shippers, and it publishes no tariffs of rates for shippers. ART'S sole activity in the transportation field is to rent railroad refrigerator cars to operating railroads for their use in performing their own transportation service for their own shippers under their own tariffs and shipping documents.

"ART has no rental agreement with railroads operating in Oregon. However, under the interchange procedures applicable to railroads today, some of its cars are interchanged onto railroads operating in Oregon and thereby do travel to, into, and through Oregon. Under its rental contracts and the interchange rules, a railroad using an ART car pays a fixed rate per mile of its use. Monthly, each using railroad reports to ART the mileage traveled by each car used by it. These reports and the rental payments are sent directly to St. Louis. Light or running repairs on ART cars are made by the using railroad, and some such repairs are made in Oregon by railroads serving this state which have the use of cars under interchange arrangements with ART'S lessees. All other repairs are made outside of Oregon.

"ART cars are delivered to the contracting railroads at certain junction points, none of which is in Oregon, and thereafter, until the cars are returned to ART at a junction point, ART has no control over their routing, movement, interchange or other use. The cars are used as are any other cars of the using railroad.

"ART files with the commission all required property tax reports and pays Oregon property tax upon its cars in Oregon as a centrally assessed utility pursuant to ORS 308.505 et seq."

The tax was imposed under ORS 318.020, which provides as follows:

"(1) There hereby is imposed upon every corporation for each taxable year a tax at the rate of eight percent upon its net income derived from sources within this state after August 3, 1955, other than income for which the corporation is subject to the tax imposed by the Corporation Excise Tax Law of 1929 (ORS chapter 317) according to or measured by its net income. For tax years beginning on and after January 1, 1957, the tax rate shall be six percent.

"(2) Income from sources within this state includes income from tangible or intangible property located or having a situs in this state and income from any activities carried on in this state, regardless of whether carried on in intrastate, interstate or foreign commerce."

Defendant assessed the tax upon the ground that the income received by plaintiff for the mileage its cars travel in Oregon is "income from tangible * * * property located or having a situs in this state" and is, therefore, "income derived from sources within this state" under ORS 318.020.

Plaintiff contends that ORS 318.020 does not apply because it has no property "located or having a situs" in Oregon, and does not carry on any activity in this state. Plaintiff further contends that if ORS 318.020 was intended to apply to its property the statute would violate the due process clause of the Fourteenth Amendment. In short, plaintiff argues that there is no nexus between the tax and the transactions within Oregon for which the tax is an exaction. The Oregon Tax Court concluded that the required nexus was lacking. The court's reasoning was as follows:

"A review of the cases brings forth, from those cases in which sufficient nexus has been found, the presence of one salient and determinative feature which is not found in this case. In each of those cases finding sufficient nexus, there was, within the borders of the taxing state, a person or persons connected with and engaged in business activities and transactions on behalf of, the proposed taxpayer. In the instant case there is no such person or activity in Oregon. * * * Thus the required nexus between tax and transaction fails for want of one of the elements which due process requires.

* * * The mere presence of ART'S property here on January 1 subjects it to property tax, which it pays. However, liability for property tax does not create, *ipso facto*, liability for income tax.

"The benefits conferred by the state in return for the property tax are not sufficient to support income tax liability.

" ' * * * The tax on each [on property and on income] is predicated upon different governmental benefits; the protection offered to the property in one state does not extend to the receipt and enjoyment of income from it in another.' New York ex rel. Cohn v. Graves, 300 U.S. 308, 314, 57 S.Ct. 466, 81 L.Ed. 666, 671, 108 A.L.R. 721, 724 (1937).

* * * Thus, the sending of solicitors, sales engineers, and other personnel into a state to solicit or otherwise further the acquisition of income creates a sufficient nexus to render the income which they create or further by their activity taxable under proper allocation procedures, because the state protects these agents of the taxpayer and creates and maintains conditions under which an income-producing relationship can be established or fostered. But after the income-

producing relationship has been established by the consummation of a lease and the transitory property which is the subject of the transaction has been delivered to the lessee, all outside of the taxing state, the mere receipt of income from the lease of that transitory personal property during the time that it is brought into the taxing state by the bailee of its lessee, in the course of the business of this bailee, under an arrangement for the interchange of railroad cars with the lessee, does not create that nexus upon which state income taxation of the nonresident lessor can be constitutionally based. There is nothing that this state does or provides which has a connection with that income as such and for which it can exact its tax, especially having already exacted its property tax for the protection of the plaintiff's income-producing property."

We cannot accept the lower court's concept of nexus necessary to sustain the constitutionality of the tax imposed upon plaintiff. We do not regard it as essential to the existence of a nexus that the taxpayer, through its agents, *directly* engage in some form of physical activity within the state in furtherance of a business purpose. The connection between the taxing state and the out-of-state taxpayer necessary to establish nexus is essentially an economic rather than a physical relationship. * * *

The nexus exists whenever the corporation takes advantage of the economic milieu within the state to realize a profit. The state is entitled to tax if the benefits it provides are a substantial economic factor in the production of the taxpayer's income. These benefits are found in the maintenance of conditions essential to the production or marketing of goods. They may be realized simply in the protection of the taxpayer's property used in the production of income.

We do not mean to say that nexus exists in every case where Oregon's economy can be said to have contributed to the production of income. Income, no matter where received, ordinarily is the product of economic influences operating from many sources, some far back in the chain of economic cause and effect. To establish nexus it is necessary to show that the taxpayer has, in the conduct of his business, taken advantage of the economy of the taxing state to produce the income which is subjected to tax. This is readily seen where, as in the instant case, the taxpayer's property itself is employed in the taxing state to produce income. Nexus may be found even where neither property nor personnel of the taxpayer is employed within the taxing state if it can be said that the state substantially contributes to the production of the taxpayer's income. Thus, apart from federal legislation,[1] it would seem to us that income derived from the sale of goods in Oregon by a non-resident corporation relying entirely upon radio or television advertising would be taxable in this state.[2]

1. Such as Pub.L. 86–272, 73 Stat. 555 (1959) which prohibits the imposition of an income tax upon sellers of tangible personal property whose only business activity within the taxing state consists of the solicitation of orders.

2. " * * * Should not the exploitation of a state's markets for the capture of

Refrigerator cars are used to ship perishables from Oregon to markets in other states and to bring perishables to the markets in this state. If plaintiff itself carried on the business of moving perishables in and out of Oregon, it would be clear that the profit earned by it would be subject to the corporate income tax. Where plaintiff does not directly engage in the business of transporting the goods, but reaps its profit from the use of its equipment by others, although the rental for its equipment cannot be deemed "income from [an activity] carried on in this state" (ORS 318.020), nevertheless the source of its profit in the economic setting in Oregon is clear and it is equally clear that the income is derived from plaintiff's property which is used in this state and to that extent is "located" here. The fact that plaintiff's cars are operated by plaintiff's lessees (or their bailees) rather than by plaintiff's own agents is not significant. Whether the income derived from property located in a state comes to the owner indirectly in the form of rent under a lease or directly in the form of income from its own use of its property, the source of the income is the same, and it is the taxing state that has provided the source by providing and maintaining the economic setting out of which the owner reaps its profit. This is the basis for the decision in Warner Bros. Pictures v. District of Columbia, 83 U.S.App.D.C. 158, 168 F.2d 157 (1948) where it was held that a non-resident lessor of films was taxable on the rentals received from its lessee within the District of Columbia which assessed the tax. The court said "the sums received by Warner [the non-resident owner] came from District sources because the location of personal property which is the subject of hire betrays the source of the owner's income derived from the hire." (168 F.2d at 159).

Plaintiff has regularly paid a property tax to Oregon on the assumption that its cars are located or have a situs in this state for property tax purposes. Plaintiff argues, however, that situs for property tax purposes does not establish situs for income tax purposes. The lower court took the same view upon the ground that "the benefit conferred by the state with respect to income taxation is not the same protection of the income-producing property for which the property tax is exacted, but rather is the protection of the receipt and enjoyment of income or the maintenance of conditions under which the acquisition of that income can be accomplished or materially furthered." We do not

profits be enough for that state to demand something in return, thus satisfying the requisites of the due process clause? Several hundred traveling salesmen, no matter how avidly they hawk their wares, are not nearly as effective a 'nexus' for an exploitation or invasion of a consumer market as a Dinah Shore or a Pat Boone as they croon their sponsor's products into the hands of thousands of purchasers on interstate television and radio. Is the state of market to be denied a tax from either the out-of-state seller or the broad-casting company because the contacts of such out-of-state sellers and broadcasters are ethereal only? Or, should a well known milk company be permitted to milk the consumer market with the sonorous singing of ballads by hillfolk and western singers without paying its tithe to the state of market on the ground that the interstate radio and television milking process is too ethereal?" Hartman, State Taxation of Corporate Income from a Multistate Business, 13 Vanderbilt L.Rev. 21, 43 (1959).

believe that the lower court's distinction is sound. Both the income tax and the property tax may be exacted from the same taxpayer for the same form of a "protection." For example, the property tax may be justified upon the ground that property receives police protection from local government and the income tax may be justified on the ground that the property receives police protection from the state government.

Adopting the language of the lower court, it could be said that the state's police protection is in part "the maintenance of conditions under which the acquisition of that income can be accomplished or materially furthered," assuming, of course, it can be shown that the owner derives income from the protected property.

We hold that the plaintiff's cars had a "situs" in Oregon within the meaning of ORS 318.020 and that since the cars were used in the exploitation of the market in Oregon from which plaintiff derived income through its rental of the cars, there was a sufficient nexus to satisfy the due process requirement of the Fourteenth Amendment.

There is support for our position in at least two states.[3] A contrary view is indicated in several cases.[4] The question before us has not yet been passed upon by the United States Supreme Court. It is now firmly established that a state may tax the net income of a corporation engaged exclusively in interstate commerce.[5] We would expect the United States Supreme Court to hold, as we do, that due process nexus is established even though the taxpayer has no offices or agents within the taxing state if it could be shown that Oregon's economy was a substantial economic factor in the production of the taxpayer's income subject to tax.[6]

The decree of the lower court is reversed.

3. Commissioner of Revenues v. Pacific Fruit Express Co., 227 Ark. 8, 296 S.W.2d 676 (1957); Oklahoma Tax Com'n v. American Refrigerator Tr. Co., 349 P.2d 746 (Okl.1960). Comment, 11 Vanderbilt L.Rev. 257 (1957).

4. Williams v. American Refrigerator Transit Co., 91 Ga.App. 522, 86 S.E.2d 336 (1955); Kentucky Tax Com'n v. American Refrigerator Transit Co., 294 S.W.2d 554 (Ky.1956).

5. Northwestern States Portland Cement Co. v. Minnesota, 358 U.S. 450, 79 S.Ct. 357, 3 L.Ed.2d 421, 67 A.L.R.2d 1292 (1959) (net income from manufacture and sale of goods). Certiorari has been denied in cases where the activity carried on by the taxpayer in the taxing state was of relatively slight significance in the production of income. In Brown Forman Distillers Corp. v. Collector of Revenue, 234 La. 651, 101 So.2d 70 (1958) the taxpayer's only activity in the taxing state was the maintenance of representatives to receive orders and the presence of certain promotional representatives. In International Shoe Co. v. Fontenot, 236 La. 279, 107 So.2d 640 (1959) the taxpayer's activity consisted of the regular and systematic solicitation of orders for its product by fifteen salesmen. In both cases, the Louisiana Supreme Court held that there was no undue burden on interstate commerce and no violation of the Fourteenth Amendment.

6. " * * * The * * * controlling question is whether the state has given anything for which it can ask return." Wisconsin v. J.C. Penney Co., 311 U.S. 435, 444, 61 S.Ct. 246, 250, 85 L.Ed. 267 (1949).

" * * * It is probable, however, that the maintenance of an office is not necessary in order to provide due process and that an apportioned tax on the net income of a corporation which sends only drummers into the state will be held valid, applying the principles of International Shoe Co. v. Washington, [326 U.S. 310, 66 S.Ct. 154, 90 L.Ed. 95, 161 A.L.R. 1057 (1945)]." Note, 47 Calif.L.Rev. 388 at 392 (1959).

Notes and Problems

A. The court's statement as to the power of the States to impose income taxes on out-of-state enterprises deriving income from the State is one of the most sweeping statements in the books.

> Nexus may be found even where neither property nor personnel of the taxpayer is employed within the taxing state if it can be said that the state substantially contributes to the production of the taxpayer's income. Thus, apart from federal legislation, it would seem to us that income derived from the sale of goods in Oregon by a non-resident corporation relying entirely upon radio or television advertising would be taxable in this state.

In National Bellas Hess, Inc. v. Department of Revenue, 386 U.S. 753, 87 S.Ct. 1389 (1967), set out in Chapter 10, pp. 812–20 infra, the Court, in delineating restraints on a State's jurisdiction to impose a use tax collection duty on an out-of-state vendor, held that a State may not impose such a duty on a vendor whose only connection with customers in the State is by common carrier or the United States mail. This was so notwithstanding more than $2 million in sales to in-state customers over a 15–month period. Can the Oregon court's approach to due process nexus requirements in income taxation be reconciled with the Supreme Court's views as expressed in *National Bellas Hess?* See p. 825 infra where the *National Bellas Hess* case and the controversy as to whether the decision rests on the Commerce Clause, and not the Due Process Clause, are treated.

B. As noted in the *American Refrigerator Transit* opinion, the courts of Kentucky and Georgia have held that their States' income tax statutes did not reach the taxpayer involved in the Oregon case. See note 4 of the opinion. In the Kentucky case, the court found that the contract for the lease of the taxpayer's refrigerated cars was the source of its income and that the income had "no relation to a subject within the taxing government," despite the fact that the statute taxed all income "derived from * * * property located" in the State. In the Georgia case, the court found that the taxpayer was not doing business in Georgia and that, without any business income in the State, there could be no apportionment for tax purposes.

While the taxpayer-lessor avoided taxation in Kentucky and Georgia, the implications of the holdings in those cases may have repercussions on taxation by the State in which the taxpayer maintains its principal office. This result is illustrated by the decision in Commission v. Truck Rental Co., Pa.Com.Pl. (Dauphin Co. 1956), CCH ¶ 200–074, P–H ¶ 10,834.12, in which a Pennsylvania corporation maintaining its only offices in that State was engaged in leasing trucks for use by its lessees in various States. The leases were executed in Pennsylvania and all rentals were received in that State. In applying the receipts factor of the State's three-factor formula under the Pennsylvania net income tax, the corporation sought to exclude from Pennsylvania receipts rentals for out-of-state use of its trucks. The court rejected this contention, holding that the taxpayer was not entitled to any out-of-state apportionment because it conducted all its business in Pennsylvania. The rule that a taxpayer is not entitled to apportion or allocate its income or receipts unless it does business or maintains a bona fide office in another State is embodied in many statutes. See Chapter 9, subd. C, § 1 infra, and see, e.g., L.C.L. Corp. v. State Tax Commission, 8 A.D.2d 658, 184 N.Y.S.2d 940 (3d Dept.1959), in which a lessor to railroads of shipping containers used on freight cars by shippers in many States was denied any out-of-state apportionment under the New York franchise tax because it failed to satisfy the statutory condition precedent to such apportionment, i.e., the maintenance of a bona fide place of business outside the taxing State.

(a) The Challenge by the States to the Physical Presence Requirement of Jurisdiction to Tax

As the *AVCO* and *American Refrigerator* cases reveal, increasingly the states are pressing jurisdiction to tax out-of-state enterprises beyond the physical presence rule. They argue that radical changes have taken place in the methods of marketing goods and services in this country that no longer make physical presence in a State an acceptable requirement for jurisdiction to tax.

(i) *The insurance premium tax cases.* A number of cases have been decided that deal with the constitutionality of insurance premiums taxes in which the insurer had less than the usual presence required for taxation of out-of-state vendors of other products or services. Because they shed some light on the current challenges being made by the States to the physical presence requirement for taxation of non-insurers, those cases are here summarized.

In Ministers Life and Casualty Union v. Haase, 30 Wis.2d 339, 141 N.W.2d 287, appeal dismissed 385 U.S. 205, 87 S.Ct. 407 (1966), an insurance company organized in Minnesota and conducting a mail order business in life, accident, and health insurance, brought a declaratory judgment suit attacking the constitutionality of the Wisconsin comprehensive insurance regulatory and tax law. The statute imposed a three percent tax on the premiums of insurance business done in the State by unauthorized insurers, as compared with a two percent tax on authorized insurers, with secondary liability for the tax (with some exceptions) on the insured. The company had no soliciting agents in Wisconsin; it solicited business by mail and advertisements in national church and other religious publications. In the case of individual policies, upon receiving an inquiry at its home office in Minneapolis, Ministers mailed an application to the prospect who filled it out and mailed it back to Ministers. This application was usually accompanied by the first premium. The policy was prepared, signed, and mailed to the applicant from its home office. Under its articles of incorporation, a person became a member of Ministers upon delivery and acceptance of the policy and the applicant was given an opportunity to examine the policy upon its receipt; if unsatisfactory, he could reject it and mail it back and his premium would be refunded. All the mailing of notices of premium and other mailing was done at the home office of Ministers and all premiums were payable and received there. Medical reports were obtained, where necessary, from local doctors who were paid by Ministers.

In selling group-life, accident or health policies, a leader was selected by the group and he or she negotiated with Ministers by mail, received literature and forms, and enrolled members. Premium notices were sent by the company to the group leader who collected the premiums and remitted them to the company. No compensation was paid to the group leader. Claims for accidental death occurring during the contestable period were investigated for the company by a national investigative agency. All claims were paid by the company's home office on proof of claim forms furnished by the company.

In the mid-nineteenth century case of Paul v. Virginia, 75 U.S. (8 Wall.) 168 (1869), insurance was held not to constitute "commerce"; as a consequence, out-of-state insurance companies had no Commerce Clause protection against State taxation. See Chapter 6, subd. C, § 1 supra. After the Supreme Court held in 1944 that insurance is inter-state commerce and is subject to Congressional regulation, Congress adopted the McCarran Act, which reestablished the power of the States to tax insurers without reference to the Commerce Clause. The Due Process Clause remained, however, as a constitutional barrier to State taxation.

Subsequent to the adoption of the McCarran Act, the Supreme Court was faced in State Bd. of Ins. v. Todd Shipyards, 370 U.S. 451, 82 S.Ct. 1380 (1962), with the question whether the Due Process Clause precluded Texas from taxing the insured on premiums paid to insurers who were not licensed to do business in Texas, where the "only connection between Texas and the insurance transactions is the fact that the property covered by the insurance is physically located in Texas." There, the entire transaction leading to, and the issuance of the insurance, had been handled outside the taxing State; the insurer did not solicit business in Texas, it had no employees, agents or place of business in the State; the adjustment and payment of losses took place outside the State. The Court held that the tax was repugnant to the Due Process Clause, and, relying on the Congressional Committee Report accompanying the McCarran Act, which stated that the legisla-tion was not intended to abrogate the limitations set out in three specifically cited earlier decisions dealing with the Due Process issue, it found that *Todd Shipyards* fitted neatly into those cases.

The Wisconsin court distinguished the *Todd Shipyards* case, and sustained the tax on the ground that:

> Here, we have a systematic solicitation of insurance by mail, not sporadic but continuous, and in addition, group leader's solicitations. We need not consider group leaders as agents but even Ministers should admit they are significant contacts which were encouraged to work for Ministers' benefit and which were relied upon as a method of doing business. Besides, Ministers utilizes the necessary services of investigatory agencies and doctors in the state for underwriting and

claim-settlement purposes, carefully avoiding designating them agents but securing the same results. Ministers has "realistically entered the state looking for and obtaining business." [141 N.W.2d at 295.] [9]

The New Jersey Supreme Court sustained a premium tax in a case in which the out-of-state insurer did not engage in solicitation, even by mail order, of insurance in the State. In Howell v. Rosecliff Realty Co., 52 N.J. 313, 245 A.2d 318 (1968), an action was brought by the Commissioner of Banking and Insurance to collect the New Jersey three percent tax in insurance premiums paid to underwriters of New Jersey risks. Rosecliff, a New Jersey corporation with its principal place of business at Fort Lee, New Jersey, owned and operated Palisades Amusement Park in New Jersey; the insurance risks at issue related to the ownership of the property covering the amusement park and the operation of the business at the park, including public and garage keeper's liability, fire and extended coverage, burglary, theft, and employee security.

The insurers were all of London, and were unauthorized to write insurance on New Jersey risks (except in limited circumstances not here relevant to issue certain insurance through a "licensed surplus agent"); they maintained no offices, employees, or property in the State. The contracts of insurance on which the tax was levied were negotiated in New York City, through a New York broker, and the premiums were paid in New York by Rosecliff's check on a New York bank.

When a loss occurred, other than in the case of public liability, Rosecliff notified the broker at the latter's New York City office, who, in turn, informed the insurer; the latter then assigned an adjuster to the loss. The only major claim of any kind during the year at issue grew out of a fire at Fun House. The adjuster assigned by the insurer was an independent contractor, located in New York, who went to the amusement park to inspect the damage with the broker. Thereafter, negotiations with the adjuster followed in New York City, with the broker and a New York accountant retained by Rosecliff acting for the company. The loss, when finally determined, was paid in New York to Rosecliff's broker by check on a New York bank; the broker then issued its check to Rosecliff (presumably by mail from New York to Fort Lee, but this fact was not stated). The same procedure as to payment was followed when minor losses occurred.

9. The California Supreme Court reached a similar conclusion in affirming the power of the California Insurance Commission to debar a mail order insurer from soliciting insurance in the State without a license and attendant regulation by the Commission. People v. United Nat. Life Ins. Co., 66 Cal.2d 577, 58 Cal.Rptr. 599, 427 P.2d 199, appeal dismissed 389 U.S. 330, 88 S.Ct. 506 (1967). The operation of United National did not involve the utilization of group leaders as was true in the case of Ministers Life. See also Illinois Commercial Men's Ass'n v. State Bd. of Equalization, 34 Cal.3d 839, 671 P.2d 349, 196 Cal.Rptr. 198 (1983), appeal dismissed 466 U.S. 933, 104 S.Ct. 1901 (1984), in which the California Supreme Court sustained a gross premiums tax on an out-of-state insurer that solicited business by mail from outside the State, but utilized independent contractors to perform functions incident to the administration of claims.

To deal with accidents occurring at the amusement park, Rosecliff maintained a register of each occurrence, in which it recorded relevant information. During the park season, a representative of the adjustment firm designated by the insurer, an independent contractor located in New York, visited the park at least once or twice a week, and copied the information set out in the register. The adjuster visited or telephoned the victim of the accident at his home, and he, of course, was frequently a New Jersey resident. Many claims were settled by the adjuster directly with the claimant, some at the latter's home in New Jersey, and, in those cases, releases could be executed by the claimant at his home. Where a lawyer represented the claimant, Rosecliff turned all "lawyer letters" over to the adjuster, and the adjuster picked up the dealings with counsel. When litigation ensued, the insurer undertook the defense of the case, through attorneys who were ordinarily New Jersey lawyers; and the legal proceedings took place in that State. Public liability accounted for the largest part of the premiums at issue—approximately $100,000.

Chief Justice Weintraub, one of the most highly regarded State Supreme Court judges in the country while he was on the bench, writing for the New Jersey Supreme Court, reviewed the facts relating to the public liability policy and said:

> The insurers are obliged to investigate, to settle, to defend, and to pay. The stipulation of facts * * * reveals intensive activity in that regard. It is no answer to say, as Rosecliff does, that the insurers engage 'independent contractors' to perform contracts for them; the fact remains that the obligation is the insurers' to perform, and it is irrelevant to the subject of taxation whether they perform through employees or through individuals who, as to the insurers, have the status of contractors. [245 A.2d at 325.]

The other policies involved no such extensive activity on the insurer's part, but the court noted that the adjuster came to the amusement park in connection with the fire loss, a practice which it observed would be normal, and concluded that "such acts within the State would themselves be enough to support the tax." Chief Justice Weintraub concluded:

> * * * Rosecliff is a New Jersey corporation, earns in this State the money with which it pays the premiums, draws its premium checks here, and * * * realistically, the policies are an integral part of the total business operation conducted in this State alone. [Id. at 326.]

Suppose Congress had not waived the Commerce Clause protection of multistate insurance companies. Would the premium taxes in the cases discussed above have been invalidated? Cf. the above noted *National Bellas Hess* use tax collection case, Chapter 10, pp. 812–20 infra, as applied to mail order houses. What bearing does the extent of the taxpayer's presence in a State, through people or property, have on the Commerce Clause issues? See J. Hellerstein, "Federal Constitutional Limitations on State Taxation of Multistate Banks," Report of

Study under P.L. 91–156, "State and Local Taxation of Banks," App. 11, prepared by Board of Governors, Federal Reserve System, Senate Committee on Banking, Housing & Urban Affairs (92nd Cong. 1st Sess., 1971); McCray, "Overturning *Bellas Hess:* Due Process Considerations," 1985 B.Y.U.L. Rev. 265; and McCray, "Commerce Clause Sanctions Against Taxation on Mail Order Sales: A Re–Evaluation," 17 Urb.Law. 529 (1985).

(ii) *Licensing of television films to local broadcasters.* In Matter of Heftel Broadcasting Honolulu, Inc., 57 Haw. 175, 554 P.2d 242 (1976), certiorari denied 429 U.S. 1073, 97 S.Ct. 811 (1977), the court held, inter alia, that Hawaii's privilege tax could be applied to foreign corporations that had licensed the use of television films to local broadcasters without violating constitutional nexus requirements, even though the agreed facts disclosed "that *all* activities [including transfer of possession of the films] of the licensors occurred on the mainland." The case is considered in more detail in Section 3 infra.

(iii) In pressing their view that physical presence in a State should no longer be regarded as a sine qua non of jurisdiction to impose an income or franchise tax on a foreign corporation whose activities or operations extend to the State, the States contend that regular, systematic exploitation of a State's market for goods or services, coupled with solicitation of business from customers in the State, ought to be sufficient to satisfy the Due Process Clause.[10] They contend that the radical changes that have taken place in the method of marketing goods and services since the traditional due process State tax principles were established call for an adaptation of those principles to the modern era.

The argument of the States may be illustrated by the story that the father of one of the authors and the grandfather of the other used to tell of solicitation for business in an earlier era. In the 1890's in Denver, he began his jewelry business by peddling jewelry and soliciting watch repairs by riding a bicycle in the outskirts of the city. When he was able to raise the capital, he graduated to a horse and buggy. He obviously did his marketing by his physical presence. As salesmen substituted the automobile, and then the airplane, for the bicycle or horse and buggy, physical presence still remained central to the exploitation of the market.

But all that has changed significantly in recent times. A large part of the solicitation done today in and around Denver, the Rocky Mountain region, and over the country, is carried on without a physical presence. It is done through newspapers, the mails and radio, and more recently the telephone with the great expansion of the use of the

---

10. In some industries, different factors may be relied on. Thus, the States may seek to tax a television station that broadcasts to viewers in neighboring States in which the State maintains no business establishment, property, employees, or agents and does no solicitation for advertising or viewers.

toll-free 800-number telephone call.[11] Most recently and most pervasively of all, marketing is done by television.

Consequently, the markets of the country are now being exploited by solicitation without employees, offices or inventory, or other property in the State. Moreover, the miracle of the electronics age, the computer, frequently makes it unnecessary to maintain local warehouses in many of the States, which was often the key to developing a market in many industries in earlier times. The computer has made possible centralized order taking, centralized warehousing, and centralized order fulfilment.

The question the States are posing is whether the physical presence jurisdictional requirement is still viable in this era of high technology, or whether it should be regarded as a relic of the bicycle, horse and buggy, and automobile eras of solicitation. Should we instead recognize as alternative bases for jurisdiction to tax the regular exploitation of a State's market by mail, newspaper, telephone, or telecommunication?

P.L. 86–272 prohibits the State from taxing out-of-state sellers of tangible personal property, who have no physical presence in the State and whose activities do not exceed the statutory minimum. See Section 2 infra. However, there are many industries not covered by P.L. 86–272, in which jurisdiction to tax without the traditional physical presence is very much an issue among the States. That includes consumer loan companies, banks and other financial institutions that make regular, recurring loans in States in which they have no physical presence, out-of-state radio and television stations whose broadcasts regularly reach a listening audience in the State, brokerage and investment businesses, computer and other service centers, franchisers, and a whole host of other businesses.

SECTION 2. CONGRESSIONAL ACTION RESTRICTING THE POWER OF STATE TAXATION OF INTERSTATE BUSINESSES. PUBLIC LAW 86–272

In Chapter 6, materials relating to the power of Congress to broaden and restrict State taxation under the Commerce Clause are set out. See pp. 326–31 supra. This section is devoted to the most important piece of legislation that Congress has enacted limiting the States' power to tax interstate business—Public Law 86–272.

The *Northwestern Portland Cement* and *Stockham Valves* cases, Ch. 6, pp. 229–46 supra, produced widespread alarm and protest among businesses. The most dire consequences to business and, indeed, the entire nation were predicted. Two Senate Committees promptly held

---

11. See Yarrow, "The Revolution Wrought by Toll–Free Calls," New York Times, Feb. 12, 1987, p. C1, in which it is stated:

  Four billion toll-free calls, worth $4 billion in revenues to A.T. & T., were answered last year by an invisible army of

far-flung phone operators. Last year's total accounted for about 20 percent of all long-distance calls and one-eighth of long-distance revenues in the United States.

There were 400,000 800 numbers in use.

hearings, and there was vociferous demand for immediate Congressional action. Congress reacted with astonishing speed and for the first time in its history adopted an act restricting the power of the States to tax interstate businesses.[12]

PUBLIC LAW 86–272, 73 STAT. 555

Title I—Imposition of Minimum Standard

Sec. 101. (a) No State, or political subdivision thereof, shall have power to impose, for any taxable year ending after the date of the enactment of this Act, a net income tax on the income derived within such State by any person from interstate commerce if the only business activities within such State by or on behalf of such person during such taxable year are either, or both, of the following:

(1) the solicitation of orders by such person, or his representative, in such State for sales of tangible personal property, which orders are sent outside the State for approval or rejection, and, if approved, are filled by shipment or delivery from a point outside the State; and

(2) the solicitation of orders by such person, or his representative, in such State in the name of or for the benefit of a prospective customer of such person, if orders by such customer to such person to enable such customer to fill orders resulting from such solicitation are orders described in paragraph (1).

(b) The provisions of subsection (a) shall not apply to the imposition of a net income tax by any State, or political subdivision thereof, with respect to—

(1) any corporation which is incorporated under the laws of such State; or

(2) any individual who, under the laws of such State, is domiciled in, or a resident of, such State.

(c) For purposes of subsection (a), a person shall not be considered to have engaged in business activities within a State during any taxable year merely by reason of sales in such State, or the solicitation of orders for sales in such State, of tangible personal property on behalf of such person by one or more independent contractors, or by reason of the maintenance of an office in such State by one or more independent contractors whose activities on behalf of such person in such State consist solely of making sales, or soliciting orders for sales, of tangible personal property.

---

12. P.L. 86–272 (1959), 73 Stat. 555, 15 U.S.C.A. § 381. See Hearings Before Select Committee on Small Business of United States Senate (86th Cong. 1st Sess., April–May 1959), "State Taxation of Interstate Income," and S.Rep. No. 453 id.; Hearings Before Committee on Finance of United States Senate, "State Taxation of Interstate Commerce" (86th Cong. 1st Sess.) on S.J.Res. 113, S. 2213 and 2281 (July 1959) and S.Rep. No. 658.

These hearings contain valuable background materials as well as extensive statements of the conflicting views of businessmen and State tax administrators.

(d) For purposes of this section—

(1) the term "independent contractor" means a commission agent, broker, or other independent contractor who is engaged in selling, or soliciting orders for the sale of, tangible personal property for more than one principal and who holds himself out as such in the regular course of his business activities; and

(2) the term "representative" does not include an independent contractor.

Sec. 102. (a) No State, or political subdivision thereof, shall have power to assess, after the date of the enactment of this Act, any net income tax which was imposed by such State or political subdivision, as the case may be, for any taxable year ending on or before such date, on the income derived within such State by any person from interstate commerce, if the imposition of such tax for a taxable year ending after such date is prohibited by section 101.

(b) The provisions of subsection (a) shall not be construed—

(1) to invalidate the collection, on or before the date of the enactment of this Act, of any net income tax imposed for a taxable year ending on or before such date, or

(2) to prohibit the collection, after the date of the enactment of this Act, of any net income tax which was assessed on or before such date for a taxable year ending on or before such date.

Sec. 103. For purposes of this title, the term "net income tax" means any tax imposed on, or measured by, net income.

Sec. 104. If any provision of this title or the application of such provision to any person or circumstance is held invalid, the remainder of this title or the application of such provision to persons or circumstances other than those to which it is held invalid, shall not be affected thereby.

[Title II provides for the making by the Committee on the Judiciary of the House and the Committee on Finance of the Senate of "full and complete studies of all matters pertaining to the taxation by the States of income derived within the States from the conduct of business activities which are exclusively in furtherance of interstate commerce or which are a part of interstate commerce, for the purpose of recommending to the Congress proposed legislation providing uniform standards to be observed by the States in imposing income taxes on income so derived."]

(a) Constitutionality of Public Law 86–272

The constitutionality of Public Law 86–272 is considered in Chapter 6, Subd. C, § 2 supra.

(b) Analysis of Public Law 86–272

The legislation denies to the States the power to impose taxes on or measured by net income derived within the State from interstate commerce if the "only business activities carried on within the State" are the solicitation of orders for sales of tangible personal property, where the orders are sent outside the State for approval or rejection and are filled by shipment or delivery from a point outside the State.

The legislation is carefully circumscribed and is limited to:

(1) *Selling tangible personal property.* The statute appears to exclude from its immunity airlines, railroads, pipelines, trucking, bus and other aspects of the transportation industry, and radio and television. Many questions arise in the penumbral area between sales and services. Is the sale of machines which the vendor installs in the State a sale or a sale and installation service? And does the installation activity, whether or not a service, take the case outside the minimum standards of immunity? Or will the courts develop a rule of ignoring incidental minor services? If so, nice lines may be drawn between "incidental installation" and extensive installation, such as the erection of the steel framework of a building out of girders fabricated outside the State.

(2) *Solicitation and related activities.* Solicitation of orders is an immune activity under the statute. The statute does not, however, grant explicit immunity to collecting any part of the purchase price from the customer. Controversy as to the scope of solicitation has produced extensive litigation. Suppose the door-to-door canvasser, as is often the case, collects a deposit from the customer. Does this mean the immunity will be lost? Unless there is immunity for activities incidental to solicitation to cover such deposits, or the handling of complaints, checking on credit, and so forth, any one of these activities may produce taxability. Some courts have developed a rule that normal incidental activities of solicitation are immune from tax.

(3) *Local warehousing.* Local warehousing and delivery of goods out of a local warehouse are clearly beyond the pale of the minimum standards set up for immunity. Instead, shipment must be made from a point outside the State. Presumably, the protected area includes not only delivery by common carrier or the post office, but also by the vendor's trucks, for the test appears to be the point of origin of the shipment. Query, however, as to delivery by the vendor to the local salesman for him to make delivery to the customer. Does this constitute a continuous shipment from outside the State to the customer, or is it a local delivery not protected by the statute?

(4) *Sales office.* The legislative history of the statute leaves little doubt that the maintenance of a sales office within the State designed to serve local solicitors takes the taxpayer outside the area of immunity from taxation, although some commentators have raised questions as to whether the language of the statute accomplishes that result. This means that both Northwestern Portland Cement Co. and Stockham Valves, operating as they did during the years before the Supreme Court decision, are presumably still taxable by Minnesota and Georgia. This restriction raises some perplexing questions. Any kind of office— if the taxpayer more or less permanently maintains an employment office, a purchasing office, a repair shop, a garage or terminal—any

one of these—would appear to be enough to end the statutory immunity. Suppose the out-of-state vendor rents a hotel suite, which the salesman uses for a few days or few weeks on his periodic trips to the State. Does this constitute the maintenance of an office or other activities beyond the immunity granted? It is unlikely that the statute would receive so narrow a construction. But if a local salesman makes his home in effect the business and display office of his out-of-state employer and is in one way or another recompensed for it, it is a little hard to see why such activity should be treated any differently from the company's own directly maintained office in the State.

(5) *Domestic corporations.* The law does not seek to restrict the State's powers to tax either domestic corporations or individuals domiciled in the State.

(6) *Independent sales representatives.* The immunity statute is extended to cover the use of sales representatives, that is, persons who are not employees but are independent contractors soliciting orders or making sales of tangible property for the out-of-state vendor. To qualify, these brokers or independent sales representatives must represent more than one principal and hold themselves out as such sales representatives. Unlike the employee salesman, the independent broker *may complete sales in the State,* that is, at least accept orders; and the maintenance by the independent sales representative of his own sales office will not affect immunity. It is apparent that this difference in treatment between the independent broker-solicitor and the employee solicitor can give rise to all sorts of manipulation to seek to transform employee-salesmen into independent contractors. This is an illustration of the frequently recurring situation in which tax considerations tend to encourage one form of business operation over another— here the independent broker-solicitor, as distinguished from the employee-salesman.

UNITED STATES TOBACCO COMPANY v. COMMONWEALTH OF PENNSYLVANIA

Supreme Court of Pennsylvania, 1978.
478 Pa. 125, 386 A.2d 471, certiorari denied, 439 U.S. 880, 99 S.Ct. 217.

OPINION

MANDERINO, JUSTICE.

This case presents the important question of whether Pennsylvania's Corporation Income Tax can be validly applied to a foreign corporation which is engaged solely in interstate commerce but solicits business in this Commonwealth through the use of field representatives.

The relevant facts are not in dispute. Appellant, United States Tobacco Company, is a New Jersey Corporation engaged in the manufacture and sale of tobacco products. Its products are sold exclusively in interstate commerce, in part to Pennsylvania customers. For the time period in question, appellant had no manufacturing plants in

Pennsylvania, no warehouses or other structures in which inventory was stored, no offices in this state, maintained no bank accounts nor kept any corporate records, and held no corporate meetings in Pennsylvania.

Appellant's sole contact with Pennsylvania is through ten so-called "missionary representatives." These representatives, furnished with company cars, visit independent wholesalers to inform them of company activities and promotions, and sometime take orders for appellant's products. Orders obtained are sent to Greenwich, Connecticut for approval or rejection, and if approved, are filled by shipment from a point outside Pennsylvania. The representatives do not have the authority to accept an order, have no agency powers whatsoever, and no authority to adjust or settle claims, collect accounts receivable, or otherwise handle any money belonging to or due appellant.

These representatives also visit various retail outlets. On these visits, the representatives carry samples of new products. These samples are purchased from wholesalers in Pennsylvania at the wholesale price. If a retailer agrees to purchase those samples, the retailer pays the representative the same price. Hence, no profit is realized on these incidental sales. Representatives also check the retailer's existing inventory of appellant's tobacco products to determine if the products are fresh and attractively displayed. The representatives set up counter displays and sometimes give the retailers free samples of appellant's products in exchange for more extensive counter space. The representatives maintain daily reports of their activities.

These retailers order their products directly from the independent wholesalers who, in turn, send their own orders to appellant's headquarters outside Pennsylvania.

Appellant's solicitation activities were previously the subject of litigation in this Commonwealth, and it was determined that its activities did not create a constitutional taxable nexus, Commonwealth v. United States Tobacco Co., 70 Dauph. 217 (1957). The matter at that time did not reach this Court.

Pursuant to Article V of the Tax Reform Code of 1971, as amended, 72 P.S. §§ 7501–7506 (Supp.1977–78), which imposes on corporations "carrying on activities" in Pennsylvania a tax based on taxable income derived from sources in the Commonwealth, the Commonwealth settled appellant's Corporation Income Tax for the year 1971 in the amount of $70,878.52. On August 13, 1974, the Resettlement Board denied appellant's petition for resettlement. The Board of Finance and Review subsequently sustained the settlement, as did the Commonwealth Court. United States Tobacco Co. v. Commonwealth, 22 Pa.Cmwlth. 211, 348 A.2d 755 (1975). [This decision is cited in the Casebook at p. 355]. Appellant then exercised its right of appeal to this Court. See The Appellate Court Jurisdiction Act of 1970, § 203, 17 P.S. § 211.203 (Supp.1977–78).

Throughout this entire litigation appellant has presented three issues for resolution. Appellant claims (1) that imposing Pennsylvania's Corporation Income Tax against appellant, a foreign corporation engaged solely in the solicitation of orders for sale in interstate commerce, violates federal statutory law exempting such activity from this kind of state taxation; (2) that because of appellant's minimal contacts with Pennsylvania, Pennsylvania's Corporation Income Tax is unconstitutional as applied to appellant; and (3) that if appellant is subject to this state tax, Pennsylvania's "add back" of corporation income tax, after apportioning appellant's income to Pennsylvania activities to determine appellant's ultimate tax liability, is void for want of statutory authority, or alternatively, is unconstitutional because it taxes more of appellant's income than Pennsylvania can legally reach.

We agree with appellant that federal statutory law exempts it from Pennsylvania's Corporation Income Tax, and reverse the order of the Commonwealth Court directing appellant to pay the tax. We therefore need not address appellant's constitutional arguments, nor do we address the issues relating to the computation (add back) of appellant's ultimate tax liability. * * *

[The court next traced the familiar historical background leading up to the Supreme Court's decisions in Northwestern States Portland Cement Co. v. Minnesota and T.V. Williams v. Stockham Valves and Fittings, Inc., pp. 229–46 supra.]

* * *

* * * Section 381 defines the lower limit of a state's taxing power. If a foreign corporation presumptively covered by the Act engages solely in the solicitation of orders, either by soliciting orders for the direct benefit of the foreign corporation (§ 381(a)(1)) or by soliciting orders which benefit an independent customer, wholesaler, or distributor (§ 381(a)(2)), or both, a state may not impose on that out-of-state business any tax based on or measured by net income. 15 U.S.C. § 383 (1970). If the interstate corporation is involved in something more than solicitation, a state may validly tax that portion of the corporation's taxable income attributable to activity within the state. It is undisputed that appellant meets all the other statutory criteria for tax exempt status; thus our decision turns on whether appellant's activities in Pennsylvania are solicitation or something more than solicitation.

This Court has never had occasion to construe § 381, and the United States Supreme Court's only opinion addressed to the statute is uninstructive on the proper interpretation of "solicitation" as it appears in the Act. See Heublein v. South Carolina Tax Comm'n, 409 U.S. 275, 93 S.Ct. 483, 34 L.Ed.2d 472 (1972). In *Heublein,* the taxpayer was required to maintain a local representative in the taxing state in order to comply with state liquor regulations. This representative's functions included contacting local retailers to inform them of new company products. South Carolina law, however, required that shipments of liquor into the state be sent to this representative, who then transferred the shipments to a local wholesaler. The Court did not have to reach the issue of whether the representative's sales activities were limited to solicitation. In its view, the shipment of liquor to the representative, and subsequent transfer to a local wholesaler, "was neither 'solicitation' nor the filling of orders 'by shipment or delivery from a point outside the State' within the meaning of § 381." 409 U.S. at 278–79, 93 S.Ct. at 486, 34 L.Ed.2d at 477.

Opinions from sister states, although by no means uniform in their construction, are helpful in determining whether Congress sought to insulate from state income taxes the type of activity engaged in by appellant. In the most recent state court decision to consider § 381, a New York appellate court, on facts similar to the case before us, held that the foreign corporation was exempt from a New York tax measured by income attributable to New York sales. Gillette Co. v. State Tax Comm'n, 56 A.D.2d 475, 393 N.Y.S.2d 186 (1977) (appeal pending, N.Y.Ct.Appeals *). Gillette had no place of business in New York, did no manufacturing there, had no inventory in New York save for samples carried by its salesmen, and filled all orders from outside the state. Like appellant here, Gillette sold its products to a wholesaler who in turn sold its products to retail chains. The activity which the Tax Commission argued went beyond solicitation involved the interaction between Gillette's representatives and these retailers:

> "[T]he salesman tells the retailer of changes in products and of new promotions in the hope the retailer will order the new or promoted item from the * * * wholesaler. The salesman also reviews the retailer's display of Gillette products to insure they are attractively arranged and in saleable condition. It is this last activity which the respondent commission focuses on as more than solicitation, characterizing it rather than 'merchandising'."

Id. at 478, 393 N.Y.S.2d at 188.

The tax commission argued, in short, that advising retailers on display techniques, in order to make the product more attractive to the ultimate consumer, was actually a post-sale activity and hence was not solicitation.

The court reviewed the legislative history of § 381, the precise statutory language, and the various state court decisions which have construed the federal law, including the Commonwealth Court's opinion in the instant case. Finding the rationale offered by the Pennsylvania Commonwealth Court to be "unconvincing," id. at 480, 393 N.Y.S.2d at 190, the court rejected the tax commission's argument that Gillette was doing more than solicitation as envisioned by § 381:

> "[A]lthough it is not possible to state a general rule demarcating solicitation from merchandising, certainly where, as here, the com-

---

* [This decision has since been affirmed. See p. 400, infra.]

plaining taxpayer owns no real or personal property (except salesmen's samples) in the State and makes no repairs on its goods after sale, the purpose of P.L. 86–272 would be frustrated by permitting the tax. Advice to retailers on the act of displaying goods to the public can hardly be more thoroughly solicitation, i.e., in this context, an effort to induce purchase of Gillette products. Making the evanescent distinctions which would be necessary to justify the imposition of the tax upon petitioner herein would, if indulged in by the several states, tend to 'Balkanize the American economy', a result which it was Congress's purpose to prevent."

Id. at 482, 393 N.Y.S.2d at 191.

Accord, State ex rel. CIBA Pharmaceutical Products, Inc. v. State Tax Comm'n, 382 S.W.2d 645 (Mo.1964) (granting § 381 immunity from state tax where seller's representatives visit prospective customers, explain seller's products, and leave literature and samples of seller's product, all in an effort to persuade doctors to write prescriptions for seller's products); Coors Porcelain Co. v. State, 183 Colo. 325, 517 P.2d 838 (1973) (granting immunity where seller's representatives, *inter alia,* demonstrated seller's products, negotiated customer prices, and were supplied with company automobiles). See also International Shoe Co. v. Cocreham, 246 La. 244, 164 So.2d 314, cert. denied sub nom. Mouton v. International Shoe Co., 379 U.S. 902, 85 S.Ct. 193, 13 L.Ed.2d 177 (1964); Oklahoma Tax Comm'n v. Brown–Forman Distillery Corp., 420 P.2d 894 (Okl.1966).

Illustrative of cases denying § 381 immunity is Clairol, Inc. v. Kingsley, 109 N.J.Super. 22, 262 A.2d 213, aff'd, 57 N.J. 199, 270 A.2d 702 (1970), dismissed for want of a substantial federal question, 402 U.S. 902, 91 S.Ct. 1337, 28 L.Ed.2d 643 (1971). * * * See also Miles Laboratories, Inc. v. Department of Revenue, 274 Or. 395, 546 P.2d 1081 (1976) (denying § 381 immunity where salespeople maintained stock to replace damaged merchandise, serviced accounts, and arranged advertising displays); Hervey v. AMF Beaird, Inc., 250 Ark. 147, 464 S.W.2d 557 (1971) (since "solicitation of orders" must be narrowly construed, fact that company's representatives make regular checks of customers' inventories of company's equipment goes beyond solicitation of orders); Olympia Brewing Co. v. Department of Revenue, 266 Or. 309, 511 P.2d 837 (1973) (agreeing with Oregon tax court that presence of interstate company's beer kegs in taxing state stripped company of § 381 immunity; expressing no opinion on tax court's determination that regular inspections of supply of seller's beer to check for shortages, and efforts to induce attractive displays of seller's products, were essentially solicitation).

Comparing those cases granting § 381 immunity with those denying the same illustrates two principles of primary importance. First, each claimed § 381 exemption from a state income tax must be judged on its individual facts. The totality of the solicitors' or representatives' activities must be considered, and any nexus with the taxing state that

cannot accurately be characterized as "solicitation of orders" is sufficient to remove the protection of § 381: e.g., maintaining personal
property in the state (Olympia Brewing, supra), employing technicians
instead of salespeople (Clairol, supra), or having representatives collect
deposits on merchandise ordered or balances of payment on merchandise delivered. Herff Jones Co. v. State Tax Comm'n, 247 Or. 404, 430
P.2d 998 (1967). No such activities were involved in Gillette, supra, nor
are such activities involved in the instant case. Second, and perhaps
more instrumental in the disposition of these cases, is that much
depends on the breathing space courts are willing to accord the term
"solicitation": The courts of Oregon and Arkansas have expressly given
"solicitation" a narrow construction, see Hervey v. AMF Beaird, Inc.,
250 Ark. 147, 153–57, 464 S.W.2d 557, 561–62 (1971) (citing cases),
whereas the *Gillette* court decided that Congress intended that "solicitation" was not to be construed so that any activity beyond an actual
request to buy a product would remove § 381's protection. It is this
question—the proper construction of "solicitation"—to which we now
turn.

The text of § 381 gives no indication of how narrowly or broadly
"solicitation" should be construed when assessing the taxability of any
particular set of circumstances. It is not clear whether factors such as
the presence of sample goods, furnishing solicitors with automobiles, or
supervision over or assistance with displays are activities merely incidental to "solicitation" and hence within the statute, or whether they
are distinct activities which, either independently or in conjunction
with other activities including solicitation, justify imposition of a tax.
See Developments in the Law—Federal Limitations on State Taxation
of Interstate Business, 75 Harv.L.Rev. 953, 1007–1010 (1962). We do
have several aids, however, in addition to the background provided by
sister state decisions, to assist us in this task. Of primary importance
in the proper construction of "solicitation" is § 381's legislative history,
for we cannot forget that "it is essential that we place the words of a
statute in their proper context by resort to the legislative history."
Tidewater Oil Co. v. United States, 409 U.S. 151, 157, 93 S.Ct. 408, 413,
34 L.Ed.2d 375, 383 (1972).

We think it highly significant that the Senate Report in support of
§ 381 specifically referred to the United States Supreme Court's refusal
to review, in Brown–Forman, supra, the Louisiana Supreme Court's
decision, which, on facts similar to the case at bar, upheld the state's
power to tax an interstate corporation. See S.Rep. No. 658, 86th Cong.,
1st Sess., at 2; U.S.Code Cong. & Admin.News 1959, p. 2549:

> "Persons engaged in interstate commerce are in doubt as to the
> amount of local activities within a State that will be regarded as
> forming a sufficient 'nexus', that is, connection, with the State to
> support the imposition of a tax on net income from interstate opera-
> tions * * *. [There is] a general apprehension in the business
> community that sales within a State obtained through the mere
> solicitation of orders within the State by an out-of-State company

having no other activities within the State would subject the out-of-State company to the imposition of an income tax by the State on earnings of the company 'properly apportioned' to the State. This apprehension is apparently strengthened by the decision of the Louisiana Supreme Court in the *Brown–Forman* case, which the U.S. Supreme Court refused to review. There the activities of the corporation within the State were apparently limited to the presence of 'missionary men' engaged in solicitation."

In *Brown–Forman,* the foreign corporation's "missionary men," like appellant's representatives, not only sought to procure initial orders for the company's products, but also were involved in obtaining optimum counter displays for those products. 234 La. at 653, 101 So.2d at 70. When Congress enacts legislation exempting "solicitation" by an interstate corporation from a state's net income tax, and does so in response to a case where the "solicitation" involved activity incidental to the initial contact between seller and prospective buyer, we as state courts are bound to give foreign corporations § 381 immunity even though their representatives engage in activities incidental to the initial contact between buyer and seller. The question is one of degree. The foregoing analysis, however, constrains us to disagree with those courts which have concluded that Congress intended "solicitation" to be narrowly construed. Cal–Roof Wholesale Co. v. State Tax Comm'n, 242 Or. 435, 410 P.2d 233 (1967); Hervey v. AMF Beaird, Inc., 250 Ark. 147, 464 S.W.2d 557 (1971) (citing *Cal–Roof*).

Indeed, our own experience with the word solicitation supports our view that Congress saw "solicitation" as involving sundry activities so long as those activities were closely related to the eventual sale of a product. Although this Court has never construed the word "solicitation" in the framework of § 381, we have had occasion to consider the term in other contexts. In Business Tax Bureau of the School Dist. of Philadelphia v. American Cyanamid Co., 426 Pa. 69, 231 A.2d 116 (1967), we discussed solicitation in the context of what constitutes "doing business" for purposes of a general business tax. See also Shambe v. Delaware & Hudson R.R., 288 Pa. 240, 135 A.2d 755 (1927). In those cases, we had to determine what activities would amount to something more than "solicitation" such that the taxpayer would be subject to the tax. We have said that acts of courtesy performed by business solicitors, in order to satisfy or accommodate customers, did not go beyond solicitation; nor was it relevant that the solicitors were provided facilities to carry on their solicitations. See 426 Pa. at 76, 231 A.2d at 119, 231 A.2d 116, citing Lutz v. Foster & Kester Co., 367 Pa. 125, 129–30, 79 A.2d 222, 224 (1951). The import of these decisions is that "solicitation" does not stop at the moment a prospective customer (or wholesaler) is asked to consider purchasing the seller's goods: other practices incident to the initial contact between buyer and seller, such as advice on making the product attractive to the ultimate consumer, also fall under the rubric "solicitation."

We therefore conclude that § 381 exempts appellant from Pennsylvania's corporation income tax. Appellant's only contacts with this state—visiting retail outlets, introducing new products, and advising retailers on making attractive displays of appellant's products—are inextricably related to solicitation. Subsection (2) of § 381(a) envisioned precisely the kind of sales activities engaged in by appellant's representatives: an effort to generate sales at the retail level so that appellant's direct customers (Pennsylvania wholesalers) will order more of appellant's products to be able to satisfy the retailers' needs. We agree with the New York court in *Gillette* that making evanescent distinctions between "solicitation" and "solicitation plus" or "merchandising," when the activities in question were all incident to soliciting business, would defeat the very purpose of § 381. Solicitation cannot mean that a foreign corporation may do no more than send salespeople into another state who leave brochures describing their employer's products, hoping the prospective customer will then take the initiative to contact the employer for a possible sale. A company which sends ten "missionary representatives" into a state to "solicit orders" cannot hope to solicit those orders by having those ten persons call on every consumer to buy its product. All of the activities of appellant's representatives were a kind of solicitation activity—as much so as the exchanging of friendly amenities between a solicitor and the potential customer.

We also think it insignificant that appellant furnishes its solicitors with automobiles. See Coors Porcelain Co. v. State, supra, 517 P.2d 838 (Colo.1973). Congress could hardly have intended to exempt only walking solicitors. We do not think Congress intended factors such as how the solicitors get from customer to customer to be determinative of which interstate corporations enjoy § 381 immunity. The representatives' means of transportation does not change the character of their promotional activities. In our view, appellant's activities in Pennsylvania are confined to "solicitation" within the meaning of § 381.

* * *

Order reversed and the case is remanded for proceedings consistent with this opinion.

JONES, former C.J., did not participate in the decision of this case.

ROBERTS, J., filed a dissenting opinion in which EAGEN, C.J., joined.

ROBERTS, JUSTICE, dissenting.

Through an unjustified interpretation of a federal statute, the majority allows appellant, United States Tobacco Co., to escape taxation on income unquestionably earned through its activities in Pennsylvania. In reaching this conclusion, the majority overlooks a controlling decision of the United States Supreme Court, Clairol, Inc. v. Kingsley, 402 U.S. 902, 91 S.Ct. 1337, 28 L.Ed.2d 643 (1971), dismissing for want of a substantial federal question, 57 N.J. 199, 270 A.2d 702 (per curiam), aff'g 109 N.J.Super. 22, 262 A.2d 213 (1970). Today's result will allow foreign corporations with income fairly attributable to activities in Pennsylvania to escape Pennsylvania taxation, thus placing a heavy and unfair burden upon domestic taxpayers, both corporate and individual. I dissent.

*　*　*

On almost identical facts, the New Jersey courts held Clairol, Inc. taxable in New Jersey. Clairol, Inc. v. Kingsley, 109 N.J.Super. 22, 262 A.2d 213, aff'd, 57 N.J. 199, 270 A.2d 702 (1970) (solicitors performed other marketing duties such as rotating stock for freshness, setting up counter displays, etc.). The United States Supreme Court dismissed Clairol's appeal for want of a substantial federal question. 402 U.S. 902, 91 S.Ct. 1337, 28 L.Ed.2d 643 (1971). Such a dismissal is a decision by the Supreme Court on the merits of the particular factual situation which the case presents. Hicks v. Miranda, 422 U.S. 332, 343–45, 95 S.Ct. 2281, 2289, 45 L.Ed.2d 223 (1975). Because I see no substantial difference from the facts in *Clairol* and the facts of the instant case, I believe that *Clairol* controls our interpretation of Section 381.* See also Zucht v. King, 260 U.S. 174, 43 S.Ct. 24, 67 L.Ed. 194 (1922) (appeal will be dismissed when state court decision on federal question is clearly correct).

My interpretation of the word "solicitation" is also consistent with the rule that Congress is presumed to respect state sovereignty and traditional state powers unless, and only to the extent, that it explicitly limits those powers. Employees of Department of Public Health and Welfare v. Missouri, 411 U.S. 279, 284–85, 93 S.Ct. 1614, 1618, 36 L.Ed. 2d 251 (1973); 3 Sutherland, Statutory Interpretation § 62.01 at 64 n. 8 (Sands ed. 1974). We should thus interpret Section 381 to impose as few limitations upon the traditional state power to impose taxes as is consistent with the clear language of the section. Such a construction compels us to conclude that "solicitation" does not include appellant's marketing techniques.

Because appellant's representatives marketed and immediately distributed products in Pennsylvania, rather than merely solicited orders to be filled from out of state, 15 U.S.C. § 381 does not immunize appellant from taxation in Pennsylvania. I dissent.

EAGEN, C.J., joins in this dissenting opinion.

* Cases from other jurisdictions also support this distinction between mere solicitation and marketing. Two other states have explicitly construed "solicitation" to exclude even the incidentals of solicitation. Miles Laboratories v. Department of Revenue, 274 Or. 395, 546 P.2d 1081 (1976) (setting up counter displays, etc., not "solicitation"; particularly noteworthy because Oregon's tax scheme allowed domestic taxpayers to escape from taxation of income earned out of state in states where it failed the § 381 test); Herff Jones Co. v. State Tax Comm'n, 247 Or. 404, 430 P.2d 998 (1967) (corporation held taxable where collection of funds was the only activity beyond solicitation); Hervey v. AMF Beaird, Inc., 250 Ark. 147, 464 S.W.2d 557 (1971). Contra, State ex rel. Ciba Pharmaceuticals, Inc. v. State Tax Comm'n, 382 S.W.2d 645 (Mo.1964) (pre-*Clairol*) (incidentals of solicitation did not go beyond exemption of § 381). Similarly, those other cases granting exemptions under § 381 have involved corporations whose in-state activity did not go beyond narrow solicitation. Oklahoma Tax Comm'n v. Brown–Forman Distillers Corp., 420 P.2d 894 (Okl.1966) (stipulated facts); International Shoe Co. v. Cocreham, 246 La. 244, 164 So.2d 314 (1964), cert. denied, 379 U.S. 902, 85 S.Ct. 193 (1964).

Notes and Problems

A. The New York Court of Appeals summarily affirmed the Appellate Division's decision in Gillette Co. v. State Tax Commission, 45 N.Y.2d 846, 410 N.Y.S.2d 65, 382 N.E.2d 764 (1978), which the Pennsylvania Supreme Court discussed in the *United States Tobacco* case.

B. In Clairol, Inc. v. Kingsley, 109 N.J.Super. 22, 262 A.2d 213 (1970), affirmed 57 N.J. 199, 270 A.2d 702 (1970), appeal dismissed 402 U.S. 902, 91 S.Ct. 1377 (1971), noted in both the majority and dissenting opinions of the *United States Tobacco* case, the activities of the well-known hair products company's "detail men" who "rearrange a promotion," or "make up a little display on the counter," "or take an inventory of the store's stock of products" were held to fall outside the protected scope of solicitation. Testimony in the case revealed that the company's detail men

> who call on beauty salons have a technical background and * * * do very little as far as order taking. In other words, their big function is going into the local beauty salon to tell them how to use Clairol products. * * * And maybe in teaching them new techniques possibly.

109 N.J.Super. at 30. Although such servicing and teaching operations will affect future orders, to treat such operations as merely "incident" to solicitation stretches the term beyond its normally understood scope.

C. *The Oregon Cases.* The Oregon courts have thus far been the most fruitful source of interpretation of P.L. 86–272. See Smith, Kline & French Laboratories, Inc. v. State Tax Commission, 241 Or. 50, 403 P.2d 375 (1965); Atlas Foundry v. State Tax Commission, 2 Or.Tax R. 200 (1965); Briggs & Stratton Corp. v. State Tax Commission, 3 Or.Tax R. 174 (1968).

Beginning with Herff Jones Co. v. State Tax Commission, 247 Or. 404, 430 P.2d 998 (1967), the Oregon Supreme Court narrowed its view of what constitutes solicitation under the statute. It held that the collection of deposits and balances exceeded the allowable limits of solicitation by the salesmen. 430 P.2d at 1001–02. See also Olympia Brewing Co. v. Department of Revenue, 266 Or. 309, 310, 511 P.2d 837, 838 (1973), cert. denied 415 U.S. 976, 94 S.Ct. 1561 (1974), in which it was held that "the fact that plaintiff maintained in Oregon personal property in the form of beer kegs which were used by retailers in dispensing draft beer subjected plaintiff to the Oregon tax." The Oregon court has likewise applied its view of solicitation in cases involving the right of a taxpayer to apportion its income. See Note F infra.

D. *Limitation of Solicitation to Acts Preceding the Taking of an Order.** The Oregon Supreme Court approved and applied the interpretation of "solicitation" that had been developed by the Oregon Tax Court, in which a distinction was drawn between pre-sale and post-sale activities. " '[S]olicitation' should be limited to those generally accepted or customary acts in the industry which lead to the placing of orders, not those which

---

* The first paragraph of this note is based on J. Hellerstein, State Taxation I, Corporate Income and Franchise Taxes ¶ 6.11[1] (1983). Used with the consent of the copyright owner and publisher.

follow as a natural result of the transaction, such as collections, servicing complaints, technical assistance and training." Miles Laboratories, Inc. v. Department of Revenue, 274 Or. 395, 400, 546 P.2d 1081, 1083 (1976). Applying that standard, the salesmen's replacing of damaged goods was found to take *Miles Laboratories* out from under the statutory umbrella. The court enumerated various types of other activities that had likewise been held in its earlier decisions to transcend solicitation:

> Examples of such fatal, "non-solicitous" activity are: giving "spot credit," accepting orders, collecting delinquent accounts and picking up returned goods within the taxing state, collecting deposits and advances on orders within the taxing state, pooling and exchanging technical personnel in a complex mutual endeavor, maintaining personal property (beer kegs) and associated local business activity for purposes not related to soliciting orders within the taxing state. [274 Or. at 399, 546 P.2d at 1083.]

The North Dakota Supreme Court has adopted the Oregon view. In Drackett Products Co. v. Conrad, 370 N.W.2d 723 (N.D.1985), it was held that "a business exceeds the mere 'solicitation of orders' for purposes of tax exemption under 15 U.S.C. § 381 if its activities go beyond acts necessary for and leading to the placing of orders." 370 N.W.2d at 726. The following local activities of the taxpayer's sales representative, in addition to the solicitation of orders, were found to deprive the taxpayer of the protection of P.L. 86–272: replacing damaged merchandise, checking inventory, pricing items for resale by wholesalers to retailers, tracing late shipments, selling and installing aisle displays, and monitoring product shelf placement. See also Hervey v. AMF Beaird, 250 Ark. 147, 464 S.W.2d 557 (1971), in which the court relied on *Clairol* and the Oregon cases in holding that activities such as checking customers' inventories exceeded solicitation. The court also indicated that sales of goods on a consignment basis would subject the taxpayer to the State's power of taxation. Accord, on the consignment issue, Consolidated Accessories Corp. v. Franchise Tax Bd., 161 Cal.App.3d 1036, 208 Cal.Rptr. 74 (1984).

Other courts, however, have rejected the limitation of the scope of solicitation to the point an order is taken. The Pennsylvania and New York courts have held that verification of destruction of damaged merchandise, and coordinating delivery of merchandise for special promotions, fall within the protection of P.L. 86–272. See the *United States Tobacco Co.* and *Gillette cases,* pp. 391 and 394 supra. In Indiana Department of Revenue v. Kimberly–Clark Corp., 275 Ind. 378, 416 N.E.2d 1264 (1981), the Indiana court likewise rejected the rule that solicitation ends when the order is taken, and ruled that the types of activities at issue in the *United States Tobacco* and *Gillette* cases "may be properly characterized as 'inextricably related to solicitation,' or as 'acts of courtesy,'" that are embraced within the statutory protection. See also, Matthew Bender & Co., Inc. v. Comptroller of Treasury, 67 Md.App. 693, 509 A.2d 702 (1986) (recognizing but finding it unnecessary to resolve the conflict among the courts).

E. *Other Issues Arising Under P.L. 86–272.* The Alaska Supreme Court held that a Seattle-based fisherman who delivered his catch to

Alaska processors on the basis of contractual arrangements made in Washington was not protected by P.L. 86–272 because

> in order to qualify for the exemption, a business must solicit orders, which are sent out of state for approval, and then make deliveries into the state. Since [the taxpayer's] acts concern only the third part of the described activity, deliveries, it does not come within the statutory exemption.

Sjong v. State, 622 P.2d 967, 968 (Alaska 1981). Is this interpretation of P.L. 86–272 consistent with its purpose of immunizing out-of-state vendors of tangible personal property from State income taxation whose activities in the State do not go beyond the statutory minimum?

Matthew Bender Co., the publisher of legal texts, solicited orders for its publications through salesmen working on a commission basis and through the mails. The orders were sent back to Matthew Bender's principal office in New York for acceptance. In addition Matthew Bender employed a Maryland printer on a continuing basis to print its publications. In this connection it occasionally sent representatives into Maryland to consult with the printer's staff. It also provided the printer with paper that the printer stored for use in printing Matthew Bender's texts. In holding that the taxpayer was not subject to the Maryland income tax, the Maryland Tax Court distinguished cases in which the taxpayer's activities were found to fall outside the protection of P.L. 86–272 because of activities exceeding, but related to, its solicitation of orders in the State:

> In contrast, in the instant case, Matthew Bender's solicitation and printing operations are completely unrelated. Petitioner placed orders for printing jobs with a Maryland firm, as it did with six or seven other printers throughout the country. The finished product was not sold directly to Maryland customers, but, instead, was shipped back to Petitioner's principal place of business in New York. It does not appear to this Court that Congress intended a totally unrelated aspect of a corporation's business to combine with solicitation so as to yield tax liability in a given state.

Matthew Bender Co. v. Comptroller of Treasury, Md.Tax Ct., Oct. 22, 1984, P–H ¶ 13,107 at 13,141–42. Is this a proper construction of the statute? See Matthew Bender & Co., Inc. v. Comptroller of Treasury, 67 Md.App. 693, 509 A.2d 702 (1986). Why should the fact that the printing in Maryland was unrelated to solicitation in the State preclude taxation? Cf. National Geographic Society v. State Board of Equalization, Chapter 10, p. 820 infra. That issue aside, should the fact that the visits to Maryland and the keeping of paper in the State related to the independent printer's operation in the State prevent the attribution of those actions to the publisher for purposes of P.L. 86–272? Compare the regular visits to New York and Los Angeles apparel manufacturers by buyers of department stores from various States. Their visits have not been regarded as subjecting the department stores to tax.

    F. *P.L. 86–272 and the Right of a Corporation to Apportion Its Income.* Under the laws of many States, a taxpayer is entitled to apportion or allocate its income only if its income is taxable by another State, regardless of whether that State has exercised its taxing power. See UDITPA §§ 2 and 3, Chapter 9, subd. C, § 6 infra; see also Chapter 9, subd. C, § 1 infra. As a consequence, the issue has arisen in income apportionment and allocation cases whether foreign corporations are taxable in a State that does not in fact tax them. In such cases the taxing authorities contend that P.L. 86–272 prevents taxation by other States, whereas taxpayers argue that their activities in other States exceed the minimum threshold established by P.L. 86–272 and, accordingly, that they are entitled to apportion or allocate their income.

The Oregon court has applied its restrictive view of P.L. 86–272 to apportionment cases by holding that the taxpayer is subject to the taxing powers of other States. In one case it concluded that the corporation was subject to the taxing powers of other States because of the following activities, which would normally be treated as customary incidents to solicitation:

> In addition to his principal activity, soliciting orders, the Washington salesman on numerous occasions collected delinquent accounts, made pick-ups of merchandise which customers desired to return, and customarily carried with him a supply of small items which he sold and delivered within the State of Washington. Also, he was authorized to and did on some occasions give spot credit and accept orders rather than submit them to the home office in Oregon for approval. [Cal–Roof Wholesale, Inc. v. State Tax Comm'n, 242 Or. 435, 436, 410 P.2d 233, 234 (1966).]

For other Oregon P.L. 86–272 apportionment cases, see Iron Fireman Co. v. State Tax Comm'n, 251 Or. 227, 445 P.2d 126 (1968); Miles Laboratories, Inc. v. Department of Revenue, 274 Or. 395, 546 P.2d 1081 (1976).

In John Ownbey Co. v. Butler, 211 Tenn. 366, 365 S.W.2d 33 (1963), the Tennessee State Tax Commissioner relied on P.L. 86–272 to deny out-of-state apportionment to several corporations that for a number of years prior to the enactment of the Federal legislation had been permitted to apportion their incomes. The case came up under the Tennessee "excise tax" on "net earnings" arising "from business done in the State."

A manufacturer of school supplies, an appliance manufacturer, and a vendor of custom made suits made by contractors, all authorized to do business only in Tennessee, used their own salesmen or sales representatives to solicit orders in other States, for acceptance in Tennessee and delivery across State lines. Two of the corporations shipped the goods directly to their customers, but the appliance manufacturer shipped them to its manufacturer's representative, who stored them in a warehouse and then delivered them to the customer. Another taxpayer involved in the same set of cases manufactured and sold clothing to the United States Government, and delivered it at designated out-of-Tennessee government installations.

The court held that the Tennessee tax was properly imposed on all the taxpayers, relying in part on P.L. 86–272 for the conclusion that the corporations were not taxable in any other State and stating that "all the corporate earnings are inevitably realized at the respective Tennessee offices."

Is this conclusion sound in the case of the vendor that shipped its goods to the out-of-state agent for warehousing and delivery to the customers? In the case of the custom suit dealer, was the measuring by the salesmen of the customers for their suits within the minimal activities protected by the Congressional act? Although the *John Ownbey* case was followed in Signal Thread Co. v. King, 222 Tenn. 241, 435 S.W.2d 468 (1968), in a more recent case the Tennessee Supreme Court took a broader view of the right of a corporation to apportion its income. Howard Cotton Co. v. Olsen, 675 S.W.2d 154 (Tenn.1984). While the court made no mention of P.L. 86–272 or the *John Ownbey* case, it held that a Tennessee cotton broker with no business locations outside the State and all of whose employees were located in Memphis was entitled to apportion its income, in large part due to its "millions of dollars worth of cotton * * * warehoused in public warehouses in other states." 675 S.W.2d at 16.

In Coors Porcelain Co. v. State, 183 Colo. 325, 517 P.2d 838 (1973), a Colorado based manufacturer of porcelain and ceramic products was denied apportionment on the ground that its out-of-state activities did not exceed the minimum threshold established by P.L. 86–272. Coors maintained sales employees and agents, including regional sales managers, located in other States, and their practices were described as follows:

> Orders are mailed either from the agent or from a customer to Golden, Colorado, from which point the orders are approved and shipped. Some agents buy directly and resell to their customers; some merely solicit the orders from customers and Coors ships directly to the customer and pays a commission to the agent. * * *

> Each field representative maintains his own business office in the locality wherein he resides. Coors supplies each field representative with a business automobile and also places advertisements in the local telephone directory listing the local representative's business telephone. Coors does not consistently maintain warehouses or stocks of products, parts or supplies outside of Colorado, but its out of state representatives do consistently maintain sample materials owned by Coors and on occasion they possess Coors products for shipment to the customer and also retain Coors products which have been rejected by the customer upon delivery. [183 Colo. at 327–29, 517 P.2d at 839–40.]

Query: If the activities carried on by Coors outside Colorado had been carried on by a foreign corporation in Colorado, would the court have sustained the taxpayer's contention that it was immune from taxation under P.L. 86–272?

A Georgia case presented an interesting question as to the interplay between a State's standards of what constitutes "doing business" in other States and P.L. 86–272. Hawes v. William L. Bonnell Co., 116 Ga.App. 184, 156 S.E.2d 536 (1967). The court found that the activities of a Georgia manufacturer of aluminum products satisfied the State's requirement for the right to apportion income and rejected the contention of the taxing authority that the State rules should be conformed to P.L. 86–272, by saying:

> The federal act at best only impliedly modified the [Georgia] act insofar as a foreign corporation's activities within the state are con-

cerned. The fact that attempting to tax a foreign corporation under that provision might now run afoul of the federal statute would not affect the provision as to Georgia corporations with described activities in other states. The federal law does not endeavor to pre-empt that area. It did not in any manner relate to the act's provisions insofar as a domestic corporation is concerned.

The Revenue Department argues that they apply complete reciprocity and that it is a bad policy to allow a corporation an exemption for certain activities which are no longer taxable in a foreign state. If this be true it is a matter for the remedial power of the legislature, not the courts. * * *

Thus, despite the apparent anomaly of treatment under the statute, * * * we hold that the taxpayer is doing business outside Georgia and is entitled to apportion its income. [156 S.E.2d at 541–42.]

In Tonka Corp. v. Commissioner, 284 Minn. 185, 169 N.W.2d 589 (1969), the taxpayer's right to an apportionment was considered in the light of the independent contractor provision of P.L. 86–272. The taxpayer was a Minnesota corporation engaged in the manufacture and sale of toy metal vehicles. Although the agreements between Tonka and its out-of-state representatives referred to the latter as independent contractors, the court concluded that the evidence supported a finding that Tonka's sales representatives were more like employees than independent contractors. Since these representatives maintained a sales office in New York, their activities exceeded the solicitation standards of the Congressional Act; hence the taxpayer was entitled to apportion its income.

C. *References.* Detailed discussions of the cases arising under P.L. 86–272 are contained in J. Hellerstein, State Taxation I, Corporate Income and Franchise Taxes ¶ 6.10 et seq. (1983); Tatarowicz, "State Judicial and Administrative Interpretations of U.S. Public Law 86–272," 38 Tax Law. 293 (1985); Sweeney, "State Taxation of Interstate Commerce Under Public Law 86–272," 1984 B.Y.L.U.L.Rev. 169; Hartman, " 'Solicitation' and 'Delivery' Under Public Law 86–272: An Uncharted Course," 29 Vand.L.Rev. 353 (1976); Note, "Public Law 86–272: Legislative Ambiguities and Judicial Difficulties," 27 Vand.L.Rev. 313 (1974). See also Hartman, "State Taxation of Corporate Income from a Multi–State Business," 13 Vand.L. Rev. 21 (1959); Kust, "State Taxation & Interstate Income: New Developments of an Old Problem," Tax Exec. 45 (1959); Dane, "What Is The Future of Public Law 86–272," 1960 Nat.Tax Ass'n Procs. 192. For a critical treatment of Public Law 86–272 and an advocacy of the adoption of the NCCUSL Uniform Act, see Wagner & Del Duca, "Uniformity or Preferential Tax Immunity," 48 A.B.A.J. 532 (1962). There is a comprehensive treatment of the case law, as well as an analysis of Public Law 86–272, in "Federal Limitations on State Taxation of Interstate Business," 75 Harv.L. Rev. 953 (1962). P.L. 86–272 is analyzed in W. Beaman, Paying Taxes to Other States, ch. 6, "Minimum Nexus for Direct Net Income Taxes" (1963).

SECTION 3. WHAT CONSTITUTES "DOING BUSINESS" UNDER THE STATE TAXING STATUTES

A. To inquire whether a foreign corporation is "doing business" within a particular State, or has contact with a particular State, has significance only in terms of the particular purposes of the inquiry. Thus, the term "doing business" is used in State statutes in three distinct situations: (1) statutes which require foreign corporations to "qualify" in order to transact local business; (2) statutes directed to the amenability of the foreign corporation to suit and service of process; and (3) statutes imposing excise taxes upon foreign corporations for the privilege of doing local business.[13] Nevertheless, the problems presented in each of the three areas involve different considerations, which ought to govern the results. The dissenting opinion in Eli Lilly and Company v. Sav-on-Drugs, 366 U.S. 276, 81 S.Ct. 1316 (1961), which dealt with qualification to transact local business, argued that the majority uncritically blended the decisions in all three types of cases. See also Allenberg Cotton Co. v. Pittman, 419 U.S. 20, 95 S.Ct. 260 (1974), with respect to whether local contacts sufficient to require a foreign corporation to qualify to do business is a different question from whether such contacts would justify taxation of the corporation.

B. Many problems have arisen as to what constitutes the doing or carrying on of business within the meaning of State taxing statutes. The ownership of property in the State (which is sometimes explicitly made a basis for taxation by the statute) actively used in the trade or business normally gives rise to tax. The issue has arisen as to whether a foreign corporation is doing business in a State in which it warehouses goods in public warehouses. In Sealed Power Corporation v. Stokes, 174 Tenn. 493, 127 S.W.2d 114 (1939), the court sustained a doing business tax on a corporation using public warehouses in the State to store and distribute goods, where orders were filled out of these warehouses by direct shipment to the customers on instruction from the taxpayer's out-of-state office. Accord: R.J. Reynolds Tobacco Co. v. Carson, 187 Tenn. 157, 213 S.W.2d 45 (1948).

In Matter of Heftel Broadcasting Honolulu, Inc., 57 Hawaii 175, 554 P.2d 242 (1976), certiorari denied 429 U.S. 1073, 97 S.Ct. 811 (1977), CBS, in a test suit, challenged the application of Hawaii's privilege tax to foreign corporations that had licensed the use of television films to local broadcasters. The agreed facts disclosed "that *all* activities [including transfer of possession of the films] of the licensors occurred on the mainland." CBS contended that the mere physical presence of its films in the State and their rental was insufficient to constitute "engaging in business" in the State under the statute, H.R.S. §§ 237–2,

---

13. Prior to the decision in Complete Auto Transit, Inc. v. Brady, 430 U.S. 274, 97 S.Ct. 1076 (1977), many Commerce Clause cases dealt with the question as to whether the business being done was exclusively in interstate commerce. See Chapter 6, subd. A supra. If the conduct of an exclusively interstate business was being taxed, the Commerce Clause was infringed. That is no longer the law. Id.

–13(10), CCH ¶¶ 92–802, 92–849, P–H ¶¶ 22,210.5, 22,270.100. The Hawaii Supreme Court rejected this argument and declared:

> Of significance in this case, as we see it, is that in essence what CBS leased * * * were not only the film prints but, more importantly, also the intangible telecast rights of the films. These telecast rights were wholly consumable and *only consumable in Hawaii* within specific time limits. And both CBS and KGMB–TV exercised continuing dominion over such telecast rights. So even though the agreement was consummated on the mainland, it was done so with the intent that performance would occur almost entirely in Hawaii. Furthermore, unlike a sale of goods that takes place on the mainland with the goods being transported here, the license agreement continued into this State wherein it was a source of income to the licensor. Thus * * * CBS was engaged in local "business" within the meaning of chapter 237. [554 P.2d at 246–47 (footnotes omitted, emphasis in original).]

The court also rejected CBS' Commerce Clause and Due Process Clause objections to the tax.

C. *Doing Business Through Independent Contractors.* Solicitation by an independent contractor does not ordinarily subject the seller to franchise taxes. District of Columbia v. Cities Service Oil Co., 258 F.2d 426 (D.C.Cir.1958); W.J. Dickey & Sons v. State Tax Commission, 212 Md. 607, 131 A.2d 277 (1957). Cf., however, the Supreme Court's holding as a constitutional matter that sales through an independent contractor do not relieve the vendor of his duty to collect a State use tax. Scripto, Inc. v. Carson, p. 818 infra. Once the Court finds, however, that local solicitation, advertising, or promotion are carried on through the seller's agents, tax liability will ordinarily result. Ruppert v. Morrison, 117 Vt. 83, 85 A.2d 584, (1952) discussed in 1952 Ann. Survey Am.Law 206 (1953); Pekao Trading Corp. v. Bragalini, 9 A.D.2d 559, 189 N.Y.S.2d 241 (Sup.Ct., 3rd Dep't 1959), aff'd 8 N.Y.2d 903, 168 N.E.2d 823, 204 N.Y.S.2d 147, appeal dismissed 364 U.S. 478, 81 S.Ct. 243 (1960).

In Minnesota Tribune Co. v. Commissioner of Taxation, 228 Minn. 452, 37 N.W.2d 737 (1949), a domestic corporation owning stock of a foreign corporation was held to be the agency through which the foreign corporation conducted business in the State and hence was subject to a franchise tax. Accord: Alpha Corporation v. Multnomah County, 182 Or. 671, 189 P.2d 988 (1948).

This is contrary to the usual holding, in which the separateness of the business of the various corporate entities is recognized; activities of the out-of-state parent corporation in the taxing State in supervising the activities of a local subsidiary, or in protecting its interest, are normally treated as incidents to stock ownership that do not constitute doing business within the State. Nationwide Corp. v. Schneider, 7 Ohio St.2d 59, 218 N.E.2d 611 (1966). See 18 A.L.R.2d 202.

D. *Investment Companies and Holding Companies.* In a number of cases the courts have held that investment companies and other corporations actively engaged in buying and selling securities for their own investment are doing business within the meaning of the taxing statutes in the State in which such activities take place. People ex rel. Tobacco & Allied Stocks v. Graves, 250 App.Div. 149, 294 N.Y.S. 995 (1937), aff'd 277 N.Y. 723, 14 N.E.2d 821 (1938); Argonaut Consolidated Mining Co. v. Anderson, 42 F.2d 219 (S.D.N.Y.1930), aff'd 52 F.2d 55 (2d Cir.1931) cert. denied 284 U.S. 682, 52 S.Ct. 200 (1931); People ex rel. North American Co. v. Miller, 90 App.Div. 560, 86 N.Y.S. 386 (3rd Dept. 1904), aff'd 182 N.Y. 521, 74 N.E. 1124 (1905) (foreign corporation; active investment company); Queens Run Refractories Co. v. Commonwealth, 270 Mass. 19, 169 N.E. 515 (1930); see also People ex rel. Manhattan Silk Co. v. Miller, 125 App.Div. 296, 109 N.Y.S. 866 (3rd Dept.1908), aff'd 197 N.Y. 577, 91 N.E. 1119 (1910) (foreign corporation; served as purchasing agent for its subsidiaries).

An issue has arisen in this area as a result of the great growth of mutual funds and other investment companies. Are such companies "doing business" and, therefore, taxable in the States in which they sell investment certificates or other stock interests in the companies? For an affirmative answer to this question, see Ramsey v. Investors Diversified Services, Inc., 248 S.W.2d 263 (Tex.Civ.App.1952); Investors Syndicate of America v. Allen, 198 Tenn. 288, 279 S.W.2d 497 (1955).

The place where the directors hold their meetings is typically not decisive in determining the taxability of investment or holding companies; the State in which the policies of the investment company are carried out is accorded greater weight in determining tax liability. Arkansas Fuel Oil Corp. v. Fontenot, 225 La. 166, 72 So.2d 465 (1954), appeal dismissed 348 U.S. 804, 75 S.Ct. 46 (1954); Standard Carloading Corp. v. Glander, 152 Ohio St. 404, 89 N.E.2d 575 (1949); Commonwealth v. Eagles Corp., 354 Pa. 493, 47 A.2d 661 (1946).

E. *Liquidating Corporations.* The Arkansas corporate income tax is imposed "with respect to carrying on or doing business." Ark.Stat. Ann. § 84–2004, CCH ¶ 94–473, P–H ¶ 12,420.5. An Arkansas corporation filed its certificate of dissolution with the Secretary of State and later in the same day, pursuant to a plan of liquidation, sold its assets for more than book value. The company did not report the profit as income and its position was sustained on the ground that a dissolved corporation, in selling its assets for the purposes of liquidation, is not carrying on or doing business within the meaning of the income tax law. Larey v. Mountain Valley Spring Co., 245 Ark. 689, 434 S.W.2d 820 (1968).

F. *Doing Business in No State Within the Meaning of Taxing Statutes.* Typically, a foreign corporation which attacks a "doing business" tax seeks to establish that it is doing business only in some other State. Is it possible for a corporation, not in liquidation and carrying on the business for which it was organized, to defeat a doing business tax on the theory that it is not doing business in any State within the meaning of the taxing statute? The leading case answering the question in the affirmative is People ex rel. Manila Electric R.R. & Lighting Corp. v. Knapp, 229 N.Y. 502, 128 N.E. 892 (1920), in which it was held that a foreign holding company, with its principal office in New York, whose officers were paid no salaries, and whose affairs were controlled by a management company, was not doing business for purposes of the New York franchise tax, even though it aided its subsidiaries financially and exercised some control over their affairs. See also Elsner v. United American Utilities, Inc., 21 Del.Ch. 73, 180 A. 589 (1935), aff'd sub nom. State of New York v. Mahaffy, 22 Del.Ch. 405, 12 A.2d 389 (1936); United States Rubber Co. v. Query, 19 F.Supp. 191 (E.D.S.C.1937); Welch Holding Co. v. Galloway, 161 Or. 515, 89 P.2d 559 (1939). For cases reflecting a contrary view, see Minnesota Tribune Co. v. Comm. of Taxation, 228 Minn. 452, 37 N.W.2d 737 (1949); Commonwealth v. American Gas Co., 352 Pa. 113, 42 A.2d 161 (1945); Bankers Holding Corp. v. Maybury, 161 Wash. 681, 297 P. 740 (1931); Rhode Island Hospital Trust Co. v. Rhodes, 37 R.I. 141, 91 A. 50 (1914).

Similar problems arose under the Federal Corporation Tax Act of 1909, which imposed a tax on the income of "every corporation * * * engaged in business * * * with respect to the carrying on or doing of business." Under that Act it was held that where corporations discontinue operating, lease their businesses and properties to others, and simply collect the rents (Zonne v. Minneapolis Syndicate, 220 U.S. 187, 31 S.Ct. 361 [1911]), or invest and reinvest in securities (McCoach v. Minehill Ry., 228 U.S. 295, 33 S.Ct. 419 [1913]), they are not "doing business."

In Edwards v. Chile Copper Co., 270 U.S. 452, 46 S.Ct. 345 (1926), a holding company formed for the purpose of issuing bonds on the security of its subsidiary's stock (because the subsidiary was forbidden to pledge its assets directly, and, therefore, could not raise new money), and existing solely as the medium by which the subsidiary obtained new cash, was held to be "doing business" within the Federal Corporation Tax Act in an opinion in which Justice Holmes stated that the corporation "was organized for profit and was doing what it principally was organized to do in order to realize profit. The case must be exceptional when such activities of such corporations do not amount to doing business in the sense of the statutes. * * * The activities and situation must be judged as a whole. Looking at them as a whole we see that the plaintiff was a good deal more than a conduit for the Chile Exploration Company. It was its brain or at least the efferent nerve without which that company could not move. The plaintiff owned and by indirection governed it, and was its continuing support, by advances from time to time in the plaintiff's discretion." (270 U.S. at 455, 456.) See also Phillips v. International Salt Co., 274 U.S. 718, 47 S.Ct. 589 (1927).

The Federal capital stock tax, which was imposed on "every domestic corporation with respect to carrying on or doing business," resulted in a mass of litigation as to what constitutes doing business. These cases are collected in P–H Fed.Tax Serv. ¶ 52,613.

ASSIGNMENT

Many States have refrained from exercising their full constitutional powers to tax foreign corporations doing business in the State. The New York Legislature, for example, to safeguard the position of New York City as the nation's financial center, has expressly provided that a foreign corporation "shall not be deemed to be doing business, employing capital, owning or leasing property, or maintaining an office in this state, for the purposes of this article, by reason of (a) the maintenance of cash balances with banks or trust companies in this state, or (b) the ownership of shares of stock or securities kept in this state, if kept in a safe deposit box, safe, vault or other receptacle rented for the purpose, or if pledged as collateral security, or if deposited with one or more banks or trust companies, or brokers who are members of a recognized security exchange, in safekeeping or custody accounts, or (c) the taking of any action by any such bank or trust company or broker, which is incidental to the rendering of safekeeping or custodian service to such corporation, or (d) the maintenance of an office in this state by one or more officers or directors of the corporation who are not employees of the corporation if the corporation otherwise is not doing business in this state, and does not employ capital or own or lease property in this state, or (e) the keeping of books or records of a corporation in this state if such books or records are not kept by employees of such corporation and such corporation does not otherwise do business, employ capital, own or lease property or maintain an office in this state, or (f) any combination of the foregoing activities." N.Y.Tax Law § 209–2, CCH ¶ 93–892, P–H ¶ 12,015.15.

Examine the statutes and regulations, if any, issued under your State's corporate franchise, capital stock, business income, or similar tax and prepare a report indicating the extent to which your State seeks to subject to tax foreign corporations:

    (a) selling goods or soliciting orders for sales in the State;

    (b) maintaining a sales or other office in the State;

    (c) carrying on the activities quoted above from the New York statute;

    (d) holding directors' or stockholders' meetings in the State.

Consider, also, whether your State imposes a second tier direct net income tax. If so, examine the differences in the two taxes.

References. The possible exposure of banks and other lending institutions to State franchise or income taxation is discussed in McCray, "State Taxation of Interstate Banking," 21 Ga.L.Rev. 283 (1986); J. Hellerstein, "Federal Constitutional Limitations on State Taxation of Multistate Banks," App. 11, Report of Board of Governors, Federal Reserve System, Senate Banking, Housing and Urban Affairs Committee (92d Cong., 2d Sess.1972).

Chapter 9

CORPORATE FRANCHISE, CAPITAL STOCK, AND INCOME TAXES

The most distinctive type of State tax on business, presenting many of the most difficult legal problems in the field, is the franchise, capital stock, or business income tax. Typically, these are levies on doing business, holding property, the grant of authority to do business, the privilege of existing as a domestic corporation, or carrying on other activities within the State. The "doing business" problem, i.e., the subject of many such levies, is considered in Chapter 8, § 3 supra. The problems dealt with in this chapter have to do principally with the measures of corporate franchise, capital stock, and business income taxes, and, particularly, with apportionment and allocation issues. With the inevitable overlapping of legal materials, some apportionment issues have already been adverted to in the chapters dealing with the Commerce Clause and Jurisdiction to Tax. See Chapters 6 and 8 supra. Here, however, it is intended to make a detailed study of the more important apportionment and allocation problems arising in the application of State levies.

A. CAPITAL STOCK TAXES

SECTION 1. INTRODUCTION *

"The capital stock tax, which has had a long history in State taxation, has its roots in the property tax.[1] The earliest form of general corporation tax in this country, the corporate excess tax, was not a special tax but a modification of the general property tax. It was a levy on the value of a corporate business in excess of the value of its assets. The excess included goodwill, going business value, and other

---

* This note is taken from J. Hellerstein, State Taxation I, Corporate Income and Franchise Taxes ¶ 11.1, pp. 691–92 (1983). Used with the consent of the copyright owner and publisher.

1. For an historical account of the development of capital stock taxation in this country, see Part IV "Historical Note," at page 197.

factors that are reflected in the market value of the corporation's stock. At first, this intangible "corporate excess" value was assessed and taxed to the shareholders. Subsequently, it was levied on the corporations themselves. This form of corporate taxation has largely given way to the capital stock tax.[2]

"The capital stock tax is typically an annual franchise tax, imposed on domestic corporations for the privilege of existing as a corporation, and on foreign corporations for the privilege of doing business, or the actual conduct of business, within the taxing State. It is usually measured by the value of the business as a going enterprise, determined on a book value basis, although in some States an attempt is made to utilize the market value.[3]

"The capital stock tax is to be distinguished from organization or entrance fees or taxes. During the nineteenth century, it was customary for the States to collect flat fees to cover the costs of incorporation. After the Civil War, these fees were gradually increased and evolved into taxes. These levies are typically based on the par value of authorized stock, and a flat rate on each share of authorized no-par value stock. They are collected at the time the incorporation papers are filed; and upon the subsequent filing of a certificate increasing the corporation's authorized capital, an additional tax is collected.

"In 1894, Ohio extended this principle to foreign corporations by imposing a tax on the grant of a license to do business in the State, measured by the amount of capital stock to be employed in the State. This type of entrance tax spread throughout the country. In some States, there is a flat duty, which may more nearly resemble a fee than a tax. Many States, however, measure the tax by the amount of authorized or issued capital stock apportioned to the State. Unlike the corporate franchise tax, entrance taxes are not annually recurring levies. They come into play after the initial entrance only if the amount of authorized or issued capital is increased, or if the amount of property or volume of business in the State, or other apportionment factors, increase.[4]" J. Hellerstein, State Taxation I, Corporate Income and Franchise Taxes ¶ 11.1, pp. 691–92 (1983).

SECTION 2. CAPITAL STOCK TAXES MEASURED BY AUTHORIZED CAPITAL STOCK

In Looney v. Crane, 245 U.S. 178, 38 S.Ct. 85 (1917), Texas franchise and permit taxes, measured by authorized capital stock, were set aside as applied to a foreign corporation engaged in interstate and intrastate business because they imposed "direct burdens upon interstate commerce and moreover exerted the taxing authority of the State

---

2. For a brief history of corporate excess and the capital stock taxes in this country, see *State and Local Taxation* 391 et seq., and 3 Willis Comm.Rep. at 904–907.

3. Current capital stock taxes are listed in Table of Capital Values Taxes, P–H All States Guide ¶ 240.

4. See *State and Local Taxation* 393; W. Beaman, *Paying Taxes to Other States* 16–1 (1963) (entrance taxes).

over property and rights which were wholly beyond the confines of the State and not subject to its jurisdiction and therefore constituted a taking without due process." 245 U.S. at 187.

In Hump Hairpin Co. v. Emmerson, 258 U.S. 290, 42 S.Ct. 305 (1922), an Illinois franchise tax was imposed on a foreign manufacturing corporation, measured by authorized capital stock allocated to the State. Of the 6,000,000 shares of capital stock authorized, 5,500,000 had been issued. The basis for the allocation was property located and business done within and without the State. Because all the corporation's tangible assets were located in Illinois, where its principal office was located, to which its salesmen were attached, and where all orders were accepted, the Court upheld the levy even though not all the authorized stock was issued and the corporation made sales in interstate commerce. The Court noted that if the tax had been "computed on the property admitted to have been in use in the State," as distinguished from a levy on allocated authorized capital stock, "it would be but slightly less than the tax collected." 258 U.S. at 295, 296.

In Air–Way Electric Appliance Corporation v. Day, 266 U.S. 71, 45 S.Ct. 12 (1924), the Court invalidated an Ohio franchise tax, measured by the authorized capital stock of a foreign corporation allocated to the State. While the corporation had 400,000 shares of authorized no par value stock, it had only 50,485 issued and outstanding. The allocation to Ohio was made on the basis of the ratio of Ohio property and business to the corporation's total property and business. The corporation was engaged in both interstate and intrastate business in Ohio. The Court held that the tax violated the Commerce Clause, because a levy on authorized stock amounting to eight times the number of issued shares, the latter being represented by property, a part of which was used in interstate commerce, "necessarily amounts to a tax and direct burden upon all the property and business including the interstate commerce of the plaintiff." 266 U.S. at 82–83. The Court also held that the tax violated the Equal Protection Clause because "the mere number of authorized non-par value shares is not a reasonable basis for the classification of foreign corporations for the purpose of determining the amount of such annual fees. Such a classification is not based on anything having relation to the purpose for which it is made." Id. at 85.

In Roberts & Schaefer Co. v. Emmerson, 271 U.S. 50, 46 S.Ct. 375 (1926), the Court considered an attack by a domestic corporation on a franchise tax measured by authorized capital stock. The corporation had 10,000 shares of authorized no-par value stock. Under the statute par value stock was taxed at five cents per $100 of par value, whereas no-par value stock was taxed at five cents per share. The plaintiff, which did all its business in Illinois, relied on Air–Way Electric Appliance Corporation v. Day, supra, in attacking the levy. In rejecting the argument that authorized stock may not be used as a measure of the tax, the Court distinguished between a domestic and a foreign corporation, saying, "We cannot say that a State may not impose a franchise tax on a domestic corporation, measured by its authorized capital stock." 271 U.S. at 54.

The Court also rejected the contention that it was unreasonable to tax no-par stock at five cents per share, as compared with par value stock at five cents per $100, thereby arbitrarily assuming that each share of no-par stock was represented by $100 of property. The Court pointed out that the corporation's power to issue stock is derived from the State of Illinois; that the tax is not a property tax but "a tax on the corporate franchise, which includes the privilege, whether exercised or not, of issuing and using when issued, a particular kind of stock known as 'no-par value stock.'" Id. at 55–56. On examination, it was found that there are "differences of practical importance between the two classes of stock" sufficient to warrant a separate classification.

SECTION 3.   CAPITAL STOCK TAXES MEASURED BY ISSUED CAPITAL STOCK

In New York v. Latrobe, 279 U.S. 421, 49 S.Ct. 377 (1929), the Court sustained a New York State "annual license fee" or "franchise tax" collected as a condition of obtaining a certificate of authority to do business in the State, which was imposed on a foreign corporation and measured by issued capital stock allocated to the State. The tax was imposed at a flat rate per share of no-par value stock on the number of shares allocated to the State. The Court rejected the contention that under the *Air–Way Electric Appliance* case the use of a fixed rate of six cents per share allocated to the State infringes on the Equal Protection Clause. Here, said the Court, issued capital stock, not authorized stock, is the basis for the levy. The tax is, therefore, not based on authority to issue stock, an authority obtained from the State of incorporation, but on shares issued and used in the business in the State. Moreover, the State is justified in taxing no-par stock at a fixed rate per share and par value stock at par. Accord, as applied to a corporation engaged in interstate commerce, Western Cartridge Co. v. Emmerson, 281 U.S. 511, 50 S.Ct. 383 (1930); Southern Pacific Co. v. State Corp. Comm'n, 41 N.M. 556, 72 P.2d 15 (1937), in which the court upheld different treatment for par and no-par value issued stock. For cases dealing with the capital stock measure and its apportionment, see pp. 468–72 infra.

B.   THE CORPORATE INCOME TAX MEASURE

SECTION 1.   CONFORMITY TO THE FEDERAL INCOME TAX

The outstanding characteristic of State corporate net income measures is their broad conformity to the measure of the Federal corporation income tax.[5] Alaska at one time went even further by imposing a piggy-back tax, at the rate of 18 percent of the Federal income tax, payable on income from Alaska sources. That tax was abandoned by Alaska in 1972 for a statute that essentially incorporates by reference the provisions of the Internal Revenue Code determining taxable income.[6] No other State has adopted the piggy-back method with respect to its corporate net income tax, either because of concern as to the constitutionality of such a tax, or because their legislatures have been unwilling to surrender completely to Congress the power to determine State corporate income tax policy.

Pressure from taxpayers for easing compliance and auditing burdens has been the prime force responsible for the very wide conformity of the State corporate net income measures to Federal taxable income, before allocation, apportionment, or other method of division of the income. The most efficient and simplest method of achieving Federal conformity, without complete piggy-backing, is to incorporate by reference in the State statute the current key Federal income tax terms, such as "gross income" and "taxable income," and then make such specific adjustments as State policy may dictate. Many States have adopted that type of conformity.[7]

Some legislatures have been unwilling to incorporate by reference the provisions of the Internal Revenue Code applicable to the taxable year as the starting point for determining the State corporate net income base. There are several reasons for this reluctance. First, there are concerns among lawyers that such legislation would constitute an unconstitutional delegation to Congress of legislative powers, and that the incorporation by reference may run afoul of the provisions of State constitutions that require clear identification of the precise law being enacted. See Chapter 13, § 1 infra. Second, as a matter of policy, legislators may be unwilling to empower Congress to change the State's tax laws, without their having had an opportunity to review the changes. To be sure, the State legislature can always reject any amendment to the Internal Revenue Code, but that is a cumbersome procedure requiring affirmative action by the legislature, and it may mean a time lag.

Incorporation of the terminology of the Internal Revenue Code as it exists at the effective date of the State conformity act can be accomplished without any constitutional defect by the clumsy but constitutionally comforting expedient of attaching to the legislation a reprint of the provisions of the IRC being enacted.[8] However, since that expedient does not resolve the constitutionality of incorporating future Congressional changes in the Federal income tax, some States have limited

5. See Chart, Federal Income Tax Rules Used in the States, P–H All States Guide ¶ 221.

6. See Alaska Stat. § 4320.021, CCH ¶ 96–868, P–H ¶ 12,213.

7. See note 5 supra.

8. See, e.g., N.Y.Laws of 1966, General City Law, Art. 2–D, § 1(c); CCH ¶ 193–571x, P–H ¶ 83,501.

their conformity to the Federal income tax provisions as they exist at the date of the adoption of the State act.

The States were jolted into a realization of the risks to State revenues that are entailed in adopting the moving Federal tax base by President Ronald Reagan's drastic Federal income tax-cutting program effected in 1981. To illustrate, sharp increases in depreciation under the Accelerated Cost Recovery System (the 15–10–5–3 year depreciable life plan) would in turn apply to the many States that follow Federal depreciation rules. A conference of State governors and State legislators was informed that under the new depreciation rules, the States would lose an estimated $500 million in corporate income taxes in 1981, $1.6 billion in 1982 and by 1986, the revenue loss would increase to $8.8 billion.[9] As a consequence, Governor Hugh L. Carey of New York recommended in his 1982 State of the State Message to the Legislature that New York amend its tax laws to prevent the Federal depreciation and some other Federal tax reducing measures from applying to the State's income based taxes and the proposals were enacted by the Legislature.[10] Similar measures have been adopted in other States.[11]

The Federal Tax Reform Act of 1986 likewise had significant repercussions on State corporate and individual income taxes, but this time the result was to increase revenues. The reduction in depreciation and medical expense allowances, the disallowance of the deduction for State and local sales taxes, the repeal of the partial exclusion of capital gains, and other revenue producing changes were offset for Federal, but not State, income tax purposes by sharp reductions in the tax rates. As a consequence the States found themselves with large unexpected surpluses. Governor Mario Cuomo of New York announced his plan to seek legislation that would return to State taxpayers the $1.67 billion in annual excess taxes that he estimated the State would collect because of the changes in the Federal tax law. New York Times, Feb. 20, 1987. The National Association of State Budget Offices, which conducted a survey, reported that 20 States, including New York, were expected to increase personal exemptions and standard deductions and reduce the number of tax brackets and tax rates, as a result of the changes in the Federal income tax law. New York Times, Feb. 25, 1987. Only $905 million of the total expected windfall of $5.6 billion was expected to be kept by the States and used for public services. Id.

9. See N.Y.Times, Feb. 22, 1981.

10. Id. Jan. 7, 1982; N.Y.Laws of 1982, ch. 55 amending § 208(g) Tax Law.

11. See P–H All States Guide, "How States Line Up on New Fed. ACRS Depreciation," Rep.Bull. 10, March 9, 1982.

C. APPORTIONMENT AND ALLOCATION OF PROPERTY, RECEIPTS, AND INCOME

INTRODUCTORY NOTE

Apportionment and allocation of property, receipts, and income are among the most troublesome and difficult areas of State taxation.[12] Our problem relates to taxpayers doing business or maintaining property in several States and, accordingly, subject to tax in the various States. How do we determine the portion of the total value of the corporation's capital stock, or the portion of the gross receipts or net income of the individual, partnership, or corporation which should be included in the measure of each State's tax?

One method, termed "specific allocation," is to attempt to trace the property, or receipt, or income to the State of its source, and to include the item in full in the measure of that State's tax. Thus, in a corporate capital stock tax, which ordinarily employs as its measure the value of the corporation's assets in the State, the real and tangible personal property located in the State would be treated as a part of the corporation's property used and allocated to the State. Where, however, the property is intangible, the problem is more difficult. Suppose the intangible is an account receivable owed to the taxpayer, which maintains its plant and executive offices in State A, by a customer in State B, and arising out of a sale of goods manufactured in and shipped from State A. If both States tax the account receivable in full, the corporation dividing its operations between two States would be subject to a more onerous tax burden than the local manufacturer selling its goods in one State. If only one State should include the intangible in the measure of its tax, which State should that be? State A affords the taxpayer the benefits and protection of conducting its manufacturing operations and of maintaining its executive offices in that State, and, therefore, it has a strong basis for regarding the proceeds of the manufacturer as part of the assets attributable to its State. Likewise, the State of the market, State B, can make out a persuasive case for levying the tax. It furnishes the market for the sale. The customer-debtor is located in State B, whose courts may have to be resorted to in order to enable the taxpayer to collect the amount owing. Moreover, unless State B imposes the tax on out-of-state vendors who do business

---

12. The terms "allocation" and "apportionment" are often used interchangeably in State statutes and decisions in referring to the formulary method of dividing income or other tax measures; and the term "specific allocation" is used to refer to nonformulary attribution of income to a State or States, such as the assignment of rents from mobile tangible personal property to the various States in which the property is issued by the lessee. Increasingly, however, the term specific allocation is being used to refer to the attribution of a particular type of income or receipt or property or the like to a designated State, whereas apportionment refers to the division of the tax base by formula. That is the terminology employed in the editorial materials in this work. The Uniform Division of Income for Tax Purposes Act ("UDITPA") uses the terms allocation and apportionment. See Chapter 9, subd. C, § 6 infra.

in State B, they may have a competitive advantage over local manufacturer-vendors, since State A may not in fact impose a similar tax.

Similar and indeed more complex problems are presented by gross receipts and income taxes. T manufactures goods in State A, where it maintains its executive offices. It warehouses the goods in State B and sells them in States A, B, C, and D. Where does the sale "take place"? In State A, where the order is accepted, or in State B, where the stock of goods is located from which the order is filled, or in State C or D where the goods are delivered to the customers? Whatever the law of contracts as to where the contract is made, or the law of sales as to where title passes—considerations which may have some bearing on the constitutional power of the States to impose certain laws—these considerations would appear to have little importance in determining State fiscal policy as to how the receipt or income should be taxed. Each State, A, B, C, and D, would appear to have a legitimate claim to a portion of the receipt or income.

It is because of such competing claims of the States, the difficulty of fixing a single basis of intangible assets and of attaching the entire proceeds of sales to a single State, that specific allocation of intangible assets under capital stock taxes and specific allocation of the proceeds of sales under net income taxes have been largely rejected by the States. Specific allocation, however, is applied in many States to rents and royalties from real estate, including oil and mineral royalties, and from tangible personal property; patents and copyright royalties; dividends and interest; capital gains and losses; and, in some States, to compensation for services.[13]

The operating income of a manufacturer, wholesaler, or retailer cannot be satisfactorily allocated by source. To deal with this problem, apportionment by the formula method has been developed.

The theory of apportionment by formula is that certain factors or elements of a business will fairly reflect the portion of the measure of the tax allocable to a State. Thus, in capital stock taxes, which employ essentially a property measure, an apportionment method used in some States is a single-factor formula of the ratio of the corporation's real and tangible personal property within the State to the corporation's entire real and tangible personal property, wherever located. For example, suppose the value of T's entire real and personal property is valued at $1,000,000 and its factory and inventory and other tangibles within the State are valued at $750,000. Seventy-five per cent of its capital stock will be allocated to the taxing State, there to be taxed. If all the other States in which T does business utilize a similar method of allocation and find the same values for T's property and capital stock,

---

13. This problem is extensively discussed in G. Altman & F. Keesling, Allocation of Income in State Taxation (2d ed. 1950). For an overall treatment of apportionment, allocation, and separate accounting, see J. Hellerstein, State Taxation I, Corporate Income and Franchise Taxes ch. 8 (1983).

T's entire capital stock will be taxed, in full, but only once, by all the States in which it does business.

While the single-factor property formula is sometimes still used in apportioning capital stock taxes, it has been generally discarded in apportioning net income and, in many States, in apportioning capital stock. The most widely used formula, the so-called Massachusetts formula, employs three factors: real and tangible personal property, payroll, and sales. Typically, the three factors are averaged, so that if a corporation has 40 percent of its property, 30 percent of its payroll and 50 percent of its sales in the State, its allocation percentage will be 40; and it will allocate 40 percent of its income or capital stock or other measure of the tax to the State.

A broad consensus has developed over the country that, for most manufacturing and mercantile businesses, averaging of the ratios of property, payroll, and sales or gross receipts within the State to the totals throughout the business typically produces an equitable and workable division of a net income tax measure.[14] To be sure, this consensus has taken decades to develop and there have been influential advocates of very different formulas. In 1964, the Willis Committee, on the basis of the most comprehensive study of State taxation of inter-

---

14. The development of apportionment methods since the inception of the modern corporate income tax, at the end of the first decade of the twentieth century, has been greatly influenced by the work of the committees of the National Tax Association (N.T.A.). As far back as 1917, Professor T.S. Adams of Yale University, one of the country's pioneers in public finance, wrote:

> Eventually the difficult problem of allocation will have to be solved more scientifically. What is most needed is a uniform rule. Just what rule shall be selected is less important than the general adoption of the same rule by competing jurisdictions. Eventually the federal government (through the Interstate Commerce Commission or the Federal Trade Commission or both) should lay down general rules for this important department of American business. An equally efficacious remedy would be found in the adoption of some common rule by the Congress of States whose organization has just been effected; or by the passage, voluntarily, of uniform legislation upon this subject by the several state legislatures. [1917 N.T.A. Procs. 185, 194.]

In 1921, an N.T.A. committee prepared a model bill for the taxation of business income, which apportioned net income on the basis of tangible property and gross re-

ceipts. 6 N.T.A.Bull. 110, 118 (1921). By 1939, a committee of the Association recommended the use of the three-factor Massachusetts formula, consisting of tangible property, payrolls, and sales, as the most acceptable method of apportioning business net income. 1939 N.T.A.Procs. 205. For other reports of N.T.A. committees relating to apportionment and allocation, see "Report of Committee on Standardization and Simplification of Business Taxes," 1929 N.T.A.Procs. 152; "Report of Committee on Uniformity and Reciprocity in State Taxing Legislation," 1933 id. at 259; "Preliminary Report of Committee of N.T.A. on Allocation of Income," 1938 id. at 486; "Report of Committee of N.T.A. on Allocation of Income," 1939 id. at 190; "Preliminary Report of Committee on Tax Situs and Allocation," 1949 id. at 239; "Second Preliminary Report of the Committee on Tax Situs and Allocation," 1950 id. at 349; "Final Report of the Committee on Tax Situs and Allocation," 1951 id. at 456. For major studies of apportionment and allocation, see Ford, "The Allocation of Corporate Income for the Purpose of State Taxation," N.Y. State Tax Commission, Spec. Rep. No. 6 (1933); G. Altman & F. Keesling, note 13 supra; W. Beaman, Paying Taxes to Other States (1963); Willis Comm. Rep. (1964–1965); Hartman, "State Taxation of Corporate Income from a Multistate Business," 13 Vand.L.Rev. 21 (1959).

state commerce in our history,[15] recommended the abandonment of the gross receipts or sales factor for the two-factor property-payroll formula. There are economists who strongly oppose the use of a sales factor in the formula, on the ground that wealth is not created by selling but only by production and the rendition of services.[16] The Willis Committee proposed the elimination of the sales or receipts factor largely because of the burdens and costs of compliance and administration.[17] Its recommendation evoked a storm of virtually unanimous protest from State taxing authorities.[18] The theoretical basis suggested by Professor Lowell Harriss and other economists has been rejected by many students of income taxation on the ground that a State which provides a market for goods is furnishing a key link in the chain of income production; and that since the other two factors, property and payroll, weight the apportionment heavily in favor of the manufacturing States, the use of a sales factor and the destination rule of apportionment of sales receipts, is necessary to provide market States which do not have heavy manufacturing industries with an equitable portion of interstate net income.[19]

The reaction of the business community to the Willis Committee proposal was at best lukewarm, and the leading spokesmen for manufacturers and other national businesses in State tax matters either failed to support or opposed the two-factor formula on the grounds (at least as publicly stated) that the abandonment of the widely used sales factor ought not be imposed on the States by Federal intervention, and that it would shift tax burdens among the States.[20]

15. The Special Subcommittee on State Taxation of Interstate Commerce (the Willis Committee) was established by Congress in enacting P.L. 86–272, which it regarded as a stop-gap measure. After four years of extensive investigation, the Committee published its two-volume, 1100–page comprehensive study of State taxes based on net income, and a year later a third volume dealing with sales and use taxes, capital stock taxes, and gross receipts taxes.

16. See Harriss, "Economic Aspects of Interstate Apportionment of Business Income," 37 Taxes 327 (1959); for others who advocate the elimination of a receipts or sales factor, see Studenski and Glasser, "New Threat in State Business Taxation," 36 Harv.Bus.Rev. 77 (November–December 1958); Murphy, "State Taxation of Interstate Commerce," Hearings Before Select Committee on Small Business (86th Cong. 1st Sess., 1959) 327–328; Barber, "A Suggested Shot at a Gordian Knot of Income Apportionment," 13 Nat.Tax.J. 243 (1960); Drabkin, "The Role of Myth in State Taxation of Interstate Business," State and Local Taxes on Business 55 (Tax.Inst.Sympos. 1964).

17. 4 Willis Comm.Rep. 1144 et seq.

18. See Hearings Before the Special Subcommittee on State Taxation of Interstate Commerce (the Willis Committee), House Committee on the Judiciary (89th Cong., 2d Sess., on HR 11798 (Interstate Taxation Act) and companion bills, passim (1966).

19. See J. Hellerstein, "Allocation and Nexus in State Taxation of Interstate Businesses," in State and Local Taxes on Business, Symposium of Tax Inst. of America 67 (1964), reprinted in 20 Tax L.Rev. 259 (1965); Kust, "State Taxation of Interstate Income: New Dimensions of an Old Problem," 12 Tax Exec. 45 (1959); Hartman, "State Taxation of Corporate Income from a Multistate Business," 13 Vand.L.Rev. 21 (1959); Barnes, "Prerequisites of a Federal Statute Regulating State Taxation of Interstate Commerce," 46 Va.L.Rev. 1269 (1960); Brieske, "One Area of Agreement—A Uniform Allocation Formula," 1963 N.T.A. Procs. 292. The rationale back of the three-factor Massachusetts formula is discussed in "Second Preliminary Report, Committee on Tax Situs and Allocation," 1950 N.T.A.Procs. 349 et seq.

20. See statements of the Chamber of Commerce of the United States in "Hear-

Despite the use of a sales or gross receipts factor in their apportionment formulas, a good many States—particularly the smaller, less industrialized ones whose markets were exploited by manufacturers and wholesalers which maintained their factories, warehouses, commercial centers, and employees in other States in the Northeast and Midwest before the great expansion in recent decades of industrial and commercial activities in the South and the Pacific Coast—received little or no revenues from such out-of-state corporations. This was due, to a large extent, to the Supreme Court's interpretation of the Commerce Clause (and, to a lesser extent, the Due Process Clause) of the Constitution as imposing restrictions on State business taxation of foreign corporations, which many of the States affected and commentators regarded as unduly severe. In 1959, the Supreme Court liberalized its approach to the Commerce Clause in the *Northwestern States Portland Cement* and the *Stockham Valves* cases,[21] which for the first time, at least clearly and explicitly, made it possible for the States to levy direct net income taxes, as distinguished from franchise taxes measured by net income or capital stock, on a large number of foreign manufacturing and mercantile corporations conducting their businesses across State lines. To be sure, Congress responded with unusual alacrity to the protest of spokesmen for business organizations, and enacted, for the first time in our history, legislation which imposed jurisdictional restrictions on State income taxation of such businesses.[22] Nevertheless, a very considerable broadening of the State taxing powers over interstate commerce had taken place.

To translate this broadened taxing power into revenue dollars from multistate corporations required the use by the market States of a sales or receipts factor, along with the destination test of sales attribution. Without the sales factor, coupled with the destination test, the broadened taxing powers would have been largely a Pyrrhic victory for the States.[23] This infirmity in the statutes was rapidly cured by the prompt adoption by many States of the Uniform Division of Income for Tax Purposes Act (UDITPA), which employs a three-factor formula and the destination test of the attribution of sales, i.e., sales of goods are generally attributed to a State if the property is delivered or shipped to a purchaser within the State regardless of the f.o.b. point or other conditions of the sale.[24]

In recent years, some States, including Florida, Massachusetts, Minnesota, New York, and Wisconsin, have distorted the original

---

ings Before the Subcommittee on State Taxation of Interstate Commerce ("Mondale Committee"), Senate Finance Committee (93rd Cong. 1st Sess., Sept. 18–19, 1973) [hereinafter cited as "Mondale Comm. Hearings"] at 86 et seq.; and the National Association of Manufacturers, id. at 260 et seq.; see also Kust, "State Taxation of Interstate Commerce—An Obdurate Issue," 92 Tax Exec. (April 1973), reprinted in Mondale Comm. Hearings at 92 et seq.

21. Chapter 6, subd. C, § 2 supra.

22. P.L. 86–272, Chapter 8, § 2 supra.

23. See note 19 supra.

24. For a vigorous statement of opposition to the use of the state-of-destination rule as resulting in the taxation of extraterritorial values, see Britten, "Taxation Without Representation Modernized," 46 A.B.A.J. 369, 526 (1960).

purpose of the sales destination test by giving greater weight to the sales factor than the property and payroll factors, in order to reduce their taxes on in-state manufacturers and mercantile companies and at the same time to offset some or all of the lost revenues (or to augment their revenues) by added taxes on out-of-state taxpayers selling goods in the local market. Such an allocation is open to the criticism that it weights the sales factor at the expense of the other two factors in the three-factor formula. In other States, manufacturing costs have been substituted for the payroll factor; other variations obtain in various States. See notes to Table 1, Chapter 9, subd. C, § 6 infra.

References. There are comprehensive surveys of the allocation and apportionment practices of the States, as they existed in 1963, in 2 Willis Comm.Rep. passim, and W. Beaman, Paying Taxes to Other States, ch. 7 (1963).

For analysis of the current allocation and apportionment practices of the States see J. Hellerstein, State Taxation I, Corporate Income and Franchise Taxes, chs. 9 and 10 (1983). For tables of the current factors, see State Apportionment and Allocation, P–H All States Guide ¶¶ 223– 226A.

SECTION 1. THE RIGHT TO APPORTION OR ALLOCATE THE MEASURE OF THE TAX

Notes and Problems

A. *The Doing Business Out-of-State Requirement.* Apportionment and allocation under the statutes are not permitted in some States unless the taxpayer is "doing business" outside the State or carries on "trade or business * * * partly within and partly without the State." See the Iowa corporate income tax, Iowa Code Ann. § 422.33(1), CCH ¶ 92–406, P–H ¶ 12,135.5; the Tennessee corporate earnings tax, Tenn.Code Ann. § 67–4– 909, CCH ¶ 132–480, P–H ¶ 25,295; Montag Bros. v. State Revenue Comm'n, 50 Ga.App. 660, 179 S.E. 563 (1935), affirmed 182 Ga. 568, 186 S.E. 558 (1936); Rock Island Refining Co. v. State Tax Comm'n, 193 Okl. 468, 145 P.2d 194 (1943), appeal dismissed 322 U.S. 711, 64 S.Ct. 1159 (1944).

In some States, the courts have sustained the action of tax administrators in requiring proof of actual payment of franchise or similar taxes by a corporation claiming to be doing business in another State as a condition to permitting apportionment. Roane Hosiery, Inc. v. King, 214 Tenn. 441, 381 S.W.2d 265 (1964). One court has gone even further by holding that proof of actual payment of a franchise tax to the District of Columbia did not establish that the corporation was doing business outside the State; the court denied it apportionment of its income. E.F. Johnson Co. v. Commissioner of Taxation, 302 Minn. 236, 224 N.W.2d 150 (1974), appeal dismissed 421 U.S. 982, 95 S.Ct. 1985 (1975). In that case, the taxpayer maintained offices only in Minnesota, where its manufacturing plant was located. It sold its products throughout the country through manufacturers' representatives, who were independent contractors, and solicited orders for several companies. The extensive "non-solicitation" services rendered by the manufacturers' representatives to the taxpayer's customers, including assisting them in preparing specifications for custom-made articles, credit checking, collection of accounts, and leveling inventories between various distributors, strongly suggest that the company was "doing business" in other States within the usual definition of that term. The court relied on the rule that the right of apportionment does not accrue from activities of independent contractors outside the State. Cf. Irvine Co. v. McColgan, 26 Cal.2d 160, 157 P.2d 847 (1947), in which apportionment was denied a corporation that grew citrus crops and other products in California; the crops were cleaned, graded, packed, marketed and shipped to other States by cooperative market associations, whose activities in other States did not give the corporation the right of apportionment.

B. *Maintenance of an Out-of-State Office.* A stricter rule than the doing or transacting of business in another State as a condition precedent to the right to apportion or allocate for corporate franchise or income tax purposes obtains in some States through the requirement that the corporation have a regular place of business outside the State. See N.J.Rev.Stat. § 54:10A–6, CCH ¶ 94–053, P–H ¶ 16,150.

An interesting decision dealing with what constitutes the maintenance of an office outside the State was handed down by Mr. Justice Cohen, who has written a number of searching opinions for the Pennsylvania Supreme Court in apportionment and allocation cases. In Commonwealth v. Hellertown Mfg. Co., 438 Pa. 134, 264 A.2d 382 (1970), the taxpayer, a wholly owned subsidiary of Champion Spark Plug Company, challenged the denial by the Pennsylvania tax administrators of apportionment under the State's corporate net income tax. The issues were (1) whether Hellertown was "transacting" business outside the State, so as to be entitled to apportion, and (2) if so, whether it "negotiated" or "effected" sales outside the State for purposes of the then sales office negotiation rule for the attribution of receipts from sales.

The factual pattern presented by the case is one that has become increasingly common in recent years with the rapid growth of vertically integrated enterprises. Hellertown's sole business was the manufacture of spark plugs, all of which it sold to Champion. The taxpayer's factory was located and all its production operations were conducted in Pennsylvania under the direction of the resident general manager of manufacturing, who was an assistant secretary of the company. All other activities and the general direction and governance of the company's affairs were conducted in Toledo, Ohio, by the taxpayer's other officers, all of whom held the same offices of Champion. The parent company owned an office building in Toledo, where the officers had their offices. The entire business of Hellertown, including administration, labor negotiations, budget, accounting, research and design, engineering and management services, and the like— other than the factory operations—was carried on in Toledo by personnel of Champion, for which the parent was paid a "management fee" of approximately $550,000 for one of the years at issue, computed as 15 percent of the direct costs of Hellertown's manufacturing operations.

All orders for spark plugs were received from Champion's customers at Toledo, where Champion employees decided whether to fill them from Hellertown's inventory and operations or from one of Champion's other production facilities. Hellertown shipped the goods directly to the customers of Champion, which handled credit, billing, and collections. Hellertown was authorized to do business in Ohio, and there paid franchise tax.

Adopting a "practical and not a technical test" of the meaning of "transacting business," the court stated:

> If the taxpayer is present (e.g., through administrative functioning, property ownership or sales activity) in some fashion outside of Pennsylvania and if this presence is related to its actual business activity, it is transacting business outside of Pennsylvania. This conclusion follows without reference to whether or not the taxpayer is "doing business" elsewhere as that term is customarily used, is registered to do business in another state in accordance with that state's corporation laws or pays a privilege tax to that state.

> Here, it is unquestioned that Hellertown's administrative machinery and executive policies are operated and established by its officers at Toledo, Ohio. These activities are as essential to Hellertown's manufacturing activity as are the actual production operations at its plant and are equally a part of its "business." Consequently, we have no problem in concluding that not all of Hellertown's business is transacted in Pennsylvania and that it is entitled to use the allocation fractions. [264 A.2d at 386.]

The court also held that Hellertown maintained an office in Toledo and was entitled to treat its sales as having been negotiated or effected in Toledo, through the activities of the joint officers of the two companies and of the employees of Champion who handled sales and for whose services Hellertown paid a management fee. Mr. Justice Cohen stated:

> Finally, the payment from Hellertown to Champion was clearly not a sales commission; rather, it was a conglomerate payment for many services. Even assuming we cannot resolve the issue of whether or not any part of Hellertown's management fee constituted rent (payment for the use of premises by its officers), we nevertheless, must face the issue presented by the word "maintained." It is our conclusion that where part of a corporation's own business activity is carried on at a defined location and where that corporation reimburses or otherwise pays the actual owner or lessor a fee for the latter's services to it at that location, the corporation is participating in the maintenance of those premises because it is, at least in part, responsible for the upkeep of those premises. Any other conclusion, we believe, would fail to account properly for the 1939 change from "owned or rented" to "maintained." Therefore, we hold that the Toledo premises were maintained within the meaning of the Act by Hellertown. [264 A.2d at 388.]

C. The State laws imposing a condition on the right to apportion or allocate capital stock, net income, and other tax bases developed during an era in our constitutional history when the prevailing Supreme Court doctrine was that a foreign corporation engaged in interstate commerce was not subject to a State franchise tax—the type of corporate levy employed by most States—unless it was doing an intrastate business within the State. See Chapter 6, subd. A, § 1 supra. But in recent decades those decisions were whittled away with the most significant development prior to 1977 being the Court's holding such decisions inapplicable to a direct net income tax. See Chapter 6, subd. A, § 4(a) supra. As a consequence, some States now supplement their franchise taxes by an alternative direct net income tax. In 1977, the Court abandoned altogether the doctrine that a privilege tax upon an exclusively interstate business was per se invalid. See Chapter 6, subd. A, § 4(b) supra.

Some States have adapted their apportionment provisions to the broadening of the taxing powers of the States. Thus in a number of States a corporation may apportion and allocate the tax base, following the pattern of P.L. 86–272 (see Chapter 8, § 2 supra), if it is subject to the power of another State to levy a corporate franchise or income tax, irrespective of whether such power has been exercised. See Mass.Laws Ann., ch. 63, § 38, CCH ¶ 91–289, P–H ¶ 12,405; Hawes v. William L. Bonnell Co., 116 Ga.App. 184, 156 S.E.2d 536 (1967); Blackmon v. Habersham Mills, Inc., 233 Ga. 501, 212 S.E.2d 337 (1975); Commonwealth v. Greenville Steel Car Co., 469 Pa. 444, 366 A.2d 569 (1976). Compare with the *Greenville Steel Car* case the decisions of the Pennsylvania courts under the prior statutes. Commonwealth v. Tube City Iron & Metal Co., 432 Pa. 600, 248 A.2d 225 (1968).

Query: should the traditional rules requiring doing business outside the State, or maintaining an office outside the State, as a sine qua non to apportionment and allocation, survive the broadened power of the States to tax? Suppose a Delaware corporation maintains a business establishment and employees in Georgia and Texas. Texas has no corporate net income tax, but it does have a capital stock tax. May Georgia measure its income tax on the corporation by its entire net income in view of the fact that no other State taxes the income? Is the failure of one State to exercise its constitutional power to tax a corporation relevant to the constitutional power of another State to tax the corporation?

See Annot., 167 A.L.R. 943.

SECTION 2. APPORTIONMENT BY FORMULA: FEDERAL CONSTITUTIONAL LIMITATIONS

(a) Property Taxes

NORFOLK AND WESTERN RAILWAY COMPANY v. MISSOURI STATE TAX COMMISSION

Supreme Court of the United States, 1968.
390 U.S. 317, 88 S.Ct. 995.

MR. JUSTICE FORTAS delivered the opinion of the Court.

This case brings before us, once again, troublesome problems arising from state taxation of an interstate commercial enterprise. At issue is a tax assessment pursuant to a Missouri statute specifying the manner in which railroad rolling stock is to be assessed for the State's ad valorem tax on that property.[1]

1. The tax in question applies to "all real property * * * [and] tangible personal property * * * owned, hired or leased by any railroad company * * * in this state." Intangible personal property

In 1964 the Norfolk & Western Railway Co. (N & W), a Virginia corporation with interstate rail operations, leased all of the property of appellant Wabash Railroad Company. The Wabash owned substantial fixed property and rolling stock, and did substantial business in Missouri as well as in other States. Prior to the lease, N & W owned no fixed property and only a minimal amount of rolling stock in Missouri. N & W is primarily a coal-carrying railroad. Much of its equipment and all of its specialized coal-carrying equipment are generally located in the coal regions of Virginia, West Virginia, and Kentucky, and along the coal-ferrying routes from those regions to the eastern seaboard and the Great Lakes. Scarcely any of the specialized equipment ever enters Missouri. According to appellants, the Wabash property in Missouri was leased by N & W in order to diversify its business, not to provide the opportunity for an integrated through movement of traffic.

By the terms of the lease, the N & W became obligated to pay the 1965 taxes on the property of the Wabash in Missouri and elsewhere.[2] Upon receiving notice of the 1965 assessment from the appellee Missouri Tax Commission, the N & W filed a request for an adjustment and hearing before the Commission. The hearing was held, and the Commission sustained its assessment against the taxpayer's challenge. On judicial review, the Commission's decision was affirmed without opinion by the Circuit Court of Cole County, and then by the Supreme Court of Missouri. Appellants filed an appeal in this Court, contending that the assessment in effect reached property not located in Missouri and thus violated the Due Process Clause and the Interstate Commerce Clause of the United States Constitution. We noted probable jurisdiction. 389 U.S. 810, 88 S.Ct. 84, 19 L.Ed.2d 63 (1967).

I.

The Missouri property taxable to the N & W was assessed by the State Tax Commission at $31,298,939. Of this sum, $12,177,597 relates to fixed property within the State, an assessment that is not challenged by appellants. Their attack is aimed only at that portion of the assessment relating to rolling stock, $19,981,757.[3]

With respect to the assessment of rolling stock, the Commission used the familiar mileage formula authorized by the Missouri statute. In relevant part, this provides (§ 151.060(3)):

> " * * * when any railroad shall extend beyond the limits of this state and into another state in which a tax is levied and paid on the rolling stock of such road, then the said commission shall assess,

is explicitly exempted from this tax. Mo. V.A.S. § 151.010.

2. As of January 1, 1966, the N & W purchased the Wabash rolling stock that it had previously leased, while continuing to lease Wabash fixed property. This change in the relationship between N & W and the Wabash has no effect on the issues presented to us. Our analysis would apply both before and after the purchase of the Wabash rolling stock.

3. The Commission deducted from the sum of these two figures $860,415, representing an "economic factor" which is allowed to all railroads in varying amounts. Exactly the same deduction had been allowed the Wabash in each of the three preceding years.

equalize and adjust only such proportion of the total value of all the rolling stock of such railroad company as the number of miles of such road in this state bears to the total length of the road as owned or controlled by such company."

The Commission arrived at the assessment of rolling stock by first determining the value of all rolling stock, regardless of where located, owned or leased by the N & W as of the tax day, January 1, 1965. Value was ascertained by totaling the original cost, less accrued depreciation at 5% a year up to 75% of cost, of each locomotive, car, and other piece of mobile equipment. To the total value, $513,309,877, was applied an "equalizing factor" of 47%, employed in assessing all railroad property in an attempt to bring such assessments down to the level of other property assessments in Missouri. The Commission next found that 8.2824% of all the main and branch line road (excluding secondary and side tracks) owned, leased, or controlled by the N & W was situated in Missouri. This percentage was applied to the equalized value of all N & W rolling stock, and the resulting figure was $19,981,757.

There is no suggestion in this case that the Commission failed to follow the literal command of the statute. The problem arises because of appellants' contention that, in mechanically applying the statutory formula, the Commission here arrived at an unconscionable and unconstitutional result. It is their submission that the assessment was so far out of line with the actual facts of record with respect to the value of taxable rolling stock in the State as to amount to an unconstitutional attempt to exercise state taxing power on out-of-state property.

Appellants submitted evidence based upon an inventory of all N & W rolling stock that was actually in Missouri on tax day. The equalized value of this rolling stock, calculated on the same cost-less-depreciation basis employed by the Commission, was approximately $7,600,000, as compared with the assessed value of $19,981,000. Appellants also submitted evidence to show that the tax-day inventory was not unusual. The evidence showed that, both before and in the months immediately after the Wabash lease, the equalized value of the N & W rolling stock actually in Missouri never ranged far above the $7,600,000 figure. In the preceding year, 1964, the rolling stock assessment against the Wabash was only $9,177,683, and appellants demonstrated that neither the amount of rolling stock in Missouri nor the Missouri operations of the N & W and Wabash had materially increased in the intervening period.[4] The assessment of the fixed properties (for which no mileage formula was applied) hardly increased between 1964 and 1965. In 1964, prior to the lease, the fixed properties in Missouri were assessed at $12,092,594; in 1965, after the lease, the assessment was $12,177,597.

---

4. Appellants further argue that the arbitrariness of the result reached here is shown by the fact that if the rolling stock in Missouri had been taxable to the Wabash in 1965, rather than to N & W, the application of the formula to the same rolling stock would have resulted in an assessment of little more than half of that which was actually levied ($10,103,340).

The Supreme Court of Missouri concluded that the result reached by the Commission was justifiable. It pointed out that the statutory method used by the Commission proceeds on the assumption that "rolling stock is substantially evenly divided throughout the railroad's system, and the percentage of all units which are located in Missouri at any given time, or for any given period of time, will be substantially the same as the percentage of all the miles of road of the railroad located in Missouri." It then held that the valuation found by the Commission could be justified on the theory of "enhancement," although the Commission had not referred to that principle. The Court described the theory as follows:

> "The theory underlying such method of assessment is that rolling stock regularly employed in one state has an enhanced or augmented value when it is connected to, and because of its connection with, an integrated operational whole and may, therefore, be taxed according to its value as part of the system, although the other parts be outside the state;—in other words, the tax may be made to cover the enhanced value which comes to the property in the state through its organic relation to the system. Pullman Co. v. Richardson, 261 U.S. 330, 338, 43 S.Ct. 366, 67 L.Ed. 682."

The court correctly noted, however, that "even if the validity of such methods be conceded, the results, to be valid must be free of excessiveness and discrimination." It concluded that in the present case, the result reached by the Commission was justifiable. We disagree. In our opinion, the assessment violates the Due Process and Commerce Clauses of the Constitution.

II.

Established principles are not lacking in this much discussed area of the law. It is of course settled that a State may impose a property tax upon its fair share of an interstate transportation enterprise. * * * That fair share may be regarded as the value, appropriately ascertained, of tangible assets permanently or habitually employed in the taxing State, including a portion of the intangible, or "going-concern," value of the enterprise. Railway Express Agency v. Commonwealth of Virginia, 347 U.S. 359, 364, 74 S.Ct. 558, 561, 98 L.Ed. 757 (1954); Cudahy Packing Co. v. State of Minnesota, 246 U.S. 450, 455, 38 S.Ct. 373, 375, 62 L.Ed. 827 (1918); Adams Express Co. v. Ohio State Auditor, 166 U.S. 185, 218–225, 17 S.Ct. 604, 605, 607, 41 L.Ed. 965 (1897). The value may be ascertained by reference to the total system of which the intrastate assets are a part. As the Court has stated the rule, "the tax may be made to cover the enhanced value which comes to the [tangible] property in the state through its organic relation to the [interstate] system." Pullman Co. v. Richardson, 261 U.S. 330, 338, 43 S.Ct. 366, 368, 67 L.Ed. 682 (1923). Going-concern value, of course, is an elusive concept not susceptible of exact measurement. Rowley v. Chicago & N.W.R. Co., 293 U.S. 102, 109, 55 S.Ct. 55, 58, 79 L.Ed. 222 (1934); Nashville, Chattanooga & St. Louis R. Co. v. Browning, 310 U.S. 362, 365–366, 60 S.Ct. 968, 970, 84 L.Ed. 1254 (1940). As a consequence, the States have been permitted considerable latitude in devising formulas to measure the value of tangible property located within their borders. Union Tank Line Co. v. Wright, 249 U.S. 275, 282, 39 S.Ct. 276, 278, 63 L.Ed. 602 (1919). Such formulas usually involve a determination of the percentage of the taxpayer's tangible assets situated in the taxing State and the application of this percentage to a figure representing the total going-concern value of the enterprise. See, e.g., Rowley v. Chicago & N.W.R. Co., 293 U.S. 102, 55 S.Ct. 55, 79 L.Ed. 222 (1934); Pittsburgh, Cincinnati, Chicago and St. Louis R. Co. v. Backus, 154 U.S. 421, 14 S.Ct. 1114, 38 L.Ed. 1031 (1894). A number of such formulas have been sustained by the Court, even though it could not be demonstrated that the results they yielded were precise evaluations of assets located within the taxing State. See, e.g., Nashville, C. & St. L.R. Co. v. Browning, 310 U.S. 362, 365–366, 60 S.Ct. 968, 970, 84 L.Ed. 1254 (1940).

On the other hand, the Court has insisted for many years that a State is not entitled to tax tangible or intangible property that is unconnected with the State. Delaware R. Tax, 18 Wall. 206, 229, 21 L.Ed. 888 (1873); Fargo v. Hart, 193 U.S. 490, 499, 24 S.Ct. 498, 500, 48 L.Ed. 761 (1904). In some cases the Court has concluded that States have, in fact, cast their tax burden upon property located beyond their borders. Fargo v. Hart, 193 U.S. 490, 499–503, 24 S.Ct. 498, 500, 501, 48 L.Ed. 761 (1904); Union Tank Line Co. v. Wright, 249 U.S. 275, 283–286, 39 S.Ct. 276, 278, 279, 63 L.Ed. 602 (1919); Wallace v. Hines, 253 U.S. 66, 69–70, 40 S.Ct. 435, 436, 64 L.Ed. 782 (1920); Southern R. Co. v. Commonwealth of Kentucky, 274 U.S. 76, 81–84, 47 S.Ct. 542, 544–545, 71 L.Ed. 934 (1927). The taxation of property not located in the taxing State is constitutionally invalid, both because it imposes an illegitimate restraint on interstate commerce and because it denies to the taxpayer the process that is his due.[5] A State will not be permitted, under the shelter of an imprecise allocation formula or by ignoring the peculiarities of a given enterprise, to "project the taxing power of the state plainly beyond its borders." Nashville, Chattanooga & St. Louis R. Co. v. Browning, 310 U.S. 362, 365, 60 S.Ct. 968, 970, 84 L.Ed. 1254 (1940). Any formula used must bear a rational relationship, both on its face and in its application, to property values connected with the taxing State. Fargo v. Hart, 193 U.S. 490, 499–500, 24 S.Ct. 498, 500, 48 L.Ed. 761 (1904).[6]

5. We have said: "The problem under the Commerce Clause is to determine 'what portion of an interstate organism may appropriately be attributed to each of the various states in which it functions.' Nashville, Chattanooga & St. Louis R. Co. v. Browning, 310 U.S. 362, 365, 60 S.Ct. 968, 970, 84 L.Ed. 1254. So far as due process is concerned, the only question is whether the tax in practical operation has relation to opportunities, benefits, or protection conferred or afforded by the taxing State. See State of Wisconsin v. J.C. Penney Co., 311 U.S. 435, 444, 61 S.Ct. 246, 249, 85 L.Ed. 267, 130 A.L.R. 1229. Those requirements are satisfied if the tax is fairly apportioned to the commerce carried on within the State." Ott v. Mississippi Barge Line, 336 U.S. 169, 174, 69 S.Ct. 432, 434, 93 L.Ed. 585 (1949). Neither appellants nor appellee contend that these two analyses bear different implications insofar as our present case is concerned.

6. As the Court stated in Wallace v. Hines, 253 U.S. 66, at 69, 40 S.Ct. 435, at 436, 64 L.Ed. 782: "The only reason for allowing a state to look beyond its borders

III.

Applying these principles to the facts of the case now before us, we conclude that Missouri's assessment of N & W's rolling stock cannot be sustained. This Court has, in various contexts, permitted mileage formulas as a basis for taxation. See, e.g., Pittsburgh, Cincinnati, Chicago & St. Louis R. Co. v. Backus, 154 U.S. 421, 14 S.Ct. 1114, 38 L.Ed. 1031 (1894). A railroad challenging the result reached by the application of such a formula has a heavy burden. See Butler Brothers v. McColgan, 315 U.S. 501, 507, 62 S.Ct. 701, 704, 86 L.Ed. 991 (1942); Norfolk & Western R. Co. v. State of North Carolina ex rel. Maxwell, 297 U.S. 682, 688, 56 S.Ct. 625, 628, 80 L.Ed. 977 (1936). It is confronted by the vastness of the State's taxing power and the latitude that the exercise of that power must be given before it encounters constitutional restraints. Its task is to show that application of the mileage method in its case has resulted in such gross overreaching, beyond the values represented by the intrastate assets purported to be taxed, as to violate the Due Process and Commerce Clauses of the Constitution. Cf. Capitol Greyhound Lines v. Brice, 339 U.S. 542, 547, 70 S.Ct. 806, 809, 94 L.Ed. 1053 (1950). But here the appellants have borne that burden, and the State has made no effort to offset the convincing case that they have made.

Here, the record shows that rigid application of the mileage formula led to a grossly distorted result. The rolling stock in Missouri was assessed to N & W at $19,981,757. It was practically the same property that had been assessed the preceding year at $9,177,683 to the Wabash. Appellants introduced evidence of the results of an actual count of the rolling stock in Missouri. On the basis of this actual count, the equalized assessment would have been less than half of the value assessed by the state commission. The commission's mileage formula resulted in postulating that N & W's rolling stock in Missouri constituted 8.2824% of its rolling stock. But appellants showed that the rolling stock usually employed in the State comprised only about 2.71% by number of units (and only 3.16% by cost-less-depreciation value) of the total N & W fleet.

Our decisions recognize the practical difficulties involved and do not require any close correspondence between the result of computations using the mileage formula and the value of property actually located in the State, but our cases certainly forbid an unexplained discrepancy as gross as that in this case.[7] Such discrepancy certainly

when it taxes the property of foreign corporations is that it may get the true value of the things within it, when they are part of an organic system of wide extent, that gives them a value above what they otherwise would possess. The purpose is not * * * to open to taxation what is not within the State. Therefore no property of * * * an interstate road situated elsewhere can be taken into account unless it

can be seen in some plain and fairly intelligible way that it adds to the value of the road and the rights exercised in the State."

7. "If the ratio of the value of the property in [the State] to the value of the whole property of the company be less than that which the length of the road in [the State] bears to its entire length * * * a tax imposed upon the property in [the State] means that the impact of the state tax is not confined to intrastate property even within the broad tolerance permitted. The facts of life do not neatly lend themselves to the niceties of constitutionalism; but neither does the Constitution tolerate any result, however distorted, just because it is the product of a convenient mathematical formula which, in most situations, may produce a tolerable product.

The basic difficulty here is that the record is totally barren of any evidence relating to enhancement or to going-concern or intangible value, or to any other factor which might offset the devastating effect of the demonstrated discrepancy. The Missouri Supreme Court attempted to justify the result by verbal reference to "enhanced" value, but the Missouri Commission made no effort to show such value or to measure the extent to which it might be attributed to the rolling stock in the State. In fact, N & W showed that it is chiefly a coal-carrying railroad, 70% of whose 1964 revenue was derived from coal traffic. It demonstrated that its coal operations require a great deal of specialized equipment, scarcely any of which ever enters Missouri. It showed that traffic density on its Missouri tracks was only 54% of traffic density on the N & W system as a whole. Finally, it proved that the overwhelming majority of its rolling stock regularly present in Missouri was rolling stock it had leased from the Wabash. As long ago as Pittsburgh, Cincinnati, Chicago & St. Louis R. Co. v. Backus, 154 U.S. 421, 14 S.Ct. 1114, 38 L.Ed. 1031 (1894), we indicated that an otherwise valid mileage formula might not be validly applied to ascertain the value of tangible assets within the taxing State in exceptional situations, for example, "where, in certain localities, the company is engaged in a particular kind of business, requiring for sole use in such localities an extra amount of rolling stock." Id., at 431, 14 S.Ct. at 1119.

The Missouri Supreme Court did not challenge the factual data submitted by the N & W. Its decision that this data did not place this case within the realm of "exceptional situations" recognized by this Court was apparently based on the conclusion that the lease transaction between Wabash and the N & W had increased the value of tangible assets formerly belonging to the two separate lines. This may be true, but it does not follow that the Constitution permits us, without evidence as to the amount of enhancement that may be assumed, to bridge the chasm between the formula and the facts of record. The difference between the assessed value and the actual value as shown by the evidence to which we have referred is too great to be explained by the mere assertion, without more, that it is due to an assumed and nonparticularized increase in intangible value. See Wallace v. Hines, 253 U.S. 66, 69, 40 S.Ct. 435, 436, 64 L.Ed. 782 (1920).

As the Court recognized in Fargo v. Hart, 193 U.S. 490, 499, 24 S.Ct. 498, 500, 48 L.Ed. 761 (1904), care must be exercised lest the

according to the ratio of the length of the whole road must necessarily fall upon property out of the State." Delaware Railroad Tax, 18 Wall. 206, 230–231, 21 L.Ed. 888 (1873).

mileage formula "be made a means of unlawfully taxing the privilege, or property outside the state, under the name of enhanced value or goodwill, if it is not closely confined to its true meaning. So long as it fairly may be assumed that the different parts of a line are about equal in value a division by mileage is justifiable. But it is recognized in the cases that if for instance a railroad company had terminals in one state equal in value to all the rest of the line through another, the latter state could not make use of the unity of the road to equalize the value of every mile. That would be taxing property outside of the state under a pretense." We repeat that it is not necessary that a State demonstrate that its use of the mileage formula has resulted in an exact measure of value. But when a taxpayer comes forward with strong evidence tending to prove that the mileage formula will yield a grossly distorted result in its particular case, the State is obliged to counter that evidence or to make the accommodations necessary to assure that its taxing power is confined to its constitutional limits. If it fails to do so and if the record shows that the taxpayer has sustained the burden of proof to show that the tax is so excessive as to burden interstate commerce, the taxpayer must prevail.

IV.

Accordingly, we conclude that, on the present record, Missouri has in this case exceeded the limits of her constitutional power to tax, as defined by the Due Process and Commerce Clauses. It will be open to the Missouri Supreme Court, so far as our action today is concerned, to remand the case to the appropriate tribunal to reopen the record for additional evidence to support the assessment. We vacate the judgment of the Supreme Court of Missouri and remand the cause to it for further proceedings not inconsistent with our decision.

Vacated and remanded.

MR. JUSTICE BLACK, dissenting.

It is established law, as the Court apparently recognizes in its opinion, that an interstate company challenging a state apportionment of the company's property taxable in the State has the heavy burden of proving by "clear and cogent proof" that the apportionment is grossly and flagrantly excessive. See, e.g., Railway Express Agency v. Commonwealth of Virginia, 358 U.S. 434, 444, 79 S.Ct. 411, 417, 3 L.Ed.2d 450, and cases cited. I agree with the Supreme Court of Missouri that the railroad here failed to meet that burden and would therefore affirm its judgment. See its opinion at Mo., 426 S.W.2d 362.

It is true that most of the cars used in Missouri by N & W were owned by the Wabash Railroad and that before transfer to N & W they had been assessed at $9,179,688 as against the assessment here of $19,981,000. But this, of course, does not prove that the higher assessment was too much. For as the Supreme Court of Missouri pointed out, this Court has held that "a mere increase in the assessment does not prove that the last assessment is wrong. Something more is necessary before it can be adjudged that the assessment is illegal and excessive * * *." Pittsburgh, Cincinnati, Chicago & St. Louis R. Co. v. Backus, 154 U.S. 421, 432, 14 S.Ct. 1114, 1119, 38 L.Ed. 1031. The court below held, and this Court agrees, that in pricing the value of the rolling stock the Commission was authorized to consider intangible values, such as goodwill and values added because of the enhancement to the property in Missouri brought about by being merged into the entire N & W system. This consideration of enhanced value is not new (see, e.g., Pullman Co. v. Richardson, 261 U.S. 330, 338, 43 S.Ct. 366, 368, 67 L.Ed. 682), and, as the Court points out, it is because of this intangible factor of enhancement that States are allowed wide discretion in determining the value of tangible property located within their borders. Thus, mileage formulas, such as the one used here, have generally been upheld. As this Court said in Nashville, C. & St. Louis R. Co. v. Browning, 310 U.S. 362, "In basing its apportionment on mileage, the Tennessee Commission adopted a familiar and frequently sanctioned formula [cases cited]." 310 U.S. at 365, 60 S.Ct. at 970. It has never been contended that mileage formulas are completely accurate, but because States must consider such intangibles as enhancement value, these formulas are allowed except where the taxpayer can show, as the Court puts it, "that application of the mileage method in its case has resulted in such gross overreaching, beyond the values represented by the intrastate assets purported to be taxed, as to violate the Due Process and Commerce Clauses of the Constitution." I do not believe that appellant has made such a showing here. The fatal flaw with the appellant's case is that it has not proved that the tax is excessive when possible enhancement of value due to the merger is considered. The Court's opinion admits as much when it says that "the record is totally barren of any evidence relating to enhancement or going-concern or intangible value, or to any other factor * * *." Where I differ with the Court is that I believe the burden of proof is on the railroad to show that the tax is excessive under all considerations rather than on the Commission to show sufficient enhancement of value to justify the tax.

This Court has recognized before, and indeed the majority pays lipservice to the fact today, that it is impossible for a State to develop tax statutes with mathematical perfection. Indeed, as was stated in International Harvester Co. v. Evatt, 329 U.S. 416, 67 S.Ct. 444, 91 L.Ed. 390: "Unless a palpably disproportionate result comes from an apportionment, a result which makes it patent that the tax is levied upon interstate commerce rather than upon an intrastate privilege, the Court has not been willing to nullify honest state efforts to make apportionments." 329 U.S. at 422–423, 67 S.Ct. at 447. And the "burden is on the taxpayer to make oppression manifest by clear and cogent evidence." Norfolk & Western R. Co. v. State of North Carolina ex. rel. Maxwell, 297 U.S. 682, 688, 56 S.Ct. 625, 628, 80 L.Ed. 977. Since appellant here did not prove that the *enhanced value* * of its

---

* There is a familiar principle of valuation in such tax cases. See Fargo v. Hart, 193 U.S. 490, 499, 24 S.Ct. 498, 500, 48 L.Ed. 761; Galveston, Harrisburg & San

rolling stock was less than the tax assessment, or that the State was imposing on it taxes that were exorbitant on the full value of all its property, cf. Capitol Greyhound Lines v. Brice, 339 U.S. 542, 70 S.Ct. 806, 94 L.Ed. 1053, I would affirm the decision of the Missouri Supreme Court.

Notes and Problems

Railroads, bus lines, airlines, and other interstate utilities present a host of special problems which have resulted in the adoption of mileage, tonnage, freight or passenger mile, and other methods of apportionment and allocation of receipts, income, and other tax measures adapted to these industries. See Section 5 infra.

(b) Taxes Measured by Net Income

Notes and Problems

A. In Underwood Typewriter Co. v. Chamberlain, 254 U.S. 113, 41 S.Ct. 45 (1920), the Court for the first time addressed a constitutional challenge to a State income tax apportionment, and in so doing it established its basic approach to such challenges. Underwood was a Delaware corporation that did all its manufacturing in Connecticut, had its main office in New York, and maintained branch offices over the country through which it sold, leased, and repaired typewriters, accessories, and supplies. Connecticut imposed a tax on manufacturing companies at the rate of two percent of the net income from business carried on in the State during the preceding year. The statute provided for an apportionment of net income to the State in the ratio of the fair cash value of the taxpayer's real and tangible personal property within the State to the fair cash value of all its real and tangible personal property wherever located. The apportionment for the tax year at issue attributed 47 percent of the approximately $1,336,000 of the company's net income to Connecticut, or some $630,000. The taxpayer contended that the tax violated the Due Process Clause because "it is imposed on income arising from business conducted beyond the boundaries of the state." Mr. Justice Brandeis, who delivered the opinion, noted that the taxpayer "rests solely upon the showing that of its net profits $1,293,643.95 was received in other states and only $42,942.18 in Connecticut," and said:

> But this showing wholly fails to sustain the objection. The profits of the corporation were largely earned by a series of transactions beginning with manufacture in Connecticut and ending with sale in other states. In this it was typical of a large part of the manufacturing business conducted in the state. The Legislature, in attempting to put upon this business its fair share of the burden of taxation, was faced with the impossibility of allocating specifically the profits earned by the processes conducted within its borders. It, therefore, adopted a method of apportionment which, for all that appears in this record,

Antonio R. Co. v. State of Texas, 210 U.S. 217, 225, 28 S.Ct. 638, 639, 52 L.Ed. 1031; United States Express Co. v. State of Minnesota, 223 U.S. 335, 337, 32 S.Ct. 211, 212, 56 L.Ed. 459; Union Tank Line Co. v. Wright, 249 U.S. 275, 282, 39 S.Ct. 276, 278, 63 L.Ed. 602.

reached, and was meant to reach, only the profits earned within the state. "The plaintiff's argument on this branch of the case," as stated by the Supreme Court of Errors, "carries the burden of showing that 47 per cent. of its net income is not reasonably attributable, for purposes of taxation, to the manufacture of products from the sale of which 80 per cent. of its gross earnings was derived after paying manufacturing costs." The corporation has not even attempted to show this; and for aught that appears the percentage of net profits earned in Connecticut may have been much larger than 47 per cent. There is, consequently, nothing in this record to show that the method of apportionment adopted by the state was inherently arbitrary, or that its application to this corporation produced an unreasonable result. [254 U.S. at 120–21.]

B. *Apportionment of Net Income to Loss State.* In Bass, Ratcliff & Gretton, Ltd. v. State Tax Commission, 266 U.S. 271, 45 S.Ct. 82 (1924), an often cited decision on the formula method of apportioning income, an English company engaged in brewing ale in England sold its product both in England and in the United States. The company maintained sales offices in Chicago and New York. Its Federal income tax return showed a loss from United States operations, although the business as a whole operated at a profit. The New York State Tax Commission, in accordance with the State's franchise tax formula, assigned to the State the portion of the total net income of the business which the value of certain assets within New York bore to the total value of such assets everywhere located. The company contended that the Tax Commission was attempting to assign income derived from its operations outside the United States to New York, when it actually operated at a loss in that State. In upholding the Tax Commission, the Court took the position that since the business profits were derived from the operations of the company as a whole, a portion could be attributed to New York through the selective property allocation method utilized.

C. *Effect of Property Allocation Where Sales in State are Small.* In Maxwell v. Kent–Coffey Mfg. Co., 204 N.C. 365, 168 S.E. 397, 90 A.L.R. 476 (1933), aff'd without opinion 291 U.S. 642, 54 S.Ct. 437 (1933), the Court upheld a tax on a Delaware corporation conducting a manufacturing business in North Carolina. The percentage of its net income attributable to North Carolina was ascertained by taking the ratio of the fair cash value of its real and tangible property in the State to the fair cash value of its property everywhere, with no deductions allowed for encumbrances. Since 99.2 percent of the real and tangible property was located in North Carolina, the tax was measured by 99.2 percent of the entire net income. The taxpayer established that only .002 percent of its total sales were made within North Carolina. The result was that a corporation selling only .002 percent of its products in the State was taxed on 99.2 percent of its net income. Nevertheless, the Court held that the evidence was not sufficient to show that the method of apportionment adopted by the State was inherently arbitrary, or that its application produced an unreasonable result. This case suggests the unfairness which may result from a simple property allocation of a receipts or income tax. If all the States allocated such taxes by a real and tangible personal property allocation method,

Michigan, for example, with its heavy concentration of automobile plants, might obtain an allocation of the lion's share of the receipts and income derived from the manufacture and sale of automobiles in markets throughout the country.

D. Taxpayers' attempts to set aside apportionments as attributing out-of-state income or receipts to the taxing States are frequently frustrated by courts' conclusions that the taxpayers' proof falls short. A flagrant example of the tendency of some courts to dismiss taxpayers' challenges on that ground was reflected in Federated Department Stores v. Gerosa, 16 N.Y.2d 320, 266 N.Y.S.2d 378, 213 N.E.2d 677 (1965), appeal dismissed 385 U.S. 454, 87 S.Ct. 611 (1967). The case arose under the now repealed New York City tax on the doing of business in the city, measured by gross receipts. Wholly intra-state receipts were taxed in full; wholly out-of-state receipts were excluded from the tax base. Only allocable receipts, i.e., those involving goods moving between New York City and other States were apportioned. Having carved out allocable receipts, the numerators of the formula purported to consider only property and payroll within the city attributable to the allocable receipts, whereas the denominators took into account property and payroll attributable to both allocable and wholly non-taxable receipts. Despite the court's agreement with the contention of the department store chain involved in the case that under the formula "the tax tends to increase as taxpayer's out-of-state and hence wholly non-taxable receipts increase when the relative amounts of property and wages are constant" (266 N.Y.S.2d at 382), relief was denied because "petitioner has not demonstrated unfairness in the actual impact on it of the tax assessments of which it complains." 266 N.Y.S.2d at 384.

HANS REES' SONS, INC. v. NORTH CAROLINA EX REL. MAXWELL

Supreme Court of the United States, 1931.
283 U.S. 123, 51 S.Ct. 385.

Mr. Chief Justice Hughes delivered the opinion of the Court.

The appellant, Hans Rees' Sons, Inc., a corporation organized under the laws of New York, began this action by an application to the commissioner of revenue of the state of North Carolina for the readjustment of the income tax assessed against the appellant by that state. The assessment was for the years 1923, 1924, 1925, and 1926, in accordance with the applicable state laws, and the controversy related to the proper allocation of income to the state of North Carolina. The commissioner of revenue made his findings of fact and conclusions of law, the appellant's exceptions were overruled, and the prayer for revision of the taxes was disallowed. Appeal, waiving a jury, was taken to the superior court of Buncombe county, N.C. On the trial in that court, evidence was introduced by the appellant with respect to the course of business and the amount and sources of income for the years in question. The appellant admitted that "(a) in assessing the tax the Commissioner of Revenue followed the statutory method; * * * (b) that the valuation of the real estate and tangible property of the taxpayer 'both within and without the State' is correct; (c) that the total net income used as a basis for the calculation of the tax is correct; (d) that the allocation of the net income for purposes of taxation was in full accord with the statute." The contention of the appellant was that the income tax statute as applied to the appellant, upon the facts disclosed, was arbitrary and unreasonable, and was repugnant to the commerce clause and to section 1 of the Fourteenth Amendment of the Federal Constitution. The superior court struck out the testimony offered by the appellant, as being immaterial, and held that the statute, as applied did not violate constitutional rights. The judgment dismissing the action was affirmed by the Supreme Court of the state, 199 N.C. 42, 153 S.E. 850, 853. The case comes here on appeal.

As to the portions of the taxes for the years in question, which had been paid by the appellant voluntarily and as to which recovery was denied upon that ground, no question is raised here.

The Supreme Court of the state sustained the ruling of the trial court in striking out the evidence offered by the appellant, but held that, if the evidence were deemed to be competent, it would not change the result. The case may therefore be viewed as though the evidence had been received and held to have no bearing on the validity of the statute. * * * The evidence was thus summarized by the state court.

"This evidence tended to show that the petitioner [the appellant here] was incorporated in the state of New York in 1901 and is engaged in the business of tanning, manufacturing, and selling belting and other heavy leathers. Many years prior to 1923 it located a manufacturing plant at Asheville, N.C., and, after this plant was in full operation, dismantled and abandoned all plants which it had heretofore operated in different states of the Union. The business is conducted upon both wholesale and retail plans. The wholesale part of the business consists in selling certain portions of the hide to shoe manufacturers and others in carload lots. The retail part of the business consists in cutting the hide into innumerable pieces, finishing it in various ways and manners, and selling it in less than carload lots. In order to facilitate sales a warehouse is maintained in New York from which shipments are made of stock on hand to various customers. The tannery at Asheville is used as the manufacturing plant and a supply house, and, when the quantity or quality of merchandise required by a customer is not on hand in the New York warehouse, a requisition is sent to the plant at Asheville to ship to the New York warehouse or direct to the customer. The sales office is located in New York, and the salesmen report to that office. Sales are made throughout this country and in Canada and Continental Europe. Some sales are also made in North Carolina. Certain finishing work is done in New York. The evidence further tended to show that "between forty and fifty per cent. of the output of the plant in Asheville is shipped from the Asheville tannery to New York. The other sixty per cent. is shipped direct on orders from New

York. ＊ ＊ ＊ Shipment is made direct from Asheville to the customer."

"The petitioner also offered evidence to the effect that the income from the business was derived from three sources, to wit: (1) buying profit; (2) manufacturing profit; (3) selling profit. It contends that buying profit resulted from unusual skill and efficiency in taking advantage of fluctuations of the hide market; that manufacturing profit was based upon the difference between the cost of tanning done by contract and the actual cost thereof when done by the petitioner at its own plant in Asheville, and that that selling profit resulted from the method of cutting the leather into small parts so as to meet the needs of a given customer.

"Without burdening this opinion with detailed compilations set out in the record, the evidence offered by the petitioner tends to show that, for the years 1923, 1924, 1925, and 1926, the average income having its source in the manufacturing and tanning operations within the state of North Carolina was 17 per cent."

According to the assessments in question, as revised by the commissioner of revenue and sustained, there was allocated to the state of North Carolina, pursuant to the prescribed statutory method, for the year 1923, 83+ per cent of the appellant's income; for 1924, 85+ per cent; for 1925, 66+ per cent; and for 1926, 85+ per cent.

The applicable statutory provisions, as set forth by the state court, are as follows:

"Every corporation organized under the laws of this State shall pay annually an income tax, equivalent to four per cent. of the entire net income as herein defined, received by such corporation during the income year; and every foreign corporation doing business in this State shall pay annually an income tax equivalent to four per cent. of a proportion of its entire income to be determined according to the following rules:

"(a) In case of a company other than companies mentioned in the next succeeding section, deriving profits principally from the ownership, sale or rental of real estate or from the manufacture, purchase, sale of, trading in, or use of tangible property, such proportion of its entire net income as the fair cash value of its real estate and tangible personal property in this State on the date of the close of the fiscal year of such company in the income year is to the fair cash value of its entire real estate and tangible personal property then owned by it with no deductions on account of encumbrances thereon.

"(b) In case of a corporation deriving profits principally from the holding or sale of intangible property, such proportion as its gross receipts in this State for the year ended on the date of the close of its fiscal year next preceding is to its gross receipts for such year within and without the State.

"(c) The words "tangible personal property" shall be taken to mean corporeal personal property, such as machinery, tools, implements, goods, wares and merchandise and shall not be taken to mean money deposits in bank, shares of stock, bonds, notes, credits or evidence of an interest in property and evidences of debt."

* * *

[The Court thereupon discussed Underwood Typewriter Co. v. Chamberlain, p. 434 supra, and Bass, Ratcliff & Gretton, Ltd. v. State Tax Commission, p. 435 supra.]

In the instant case, the state court, having considered these decisions, held that the statute of North Carolina was valid upon its face, and sought to justify its view that the evidence offered by the appellant was without effect, upon the following grounds:

"The fallacy of this conclusion" (that is, the appellant's contention that the application of the statute had been shown to be unreasonable and arbitrary, and hence repugnant to the Federal Constitution) "lies in the fact that the petitioner undertakes to split into independent sources income which the record discloses was created and produced by a single business enterprise. Hides were bought for the purpose of being tanned and manufactured into leather at Asheville, N.C., and this product was to be shipped from the plant and sold and distributed from New York to the customer. The petitioner was not exclusively a hide dealer or a mere tanner or a leather salesman. It was a manufacturer and seller of leather goods, involving the purchase of raw material and the working up of that raw material into acceptable commercial forms, for the ultimate purpose of selling the finished product for a profit. Therefore, the buying, manufacturing, and selling were component parts of a single unit. The property in North Carolina is the hub from which the spokes of the entire wheel radiate to the outer rim." And, in its final conclusion, the state court said that, if it were conceded that the evidence offered by the appellant was competent, still, as it showed that the appellant "was conducting a unitary business as contemplated and defined by the courts of final jurisdiction," it was "not permissible to lop off certain elements of the business constituting a single unit, in order to place the income beyond the taxing jurisdiction of this state."

We are unable to agree with this view. Evidence which was found to be lacking in the Underwood and Bass cases is present here. These decisions are not authority for the conclusion that, where a corporation manufactures in one state and sells in another, the net profits of the entire transaction, as a unitary enterprise, may be attributed, regardless of evidence, to either state. In the Underwood case, it was not decided that the entire net profits of the total business were to be allocated to Connecticut because that was the place of manufacture, or, in the Bass case, that the entire net profits were to be allocated to New York because that was the place where sales were made. In both instances, a method of apportionment was involved which, as was said in the Underwood case, "for all that appears in this record, reached, and was meant to reach, only the profits earned within the state." The difficulty with the evidence offered in the Underwood case was that it failed to establish that the amount of net income with which the corporation was charged in Connecticut under the method adopted was not reasonably attributable to the processes conducted within the borders of that State; and in the Bass case, the court found a similar defect in proof with respect to the transactions in New York.

Undoubtedly the enterprise of a corporation which manufactures and sells its manufactured product is ordinarily a unitary business, and all the factors in that enterprise are essential to the realization of profits. The difficulty of making an exact apportionment is apparent, and hence, when the state has adopted a method not intrinsically arbitrary, it will be sustained until proof is offered of an unreasonable and arbitrary application in particular cases. But the fact that the corporate enterprise is a unitary one, in the sense that the ultimate gain is derived from the entire business, does not mean that for the purpose of taxation the activities which are conducted in different jurisdictions are to be regarded as "component parts of a single unit" so that the entire net income may be taxed in one state regardless of the extent to which it may be derived from the conduct of the enterprise in another state. As was said in the Bass case with regard to "the unitary business of manufacturing and selling ale" which began with manufacturing in England and ended in sales in New York, that state "was justified in attributing to New York a just proportion of the profits earned by the Company from such unitary business." And the principle that was recognized in National Leather Company v. Massachusetts, supra, was that a tax could lawfully be imposed upon a foreign corporation with respect to "the proportionate part of its total net income which is attributable to the business carried on within the State." When, as in this case, there are different taxing jurisdictions, each competent to lay a tax with respect to what lies within, and is done within, its own borders, and the question is necessarily one of apportionment, evidence may always be received which tends to show that a state has applied a method, which, albeit fair on its face, operates so as to reach profits which are in no just sense attributable to transactions within its jurisdiction.

Nor can the evidence be put aside in the view that it merely discloses such negligible criticisms in allocation of income as are inseparable from the practical administration of a taxing system in which apportionment with mathematical exactness is impossible. The evidence in this instance, as the state court puts it, "tends to show that for the years 1923, 1924, 1925, and 1926, the average income having its source in the manufacturing and tanning operations within the State of North Carolina was 17 per cent," while under the assessments in question there was allocated to the state of North Carolina approximately 80 per cent of the appellant's income.

An analysis has been submitted by the appellant for the purpose of showing that the percentage of its income attributable to North Carolina, for the years in question, did not in any event exceed 21.7 per cent.

As pointed out by the state court, the appellant's evidence was to the effect that the income from its business was derived from three sources, buying profit, manufacturing profit, and selling profit. The appellant states that its sales were both wholesale and retail; that the profits from the wholesale business were in part attributable to the manufacturing in Asheville and in part to the selling in New York but that the appellant's accountants made no attempt to separate this, and that the entire wholesale profit was credited to manufacturing and allocated to North Carolina. Similarly, it is said that no attempt was made to separate profits from manufacturing in New York from profits derived from manufacturing in Asheville, and that all manufacturing profits were allocated to North Carolina. It is insisted that, in the retail part of the business, the leather is cut into small pieces and finished in particular ways and supplied in small lots to meet the particular needs of individual customers and that this part of the business is essential to the retail merchandising business conducted from the New York office. The so-called "buying profit" is said to result from the skill with which hides are bought, and the contention is that these buying operations were not conducted in North Carolina. If as to the last it be said that the buying of raw material for the manufacturing plant should be regarded as incident to the manufacturing business, and as reflected in the value at wholesale of the manufactured product as turned out at the factory, still it is apparent that the amount of the asserted buying profit is not enough to affect the result so far as the constitutional question is concerned.

For the present purpose, in determining the validity of the statutory method as applied to the appellant, it is not necessary to review the evidence in detail, or to determine as a matter of fact the precise part of the income which should be regarded as attributable to the business conducted in North Carolina. It is sufficient to say that, in any aspect of the evidence, and upon the assumption made by the state court with respect to the facts shown, the statutory method, as applied to the appellant's business for the years in question operated unreasonably and arbitrarily, in attributing to North Carolina a percentage of income out of all appropriate proportion to the business transacted by the appellant in that state. In this view, the taxes as laid were beyond the state's authority. Shaffer v. Carter, 252 U.S. 37, 52, 53, 57, 40 S.Ct. 221, 64 L.Ed. 445.

For this reason the judgment must be reversed, and the cause remanded for further proceedings not inconsistent with this opinion. It is so ordered.*

* [This case is noted in 40 Yale L.J. 1273 (1931); 9 N.C.L.Rev. 470 (1931); 5 U.Cin.L. Rev. 496, (1931); 6 St. John's L.Rev. 179 (1931).]

BUTLER BROS. v. McCOLGAN

Supreme Court of the United States, 1942.
315 U.S. 501, 62 S.Ct. 701.

MR. JUSTICE DOUGLAS delivered the opinion of the Court.

This is an appeal (Judicial Code § 237(a) 28 U.S.C.A. § 344(a)) from a final judgment of the Supreme Court of California sustaining the validity of a statute of California against the claim that as construed and applied to appellant it violated the Fourteenth Amendment. 17 Cal.2d 664, 111 P.2d 334. The statute in question is the Bank and Corporation Franchise Tax Act * * * which provides for an annual corporate franchise tax payable by a corporation doing business within the State. The tax is measured by the corporation's net income and is at the rate of four per cent "upon the basis of its net income" for the preceding year. The minimum annual tax is $25. Sec. 10 prescribes the method for computing the net income on which the tax is laid. It provides in part:

> "If the entire business of the bank or corporation is done within this State, the tax shall be according to or measured by its entire net income; and if the entire business of such bank or corporation is not done within this State, the tax shall be according to or measured by that portion thereof which is derived from business done within this State. The portion of net income derived from business done within this State, shall be determined by an allocation upon the basis of sales, purchases, expenses of manufacture, pay roll, value and situs of tangible property, or by reference to these or other facts, or by such other method of allocation as is fairly calculated to assign to the State the portion of net income reasonably attributable to the business done within this State and to avoid subjecting the taxpayer to double taxation."

The tax in dispute is for the calendar year 1936. Appellant paid the minimum tax of $25, asserting that it operated in California during 1935 at a loss of $82,851. The tax commissioner made an additional assessment of $3,798.43 which appellant paid, together with interest, under protest. This suit was brought to recover back the amount so paid on the theory that the method of allocation employed by the tax commissioner attributed to California income derived wholly from business done without that State.

The facts are stipulated and show the following. Appellant is an Illinois corporation qualified to do business in California. Its home office is in Chicago, Ill. It is engaged in the wholesale dry goods and general merchandise business, purchasing from manufacturers and others and selling to retailers only. It has wholesale distributing houses in seven states, including one at San Francisco, California. Each of its houses in the seven states maintains stocks of goods, serves a separate territory, has its own sales force, handles its own sales and all solicitation, credit and collection arrangements in connection therewith, and keeps its own books of account. For the period in question, all receipts from sales in California were credited to the San Francisco house. Appellant maintains a central buying division through which goods for resale are ordered, the goods being shipped by manufacturers to the houses for which they are ordered. All purchases made by appellant for sale at its various houses are made through that central buying division. The cost of the goods and the transportation charges are entered on the books of the house which receives the goods. No charges are made against any house for the benefit of appellant or any of its other houses by reason of the centralized purchasing. But the actual cost of operating the centralized buying division is allocated among the houses. The greater part of appellant's other operating expenses is incurred directly and exclusively at the respective houses. Certain items of expense are incurred and paid by appellant for the benefit of all the houses and allocated to them. No question exists as to the accuracy of the amounts of such expense or the method of allocation. The latter admittedly followed recognized accounting principles. For the year 1935 the amount of such allocated expense charged to the San Francisco house was $100,091. For purposes of this suit it was agreed that approximately 75% of that amount would have been incurred even though the San Francisco house was not operated. The accuracy and propriety of the basis of allocation of those common expenses for 1935 were admitted. Included in such expenses were executive salaries, certain accounting expenses, the cost of operating a central buying division, and a central advertising division. Except for such common expenses, each house is operated independently of each other house. Appellant computed its income from the San Francisco house for the period in question by deducting from the gross receipts from sales in California the cost of such merchandise, the direct expense of the San Francisco house, and the indirect expense allocated to it. By that computation a loss of $82,851 was determined. In the year 1935 the operations of all houses of appellant produced a profit of $1,149,677. The tax commissioner allocated to California 8.1372 per cent of that amount. That percentage was determined by averaging the percentages which (a) value of real and tangible personal property (b) wages, salaries, commissions and other compensation of employees, and (c) gross sales, less returns and allowances, attributable to the San Francisco house bore to the corresponding items of all houses of appellant. No other factor or method of allocation was considered. The propriety of the use of that formula is not questioned if by reason of the stipulated facts a formula for allocation to California of a portion of appellant's income from all sources is proper.

The stipulation also states that in the year 1935 the total sales made by appellant at all its houses amounted to $66,326,000, of which $5,206,000 were made by the San Francisco house. The purchases made for the account of that house were substantially in the same proportion to total purchases. By reason of the volume of purchases made by appellant "more favorable prices are obtained than would be obtainable in respect of purchases for the account of any individual house." The addition of purchases "in an amount equal to the purchases made for the account of the San Francisco house results in no more favorable prices than could be obtainable in respect of purchases in an amount equal to the purchases which would be made" by appellant for its other houses if the San Francisco house was not in existence; and "a reduction in the volume of purchases in an amount equal to the purchases made for the San Francisco house would result in no less favorable prices being obtainable in respect of the purchases which would be made for the remaining houses" of appellant.

Hans Rees' Sons, Inc. v. North Carolina, 283 U.S. 123, 51 S.Ct. 385, constitutes appellant's chief support in its attack on the formula employed and the tax imposed by California. Appellant maintains that the use of the formula in question, resulted in converting a loss of $82,851 into a profit of over $93,500 and that the difference of some $175,000 has either been created out of nothing or has been appropriated by California from other states.

We take a different view. We read the statute as calling for a method of allocation which is "fairly calculated" to assign to California that portion of the net income "reasonably attributable" to the business done there. The test, not here challenged which has been reflected in prior decisions of this Court, is certainly not more exacting. Bass, Ratcliff & Gretton, Ltd. v. Tax Commission, 266 U.S. 271, 45 S.Ct. 82; Ford Motor Co. v. Beauchamp, 308 U.S. 331, 60 S.Ct. 273. Hence if the formula which was employed meets those standards, any constitutional question arising under the Fourteenth Amendment is at an end.

One who attacks a formula of apportionment carries a distinct burden of showing by "clear and cogent evidence" that it results in extraterritorial values being taxed. See Norfolk & Western Ry. Co. v. North Carolina, 297 U.S. 682, 688, 56 S.Ct. 625. This Court held in Hans Rees' Sons, Inc. v. North Carolina, supra, p. 135, that that burden had been maintained on a showing by the taxpayer that "in any aspect of the evidence" its income attributable to North Carolina was "out of all appropriate proportion to the business" transacted by the taxpayer in that State. No such showing has been made here.

It is true that appellant's separate accounting system for its San Francisco branch attributed no net income to California. But we need not impeach the integrity of that accounting system to say that it does not prove appellant's assertion that extraterritorial values are being taxed. Accounting practices for income statements may vary considerably according to the problem at hand. Sanders, Hatfield & Moore, A Statement of Accounting Principles (1938), p. 26. A particular accounting system, though useful or necessary as a business aid, may not fit the different requirements when a State seeks to tax values created by business within its borders. Cf. Hamilton, Cost as a Standard for Price, 4 Law & Contemporary Problems 321. That may be due to the fact, as stated by Mr. Justice Brandeis in Underwood Typewriter Co. v. Chamberlain, 254 U.S. 113, 121, 41 S.Ct. 45, that a State in attempting to place upon a business extending into several States "its fair share of the burden of taxation" is "faced with the impossibility of allocating specifically the profits earned by the processes conducted within its borders." Furthermore, the particular system used may not reveal the facts basic to the State's determination. Bass, Ratcliff & Gretton, Ltd. v. Tax Commission, supra, p. 283. In either aspect of the matter the results of the accounting system employed by appellant do not impeach the validity or propriety of the formula which California has applied here.

At least since Adams Express Co. v. Ohio, 165 U.S. 194, 17 S.Ct. 305, this Court has recognized that unity of use and management of a business which is scattered through several States may be considered when a State attempts to impose a tax on an apportionment basis. As stated in Hans Rees' Sons, Inc. v. North Carolina, supra, p. 133, " * * * the enterprise of a corporation which manufactures and sells its manufactured product is ordinarily a unitary business, and all the factors in that enterprise are essential to the realization of profits." And see Bass, Ratcliff & Gretton, Ltd. v. Tax Commission, supra, p. 282. By the same token, California may properly treat appellant's business as a unitary one. Cf. Great Atlantic & Pacific Tea Co. v. Grosjean, 301 U.S. 412, 57 S.Ct. 772. There is unity of ownership and management. And the operation of the central buying division alone demonstrates that functionally the various branches are closely integrated. Admittedly, centralized purchasing results in more favorable prices being obtained than if the purchases were separately made for the account of any one branch. What the savings were and what portion is fairly attributable to the volume contributed by the San Francisco branch do not appear. But the concession that a reduction or addition of purchases "in an amount equal to the purchases made for the San Francisco house" would not result in higher or lower purchase prices respectively does not aid appellant's case. There is no justification on this record for singling out the San Francisco branch rather than another and concluding that it made no contribution to those savings. As aptly stated by the Supreme Court of California, "If the omission of the California sales would have no effect on the purchasing power, the omission of sales in an equal amount wherever made would likewise have no effect on the company's ability to purchase at a saving. Thus, by proceeding in turn from state to state, it could be shown that none of the sales in any of the states should be credited with the income resulting from the purchasing of goods in large quantities." Nor are there any facts shown which permit the conclusion that the other advantages of centralized management (Great Atlantic & Pacific Tea Co. v. Grosjean, supra) are attributable to other branches but not to the one in California. The fact of the matter is that appellant has not shown the precise sources of its net income of $1,149,677. If factors which are responsible for that net income are present in other States but not present in California, they have not been revealed. At least in absence of that proof, California was justified in assuming that the San Francisco branch contributed its aliquot share to the advantages of centralized management of this unitary enterprise and to the net income earned.

We cannot say that property, pay roll, and sales are inappropriate ingredients of an apportionment formula. We agree with the Supreme Court of California that these factors may properly be deemed to reflect "the relative contribution of the activities in the various states to the production of the total unitary income," so as to allocate to California its just proportion of the profits earned by appellant from this unitary business. And no showing has been made that income unconnected with the unitary business has been used in the formula.

* * *

Affirmed.

Notes and Problems

A. *The History of the Use of Separate Accounting.* When corporation income taxation first developed in this country, separate accounting for multistate operations was regarded as the most precise and accurate method of determining the income derived from various States. Consequently the usual practice under the early State income taxes was to permit corporations to use separate accounting, if they maintained accounting records enabling them to ascertain with reasonable accuracy the net income in each of the States in which they operated. "Report of Committee on the Apportionment between States of Taxes on Mercantile and Manufacturing Business," 1922 N.T.A. Procs. 198, 214–15. Indeed, for several decades, the Committees of the National Tax Association preferred separate accounting for corporate income taxes, if the taxpayer's records were maintained in a manner adequate to permit a State-by-State breakdown of data. "Report of the Committee of the National Tax Association on Allocation of Income," 1939 N.T.A. Procs. 190, 204. This was not, however, without dissent. See Keesling, id. at 220. A survey by the N.T.A. Committee in 1939 disclosed that a majority of the corporate respondents preferred apportionment by formula to separate accounting. See McColgan, id. at 220–30. Many statutes prescribe apportionment where business is conducted within and without the States, and authorize separate accounting or adjustment of the factors or "any other method to effectuate an equitable allocation and apportionment" only if the prescribed methods do not "fairly represent the extent of the taxpayer's business activity in this state." (Quoted from UDITPA § 18, set out in Section 6 infra.) The courts have interpreted such provisions as preferring formulary apportionment to separate accounting. See Section 4 infra.

Nevertheless, from the outset the disproportionate expense of separate accounting was recognized to be a seriously deterring factor in its use. As one N.T.A. Committee put it, "[separate accounting] is very expensive and in most cases would probably be so costly that the tax found to be due" by formulary apportionment "would be less than the cost of arriving at the tax if this method were used." It was found that "a system of separate accounts for branches or subsidiaries is, in the majority of cases, impracticable." Gerstenberg, "Allocation of Business Income," 1931 N.T.A. Procs. 301, 306.

Over the years, separate accounting has also come in for increased criticism on the merits. As one study concludes, except in cases in which separate, non-unitary businesses are conducted by a corporation, "determination by the separate accounting method of the economic effect within prescribed geographical limits of any particular phase of a unitary business is artificial and extremely awkward." See Cohen, "Apportionment and Allocation Formulae and Factors Used by States in Levying Taxes Based on or Measured by Net Income of Manufacturing, Distributive and Extractive Corporations," a research report prepared for the Controllership Foundation (1954); and J. Hellerstein, "The Unitary Business Principle and Multicorporate Enterprises: An Examination of the Major Controversies," 27 Tax Executive 313 (1975). For the argument in support of separate accounting as the most satisfactory method of dividing the income of multicorporate structured unitary businesses, see Miller, "State Income Taxation of Multiple Corporations and Multiple Businesses," Tax Foundation Seminar on Taxation of Interstate Business (April 16–17, 1970); and "Industry Statement on Proposed Interstate Tax Legislation," Mondale Comm. Hearings 260, 281–83. As multistate businesses have expanded and have come to dominate the economies of all 50 States in which they manufacture, produce, process, warehouse, and market a large number and variety of products, separate accounting for unitary business has become even less viable, less warranted in principle, and, as a consequence, it is now seldom used in State corporate income taxation. 1 Willis Comm.Rep. 160–67.

B. *Distributing Profits Under Separate Accounting.* The taxpayer in the *Hans Rees'* case offered to establish the portion of the profit allocable to buying, to manufacturing, and to selling. What methods are available for apportioning the profit of a unitary business which buys, manufactures, and sells? Two methods often used to separate the manufacturing profit from selling profit are these:

(1) Ascertain the actual cost of manufacturing and add a "reasonable" profit determined by reference to profit made by other corporations, by the opinions of businessmen, and so forth. The goods are then deemed to have been sold by the manufacturing department to the selling department at the price indicated. Specific costs of each department are determined and overhead, administrative, and other general expenses are charged to the various departments. Thereupon, the allocable profit is determined.

(2) Ascertain the price at which the articles manufactured may be purchased from other manufacturers in the quantities desired. Utilize this figure as the cost of goods and otherwise proceed as indicated in (1) above.

Do such methods produce a satisfactory norm for drawing the line between manufacturing costs at which the goods can be bought elsewhere, manufacturing profit, selling costs, and selling profits? Is it possible with any degree of accuracy to obtain truly comparable prices at which the goods can be bought elsewhere—consider quantities, delivery dates, terms of payment, devotion of the entire output to a single customer? Is it possible, without speculation and arbitrary assumptions, to establish a reasonable markup over manufacturing costs as the manufacturer's share of an integrated sales operation? What source data will be used which will not suffer from the same defects as the taxpayer's own records?

Even if a satisfactory constructive profit can be allocated to each branch of the business, i.e., manufacturing, selling, and so on, does not the entire method proceed on a false assumption that the business should be treated as if it sells not to the trade but to an intermediary (i.e., the taxpayer), which in turn resells? For a basic study of the problems involved in separate accounting, see Ford, The Allocation of Corporate Income for the Purpose of State Taxation, N.Y. State Tax Comm., Spec.Rep. No. 6 (1933).

C. *Allocation of Receipts from Sales Under the Separate Accounting Method.* Under the separate accounting method, a taxpayer which buys and sells goods normally charges each branch of the business with the actual cost of the merchandise sold. The following illustration (taken from G. Altman & F. Keesling, Allocation of Income in State Taxation 96 [2d ed. 1950]) raises an important question as to the soundness of this method of cost allocation. X, a dealer in mules, has a customer in New Jersey, A, who wants to buy a mule, for which he will pay $100. X can purchase a mule in Missouri, but it will cost him $100 delivered to A. He scouts around and finds B, in New York, who also wants to buy a mule, but B will pay only $75. X then finds that he can buy two mules in Missouri for a total price of $150, including delivery to A and B. X makes the deals and realizes a total profit of $25. X, a resident of Connecticut, does business in both New York and New Jersey and is subject to income tax in both states. To which State or States should the $25 profit be allocated?

D. *Higher Cost of Doing Business in the State as a Basis for Substituting Separate Accounting for Apportionment Formula.* In a later California case one of the lawyers who represented the State in the *Butler Bros.* case sought to compel the Franchise Tax Board to permit the use of separate accounting, arguing that the defect in the evidence in the former case was here cured, namely, that the taxpayer had here demonstrated that the formula produced "unreasonable results by assigning to this state extraterritorial values." John Deere Plow Co. v. Franchise Tax Board, 38 Cal.2d 214, 238 P.2d 569 (1951), appeal dismissed 343 U.S. 939, 72 S.Ct. 1036 (1952). The plaintiff, an Illinois corporation, the parent company of a group of corporations operating a large far-flung national business in manufacturing and selling plows and other agricultural equipment, attacked California's three-factor Massachusetts-type allocation formula by a persuasive showing that its California operations were considerably more expensive and less profitable than its operations generally. The trial court upheld the factual contentions made but nevertheless denied the claim for a determination of the tax on a separate accounting basis. In upholding this judgment, the California Supreme Court pointed out that the formula "is not framed on the assumption that there must be uniformity of operating revenues and expenses in the relative functions of the various units contributing to the earnings of an integrated, multistate business," and concluded that the attack on the formula by proof of the higher costs and the less profitable nature of the California business misconceives the whole purport of the unit rule of assessment, which rests on the principle that "where a business is unitary in character, so that its separate parts cannot be fairly considered by themselves and the whole business in the several states derives a value from the unity of use, allocation of income upon a reasonable formula is properly sustained." See 38 Cal.2d at 228, 238 P.2d at 577.

E. *Disparities in Wage and Property Costs in Various Jurisdictions as Distorting Apportionment.** "Taxpayers also contend that the existence of substantial disparities in wage rates and property costs in the various jurisdictions in which a multistate or multinational unitary business operates requires a modification or rejection of the standard formula. This type of challenge to formulary apportionment does not depend on the use of a technique, such as separate accounting, which departs from the formulary approach adopted by the State legislature, or promulgated by the tax administrator. Instead, the taxpayer's contention is that with respect to two of the factors, property and payroll, the formula itself is based on the premise that every dollar of payroll spent and every dollar of property cost incurred in one State will produce roughly the same amount of income as a dollar of property or payroll expended in the other jurisdictions in which the corporation may be taxed. A substantial overage of State A's wage and property costs, as compared to those prevailing in other States, perverts this premise, with the consequence, as taxpayers contend, that State A thereby taxes income that is attributable to other taxing jurisdictions under the rationale of the formula itself.[25]

"The major problem with this type of demonstration is one of proof. A showing, for example, that wage rates are higher in the taxpayer's manufacturing plants in the Northeast than in the South does not establish distortion of income. Labor productivity, which may depend not only on the comparative skill and efficiency of workers in the various plants, but also on the character and efficiency of the machinery being used; energy, environmental protection costs, and the like must be taken into account. Consequently, unit labor costs and unit property costs, i.e., the labor and property costs of producing a single unit of the same article in the plants located in varying taxing jurisdictions, must be established. Moreover, if one plant produces, for example, one model or type of automobile and other

* This note is taken from J. Hellerstein, State Taxation I, Corporate Income and Franchise Taxes ¶ 8.10[5], pp. 373–74 (1983). Used with the consent of the copyright owner and publisher.

25. It may be contended that proof of higher wages and property costs in the taxing State than in other States does not show misattribution of income if, as here contended, source of income is not the only yardstick of proper income attribution. That does not follow, for if jurisdiction to tax is based on the benefits and protection extended by the State and the costs of public services, the use of wage and property factors to measure income attribution would presumably be based on the premise that comparative wage and property costs are reasonable measures of comparative benefits, protection, and cost of public service in the various States. The validity of that premise is undermined if there are marked differences in wage rates or property costs, at least on a unit of production basis.

plants produce different models or types of automobiles, if one produces subcompacts in large volume and another large luxury cars in smaller volume, the unit wage and property costs may not be comparable. And the comparability problem would be greatly magnified if the taxpayer produces a variety of products, such as television sets in one State, tape recorders in another, and stereophonic equipment in still other States." J. Hellerstein, State Taxation I, Corporate Income and Franchise Taxes ¶ 8.10[5], pp. 373–74 (1983).

F. *Invocation of Separate Accounting by Tax Administrators.* In Texas Co. v. Cooper, 236 La. 380, 107 So.2d 676 (1958), an oil company sought the use of the State's three-factor apportionment formula under the Louisiana income tax. Under the statute, the Collector may resort to separate accounting if this method will more equitably determine net income from sources within the State, but he must bear the burden of showing that the formula would produce a "manifestly unfair result." The taxpayer's principal business in the State was the production of crude oil from its wells and leases; it used most of the oil in its refineries outside the State, but it sold some crude in the market in Louisiana. The taxpayer argued that the Collector had erred in utilizing separate accounting in making the assessment, since it was a unitary business whose Louisiana net income could not properly be determined except by formula. Declaring that there is no authority requiring it to treat the oil business as unitary, the court sustained the Collector. It resorted to the sales of crude oil on the local market as the means of establishing the profit attributable to every barrel of oil produced by the taxpayer in Louisiana as it leaves the State for refining elsewhere by the taxpayer.

Does such a method—measuring the profit on sales of crude oil on the local market of a comparatively small portion of a producer's output—fairly determine the profit allocable to the Louisiana oil production in the operation of an integrated producer-refiner-distributor, which sells the final products—gasoline, fuel oil, lubricating oil, and other products—throughout the country and abroad under the Texaco trade-name? There is little doubt that if the taxpayer sought to compel separate accounting under the Louisiana statutory standards, it would fail.

G. *The Acceptance of Separate Accounting in Some States.* Not all States are as unreceptive to separate accounting as California. A Mississippi case reflects the rule in some States that separate accounting is preferred and that formulary apportionment will be accepted only where separate accounting is not applicable for lack of adequate records or otherwise. In McWilliams Dredging Co. v. McKeigney, 227 Miss. 730, 86 So.2d 672 (1956), appeal dismissed, 352 U.S. 807, 77 S.Ct. 57 (1956), the taxpayer, whose principal office was in New Orleans, was engaged in dredging operations in Mississippi and other States. The taxpayer sought to report its net income on a formulary basis; the regulations required the use of separate accounting if the taxpayer's system of accounts accurately reflected its net income earned in Mississippi and provided that the "use of an apportionment formula will be discouraged." The court found that the taxpayer had failed to sustain the burden of establishing that the separate accounting determination made by the tax commission, from the taxpayer's records, taxed extraterritorial values. Mississippi's preference for separate accounting continues to be reflected in its statutes. Miss.Code Ann. § 27–7–23(c)(2)(B), CCH ¶ 92–532k, P–H ¶ 12–154K.24. See also Magnolia Petroleum Co. v. Okla. Tax Comm., 190 Okla. 172, 121 P.2d 1008 (1941), and Palestin, "Interstate Taxation: Non–Unitary Corporation—Should Statutory Apportionment Yield to Separate Accounting?," 1965 N.T.A. Procs. 531; and note the advocacy of separate accounting by spokesmen for multinational corporations, as applying to income from operations abroad. See Section 10, infra.

H. *Single–Factor Gross Receipts Formula for Apportioning Income.* In General Motors Corp. v. District of Columbia, 380 U.S. 553, 85 S.Ct. 1156 (1965), the Supreme Court considered an attack upon the single-factor sales formula promulgated by the District's Tax Commissioners. The formula was adopted by the Commissioners pursuant to a statute authorizing them to prescribe apportionment and allocation regulations determining "the portion of the net income of the corporation * * * as is fairly attributable to any trade or business carried on or engaged in within the District." 380 U.S. at 554, 85 S.Ct. at 1157. The formula provided that if income is derived from the manufacture and sale, or purchase and sale of tangible personal property, the income was to be apportioned to the District in the percentage of District sales to sales everywhere.

General Motors, which manufactured motor vehicles, parts, and accessories outside the District and sold them within the District challenged its tax based on the formula as unauthorized by the statute and as violative of the Due Process and Commerce Clauses. The Court agreed with the taxpayer's statutory argument, i.e., that in a case in which "the company carries on business both inside and outside the District," the statute requires that some portion of the income derived from the sales made in the District "be deemed to arise from sources outside the District," and must accordingly be apportioned outside the District. 380 U.S. at 559, 85 S.Ct. at 1160.

Although the Court explicitly disavowed deciding the case on constitutional grounds, it stated:

> The conclusion which we reach by analysis of the plain language of the statute also finds support in the consequences which a contrary view would have for the overall pattern of taxation of income derived from interstate commerce. The great majority of States imposing corporate income taxes apportion the total income of a corporation by application of a three-factor formula which gives equal weight to the geographical distribution of plant, payroll, and sales. The use of an apportionment formula based wholly on the sales factor, in the context of general use of the three-factor formula, will ordinarily result in multiple taxation of corporate income.

380 U.S. at 559, 85 S.Ct. at 1160. Furthermore, the Court went on to observe that "[t]he standard three-factor formula can be justified as a rough, practical approximation of the distribution of either a corporation's sources of income or the social costs which it generates" whereas "the geographical distribution of a corporation's sales is, by itself, of dubious significance in indicating the locus of either factor." 380 U.S. at 561, 85

S.Ct. at 1161. Although some observers understandably read these remarks as casting doubt on the constitutionality of a single-factor sales formula for apportioning net income, see J. Hellerstein, "State Tax Discrimination Against Out-of-Staters," 30 Nat'l Tax J. 113, 122 (1977), the Court repudiated the constitutional overtones of *General Motors* in *Moorman Manufacturing Co. v. Bair,* which follows.

MOORMAN MANUFACTURING CO. v. BAIR

Supreme Court of the United States, 1978.
437 U.S. 267, 98 S.Ct. 2340.

MR. JUSTICE STEVENS delivered the opinion of the Court.

The question in this case is whether the single-factor sales formula employed by Iowa to apportion the income of an interstate business for income tax purposes is prohibited by the Federal Constitution.

I

Appellant, Moorman Manufacturing Company, is an Illinois corporation engaged in the manufacture and sale of animal feeds. Although the products it sells to Iowa customers are manufactured in Illinois, appellant has over 500 salesmen in Iowa and it owns six warehouses in the State from which deliveries are made to Iowa customers. Iowa sales account for about 20% of appellant's total sales.

Corporations, both foreign and domestic, doing business in Iowa are subject to the State's income tax. The taxable income for federal income tax purposes, with certain adjustments, is treated as the corporation's "net income" under the Iowa statute. If a corporation's business is not conducted entirely within Iowa, the statute imposes a tax only on the portion of its income "reasonably attributable" to the business within the State.

There are essentially two steps in computing the share of a corporation's income "reasonably attributable" to Iowa. First, certain income, "the geographical source of which is easily identifiable," is attributed entirely to a particular State.[1] Second, if the remaining income is derived from the manufacture or sale of tangible personal property, "the part thereof attributable to business within the state shall be in that proportion which the gross sales made within the state bear to the total gross sales." [2] This is the single-factor formula that appellant challenges in this case.

1. The statute provides:

"Interest, dividends, rents and royalties (less related expenses) received in connection with business in the state, shall be allocated to the state, and where received in connection with business outside the state, shall be allocated outside of the state." Iowa Code § 422.33(1)(a).

In describing this section, the Iowa Supreme Court stated that "certain income, the geographical source of which is easily identifiable, is allocated to the appropriate state." 254 N.W.2d 737, 739. Thus, for example, rental income would be attributed to the State where the property was located. And in appellant's case, this section operated to exclude its investment income from the tax base.

2. Iowa Code § 422.33(1)(b).

If the taxpayer believes that application of this formula subjects it to taxation on a greater portion of its net income than is "reasonably attributable" to business within the State, it may file a statement of objections and submit an alternative method of apportionment. If the evidence submitted by the taxpayer persuades the Director of Revenue that the statute is "inapplicable and inequitable" as applied to it, he may recalculate the corporation's taxable income.

During the fiscal years 1949 through 1960, the State Tax Commission allowed appellant to compute its Iowa income on the basis of a formula consisting of three, equally weighted factors—property, payroll and sales—rather than the formula prescribed by statute.[3] For the fiscal years 1961 through 1964, appellant complied with a directive of the State Tax Commission to compute its income in accordance with the statutory formula. Since 1965, however, appellant has resorted to the three-factor formula without the consent of the Commission.

In 1974, the Iowa Director of Revenue revised appellant's tax assessment for the fiscal years 1968 through 1972. This assessment was based on the statutory formula, which produced a higher percentage of taxable income than appellant, using the three-factor formula, had reported on its return in each of the disputed years.[4] The higher percentages, of course produced a correspondingly greater tax obligation for those years.[5]

After the Tax Commission had rejected Moorman's appeal from the revised assessment, appellant challenged the constitutionality of the single-factor formula in the Iowa District Court for Polk County. That court held the formula invalid under the Due Process Clause and the Commerce Clause. The Supreme Court of Iowa reversed, holding that an apportionment formula that is necessarily only a rough approximation of the income properly attributable to the taxing State is not subject to constitutional attack unless the taxpayer proves that the formula has produced an income attribution "out of all proportion to the business transacted" within the State. The court concluded that appellant had not made such a showing.

3. The operation of the two formulas may be briefly described. The single-factor sales formula yields a percentage representing a ratio of gross sales in Iowa to total gross sales. The three-factor formula yields a percentage representing an average of three ratios: property within the State to total property, payroll within the State to total payroll, and sales within the State to total sales.

These percentages are multiplied by the adjusted total net income to arrive at Iowa taxable net income. This net income figure is then multiplied by the tax rate to compute the actual tax obligation of the taxpayer.

4. For those years the two formulas resulted in the following percentages:

Fiscal Year Ended	Sales Factor Percentage	Three–Factor Percentage
3/31/68	21.8792%	14.1088%
3/31/69	21.2134%	14.3856%
3/31/70	19.9492%	14.0200%
3/31/71	18.9544%	13.2186%
3/31/72	18.6713%	12.2343%

For a description of how these percentages are computed, see n. 3, supra.

5. Thus, in 1968, for example, Moorman's three-factor computation resulted in a tax of $81,466, whereas the Director's single-factor computation resulted in a tax of $121,363.

We noted probable jurisdiction of Moorman's appeal, 434 U.S. 953, 98 S.Ct. 478, 54 L.Ed.2d 311 and now affirm.

II

Appellant contends that Iowa's single-factor formula results in extraterritorial taxation in violation of the Due Process Clause. This argument rests on two premises: first, that appellant's Illinois operations were responsible for some of the profits generated by sales in Iowa; and, second, that a formula that reaches any income not in fact earned within the borders of the taxing State violates due process. The first premise is speculative and the second is foreclosed by prior decisions of this Court.

Appellant does not suggest that it has shown that a significant portion of the income attributed to Iowa in fact was generated by its Illinois operations; the record does not contain any separate accounting analysis showing what portion of appellant's profits was attributable to sales, to manufacturing, or to any other phase of the company's operations. But appellant contends that we should proceed on the assumption that at least some portion of the income from Iowa sales was generated by Illinois activities.

Whatever merit such an assumption might have from the standpoint of economic theory or legislative policy, it cannot support a claim in this litigation that Iowa in fact taxed profits not attributable to activities within the State during the years 1968 through 1972. For all this record reveals, appellant's manufacturing operations in Illinois were only marginally profitable during those years and the high volume sales to Iowa customers from Iowa warehouses were responsible for the lion's share of the income generated by those sales. Indeed, a separate accounting analysis might have revealed that losses in Illinois operations prevented appellant from earning more income from exploitation of a highly favorable Iowa market. Yet even were we to assume that the Illinois activities made some contribution to the profitability of the Iowa sales, appellant's claim that the Constitution invalidates an apportionment formula whenever it may result in taxation of some income that did not have its source in the taxing State is incorrect.

The Due Process Clause places two restrictions on a State's power to tax income generated by the activities of an interstate business. First, no tax may be imposed, unless there is some minimal connection between those activities and the taxing State. National Bellas Hess, Inc. v. Department of Revenue, 386 U.S. 753, 756, 87 S.Ct. 1389, 1390, 18 L.Ed.2d 505. This requirement was plainly satisfied here. Second, the income attributed to the State for tax purposes must be rationally related to "values connected with the taxing state." Norfolk & Western R. Co. v. Missouri, 390 U.S. 317, 325, 88 S.Ct. 995, 1001, 19 L.Ed.2d 1201.

Since 1934 Iowa has used the formula method of computing taxable income. This method, unlike separate accounting, does not purport to identify the precise geographical source of a corporation's profits; rather, it is employed as a rough approximation of a corporation's income that is reasonably related to the activities conducted within the taxing State. The single-factor formula used by Iowa, therefore, generally will not produce a figure that represents the actual profits earned within the State. But the same is true of the Illinois three-factor formula. Both will occasionally over-reflect or under-reflect income attributable to the taxing State. Yet despite this imprecision, the Court has refused to impose strict constitutional restraints on a State's selection of a particular formula.[6]

Thus, we have repeatedly held that a single-factor formula is presumptively valid. * * * [discussing the *Underwood Typewriter* case, p. 434 supra].

In individual cases, it is true, the Court has found that the *application* of a single-factor formula to a particular taxpayer violated due process. See Hans Rees' Sons v. North Carolina, 283 U.S. 123, 51 S.Ct. 385, 75 L.Ed. 879; Norfolk & Western R. Co. v. State Tax Commission, 390 U.S. 317, 88 S.Ct. 995, 19 L.Ed.2d 1201. In *Hans Rees'*, for example, the Court concluded that proof that the formula produced a tax on 83% of the taxpayer's income when only 17% of that income actually had its source in the State would suffice to invalidate the assessment under the Due Process Clause. But in neither *Hans Rees'* nor *Norfolk & Western* did the Court depart from the basic principles that the States have wide latitude in the selection of apportionment formulas and that a formula-produced assessment will only be disturbed when the taxpayer has proved by "clear and cogent evidence" that the income attributed to the State is in fact "out of all appropriate proportion to the business transacted * * * in that State," 283 U.S., at 135, 51 S.Ct., at 389, or has "led to a grossly distorted result." 390 U.S., at 326, 88 S.Ct., at 1002.

* * *

[The Court also discussed *General Motors Corp. v. District of Columbia*, see p. 451 supra, and concluded that] the Court in *General Motors* made clear that it did "not mean to take any position on the constitutionality of a state income tax based on the sales factor alone." 380 U.S., at 561, 85 S.Ct., at 1161.

The Iowa statute afforded appellant an opportunity to demonstrate that the single-factor formula produced an arbitrary result in its case. But this record contains no such showing and therefore the Director's assessment is not subject to challenge under the Due Process Clause.[9]

---

6. See, e.g., Underwood Typewriter Co. v. Chamberlain, 254 U.S. 113, 41 S.Ct. 45, 65 L.Ed. 165; Bass, Ratcliff & Gretton, Ltd. v. State Tax Comm'n, 266 U.S. 271, 45 S.Ct. 82, 69 L.Ed. 282; Ford Motor Co. v. Beauchamp, 308 U.S. 331, 60 S.Ct. 273, 84 L.Ed. 640.

9. In his concurring opinion, Justice McCormick of the Iowa Supreme Court made this point:

III

Appellant also contends that during the relevant years Iowa and Illinois imposed a tax on a portion of the income derived from the Iowa sales that was also taxed by the other State in violation of the Commerce Clause. Since most States use the three-factor formula that Illinois adopted in 1970, appellant argues that Iowa's longstanding single-factor formula must be held responsible for the alleged duplication and declared unconstitutional. We cannot agree.

In the first place, this record does not establish the essential factual predicate for a claim of duplicative taxation. Appellant's net income during the years in question was approximately $9 million. Since appellant did not prove the portion derived from sales to Iowa customers, rather than sales to customers in other States, we do not know whether Illinois and Iowa together imposed a tax on more than 100% of the relevant net income. The income figure that appellant contends was subject to duplicative taxation was computed by comparing gross sales in Iowa to total gross sales. As already noted, however, this figure does not represent *actual* profits earned from Iowa sales. Obviously, all sales are not equally profitable. Sales in Iowa, although only 20% of gross sales, may have yielded a much higher percentage of appellant's profits. Thus, profits from Iowa sales may well have exceeded the $2.5 million figure that appellant contends was taxed by the two States. If so, there was no duplicative taxation of the net income generated by Iowa sales. In any event, on this record its existence is speculative.[11]

Even assuming some overlap, we could not accept appellant's argument that Iowa, rather Illinois, was necessarily at fault in a constitutional sense. It is of course true that if Iowa had used Illinois' three-factor formula, a risk of duplication in the figures computed by the two States might have been avoided. But the same would be true had Illinois used the Iowa formula. Since the record does not reveal the sources of appellant's profits, its Commerce Clause claim cannot rest on the premise that profits earned in Illinois were included in its

"In the present case, Moorman did not attempt to prove the amount of its actual net income from Iowa activities in the years involved. Therefore no basis was presented for comparison of the corporation's Iowa income and the income apportioned to Iowa under the formula. In this era of sophisticated accounting techniques, it should not be impossible for a unitary corporation to prove its actual income from activities in a particular state. However, Moorman showed only that its tax liability would be substantially less if Iowa employed a three-factor apportionment formula. We have no basis to assume that the three-factor formula produced a result equivalent to the corporation's actual income from Io-wa activities. Having failed to establish a basis for comparison of its actual income in Iowa with the income apportioned to Iowa under the single-factor formula, Moorman did not demonstrate that the single-factor formula produced a grossly unfair result. Thus it did not prove unconstitutionality of the formula as applied." 254 N.W.2d, at 757.

11. Since there is no evidence in the record regarding the percentages of its total net income taxed in the other States in which it did business during those years, any claim that appellant was taxed on more than 100% of its total net income would also be speculative.

Iowa taxable income and therefore the Iowa formula was at fault for whatever overlap may have existed. Rather, the claim must be that even if the presumptively valid Iowa formula yielded no profits other than those properly attributable to appellant's activities within Iowa, the importance of avoiding any risk of duplication in the taxable income of an interstate concern justifies invalidation of the Iowa statute.

Appellant contends that to the extent this overlap is permitted the corporation that does business in more than one State shoulders a tax burden not shared by those operating entirely within a State.[12] To alleviate the burden, appellant invites us to hold that the Commerce Clause itself, without implementing legislation by Congress, requires Iowa to compute corporate net income under the Illinois equally weighted, three-factor formula. For the reasons that follow, we hold that the Constitution does not require such a result.

The only conceivable constitutional basis for invalidating the Iowa statute would be that the Commerce Clause prohibits any overlap in the computation of taxable income by the States. If the Constitution were read to mandate such precision in interstate taxation, the consequences would extend far beyond this particular case. For some risk of duplicative taxation exists whenever the States in which a corporation does business do not follow identical rules for the division of income. Accepting appellant's view of the Constitution, therefore, would require extensive judicial law-making. Its logic is not limited to a prohibition on use of a single-factor apportionment formula. The asserted constitutional flaw in that formula is that it is different from that presently employed by a majority of States and that difference creates a risk of duplicative taxation. But a host of other division of income problems create precisely the same risk and would similarly rise to constitutional proportions.

Thus, it would be necessary for this Court to prescribe a uniform definition of each category in the three-factor formula. For if the States in which a corporation does business have different rules regarding where a "sale" takes place, and each includes the same sale in its three-factor computation of the corporation's income, there will be duplicative taxation despite the apparent identity of the formulas

12. Appellant also contends that the Iowa formula discriminates against interstate commerce in violation of the Commerce Clause and the Equal Protection Clause, because an Illinois corporation doing business in Iowa must pay tax on a greater portion of its income than a local Iowa company, and an Iowa company doing business in Illinois will pay tax on less of its income than an Illinois corporation doing business in Iowa. The simple answer, however, is that whatever disparity may have existed is not attributable to the Iowa statute. It treats both local and foreign concerns with an even hand; the alleged disparity can only be the consequence of the combined effect of the Iowa *and* Illinois statutes, and Iowa is not responsible for the latter.

Thus, appellant's "discrimination" claim is simply a way of describing the potential consequences of the use of different formulas by the two States. These consequences, however, could be avoided by the adoption of any uniform rule; the "discrimination" does not inhere in either State's formula.

employed.[13] A similar risk of multiple taxation is created by the diversity among the States in the attribution of "non-business" income, generally defined as that portion of a taxpayer's income that does not arise from activities in the regular course of its business.[14] Some States do not distinguish between business and nonbusiness income for apportionment purposes. Other States, however, have adopted special rules that attribute nonbusiness income to specific locations. Moreover, even among the latter, there is diversity in the definition of nonbusiness income and in the designation of the locations to which it is deemed attributable. The potential for attribution of the same income to more than one State is plain.[15]

The prevention of duplicative taxation, therefore, would require national uniform rules for the division of income. Although the adoption of a uniform code would undeniably advance the policies that underlie the Commerce Clause, it would require a policy decision based on political and economic considerations that vary from State to State. The Constitution, however, is neutral with respect to the content of any uniform rule. If division of income problems were to be constitutionalized, therefore, they would have to be resolved in the manner suggested by appellant for resolution of formula diversity—the prevalent practice would be endorsed as the constitutional rule. This rule would at best be an amalgam of independent State decisions, based on considerations unique to each State. Of most importance, it could not reflect the national interest, because the interests of those States whose policies are subordinated in the quest for uniformity would be excluded from the calculation.

While the freedom of the States to formulate independent policy in this area may have to yield to an overriding national interest in uniformity, the content of any uniform rules to which they must subscribe should be determined only after due consideration is given to the interests of all affected States. It is clear that the legislative power granted to Congress by the Commerce Clause of the Constitution would amply justify the enactment of legislation requiring all States to adhere to uniform rules for the division of income. It is to that body, and not this Court, that the Constitution has committed such policy decisions.

---

13. Thus, while some States such as Iowa assign sales by destination, "sales can be assigned to the state * * * of origin, the state in which the sales office is located, the state where an employee of the business making the sale carries on his activities or where the order is first accepted, or the state in which an interstate shipment is made." Note, State Taxation of Interstate Businesses and the Multistate Tax Compact: The Search for a Delicate Uniformity, 11 Colum.J.Law & Soc.Prob. 231, 237 n. 20 (1975) (citation omitted).

14. See, e.g., Uniform Division of Income for Tax Purposes Act § 1(a).

15. Thus, one State in which a corporation does business may consider a particular type of income business income and simply include it in its apportionment formula; a second State may deem that same income nonbusiness income and attribute it to itself as the "commercial domicile" of the company; and a third State, though also considering it nonbusiness income, may attribute it to itself as the "legal domicile" of the company. See Note, supra n. 13, at 239.

Finally, it would be an exercise in formalism to declare appellant's income tax assessment unconstitutional based on speculative concerns with multiple taxation. For it is evident that appellant would have had no basis for complaint if, instead of an income tax, Iowa had imposed a more burdensome gross receipts tax on the gross receipts from sales to Iowa customers. In Standard Pressed Steel Co. v. Department of Revenue, 419 U.S. 560, 95 S.Ct. 706, 42 L.Ed.2d 719, the Court sustained a tax on the entire gross receipts from sales made by the taxpayer into Washington State. Because receipts from sales made to States other than Washington were not included in Standard Steel's taxable gross receipts, the Court concluded that the tax was " 'apportioned exactly to the activities taxed.' " Id., at 564, 95 S.Ct. at 709.

In this case appellant's actual income tax obligation was the rough equivalent of a 1% tax on the entire gross receipts from its Iowa sales. Thus, the actual burden on interstate commerce would have been the same had Iowa imposed a plainly valid gross receipts tax instead of the challenged income tax. Of more significance, the gross receipts tax sustained in *Standard Pressed Steel* and General Motors Corp v. Washington, 377 U.S. 436, 84 S.Ct. 1564, 12 L.Ed.2d 430, is inherently more burdensome than the Iowa income tax. It applies whether or not the interstate concern is profitable and its imposition may make the difference between profit and loss. In contrast, the income tax is only imposed on enterprises showing a profit and the tax obligation is not heavy unless the profits are high.

Accordingly, until Congress prescribes a different rule, Iowa is not constitutionally prohibited from requiring taxpayers to prove that application of the single-factor formula has produced arbitrary results in a particular case.

The judgment of the Iowa Supreme Court is affirmed.

MR. JUSTICE BRENNAN, dissenting.

I agree with the Court that, for purposes of constitutional review, there is no distinction between a corporate income tax and a gross receipts tax. I do not agree, however, that Iowa's single-factor sales apportionment formula meets the Commerce Clause requirement that a State's taxation of interstate business must be "fairly apportioned to the commerce carried on within the taxing state." Western Live Stock v. Bureau of Revenue, 303 U.S. 250, 256, 58 S.Ct. 546, 549, 82 L.Ed. 823 (1938). As I have previously explained, where a sale

> "exhibits significant contacts with more than one State * * * it is the commercial activity within the State, and not the sales volume, which determines the State's power to tax, and by which the tax must be apportioned. While the ratio of in-state to out-of-state sales is often taken into account as one factor among others in apportioning a firm's total net income, see, e.g., the description the 'Massachusetts Formula' in Note, 75 Harv.L.Rev. 953, 1011 (1962), it nevertheless remains true that if commercial activity in more than one State results in a sale in one of them, that State may not claim as all its own the gross receipts

to which the activity within its borders has contributed only a part. Such a tax must be apportioned to reflect the business activity within the taxing State." General Motors Corp. v. Washington, 377 U.S. 436, 450–451, 84 S.Ct. 1564, 1573, 12 L.Ed.2d 430 (1964) (Brennan, J., dissenting).

I would therefore reverse.

MR. JUSTICE BLACKMUN, dissenting.

The unspoken, but obvious, premise of the majority opinion is the fear that a Commerce Clause invalidation of Iowa's single-factor sales formula will lead the Court into problems and difficulties in other cases yet to come. I reject that premise.

I agree generally with the content of MR. JUSTICE POWELL's opinion in dissent. I join that opinion because I, too, feel that the Court has a duty to resolve, not to avoid, these problems of "delicate adjustment," Boston Stock Exchange v. State Tax Comm'n, 429 U.S. 318, 329, 97 S.Ct. 599, 606, 50 L.Ed.2d 514 (1977), and because the opinion well demonstrates that Iowa's now anachronistic single-factor sales formula runs headlong into overriding Commerce Clause considerations and demands.

Today's decision is bound to be regressive. Single-factor formulas are relics of the early days of state income taxation. The three-factor formulas were inevitable improvements and, while not perfect, reflect more accurately the realities of the business and tax world. With their almost universal adoption by the States, the Iowa system's adverse and parochial impact on commerce comes vividly into focus. But with its single-factor formula now upheld by the Court, there is little reason why other States, perceiving or imagining a similar advantage to local interests, may not go back to the old ways. The end result, in any event, is to exacerbate what the Commerce Clause, absent governing congressional action, was devised to avoid.

MR. JUSTICE POWELL, with whom MR. JUSTICE BLACKMUN joins, dissenting.

It is the duty of this Court "to make the delicate adjustment between the national interest in free and open trade and the legitimate interest of the individual States in exercising their taxing powers." Boston Stock Exchange v. State Tax Commission, 429 U.S. 318, 329, 97 S.Ct. 599, 606, 50 L.Ed.2d 514 (1977). This duty must be performed with careful attention to the settings of particular cases and consideration of their special facts. See Raymond Motor Transp., Inc. v. Rice, 434 U.S. 429, 447–448 n. 25, 98 S.Ct. 787, 797, 54 L.Ed.2d 664 (1978). Consideration of all the circumstances of this case leads me to conclude that Iowa's use of a single-factor sales formula to apportion the net income of multistate corporations results in the imposition of "a tax which discriminates against interstate commerce * * * by providing a direct commercial advantage to local business." Northwestern States

Portland Cement Co. v. Minnesota, 358 U.S. 450, 458, 79 S.Ct. 357, 362, 3 L.Ed.2d 421 (1959). I therefore dissent.

I

Iowa's use of a single-factor sales apportionment formula—though facially neutral—operates as a tariff on goods manufactured in other States and as a subsidy to Iowa manufacturers selling their goods outside of Iowa. Because 44 of the 45 other States which impose corporate income taxes use a three-factor formula involving property, payroll, and sales, Iowa's practice insures that out-of-state businesses selling in Iowa will have higher total tax payments than local businesses. This result follows from the fact that Iowa attributes to itself all of the income derived from sales in Iowa, while other taxing States—using the three-factor formula—are also taxing some portion of the same income through attribution to property or payroll in those States.

This surcharge on Iowa sales increases to the extent that a business' plant and labor force are located outside Iowa. It can be avoided altogether only by locating all property and payroll in Iowa; an Iowa manufacturer selling only in Iowa will never have any portion of its income attributed to any other State. And to the extent that an Iowa manufacturer makes its sales in States other than Iowa, its overall state tax liability will be reduced. Assuming comparable tax rates, its liability to other States, in which sales constitute only one-third of the apportionment formula, will be far less than the amount it would have owed with a comparable volume of sales in Iowa, where sales are the exclusive mode of apportioning income. The effect of Iowa's formula, then, is to penalize out-of-state manufacturers for selling in Iowa and to subsidize Iowa manufacturers for selling in other States.

This appeal requires us to determine whether these economic effects of the Iowa apportionment formula violate either the Due Process Clause or the Commerce Clause. I now turn to those questions.

II

For the reasons given by the Court, * * * I agree that application of Iowa's formula does not violate the Due Process Clause. The decisions of this court make it clear that arithmetical perfection is not to be expected from apportionment formulae. International Harvester Co. v. Evatt, 329 U.S. 416, 67 S.Ct. 444, 91 L.Ed. 390 (1947). It has been said that the "apportionment theory is a mongrel one, a cross between desire not to interfere with state taxation and desire at the same time not utterly to crush out interstate commerce." Northwest Airlines, Inc. v. Minnesota, 322 U.S. 292, 306, 64 S.Ct. 950, 957, 88 L.Ed. 1283 (1944) (Jackson, J., concurring). It owes its existence to the fact that with respect to a business earning income through a series of transactions beginning with manufacturing in one State and ending with a sale in another, a precise—or even wholly logical—determination of the State in which any specific portion of the income was earned is impossible. Underwood Typewriter Co. v. Chamberlain, 254 U.S. 113, 120–121, 41 S.Ct. 45, 46–47, 65 L.Ed. 165 (1920).

Hence, the fact that a particular formula—like the one at issue here—may permit a State to tax some income actually "located" in another State is not in and of itself a basis for finding a due process violation.[3] Were it otherwise, any formula deviating in the smallest detail from that used in other States would be invalid. Because there is no ideal means of "locating" any State's rightful share, such uniformity cannot be dictated by this Court. Hence, the decisions of this Court properly require the taxpayer claiming a due process violation to show that the apportionment is "out of all appropriate proportion to the business transacted." Hans Rees' Sons, Inc. v. North Carolina ex rel. Maxwell, 283 U.S. 123, 135, 51 S.Ct. 385, 389, 75 L.Ed.2d 879 (1931). As petitioner has failed to make any such showing, I agree with the Court that no due process violation has been made out here.

This conclusion does not *ipso facto* mean that Commerce Clause strictures are satisfied as well. This Court's decisions dealing with state levies that discriminate against out-of-state business, as Iowa's formula does, compel a more detailed inquiry.

III

A

It is a basic principle of Commerce Clause jurisprudence that "[n]either the power to tax nor the police power may be used by the state of destination with the aim and effect of establishing an economic barrier against competition with the products of another state or the labor of the residents."

* * *

One form of such unreasonable restrictions is "discriminating State legislation." Welton v. Missouri, 91 U.S. 275, 280, 23 L.Ed. 347 (1876). This Court consistently has struck down state and local taxes which unjustifiably benefit local businesses at the expense of out-of-state businesses.

* * *

3. This does not mean, as the Court suggests * * * that this Court is disabled from ever determining whether a particular apportionment formula imposes multiple burdens upon or discriminates against interstate commerce. See General Motors Corp. v. District of Columbia, 380 U.S. 553, 85 S.Ct. 1156, 14 L.Ed.2d 68 (1965); Bass, Ratcliff & Gretton, Ltd. v. State Tax Comm'n, 266 U.S. 271, 45 S.Ct. 82, 69 L.Ed. 282 (1924); Underwood Typewriter Co. v. Chamberlain, 254 U.S. 113, 41 S.Ct. 45, 65 L.Ed. 165 (1920). Regardless of which formula more accurately locates the State in which any particular segment of income is earned, it is a mathematical fact that the use of different formulae may result in taxation on more than 100% of the corporation's income under the State's own definitions, as well as in skewed tax effects. See, n. 2, supra. When this result has a predictably burdensome or discriminatory effect, Commerce Clause scrutiny is triggered. See Part III, infra. The effects of the challenged formula upon the particular corporation's income is strictly related only to inquiry under the Due Process Clause, since Commerce Clause analysis focuses on the impact upon commerce in general.

This ban applies not only to state levies that by their terms are limited to products of out-of-state business, or which explicitly tax out-of-state sellers at higher rates than local sellers. It also reaches those taxes that "in their practical operation [work] discriminatorily against interstate commerce to impose upon it a burden, either in fact or by the very threat of its incidence." Nippert v. Richmond, supra, 327 U.S., at 425, 66 S.Ct., at 590. For example, this Court has invalidated a facially neutral fixed-fee license tax collected from all local and out-of-state "drummers," where it appeared the tax fell far more heavily upon out-of-state businesses, since local businesses had little or no occasion to solicit sales in that manner. * * * Thus, the constitutional inquiry relates not simply to the form of the particular tax, but to its effect on competition in the several States.

As indicated in Part I above, application of Iowa's single-factor-sales apportionment formula, in the context of general use of three-factor formulae, inevitably handicaps out-of-state businesses competing for sales in Iowa. The handicap will diminish to the extent that the corporation locates its plant and labor force in Iowa, but some competitive disadvantage will remain unless all of the corporate property and payroll are relocated in Iowa.[4] In the absence of congressional action, the Commerce Clause constrains us to view the State's interest in retaining this particular levy as against the constitutional preference for an open economy. * * *

B

Iowa's interest in any particular level of tax revenues is not affected by the use of the single-factor sales formula. It cannot be predicted with certainty that its application will result in higher revenues than any other formula. If Iowa needs more revenue, it can adjust its tax rates. That adjustment would not have the discriminatory impact necessarily flowing from the choice of the single-factor sales formula. Hence, if Iowa's choice is to be sustained, it cannot be by virtue of the State's interest in protecting its fisc or its power to tax. No other justification is offered. If we are to uphold Iowa's apportionment formula, it must be because no consistent principle can be developed that could account for the invalidation of the Iowa formula, yet support application of other States' imprecise formulae.

It is argued that since this Court on several occasions has upheld the use of single-factor formulae, Iowa's scheme cannot be regarded as

---

4. The clog on commerce present here is similar to the risk of imposing "multiple burdens" on interstate commerce against which the Court has warned in various decisions. See, e.g., Western Live Stock v. Bureau of Revenue, 303 U.S. 250, 255–256, 58 S.Ct. 546, 548–549, 82 L.Ed. 823 (1938); J.D. Adams Mfg. Co. v. Storen, 304 U.S. 307, 311–312, 58 S.Ct. 913, 915–916, 82 L.Ed. 1365 (1938); Gwin, White & Prince, Inc. v. Henneford, 305 U.S. 434, 439, 59 S.Ct. 325, 83 L.Ed. 272 (1939); Northwestern States Portland Cement Co. v. Minnesota, 358 U.S. 450, 458, 79 S.Ct. 357, 362, 3 L.Ed.2d 421 (1959). Compare Evco v. Jones, 409 U.S. 91, 93 S.Ct. 349, 34 L.Ed.2d 325 (1972), with General Motors Corp. v. Washington, 377 U.S. 436, 84 S.Ct. 1564, 12 L.Ed.2d 430 (1964). In this case, Iowa corporations will not risk additional burdens when they make out-of-state sales.

suspect simply because it does not embody the prevalent three-factor theory. Consideration of the decisions dealing with single-factor formulae, however, reveals that each is distinguishable.

* * *

[After discussing the *Underwood Typewriter* and *Bass, Ratcliff* cases, pp. 434–35 supra, Justice Powell turned to other single-factor apportionment formula cases].

Somewhat more troublesome is Ford Motor Co. v. Beauchamp, 308 U.S. 331, 60 S.Ct. 273, 84 L.Ed. 640 (1939). In that case, the Court sustained Texas' use of a single-factor sales formula to apportion the outstanding capital stock, surplus, undivided profits, and long-term obligations of corporations subject to the state franchise tax. While this case may be seen as standing for the proposition that single-factor sales formulae are not *per se* illegal, it is not controlling in the present case.[7] In *Ford Motor Co.,* as in *Underwood Typewriter* and *Bass,* there was no showing of virtually universal use of a conflicting type of formula for determining the same tax. Thus it could not be said that the Texas formula inevitably imposed a competitive disadvantage on out-of-state corporations. Discrimination not being shown, there was no basis for invalidating the Texas scheme under the Commerce Clause.

The opposite is true here. In the context of virtually universal use of the basic three-factor formula, Iowa's use of the single-factor sales formula necessarily discriminates against out-of-state manufacturers. The only remaining question, then, is whether Iowa's scheme may be saved by the fact that its discriminatory nature depends on context: If other States were not virtually unanimous in their use of an opposing formula, past decisions would make it difficult to single out Iowa's scheme as more offensive than any other.

D

On several occasions, this Court has compared a state statutory requirement against the practice in other States in determining the statute's validity under the Commerce Clause. In Southern Pacific Co. v. Arizona ex rel. Sullivan, 325 U.S. 761, 65 S.Ct. 1515, 89 L.Ed. 1915 (1945), the Court struck down a state statute limiting passenger trains to 14 cars and freight trains to 70 cars. Noting that only one State other than Arizona enforced a restriction on train lengths, the *Southern Pacific* Court specifically considered the Arizona law against the background of the activities in other States.

* * *

---

7. Although overruling *Ford Motor Co.* would not be necessary in this case, the time may be ripe for its reconsideration. See, e.g., J. Hellerstein, State and Local Taxation 324 (3d ed. 1969). As suggested in General Motors Corp. v. District of Columbia, 380 U.S. 553, 561, 85 S.Ct. 1156, 1161, 14 L.Ed.2d 68 (1965), a sales-only formula is probably the most illogical of all apportionment methods, since "the geographic distribution of a corporation's sales is, by itself, of dubious significance in indicating the locus of either" a corporation's sources of income or the social costs it generates.

The Court also looked to the practices of other States in holding unconstitutional Illinois' mudguard requirement in Bibb v. Navajo Freight Lines, Inc., 359 U.S. 520, 79 S.Ct. 962, 3 L.Ed.2d 1003 (1959).

* * *

[Justice Powell referred to *General Motors Corp. v. District of Columbia,* which is treated at p. 451 supra, and emphasized the Court's reference to the widespread use of the three-factor formula, quoting the Court's statement that the]

> "use of an apportionment formula based wholly on the sales factor, in the context of general use of the three-factor approach, will ordinarily result in multiple taxation of corporate net income * * *. In any case, the sheer inconsistency of the District formula with that generally prevailing may tend to result in the unhealthy fragmentation of enterprise and an uneconomic pattern of plant location, and so presents an added reason why this Court must give proper meaning to the relevant provisions of the District Code." Id., at 559–560, 85 S.Ct. at 1160.

The *General Motors* Court, then, expressly evaluated the single-factor sales formula in the context of general use of the three-factor method and concluded that the former created dangers for interstate commerce.

These cases lead me to believe that it is not only proper but essential to determine the validity of the Iowa formula against the background of practices in the other States. If one State's regulatory or taxing statute is significantly "out of line" with other States' rules, *Bibb,* 359 U.S., at 530, 79 S.Ct. at 968, and if by virtue of that departure from the general practice it burdens or discriminates against interstate commerce, Commerce Clause scrutiny is triggered, and this Court must invalidate it unless it is justified by a legitimate local purpose outweighing the harm to interstate commerce, Pike v. Bruce Church, Inc., supra, 397 U.S. at 142, 90 S.Ct. at 847; accord, Hughes v. Alexandria Scrap Corp., 426 U.S. 794, 804, 96 S.Ct. 2488, 2495, 49 L.Ed.2d 220 (1976). There probably can be no fixed rule as to how nearly uniform the countervailing state policies must be; that is, there can be no rule of 26 States, of 35, or of 45. Commerce Clause inquiries generally do not run in such precise channels. The degree of conflict and its resulting impact on commerce must be weighed in the circumstances of each case. But the difficulty of engaging in that weighing process does not permit this Court to avoid its constitutional duty and allow an individual State to erect "an unreasonable clog upon the mobility of commerce," Baldwin v. G.A.F. Seelig Inc., 294 U.S., at 527, 55 S.Ct. at 502, by taking advantage of the other States' commendable trend toward uniformity.

Such is the case before us. Forty-four of the 45 States, other than Iowa, that impose a corporate income tax utilize a similar three-factor apportionment formula.[9] The 45th State, West Virginia, uses a two-

---

9. There are differences in definitions of the three factors among the States that use a three-factor formula. See, e.g., J. Hellerstein, State and Local Taxation 309–310, and n. 7 (3d ed. 1969); Note, State Taxation of Interstate Businesses and the

factor formula based on property and payroll. Those formulae individually may be no more rational as means of apportioning the income of a multistate business than Iowa's single-factor sales formula. But see General Motors, Inc. v. District of Columbia, 380 U.S., at 561, 85 S.Ct. at 1161. Past decisions upheld differing formulae because of this inability to determine that any of the various methods of apportionment in use was the best; so long as a State's choice was not shown to be grossly unfair, it would be upheld. Compare *Underwood Typewriter*, supra, with *Hans Rees' Sons*, supra. The more recent trend toward uniformity, however, permits identification of Iowa's formula, like the mudguard requirement in *Bibb*, as "out of line," if not *per se* irrational. Since Iowa's formula inevitably discriminates against out-of-state sellers, and since it has not been justified on any fiscal or administrative basis, I would hold it invalid under the Commerce Clause.

Notes and Problems

A. In *Moorman*, the Court faulted the taxpayer for failing to show that "a significant portion of the income attributed to Iowa in fact was generated by its Illinois operations" and for failing to provide "any separate accounting analysis showing what portion of appellant's profits was attributable to sales, to manufacturing, or to any other phase of the company's operations." In Exxon Corp. v. Wisconsin Dept. of Revenue, 447 U.S. 207, 100 S.Ct. 2109 (1980), the taxpayer attacked the application of Wisconsin's three-factor formula to its income on the basis of detailed separate accounting evidence that purportedly demonstrated that significantly less income was earned in the State than was apportioned to the State by the formula. In the course of rejecting the taxpayer's claim, which relied on the above quoted language from *Moorman,* the Court denigrated its remarks in *Moorman* as "dicta" and declared:

> In *Moorman* we simply noted that the taxpayer had made no showing that its Illinois operations were responsible for profits from sales in Iowa. This hardly leads to the conclusion, urged by Exxon here, that a taxpayer's separate functional accounting, if it purports to separate out income from various aspects of the business, must be accepted as a matter of constitutional law for state tax purposes. Such evidence may be helpful, but *Moorman* in no sense renders such accounting conclusive.

447 U.S. at 223, 100 S.Ct. at 2120. The *Exxon* case is noted in more detail at pp. 528–29 infra.

Miltistate Tax Compact: The Search for a Delicate Uniformity, 11 Colum.J. of Law & Soc.Prob. 231, 235–238 (1975). Such differences may tend in less dramatic fashion to impose burdens on out-of-state businesses not entirely dissimilar to the one presented here. It may be that any such effects do not work inevitably in one direction, as does the burden imposed here, or they may be *de minimis* in Commerce Clause terms. In any event, they are not presently before us. It suffices to dispose of this case that nearly all the other States use a basic three-factor formula, while Iowa clings to its sales-only method.

B. *The Weaknesses of Separate Accounting as a Basis for Challenging Unitary Apportionment.* * "Historically, separate accounting was the method preferred by both tax administrators and taxpayers for dividing the income of corporations doing business within and without the State, but the method was largely abandoned because it was found too expensive in record keeping and unworkable in practice.[26] The Achilles heel of separate accounting is the inability to establish fair arm's length prices for goods transferred, or basic operational services rendered, between controlled branches or subsidiaries of an enterprise.[27] Taxpayers have long contended that the transfer price problem of multinational enterprises is effectively handled by the IRS in auditing Federal income tax returns that require a separation of foreign from U.S. source income, and that under Section 482 of the Internal Revenue Code, fair arm's length prices are regularly established.[28] That argument has been dealt a body blow by the General Accounting Office (GAO), which recently published a report of its study of the determination of transfer prices by the IRS under Section 482. The GAO concluded that the current system is not working satisfactorily, and recommended that the Treasury study the possible substitution of unitary apportionment for the current separate accounting method under Section 482.[29]

"Separate accounting is also vulnerable on its merits when applied to a unitary business because, as I have suggested elsewhere, as in Alice in Wonderland, it operates in a universe of unreality.[30] For the essence of the separate accounting technique of dividing the income of a unitary business is to ignore interdependence and integration of the business operations conducted in the various taxing jurisdictions and treat them, instead, as if they were separate, independent, and nonintegrated. Thus, a business that owns and operates its own rubber plantations, produces rubber and related raw materials, manufactures a variety of products, ranging from tires, automobile and airplane parts to raincoats and galoshes, and sells them to manufacturers, wholesalers, and retailers, is a very different enterprise from the sum total of a rubber plantation owner, a rubber products manufacturer and a wholesaler, each separate, unaffiliated, and independent, and each owning and operating one piece of the business. The differences between such separate businesses and the national and multina-

---

* This note is taken from J. Hellerstein, State Taxation I, Corporate Income and Franchise Taxes ¶ 8.10[2], pp. 367–68 (1983). Used with the consent of the copyright owner and publisher.

26. See J. Hellerstein's "Recent Developments in State Tax Apportionment and the Circumscription of Unitary Business," 21 Nat'l Tax J. 487 (1968); *State and Local Taxation,* at 512 et seq.

27. Id.

28. See Miller, "State Income Taxation of Multiple Corporations and Multiple Businesses," Tax Foundation Seminar on *Taxation of Interstate Businesses* (April 16–17, 1970).

29. Comptroller General of the United States, General Accounting Office, Report to the House Ways and Means Committee, on the Internal Revenue Service's administration of Section 482 of the Internal Revenue Code, at i-ix (Sept. 30, 1981); see also ¶ 8.10[7]. See the recent study by a New Zealand barrister and solicitor, Harley, "International Division of the Income Tax Base of Multinational Enterprise: An Overview," Tax Notes, Dec. 28, 1981, at 1563.

30. See J. Hellerstein, "The Unitary Business Principle and Multicorporate Enterprises: An Examination of the Major Controversies," 27 Tax Executive 313, 317 (1975).

tional unitary businesses that dominate our economy are crucial and, to a considerable extent, the wealth, power, and profits of the latter group are attributable to the very fact that they are integrated, unitary businesses. That is why separate accounting, which ignores the unitary character of businesses, is not in general a satisfactory method of division of taxable income among the States." J. Hellerstein, State Taxation I, Corporate Income and Franchise Taxes ¶ 8.10[2], pp. 367–68 (1983).

C. *Minimum Allocation Percentage.* May a State use a minimum apportionment percentage? In Gulf Oil Corp. v. Joseph, 307 N.Y. 342, 121 N.E.2d 360 (1954), appeal dismissed 348 U.S. 923, 75 S.Ct. 339 (1955), the court considered the application of the former New York City gross receipts tax to an oil company conducting both an intrastate and interstate business. The receipts factor of the city's three-factor formula broke down receipts into three categories: wholly taxable, allocable, and non-taxable; the latter were excluded from the computation. The numerator of the receipts factor consisted of wholly taxable receipts plus one-third of allocable receipts, i.e., those arising from sales involving interstate commerce; and the denominator included all the allocable receipts. When the receipts factor, as thus determined, was averaged with the property and payroll factors, if the resultant average was less than $33\frac{1}{3}$ percent, it was increased to that figure, and if it exceeded $66\frac{2}{3}$ percent, it was reduced to that figure. In the *Gulf* case the resultant fractions were slightly under $33\frac{1}{3}$ percent— by one to three percentage points—and the court held that "the comptroller in using such minimum figures acted arbitrarily and out of harmony with the declared legislative purpose of taxing only that part of the interstate receipts which is properly attributable and allocable to the doing of business in the city. In setting up minimum figures no attempt at rough approximation or apportionment has been made by the comptroller." 307 N.Y. at 349, 121 N.E.2d at 361–362. The court was of the view that an "unfair apportionment by one State could result in the risk of multiple taxation which would discriminate against petitioner as one engaged in interstate commerce." The matter was remitted to the comptroller for the purpose of making a fair apportionment. As a result of this decision, the New York City regulations were amended—to produce the complicated formula referred to in the discussion of the *Federated Department Store* case, p. 436 supra.

(c) Capital Stock Taxes

Notes and Problems

A. In Ford Motor Co. v. Beauchamp, 308 U.S. 331, 60 S.Ct. 273 (1939), which was cited by the majority in *Moorman* and discussed by Justice Powell in his dissenting opinion in that case, the Court sustained the power of a State to apportion a capital stock tax under a single-factor gross receipts formula. Ford Motor Company, which had its principal motor vehicle manufacturing plants in Michigan, maintained an assembly plant in Texas, where most of the vehicles sold in that State were assembled. Approximately $34 million of Ford's total sales of about $888 million, or 3.85 percent, were made within the State. As a consequence, the receipts formula resulted in the attribution to Texas of some $23 million of the company's total capital of about $600 million. The actual value of all of Ford's physical assets located in Texas was somewhat over $3 million. The Court described the tax as a "payment for the privilege of carrying on business in Texas" (308 U.S. at 336, 60 S.Ct. at 276), and held that the apportionment did not violate the Due Process or Commerce Clause. The Court declared that "in a unitary enterprise property outside the state, when correlated in use with property within the state, necessarily affects the worth of the privilege within the state." Id.

The incongruity of apportioning capital stock by reference to gross receipts is shown by the *Ford* case. The measure of a capital stock tax is essentially property, tangibles and intangibles. Indeed, this type of tax grew up in this country essentially as a tool for measuring the value of intangible corporate assets that were escaping property taxes. The use of the sales receipts ratio to measure property values borders on the capricious. Ford Motor Company has very large physical plants in Michigan. The effect of the type of apportionment permitted in the *Ford* case is to permit other States in effect to include in the measure of their capital stock taxes the value of plants located in Michigan.

This is the obverse of the use of a single-factor property formula to apportion a net income measure, the type of apportionment approved in the *Underwood* and *Kent–Coffey* cases (see pp. 434–35 supra). It would be entirely fortuitous if a single-factor property formula fairly reflected net profits in a multistate business. Hence, in addition to the built-in arbitrariness inherent in any single-factor formula designed to measure net income or capital stock, the formulas in the cases under consideration suffer from the weakness that there is little rational relationship between the apportionment technique and the measure of the tax. In Certified Credit Corp. v. Bowers, 174 Ohio St. 239, 188 N.E.2d 594 (1963), appeal dismissed 375 U.S. 84, 84 S.Ct. 217 (1963), the taxpayer urged this point in attacking an apportionment of an Ohio capital stock tax as violating the Due Process Clause. The capital stock of a small loan company was apportioned under a single-factor gross receipts formula. Its contention that the amount of capital stock employed in a State ought to be measured by the proportion of its property in the State, not by a receipts ratio, was rejected.

B. *Inclusion in the Capital Stock Base of Minority Stock Holdings in Other Corporations.* The Michigan Supreme Court held, in a case whose rationale has since been relied on by a number of State taxing authorities, that minority stock holdings in other corporations, which contributed to the taxpayer's overall business, are properly includible in the measure of the taxpayer's capital stock base. Cleveland–Cliffs Iron Co. v. Michigan Corporation and Securities Commission, 351 Mich. 652, 88 N.W.2d 564 (1958). The taxpayer, an Ohio corporation whose executive, general business, sales, and principal accounting offices were located in Cleveland, owned and operated extensive iron ore, timber lands and other properties located in Michigan. It shipped iron ore, stone, and grain, and operated its own fleet of ships in the Great Lakes, shipping to customers in a number of States. Cleveland–Cliffs also engaged in a substantial coal business, purchasing the coal from mines in Kentucky, Pennsylvania, Ohio, West Virginia, and Illinois, and carrying the coal in its vessels for sale to its customers in

Michigan and other States. The taxpayer was authorized to do business in Michigan, where the office of the general manager and all its iron mines, a land and lumbering office, and a local coal sales office were located.

The Michigan tax imposed on foreign corporations for the privilege of doing business in the State was measured by the taxpayer's capital stock and surplus and was apportioned to the State under a three-factor Massachusetts formula comprising property, payroll, and sales. The taxing authority included in the tax base the book value of the taxpayer's minority stock holdings in six major steel companies, including Inland Steel, Republic Steel, and Youngstown Sheet and Tube Company. The book value of the stocks totalled $27,000,000 and comprised some 27 percent of the taxpayer's total assets.

In rejecting the taxpayer's contention that the stocks in question "do not form an integral part of the activities of Cleveland–Cliffs in Michigan," the court relied on the findings of the Corporation Tax Appeal Board:

> "13. That the appellant's steel stocks in its investment portfolio were used for its over-all business, including its Michigan business, in the following specific particulars in 1951–1952: as an asset for general credit purposes; by using the dividend income that went into the general corporate account as working capital; by sales and use of the proceeds of the sales for the years 1951 and 1952 as part of working capital; and by the use of the sale proceeds and dividend income for various capital outlays, including the acquisition of fifty per cent. interest in the Humboldt Mines in Michigan, and the investment in Michigan in additional mining equipment and development regarding low grade ores." [88 N.W.2d at 570.] *

If the value of the taxpayer's holdings was properly includible in the taxpayer's capital stock base, should the taxpayer have been permitted to include the property, payroll, and receipts of the underlying corporations in valuing its own apportionment to the extent of its proportionate ownership of the stocks of those companies? Presumably, the consequence would have been to reduce the taxpayer's Michigan apportionment percentage, since the corporations in question appear to have conducted their business entirely or principally outside Michigan. Unless that is done, the apportionment tends to produce a disproportionately high apportionment to the State. Distortion may be inherent in formulas in which the measure of the tax takes into account items not taken into account by the apportionment. The Michigan statute contained a provision directing the State Tax Commission to vary the statutory formula in cases in which the application of the formula "does not properly reflect the activity, business, receipts and capital of a taxpayer reasonably attributable to the state * * *" Section 5e of the Michigan franchise tax act, Mich.Comp.Laws Ann. § 450.305e, set out in the court's opinion at 88 N.W.2d at 573. Should the court have directed the Commission to resort to § 5e by varying the statutory formula in the manner indicated? See Section 4 infra.

For a consideration of the combined method of apportionment as applied to an affiliated group of corporations, see Sections 8 and 9 infra.

---

* [The case is discussed in 35 U.Detroit L.J. 623 (1958)].

C. *Effects of Inclusion in Capital Stock Measure of Value of Invest-*
ment in Subsidiaries and Exclusion of Subsidiaries' Receipts, Assets and
Other Factors From Apportionment. The problem presented in the *Cleve-*
land–Cliffs case is accentuated where a series of integrated business
activities are carried on by a parent corporation and a group of subsidiary
corporations. Such a case was presented by Household Finance Corporation v. State Tax Commission of Maryland, 212 Md. 80, 128 A.2d 640 (1957),
noted in 17 Md.L.Rev. 327 (1957), in which the court considered the
application of Maryland's capital stock tax to a foreign small loan company. Household is a Delaware corporation with its principal offices in
Chicago and with regional offices in various parts of the United States and
Canada. Its business is that of making installment cash loans to consumers. During 1952, the year in question, the taxpayer owned all, or substantially all, of the capital stock of ten subsidiary corporations, nine of which
carried on the same type of business as the parent company. The parent
operated in Maryland through its own direct branches without the subsidiaries. Household's consolidated balance sheet, as of the end of the taxable
year, showed assets of approximately $340,000,000, consolidated gross in-
come of $75,000,000 and consolidated net income of about $13,000,000.

The Maryland statute imposes a capital stock tax measured by the full
cash value of the capital stock. In the case of foreign finance corporations,
there is to be assessed so much of the capital stock "as represents the
business done in this State." The tax was assessed on the basis of the
single-factor gross receipts formula thus set out in the statute (to be utilized
"in the absence of clear evidence to the contrary") as applied to the value of
the capital stock of Household, which took into account the value of the
investment in the subsidiaries. The court analyzed the action taken by the
State Tax Commission as follows:

> What the Commission actually did can be described in terms of
> fractions. It was simply this: the Commission, in constructing the
> fraction to calculate business done within and without the State, used
> as the numerator total gross receipts within the State; and, in deter-
> mining the denominator, used, not total gross receipts of the parent
> company (excluding intercompany transactions) plus total gross re-
> ceipts of subsidiaries, but total gross receipts of the parent, plus
> interest, supervision fees and dividends paid to it by the subsidiaries.
> [212 Md. at 97, 128 A.2d at 649.]

In holding that this action was erroneous, the court declared:

> We have just determined that Household's business is unitary, and
> we have upheld the Commission's valuation of it as such, for the
> Commission has taken the appraisal of the market and the market
> makes its appraisal of the business as a unit vary largely on the basis
> of the consolidated assets, liabilities and earnings of the parent and its
> subsidiaries, as well as on the basis of yield. In allocating the value of
> the property and business of the entity attributable to Maryland, the
> statutes under which the Commission is acting require the exclusion of
> business and property outside of Maryland. These statutes further
> provide a presumption that "in the absence of clear evidence to the
> contrary" the proper basis of apportionment is the ratio of gross

receipts or earnings in Maryland to gross receipts or earnings outside of Maryland (subject to an exception not here pertinent). We think that the record affords clear evidence that the presumption is not correct in this case, from which it follows that it should not have been applied.

In a few words, the basis for our view is this: if the Commission sees fit to arrive at the total value of a unitary enterprise on a consolidated basis, it cannot in fairness apportion that value as between Maryland and other jurisdictions on a basis which is inconsistent with, and which rejects, an element used in building up that value. Here, of course, that element is the earnings of the subsidiaries. They have been discarded and the gross earnings of the parent company only have been used for the apportionment. The result has been to produce a considerably larger apportionment of value to Maryland than would have been reached if the gross earnings of subsidiaries, rather than the gross income which—on an intercompany basis—the parent company derived from them had been used in determining the ratio of gross receipts in Maryland to gross receipts outside of Maryland. [212 Md. at 97–98, 128 A.2d at 649.]

The case was remanded for further action by the tax commission. How should the distorting effects of including the investments in the out-of-state operating subsidiaries in the measure of the tax, without including the underlying receipts of the subsidiaries in the denominator of the gross receipts formula, have been cured? By separate accounting? By a consolidated report of the parent and subsidiaries?

The Missouri Supreme Court gave the same taxpayer relief under its capital stock tax by excluding from the capital stock measure the value of the company's investments in loans to the subsidiaries. Household Finance Corp. v. Robertson, 364 S.W.2d 595 (Mo.1963). The New Jersey courts, however, reached contrary results in Household Finance Corp. v. Director of Taxation, 36 N.J. 353, 177 A.2d 738 (1962), appeal dismissed, 371 U.S. 13, 83 S.Ct. 41 (1962). No relief was granted from the application of a single-factor gross receipts apportionment to the value of Household's capital stock. See also the provision in the Ohio property factor, used in apportioning the base of the capital stock tax, that investments in the stock of, or loans to, 51 percent or more owned subsidiaries "shall be allocated in and out of the state in accordance with the value of the physical property [of the subsidiary] in and out of the state." Ohio Rev.Code Ann. § 5733.05, CCH ¶ 94–359, P–H ¶ 16,220.25; Armour & Co. v. Kosydar, 46 Ohio St.2d 450, 349 N.E.2d 301 (1976). Compare the New York franchise tax provision for allocating investments in stocks and securities by reference to the New York apportionment factors of the corporation whose stocks or securities are held. N.Y.Tax Law § 210.3(b)(1), CCH ¶ 93–910, P–H ¶ 12,020.53.

SECTION 3. ALLOCATION AND APPORTIONMENT METHODS USED BY THE STATES

INTRODUCTORY NOTE

Forty-five out of the forty-six States (including the District of Columbia) which levy corporate taxes measured by net income have adopted the so-called Massachusetts three-factor apportionment formula, consisting of property, payroll, and receipts.[31] In many of the States, particularly a number of those which have enacted the major features of the Uniform Division of Income for Tax Purposes Act (UDITPA),[32] its provisions are available at the election of the taxpayer as an optional alternative to the State's regular apportionment formula. There is some diversity in the language of the statutes of the various States defining and applying the three factors, and that is true also in the case of a few States which have adopted the general provisions of UDITPA.[33]

(a) Property Factor

Real and Tangible Personal Property. The property factor normally relates only to real and tangible personal property.[34] Historically, the exclusion from the property factor of stocks, bonds, patents, and other intangibles grew out of the application to taxation of the doctrine of *mobilia sequuntur personam*, under which intangibles were regarded as having a taxable situs at the domicile of the owner. See Section 12, Introductory Note infra. As a consequence, for property tax purposes intangibles were taxed by the State of the owner's domicile, and this principle was extended by many States to their income taxes. Id. When apportionment and allocation methods were developed, it fitted

31. See Table 1, Section 6 infra; 1 Willis Comm.Rep. 170 et seq.

32. UDITPA was developed by the National Conference of Commissioners on Uniform State Laws, and it was approved by the 66th Annual Conference in July 1957 and by the House of Delegates of the American Bar Association during the same year. See Pierce, "The Uniform Division of Income for State Tax Purposes," 35 Taxes 747 (1957), for a brief analysis of the provisions of the Model Act by one of its draftsmen. See also Wilkie, "Uniform Division of Income for Tax Purposes," 37 Taxes 65 (1959); Conlon, "The Apportionment of Multi–State Business Income: The NCCUSL Division of Income Act," 12 Tax Executive 220 (1960); Cox, "The NCCUSL Uniform Apportionment Formula," 42 Taxes 530 (1964).

33. See Table 1, Section 6 infra; 1 Willis Comm.Rep. 194–95. Thus, Pennsylvania, which has adopted most of the provisions of UDITPA, did not enact the throwback rule. Pa.Tax Reform Code § 401.2(a)(15), Pa.Stat.Ann. tit. 72

§ 7401.2(a)(15), CCH ¶ 100–670, P–H ¶ 12,300.140. See, however, the use of the "throwout rule" for sales in Pennsylvania. Note C, p. 485 infra. When Florida adopted a corporate income tax in 1971, it modified Article IV of the Multistate Tax Compact (which it had previously adopted) by giving double weight to the sales factor. Fla.Stat.Ann. § 220.15, CCH ¶ 94–487, P–H ¶ 12,040.25. More recently, Massachusetts, the cradle of the equally weighted three-factor formula, has likewise modified its formula so as to tax out-of-state vendors more heavily by double-weighting its receipts factor.

34. For discussions of the property factor, see Roesken, "The Property Factor in State Income Tax Allocation," 24 Taxes 473 (1946) and "The Property Factor in State Franchise Taxation," id. at 1043; Summerwell, "State Allocation Factors: Property Factor," 7 Tax Exec. 30 (1955); Morss, "Apportioning Corporate Income Among States for Tax Purposes," 42 Taxes 261 (1964).

into this pattern of the law to allocate income from intangibles to the State of the owner's domicile and, accordingly, to exclude intangibles from the property factor.[35] Moreover, the selection of the State to which intangibles are to be attributed, if they are included in the property factor, is fraught with exceptional complications.

Rented Property. Traditionally, rented property was not taken into account in the property factor; only property owned by the taxpayer was counted. This tended to create unwarranted discrepancies between taxpayers which owned the plants, stores, or office buildings they used in their operations, and those which leased the property.[36] With the extensive growth of sale lease-backs and the widespread use of leasing, in form if not in substance, of trucks, airplanes, duplicating equipment, computers, and other personalty, many States changed their laws so as to include in the property factor rented property used in the business.[37] The value of rented property is usually determined by a multiple of net rents (gross rents paid less rents received on subrentals of the property), such as five to eight times the rent.

Property in Transit and Mobile Property. Property in transit between the States on the date as of which the apportionment is made is treated in a variety of ways by the States. In some States, inventory in transit between the taxing State and any other State is excluded from both the numerator and the denominator of the factor. If the inventory is being transported between States other than the taxing State, it is excluded from the latter's property numerator, but it is included in the denominator. In other States, inventory in transit is taken into account in the numerator if the destination of the goods is in the taxing State, provided the taxpayer regularly includes in the denominator of the property factor goods in transit between the States. Most State statutes and regulations are, however, silent on the point.[38]

A related question arises in the case of mobile property, such as trucks, automobiles, construction equipment, and airplanes used in the conduct of the taxpayer's business. Some States apportion the value of the equipment to the numerator to the extent the equipment is used in the States, by methods such as percentage, mileage, or time factors, and include the full value of the property in the denominator.[39] The language of most State statutes, including UDITPA, which defines the property factor as the ratio of "the taxpayer's real and tangible person-

35. See 1 Willis Comm.Rep. 171. This rule has its exceptions, however. The property fraction of the two-factor formula used in apportioning capital stock, under the Ohio franchise tax, includes intangibles. For problems arising under this apportionment formula, see Armour & Co. v. Kosydar, 46 Ohio St.2d 450, 349 N.E.2d 301 (1976); Miami Valley Broadcasting Corp. v. Kosydar, 48 Ohio St.2d 10, 355 N.E.2d 812 (1976).

36. See Edelman, "Should Rented Property be Included in the Property Allocation Factor?," 1949 N.T.A.Procs. 185.

37. Id., and see Table 1, Section 6 infra.

38. For the treatment of inventory in transit by various States, see the State-by-State summary in 2 Willis Comm.Rep., App. A.

39. Id.

al property owned or rented and used in this state during the tax period to the total everywhere" appears to lend itself to such apportionment.[40]

Valuation of Property. The value of the property is determined under the statutes of some States at fair market value, under others at book cost less accrued depreciation, and others at undepreciated original or book cost.[41] The National Commission on Uniform State Laws, which drafted UDITPA, justified its use of undepreciated book cost, although "admittedly arbitrary," on the ground of ease of compliance.[42] This figure is usually readily ascertainable, and its use eliminates "any differences due to varying methods of depreciation."[43] Moreover, since the same standard applies to both in-state and out-of-state property, any distortion resulting from the use of undepreciated cost would not ordinarily be significant. Most statutes provide that property values are to be determined by averaging values at the beginning and end of the taxable year, but the tax administrator is usually authorized, in appropriate cases, to permit or require monthly or other averaging of values over the year.[44]

(b) Payroll Factor

All the States which impose corporate taxes measured by net income, with the exception of Iowa, use a payroll factor, either in the regular State formula, or in the optional formula allowed. The payroll factor, which is somewhat more varied over the country than the property factor, raises fewer controversial questions. "Compensation," the usual statutory term used, is defined by UDITPA as "wages, salaries, commissions and any other form of remuneration paid to employees for personal services,"[45] and other State laws adopt essentially the same language.[46] These provisions are modeled after the definition of wages in the Federal Unemployment Tax Act and are generally construed in accordance with the interpretation of that Act by the Internal Revenue Service, as embracing all compensation for services as an employee, whether paid in cash or in kind, which is treated as gross income for Federal income tax purposes.[47]

The attribution of payroll to the taxing State is derived by most of the statutes, including the UDITPA payroll provisions,[48] from the Model Unemployment Compensation Act. Under that Act, the wages

40. UDITPA § 10. See Section 6 infra.

41. 1 Willis Comm.Rep. 172–74.

42. See notes to UDITPA, Section 6 infra.

43. Id.

44. See note 41 supra.

45. UDITPA § 1(c).

46. The New York franchise tax, for example, includes in the payroll factor "wages, salaries and other personal service compensation * * * of employees within the state, except general executive officers * * *" N.Y. Tax Law § 210.3(a)(3), CCH ¶ 93–908, P–H ¶ 12.020.45.

47. The State payroll factors are generally derived from the Model Unemployment Compensation Act, which is integrated with the Federal Unemployment Tax Act. The IRS rulings are digested in Bulletin Index–Digest System, Service Three, Employment Taxes, Basic Volume 1953–72, IRS Pub. No. 643 (Rev. 12–72) and Supplements.

48. UDITPA § 13, Section 6 infra.

or salary of an employee are attributed to the State if (1) the services are performed entirely within the State; or (2) the services are performed both within and without the State and (a) the base of operations, or, if there is no base of operations, the place from which the service is directed or controlled, is in the State, or (b) the base of operations, or the place from which the service is directed or controlled, is not in any State in which the employee performs services, but his residence is in the State.[49]

This test does not fractionate the compensation of any individual employee who renders services in more than one State, as is done, for example, in some States with respect to the property factor in dealing with construction equipment and other movable property. Under such rules, only the percentage of the value of the property, determined on a time basis within and without the State, is attributed to the taxing State.[50] Under the payroll test of the Model Unemployment Compensation Act, the entire compensation of an individual employee is attributed to the State, or none is attributed. The State unemployment insurance tax returns thus provide the State-by-State breakdown of the data required for the income tax apportionment purposes.

Not all States, however, have adopted the Model Unemployment Compensation Act provisions.[51] Thus, the former Pennsylvania statute provided that the numerator of the wage fraction shall include all compensation to employees "not chiefly situated at, connected with, or sent out from, premises for the transaction of business, owned or rented by the corporation outside" the State. Pa.Stat.Ann. tit. 72 § 3420b (1964); Commonwealth v. Continental Rubber Works, 347 Pa. 514, 32 A.2d 878 (1943).[52] The highest court of the State (per Cohen, J.) construed the "chiefly situated at, connected with, or sent out from" test as being measured by "control. ＊ ＊ ＊ If the employee is controlled or directed or supervised by or reports to an office outside Pennsylvania, his wages are to be assigned outside Pennsylvania because of this connection," regardless of residence in Pennsylvania or "simply because they spend all of their time there." Commonwealth v. General Foods Corp., 429 Pa. 266, 277–78, 239 A.2d 359, 365 (1971).

49. UDITPA § 14; Ohio Rev.Code Ann. § 5733.05(B)(2)(b), CCH ¶ 94–366, P–H ¶ 16,220.65. The New Jersey statute contains the payroll attribution provision summarized in the text, but adds a further category with respect to which an employee's compensation is attributed to the State: "Contributions are not required and paid with respect to such services under an unemployment compensation law of any other State." N.J.Stat.Ann. § 54:10A–7, CCH ¶ 94–062, P–H ¶ 16,160.

50. Cal.Reg. 25129(a), CCH ¶ 12–575, P–H ¶ 11,537L.

51. See, e.g., N.Y. Tax Law § 210.3(a)(3), CCH ¶ 93–908, P–H ¶ 12,020.45. See Charts of Payroll—How Apportioned, Payroll—What Pay Is Apportioned, P–H All States Guide ¶¶ 225, 226.

52. The negative form in which the statute is framed is not uncommon; its purpose is to attribute the residue or doubtful items to the taxing State; compare the throwback rule, Note C, p. 485 infra. This so-called "residue theory of allocation" was discussed in the *General Foods* case and considered proper by Mr. Justice Cohen.

In some States compensation paid to executive officers is not taken into account in the payroll factor,[53] presumably on the theory that high executive salaries tend to distort the payroll factor.[54]

(c) Receipts or Sales Factor

The receipts or sales factor has been at the center of the major controversies which have arisen in the implementation of the apportionment factors. All of the States which have on their statute books corporate taxes measured by net income, use a receipts or sales factor.[55] The terminology varies; UDITPA and some non-UDITPA State statutes use the narrow term "sales factor," and two other States use the term "gross sales," but the factor has a much broader scope than receipts from sales of property. It covers income from services, rentals, royalties, and business operations generally.[56] The inept term "sales factor" may have been adopted because the three-factor formula had its origin in, and was designed for, mercantile and manufacturing companies.[57] Other States use the more appropriate term "receipts" to cover the factor.[58] Georgia uses the term "gross receipts" but includes in the determination of the fraction only receipts from sales of tangible personal property,[59] as does Ohio, which uses "sales" as the factor.[60]

The Willis Committee in 1963 found that four different methods were in use in most of the States for determining the receipts to be included in the numerator of the State's receipts factor: (1) *the destination test,* attribution of the sales receipts to the State in which the goods are shipped to the customer, or in which they are delivered to the customer; (2) *the origin test,* attribution to the State of the factory, warehouse or office from which the goods are shipped; (3) *the sales office negotiation test,* attribution to the State of the sales office from or through which the sale was principally negotiated; (4) *the sales activity test,* attribution to the State in which the sales employees principally conducted selling activities. See 1 Willis Comm.Rep., Table 7–2, at 182–83.

A. *Sales Destination Test.* The destination test of attribution of receipts from sales of tangible personal property has spread so rapidly since 1964 that it is now in use in whole or in part in 45 of the 46 jurisdictions (45 States and the District of Columbia) that employ a sales or receipts factor in their apportionment formulas. (Table 2, Section 6 infra.) Connecticut, Massachusetts, Utah, and Wisconsin are among the States that use the sales office test of attribution (at least in part). Vermont is the only State which uses the origin test as its basic

---

53. See note 51 supra.

54. Id.

55. See Table 1, Section 6 infra; and the State-by-State summary in 2 Willis Comm.Rep., App. J, A233, and 1 Willis Comm.Rep. 180.

56. UDITPA § 1(g).

57. See Section 5 infra.

58. Conn.Gen.Stat. § 12–218, CCH ¶ 91–404, P–H ¶¶ 12,020 et seq.

59. O.C.G.A. § 48–7–31(d)(2)(c), CCH ¶ 95–554, P–H ¶ 12,055.105.

60. Ohio Rev.Code Ann. §§ 5733.05(B)(2), 5733.05(B)(2)(c), CCH ¶¶ 94–363, 94–368, P–H ¶¶ 16,220.45, 16,220.85.

rule of attribution, although many States attribute receipts to the State of origin when the "throwback" or similar rule comes into play.[61]

The destination method of attributing receipts from the sale of tangible personal property has been adopted by most States that levy taxes measured by net income, through the enactment of UDITPA or otherwise. In a case arising under a Georgia statute which utilized that method, a taxpayer raised Due Process and Commerce Clause objections to the inclusion in the Georgia receipts numerator of receipts from sales negotiated and contracted for outside the State, although no goods were shipped to customers located in Georgia. The corporation maintained operating divisions in Georgia, where it had employees, sales offices, warehouses and inventories of goods. The court dismissed the contentions, finding adequate nexus with the Georgia operations to warrant the apportionment. United States Steel Corp. v. Undercofler, 220 Ga. 553, 140 S.E.2d 269 (1965).

B. *Origin Test.* Attribution of receipts from sales to the State of origin has its major current importance under the throwback rule. As set out in UDITPA, the State of origin, for purposes of the throwback rule, is defined as the State from which:

> the property is shipped from an office, store, warehouse, factory or other place of storage in this state. [§ 16(b).]

Contrast the foregoing provision with the rule that formerly prevailed in New York, under which receipts were attributed to the State from which they were shipped only if the place of shipment constituted a "regular place of business" of the taxpayer. As a consequence, goods shipped from a public warehouse, where they were stored, did not qualify as a "regular place of business," so that the origin attribution rule applied. American Chicle Co. v. State Tax Comm'n, 11 A.D.2d 256, 203 N.Y.S.2d 282 (3rd Dept.1960), appeal denied 8 N.Y.2d 1119, 209 N.Y.S.2d 798, 171 N.E.2d 882 (1960), appeal dismissed 368 U.S. 17, 82 S.Ct. 136 (1961). No such qualification is included in UDITPA's definition of the State of origin.

C. *Sales Negotiation Office Test of Attribution of Receipts.* Many States which formerly used the sales negotiation office test for attributing receipts from sales of tangible personal property have in recent years substituted the sales destination rule. The abandonment of the sales negotiation office test has occurred both because of the increasing recognition of the claim of the market State to a portion of the tax and because of the serious administrative difficulties encountered in applying the former rule. For an illustration of these difficulties, see Commonwealth v. General Foods Corp., 429 Pa. 266, 239 A.2d 359 (1968), and Commonwealth v. Hellertown Mfg. Co., 438 Pa. 134, 264 A.2d 382 (1970). For other cases construing sales negotiation provisions, see Grain Belt Breweries, Inc. v. Commissioner of Taxation, 309 Minn. 190, 243 N.W.2d 322 (1976); Commissioner of Corporations and

---

61. See Note C, p. 485 infra.

Taxation v. Ford Motor Co., 308 Mass. 558, 33 N.E.2d 318 (1941); California Packing Corp. v. State Tax Comm., 97 Utah 367, 93 P.2d 463 (1939); Glove–Union, Inc. v. Department of Taxation, 20 Wis.2d 213, 121 N.W.2d 894 (1963); Gross Income Tax Div. v. Owens–Corning Fiberglas Corp., 253 Ind. 102, 251 N.E.2d 818 (1969). *Caveat:* A number of the States whose laws were at issue in the cases cited, including Pennsylvania, have substituted the sales destination test.

INTERNATIONAL HARVESTER CO. v. EVATT

Supreme Court of the United States, 1947.
329 U.S. 416, 67 S.Ct. 444.

MR. JUSTICE BLACK delivered the opinion of the Court.

The Supreme Court of Ohio affirmed a decision of that State's Board of Tax Appeals fixing the amount owed by appellant for its State corporation franchise tax for the years 1935 to 1940, inclusive. * * *

Section 5495 of the Ohio Gen.Code provides that each foreign corporation authorized to do business in the State must pay a tax or fee for the "privilege of doing business" or "owning or using a part or all of its capital or property" or "holding a certificate * * * authorizing it to do business in the state." It is not denied that appellant owed a franchise tax under this section for it held a certificate to do business in Ohio during all the years in question. It also owned and operated two large factories at Springfield, Ohio, which produced millions of dollars worth of goods. And it operated four branch selling establishments associated with four warehouses, and fourteen retail stores, all located at various places in Ohio, which stored and sold goods produced at the Ohio factory.

But appellant also owns and operates sixteen factories, nearly a hundred selling agencies, and numerous retail stores in other states. Goods produced at its Ohio factories are not only sold in Ohio, but in addition, are shipped for storage to out-of-Ohio warehouses to be sold by out-of-Ohio selling agencies to out-of-Ohio customers. Some are shipped directly to out-of-Ohio customers on orders from out-of-Ohio selling agencies. Conversely, goods manufactured by appellant out-of-Ohio are shipped to its Ohio warehouses, and sold by its Ohio selling agencies to Ohio customers. Appellant's claim is that the amount of the tax assessed against it has been determined in such manner that a part of it is for sales made outside Ohio and another part for interstate sales. These consequences result, appellant argues, from the formula used by Ohio in determining the amount and value of Ohio manufacturing and sales, as distinguished from interstate and out-of-state sales.

The tax is computed under the Ohio statute in the following manner: Section 5498 prescribes the formula used in determining what part of a taxpayer's total capital stock represents business and property conducted and located in Ohio. To determine this the total value of issued capital stock [1] is divided in half. One half is then multiplied by a fraction, the numerator of which is the value of all the taxpayer's Ohio property, and the denominator of which is the total value of all its property wherever owned. The other half is multiplied by another fraction whose numerator is the total value of the "business done" in the State and whose denominator is country-wide business. Addition of these two products gives the tax base, which, when multiplied by the tax rate of $\frac{1}{10}$ of 1%, produces the amount of the franchise tax.

In the "business done" numerator the State included as a part of Ohio business an amount equal to the sales proceeds of a large part of the goods manufactured at appellant's Ohio plants, no matter where the goods had been sold or delivered.[2] A part of the measure of the tax is consequently an amount equal to the sales price of Ohio-manufactured goods sold and delivered to customers in other states. Appellant contends that the State has thus taxed sales made outside of Ohio in violation of the Due Process clause. A complete answer to this due process contention is that Ohio did not tax these sales. Its statute imposed the franchise tax for the privilege of doing business in Ohio for profit. The State supreme court construed the statute as imposing the tax on corporations for engaging in business such as that in which taxpayer engaged. One branch of that business was manufacturing. It has long been established that a state can tax the business of manufacturing. The fact that it chose to measure the amount of such a tax by the value of the goods the factory has produced, whether of the current or a past year, does not transform the tax on manufacturers to something else. American Mfg. Co. v. St. Louis, 250 U.S. 459, 39 S.Ct. 522. * * *

In the Ohio "business done" numerator, we assume the State also included sales made by Ohio branches to Ohio customers of goods manufactured and delivered to those Ohio customers from out-of-Ohio factories.[3] Appellant's business practice was to conduct and account for its sales agencies' activities separately and distinctly from its factory operations. The State followed this distinction. It treated the sales agencies as conducting one type of business and the factories another. Thus it measured the value of the Ohio sales agencies' business by the total amount of the preceding year's Ohio sales of goods manufactured outside Ohio as well as those manufactured in Ohio. Here again, appellant's contention that this resulted in taxing out-of-state or inter-

1. Section 5498 also sets out in some detail the factors to be considered, and those not to be considered, in calculating the total value of a taxpayer's issued and outstanding stock. These provisions are not here at issue.

2. Rule 275, Tax Commissioner of Ohio, Oct. 13, 1939, exempted from the computation all goods manufactured by appellant in Ohio, but shipped to appellant's out-of-Ohio warehouses before sale.

3. The State contends here that it did not include in the "business-done" numerator an amount equal to the proceeds from sales by Ohio branches to Ohio customers of goods which were shipped to the Ohio customers from factories outside Ohio. Appellant insists that it did. We need not resolve this controversy, for we think the result is the same whichever view is taken.

state transactions or sales in violation of the Due Process clause is wholly without substance. The Ohio sales agencies' business and their sales to Ohio customers were intrastate activities. International Harvester Co. v. Department of Treasury et al., 322 U.S. 340, 64 S.Ct. 1019. What effect inclusion of this element in the "business done" numerator would have were these transactions not intrastate is a question we need not now decide.

What we have said disposes of the only ground urged to support the due process contention. It also answers most of the argument made against the Ohio statute on the ground that its application to appellant unduly burdens interstate commerce and therefore violates the Commerce Clause. Of course, the Commerce Clause does not bar a state from imposing a tax based on the value of the privilege to do an intrastate business merely because it also does an interstate business. Ford Motor Co. v. Beauchamp, 308 U.S. 331, 336, 60 S.Ct. 273, 276. Nor does the fact that a computation such as that under Ohio's law includes receipts from interstate sales affect the validity of a fair apportionment.

* * *

Plainly Ohio sought to tax only what she was entitled to tax, and there is nothing about application of the formula in this case that indicates a potentially unfair result under any circumstances. It is not even contended here that the amount of these taxes could be considered to bear an unjust or improper relation to the value of the privilege of doing business in Ohio if the legislature had imposed a flat franchise tax of the same amounts for the respective years which application of this formula has produced.

* * * Furthermore, this Court has long realized the practical impossibility of a state's achieving a perfect apportionment of expansive, complex business activities such as those of appellant, and has declared that "rough approximation rather than precision" is sufficient. Illinois Central Ry. v. Minnesota, 309 U.S. 157, 161, 60 S.Ct. 419. Unless a palpably disproportionate result comes from an apportionment, a result which makes it patent that the tax is levied upon interstate commerce rather than upon an intrastate privilege, this Court has not been willing to nullify honest state efforts to make apportionments. See cases collected in opinion of Mr. Chief Justice Stone, dissenting, Northwest Airlines v. Minnesota, 322 U.S. 292, 325, 64 S.Ct. 950. A state's tax law is not to be nullified merely because the result is achieved through a formula which includes consideration of interstate and out-of-state transactions in their relation to the intrastate privilege. Since it has not been demonstrated that the apportionment here achieves an unfair result, cf. Hans Rees' Sons, Inc. v. North Carolina, 283 U.S. 123, 134, 135, 51 S.Ct. 385, and since it is assessed only against the privilege of doing local Ohio business of manufacturing and selling we do not come to the question, argued by appellant, of possible multiplication of this tax by reason of its imposition by other states. None of them can tax the privilege of operating factories and sales agencies in Ohio.

Affirmed.

MR. JUSTICE RUTLEDGE, concurring.

I concur in the opinion and judgment of the Court. But I desire to add that, in the due process phase of the case, I find no basis for conclusion that any of the transactions included in the measure of the tax was so lacking in substantial fact connections with Ohio as to preclude the state's use of them, cf. McLeod v. Dilworth Co., 322 U.S. 327, 64 S.Ct. 1023, dissenting opinion at 352–357, if indeed a limitation of this sort were material to an apportionment found on the whole to be fairly made. For the rest, as the Court holds, the apportionment clearly is valid.*

Notes and Problems

A. The opinion of the Ohio court discloses that the tax commissioner excluded from Ohio sales the goods manufactured in the State, but delivered to and sold from warehouses located outside the State. 146 Ohio St. 58, 64 N.E.2d 53 (1945). In a later case, the State court upheld the tax commissioner's inclusion in the Ohio "business done" numerator of receipts from sales made by out-of-state sales offices to out-of-state customers, but filled by deliveries from Ohio out of stocks of goods manufactured within the State. Wheeling Steel Corp. v. Porterfield, 21 Ohio St.2d 57, 255 N.E.2d 257 (1970). Is this result within the State's constitutional powers as delineated in the *International Harvester* case? If not, would such inclusion be within the State's taxing power if the tax were levied on the privilege of manufacturing in the State, measured by apportioned capital stock? Cf. American Manufacturing Co. v. St. Louis, 250 U.S. 459, 39 S.Ct. 522 (1919).

Suppose, also, in the principal case with respect to goods shipped into Ohio, that instead of operating through branches located in the State, salesmen had been sent into the State to solicit orders which were forwarded to warehouses outside the State and there accepted and filled. Such an apportionment would be a typical example of the widely accepted sales origin test and would presumably encounter no Federal constitutional barrier.

Can the use by the same State of both the origin and destination test of sales be justified? Aside from the dubious fiscal policy such apportionment

* [This case is noted in 56 Yale L.J. 898 (1947). The Ohio capital stock tax "business done" fraction has produced a considerable amount of litigation. The statute measures the business done in the State of a corporation engaged in selling goods by the ratio of sales of tangible personal property in the State to such sales everywhere. However, in the case of a corporation whose "business does not consist" in the making of such sales but "in such activities as receiving commissions, rents, interest, dividends and fees," the business done is "determined by allocating such business activities in and out of Ohio according to their situs." For the refined distinctions drawn by the Ohio Supreme Court in construing these provisions in cases involving taxpayers which engage in both categories of business activities described above, see Westinghouse Electric Corp. v. Porterfield, 23 Ohio St.2d 50, 261 N.E.2d 272 (1970); Gulf Oil Corp. v. Kosydar, 44 Ohio St.2d 208, 339 N.E.2d 820 (1975).]

would involve, does the use of the dual tests make the levy repugnant to the Due Process or Commerce Clauses on the ground that such apportionment, by its very nature, attributes to the taxing State extraterritorial income or capital stock and subjects interstate business to a risk of multiple tax burdens not borne by intrastate business?

B. *Dock Pickup Sales.* Problems arise in defining and identifying the State of destination of sales. UDITPA provides that sales of tangible personal property are in the State if "the property is delivered or shipped to a purchaser other than the United States government, within this state regardless of the f.o.b. point or other conditions of the sale * * *" UDITPA § 16. Suppose the seller in State A delivers the goods at its "docks" in State A to the purchaser who immediately transports them to its place of business in State B? Would State A or State B be the State of destination under UDITPA?

Some courts that have considered this problem under UDITPA and similar sales destination provisions have concluded that dock sales to out-of-state purchasers do not constitute in-state sales. In Department of Revenue v. Parker Banana Co., 391 So.2d 762 (Fla.App.1980), the taxpayer was engaged in importing bananas to Tampa in refrigerated ships and selling them to wholesalers. All of Parker's purchasers arranged their own pickup and transportation. Parker delivered the bananas directly from the ship's hold to trucks sent by or on behalf of purchasers. Some purchasers sent their own trucks and others used common or contract carriers. In applying the language of UDITPA to this set of facts, the Department of Revenue contended that out-of-state purchasers "who arrange to pick up their bananas other than by common carrier take delivery as a matter of law at dockside in Tampa." 391 So.2d at 763. The court disagreed, declaring:

> In our view, the words "within this state" must refer to the word "purchaser" if the legislative intent is observed. Under our construction of the apportionment statute, *a sale is in this state if the sale is to a Florida purchaser and that, in turn, depends on the destination of the goods sold.* It matters not whether delivery or shipment occurs in Florida or out of Florida. Our interpretation of the statute accords with the legislative intent to assign to Florida for tax purposes a portion of net income attributable to sales by the taxpayer *in the Florida market* as determined by the destination of the goods. [Id. (emphasis in the second sentence supplied).]

Courts in Minnesota and Wisconsin have likewise concluded that dock sales to out-of-state purchasers are not in-state sales under UDITPA's sales destination provision. Olympia Brewing Co. v. Commissioner, 326 N.W.2d 642 (Minn.1982); Pabst Brewing Co. v. Wisconsin Dept. of Revenue (Dane County Circuit Court, Jan. 31, 1984), CCH ¶ 202–304; see also Strickland v. Patcraft Mills, Inc., 251 Ga. 43, 302 S.E.2d 544 (1983) (sales destination language varies from UDITPA). In these cases, the courts took the position that the purpose of the sales destination provision was more faithfully served by attributing the sale to the final destination of the goods and that the terms of delivery should not control the sales attribution rule.

The sales destination provisions of some States differ from those of UDITPA and are more detailed.[62] Thus, the Louisiana statute includes in the sales factor numerator "all goods received in this state by the purchaser," and provides for attribution to the State if the "goods are ultimately received [in the State] after all transportation including transportation by the taxpayer has been completed." Where the goods delivered to the taxpayer's trucks outside the State are immediately transported by the purchaser to its place of business in the State, the Louisiana regulations treat the destination as being within the State.[63] See also Dupps Co. v. Lindley, 62 Ohio St.2d 305, 405 N.E.2d 716 (1980) (construing Ohio's "ultimately received" provision to attribute sales of heavy equipment picked up at the manufacturer's plant in Ohio by out-of-state customers as out-of-state sales); House of Seagram, Inc. v. Porterfield, 27 Ohio St.2d 97, 271 N.E.2d 827 (1971) (construing Ohio's provision to attribute to Ohio sales of liquor by a New York dealer to an Ohio purchaser, where the purchaser sent its trucks to New York to pick up the goods).

Despite the *Parker Banana* case and other similar decisions, the UDITPA statute can be fairly construed as attributing dock sales to the State where the purchaser picks up the goods. This is apparently the position taken in the Multistate Tax Commission regulations, which provide that "[p]roperty is delivered or shipped to a purchaser within this state if the shipment terminates in this state, even though the property is subsequently transferred by the purchaser to another state." MTC Reg. IV.16.(a).(3), CCH All States Guide ¶ 352, P–H All States Guide ¶ 662. This is also the position taken by New York and California. New York Tax Reg. § 4–4.2, P–H ¶ 11,203; Legal Ruling No. 348, California Franchise Tax Bd., Feb. 21, 1973, CCH at p. 12,047.

*The question as to what is the destination of the goods in a dock-pickup sale is "a question of degree that can be fairly answered either way. Consequently, in determining what is the destination of the goods, the decisive consideration ought to be the facilitation of simple and inexpensive taxpayer compliance and administration by the taxing authorities. For we are here dealing with a vast number of transactions that occur annually over the country, and it is unlikely that any significant shift of revenues among the States will be produced by whatever rule is adopted as to the destination of the goods in the types of transactions under discussion.

"The MTC construction of UDITPA enables the vendor to classify the destination of sales by the buyer's invoice address, without making it necessary for him to examine the facts as to the purchaser's reshipment or transshipment of the goods, except for reshipments by common carrier, which should not be difficult to identify. The Louisiana *ultimately received* rule and the Florida court's construction of UDITPA introduce time-consuming and burdensome complexities that would require vendors to examine into the course of goods after they are turned over to the

62. La.Rev.Stat. § 47:245, CCH ¶ 93–121, P–H ¶ 12,648; Del.Code Ann. tit. 30, § 1903(b)(6)(C), CCH ¶ 92–329, P–H ¶ 12,110.75.

63. La. reg., art. 47:245.4C3, CCH ¶ 12–437, P–H ¶ 11,426.10.

* The ensuing discussion in this note is taken from J. Hellerstein, State Taxation I, Corporate Income and Franchise Taxes ¶ 9.17[1][a], pp. 587–88 (1983). Used with the consent of the copyright owner and publisher.

customer, the local trucker, or the like. These practical considerations ought to outweigh the Florida court's desire, albeit a legitimate one, to attribute sales to the market for the goods, which is typically likely to be the State of ultimate destination."[64] J. Hellerstein, State Taxation I, Corporate Income and Franchise Taxes ¶ 9.17[1][a], pp. 587–88 (1983).

See Nackenson, "Attribution of Dock Pick–Up Sales: the Olympia Brewing Case," 2 Interstate Tax Rep., Feb. 1983, p. 12; Reich, "Dock Sales—the New State Income Tax Background," 1 J. State Tax. 42 (1982).

C. *Throwback and Throwout Rules.* In order to prevent any part of the tax base from falling into the "no-man's land" of non-taxation by any State, UDITPA contains a so-called "throwback" rule. The sales factor provides for attribution to the State of origin of sales of tangible personal property, in cases in which "the taxpayer is not taxable in the state of the purchaser." The term "taxable in the state of the purchaser" has been interpreted as referring to the power of the purchaser's State to tax the vendor, whether or not the power has been exercised. Miles Laboratories, Inc. v. Department of Revenue, 274 Or. 395, 546 P.2d 1081 (1976).

In Covington Fabrics Corp. v. South Carolina Tax Commission, 264 S.C. 59, 212 S.E.2d 574 (1975), appeal dismissed, 423 U.S. 805, 96 S.Ct. 14 (1975), the throwback rule was sustained on a challenge to its constitutionality. The rule is based on the premise that, while the State of origin of a shipment of goods is not justified in increasing its apportionment of net income of an interstate seller, if a State which has the power to tax chooses not to exercise it, such an increase is justified if the State of destination lacks the constitutional power to subject the vendor to its income tax. A destination State which is empowered to tax the interstate seller may impose other heavier taxes to compensate for its non-taxation of the income of the seller, or it may choose, as a matter of fiscal policy or business climate, not to tax such out-of-state sellers. However, if the destination State lacks the power to levy the tax, because of limitations imposed by the Federal Constitution or Congressional legislation, the attribution of the sale for receipts factor purposes to some State is justified. Else, the taxpayer will obtain a windfall. See Dexter, Mondale Comm. Hearings 405; Turlington, id. at 322, 323; Corrigan, "Interstate Corporate Income Taxation—Recent Revolutions and a Modern Response," 29 Vand.L.Rev. 423, 429–30 (1976). Some of the States which have enacted the major provisions of UDITPA have excluded or modified the throw-back provisions. See Receipts in Apportionment Numerators (chart), P–H All States Guide ¶ 224.

An alternative "throwout" method for dealing with the so-called "no-man's land" income has been recommended by some tax administrators and was used, on a limited basis, in at least one State (Pennsylvania). Under the "throwout" rule, if a taxpayer corporation is not subject to income tax in the destination State, the receipts from the sales whose destination is such a State would not be included in either the numerator or the denominator of the sales or receipts factor. Such a rule would result

---

64. The types of inquiry that vendors and customers are required to make in the transactions under discussion are indicated by the Louisiana regulation set out in note 373 supra. [The regulation is cited in note 63 supra.]

in "full accountability" for all the taxpayer's income to the States in which the corporation is taxable, if all the States choose to exercise their taxing powers. See Clarke, Mondale Comm. Hearings 313, 315–316. For industry legislative proposals which would prevent the States from using the throwback or throwout rules, or otherwise modify the receipts factor so as to eliminate "no-man's land" receipts from the factor, see "Industry Statement on Proposed Interstate Tax Legislation," Mondale Comm. Hearings 274.

The Pennsylvania Department of Revenue's use of the throwout rule was initially sustained by the State Supreme Court as a proper exercise of the power to vary the statutory formula under the State's relief provision. Hellertown Manufacturing Co. v. Commonwealth, 480 Pa. 358, 390 A.2d 732 (1978). Six years later, however, the court overruled its earlier decision and held that the tax administrator lacked authority under Pennsylvania's version of UDITPA to modify the State's apportionment provisions in this fashion. Paris Manufacturing Co., Inc. v. Commonwealth, 505 Pa. 15, 476 A.2d 890 (1984). For a consideration of the apportionment relief or variation provisions, see Section 4 infra.

Does the throwback rule of UDITPA apply to sales destined to customers located in foreign countries? See UDITPA § 1(h). If it does, are United States standards, based on our jurisdictional traditions and concepts and in part on the Constitution of the United States, to be employed in determining taxability in foreign countries? Should P.L. 86–272 be taken into account? See Appeal of Dresser Industries, Cal.State Bd. of Equalization, June 29, 1982, CCH ¶ 400–376, P–H ¶ 13,107–F (U.S. jurisdictional standards, but not P.L. 86–272, should be taken into account in determining whether a foreign country has jurisdiction to tax for purposes of the throwback rule); contra Scott & Williams, Inc. v. Board of Taxation, 117 N.H. 189, 372 A.2d 1305 (1977) (jurisdiction of foreign country to tax, for purposes of throwback rule, must be determined by laws of the country in question). See generally Clarke, Mondale Comm. Hearings 313, 316; Powers, "P.L. 86–272 and the Throwback Rule: The *Dresser* Decision", 2 Interstate Tax Rep., Dec. 1982, p. 1; J. Hellerstein & W. Hellerstein, State Taxation I, Corporate Income and Franchise Taxes, 1987 Cum.Supp. ¶ 9.17[1][b][i].

For various analyses of the throwback and throwout rules, see Peters & Leegstra, "How to Deal with the Sales Factor in the State's Income Tax Apportionment Formula," State Tax Ideas, P–H ¶ 100.7 (1983); Savoie & Burr, "The Throwback Rule: Concepts, Components and Planning Opportunities", 25 J. State Tax. 19 (1983); Pfeffer "Minimizing the Effect of the Throwback Rule", 1 Interstate Tax Rep., Feb. 1982, p. 8.

Sales to the Federal government are also subject to the UDITPA rule of throwback to the State of origin, on the theory that "they are not necessarily attributable to a market existing in the state to which the goods are originally shipped." The quotation is from the official commentary on Section 16 by the draftsmen of UDITPA. Does throwback to the State of origin produce a disproportionate attribution of income from defense and other governmental contracts to the manufacturing States? Would a throwout rule produce more satisfactory attribution of the income among the States involved? See Wilkie, "Uniform Division of Income for Tax Purposes," 37 Taxes 65 (1959).

D. *Drop Shipments.* T, a corporation engaged in business in Illinois and some other States, made sales of goods to customers in State X, in which T is not subject to the State's power to impose an income tax. T orders the goods in question from a supplier located in State Y, in which T is likewise not taxable, and, at T's request, the supplier delivers the goods directly to T's customer in State X. Are the receipts from such so-called "drop shipment" sales includable in the numerator of the sales factor of Illinois' UDITPA-based apportionment formula? Recall that the language of UDITPA provides for a throwback to the State of origin only when "the property is shipped from * * * this state." UDITPA § 16(b). Although the Illinois court answered the question in the affirmative in reliance on UDITPA's relief provision (see Section 4 infra), GTE Automatic Electric, Inc. v. Allphin, 68 Ill.2d 326, 12 Ill.Dec. 134, 369 N.E.2d 841 (1977), the court's opinion is open to criticism. See W. Hellerstein, "Construing the Uniform Division of Income for Tax Purposes Act: Reflections on the Illinois Supreme Court's Reading of the 'Throwback' Rule," 45 U.Chi.L.Rev. 768 (1978). In a similar case, the Colorado Supreme Court refused to countenance resort by the Department of Revenue to the State's equitable apportionment provision to read a "throwback" rule into the apportionment. Miller International, Inc. v. State, Dept. of Revenue, 646 P.2d 341 (Colo.1982).

E. *Receipts From Services: The Basic Rules.* The receipts factors of the State apportionment provisions typically include receipts from the rendition of services, although a few States take such receipts out of the apportionment and allocate them to the State in which the services are rendered. See 1 Willis Comm.Rep. 204–15, 188; Hartman, "State Taxation of Corporate Income from a Multistate Business," 13 Vand.L.Rev. 21 (1959). Prior to the adoption of UDITPA, receipts from services were included in the numerator of the receipts factors of many States to the extent that the services were there performed. See 1 Willis Comm.Rep. 180, 188–189; "Final Report of the Committee on Tax Situs and Allocation," 1951 N.T.A. Procs. 456, 463. That rule still obtains in a number of States so that if a lump sum is received by the taxpayer for services rendered both within and without the State, the allocation is made on a comparative time base, the relative values of the services in the various States, and similar factors.[65]

UDITPA contains no separate provision dealing with either the allocation or apportionment of receipts or income from the rendition of services. Section 6 infra. Section 4 of the Uniform Act, which provides for allocation of specific types of rents and royalties, interest, dividends, and the like, to the extent that they constitute non-business income, does not refer to service income. As a consequence, receipts from the rendition of services are dealt with by UDITPA only through the general definition of "business income" and the catch-all attribution to the taxing State of "sales other than sales of tangible personal property." (Verify this conclusion for yourself by tracing through §§ 1(a) and 1(c), 4–8, 15 and 17.) Hence,

---

65. See, e.g., N.Y. Franchise Tax Reg.   Reg. 18:7–8.10, CCH ¶ 5–819b, P–H § 4–4.1, CCH ¶ 9–640, P–H ¶ 11,201; N.J.   ¶ 11,315.

receipts from services fall within the numerator of the State's sales fraction if "the income-producing activity is performed in this state," or if performed in more than one State and "a greater proportion of the income-producing activity is performed in this state than in any other state." The test of the proportion of income-producing activity within a State is its cost of performance. UDITPA § 17.

Does UDITPA provide an acceptable basis for attributing receipts from services? Would a more equitable result be obtained by fractionating the receipts from services on a time or cost basis, so that where substantial work is done in more than one State, each State would benefit? See Wilkie, "Uniform Division of Income for Tax Purposes," 37 Taxes 65, 73 (1959).

The UDITPA rule is likely to raise questions in determining whether a taxpayer performing services in more than one State is engaging in a single "income-producing activity," or in several such activities, and in fixing the State in which the "greater proportion of the income-producing activity is performed."

The experience of the States over the years with apportionment and allocation of service income indicates the virtue of a statutory standard that employs a variety of factors, which can be adapted to the broad diversity of business operations. The draftsmen of UDITPA were aware of this problem and expressed the view that the adjustment or relief provision of UDITPA could be resorted to in order to deal with what it regarded as exceptional situations. See Pierce, "The Uniform Division of Income for State Tax Purposes," 35 Taxes 747 (1957).

F. *A Possible Gap in UDITPA.* Suppose income from a particular type of services is held not to constitute "business income" under UDITPA. Is such income taken out of the apportionment and allocated; if so, to which State? Examine UDITPA § 4. If such service income is not allocable, is it apportioned? Examine UDITPA § 9. Is service income which is non-business income excluded from tax by UDITPA? See Wilkie, supra.

G. *Application of UDITPA to Non–Manufacturing Non–Mercantile Businesses.* One of the major criticisms to be made of UDITPA and other statutory formulas in force in many States is that they were developed to fit the needs of mercantile, manufacturing, and producing companies, but that they are applied, in some States at least, to other businesses to which they are ill-adapted and produce distorted results. See Section 5 infra, for a consideration of this problem and of statutes which give the tax administrator power to promulgate varying apportionment methods so as to adapt them to the characteristics of the enterprise. Some of the cases noted below illustrate the Procrustean results of the failure to vary apportionment methods so as to adapt them to the needs of businesses and industries whose relevant characteristics are markedly different from manufacturing, mercantile and producing enterprises.

H. *Advertising Receipts: Magazine Publication.* The treatment of advertising receipts of magazine publishers and radio and television broadcasters raises problems peculiar to those industries. In McCall Corp. v. Joseph, 284 A.D. 484, 132 N.Y.S.2d 38 (1st Dept.1954), the City of New York sought to include in the gross receipts measure of its tax on doing business the taxpayer's entire magazine advertising revenues as attributable to its New York office. The court held the regulation invalid because local activities in Ohio, where the taxpayer maintained the printing plant in which its magazines were printed, contributed to the advertising receipts. As a result of this decision, the New York City regulations (Article 231) were amended so as to set up a special apportionment formula for receipts from advertising, where the publication is printed at a plant owned by the taxpayer outside the State.

Subsequently, the New Yorker Magazine challenged an assessment under the same tax, based on all its advertising receipts, except those solicited by its only out-of-city advertising office in Chicago. This time the assessment was sustained; the new regulation did not apply to the New Yorker because it did not own an out-of-state printing plant. While its magazine is printed and mailed in Connecticut, those operations were carried on by independent contractors under directions from the taxpayer's editorial and other staff in New York City. New Yorker Magazine, Inc. v. Gerosa, 3 N.Y.2d 362, 165 N.Y.S.2d 469, 144 N.E.2d 367 (1957), appeal dismissed, 356 U.S. 339, 78 S.Ct. 777 (1958). Is this decision justified by Western Live Stock v. Bureau of Revenue, 303 U.S. 250, 58 S.Ct. 546 (1938), relied on by the New York court, which held that a State may measure a tax on the local publication of a newspaper by the entire advertising receipts derived from a magazine circulated across State lines?

A subsequent case involving the apportionment of magazine advertising receipts arose under the New York State franchise tax measured by net income. Conde Nast Publications, Inc. v. State Tax Comm'n, 51 A.D.2d 17, 378 N.Y.S.2d 132, appeal dismissed 39 N.Y.2d 889, 386 N.Y.S.2d 393, 352 N.E.2d 580 (1976). The publisher of Vogue, House and Garden, and other magazines maintained offices in New York and a number of other States from which advertising was solicited. The magazines were printed in Iowa and Ohio, from which they were mailed to subscribers, or were distributed by an independent distributor. The taxpayer had attributed its advertising receipts to New York, on the basis of the ratio of the circulation of its magazines in the State to their total circulation, on the theory that advertising is a service, which is performed when the advertisements are read by a potential purchaser of the advertised product.

The State Tax Commission rejected the categorization of the advertising revenues as receipts from "services performed" and, instead, applied the New York catch-all provision, which includes in the numerator of the receipts factor "all other business receipts earned within the state." N.Y. Tax Law § 210.3(a)(2)(D), CCH ¶ 93–908, P–H ¶ 12,020.38. The court sustained the action of the Commission in attributing to the State all receipts from advertising contracts solicited and serviced by the New York office. That rule was, however, overruled by the New York Legislature, which amended the State's corporate franchise tax statute so as to provide that a taxpayer engaged in the business of publishing newspapers and periodicals shall attribute to New York receipts from advertising in the newspapers or periodicals only to the extent that the newspapers or periodicals are delivered in the State. N.Y.Tax Law § 210.3(a)(2)(B), as amended by 1981 N.Y.Laws, CCH ¶ 93–908, P–H ¶ 12,020.38.

In a case in which a newspaper edited and published in the District of Columbia had substantial sales and newsgathering activities outside the District, a District of Columbia court held that receipts from advertising in the newspaper should be apportioned by reference to the location of the subscribers. District of Columbia v. Evening Star Newspapers Co., 273 F.2d 95 (D.C.Cir.1959). Solicitation of advertising and subscriptions was carried on in Virginia and Maryland by employees of the Star. But see Broadcasting Publications, Inc. v. District of Columbia, 313 F.2d 554 (D.C. Cir.1962).

The cases dealing with the apportionment of the receipts from magazine advertising are treated in J. Hellerstein, State Taxation I, Corporate Income and Franchise Taxes ¶ 10.3[1] (1983).

I. *Advertising Receipts: Television and Radio Broadcasting.* Radio and television advertising raise closely related questions. The problem may be illustrated by a broadcasting case involving a corporation whose executive offices were located in New York and which owned and operated radio and television stations in several States. In re Capital Cities Communications, Inc. v. State Tax Comm'n, 65 A.D.2d 25, 411 N.Y.S.2d 46 (3d Dep't 1978). One of the stations maintained its studios and transmitting facilities entirely within New York, another station maintained them entirely outside the State, and still others had such facilities in New York and other States. At issue was the attribution, under the receipts factor of the New York three-factor formula, of the broadcasting fees received by the stations from advertisers and sponsors. The statute attributes to the State receipts from "services performed within this state"; under its regulations, the State Tax Commission attributes a lump sum payment for "services within and without New York * * * on the basis of the relative values of, or amounts of time spent in the performance of, such services within and without New York, or by some other reasonable method." [66]

In its returns for the first year at issue, the taxpayer had attributed all the broadcasting fees to the State in which its studios were located, but for the later years it attributed to New York the percentage of its receipts that the in-state listening audience of the stations bore to their total listening audience, as determined by a standard industry research organization. The auditors attributed to the State all the broadcasting fees of the stations whose studios and transmission facilities were located entirely in New York, and no part of the fees of the stations that had no studios or transmission facilities in the State. The receipts of the various stations that had either studios or transmission facilities both within and without New York were attributed, under a separate three-factor formula, consisting of the ratio of New York property, wages, and rents paid to the totals. The State Tax Commission sustained the assessment on an administrative appeal. Should the holding be rejected on the ground that advertising is a service?

66. N.Y. Tax Law § 210.3(a)(2)(B), CCH ¶ 93–908, P–H ¶ 12,020.38; N.Y. Franchise Tax Reg. § 4–4.3(f)(1), CCH ¶ 9–642, P–H ¶ 11,205.20.

This decision was reversed by the same New York court that had passed on the magazine cases (see Note H supra), on the ground that there was no justification under the statute for determining the receipts factor by an amalgam of property and wage factors under a statute that called for three separate factors, including a receipts factor. In re Capital Cities Communications, Inc. v. State Tax Comm'n, supra. The court stated:

> We do not here decide that petitioner's "audience location method" is the proper measure of receipts under the statute. Indeed, we have upheld the respondent's rejection of a similar proposed method of allocating receipts in the magazine industry (Matter of Conde Nast Pub. v. State Tax Comm., 51 A.D.2d 17, 378 N.Y.S.2d 132, app. dsmd. 39 N.Y.2d 942, 386 N.Y.S.2d 1029, 352 N.E.2d 897). Our decision is that in calculating petitioner's business allocation percentage under paragraph (a) of subdivision 3 of section 210 of the Tax Law, the respondent must ascertain the percentage of petitioner's business receipts allocable to New York State independently of its allocation of property and payroll. The precise manner of thus allocating such receipts is within the unique province of the respondent. [65 A.D.2d at 28.]

Thereafter, the New York State Tax Commission exercised its power to determine the "precise manner of * * * allocating" the advertising receipts by adopting the audience location method of attributing advertising receipts from radio and TV. N.Y. Franchise Tax Reg. § 4–4.3(f)(2), CCH ¶ 9–642, P–H ¶ 11,205.20.

The audience location method for attributing receipts of broadcasters of motion picture, television film, and television network broadcasting has been adopted in California,[67] New Jersey, and some other States.[68] For a

67. (3) Sales Factor Numerator. The numerator shall include all gross receipts of the taxpayer from sources within this state including the following:

(A) Gross receipts from films in release to theaters and television stations located in this state.

(B) Gross receipts from films in release to or by a television network for network telecast shall be attributed to this state in the ratio that the audience for such network stations (owned and affiliated) located in California bears to the total audience for all such network stations (owned and affiliated) everywhere. The audience shall be determined by rate card values published annually in the *Television & Cable Factbook,* Vol. I, "Stations Volume," Television Digest, Inc., Washington, D.C., if available, or by other published market surveys, or, if none is available, by population data published by the U.S. Bureau of the Census.

(C) Gross receipts from films in release to subscription television telecasters shall be attributed to this state in the ratio that the subscribers for such telecaster located in California bears to the total subscribers of such telecaster everywhere. If the number of subscribers cannot be determined accurately from records maintained by the taxpayer, the ratio shall be determined on the basis of the applicable year's statistics on subscribers published in *Cable Vision,* International Thompson Communications Inc., Denver, Colorado, if available, or by other published market surveys, or, if none is available, by population data published by the U.S. Bureau of the Census for all states in which the telecaster has subscribers.

(D) Receipts from sales and rentals of video cassettes and discs shall be included in the sales factor as provided in Regulations 25135 and 25136.

Reg. 25137–8, CCH ¶ 14–834–H, P–H ¶ 11,538–K.1300

68. The Director of the Division of Taxation of New Jersey adopted an audience factor in apportioning receipts from advertising of television stations under the State's corporate franchise tax. The New

critique of the decisions that supports the audience ratio for attributing receipts from magazine, radio and TV advertising, see J. Hellerstein, State Taxation I, Corporate Income and Franchise Taxes, ¶ 10.4 (1983).

A more artificial approach, growing out of the application of traditional concepts of situs of intangibles, was applied to receipts from television and radio advertising in an Ohio capital stock tax case. Miami Valley Broadcasting Corp. v. Kosydar, 48 Ohio St.2d 10, 355 N.E.2d 812 (1976). The Ohio franchise tax, measured by capital stock, is apportioned by a two-factor formula, consisting of a "property fraction" (which, unlike most proeprty factors, takes intangible property into account) and a "business done fraction." The statute provides that where the "business consists of such activities as receiving commissions, rents, interest, dividends and fees, the [business done] fraction shall be determined by allocating such business activities in and out of this state according to their situs."

The taxpayer, a wholly-owned subsidary of a Georgia corporation, operated radio and television stations in Dayton, Ohio. It maintained offices in New York, along with the parent company, where all the contracts for national network sales were made with advertising agencies, through the taxpayer's New York based sales representative, an independent contractor. Billings were received and payments were all handled in New York. The court held "it is the situs or place of *receiving* the rents, commissions or fees that determine the allocation within and without Ohio" (court's emphasis), and, accordingly, that the receipts from the national sales and network broadcasts and telecasts by the Ohio stations were not includible in the Ohio business done factor. Receipts from local sales of radio or television broadcasts and from sales of broadcasts made, handled and paid to the taxpayer's own sales and other offices in Dayton to Ohio-located advertisers were attributable to Ohio. Is this formalistic, legal situs standard an acceptable mode of dividing the advertising revenues of radio and television broadcasting?

J. *Motion Picture Lease or Rental Receipts.* Payments of film rentals by exhibitors to a major motion picture producer were held by the Georgia Court of Appeals to constitute receipts from sales, not rentals from property, for apportionment purposes. Twentieth Century–Fox Film Corp. v. Phillips, 76 Ga.App. 825, 47 S.E.2d 183 (1948). As a consequence, under the then Georgia sales office negotiation rule, receipts from the exhibition of the films by motion picture houses in Florida, Tennessee, and Alabama were attributed to the taxpayer's regional sales office in Georgia. In rejecting the taxpayer's contention that the payments constituted rents from the use of property outside the State and, hence, were not includible in the numerator of the receipts factor, the court said:

Jersey Tax Court set aside the use of the audience factor, not on the merits, but on the ground that the procedure prescribed for the adoption of administrative rules required by the State's Administrative Procedure Act had not been complied with. Metromedia, Inc. v. Tax Division, 3 N.J. Tax 397 (1981), P–H ¶ 10–410.12.

The listening audience ratio test was applied in apportioning a Tennessee excise tax imposed on an in-state broadcasting station, whose programs reached audiences in several other States. WDOD Broadcasting Corp. v. Stokes, 180 Tenn. 677, 177 S.W.2d 837 (1941). The taxpayer did not contest the apportionment.

It is the opinion of this Court that in using the word "sales" in Code Ann. § 92–3113(3)(c), the legislature did not intend to define or limit the levy of the tax, but the evident purpose of such section is to provide methods of calculation for apportioning to the State the business income of the corporation reasonably attributable to the property owned and business done within the State; and further that the legislature in using the word "sales" intended to include within its meaning and application the marketing, or distribution for public consumption, of the merchandise of a business, held, owned, used, or sold in connection with the regular course of business in this State and thereby subject to the taxable jurisdiction of this State for however brief period of time, and not excepted from the apportionable part of the income of the business as gains from property held for investment or from property not held, owned, or used in connection with the regular course of business by Code Ann. § 92–3113(1, 2), whether the marketing or distribution for public consumption be termed a sale, a lease, a rental, or otherwise; and that to hold otherwise would contravene the manifest intent of the Legislature clearly expressed by the history and entirety of the Act.

In Warner Bros. Pictures, Inc. v. District of Columbia, 168 F.2d 157 (D.C.Cir.1948), a motion picture producer, receiving a percentage of the film rentals paid by District of Columbia exhibitors to the producer's subsidiary-distributing corporation, was held subject to the District of Columbia income tax on such receipts. Where goods are sold, the manufacturer is ordinarily not subject to taxes by the State in which its distributing subsidiary sells the goods. Should the result be different where the nature of the product requires the use of a license or rental? Cf. Matter of Heftel Broadcasting Honolulu, Inc., discussed in Chapter 8, pp. 406–07 supra.

K. *Rents and Royalties From Real and Tangible Personal Property.* Prior to the emergence of UDITPA, the States generally allocated rents and royalties from real and tangible personal property to the State in which the property was located. The Willis Committee reported (as of 1963) that 29 States allocated rents and royalties from real estate and that 27 of the 29 States allocated such rent and royalties to the State in which the property was located. 1 Willis Comm.Rep. 206–07. In a few States, such rents and royalties were apportioned, and those States usually included the receipts in the numerator of their receipts factors if the property was located in the State. In making the allocation or apportionment of rents and royalties from mobile tangible personal property, or other tangibles which are situated in more than one State during the taxable year, the usual rule was to attribute the income or receipts to a State to the extent of its use within the State. These allocation and apportionment principles are currently in effect in most of the States that have not adopted the UDITPA treatment of such rents and royalties.

UDITPA follows the traditional rule of allocation of rents and royalties to the State of the location of real property if they constitute non-business income; but if they constitute business income, rentals and royalties from real property are apportioned. UDITPA §§ 4 and 9. The attribution of rents and royalties which constitute business income is governed by the omnibus provisions of the UDITPA sales factor. Hence, such rents and royalties come into the numerator of a State's sales factor only if the greater proportion of the "income-producing activity is performed in this state." Id. § 17.

Suppose that T, a real estate company whose commercial domicile is in Denver, owns an office building in Omaha. The operations of the building, including leasing, maintenance, collection of the rents and the like, are handled by an Omaha independent managing agent, under contract with T. All of T's own activities relating to the building are carried on at its Denver office. The rents received by T would be classified as business income under UDITPA, which has been enacted by both Colorado and Nebraska. See Section 6 infra.

The Multistate Tax Commission's regulations interpreting UDITPA (which do not have the standing of regulations in any State until adopted by the State) take the position that "activities performed on behalf of a taxpayer, such as those conducted on its behalf by an independent contractor," are not to be taken into account in determining where income producing activity takes place. See MTC Reg. IV.17(2), CCH All States Guide ¶ 352, P–H All States Guide ¶ 664.15. If this is a proper construction of the statute, the rentals derived from the Nebraska building would be attributed to Colorado. Is this an acceptable result? Is it a sufficient answer to Nebraska's claim to inclusion of the rentals in its receipts factor that the value of the property is included in that State's property factor? Should the UDITPA rule of allocating non-business rentals to the State in which real property is located be made applicable also to business rentals? UDITPA § 5.

SECTION 4. RELIEF PROVISIONS FOR VARYING STATUTORY FORMULAS

A. Most statutes prescribing the use of apportionment formulas provide for variations if the "provisions * * * do not fairly represent the extent of the taxpayer's business activity in this state" (quoted from UDITPA § 18). In such cases, the statutes usually authorize the tax administrator, on his own initiative or on petition by the taxpayer, to apply separate accounting, exclude or add one or more factors, or use "any other method to effectuate an equitable allocation and apportionment of the taxpayer's income." Id. It has been held that if the taxpayer makes a showing that the statutory methods do not "fairly reflect" its income or other base attributable to the State, the granting of relief is mandatory on the tax administrator. F.W. Woolworth Co. v. Director, Div. of Taxation, 45 N.J. 466, 213 A.2d 1 (1965); F.W. Woolworth Co. v. Commissioner of Taxes, 130 Vt. 544, 298 A.2d 839 (1972), 133 Vt. 93, 328 A.2d 402 (1974); United States Steel Corp. v. State Tax Comm'n, Idaho CCH ¶ 14–510 (Idaho D.Ct., Ada Cty.1975). For the variation in the statutory method granted by the New Jersey Director of Taxes following the above decision in the New Jersey Woolworth case, see N.J.Corp.Bus.Tax Regs. 18:7–10.2 and 18:7–10.3, CCH ¶¶ 5–840, 5–843, P–H ¶¶ 11,352–53. For an unsuccessful effort by a taxpayer to invoke such a provision, see Payne & Dolan of Wis., Inc.

v. Department of Treasury, 138 Mich.App. 418, 360 N.W.2d 208 (1984); and for a decision holding that the tax administrator was unjustified in departing from the statutory method, because of his failure to show that the prescribed methods were inappropriate, see First Republic Corp. of America v. Norberg, 116 R.I. 414, 358 A.2d 38 (1976).

B. The Virginia Supreme Court passed on that State's relief provision in Commonwealth v. Lucky Stores, Inc., 217 Va. 121, 225 S.E. 2d 870 (1976). The taxpayer was a California-based corporation whose corporate and central headquarters were located in that State; it operated some 400 supermarkets, discount centers and other department stores, including two in Virginia, throughout the country, all as branches of a single corporate entity. The stores were operated through regional offices. The taxpayer produced its own milk, meat, and bakery goods, but none of these products was sold by the Virginia stores. Food and beverages, major appliances, paint and other products sold by the stores were purchased locally, although there was a joint warehouse for the Virginia and Maryland stores' appliances in Maryland. Some ten to twenty percent of the gross receipts from the Virginia stores' sales consisted of sales of apparel, which was purchased and priced in New York City by a staff of buyers who served the company nationwide. Accounting for purchases, invoices, and payment was handled centrally in California.

The Commissioner denied the taxpayer's application for an alternative method of division of income, and that action was sustained by the court, which described the taxpayer's contention as follows:

> The main thrust of Lucky's effort to demonstrate that use of the statutory formula produced a tax on income not reasonably attributable to business in Virginia was the attempt to show that Virginia's share of Lucky's taxable income under the statutory formula exceeded that resulting from separate accounting. [225 S.E.2d at 876.]

The court properly held that such "a showing," which is frequently made by taxpayers seeking a variation from the statutory method, is "insufficient to prove Virginia has 'reached out' to tax income earned elsewhere." Id. Such evidence, as a basis for relief, is based on the premise that the income of a taxpayer "reasonably attributable" to the State is more accurately shown by separate accounting than by the statutory formula—a premise rejected by the legislature in enacting the statute. To succeed in obtaining a variance, the taxpayer should be required to establish, by evidence other than resort to the separate accounting method, that distortion results from the statutory method. Consequently, in the *Lucky Stores* case, once the court concluded (relying on the *Butler Bros.* case, p. 442 supra) that the Virginia stores were part of a unitary business, it followed that separate accounting was inappropriate under the Virginia statute. Cf. Donald M. Drake Co. v. Department of Revenue, 263 Or. 26, 500 P.2d 1041 (1972).

The court also stated that a variation in the results of the statutory formula, as compared with separate accounting, of only one percent in allocation of income was too small to warrant invocation of the provision. On the facts, there was a swing of $500,000 for 1970, a $250,000 profit under the statutory formula, as compared with a $250,000 loss under direct accounting; and for 1971, there was a swing of $264,000; $39,000 in deficiency in taxes for the two years were at issue. Is the premise back of this rationale, that, "[u]nless a gross disparity in percentages results, the statutory formula must be upheld" (225 S.E.2d at 876) sound? Are only "gross" percentages of misattribution of out-of-state income precluded by the Due Process and Commerce Clauses? Can the court's quantitative yardstick of constitutionality be regarded as an acceptable standard, in view of the recognition that any method of dividing income can only be an approximation? See Section 2(b) supra.

The Michigan Court of Appeals has taken the position that use of an alternative to the formulary apportionment cannot be justified even on the basis of a "gross disparity" in the results between the different methods because this does not necessarily show that the method proposed under the relief provision "more accurately reflects the corporate taxpayer's unitary business in the state." Donovan Construction Co. v. Michigan Dept. of Treasury, 126 Mich.App. 11, 21 n. 2, 337 N.W.2d 297, 300 n. 2 (1983). The critical question in Michigan is qualitative: "Only if formulary apportionment does not fairly represent *the extent of business activity in the state* may a different method, such as separate accounting, be employed." Id. (emphasis supplied). See Jones & Laughlin Steel Corp. v. Department of Treasury and Wilson Foods Corp. v. Department of Treasury, 145 Mich.App. 405, 377 N.W.2d 397 (1985).

By way of contrast, the highest court of Kansas upheld the tax director's reliance on that State's UDITPA relief provisions, in applying separate accounting to the income of a wholly owned subsidiary of Standard Oil Company of Indiana, in lieu of the combined apportionment method sought by the taxpayer. Amoco Production Co. v. Armold, 213 Kan. 636, 518 P.2d 453 (1974). The taxpayer, Amoco, was engaged in the exploration and production of crude oil and natural gas in 21 States, including Kansas; as the principal source of crude oil for Standard and its subsidiaries, Amoco would appear to have been part of an integrated unitary oil enterprise. Nevertheless, the court sustained the tax director's use of the separate accounting method applied to Amoco on the basis of the relief provision, stating that "the majority of this court is unable to say an apportionment of 2.78 or 2.71 percent of Amoco's business income fairly represents the extent of its business activities in Kansas, when those activities actually generated a grossly disproportionate 23 or 24 percent of its total net income." 518 P.2d at 464.

The Kansas court thus appears to have relied for its conclusion as to the percentage of income "actually generated" within the State on the tax director's separate accounting figures, a reliance which was criticized and rejected in the *Lucky Stores* case. Three Justices dissented in the Kansas case on the ground that "the use of any method other than apportionment should be exceptional," and that by the use of separate accounting figures, the director had not borne his burden of providing "a factual basis" for his contention that the preferred apportionment method "does not clearly reflect the extent of the taxpayer's Kansas business activity." 518 P.2d at 468. Cynical tax counsel for multistate enterprises may be inclined to regard the crucial difference between the two decisions to be that in the Virginia case the taxpayer sought a variation from the statutory formula, whereas in the Kansas case, it was the tax director who sought the variation.

C. *Disparity Between Factors as a Basis for Relief.* Taxpayers have sought relief under the equitable apportionment provisions based on disparities between the different factors of the three-factor apportionment formula. In GATX Corp. v. Limbach, 21 Ohio App.3d 59, 486 N.E.2d 840 (1984), the taxpayer, which was engaged primarily in the business of leasing railroad rolling stock, also manufactured railroad cars for use in its leasing business. Its single manufacturing facility was located in Ohio. GATX sought relief from the application of the three-factor formula to its Ohio income tax base on the ground that inclusion of the wage factor resulted in distortion of its income "since the sales factor ＊ ＊ ＊ was 1.10 percent, the property factor was 3.01 percent, and the wage factor was 27.84 percent." 486 N.E.2d at 842. The Court of Appeals granted the taxpayer's request under the relief provision to eliminate the payroll factor because of its view that "the payroll factor which is thirteen times the property factor and twenty-seven times the sales factor puts the entire apportionment formula out of focus." Id. at 843. Is the Ohio court's view that a disparity between different factors provides a basis for relief under the equitable apportionment provisions warranted? Compare Paris Manufacturing Co., Inc. v. Commonwealth and Doe Spun, Inc. v. Commonwealth, 505 Pa. 15, 476 A.2d 890, 893 (1984), where the Pennsylvania Supreme Court rejected "the assertion that mere disparity between the magnitudes of the property, payroll, and sales fractions is, in itself, indicative of a failure of the apportionment fairly to reflect the loci of business activities."

D. Is it within the province of a tax administrator to utilize the relief provision to substitute the origin test for the destination test of attribution of receipts from sales of property? The Utah Commission did so in Kennecott Copper Corp. v. State Tax Comm'n, 27 Utah 2d 119, 493 P.2d 632 (1972), appeal dismissed 409 U.S. 973, 93 S.Ct. 323 (1972), and was upheld in its action, apparently on the ground that the destination test "tended to greatly diminish the amount of the franchise taxes due." The consequence was to attribute some $158 million of Kennecott's total of approximately $400 million of sales of copper to Utah, where the copper was mined and from which it was shipped, instead of the $3.3 million of sales made to Utah destinations. A dissenting opinion called this action by the Commission a "defiance of express legislative policy and in disregard of the balancing purpose of the sales factor in a production jurisdiction." 493 P.2d at 637.[69] See also Deseret Pharmaceutical Corp. v. State Tax Comm'n, 579 P.2d 1322 (Utah 1978) where the court sanctioned a deviation from the three-factor formula at the behest of the taxing authorities on the ground that income would otherwise be apportioned to States where the taxpayer was not taxable, notwithstanding the fact that the legislature had rejected the throwback rule (see p. 485 supra) in enacting its version of UDITPA.

SECTION 5. METHODS OF APPORTIONMENT FOR SPECIAL INDUSTRIES

The three-factor Massachusetts property, payroll, and receipts factor was developed for mercantile and manufacturing businesses. See "Model Business Income Tax," 6 N.T.A.Bull. 113 (Nov. 1920). In a 1939 survey of the operation of the formula, the N.T.A. Committee on Allocation of Income pointed out: "It is obvious, however, from the studies conducted by the present Committee * * * that such a formula would not be suited to taxpayers other than those engaged in manufacturing or conducting mercantile businesses." 1939 N.T.A. Procs. 190, 205. Nevertheless, because of the failure of some statutes to restrict the formula to such business, or to enact, or authorize tax administrators to promulgate, methods especially adapted to the characteristics of non-manufacturing and non-mercantile business, awkward and inappropriate apportionment under the general formula has sometimes resulted. See, for example, American Airlines, Inc. v. Porterfield, 21 Ohio St.2d 272, 257 N.E.2d 348 (1970).

The general statutory formula is usually made explicitly inapplicable to public utilities engaged in transportation or communication and to electric and gas utilities.[70] The same is true in many States of insurance companies, which are typically taxed on their gross premiums attributable to the State. See, e.g., Guardian Life Ins. Co. v. Chapman, 302 N.Y. 226, 97 N.E.2d 877 (1951).

Special formulas adapted to the characteristics of railroads, trucks and airlines (as they came into being), have been developed over the decades, starting with crude mileage allocations of the tax base and moving to more sophisticated methods, such as ton miles of freight and passenger miles. See Mott, "Report of the Committee on Railroad Allocation," Procs. 15th Ann.Conf.Nat'l Ass'n of Tax Administrators 27

---

69. Kennecott Copper Corporation was also indirectly involved in the *Chase Brass & Copper Co.* case decided by the California courts two years before the Utah decision. See p. 512 infra. The income of Chase Brass & Copper was held properly apportionable as part of a unitary business with its parent company, Kennecott. Since California used the sales destination test in making the apportionments, business spokesmen have used the two cases as a "horrible example" of the whipsawing of taxpayers which can flow from the diversity of State apportionment and allocation methods. See "Industry Statement on Proposed Interstate Tax Legislation," Mondale Comm. Hearings 270.

70. See UDITPA § 2; N.J.Corp.Bus. Tax, N.J.Stat.Ann. § 54:10A–3, CCH ¶ 94–031, P–H ¶ 16,120.

(1947); id. Procs. 17th Ann.Conf.Nat'l Ass'n of Tax Administrators 60 (1949); Report of Civil Aeronautics Board, "Multiple Taxation of Air Commerce," H.R.Doc. 141 (79th Cong. 1st Sess.1945). There is an excellent study of the problems and a recommendation for a model uniform formula in Wilkie, "Income Apportionment of Unitary Public Utility Corporations," 15 Tax L.Rev. 467 (1960). In recent years, in apportionment of the tax bases of airlines, attention has been given to such factors as time spent by planes in airports and the percentage of flight time within the State, along with passenger and plane ton miles. See the work of the Committee on Taxation of Airlines, Nat'l Ass'n of Airlines.

Apportionment or allocation of the income of savings and loan associations and other depositories has become a controversial issue of major significance, since Congress enacted legislation, beginning in 1969, modifying the long-standing immunities from franchise, income, and similar State taxes as applied to national banks organized in other States.[71] See Chapter 15, § 7, infra.

Pennsylvania has developed a two-part single-factor gross receipts formula to apportion the income of regulated investment companies. The numerator consists of receipts from sales by a corporation of its own shares of stock to Pennsylvania investors, plus receipts from sales of portfolio securities, where an order for the sale is placed with, or credited to, offices of registered security dealers in the State; and the denominator consists of the total of all receipts from sales of the corporation's own shares and its portfolio.[72] Compare the New York method of apportioning investment income by reference to the New York apportionment fraction of the corporations whose stocks are held.[73]

Detailed consideration of the division of income of special industries is beyond the scope of this book; such consideration is provided in J. Hellerstein, State Taxation I, Corporate Income and Franchise Taxes ch. 10 (1983).

WILLIS COMMITTEE CONCLUSIONS CONCERNING APPORTIONMENT AND ALLOCATION

In the summary of its findings, the Willis Committee Report declared:

> In summary, the present system for the division of income is characterized by diversity and complexity. These characteristics are most extreme where income is assigned to a location apart from the

71. Conflicting views as to how the income of out-of-state based depositories should be apportioned or allocated are set forth in "State and Local 'Doing Business' Taxes on Out-of-State Financial Depositories," Report of a study under P.L. 93–100, Advisory Commission on Intergovernmental Relations, Senate Banking, Housing and Urban Affairs Committee (94th Cong., 1st Sess., May 1975).

72. Pa. Tax Reform Code § 401.3, Pa. Stat.Ann. tit. 72, § 7401.3, CCH ¶ 100–681, P–H ¶ 12,300.190.

73. N.Y. Tax Law § 210.3(b), CCH ¶ 93–910, P–H ¶¶ 12,020.53, 12,020.69.

locations of employees and tangible assets. No consistent and coherent technique for relating the accounting concept of net income to geographical location has been achieved. The variety of techniques found in the present system requires extraordinarily complex accounting by the taxpayer who divides income. For any company to attempt to meet the literal requirements of all of these rules would clearly result in unacceptably high compliance costs. As will be seen in later chapters, much of this variety is disregarded in practice and a lower order of compliance cost is incurred. The lack of consistency in the rules for the division of income also raises the possibility of overtaxation and undertaxation, and a later chapter will show that this problem in fact occurs today.

The present system for division of income is on its face overwhelming. It will surprise no one familiar with it that in practice it works badly. [I Willis Comm.Rep. 249.]

SECTION 6. STATUTORY APPORTIONMENT AND ALLOCATION PROVISIONS

UNIFORM DIVISION OF INCOME FOR TAX PURPOSES ACT *

Sec. 1. As used in this Act, unless the context otherwise requires:

(a) "Business income" means income arising from transactions and activity in the regular course of the taxpayer's trade or business and includes income from tangible and intangible property if the acquisition, management, and disposition of the property constitute integral parts of the taxpayer's regular trade or business operations.

(b) "Commercial domicile" means the principal place from which the trade or business of the taxpayer is directed or managed.

(c) "Compensation" means wages, salaries, commissions and any other form of remuneration paid to employees for personal services.

COMMENT

This definition is derived from the Model Unemployment Compensation Act which has been adopted in all states.

(d) "Financial organization" means any bank, trust company, savings bank, [industrial bank, land bank, safe deposit company], private banker, savings and loan association, credit union, [cooperative bank], investment company, or any type of insurance company.

(e) "Non-business income" means all income other than business income.

(f) "Public utility" means [any business entity which owns or operates for public use any plant, equipment, property, franchise, or license for the transmission of communications, transportation of goods

---

* [The Uniform Act (UDITPA) was drafted by the National Conference of Commissioners on Uniform State Laws and approved at their 66th Annual Conference in July, 1957. The Comments of the Commissioners are included.]

or persons, or the production, storage, transmission, sale, delivery, or furnishing of electricity, water, steam, oil, oil products or gas.]

COMMENT

It is expected that "public utility" will be defined to include all taxpayers subject to the control of the state's regulatory bodies on the theory that separate legislation will provide for the apportionment and allocation of the income of such taxpayers.

(g) "Sales" means all gross receipts of the taxpayer not allocated under sections 4 through 8 of this Act.

(h) "State" means any state of the United States, the District of Columbia, the Commonwealth of Puerto Rico, any territory or possession of the United States, and any foreign country or political subdivision thereof.

Sec. 2. Any taxpayer having income from business activity which is taxable both within and without this state, other than activity as a financial organization or public utility or the rendering of purely personal services by an individual, shall allocate and apportion his net income as provided in this Act.

Sec. 3. For purposes of allocation and apportionment of income under this Act, a taxpayer is taxable in another state if (1) in that state he is subject to a net income tax, a franchise tax measured by net income, a franchise tax for the privilege of doing business, or a corporate stock tax, or (2) that state has jurisdiction to subject the taxpayer to a net income tax regardless of whether, in fact, the state does or does not.

Sec. 4. Rents and royalties from real or tangible personal property, capital gains, interest, dividends, or patent or copyright royalties, to the extent that they constitute non-business income, shall be allocated as provided in sections 5 through 8 of this Act.

Sec. 5. (a) Net rents and royalties from real property located in this state are allocable to this state.

(b) Net rents and royalties from tangible personal property are allocable to this state:

(1) if and to the extent that the property is utilized in this state, or

(2) in their entirety if the taxpayer's commercial domicile is in this state and the taxpayer is not organized under the laws of or taxable in the state in which the property is utilized.

(c) The extent of utilization of tangible personal property in a state is determined by multiplying the rents and royalties by a fraction, the numerator of which is the number of days of physical location of the property in the state during the rental or royalty period in the taxable year and the denominator of which is the number of days of physical location of the property everywhere during all rental or royalty periods in the taxable year. If the physical location of the property during the rental or royalty period is unknown or unascertainable by the taxpayer tangible personal property is utilized in the state in which the property was located at the time the rental or royalty payer obtained possession.

Sec. 6. (a) Capital gains and losses from sales of real property located in this state are allocable to this state.

(b) Capital gains and losses from sales of tangible personal property are allocable to this state if

(1) the property had a situs in this state at the time of the sale, or

(2) the taxpayer's commercial domicile is in this state and the taxpayer is not taxable in the state in which the property had a situs.

(c) Capital gains and losses from sales of intangible personal property are allocable to this state if the taxpayer's commercial domicile is in this state.

Sec. 7. Interest and dividends are allocable to this state if the taxpayer's commercial domicile is in this state.

Sec. 8. (a) Patent and copyright royalties are allocable to this state:

(1) if and to the extent that the patent or copyright is utilized by the payer in this state, or

(2) if and to the extent that the patent or copyright is utilized by the payer in a state in which the taxpayer is not taxable and the taxpayer's commercial domicile is in this state.

(b) A patent is utilized in a state to the extent that it is employed in production, fabrication, manufacturing, or other processing in the state or to the extent that a patented product is produced in the state. If the basis of receipts from patent royalties does not permit allocation to states or if the accounting procedures do not reflect states of utilization, the patent is utilized in the state in which the taxpayer's commercial domicile is located.

(c) A copyright is utilized in a state to the extent that printing or other publication originates in the state. If the basis of receipts from copyright royalties does not permit allocation to states or if the accounting procedures do not reflect states of utilization, the copyright is utilized in the state in which the taxpayer's commercial domicile is located.

Sec. 9. All business income shall be apportioned to this state by multiplying the income by a fraction, the numerator of which is the property factor plus the payroll factor plus the sales factor, and the denominator of which is three.

Sec. 10. The property factor is a fraction, the numerator of which is the average value of the taxpayer's real and tangible personal property owned or rented and used in this state during the tax period and the denominator of which is the average value of all the taxpayer's real and tangible personal property owned or rented and used during the tax period.

Sec. 11. Property owned by the taxpayer is valued at its original cost. Property rented by the taxpayer is valued at eight times the net annual rental rate. Net annual rental rate is the annual rental rate paid by the taxpayer less any annual rental rate received by the taxpayer from sub-rentals.

COMMENT

This section is admittedly arbitrary in using original cost rather than depreciated cost, and in valuing rented property as eight times the annual rental. This approach is justified because the act does not impose a tax, nor prescribe the depreciation allowable in computing the tax, but merely provides a basis for division of the taxable income among the several states. The use of original cost obviates any differences due to varying methods of depreciation, and has the advantage that the basic figure is readily ascertainable from the taxpayer's books. No method of valuing the property would probably be universally acceptable.

Sec. 12. The average value of property shall be determined by averaging the values at the beginning and ending of the tax period but the [tax administrator] may require the averaging of monthly values during the tax period if reasonably required to reflect properly the average value of the taxpayer's property.

Sec. 13. The payroll factor is a fraction, the numerator of which is the total amount paid in this state during the tax period by the taxpayer for compensation, and the denominator of which is the total compensation paid everywhere during the tax period.

Sec. 14. Compensation is paid in this state if:

(a) the individual's service is performed entirely within the state; or

(b) the individual's service is performed both within and without the state, but the service performed without the state is incidental to the individual's service within the state; or

(c) some of the service is performed in the state and (1) the base of operations or, if there is no base of operations, the place from which the service is directed or controlled is in the state, or (2) the base of operations or the place from which the service is directed or controlled is not in any state in which some part of the service is performed, but the individual's residence is in this state.

COMMENT

This section is derived from the Model Unemployment Compensation Act. This is the same figure which will be used by taxpayers for unemployment compensation purposes.

Sec. 15. The sales factor is a fraction, the numerator of which is the total sales of the taxpayer in this state during the tax period, and the denominator of which is the total sales of the taxpayer everywhere during the tax period.

Sec. 16. Sales of tangible personal property are in this state if:

(a) the property is delivered or shipped to a purchaser, other than the United States government, within this state regardless of the f.o.b. point or other conditions of the sale; or

(b) the property is shipped from an office, store, warehouse, factory, or other place of storage in this state and (1) the purchaser is the United States government or (2) the taxpayer is not taxable in the state of the purchaser.

COMMENT

Sales to the United States Government are treated separately because they are not necessarily attributable to a market existing in the state to which the goods are originally shipped.

Sec. 17. Sales, other than sales of tangible personal property, are in this state if:

(a) the income-producing activity is performed in this state; or

(b) the income-producing activity is performed both in and outside this state and a greater proportion of the income-producing activity is performed in this state than in any other state, based on costs of performance.

Sec. 18. If the allocation and apportionment provisions of this Act do not fairly represent the extent of the taxpayer's business activity in this state, the taxpayer may petition for or the [tax administrator] may require, in respect to all or any part of the taxpayer's business activity, if reasonable:

(a) separate accounting;

(b) the exclusion of any one or more of the factors;

(c) the inclusion of one or more additional factors which will fairly represent the taxpayer's business activity in this state; or

(d) the employment of any other method to effectuate an equitable allocation and apportionment of the taxpayer's income.

COMMENT

It is anticipated that this act will be made a part of the income tax acts of the several states. For that reason, this section does not spell out the procedure to be followed in the event of a disagreement between the taxpayer and the tax administrator. The income tax acts of each state presumably outline the procedure to be followed.

Sec. 19. This Act shall be so construed as to effectuate its general purpose to make uniform the law of those states which enact it.

Sec. 20. This Act may be cited as the Uniform Division of Income for Tax Purposes Act.

Notes

A. Some 25 states and the District of Columbia may be regarded as having adopted UDITPA, either *in haec verba* or in substantially the form of the Model Act as prepared by the National Conference of Commissioners on Uniform State Laws. See CCH All States Guide ¶ 10–000. The Multistate Tax Compact (see Section 14 infra) embodies UDITPA so that a number of States enacted the Uniform Act by adopting the Compact.

Caveat: The State statutes should be examined carefully for differences from the model UDITPA as approved by the National Conference. See, for example, the variations in the Alabama, Florida, Massachusetts, New Hampshire, and Oklahoma versions of UDITPA.

References. For overall comments on UDITPA see Cox, "NCCUSL Uniform Apportionment Formula," 42 Taxes 530 (1964); Conlon, "The Apportionment of Multi–State Business Income: The NCCUSL Division of Income Act," 12 Tax Exec. 220 (1960); Pierce, "The Uniform Division of Income for State Tax Purposes," 35 Taxes 747 (1957); Lynn, "The Uniform Division of Income for Tax Purposes Act," 19 Ohio St.L.J. 41 (1958); Wilkie, "Uniform Division of Income for Tax Purposes," 37 Taxes 65 (1959).

TABLE 1

Income Apportionment Elements *

Multistate operations. This chart shows factors—property, receipts, payroll and other components, states use to fix taxable net income of multistate businesses. Also shown— income, separately or specifically allocated, rather than apportioned by ratios or percentage formulas.

	FACTORS OF APPORTIONMENT FRACTIONS				ITEMS SEPARATELY ALLOCATED	SEPARATE ACCOUNTING ALLOWED?
STATE Col. A	Property Col. B	Receipts Col. C	Payroll Col. D	Others Col. E	Col. F	Col. G(2)
ALA.(1,6)	Yes	Yes	Yes	(6–7)	(1–5)	Yes(2)
ALASKA(9)	Yes	Yes	Yes	(6)	(1–5)	Yes
ARIZ.(6)	Yes	Yes	Yes		(1–5)	Yes
ARK.(6,9)	Yes	Yes	Yes	(4,6)	(1–5)	Yes
CALIF.(6,9)	Yes	Yes	Yes	(4)	(1–5)	Yes
COLO.(9)	Yes	Yes	No		(20)	Yes
CONN.(4)	Yes	Yes(3,4)	Yes	(4.6)		Yes
DEL.	Yes	Yes	Yes	(7)	(1–5,9,15)	Yes
D.C.(6,9)	Yes	Yes	Yes	(4)	(1–5)	Yes
FLA.(4)	Yes(1)	Yes(2)	Yes(3)	(4,6)	(1–5)	Yes
GA.	Yes	Yes	Yes	(4–6)	(2–5,7)	Yes
HAW.(6,9)	Yes	Yes	Yes	(6,15)	(1–5)	Yes
IDAHO(6,9)	Yes	Yes	Yes	(4)	(1–5)	Yes
ILL.	Yes	Yes(3)	Yes	(6)	(1–5)	Yes
IND.(6,11)	Yes	Yes	Yes		(1–5)	Yes
IOWA	No	Yes	No	(3,6)	(1–5)	Yes
KAN.(6,9)	Yes	Yes	Yes	(4,6)	(1–5)	Yes
KY.	Yes	Yes(3)	Yes	(6)	(1–3,5)	Yes
LA.	Yes	Yes	Yes	(4,6)	(1–5,11)	Yes
ME.(6,7,8)	Yes	Yes	Yes		(1–5)	Yes
MD.	Yes	Yes	Yes	(5)	(10)	Yes(3)
MASS.	Yes	Yes(3)	Yes	(5)	(4)	Yes
MICH.(6,9,12)	Yes	Yes	Yes	(4,6,13)	(19)	Yes
MINN.(3, 9)	Yes	Yes(5)	Yes	(16)	(1–5,8,14,15)	Yes
MISS.(5)	Yes	Yes(1)	Yes	(5,6)	(1–5)	Yes
MO.(9)	No	Yes	No	(4,6)	(1–5)	Yes
MONT.(6,8,9)	Yes	Yes	Yes		(1–5)	Yes
NEB.(4,7)	Yes	Yes(6)	Yes	(7)		Yes
N.H.	Yes	Yes	Yes	(7)		No
N.J.	Yes	Yes	Yes	(9)	(1,4)	No
N.M.(6,9)	Yes	Yes	Yes	(6,12)	(1–5)	Yes(4)
N.Y.(4)	Yes	Yes(3)	Yes	(8)	(1–5,9)	(1,2)
N.C.(6,8)	Yes	Yes	Yes	(4,6)	(1–5,7)	Yes
N.D.(6,7,9)	Yes	Yes	Yes	(16)	(1–5)	Yes
OHIO(10)	Yes	Yes(3)	Yes	(6,9)	(2–4,8,21)	Yes
OKLA.(6)	Yes	Yes	Yes(2)	(6)	(1–5,6,10,13)	Yes
ORE.(6,8,9)	Yes	Yes	Yes	(4,6)	(1–5)	Yes
PA.(6)	Yes	Yes	Yes	(14)	(1–3,5)	Yes
R.I.	Yes	Yes	Yes			(1)
S.C.(6)	Yes	Yes	Yes	(10)	(2–5,8,12,15,16)	Yes
TENN.(6)	Yes	Yes	Yes(5)	(4,6)	(1–5)	Yes
UTAH(6,8,9)	Yes	Yes	Yes		(1–5)	Yes
VT.	Yes	Yes	Yes	(7)	(1–3,17)	Yes
VA.(6)	Yes	Yes	Yes	(4,5,16)	(4)	Yes
W.Va.(7)	Yes	Yes(3)	Yes	(6)	(1–5)	Yes
WIS.(4,8)	Yes(1)	Yes(2)	Yes(3,4)	(2–4,6)	(15,18)	Yes

* From Prentice–Hall, State and Local Taxes, All States Guide ¶ 223 (10–20–87), reprinted with the permission of Prentice–Hall, Inc.

NOTES to chart (corresponding to number in parentheses in the chart):

Col. A. (1) Domestic corporations and residents can't allocate. (2) Gross income tax allows no allocation. (3) Ratio computed under Columns B, C and D can't exceed sum of 15% of property percentage (Col. B), 70% of sales percentage (Col. C) and 15% of payroll percentage (Col. D). Entire income of unitary business is apportioned. (4) Disallows equally weighted 3–factor formula. In Neb., eff. for tax yrs. starting after 12–31–87 unitary business' property-payroll factors' weight decreases and sales' increases until sales factor is sole factor for tax yrs. starting after 12–31–91 (after that see col. C). (5) Mfr.-wholesalers use property-payroll factors (denominator is 3); Mfr.-retailers use sales, plus property-payroll (denominator is 2); retailing renting, servicing & merchandising use single sales factor. (6) Uniform Div. of Income for Tax Purposes Act (UDITPA) is substantially adopted. (7) Applies only to corporations. In Nebr. only unitary businesses can apportion. (8) Only for corporations and non-resident individuals. (9) State has adopted Multistate Tax Compact (MTC), including 3–factor formula. Taxpayer may elect to allocate by 3–factor formula. Minn. disallows use of equally weighted 3–factor formula. (10) For corporation (income) franchise tax, personal income tax. (11) Foreign corps. don't consider out-US factors (property-sales-payroll). In Ind., note (2) also applies. (12) Chart entries apply to Single Business Tax.

Col. B. (1) Factor represents 25% of formula.

Col. C. (1) Sole factor only for retailing, renting, servicing & merchandising. (2) Factor is 50% of formula. (3) Sales factor used twice. In Ill. eff. for tax years ending after 12–31–86; in Ky. eff. for tax years begun after 7–31–85; in W.Va. eff. 7–1–85. (4) Sole factor for businesses, other than mfg. or sale of tangibles. (5) Sole factor only for retailing goods or services in response to phone or mail orders and entire property-payroll in Minn. (6) Sole factor in Neb. for unitary businesses (eff. for tax yrs. starting after 12–31–91).

Col. D. (1) Mfg. labor only, direct and indirect. (2) Includes services related to unitary business, but excludes compensation as general or administrative expense. (3) Factor is 25% of formula. (4) Payroll factor replaces cost factor. (5) See footnote (6), Col. A.

Col. E. (1) Purchases factor may be used for purchasing businesses. (2) Manufacturers' costs. (3) For businesses other than manufacture or sale of tangible personalty, Dir. may make rules. (4) Special provisions apply to some or all carriers. (5) Special provisions for construction cos. (6) Special provisions for specialized businesses (e.g., utility, oil & gas insurance, financial and service businesses, etc.). (7) Such other factors as Admr. deems applicable. (8) 3–factor formula for business income and capital; investment income and capital separately treated. (9) Use assets (in N.J.) and net worth (Ohio) allocation if producing greater percentage than average of Col. B, C and D. (10) Single factor (gross receipts) formula for income other than from mfg., producing, collecting, processing, buying, selling, distributing, or dealing in tangible personalty. (11) Wages not a separate factor for sellers but part of mfr.'s production cost factor. (12)

Operating expenses. (13) Special provisions for small instate sales. (14) Special provisions for transportation, pipeline, natural gas and water transportation cos. (15) Haw.—2 factors for mfrs.-producers (property-payroll). (16) Special provisions for financial business.

Col. F. (1) Capital gains; in Pa., "gains". (2) Rents. (3) Royalties (in S.C. limited to tangibles). (4) Dividends (in Mass. & NJ not included in tax base; in Ohio, if not deducted or excluded for corporate net income, and specifically includes distributions). (5) Interest. (6) Special rules apply to life insurance cos. (7) Gain on sale of assets not connected with business. (8) Income from personal services. (9) Income from sale of realty. In Del., DC also, gain from sale of tangible personalty. (10) If business not unitary, net income allocated to state where activity conducted. (11) Income from construction, repairs and similar services. (12) Gain or loss on realty sale. (13) Net income of certain manufacturing or processing enterprises. (14) Farm income. (15) Gain or loss from intangibles. (16) Investments in subsidiaries, not included in base. (17) Income from any trade, business, all instate. (18) Nonbusiness income or loss from rental and royalties from or sales of tangibles follow property situs; income or gains from intangibles earned by personal holding co. (IRC § 542 as of 12–31–74) are allocated to taxpayer's residence. (19) Single Business tax allows deduction from base: dividends, interest, royalties and certain capital losses. (20) If electing MTC method, items (1) thru (5) are allocated. (21) Allocate capital gains from disposition of dividend-producing intangibles; others subject to apportionment (Ohio).

Col. G. (1) No specific provision. (2) Separate accounting, if allowed, may require official approval. (3) Denied unitary businesses. (4) May be used for 5 consecutive tax years.

TABLE 2

Receipts in Apportionment Numerators *

STATE Col. A(1)	OFFICE WHERE NE- GOTIATED Col. B	PROPERTY AT TIME OF ORDER Col. C	RECEIPT OR ACCEPT- ANCE OF ORDER Col. D	DELIVERY PLACE Col. E	SHIPMENT ORIGIN Col. F	OTHER Col. G
ALA.				X	X(2,3)	X(9)
ALASKA				X	X(2,3)	X(3,9)
ARIZ.				X	X(2,3)	X(3,9)
ARK.				X(7)	X(2,3)	X(7)
CALIF.				X	X(2,3)	X(3,9)
COLO.(5)				X(8)	X(10)	X(4,15)
CONN.	X			X(6,10)		X(2,16)
DEL.				X(1)		X(2)
D.C.		(2)		X(6)	X(2,3)	X(3,9)
FLA.				X(6)	(11)	X(3,4,9)
GA.				X(1)		
HAW.				X(7)	X(2,3)	X(3,9)
IDAHO				X(7)	X(2,3)	X(3,9)
ILL.				X(7)	X(8)	X(3,9)
IND.				X(7)	X(2,3)	X(3,9)
IOWA				X(1,6)		
KAN.				X(7)	X(2,3)	X(3,9)
KY.				X(7)	X(2)	X(3,9)
LA.				X		
ME.				X(7)	X(2,3)	X(3,9
MD.				X(7)		X(3,9)
MASS.	X(3)			X	X(1)	X(3,9,14)
MICH.				X	X(2,3)	X(3,9)
MINN.(5)				X(2)		X(17)
MISS.(4)				X(7)	X(2,3)	X(18)
MO.(5)			X(2)	X	X	X(5)
MONT.				X(7)	X(2,3)	X(3,9)
NEB.				X(7)	X(2,3)	X(3,9)
N.H.				X(7)	X(2,3)	X(3,9)
N.J.		X(3)		X(5)		X(2,4)
N.M.				X(7)	X(2,3)	X(3,9)
N.Y.				X		X(2,4,13)
N.C.				X(9)		X(2,6)
N.D.				X(7)	X(2,3)	X(3,9)
OHIO	X(1)			X(9)		X(3,9)
OKLA.				X(7)	X(2,3)	X(10)
ORE.				X	X(2,3)	X(3,9)
PA.				X		X(3,9)
R.I.				X(11)		X(2,4,19)
S.C.				X(1)	X(2,3,11)	X(3,8,9)
TENN.	X(2)			X(7)	X(2)	X(3,9)
UTAH	X(2)			X(7)	X(2,3)	X(3,9)
VT.		X(1)	X(1)	X(7)	X	X(2,3)
VA.(3)				X(9)	(9)	(16)
W.VA.				X(7)	X(2,3)	X(3,9)
WIS.	X(2)			X(7)	X(2,3,7)	X(3,12)

* From Prentice–Hall, State and Local Taxes, All States Guide ¶ 224 (10–20–87), reprinted with the permission of Prentice–Hall, Inc.

NOTES to chart (corresponding to parenthetical numbers in chart):

Col. A. (1) For member states of Multistate Tax Compact, see ¶ 223. (2) (Reserved.) (3) Limited to sales connected with US business and if income is Fed taxable. (4) Not for mfrs. principally in wholesaling. (5) Multistate Tax Compact rules can be elected instead of rules shown. Minn. disallows option (eff. for tax yrs. begun after 12–31–86).

Col. B. (1) Location of solicitation controls if sales other than tangible personalty. (2) Sales through or by instate offices, agencies or branches and taxpayer not taxed in buyer's state. In Wisc., if goods shipped directly by 3rd party to buyer. (3) Sales not negotiated or effected by agents or agencies chiefly at, connected with or sent out from business premises outstate.

Col. C. (1) Property instate on receipt or appropriation to order, or not at taxpayer's outstate business place when order received or accepted instate. (2) If taxpayer not taxed in destination state (repealed eff. 2–28–87). (3) If coupled with delivery instate.

Col. D. (1) See Col. C. (2) One element of sale.

Col. E. (1) Deliveries in state, excluding deliveries for out-shipment. In S.C. except sales to U.S. (2) Property (except beer, liquor, wine or tobacco products if buyer can sell only in state of domicile) received by buyer at point in state (dock sales) regardless of FOB point or final destination (excluding deliveries to common carrier or foreign vessel for buyers outstate). (3–4) (Reserved). (5) See Col. C. (6) Or inshipments, regardless of F.O.B. point or other sales condition. In Fla. except if made by common or contract carrier. Eff. 2–28–87 in D.C. (was note (9) applied). (7) Deliveries to instate buyer (other than U.S.) and note (6) applies. (8) Note (6) applies and regardless of taxability of corporation in the state or foreign country where goods delivered or shipped. If electing MTC method, note (7) applies. (9) Deliveries to buyer or designee in state, excluding deliveries for outshipments. (10) Not inshipments to DISCs electing under IRC § 992. (11) Not inshipments to FSCs.

Col. F. (1) See Col. G entry for state. (2) If purchaser is U.S. government. In D.C., eff. 2–28–87. (3) If taxpayer is not taxable in purchaser's state. (4) See Col. G(10). (5) Taxpayer isn't doing business in state of destination. (6) Footnotes (2) and (3) apply. (7) Only 50% of tangible personalty sales under "throwback" rule is in numerator. (8) Footnotes (2) and (3) apply. Outshipments not local sales if from premises of person independently contracting with seller for printing of newspapers, periodicals or books. (9) In Va. note (3) applied for yrs. begun pre–1981. (10) If electing MTC, notes (2) and (3) apply. (11) Sales in situations where notes (2) and (3) apply are S.C. sales to extent of 75% for taxpayer's 1st fiscal year (fy) starting after 1984; 50% for 2nd fy; 25%, 3rd; zero (not in numerator) after 3rd fy.

Col. G. (1) (Reserved.) (2) Receipts from instate sources. (3) For sale of intangibles, allocate instate if income-producing (earnings-producing, in Tenn.) activity is instate or Col. G(9) applies. (4) Receipts from instate services and rentals or royalties on property in or used in state. (5) All sales or business transacted in state and half transacted in and outside. (6)

Services instate (in Miss. & N.C., if income-producing activities are instate).
(7) If income producing activity is instate for nontangibles; if multistate,
Ark. share is same formula percentage used in allocating income of year.
(8) Personalty rentals not separately allocated. (9) For sales other than
sales of tangible personalty, state with largest share of costs of performance. (10) Though sales of intangibles are included in 3–factor apportionment, there's no provision indicating which go in numerator. (11) If not
taxed in purchaser's state. "Purchaser" includes U.S. (12) For intangibles
and services allocate between states in ratio of local-to-local production
costs. (use or consumption of benefits in Minn. eff. for tax yrs. begun after
12–31–86). (13) Sales of closed-circuit or CATV rights to events instate
(employee's performance as entertainers or artists); publishers' receipts
from sale of advertising in newspapers or periodicals delivered instate. (14)
Note (11) applies but deliveries in foreign countries and sales to U.S. for
resale to foreign govts. are treated as taxable in buyer's state. (15) Gain
from intangibles sale, interest and dividends, if commercial domicile in-
state. (16) Gain from intangibles sale and interest if managed or controlled
instate; gain from tangibles located instate; note (4) also applies. (17)
Sales by or thru DISCs are excluded. Note (12) also applies. (18) Construction contractors include receipts allocable for Miss. sales tax purposes; note
(4) & (6) also apply. (19) Net Income from sale of non-inventory and capital
assets, income from sale of securities or financial obligations. Notes (2) &
(4) apply except "gross income" from such receipts are used.

References. J. Hellerstein, State Taxation I, Corporate Income and
Franchise Taxes chs. 8–10 (1983); Hartman, "State Taxation of Income
from a Multi-state Business," 3 Vand.L.Rev. 21 (1959); G. Altman & F.
Keesling, Allocation of Income in State Taxation (2d ed. 1950); Silverstein,
"Problems of Apportionment in Taxation of Multistate Business," 4 Tax
L.Rev. 207 (1949); Cohen, "Apportionment and Allocation Formulae and
Factors Used by States in Levying Taxes Based on or Measured by Net
Income of Manufacturing, Distributive and Extractive Corporations," Rep.
of Controllership Foundation, Inc. (N.Y.1954); Cohen, "State Tax Alloca-
tions and Formulas which Affect Management Operating Decisions," 1
J.Tax. (1954).

SECTION 7. DELINEATION OF THE SCOPE OF A UNITARY ENTERPRISE

INTRODUCTORY NOTE

With the growth of apportionment by formula and the frequent
frustration of the efforts of multistate enterprises to obtain separate
accounting, either from tax administrators or the courts, the focus of
the controversy has shifted: how far does the unitary enterprise extend? With vertically integrated businesses, attempts have been made,
typically by taxpayers but at times by taxing administrators, to separate parts of the business carried on in other States from the activities
carried on within the taxing State. And as businesses have diversified,
they have sought to separate operations in one aspect of the enterprise
from others.

It is generally recognized that the unitary apportionment method is inapplicable to separate businesses.[74] Thus, in California, which has been the leading State exponent of a broad definition of the unitary business, the rule obtains that separate businesses may not be included within a single unitary apportionment. This qualification is essential since the California unitary doctrine would otherwise lump together in the formulary apportionment businesses totally independent in their operations. This is a problem that has plagued both taxpayers and tax administrators, and has led to such probings as whether a "company which manufactures insecticides in California, fertilizers in West Virginia and chemicals for use in textile manufacturing in Georgia [is] engaged in three separate businesses, or is * * * engaged in the single business of manufacturing chemicals?"[75]

CHASE BRASS AND COPPER CO. v. FRANCHISE TAX BD.

California Court of Appeal, First District, Division 4, 1970.
10 Cal.App.3d 496, 95 Cal.Rptr. 805.

DEVINE, PRESIDING JUSTICE.

Franchise Tax Board of the State of California (herein, the Board) appeals from a portion of a judgment in the amount of $231,257.32 plus interest, which was awarded to plaintiff in this lawsuit to recover taxes paid under protest. The taxes are upon the franchise to do business in California during the years 1954, 1955 and 1956; but in order to make the reading easier, operations and relationships among companies are sometimes narrated, in this opinion, in the present tense.

Plaintiff, Chase Brass and Copper Co., Incorporated, is a wholly owned subsidiary of Kennecott Copper Corporation. The principal question is whether plaintiff's business is unitary or nonunitary with Kennecott, and a lesser question is whether plaintiff's business is unitary with any of Kennecott's other subsidiary corporations. If the business be unitary, a much larger franchise tax would be imposed than if the business be nonunitary. It is not always unfavorable as to tax for a corporation to conduct a unitary business; for example, in the leading cases of Superior Oil Co. v. Franchise Tax Board, 60 Cal.2d 406, 34 Cal.

---

74. The California doctrine proceeds on the premise that "It is only where the activities within and without the state constitute inseparable parts of a single business that the classification of unitary should be used." Keesling & Warren, "The Unitary Concept in the Allocation of Income," 12 Hastings L.J. 42, 48 (1960). The California regulations provide that where a taxpayer has more than one trade or business, "[t]he income of each business is then apportioned by an apportionment formula which takes into consideration the instate and outstate factors which relate to the trade or business the income of which is being apportioned." Reg. 25120, Cal. CCH ¶ 14–815, P–H ¶ 11,536–L.10.

75. Keesling & Warren, "California's Uniform Division of Income for Tax Purposes Act," 15 U.C.L.A.L.Rev. 156, 172 (1967). This aspect of the California unitary approach has been used by critics of formulary apportionment to emphasize its ambiguities and uncertainties. See also Miller, "State Income Taxation of Multiple Corporations and Multiple Businesses," Tax Foundation Seminar on Taxation of Interstate Business 4 (April 16–17, 1970).

Rptr. 545, 386 P.2d 33, and Honolulu Oil Corp. v. Franchise Tax Board, 60 Cal.2d 417, 34 Cal.Rptr. 552, 386 P.2d 40, the corporations asserted, successfully, that their California operations were unitary with those conducted outside the state.

In the case before us, plaintiff computed its California income, using an allocation formula which is applied to nonunitary enterprises and which takes into account sales, property and payroll within the state as compared with those existing outside. The Board disagrees with this method of computation; it has assessed taxes at a much higher figure on the "unitary business" theory.

The Corporations

The parent is Kennecott Copper Corporation (called Kennecott herein), the nation's largest producer of copper, a New York corporation. It does no business in California. It mines, smelts and refines copper, gold, silver and molybdenite. The metals are mined in Utah, Nevada, Arizona and New Mexico. Metals other than copper are sold in operations completely unrelated to plaintiff. Copper is not fabricated by Kennecott, but is sold through a subsidiary of Kennecott, Kennecott Sales Corporation.

Braden Copper Company, a Maine corporation, wholly owned by Kennecott, operates mines in Chile. Ordinarily, it sold copper to the government of Chile and to purchasers in the world market, but not to buyers in the United States. In the years relevant hereto, however, because of shortages, it did sell, through Kennecott Sales Corporation, in this country. Plaintiff was a buyer. Braden does not fabricate; it sells fungible copper.

Bear Creek Mining Company, a Delaware corporation, owned by Kennecott, explored for metals in California in the relevant years, but made no significant discoveries. It is the third company in the mining group consisting of Kennecott, Braden, and Bear Creek.

The procedure beyond mining and refining of copper, sales, is committed to Kennecott Sales Corporation (herein, Kennecott Sales), a New York corporation, wholly owned by Kennecott, which in 1934 took over the sales and activity theretofore assigned by Kennecott and Braden to an independent agency. The sale of copper by Kennecott and by Braden within the United States is done by Kennecott Sales. No sales are made in California; Kennecott does no business here. Its sales of copper which enters this state are completed elsewhere. Kennecott Sales charges Kennecott a commission on the sales.

Kennecott Wire and Cable Co. (herein, Kennecott Wire), a Rhode Island corporation, owned by Kennecott, manufactures copper rod, wire and cable for transmission of electricity. It uses refined primary copper, all of which it buys from Kennecott or Braden through Kennecott Sales. Its sales operation in California is largely through plaintiff. Kennecott Wire did not do business in California in the relevant years.

Finally, there is plaintiff, Chase Brass and Copper Co., Incorporated, a Connecticut corporation, wholly owned by Kennecott. Like Kennecott Wire, it is a manufacturer. Its products are brass (made of copper and zinc), bronze (copper and alloys, mostly tin), and copper rod, sheet, wire and tube. The manufacture is done entirely outside California. Copper is bought from Kennecott Sales, derived from Kennecott and Braden, to the extent of 80 to 84 percent of Chase's needed supply. Within California, Chase warehouses and sells its products and those of Kennecott Wire.

THE FRANCHISE TAX LAW

When a corporation engages in multistate business, including business in California, and the business is unitary, there must be an allocation of income by formula. Separate accounting is not allowable, although it is usable for a corporation which, by operating here and elsewhere, conducts a nonunitary business. In the case of Chase itself, it was always recognized by the company that its own business is unitary, wherefore its own computation of the franchise tax was done according to formula. But the Board contends that the geographic unitary character of Chase is not all that is to be considered; there must also be taken into account the whole intercorporate parentage and affiliation of the Kennecott family. Mainly, it is the vertical aspect which is put before us: the relationship of Chase to Kennecott Sales, to Braden and to Kennecott. Secondarily, there is to be considered the horizontal relationship of Chase to Kennecott Wire.

Intercorporate unitary character of business, in which the activities of the parent are considered, under an appropriate factual situation, is a valid concept for taxing purposes. (Edison California Stores v. McColgan, 30 Cal.2d 472, 183 P.2d 16.) This holding of the Edison Stores case was but a logical sequence of the holding in Butler Brothers v. McColgan, 17 Cal.2d 664, 111 P.2d 334, in which a single company had operated through wholly controlled branches. In both cases, there were strong and embracing central controls. The general test which we are to apply is this: "If the operation of the portion of the business done within the state is dependent upon or contributes to the operation of the business without the state, the operations are unitary." (Edison California Stores v. McColgan, supra, 30 Cal.2d at p. 481, 183 P.2d at p. 21; Superior Oil Co. v. Franchise Tax Board, 60 Cal.2d 406, 412, 34 Cal. Rptr. 545, 386 P.2d 33.) A more particular statement of the test is that a business is unitary if these circumstances are present: "(1) Unity of ownership; (2) Unity of operation as evidenced by central purchasing, advertising, accounting and management divisions; and (3) Unity of use of its centralized executive force and general system of operation." (Butler Brothers v. McColgan, supra, 17 Cal.2d at p. 678, 111 P.2d at p. 341; Superior Oil Co. v. Franchise Tax Board, supra, 60 Cal.2d at p. 412, 34 Cal.Rptr. 545, 386 P.2d 33.)

* * *

UNITY OF OWNERSHIP

As is usual in disputes of this kind, ownership of one corporation by another is present. This means, of course, that the owner (its stockholders and directors) expects, or at least hopes, that its subsidiary will make a profit. But more is required for a business to be unitary, that is, fulfillment of the other two tests.

UNITY OF OPERATION

Although there is not a clear demarcation between what is "operation" and what is "use," in general it may be said that the acts falling within the category of "operation" are the staff functions, and those within "use" are the line functions.

The staff functions of a vertically integrated enterprise probably are not so markedly unitary as they are in a horizontally integrated business. This is so because, in the case of horizontal integration, functions such as central control of advertising of the same product, central purchasing, and the like are designed to give advantages to the business despite geographic differences. In the case of vertical integration involving various steps in the production and distribution, integration of staff functions probably will be considerably less. Nevertheless, when we consider each of the functions of Chase coming under the heading "Unity of Operation," in connection with those of its parent, Kennecott, we find considerable cooperation.

Purchasing: Under this heading, we consider the buying of items other than the purchase of copper, because copper buying is an essential "line" function. As to the auxiliary supplies, it is stipulated that Chase had its own purchasing department staffed by its own personnel. But Kennecott does some "minor" purchasing for Chase. In some instances, insurance was purchased for two or more companies in order to obtain a more favorable rate or better coverage or a better spread of risk. There was no intercompany coverage on basic industrial policies such as fire, fire use and occupancy, workmen's compensation, public liability, automobile liability and fire, sickness and accident, hospitalization and surgical, and certain types of bonds.

Advertising: Chase maintains its own advertising program and budget. The name and trademark of Chase are predominant in its advertisements, but these often contain a statement that Chase is a subsidiary of Kennecott. When Chase places advertising through an advertising agency, it uses the same agency that is used by Kennecott.

Accounting: Kennecott and Chase keep separate books of account, but the two use the same accounting firm. Kennecott prepared consolidated tax accounts for Chase.

Legal: Chase has its own legal staff and on occasion employs its own outside counsel. Presentation of the protest of Chase before the Franchise Tax Board in these proceedings was handled by Kennecott employees.

Financing: In 1955, Chase's mill at Waterbury, Connecticut, was severely damaged by flood. Kennecott made loans to Chase, in the amount of $10,000,000, for rehabilitation of the plant. The prime bank rate of interest, which was then three and a half percent, was charged. The loan, including interest, was repaid within four years. We find this to be substantial evidence of unity of operation. It may be that Chase could have borrowed the money from lending institutions, but the fact remains that it could turn readily to its parent for help. It must have been deemed advantageous to the over-all management to have handled the transaction in this way, otherwise a separate arrangement would have been made.

Retirement Plan: There is a common retirement plan for salaried employees, which is administered by Kennecott, because when it was installed it appeared to be more economical and because it assures salaried employees in each company the same treatment as those in other Kennecott companies.

UNITY OF USE

Unity of use relates to executive forces and operational systems. (Superior Oil Co. v. Franchise Tax Board, 60 Cal.2d 406, 415, 34 Cal. Rptr. 545, 386 P.2d 33.)

Executive Forces: The integration of executive forces is an element of exceeding importance. It is top level management which is credited (or, in case of failure or indifferent results, debited) with the effects of corporate enterprises. Chief executives of large organizations are regarded as highly prized acquisitions. They are induced to join a corporation, or to remain with it, and to exert their best efforts, not only by generous salaries, but also in many cases by incentive plans of various kinds. For a subsidiary corporation to have the assistance and direction of high executive authority of such a corporation as Kennecott is an invaluable resource. The stipulation of facts reads: "The day to day operations of the subsidiaries were the concern of the executives of the subsidiaries and were handled by various subordinate employees of the subsidiaries. The Board of Directors of Kennecott was primarily interested in, and devoted the majority of its time to, the larger problems facing the copper industry in general, including the development and maintenance of its fabricating subsidiaries. The President of Kennecott was concerned with basic problems and policies of the subsidiaries. The executives of the subsidiaries reported to the President of Kennecott with respect to major policy matters." The "major policy matters" are what count in our estimation of integration. Day to day operations are made at various levels by many executives in any organization. They are made, no doubt, by a multitude of officials of Kennecott and its subsidiaries. Major policy is another thing. This was the concern of Kennecott.

Not only was there opportunity for control at the highest levels. The salaries of Chase's executives (and of those of Kennecott Wire) who earned more than $15,000 a year were subject to review by Kennecott.

Exercising regulation of salaries of Chase's executives, even of those who were compensated at a not particularly sizable figure, Kennecott could control costs of management. Besides, these executives could hardly fail to recognize that their compensation was dependent upon the decision of Kennecott's salary committee.

It is true that the President of Chase had a complete staff and line organization under his direction, but executive control at the highest level was in Kennecott.

Chase and Kennecott Wire: Inextricably bound to Chase's vertical relationship with Kennecott is its horizontal tie with Kennecott Wire. In fact, the relationships between Chase and Kennecott Wire, described in this paragraph, are evidence of the central control of these sibling corporations by their parent, Kennecott. Who would decide the extent of the horizontal relationships and whether the joint activities were mutually advantageous to the siblings, and commonly so to the parent, but the parent itself? Kennecott Wire, like Chase, is a manufacturer. Since 1944, Chase has taken over the sales of the major part of the products of Kennecott Wire. Chase warehouses the products of Kennecott Wire; Chase salesmen call on prospective wire and copper customers. If the salesmen obtain orders, they send them to Kennecott Wire. The orders are filled and shipped in the name of Chase. Chase receives a discount on the products sold. Chase does much of the accounting and reviews the taxes for Kennecott Wire. The former president and the general sales manager of Kennecott Wire had been Chase employees. Although the products, all of them composed to some extent of copper, are different, the activities clearly show a unitary business. (RKO Teleradio Pictures, Inc. v. Franchise Tax Board, 246 Cal.App.2d 812, 55 Cal.Rptr. 299.) Respondent argues that unity of ownership is absent. In form this is correct, but in substance the unity of ownership is present because Kennecott is the sole owner of Chase and of Kennecott Wire.

Purchase of Copper: Kennecott sells about 20 percent of its total copper production to Chase through Kennecott Sales. During the relevant years, there was an industry-wide copper shortage so that Kennecott would have had no difficulty in selling copper to others. This does not mean, however, that there was no contribution at all to Kennecott by Chase except the profits which Chase might make and which would redound to the benefit of Kennecott as sole stockholder. Although the three years, 1954, 1955 and 1956, are the only ones involved in the present case, these years are not the only ones in which the two corporations have been interested for their anticipated prosperity. Chase has been owned by Kennecott since 1929. To have a buyer of a substantial portion of the parent's production throughout the years must be assumed to be an advantage.

It is the position of respondent that Chase gained no particular advantage during the years in question by reason of the parentage of Kennecott. Kennecott sold to Chase at exactly the same price as that which it charged Chase's competitors. Moreover, during the period of shortage an allocation was made based on prior sales. Respondent does not contend that price equality was the result of benevolence toward other consumers, including competing companies. The equality was under compulsion of the Robinson–Patman Act (15 U.S.C.A. § 13a). But it is argued that under these conditions Chase is no more unitary with Kennecott than is, for example, another large buyer from Kennecott, Revere Copper & Brass Company. Here, again, however, we remark that the three years are not the only ones to be considered. The percentage which governed the amount of copper allocable to Chase was built over the years.

The fact of the sales alone, however, whether specially advantageous to Kennecott or to Chase, does not determine the business to be unitary. The factors described under headings above, and particularly those relating to control of major policy, together with the subject of sales, bring us to the conclusion that the business among Kennecott, Kennecott Sales and Chase is unitary.

Except for the matter of sales and joint ownership, Braden and Chase are not unitary. We support the conclusion of the trial judge to this extent. As to Bear Creek, too, there is no such relationship as would allow formula computation of the taxes on the unitary theory. We agree with respondent on another point, namely, that Kennecott's sales of gold, silver and molybdenite metals, which are not bought by Chase or Kennecott Wire, are not part of the unitary business. The fact that these metals come from the same ore as that which produces copper is not sufficient to cause their sales to be included in the computations which are to follow.

The Board concedes that there is error in the property factor as it was applied, because of the decision in McDonnell Douglas Corp. v. Franchise Tax Board, 69 Cal.2d 506, 72 Cal.Rptr. 465, 446 P.2d 313; wherefore, the case must be remanded in any event. Our decision requires further revisions of the formula.

We reverse the judgment, with directions to the trial court to proceed in accordance with this opinion.*

RATTIGAN and CHRISTIAN, JJ., concur.

Notes and Problems **

A. *The California Approach to the Scope of the Unitary Business.* "A high-water mark of the California Supreme Court's delineation of the scope of a unitary business was reached in the *Superior Oil* and *Honolulu Oil*

---

* [Rehearing denied 10 Cal.App.3d 505, 95 Cal.Rptr. 810 (1970). The United States Supreme Court dismissed the taxpayer's appeal for want of jurisdiction; treating the papers whereon the appeal was taken as a petition for writ of certiorari, the Court denied the petition. 400 U.S. 961, 91 S.Ct. 365 (1970).]

** [The ensuing discussion of the unitary business is largely taken from J. Hellerstein, State Taxation I, Corporate Income and Franchise Taxes p. 404 et seq. (1983). Used with the consent of the copyright owner and publisher.]

cases, in which segments of an oil producing business conducted in different States were found to be unitary, even though there was no flow of products between the States.[76] Superior Oil Co., which was engaged in producing and selling petroleum and petroleum products in eight States, including California, sought unitary treatment since it had sustained losses in its operations in Arkansas and Louisiana; under the unitary method, it was able to offset the income earned in California by those losses. Superior was not an integrated oil company, since it did no refining or processing (except on a minor scale).[77] It sold its crude petroleum typically at the well site to other oil companies, which refined and processed it for retail distribution and sale. All its crude oil mined in California was sold within the State, and all crude oil mined outside the State was sold outside California. The executive offices of the company were located in Los Angeles, which also handled accounting, purchasing of equipment and supplies, and insurance matters for the entire enterprise.

"The Franchise Tax Board assessed the tax under a separate accounting method, using Superior's net income determined by reference to its operations, receipts, and expenses in California alone. The trial court found:

> California business operations contributed substantially to the out-of-state portion of its business in areas relating to executive policy making, administrative control, coordination of exploration activities, well production and land acquisition, training of technical personnel, specific scientific and technical development and testing laboratories, drilling operations and drilling equipment, manufacturing and sales, accounting, tax returns, personnel, insurance and purchasing.

> The court also found that "Superior's California operations were substantially dependent upon the out-of-state operations" in areas relating to the borrowing of substantial funds on assets located outside of California in order to finance projects within California, the transfer of company funds from sources outside of California to finance projects within California, legal counseling provided by the chief counsel located in Texas and other attorneys in Washington, D.C., the supplying and control of tubular materials from Superior's Texas office and transfer of other materials to California from company sources outside of California, fiscal control from Superior's Texas office for half of the year in question, geophysical technical information and services supplied to California from the company's Texas laboratories, certain land-lease controls supplied by offices in Texas, the transfer of valuable drilling equipment from out-of-state for California operations, the transfer of skilled personnel from out-of-state for purposes of performing services in California, and the supply, on a daily basis, of technical

76. Superior Oil Co. v. Franchise Tax Bd., 60 Cal.2d 406, 386 P.2d 33, 34 Cal. Rptr. 545 (1963). The essential facts were the same in the companion case of Honolulu Oil Corp. v. Franchise Tax Bd., 60 Cal.2d 417, 386 P.2d 40, 34 Cal.Rptr. 552 (1963). For a defense of the holdings in the *Superior Oil* and *Honolulu* cases, see Keesling, "A Current Look at Combined Report and Uniformity in Allocation Practices," 42 J.Tax'n 106 (1975); cf. also Boren, note 326 supra 18 U.C.L.A.L.Rev. at 532–533.

77. See note 312 supra for a definition of the term "integrated oil company." [Footnote references to other portions of the treatise from which this Note is taken have been retained. Eds.]

and other information to the company's California offices in order that executive and policy decisions could be made and over-all control exercised.[78]

"The State argued, awkwardly for a taxing authority that has pressed the unitary business conception to the limit when the result was to produce larger taxes, that 'the employment of an allocation formula is justified only when the various local operations are so essential to the overall operations that it is impossible to make separate accounting computations.'[79] The court rejected this position and held that the business was unitary and that the taxpayer was entitled to formulary apportionment, declaring:

> It is only through a multitude of individual operations which precede and make possible the outflow of petroleum at a producing well that Superior is able to obtain possession of a product which it can market. While the actual recovery and sale of the crude oil are, perhaps, local activities, nevertheless very extensive interstate transactions are theretofore involved in the other individual operations which make such production possible. The evidence here reveals that such essential factors as land acquisition, exploration, technology, testing, availability of equipment and personnel, financing and many others are definitely interstate in character. It must also be considered that each producing well in a particular state is the end product of interstate activities which may involve many other unproductive wells in many other states. Superior's products are thus acquired for the local market only as the result of interstate transactions. * * *"[80]

J. Hellerstein, State Taxation I, Corporate Income and Franchise Taxes ¶ 8.11[3][a][i], pp. 404–06 (1983).

The same result was reached on essentially similar facts in the companion *Honolulu Oil* case. For a case more or less following the approach taken in the California cases, see Phillips v. Sinclair Refining Co., 76 Ga. App. 674, 44 S.E.2d 671 (1947), in which the taxpayer failed in its effort to separate its pipeline department from its business of refining and marketing petroleum products. In Western Contracting Corp. v. State Tax Commission, 18 Utah 2d 23, 414 P.2d 579 (1966), an Iowa based construction company, with its executive offices located in that State, performed profitable stripping operations for a copper company located in Utah, but suffered substantial losses during the taxable year in construction contracts in other States. As in the *Superior Oil* case, the State Tax Commission sought to employ separate accounting, but was rebuffed; the business was found to be unitary and since the court found that the taxing statute "clearly expresses a preference for the statutory formula," it held that the taxpayer was entitled to compute its Utah tax under the formula.

B. *Varying Views of the Scope of the Unitary Business.* The definition of unitary business used by the Oregon Tax Commission is set out in John. I. Haas Inc. v. Ellis, 227 Or. 170, 361 P.2d 820 (1961):

---

78. Superior Oil Co. v. Franchise Tax Bd., note 335 [casebook note 76] supra, 60 Cal.2d at 412–413.

79. Id. 60 Cal.2d at 412.

80. Id. 60 Cal.2d at 415.

* * * The term "unitary business" means that the taxpayer to which it is applied is carrying on a business, the component parts of which are *too closely connected and necessary to each other to justify division or separate consideration as independent units.* * * * Basically, if the operation of a business within Oregon *is dependent on* or *contributes to* the operation of the business outside the state, the entire operation is unitary in character, and the income from Oregon activities will be determined by the apportionment method. [361 P.2d at 822.]

See also the extensive analyses of the unitary business concept by Judge Carlisle B. Roberts of the Oregon Tax Court in Coca–Cola Co. v. Department of Revenue, 5 Or.Tax 405, CCH ¶ 203–033, P–H ¶ 10,650.10 (1974), affirmed 271 Or. 517, 533 P.2d 788 (1975), and by the Ada County District Court of Idaho in United States Steel Corp. v. State Tax Comm'n, CCH ¶ 14–510 (1975).

In Webb Resources, Inc. v. McCoy, 194 Kan. 758, 401 P.2d 879 (1965), the taxpayer carried on business in Kansas and five other Western States exploring and drilling for oil, and producing oil, gas and other liquid hydrocarbons. Its main office was located in Denver, Colorado, from which it managed its business with its officers and staff of geologists and supervisors. It had 84 producing wells in Kansas, and all the oil and gas produced in Kansas was sold to other companies within the State. Here, as in the California cases, it was the taxpayer that sought a unitary apportionment under the statutory formula, but the court sustained the action of the Director of Revenue in using separate accounting. It declared:

It cannot be said that the business of the taxpayer of exploring and drilling for, finding, producing and selling oil and gas is of such a unitary character in its multi-state operations as to require the application of the formula method of income allocation to Kansas. [401 P.2d at 890.]

Despite the differences between the Kansas result and that reached in *Superior Oil,* the judicial verbalizations of the tests of unitary business are not essentially different in the two States. In Crawford Mfg. Co. v. State Comm'n of Revenue and Taxation, 180 Kan. 352, 304 P.2d 504 (1956), the court said:

A multi-state business is unitary when the operations conducted in one state benefit and are benefited by the operations conducted in another state or states. The essential test to be applied is whether or not the operation of the portion of the business within the state is dependent upon or contributory to the operation of the business outside the state. If there is such relationship, the business is unitary. Stated another way, the test is whether a business' various parts are interdependent and of mutual benefit so as to form one business rather than several business entities and not whether the operating experience of the parts is the same in all places. [304 P.2d at 510.]

C. *Wholesaling and Retailing.* "The leading case dealing with the application of unitary apportionment to mercantile businesses is the Supreme Court's decision in *Butler Brothers,* involving a wholesaler that bought goods in one State through its central purchasing division and sold them through its regional distributing houses in other States.[81] The Court sanctioned California's apportionment of the income of the in-state and out-of-state operations, even though the taxpayer's separate accounting analysis disclosed that the San Francisco regional distributing house suffered a loss. The Court did not impugn the taxpayer's cost analysis, which disclosed that the central buying division charged out the goods at cost plus transportation charges. The expense of operating the centralized buying division was allocated among the houses. Admittedly, because of the volume of purchases, 'more favorable prices are obtained than would be obtainable in respect of purchases for the account of any individual house.'[82] The taxpayer contended that the addition of the purchases made for the San Francisco house did not result in more favorable prices than the overall volume purchases would have been without the San Francisco house, and that the apportionment 'resulted in converting a loss of $82,851 into a profit of over $93,500 and that the difference of some $175,000 has either been created out of nothing or has been appropriated by California from other states.'[83]

"The Court rejected this argument, pointing out that there was no justification for singling out the San Francisco branch, rather than any other distributing house, in concluding that it made no contribution to the savings on volume purchasing. If the omission of the California sales would have had no effect on producing the savings, presumably by proceeding in turn from State to State, it could be demonstrated that no State should be credited with quantity purchasing savings. The Court accordingly concluded:

> We cannot say that property, pay roll, and sales are inappropriate ingredients of an apportionment formula. We agree with the Supreme Court of California that these factors may properly be deemed to reflect 'the relative contribution of the activities in the various states to the production of the total unitary income,' so as to allocate to California its just proportion of the profits earned by appellant from this unitary business. And no showing has been made that income unconnected with the unitary business has been used in the formula.[84]

"The Minnesota courts have also handed down a series of decisions holding multistate mercantile businesses unitary. Western Auto Supply, a foreign corporation engaged in the retail and wholesale merchandising of automotive parts and accessories and other merchandise, operated 250 retail stores in thirty States and the District of Columbia, eight of which were located in Minnesota.[85] The company also sold automotive parts and accessories to some 1900 wholesalers in various States, including Minnesota. The general executive and management functions of the taxpayer were handled principally in Kansas City, Missouri; no such activities were carried on in Minnesota. All purchases of goods for both retail and wholesale sales were made by a centralized department of the taxpayer in

81. Butler Bros. v. McColgan, 17 Cal.2d 644, 678, 111 P.2d 334, 341 (1941), aff'd, 315 U.S. 501, 62 S.Ct. 701 (1942).

82. Id. 315 U.S. at 506.

83. Id.

84. Id. 315 U.S. at 508.

85. Western Auto Supply Co. v. Commissioner of Taxation, 245 Minn. 346, 71 N.W.2d 797 (1955).

Kansas City. The goods ordered for both divisions of the business were shipped by manufacturers and jobbers to the taxpayer's warehouses, none of which was located in Minnesota. From the warehouses, the goods were shipped to the company's retail stores, or they were sold and delivered to dealers' stores. Dealer stores displayed signs showing that they carried Western Auto Supply's line.

"The taxpayer sought a separate accounting for its Minnesota income on the ground that 'its business as operated by it is not sufficiently homogeneous to justify applying the multiple formula.'[86] The claim was also made that no part of the wholesale business was conducted in Minnesota, since there was no warehouse in the State from which goods were shipped to Minnesota dealers and the dealers ordered the goods directly from the company's out-of-state warehouses. In holding that the retail and wholesale divisions of the company's business constituted a single unitary business and were properly apportioned on a unitary basis, the court said:

> The taxpayer's contention, however, that none of its wholesale business is conducted in Minnesota, even if this were the fact and it were also the fact that the operating experience of the retail store is not identical or the same everywhere, becomes irrelevant as far as the question of homogeneity or unitary character of the taxpayer's business is concerned.
>
> *   *   *
>
> It is not required, as the taxpayer contends, that the taxpayer have a portion of all parts of its business in the taxing state before the state may apply the formula method of apportionment. Various parts of its business may be carried on exclusively in different states without destroying its unitary nature if these parts are of mutual benefit to one another.[87]

"Declaring that 'the test of whether a business is unitary is whether its various parts are interdependent and of mutual benefit so as to form one business unit rather than separate business entities,' the court concluded:

> The taxpayer, in its analysis of the sources of its profits, treats its business as if it were made up of independent, separate business units. The fact remains that the buying profit and the administrative profit which its business reflects were not created solely by activities in the state of the taxpayer's home office or in states where its warehouses are located. It was created by the operation of the entire business unit, through the coordinated and standardized activity of numerous stores throughout the country which made possible the central purchasing, the central management, the warehousing as carried on, and the advertising methods adopted. The stores in Minnesota contributed in part to make all this possible, and the multiple-formula method simply allocates a fair share of the profit to Minnesota, a share corresponding to the contribution of the taxpayer's Minnesota operation (measured by its Minnesota property, payroll, and sales activity) to the existence and operation of the taxpayer's entire business unit.[88]

86. Id. 245 Minn. at 355.

87. Id. 245 Minn. at 355, 356.

88. Id. 245 Minn. at 358. Accord, Walgreen Co. v. Commissioner of Taxation, 258 Minn. 522, 104 N.W.2d 714 (1960); see also

"In a subsequent case, the Minnesota court sustained the treatment of the income of a corporation that operated six retail stores, three in the Minneapolis–St. Paul area and three in the Chicago area, as a unitary business, even though there was not centralized purchasing for the in-state and out-of-state stores.[89]   Each of the Minnesota stores had its own purchasing office, its own merchandise manager and buyers, and its own buying offices in New York, and there was no central warehousing of goods. The Minnesota Board of Tax Appeals in holding the business unitary had found

> that frequent consultations between the management of the Chicago and Minnesota stores were held concerning fast-moving items and overall policy; that slow-moving merchandise in one store or area would occasionally be shipped to other stores for possible better and faster disposition; that although many lines of merchandise carried in the Chicago stores differed from those carried in the Minnesota stores, the basic lines in men's and women's clothing and in men's shoes were the same; that because of this, price concessions resulted due to volume purchases and there was faster service on reorders and greater advertising allowances by the manufacturer.[90]

"The court relied on these findings to sustain the Commissioner's action on the ground that they

> demonstrated clearly interdependence and mutual benefit between the in-state portion of taxpayer's operation and the out-state portion.

* * *

It was pointed out in Butler Bros. v. McColgan * * * that the benefits of lower prices through volume purchases are enough in and of themselves to render a business unitary for the purposes of allocation.[91]

Commonwealth of Va. v. Lucky Stores, Inc., 217 Va. 121, 225 S.E.2d 870 (1976).

89. Maurice L. Rothschild & Co. v. Commissioner of Taxation, 270 Minn. 245, 133 N.W.2d 524 (1965).

90. Id. 270 Minn. at 250.

91. Id. 270 Minn. at 257–258. The taxpayer cited the Minnesota Skelly Oil case (see ¶ 8.11[2][a] supra) in contending that it operated two separate businesses, "the sale of clothing at retail in *Minnesota* and the sale of clothing at retail in *Illinois*." (Id. 270 Minn. at 258, emphasis in original.) In *Skelly Oil*, the court had held that the company was engaged in two separate businesses, (1) the production and refining of crude oil; and (2) the marketing of oil and oil products, and that since no part of the production (or refining), but only marketing, took place in Minnesota, it was improper to include the company's income from production in the apportionable base of the State tax. In the *Rothschild* case, the court said:

> We held in the *Skelly* case that the determination of the Board of Tax Ap-

peals that part of taxpayer's production income was apportionable to Minnesota had no support in the findings and that the evidence and the record as a whole did not reasonably support such a determination. We therefore held that the board reached sound conclusions in determining that Skelly's production operations and its manufacturing and marketing operations constituted separate businesses. In the instant case, however, the board's finding that taxpayer's business was unitary had support in the evidence of some interdependence of various parts of its business and of benefits flowing between various parts. We conclude that the Skelly case is not applicable here.

Id. This manner of distinguishing the *Skelly* case suggests that the Minnesota court may now be disenchanted with its holding that Skelly's production and refining were not unitary with its business of marketing the products flowing from the production and refining. For the 1982 amendment to the Minnesota statute

"The most recent decision of the Minnesota Supreme Court sustaining a unitary apportionment of a retail business that lacked centralized purchasing was defended on the ground that although 'the various divisions within the Associated Dry Goods are not necessarily dependent upon one another * * * they are certainly contributing to the success of the operation of one another'."[92] J. Hellerstein, State Taxation I, Corporate Income and Franchise Taxes ¶ 8.11[3][a][ii], pp. 408–12 (1983).

D. *Types of Businesses.* A Minnesota case held that the profit from the sale of out-of-state land is not apportionable to the State, because the operations were not part of the taxpayer's "usual" and "normal" business; the land had been held for use as expansion sites of the business. Target Stores, Inc. v. Commissioner of Revenue, 309 Minn. 267, 244 N.W.2d 143 (1976). On the other hand, the highest court of New Hampshire has treated the profit from a sale of out-of-state land, formerly used in the taxpayer's unitary business but for several years held for investment purposes, as apportionable. Johns–Manville Products Corp. v. Commissioner of Revenue Administration, 115 N.H. 428, 343 A.2d 221 (1975), appeal dismissed 423 U.S. 1069, 96 S.Ct. 851 (1976); cf. Commonwealth v. Emhart Corp., 443 Pa. 397, 278 A.2d 916, appeal dismissed 404 U.S. 981, 92 S.Ct. 451 (1971). However, a securities portfolio held by an investment company, which owned a single piece of real estate in Pennsylvania, was determined not to be part of the unitary business in the State for Pennsylvania capital stock tax apportionment purposes. Commonwealth v. Kirby Estates, Inc., 432 Pa. 103, 246 A.2d 120 (1968).

E. *The Pennsylvania "Multiform Business" Doctrine.* Under the "multiform business doctrine" enunciated by the Pennsylvania Supreme Court in Commonwealth v. Columbia Gas & Electric Corp., 336 Pa. 209, 8

which defines "unitary business," see note 356 [casebook note 92] infra.

92. See Associated Dry Goods Corp. v. Commissioner of Taxation, [Minn.Tax Ct., 1974, CCH ¶ 200–675, P–H ¶ 13,164, aff'd, 306 Minn. 532, 235 N.W.2d 821 (1975), cert. denied 425 U.S. 999, 96 S.Ct. 2216 (1976).] The Tax Court utilized the test of unitary business as enunciated by the Minnesota Supreme Court in the *Western Auto Supply* case, note 349 [casebook note 85] supra. In the *Associated Dry Goods* case, the Tax Court found that each of the taxpayer's fifteen retail divisions (each division operated one or more stores) "operates as an autonomous unit with local management in complete charge of day-to-day operations," (subject to the overall control of the taxpayer's central office). All the divisions had the benefit of a large market research division in the company's New York office, technical advice concerning other operating matters and centralized financing. It was those features of the enterprises that the Tax Court apparently relied on in holding that the various divisions were unitary because they are "contributing to the suc-cess of the operation of one another." The decision of the Minnesota Tax Court was affirmed by an equally divided State supreme court.

The Minnesota statute was amended in 1982 so as to incorporate directly into the statute the broad California view of the meaning of a unitary business. The provision is as follows:

The term "unitary business" shall mean a number of business activities or operations which are of mutual benefit, dependent upon, or contributory to one another, individually or as a group. Unity shall be presumed whenever there is unity of ownership, operation, and use, evidenced by centralized management or executive force, centralized purchasing, advertising, accounting, or other controlled interaction. Unity of ownership will not be deemed to exist unless the corporation owns more than 50 percent of the voting stock of the other corporation.

Minn.Stat., Subd. D, § 290.17 (1981 Supp.), as amended, CCH ¶ 94–067.

A.2d 404 (1939), distinct or disparate operations of a corporation conducted outside the taxing State are excluded from the unitary apportionment. In Commonwealth v. Advance–Wilson Industries, Inc., 456 Pa. 200, 317 A.2d 642 (1974), the doctrine was applied to a foreign corporation, domiciled in New York, which, in Pennsylvania, manufactured and sold ceramic tiles used in the building trade, through its Keystone Division; the company's certificate of authority to do business in the State permitted it to manufacture and deal in building materials. The taxpayer also had an Electrolyzing Division which was engaged in applying an electrolyzing process to worn machines and machine parts, which was carried on in a number of States other than Pennsylvania. Neither division was separately incorporated. The court, having found that there was no flow of money between the two divisions, no sales or purchases and no accounting transactions or the like between the divisions, held that the Electrolyzing Division was not part of the taxpayer's unitary business carried on in Pennsylvania, saying, per Cohen, J.:

> The Commonwealth first argues that the businesses conducted by appellee were not independent because certain administrative and other functions were performed for the two divisions by the home office, and profits from each division were remitted to the home office of the corporation. However, the following excerpts from our opinion in Commonwealth v. ACF Industries, Inc., supra [441 Pa. 129, 271 A.2d 273 (1970)], dispose of this contention: "[W]e must focus upon the relationship between the Pennsylvania activity and the outside one, not the common relationships between these and the central corporate structure. Only if the impact of the latter on the operating units or activities is so pervasive as to negate any claim that they function independently from each other do we deny exclusion in this context." 441 Pa. at 142.

> "[C]ontributions of unrelated activities to the corporate whole do not vitiate a claim for exclusion. * * * it is the interrelationship between the activities themselves which is the critical factor." 411 Pa. at 139. "[P]erformance by the corporate whole of policy, administrative, research and similar functions for otherwise independently operating units does not vitiate multiformity any more than does their common but independent contribution of benefits to the corporate whole." 441 Pa. at 142. "[T]he factors relied upon to characterize the enterprise as unitary are precisely those things which do not involve the interrelationship between operating divisions but rather the interrelationship between each division and the corporate superstructure—factors which would likely appear in every case, no matter how independently each division operated from the other." 441 Pa. at 140. [456 Pa. at 203–04.]

See also Logan Clay Products Co. v. Commonwealth, 11 Pa.Cmwlth.Ct. 629, 315 A.2d 346 (1974).

Compare the multiform business doctrine with the basic operations interdependence test of unitary business, discussed at p. 568 infra. In the *ACF Industries* case, supra, the court referred to J. Hellerstein, "Recent Developments in State Tax Apportionment and the Circumscription of Unitary

Business," 21 Nat.Tax J. 487 (1968), in which the operational interdependence doctrine is articulated, and commented:

> While we are not prepared at this stage (and need not in this case) to go as far as Hellerstein in permitting exclusion of a business activity outside the state identical to one carried on inside the state where each operates independently of the other (as he says appears in the case of Superior Oil Co. v. Franchise Tax Board, 34 Cal.Repr. 545, 386 P.2d 33 (1963) cited in the article), we otherwise feel his analysis is a valid one. We note, also, that in the *Superior Oil* case, non-California assets were used to obtain funds to support California operations and non-California operating funds were transferred to California to finance projects there. To this extent we have customarily found an interdependence of business activities and have not considered such factors simply additional "centralized operations" properly carried out by the corporate executive office (as we agree are the legal, accounting and research activities) without infringing on otherwise multiform activities. Because of this feature of the *Superior Oil* case we leave open the principle suggested by Hellerstein insofar as it would apply to a company doing outside of Pennsylvania what it does in Pennsylvania but in a truly independent way. [441 Pa. at 143.]

F. *The Scope of the Unitary Business as Defined by the Supreme Court in Dealing With Constitutional Challenges to Apportionment.* In the early 1980's, the Supreme Court handed down five significant decisions bearing on the scope of the unitary business. Mobil Oil Corp. v. Commissioner of Taxes, 445 U.S. 425, 100 S.Ct. 1223 (1980), which involved the apportionment of foreign source dividends is printed at p. 610 infra. Exxon Corp. v. Wisconsin Dept. of Revenue, 447 U.S. 207, 100 S.Ct. 2109 (1980), Asarco Inc. v. Idaho State Tax Com'n, 458 U.S. 307, 102 S.Ct. 3103 (1982) and F.W. Woolworth Co. v. Taxation and Revenue Dep't, 458 U.S. 354, 102 S.Ct. 3128 (1982) are treated in this section. Container Corp. of America v. Franchise Tax Bd., 463 U.S. 159, 103 S.Ct. 2933 (1983), which deals with the apportionment of income of a combined group of corporations on a worldwide basis, is printed at p. 578 infra.

The Commerce and Due Process Clauses forbid the State from including in its apportionable tax base income generated by out-of-state activities with which it lacks a minimum connection. If, however, a taxpayer is conducting a unitary business partly within and partly without a State, the State has the requisite constitutional connection with the out-of-state activities to justify its taxing an apportioned share of the income generated by the in-state and out-of-state activities. As the Supreme Court declared in *Mobil,* "the linchpin of apportionability in the field of state income taxation is the unitary business principle." 445 U.S. at 439, 100 S.Ct. at 1232. The unitary business principle therefore has constitutional content insofar as it provides the predicate for the minimum connection the State must have with the income that it seeks to include in its apportionable tax base.

In Exxon Corp. v. Wisconsin Dep't of Revenue, supra, Exxon,[93] the nation's largest oil company, was engaged in exploration, production, refining, and marketing of petroleum and petroleum products throughout the United States and foreign countries. The only activity that Exxon carried on in Wisconsin, however, was the marketing of petroleum and related products. Exxon challenged the constitutionality of Wisconsin's application of its three-factor apportionment formula to all of the company's operating income. It claimed that it was carrying on only a marketing business in Wisconsin and that the State therefore had no basis for including income from exploration, production, and refining in its apportionable tax base. It also claimed that it had demonstrated by separate accounting the precise sources of its income and that the apportionment formula produced a grossly distorted result.

With respect to this contention, the Supreme Court declared:

> The Wisconsin Supreme Court rejected [Exxon's] contention that its separate functional accounting proved that its exploration and production income was earned totally outside Wisconsin, noting that "the idea of separate functional accounting seems to be incompatible with the 'very essence of formulary apportionment, namely, that where there are integrated, interdependent steps in the economic process carried on by a business enterprise, there is no logical or viable method for accurately separating out the profit attributable to one step in the economic process from other steps.'" Id., at 726, 281 N.W.2d, at 109, quoting Hellerstein, State and Local Taxation 400 (3d ed. 1969). The court concluded that the State was acting within constitutional limitations despite [Exxon's] evidence based on separate functional accounting. [447 U.S. at 218–19.]

In holding that Exxon was carrying on a unitary business from wellhead to gas pump—rather than simply a marketing business—in the State, the Supreme Court stressed a number of factors in support of its conclusion. It noted that Exxon was a corporate entity with centralized management, supervision of the Wisconsin marketing district was exercised from regional and national headquarters. Centralized corporate staff departments provided a wide range of services for the entire corporation. Moreover, although Exxon's Wisconsin activities were limited to marketing, the Court pointed out that these activities were interdependent with the company's integrated operations at the national level, and that the whole derived benefit from the sum of the parts, including marketing. In particular, Exxon employed centralized purchasing to enhance companywide profits, intradepartmental coordination to achieve operating efficiencies, nationwide distribution and uniform brand names, advertising, credit cards, and packaging to facilitate sales, and a host of other important links between its three principal operating departments to provide "an assured supply of raw materials[,] * * * stable outlet[s] for products[,] * * * and greater profit stability," for the entire enterprise. 447 U.S. at 225, 100 S.Ct. at 2121 (quoting the record testimony of an Exxon vice president). In

---

93. Exxon was actually the legal successor to Humble Oil & Refining Co., the original taxpayer during the years at issue, 1965–68. We will follow the Supreme Court's opinion in referring to the taxpayer by its present name.

the Court's view, Exxon was a "highly integrated business which benefits from an umbrella of centralized management and controlled interaction." Id. at 224.

Exxon was also unsuccessful in South Carolina in seeking to separate for apportionment purposes its out-of-state exploration and production operations from its in-state refining and marketing. Exxon Corp. v. South Carolina Tax Commission, 273 S.C. 594, 258 S.E.2d 93 (1979), appeal dismissed for want of a substantial Federal question, 447 U.S. 917, 100 S.Ct. 3005 (1980).

ASARCO INC. v. IDAHO STATE TAX COMMISSION *

Supreme Court of the United States, 1982.
458 U.S. 307, 102 S.Ct. 3103.

JUSTICE POWELL delivered the opinion of the Court.

The question is whether the State of Idaho constitutionally may include within the taxable income of a nondomiciliary parent corporation doing some business in Idaho a portion of intangible income—such as dividend and interest payments, as well as capital gains from the sale of stock—that the parent receives from subsidiary corporations having no other connection with the State.

I

This case involves corporate income taxes that appellee Idaho sought to levy on appellant ASARCO Inc. for the years 1968, 1969, and 1970. ASARCO is a corporation that mines, smelts, and refines in various states nonferrous metals such as copper, gold, silver, lead, and zinc. It is incorporated in New Jersey and maintains its headquarters and commercial domicile in New York. ASARCO's primary Idaho business is the operation of a silver mine. It also mines and sells other metals and operates the administrative office of its northwest mining division in Idaho. According to the State's tax calculations, approximately 2.5% of ASARCO's total business activities take place in Idaho. App. 59, 67, and 75.

During the years in question, ASARCO received three types of intangible income of relevance to this suit.[1] First, it collected dividends from five corporations in which it owned major interests: M.I.M. Holdings, Ltd.; General Cable Corp.; Revere Copper and Brass, Inc.; ASARCO Mexicana, S.A.; and Southern Peru Copper Corp.[2] Second,

---

* [Some footnotes have been omitted.]

1. ASARCO also received other intangible income, but the proper tax treatment of that income is not at issue in this case.

2. M.I.M. Holdings, Ltd. is a publicly owned corporation engaged in the mining, milling, smelting, and refining of nonferrous metals in Australia and England. ASARCO owned about 53% of M.I.M.'s stock during the period in question. General Cable Corp. and Revere Copper and Brass, Inc. are publicly owned companies that respectively fabricate cables and manufacture copper wares. ASARCO owned about 34% of the stock of each. ASARCO Mexicana, S.A., engages in Mexico in the same general line of business as does ASARCO in the United States. ASARCO owned 49% of Mexicana. Southern Peru Copper Corp. mines and smelts copper in

ASARCO received interest income from three sources: from Revere's convertible debentures; from a note received in connection with a prior sale of Mexicana stock; and from a note received in connection with a sale of General Cable Stock. Third, ASARCO realized capital gains from the sale of General Cable and M.I.M. stock.

In 1965, Idaho adopted its version of the Uniform Division of Income for Tax Purposes Act (UDITPA). See Idaho Code § 63–3027 (1976 and 1981 Supp.); 7A Uniform Laws Annotated 91–1978. Under this statute, Idaho classifies corporate income from intangible property as either "business" or "nonbusiness" income. "Business" income is defined to include income from intangible property when "acquisition, management, or disposition [of the property] constitute[s] integral or necessary parts of the taxpayers' trade or business operations." Idaho apportions such "business" income according to a three-factor formula and includes this apportioned share of "business" income in the taxpayer's taxable Idaho income. "Nonbusiness" income, on the other hand, is defined as "all income other than business income." Idaho Code § 63–3027(a)(4) (Supp.1981). Idaho allocates intangible "nonbusiness" income entirely to the State of the corporation's commercial domicile instead of apportioning it among the States in which a corporate taxpayer owns property or carries on business.

Idaho is a member of the Multistate Tax Compact, an interstate taxation agreement concerning state taxation of multistate businesses. * * *

In 1971, the Multistate Tax Commission audited ASARCO's tax returns for the years in question on behalf of six States, including Idaho. The auditor recommended adjusting ASARCO's tax computations in several respects. As accepted by the Idaho State Tax Commission and as relevant to the present dispute, the auditor first "unitized"—or treated as one single corporation—ASARCO and six of its *wholly* owned subsidiaries.[8] * * * The propriety of this treatment of the six wholly owned subsidiaries is not an issue before us.

The auditor found the situation to differ with respect to ASARCO's interest in M.I.M., General Cable, Revere, Mexicana, and Southern Peru. This judgment planted the seed of the current dispute. As to these five companies, the auditor determined that the links with ASARCO were not sufficient to justify unitary treatment. Nonetheless, he found that ASARCO's receipt of dividends from each of these did constitute "business" income to ASARCO. See n. 4, supra. The auditor similarly classified the interest and capital gains income at issue in this case. These categories of income also were added in ASARCO's

Peru. ASARCO owned about 51.5% of Southern Peru during the time at issue.

8. Idaho law provides that "two * * * or more corporations the voting stock of which is more than fifty percent * * * owned directly or indirectly by a common owner or owners may, when necessary to accurately reflect income, be considered a single corporation." Idaho Code § 63–3027(s) (Supp.1981).

* * *

total income to be apportioned among the various States in which ASARCO was subjected to an income tax.

The Idaho State Tax Commission * * * upheld the auditor's conclusion that the dividends presently at issue were properly treated as apportionable "business" income. It consequently assessed tax deficiencies against ASARCO of $92,471.88 for 1968, $111,292.44 for 1969, and $121,750.76 for 1970, plus interest.

On ASARCO's petition for review, the state district court * * * overruled the Commission's determination that the disputed dividends, interest, and capital gains constituted "business" income, on the reasoning that this income did not come from property or activities that were "an integral part of [ASARCO's] trade or business." Idaho Code § 63–3027(a)(1) (Supp.1981). In the court's view, "if the dividend income from other corporations is an integral part of the business of [ASARCO] * * * they should be unitized and all matters considered and [,] if they are not [,] * * * the income is not business income but is [nonapportionable] non business income." App. to Juris. Statement 37.

The Commission, but not ASARCO, appealed to the Idaho Supreme Court. That court held that the trial court had erred by excluding from "business" income ASARCO's receipt of dividends, interest, and capital gains as a result of its owning stock in the five corporations. American Smelting and Refining Co. v. Idaho State Tax Comm'n, 99 Idaho 924, 935–937, 592 P.2d 39, 50–52 (1979). In response to ASARCO's constitutional arguments, the court decided that this tax treatment withstood attack under the Commerce and Due Process Clauses. We vacated and remanded the case for reconsideration in light of our decision in Mobil Oil Corp. v. Commissioner of Taxes of Vermont, 445 U.S. 425 (1980). ASARCO Inc. v. Idaho Tax Comm'n, 445 U.S. 939 (1980). The Idaho Supreme Court reinstated its previous opinion in a brief *per curiam* order on March 4, 1981. We noted probable jurisdiction, ___ U.S. ___ (1981), and we now reverse.

II

* * *

Our application of this general principle that "A state may not tax value earned outside its borders" [11] in this case is guided by two of our recent decisions. In Mobil Oil Corp. v. Commissioner of Taxes of Vermont, [p. 610 infra], * * * our analysis * * * began with the observation that Mobil's principal dividend payors were part of Mobil's integrated petroleum business. Although Mobil was "unwilling to concede the legal conclusion" that activities by these dividend payors formed part of Mobil's " 'unitary business,' " it "offered no evidence that would undermine the conclusion that most, if not all, of its subsidiaries and affiliates contribute[d] to [Mobil's] worldwide petroleum enterprise." 445 U.S., at 435.

11. See Rudolph, State Taxation of Interstate Business: The Unitary Business Concept and Affiliated Corporate Groups, 25 Tax L.Rev. 171, 181 (1970).

The Court next stated that due process limitations on Vermont's attempted tax would be satisfied if there were "a 'minimal connection' between the interstate activities and the taxing State, and a rational relationship between the income attributed to the State and the intrastate values of the enterprise." * * * And we said that these limitations would not be contravened by state apportionment and taxation of income that was determined by geographic accounting to have arisen from a different State "so long as the intrastate and extrastate activities formed part of *a single unitary business.*" 445 U.S., at 438 (emphasis added).

The *Mobil* Court explicated the limiting "unitary business" principle by observing that geographic accounting, in purporting to isolate income received in various States, "may fail to account for contributions to income resulting from functional integration, centralization of management, and economies of scale." Ibid. * * *

> "[Mobil] has made no effort to demonstrate that the foreign operations of its subsidiaries and affiliates are distinct in any business or economic sense from its petroleum sales activities in Vermont. Indeed, all indications in the record are to the contrary, since it appears that these foreign activities are part of [Mobil's] integrated petroleum enterprise. In the absence of any proof of *discrete business enterprise,* Vermont was entitled to conclude that the dividend income's foreign source did not destroy the requisite nexus with in-state activities." Id., at 439–440 (emphasis added and footnote omitted).

We consequently rejected Mobil's constitutional challenge to Vermont's tax. * * *

We soon had occasion to reiterate these principles. Three months after *Mobil,* we decided Exxon Corp. v. Wisconsin Dept. of Revenue, 447 U.S. 207 (1980). * * *

Examining the facts, the Court found that Exxon was "a highly integrated business which benefits from an umbrella of centralized management and controlled interaction." Id., at 224. We rejected the company's protest because "[w]e agree[d] with the Wisconsin Supreme Court that Exxon [was] such a unitary business and that Exxon has not carried its burden of showing that its functional departments are 'discrete business enterprises' * * *." Ibid.[14]

14. The unitary business principle applied in *Mobil* and *Exxon* is not new. It has been a familiar concept in our tax cases for over 60 years. See United States Steel Corp. v. Multistate Tax Commission, 434 U.S. 452, 473 n. 25, 474 n. 26 (1978); General Motors Corp. v. Washington, 377 U.S. 436, 439 (1964); Northwestern States Portland Cement Co. v. Minnesota, 358 U.S. 450, 460 (1959); Butler Bros. v. McColgan, 315 U.S. 501, 508 (1942); Ford Motor Co. v. Beauchamp, 308 U.S. 331, 336 (1939); Norfolk & Western R. Co. v. North Carolina, 297 U.S. 682, 684 (1936); Hans Rees' Sons v. North Carolina, 283 U.S. 123, 132–133 (1931); Bass, Ratcliff & Gretton, Ltd. v. State Tax Commission, 266 U.S. 271, 282 (1924). Cf. Burnet v. Aluminum Goods Mfg. Co., 287 U.S. 544, 550 (1933); Underwood Typewriter Co. v. Chamberlain, 254 U.S. 113, 120–121 (1920); Wallace v. Hines, 253 U.S. 66, 69 (1920); Fargo v. Hart, 193 U.S. 490, 499–500 (1904); Adams Express Co. v. Ohio, 166 U.S. 185, 219, 222, 223–224 (1897).

A review of our cases before *Mobil* made plain that "[f]ormulary apportionment,

III

In this case, ASARCO claims that it has succeeded, where the taxpayers in *Mobil* and *Exxon* failed, in proving that the dividend payors at issue are not part of its unitary business, but rather are "discrete business enterprises." 447 U.S., at 224. We must test this contention on the record before us.

A

The closest question is posed by ASARCO's receipt of dividends from Southern Peru. ASARCO is one of Southern Peru's four shareholders, holding 51.5% of its stock.[15] Southern Peru produces smelted but unrefined "blister copper" in Peru, and sells 20–30% of its output to the Southern Peru Copper Sales Corp.[16] The remainder of Southern Peru's output is sold under contracts to its shareholders in proportion to their ownership interests. Southern Peru sold about 35% of its output to ASARCO, App. 89, at prices determined by reference to average representative trade prices quoted in a trade publication and over which the parties had no control.[17] App. 125–126; 99 Idaho, at 920, 592 P.2d, at 43.

ASARCO's majority interest, if asserted, could enable it to control the management of Southern Peru. The Idaho State Tax Commission, however, found that Southern Peru's "remaining three shareholders, owning the remainder of the stock, refuse[d] to participate in [Southern Peru] unless assured that they would have a way to assure that management would not be completely dominated by ASARCO." App. to Juris. Statement 55. Consequently ASARCO entered a manage-

which takes into account the entire business income of a multistate business in determining the income taxable by a particular state, is constitutionally permissible only in the case of a unitary business." Rudolph State Taxation of Interstate Business: The Unitary Business Concept and Affiliated Corporate Groups, 25 Tax L.Rev. 171, 183–184 (1970).

15. The other shareholders are Phelps Dodge, 16%; Newmont Mining, 10.25%; and Cerro Copper, 22.25%. App. 86. Either these large companies or their parents were traded on the New York Stock Exchange at the time in question.

16. Southern Peru Copper Sales Corporation in turn sells the copper to European customers. These European sales are handled in this manner to preserve Southern Peru's favorable federal tax status as a Western Hemisphere Trading Corporation.

Southern Peru Copper Sales Corporation's stock is owned in the same manner as is Southern Peru's. Unlike Southern Peru, however, Southern Peru Copper Sales Corporation has no employees of its own. Sales are generally transacted by

ASARCO's New York office, for which that office earns a sales commission. App. 86.

17. These sales ranged between $44 and $65 million for the years in question. App. 89. There was evidence that ASARCO could replace this output contact "[w]ithin a short time" if it were lost, and that loss of ASARCO's ownership in Southern Peru would not cause the loss of the output contract. Id., at 128.

Southern Peru has a "staff that you'd expect a major corporation to have." Id., at 122. ASARCO provided Southern Peru with purchasing service outside of Peru, traffic service for its exports and imports outside of Peru, and preparation service for its United States tax return. Id., at 123–124. The contract for ASARCO's purchasing services provided for payment of this service on the basis of a fixed fee plus a commission based on the dollar volume of purchases. Id., at 124. ASARCO received separate "negotiated fair fee[s]" for its tax and traffic services. Ibid. Southern Peru has its own purchasing, traffic, and tax departments in Peru. Id., at 123.

ment agreement giving it the right to appoint six of Southern Peru's 13 directors. The other three shareholders also appointed six directors. Ibid. The thirteenth and final director is appointed by the joint action of either the shareholders or the first 12 directors. Ibid.; App. 121. Southern Peru's by-laws provide that eight votes are required to pass any resolution, App. 121, and its articles and by-laws can be changed only by unanimous consent of the four stockholders.

In its unreported opinion, the state trial court concluded that this management contract "insures that [ASARCO] will not be able to control [Southern Peru]." App. to Juris. Statement 43. It likewise found that Southern Peru "operates independently of [ASARCO]." Id., at 42. The court reached this conclusion after hearing testimony that ASARCO did not "control Southern Peru in any sense of that term," App. 121, and that Southern Peru did not "seek direction or approval from ASARCO on major decisions." Id., at 124. Idaho does not dispute any of these facts. In view of the findings and the undisputed facts, we conclude that ASARCO's Idaho silver mining and Southern Peru's autonomous business are insufficiently connected to permit the two companies to be classified as a unitary business.

B

Under the principles of our decisions, the relationship of each of the other four subsidiaries to ASARCO falls far short of bringing any of them within its unitary business. M.I.M. Holdings engages in the mining, milling, smelting, and refining of copper, lead, zinc, and silver in Australia. The company also operates a lead and zinc refinery in England. During the years in question M.I.M. sold only about 1% of its output to ASARCO, for sums in the range of $0.2 to $2.2 million. App. 43–47. It appears that these sales were on the open market at prevailing market rates. ASARCO owns 52.7% of M.I.M.'s stock, and the rest is widely held. Although ASARCO has the control potential to manage M.I.M., no claim is made that it has done so.[18] As an ASARCO executive explained, it never even elected a member of M.I.M.'s board:

> "This company has been very successful in staffing the corporation with Australian people and [they have] been able to run this company by themselves and, therefore, in consequence of the nationalistic feeling which develops in most of such developing countries we have not exercised any right we might have to elect a director to the board of the company." App. 132.

In addition to foregoing its right to elect directors, ASARCO similarly has taken no part in the selection of M.I.M.'s officers—a function of the board of directors. Nor do the two companies have any common directors or officers. Id., at 34, 40. The state trial court found that M.I.M. "operates entirely independently of and has minimal contact with" ASARCO. App. to Juris. Statement 43. As the business relation also is nominal, it is clear that M.I.M. is merely an investment.

---

18. M.I.M. did use an ASARCO melting furnace patent for which it pays a price "the same that would be paid by any other company using it." App. 133.

See, e.g., Keesling and Warren, The Unitary Concept in the Allocation of Income, 12 Hastings L.Rev. 42, 52–53 (1960).

General Cable and Revere Copper, large publicly owned companies, fabricate metal products. Both are ASARCO customers.[19] But ASARCO held only minority interests, owning approximately 34% of the outstanding common shares of each. The remaining shares—listed on the New York Stock Exchange—are widely held. App. 135. The two companies occupy parallel positions with respect to ASARCO as a result of a 1961 Department of Justice antitrust suit against ASARCO. The suit was based on ASARCO's interests in each. In 1967, ASARCO consented to a decree that prohibited it from maintaining common officers in these companies, voting its stock in them, selling the companies copper at prices below those quoted to their competition, and from acquiring stock in any other copper fabricator. App. 96. Neither Revere's nor General Cable's management seeks direction or approval from ASARCO on operational or other management decisions.[20] Id., at 137.

Mexicana mines and smelts lead and copper in Mexico. Originally it was a wholly owned subsidiary of ASARCO, but a change in Mexican law required ASARCO to divest itself of 51% of Mexicana's stock in 1965. This stock is now publicly held by Mexican nationals. The record does not reveal whether ASARCO and Mexicana have any common directors. The state trial court found, however, that Mexicana "operates independently of [ASARCO]," App. to Juris. Statement 43, and the Idaho Supreme Court stated that "Mexicana does not seek approval from ASARCO concerning major policy decisions. ＊ ＊ ＊" 99 Idaho, at 929, 592 P.2d, at 44.[21]

---

19. For the years in question, Revere's purchases averaged 3–4% of ASARCO's sales and totalled from $17 to $29 million. App. 27. Revere in turn sold ASARCO from 1 to 2% of its total output, which totalled $4–$6 million. Id., at 43–47. General Cable's purchases accounted for approximately 6% of ASARCO's sales and ranged from $31 to $47 million. Id., at 27. ASARCO's purchases from General Cable averaged .1% of General Cable's total sales and ranged between $.3 and $.5 million. Id., at 43–47.

20. Both Revere and General Cable utilized ASARCO's stock transfer department on a contract basis, and Revere licensed one patent from ASARCO for a "fair price." Id., at 136.

In 1970, ASARCO was compelled, apparently by the Department of Justice, to divest itself of all its General Cable stock. App. 95.

21. ASARCO sold Mexicana none of its output in 1968 and insignificant amounts (totalling $24,169 and $14,902) in 1969 and 1970. App. 27. Mexicana apparently did

not sell ASARCO any of its output during the time in question. Id., 43–47. For a commission, ASARCO does act as a contract sales agent for Mexicana in the United States. App. 131. This contract would continue if ASARCO lost its investment interest in Mexicana. Ibid. ASARCO also provides technical services to Mexicana for a fee. Id., at 130; 99 Idaho, at 929, 592 P.2d, at 44.

The dissent's perception of some of the facts differs substantially from the records. It speculates that ASARCO's unitary business experience "must" have aided ASARCO's stock investments, post, at 6, despite the undisputed trial court finding that ASARCO's stock investments were "not integral to nor a necessary part of [ASARCO's] business operation ＊ ＊ ＊." App. to Juris. Statement 44. See also id., at 43. It maintains that—"[f]or all we know"—ASARCO's stock investments were *interim* uses of idle funds "accumulated for the future operation of [ASARCO's] own primary business." Post, at 7. The trial court, however, found that ASARCO "has

C

Idaho does not dispute the foregoing facts. Neither does it question that a unitary business relationship between ASARCO and these subsidiaries is a necessary prerequisite to its taxation of the dividends at issue. E.g., Brief for Appellee 10 ("When income is earned from activities which are part of a unitary business conducted in several states, then the requirement that the income bear relation to the benefits and privileges conferred by the several states has been met."). See also Tr. of Oral Arg. 25 ("[W]hen intangible assets such as, for example, shares of stock, are found to be a part of a taxpayer's own unitary business, * * * there is no logical or constitutional reason why the income from those same intangibles should be treated any differently than any other business income that that taxpayer might earn."). Rather the State urges that we expand the concept of a "unitary business" to cover the facts of this case.

Idaho's proposal is that corporate *purpose* should define unitary business. It argues that intangible income should be considered a part of a unitary business if the intangible property (the shares of stock) is "acquired, managed or disposed of for purposes relating or contributing to the taxpayer's business." Brief for Appellee 4. See also Tr. of Oral Arg. 25 (urging that income from intangible property be considered part of a unitary business when the intangibles contribute to or relate to or are in some way in furtherance of the taxpayer's own trade or business). Idaho asserts that "[i]t is this integration—i.e., between the business use of the intangible asset (the shares of stock) and ASARCO's mining, smelting, and refining business—which makes the income part of the unitary business." Brief for Appellee 4.

This definition of unitary business would destroy the concept. The business of a corporation requires that it earn money to continue operations and to provide a return on its invested capital. Consequently *all* of its operations, including any investment made, in some sense can be said to be "for purposes related to or contributing to the [corporation's] business." When pressed to its logical limit, this conception of the "unitary business" limitation becomes no limitation at all. When less ambitious interpretations are employed, the result is simply arbitrary.[22]

never been required to utilize its stock as security for borrowing of working capital, acquiring stock or securities in other companies or to support any bond issues." App. to Juris. Statement 41. Moreover, ASARCO was found to have "sufficient cash flow from mining to provide operating capital for all mining operations without reliance upon cash flow from * * * income from intangibles." Ibid.

The dissent also describes the five companies as "captive suppliers and customers. * * *" Post, at 12. This description is at odds with the undisputed facts. See supra, at 13–17.

22. Cf. Keesling and Warren, California's Uniform Division of Income for Tax Purposes Act, pt. 1, 15 U.C.L.A.L.Rev. 156, 172 (1967).

* * *

Justice O'Connor's dissent views the Court's decision as "prohibiting apportioned taxation of investment income by non-domiciliary states". Post, at 15, et seq. This reflects a serious misunderstanding of our decision today and the cases on which

We cannot accept, consistently with recognized due process standards, a definition of "unitary business" that would permit nondomiciliary States to apportion and tax dividends "[w]here the business activities of the dividend payor have nothing to do with the activities of the recipient in the taxing State. ＊ ＊ ＊"[23] Mobil Oil Corp. v. Commissioner of Taxes of Vermont, 445 U.S., at 442. In such a situation, it is not true that "the state has given anything for which it can ask return." Wisconsin v. J.C. Penney Co., 311 U.S., at 444.

Justice Holmes stated long ago that "the possession of bonds secured by mortgages of lands in other States, or of a land-grant in another State of other property that adds to the riches of the corporation but does not affect the [taxing State's] part of the [business] is not sufficient ground for the increase of the tax—whatever it may be ＊ ＊ ＊." Wallace v. Hines, 253 U.S. 66, 69–70 (1920). In this case, it is plain that the five dividend-paying subsidiaries "add to the riches" of ASARCO. But it is also true that they are "discrete business enterprises" that—in "any business or economic sense"—have "nothing to do with the activities" of ASARCO in Idaho. Mobil, supra, at 439–442. Therefore there is no "rational relationship between the [ASARCO dividend] income attributed to the State and the intrastate values of the enterprise. Moorman Mfg. Co. v. Bair, 437 U.S. 267, 272–273 (1978)." Mobil, supra, at 437. Idaho's attempt to tax a portion of these dividends can be viewed as "a mere effort to reach profits earned elsewhere under the guise of legitimate taxation." Bass, Ratcliff & Gretton, Ltd. v. State Tax Commission, 266 U.S., at 283. The Due Process Clause bars such an effort to levy upon income that is not properly "within the reach of [Idaho's] taxing power." Connecticut General Life Ins. Co. v. Johnson, 303 U.S., at 80.[24]

we rely. The case we follow primarily is *Mobil.* It sustained the taxation of investment income after applying enunciated principles carefully to the facts of the case. In this case we have applied the same principles but have reached a different result because the facts differ in critical respects. As we have said elsewhere, the application of the unitary-business principle requires in each case a careful examination both of the way in which the corporate enterprise is structured and operates, and of the relationship with the taxing state.

23. The dissent, argues that our reliance on the Due Process Clause is inappropriate. It also says that our holding that Idaho has exceeded its jurisdiction to tax somehow "strip[s] Congress of the authority" to authorize or regulate state taxation. Post, at 2. See also id., at 20–21, 23. In analyzing the validity of Idaho's tax, we follow long-established precedent in relying on the Due Process Clause of the Fourteenth Amendment. See, e.g., *Exxon,* 447

U.S., at 219, 221–225, 226, 227; *Mobil,* 445 U.S., at 436–442; Butler Bros. v. McColgan, 315 U.S. 501, 507, 508 (1942); Underwood Typewriter Co. v. Chamberlain, 254 U.S. 113, 120–121 (1920). In view of our decision on due process, it is unnecessary to address petitioner's Commerce Clause argument. In any event, it is elementary that the "states ＊ ＊ ＊ are subject to limitations on their taxing powers that do not apply to the federal government." F.W. Woolworth Co. v. Taxation & Revenue Dept., — U.S. —, — (1982). Cf. Insurance Corp. of Ireland, Ltd. v. Compagnie Des Bauxites de Guinee, — U.S. —, — (1982) (slip op. at 4) (POWELL, J., concurring). The question of federal authority to legislate in this area—whether to lay taxes or to delegate such power—is not presented in this case, and we imply no view as to it.

24. The dissenting opinion reflects profound—though unexpressed—dissatisfaction with the unitary business principle, even though it was firmly established by

IV

In addition to the disputed dividend income, Idaho also has sought to tax certain ASARCO interest and capital gains income. The interest income arose from a note ASARCO received from its sale of Mexicana stock and from a Revere convertible debenture, as well as in connection with ASARCO's 1970 disposition of its General Cable stock. See n. 21, supra. The General Cable stock sale also generated capital gains for ASARCO, as did ASARCO's sale of a portion of its stock in M.I.M.

Idaho and ASARCO agree that interest and capital gains income derived from these companies should be treated in the same manner as the dividend income. Brief for Appellant 27; Brief for Appellee 21. Cf. 99 Idaho, at 937, 592 P.2d, at 52 ("In our view the same standard applies to the question whether gains from the sale of stock are business income as applies to the question whether dividends from stock are business income."). We also agree. "One must look principally at the underlying activity, not at the form of investment, to determine the propriety of apportionability." Mobil, supra, at 440. Changing the form of the income "works no change in the underlying economic realities of [whether] a unitary business [exists], and accordingly it ought not to affect the apportionability of income the parent receives." Id., at 441. We therefore hold that Idaho's attempt to tax this income also violated the Due Process Clause.

more than half a dozen decisions of this Court prior to *Mobil* and *Exxon.* See n. 13, supra. The dissent purports to rely on these recent cases, and yet its basic arguments—in practical effect—would seriously undermine their force as precedents. It relies primarily on considerations quite different from those identified as controlling in *Mobil* and *Exxon.* The dissent does not deny that ASARCO's subsidiaries were discrete business enterprises; rather it submits that they were engaged "in the same general line of business". Post, at 6. It notes—though the relevance is not obvious—that the management of ASARCO had special knowledge of the types of business engaged in by these subsidiaries. Post, at 6–7. The dissent also perceives a relationship between Idaho and the investment income simply because ASARCO has the use in its business of income from whatever source it may be derived. Post, at 7–10. Finally, it emphasizes the limited amount of open market buying and selling of products between ASARCO and the companies in which it has invested funds. See Part IIIA and B, supra.

In *Mobil,* in applying the unitary-business principle, the Court stated that the question is whether "the [investment] income was earned in the course of activities unrelated to the sale of petroleum products" in the State seeking to tax the income. Our decision went against Mobil Oil Corporation because we found that its "foreign activities [were] part of appellant's integrated petroleum enterprise", and because the subsidiaries in question were not shown to operate as "discrete business enterprise[s]". Mobil Oil Corp. v. Commissioner, 445 U.S., at 439. In this case, in sharp contrast, the record establishes that each of the three partial subsidiaries in question operated a "discrete business enterprise" having "nothing to do with the activities of [ASARCO] in the taxing state." Id., at 442.

As we recognize in the Court's opinion, these cases are decided on their facts in light of established general principles. The most comprehensive discussion of the factors that are relevant is contained in our recent decisions in *Mobil* and *Exxon.* In both of those cases, that we follow today, the states prevailed because it was clear that the corporations operated unitary businesses with a continuous flow and interchange of common products. ASARCO has proved that these essential factors are wholly absent in this case. It is late in the day to confuse this important area of state tax law by rewriting the standards of *Mobil* and *Exxon.*

V

For the reasons stated, the judgment of the Supreme Court of Idaho is reversed.

CHIEF JUSTICE BURGER, concurring [in both *ASARCO* and *Woolworth* p. 551 infra].

I join the Court's opinions in these cases in reliance on the Court's express statement that the Court's holdings do not preclude future Congressional action in this area.

JUSTICE O'CONNOR, with whom JUSTICE BLACKMUN and JUSTICE REHNQUIST join, dissenting.

The Court today declares that the Due Process Clause of the Constitution forbids a State from taxing a proportionate share of the investment income of a nondomiciliary corporation doing business within its borders. In so doing, the Court groundlessly strikes down the eminently reasonable assertion of Idaho's taxing power at issue in this case. Far more dismaying, however, is that the Court's reliance on the Due Process Clause may deprive Congress of the authority necessary to rationalize the joint taxation of interstate commerce by the 50 States.

Today, the taxpayer wins. Yet in the end, today's decision may prove to be a loss for all concerned—interstate businesses themselves, which the Commerce Clause guarantees the opportunity to serve the country's needs unimpeded by a parochial hodge-podge of overlapping and conflicting tax levies; the Nation, which demands a prosperous interstate market; and the States, which deserve fair return for the advantages they afford interstate enterprise. For while this Court has the authority to invalidate a specific state tax, only Congress has both the ability to canvass the myriad facts and factors relevant to interstate taxation and the power to shape a nationwide system that would guarantee the States fair revenues and offer interstate businesses freedom from strangulation by multiple paperwork and tax burdens. Unfortunately, by apparently stripping Congress of the authority to do the job, the Court delays the day when a uniform system responsive to the needs of all can be fashioned.

The Court has strayed "beyond the extremely limited restrictions that the Constitution places" on the taxing power of the States, "inject[ed itself] in a merely negative way into the delicate processes of fiscal policy-making," and regrettably "imprison[ed] the taxing power of the states within formulas that are not compelled by the Constitution." Wisconsin v. J.C. Penney Co., 311 U.S. 435, 445 (1940). I respectfully dissent.

I

*   *   *

*   *   * [T]he "linchpin" of apportioned state taxation is the concept of an organic, unitary business. Mobil Oil Corp. v. Commissioner of Taxes, supra, at 439. The constitutionality of a state tax levied on extraterritorial business operations thus turns on whether the out-of-state business activity can be characterized as a separate business with no in-state contacts or whether instead it is a part of a unitary enterprise doing business in the State. In the case before us, the Court first errs when it attempts to determine whether or not ASARCO's investments were part of ASARCO's unitary nonferrous metals business.

II

ASARCO realized capital gains, dividends, and interest income from its ownership of securities issued by five foreign subsidiaries. The issue for the Court is whether that income was earned by ASARCO's unitary nonferrous metals business, and therefore was subject to Idaho's taxes, or instead was earned by a separate investment business unrelated to ASARCO's operations in Idaho, and therefore was constitutionally exempt from taxation by that State. As always, of course, the State's taxation of the company's income is presumptively constitutional. To overcome that presumption, ASARCO has the "distinct burden of showing by 'clear and cogent evidence'" that Idaho's scheme "results in extraterritorial values being taxed." Exxon Corp. v. Wisconsin Department of Revenue, supra, at 221 (quoting Butler Bros. v. McColgan, 315 U.S. 501, 507 (1942)) (quoting Norfolk & Western R. Co. v. North Carolina ex rel. Maxwell, 297 U.S. 682, 688 (1936)).

According to the Court, ASARCO has met this burden by showing that during the relevant tax years its holdings in the five subsidiaries were passive investments not functionally integrated with ASARCO's nonferrous metals business. On this basis, the Court concludes that ASARCO's holdings were, in effect, part of a separate investment business having too little to do with ASARCO's unitary nonferrous metals business to support apportioned taxation.

Both common sense and business reality dictate a different result. ASARCO, far from showing that its investment holdings were part of an "unrelated," [2] "discrete business enterprise," [3] "hav[ing] nothing to do with the activities" [4] of its unitary nonferrous metals business, has failed in at least three ways to bear its "distinct burden" of demonstrating that Idaho's tax was unconstitutionally levied.

A

First, even accepting *arguendo* the Court's conclusion that the contested income was derived from passive investments, ASARCO has failed to show that its investment decisionmaking was segregated from its nonferrous metals business. ASARCO cannot deny that the subsidiary companies in which it invested were participants in the nonferrous metals industry, the very industry in which ASARCO played a major operational role. As the Court acknowledges, ASARCO "mine[d],

---

2. Mobil Oil Corp. v. Commissioner of Taxes, supra, at 439.

3. Exxon Corp. v. Department of Revenue, supra, at 224.

4. Mobil Oil Corp. v. Commissioner of Taxes, supra, at 442.

smelt[ed], and refine[d] * * * nonferrous metals such as copper, gold, silver, lead, and zinc," ante, at 1, while one of its subsidiaries "engaged in the mining, milling, smelting, and refining of nonferrous metals," ante, at 2, n. 2, another engaged "in the same general line of business" as did ASARCO in the United States, ante, at 2, n. 2, a third "mine[d] and smelt[ed] copper," ante, at 2, n. 2, and the last two were important "ASARCO customers," ante, at 16, fabricating, respectively, cables and copper wares, ante, at 2, n. 2. In short, ASARCO invested not in "unrelated business[es]," such as hotel chains and breweries, but in companies participating in the nonferrous metals markets. Exxon Corp. v. Department of Revenue, at 224 (quoting Mobil Oil Corp. v. Commissioner of Taxes, supra, at 442).

ASARCO invested in these nonferrous metals companies with a well-founded confidence that few other investors could muster, since much of what it had learned in operating its own nonferrous metals business must have been invaluable in evaluating the prospects for other companies engaged in similar businesses and markets worldwide. Put another way, it would have been a perverse act of self-denial for ASARCO to ignore its intimate knowledge of world markets, refining and smelting technology, mining operations, and geological reserves when it decided whether and how to invest in the five companies of concern here. Thus, the investment decisions ASARCO made regarding the securities of these five participants in the nonferrous metals markets undoubtedly depended heavily on ASARCO's knowledge of its own business.

In fact, during the course of this litigation, ASARCO has admitted as much. * * *

* * * [I]n its brief to the Supreme Court of Idaho ASARCO flatly stated that "[i]t invests its shareholders' money in businesses in which it has expertise and distributes the investment return in the form of dividends to its shareholders." Record 521.

In sum, far from showing by "clear and cogent evidence" that its investment decisions regarding other nonferrous metal suppliers and users were segregated from the resources of information and expertise developed in its own nonferrous metals business, ASARCO itself provided evidence that its investment decisionmaking was part of an indivisible, unitary nonferrous metals business. This alone warrants affirming the Idaho Supreme Court's due process ruling.

B

Second, again assuming *arguendo* that the contested investments were in fact passive, ASARCO has failed to show that its holdings were divorced from its management of the financial requirements of its nonferrous metals business. For all we know, ASARCO's investments were triggered by its need to obtain a return on idle financial resources accumulated for the future operation of its own primary business.

ASARCO does not, and could not, contend that all its investment income is *per se* beyond the taxing power of the nondomiciliary States in which it operates. Rather, it concedes that the Due Process Clause permits Idaho to tax, on an apportioned basis, the income ASARCO earned on short term investments of its working capital.[5] After all, an appropriate amount of liquid working capital is necessary to the day-to-day operation of a business, and any return earned from its temporary investment is a byproduct of the operation of the business. ASARCO thus admits that Idaho could tax a portion of the income realized from an investment in, say, short term commercial paper, even though the underlying operations of the issuing companies were far less related to ASARCO's nonferrous metals business than the operations of the five subsidiaries at issue here.

The interim investment of retained earnings prior to their commitment to a major corporate project, however, merely recapitulates on a grander scale the short term investment of working capital prior to its commitment to the daily financial needs of the company. Just as companies prefer to maintain a cushion of working capital rather than resort to the short term capital markets on an hourly basis for the money necessary to operate their businesses, many enterprises prefer to acquire the capital necessary for the expansion and replacement of plants and equipment by creating long term funds, rather than resort to the vagaries of the capital markets. In order to prevent the accumulating capital from sitting idle, such funds are usually invested in financial assets with a degree of liquidity appropriate to the money's intended ultimate use.[6] Any return ASARCO earned on such investments plainly would be functionally related to the conduct of its nonferrous metals business and, therefore, taxable by Idaho on an apportioned basis as unitary business income.

Such investment of idle funds, after all, mirrors the borrowing of funds a company lacks. Undoubtedly, ASARCO would be quick to assert that any long term borrowing recorded on the liability side of its

---

5. ASARCO states that it "has not contested Idaho's right to treat interest income from temporary deposits of [its] working capital funds as apportionable business income derived in the ordinary course of [its] Unitary Business activities." Brief for Appellant 26. See also Tr. of Oral Arg. 6–7.

6. This process is analogous to the leasing of idle physical assets until they are needed in the business. By analogy to ASARCO's investment of its working capital in short term securities, for example, a company might lease time on one of its computers to outsiders on an hourly basis in order to keep the computer fully occupied during slack periods. Similarly, in analogy to the interim investment of retained earnings, a company might lease for a term of years the areas of its office buildings into which it intends ultimately to expand. It could hardly be claimed that by so doing the company had opened up a separate and unrelated leasing business. To the contrary, the income from such leases would be functionally related to the company's unitary business and, therefore, taxable on an apportioned basis by a State in which the company did business. Accordingly, it is hard to see why a company that rents out idle money rather than idle physical assets should be treated differently under the Due Process Clause, and harder still to see why the Constitution would treat short term investments of working capital differently than longer term investments of retained earnings.

balance sheet is an integral part of its unitary business justifying the deduction of interest expense in the computation of apportionable net income. If so, ASARCO cannot contend that the long term investments recorded on the asset side of its balance sheet are automatically separate from its unitary business, thereby justifying the exclusion of the revenues received from apportionable net income. The same principles apply whether the money is going in or coming out.

Thus, because investments of ASARCO's working capital are functionally integrated with its unitary nonferrous metals business, and because ASARCO failed to show by "clear and cogent evidence" the facts necessary to distinguish, on a principled basis, its investments in the securities of the five subsidiaries at issue here,[7] the Idaho Supreme Court correctly concluded that apportioned taxation of ASARCO's contested investment income does not violate the Due Process Clause.

C

Finally, the Court errs even in its fundamental determination that ASARCO's holdings were passive investments unrelated to ASARCO's operational business. In fact, the disputed investments actively contributed to ASARCO's nonferrous metals business.

To begin with, ASARCO had effective operational control of at least three of the five subsidiaries. ASARCO's commanding 52.7% interest in M.I.M. Holdings, Ltd., uncontestably gave it full control of that company. Although ASARCO did not wield quite the same power over Southern Peru Copper, its 51.5% interest nonetheless gave it unilateral veto power over all corporate decisions, including those supported unanimously by all other shareholders.[8] Finally, in the case of ASARCO Mexicana, the record discloses only that ASARCO had been forced to sell 51% of its initial 100% interest to Mexican nationals, retaining a 49% interest for itself. ASARCO has made no showing that it is not the principal investor in Mexicana and thus able to control the company. In sum, ASARCO undoubtedly was the dominant factor in at least three of the five subsidiaries under consideration here, with the power to use them to advantage in its nonferrous metals business.[9]

---

7. Of course, had ASARCO attempted to do so, it might have been able to make such a showing. ASARCO did argue, and the trial court found, that it had "never been required to utilize its stock as security for borrowing of working capital, acquiring stock or securities in other companies or to support any bond issues." Record 326.

8. Under the management agreement between ASARCO and the other three shareholders of Southern Peru, ASARCO has the right to appoint six of the company's 13 directors, the other three shareholders together have the right to appoint another six, and the 13th and final director is appointed by the first 12 directors or by joint action of all the shareholders. Southern Peru's by-laws, which can be changed only by unanimous consent, provide that eight votes are needed to pass any resolution. App. to Juris. Statement 55; App. 121.

9. ASARCO also dominated Revere Copper and General Cable. While ASARCO owned only 34% interests in each company, the remaining shares of each were "widely held," ante, at 16, so that ordinarily ASARCO would be assured control of each company and almost never face effective opposition to its wishes.

Prior to the tax years in question, however, the Justice Department brought an

The Court, however, minimizes the significance of this control, emphasizing that ASARCO did not openly and aggressively assert its control during the tax years in question and concluding that ASARCO's subsidiaries did not contribute to its nonferrous metals business.

The Court's result is hard to understand in view of our decision just two years ago in Exxon Corp. v. Wisconsin Dept. of Revenue, supra. In summarizing our result in *Exxon,* we asserted that the "important link" establishing the unity of Exxon's business "most clearly" was based on two factors. 447 U.S., at 224.

First, we noted that "placing individual segments under one corporate entity * * * provide[s] greater profits stability" because "nonparallel and nonmutual economic factors which may affect one department may be offset by the factors existing in another department." Id., at 225 (quoting the testimony of an Exxon senior vice president). ASARCO's ownership of subsidiaries doing business in precisely ASARCO's line of work in two different geographical markets, M.I.M. Holdings in Australia and ASARCO Mexicana in Mexico, undoubtedly provided exactly that sort of advantage; economic conditions in Australia and Mexico do not track those in the United States, so that when the nonferrous metals business is in the doldrums in one country, it maybe prospering in another. But, unlike the *Exxon* Court, today's Court is blind to the significance to the "profits stability" of ASARCO's nonferrous metals business of its subsidiaries in unrelated geographical markets.

antitrust suit against ASARCO related to its holdings in General Cable and Revere Copper. The suit culminated in a consent decree issued in 1967 forbidding ASARCO to sell to General Cable and Revere Copper at prices lower than ASARCO sold to other customers and preventing ASARCO from voting its stock in either company. In 1970, the last of the three tax years at issue here, the decree was modified and "ASARCO was compelled * * * to divest itself of all its General Cable stock." Ante, at 17, n. 20.

ASARCO argues that the 1967 consent decree, which was issued before the tax years of concern here, prevented General Cable and Revere Copper from being a part of ASARCO's unitary business. To the contrary, however, the antitrust suit and consent decree strongly suggest that General Cable and Revere Copper were entangled in ASARCO's unitary business, perhaps unlawfully so. On the present record, ASARCO has not borne the burden of showing that the 1967 decree severed enough of the connections between ASARCO and the two subsidiaries to transform ASARCO's holdings from active components of its unitary business to passive investments. At least with respect to General Cable, the modification in 1970 (the last tax year in issue here) of the consent decree so that ASARCO was required to sell its holdings in the company indicates the contrary, since divestiture would scarcely be necessary if the business of the two companies had been unrelated. Moreover, the mere fact that ASARCO traded with General Cable and Revere Copper at market rates does not compel the conclusion that ASARCO's investments in those companies were part of its unitary business. In *Exxon,* for example, we concluded that the fact that "wholesale market values" were assigned "to interdepartmental transfers of products and supplies," 447 U.S., at 225, did not undermine the unitary nature of Exxon's business.

Although I believe that ASARCO's showing was insufficient to establish that General Cable and Revere Copper were not under its control for purposes of determining the constitutional limits of Idaho's taxation, for simplicity in what follows I assume only that ASARCO was a major investor in these two subsidiaries.

Second, in *Exxon* we noted that the vertical relationship between the various departments in Exxon's business provided both "an assured supply of raw materials" and an "assured and stable outlet for products" so that Exxon could "minimiz[e]" the "risk of disruptions" "due to [the] supply and demand imbalances that may occur from time to time." Ibid. The *Exxon* Court's recognition of the business importance of captive suppliers and customers merely confirmed our earlier decision in *Mobil Oil,* in which we affirmed Vermont's apportioned taxation of the more than $115 million in dividend income Mobil had received from its 10% interest in the Arabian American Oil Company. 445 U.S., at 457, n. 10 (STEVENS, J., dissenting). Mobil's 10% investment, apart from providing handsome dividends, apparently had helped to assure Mobil of supplies of crude oil for its petroleum business. By contrast, the Court today inexplicably invalidates Idaho's taxation of ASARCO's dividend income from its five-fold greater 51.5% interest in Southern Peru Copper Corp., an investment that evidently helped to assure ASARCO of supplies of unrefined copper, since 35% of the entire copper output of Southern Peru was sold to ASARCO.[10]

Apparently, the Court no longer believes it significant that the subsidiaries in which a parent has major holdings "minimiz[e]" the "risk of disruptions" "due to [the] supply and demand imbalances that may occur from time to time," Exxon Corp. v. Department of Revenue, 447 U.S., at 225, by providing "assured suppl[ies]" and "stable outlet[s]," ibid., unless the subsidiaries are actively managed on a day-to-day basis. The Court evidently would find that ASARCO's subsidiaries were part of ASARCO's unitary business only if ASARCO experienced a "supply and demand imbalanc[e]" sufficiently severe to force it to exercise day-to-day control of its captive subsidiaries. In this regard, the Court's position is akin to the view that a paid-up fire insurance policy is a worthless asset unless smoke is in the air.

In sum, despite ASARCO's failure on each of the three counts just discussed to bear its "distinct burden" of showing that its investments are unrelated to its nonferrous metals business, the Court rules that Idaho cannot tax the investment income at issue here. In so doing, the Court unwisely substitutes for the multifaceted analysis used to determine whether the businesses in *Mobil Oil* and *Exxon* were unitary the oversimplified test of active operational control. The result is that the Court has ignored business advantages to ASARCO more than sufficient to establish that its holdings in its subsidiaries were part of its unitary business. In consequence, the Court wrongly concludes that ASARCO has borne the "distinct burden" of showing that its holdings

10. Just as inexplicably, the Court reverses Idaho's apportioned tax on ASARCO's dividend income from its 34% interests in Revere Copper & Brass and in General Cable Corp., companies that were "major customers" of ASARCO buying tens of millions of dollars of goods from ASARCO each year.

in the five affected subsidiaries are not functionally related to the income of its operational nonferrous metals business.[11]

Trying to justify that result, the Court suggests that for it to hold otherwise "would destroy the concept" of a unitary business by expanding the idea until it "becomes no limitation at all" on the power of the States to tax. Ante, at 19. In actuality, the Court's decision today shrinks the concept beyond all recognition. Thus it is the Court's holding, not Idaho's tax, that menaces the unitary business principle. The "linchpin" is loose from the axle.

III

As a natural consequence of its decision that Idaho cannot tax ASARCO's investment income, the Court simultaneously, if implicitly, rules out taxation of the disputed income by any other nondomiciliary State in which ASARCO conducts its nonferrous metals business, absent a special connection between the would-be taxing State and ASARCO's investments.[12] By the process of elimination, then, the Court's holding provides a partial answer to the question of which State or States the Constitution permits to tax this income. The answer the Court gives, however, demonstrates how ill-advised is the course on which it embarks. By its analysis, the Court leaves open three possible choices regarding which States, if any, may tax ASARCO's contested income. Each of these possibilities suffers from crippling defects, pointing to the conclusion that the Court errs in prohibiting apportioned taxation of investment income by nondomiciliary States.

A

First, there is the disturbing possibility that no State could satisfy the requirements of the Due Process Clause as interpreted today by the Court, so that the contested income would be, in the words of state tax administrators, "nowhere income." [13] If so, today's holding casts a deep shadow on the ability of the States to tax their fair share of the corporate income they help to produce by providing an "orderly, civilized society." Even more disturbing, given such an interpretation, the Court's decision endangers even federal taxation of passive investment

---

11. The Court suggests that my "perception of some of the facts" necessary to reach this conclusion "differs substantially from the record." Ante, at 17, n. 21. In fact, however, my view of the facts differs from neither the record nor, I think, that of the Court. As should be apparent, my disagreement with the Court is based, not on the facts, but on the constitutional significance to be given those facts.

12. The Court is careful not to extend the reach of its holding to domiciliary States. It states the question presented as "whether the State of Idaho constitutionally may include within the taxable income of a *non* domiciliary parent corporation * * * a portion of intangible income * * * that the parent receives from subsidiary corporations having no other connection with the State." Ante, at 1 (emphasis added). As its holding, the Court asserts that it "cannot accept * * * a definition of 'unitary business' that would permit *non* domiciliary States to apportion and tax dividends '[w]here the business activities of the dividend payor have nothing to do with the activities of the recipient in the taxing State. * * * ' " Ante, at 20 (citation omitted) (emphasis added).

13. See Dexter, Taxation of Income from Intangibles of Multistate–Multinational Corporations, 29 Vand.L.Rev. 401, 403 (1976).

income, since the Federal Government's contacts with the income at issue here obviously cannot exceed the sum of the contacts of the various States. Presumably, the Court's opinion should not be read as erecting so high a hurdle to state and federal taxation.

B

Second, there is the possibility that only a domiciliary State or States could tax the disputed income. In *Mobil Oil,* the Court stated that "[t]axation by apportionment *and* taxation by allocation to a single situs are theoretically incommensurate, and if the latter method is constitutionally preferred, a tax based on the former cannot be sustained." 445 U.S., at 444–445 (emphasis added). If so, the converse may also be true: if taxation by apportionment is constitutionally condemned, taxation by allocation to a single situs may be constitutionally preferred. The Court's decision today thus could be read as broadly hinting that a domiciliary State enjoys a preference of constitutional dimension justifying its—and only its—taxation of income such as that derived from ASARCO's investments.

Perhaps such a preference could find some blessing in tradition, but certainly not in logic or in the recent opinions of this Court. In *Mobil Oil* itself, the Court declared:

> "We find no adequate justification * * * for such a preference. Although a fictionalized situs for intangible property sometimes has been invoked to avoid multiple taxation of ownership, there is nothing talismanic about the concepts of 'business situs' or 'commercial domicile' that automatically renders those concepts applicable when taxation of income from intangibles is at issue. The Court has observed that the maxim *mobilia sequuntur personam,* upon which these fictions of situs are based, 'states a rule without disclosing the reasons for it.' The Court has also recognized that 'the reason for a single place of taxation no longer obtains' when the taxpayer's activities with respect to the intangible property involve relations with more than one jurisdiction. * * * Moreover, cases upholding allocation to a single situs for property tax purposes have distinguished income tax situations where the apportionment principle prevails." 445 U.S., at 445 (citations omitted).

The Court thus made clear only two years ago that a State of domicile cannot expect automatically to meet the due process requirements for the taxation of investment income. As with a nondomiciliary State, a domiciliary State may tax investment income only if it confers benefits on or affords protection to the investment activity. Mere assertion of the arbitrary legal fiction that intangible property is located at its owner's domicile no longer suffices to repel a reluctant taxpayer's due process attack.

The principal functional basis on which this Court has justified taxation by the commercial domicile, moreover, actually supports the fully apportioned taxation of investment income that today's decision rules out, rather than taxation by allocation to a single situs. In

Wheeling Steel Corp. v. Fox, 298 U.S. 193 (1936), for example, we sustained an ad valorem tax on accounts receivable and bank deposits levied by the State in which the taxpayer maintained "the actual seat of its corporate government," 298 U.S., at 212, for the reason that the intangibles at issue had become "integral parts of some local business," id., at 210 (quoting Farmers Loan & Trust Co. v. Minnesota, 280 U.S. 204, 213 (1930)). Thus, other than the arbitrary fiction that intangible property is "located" at the domicile of its owner, the underlying jurisdictional basis for taxation at the commercial domicile is grounded in the fact that intangibles are an "integral part" of the business. This justification supports the principle of apportionment rather than allocation solely to the single domiciliary State. After all, if intangibles are an "integral part" of the unitary business in the domiciliary State, they also are related to the business of the corporation elsewhere. It hardly makes sense to allocate income to the commercial domicile on the theory that business activity at the commercial domicile promotes the unitary business everywhere, and then to ignore those connections and to disregard the claims of the other States in which the unitary business operates. See Dexter, Taxation of Income from Intangibles of Multistate–Multinational Corporations, 29 Vand.L.Rev. 401, 416 (1976).

In short, unless the Court is prepared to abandon the unitary business principle as applied to investment income and to read into the Constitution the arbitrary legal fiction that intangibles are situated at the domicile of their owner, the Court will be unable to sustain a domiciliary State's allocation of all passive investment income to itself against due process attack.

C

We thus arrive at the only remaining possibility. The Court's holding today, taken with past decisions, may imply that ASARCO's investments must be treated as though ASARCO were not only running its nonferrous metals business but also running as another, separate business a sort of mutual fund or holding company specializing in the worldwide nonferrous metals industry. The income from this fictitious separate business would then be taxable on an apportioned basis by those States in which the business was carried out, just as ASARCO's unitary nonferrous metals business could be taxed on an apportioned basis by those States in which that business is conducted.

If so, the Constitution apparently requires that a very small tail be permitted to wag a very big dog. For in the case of companies like ASARCO with tens or hundreds of millions of dollars of dividend income generated by a handful of long term investments, vast differences in state revenues may turn on whether the quarterly dividend checks sent from "passive" subsidiaries are sent to a clerk in a company office in one State rather than another. Surely it is highly anomalous that the Due Process Clause should require the dividend income of a far-flung interstate business selectively to be attributed solely to the State or two in which a few minimal securities management functions are carried out, rather than apportioned among all the States whose "civilized society," has made the income-generating wealth of the larger enterprise possible.

Moreover, if such a requirement were judicially imposed it would create potentially staggering practical difficulties for taxpayers, state tax administrators, and, ultimately, the courts. For despite the Court's easy conclusion today that ASARCO's supposedly discrete investment business is distinct from ASARCO's operational nonferrous metals business, it is unlikely in practice that the two could be so readily disentangled. Imagine, for example, that the dividend checks were received and the management decisions regarding ASARCO's investments were made at ASARCO's corporate headquarters in one State, while the expertise and information relied on to make those decisions were drawn from corporate sources in many States. In apportioning the income of this purportedly separate investment business among the States, the question inescapably would arise as to what limits the Constitution places on how little of the taxable values at ASARCO's headquarters the expertise and information producing States could allocate to ASARCO's investment business as opposed to the theoretically distinct operational nonferrous metals business. Stating the question suffices to show that it reintroduces just the sort of insoluble problem of dividing businesses that the unitary business principle was designed to avoid. Thus, if the Court does not abandon the separate business theory that it endorses today, it merely will have substituted the vexing constitutional problem of how to apportion businesses for today's problem of how to apportion taxes.

In sum, the Court has erred. Without a well-founded Constitutional mandate, it has straightjacketed the States' ability to develop fair systems of apportionment, prematurely ending the evolutionary process begun by the Uniform Division of Income for Tax Purposes Act and the Multistate Tax Commission. By limiting the apportionment concept by restrictions not found anywhere in the Constitution, moreover, the Court has committed itself to a path leading to more constitutional problems and greater involvement by this Court in the intricacies of interstate taxation.

IV

The Court's error, moreover, is compounded by its decision to invoke the Due Process Clause as the source of its authority, despite the ready availability of the Commerce Clause.[14] For unlike a Commerce

---

14. This Court's authority to invalidate state legislation because it interferes with interstate commerce is inferred from the Constitution's grant to *Congress* of the authority to regulate interstate commerce. Art. I, § 8, cl. 3. For this reason, Congress may "confe[r] upon the States an ability to restrict the flow of interstate commerce that they would not otherwise enjoy." Lewis v. BT Investment Managers, Inc.,

447 U.S. 27, 44 (1980) (citations omitted). Consistent with this principle, it has long been established that Congress generally has the power to "overrule" a decision of this Court invalidating state legislation on Commerce Clause grounds. Compare Leisy v. Hardin, 135 U.S. 100 (1890), with In re Rahrer, 140 U.S. 545 (1891). By contrast, Congress generally cannot waive a ruling of this Court decided under the Due

Clause ruling which is susceptible to repair by Congress, today's due process decision may be beyond Congress' power to correct.

This constitutional shortsightedness overlooks the fact that Congress, not this Court, holds the ultimate responsibility for maintaining a healthy system of interstate commerce. Moreover, it is Congress, not this Court, which has the institutional tools to deal with these complex problems. Congress itself is only too aware of the limitations under which the judiciary operates when it attempts to deal with the knotty problems of state taxation of multistate enterprises within a federal system. [The opinion quotes from the report of the Willis Committee. H.R.Rep. No. 1480, 88th Cong., 2d Sess., pp. 11–12 (1964).] * * *

Nor is Congress alone in recognizing the limitations of the judiciary in this field. Many Justices of this Court have acknowledged "the weakness of the judicial process in these tax questions where the total problem * * * reaches us only in installments." Northwest Airlines, Inc. v. Minnesota, 322 U.S. 292, 307 (1944) (Jackson, J., concurring). * * * Surely in a case such as the one before us, Congress, unconfined by "the narrow scope of judicial proceedings," Pennsylvania v. Wheeling & Belmont Bridge Co., 13 How. 518, 592 (1851) (Taney, C.J., dissenting), is in a better position "in the exercise of its plenary constitutional control over interstate commerce, not only [to] consider whether such a tax as now under scrutiny is consistent with the best interests of our national economy, but * * * also on the basis of full exploration of the many aspects of a complicated problem [to] devise a national policy fair alike to the States and our Union." McCarroll v. Dixie Greyhound Lines, Inc., 309 U.S. 176, 189 (1940) (Black, J., dissenting). But it is just this sort of congressional action which today's due process decision appears to preclude. This Court should not so confidently preempt the Congress.

V

In sum, the Court has focused its attention solely on the question whether ASARCO's interests in its subsidiaries represented active investments and concludes they did not. The Court then permits this

Process Clause. Accordingly, this Court's "threshold" for invalidating state legislation should be considerably higher under the Due Process Clause than under the Commerce Clause.

In the present case, the Court could have reached its result by relying on the Commerce Clause. Our cases establish that analysis of the validity of state taxation under the Commerce Clause is similar to analysis under the Due Process Clause. The test under the Commerce Clause is whether the tax "is applied to an activity with a substantial nexus with the taxing State, is fairly apportioned, does not discriminate against interstate commerce, and is fairly related to the services provid-

ed by the State." Mobil Oil Corp. v. Commissioner of Taxes, supra, at 443 (quoting Complete Auto Transit, Inc. v. Brady, 430 U.S. 274, 279 (1977)). In his dissent in *Mobil Oil,* Justice STEVENS explained how a violation of the Due Process Clause could also be a violation of the Commerce Clause: "[I]f, in a particular case, use of an allocation formula has the effect of taxing income earned by an interstate entity outside the State, it could alternatively be said to have the effect of taxing the income earned by that entity inside the State at a rate higher than that used for a comparable, wholly intrastate business, a discrimination that violates the Commerce Clause." Id., at 452, n. 4.

initial erroneous result to derail its analysis. Instead of continuing, the Court fails to consider the possibility that ASARCO's investment decisionmaking was not segregated from its operational nonferrous metals business; fails to consider the possibility that ASARCO's investments were simply an interim use of long term funds accumulated for ultimate use elsewhere in the business; fails to consider the possibility that ruling out apportioned taxation of income earned from intangibles may imply that such income is "nowhere income"; fails to consider the possibility that its ruling may be inconsistent with the unitary business principle because it suggests that income from intangibles may be taxed only by a domiciliary State; and fails to consider the possibility that it may be as difficult to apportion a business as to apportion income for constitutional purposes. Finally, and most distressingly, the Court fails to consider its own limitations and Congress' constitutional prerogatives. Had the Court given the intricate questions presented by this case the attention they deserve, it might have reached a different result. I respectfully dissent.

F.W. WOOLWORTH CO. v. TAXATION AND REVENUE DEPARTMENT OF NEW MEXICO *

Supreme Court of the United States, 1982
458 U.S. 354, 102 S.Ct. 3128

JUSTICE POWELL delivered the opinion of the Court.

The question is whether the Due Process Clause permits New Mexico to tax a portion of dividends that appellant F.W. Woolworth Co. received from foreign subsidiaries that do no business in New Mexico. We also must decide whether New Mexico may include within Woolworth's apportionable New Mexico income a sum, commonly known as "gross-up," that Woolworth calculated in order to claim a foreign tax credit on its federal income tax.

I

Woolworth's principal place of business and commercial domicile is in New York. It engages in retail business through chains of stores located in the United States, Puerto Rico, and the Virgin Islands. It sells a wide spectrum of merchandise, including dry goods, hardware, small appliances, confections, packaged goods, and fountain items. In the fiscal year ending January 31, 1977, Woolworth's gross domestic sales totalled approximately $2.5 billion, with New Mexico sales amounting to approximately $13 million—or about 0.5% of the gross figure. App. 57.

Woolworth owns four foreign subsidiaries of relevance to this suit. Three are wholly-owned: F.W. Woolworth Gmbh, in Germany; F.W. Woolworth, Ltd., in Canada; and F.W. Woolworth, S.A. de C.V. Mexico. F.W. Woolworth Co., Ltd., is an English corporation of which Woolworth owns 52.7%, with the remainder held and traded publicly.

_____
* [Some footnotes have been omitted.]

These four corporations also engage in chain store retailing.[1] Together they paid Woolworth approximately $39.9 million in dividends during the fiscal year in question.

New Mexico adopted a version of the Uniform Division of Income for Tax Purposes Act in 1965, N.M.Stat.Ann. §§ 7–4–1–7–4–21 (1981), and joined the Multistate Tax Compact in 1967. *Id.*, §§ 7–5–1–7–5–7. See ASARCO Inc. v. Idaho State Tax Comm'n, ante, at 4; United States Steel Corp. v. Multistate Tax Comm'n, 434 U.S. 452 (1978). Consequently the State distinguishes between "business" income, which it apportions between it and other States for tax purposes, and "nonbusiness" income, which it generally allocates to a single State on the basis of commercial domicile. Woolworth reported its dividend income of $39.9 million from its German, Canadian, Mexican, and English subsidiaries as "nonbusiness" income, none of which was to be allocated to New Mexico. Woolworth also treated as "nonbusiness" income a $1.6 million gain from a hedging transaction in British pounds. This transaction was undertaken for the purpose of insuring the payment of the British subsidiary's dividend against currency fluctuations. See App. 52–54. Similarly, Woolworth did not report as New Mexico "business" income $25.5 million of "gross-up" that it never actually received but that the Federal Government (for purposes of calculating Woolworth's federal foreign tax credit pursuant to 26 U.S.C. §§ 78, 901(a), and 902(a)) *deemed* Woolworth to have received from its foreign subsidiaries.

On audit, the New Mexico Taxation and Revenue Department determined that, under state law, Woolworth should have included in its apportionable New Mexico income the dividends from its four foreign subsidiaries, the foreign exchange gain, and the $25.5 million gross-up figure. These additions increased Woolworth's apportioned New Mexico income from $84,622 to $401,518. App. 69. The Department denied Woolworth's protest,[7] but this decision was reversed on appeal by the New Mexico Court of Appeals. F.W. Woolworth Co. v. Bureau of Revenue, 95 N.M. 542, 624 P.2d 51 (1979).

As a matter of state law, the court of appeals excluded from apportionable New Mexico income Woolworth's receipt of the dividends at issue. The court stated that "[t]here is no indication that the income from Woolworth's long-standing investments [in its subsidiaries] was used either in taxpayer's unitary domestic business or in its business conducted in New Mexico. * * * " 95 N.M., at 545, 624 P.2d, at 54.

---

1. The English subsidiary operates about 2,000 stores, App. 39, the Canadian company about 500, App. 24, and the Mexican about 12. App. 28. The record does not specify the number of stores the German company owns, but the company may be between the English and Canadian operations in size.

7. Only one witness—Woolworth's tax manager—appeared before the Department's hearing examiner. The State introduced as evidence Woolworth's tax return, a notice of assessment, its worksheets, Woolworth's protest, and tax regulations. Woolworth introduced a one page diagram of its corporate structure. See App. B to Brief for Appellee. The testimony given before the examiner and referred to in this opinion is uncontroverted unless otherwise noted.

*   *   * [The Court's discussion of the gross-up issue at this and other points in the opinion is omitted, other than its conclusion infra, has been omitted].

The New Mexico Supreme Court reversed over one dissent. Taxation and Revenue Dept. v. F.W. Woolworth Co., 95 N.M. 519, 624 P.2d 28 (1981). On the question whether Woolworth's receipt of dividends from its subsidiaries constituted apportionable New Mexico income, the court observed that, "[r]egrettably, it needs to be said that the State did a very poor job of inquiring into and developing the facts in this case." 95 N.M., at 524, 624 P.2d, at 33. The court nonetheless found substantial evidence to support the findings that the subsidiaries' dividend payments met the State's statutory test for inclusion in Woolworth's apportionable New Mexico income. On the constitutional issue, the court identified the "key question" after our decision in Mobil Oil Corp. v. Commissioner of Taxes, 445 U.S. 425 (1980), as "whether those dividends were income earned in a unitary business." 95 N.M., at 528, 624 P.2d, at 37. The court stated:

> "The [dividend] income [from Woolworth's subsidiaries] is obviously related to the mutual activities of the parent and its affiliates. The control over the subsidiaries, the interdependence, the history of the relationships, the placing of the [dividend] money in [Woolworth's] general operating account, all point to functional integration and reveal an underlying unitary business for our purposes here." 95 N.M., at 529, 624 P.2d, at 38.

*   *   *

II

*   *   *

Woolworth owns all the stock of three of its dividend payors and a 52.7% majority interest in the fourth. As a result, Woolworth (at least with respect to the three wholly owned companies) elects all of the subsidiaries' directors. It potentially has the authority to operate these companies as integrated divisions of a single unitary business. Our decision in *ASARCO* makes clear, however, that the *potential* to operate a company as part of a unitary business is not dispositive when, looking at "the 'underlying economic realities of a unitary business,' " the dividend income from the subsidiaries *in fact* is "derive[d] from 'unrelated business activity' which constitutes a 'discrete business enterprise.' " Exxon, 447 U.S., at 223–224, quoting Mobil, 445 U.S., at 441, 442, 439. See ASARCO, ante, at 15–16 (holding that a 52.7%–owned subsidiary is not part of its parent's unitary business).

A

The state supreme court in important part analyzed this case under a different legal standard. After stating that the existence of a unitary business relationship was the "key question," the court proceeded to resolve this question largely by emphasizing the potentials of the relationship between Woolworth and its subsidiaries:

"The possession of large assets by subsidiaries is a business advantage of great value to the parent; 'it may give credit which will result in more economical business methods; it may give a standing which shall facilitate purchases; it may enable the corporation to enlarge the field of its activities and in many ways give it business standing and prestige.' Flint v. Stone Tracy Co., 220 U.S. 107, 166 (1911)." 95 N.M., at 529, 624 P.2d, at 38.

This reliance on the *Flint* case was error. *Flint* upheld a *federal* excise tax levied on corporate income.[10] The States, of course, are subject to limitations on their taxation powers that do not apply to the Federal Government. As relevant here, "the income attributed to [a] State for tax purposes must be rationally related to 'values connected with the taxing State.' Norfolk & Western R. Co. v. State Tax Comm'n, 390 U.S. 317, 325." Moorman Mfg. Co. v. Bair, 437 U.S. 267, 273 (1978). The state court's reasoning would trivialize this due process limitation by holding it satisfied if the income in question "adds to the riches of the corporation * * *." Wallace v. Hines, 253 U.S. 66, 70 (1920). Income, from whatever source, always is a "business advantage" to a corporation. Our cases demand more. In particular, they specify that the proper inquiry looks to "the underlying unity or diversity of business enterprise," Mobil, 445 U.S., at 440, not to whether the nondomiciliary parent derives some economic benefit—as it virtually always will—from its ownership of stock in another corporation. See ASARCO, ante, at 17–20.[11]

B

In *Mobil* we emphasized, as relevant to the right of a State to tax dividends from foreign subsidiaries, the question whether "contributions to income [of the subsidiaries] result[ed] from functional integration, centralization of management, and economies of scale." 445 U.S., at 438. If such "factors of profitability" arising "from the operation of the business as a whole" exist and evidence the operation of a unitary business, a State can gain a justification for its tax consideration of value that has no other connection with that State. Ibid. We turn now to consider the extent, if any, to which these factors exist in this case.

There was little functional integration. Woolworth's subsidiaries engaged exclusively in the business of retailing—the purchase of wholesale goods for resale to final consumers. This type of business differs significantly from the "highly integrated business" of locating, process-

---

10. The tax did *not* apply to a corporation's receipt of dividends from other companies subjected to the tax. 220 U.S., at 144–145.

11. The hearing examiner and the New Mexico Supreme Court also thought it significant that Woolworth had commingled its dividends with its general funds and had used them for general corporate operating purposes. See 95 N.M., at 529, 624 P.2d, at 38; note 9, supra. This analysis likewise subverts the unitary business limitation. *All* dividend income—irrespective of whether it is generated by a "discrete business enterprise," Mobil, 445 U.S., at 439—would become part of a unitary business if the test were whether the corporation commingled dividends from other corporations, whether subsidiaries or not.

ing, and marketing a resource (such as petroleum) that we previously have found to constitute a unitary business. Exxon, 447 U.S., at 224. See also id., at 226 (describing "a unitary stream of income, of which the income derived from internal transfers of raw materials from exploration and production to refining is a part"); Mobil, 445 U.S., at 428. Consistent with this distinction, the evidence in this case is that *no* phase of any subsidiary's business was integrated with the parent's. With respect to "who makes the decision for seeing to the merchandise, [store] site selection, advertising and accounting control," the undisputed testimony stated "[e]ach subsidiary performs these functions autonomously and independently of the parent company." App. 12.[12] "Each subsidiary has a complete accounting department and a financial staff." Id., at 14. Each had its own outside counsel. App. to Juris. Statement 34. It further appears that Woolworth engaged in no centralized purchasing, manufacturing, or warehousing of merchandise.[13] The parent had no central personnel training school for its foreign subsidiaries. Id., at 34. And each subsidiary was responsible for obtaining its own financing from sources other than the parent.[14] In sum, the record

12. The testimony before the Department's hearing officer, see n. 7, supra, focused primarily on the English and German subsidiaries. With respect to the Mexican and Canadian subsidiaries, the evidence was confined to the following:

"Q. Now, I would like to[,] without repeating every question if I may[,] ask a summary question concerning the Canadian and the Mexican subsidiaries, we are talking about decisions concerning merchandise mix, site selection, advertising, accounting, training of personnel, and of those items[,] would you say there is a similarity between the relationship of the U.S. parent to Canada as there is to the German and the English subsidiaries to the extent to which these things are decentralized?

"A. Yes, there is a distinct similarity or philosophy involved in the ownership of these companies." App. 18.

The State did not undertake to controvert the implications of this statement, and neither of the courts below found any difference in the relationships between the parent and each of the four subsidiaries. We thus must assume that the relationship between the parent and the Mexican and Canadian subsidiaries paralleled that between the parent and the English and German subsidiaries in material respects.

13. The New Mexico Supreme Court did state that "[t]here is some flow back and forth of goods" between the parent and the subsidiaries. 95 N.M., at 524, 624 P.2d, at 33. It cited no evidence in support of this statement. Neither the Department's

hearing officer nor the Court of Appeals made such a finding. The testimony in the record was that there were not "any intercompany sales of inventory." App. 13.

The Woolworth witness also stated that, with respect to certain types of goods manufactured by other of the parent's subsidiaries, he lacked actual knowledge of whether there were intercompany sales. He continued that the idea was "inconceivable to me because of the autonomous operation of the company and the lack of coordination and other facets." App. 43. Upon further questioning, the witness conceded that he did not "really know where [the English subsidiary's managers] buy their merchandise." But he affirmed his knowledge that the English company's sales to and purchases from the parent were "virtually nil." Id., at 44. When questioned whether Woolworth utilized a central buying office for it and its subsidiaries, the witness replied that it did not. Id., at 14. No other evidence indicated that the parent and the subsidiaries engaged in any joint manufacturing, purchasing, or warehousing functions. Nor did the New Mexico courts find otherwise.

14. Woolworth had no outstanding debts from its English subsidiary, App. to Juris. Statement 35, and it had not reinvested its dividends in that company. App. 51. The parent had reinvested dividends in the German company, id., at 52, but the last additional capital contribution by the parent that the witness could recall, id., at 46, was a $400,000 transfer made

is persuasive that Woolworth's operations were not functionally integrated with its subsidiaries.

We now consider the extent to which there was centralization of management or achievement of other economies of scale. It appears that each subsidiary operated as a distinct business enterprise at the level of fulltime management. With one possible exception,[15] none of the subsidiaries' officers during the year in question was a current or former employee of the parent. App. to Juris. Statement 34. The testimony was that the subsidiaries "figure their operations are independent, autonomous." App. 13. Woolworth did not "rotate or train personnel to operate stores in those countries. There is no exchange of personnel." Ibid. There was no "training program that is central to transmit the Woolworth idea of merchandising[,] such as it may be[,] to the foreign subsidiaries." Id., at 15. The subsidiaries "proceed * * * with their own programs, either formal or informal. They develop their own managers and instruct them in their methods of operation." Ibid.

This management decentralization was reflected in the fact that each subsidiary possessed autonomy to determine its own policies respecting its primary activity—retailing. According to the hearing examiner:

> "Each of the four subsidiaries are responsible for determining the size and location of retail stores, the market conditions in their own territory and the mix of items to be sold. The German subsidiary emphasizes soft goods such as dresses and coats. It sells no food. The English subsidiary operates restaurants in its stores and also operates supermarkets. Each subsidiary attempts to cater to local tastes and needs. The inventory of each subsidiary consists, in large part, of home country produced items. This purchase-at-home practice is consistent with the policy of the taxpayer. A number of inventory items are purchased from the Orient or other places but there is no evidence that the subsidiaries purchase, or are required to purchase, inventory items from any particular source." App. to Juris Statement 33–34.

Importantly, the Department's hearing officer found that Woolworth had "no department of section, as such, devoted to overseeing the foreign subsidiary operations." App. to Juris. Statement 34.[16] Neither the parent corporation nor any of the subsidiaries consolidates its tax return with any of the other companies. App. 37–38. The tax

after the German company was demolished during World War II. Id., at 30. See App. to Juris. Statement 35.

15. The hearing examiner found that "[i]n the taxable year involved, none of the four [subsidiaries'] officers were currently or formerly employees of the parent." App. to Juris. Statement 34. Without explanation, he also later stated that "[a]t least one officer of the Canadian subsidiary [was] also an officer of the [parent]." Id., at 34.

One officer from the Mexican subsidiary was a participant in Woolworth's profit sharing plan. Woolworth paid the employee's share of this plan. Ibid.

16. Woolworth had one vice president "who is the liaison man with the smaller foreign subsidiaries," ibid., such as the Spanish and Mexican subsidiaries. App. 50. The testimony was that this liaison man "from time to time may have contact with the major subsidiaries * * *." Ibid.

manager for Woolworth stated that he did not review the subsidiaries' tax returns or consult with them on decisions affecting taxes. Id., at 14. There was no "policy of the parent that all of the managers of all the operations get together periodically to discuss the overall Woolworth operations." Id., at 35.

There were some managerial links. Woolworth maintained one or several common directors with some of the subsidiaries. There also was irregular in-person and "frequent" mail, telephone, and teletype communication between the upper echelons of management of the parent and the subsidiaries. App. to Juris. Statement 34. Decisions about major financial decisions, such as the amount of dividends to be paid by the subsidiaries and the creation of substantial debt, had to be approved by the parent. Id., at 35. Woolworth's published financial statements, such as its annual reports, were prepared on a consolidated basis.[22] Ibid.

We conclude, on the basis of undisputed facts, that the four subsidiaries in question are not a part of a unitary business under the principles articulated in *Mobil* and *Exxon,* and today reiterated in *ASARCO.* Except for the type of occasional oversight—with respect to capital structure, major debt, and dividends—that any parent gives to an investment in a subsidiary, there is little or no integration of the business activities or centralization of the management of these five corporations. Woolworth has proved that its situation differs from that in *Exxon,* where the corporation's Coordination and Services Management office was found to provide for the asserted unitary business.

> "long-range planning for the company, maximization of overall company operations, development of financial policy and procedures, financing of corporate activities, maintenance of the accounting system, legal advice, public relations, labor relations, purchase and sale of raw crude oil and raw materials, and coordination between the refining and other operating functions so as to obtain an optimum short range operating program." 447 U.S., at 207.

In this case the parent company's operations are not interrelated with those of its subsidiaries so that one's "stable" operation is important to the other's "full utilization" of capacity. 447 U.S., at 218. See also id., at 225. The Woolworth parent did not provide "many essential

---

22. The English subsidiary was not included in the consolidated statements. App. to Juris. Statement 35. Cf. Keesling and Warren, The Unitary Concept in the Allocation of Income, 12 Hastings L.J. 42, 52 (1960) ("Central accounting, for instance, may result in some savings, but in most instances the amount is trifling in comparison with the income involved. Alone considered, it is too weak a connecting link to bind into one business, what would otherwise, from an operational standpoint, be considered separate businesses.").

As noted, there was no centralized tax department and no consolidation of tax returns.

In addition to the links set forth in the text, it is plain that the parent and the four subsidiaries all utilize the same general "F.W. Woolworth" corporate name. There is no record information on the significance of the use of this common name. Neither the Department nor the New Mexico Supreme Court gave any weight to use of a common corporate name when sustaining the tax at issue.

corporate services" for the subsidiaries, and there was no "centralized purchasing office * * * whose obvious purpose was to increase overall corporate profits through bulk purchases and efficient allocation of supplies among retailers." Id., at 224.[23] And it was not the case that "sales were facilitated through the use of a uniform credit card system, uniform packaging, brand names, and promotional displays, all run from the national headquarters." Ibid. See also Mobil, 445 U.S., at 428, 435.

There is a critical distinction between a retail merchandising business as conducted by Woolworth and the type of multinational business—now so familiar—in which refined, processed, or manufactured products (or parts thereof) may be produced in one or more countries and marketed in various countries, often worldwide.[25] In operations of this character there is a flow of international trade, often an interchange of personnel, and substantial mutual interdependence. The uncontradicted evidence demonstrates that Woolworth's international retail business is not comparable. There is no flow of international business. Nor is there any integration or unitary operation in the sense in which our cases consistently have used these terms.

In *Mobil,* we recognized that

"all dividend income received by corporations operating in interstate commerce is [not] necessarily taxable in each State where that corporation does business. Where the business activities of the dividend payor have nothing to do with the activities of the recipient *in the taxing state,* due process considerations might well preclude apportionability, because there would be no underlying unitary business."

445 U.S., at 441–442.

This is such a case. Each of the foreign subsidiaries at issue operates a "discrete business enterprise," Mobil, 445 U.S., at 439, with a notable absence of any "umbrella of centralized management and controlled interaction." Exxon, 447 U.S., at 224. New Mexico, in taxing a portion of dividends received from such enterprises, is attempting to reach "extraterritorial values," Mobil, 445 U.S., at 442, wholly unrelated to the business of the Woolworth stores in New Mexico. As a result, a "showing has been made that income unconnected with the unitary business has been used in the" levy of New Mexico tax. Butler Bros. v. McColgan, 315 U.S. 501, 509 (1942). We conclude that this tax does not bear the necessary relationship "to opportunities, benefits, or protection conferred or afforded by the taxing State. See Wisconsin v.

23. Cf. Butler Bros. v. McColgan, 315 U.S. 501, 508 (1942).

25. See Hans Rees' Sons v. North Carolina, 283 U.S. 123, 133 (1931) ("Undoubtedly, the enterprise of a corporation which manufactures and sells its manufactured product is ordinarily a unitary business, and all the factors in that enterprise are essential to the realization of profits."); Hellerstein, Recent Developments in State

Tax Apportionment and the Circumscription of Unitary Business, 21 Natl. Tax J. 487, 496 (1968) ("Manufacturing or purchasing goods in one state and selling in another, and transportation and communication between states are typical of cases considered unitary."), G. Altman and F. Keesling, Allocation of Income in State Taxation 101–102 (1946).

J.C. Penney Co., 311 U.S. 435, 444." Norfolk & W.R. Co. v. Missouri State Tax Comm'n, 390 U.S. 317, 325, n. 5 (1968), quoting Ott v. Mississippi Valley Barge Line Co., 336 U.S. 169, 174 (1969). New Mexico's tax thus fails to meet established due process standards.

III

We need not be detained by New Mexico's reaching out to tax "gross-up" amounts that even the Supreme Court of New Mexico recognized as "fictitious." 95 N.M., at 522, 624 P.2d, at 31. The gross-up computation is a figure that the Federal Government "deems" Woolworth to have received for purposes of part of Woolworth's federal foreign tax credit calculation. It "is treated [for this purpose] as a dividend in the same manner as a dividend actually received by the domestic corporation from a foreign corporation." H.R.Rep. No. 1447, 87th Cong., 2d Sess., A83 (1962). See also S.Rep. No. 1881, 87th Cong., 2d Sess., 227 (1962). In this case the foreign tax credit arose from the taxation by foreign nations of Woolworth foreign subsidiaries that had no unitary business relationship with New Mexico. New Mexico's effort to tax this income "deemed received"—with respect to which New Mexico contributed nothing—also must be held to contravene the Due Process Clause.

IV

The judgment of the Supreme Court of New Mexico is reversed.

[For Chief Justice Burger's concurring opinion, see his concurrence in the *ASARCO* case p. 539 supra.]

JUSTICE O'CONNOR, with whom JUSTICE BLACKMUN and JUSTICE REHN-QUIST join, dissenting.

The $39.9 million in dividend income at issue in this case was earned by four foreign subsidiaries of F.W. Woolworth Co.: F.W. Woolworth Gmbh (Germany), F.W. Woolworth, Ltd. (Canada), F.W. Woolworth, S.A. de C.V. (Mexico), and F.W. Woolworth Co., Ltd. (England). F.W. Woolworth Co. wholly owned its German, Canadian, and Mexican subsidiaries, and had a 52.7% interest in its English subsidiary. During the tax year in question the subsidiaries apparently operated somewhat autonomously in their respective markets, but "mail, telephone, and teletype communication between the upper echelons of management of the parent and the subsidiaries" was " 'frequent.' " Ante, at 13–14 (footnote omitted) (quoting App. to Juris. Statement 34). Moreover, "[d]ecisions about major financial decisions, such as the amount of dividends to be paid by the subsidiaries and the creation of substantial debt, had to be approved by the parent," and "Woolworth's published financial statements, such as its annual reports, were prepared on a consolidated basis." Ante, at 14. (citations and footnotes omitted).

These controlled subsidiaries, operating in geographically diverse markets in the same line of business as F.W. Woolworth itself, were simply not "unrelated,"[1] "discrete business enterprise[s]",[2] "hav[ing] nothing to do with the activities"[3] of F.W. Woolworth in New Mexico. Because I disagree with the redefinition of the limits of a unitary business adopted today by the Court, and for the reasons expressed in my dissent in No. 80–2015, ASARCO, Inc. v. Idaho State Tax Commission, ante, which was argued in tandem with this case, I respectfully dissent.

References. See J. Hellerstein, State Taxation I, Corporate Income and Franchise Taxes, "Intervention by the Supreme Court in apportionment controversies," ¶ 8.11[4] (1983); W. Hellerstein, "State Taxation of Multijurisdictional Corporations, Part II: Reflections on *ASARCO* and *Woolworth*," 81 Mich.L.Rev. 157 (1982); Peters, "Apportioning Multistate Income in *Exxon*: Analyzing the Decision; the Implications," 53 J. Tax. 246 (1980); Von Lehe, "*Exxon* and Its Impact on the *Hans Rees'* Doctrine", 1 Interstate Tax Rep. No. 9, Dec. 1981, p. 1; Dexter, "The Unitary Concept of State Income Taxation of Multistate—Multinational Business", 10 Urb.Law. 181 (1978).

In the aftermath of the recent Supreme Court decisions, there have been a number of State court decisions dealing with the delineation of a unitary business. See, as well as the Court's important decision in Container Corp. of America v. Franchise Tax Bd., 463 U.S. 159, 103 S.Ct. 2933 (1983), pp. 578–606 infra, which also deals with the scope of the unitary business in detail, and J. Hellerstein & W. Hellerstein, Cumulative Supplement to J. Hellerstein, State Taxation I, Corporate Income and Franchise Taxes ¶ 8.11[11] (1983).

ASH GROVE CEMENT COMPANY v. DEPARTMENT OF REVENUE

Oregon Tax Court, January 19, 1977.
7 OTR 6.

CARLISLE B. ROBERTS, JUDGE.

Plaintiff is a Delaware corporation with headquarters in Kansas City, Missouri, engaged in business in the State of Oregon and subject to ORS chapter 317, the Corporation Excise Tax Law of 1929. This act imposes a tax upon the privilege of carrying on or doing business in this state. The tax is measured by the plaintiff's net income attributable to business activity in Oregon (ORS 317.070(1)), as determined by the provisions of the Uniform Division of Income for Tax Purposes Act, ORS 314.605–314.670. The uniform act provides for allocation of a multistate corporation's income when it does business in this state and it specifically prescribes formulas for use in apportioning business income earned in operations involving more than one state, including Oregon. Such formulas seek a rough justice which, unfortunately, is

1. Mobil Oil Corp. v. Commissioner of Taxes, 445 U.S. 425, 439 (1980).

2. Exxon Corp. v. Department of Revenue, 447 U.S. 207, 224 (1980).

3. Mobil Oil Corp. v. Commissioner of Taxes, supra, at 442.

often the best standard that can be achieved in taxation. Norfolk & W.R. Co. v. North Carolina, 297 U.S. 682, 56 S.Ct. 625, 80 L.Ed. 977 (1936).

ORS 314.670 takes cognizance of the possibility of a failure of the generally applicable formulas fairly to represent the Oregon business activity and it permits the use of a special formula or method in a particular instance, including the use of separate accounting for the Oregon business activity.

The issue presented can be paraphrased by a quotation taken from Butler Bros. v. McColgan, 17 Cal.2d 664, 667–668, 111 P.2d 334, 336 (1941):

> "The sole question to be determined on this appeal is whether it is lawful and proper for the respondent, as franchise tax commissioner, to insist upon use of the formula for allocation of income in a case such as this, or whether the company is entitled to use the separate accounting of its San Francisco house to determine its net income in the state of California. The answer to this question depends entirely on the nature of the business conducted within and without the state by appellant, a foreign corporation. It is only if its business within this state is truly separate and distinct from its business without this state, so that the segregation of income may be made clearly and accurately, that the separate accounting method may properly be used. Where, however, interstate operations are carried on and that portion of the corporation's business done within the state cannot be clearly segregated from that done outside the state, the unit rule of assessment is employed as a device for allocating to the state for taxation its fair share of the taxable values of the taxpayer. (Citations omitted.) * * * "

Plaintiff appealed to the defendant, seeking to report its Oregon income on a separate accounting basis for the calendar years 1966, 1967, and 1969 through 1973. The defendant's Order No. I 76–7, dated March 5, 1976, denied the plaintiff's request and sustained the income tax auditor's requirement that the plaintiff corporation report its total business activity on the unitary method of computation, utilizing the three-factor formula for apportionment specified in ORS 314.650. Plaintiff paid its taxes as required by this method but appealed to this court from the defendant's order, seeking a reversal of the denial of separate accounting of most of its Oregon business activity for the tax years 1969 to 1973, inclusive, and for a refund of taxes the corporation deemed overpaid by the requirement to report on the unitary basis. (The tax years 1966 and 1967, in issue at the departmental hearing, were not pleaded in this court.)

In cases such as this, involving the question of segregated versus unitary accounting, it has often been observed that "the facts are all important." Norfolk & Western R. Co. v. Missouri Tax Com., 390 U.S. 317, 88 S.Ct. 995, 19 L.Ed.2d 1201 (1968); Hines Lumber Co. v. Galloway, 175 Or. 524, 539, 154 P.2d 539, 544 (1944); Hamilton Management Corp. v. Com., 3 OTR 154, 156 (1968).

The plaintiff's first predecessor in interest began as a Missouri corporation in 1882, manufacturing and selling lime products. Many years later, a cement business was developed. The parties have stipulated, *inter alia:*

"7. During the period 1969–1973 Ash Grove's principal business was the manufacture and sale of cement. About 85% of its gross receipts each year related to cement sales.

"8. Ash Grove also has two lime manufacturing plants within its corporate structure: one in Springfield, Missouri and one in Portland, Oregon.

"9. The Springfield plant began operations at the turn of the twentieth century. Its manufacturing facility is in Springfield and the sales from that plant are made in Missouri, Kansas, Nebraska, Iowa, South Dakota, North Dakota, Minnesota, Arkansas, Oklahoma, Colorado and Texas. A few sales are also made each year in Illinois, Ohio and New Jersey.

"10. Over the years some lime products from the Springfield plant were shipped into Oregon, Washington, California and British Columbia (hereinafter referred to collectively as the 'Northwest Territory'). However, it was recognized that there was a potentially large market for lime in the Northwest Territory. The wood processing industry and the road building process were two areas that looked particularly good as potential users of lime. Accordingly, a 4.5 million dollar lime plant was constructed at Portland, Oregon and was put into operation in 1964.

"11. Lime manufactured in the Portland plant is sold exclusively to customers in Oregon, Washington, California and British Columbia (the 'Northwest Territory').

"12. The following annual amounts of lime have been sold from the Portland plant in the Northwest Territory (by years and tons sold): 1965, 46,286; 1966, 55,807; 1967, 43,680; 1968, 51,191; 1969, 48,766; 1970, 47,775; 1971, 49,450; 1972, 51,223; 1973, 60,907; 1974, 65,604.

"13. During the period 1969–1973 Ash Grove continued to supply customers in the Northwest Territory from its Springfield plant with lime products that the Portland plant did not make, namely, pulverized quick lime and slik lime. Sales of these two types of lime were made to Ocean Cement Ltd. and Dealers Supply Company, neither of which purchases products from the Portland plant.

"14. The following annual amounts of pulverized quick lime and slik lime from the Springfield plant were sold in the Northwest Territory (by years and tons sold): 1965, 5,877; 1966, 5,037; 1967, 4,605; 1968, 4,452; 1969, 3,670; 1970, 2,362; 1971, 1,926; 1972, 1,490; 1973, 891; 1974, 648.

"15. Ash Grove has always been reluctant to continue these lime sales in the Northwest Territory from the Springfield plant. Shipping costs make the profit margin thin, and the same lime can be more profitably sold in its regular Midwest Territory. However, the Northwest customers for this type of lime are unable to secure the same quality and type of lime elsewhere, so the sales continue but in a steadily diminishing volume.

"16. Sales from the Springfield [Missouri] plant (in dollars) can be analyzed as follows:

Year	Northwest Sales	Other Sales	Total Sales
1965	$129,088	$1,644,224	$1,773,312
1966	121,465	1,714,180	1,835,645
1967	116,844	1,727,497	1,844,341
1968	112,573	1,951,910	2,064,483
1969	101,766	2,016,005	2,117,771
1970	63,091	2,340,278	2,403,369
1971	52,035	2,141,570	2,193,605
1972	45,355	2,086,729	2,132,084
1973	27,899	2,575,916	2,603,815
1974	32,570	3,238,527	3,271,097

"17. During 1969–1973 Ash Grove also sold small amounts of hydrate lime to Dealers Supply Company in retail size 10–pound bags from its Springfield plant. During that period the Portland plant did not have the facilities to pack and ship retail size 10–pound bags of hydrate lime.

"18. Ash Grove makes no cement sales in the Northwest Territory. None of the customers to which it sells cement (all in the Midwest) is a customer of Ash Grove's Portland lime plant."

The testimony shows, and the court finds, that the plaintiff's midwestern cement plants in Louisville, Nebraska, and Chanute, Kansas, its lime plant in Springfield, Missouri, and its headquarters in Kansas City, Missouri, constitute the operating and administrative activities of a typical multistate corporation which is properly required to make its income tax reports to a number of states under provisions for allocation and apportionment similar to those set out in the Uniform Division of Income for Tax Purposes Act (ORS 314.605 to 314.670). The parties agree that, as to that part of the business, various factors are so intertwined that it is not feasible to determine the source of net income between several states except through the use of an approved formula. (This includes sales from the Midwest to the "Northwest Territory," including Oregon, although these are very small from Oregon's standpoint.)

However, the record shows that the situation is quite different with respect to the lime plant in Portland, Oregon. It is physically removed from the midwestern complex (1,800 miles). Freight charges enhance the separation. (It is uneconomical for the several plants in the

Midwest to interchange raw materials or finished products with the Portland plant.)

Although several of the Kansas City officers regularly visit and consult with the Portland management, the autonomy of the latter is very substantial. (The court recognizes that the power is in Kansas City and changes could be made at any time.) Portland does its own basic accounting, hires and discharges personnel as needed, has its own local law firm to advise it, makes its own purchases (except paper bags), and has its own sales department. The costs of the few services rendered to the Portland plant by the Kansas City headquarters and its staff are easily separable and chargeably (but actually were not charged to Portland in the years considered in this case).

The strongest link by way of services between Kansas City and Portland was the former's provision of accounting aids through use of the Kansas City computer. (This not only aided Portland mechanically but gave the top management important data essential to overall supervision.) But separability of activities was still maintained during the computer use and no charge was made to Portland for it. Income attributable to Oregon was not affected.

The most important aspect of this suit is that plaintiff was able to demonstrate to the court's satisfaction that the Oregon activities during the years in question gave rise to an income tax net loss. There was no income with which to measure the tax.[1] See Utah Const. & Mining v. Tax Com., 255 Or. 228, 465 P.2d 712 (1970), and John I. Haas, Inc. v. Tax Com., 227 Or. 170, 192, 361 P.2d 820, 830 (1961).

It appears to the court that the defendant has based its position upon the following proposition: (1) the plaintiff, a foreign corporation, was doing business in Oregon during the years in question; (2) the plaintiff is a unitary corporation; and (3) ergo, even though plaintiff suffers losses in its business transacted in Oregon but has an overall net income after deducting losses from the Portland operation (and possibly elsewhere), allocation and apportionment of the income must follow and the amounts demanded by the state have been properly paid to Oregon in reliance upon the statutory allocation formula found in ORS 314.650–314.665. The word "unitary" expresses a conclusion which requires careful examination.

The necessity and justification for the use of allocation formulas for determination of corporate income attributable to a particular state are found in the typical factual situations; e.g., to attribute to the state the aliquot corporate profits earned through steps in a vertical process, a series of transactions which may begin upon obtaining raw materials in one or more states, to be turned to manufactured goods in another state

---

1. In its published rule, OAR 150–314.–615–(D), defendant has stated: " * * * Whether the Oregon activities engaged in for a financial profit actually result in a financial profit *or loss* is not determinative. * * * " (Emphasis supplied.) This is a correct statement in context, but must be used with caution unless the facts unquestionably require apportionment and allocation.

and ending with sales in several other states, from which the ultimate gain is derived by the taxpayer. Underwood Typewriter Co. v. Chamberlain, 254 U.S. 113, 41 S.Ct. 45, 65 L.Ed. 165, 3 AFTR 3087 (1920). Another example is that of a multistate corporation which obtains unusually favorable inventory prices through very large purchases, made by a central buying division, and then places its goods in numerous outlets in several states. With such large purchases, markdowns in prices may be necessary to dispose of residues and some outlets may show a bookkeeping loss. The corporation, nevertheless, may be denied separate tax reporting of an alleged loss, indicated by its separate accounting, if it fails to prove by clear and cogent evidence that extraterritorial values have been taxed. Butler Brothers v. McColgan, 315 U.S. 501, 62 S.Ct. 701, 86 L.Ed. 991 (1942). As stated in Hellerstein, Recent Developments in State Tax Apportionment and the Circumscription of Unitary Business, XXI Nat'l Tax J (No. 4, December 1968), at 500, it is improper to disregard

> " * * * the underlying reasons for the development of formulary apportionment, namely, that there is no viable way of separately accounting for the profits of a business where interdependent operating functions that produce the profits of the enterprise are carried on in more than one state. Thus, to take a simple case, where goods are manufactured in State A and sold in State B, efforts to account separately for the profit from these interdependent operations have floundered on the inability to find acceptable methods of breaking up the profit realized into a 'manufacturing' profit and a 'selling' profit. * * * "

Lacking the clear evidence which was presented in this suit, and conscious that several states can justly claim that activities protected by them were essential to the final realization of income, experience has shown that an acceptable allocation formula must be used in most situations.

*   *   *

It must be constantly held in mind that Oregon seeks to measure its tax only upon net income attributable to Oregon. ORS 317.070(1). If no corporate profit can be found which can be attributed to Oregon, then only the minimum tax of $10 can be imposed upon a corporation over which the state has some jurisdiction. ORS 317.090; Hines Lumber Co. v. Galloway, supra.

Butler Brothers failed to meet its burden of proof. That is not the situation in the present suit. The separability of the Oregon lime plant from the midwestern parent complex has been well demonstrated. The exclusion from the balance sheet of any charges for the corporation's contribution of services to the Portland plant (which were shown to be inconsiderable, if not de minimis) makes possible a bona fide separate accounting in this instance. The record is replete with uncontradicted testimony that the Portland plant contributed nothing to the parent. The Portland plant operated at a loss throughout 1969–1973. After the initial capital investment, Kansas City and the midwestern manufacturing complex, during the years in question, contributed minimal services of central advertising and bag purchasing which, if charged to the Portland plant, would merely have enlarged its loss. (The Portland plant was able to operate independently because its depreciation reserves gave it a cash flow.)

The defendant's administrative rule, published as OAR 150–314.–615–(E), reflects Hamilton Corp. v. Tax Com., 253 Or. 602, 457 P.2d 486 (1969), and takes cognizance that:

> "[a] taxpayer may have more than one 'trade or business.' In such cases, it is necessary to determine the business income attributable to each separate trade or business. The income of each business is then apportioned by an apportionment formula which takes into consideration the instate and outstate factors which relate to the trade or business the income of which is being apportioned."

The ruling then sets out indicia of a single trade or business, all of which were adverted to in the testimony and have been considered by this court in this suit.

The first indicator is captioned: "same type of business." This is applicable here (considering the Missouri lime plant and the Portland lime plant), but is overcome by geographical location, source and ownership of supply (third-party owned British Columbia lime for Portland, plaintiff's own Springfield lime deposits for Springfield), different customers, and the like. The very small percentage of Portland's business in relation to plaintiff's total business and the small percentage of plaintiff's lime business done by Portland aids segregation in accounting, also.

The second indicator listed by OAR 150–314.615–(E) is described as "steps in a vertical process" and is not applicable here.

The third is "strong centralized management." As stated above, the facts could change in any year, but during 1969 to 1973, inclusive, management provided little in services that the Portland plant could not have acquired from third persons at a reasonable fee, readily determined.[2]

This factual situation is readily distinguishable from that in Coca Cola Co. v. Dept. of Rev., 5 OTR 405 (1974), aff'd, 271 Or. 517, 533 P.2d 788 (1975), involving the use of a syrup, based on a secret formula, absolutely controlled by the parent organization, coupled with the parent's active, extensive control and supervision of quality of product, advertising, method of marketing, research and development, maintenance and audit of books and records, as well as the geographical area to be served (which was not solely on the basis of freight rates). The factors of contribution and dependency were plain, and the Oregon business, even under its separate accounting, made a profit.

---

2. Plaintiff is most vulnerable here because of the importance in this context of centralized management. However, plaintiff can only be taxed the statutory minimum in Oregon for 1969 to 1973 because it has demonstrated that it has no income by which a tax could be measured.

It is true that experience has shown that allocation and apportionment formulas must be used with much greater frequency than separate accounting. Segregated accounting may be "unusual." Hence, apportionment of income (unitary reporting) is deemed, prima facie, as the method for income tax accounting of multistate corporations, under present law. Donald M. Drake Co. v. Dept. of Rev., 263 Or. 26, 31, 500 P.2d 1041, 1043 (1972), aff'g 4 OTR 552 (1971). Courts recognize that accounting can be arbitrary, that the business done within this state can be "managed," and that it is often impossible to unravel the accounts of a profitable interstate business. However, ORS 314.670 is applicable to the facts presented by Ash Grove. That statute provides:

"If the allocation and apportionment provisions of ORS 314.610 to 314.665 do not fairly represent the extent of the taxpayer's business activity in this state [as a basis for taxation], the taxpayer may petition for and the department may permit, or the department may require, in respect to all or any part of the taxpayer's business activity, if reasonable:

"(1) *Separate accounting;*

"(2) The exclusion of any one or more of the factors;

"(3) The inclusion of one or more additional factors which will fairly represent the taxpayer's business activity in this state; or

"(4) The employment of any other method to effectuate an equitable allocation and apportionment of the taxpayer's income." (Emphasis supplied.)

On the basis of the record herein, this court is convinced that the tax assessed by the state in this instance would have to be paid from income properly attributable to other states. See Wah Chang Corp. v. Commission, 2 OTR 31 (1964).

The court finds that the plaintiff's Portland lime plant, in 1969 to 1973, inclusive, should be treated as a separate business of the plaintiff.

In the light of the foregoing decision, the plaintiff's second cause of suit, based upon the Commerce Clause and Due Process Clause of the U.S. Constitution, is moot.

* * * The plaintiff is entitled to and should utilize separate accounting for corporation excise tax purposes for those years. Defendant shall assess taxes for the years in question at the statutory amount of $10 per year and refund overpayments of tax with interest pursuant to ORS 314.415.[3] Plaintiff is awarded its statutory court costs and disbursements.

3. The testimony indicates that Ash Grove's Oregon plant began to enjoy profits in 1974 and 1975 and, presumably, thereafter. If other facts remain unchanged, it can be argued that the Portland operation should continue to file a separate return in future years, with apportionment between the several states in the "Northwest Territory." However, under the decision of this case and the authorities on which it is based, there is implicit recognition that each tax year must be considered on its own set of facts, with the presumption that the apportionment accounting of the total corporation is the preferred method of reporting unless the taxpayer proves otherwise.

Notes and Problems

A. *Substantial Interdependence of Basic Operations as a Requirement of the Unitary Business.* The *Ash Grove Cement* case appears to lend credence to the view that a substantial flow of goods or the rendition of substantial basic operational services is an essential requirement of a unitary manufacturing business. See also the decisions of the Pennsylvania Supreme Court noted at Note E, pp. 525–27 supra. In Container Corp. of America v. Franchise Tax Bd., p. 578 infra, the Supreme Court rejected the basic operations interdependence test *as a constitutional requirement,* saying:

> Finally, appellant urges us to adopt a bright-line rule requiring as a prerequisite to a finding that a mercantile or manufacturing enterprise is unitary that it be characterized by "a substantial flow of goods." Brief for Appellant 47. We decline this invitation. The prerequisite to a constitutionally acceptable finding of unitary business is a flow of *value,* not a flow of goods. As we reiterated in *F.W. Woolworth,* a relevant question in the unitary business inquiry is whether " 'contributions to income [of the subsidiaries] result[ed] from functional integration, centralization of management, and economies of scale.'" 458 U.S., at 364, 102 S.Ct., at 3135, quoting *Mobil,* 445 U.S., at 438, 100 S.Ct., at 1232. "[S]ubstantial mutual interdependence," *F.W. Woolworth,* supra, 458 U.S., at 371, 102 S.Ct., at 3139, can arise in any number of ways; a substantial flow of goods is clearly one but just as clearly not the only one. [463 U.S. at 178–79.]

The Court also noted:

> As we state supra, at 168–170, there is a wide range of constitutionally acceptable variations on the unitary business theme. Thus, a leading scholar has suggested that a "flow of goods" requirement would provide a reasonable and workable bright-line test for unitary business, see Hellerstein, Recent Developments in State Tax Apportionment and the Circumscription of Unitary Business, 21 Nat.Tax J. 487, 501–502 (1968); Hellerstein, Allocation and Apportionment of Dividends and the Delineation of the Unitary Business, 14 Tax Notes 155 (Jan. 25, 1982), and some state courts have adopted such a test, see, e.g., Commonwealth v. ACF Industries, Inc., 441 Pa. 129, 271 A.2d 273 (1970). But see, *e.g.,* McLure, Operational Interdependence Is Not the Appropriate "Bright Line Test" of a Unitary Business—At Least Not Now, 18 Tax Notes 107 (Jan. 10, 1983). However sensible such a test may be as a policy matter, however, we see no reason to impose it on all the States as a requirement of constitutional law. Cf. Wisconsin v. J.C. Penney Co., 311 U.S. 435, 445, 61 S.Ct. 246, 250, 85 L.Ed. 267 (1940). [463 U.S. at 178 n. 17.]

For other writings dealing with the test, see "Interdependence of basic operating functions as a prerequisite of unitary producing, manufacturing or mercantile business," in J. Hellerstein, State Taxation I, Corporate Income and Franchise Taxes ¶ 8.11[5] (1983); J. Hellerstein, "The Basic Operations Interdependence Requirement of a Unitary Business: A Reply to Charles E. McLure, Jr.," Tax Notes Feb. 28, 1983, at 723; McLure, "The

Basic Operational Interdependence Test of a Unitary Business: Rejoinder," Tax Notes, Oct. 10, 1983, at 91.

B. *The Unitary Business Principle and "Separate Businesses"*. It is well established that separate businesses may not be included in an overall apportionment of a single corporation or to a group of affiliated corporations on a combined basis. This follows from the concept that a "separate business" is not part of a unitary business. Consequently, many unitary business controversies are approached by the courts, as in the *Ash Grove* case, in terms of whether a branch or a subsidiary is engaged in a "separate business" from the rest of the enterprise.

However, that approach has its shortcomings. As one of the co-authors has suggested: *

"Couching of the unitary business problem in terms of whether a 'separate business' is carried on in the State has tended to emphasize the similarity or dissimilarity in the nature of the lines of business being conducted in various areas, or the products created and sold, or the services handled. Thus, the MTC regulations provide that 'a taxpayer is generally engaged in a single trade or business when all of its activities are in the same general line.' [94]

"The focus on the line of business or products being handled in determining the separateness of businesses [95] has led to speculations, such as those of Keesling and Warren:

Is the growing of oranges a different kind of business than the growing of grapefruit, or are they one business inasmuch as both oranges and grapefruit are citrus fruits? Is a company which manufactures insecticides in California, fertilizers in West Virginia and chemicals for use in textile manufacturing in Georgia engaged in three separate businesses, or is it engaged in the single business of manufacturing chemicals? Again, is a company which operates oil wells in California and mines in a number of other states engaged in two different businesses or in the single business of extracting mineral substances from the earth? [96]

"The difficulty with drawing lines between separate and unitary businesses by distinguishing different 'kinds' of businesses, although espoused

---

* The following material is taken from J. Hellerstein, State Taxation I, Corporate Income and Franchise Taxes ¶ 8.11[8], pp. 454–57 (1983). Used with the consent of the copyright owner and publisher.

94. Reg. IV.1.(b). The following example of separate businesses is given in the MTC regulations;

The taxpayer is a conglomerate with three operating divisions. One division is engaged in manufacturing aerospace items for the federal government. Another division is engaged in growing tobacco products. The third division produces and distributes motion pictures for theatres and television. Each division operates independently; there is no strong central management. Each division operates in this state as well as in other states. In this case, it is fair to conclude that the taxpayer is engaged in three separate "trades or businesses."

95. See also Honolulu Oil Corp. v. Franchise Tax Bd., 60 Cal.2d 417, 424, 386 P.2d 40, 34 Cal.Rptr. 552 (1963), in which in referring to the corporation's business of producing and selling crude oil in several States, the court said: "Honolulu is not operating two distinct types of businesses. * * *" See ¶ 8.11[3][a] for a discussion of the case and criticism of its holding that the business was unitary.

96. Keesling and Warren, "California's Uniform Division of Income for Tax Purposes Act," 15 U.C.L.A.L.Rev. 156, 172 (1967).

by Keesling in his earlier writing,[97] has apparently been one of the factors that caused him to abandon the effort altogether, and to argue in his more recent writing that 'all income from commonly-owned business activities should be combined and apportioned by a single formula without inquiring as to whether such activities are unitary or separate. * * *'[98]   A leading spokesman for multicorporate structured business, likewise despairing of distinguishing separate from unitary businesses, goes to the opposite extreme and concludes that the unitary business approach should be abandoned altogether and that separate accounting should be substituted for apportionment of the income of multicorporate enterprises.[99]

"Both these analysts come out with the wrong answers, because in our view they ask the wrong question.[100]   Whether the businesses differ in the nature of their products, lines, and services should be irrelevant in deciding whether unitary apportionment is appropriate.   Such an inquiry is not directed to the fundamental question presented in deciding whether a unitary business exists, i.e., the extent of interdependence, integration, and interrelation of their basic operations.

97.   See G. Altman & F. Keesling, [Allocation of Income in State Taxation (2d ed. 1950).   Altman and Keesling take the position that corporations engaged in more than one State in manufacturing and selling, buying and selling, or transportation and communication are ordinarily to be regarded as unitary businesses. Id. at 100–102.   They give as illustrations of separate, nonunitary businesses a chain of bakeries in which the buying and selling are local to each State, and a chain of hotels. Id.]

98.   See Keesling, "A Current Look at the Combined Report and Uniformity in Allocation Practices," 42 J.Tax. 106, 109 (1975); and Keesling & Warren, "The Unitary Concept in the Allocation of Income," 12 Hastings L.J. 42, 46 (1960).

99.   See Miller, "State Income Taxation of Multiple Corporations and Multiple Businesses," Tax Foundation Seminar on Taxation of Interstate Business (April 16–17, 1970).

100.   Miller does, however, make the following comment on the treatment of separate businesses under the basic operations test of a unitary business:

Without attempting to assess the validity of this thesis, i.e., that a 'unitary' business is to be characterized primarily by interdependence of 'operating' functions, it is significant that, even if generally accepted, this thesis would leave unresolved the many questions which typically arise in attempting to determine whether and how 'operating' functions should be grouped into a series of separate businesses rather than a single business.

For example, a manufacturer of air conditioning equipment may produce single-room window units, larger units to cool one-family homes, and still larger units to cool entire high-rise apartment houses.   Should the classification of these activities into one, two, or three businesses depend on whether or not the several products (i) are manufactured at one rather than at separate factories, (ii) utilize similar or dissimilar productive processes and components, (iii) are sold under a single brand name or several names, or (iv) are marketed through one or several channels of distribution?

Id. at 5–6.

To respond to Miller's hypothetical cases, manufacturing qualifies as a basic operation.   Whether the three sizes and types of air-conditioning equipment are manufactured at one rather than separate factories, whether similar or dissimilar processes or components are used, whether a single brand name or several names are used for the various units, are irrelevant to the issue.   The right questions to be asked are whether there is flow of raw materials, components and products or operating services between the factories, or between the manufacturer's purchasing department and the various factories.   As for selling, which is a basic operational function, the method of marketing would be a crucial factor.   If all three types of air conditioners were sold through the manufacturer's central sales division, the operations of the various factories in producing all three types of air conditioners would be part of the unitary business.

"This point may be illustrated by applying the test of interdependence of basic operations to Keesling's teasing examples in exploring the line between separate and unitary businesses. If the California insecticide manufacturer obtains a substantial part of the basic chemicals it uses in producing the insecticides from either its fertilizer or textile chemical division, the requisite operational interdependence would exist; and if not, and if no other substantial basic operations are carried on between the various divisions, the insecticide, fertilizer, and textile chemical operations would not constitute parts of a unitary business. Whether the insecticide or the fertilizer business should be regarded as *separate lines of business* from the chemical business, or as parts of the chemical business, is a semantic formulation that is irrelevant to the real issues presented in defining the scope of a unitary business." J. Hellerstein, State Taxation I, Corporate Income and Franchise Taxes ¶ 8.11[8], pp. 454–57 (1983).

SECTION 8. COMBINED APPORTIONMENT AND ALLOCATION WITH RESPECT TO MULTICORPORATE ENTERPRISES

Notes and Problems

A. *Application of Unitary Method to Multicorporate Enterprise.* The unitary business doctrine had its origin in the nineteenth century "unit rule," which was developed in the taxation of interstate railroads and telegraph and express companies operated by a single corporation. See Sanford v. Poe, 165 U.S. 194, 17 S.Ct. 305 (1897) and the cases cited in Norfolk and Western Railway Co. v. Missouri State Tax Commission, p. 425 supra. During the current century, that rule, now termed the "unitary business doctrine," was first applied to manufacturing and mercantile businesses conducted in various States as branches or departments of a single corporation. Edison California Stores, Inc. v. McColgan, 176 P.2d 697 (Cal.1947), on rehearing 30 Cal.2d 472, 183 P.2d 16 (1947), was the pioneer case holding that the unitary method was likewise appropriate in the case of apportioning the income of an enterprise conducted through controlled subsidiaries, if the business is unitary. There, a Delaware corporation owned a chain of retail stores selling shoes and accessories, each store being organized as a separate subsidiary corporation in the State in which it did business. The parent corporation manufactured no goods, but conducted at St. Louis central management, purchasing, distributing, advertising, and administrative departments. The California subsidiary, which carried on a purely intrastate business, paid for the goods and services received at the parent company's cost, plus overhead charges.

The taxpayer sought to have its franchise tax, which was measured by apportioned net income, assessed by a separate accounting method, offering in support of its application evidence of actual costs and actual California net income. The accuracy of these figures was not assailed. Nevertheless, the application was rejected and the tax commissioner instead applied a formula—made up of three factors, sales, property and payroll—to the business of the entire chain in order to obtain the net income apportionable to California. The use of the formula produced a tax which apportioned to California a percentage of the chain's profits which was slightly lower than the California percentage of the total sales, whereas a substantially lower figure was produced by the separate accounting method sought by the taxpayer. The application of the unitary business approach to the separate corporations was upheld by the court.

The same view was adopted in Zale–Salem, Inc. v. State Tax Comm'n, 237 Or. 261, 391 P.2d 601 (1964); Interstate Finance Corp. v. Wisconsin Department of Taxation, 28 Wis.2d 262, 137 N.W.2d 38 (1965); see Gulf Oil Corp. v. Clayton, 267 N.C. 15, 147 S.E.2d 522 (1960).

B. *Combined and Consolidated Reports and the Use of the Combination Method in Apportioning the Taxpayer's Base.* The division of income of a group of controlled corporations has taken on major importance for Federal income tax purposes as multinational businesses operating through subsidiaries have expanded.[101] In the early days of State franchise taxation measured by net income, and later under direct corporate net income taxes as they developed, the States relied on provisions somewhat similar to I.R.C. § 482, in order to attempt to prevent the siphoning off of income to out-of-state affiliated or controlled corporations, through non-arm's-length pricing and other arrangements. Recent experience in the Federal income tax field has demonstrated the great difficulties in establishing arm's-length income and deduction allocations as between United States corporations and their foreign subsidiaries.[102] The experience of the States with this type of technique proved unsatisfactory. See Palmolive Company v. Conway, 43 F.2d 226 (D.C.W.D.Wis.1930), affirmed 56 F.2d 83 (7th Cir.), certiorari denied 287 U.S. 601, 57 S.Ct. 7 (1932); Buick Motor Co. v. City of Milwaukee, 48 F.2d 801 (7th Cir.1931), affirming 43 F.2d 385 (E.D.Wis. 1930), certiorari denied 284 U.S. 655, 52 S.Ct. 34 (1931); People ex rel. Studebaker Corp. v. Gilchrist, 244 N.Y. 114, 155 N.E. 68 (1926); Addison Miller Inc. v. Commissioner of Taxation, 249 Minn. 24, 81 N.W.2d 89 (1957). The *Palmolive* case is noted in 7 Wis.L.Rev. 250 (1932); 31 Col.L.Rev. 719 (1931); 80 U. of Pa.L.Rev. 892 (1932).

The central controversy has to do with the use of combined or consolidated reports, or the determination of the liability of a taxpayer which has filed a separate return, on a combined basis in cases in which the unitary business includes corporations not taxable in the State. Many States permit or require such reporting for affiliates of a unitary business all of which are taxable in the State.[103] Some States have adopted explicit

---

101. See the growing literature relating to Section 482 of the Internal Revenue Code and the frequent modifications of the Treasury Regulations. Comptroller General of the United States, General Accounting Office, Report to the Chairman of the House Ways and Means Committee (GAO § 482 Report), dealing with the administration by the Internal Revenue Service of I.R.C. § 482; "Criteria for the Allocation of Items of Income and Expense Between Related Corporations in Different States," Studies in International Fiscal Law, Int'l Fiscal Ass'n, General Report by Surrey and Tillinghast I/29 et seq. (Washington 1971); Mansfield, Cohen and Surrey, "Spe-

cial Report on Section 482," 28 J.Tax. 66 (1968).

102. Report of the Comptroller General, note 101 supra; Note, "Multinational Corporations and Income Allocation under Section 482 of the Internal Revenue Code," 89 Harv.L.Rev. 1202 (1976); Fuller, "Section 482 Revisited," 31 Tax L.Rev. 475 (1976).

103. See N.Y.Tax Law § 211.4, CCH ¶ 92–391, P–H ¶ 12,025.20; Va.Code Ann. § 58.1–442, CCH ¶ 94–087h–j, P–H ¶ 12,726; State Tax Comm'n v. La Touraine Coffee Co., 361 Mass. 773, 282 N.E.2d 643 (1972).

provisions authorizing tax administrators, under broader standards than the existence of non-arm's-length arrangements or transactions, to require or permit the filing of combined or consolidated reports, which include the tax base and apportionment factors of affiliates that are not taxable in the State.[104] Since combined apportionment has been recognized as applicable only to the unitary business, a controlled subsidiary conducting a separate business is not includible within the combination, at least as administrative practice and judicial decision have developed.

In other States, the general powers of the tax administrator to determine the income or other tax base properly attributable to the State have been the basis for apportionment on a combined basis; indeed, the decisions in *Edison California Stores* and *Zale–Salem,* supra, were based on such general statutory provisions.

A good deal of impetus to the use of the combined method of apportionment has been given in recent years by the Multistate Tax Commission (MTC, the administrative arm of the Multistate Tax Compact). See Corrigan "Interstate Corporate Income Taxation—Recent Revolutions and a Modern Response," 29 Vand.L.Rev. 423, 439–441 (1976).

There is a growing trend over the country to apply the combined method broadly by including the tax base and factors of all the corporations which are part of the unitary enterprise conducted within the United States. See Peters, "Use of Combined Reporting Required by Increasing Number of States," 41 J.Tax. 375 (1974). In 1987 the method was employed by more than 20 States with respect to multistate business. See CCH Multistate Corporate Income Tax Guide 185 (Chart). Although some courts found that combined reporting is not authorized by the State's statute, see Polaroid Corp. v. Commissioner of Revenue, 393 Mass. 490, 472 N.E.2d 259 (1984), Universal Manufacturing Corp. v. Brady, 320 So.2d 784 (Miss.1975); American Bakeries Co. v. Johnson, 259 N.C. 419, 131 S.E.2d 1 (1963), in recent years the courts have tended to sustain the taxing authorities' power to require combined reporting. PMD Investment Co. v. State, 216 Neb. 553, 345 N.W.2d 815 (1984); Pioneer Container Corp. v. Beshears, 235 Kan. 745, 684 P.2d 396 (1984); Joslin Dry Goods Co. v. Dolan, 200 Colo. 291, 615 P.2d 16 (1980). As a result of 1978 changes in the statute, the Mississippi State Law Commission may now permit or require consolidated income tax

---

104. See, e.g., the current Alaska, California, and Oregon provisions. Thus the California statute provides: "In the case of a corporation liable to report under this part owning or controlling, either directly or indirectly, another corporation, or other corporations, and in the case of a corporation liable to report under this part and owned or controlled, either directly or indirectly, by another corporation, the Franchise Tax Board may require a consolidated report showing the combined net income or such other facts as it deems necessary. The Franchise Tax Board is authorized and empowered, in such manner as it may determine, to assess the tax against either of the corporations whose net income is involved in the report upon the basis of the combined entire net income and such other information as it may possess, or it may adjust the tax in such other manner as it shall determine to be equitable if it determines it to be necessary in order to prevent evasion of taxes or to clearly reflect the net income earned by said corporation or corporations from business done in this State." Cal.Rev. and Tax Code Ann. § 25104, CCH ¶ 104–888, P–H ¶ 12,562. The statute defines "ownership or control" as owning directly or indirectly more than 50 percent of the voting stock of the taxpayer. Cal.Rev. and Tax Code Ann. § 25105, CCH ¶ 104–889, P–H ¶ 12,563.

returns to be filed by a group of affiliated corporations. This change nullifies the decision in Universal Manufacturing Corp. v. Brady, supra.

Generally, the combined method may be used by the tax administrator so as to include nontaxable corporations if intercompany arrangements or agreements distort the taxpayer's income. See, e.g., Wurlitzer Co. v. State Tax Comm'n, 35 N.Y.2d 100, 358 N.Y.S.2d 762, 315 N.E.2d 805 (1974).

C. Virtually all corporation tax laws grant the administrator broad powers to prescribe methods of reporting and to vary the statutory formula, in cases in which the formula does not "fairly represent the extent of the taxpayer's business activity in this state" (quoted from UDITPA § 18). The courts of some States have held that this provision empowers the tax administrator to apply the combined method of apportionment to a multicorporate unitary business. See Caterpillar Tractor Co. v. Lenckos, 77 Ill. App.3d 90, 395 N.E.2d 1167 (1979), aff'd, 84 Ill.2d 102, 417 N.E.2d 1343 (1981); Montana Dep't of Revenue v. American Smelting & Refining Co., 117 Mont. 316, 567 P.2d 901 (1977), appeal dismissed, 434 U.S. 1042, 98 S.Ct. 884 (1978). In Massachusetts, however, the existence of such authority to make an equitable determination of income attributable to the State did not warrant the determination of the tax on a combined basis. Despite the language of the statute granting the commissioner the power "equitably [to] determine" the net income of parent and subsidiary "by reasonable rules of apportionment of the combined income of the subsidiary," the court held, in the light of the legislative history, that the commission had no power to require combined reporting, at least in the absence of a determination that dealings between the parent and subsidiaries were not at arm's length. See Polaroid Corp. v. Commissioner of Revenue, supra. Examine the statutes of your State and consider whether such provisions afford the tax administrator a sufficient basis for requiring combined reports, or for determining tax liability on a combined basis.

D. Does the Due Process Clause or the Commerce Clause prohibit the inclusion in the combined apportionment of the income and factors of a corporation that is not taxable within the State? It has been contended that members of the controlled group which are not taxable in the State, in effect, are being taxed by such an apportionment. See Garrison, "Toward a Consensus on Apportionable vs. Allocable Income," 38 Tax Exec. 41, 45 (1975); Cahoon, Mondale Comm. Hearings 237. The premise that nontaxable corporations are being taxed by the use of combined apportionment underlies the reasoning of cases such as *Universal Manufacturing Corp.*, Note B, supra. Consider, in this connection, the Supreme Court's holdings that income which cannot be taxed directly may be used as a tax measure (Underwood Typewriter Co. v. Chamberlain, Butler Bros. v. McColgan, International Harvester Co. v. Evatt, pp. 435, 442, and 479 supra); that death and income tax rates may be determined by taking into account assets and income outside the territorial jurisdiction of the State (Maxwell v. Bugbee, p. 111 supra, and Wheeler v. State of Vermont, p. 947 infra); and the Court's dismissal of the appeal in the *Chase Brass & Copper* case for "want of jurisdiction," p. 518 supra.

E. Under the New York corporate franchise tax statute, the State Tax Commission is granted the "discretion" to require or permit the filing of a combined report in the case of a taxpayer which owns or controls, directly or indirectly, substantially all the stock of one or more other corporations, or in the case in which substantially all the taxpayer's stock is owned or controlled, directly or indirectly, by one or more other corporations or interests. N.Y.Tax Law § 211.4, CCH ¶ 93–974, P–H ¶ 12,025.20. Only corporations subject to the New York tax may be included in a combined report, unless the inclusion of non-taxpayers is deemed necessary by the Commission "in order properly to reflect the tax liability" under the statute, in view of intercompany agreements, arrangements or transactions. The term "substantially" all the stock has been construed by the Commission to mean 80 percent or more of the voting stock. Reg. § 6–2.2(a)(2), CCH ¶ 9–702, P–H ¶ 11,337.5.

Until comparatively recently, the discretionary powers to require or permit combined reports were invoked very charily; but in the past few years, the Commission has begun to impose combined reports with greater frequency, in cases of a manufacturer and a sales subsidiary, or an automobile manufacturer and a credit company subsidiary, and the like. See Campbell Sales Co. v. State Tax Comm'n, 68 N.Y.2d 617, 505 N.Y.S.2d 54 (1986); Wurlitzer Co. v. State Tax Comm'n, 35 N.Y.2d 100, 358 N.Y.S.2d 762, 315 N.E.2d 805 (1974); Petition of Chrysler Financial Corp., CCH ¶ 997–515.538, P–H ¶ 10.510.140 (N.Y.State Tax Comm'n 1975); Fedders Corp. v. State Tax Comm'n, 45 A.D.2d 359, 357 N.Y.S.2d 719 (3rd Dep't 1974).

Taxpayers seeking permission to file combined reports have encountered considerable reluctance on the Commission's part to grant the requests. In denying permission, the Commission has relied, and in at least one case a State court has acquiesced in its reliance, on the following legal position:

> A combined return would produce a distorted result, in that losses of unprofitable corporations would be offset against the income of the other corporations. [Annel Holding Corp. v. Procaccino, 77 Misc.2d 886, 355 N.Y.S.2d 237 (Sup.Ct., Albany Cty.1974); Matter of N.K. Winston Corp., CCH ¶ 7–515.40, P–H ¶ 10.510.100 (N.Y.State Tax Comm'n 1974); Matter of Dale Funding Corp., CCH ¶ 97–515.43–952, P–H ¶ 10.510.90 (N.Y.State Tax Comm'n 1974).]

Can this position be squared with the concept on which combined reporting for multicorporate unitary enterprises appears to be premised, i.e., that in order to *avoid* the distortion of income, the income and apportionment factors of the entire enterprise that is unitary must be taken into account? The Appellate Division for the Third Department appears to have repudiated the holdings referred to above by ruling that where a parent company and its subsidiary constitute a unitary business, in view of their extensive intercompany transactions, the Commission abused its discretionary power by rejecting a combined report of the taxpayers on the ground that the "net loss [of one of the subsidiaries] was primarily due to its own operations and not the inter-company transactions." Sapolin Paints Inc. v. Tully, 55 A.D.2d 759, 390 N.Y.S.2d 220 (3rd Dep't 1976). More recent decisions by the New York courts have continued to find denials by the Commission of permission to file combined reports arbitrary and capricious. Coleco Industries, Inc. v. State Tax Comm'n, 92 A.D.2d 1008, 461 N.Y.S.2d 462 (3d Dept. 1983); American Intern. Group, Inc. v. Tully, 89 A.D.2d 687, 453 N.Y.S.2d 797 (3d Dep't 1982), affirmed 59 N.Y.2d 832, 464 N.Y.S.2d 755 (1983).

The State's combined report regulations, which set forth the principles guiding the Commission in permitting or requiring combined reports, adopt in essence a basic operations interdependence test. Their substantial revision in 1976, coupled with the decisions in the cases cited above could conceivably mark a liberalization in the Commission's posture toward granting taxpayers permission to file combined reports. Franchise Tax Reg. § 6–2.1, CCH ¶ 9–701, P–H ¶ 11,335.

References. Olson, "Taxation: Allocation of Income of an Interstate Business Under the California Franchise Tax: the Unitary Business," 52 Cal.L.Rev. 430 (1964); Rudolph, "State Taxation of Interstate Business: The Unitary Business Concept and Affiliated Corporate Groups," 25 Tax.L. Rev. 171 (1970); Lavelle, "What Constitutes a Unitary Business," 25 So.Cal. Tax Inst. 239 (1973); Keesling, "A Current Look at the Combined Report and Uniformity in Allocation Practices," 42 J.Tax. 106 (1975); Nackenson, "Domestic Taxpayer Challenges Kansas Combined Reporting," 2 Interstate Tax Rep., Sept. 1982, p. 14.

SECTION 9. PROPOSED CONGRESSIONAL LEGISLATION RESTRICTING USE OF THE COMBINED METHOD OF APPORTIONING THE TAX AS APPLIED TO MULTICORPORATE ENTERPRISES

In 1959, Congress enacted P.L. 86–272, which was designed as a stop-gap measure, pending further Congressional study, and dealt only with the jurisdiction of State and local governments to tax interstate businesses. Six years later, the Willis Committee, after an exhaustive study, recommended further stringent curbs on State and local income, capital stock, gross receipts, and sales and use taxes, as applied to interstate commerce, including restrictions on apportionment and allocation.[105] Since then, there has been a steady stream of bills introduced in virtually every session of Congress and a Senate Committee has held hearings, but thus far no new legislation has emerged from Congress.[106]

In essence, a political stalemate developed, because of the sharp divergences of views between major multistate and multinational corporations, spearheaded by the Committee on State Taxation of the Council of State Chambers of Commerce (COST), on the one hand, and the States, led by the National Association of State Tax Administrators (NATA) and the MTC, on the other.[107] The application of the combined

105. H.R. 11798, 89th Cong., 1st Sess. (1965).

106. For the history of the proposed legislation, see the Mondale Committee Hearings; Kust, "State Taxation of Interstate Business—An Obdurate Issue," The Tax Executive (April 1973), reprinted in Mondale Comm. Hearings 92 et seq.; J. Hellerstein, "State Taxation Under the

Commerce Clause: An Historical Perspective," 29 Vand.L.Rev. 335 (1976).

107. The Mondale Committee Hearings set out the views of various parties to the controversies. The COST-supported bill was S. 1245, 93rd Cong., 1st Sess. (1973) (the Mathias bill), which was modified by Senator Mathias in S. 2080, 94th Cong., 1st Sess. (1975); see the arguments for this bill

method of apportioning the income of taxable corporations by including the income of non-taxable affiliates, and the apportionment of dividends, as distinguished from allocation to the taxpayer's commercial domicile, are among the key controversial issues. For the legislative developments following the *Container* case, p. 578 infra, see Section 10, note D infra.

SECTION 10. APPORTIONMENT AND ALLOCATION OF INCOME ON A WORLDWIDE BASIS

INTRODUCTORY NOTE

A controversy has developed as to the propriety of applying unitary apportionment principles to foreign operations. On the merits, unitary apportionment may become a questionable yardstick as a fair measure of a State's share of the earnings of an enterprise, when it is extended worldwide. Some companies may earn considerably higher rates of profit abroad than in the United States; relative ratios of property, payroll, and receipts may be an extremely crude method of ascribing profits actually earned in the various countries. The large differences in wage rates paid in the United States and many foreign countries, particularly in Latin America, Africa, and Asia, where wage scales for the same type of work may amount to as little as one-fifth or one-tenth of those in the United States, tend to produce serious distortions in the apportionment.[108] Of course, the monetary wage rates need to be adjusted for differences in productivity, but it appears likely that in some industries unit wage costs vary so markedly as to result in such distortion.

The underlying premise of formulary apportionment under the Massachusetts three-factor formula is that (using UDITPA as illustrative), by and large, every dollar of wages or property spent in one taxing jurisdiction, along with receipts from sales in the area, will produce the same amount of profit in all taxing jurisdictions. Wide disparities in unit labor or unit property costs between taxing jurisdictions tend to attribute to the high wage-property cost jurisdictions, such as the United States, income which is attributable to other jurisdictions. A margin of tolerance for disparities in wage and property costs

in Cahoon and Brown, "The Interstate Tax Dilemma—A Proposed Solution," 26 Nat. Tax J. 187 (1973). The Magnuson bill, S. 2092, 93rd Cong., 1st Sess. (1973), which was developed by the so-called Ad Hoc Committee (see Kinnear, Mondale Comm. Hearings 326), and Kust, "A New Venture in Federalism—Toward a Solution to State Taxation of Multistate Business," The Tax Executive (Jan. 1971), reprinted in Mondale Comm. Hearings 97 et seq.) was generally supported by the National Association of Tax Administrators. See Clarke,

id. at 310. For an explanation of the major features of the cited bills, see J. Hellerstein, note 106 supra, at 340–41. See also Nemeth and Agee, "State Taxation of Multistate Business: Resolution or Stalemate?," 48 Taxes 237 (1970).

108. See, for example, the hourly earnings rates of wage earners in manufacturing industries of various countries, Table 179, United Nations Statistical Yearbook (1976), based on data from the International Labour Office.

has been found constitutionally acceptable in the operation of apportionment formulas, as applied to interstate business, in view of the judicial recognition that any method of division of income is at best an approximation. John Deere Plow Co. v. Franchise Tax Bd., 38 Cal.2d 214, 238 P.2d 569 (1951), appeal dismissed, 343 U.S. 939, 72 S.Ct. 1036 (1952); Virginia Electric and Power Co. v. Currie, 254 N.C. 17, 118 S.E.2d 155, appeal dismissed 367 U.S. 910, 81 S.Ct. 1919 (1961). But once the differences exceed any reasonable measure of tolerance, the application of the formula ought to be vulnerable to constitutional challenge, unless the State grants a variation from the standard formula under the relief provision of the statute.

Moreover, the difficulties of obtaining accurate and verifiable data from foreign countries as to assets, payroll, and sales are multiplied; accounting techniques and methods frequently vary sharply from those prevailing in the United States, especially in the case of subsidiaries or branches of United States corporations operating in the developing countries. The question whether these differences between worldwide apportionment and that method as confined to the borders of the United States require a rejection of worldwide apportionment on Due Process and Commerce Clause grounds as inherently tending to arbitrary and capricious distortion of the tax base, and as imposing undue compliance burdens on multinational enterprises, lie at the heart of the *Container* case. See J. Hellerstein, "The Unitary Business Principle and Multicorporate Enterprises: An Examination of the Major Controversies," 37 Tax Exec. 313 (1975); Miller, "State Income Taxation of Multiple Corporations and Multiple Businesses," Tax Foundation Seminar (April 16–17, 1970); J. Hellerstein, State Taxation I, Corporate Income and Franchise Taxes ¶¶ 8.10[6], [8] (1983).

CONTAINER CORPORATION OF AMERICA v. FRANCHISE TAX BOARD

Supreme Court of the United States.
463 U.S. 159, 103 S.Ct. 2933, 1983, rehearing denied
464 U.S. 909, 104 S.Ct. 265.

JUSTICE BRENNAN delivered the opinion of the Court.

This is another appeal claiming that the application of a state taxing scheme violates the Due Process and Commerce Clauses of the Federal Constitution. California imposes a corporate franchise tax geared to income. In common with a large number of other States, it employs the "unitary business" principle and formula apportionment in applying that tax to corporations doing business both inside and outside the State. Appellant is a Delaware corporation headquartered in Illinois and doing business in California and elsewhere. It also has a number of overseas subsidiaries incorporated in the countries in which they operate. Appellee is the California authority charged with administering the State's franchise tax. This appeal presents three questions for review: (1) Was it improper for appellee and the state courts to find that appellant and its overseas subsidiaries constituted a "unitary business" for purposes of the state tax? (2) Even if the unitary business finding was proper, do certain salient differences among national economies render the standard three-factor apportionment formula used by California so inaccurate as applied to the multinational enterprise consisting of appellant and its subsidiaries as to violate the constitutional requirement of "fair apportionment"? (3) In any event, did California have an obligation under the Foreign Commerce Clause, U.S. Const., Art. I, § 8, cl. 3, to employ the "arm's-length" analysis used by the Federal Government and most foreign nations in evaluating the tax consequences of intercorporate relationships?

I

A

Various aspects of state tax systems based on the "unitary business" principle and formula apportionment have provoked repeated constitutional litigation in this Court. See, e.g., ASARCO Inc. v. Idaho State Tax Comm'n, 458 U.S. 307, 102 S.Ct. 3103, 73 L.Ed.2d 787 (1982); F.W. Woolworth Co. v. Taxation & Revenue Dept., 458 U.S. 354, 102 S.Ct. 3128, 73 L.Ed.2d 819 (1982); Exxon Corp. v. Wisconsin Dept. of Revenue, 447 U.S. 207, 100 S.Ct. 2109, 65 L.Ed.2d 66 (1980); Mobil Oil Corp. v. Commissioner of Taxes, 445 U.S. 425, 100 S.Ct. 1223, 63 L.Ed.2d 510 (1980); Moorman Mfg. Co. v. Bair, 437 U.S. 267, 98 S.Ct. 2340, 57 L.Ed.2d 197 (1978); General Motors Corp. v. Washington, 377 U.S. 436, 84 S.Ct. 1564, 12 L.Ed.2d 430 (1964); Butler Bros. v. McColgan, 315 U.S. 501, 62 S.Ct. 701, 86 L.Ed. 991 (1942); Bass, Ratcliff & Gretton, Ltd. v. State Tax Comm'n, 266 U.S. 271, 45 S.Ct. 82, 69 L.Ed. 282 (1924); Underwood Typewriter Co. v. Chamberlain, 254 U.S. 113, 41 S.Ct. 45, 65 L.Ed. 165 (1920).

Under both the Due Process and the Commerce Clauses of the Constitution, a State may not, when imposing an income-based tax, "tax value earned outside its borders." ASARCO, supra, 458 U.S., at 315, 102 S.Ct., at 3108. In the case of a more-or-less integrated business enterprise operating in more than one State, however, arriving at precise territorial allocations of "value" is often an elusive goal, both in theory and in practice. See Mobil Oil Corp. v. Commissioner of Taxes, supra, 445 U.S., at 438, 100 S.Ct., at 1232; Butler Bros. v. McColgan, supra, 315 U.S., at 507–509, 62 S.Ct., at 704–705; Underwood Typewriter Co. v. Chamberlain, supra, 254 U.S., at 121, 41 S.Ct., at 47. For this reason and others, we have long held that the Constitution imposes no single formula on the States, Wisconsin v. J.C. Penney Co., 311 U.S. 435, 445, 61 S.Ct. 246, 250, 85 L.Ed. 267 (1940), and that the taxpayer has the " 'distinct burden of showing by "clear and cogent evidence" that [the state tax] results in extraterritorial values being taxed. * * *' " Exxon Corp., supra, 447 U.S., at 221, 100 S.Ct., at 2119, quoting Butler Bros. v. McColgan, supra, 315 U.S., at 507, 62 S.Ct., at

704, in turn quoting Norfolk & Western R. Co. v. North Carolina ex rel. Maxwell, 297 U.S. 682, 688, 56 S.Ct. 625, 628, 80 L.Ed. 977 (1936).

One way of deriving locally taxable income is on the basis of formal geographical or transactional accounting. The problem with this method is that formal accounting is subject to manipulation and imprecision, and often ignores or captures inadequately the many subtle and largely unquantifiable transfers of value that take place among the components of a single enterprise. See generally Mobil Oil Corp., supra, 445 U.S., at 438–439, 100 S.Ct., at 1232, and sources cited. The unitary business/formula apportionment method is a very different approach to the problem of taxing businesses operating in more than one jurisdiction. It rejects geographical or transactional accounting, and instead calculates the local tax base by first defining the scope of the "unitary business" of which the taxed enterprise's activities in the taxing jurisdiction form one part, and then apportioning the total income of that "unitary business" between the taxing jurisdiction and the rest of the world on the basis of a formula taking into account objective measures of the corporation's activities within and without the jurisdiction. This Court long ago upheld the constitutionality of the unitary business/formula apportionment method, although subject to certain constraints. See, e.g., Hans Rees' Sons, Inc. v. North Carolina ex rel. Maxwell, 283 U.S. 123, 51 S.Ct. 385, 75 L.Ed. 879 (1931); Bass, Ratcliff & Gretton, Ltd. v. State Tax Comm'n, supra; Underwood Typewriter Co. v. Chamberlain, supra. The method has now gained wide acceptance, and is in one of its forms the basis for the Uniform Division of Income for Tax Purposes Act (Uniform Act), which has at last count been substantially adopted by 23 States, including California.

B

Two aspects of the unitary business/formula apportionment method have traditionally attracted judicial attention. These are, as one might easily guess, the notions of "unitary business" and "formula apportionment," respectively.

(1)

The Due Process and Commerce Clauses of the Constitution do not allow a State to tax income arising out of interstate activities—even on a proportional basis—unless there is a " 'minimal connection' or 'nexus' between the interstate activities and the taxing State, and 'a rational relationship between the income attributed to the State and the intrastate values of the enterprise.' " Exxon Corp. v. Wisconsin Dept. of Revenue, supra, 447 U.S., at 219–220, 100 S.Ct., at 2118, quoting Mobil Oil Corp. v. Commissioner of Taxes, supra, 445 U.S., at 436, 437, 100 S.Ct., at 1231. At the very least, this set of principles imposes the obvious and largely self-executing limitation that a State not tax a purported "unitary business" unless at least some part of it is conducted in the State. See Exxon Corp., supra, 447 U.S., at 220, 100 S.Ct., at 2118; Wisconsin v. J.C. Penney Co., supra, 311 U.S., at 444, 61 S.Ct., at

249. It also requires that there be some bond of ownership or control uniting the purported "unitary business." See ASARCO, supra, 458 U.S., at 316–317, 102 S.Ct., at 3109.

In addition, the principles we have quoted require that the out-of-state activities of the purported "unitary business" be related in some concrete way to the in-state activities. The functional meaning of this requirement is that there be some sharing or exchange of value not capable of precise identification or measurement—beyond the mere flow of funds arising out of a passive investment or a distinct business operation—which renders formula apportionment a reasonable method of taxation. See generally ASARCO, supra, at 317, 102 S.Ct., at 3115; Mobil Oil Corp., supra, 445 U.S., at 438–442, 100 S.Ct., at 1232–1234. In Underwood Typewriter Co. v. Chamberlain, supra, we held that a State could tax on an apportioned basis the combined income of a vertically integrated business whose various components (manufacturing, sales, etc.) operated in different States. In Bass, Ratcliff & Gretton, supra, we applied the same principle to a vertically integrated business operating across national boundaries. In Butler Bros. v. McColgan, supra, we recognized that the unitary business principle could apply, not only to vertically integrated enterprises, but also to a series of similar enterprises operating separately in various jurisdictions but linked by common managerial or operational resources that produced economies of scale and transfers of value. More recently, we have further refined the "unitary business" concept in Exxon Corp. v. Wisconsin Dept. of Revenue, 447 U.S. 207, 100 S.Ct. 2109, 65 L.Ed.2d 66 (1980), and Mobil Oil Corp. v. Commissioner of Taxes, 445 U.S. 425, 100 S.Ct. 1223, 63 L.Ed.2d 510 (1980), where we upheld the States' unitary business findings, and in ASARCO Inc. v. Idaho State Tax Comm'n, 458 U.S. 307, 102 S.Ct. 3103, 73 L.Ed.2d 787 (1982), and F.W. Woolworth Co. v. Taxation & Revenue Dept., 458 U.S. 354, 102 S.Ct. 3128, 73 L.Ed.2d 819 (1982), in which we found such findings to have been improper.

The California statute at issue in this case, and the Uniform Act from which most of its relevant provisions are derived, track in large part the principles we have just discussed. In particular, the statute distinguishes between the "business income" of a multijurisdictional enterprise, which is apportioned by formula, Cal.Rev. & Tax.Code Ann. §§ 25128–25136 (West 1979), and its "nonbusiness" income, which is not.[1] Although the statute does not explicitly require that income from distinct business enterprises be apportioned separately, this requirement antedated adoption of the Uniform Act,[2] and has not been abandoned.[3]

1. Certain forms of nonbusiness income, such as dividends, are allocated on the basis of the taxpayer's commercial domicile. Other forms of nonbusiness income, such as capital gains on sales of real property, are allocated on the basis of situs. See Cal.Rev. & Tax.Code Ann. §§ 25123–25127 (West 1979).

2. See generally Honolulu Oil Corp. v. Franchise Tax Board, 60 Cal.2d 417, 34 Cal.Rptr. 552, 386 P.2d 40 (1963); Superior Oil Corp. v. Franchise Tax Board, 60 Cal.2d 406, 34 Cal.Rptr. 545, 386 P.2d 33 (1963).

3. See the opinion of the California Court of Appeal in this case, 117 Cal.App. 3d 988, 990–991, 993–995, 173 Cal.Rptr.

A final point that needs to be made about the unitary business concept is that it is not, so to speak, unitary: there are variations on the theme, and any number of them are logically consistent with the underlying principles motivating the approach. For example, a State might decide to respect formal corporate lines and treat the ownership of a corporate subsidiary as *per se* a passive investment.[4] In Mobil Oil Corp., 445 U.S., at 440–441, 100 S.Ct., at 1233, however, we made clear that, as a general matter, such a *per se* rule is not constitutionally required:

> "Superficially, intercorporate division might appear to be a[n] * * * attractive basis for limiting apportionability. But the form of business organization may have nothing to do with the underlying unity or diversity of business enterprise." Id., at 440, 100 S.Ct., at 1233.

Thus, for example, California law provides:

> "In the case of a corporation * * * owning or controlling, either directly or indirectly, another corporation, or other corporations, and in the case of a corporation * * * owned or controlled, either directly or indirectly, by another corporation, the Franchise Tax Board may require a consolidated report showing the combined net income or such other facts as it deems necessary." Cal.Rev. & Tax.Code Ann. § 25104 (West 1979).[5]

Even among States that take this approach, however, only some apply it in taxing American corporations with subsidiaries located in foreign countries.[6] The difficult question we address in Part V of this opinion

121, 123, 124–126 (1982). See also Cal.Rev. & Tax.Code Ann. § 25137 (West 1979) (allowing for separate accounting or other alternative methods of apportionment when total formula apportionment would "not fairly represent the extent of the taxpayer's business activity in this state").

4. We note that the Uniform Act does not speak to this question one way or the other.

5. See also Cal.Rev. & Tax.Code Ann. § 25105 (West 1979) (defining "ownership or control"). A necessary corollary, of course, is that intercorporate dividends in a unitary business *not* be included in gross income, since such inclusion would result in double-counting of a portion of the subsidiary's income (first as income attributed to the unitary business, and second as dividend income to the parent). See § 25106.

Some States, it should be noted, have adopted a hybrid approach. In *Mobil* itself, for example, a nondomiciliary State invoked a unitary business justification to include an apportioned share of certain corporate dividends in the gross income of the taxpayer, but did not require a combined return and combined apportionment. The Court in *Mobil* held that the taxpayer's objection to this approach had not been properly raised in the state proceedings. 445 U.S., at 441, n. 15, 100 S.Ct., at 1233, n. 15. Justice Stevens, however, reached the merits, stating in part: "Either Mobil's worldwide 'petroleum enterprise' is all part of one unitary business, or it is not; if it is, Vermont must evaluate the entire enterprise in a consistent manner." Id., at 461, 100 S.Ct., at 1243 (citation omitted). See id., at 462, 100 S.Ct., at 1244 (Stevens, J., dissenting) (outlining alternative approaches available to State); cf. The Supreme Court, 1981 Term, 96 Harv.L.Rev. 62, 93–96 (1982).

6. See generally General Accounting Office Report to the Chairman, House Committee on Ways and Means: Key Issues Affecting State Taxation of Multijurisdictional Corporate Income Need Resolving 31 (1982).

is whether, for reasons not implicated in *Mobil*,[7] that particular variation on the theme is constitutionally barred.

(2)

Having determined that a certain set of activities constitute a "unitary business," a State must then apply a formula apportioning the income of that business within and without the State. Such an apportionment formula must, under both the Due Process and Commerce Clauses, be fair. See Exxon Corp., supra, 447 U.S., at 219, 227–228, 100 S.Ct., at 2118, 2122–2123; Moorman Mfg. Co., 437 U.S., at 272–273, 98 S.Ct., at 2343–2344; Hans Rees' Sons, Inc., 283 U.S., at 134, 51 S.Ct., at 389. The first, and again obvious, component of fairness in an apportionment formula is what might be called internal consistency—that is, the formula must be such that, if applied by every jurisdiction, it would result in no more than all of the unitary business income being taxed. The second and more difficult requirement is what might be called external consistency—the factor or factors used in the apportionment formula must actually reflect a reasonable sense of how income is generated. The Constitution does not "invalidat[e]·an apportionment formula whenever it *may* result in taxation of some income that did not have its source in the taxing State * * *." Moorman Mfg. Co., supra, 437 U.S., at 272, 98 S.Ct., at 2344 (emphasis added). See Underwood Typewriter Co., 254 U.S., at 120–121, 41 S.Ct., at 46–47. Nevertheless, we will strike down the application of an apportionment formula if the taxpayer can prove "by 'clear and cogent evidence' that the income attributed to the State is in fact 'out of all appropriate proportions to the business transacted * * * in that State,' [Hans Rees' Sons, Inc.,] 283 U.S., at 135, 51 S.Ct., at 389, or has 'led to a grossly distorted result,' [Norfolk & Western R. Co. v. State Tax Comm'n, 390 U.S. 317, 326, 88 S.Ct. 995, 1001, 19 L.Ed.2d 1201 (1968)]." Moorman Mfg. Co., supra, 437 U.S., at 274, 98 S.Ct., at 2345.

California and the other States that have adopted the Uniform Act use a formula—commonly called the "three-factor" formula—which is based, in equal parts, on the proportion of a unitary business' total payroll, property, and sales which are located in the taxing State. See Cal.Tax & Rev.Code Ann. §§ 25128–25136 (West 1979). We approved the three-factor formula in Butler Bros. v. McColgan, 315 U.S. 501, 62 S.Ct. 701, 86 L.Ed. 991 (1942). Indeed, not only has the three-factor formula met our approval, but it has become, for reasons we discuss in more detail infra, at 2949, something of a benchmark against which other apportionment formulas are judged. See Moorman Mfg. Co.,

7. *Mobil* did, in fact, involve income from foreign subsidiaries, but that fact was of little importance to the case for two reasons. First, as discussed in n. 5, supra, the State in that case included *dividends* from the subsidiaries to the parent in its calculation of the parent's apportionable taxable income, but did not include the underlying income of the subsidiaries themselves. Second, the taxpayer in that case conceded that the dividends could be taxed *somewhere* in the United States, so the actual issue before the Court was merely whether a particular State could be barred from imposing some portion of that tax. See 445 U.S., at 447, 100 S.Ct., at 1236.

supra, at 282, 98 S.Ct., at 2349 (BLACKMUN, J., dissenting); cf. General Motors Corp. v. District of Columbia, 380 U.S. 553, 561, 85 S.Ct. 1156, 1161, 14 L.Ed.2d 68 (1965).

Besides being fair, an apportionment formula must, under the Commerce Clause, also not result in discrimination against interstate or foreign commerce. See Mobil Oil Corp., supra, 445 U.S., at 444, 100 S.Ct., at 1235; cf. Japan Line, Ltd. v. County of Los Angeles, 441 U.S. 434, 444–448, 99 S.Ct. 1813, 1819–1821, 60 L.Ed.2d 336 (1979) (property tax). Aside from forbidding the obvious types of discrimination against interstate or foreign commerce, this principle might have been construed to require that a state apportionment formula not differ so substantially from methods of allocation used by other jurisdictions in which the taxpayer is subject to taxation so as to produce double taxation of the same income, and a resultant tax burden higher than the taxpayer would incur if its business were limited to any one jurisdiction. [At least in the interstate commerce context, however, the anti-discrimination principle has not in practice required much in addition to the requirement of fair apportionment. In Moorman Mfg. Co. v. Bair, supra, in particular, we explained that eliminating all overlapping taxation would require this Court to establish not only a single constitutionally mandated method of taxation, but also rules regarding the application of that method in particular cases. 437 U.S., at 278–280, 98 S.Ct., at 2347–2348. Because that task was thought to be essentially legislative, we declined to undertake it, and held that a fairly apportioned tax would not be found invalid simply because it differed from the prevailing approach adopted by the States.] As we discuss infra, at 2950–2952, however, a more searching inquiry is necessary when we are confronted with the possibility of international double taxation.

II

A

Appellant is in the business of manufacturing custom-ordered paperboard packaging. Its operation is vertically integrated, and includes the production of paperboard from raw timber and wastepaper as well as its composition into the finished products ordered by customers. The operation is also largely domestic. During the years at issue in this case—1963, 1964, and 1965—appellant controlled 20 foreign subsidiaries located in four Latin American and four European countries. Its percentage ownership of the subsidiaries (either directly or through other subsidiaries) ranged between 66.7% and 100%. In those instances (about half) in which appellant did not own a 100% interest in the subsidiary, the remainder was owned by local nationals. One of the subsidiaries was a holding company that had no payroll, sales, or property, but did have book income. Another was inactive. The rest were all engaged—in their respective local markets—in essentially the same business as appellant.

Most of appellant's subsidiaries were, like appellant itself, fully integrated, although a few bought paperboard and other intermediate products elsewhere. Sales of materials from appellant to its subsidiaries accounted for only about 1% of the subsidiaries' total purchases. The subsidiaries were also relatively autonomous with respect to matters of personnel and day-to-day management. For example, transfers of personnel from appellant to its subsidiaries were rare, and occurred only when a subsidiary could not fill a position locally. There was no formal United States training program for the subsidiaries' employees, although groups of foreign employees occasionally visited the United States for 2–6 week periods to familiarize themselves with appellant's methods of operation. Appellant charged one senior vice president and four other officers with the task of overseeing the operations of the subsidiaries. These officers established general standards of professionalism, profitability, and ethical practices and dealt with major problems and long-term decisions; day-to-day management of the subsidiaries, however, was left in the hands of local executives who were always citizens of the host country. Although local decisions regarding capital expenditures were subject to review by appellant, problems were generally worked out by consensus rather than outright domination. Appellant also had a number of its directors and officers on the boards of directors of the subsidiaries, but they did not generally play an active role in management decisions.[8]

Nevertheless, in certain respects, the relationship between appellant and its subsidiaries was decidedly close. For example, approximately half of the subsidiaries' long-term debt was either held directly, or guaranteed, by appellant. Appellant also provided advice and consultation regarding manufacturing techniques, engineering, design, architecture, insurance, and cost accounting to a number of its subsidiaries, either by entering into technical service agreements with them or by informal arrangement. Finally, appellant occasionally assisted its subsidiaries in their procurement of equipment, either by selling them used equipment of its own or by employing its own purchasing department to act as an agent for the subsidiaries.[9]

8. There were a number of reasons for appellant's relatively hands-off attitude toward the management of its subsidiaries. First, it comported with the company's general management philosophy emphasizing local responsibility and accountability; in this respect, the treatment of the foreign subsidiaries was similar to the organization of appellant's domestic geographical divisions. Second, it reflected the fact that the packaging industry, like the advertising industry to which it is closely related, is highly sensitive to differences in consumer habits and economic development among different nations, and therefore requires a good dose of local expertise to be successful. Third, appellant's policy was designed to appeal to the sensibilities of local customers and governments.

9. There was also a certain spillover of good-will between appellant and its subsidiaries; that is, appellant's customers who had overseas needs would on occasion ask appellant's sales representatives to recommend foreign firms, and, where possible, the representatives would refer the customers to appellant's subsidiaries. In at least one instance, appellant became involved in the actual negotiation of a contract between a customer and a foreign subsidiary.

B

During the tax years at issue in this case, appellant filed California franchise tax returns. In 1969, after conducting an audit of appellant's returns for the years in question, appellee issued notices of additional assessments for each of those years. The respective approaches and results reflected in appellant's initial returns and in appellee's notices of additional assessments capture the legal differences at issue in this case.[10]

In calculating the total unapportioned taxable income of its unitary business, appellant included its own corporate net earnings as derived from its federal tax form (subject to certain adjustments not relevant here), but did not include any income of its subsidiaries. It also deducted—as it was authorized to do under state law, see supra, at 2941, and n. 1—all dividend income, non-business interest income, and gains on sales of assets not related to the unitary business. In calculating the share of its net income which was apportionable to California under the three-factor formula, appellant omitted all of its subsidiaries' payroll, property, and sales. The results of these calculations are summarized in the margin.[11]

The gravamen of the notices issued by appellee in 1969 was that appellant should have treated its overseas subsidiaries as part of its unitary business rather than as passive investments. Including the overseas subsidiaries in appellant's unitary business had two primary effects: it increased the income subject to apportionment by an amount equal to the total income of those subsidiaries (less intersubsidiary dividends, see n. 5, supra), and it decreased the percentage of that income which was apportionable to California. The net effect, however, was to increase appellant's tax liability in each of the three years.[12]

---

10. After the notices of additional tax, there followed a series of further adjustments, payments, claims for refunds, and assessments, whose combined effect was to render the figures outlined in text more illustrative than real as descriptions of the present claims of the parties with regard to appellant's total tax liability. These subsequent events, however, did not concern the legal issues raised in this case, nor did they remove either party's financial stake in the resolution of those issues. We therefore disregard them for the sake of simplicity.

11.

	Total income of unitary business	Percentage attributed to California	Amount attributed to California	Tax (5.5%)
1963	$26,870,427.00	11.041	$2,966,763.85	$163,172.01
1964	28,774,320.48	10.6422	3,062,220.73	168,422.14
1965	32,280,842.90	9.8336	3,174,368.97	174,590.29

See Exhibit A–7 to Stipulation; Record 36, 76, 77, 79, 104, 126.

12. According to the notices, appellant's actual tax obligations were as follows:

	Total income of unitary business	Percentage attributed to California	Amount attributed to California	Tax (5.5%)
1963	$37,348,183.00	8.6886	$3,245,034.23	$178,476.88
1964	44,245,879.00	8.3135	3,673,381.15	202,310.95
1965	46,884,966.00	7.6528	3,588,012.68	197,340.70

See Exhibit A–7 to Stipulation; Record 76, 77, 79.

Appellant paid the additional amounts under protest, and then sued in California Superior Court for a refund, raising the issues now before this Court. The case was tried on stipulated facts, and the Superior Court upheld appellee's assessments. On appeal, the California Court of Appeal affirmed, 117 Cal.App.3d 988, 173 Cal.Rptr. 121 (1981), and the California Supreme Court refused to exercise discretionary review. We noted probable jurisdiction. 456 U.S. 960, 102 S.Ct. 2034, 72 L.Ed.2d 483 (1982).

III

A

We address the unitary business issue first. As previously noted, the taxpayer always has the "distinct burden of showing by 'clear and cogent evidence' that [the state tax] results in extraterritorial values being taxed." Supra, at 2939–2940. One necessary corollary of that principle is that this Court will, if reasonably possible, defer to the judgment of state courts in deciding whether a particular set of activities constitutes a "unitary business." As we said in a closely related context in Norton Co. v. Department of Revenue, 340 U.S. 534, 71 S.Ct. 377, 95 L.Ed. 517 (1951):

"The general rule, applicable here, is that a taxpayer claiming immunity from a tax has the burden of establishing his exemption.

"*This burden is never met merely by showing a fair difference of opinion which as an original matter might be decided differently.* * * * Of course, in constitutional cases, we have power to examine the whole record to arrive at an independent judgment as to whether constitutional rights have been invaded, but that does not mean that we will re-examine, as a court of first instance, findings of fact supported by substantial evidence." Id., at 537–538, 71 S.Ct., at 380 (footnotes omitted; emphasis added).[13]

See id., at 538, 71 S.Ct., at 380 (concluding that, "in light of all the evidence, the [state] judgment [on a question of whether income should be attributed to the State] was within the realm of permissible judgment"). The legal principles defining the constitutional limits on the unitary business principle are now well established. The factual records in such cases, even when the parties enter into a stipulation, tend to be long and complex, and the line between "historical fact" and "constitutional fact" is often fuzzy at best. Cf. ASARCO, 458 U.S., at 326–328, nn. 22, 23, 102 S.Ct., at 3114–3115, nn. 22, 23. It will do the cause of legal certainty little good if this Court turns every colorable claim that a state court erred in a particular application of those principles into a *de novo* adjudication, whose unintended nuances would then spawn further litigation and an avalanche of critical comment.[14]

---

13. This approach is, of course, quite different from the one we follow in certain other constitutional contexts. See, e.g., Brooks v. Florida, 389 U.S. 413, 88 S.Ct. 541, 19 L.Ed.2d 643 (1967); New York Times Co. v. Sullivan, 376 U.S. 254, 285, 84 S.Ct. 710, 728, 11 L.Ed.2d 686 (1964).

14. It should also go without saying that not every claim that a state court erred in making a unitary business finding will pose a substantial federal question in the first place.

Rather, our task must be to determine whether the state court applied the correct standards to the case; and if it did, whether its judgment "was within the realm of permissible judgment." [15]

B

In this case, we are singularly unconvinced by appellant's argument that the State Court of Appeal "in important part analyzed this case under a different legal standard," F.W. Woolworth, 458 U.S., at 363, 102 S.Ct., at 3134, from the one articulated by this Court. Appellant argues that the state court here, like the state court in *F.W. Woolworth,* improperly relied on appellant's mere *potential* to control the operations of its subsidiaries as a dispositive factor in reaching its unitary business finding. In fact, although the state court mentioned that "major policy decisions of the subsidiaries were subject to review by appellant," 117 Cal.App.3d, at 998, 173 Cal.Rptr., at 127, it relied principally, in discussing the management relationship between appellant and its subsidiaries, on the more concrete observation that "[h]igh officials of appellant gave directions to subsidiaries for compliance with the parent's standard of professionalism, profitability, and ethical practices." Id., at 998, 173 Cal.Rptr., at 127–128.[16]

Appellant also argues that the state court erred in endorsing an administrative presumption that corporations engaged in the same line of business are unitary. This presumption affected the state court's reasoning, but only as one element among many. Moreover, considering the limited use to which it was put, we find the "presumption" criticized by appellant to be reasonable. Investment in a business enterprise truly "distinct" from a corporation's main line of business often serves the primary function of diversifying the corporate portfolio and reducing the risks inherent in being tied to one industry's business

15. *ASARCO* and *F.W. Woolworth* are consistent with this standard of review. *ASARCO* involved a claim that a parent and certain of its partial subsidiaries, in which it held either minority interests or bare majority interests, were part of the same unitary business. The State Supreme Court upheld the claim. We concluded, *relying on factual findings made by the state courts,* that a unitary business finding was impermissible because the partial subsidiaries were not realistically subject to even minimal control by ASARCO, and were therefore passive investments in the most basic sense of the term. 458 U.S., at 320–324, 102 S.Ct., at 3111–3113. We held specifically that to accept the State's theory of the case would not only constitute a misapplication of the unitary business concept, but would "destroy" the concept entirely. Id., at 326, 102 S.Ct., at 3114.

F.W. Woolworth was a much closer case, involving one partially owned subsidiary

and three wholly owned subsidiaries. We examined the evidence in some detail, and reversed the state court's unitary business finding, but only after concluding that the state court had made specific and crucial legal errors, not merely in the conclusions it drew, but in the legal standard it applied in analyzing the case. 458 U.S., at 363–364, 102 S.Ct., at 3134–3135.

16. In any event, although potential control is, as we said in *F.W. Woolworth,* not "*dispositive*" of the unitary business issue, id., at 362, 102 S.Ct., at 3134 (emphasis added), it is *relevant,* both to whether or not the components of the purported unitary business share that degree of common ownership which is a prerequisite to a finding of unitariness, and also to whether there might exist a degree of implicit control sufficient to render the parent and the subsidiary an integrated enterprise.

cycle. When a corporation invests in a subsidiary that engages in the same line of work as itself, it becomes much more likely that one function of the investment is to make better use—either through economies of scale or through operational integration or sharing of expertise—of the parent's existing business-related resources.

* * *

[The Court discusses the proposed "bright-line rule" that a mercantile or manufacturing enterprise is not unitary unless there is substantial interdependence of basic operations by a flow of goods or services among the companies. The Court rejected the test as a constitutional mandate. The portion of the opinion dealing with that issue is set out at p. 568 supra.]

C

The State Court of Appeal relied on a large number of factors in reaching its judgment that appellant and its foreign subsidiaries constituted a unitary business. These included appellant's assistance to its subsidiaries in obtaining used and new equipment and in filling personnel needs that could not be met locally, the substantial role played by appellant in loaning funds to the subsidiaries and guaranteeing loans provided by others, the "considerable interplay between appellant and its foreign subsidiaries in the area of corporate expansion," 117 Cal. App.3d, at 997, 173 Cal.Rptr., at 128, the "substantial" technical assistance provided by appellant to the subsidiaries, id., at 998–999, 173 Cal. Rptr., at 127–128, and the supervisory role played by appellant's officers in providing general guidance to the subsidiaries. In each of these respects, this case differs from *ASARCO* and *F.W. Woolworth*,[18] and clearly comes closer than those cases did to presenting a "functionally integrated enterprise," Mobil, supra, 445 U.S., at 440, 100 S.Ct., at 1233, which the State is entitled to tax as a single entity. We need not decide whether any one of these factors would be sufficient as a constitutional matter to prove the existence of a unitary business. Taken in combination, at least, they clearly demonstrate that the state court reached a conclusion "within the realm of permissible judgment." [19]

18. See n. 15, supra. See also, e.g., F.W. Woolworth, 458 U.S., at 365, 102 S.Ct., at 3135–3136 ("*no* phase of any subsidiary's business was integrated with the parent's"), ibid. (undisputed testimony stated that each subsidiary made business decisions independently of parent); id., at 366, 102 S.Ct., at 3135 ("each subsidiary was responsible for obtaining its own financing from sources other than the parent"); ibid. ("With one possible exception, none of the subsidiaries' officers during the year in question was a current or former employee of the parent.") (footnote omitted).

19. Two of the factors relied on by the state court deserve particular mention. The first of these is the flow of capital resources from appellant to its subsidiaries through loans and loan guarantees. There is no indication that any of these capital transactions were conducted at arm's length, and the resulting flow of value is obvious. As we made clear in another context in Corn Products Refining Co. v. Commissioner, 350 U.S. 46, 50–53, 76 S.Ct. 20, 23–24, 100 L.Ed. 29 (1955), capital transactions can serve either an investment function or an operational function. In this case, appellant's loans and loan guarantees were clearly part of an effort to ensure that "[t]he overseas operations of [appellant] continue to grow and to become a more substantial part of the company's strength and profitability." Container

IV

We turn now to the question of fair apportionment. Once again, appellant has the burden of proof; it must demonstrate that there is " 'no rational relationship between the income attributed to the State and the intrastate values of the enterprise.' " Exxon Corp., 447 U.S., at 220, 100 S.Ct., at 2118, quoting Mobil, supra, 445 U.S., at 437, 100 S.Ct., at 1231, by proving that the income apportioned to California under the statute is "out of all appropriate proportion to the business transacted by the appellant in that State," Hans Rees' Sons, Inc., 283 U.S., at 135, 51 S.Ct., at 389.

Appellant challenges the application of California's three-factor formula to its business on two related grounds, both arising as a practical (although not a theoretical) matter out of the international character of the enterprise. First, appellant argues that its foreign subsidiaries are significantly more profitable than it is, and that the three-factor formula, by ignoring that fact and relying instead on indirect measures of income such as payroll, property, and sales, systematically distorts the true allocation of income between appellant and the subsidiaries. The problem with this argument is obvious: the profit figures relied on by appellant are based on precisely the sort of formal geographical accounting whose basic theoretical weaknesses justify resort to formula apportionment in the first place. Indeed, we considered and rejected a very similar argument in *Mobil,* pointing out that whenever a unitary business exists,

> "separate [geographical] accounting, while it purports to isolate portions of income received in various States, may fail to account for contributions to income resulting from functional integration, centralization of management, and economies of scale. Because these factors of profitability arise from the operation of the business as a whole, it becomes misleading to characterize the income of the business as having a single identifiable 'source.' Although separate geographical accounting may be useful for internal auditing, for purposes of state taxation it is not constitutionally required." 445 U.S., at 438, 100 S.Ct., at 1232 (citation omitted).

Corporation of America, 1964 Annual Report 6, reproduced in Exhibit I to Stipulation of Facts. See generally id., at 6–9, 11.

The second noteworthy factor is the managerial role played by appellant in its subsidiaries' affairs. We made clear in *F.W. Woolworth Co.* that a unitary business finding could not be based merely on "the type of occasional oversight—with respect to capital structure, major debt, and dividends—that any parent gives to an investment in a subsidiary. . . ." 458 U.S., at 369, 102 S.Ct., at 3138. As *Exxon* illustrates, however, mere decentralization of day-to-day management responsibility and accountability cannot defeat a unitary business finding. 447 U.S., at 224, 100 S.Ct., at 2120. The difference lies in whether the management role that the parent does play is grounded in its own operational expertise and its overall operational strategy. In this case, the business "guidelines" established by appellant for its subsidiaries, the "consensus" process by which appellant's management was involved in the subsidiaries' business decisions, and the sometimes uncompensated technical assistance provided by appellant, all point to precisely the sort of operational role we found lacking in *F.W. Woolworth.*

Appellant's second argument is related, and can be answered in the same way. Appellant contends:

> "The costs of production in foreign countries are generally significantly lower than in the United States, primarily as a result of the lower wage rates of workers in countries other than the United States. Because wages are one of the three factors used in formulary apportionment, the use of the formula unfairly inflates the amount of income apportioned to United States operations, where wages are higher." Brief for Appellant 12.

Appellant supports this argument with various statistics that appear to demonstrate, not only that wage rates are generally lower in the foreign countries in which its subsidiaries operate, but also that those lower wages are not offset by lower levels of productivity. Indeed, it is able to show that at least one foreign plant had labor costs per thousand square feet of corrugated container that were approximately 40% of the same costs in appellant's California plants.

The problem with all this evidence, however, is that it does not by itself come close to impeaching the basic rationale behind the three-factor formula. Appellant and its foreign subsidiaries have been determined to be a unitary business. It therefore may well be that in addition to the foreign payroll going into the production of any given corrugated container by a foreign subsidiary, there is also California payroll, as well as other California factors, contributing—albeit more indirectly—to the same production. The mere fact that this possibility is not reflected in appellant's accounting does not disturb the underlying premises of the formula apportionment method.

Both geographical accounting and formula apportionment are imperfect proxies for an ideal which is not only difficult to achieve in practice, but also difficult to describe in theory. Some methods of formula apportionment are particularly problematic because they focus on only a small part of the spectrum of activities by which value is generated. Although we have generally upheld the use of such formulas, see, e.g., Moorman Mfg. Co. v. Bair, 437 U.S. 267, 98 S.Ct. 2340, 57 L.Ed.2d 197 (1978); Underwood Typewriter Co. v. Chamberlain, 254 U.S. 113, 41 S.Ct. 45, 65 L.Ed. 165 (1920), we have on occasion found the distortive effect of focusing on only one factor so outrageous in a particular case as to require reversal. In Hans Rees' Sons, Inc. v. North Carolina ex rel. Maxwell, supra, for example, an apportionment method based entirely on ownership of tangible property resulted in an attribution to North Carolina of between 66% and 85% of the taxpayer's income over the course of a number of years, while a separate accounting analysis purposely skewed to resolve all doubts in favor of the State resulted in an attribution of no more than 21.7%. We struck down the application of the one-factor formula to that particular business, holding that the method, "albeit fair on its face, operates so as to reach profits which are in no just sense attributable to transactions within its jurisdiction." Id., at 134, 51 S.Ct., at 389.

The three-factor formula used by California has gained wide approval precisely because payroll, property, and sales appear in combination to reflect a very large share of the activities by which value is generated. It is therefore able to avoid the sorts of distortions that were present in *Hans Rees' Sons, Inc.*

Of course, even the three-factor formula is necessarily imperfect.[20] But we have seen no evidence demonstrating that the margin of error (systematic or not) inherent in the three-factor formula is greater than the margin of error (systematic or not) inherent in the sort of separate accounting urged upon us by appellant. Indeed, it would be difficult to come to such a conclusion on the basis of the figures in this case: for all of appellant's statistics showing allegedly enormous distortions caused by the three-factor formula, the tables we set out at nn. 11, 12, supra, reveal that the percentage increase in taxable income attributable to California between the methodology employed by appellant and the methodology employed by appellee comes to approximately 14%, a far cry from the more than 250% difference which led us to strike down the state tax in *Hans Rees' Sons, Inc.*, and a figure certainly within the substantial margin of error inherent in any method of attributing income among the components of a unitary business. See also Moorman Mfg. Co., supra, 437 U.S., at 272–273, 98 S.Ct., at 2343–2344; Ford Motor Co. v. Beauchamp, 308 U.S. 331, 60 S.Ct. 273, 84 L.Ed. 304 (1939); Underwood Typewriter Co., supra, 254 U.S., at 120–121, 41 S.Ct., at 46–47.

V

For the reasons we have just outlined, we conclude that California's application of the unitary business principle to appellant and its foreign subsidiaries was proper, and that its use of the standard three-factor formula to apportion the income of that unitary business was fair. This proper and fair method of taxation happens, however, to be quite different from the method employed both by the Federal Government in taxing appellant's business, and by each of the relevant foreign jurisdictions in taxing the business of appellant's subsidiaries. Each of these other taxing jurisdictions has adopted a qualified separate accounting approach—often referred to as the "arm's-length" approach—

---

20. First, the one-third-each weight given to the three factors is essentially arbitrary. Second, payroll, property, and sales still do not exhaust the entire set of factors arguably relevant to the production of income. Finally, the relationship between each of the factors and income is by no means exact. The three-factor formula, as applied to horizontally linked enterprises, is based in part on the very rough economic assumption that rates of return on property and payroll—as such rates of return would be measured by an ideal accounting method that took all transfers of value into account—are roughly the same in different taxing jurisdictions. This assumption has a powerful basis in economic theory: if true rates of return were radically different in different jurisdictions, one might expect a significant shift in investment resources to take advantage of that difference. On the other hand, the assumption has admitted weaknesses: an enterprise's willingness to invest simultaneously in two jurisdictions with very different true rates of return might be adequately explained by, for example, the difficulty of shifting resources, the decreasing marginal value of additional investment, and portfolio-balancing considerations.

to the taxation of related corporations.[21] Under the "arms-length" approach every corporation even if closely tied to other corporations, is treated for most—but decidedly not all—purposes as if it were an independant entity dealing at arm's length with its affiliated corporations, and subject to taxation only by the jurisdictions in which it operates and only for the income it realizes on its own books.

If the unitary business consisting of appellant and its subsidiaries were entirely domestic, the fact that different jurisdictions applied different methods of taxation to it would probably make little constitutional difference, for the reasons we discuss supra, at 2943. Given that it is international, however, we must subject this case to the additional scrutiny required by the Foreign Commerce Clause. See Mobil Oil Corp., 445 U.S., at 446, 100 S.Ct., at 1236; Japan Line, Ltd., 441 U.S., at 446, 99 S.Ct., at 1820; Bowman v. Chicago & N.W.R. Co., 125 U.S. 465, 482, 8 S.Ct. 689, 696, 31 L.Ed. 700 (1888). The case most relevant to our inquiry is *Japan Line.*

A

Japan Line involved an attempt by California to impose an apparently fairly apportioned, nondiscriminatory, ad valorem property tax on cargo containers which were instrumentalities of foreign commerce and which were temporarily located in various California ports. The same cargo containers, however, were subject to an unapportioned property tax in their home port of Japan. Moreover, a convention signed by the United States and Japan made clear, at least, that neither National Government could impose a tax on temporarily imported cargo containers whose home port was in the other nation. We held that "[w]hen a State seeks to tax the instrumentalities of foreign commerce, two additional considerations, beyond those articulated in [the doctrine governing the Interstate Commerce Clause], come into play." 441 U.S., at 446, 99 S.Ct., at 1820. The first is the enhanced risk of multiple taxation. Although consistent application of the fair apportionment standard can generally mitigate, if not eliminate, double taxation in the domestic context,

> "neither this Court nor this Nation can ensure full apportionment when one of the taxing entities is a foreign sovereign. If an instrumentality of commerce is domiciled abroad, the country of domicile may have the right, consistently with the custom of nations, to impose a tax on its full value. If a State should seek to tax the same instrumentality on an apportioned basis, multiple taxation inevitably results. * * * Due to the absence of an authoritative tribunal capable of ensuring that the aggregation of taxes is computed on no more than one full value, a state tax, even though 'fairly apportioned' to reflect an instrumentality's presence within the State, may subject foreign commerce ' "to the risk of a double tax burden to which [domestic]

---

21. The "arm's-length" approach is also often applied to geographically distinct divisions of a single corporation.

commerce is not exposed, and which the commerce clause forbids." ' " Id., at 447–448, 99 S.Ct., at 1821, quoting Evco v. Jones, 409 U.S. 91, 94, 93 S.Ct. 349, 351, 34 L.Ed.2d 325 (1972), in turn quoting J.D. Adams Mfg. Co. v. Storen, 304 U.S. 307, 311, 58 S.Ct. 913, 916, 82 L.Ed. 1365 (1938) (footnote omitted).

The second additional consideration that arises in the foreign commerce context is the possibility that a state tax will "impair federal uniformity in an area where federal uniformity is essential." 441 U.S., at 448, 99 S.Ct., at 1821.

> "A state tax on instrumentalities of foreign commerce may frustrate the achievement of federal uniformity in several ways. If the State imposes an apportioned tax, international disputes over reconciling apportionment formulae may arise. If a novel state tax creates an asymmetry in the international tax structure, foreign nations disadvantaged by the levy may retaliate against American-owned instrumentalities present in their jurisdictions. * * * If other States followed the taxing State's example, various instrumentalities of commerce could be subjected to varying degrees of multiple taxation, a result that would plainly prevent this Nation from 'speaking with one voice' in regulating foreign commerce." Id., at 450–451, 99 S.Ct., at 1822–1823 (footnote omitted).

On the basis of the facts in *Japan Line,* we concluded that the California tax at issue was constitutionally improper because it failed to meet either of the additional tests mandated by the Foreign Commerce Clause. Id., at 451–454, 99 S.Ct., at 1823–1824.

This case is similar to *Japan Line* in a number of important respects. First, the tax imposed here, like the tax imposed in *Japan Line,* has resulted in actual double taxation, in the sense that some of the income taxed without apportionment by foreign nations as attributable to appellant's foreign subsidiaries was also taxed by California as attributable to the State's share of the total income of the unitary business of which those subsidiaries are a part.[22] Second, that double taxation stems from a serious divergence in the taxing schemes adopted by California and the foreign taxing authorities. Third, the taxing method adopted by those foreign taxing authorities is consistent with accepted international practice. Finally, our own Federal Government, to the degree it has spoken, seems to prefer the taxing method adopted

---

22. The stipulation of facts indicates that the tax returns filed by appellant's subsidiaries in their foreign domiciles took into account "only the applicable income and deductions incurred by the subsidiary or subsidiaries in that country and not . . . the income and deductions of [appellant] or the subsidiaries operating in other countries." App. 72. This does not conclusively demonstrate the existence of double taxation because appellant has not produced its foreign tax returns, and it is entirely possible that deductions, exemptions, or adjustments in those returns eliminated whatever overlap in taxable income resulted from the application of the California apportionment method. Nevertheless, appellee does not seriously dispute the existence of actual double taxation as we have defined it, Brief for Appellee 114–121, but cf. Tr. of Oral Arg. 28–29, and we assume its existence for the purposes of our analysis. Cf. Japan Line, 441 U.S., at 452, n. 17, 99 S.Ct., at 1823, n. 17.

by the international community to the taxing method adopted by California.[23]

Nevertheless, there are also a number of ways in which this case is clearly distinguishable from *Japan Line*.[24] First, it involves a tax on income rather than a tax on property. We distinguished property from income taxation in Mobil Oil Corp., 445 U.S., at 444–446, 100 S.Ct., at 1235–1236, and Exxon Corp., 447 U.S., at 228–229, 100 S.Ct., at 2122–2123, suggesting that "[t]he reasons for allocation to a single situs that often apply in the case of property taxation carry little force" in the case of income taxation. 445 U.S., at 445, 100 S.Ct., at 1235. Second, the double taxation in this case, although real, is not the "inevitabl[e]" result of the California taxing scheme. Cf. Japan Line, 441 U.S., at 447, 99 S.Ct., at 1820. In *Japan Line*, we relied strongly on the fact that one taxing jurisdiction claimed the right to tax a given value in full, and another taxing jurisdiction claimed the right to tax the same entity in part—a combination resulting necessarily in double taxation. Id., at 447, 452, 455, 99 S.Ct., at 1820, 1823, 1825. Here, by contrast, we are faced with two distinct methods of allocating the income of a multinational enterprise. The "arm's-length" approach divides the pie on the basis of formal accounting principles. The formula apportionment method divides the same pie on the basis of a mathematical generalization. Whether the combination of the two methods results in the same income being taxed twice or in some portion of income not being taxed at all is dependent solely on the facts of the individual case.[25] The third difference between this case and *Japan Line* is that the tax here falls, not on the foreign owners of an instrumentality of foreign commerce, but on a corporation domiciled and headquartered in the United States. We specifically left open in *Japan Line* the application of that case to "domestically owned instrumentalities engaged in foreign commerce," id., at 444, n. 7, 99 S.Ct., at 1819, n. 7, and—to the extent that corporations can be analogized to cargo containers in the first place—this case falls clearly within that reservation.[26]

In light of these considerations, our task in this case must be to determine whether the distinctions between the present tax and the tax at issue in *Japan Line* add up to a constitutionally significant differ-

23. But see infra, at 2956–2957 (discussing whether state scheme is preempted by federal law).

24. Note that we deliberately emphasized in *Japan Line* the narrowness of the question presented: "whether instrumentalities of commerce that are owned, based, and registered abroad and that are used exclusively in international commerce, may be subjected to apportioned ad valorem property taxation by a State." 441 U.S., at 444, 99 S.Ct., at 1819.

25. Indeed, in Chicago Bridge & Iron Co. v. Caterpillar Tractor Co., No. 81–349, which was argued last Term and carried over to this Term, application of worldwide combined apportionment resulted in a refund to the taxpayer from the amount he had paid under a tax return that included neither foreign income nor foreign apportionment factors.

26. We have no need to address in this opinion the constitutionality of combined apportionment with respect to state taxation of domestic corporations with foreign parents or foreign corporations with either foreign parents or foreign subsidiaries. See also n. 32, infra.

ence. For the reasons we are about to explain, we conclude that they do.

B

In *Japan Line*, we said that "[e]ven a slight overlapping of tax—a problem that might be deemed *de minimis* in a domestic context—assumes importance when sensitive matters of foreign relations and national sovereignty are concerned." Id., at 456, 99 S.Ct., at 1825 (footnote omitted). If we were to take that statement as an absolute prohibition on state-induced double taxation in the international context, then our analysis here would be at an end. But, in fact, such an absolute rule is no more appropriate here than it was in *Japan Line* itself, where we relied on much more than the mere fact of double taxation to strike down the state tax at issue. Although double taxation in the foreign commerce context deserves to receive close scrutiny, that scrutiny must take into account the context in which the double taxation takes place and the alternatives reasonably available to the taxing State.

In *Japan Line*, the taxing State could entirely eliminate one important source of double taxation simply by adhering to one bright-line rule: do not tax, to any extent whatsoever, cargo containers "that are owned, based, and registered abroad and that are used exclusively in international commerce * * *." Id., at 444, 99 S.Ct., at 1819. To require that the State adhere to this rule was by no means unfair, because the rule did no more than reflect consistent international practice and express federal policy. In this case, California could try to avoid double taxation simply by not taxing appellant's income at all, even though a good deal of it is plainly domestic. But no party has suggested such a rule, and its obvious unfairness requires no elaboration. Or California could try to avoid double taxation by adopting some version of the "arm's-length" approach. That course, however, would not by any means guarantee an end to double taxation.

As we have already noted, the "arm's-length" approach is generally based, in the first instance, on a multicorporate enterprise's own formal accounting. But, despite that initial reliance, the "arm's-length" approach recognizes, as much as the formula apportionment approach, that closely related corporations can engage in a transfer of values that is not fully reflected in their formal ledgers. Thus, for example, 26 U.S.C. § 482 provides:

> "In any case of two or more * * * businesses (whether or not incorporated, whether or not organized in the United States, and whether or not affiliated) owned or controlled directly or indirectly by the same interests, the Secretary [of the Treasury] may distribute, apportion, or allocate gross income, deductions, credits, or allowances between or among such * * * businesses, if he determines that such distribution, apportionment, or allocation is necessary in order to

prevent evasion of taxes or clearly to reflect the income of any of such * * * businesses." [27]

And, as one might expect, the United States Internal Revenue Service has developed elaborate regulations in order to give content to this general provision. Many other countries have similar provisions.[28] A serious problem, however, is that even though most nations have adopted the "arm's-length" approach in its general outlines, the precise rules under which they reallocate income among affiliated corporations often differ substantially, and whenever that difference exists, the possibility of double taxation also exists.[29] Thus, even if California were to adopt some version of the "arm's-length" approach, it could not eliminate the risk of double taxation of corporations subject to its franchise tax, and might in some cases end up subjecting those corporations to more serious double taxation than would occur under formula apportionment.[30]

27. Cf. Treasury Department's Model Income Tax Treaty of June 16, 1981, Art. 9, reprinted in CCH Tax Treaties ¶ 158 (1981) (hereinafter Model Treaty) ("Where * * * an enterprise of a Contracting State participates directly or indirectly in the management, control or capital of an enterprise of the other Contracting State * * * and * * * conditions are made or imposed between the two enterprises in their commercial or financial relations which differ from those which would be made between independent enterprises, then any profits which, but for those conditions would have accrued to one of the enterprises, but by reason of those conditions have not so accrued, may be included in the profits of that enterprise and taxed accordingly"); J. Bischel, Income Tax Treaties 219 (1978) (hereinafter Bischel).

28. See generally G. Harley, International Division of the Income Tax Base of Multinational Enterprise 143–160 (1981) (hereinafter Harley); Madere, International Pricing: Allocation Guidelines and Relief from Double Taxation, 10 Tex.Int'l L.J. 108, 111–120 (1975).

29. See Surrey, Reflections on the Allocation of Income and Expenses Among National Tax Jurisdictions, 10 L. & Policy Int'l Bus. 409 (1978); Bischel 459–461, 464–466; B. Bittker & J. Eustice, Federal Income Taxation of Corporations and Shareholders ¶ 15.06 (4th ed. 1979); Harley 143–160.

30. Another problem arises out of the treatment of intercorporate dividends. Under formula apportionment as practiced by California, intercorporate dividends attributable to the unitary business are, like many other intercorporate transactions, considered essentially irrelevant and are

not included in taxable income. See n. 5, supra. If the "arm's-length" method were entirely consistent, it would tax intercorporate dividends when they occur, just as all other investment income is taxed. (In which State that dividend could be taxed is not particularly important, since the issue here is international rather than interstate double taxation. See *Mobil,* 445 U.S., at 447–448, 100 S.Ct., at 1237.) It could also be argued that this would not, strictly speaking, result in double taxation, since the income taxed would be income "of" the parent rather than income "of" the subsidiary. The effect, however, would often be to penalize an enterprise simply because it has adopted a particular corporate structure. In practice, therefore, most jurisdictions allow for tax credits or outright exemptions for intercorporate dividends among closely tied corporations, and provision for such credits or exemptions is often included in tax treaties. See generally Model Treaty, Art. 23; Bischel 2. No suggestion has been made here that appellant's dividends from its subsidiaries would have to be exempt entirely from domestic state taxation. And the grant of a credit, which is the approach taken by federal law, see 26 U.S.C. § 901 et seq., does not in fact entirely eliminate effective double taxation: the same income is still taxed twice, although the credit insures that the total tax is no greater than that which would be paid under the higher of the two tax rates involved. Moreover, once the Federal Government has allowed a credit for foreign taxes on a particular intercorporate dividend, we are not persuaded why, as a logical matter, a State would have to grant another credit of its own, since the federal credit would have already vindicated the goal of not subjecting the taxpayer to a

That California would have trouble avoiding double taxation even if it adopted the "arm's-length" approach is, we think, a product of the difference between a tax on income and a tax on tangible property. See supra, at 2952. Allocating income among various taxing jurisdictions bears some resemblance, as we have emphasized throughout this opinion, to slicing a shadow. In the absence of a central coordinating authority, absolute consistency, even among taxing authorities whose basic approach to the task is quite similar, may just be too much to ask.[31] If California's method of formula apportionment "inevitably" led to double taxation, see supra, at 2952, that might be reason enough to render it suspect. But since it does not, it would be perverse, simply for the sake of avoiding double taxation, to require California to give up one allocation method that sometimes results in double taxation in favor of another allocation method that also sometimes results in double taxation. Cf. Moorman Mfg. Co., 437 U.S., at 278–280, 98 S.Ct., at 2347–2348.

It could be argued that even if the Foreign Commerce Clause does not require California to adopt the "arm's-length" approach to foreign subsidiaries of domestic corporations, it does require that whatever system of taxation California adopts must not result in double taxation in any particular case. The implication of such a rule, however, would be that even if California adopted the "arm's-length" method, it would be required to defer, not merely to a single internationally accepted bright-line standard, as was the case in *Japan Line*, but to a variety of § 482–type reallocation decisions made by individual foreign countries in individual cases. Although double taxation is a constitutionally disfavored state of affairs, particularly in the international context, *Japan Line* does not require forbearance so extreme or so one-sided.

C

We come finally to the second inquiry suggested by *Japan Line* — whether California's decision to adopt formula apportionment in the international context was impermissible because it "may impair federal uniformity in an area where federal uniformity is essential," 441 U.S., at 448, 99 S.Ct., at 1821, and "prevents the Federal Government from 'speaking with one voice' in international trade," id., at 453, 99 S.Ct., at 1824, quoting Michelin Tire Corp. v. Wages, 423 U.S. 276, 285, 96 S.Ct.

higher tax burden that it would have to bear if its subsidiary's income were not taxed abroad.

31. At the federal level, double taxation is sometimes mitigated by provisions in tax treaties providing for intergovernmental negotiations to resolve differences in the approaches of the respective taxing authorities. See generally Model Treaty, Art. 25; 2 New York University, proceedings of the Fortieth Annual Institute on Federal Taxation § 31.03[2] (1982) (hereinafter N.Y.U. Institute). But cf. Owens, United States

Income Tax Treaties: Their Role in Relieving Double Taxation, 17 Rutgers L.Rev. 428, 443–444 (1963) (role of such provisions procedural rather than substantive). California, however, is in no position to negotiate with foreign governments, and neither the tax treaties nor federal law provides a mechanism by which the Federal Government could negotiate double taxation arising out of state tax systems. In any event, such negotiations do not always occur, and when they do occur they do not always succeed.

535, 540, 46 L.Ed.2d 495 (1976). In conducting this inquiry, however, we must keep in mind that if a state tax merely has foreign resonances, but does not implicate foreign affairs, we cannot infer, "[a]bsent some explicit directive from Congress, . . . that treatment of foreign income at the federal level mandates identical treatment by the States." Mobil, 445 U.S., at 448, 100 S.Ct., at 1237. See also Japan Line, 441 U.S., at 456, n. 20, 99 S.Ct., at 1825, n. 20; Michelin Tire Corp., supra, 423 U.S., at 286, 96 S.Ct., at 541. Thus, a state tax at variance with federal policy will violate the "one voice" standard if it *either* implicates foreign policy issues which must be left to the Federal Government *or* violates a clear federal directive. The second of these considerations is, of course, essentially a species of pre-emption analysis.

(1)

The most obvious foreign policy implication of a state tax is the threat it might pose of offending our foreign trading partners and leading them to retaliate against the Nation as a whole. 441 U.S., at 450, 99 S.Ct., at 1822. In considering this issue, however, we are faced with a distinct problem. This Court has little competence in determining precisely when foreign nations will be offended by particular acts, and even less competence in deciding how to balance a particular risk of retaliation against the sovereign right of the United States as a whole to let the States tax as they please. The best that we can do, in the absence of explicit action by Congress, is to attempt to develop objective standards that reflect very general observations about the imperatives of international trade and international relations.

This case is not like *Mobil,* in which the real issue came down to a question of interstate rather than foreign commerce. 445 U.S., at 446–449, 100 S.Ct., at 1236–1237. Nevertheless, three distinct factors, which we have already discussed in one way or another, seem to us to weigh strongly against the conclusion that the tax imposed by California might justifiably lead to significant foreign retaliation. First, the tax here does not create an *automatic* "asymmetry," Japan Line, supra, 441 U.S., at 453, 99 S.Ct., at 1824, in international taxation. See supra, at 2952, 2954–2955. Second, the tax here was imposed, not on a foreign entity as was the case in *Japan Line,* but on a domestic corporation. Although, California "counts" income arguably attributable to foreign corporations in calculating the taxable income of that domestic corporation, the legal incidence of the tax falls on the domestic corporation.[32] Third, even if foreign nations have a legitimate interest in reducing the tax burden of domestic corporations, the fact remains that appellant is without a doubt amenable to be taxed in california in one way or another, and that the amount of tax it pays is much more the function of California's tax rate than of its allocation method. Although a

---

32. We recognize that the fact that the legal incidence of a tax falls on a corporation whose formal corporate domicile is domestic might be less significant in the case of a domestic corporation that was owned by foreign interests. We need not decide here whether such a case would require us to alter our analysis.

foreign nation might be more offended by what it considers unorthodox treatment of appellant than it would be if California simply raised its general tax rate to achieve the same economic result, we can only assume that the offense involved in either event would be attenuated at best.

A state tax may, of course, have foreign policy implications other than the threat of retaliation. We note, however, that in this case, unlike *Japan Line,* the Executive Branch has decided not to file an *amicus curiae* brief in opposition to the state tax.[33] The lack of such a submission is by no means dispositive. Nevertheless, when combined with all the other considerations we have discussed, it does suggest that the foreign policy of the United States—whose nuances, we must emphasize again, are much more the province of the Executive Branch and Congress than of this Court—is not seriously threatened by California's decision to apply the unitary business concept and formula apportionment in calculating appellant's taxable income.

(2)

When we turn to specific indications of congressional intent, appellant's position fares no better. First, there is no claim here that the federal tax statutes themselves provide the necessary pre-emptive force. Second, although the United States is a party to a great number of tax treaties that require the Federal Government to adopt some form of "arm's-length" analysis in taxing the domestic income of multi-national enterprises,[34] that requirement is generally waived with respect to the taxes imposed by each of the contracting nations on its own domestic corporations.[35] This fact, if nothing else, confirms our view that such taxation is in reality of local rather than international concern. Third, the tax treaties into which the United States has entered do not generally cover the taxing activities of subnational governmental units such as States,[36] and in none of the treaties does the restriction on "non-arm's length" methods of taxation apply to the States. Moreover, the Senate has on at least one occasion, in considering a proposed treaty, attached a reservation declining to give its consent to a provision in the treaty that would have extended that restriction to the States.[37] Finally, it remains true, as we said in *Mobil,* that "Congress has long debated, but has not enacted, legislation designed to regulate

33. The Solicitor General did submit a memorandum opposing worldwide formula apportionment by a State in Chicago Bridge & Iron Co. v. Caterpillar Tractor Co., No. 81–349, a case that was argued last Term, and carried over to this Term. Although there is no need for us to speculate as to the reasons for the Solicitor General's decision not to submit a similar memorandum or brief in this case, cf. Brief for National Governors' Association et al. as Amici Curiae 6–7, there has been no indication that the position taken by the Government in *Chicago Bridge & Iron Co.* still represents its views, or that we should regard the brief in that case as applying to this case.

34. See generally Model Treaty, Art. 7(2); Bischel 33–38, 459–461.

35. See Model Treaty, Art. 1(3); Bischel 718; N.Y.U. Institute § 31.04[3].

36. See Bischel 7.

37. See 124 Cong.Rec. 18400, 19076 (1978).

state taxation of income."   445 U.S., at 448, 100 S.Ct., at 1237.[38]   Thus, whether we apply the "explicit directive" standard articulated in *Mobil,* or some more relaxed standard which takes into account our residual concern about the foreign policy implications of California's tax, we cannot conclude that the California tax at issue here is pre-empted by federal law or fatally inconsistent with federal policy.

VI

The judgment of the California Court of Appeal is

Affirmed.

JUSTICE STEVENS took no part in the consideration or decision of this case.

JUSTICE POWELL, with whom THE CHIEF JUSTICE and JUSTICE O'CONNOR join, dissenting.

The Court's opinion addresses the several questions presented in this case with commendable thoroughness.   In my view, however, the California tax clearly violates the Foreign Commerce Clause—just as did the tax in Japan Line, Ltd. v. County of Los Angeles, 441 U.S. 434, 99 S.Ct. 1813, 60 L.Ed.2d 336 (1979).   I therefore do not consider whether appellant and its foreign subsidiaries constitute a "unitary business" or whether the State's apportionment formula is fair.

With respect to the Foreign Commerce Clause issue, the Court candidly concedes: (i) "double taxation is a constitutionally disfavored state of affairs, particularly in the international context," ante, at 2955; (ii) "like the tax imposed in *Japan Line,* [California's tax] has resulted in actual double taxation," ante, at 2951; and therefore (iii) this tax "deserves to receive close scrutiny," ante, at 2953.   The Court also concedes that "[t]his case is similar to *Japan Line* in a number of important respects," ante, at 2951, and that the Federal Government "seems to prefer the ["arm's-length"] taxing method adopted by the international community," ante, at 2952.   The Court identifies several distinctions between this case and *Japan Line,* however, and sustains the validity of the California tax despite the inevitable double taxation and the incompatability with the method of taxation accepted by the international community.

In reaching its result, the Court fails to apply "close scrutiny" in a manner that meets the requirements of that exacting standard of review.   Although the facts of *Japan Line* differ in some respects, they are identical on the critical questions of double taxation and federal uniformity.   The principles enunciated in that case should be controlling here: a state tax is unconstitutional if it either "creates a substantial risk of international multiple taxation" or "prevents the Federal Government from 'speaking with one voice when regulating commer-

---

38. There is now pending one such bill of which we are aware. See H.R. 2918, 98th Cong., 1st Sess. (1983).

cial relations with foreign governments.' " 441 U.S., at 451, 99 S.Ct., at 1823.

I

It is undisputed that the California tax not only "creates a substantial risk of international multiple taxation," but also "has resulted in actual double taxation" in this case. See ante, at 2951. As the Court explains, this double taxation occurs because California has adopted a taxing system that "serious[ly] diverge[s]" from the internationally accepted taxing methods adopted by foreign taxing authorities. Ante, at 2952. The Court nevertheless upholds the tax on the ground that California would not necessarily reduce double taxation by conforming to the accepted international practice.[1] Ante, at 2953–2955. This argument fails to recognize the fundamental difference between the current double taxation and the risk that would remain under an "arm's-length" system. I conclude that the California tax violates the first principle enunciated in *Japan Line*.

At present, double taxation exists because California uses an allocation method that is different in its basic assumptions from the method used by all of the countries in which appellant's subsidiaries operate. The State's formula has no necessary relationship to the amount of income earned in a given jurisdiction as calculated under the "arm's-length" method. On the contrary, the formula allocates a higher proportion of income to jurisdictions where wage rates, property values, and sales prices are higher. See J. Hellerstein & W. Hellerstein, State and Local Taxation 538–539 (4th ed. 1978). To the extent that California is such a jurisdiction, the formula inherently leads to double taxation.

Appellant's case is a good illustration of the problem. The overwhelming majority of its overseas income is earned by its Latin American subsidiaries. See App. 112. Since wage rates, property values, and sales prices are much lower in Latin America than they are in California, the State's apportionment formula systematically allocates a much lower proportion of this income to Latin America than does the internationally accepted "arm's-length" method.[2] Correspondingly, the formula allocates a higher proportion of the income to California, where it is subject to state tax. As long as the three factors remain higher in

---

1. The Court also appears to attach some weight to its view that California is unable "simply [to] adher[e] to one bright-line rule" to eliminate double taxation. See ante, at 2953. From California's perspective, however, a bright-line rule that avoids Foreign Commerce Clause problems clearly exists. The State simply could base its apportionment calculations on appellant's United States income as reported on its federal return. This sum is calculated by the "arm's-length" method, and is thus consistent with international practice and federal policy. Double taxation is avoided to the extent possible by international negotiation conducted by the Federal Government. California need not concern itself with the details of the international allocation, but could apportion the American income using its three-factor formula.

2. Although there are a few foreign countries where wage rates, property values, and sales prices are higher than they are in California, appellant's principal subsidiaries did not operate in such countries.

California, it is inevitable that the State will tax income under its formula that already has been taxed by another country under accepted international practice.

In the tax years in question, for example, over 27% of appellant's worldwide income was earned in Latin America and taxed by Latin American countries under the "arm's-length" method. See ibid. Latin American wages, however, represented under 6% of the worldwide total; Latin American property was about 20% of the worldwide total; and Latin American sales were less than 14% of the worldwide total. See id., at 109–111. As a result, roughly 13% of appellant's worldwide income—less than half of the "arm's-length" total—was allocated to Latin America under California's formula. In other words, over half of the income of appellant's largest group of subsidiaries was allocated elsewhere under the State's formula. In accordance with international practice, all of this income had been taxed in Latin America, but the California system would allow the income to be taxed a second time in California and other jurisdictions. This problem of double taxation cannot be eliminated without either California or the international community changing its basic tax practices.

If California adopted the "arm's-length" method, double taxation could still exist through differences in application.[3] California and Colombia, for example, might apply different accounting principles to a given intracorporate transfer. But these types of differences, although presently tolerated under international practice, are not inherent in the "arm's-length" system. Moreover, there is no reason to suppose that they will consistently favor one jurisdiction over another. And as international practice becomes more refined, such differences are more likely to be resolved and double taxation eliminated.

In sum, the risk of double taxation can arise in two ways. Under the present system, it arises because California has rejected accepted international practice in favor of a tax structure that is fundamentally different in its basic assumptions. Under a uniform system, double taxation also could arise because different jurisdictions—despite their agreement on basic principles—may differ in their application of the system. But these two risks are fundamentally different. Under the former, double taxation is inevitable. It cannot be avoided without changing the system itself. Under the latter, any double taxation that exists is the result of disagreements in application. Such disagreements may be unavoidable in view of the need to make individual judgments, but problems of this kind are more likely to be resolved by international negotiation.

On its face, the present double taxation violates the Foreign Commerce Clause. I would not reject, as the Court does, the solution to this

---

3. Similarly, there could be double taxation if the entire international community adopted California's method of formula apportionment. Different jurisdictions might apply different accounting principles to determine wages, property values, and sales. Indeed, any system that calls for the exercise of any judgment leaves the possibility for some double taxation.

constitutional violation simply because an international system based on the principle of uniformity would not necessarily be uniform in all of the details of its operation.

II

The Court acknowledges that its decision is contrary to the Federal Government's "prefer[ence for] the taxing method adopted by the international community." Ante, at 2952. It also states the appropriate standard for assessing the State's rejection of this preference: "a state tax at variance with federal policy will violate the 'one voice' standard if it *either* implicates foreign policy issues which must be left to the Federal Government *or* violates a clear federal directive." Ante, at 2955 (emphasis in original). The Court concludes, however, that the California tax does not prevent the Federal Government from speaking with one voice because it perceives relevant factual distinctions between this case and *Japan Line*. I conclude that the California taxing plan violates the second principle enunciated in *Japan Line*, despite these factual distinctions, because it seriously "implicates foreign policy issues which must be left to the Federal Government."

The Court first contends that "the tax here does not create an *automatic* 'asymmetry.'" Ante, at 2955 (emphasis in original) (quoting Japan Line, 441 U.S., at 453, 99 S.Ct., at 1824). This seems to mean only that the California tax does not result in double taxation in every case. But the fundamental inconsistency between the two methods of apportionment means that double taxation is inevitable. Since California is a jurisdiction where wage rates, property values, and sales prices are relatively high, double taxation is the logical expectation in a large proportion of the cases. Moreover, we recognized in *Japan Line* that "[e]ven a slight overlapping of tax—a problem that might be deemed *de minimis* in a domestic context—assumes importance when sensitive matters of foreign relations and national sovereignty are concerned." Id., at 456, 99 S.Ct., at 1825.

The Court also relies on the fact that the taxpayer here technically is a domestic corporation. See ante, at 2955. I have several problems with this argument. Although appellant may be the taxpayer in a technical sense, it is unquestioned that California is taxing the income of the foreign subsidiaries. Even if foreign governments are indifferent about the overall tax burden of an American corporation, they have legitimate grounds to complain when a heavier tax is calculated on the basis of the income of corporations domiciled in their countries. If nothing else, such a tax has the effect of discouraging American investment in their countries.

The Court's argument is even more difficult to accept when one considers the dilemma it creates for cases involving foreign corporations. If California attempts to tax the American subsidiary of an overseas company on the basis of the parent's worldwide income, with the result that double taxation occurs, I see no acceptable solution to the problem created. Most of the Court's analysis is inapplicable to such a case. There can be little doubt that the parent's government would be offended by the State's action and that international disputes, or even retaliation against American corporations, might be expected.[4] It thus seems inevitable that the tax would have to be found unconstitutional—at least to the extent it is applied to foreign companies. But in my view, invalidating the tax only to this limited extent also would be unacceptable. It would leave California free to discriminate against a Delaware corporation in favor of an overseas corporation. I would not permit such discrimination[5] without explicit congressional authorization.

The Court further suggests that California could impose the same tax burden on appellant under the "arm's-length" system simply by raising the general tax rate. See ante, at 2956. Although this may be true in theory, the argument ignores the political restraints that make such a course infeasible. If appellant's tax rate were increased, the State would be forced to raise the rate for all corporations.[6] If California wishes to follow this course, I see no constitutional objection. But it must be accomplished through the political process in which corporations doing business in California are free to voice their objections.

Finally, the Court attaches some weight to the fact that "the Executive Branch has decided not to file an *amicus curiae* brief in opposition to the state tax." Ibid. The Court, in a footnote, dismisses the Solicitor General's memorandum in Chicago Bridge & Iron Co. v. Caterpillar Tractor Co., No. 81–349, despite the fact that it is directly on point and the case is currently pending before the Court. See ante, at 2956, n. 33. In this memorandum, the Solicitor General makes it clear beyond question what the Executive Branch believes: "imposition of [a state tax] on the apportioned combined worldwide business income of a unitary group of related corporations, including foreign corporations, impairs federal uniformity in an area where such uniformity is essential."[7] Memorandum for United States as *Amicus Curiae* in Chicago Bridge & Iron Co. v. Caterpillar Tractor Co., O.T.1982, No. 81–

---

4. This is well illustrated by the protests that the Federal Government already has received from our principal trading partners. Several of these are reprinted or discussed in the papers now before the Court. See, e.g., App. to Brief for Committee on Unitary Tax as *Amicus Curiae* 7 (Canada); id., at 9 (France); id., at 13–16 (United Kingdom); id., at 17–19 (European Economic Community); App. to Brief for International Bankers Association in California et al. as *Amici Curiae* in Chicago Bridge & Iron Co. v. Caterpillar Tractor Co., O.T.1982, No. 81–349, pp. 4–5 (Japan); Memorandum for United States as *Amicus Curiae* in Chicago Bridge & Iron Co. v. Caterpillar Tractor Co., O.T.1982, No. 81–349, p. 3 ("[A] number of foreign governments have complained—both officially and unofficially—that the apportioned

combined method . . . creates an irritant in their commercial relations with the United States. Retaliatory taxation may ensue . . ."); App. to id., at 2a–3a (United Kingdom); id., at 8a–9a (Canada).

5. California is, of course, free to tax its own corporations more heavily than it taxes out-of-state corporations.

6. The State could not raise the tax rate for appellant alone, or even for corporations engaged in foreign commerce, without facing constitutional challenges under the Equal Protection or the Commerce Clause.

7. *Chicago Bridge & Iron*, it might be noted, is a case in which the state tax is imposed on an American parent corporation.

349, p. 2. I recognize that the Government may change its position from time to time, but I see no reason to ignore its view in one case currently pending before the Court when considering another case that raises exactly the same issue. The Solicitor General has not withdrawn his memorandum, nor has he supplemented it with anything taking a contrary position. As long as *Chicago Bridge & Iron* remains before us, we must conclude that the Government's views are accurately reflected in the Solicitor General's memorandum in that pending case.

In sum, none of the distinctions on which the Court relies is convincing. California imposes a tax that is flatly inconsistent with federal policy. It prevents the Federal Government from speaking with one voice in a field that should be left to the Federal Government.[8] This is an intrusion on national policy in foreign affairs that is not permitted by the Constitution.

III

In *Japan Line* we identified two constraints that a state tax on an international business must satisfy to comply with the Foreign Commerce Clause. We explicitly declared that "[i]f a state tax contravenes either of these precepts, it is unconstitutional." 441 U.S., at 451, 99 S.Ct., at 1823. In my view, the California tax before us today violates *both* requirements. I would declare it unconstitutional.

Notes and Problems

A. The *Container* case is extensively analyzed in J. Hellerstein & W. Hellerstein, ¶¶ 8.10[7A], [10] Cumulative Supplement to J. Hellerstein, State Taxation I, Corporate Income and Franchise Taxes (1983). There has been a veritable snowstorm of comments on the *Container* case and its implications in the tax journals and law reviews. See the thoughtful analysis of the case in an article by John D. Whiteknack, who argued the *Chicago Bridge & Iron Co.* case both in the Illinois courts and the U.S. Supreme Court, in "State Tax Litigation After the *Container* Decision: The Potential Breaks for Foreign Multinationals," Tax Notes, Sept. 5, 1983, p. 771; see also "The Supreme Court 1982 Term," 97 Harv.L.Rev. 70, 112 (1983); Hreha & Seago, "Domestic and Foreign Aspects of the *Container* Decision," 2 J. of St. Tax. 101 (1983); Peters, "Supreme Ct. in *Container* Upholds State's Broad Power Under Unitary Taxation Method," 59 J. of Tax'n 300 (1983); Feinschreiber, "The *Container* 'Flow of Value' Test and Unitary Taxation," 3 Interstate Tax Rep. 12 (Aug.1983); DeLap, "From *Moorman* to *Chicago Bridge:* U.S. Supreme Court Decisions Relating to 'Unitary' Taxation," 2 J. of St. Tax. 197 (1983); Kaplan, "The Unitary Tax Debate, The United States Supreme Court, and Some Plain English," 10 J. of Corp. Tax. 283 (1984).

For the impact of *Container* on State court decisions dealing with the delineation of the scope of a unitary business for apportionment purposes,

---

8. The Court relies on the absence of a "clear federal directive." See ante, at 2955, 2956–2957. In light of the Government's position, as stated in the Solicitor General's memorandum, see supra, at 2960, the absence of a more formal statement of its view is entitled to little weight.

see J. Hellerstein & W. Hellerstein ¶ 8.11[11] Cumulative Supplement supra.

B. In Chicago Bridge & Iron Co. v. Caterpillar Tractor Co., 456 U.S. 958, 102 S.Ct. 2032 (1982) (Chicago Bridge & Iron Co. was one of the intervenors in *Caterpillar Tractor Co. v. Lenckos,* which challenged worldwide apportionment of Caterpillar's income), the Solicitor General of the United States filed a brief amicus curiae, in which he contended that worldwide apportionment of corporate income was unconstitutional. (For the history of the *Caterpillar* case, which was dismissed following the decision in *Container* (463 U.S. 1220, 103 S.Ct. 3562 (1983)), see J. Hellerstein & W. Hellerstein ¶ 8.10[7A][b] Cumulative Supplement supra.

C. *Worldwide Apportionment of the Income of U.S. Operating Subsidiaries of a Foreign Parent Company.* In *Container,* the Court did not pass on "the constitutionality of combined apportionment with respect to state taxation of domestic corporations with foreign parents or foreign corporations with either foreign parents or foreign subsidiaries." Note 26, p. 595 supra. In his brief amicus filed in the *Caterpillar* case, Note B supra, the Solicitor General took the position that, regardless of the Court's decision as to the power of the States to apportion the income of a U.S. parent company or its subsidiaries on a worldwide combined basis, such apportionment of the income of a U.S. subsidiary of a foreign corporation should be held to be beyond the constitutional power of the States. The Solicitor General argued:

> It may well be that the multiple tax burdens and the impairment to federal uniformity in international trade caused by the state apportionment method will be more easily demonstrated in a case involving a corporate group with a foreign parent. In that case, there will be, in addition to the considerations we have already pointed out, other burdens that the state unitary method will impose on international trade and foreign relations. For example, a foreign parent corporation with no direct U.S. activities would generally maintain its financial accounts according to local (i.e. foreign) accounting principles and in the local currency. Conversion of such accounts to conform to U.S. accounting principles and to the individual states' tax accounting rules, as well as conversion of all entries into U.S. dollars (which are required for apportionment under the state unitary method), pose a severe administrative and financial burden on the foreign parent corporation and other foreign affiliates. Moreover, there will be further burdens on international trade resulting from the demands by state tax authorities that the foreign corporation produce and explain its records of business transactions that are entirely unrelated to activities within the United States. [See Sol.Gen.Br. pp. 22–23, Chicago Bridge & Iron Co. v. Caterpillar Tractor Co., 463 U.S. 1220, 103 S.Ct. 3562 (1983).]

That position is being tested in cases pending in the State and Federal Courts. In Barclays Bank Int'l Ltd. v. Franchise Tax Bd., Nos. 325059, 325061, Cal.Super.Ct., Sacramento County, June 18, 1987, the court ruled that California's worldwide combined method of reporting was unconstitutional as applied to a group of multinational corporations with a foreign parent. The court held that because the impact of

California's tax "falls on ✳ ✳ ✳ the foreign parent rather than on a domestic parent," id. slip. op. at 28, worldwide combined reporting infringes on the exclusive power of the Federal government to regulate foreign affairs. The court also found that the tax burdened foreign commerce by violating the requirement of *Japan Line* that mandates "federal uniformity in an area where federal uniformity is essential." Finally, the court concluded that there was de facto discrimination against foreign commerce because of the burdens imposed on foreign-based multinationals to comply with worldwide combined reporting. "[O]nly a foreign multi-national is put in th[e] position of either foregoing available tax reporting benefits ✳ ✳ ✳ or spending inordinate sums to be in a position to file properly." Id. at 34. At this writing, the court's decision has been appealed, and the California Attorney General announced that the State would continue to apply worldwide combination to foreign-based multinationals while the appeal was pending. Daily Tax Rep. (BNA), June 25, 1987, p. G6. See also Alcan Aluminum. Ltd. v. Franchise Tax Board (unreported) (N.D.Ill.1985) (appeal pending). For the procedural difficulties that foreign parent companies that are not taxpayers in the States whose tax is being challenged have experienced in attacking worldwide apportionment, and a consideration on the merits of the constitutionality of worldwide apportionment of the income of U.S. operating subsidiaries of a foreign parent company, see J. Hellerstein & W. Hellerstein, ¶ 8.13[1] Cumulative Supplement and Whitenack, cited in Note A supra; Javaras & Brown, "Litigation Prospects After *Container:* The Foreign Parent Issue," Tax Notes, Dec. 19, 1983, p. 1027.

D. *Proposed Congressional Legislation Restricting Use of Combined Method of Apportionment and Limiting State Taxation of Foreign Source Income: Post–Container Developments.* The Supreme Court's decision in *Container* gave rise to renewed pressure on the part of business groups for the enactment of congressional legislation restricting State apportionment and taxation of foreign source income. In 1983, President Reagan established the Worldwide Unitary Taxation Working Group to address the questions raised by worldwide apportionment in the aftermath of *Container.* Although the Working Group did not reach agreement on various legislative options the Group considered, it did agree that three principles should guide the formulation of State tax policy in this area: (1) water's edge unitary combination [109] for both U.S. and foreign-based companies; (2) increased Federal administrative assistance and cooperation with the States to promote full taxpayer disclosure and accountability; and (3) competitive balance for U.S. multinationals, foreign multinationals, and purely domestic businesses. Office of the Secretary, Department of the Treasury, Final Report of the Worldwide Unitary Taxation Working Group (1984). At the same time, the Working Group failed to reach agreement on

---

109. Water's edge unitary combination restricts the application of the unitary method by the States to a specifically defined water's edge group. Although there was disagreement among the Working Group members as to the precise scope of this group, it would at a minimum include U.S. corporations included in a consolidated return for Federal income tax purposes, U.S. possessions corporations, companies incorporated in the U.S., certain tax haven corporations, and foreign corporations with a threshold of business activity in the United States.

two other issues: (1) whether so-called 80/20 corporations [110] should be included in combined reports; and (2) whether foreign source dividends paid by corporations excluded from the combined report should be included in the State tax base. Id.

The Treasury Department subsequently issued draft legislation that would require certain corporations to file annual information returns reflecting their computation of State income tax in the various States. This so-called domestic disclosure spreadsheet legislation was designed to implement the Federal Government's pledge to provide increased administrative assistance to the States and to promote full disclosure and accountability by multinational corporations in States that agreed to a water's edge approach. Thereafter, in view of the fact that the States had not "universally accepted" the principles of water's edge unitary combination and "equitable taxation of foreign source dividends," Statement by President Ronald Reagan, Nov. 8, 1985, reprinted in Tax Notes, Nov. 18, 1985, p. 3, the Treasury Department proposed legislation in accord with the President's instructions, and the legislation was immediately introduced into both Houses of Congress. S. 1974, 99th Cong., 1st Sess. (1985); H.R. 3980, 99th Cong., 1st Sess. (1985) (the "Unitary Tax Repealer Act").

The proposed legislation precludes the States from imposing corporate income taxes on a worldwide unitary basis. It imposes a water's edge limitation on combined reporting defined as including principally domestic corporations (other than 80/20 corporations), foreign corporations subject to taxation by at least one State and that exceed a specified quantitative level of activity in the United States, and certain foreign corporations located in tax havens. The legislation also prohibits the States from taxing "more than an equitable portion" of dividends received from corporations outside the water's edge group. The States will comply with this injunction if they exclude at least 85 percent of such dividends from their tax base, exclude from their tax base the portion of the dividend that effectively bears no Federal income tax after the application of the foreign tax credit, or adopt some other method that achieves results similar to the specified methods under regulations prescribed by the Treasury. Finally, the legislation is designed to satisfy the States' need for information as to how multinational enterprises report their income to other States by providing that "reporting corporations" annually file a return disclosing information relating to their income tax returns filed in other States. A "reporting corporation" is any corporation required to file a Federal income tax return and whose foreign or domestic operations exceed specified quantitative thresholds.

Although the Reagan administration initially gave every indication that it intended to push its unitary tax package, after California enacted legislation adopting a water's edge approach to combined apportionment and providing some relief from taxation of foreign source dividends, see Note E infra, the Treasury withdrew its support for Federal legislation.

110. The term "80/20 corporation," as used by the Working Group, referred to a U.S. corporation with at least 80 percent of its payroll and property outside the United States. Broadly speaking, the problem of the 80/20 corporation is the problem of how the States should tax corporations whose operations are principally foreign.

E. *State Legislative Reaction to Container.* Although the initial reaction of some State legislatures to *Container* was the adoption of expanded definitions, both conceptually and geographically, of the scope of a unitary business, a clear countertrend had emerged by the mid–1980's. The change in legislative direction was attributable in large part to the successful lobbying campaign of the business community which predicted dire economic consequences for States that jumped on (or failed to jump off) the worldwide unitary combination bandwagon. Thus, while Florida and Maine broadened their definitions of a unitary business in 1983 after *Container* was handed down, by 1987 Florida had reversed course, repealing its previous adoption of worldwide unitary combination; Arizona, Colorado, Idaho, Indiana, Oregon, and Utah had endorsed a water's edge approach to the unitary business principle; and, most significantly, California—the principal source of the controversy over worldwide unitary combination—had adopted legislation effective January 1, 1988 adopting a water's edge approach to combined apportionment and limiting its taxation of foreign source dividends. For a detailed treatment of the State legislation, see J. Hellerstein & W. Hellerstein, ¶ 8.14[2] Cumulative Supplement, Note A supra.

F. *References.* "The Supreme Court 1982 Term," 97 Harv.L.Rev. 70, 112 (1983); Kaplan, "The Unitary Tax Debate, The United States Supreme Court, and Some Plain English," 10 J.Corp.Tax. 283 (1984); and the references cited in Note A supra.

SECTION 11. CONSTITUTIONAL ASPECTS OF APPORTIONMENT OF DIVIDENDS AND OTHER INCOME FROM INTANGIBLES

MOBIL OIL CORPORATION v. COMMISSIONER OF TAXES OF VERMONT

Supreme Court of the United States, 1980.
445 U.S. 425, 100 S.Ct. 1223.

MR. JUSTICE BLACKMUN delivered the opinion of the Court.*

In this case we are called upon to consider constitutional limits on a nondomiciliary State's taxation of income received by a domestic corporation in the form of dividends from subsidiaries and affiliates doing business abroad. The State of Vermont imposed a tax, calculated by means of an apportionment formula, upon appellant's so-called "foreign source" dividend income for the taxable years 1970, 1971, and 1972. The Supreme Court of Vermont sustained that tax.

I

A

Appellant Mobil Oil Corporation is a corporation organized under the laws of the State of New York. It has its principal place of business and its "commercial domicile" in New York City. It is authorized to do business in Vermont.

* Some footnotes have been omitted.

Mobil engages in an integrated petroleum business, ranging from exploration for petroleum reserves to production, refining, transportation, and distribution and sale of petroleum and petroleum products. It also engages in related chemical and mining enterprises. It does business in over 40 of our States and in the District of Columbia as well as in a number of foreign countries.

Much of appellant's business abroad is conducted through wholly and partly owned subsidiaries and affiliates. Many of these are corporations organized under the laws of foreign nations; a number, however, are domestically incorporated in States other than Vermont. None of appellant's subsidiaries or affiliates conducts business in Vermont, and appellant's shareholdings in those corporations are controlled and managed elsewhere, presumably from the headquarters in New York City.

In Vermont, appellant's business activities are confined to wholesale and retail marketing of petroleum and related products. Mobil has no oil or gas production or refineries within the State. Although appellant's business activity in Vermont is by no means insignificant, it forms but a small part of the corporation's worldwide enterprise. According to the Vermont corporate income tax returns Mobil filed for the three taxable years in issue appellant's Vermont sales were $8,554,200, $9,175,931, and $9,589,447 respectively; its payroll in the State was $236,553, $244,577, and $254,938, respectively; and the value of its property in Vermont was $3,930,100, $6,707,534, and $8,236,792 respectively. App. 35–36, 49–50, 63–64. Substantial as these figures are, they too, represent only tiny portions of the corporation's total sales, payroll, and property.

Vermont imposes an annual net income tax on every corporation doing business within the State. Under its scheme, net income is defined as the taxable income of the taxpayer "under the laws of the United States." Vt.Stat.Ann., Tit. 32, § 5811(18) (1970 and Supp.1978).[3] If a taxpayer corporation does business both within and without Vermont, the State taxes only that portion of the net income attributable to it under a three-factor apportionment formula. In order to determine that portion, net income is multiplied by a fraction representing the arithmetic average of the ratios of sales, payroll, and property values within Vermont to those of the corporation as a whole. § 5833(a).[4]

Appellant's net income for 1970, 1971, and 1972, as defined by the Federal Internal Revenue Code, included substantial amounts received as dividends from its subsidiaries and affiliates operating abroad. Mo-

3. Section 5811(18) states in pertinent part:

" 'Vermont net income' means, for any taxable year and for any corporate taxpayer, the taxable income of the taxpayer for that taxable year under the laws of the United States, excluding income which under the laws of the United States is exempt from taxation by the states."

4. [Court's notes 4–6 omitted. Vermont uses a three factor property, payroll and sales formula].

bil's federal income tax returns for the three years showed taxable income of approximately $220 million, $308 million, and $233 million, respectively, of which approximately $174 million, $283 million, and $280 million was net dividend income. On its Vermont returns for these years, however, appellant subtracted from federal taxable income items it regarded as "nonapportionable," including the net dividends. As a result of these subtractions, Mobil's Vermont returns showed a net income of approximately $23 million for 1970 and losses for the two succeeding years. After application of Vermont's apportionment formula, an aggregate tax liability of $1,871.90 to Vermont remained for the three-year period; except for a minimum tax of $25 for each of 1971 and 1972, all of this was attributable to 1970.

The Vermont Department of Taxes recalculated appellant's income by restoring the asserted nonapportionable items to the preapportionment tax base. It determined that Mobil's aggregate tax liability for the three years was $76,418.77, and deficiencies plus interest were assessed accordingly. Appellant challenged the deficiency assessments before the Commissioner of Taxes. It argued, among other things, that taxation of the dividend receipts under Vermont's corporate income tax violated the Due Process Clause of the Fourteenth Amendment, as well as the Interstate and Foreign Commerce Clause, U.S. Const., Art. 1, § 8, cl. 3. Appellant also argued that inclusion of the dividend income in its tax base was inconsistent with the terms of the Vermont tax statute, because it would not result in a "fair" and "equitable" apportionment, and it petitioned for modification of the apportionment. See Vt.Stat. Ann., Tit. 32, § 5833(b).[8] It is evident from the transcript of the hearing before the Commissioner that appellant's principal object was to achieve the subtraction of the asserted nonapportionable income from the preapportionment tax base; the alternative request for modification of the apportionment formula went largely undeveloped. See App. 18–31.

The Commissioner held that inclusion of dividend income in the tax base was required by the Vermont statute, and he rejected appellant's Due Process Clause and Commerce Clause arguments.

Mobil sought review by the Superior Court of Washington County. That court reversed the Commissioner's ruling. It held that inclusion of dividend income in the tax base unconstitutionally subjected appellant to prohibitive multiple taxation because New York, the State of appellant's commercial domicile, had the authority to tax the dividends in their entirety. Since New York could tax without apportionment, the court concluded, Vermont's use of an apportionment formula would not be an adequate safeguard against multiple taxation. It agreed with appellant that subtraction of dividend income from the Vermont tax base was the only acceptable approach. Juris. Statement 14a.

8. [Court's note 8 omitted. The Vermont statute contains a provision for equitable adjustment of the formula that is essentially the same as Section 18 of UDITPA. See p. 504 supra].

The Commissioner, in his turn, appealed to the Supreme Court of Vermont. That court reversed the judgment of the Superior Court. 136 Vt. 545, 394 A.2d 1147 (1978). The court noted that appellant's quarrel was with the calculation of the tax base and not with the method or accuracy of the statutory apportionment formula. Id., at 547, 394 A.2d, at 1148. It found a sufficient "nexus" between the corporation and the State to justify an apportioned tax on both appellant's investment income and its operating income. The court rejected the "multiple taxation" theory that had prevailed in the Superior Court. In its view, appellant had failed to prove that multiple taxation would actually ensue. New York did not tax the dividend income during the taxable years in question, and "[i]n a conflict between Vermont's apportioned tax on Mobil's investment income and an attempt on New York's part to tax that same income without apportionment, New York might very well have to yield." Id., at 552, 394 A.2d, at 1151. Accordingly, the court held that no constitutional defect had been established. It remanded the case for reinstatement of the deficiency assessments.

The substantial federal question involved prompted us to note probable jurisdiction. 441 U.S. 941, 99 S.Ct. 2157, 60 L.Ed.2d 1043 (1979).

B

In keeping with its litigation strategy, appellant has disclaimed any dispute with the accuracy or fairness of Vermont's apportionment formula. See Juris. Statement 10; Brief for Appellant 11. Instead, it claims that dividends from a "foreign source" by their very nature are not apportionable income. This election to attack the tax base rather than the formula substantially narrows the issues before us. In deciding this appeal, we do not consider whether application of Vermont's formula produced a fair attribution of appellant's dividend income to that State. Our inquiry is confined to the question whether there is something about the character of income earned from investments in affiliates and subsidiaries operating abroad that precludes, as a constitutional matter, state taxation of that income by the apportionment method.

In addressing this question, moreover, it is necessary to bear in mind that Mobil's "foreign source" dividend income is of two distinct types. The first consists of dividends from domestic corporations, organized under the laws of States other than Vermont, that conduct all their operations, and hence earn their income, outside the United States.[12] The second type consists of dividends from corporations both

---

12. Under the Vermont tax scheme, income falling into this category is subject to apportionment only in part. Because Vermont's statute is geared to the definition of taxable income under federal law, it excludes from the preapportionment tax base 85% of all dividends earned from domestic corporations in which the taxpayer owns less than 80% of the capital stock, and 100% of all dividends earned from domestic corporations in which the taxpayer owns 80% or more of the capital stock. See § 243 of the Internal Revenue Code of 1954, as amended, 26 U.S.C. § 243; Vt.Stat.Ann., Tit. 32, § 5811(18) (1970 and Supp.1978).

organized and operating abroad. The record in this case fails to supply much detail concerning the activities of the corporations whose dividends allegedly fall into these two categories, but it is apparent, from perusal of such documents in the record as appellant's corporate reports for the years in question, that many of these subsidiaries and affiliates, including the principal contributors to appellant's dividend income, engage in business activities that form part of Mobil's integrated petroleum enterprise. Indeed, although appellant is unwilling to concede the legal conclusion that these activities form part of a "unitary business," see Reply Brief for Appellant 2, n. 1, it has offered no evidence that would determine the conclusion that most, if not all, of its subsidiaries and affiliates contribute to appellant's worldwide petroleum enterprise.

To justify exclusion of the dividends from income subject to apportionment in Vermont, Mobil offers three principal arguments. First, it argues that the dividends may not be taxed in Vermont because there is no "nexus" between that State and either appellant's management of its investments or the business activities of the payor corporations. Second, it argues that taxation of the dividends in Vermont would create an unconstitutional burden of multiple taxation because the dividends would be taxable in full in New York, the State of commercial domicile. In this context, appellant relies on the traditional rule that dividends are taxable at their "business situs," a rule which it suggests is of constitutional dimension. Third, Mobil argues that the "foreign source" of the dividends precludes state income taxation in this country, at least in States other than the commercial domicile, because of the risk of multiple taxation at the international level. In a related argument, appellant contends that local taxation of the sort undertaken in Vermont prevents the Nation from speaking with a single voice in foreign commercial affairs. We consider each of these arguments in turn.

II

It long has been established that the income of a business operating in interstate commerce is not immune from fairly apportioned state taxation. Northwestern States Portland Cement Co. v. Minnesota, 358 U.S. 450, 458–462, 79 S.Ct. 357, 362–364, 3 L.Ed.2d 421 (1959) * * *. "[T]he entire net income of a corporation, generated by interstate as well as intrastate activities, may be fairly apportioned among the States for tax purposes by formulas utilizing instate aspects of interstate affairs." Northwestern States Portland Cement Co. v. Minnesota, 358 U.S., at 460, 79 S.Ct., at 363. For a State to tax income generated in interstate commerce, the Due Process Clause of the Fourteenth Amendment imposes two requirements: a "minimal connection" between the interstate activities and the taxing State, and a rational relationship between the income attributed to the State and the intrastate values of the enterprise. * * * The requisite "nexus" is supplied if the corporation avails itself of the "substantial privilege of carrying on business" within the State; and "[t]he fact that a tax is contingent upon events brought to pass without a state does not destroy the nexus between such a tax and transactions within a state for which the tax is an exaction." Wisconsin v. J.C. Penney Co., 311 U.S. 435, 444–445, 61 S.Ct. 246, 250, 85 L.Ed. 1143 (1940).

We do not understand appellant to contest these general principles. Indeed, in its Vermont tax returns for the years in question, Mobil included all its operating income in apportionable net income, without regard to the locality in which it was earned. Nor has appellant undertaken to prove that the amount of its tax liability as determined by Vermont is "out of all appropriate proportion to the business transacted by the appellant in that State." Hans Rees' Sons v. North Carolina ex rel. Maxwell, 283 U.S. 123, 135, 51 S.Ct. 385, 389, 75 L.Ed. 879 (1931).[13] What appellant does seek to establish, in the due process phase of its argument, is that its *dividend* income must be excepted from the general principle of apportionability because it lacks a satisfactory nexus with appellant's business activities in Vermont. To carve that out as an exception, appellant must demonstrate something about the nature of this income that distinguishes it from operating income, a proper portion of which the State concededly may tax. From appellant's argument we discern two potential differentiating factors: the "foreign source" of the income, and the fact that it is received in the form of dividends from subsidiaries and affiliates.

The argument that the source of the income precludes its taxability runs contrary to precedent. In the past, apportionability often has been challenged by the contention that income earned in one State may not be taxed in another if the source of the income may be ascertained by separate geographical accounting. The Court has rejected that contention so long as the intra-state and extra-state activities formed part of a single unitary business. See Butler Bros. v. McColgan, 315 U.S. 501, 506–508, 62 S.Ct. 701, 703–704, 86 L.Ed. 991 (1942); Ford Motor Co. v. Beauchamp, 308 U.S. 331, 336, 60 S.Ct. 273, 276, 84 L.Ed. 304 (1939); cf. Moorman Mfg. Co. v. Bair, 437 U.S., at 272, 98 S.Ct., at 2344. In these circumstances, the Court has noted that separate accounting, while it purports to isolate portions of income received in various States, may fail to account for contributions to income resulting from functional integration, centralization of management, and economies of scale. Butler Bros. v. McColgan, 315 U.S., at 508–509, 62 S.Ct., at 704–705. Because these factors of profitability arise from the operation of the business as a whole, it becomes misleading to characterize the income of the business as having a single identifiable "source." Although separate geographical accounting may be useful for internal

13. Application of the Vermont three-factor formula for the three years resulted in attributing to the State the following percentages of the corporation's net income:

1970	0.146032%
1971	0.173647%
1972	0.182151%

App. 36, 50, 64.

auditing, for purposes of state taxation it is not constitutionally required.

The Court has applied the same rationale to businesses operating both here and abroad. Bass, Ratcliff & Gretton, Ltd. v. State Tax Comm'n, 266 U.S. 271, 45 S.Ct. 82, 69 L.Ed. 282 (1924), is the leading example. A British corporation manufactured ale in Great Britain and sold some of it in New York. The corporation objected on due process grounds to New York's imposition of an apportioned franchise tax on the corporation's net income. The Court sustained the tax on the strength of its earlier decision in Underwood Typewriter Co. v. Chamberlain, supra, where it had upheld a similar tax as applied to a business operating in several of our States. It ruled that the brewer carried on a unitary business, involving "a series of transactions beginning with the manufacture in England and ending in sales in New York and other places," and that "the State was justified in attributing to New York a just proportion of the profits earned by the Company from such unitary business." 266 U.S., at 282, 45 S.Ct., at 84.

As these cases indicate, the linchpin of apportionability in the field of state income taxation is the unitary business principle.[14] In accord with this principle, what appellant must show, in order to establish that its dividend income is not subject to an apportioned tax in Vermont, is that the income was earned in the course of activities unrelated to the sale of petroleum products in that State. *Bass, Ratcliff & Gretton* forecloses the contention that the foreign source of the dividend income alone suffices for this purpose. Moreover, appellant has made no effort to demonstrate that the foreign operations of its subsidiaries and affiliates are distinct in any business or economic sense from its petroleum sales activities in Vermont. Indeed all indications in the record are to the contrary, since it appears that these foreign activities are part of appellant's integrated petroleum enterprise. In the absence of any proof of discrete business enterprise, Vermont was entitled to conclude that the dividend income's foreign source did not destroy the requisite nexus with in-state activities.

It remains to be considered whether the form in which the income was received serves to drive a wedge between Mobil's foreign enterprise and its activities in Vermont. In support of the contention that dividend income ought to be excluded from apportionment, Mobil has attempted to characterize its ownership and management of subsidiaries and affiliates as a business distinct from its sale of petroleum

14. See United States Steel Corp. v. Multistate Tax Comm'n, 434 U.S. 452, 473–474, nn. 25, 26, 98 S.Ct. 799, 813, nn. 25, 26, 54 L.Ed.2d 682 (1978). For scholarly discussions of the unitary business concept see G. Altman & F. Keesling, Allocation of Income in State Taxation 97–102 (2d ed. 1950); Dexter, Taxation of Income from Intangibles of Multistate–Multinational Corporations, 29 Vand.L.Rev. 401 (1976); Hellerstein, Recent Developments in State Tax Apportionment and the Circumscription of Unitary Business, 21 Nat.Tax J. 487, 496 (1968); Keesling & Warren, The Unitary Concept in the Allocation of Income, 12 Hastings L.J. 42 (1960); Rudolph, State Taxation of Interstate Business: The Unitary Business Concept and Affiliated Corporate Groups, 25 Tax.L.Rev. 171 (1970).

products in this country. Various *amici* also have suggested that the division between parent and subsidiary should be treated as a break in the scope of unitary business, and that the receipt of dividends is a discrete "taxable event" bearing no relation to Vermont.

At the outset, we reject the suggestion that anything is to be gained by characterizing receipt of the dividends as a separate "taxable event." In Wisconsin v. J.C. Penney Co., supra, the Court observed that "tags" of this kind "are not instruments of adjudication but statements of result," and that they add little to analysis. 311 U.S., at 444, 61 S.Ct., at 250. Mobil's business entails numerous "taxable events" that occur outside Vermont. That fact alone does not prevent the State from including income earned from those events in the preapportionment tax base.

Nor do we find particularly persuasive Mobil's attempt to identify a separate business in its holding company function. So long as dividends from subsidiaries and affiliates reflect profits derived from a functionally integrated enterprise, those dividends are income to the parent earned in a unitary business. One must look principally at the underlying activity, not at the form of investment, to determine the propriety of apportionability.

Superficially, intercorporate division might appear to be a more attractive basis for limiting apportionability. But the form of business organization may have nothing to do with the underlying unity or diversity of business enterprise. Had appellant chosen to operate its foreign subsidiaries as separate divisions of a legally as well as a functionally integrated enterprise, there is little doubt that the income derived from those divisions would meet due process requirements for apportionability. Cf. General Motors Corp. v. Washington, 377 U.S. 436, 441, 84 S.Ct. 1564, 1568, 12 L.Ed.2d 430 (1964). Transforming the same income into dividends from legally separate entities works no change in the underlying economic realities of a unitary business, and accordingly it ought not to affect the apportionability of income the parent receives.[15]

---

15. In its reply brief, Mobil submits a new due process argument based on Vermont's failure to require "combined apportionment" which, while including the income of subsidiaries and affiliates as part of appellant's net income, would eliminate intercorporate transfers, such as appellant's dividend income, from that calculation. A necessary concomitant of this would be inclusion of the subsidiaries' and affiliates' sales, payroll, and property in the calculation of the apportionment formula. Reply Brief for Appellant 1–6. The result, presumably, would be advantageous to appellant, since virtually nothing would be added to the "Vermont" numerators of the apportionment factors, while there would be substantial increases in the "everywhere" denominators, resulting in a diminution of the apportionment fraction.

This argument appears to be an afterthought that was not presented to the Vermont tax authorities or to the courts of that State. The evidence in the record surely is inadequate to evaluate the effect of the proposal, its relative impact on appellant, or its potential implications. Moreover, the principal focus of this suggestion is the apportionment formula, not the apportionability of foreign source income. Appellant, we reiterate, took this appeal on the assumption that Vermont's apportionment formula was fair. At this juncture and on these facts, we need not, and do not, decide whether combined apportionment of this type is constitutionally

We do not mean to suggest that all dividend income received by corporations operating in interstate commerce is necessarily taxable in each State where that corporation does business. Where the business activities of the dividend payor have nothing to do with the activities of the recipient in the taxing State, due process considerations might well preclude apportionability, because there would be no underlying unitary business. We need not decide, however, whether Vermont's tax statute would reach extraterritorial values in an instance of that kind. Cf. Underwood Typewriter Co. v. Chamberlain, 254 U.S., at 121, 41 S.Ct., at 47. Mobil has failed to sustain its burden of proving any unrelated business activity on the part of its subsidiaries and affiliates that would raise the question of nonapportionability. See Norton Co. v. Department of Revenue, 340 U.S. 534, 537, 71 S.Ct. 377, 380, 95 L.Ed. 517 (1951); Butler Bros. v. McColgan, 315 U.S., at 507, 62 S.Ct., at 704. We therefore hold that its foreign source dividends have not been shown to be exempt, as a matter of due process, from apportionment for state income taxation by the State of Vermont.

III

In addition to its due process challenge, appellant contends that Vermont's tax imposes a burden on interstate and foreign commerce by subjecting appellant's dividend income to a substantial risk of multiple taxation. We approach this argument in two steps. First, we consider whether there was a burden on interstate commerce by virtue of the effect of the Vermont tax relative to appellant's income tax liability in other States. Next, we determine whether constitutional protections for foreign commerce pose additional considerations that alter the result.

A

The effect of the Commerce Clause on state taxation of interstate commerce is a frequently litigated subject that appears to be undergoing a revival of sorts.[17] In several recent cases, this Court has addressed the issue and has attempted to clarify the apparently conflicting precedents it has spawned. See, e.g., Moorman Mfg. Co. v. Bair, 437 U.S., at 276–281, 98 S.Ct., at 2346–2348 (1978); Washington Revenue Dept. v. Association of Wash. Stevedoring Cos., 435 U.S. 734, 743–751, 98 S.Ct. 1388, 1395–1400, 55 L.Ed.2d 682 (1978); Complete Auto Transit, Inc. v. Brady, 430 U.S. 274, 97 S.Ct. 1076, 51 L.Ed.2d 326 (1977).

required. In any event, we note that appellant's latter-day advocacy of this combined approach virtually concedes that income from foreign sources, produced by the operations of subsidiaries and affiliates, as a matter of due process is attributable to the parent and amendable to fair apportionment. That is all we decide today.

17. In particular, there has been a flurry of litigation in state courts over the Commerce Clause implications of apportioned taxation of income from intangibles.

See, e.g., Qualls v. Montgomery Ward & Co., 266 Ark. 207, 585 S.W.2d 18 (1979); American Smelting & Refining Co. v. Idaho Tax Comm'n, 99 Idaho 924, 592 P.2d 39, cert. pending, No. 78–1839; W.R. Grace & Co. v. Commissioner of Revenue, —— Mass. ——, 393 N.E.2d 330 (1979); Montana Dept. of Revenue v. American Smelting & Refining Co., Mont., 567 P.2d 901 (1977), appeal dism'd, 434 U.S. 1042, 98 S.Ct. 884, 54 L.Ed.2d 793 (1978).

In an endeavor to establish a consistent and rational method of inquiry, we have examined the practical effect of a challenged tax to determine whether it "is applied to an activity with a substantial nexus with the taxing State, is fairly apportioned, does not discriminate against interstate commerce, and is fairly related to the services provided by the State." Id., at 279, 97 S.Ct., at 1079.

Appellant asserts that Vermont's tax is discriminatory because it subjects interstate business to a burden of duplicative taxation that an intrastate taxpayer would not bear. Mobil does not base this claim on a comparison of Vermont's apportionment formula with those used in other States where appellant pays income taxes. Cf. Moorman Mfg. Co. v. Bair, supra; Western Live Stock v. Bureau of Revenue, 303 U.S. 250, 255–256, 58 S.Ct. 546, 548–549, 82 L.Ed. 823 (1938). Rather, it contends that *any* apportioned tax on its dividends will place an undue burden on that specific source of income, because New York, the State of commercial domicile, has the power to tax dividend income without apportionment. For the latter proposition, appellant cites property tax cases that hold that intangible property is to be taxed either by the State of commercial domicile or by the State where the property has a "business situs." See, e.g., First Bank Stock Corp. v. Minnesota, 301 U.S. 234, 237, 57 S.Ct. 677, 678, 81 L.Ed. 1061 (1941); Wheeling Steel Corp. v. Fox, 298 U.S. 193, 208–210, 56 S.Ct. 773, 776–777, 80 L.Ed. 1143 (1936); Louisville & Jeffersonville Ferry Co. v. Kentucky, 188 U.S. 385, 396, 23 S.Ct. 463, 467, 43 L.Ed. 513 (1903); cf. New York ex rel. Whitney v. Graves, 299 U.S. 366, 372–373, 57 S.Ct. 237, 238–239, 81 L.Ed. 285 (1937).

Insasmuch as New York does not presently tax the dividends in question, actual multiple taxation is not demonstrated on this record. The Vermont courts placed some reliance on this fact, see, e.g., 136 Vt., at 548, 394 A.2d, at 1149, and much of the debate in this Court has aired the question whether an actual burden need be shown. Compare Standard Pressed Steel Co. v. Department of Revenue, 419 U.S. 560, 563–564, 95 S.Ct. 706, 709, 42 L.Ed.2d 719 (1975), and Freeman v. Hewit, 329 U.S. 249, 256, 67 S.Ct. 274, 278, 91 L.Ed. 265 (1946), with Northwestern States Portland Cement Co. v. Minnesota, 358 U.S., at 462–463, 79 S.Ct., at 364, and Northwest Airlines, Inc. v. Minnesota, 322 U.S. 292, 64 S.Ct. 950, 88 L.Ed. 1283 (1944). See also Japan Line, Ltd. v. County of Los Angeles, 441 U.S. 434, 452, n. 17, 99 S.Ct. 1813, 1823, n. 17, 60 L.Ed.2d 336 (1979). We agree with Mobil that the constitutionality of a Vermont tax should not depend on the vagaries of New York tax policy. But the absence of any existing duplicative tax does alter the nature of appellant's claim. Instead of seeking relief from a present tax burden, appellant seeks to establish a theoretical constitutional preference for one method of taxation over another. In appellant's view, the Commerce Clause requires allocation of dividend income to a single situs rather than apportionment among the States.

Taxation by apportionment and taxation by allocation to a single situs are theoretically incommensurate, and if the latter method is constitutionally preferred, a tax based on the former cannot be sustained. See Standard Oil Co. v. Peck, 342 U.S. 382, 384, 72 S.Ct. 309, 310, 96 L.Ed. 427 (1952). We find no adequate justification, however, for such a preference. Although a fictionalized situs for intangible property sometimes has been invoked to avoid multiple taxation of ownership, there is nothing talismanic about the concepts of "business situs" or "commercial domicile" that automatically renders those concepts applicable when taxation of income from intangibles is at issue. The Court has observed that the maxim *mobilia sequuunter personam,* upon which these fictions of situs are based, "states a rule without disclosing the reasons for it." First Bank Stock Corp. v. Minnesota, 301 U.S., at 241, 57 S.Ct., at 680 (1937). The Court also has recognized that "the reason for a single place of taxation no longer obtains" when the taxpayer's activities with respect to the intangible property involve relations with more than one jurisdiction. Curry v. McCanless, 307 U.S. 357, 367, 59 S.Ct. 900, 906, 83 L.Ed. 1339 (1939). Even for property or franchise taxes, apportionment of intangible values is not unknown. See Ford Motor Co. v. Beauchamp, 308 U.S., at 335–336, 60 S.Ct., at 275–276; Adams Express Co. v. Ohio, 166 U.S. 185, 222, 17 S.Ct. 604, 606, 41 L.Ed. 965 (1897). Moreover, cases upholding allocation to a single situs for property tax purposes have distinguished income tax situations where the apportionment principle prevails. See Wheeling Steel Corp. v. Fox, 298 U.S., at 212, 56 S.Ct., at 778.

The reasons for allocation to a single situs that often apply in the case of property taxation carry little force in the present context. Mobil no doubt enjoys privileges and protections conferred by New York law with respect to ownership of its stock holdings, and its activities in that State no doubt supply some nexus for jurisdiction to tax. Cf. First Bank Stock Corp. v. Minnesota, 301 U.S., at 240–241, 57 S.Ct., at 679–680. Although we do not now presume to pass on the constitutionality of a hypothetical New York tax, we may assume, for present purposes, that the State of commercial domicile has the authority to lay some tax on appellant's dividend income as well as on the value of its stock. But there is no reason in theory why that power should be exclusive when the dividends reflect income from a unitary business, part of which is conducted in other States. In that situation, the income bears relation to benefits and privileges conferred by several States. These are the circumstances in which apportionment is ordinarily the accepted method. Since Vermont seeks to tax income, not ownership, we hold that its interest in taxing a proportionate share of appellant's dividend income is not overriden by any interest of the State of commercial domicile.

B

What has been said thus far does not fully dispose of appellant's additional contention that the Vermont tax imposes a burden on foreign commerce. Relying upon the Court's decision last Term in Japan Line, Ltd. v. County of Los Angeles, 441 U.S. 434, 99 S.Ct. 1813, 60 L.Ed.2d 336 (1979), Mobil suggests that dividends from foreign sources must be allocated to the State of commercial domicile, even if dividends from subsidiaries and affiliates operating domestically are not. By accepting the power of the State of commercial domicile to tax foreign source dividend income, appellant eschews the broad proposition that foreign source dividends are immune from state taxation. It presses the narrower contention that, because of the risk of multiple taxation abroad, allocation of foreign source income to a single situs is required at home. Appellant's reasoning tracks the rationale of *Japan Line*, that is, that allocation is required because apportionment necessarily entails some inaccuracy and duplication. This inaccuracy may be tolerable for businesses operating solely within the United States, it is said, because this Court has power to correct any gross overreaching. The same inaccuracy, however, becomes intolerable when it is added to the risk of duplicative taxation abroad, which this Court is powerless to control. Accordingly, the only means of alleviating the burden of overlapping taxes is to adopt an allocation rule.

This argument is unpersuasive in the present context for several reasons. First, it attempts to focus attention on the effect of foreign taxation when the effect of domestic taxation is the only real issue. By admitting the power of the State of commercial domicile to tax foreign source dividends *in full*, Mobil necessarily forgoes any contention that local duplication of foreign taxes is proscribed. Thus, the only inquiry of constitutional dimension is the familiar question whether taxation by apportionment at home produces significantly greater tax burdens than taxation by allocation. Once appellant's argument is placed in this perspective, the presence or absence of taxation abroad diminishes in importance.

Second, nothing about the logic of Mobil's position is limited to dividend income. The same contention could be advanced about any income arguably earned from foreign commerce. If appellant's argument were accepted, state taxing commissions would face substantial difficulties in attempting to determine what income does or does not have a foreign source.

Third, appellant's argument underestimates the power of this Court to correct excessive taxation on the field where appellant has chosen to pitch its battle. A discriminatory effect on foreign commerce as a result of multiple state taxation is just as detectable and corrigible as a similar effect on commerce among the States. Accordingly, we see no reason why the standard for identifying impermissible discrimination should differ in the two instances.

Finally, acceptance of appellant's argument would provide no guarantee that allocation will result in a lesser domestic tax burden on dividend income from foreign sources. By appellant's own admission, allocation would give the State of commercial domicile the power to tax that income in full, without regard to the extent of taxation abroad. Unless we indulge in the speculation that a State will volunteer to become a tax haven for multinational enterprises, there is no reason to suspect that a State of commercial domicile will be any less vigorous in taxing the whole of the dividend income than a State like Vermont will be in taxing a proportionate share.

Appellant's attempted analogy between this case and *Japan Line* strikes us as forced. That case involved ad valorem property taxes assessed directly upon instrumentalities of foreign commerce. As has been noted, the factors favoring use of the allocation method in property taxation have no immediate applicability to an income tax. *Japan Line* moreover, focused on problems of duplicative taxation at the international level, while appellant here has confined its argument to the wholly different sphere of multiple taxation among our States. Finally, in *Japan Line* the Court was confronted with actual multiple taxation that could be remedied only by adoption of an allocation approach. As has already been explained, in the present case we are not similarly impelled.

Nor does federal tax policy lend additional weight to appellant's arguments. The federal statutes and treaties that Mobil cites, Brief for Appellant 38–43, concern problems of multiple taxation at the international level and simply are not germane to the issue of multiple state taxation that appellant has framed. Concurrent federal and state taxation of income, of course, is a well-established norm. Absent some explicit directive from Congress, we cannot infer that treatment of foreign income at the federal level mandates identical treatment by the States. The absence of any explicit directive to that effect is attested by the fact that Congress has long debated, but has not enacted, legislation designed to regulate state taxation of income. See H.R.Rep. No. 1480, 88th Cong., 2d Sess. (1964); H.R.Rep. No. 565, 89th Cong., 1st Sess. (1965); H.R.Rep. No. 952, 89th Cong., 1st Sess. (1965); Hearings on State Taxation of Interstate Commerce, Subcommittee on State Taxation of Interstate Commerce, Senate Committee on Finance, 93d Cong., 1st Sess. (1973); cf. United States Steel Corp. v. Multistate Tax Comm'n, 434 U.S. 452, 456, n. 4, 98 S.Ct. 799, 804, n. 4, 54 L.Ed.2d 682 (1978). Legislative proposals have provoked debate over issues closely related to the present controversy. See, e.g., New York State Bar Assn. Tax Section Committee on Interstate Taxation, Proposals for Improvement of Interstate Taxation Bills (H.R. 1538 and S. 317), 25 Tax Lawyer 433 (1971). Congress in the future may see fit to enact legislation requiring a uniform method for state taxation of foreign dividends. To date, however, it has not done so.

IV

In sum, appellant has failed to demonstrate any sound basis, under either the Due Process Clause or the Commerce Clause, for establishing a constitutional preference for allocation of its foreign source dividend income to the State of commercial domicile. Because the issue has not been presented, we need not, and do not, decide what the constituent elements of a fair apportionment formula applicable to such income would be. We do hold, however, that Vermont is not precluded from taxing its proportionate share.

The judgment of the Supreme Court of Vermont is affirmed.

It is so ordered.

MR. JUSTICE STEWART and MR. JUSTICE MARSHALL took no part in the consideration or decision of this case.

MR. JUSTICE STEVENS, dissenting.

The Court today decides one substantive question and two procedural questions. Because of the way in which it resolves the procedural issues, the Court's substantive holding is extremely narrow. It is carefully "confined to the question whether there is something about the character of income earned from investments in affiliates and subsidiaries operating abroad that precludes, as a constitutional matter, state taxation of that income by the apportionment method." * * * Since that question has long since been answered in the negative, see, e.g., Bass, Ratcliff & Gretton, Ltd. v. State Tax Commission, 266 U.S. 271, 45 S.Ct. 82, 69 L.Ed. 282, the Court's principal holding is unexceptional.

The Court's substantive holding rests on the assumed premises (1) that Mobil's investment income and its income from operations in Vermont are inseparable parts of one unitary business and (2) that the entire income of that unitary business has been accurately and fairly apportioned between Vermont and the rest of the world—assuming the constitutional validity of including any foreign income in the allocation formula. The Court holds—as I understand its opinion—that Mobil "offered no evidence" challenging the first premise, and that it expressly disclaimed any attack on the second.

I disagree with both of these procedural holdings. I am persuaded that the record before us demonstrates either (1) that Mobil's income from its investments and its income from the sale of petroleum products in Vermont are not parts of the same "unitary business," as that concept has developed in this Court's cases; or (2) if the unitary business is defined to include both kinds of income, that Vermont's apportionment formula has been applied in an arbitrary and unconstitutional way. To explain my position, it is necessary first to recall the limited purpose that the unitary business concept serves in this kind of case, then to identify the two quite different formulations of Mobil's "unitary business" that could arguably support Vermont's application of its apportionment formula to Mobil's investment income, and finally to show why on this record Mobil is entitled to relief using either formulation. Because I also believe that Mobil has done nothing to waive its entitlement, I conclude that the Court's substantive holding is inadequate to dispose of Mobil's contentions.

I

It is fundamental that a State has no power to impose a tax on income earned outside of the State. The out-of-state income of a business that operates in more than one State is subject to examination by the taxing State only because of "the impossibility of allocating specifically the profits earned by the processes conducted within its borders." Underwood Typewriter Co. v. Chamberlain, 254 U.S. 113, 121, 41 S.Ct. 45, 47, 65 L.Ed. 165. An apportionment formula is an imperfect, but nevertheless acceptable, method of measuring the in-state earnings of an integrated business. "It owes its existence to the fact that with respect to a business earning income through a series of transactions beginning with manufacturing in one State and ending with a sale in another, a precise—or even wholly logical—determination of the State in which any specific portion of the income was earned is impossible." Moorman Mfg. Co. v. Bair, supra, 437 U.S., at 286, 98 S.Ct., at 2351 (POWELL, J., dissenting).

In the absence of any decision by Congress to prescribe uniform rules for allocating the income of interstate businesses to the appropriate geographical source, the Court has construed the Constitution as allowing the States wide latitude in the selection and application of apportionment formulas. See, e.g., Moorman Mfg. Co., supra, at 278–280, 98 S.Ct., at 2347–2348. Thus an acceptable formula may allocate income on the basis of the location of tangible assets, Underwood Typewriter, supra, on the basis of gross sales. Moorman, supra, or—as is more typical today—by an averaging of three factors: payroll, sales and tangible properties. * * *

The justification for using an apportionment formula to measure the in-state earnings of a unitary business is inapplicable to out-of-state earnings from a source that is unconnected to the business conducted within the State. This rather obvious proposition is recognized by the commentators [5] and is noted in our opinions. If a taxpayer proves by clear and cogent evidence that the income attributed to the State by an apportionment formula is " 'out of all appropriate proportion to the business transacted * * * in that State,' " see Moorman, supra, 437 U.S., at 274, 98 S.Ct., at 2345, the assessment cannot stand.

As Mr. Justice Holmes wrote, with respect to an Indiana property tax on the unitary business conducted by an express company:

> "It is obvious, however, that this notion of organic unity may be made a means of unlawfully taxing the privilege [of carrying on commerce among the States], or property outside the State, under the name of enhanced value or good will, if it is not closely confined to its

---

5. See, e.g., Keesling and Warren, The Unitary Concept in the Allocation of Income, 12 Hastings L.J. 42, 48 (1960):

"In applying the foregoing definitions, it must be kept clearly in mind that although in particular instances all the activities of a given taxpayer may consti-

tute a single business, in other instances the activities may be segregated or divided into a number of separate businesses. It is only where the activities within and without the state constitute inseparable parts of a single business that the classification of unitary should be used."

true meaning. So long as it fairly may be assumed that the different parts of a line are about equal in value a division by mileage is justifiable. But it is recognized in the cases that if, for instance, a railroad company had terminals in one State equal in value to all the rest of the line through another, the latter State could not make use of the unity of the road to equalize the value of every mile. That would be taxing property outside of the State under a pretense." Fargo v. Hart, 193 U.S. 490, 499–500, 24 S.Ct. 498, 500, 48 L.Ed. 761.

In this case the "notion of organic unity" of Mobil's far flung operations is applied solely for the purpose of making a fair determination of its Vermont earnings. Mobil does not dispute Vermont's right to treat its operations in Vermont as part of a unitary business and to measure the income attributable to Vermont on the basis of the three-factor formula that compares payroll, sales and tangible properties in that State with the values of those factors in the whole of the unitary business. Mobil's position, simply stated, is that it is grossly unfair to assign any part of its investment income to Vermont on the basis of those factors. To evaluate that position, it is necessary to identify the unitary business that produces the income subject to taxation by Vermont.

II

Mobil's operations in Vermont consist solely of wholesale and retail marketing of petroleum products. Those operations are a tiny part of a huge unitary business that might be defined in at least three different ways.

First, as Mobil contends, the business might be defined to include all of its operations, but to exclude the income derived from dividends paid by legally separate entities.

Second, as the Supreme Court of Vermont seems to have done, the unitary business might be defined to include not only all of Mobil's operations, but also the income received from all of its investments in other corporations, regardless of whether those other corporations are engaged in the same kind of business as Mobil, and regardless of whether Mobil has a controlling interest in those corporations.

Third, Mobil's unitary business might be defined as encompassing not only the operations of the taxpayer itself but also the operations of all affiliates that are directly or indirectly engaged in the petroleum business. The Court seems to assume that this definition justifies Vermont's assessment in this case.

Mobil does not contend that it would be unfair for Vermont to apply its three-factor formula to the first definition of its unitary business. It has no quarrel with apportionment formulas generally, not even Vermont's. But by consistently arguing that its income from dividends should be entirely excluded from the apportionment calculation, Mobil has directly challenged any *application* of Vermont's formula based on either the second or the third definition of its unitary business. I shall briefly explain why the record is sufficient to support that challenge.

III

Under the Supreme Court of Vermont's conception of the relevant unitary business—the second of the three alternative definitions just posited—there is no need to consider the character of the operations of the corporations that have paid dividends to Mobil. For Vermont automatically included all of the taxpaying entity's investment income in the tax base. Such an approach simply ignores the *raison d'etre* for apportionment formulas.

We may assume that there are cases in which it would be appropriate to regard modest amounts of investment income as an incidental part of a company's overall operations and to allocate it between the taxing State and other jurisdictions on the basis of the same factors as are used to allocate operating income.[11] But this is not such a case. Mobil's investment income is far greater than its operating income. Clearly, it is improper simply to lump huge quantities of investment income that have no special connection with the taxpayer's operations in the taxing State into the tax base and to apportion it on the basis of factors that are used to allocate operating income. The Court does not reject this reasoning; rather, its opinion at least partly disclaims reliance on any such theory.

The Court appears to rely squarely on the third alternative approach to defining a unitary business. It assumes that Vermont's inclusion of the dividends in Mobil's apportionable tax base is predicated on the motion that the dividends represent the income of what would be the operating divisions of the Mobil Oil Corporation if Mobil and its affiliates were a single, legally integrated enterprise, rather than a corporation with numerous interests in other, separate corporations that pay it dividends. * * * Theoretically, that sort of definition is unquestionably acceptable.[16] But there are at least three objections to its use in this case.

11. Because there is no necessary correlation between the levels of profitability of investment income and marketing income, if more than incidental amounts of investment income are used in an averaging formula intended to measure marketing income, inaccuracy is sure to result.

16. "It seems clear, strictly as a logical proposition, that foreign source income is no different from any other income when it comes to determining, by formulary apportionment, the appropriate share of the income of a unitary business taxable by a particular state. This does not involve state taxation of foreign source income any more than does apportionment—in the case of a multistate business—involve the taxation of income arising in other states. In both situations the total income of the unitary business simply provides the starting point for computing the in-state income taxable by the particular state. * * *

"Obviously, if the foreign source income is included in the base for apportionment, foreign property, payrolls and sales must be included in the apportionment fractions. This was recognized in Bass [Ratcliff & Gretton, Ltd. v. State Tax Commission, supra]. * * * " State Taxation, supra, at 205. [State Taxation refers to Rudolph, State Taxation of Interstate Business: The Unitary Business Concept and Affiliated Corporate Groups, 25 Tax L.Rev. 171 (1980).]

First, notwithstanding the Court's characterization of the record, it is readily apparent that a large number of the corporations in which Mobil has small minority interests and from which it derived significant dividend income would seem neither to be engaged in the petroleum business nor to have any connection whatsoever with Mobil's marketing business in Vermont.   Second the record does not disclose whether the earnings of the companies that pay dividends to Mobil are even approximately equal to the amount of the dividends.

But of greatest importance, the record contains no information about the payrolls, sales or property values of any of those corporations, and Vermont has made no attempt to incorporate them into the apportionment formula computations.   Unless the sales, payroll and property values connected with the production of income by the payor corporations are added to the denominator of the apportionment formula, the inclusion of earnings attributable to those corporations in the apportionable tax base will inevitably cause Mobil's Vermont income to be overstated.

Either Mobil's "world-wide petroleum enterprise," * * * is all part of one unitary business, or it is not; if it is, Vermont must evaluate the entire enterprise in a consistent manner.   As it is, it has indefensibly used its apportionment methodology artificially to multiply its share of Mobil's 1970 taxable income perhaps as much as tenfold.   In my judgment, the record is clearly sufficient to establish the validity of Mobil's objections to what Vermont has done here.

IV

The Court does not confront these problems because it concludes that Mobil has in effect waived any objections with respect to them. Although the Court's effort to avoid constitutional issues by narrowly constricting its holding is commendable, I believe it has seriously erred in its assessment of the procedural posture of this case.

It is true that appellant has disclaimed any dispute with "Vermont's method of apportionment."   Brief for Appellant, at 11.   And, admittedly, appellant has confused its cause by variously characterizing its attack in its main brief and reply brief.   But contrary to the Court's assertions, see nn. 1, 3, supra, appellant did not disclaim any dispute with the accuracy or fairness of the application of the formula in this case.   Mobil merely disclaimed any attack on Vermont's *method* of apportionment generally to contrast its claims in this case with the sort of challenge to Iowa's single-factor formula that was rejected in *Moorman*.

The question whether Vermont may include investment income in the apportionable tax base should not be answered in the abstract without consideration of the other factors in the allocation formula. The apportionable tax base is but one multiplicand in the formula. Appellant's challenge to the inclusion of investment income in that component necessarily carries with it a challenge to the product.

Because of the inherent interdependence of the issues in a case of this kind, it seems clear to me that Mobil has not waived its Due Process objections to Vermont's assessment. Appellant's disclaimer of a *Moorman* style attack cannot fairly be interpreted as a concession that makes its entire appeal a project without a purpose. On the contrary, its argument convincingly demonstrates that the inclusion of its dividend income in the apportionable tax base has produced a palpably arbitrary measure of its Vermont income.

In sum, if Vermont is to reject Mobil's calculation of its tax liability, two courses are open to it: (1) it may exclude Mobil's investment income from the apportionable tax base and also exclude the payroll and property used in managing the investments from the denominator of the apportionment factor; or (2) it may undertake the more difficult and risky task of trying to create a consolidated income statement of Mobil's entire unitary business, properly defined. The latter alternative is permissible only if the statement fairly summarizes consolidated earnings, and takes the payroll, sales and property of the payor corporations into account. Because Vermont has employed neither of these alternatives, but has used a method that inevitably overstates Mobile's earnings in the State, I would reverse the judgment of the Supreme Court of Vermont.

Notes and Problems

A. The *Mobil* case evoked considerable comment in the law reviews. See "The Supreme Court, 1979 Term," 94 Harv.L.Rev. 75, 117 (1980); W. Hellerstein, "State Income Taxation of Multijurisdictional Corporations: Reflections on *Mobil, Exxon,* and H.R. 5076," 79 Mich.L.Rev. 113 (1980); Peters, "Sup. Ct's *Mobil* Decision on Multistate Income Apportionment Raises New Questions," 53 J.Tax. 36 (1980); Feinschreiber, "State Taxation of Foreign Dividends after *Mobil v. Vermont,* Adjusting the Apportionment Formula", 6 Int'l. Tax J. 267 (1980); Note, "Supreme Court Decisions in Taxation: 1979 Term", 34 Tax Lawyer 423, 431 (1981); Note, "State Taxation of Foreign–Source Income: *Mobil Corp. v. Commissioner of Taxes"*, 66 Cornell L.Rev. 805 (1981); see J. Hellerstein, "Allocation and Apportionment of Dividends and the Delineation of the Unitary Business," Tax Notes, Jan. 25, 1982, p. 155.

SECTION 12. ALLOCATION OR APPORTIONMENT OF INCOME FROM INTANGIBLES

A. INTRODUCTORY NOTE

The allocation and apportionment of so-called "business" and "nonbusiness" income, and particularly of income from intangibles were, to a considerable extent, fashioned by the need to satisfy Due Process and Commerce Clause restrictions on the taxing powers of the States. The statutes were drawn in the light of the power of the States to tax income from property located and business done within their borders.[111] The income of a foreign corporation from property, however, was, at least initially, regarded as attributable to the situs of the property, and specific allocation to the situs State was widely used.

This pattern was adopted in the father of twentieth-century corporation income taxation, the 1911 Wisconsin levy. Under that statute, in the case of a corporation engaged in business within and without the State, apportionment was applied to "income * * * derived from business transacted and property located within the state," other than income "derived from rentals, stocks, bonds, securities or other evidences of indebtedness," which was specifically allocated.[112] In 1920, a Committee of the National Tax Association recommended a Model Business Income Tax Act for mercantile and manufacturing businesses in which interest, rents, and dividends were specifically allocated, whereas other income was apportioned.[113] These recommendations were adopted by many States, with the result that one commentator, writing in 1949, reported that, in most of the States that levied corporate taxes by net income, "income from rents, royalties, dividends, patents and copyrights, if not used in connection with the unitary trade or business of the taxpayer, is assigned separately as 'non-business income.'"[114]

The underlying constitutional premise on which these practices were based was that, whereas the State had the constitutional power to tax a fairly apportioned portion of the income of foreign corporations derived from *business* conducted within and without the State, income of a foreign corporation from *property* could be taxed only by the State in which the property was located.

In implementing and applying the rule of allocating income from property, the tax situs of real property, and, in turn, of rents and other income from such property, was fixed by the location of the property; and the situs of tangible personal property was established as the State

---

111. See United States Glue Co. v. Town of Oak Creek, 247 U.S. 321, 38 S.Ct. 499 (1918); Travis v. Yale & Towne Mfg. Co., 252 U.S. 60, 40 S.Ct. 228 (1920); Shaffer v. Carter, 252 U.S. 37, 40 S.Ct. 221 (1920); Chapter 11, § 4 infra; and J. Hellerstein, State Taxation I, Corporate Income and Franchise Taxes ¶ 9.8 (1983).

112. The Wisconsin statute is set out in United States Glue Co. v. Town of Oak Creek, 247 U.S. 321, 38 S.Ct. 499 (1918).

113. "Report of the Committee on the Apportionment Between States of Taxes on Mercantile and Manufacturing Business," 1922 N.T.A. Procs. 198. The reason given for this treatment was that the types of income enumerated "come from a definite source"; specific allocation is "entirely feasible," which is not true of the great mass of income of a manufacturing or mercan-

tile company—i.e., profit derived from the sale of goods.

114. Silverstein, "Problems of Apportionment in Taxation of Multistate Business," 4 Tax L.Rev. 207, 210 (1949). In 1959, two years after UDITPA had been approved by the National Conference of Commissioners on Uniform State Laws (at that time the Model Act had been adopted only by Alaska), Professor Paul J. Hartman, in summarizing the then existing rules, stated that the "classes of income said to be specifically allocable by source are designated non-business income" and generally include rents, dividends and interest, royalties from patents and copyrights, and gains and losses from the sale of capital assets. Hartman, "State Taxation of Corporate Income from a Multistate Business," 12 Vand.L.Rev. 21, 58, 80 (1959).

in which the tangibles were more or less permanently located. Id. Intangibles, which have no physical location, were governed by the rule of *mobilia sequuntur personam,* with their situs at the domicile of the owner. Income from intangibles followed the tax situs of the intangible. As the case law developed, the Supreme Court refined or amplified (depending on one's evaluation of the Court's actions) these tax rules in two major respects relevant to the taxation of income. It substituted (or added) the commercial domicile of the taxpayer for (or to) the statutory domicile as the tax situs of intangibles and the income they produced, and it created the business situs doctrine. Id.

Under the business situs doctrine, intangibles "may acquire a situs for taxation other than that of the domicile of the owner if they have become integral parts of some local business." [115] In applying the business situs doctrine to income from intangibles, some State courts viewed the income as being "derived from property." Using the conventional jurisdictional standards for taxing property, it was natural enough for courts to hold that such income is specifically allocable to the State in which the intangible has its business situs. In other States in which the statute apportioned all income or income from property having a tax situs in the State, income from intangibles having a business situs in the State was attributed to the numerator of the receipts or sales factor of the State.

Other courts, however, took a different approach to the treatment of intangibles having a business situs in the State. Intangibles having a business situs in a State are by their very nature assets used in the conduct of the business, since by definition an intangible acquires a business situs in a State only if it constitutes an integral part of a business there being conducted. As factual patterns were presented to the courts in which a taxpayer's intangibles were found to be integral parts of a general business conducted within and without the State, some courts viewed the income as being derived not from property, but from "the conduct of business" in the State. As a result, such courts held that apportionment, not specific allocation, was the proper method of dividing income derived from such intangibles.

The division of income from intangibles has emerged in recent years as one of the major controversial areas of key importance to the States and businesses, as multistate and multinational enterprises have expanded and increasingly dominate the American economy. Stocks in affiliates operating in various States, patents, trade franchises, copyrights, royalty interests, and the like are owned by large enterprises, based typically in the major cities. Hence, the apportionment or allocation of the income from such assets has taken on a new importance in the division of the income of multistate businesses. The business/nonbusiness income dichotomy adopted by UDITPA to distin-

115. Farmers Loan & Trust Co. v. Minnesota, 280 U.S. 204, 213, 50 S.Ct. 98 (1930). See also Chapter 11, § 3(a) infra.

guish between allocable and apportionable rents, royalties, interest, dividends, and capital gains has become the focal point for the controversies in this area, since most of the State statutes using a net income measure of tax have enacted UDITPA.

B. BUSINESS AND NONBUSINESS INCOME UNDER UDITPA

The Uniform Act provides:

"Business income" means income arising from transactions and activity in the regular course of the taxpayer's trade or business and includes income from tangible and intangible property if the acquisition, management, and disposition of the property constitute integral parts of the taxpayer's regular trade or business operations. [§ 1(a).]

"Nonbusiness income" means all income other than business income. [§ 1(e).]

The regulations issued by the Multistate Tax Commission (MTC), the administering arm under the Multistate Tax Compact, which embodies UDITPA, state that "[i]ncome of any type or class and from any source is business income if it arises from transactions and activity occurring in the regular course of a trade or business * * * In general all transactions and activities of the taxpayer which are dependent upon or contribute to the operations of the taxpayer's economic enterprise as a whole" are regarded as "arising in the course of, and will constitute integral parts of, a trade or business." This statement is supplemented by the enunciation of an "origin" and a "purpose" test of dependent or contributing activities. If the asset that produced the income either (a) "arises out of or was created in the regular course of the taxpayer's trade or business operations," or (b) "the purpose for acquiring * * * [the asset] is related to or incidental to such trade or business operations," the income is treated as business income. The MTC regulations also construe UDITPA as establishing a presumption in favor of apportionment, stating that "the income of the taxpayer is business income unless clearly classifiable as nonbusiness income." See MTC Apportionment Regulations, CCH All States Guide ¶ 352 P–H All States Guide ¶ 631.

The MTC apportionment and allocation regulations have been criticized by business spokesmen as so "all inclusive" as to adopt the " 'full apportionment' concept," which they contend is unjustified by the meaning of the terms "business" and "nonbusiness income" and by the history and origin of the use of those terms in the drafting of UDITPA. See Industry Statement, Mondale Comm. Hearings 269. For a defense of full apportionment by the Executive Director of the MTC, see Corrigan, "Developing Concepts in Attribution of Multistate Corporate Income," Mondale Comm. Hearings 129.

The Multistate Tax Commission is empowered "whenever any two or more party States, or subdivisions of party States, have uniform or similar provisions of law relating to an income tax, capital stock tax, gross receipts tax, sales or use tax" to "adopt uniform regulations" with respect thereto. Compact, Art. VII–1, CCH All States Guide ¶ 352, P–H All States Guide ¶ 701.

The regulations are required to be submitted to the party States, and thereupon each of the States and subdivisions to which the regulations might apply "shall consider any such regulation for adoption in accordance with its own laws and procedures." Id. at Art. VII–3, CCH All States Guide ¶ 352, P–H All States Guide ¶ 743. As of 1987, the MTC apportionment and allocation regulations were formally adopted by eleven States and were partially or informally adopted by nine States. CCH All States Guide ¶ 352. See also Dexter, "Taxation of Income from Intangibles of Multistate and Multinational Corporations," 29 Vand.L.Rev. 401, 404 (1976). *Caveat:* The regulations as adopted by any State should be examined, where they become relevant, since they may contain variations.

C. INTEREST INCOME

The Multistate Tax Commission regulations provide:

Interest. Interest income is business income where the intangible with respect to which the interest was received arises out of or was created in the regular course of the taxpayer's trade or business operations or where the purpose for acquiring and holding the intangible is related to or incidental to such trade or business operations.

Example (i): The taxpayer operates a multistate chain of department stores, selling for cash and on credit. Service charges, interest, or time-price differentials and the like are received with respect to instalment sales and revolving charge accounts. These amounts are business income.

* * *

Example (v): The taxpayer is engaged in a multistate manufacturing and selling business. The taxpayer usually has working capital and extra cash totaling $200,000 which it regularly invests in short-term interest-bearing securities. The interest income is business income.

Example (vi): In January the taxpayer sold all the stock of a subsidiary for $20,000,000. The funds are placed in an interest-bearing account pending a decision by management as to how the funds are to be utilized. The interest income is nonbusiness income. [MTC Apportionment and Allocation Regulations (Reg. IV.1(c)(3), CCH All States Guide ¶ 352, P–H All States Guide ¶ 633)].

SPERRY AND HUTCHINSON CO. v. DEPARTMENT OF REVENUE

Supreme Court of Oregon, 1974.
270 Or. 329, 527 P.2d 729.

O'CONNELL, CHIEF JUSTICE.

This is an appeal under ORS 305.425 from a decree of the Oregon Tax Court. Sperry & Hutchinson Co. v. Dept. of Rev., 5 OTR Adv.Sh. 301 (1973). The question presented is whether income received by plaintiff in the tax years 1961, 1963, 1964 and 1965 as interest on investment securities is apportionable in part to Oregon.

The Sperry & Hutchinson Company (S & H) is incorporated in New Jersey, domiciled in New York, and does business in 48 states including Oregon. S & H's primary business and the only business conducted in Oregon is the sale of a trading stamp promotional service to retailers. During the years in question this enterprise produced substantial revenues, a large part of which S & H invested in fixed income securities. Plaintiff's investment protfolio is divided into three categories: short-term [1] securities held pending use of the funds in the green stamp business; short-term securities held pending acquisition of other companies or favorable developments in the long-term money market, and long-term securities held as an investment.[2] Plaintiff reported the interest received on all three categories as allocable to its domicile rather than apportionable to all states in which it does business. The Department of Revenue held all of the interest to be apportionable,[3] and imposed an additional corporate excise tax for the years in question.

Plaintiff appealed to the Tax Court which held that the interest on the long-term and short-term securities held for investment was not apportionable, but that the interest on short-term securities used in the stamp business was apportionable. The Department of Revenue appeals from the first holding and S & H cross-appeals from the second. We affirm the Tax Court on both the appeal and cross-appeal.

The income from S & H's long-term investments are not apportionable to Oregon because neither the capital invested nor the income derived therefrom is a part of the trading stamp business conducted in this state. This is equally true both under the current Uniform Division of Income for Tax Purposes Act (ORS 314.605 to 314.670) which became effective beginning 1965 and under the pre-existing statute (ORS 314.280).[4] Both statutes impose a tax on an interstate corporation only as to income attributable to Oregon and do so through minor variations on the concept of "unitary business." We hold that

1. Securities bearing a maturity of less than 12 months.

2. The opinion of the Tax Court contains an excellent and more detailed discussion of the facts briefly set out here.

3. Department of Revenue Order No. I–71–19.

4. Oregon Laws 1963, ch. 319, § 1.

because S & H's long-term investment income was neither "closely connected or necessary"[5] under the old statute, nor "income arising from transactions * * * in the regular course of the taxpayer's" trading stamp business under the new statute,[6] the interest is not apportionable. The Department of Revenue seeks to avoid this conclusion by emphasizing that liquidation of the trading stamp enterprise would require S & H to use its long-term investment to redeem all outstanding stamps. Although this may be true, as a factual matter S & H did not draw on this portion of its investment to satisfy its stamp obligations and there is nothing in the record to indicate it shall ever be required to do so.

The short-term securities held pending favorable developments in the long-term money market or acquisition of other businesses are in precisely the same position as the long-term investments. They are not a part of the stamp business and, therefore, not apportionable to Oregon.

The short-term securities held to satisfy the needs for liquid capital in the stamp business are apportionable. These securities are purchased during periods of cash flow surplus and are liquidated when the proceeds, both interest and capital, are needed to meet business obligations during periods of cash flow deficit. Thus, this is business income "arising from transactions and activity in the regular course of the taxpayer's trade or business"[7] and is part of S & H's unitary business.[8]

S & H argues that because this income is the return on an intangible it must be allocated to the legal situs. Nothing in our former law requires such an arbitrary result and our current law expressly prohibits it.[9]

As decreed by the Tax Court, the case must be remanded to the defendant to redetermine the amount of corporate excise tax and interest due the state of Oregon by excluding from plaintiff's apportion-

---

5. Reg. 314.280(1)(B) under former ORS 314.280.

6. ORS 314.610(1).

7. ORS 314.610(1).

8. ORS 314.280; Reg. 314.280(1)(B).

9. ORS 314.610 provides:

"(1) 'Business income' means income arising from transactions and activity in the regular course of the taxpayer's trade or business and includes income from tangible and intangible property if the acquisition, the management, use or rental, and the disposition of the property constitute integral parts of the taxpayer's regular trade or business operations.

" * * *

"(5) 'Nonbusiness income' means all income other than business income."

ORS 314.625 is fully consistent with this result.

"314.625. Rents and royalties from real or tangible personal property, capital gains, interest, dividends, or patent or copyright royalties, *to the extent that they constitute nonbusiness income,* shall be allocated as provided in ORS 314.630 to 314.645." (Emphasis added.)

S & H also contends that California has reached the opposite conclusion in interpreting its similar law. This is incorrect. The California decisions holding interest income must be allocated are expressly based on a statute unique to that jurisdiction. Fibreboard Paper Products Corp. v. Franchise Tax Bd., 268 Cal.App.2d 363, 370, 74 Cal.Rptr. 46 (1968).

able income the interest received on long-term investments and such of plaintiff's short-term holdings as it can show were not used in or held for use in its trading stamp business.

Affirmed.*

Notes and Problems

A. In Montgomery Ward & Co. v. Commissioner of Taxation, 276 Minn. 479, 151 N.W.2d 294 (1967), the taxpayer, whose commercial domicile was located outside Minnesota, had accumulated some $300 million in cash out of the earnings of its nationwide general retailing business "in anticipation of a change in the economic climate which would make expansion of the business operation profitable." 276 Minn. at 480. Pending this development, the funds were invested outside Minnesota in liquid securities, the income from which was not segregated from other current operating income. The statute provided that income derived from a trade or business carried on within and without the State "including income from intangible property employed in such business" was apportionable. Id. at 481. In sustaining the Tax Commissioner's inclusion of the income from the securities in the apportionable base, the test used by the court in determining whether the securities constituted "intangible property employed in" the interstate business was whether the intangibles were part of a "unitary business." Id. at 482.

Montgomery Ward's major contention was that the income, gain, and principal of the securities at issue were not used to pay the expenses and obligations of the business activities, but instead "the primary purpose for which it acquired the intangibles was the *expansion* of its business." Id. at 483. The court referred to the facts that the intangibles were carried on the corporate balance sheet as current assets and that the income from the investments was commingled with other corporate business income in accounts used to pay ordinary business obligations, and concluded that the taxpayer had "failed to sustain its burden of proving that the intangibles were not employed in its principal business." Id. The court evidently regarded the income in controversy as on the borderline between apportionable and non-apportionable income. For, after resorting to the judicial refuge of burden of proof for disposing of hard cases, the court remanded the case to give the taxpayer an opportunity to show that "for all practical purposes some part of the amounts up to $300,000,000 held during the period in question and invested in liquid securities was not actually used or usable in its merchandising operation in any significant sense." Id. Ac-

---

* [For other decisions arising under UDITPA as to the proper classification of interest on short-term investments, see Champion International Corp. v. Bureau of Revenue, 88 N.M. 411, 540 P.2d 1300 (1975) *in accord,* and United States Steel Corp. v. State Tax Comm'n, Idaho CCH ¶ 14–510 (Idaho D.Ct., Ada Cty.1975) *per contra.* For a detailed study of the developments which led to the adoption of the business/ non-business income distinction by the draftsmen of UDITPA, see Peters, "The Distinction Between Business Income and Nonbusiness Income," 25 U.S.C. Tax Inst. Procs. 251 (1973), reprinted in Mondale Comm. Hearings 246 et seq.; Peters, "Revised Multistate Tax Commission Regs Define 'Business' and 'Non–Business' Income," 40 J.Tax. 122 (1974). See also Keesling & Warren, "California's Uniform Division of Income for Tax Purposes Act," 15 U.C.L.A.L.Rev. 156 [1967].]

cord, Qualls v. Montgomery Ward & Co., Inc., 266 Ark. 207, 585 S.W.2d 18 (1979), in which the court reached the same result under UDITPA.

D. DIVIDENDS

1. Most of the States exclude some or all dividends from the net income measure of their corporate taxes. CCH Multistate Corporate Income Tax Guide ¶ 79. The State laws usually adopt, as the starting point for the determination of the corporate income measure, taxable income as defined for Federal income tax purposes. In defining taxable income, the Internal Revenue Code allows a deduction from gross income of 100 percent of the dividends received from U.S. domestic corporations with which it could have elected to file a consolidated return, i.e., broadly speaking, 80 percent or more of whose capital stock (other than non-voting stock limited and preferred as to dividends) is owned by the group (I.R.C. §§ 243, 1501 et seq.). Eighty-five percent of the dividends received from other domestic corporations are deductible from gross income. There are variations in the case of special types of corporations (I.R.C. § 243). Dividends received from foreign corporations are taxable in full, with exceptions in the case of dividends paid by foreign corporations taxable in the United States, foreign personal holding companies, and the like.

In adjusting Federal taxable income to State taxable income (before apportionment or allocation), a good many States depart in one way or another from the Federal rules. As of 1976, a U.S. Treasury study reported that 15 States follow the Federal policy of allowing a general deduction for intercorporate dividends from essentially domestic corporations. Nine States allowed a partial deduction for intercorporate dividends received from either domestic or foreign subsidiaries, but several States granted a deduction for intercorporate dividends only if the paying corporation was taxable in the State of the receiving corporation. Six States exempted all intercorporate dividends. See Carlson, "State Taxation of Corporate Income from Foreign Sources," in Essays in International Taxation 247 et seq. (Tables 2 and 3), U.S. Treasury Dept., Tax Policy Research Study 3 (1976).

In 1963, the Willis Committee found that most of the States employing net income based taxes allocated dividends to the State of the recipient's commercial domicile, unless the stock had acquired a business situs elsewhere. Willis Comm. rep. at 204–206. In that event, in some States, the dividends were allocated to the business situs of the stock, but, in other States, if the stocks constitute an integral part of a unitary business, dividends were apportioned. Id. The widespread adoption of UDITPA in recent years has expanded the apportionment in many States to all dividends that constitute business income. See CCH Multistate Corporate Income Tax Guide ¶ 1239; Note 4 infra. Nevertheless, in a number of States the practice currently obtains of allocating all taxable dividends to the taxpayer's commercial domicile. See Note 2 infra.

2. *Allocation of Dividends to the Commercial Domicile.** The rationale behind the allocation of dividends to the State of the recipient's commercial domicile was stated by the Supreme Court of California to be that "the source of the income to the shareholders (the dividends) is the corporation's stock." Miller v. McColgan, 17 Cal.2d 432, 110 P.2d 419 (1941). Since the "source of dividends is the stock" and "shares of stock in a corporation have their situs" at the domicile of the owner, "unless they have acquired a business situs elsewhere," dividends are allocable to the State of the owner's domicile. In a subsequent decision, the same court stated the commercial domicile rule without qualifying it as to cases in which the stock has acquired a business situs elsewhere. Pacific Tel. & Tel. Co. v. Franchise Tax Bd., 102 Cal.Rptr. 782, 785–86, 498 P.2d 1030 (1972). For many years, the Franchise Tax Board followed the rule of allocating all dividends to the corporation's commercial domicile, notwithstanding California's adoption of UDITPA. The California Court of Appeal rejected the Board's position as to the apportionability of income from intangibles, by holding that capital gain realized on the sale of stock of a subsidiary that constituted part of the taxpayer's California unitary business is apportionable. Times Mirror Co. v. Franchise Tax Bd., 102 Cal.App.3d 872, 162 Cal.Rptr. 630 (2d Dist.1980). Moreover, the State Board of Equalization has ruled that with the adoption of UDITPA dividends constituting business income as defined by UDITPA (see Note 4 infra) are apportionable. Appeal of Occidental Petroleum Co., Cal. State Bd. of Equaliz., March 3, 1981, and the Franchise Tax Board now follows that decision.[116] See J. Hellerstein, State Taxation I, Corporate Income and Franchise Taxes ¶ 9.11[1], pp. 537–38 (1983). What is the rule in your State with regard to the allocation or apportionment of dividends?

3. *Allocation of Dividends to the State in Which the Dividend Paying Corporation Conducts Its Business.** In some States, it has been held that the source of dividend income is the State in which the underlying corporation conducts its business. Accordingly, in such States, dividends are allocated to the States in which the payor corporation conducts its business. See, e.g., In re Union Electric Co., 349 Mo. 73, 80, 161 S.W.2d 968 (1942); California Packing Corp. v. State Tax Com'n, 97 Utah 367, 93 P.2d 463 (1939). The New York franchise tax law is based on the concept that stock and the income it produces should be attributed to the State in which the corporation whose stock is held conducts its business. Dividends on stocks of nonsubsidiary corporations (New York does not tax dividends paid by subsidiaries) are

---

*This Note is based on J. Hellerstein, State Taxation I, Corporate Income and Franchise Taxes ¶ 9.11[1], pp. 537–38 (1983). Used with the consent of the copyright owner and publisher.

116. See generally, on the history and development of the California treatment of dividends, Boren, "Specific Allocation of Corporate Income in California: Some

Problems in the Uniform Division of Income for Tax Purposes," 30 Tax L.Rev. 607, 619 et seq. (1975).

*This Note is based on J. Hellerstein, State Taxation I, Corporate Income and Franchise Taxes ¶ 9.11[2], pp. 538–40 (1983). Used with the consent of the copyright owner and publisher.

attributed to New York by reference to the payor corporation's allocation percentage. N.Y.Tax Law § 210–3(b)(1), CCH ¶ 93–910, P–H 12,020.53. See J. Hellerstein, State Taxation I, Corporate Income and Franchise Taxes ¶ 9.11[2], pp. 538–40 (1983).

4. *Apportionment of Dividends.* Dividends are apportioned under the statutory formula by many States. See Mobil Oil Corp. v. Commissioner of Taxes, 136 Vt. 545, 394 A.2d 1147 (1978), affirmed 445 U.S. 425, 100 S.Ct. 1223 (1980); F.W. Woolworth Co. v. Director, Division of Taxation, 45 N.J. 466, 213 A.2d 1 (1965); Gulf Oil Corp. v. Clayton, 267 N.C. 15, 147 S.E.2d 522 (1966); United States Steel Corp. v. State Tax Com'n, Idaho Dist. Ct., 4th Dist., Ada County, Dec. 30, 1975, Idaho CCH ¶ 14–510. Only the last of the cited cases involved a construction of UDITPA. For the constitutionality of apportioning dividends to States other than the recipient's commercial domicile, see Section 11 supra.

Under UDITPA, dividends are allocable to the State of a recipient's corporate domicile to the extent that they constitute "nonbusiness income." UDITPA §§ 4, 7, Section 6 supra. If they constitute "business income," dividends are apportioned under the formula (§ 9); and for purposes of the sales factor, such dividends are included under the income producing activity test of Section 17.

The apportionment regulations of the Multistate Tax Commission (MTC) contain the following provisions interpreting business and nonbusiness dividend income:

> IV.1.(c).(4). **Dividends.** Dividends are business income where the stock with respect to which the dividends are received arises out of or was acquired in the regular course of the taxpayer's trade or business operations or where the purpose for acquiring and holding the stock is related to or incidental to such trade or business operations.
>
>   *   *   *
>
> Example (ii): The taxpayer is engaged in a multistate manufacturing and wholesaling business. In connection with that business the taxpayer maintains special accounts to cover such items as workmen's compensation claims, etc. A portion of the moneys in those accounts is invested in interest-bearing bonds. The remainder is invested in various common stocks listed on national stock exchanges. Both the interest income and any dividends are business income.
>
>   *   *   *
>
> Example (v): The taxpayer receives dividends from the stock of its subsidiary or affiliate which acts as the marketing agency for products manufactured by the taxpayer. The dividends are business income.
>
> Example (vi): The taxpayer is engaged in a multistate glass manufacturing business. It also holds a portfolio of stock and interest-bearing securities, the acquisition and holding of which are unrelated to the manufacturing business. The dividends and interest income received are nonbusiness income. [MTC Apportionment Regulations, CCH All States Guide ¶ 352, P–H All States Guide ¶ 633.]

United States Steel Corp. v. State Tax Comm'n., supra, construes the UDITPA dividend provision; compare, also, the construction of the related UDITPA provision dealing with business and nonbusiness interest income considered in *Sperry & Hutchinson,* p. 633 supra.

5. *A Critique of Allocation or Apportionment of Dividends.* "The controversy concerning the taxation of intercorporate dividends and the definition of business and nonbusiness income, as those terms are used in UDITPA, needs to be approached by recognizing that there are dividends and dividends. Thus, if a manufacturing company receives dividends from its wholly-owned subsidiary which is engaged principally in selling the product of the parent company, the dividends constitute a part of the profits derived from the parent-subsidiary unitary business. Such profits constitute operating income, income of the business, just as they would if the enterprise were conducted through sales branches, instead of a subsidiary. Such dividends ought to be apportioned as part of the basic operating income of the enterprise and, therefore, should fall within the UDITPA classification as business income.

"As I have already indicated [in the earlier part of the testimony], the realistic and fiscally sound tax treatment of such an enterprise is to combine or consolidate the income of the parent and selling subsidiary for purposes of unitary apportionment. The dividend issue would then disappear, since the dividends would be eliminated as an intercompany item. If, however, neither the State nor the taxpayer exercises the option granted by the type of statute which it is assumed would be in force to utilize the combined or consolidated approach, or, if for one reason or another, the taxpayer does not qualify under the statutory provision for combination, the character of the dividend income on a separate parent company basis, nevertheless, does not, in my thinking, change; it is still operating income which ought to be apportioned in taxing the recipient.

"When we turn, however, to dividends paid by nonaffiliates, or by corporations which are not integral parts of the unitary enterprise, the situation will ordinarily be different. Apart from a corporation engaged in the securities business, dividends received from investments in nonaffiliated corporations, or from affiliates in a conglomerate, which are not a part of the unitary enterprise, constitute investment income. Such income does not flow from the unitary basic operating activities, of which the taxpayer is a part. To apportion that type of dividend income by reference to factors such as the location of the taxpayer's plant and inventory of goods, the States in which its manufacturing employees and its salesmen operate, the location of its customers, would appear to me to be distorting, and simply would not reflect the activities of the taxpayer which produced the non-unitary dividends, or other factors relevant to the attribution of the dividends to particular States.

"If this conclusion is accepted, the commercial domicile rule which has been traditionally applied to income from intangibles, reflects a good deal of wisdom. For that State has the dominant claim to tax such non-operating dividend income, since the activities relating to the investment, the control and management of the stocks which produced the dividend income typically take place at the executive offices, where the financial work is carried on. Consequently, in the language of UDITPA, such investment or non-operating dividend income ought to be treated as nonbusiness income and be allocated to the commercial domicile." *

In the *Mobil Oil* case (p. 610 supra), the Supreme Court approved the principle that dividends are not apportionable to a State that is not the recipient's domicile or the State in which the stocks and the income they produce are managed and handled, unless "the dividend payors * * * are part of its [the recipient's] unitary business."

In the *ASARCO* and *Woolworth* cases (pp. 529–60 supra), the Court invalidated taxes imposed by a non-domiciliary State on dividends received by foreign corporations, on the ground that the payors were not part of the unitary business of the recipients.

There are other situations, however, not dealt with in the opinions in *Mobil, ASARCO,* or *Woolworth,* in which apportionment of dividends is also appropriate since the dividends unmistakably constitute unitary business income. These include:

(1) Dividends on temporary investments of working capital, or other current funds held for normal operating uses.

(2) Dividends received on stocks falling within the *Corn Products* doctrine. In Corn Products Refining Co. v. Commissioner, 350 U.S. 46, 76 S.Ct. 20 (1955), the general rule that capital stock held by a corporation constitutes a "capital asset" for Federal income tax purposes and generates capital gain or loss on sale or other disposition, was qualified. The capital asset rule was held inapplicable to stock bought and held, not for investment purposes, but only as an incident to the conduct of the taxpayer's business. Consequently, capital stock of a supplier acquired to assure the taxpayer's inventory sources, or the continuation of a lease of property needed to operate the business, or to obtain access to know-how and marketing techniques and the like, do not constitute capital assets. By the same token, dividends on stocks falling within the *Corn Products* doctrine ought to be treated as business income that is apportionable under UDITPA. See J. Hellerstein, State Taxation I, Corporate Income and Franchise Taxes, ¶ 9.12[2][a](ii) (1983).

[The *Corn Products* doctrine was narrowly restricted in Arkansas Best Corp. v. Commissioner of Internal Revenue, __ U.S. __, 108 S.Ct. 971 (1988), decided after this work went to press. That restriction, however, does not alter the point being made here, since the reference

---

* The quoted material is an excerpt from the testimony of Jerome R. Hellerstein before the Mondale Committee in 1973, pp. 154, 163.

to the *Corn Products* case was made merely to illustrate the types of dividends that should be apportioned as business income. The *Arkansas Best* case was not decided on the ground that the income at issue was not "business income."]

6. *Apportionment of the Factors of the Dividend Payors.* In his dissent in *Mobil Oil* (p. 627 supra), Justice Stevens stated:

> But of greatest importance, the record contains no information about the payrolls, sales or property values of any of those corporations, and Vermont has made no attempt to incorporate them into the apportionment formula computations. Unless the sales, payroll and property values connected with the production of income by the payor corporations are added to the denominator of the apportionment formula, the inclusion of earnings attributable to those corporations in the apportionable tax base will inevitably cause Mobil's Vermont income to be overstated.

> Either Mobil's "world-wide petroleum enterprise," * * * is all part of one unitary business, or it is not; if it is, Vermont must evaluate the entire enterprise in a consistent manner. As it is, it has indefensibly used its apportionment methodology artificially to multiply its share of Mobil's 1970 taxable income perhaps as much as tenfold. In my judgment, the record is clearly sufficient to establish the validity of Mobil's objections to what Vermont has done here. [445 U.S. at 460–61.]

Taxpayers, relying on Justice Stevens' dissent, are contending that if dividends are included in the apportionable base of a State tax, the payor's apportionment factors must be included in the formula. Some taxpayers invoke the Detroit formula as the proper technique for including the factors of the dividend payors. That formula is set out in J. Hellerstein, State Taxation I, Corporate Income and Franchise Taxes, p. 557, n. 267 (1983). What argument would you make to support the taxpayer's position?

7. *Allocation or Apportionment of Capital Gains and Losses.* * "In some States, capital gains and losses from sales, exchanges or other disposition of property are allocated under more or less precise statutory provisions. Thus, the Maryland statute provides that capital gains and losses from real estate located in Maryland are allocated to the State.[117] Capital gains and losses from tangible personal property are allocable to Maryland if the property had a situs in the State at the time of the disposition, or if the taxpayer's commercial domicile is in the State and the taxpayer is not taxable in the State in which the property had a situs.[118] In the case of intangibles, capital gains and losses are allocable to Maryland if the taxpayer's commercial domicile is in the State.[119] More or less similar allocation rules are followed in

---

* This note is taken from J. Hellerstein, State Taxation I, Corporate Income and Franchise Taxes ¶ 9.13 (1983). Used with the consent of the copyright owner and publisher.

117. Md.Code Ann. Art. 81, § 316, CCH ¶ 93–498(a), P–H ¶ 12,610.

118. Id.

119. Id.

some other States which use as the test of allocability whether the principal place from which the trade or business was managed was in the State.[120] It seems likely that both tests will produce the same results in most cases.

"In most States, some capital gains or losses are apportionable.[121] Under UDITPA, the dividing line between allocable and apportionable capital gains and losses depends on the nonbusiness-business income distinction, and in other States on the similar question as to whether the capital gains constitute part of the taxpayer's regular trade or business."[122] J. Hellerstein, State Taxation I, Corporate Income and Franchise Taxes ¶ 9.13 (1983).

Under UDITPA, the dividing line between allocable and apportionable gains and losses from sales or other dispositions of property depends on the business-nonbusiness income distinction. Section 4 of UDITPA defines business income as

> income arising from transactions and activity in the regular course of the taxpayer's trade or business and includes income from tangible and intangible property if the acquisition, management, and disposition of the property constitute integral parts of the taxpayer's regular trade or business.

In construing this UDITPA provision in the context of gains and losses from the sale of property, two distinct approaches have been taken by the courts. Some courts have taken the so-called "transactional" approach to the question of apportionability, holding that such gains or

---

120. Okla.Code Ann. § 2358, CCH ¶ 95–008f, P–H ¶ 12,711.25 (where an intangible has acquired a business situs outside the taxpayer's commercial domicile, the gain is allocated to the State of commercial domicile).

121. Thus, in Connecticut, gains or losses from sales of tangible assets used in the trade or business, but not for sale in the regular course of business, are allocated to the State if the property was situated in the State at the time of the sale. Conn. Gen.Stat. § 12–218(1), CCH ¶ 91–404, P–H ¶ 12,020.10. However, the statute also contains the following provision:

> Any of the foregoing classes of income or loss when derived from tangible or intangible property, the acquisition, management and disposition of which constitute integral parts of the taxpayer's regular trade or business operations, shall not be allocated as provided above in subdivisions (1) and (2), but shall be apportioned in accordance with subdivisions (3)(a), (3)(b), or (3)(c) below (Am.1961 P.A. 381).

Id. The Georgia statute provides:

> (3) Gains from the sale of tangible or intangible property not held, owned, or used in connection with the trade or

business of the corporation or held for sale in the regular course of business, shall be allocated to this State if the property sold is real or tangible personal property situated in this State or intangible property having an actual situs or a business situs within this State. Otherwise such gains shall be allocated outside this State. (Am.L.1979, Act 2.)

* * *

(e) Apportionment of income.—Net income of the classes described in subsection (c) having been separately allocated and deducted, the remainder of the net business income shall be apportioned as follows:

Ga.Code § 91A–3611, CCH ¶ 95–236, P–H ¶ 12,012.

122. In some States, all taxable income, including capital gains and losses, is apportionable. Florida is such a State. [For a case arising under the Florida statute that limits the apportionment of "out-of-State investment income" to cases in which the Florida enterprise is part of a unitary business, see Brunner Enterprises, Inc. v. Department of Revenue, 452 So.2d 550, 553 (Fla.1984).]

losses are apportionable only when the particular *transaction* giving rise to the gain or loss is in the regular course of the taxpayer's trade or business. See, e.g., General Care Corp. v. Olsen, 705 S.W.2d 642 (Tenn. 1986) (reviewing the cases); Western Natural Gas Co. v. McDonald, 202 Kan. 98, 446 P.2d 781 (1968). Other courts have taken the so-called "functional" approach to the question of apportionability, holding that gains or losses are apportionable so long as the asset giving rise to the gain or loss was used in the taxpayer's business to produce business income, even if the transaction disposing of it was unusual. See, e.g., Appeal of Centennial Equities Corp., Cal.State Bd. of Equaliz., June 27, 1984, CCH ¶ 400–904, P–H ¶ 31,110–G; Atlantic Richfield Co. v. State, 198 Colo. 413, 601 P.2d 628 (1979). Under the "transaction" approach gains or losses from the sale of assets in corporate liquidations or from other unusual dispositions of assets are allocable whereas they are apportionable under the "functional" approach, if the assets were used in the taxpayer's trade or business. Which definition of business income more closely conforms to the construction given the term by the MTC's UDITPA regulations? See Section 12, subd. B supra.

SECTION 13. INCOME FROM PATENTS, COPYRIGHTS, AND SIMILAR INTANGIBLES

XEROX CORPORATION v. COMPTROLLER OF THE TREASURY

Court of Appeals of Maryland, 1981.
290 Md. 126, 428 A.2d 1208.

MURPHY, CHIEF JUDGE: This case presents the question whether Maryland taxation of an apportioned amount of certain interest and royalty income earned by a corporation engaged in both interstate and intrastate commerce was proper under relevant statutory and constitutional standards.*

*   *   *

II. Xerox Corporation is incorporated under the laws of New York and has its principal place of business in Rochester, New York. It is divided into operating divisions, some of which are in turn combined into groups. The copier division is headquartered in New York, and the corporate headquarters and education division are located in Stamford, Connecticut. Xerox conducts business in all fifty states and the District of Columbia, and has branch offices in several territories of the United States (Puerto Rico, Guam, Samoa, and the Virgin Islands). Xerox's business consists primarily of the manufacture of copying equipment, which it sells and rents to its customers. Xerox also provides maintenance services to its customers.

The activities conducted by Xerox in Maryland are primarily in connection with the sale, rental and maintenance of its copying machines, which are manufactured in New York. Xerox has no research or development facilities in this State. Control and supervision of

---

* Some footnotes have been omitted.

(H. & H.) State & Local Tax., 5th Ed. ACB—23

Xerox's copier business activities in Maryland is exercised by personnel in a regional headquarters in Virginia. A branch office, located in the Baltimore metropolitan area, rents and sells Xerox copying machines and equipment and provides maintenance services. Xerox's education division maintains a small facility in Cheverly, Maryland, from which it distributes educational materials.

Xerox filed timely Maryland corporate income tax returns with the Comptroller for tax years 1972, 1973 and 1974. These returns reflected an apportionment of Xerox's net income to the State of Maryland from the manufacture, sale, rental and service of its machines. The apportionment was made under the Maryland apportionment formula on the basis of Xerox's property, payroll and sales in Maryland as compared to the same factors at all locations within and without Maryland. Before applying the Maryland apportionment formula, Xerox subtracted from its net income certain royalty and interest income that it had received during the tax years in question.

The royalty income was comprised of license fees that Xerox charged for use of certain of its intangible assets, i.e., patents, trademarks, copyrights and business know-how. The license fees, which were determined as a percentage of certain sales of the licensees, were received from various corporations. Approximately 86% of Xerox's royalty income came from foreign subsidiaries, with the balance coming from foreign (10%) and domestic (4%) nonaffiliated corporations. An average of almost 90% of Xerox's royalty income in each of the tax years involved was generated by fees charged to foreign subsidiaries for the use of Xerox's name. None of the licensing agreements was entered into in Maryland, nor were any of the intangible assets that generated the royalty income acquired or developed in this State. The documents evidencing Xerox's ownership of the intangible assets were kept as its facilities in Connecticut and New York. Personnel in Xerox's corporate headquarters in Connecticut and New York administered the terms of the licensing agreements and collected the licensing fees.

Xerox's ownership interest in the foreign subsidiaries that paid the license fees ranged from 15% to 100%. All of these corporations conducted their businesses entirely outside of the United States and its territories. Each was a separate corporation under foreign law and each had its own local management. Xerox received $11,368,714, $19,148,281, and $20,702,118 in license fees in 1972, 1973 and 1974, respectively.

The interest income was produced by loans that Xerox made to certain of its foreign subsidiaries. Although the subsidiaries usually borrowed money in the regular commercial market, Xerox made loans to these corporations when, for example, a subsidiary was precluded from borrowing in its own right by restrictions in existing loan agreements. The loans made by Xerox were all evidenced by formal loan documents and carried various interest rates, depending upon market conditions and the prevailing rate of interest when the loans were negotiated. The formal loan documents pertaining to these loans were executed in jurisdictions outside of the State of Maryland and were administered by personnel at Xerox's headquarters in Connecticut. For the years 1972, 1973 and 1974, the foreign subsidiaries had long-term debts outstanding in the regular commercial market of $205,617,000, $258,738,000, and $370,384,000, respectively. Indebtedness from Xerox's foreign subsidiaries to Xerox was $29,085,084, $59,324,565 and $77,669,226 at the end of tax years 1972, 1973 and 1974, respectively.

The Comptroller conducted audits of Xerox's Maryland corporate income tax returns for 1972, 1973 and 1974. Xerox's subtraction of the interest and royalty income was disallowed, and a formal assessment of $102,559 was issued in 1977. In computing the amount of tax owed by Xerox, the Comptroller modified the apportionment formula by including net interest and royalty income in the denominator of the sales factor and the net book value of Xerox's copyrights and patents in the denominator of the property factor. Xerox appealed the assessment to the Maryland Tax Court.

*   *   *

[The Maryland Tax Court sustained the assessment; that decision was affirmed by the Circuit Court for Baltimore County, which held that Mobil Oil Corp. v. Commissioner of Taxes (p. 610, supra) was controlling and required affirmance of the Tax Court's decision.]

As it did below, Xerox advances three major arguments. First, that Art. 81, §§ 280A(c)(4) and 316(c), prohibit Maryland taxation of any part of the interest and royalty income.* Second, that Maryland's taxation of the interest and royalty income offends both the federal and state constitutions. Third, that even if Maryland has the constitutional and statutory authority to tax the interest and royalty income, the formula used to determine Xerox's Maryland tax liability was constitutionally invalid.

Xerox concedes that it operates a "unitary" business in the United States and its territories, and that Maryland properly could tax a portion of the income derived from that business. Xerox contends, however, that the royalty and interest income was derived from sources totally separate and distinct from its copier business and other active business operations in which it was engaged; that the income was thus not a part of the unitary business which it conducted in part in Maryland; and that such income, therefore, was properly allocable outside of the State for tax purposes. Xerox further contends that there was a complete absence of the requisite interdependence among

---

* [The court's discussion of § 280(c)(4) has been omitted. That was a provision of the statute which had caused a good deal of litigation and has since been repealed (see the court's opinion note 1), under which interest income was excluded from the measure of the tax unless it constituted "interest earned in the conduct of a business" or in certain specified types of transactions. Xerox's contention based on § 280(A)(c)(4) was rejected by the court.]

its copier activities and royalty and interest income-generating activities. The absence of an underlying unitary business, Xerox argues, means that separate accounting rather than apportionment is mandated by § 316(c). The Comptroller suggests that the identity of the payor corporations is irrelevant to the question whether separate accounting is proper under § 316(c). The fact that Xerox conducted a unitary copier business, a part of which it conducted in Maryland, is sufficient, he urges, to preclude the use of separate accounting under § 316(c).

* * *

Even if there is no statutory bar to Maryland taxation of the interest and royalty income, Xerox contends that the due process and commerce clauses prohibit taxation of this income. It argues that the federal constitution requires a direct nexus between the income to be taxes and the taxing state, a nexus that is missing in this case. The Comptroller denies that a direct nexus is required, and submits that under traditional notions of due process there is no constitutional impediment to Maryland taxation of the interest and royalty income. In the alternative, the Comptroller argues that Xerox failed to demonstrate that it did not form a unitary business with its foreign, subsidiaries, and therefore the interest and royalty income is taxable under the Supreme Court's decision in Mobil Oil Corp. v. Commissioner of Taxes, supra.

The apportionment formula applied by the Comptroller is also attacked by Xerox on the ground that by failing to apportion its income in a rational manner, the Comptroller acted unconstitutionally. The Comptroller characterizes the use of the modified apportionment formula as fair and reasonable, and rejects each of the alternative formulas advanced by Xerox.

* * *

B. Xerox subtracted the royalty and interest income from its Maryland net taxable income on the theory that the income should be separately accounted for and allocated entirely to a specific foreign taxing jurisdiction or jurisdictions.[2] Under § 316(c), however, separate accounting is not permitted when a corporation is engaged in a unitary business.[3] Once Xerox conceded that it operated a unitary business within and without the State, it had the burden of proving by clear and cogent evidence that the interest and royalty income was unrelated to its unitary business operations. See W.R. Grace & Co. v. Commissioner of Revenue, 1979 Mass.Adv.Sh.1927, 393 N.E.2d 330 (1979); Commonwealth v. Emhart Corp., 443 Pa. 397, 278 A.2d 916, appeal dismissed, 404 U.S. 981, 92 S.Ct. 451, 30 L.Ed.2d 364 (1971).

2. For a discussion of the various methods of state taxation of income from intangibles, see Dexter, Taxation of Income from Intangibles of Multistate—Multinational Corporations, 29 Vand.L.Rev. 401 (1976).

3. If a business is allowed to separately account for all or a portion of its "business income" under § 316(c), then it may allocate that income in its entirety to a specific taxing jurisdiction or jurisdictions. No portion of a corporation's income allocated in this manner would be taxed by Maryland, unless, of course, the income was allocated to this State.

Numerous definitions of what constitutes a unitary business have been proposed. See Keesling & Warren, The Unitary Concept In the Allocation of Income, 12 Hastings L.J. 42 (1960); Rudolph, State Taxation of Interstate Business: The Unitary Business Concept and Affiliated Corporate Groups, 25 Tax L.Rev. 171 (1970). In Butler Bros. v. McColgan, 17 Cal.2d 664, 678, 111 P.2d 334, 341 (1941), aff'd, 315 U.S. 501, 62 S.Ct. 701, 86 L.Ed. 991 (1942), the Supreme Court of California focused on the presence of the following circumstances: "(1) unity of ownership; (2) unity of operation as evidenced by central purchasing, advertising, accounting and management divisions; and (3) unity of use in its centralized executive force and general system of operation." Another commonly cited definition is whether one business enterprise is dependent upon or contributory to the other. G. Altman & F. Keesling, Allocation of Income In State Taxation 101 (2d ed. 1950). In Great Lakes Pipe Line Co. v. Commissioner of Taxation, 272 Minn. 403, 138 N.W.2d 612 (1965), appeal dismissed, 384 U.S. 718, 86 S.Ct. 1886, 16 L.Ed.2d 881 (1966), the Supreme Court of Minnesota stated that "[W]hether a number of business operations having common ownership constitute a single or unitary business or several separate businesses for tax purposes depends upon whether they are of mutual benefit of one another and on whether each operation is dependent on or contributory to others." Id. at 408, 138 N.W.2d at 616.

In the present case, separate corporate entities are not involved. Xerox's copier operations and the activities that produced the royalty and interest income were conducted by a single corporation; there was unity of ownership and management. In addition, there is no suggestion that a separate corporate division, with its own officers, staff, payroll and accounting system, was in charge of the royalty and interest income-producing activities.

Xerox has attempted to meet its burden of proof by pointing to the following facts: (1) none of the licensing or loan agreements was entered into in Maryland; (2) none of the intangible assets giving rise to the royalty income was acquired or developed in Maryland, and documents evidencing ownership of these intangible assets were kept in Connecticut or New York; (3) the licensing and loan agreements were administered in Connecticut and New York. Xerox also suggests that because its copier operations generated working capital in an amount greater than its actual "general business needs" for such capital, the income in question was "not used to meet Xerox's working capital needs in its active operations." Finally, it is contended that the requisite economic interdependence among the relevant income-producing activities is lacking in this case.

In determining whether the copier operations and the activities that led to the receipt of the royalty and interest income were dependent on or contributory to each other, we must examine the nature of these business activities. Xerox's copier operations involved the manufacture, sale, rental and maintenance of copier equipment. The royalty income came from licensing agreements under which Xerox received fees for permitting the use of its trademarks, patents, copyrights and business know-how. A yearly average of approximately 90% of the royalty income was paid by foreign subsidiaries for the use of Xerox's name. Certainly, a portion of the market value of Xerox's name was attributable to active copier operations carried on in this State. Manifestly, at least some of the patents, copyrights and know-how were used in Xerox's domestic operations as well as being licensed to subsidiaries, affiliates, and nonaffiliated corporations.[4] Xerox has not shown that the capital used to develop the intangible assets did not emanate, at least in part, from its copier operations, nor has it demonstrated that the royalty income was not considered a part of working capital. Finally, the intangibles have been characterized by Xerox as "assets," and therefore improved Xerox's ability to obtain any necessary loans to be used in connection with its copier business. See generally, Household Finance v. Tax Comm., 212 Md. 80, 128 A.2d 640 (1957); Commonwealth v. Emhart Corp., supra, 443 Pa. at 404–405, 278 A.2d at 919.

The interest income was produced by substantial loans made to foreign subsidiaries. The record shows that Xerox's primary business, and in all probability primary source of income, was the manufacture, sale, rental and maintenance of copier equipment. It would appear, therefore, that at least a portion of the capital employed in making the loans, which totaled $77,669,226 in 1974, came from funds generated by Xerox's copier business. Moreover, loans were made when the foreign subsidiaries were unable to borrow in the regular commercial market. The continued vitality of the foreign subsidiaries was of obvious importance to Xerox, which had substantial stock interests in these corporations and received large royalty payments from them.

Although a more precise and properly focused record may have been desirable in this case, we conclude that Xerox has failed to meet its burden of proving that the royalty and interest income was produced by activities separate and distinct from the unitary business conducted in part in Maryland. * * * apportionment rather than separate accounting was proper under § 316(c).

C. Section 316(c) provides for taxation of "so much of the business income of the corporation as is derived from or reasonably attributable to the trade or business of the corporation carried on within this State. * * *" Xerox argues that the phrases "derived from" and "reasonably attributable to" reveal that the Legislature, in enacting § 316(c), intended to adopt a standard of taxation more restrictive than that required by the Supreme Court decisions concerning the due process and commerce clauses of the federal constitution. We find nothing in the case law or the legislative history of § 316(c) that supports Xerox's position. We agree with the lower court's conclusion that § 316(c)

---

4. For an extensive discussion of the history and operations of Xerox Corporation, see Van Dyk Research Corp. v. Xerox Corp., 478 F.Supp. 1268 (D.N.J.1979), aff'd. 631 F.2d 251 (3rd Cir.1980).

prescribes taxation of so much of a corporation's net income as is constitutionally permissible.

IV. In challenging Maryland's authority to tax an apportioned amount of its interest and royalty income, Xerox relies on the due process and commerce clauses of the federal constitution. [The court thereupon discussed Mobil Oil Corp. v. Commissioner of Taxes, p. 610, supra]. * * *

Xerox argues that this Court, as the Supreme Court did in *Mobil Oil*, should focus its due process inquiry on whether Xerox formed a unitary business with the payors of the royalty and interest income. The Supreme Court's focus in *Mobil Oil*, however, was necessitated by the fact that *dividend* income was involved. * * *

Dividend income is not involved in the present case. The appropriate due process inquiry here centers around the relationship between the activities that produced the royalty and interest income and Xerox's business activities in Maryland rather than on the relationship between Xerox and the payor corporations. This was the approach taken by the Supreme Court in Exxon Corp. v. Wisconsin Department of Revenue, 447 U.S. 207, 100 S.Ct. 2109, 65 L.Ed.2d 66 (1980), decided some three months after Mobil Oil, supra. Exxon, a vertically integrated petroleum corporation, argued that the separate functional accounting practiced for its marketing, exploration and production, and refining activities should have been respected by a State seeking to tax an apportioned amount of its total net income. The only activities conducted by Exxon in the taxing State were related to its marketing operations. The marketing operations were performed by a department that had its own management, was treated as a separate investment center, and competed with other departments for investment funds. Exxon's argument that Wisconsin could tax an apportioned amount of income derived from its marketing operations within and without the state, but could not reach any income derived from its refining or exploration and production activities, was rejected by the Court. After finding that the requisite due process nexus had been established, it said: "In order to exclude certain income from the apportionment formula, the company must prove that 'the income was earned in the course of activities unrelated to the sale of petroleum products in that state.' * * * The court looks to the 'underlying economic realities of a unitary business,' and the income must derive from 'unrelated business activity' which constitutes a 'discrete business enterprise.' " Id. at 223–24, 100 S.Ct. at 2120 (citations omitted) (quoting from Mobil Oil Corp. v. Commissioner of Taxes, supra, 445 U.S. at 439, 441, 442, 439, 100 S.Ct. at 1232, 1233, 1234, 1232). Finding that Exxon was a unitary business, the Court held that Exxon had failed to meet its burden of proof.

The first of the two parts of the due process test—the existence of a "minimal connection" or "nexus"—concerns a State's jurisdiction to tax a business's income. The second part of the test—whether there is a rational relationship between the taxing State and the intrastate values of the tax-taxpayer's enterprise—deals with constitutional limits on the application of a particular apportionment formula. Xerox does not dispute that it availed itself of the substantial privilege of doing business in Maryland. Xerox maintained several offices in this State, and its representatives sold, rented and maintained copier equipment in Maryland. The total volume of business done by Xerox in Maryland is not revealed by the record, but the nexus between Xerox and this State was clearly sufficient for imposition of an income tax. The existence of the requisite nexus means that Xerox, in order to exclude the interest and royalty income from taxation in this State, must prove that the income was derived from unrelated business activity that constitute a discrete business enterprise. Exxon Corp. v. Wisconsin Department of Revenue, supra, 447 U.S. at 224, 100 S.Ct. at 2120; Mobil Oil Corp. v. Commissioner of Taxes, supra, 445 U.S. at 439, 100 S.Ct. at 1232. We have already held that Xerox's copier activities and the activities that produced the royalty and interest income were part of a unitary business enterprise. Xerox therefore failed to meet its burden of proof.

B. Xerox argues that even if the royalty and interest income was subject to apportionment, certain modifications of the standard three-factor formula used by the Comptroller were constitutionally required. While modification of the three-factor formula is within the Comptroller's discretion under § 316(c), we cannot agree that modification was required. Once the first part of the due process test has been satisfied, the taxpayer must prove that there is no rational relationship between the portion of its income attributed to the State through application of an apportionment formula and the value of the business it conducted within the taxing State. Exxon Corp. v. Wisconsin Department of Revenue, 447 U.S. at 219–20, 100 S.Ct. at 2118; Mobil Oil Corp. v. Commissioner of Taxes, 445 U.S. at 437, 100 S.Ct. at 1231. * * * Xerox has produced no evidence regarding the value of the business it transacted within the State. We cannot say, therefore, that the factors of 2.160, 2.028, and 1.905, which were used to apportion Xerox's net income to this State for the tax years 1972, 1973, and 1974, respectively led to a "grossly distorted result" or that the assessment were [sic] "all out of appropriate proportion" to the business Xerox transacted in this State.

C. A commerce clause challenge to state taxation of income earned by a business in interstate commerce is to be evaluated by examining: "[T]he practical effect of a challenged tax to determine whether it 'is applied to an activity with a substantial nexus with the taxing State, is fairly apportioned, does not discriminate against interstate commerce, and is fairly related to the services provided by the State.'" Mobil Oil Corp. v. Commissioner of Taxes, supra, 445 U.S. at 443, 100 S.Ct. at 1234 (quoting from Complete Auto Transit, Inc. v. Brady, 430 U.S. 274, 279, 97 S.Ct. 1076, 1079, 51 L.Ed.2d 326 (1977). Xerox has alleged that Maryland taxation of the royalty and interest income violated the commerce clause. However, it has not articulated a commerce clause argument separate and distinct from its due process argument. Presumably, it is the "nexus with the taxing State" that Xerox believes is lacking in this case. We have already held, however, that a sufficient nexus was present for purposes of the due process clause, and no reasons appear to require a different result under the commerce clause.

As Maryland taxation of Xerox's royalty and interest income was proper under the relevant statutory and constitutional standards, the Comptroller's assessment of the additional tax liability was not in error. Judgment affirmed: costs to be paid by the appellant.

Notes and Problems

A. *Allocation of Royalties and Other Income From Similar Intangibles.* Royalties and other income from patents, copyrights, trade names, and similar intangibles are specifically allocated in some States to the owner's commercial domicile, under the *mobilia sequuntur personam* principle. Commonwealth v. Radio Corp. of America, 299 Ky. 44, 184 S.W.2d 250, 252 (1944); Rainier Brewing Co. v. McColgan, 94 Cal.App.2d 118, 210 P.2d 233 (1949), decided under California statute before enactment of UDITPA.

For a series of pre-UDITPA cases in California rejecting the taxpayer's contentions that income from patent licenses and copyrights on books, motion pictures, and the like should be allocated to the taxpayer's commercial domicile, see Appeal of Marcus Lesoine, Inc., Cal. SBE, July 7, 1942, CCH ¶ 12–430.15, P–H ¶ 13,006; Appeal of Houghton Mifflin Co., Cal. SBE, March 28, 1946, CCH 12–430.15, P–H ¶ 13,060; Appeal of International Business Machines, Inc., Cal. SBE, Oct. 7, 1954, CCH ¶ 12–430.15, P–H ¶ 13,143. The cases are discussed in J. Hellerstein, State Taxation I, Corporate Income and Franchise Taxes ¶ 9.9[2] (1983).

B. *Allocation to the State of Use by the Licensee.* A number of States specifically allocate royalties and other payments for the use of patents, copyrights, trademarks, and similar intangibles to the State in which, and to the extent that, the licensee uses the intangible. See 1 Willis Comm. Rep. 209; Hartman, "State Taxation of Corporate Income from a Multistate Business," 13 Vand.L.Rev. 21, 60 (1959); UDITPA § 8.

C. *Apportionment of Income From Patents, Licenses, and Similar Intangibles.* The courts of some States have upheld the apportionment of income from intangibles where "a non-domiciled taxpayer has extended his activities" to the State. The Mississippi Supreme Court applied that view in a case involving a New Jersey corporation which leased patented box-making machines and granted the lessee a license to manufacture its patented boxes. The lessees paid an initial fixed rental and a percentage of the gross of the boxes manufactured. Mississippi imposed on non-residents a tax on their net income from, inter alia, property or business carried on in the State "from sources within the State." The statute defined as income from sources within the State "rentals or royalties from property or any interest in property within the State." The taxpayer's income was apportioned to Mississippi by a single-factor gross receipts ratio; there were included in the Mississippi numerator the royalties received from the Mississippi lessees of the box-making machines and the patents.

The taxpayer challenged the assessment on the ground, among others, that Mississippi was seeking to tax an intangible interest in the form of patent rights, which was taxable only by the State of New Jersey, as the corporation's commercial domicile. The Supreme Court of Mississippi rejected this contention, declaring that it is the income from the property, and not the property itself, that was taxed and that, in any event, there is "no constitutional objection to the taxation of intangible interest by other States 'provided the taxpayer has extended his activities to other States and has availed himself of the protection of the laws of that other State.'" Stone v. Stapling Machines Co., 221 Miss. 555, 73 So.2d 123 (1954), appeal dismissed 348 U.S. 907, 75 S.Ct. 296 (1955). See also Corning Glass Works v. Department of Revenue, Ky. CCH ¶ 201–402, P–H ¶ 13,110 (Ky.Bd. of Tax Appeals 1976), in which the Board sustained the inclusion of foreign royalties received by a multinational glass products manufacturer (as well as interest and capital gains) as apportionable business income, because they were integral parts of the corporation's trade or business; and Commonwealth v. Minnesota Mining and Mfg. Co., 402 Pa. 612, 168 A.2d 560 (1961).

D. *The MTC UDITPA Regulations.*

Patent and copyright royalties. Patent and copyright royalties are business income where the patent or copyright with respect to which the royalties were received arises out of or was created in the regular course of the taxpayer's trade or business operations or where the purpose for acquiring and holding the patent or copyright is related to or incidental to such trade or business operations.

Example (i): The taxpayer is engaged in the multistate business of manufacturing and selling industrial chemicals. In connection with that business the taxpayer obtained patents on certain of its products. The taxpayer licensed the production of the chemicals in foreign countries, in return for which the taxpayer receives royalties. The royalties received by the taxpayer are business income.

Example (ii): The taxpayer is engaged in the music publishing business and holds copyrights on numerous songs. The taxpayer acquires the assets of a smaller publishing company, including music copyrights. These acquired copyrights are thereafter used by the taxpayer in its business. Any royalties received on these copyrights are business income.

Example (iii): Same as example (ii), except that the acquired company also held the patent on a type of phonograph needle. The taxpayer does not manufacture or sell phonographs or phonograph equipment. Any royalties received on the patent would be nonbusiness income. [MTC Reg. IV.1(c)(5), CCH All States Guide ¶ 352, P–H All States Tax Guide ¶ 633.]

The MTC regulations were followed by the Montana Supreme Court in holding that royalties derived from patents and copyrights developed by a mining company's research department constituted business income and were apportionable. The research and development had been undertaken for use in the company's own plant and mines. The court concluded that "[t]his income is derived from sources that are an integral part of * * * [the taxpayer's] business." Montana Dept. of Revenue v. American Refining & Smelting Co. (ASARCO), 173 Mont. 316, 567 P.2d 901 (1977), appeal dismissed for want of jurisdiction, 434 U.S. 1042, 98 S.Ct. 884 (1978).

SECTION 14. THE MULTISTATE TAX COMPACT

The Multistate Tax Compact was developed in 1967 under the aegis of the Council of State Governments, in part at least to offset the severe criticism levelled by the Willis Committee against the widespread diversity in State apportionment and allocation methods.[123] It became effective in 1967 on adoption by seven States; there are now 18 member States (and the District of Columbia), concentrated largely in the Midwest, the West, and the South, and in addition there are 10 associate member States.[124] In furtherance of the Compact's stated purpose to "promote uniformity or compatibility in significant components of tax systems," UDITPA is incorporated in the Compact.[125] The Multistate Tax Commission (MTC), composed of one member from each party State, is the governing and administering agency of the Compact. It is empowered to adopt uniform regulations relating to income, capital stock, gross receipts and sales or use taxes, if two or more party States have uniform or similar provisions; these regulations are merely advisory and not binding on any State, unless it adopts them itself. The MTC is also authorized to conduct joint audits on behalf of member States requesting them, and to issue subpoenas and seek their judicial enforcement, in order to enable the Commission to examine taxpayers' books, records and other documents.[126]

When the MTC set up a Joint Audit Program and sought to conduct such audits, it was met by a class action brought in 1972 by United States Steel Corporation and eleven other large corporations, in the United States District Court for the Southern District of New York, for a declaratory judgment to declare the Compact unconstitutional, and for an injunction against actions by the MTC under the Compact. The plaintiffs contended that the Compact violated the Compact Clause

123. The Compact is printed in CCH All States Guide ¶ 351, P–H All States Guide ¶ 701, and in 29 Vand.L.Rev. 470 et seq. (1976).

124. For the list of Compact members and associate members, see P–H All States Guide ¶ 564. Associate members are not bound by the terms of the Compact, have no voting powers, and are under no obligation to contribute to the financial support of the work of the MTC. Associate members have, however, participated in the activities carried out under the Compact and some have contributed financial support. See Annual Reports of the MTC.

125. Multistate Tax Compact, Arts. I and IV; see note 123 supra. Despite the incorporation of UDITPA in haec verba in the Compact, some of the Compact member States have enacted variations, at some points, from the provisions of UDITPA. See, e.g., the variations with respect to the throwback rule, p. 485 supra, and the double weighting of the sales factor by some States, Table 1, Col. C and notes thereto, p. 506 supra.

126. Multistate Tax Compact, Art. VI; see note 123 supra.

of the Federal Constitution (Art. I, § 10), which provides that no State shall, without consent of Congress, enter into any agreement or compact with another State or with a foreign power. They also challenged the Joint Audit Program and the Compact under the Commerce Clause, and contended, inter alia, that multistate taxpayers are denied equal protection and due process of law in the conduct of joint audits, in that they are discriminated against vis-á-vis intrastate taxpayers, because the Commission's tax auditors are selected without reference to State civil service laws, and that multistate taxpayers are denied the benefit of the confidentiality provision of State tax laws. The Supreme Court rejected all these contentions and upheld the constitutionality of the Compact. United States Steel Corp. v. Multistate Tax Com'n, 434 U.S. 452, 98 S.Ct. 799 (1978). It resolved the Compact issued by construing the Compact Clause, in accordance with the principle established by the Supreme Court in a dictum in 1893, that Congressional consent is required for the validity of a compact or agreement between States only if it "is directed to the formation of any combination tending to the increase of political power in the States, which may encroach upon or interfere with the just supremacy of the United States." [127] The Court found no such encroachment, and it dismissed the Commerce, Due Process, and Equal Protection Clause arguments as being without merit. Comments on the case appear in 64 A.B.A.J. 596 (1978) and 48 J.Tax. 368 (1978).

ASSIGNMENT

A. The following pages contain a set of facts and figures from which you are asked to prepare a franchise or corporate income tax (or other business tax) return for last year (the calendar year) for Prime Steel Co. (Prime) for the State which you have selected for study. The return should be prepared on the official forms, if they are available, as a separate return for Prime. If your State does not have a corporate tax measured by net income, please do the problem by reference to a State that does.

The return should be accompanied by a memorandum citing the article of any regulations relating to each item filled in on the return. This should be done by referring to each schedule and line on the return by its letter or number, followed by the appropriate article number of the regulations. If no regulations have been issued in your State (here called "the Home State"), or if there are no applicable regulations, reference should be made to the instructions on the return form. Any explanation which you desire to make may be added. If you find no covering regulation or instruction, that fact should be noted. In all cases in which an election is permitted, the particular method of reporting adopted by you should be justified in the memoran-

[127]. Virginia v. Tennessee, 148 U.S.
503, 519, 13 S.Ct. 728 (1893).

dum. The report may be incomplete, since not all the relevant data for all States have been supplied.

Prime, a Delaware corporation which manufactures steel products, has its plant, its executive offices, and its head sales office in the Home State. It has a regional sales office in State A, where it has a warehouse, an inventory of goods, and employees. The Home State and State A offices send salesmen to solicit business in neighboring States in which Prime is not qualified to do business. The orders received by such salesmen are forwarded for acceptance to the particular office to which the salesman is attached; the goods are shipped from the State in which the order is accepted directly to the customer. Prime is qualified to do business only in the Home State and State A (other than Delaware, in which it does no business).

Prime owns patents on a crane it developed for moving steel in its mill. It manufactured several of these cranes, which it rents out to other steel mills; it also services the rented cranes by sending its own service men to the customers' plants.

Prime owns all the capital stock of Wilson Lumber Company ("Lumber"), a non-Home State company, whose mill and lumber yard are located in a State other than the Home State. Lumber has a sales office in the Home State. It sells no products to Prime, and buys no products from Prime. Lumber's legal, tax, and accounting work are done for it by Prime's house counsel and accountants, for which Prime charges Lumber fair, arm's length amounts. Auditing for Lumber is done by Prime's auditors at reasonable rates. Lumber's employees are included in a common pension plan for both Prime and Lumber; the plan is administered by Prime.

The Board of Directors of Lumber is made up of two officers of Prime and three of the principal officers of Lumber. Lumber makes monthly written reports of its operations to Prime. Every six months the officers of Lumber come to the offices of Prime in the Home State, where Lumber's budget is reviewed with the officers of Prime. The practice has been for some years for the budget to be submitted for approval to the Board of Directors of Prime. The day-by-day operations of Lumber are handled by its own officers and employees. Unusual matters, such as labor negotiations, new products, advertising programs, and the like are discussed and cleared with Prime's officers. The President of Prime visits the lumber mill three or four times a year. Any substantial additions to, or expansion in, the plant or equipment of Lumber would, in the normal course, be reviewed by the Board of Directors of Prime in connection with its approval of the proposed budget.

The major source of Lumber's capital was Prime, which invested over the years $1,000,000 in the common stock of Lumber. In addition, there is an intercompany account between the companies, which typically has a balance owing to Prime of between $300,000 to $400,000. Lumber pays Prime the going bank rate of interest on this account.

The facts reveal the following averages for the last taxable and base year of Prime. All figures given for assets refer to average fair market value for the taxable and base year.

ASSETS

Cash

Home State	$ 100,000	
State A	25,000	$ 125,000

Inventory

Materials, goods in process and completed goods in Home State	$ 600,000	
Goods in warehouse in State A	150,000	$ 750,000

Plant and Equipment

Real Property		
Home State	500,000	
Personal Property		
Home State	1,000,000	
State A	50,000	
Cranes (rental)		
Home State	50,000	
States B and C	40,000	$1,640,000

Furniture, Fixtures, Trucks and Supplies

Home State	40,000	
State A	20,000	60,000

Notes and Accounts receivable (after reserve for bad debts)

Accounts receivable		
Home State sales	150,000	
State A sales	60,000	210,000
Open Account		
Lumber		300,000
Promissory notes of trade customers *		50,000
Stocks of Subsidiaries		
Lumber		$1,000,000
Investments **		

	Home State apportionment percentage	
Stocks		
A Corp	0	$100,000
B Corp	20	150,000
C Corp	100	25,000
D Corp	80	100,000
Bonds		
Home State Government		100,000
U.S. Government		10,000
E Corp	35	100,000

F Corp	65	$100,000	
G Corp	100	100,000	$ 785,000
		Total Assets	$4,920,000

* These are simple negotiable notes payable in less than 1 year.

** The stocks and bonds are of corporations listed on a public exchange. Prime's stock interest is a small percentage in each company.

LIABILITIES, CAPITAL, AND SURPLUS

Liabilities

Accounts Payable			$ 400,000
Bonds and Notes Payable			
Bank loan, with maturity less than 1 year		$ 250,000	
Bonds, with maturity more than 1 year		250,000	$ 500,000
Accrued Expenses			25,000
Other Liabilities			
Accrued interest on bank loan		4,000	
Accrued interest on bonds		5,000	9,000
	Total Liabilities		$ 934,000

Capital

Common Stock—30,000 shares no par value; stated value	3,000,000

Surplus

Earned Surplus	986,000
Total Liabilities and Capital	$4,920,000

GROSS INCOME

Gross Sales, less Returns and Allowances	$3,500,000	
Cost of Goods	2,400,000	
Gross Profits from Sales:		$1,100,000
Interest		
Bank accounts in Home State	5,000	
Lumber	15,000	
Promissory notes (trade customers)	2,000	
Bonds		
Home State	3,000	
U.S. Government	400	

E Corp.		$ 5,000	
F Corp.		5,000	
G Corp.		5,000	$ 40,400

Income from Cranes

	Equipment Rental	Service Income	
Home State	$10,000	$ 1,000	
States B and C	8,000	800	$ 19,800

Dividends

Lumber		$ 100,000	
A Corp.		5,000	
B Corp.		10,000	
C Corp.		5,000	
D Corp.		15,000	$ 135,000

Miscellaneous profit on sale of obsolete machinery located in Home State		10,000
Total Gross Income		$1,305,200

EXPENSES

Compensation of General Executive Officers		$ 150,000
Other Salaries and Wages		450,000
Interest		
Bank loan	$ 10,000	
Bonds ($2,500 to stockholders owning over 5% of stock)	12,500	22,500
Rent on real property located in State A		25,000
Depreciation, General Expenses and Deductible Taxes		250,000
Total Expenses		$ 897,500

ANALYSIS OF RECEIPTS FROM SALES OF GOODS

Receipts classified by state of destination of the goods

Home State	$2,000,000
State A	500,000
Other States	1,000,000

Receipts classified by location of goods at date of receipt of or appropriation to orders.

Home State plant	$2,500,000
State A warehouse	1,000,000

Receipts classified by reference to the office or branch from which the salesmen who negotiated or effected the sales were sent out and to which the salesmen are attached as well as the state in which the salesmen responsible for the sales performed the services relating thereto.

Home State	$2,500,000
State A	1,000,000

ANALYSIS OF SALARIES AND WAGES

Salaries of General Executive Officers:		$ 150,000
Home State	$120,000	
State A	30,000	
All Other Salaries and Wages:		
Home State	360,000	
State A	90,000	450,000

B. If the Home State corporate income taxes of Prime and Lumber were computed on the basis of a combined report, they would be reduced. That is because Prime is very profitable, and Lumber is losing money.

Analyze the statute, regulations and decisions of your State and prepare a memorandum dealing with the question as to whether the taxpayers would succeed in reporting their income to the Home State on a combined basis.

Chapter 10

SALES TAXATION

A. INTRODUCTION

SECTION 1. THE CLASSIFICATION OF LEVIES AS SALES TAXES

The term "sales tax" embraces a large variety of levies in vogue in this country. It includes "retail sales tax," "compensatory use tax," "gross receipts or turnover tax," "manufacturer's excise tax," and "gross income tax."

The compass of the term adopted in this work is the meaning given in R. Haig and C. Shoup's authoritative work, The Sales Tax in the American States (1934), which is that "sales tax" as used "refers to any tax which includes within its scope all business sales of tangible personal property at either the retailing, wholesaling, or manufacturing stage, with the exceptions noted in the taxing law."

Another writer defines a sales tax as being one as to which "the amount of tax payable is produced by a constant rate applied to the volume or value of commodities or services transferred or exchanged." N. Jacoby, Retail Sales Taxation 8 (1938).

Haig and Shoup * classify sales taxes as:

(a) *Retail Sales Tax,* which is imposed only on sales of tangible personal property at retail or for use or consumption. This tax also includes sales of utility services and levies on admissions.

(b) *General Sales Tax,* which reaches sales of tangible personal property both at retail and for resale, and also the acts of extracting natural resources and of manufacturing.

(c) *Gross Receipts Tax,* which has the essential elements of the general sales tax and in addition is levied upon sales of personal and professional services, and in some cases sales of intangibles.

* The excerpts from Haig and Shoup's work are reprinted with the permission of Columbia University Press.

(d) *Gross Income Taxes,* which include (a), (b), and (c), above, and in addition receipts from non-business activities such as rents, interest, salaries. [Pp. 3, 4.]

See also the definitions of a sales tax given in J. Due & J. Mikesell, Sales Taxation, ch. 1 (1983).

In W. Schultz & C. Lowell Harriss, American Public Finance (7th ed. 1959), the authors state:

> Economists distinguish five basic types of general sales tax: (1) retail sales tax; (2) single-stage excise on sales by manufacturers or wholesalers; (3) multiple-stage "gross sales" or "turnover" tax, applying to all sales by manufacturers, wholesalers, and retailers; (4) "gross income" tax, applying not only to sales of tangible commodities but also to gross income from services; finally (5) the tax on "value added" may be considered a general consumption, as well as a general business, tax. [P. 344].

There are numerous selective sales taxes, which are taxes on a specific commodity or service, in vogue in this country. Illustrations of selective sales taxes of great fiscal importance in State and local taxation are levies on tobacco and tobacco products, gasoline, and alcoholic beverages.

SECTION 2.   THE GROWING FISCAL IMPORTANCE OF STATE AND LOCAL SALES TAXES

The increasing reliance of the States on sales taxes is one of the most significant developments in State finances during recent times. Thus, in 1930 only two States imposed sales taxes covering retail sales generally; the revenues from these levies were a comparatively minor factor in the total revenue collections of the American States.[1] Mississippi, which adopted a sales tax in 1930, was the first State to turn to sales taxation as a major source of revenues. In 1987, 45 States and the District of Columbia levied general sales and use taxes. For fiscal 1986, such general sales and use taxes produced $74.8 billion, or 32.8 percent of total State tax collections. See Tables 2 and 3, pp. 6–7 supra.

Municipalities and other local subdivisions of State governments have begun to rely more heavily than in the past on sales taxes to supplement the revenues from the property tax, their traditional principal source of revenue. See Chapter 1, §§ 5 and 6 supra. In 1984, cities collected $18 billion from general and selective sales taxes.[2] These levies were used in major cities, such as New York, New Orleans, and Chicago, and the District of Columbia.

1. Treasury Department, Division of Research and Statistics, Collection from Selected State Imposed Taxes (1930–1936), Tables A, B, and C.

2. ACIR, "Significant Features of Fiscal Federalism: 1984 Edition," Table 1, at 9; Table 31, at 47; Table 33.3, at 51; Table 62, at 94 (March 1985). The local tax figures include both general and selective sales taxes. They are not broken down, as are the State tax revenues.

The figures for sales tax collections for all local governmental subdivisions are set forth in Chapter 1, § 6 supra.

A significant trend in recent years has been the integration of local with State sales taxes. In several States this has taken the form of State collection of local sales taxes; this is being done in California, Illinois, Mississippi, and New Mexico. This trend toward integration could eliminate costly and duplicate compliance and administration costs, and reduce the growing taxpayer hostility to duplicate filings with State and local governments. In 1965, the State of New York took over the administration of the New York City sales tax; since the New York State and the City taxes exist side by side, this method of administration by the State is an obviously desirable move.

References. J. Due & J. Mikesell, Sales Taxation (1983); J. Hellerstein, "Significant Sales and Use Tax Developments During the Past Half Century," 39 Vand.L.Rev. 961 (1986); McCloud, "Sales Tax and Use Tax: Historical Developments and Differing Features," 22 Duquesne L.Rev. 823 (1984); An exhaustive study of sales and use taxes, including the nature and importance of these taxes, as well as constitutional questions involved, is found in the report of the Willis Subcommittee on State Taxation of Interstate Commerce of the House Committee on the Judiciary, State Taxation of Interstate Commerce, H.R.Rep. No. 565, 89th Cong., 1st Sess., Vol. 3, p. 603 (1965).

SECTION 3. DISTRIBUTION OF THE BURDEN OF A RETAIL SALES AND USE TAX

The retail sales and use tax has been widely criticized as a regressive levy bearing most heavily on those least able to pay. Thus, in a survey made by the Nevada Legislative Counsel Bureau, the conclusion was reached that in the case of a retail sales tax, with food exempt, "the lowest income group would experience the highest ratio of tax to income, 0.57 per cent. in the case of a one per cent. tax. Between this group and the $4,000–$5,000 level, the percentage of tax to income would decline gradually to about 0.34 per cent.; above the $5,000 level, the regression would be more rapid." Survey of Sales Taxes Applicable to Nevada 59 (Bull. No. 3, May, 1948).

For a similar conclusion, see Musgrave, "Distribution of Tax Burden Under Sales and Income Taxes," 32 Bull.Nat.Tax Ass'n 16 (1946). See also Report of The Temporary National Economic Committee, "Who Pays Taxes" (Monograph No. 3, 1941).

A contrary view was reached in a Connecticut survey:

> The consumer sales tax * * * can be shown to have a substantial element of progressivity in view of the greater benefit of exemptions to taxpayers of lesser consumption as compared with those of greater consumption * * * for example * * * 78 per cent of the expenditures of a family in the lowest disposable income group is excluded from taxation by the exemption of food, housing and medical care. The same exemptions exclude only 53 per cent of the taxable expenditures of a family in the $5,000 and up disposable income group. In other words, major sales tax exemptions reduce the potential tax

liability between 61 per cent and 78 per cent for those families having annual incomes (after Federal income tax) of less than $3,000, while the reduction in tax liability for families with $3,000 and more disposable income would run downward from 60 per cent. [Report of the Connecticut Tax Survey Committee 85 (1949).]

A study made by a research associate of the New Jersey State Chamber of Commerce concluded that "a retail sales tax with food exempt is substantially proportional in burden." McGrew, "Food Exemption and Incidence of Sales Tax," 2 Nat.Tax.J. 362 (1949). See also, Brabson, "Economic Aspects of State Sales and Use Taxes," 32 Bull. Nat.Tax Ass'n 148 (1947) for a similar conclusion. The problem is also discussed in "The Pennsylvania Tax Problem (1955)," Tax Inst.Conf. (Harrisburg 1955), 121 et seq. and Pa. Regional Round Table Conference, Princeton (Supp.1957). For later studies, see Due, "Sales Taxation and Consumer," 53 Am.Econ.Rev. 1078 (1963); Morgan, "Equity Considerations of Retail Sales Taxation," 1965 Nat.Tax Ass'n Procs. 278; Rostvold, "Distribution of Property, Retail Sales, and Personal Income Tax Burdens in California," 19 Nat.Tax J. 38 (1966); J. Pechman and B. Okner, Who Bears the Tax Burden (1974); Smeeding, "Are Sales Taxes Progressive?," Institute for Research on Poverty 545–79 (1979); D. Phares, Who Pays State and Local Taxes (1980); Due, "Tax Incidence, Indirect Taxes, and Transfers—A Comment," 39 Nat. Tax J. 539 (1986).

References. For general studies of the sales tax see, J. Due & J. Mikesell, Sales Taxation (1983); J. Due, Sales Taxation (1957); Due, "Role of Sales and Excise Taxation in Overall Tax Structure," 11 J. Finance 205 (1956). The Annual Proceedings of the National Tax Association are studded with highly useful discussions of many aspects of the problem by tax administrators, lawyers, and others. The National Tax Journal concerns itself particularly with the fiscal and economic aspects of taxation, including sales and use taxes. See, e.g., Morgan, "Reappraisal of Sales Taxation: Some Recent Arguments," 16 Nat.Tax J. 89 (1963); Hamovitch, "Sales Taxation: An Analysis of the Effects of Rate Increases in Two Contrasting Cases," 19 Nat.Tax J. 411 (1966); Fox & Campbell, "Stability of the State Sales Tax Income Elasticity," 37 Nat.Tax J. 201 (1984). There are extended analyses of the sales tax cases in Lockhart, "The Sales Tax in Interstate Commerce," 52 Harv.L. Rev. 617 (1939) and Kust & Sale, "Sales and Use Taxes: State Taxation of Interstate Sales," 46 Va.L.Rev. 1290 (1960).

B. RETAIL SALES TAXES

SECTION 1. TERRITORIAL RESTRICTIONS

Notes and Problems

A. In Matter of C.G. Gunther's Sons v. McGoldrick, 255 App.Div. 139, 5 N.Y.S.2d 303 (1st Dep't 1938), affirmed 279 N.Y. 148, 18 N.E.2d 12 (1938), a New York fur merchant frequently deferred delivery of furs that it sold during the warmer months until the customer requested delivery during the colder months. The legislation authorizing New York City to impose a sales tax forbade "the imposition of a tax on any transaction [originating and/or] * * * consummated outside of the territorial limits of [the] city." The New York City tax law at issue imposed a two percent tax upon the receipts from every retail sale of tangible personal property in the city, and it defined a sale as the transfer of title or possession or both or any agreement therefor. Relying on State personal property law, which provided that "property does not pass until goods have been delivered to the buyer or reached the place agreed upon," the court concluded that

> the transactions in question involving future delivery outside the city of New York were not taxable as they were not consummated until the merchandise was delivered to the petitioner's customers outside the territorial limits of the city, including merchandise delivered in interstate commerce to points outside the State of New York. [5 N.Y.S.2d at 305.]

The City of New York does not seek to tax sales of goods "consummated" by delivery of goods outside the city. It does, however, seek to tax sales negotiated outside the city but delivered into the city. Would such a levy have violated the then-prevailing State enabling act provision noted in the *Gunther* case, which forbids the city from imposing a tax on "any transaction originating" outside the territorial limits of the city?

B. In Bloomingdale Brothers v. Chu, 119 A.D.2d 41, 505 N.Y.S.2d 258 (3d Dept.1986), the court held that the State sales tax does not apply to out-of-state purchases of merchandise by non-residents delivered, at the request of the purchasers, to third persons in New York. The taxing statute, essentially the same provision that was at issue in the *Gunther*'s case, Note A supra, defined sale as "[a]ny transfer of title or possession or both * * * in any manner or by any means * * * for a consideration, or any agreement therefor." N.Y.Tax Law § 1101[b][5], P–H ¶ 22,510.85, CCH ¶ 97–353. The court declared that "an ordinary person reading this statute * * * would conclude that the actual 'sale' occurred not in New York but in the States where the non-residents purchased the goods." 505 N.Y.S.2d at 259. Id.

A dissenting opinion reasoned as follows:

> To an ordinary person, sales effected by acceptance of orders and payments for the merchandise at a non-resident vendor's out-of-State office might well be considered to have been consummated outside the jurisdiction of New York taxing authorities. Nevertheless, for more than 40 years, it has been the settled law of this State that such transactions are subject to sales tax here if they encompass ultimate physical delivery of the goods in New York, even by common carrier (see, McGoldrick v. A.H. Du Grenier, Inc., 309 U.S. 70, 77, 60 S.Ct. 404, 405, 84 L.Ed.2d 584), and even when delivery was F.O.B. the vendor's out-of-State factory * * *
>
> * * * [T]he Legislature has broadly defined "sale" for sales tax purposes with the clear intent (1) " 'to encompass most transactions involving the transfer or use of commodities in the business world' " and (2) to defeat tax avoidance devices and to cover transactions

essentially the same as others taxed as sales and which, therefore, should be taxed as a matter of economic justice.

Viewed in the light of these undisputably expansive legislative purposes in defining "sale", I have no difficulty in concluding that the sales under review here are taxable. Tax Law § 1101(b)(5) expressly imposes the sales tax on a "transfer of title or *possession* * * * for a consideration" (emphasis supplied). Certainly, the Tax Commission could reasonably infer on the basis of the stipulated facts of direct shipment from petitioner's out-of-State stores to its customers' designees in New York that those customers bought and paid for the delivery of the goods in New York as part of their transactions. Each such customer was a "purchaser" who furnished "consideration" for "transfer of * * * possession" in New York (Tax Law § 1101[b][5]). Thus, these transactions fall literally within the definitions of Tax Law § 1101. Why, in view of the broadly encompassing statutory language, it should make a difference that the ultimate recipients of the transfer of physical possession in New York are donees/consignees of the purchasers, eludes me. Tax Law § 1101(b)(5) does not expressly require that the transfer of possession in New York be made to the purchaser, and petitioner has not cited us to any statutory language or legislative history excluding a transfer of possession to a donee/ consignee of the purchaser as a taxable event. We have previously upheld imposition of the sales tax on the basis of delivery to the New York designee of the purchaser. The majority's strained distinction between a designee who is "some type of commercial agent for the purchaser" and a designee who is a donee of the purchaser, is one that is impossible to enforce administratively in the normal commercial context of these transactions. As a practical matter, the majority's decision will enable purchasers of merchandise at out-of-State stores for delivery in New York to avoid the sales tax by the simple expedient of directing delivery to a designee. [505 N.Y.S.2d at 260–61 (citations omitted).]

C. *Territorial Restrictions as Compared With Interstate Commerce Clause.* The City of Bluefield imposed a license tax on the "opening, establishing, operating or maintaining of stores" measured by the "gross proceeds of sales of such stores." Sales were made by a licensed store which were effected in some cases by delivery outside the city but within the State and in other cases outside the State. The court held that the city could include in the measure of the tax the proceeds of the out-of-city but within-the-state deliveries, but not the proceeds of the out-of-state deliveries. The latter were held to violate the Interstate Commerce Clause. Bluefield Produce & Provision Co. v. City of Bluefield, 120 W.Va. 111, 196 S.E. 568 (1938). See Chapter 6 supra, for the question as to whether this decision is in line with the Commerce Clause decisions of the United States Supreme Court.

Compare American Bridge Co. v. Smith, 352 Mo. 616, 179 S.W.2d 12, 157 A.L.R. 798 (1944), certiorari denied 323 U.S. 712, 65 S.Ct. 37 (1944), in which the court held that the Missouri sales tax was inapplicable to sales of structural steel products manufactured outside the State in response to orders solicited in the State, where the goods were shipped f.o.b. the destination in the State. Although the court declared that the tax could have been constitutionally imposed, it held that the provision exempting sales made "in commerce between this State and any other State" precluded imposition of the tax.

SECTION 2. DEFINITION OF SALE

(a) Sales as Distinguished from Services

DUN & BRADSTREET, INC. v. CITY OF NEW YORK

Court of Appeals of New York, 1937.
276 N.Y. 198, 11 N.E.2d 728.

HUBBS, J. This is an action by appellant for an injunction and declaratory judgment to determine whether it is taxable under the local law of the city imposing a sales tax on services. * * * [The city had moved to dismiss the complaint. The lower court denied the motion, but the Appellate Division reversed on the ground that no facts were shown warranting a declaratory judgment or injunctive relief.] The allegation of the complaint is that the business of appellant is that of rendering services in furnishing information as to the financial standing of persons engaged in business.

The complaints set forth a copy of the contract entered into between appellant and its subscribers, which provides that the subscriber employs the appellant to investigate and furnish reports up to a certain number for a certain sum, and one dollar and twenty-five cents for a report on each name over and above the number specified. It also provides that the information furnished "shall be held in strict confidence," and that appellant reserves the right to terminate the subscription at any time and to recall the printed volumes loaned to the subscriber. The complaint alleges that the appellant is a mercantile agency which furnishes to its subscribers information respecting the financial standing of persons engaged in business; that each subscriber is entitled to reference books published by the company, the title to which remains in appellant; that no charge is made for the use of such reference books separate and apart from the service charge and that such reference books cannot be obtained separate and apart from the services furnished to subscribers; also that the subscriber is warned by a printed notice contained in each reference book not to rely upon the ratings contained in the book as changes in ratings vary at an average of over 5,000 each day and, therefore, that in cases involving credit, the subscriber should consult the detailed reports in the possession of appellant.

Briefly stated, the complaint alleges that the company is engaged in furnishing confidential information to its subscribers as to the financial standing and credit of persons with whom the subscribers may intend to transact business or furnish credit. In the case of Eaton, Cole

& Burnham Co. v. Avery (83 N.Y. 31) this court stated that the business of the petitioner was so well known that it would take judicial notice of it. The court then described its business substantially as it is described in the complaint in this action.

An interesting discussion of the history and development of appellant's business is contained in the case of State v. Morgan (2 S.D. 32 at p. 52, 48 N.W. 314). The questions presented for determination briefly stated are, first, do the local laws here involved require the payment of a tax upon the amount paid by subscribers for the services rendered to them by appellant.*

* * *

Section 1 of the local law, as amended, provides that when used in this local law,

"(d) The word 'receipt' means the amount of the sale price of any property or the charge for any service specified in section 2 of this Local Law * * *;

"(e) The word 'sale' or 'selling' means any transfer of title or possession or both, exchange or barter, license to use or consume, conditional or otherwise, in any manner or by any means whatsoever for a consideration, or any agreement therefor, and may include the rendering of any service specified in section 2 of this Local Law."

The only service specified in section 2 is the service rendered by public utility companies therein specified. Section 11 grants to the Comptroller power to adopt rules and regulations for carrying out the local law.

Assuming to act under the authority vested in him by the local law, the Comptroller adopted and issued Article 95 of the Rules and Regulations, which reads in part:

"Included in the receipts upon which the tax is imposed are * * * receipts by persons engaged in the business of selling a personal service, such as a tax service, financial news service and trade service and other similar service supplemented by printed matter title to which remains in the vendor."

It is contended by respondents that appellant is liable for the tax under that rule. Prior to the adoption of Article 95 of the Rules, the Comptroller had adopted and issued Articles 45 and 51 of the Rules and Regulations which by their express language exclude appellant from the payment of the tax. The rules are in direct conflict. It thus appears that respondents have been in doubt as to whether appellant and others similarly situated are subject to the tax under the local law.

It is elementary that taxing statutes when of doubtful validity or effect must be construed in favor of the taxpayers. If the local law does not by its terms impose a tax upon appellant, the Comptroller cannot by the adoption of a rule or regulation impose such a tax. * * *

---

* [The second question in the case, decided in the appellant's favor, was whether a declaratory judgment action was a proper remedy.]

Section 2 imposes a tax on the sale of tangible personal property and upon services rendered by certain public utility companies. Section 1 defines the word "receipt" in part as "the charge for any service specified in section 2." It also defines the words "sale" and "selling" and then reads, "and may include the rendering of any service specified in section 2."

It is quite apparent that the local law was not intended to impose a tax on income from services rendered except by the public utility companies named. We conclude that the appellant is not liable for a tax upon the amount received for the services which it renders to its subscribers in New York City.

We are also of the opinion that it is not liable for a tax upon the sale price of tangible personal property under section 2. It is true that in rendering services to its subscribers, it delivers to them reference books, the title of which remains in appellant, but the subscribers are expressly forbidden to let any one else see or use such books and they are notified not to rely upon the ratings given in the books but in all cases when extending credit to consult the detailed reports in the possession of appellant. No charge is made to the subscribers for the use of the reference books separate and apart from the charge for services rendered and the books cannot be obtained in any other way. The information furnished to subscribers orally, in typewriting and in the reference books is confidential and personal in character. It is not and cannot be, under the subscription contracts, disclosed to the public. The information collected by appellant at great expense is secured to enable it to furnish to its subscribers detailed information to guide them in making sales and in extending credit. The information furnished is of value to the subscribers and for it they pay but not for the paper upon which the information is conveyed or for the reference books which are only guides to assist in the rendition of appellant's service. One does not think of a telephone company as a seller of books to its subscribers. It renders a service. To make that service efficient, it furnishes its subscribers with books containing a list of its subscribers with their call numbers. "The paper is a mere incident; the skilled service is that which is required." (Burgess Co. v. Ames, 359 Ill. 427, 429, 194 N.E. 565, 566; Adair Printing Co. v. Ames, 364 Ill. 342, 4 N.E.2d 481; State v. Morgan, supra.)

Certainly it cannot be successfully contended that the local law clearly and undoubtedly makes appellant subject to a tax. * * *

The following cases are relied upon by respondents: Matter of United Artists Corp. v. Taylor (273 N.Y. 334, 7 N.E.2d 254); People ex rel. Walker Engraving Corp. v. Graves (243 App.Div. 652, 276 N.Y.S. 674, affd. 268 N.Y. 648, 198 N.E. 539); People ex rel. Foremost Studio, Inc. v. Graves (246 App.Div. 130, 284 N.Y.S. 906). In those cases it was decided that certain articles came within the act and were taxable. Those cases are clearly distinguishable upon the ground that in each the articles sold were finished products, having a market value. That type of case is distinguished in Matter of Mendoza Fur Dyeing Works, Inc. v. Taylor (272 N.Y. 275, 5 N.E.2d 818). * * *

The judgment of the Appellate Division should be reversed and that of the Special Term affirmed with costs in this court and in the Appellate Division.*

Notes and Problems

A. As originally enacted in the 1930's, most sales taxes were limited in application to the transfer of tangible personal property. In recent years, however, as State and local governments' need for revenue has grown, there has been a gradual expansion of the sales tax base in many jurisdictions to include specified services. Thus the current New York State and City sales taxes are imposed, inter alia, on:

The receipts from every sale, except for resale, of * * *

(1) The furnishing of information by printed, mimeographed or multigraphed matter or by duplicating written or printed matter in any other manner, including the services of collecting, compiling or analyzing information of any kind or nature and furnishing reports thereof to other persons, but excluding the furnishing of information which is personal or individual in nature and which is not or may not be substantially incorporated in reports furnished to other persons, and excluding the services of advertising or other agents, or other persons acting in a representative capacity, and information services used by newspapers, radio broadcasters and television broadcasters in the collection and dissemination of news. [N.Y. Tax Law § 1105(c)(1), CCH ¶ 97–397, P–H ¶ 22,525.25]

Query: Would the result in the *Dun & Bradstreet* case be the same under this provision? See Towne–Oller and Associates, Inc. v. State Tax Comm'n, 120 A.D.2d 873, 120 N.Y.S.2d 873 (3d Dept. 1986) (preparation of reports for manufacturers of health and beauty aid products taxable as information service).

WASHINGTON TIMES–HERALD, INC. v. DISTRICT OF COLUMBIA

United States Court of Appeals District of Columbia Circuit, 1954.
94 U.S.App.D.C. 154, 213 F.2d 23.

WILBUR K. MILLER, CIRCUIT JUDGE. We are asked to review a decision of the District of Columbia Tax Court under the District of Columbia Use Tax Act.[1] Petitioner, a newspaper publishing company, contracted with several syndicates for its supply of comic strips. The syndicates carry out these contracts by sending the petitioner, at intervals, fiber matrices (mats) bearing impressions of the current

---

* [The Ohio Supreme Court reached a similar result in holding that the sales of written personal credit reports by a consumer credit reporting agency to its clients were non-taxable service transactions. Credit Bureau of Miami County, Inc. v. Collins, 50 Ohio St.2d 270, 364 N.E.2d 27 (1977).]

1. 63 Stat. 124 et seq., § 47–2701 et seq., D.C.Code 1951.

sequence of strips. These mats are manufactured by the syndicates, from the original drawings, by a photo-engraving process. Petitioner uses the mats in the first of a series of operations culminating in the production of a metal plate from which the comic page is printed.[2] The petitioner pays the syndicates for the comic strip mats sums which are greatly in excess of the price of blank mats. For example, the Times–Herald purchased blank mats the size of newspaper page for twenty-two cents each, but for a mat containing six daily strips of the "Gump Family," with the right to use each strip one time, it paid the sum of $30.00.

The Tax Court held the transactions with the syndicates were sales at retail within the meaning of § 201 of the Act,[3] and upheld taxation thereof on the basis of the substantial prices paid the syndicates for mats which, had they been blank, could have been bought at a small fraction of those prices.

Section 47–2701, subd. 1(b)(3) of the Code exempts from sales and use taxes "Professional, insurance, or personal service transactions which involve sales as inconsequential elements for which no separate charges are made." An implementing Regulation [4] provides that a sale is an "inconsequential element" where the price of the tangible personal property is less than ten per cent of the amount charged for the services rendered. The Tax Court found as a fact that

> "The value and sales price of the matrices (also known as 'mats') * * * were less than ten per cent of the amount charged for the services rendered the petitioner under the contracts [with the syndicates] * * *."

This finding, which was disregarded by the Tax Court in its decision holding the transactions taxable, was a sufficient basis for reaching the opposite conclusion. The syndicates sold to the Times–Herald the right to reproduce one time the work of artists who make the drawings. They simply sold the professional and personal services of the artists whom they had under contract and in so doing transferred title to the mats, of inconsequential value, from which the drawings could be reproduced. The price was paid for the artists' work, i.e., for the right to reproduce the impressions on the mats,—not for the mats themselves. The newspaper bought the creation of the artist—not the material on which it was impressed—and the right to reproduce it. Without that right, the comic strip mats would be entirely worthless.

The transactions in question are clearly exempt under § 47–2701, subd. 1(b)(3).

Reversed.

---

2. Metal casts are made from the mats; these casts are combined in the sequence desired for the newspaper page; a mat is made of the whole page; an impression from this mat is transferred to a metal plate; this plate is put on the printing press, and the comic page is then printed.

3. Section 47–2701, subd. 1, D.C.Code 1951.

4. Section 202(b) of the Regulations Pertaining to Sales and Use Taxes, promulgated July 12, 1949, by the Commissioners of the District of Columbia.

STEPHENS, CHIEF JUDGE. I concur in the result for the following reason: I think that, in essence, what the Times–Herald contracted with the Syndicates for was a right to reproduce, once, the artist-created comic strip ideas expressed, for the purpose of reproduction, in "mat" form. That, in my view, is not a "use * * * or consumption of any tangible personal property" and is not the purchase or sale of "services" and is therefore not taxable under Section 47–2702 of the D.C.Code.

I am authorized to state that CIRCUIT JUDGES FAHY and WASHINGTON concur in the foregoing.*

Notes and Problems

A. Does the majority face the question in the case when it declares that the "sale" of the mats was an inconsequential element in the case? The issue as to whether the transaction is a "personal service" transaction is ignored by the court by its assumption that if the materials are inconsequential, the transaction is in essence one of personal service. Under the court's test—the value of the materials as compared with the services going into the final product—would the sale of a Rembrandt painting be free of sales tax, since the canvas and the paint are inconsequential elements in the cost of the article? Yet, sales tax laws typically have been construed so as to cover transactions involving works of art, originally designed dresses, and other items in which the cost of the materials used is inconsequential.

B. Compare with the principal case the statement of the court in Craig–Tourial Leather Co. Inc. v. Reynolds, 87 Ga.App. 360, 73 S.E.2d 749 (1952), in construing a similar "sales as inconsequential elements" provision in a shoe repairer's case:

> We do not think that the actual cost or monetary value of the materials used is determinative. * * * However, we think that the main consideration should be the purpose of the customer, who primarily wishes to buy the skilled services of the shoe repairman * * * Under such circumstances, the sale of various grades or qualities of materials by the shoe repairman is really incidental to and but a means of rendering the services which his customers want. [87 Ga. App. at 364–65, 73 S.E.2d at 752.]

C. The Ohio sales and use tax statute has a "personal service" exemption similar to that at issue in the *Times–Herald* case:

> * * * Other than as provided in this section, "sale" and "selling" do not include professional, insurance, or personal service transactions which involve the transfer of tangible personal property as an inconsequential element, for which no separate charges are made. [Ohio Rev. Code § 5739.01(B), CCH ¶ 95–003, P–H ¶ 22,520.4.]

In Federated Dept. Stores, Inc. v. Kosydar, 45 Ohio St.2d 1, 340 N.E.2d 840 (1976), the court was faced with the questions whether expenditures for radio and television tapes and films and free-lance art work for use in

* [The case is noted in 43 Georgetown L.Rev. 109 (1954).]

advertising constituted transactions falling within the abovequoted exception. The court first set out the governing principles:

1. In determining whether a "sale" of tangible personal property may be excepted from the sales tax by the last sentence of R.C. 5739.01(B), the proper test is to determine whether the transaction involves a consequential or inconsequential professional, insurance, or personal service. If the service rendered is inconsequential, the exception is not available and the *entire* transaction is taxable. If a consequential service *is* rendered, then it must be ascertained whether the transfer of the tangible personal property was an inconsequential element of the transaction. If so, then none of the consideration paid is taxable.

2. In determining whether a mixed transaction constitutes a consequential personal service transaction, a distinction must be made as to the *true object* of the transaction contract; that is, is the real object sought by the buyer the service *per se* or the property produced by the service.

3. Where a transaction is mixed in such a manner that the tangible personal property transferred and the service rendered are distinct consequential elements having a fixed and ascertainable relationship between the value of the property and the value of the service rendered so that both may be separately stated, there exist two separate transactions, and the one attributable to the sale of the tangible personal property is subject to taxation under R.C. 5739.01(B) while the other is not. [45 Ohio St.2d at 4–5, 340 N.E.2d at 843.]

The court concluded that the taxpayer's "real object" in the transactions was to acquire possession of the tapes, films, and art work, rather than the services performed in producing them, and it held the sales taxable. Compare Dun & Bradstreet, Inc. v. Lindley, 66 Ohio St.2d 295, 421 N.E.2d 525 (1981) in which the court, analyzing transactions similar to those discussed in Dun & Bradstreet v. City of New York, pp. 666–69 supra, declared:

[W]e find that the true object of Dun & Bradstreet's transactions with [its customer] concerned the furnishing of information ∗ ∗ ∗ The receipt of the written credit reports and access to the reference books were inconsequential elements of this service. [The customer] subscribed to Dun & Bradstreet's services to receive credit information obtained through the personal efforts and expertise of Dun & Bradstreet's employees. Therefore, the services provided by Dun & Bradstreet ∗ ∗ ∗ fall within the personal services exception of R.C. 5739.01(B). [66 Ohio St.2d at 299.]

(1) Graphic Arts

SOUTHERN BELL TELEPHONE AND TELEGRAPH COMPANY, Petitioner v. DEPARTMENT OF REVENUE, Respondent.

District Court of Appeal of Florida, First District, 1978
366 So.2d 30

BOYER, JUDGE.

By this petition, Southern Bell (petitioner here) seeks review of the decision of the Department (respondent here) determining that Southern Bell was subject to sales tax on transactions between it and artists who produced art work used in advertisements appearing in the yellow pages of Southern Bell telephone books and that the exemption contained in F.S. 212.08(7)(e) was inapplicable.

Pursuant to F.S. 212.07(9) the Department assessed a tax, penalty, and interest against Southern Bell based on alleged purchases by Southern Bell of tangible personal property on which no sales tax had been collected by the vendors. The sales tax was assessed on transactions between Southern Bell and artists who produced art work used in advertisements appearing in the yellow pages of Southern Bell telephone books.

The art work which Southern Bell acquired for use in the yellow pages fell into three different categories: (1) stock art, (2) speculative art, and (3) finished art. Southern Bell conceded in the proceedings below that it purchased stock art as tangible personal property and that those purchases were subject to the sales tax. However, Southern Bell contends that its transactions with artists who created speculative art and finished art were personal service transactions which involved sales as inconsequential elements for which no separate charges were made and thus were exempt from sales tax by virtue of F.S. 212.08(7)(e).

Prior to the final hearing, the parties entered into a stipulation of facts which defines the three types of art work. Stock art is previously created art work which is inventoried by dealers who publish catalogues describing the stock art. When Southern Bell purchases stock art, it acquires possession of papers bearing reproductions of previously prepared drawings, designs, or other representations of objects which are created by the company that sells the stock art, and are reproduced in quantity. Speculative art and finished art are created by artists with whom Southern Bell contracts. Speculative art refers to rough drawings created by artists at the specific request of the yellow pages salesperson. After a salesperson investigates the general nature of a prospective advertiser's business he gives this information to the artist who by himself or in collaboration with the salesperson creates an artistic design to show how an advertisement for the business might appear in the yellow pages. The design may be accepted or rejected by the prospective advertiser. If it is accepted, Southern Bell gives it back to the same or another artist with the request that finished art be created. Southern Bell becomes obligated to pay the artist who created the speculative art whether or not the design is accepted or rejected. The amount of the fee is measured by the size of the design and is not affected by whether or not the artist's work is used by Southern Bell. The fee is not broken down into separate amounts for the services performed and the tangible personal property transferred to Southern Bell. Finished art refers to designs which are actually photographed for use in particular yellow pages advertisements. While speculative art is a mock-up of the entire design of the advertisement, including the lettering, finished art consists of only the artistic design or illustration. Finished art is precisely drawn as opposed to being merely sketched as in the case of speculative art. Southern Bell photographs the finished art and it is the photograph—not the finished art itself—which is placed in the yellow pages advertisement. The fee for finished art is either a flat fee or based upon the amount of time spent by the artist and is not affected by the use which Southern Bell makes of finished art. The artists who prepare either speculative art or finished art furnish all the materials used in the creation of the design and the relative value of the materials used ranges from 1% to 6% of the amount paid by Southern Bell to the artist.

It is Southern Bell's position that theoretically the artists could perform the services for which they are engaged without transferring any property to Southern Bell. In the case of speculative art, the artist could accompany the yellow pages salesperson on a visit to a prospective advertiser or the prospective advertiser could accompany the salesperson to the artist's studio. In the case of finished art, Southern Bell could photograph the finished art at the studio of the artist. However, Southern Bell contends both of those methods are economically impractical.

It is the Department's contention that Southern Bell purchased title and exclusive possession to the art work, since that is the only way Southern Bell could obtain the benefit of the product.

The Administrative Hearing Officer found that the transactions involved the furnishing of personal services and that no separate charge was made for the tangible personal property which was transferred. However, the Officer concluded that since it would not be economically feasible for Southern Bell to avail itself of the artist's services without taking possession of the material on which the services were performed the transfer of tangible personal property was not an inconsequential element of the transaction. Accordingly, the Officer concluded that the personal service exemption did not apply in this case. The Department approved the recommended order. This petition for review ensued.

The Department imposed tax liability on petitioner pursuant to F.S. 212.07(9) which reads in part:

"Any person who has purchased at retail, used, consumed, distributed, or stored * * * tangible personal property, * * * and cannot prove that the tax levied by this chapter has been paid to his vendor or lessor shall be directly liable to the state for any tax, interest, or penalty due on any such taxable transactions."

Petitioner seeks an injunction from the tax pursuant to F.S. 212.08(7)(e) on the grounds that the transactions sought to be taxed by the Department are fundamentally contracts for "services". The foregoing statute provides an exemption for " * * * professional * * * or personal service transactions which involve sales as inconsequential elements for which no separate charges are made."

We agree with petitioner that the exemption set forth in F.S. 212.08(7)(e) applies to the transactions involved. When Southern Bell buys speculative and finished art, it is really purchasing the artist's idea and the fact that the idea is transmitted on tangible personal property is an inconsequential element of the transaction.

We reach this decision after considering several factors, viz:

(1) Whether or not the property to be transferred as a result of the transaction is already in existence or whether it is produced in the course of the services rendered.

(2) The value of the individual effort involved in the transaction as compared to the value of the property transferred.

(3) Finally, whether or not it is essential to the transaction that the specific tangible personal property be created.

Applying those factors to this case we find that the art work (not stock art) transferred to Southern Bell was created solely in the context of the particular transactions and not prior to them. The value of the services performed for Southern Bell was much greater than the value of the tangible personal property transferred to Southern Bell. Finally, taking possession of the material on which the services were rendered was not essential to Southern Bell's realization of the value of the artist's services because the designs created by the artist could be disassociated from the tangible personal property even though it might not have been economically feasible to do so.

Our decision finds support in this court's decision in Askew v. Bell, 248 So.2d 501 (Fla. 1st DCA 1971). In that case, the court held that a court reporter, who for a fee records a judicial or administrative proceeding, or takes down and transcribes testimony, is engaged in rendering a service and the transcript which he furnishes to the persons who employ him is a mere incident of that service. The *Askew* court held that such a transaction would be subject to sales tax only when transcripts are sold to third persons who are not parties to the proceeding for which the court reporter was engaged.

Similarly, in Nova Computing Services v. Askew, D.O.A., (the department's Case No. 76–1475: March 1, 1977), the Department enacted a rule construing computer software (punched cards, paper tape and typed sheets) to be tangible personal property and subject to sales tax. Pursuant to F.S. 120.56, Nova filed a petition challenging the validity of the rule. The Administrative Hearing Officer in that case found that when computer software is sold it is the computer information which is transferred, and that the magnetic tape or punch cards which contain the information are only the means or method of transmitting it from the originator to the user. He further found that the tangible property (i.e. punch cards) involved in the process was an inconsequential element for which no separate charges were made; the consequential element being intangible property (computer information) which was not subject to the sales tax on tangible personal property under chapter 212, Florida Statutes. Therefore, he concluded that Nova and other similar corporations were selling services to their customers which were exempt from sales tax pursuant to F.S. 212.08(7) (e).

The hearing officer's order in the above mentioned proceeding constituted final agency action and was not appealed by the Department. (A copy of that order may be obtained from the Director, Division of Administrative Hearings, Tallahassee, Florida.) Although the order is not binding on this court, we find it to be persuasive to our decision.

We conclude that the personal service exemption does apply in this case. The petition for review is granted. The final order rendered by the Department is vacated and the case is remanded to the Department to enter an order consistent with the views expressed herein.

BLACK, SUSAN H., ASSOCIATE JUDGE, concurs.

SMITH, J., dissents.

SMITH, JUDGE, dissenting:

The Department's assessment rests on a hearing officer's findings that speculative and finished art acquired by Southern Bell, like the stock art which concededly is taxable when sold, are not "inconsequential elements" of the transactions by which artists' personal services are engaged. Section 212.08(7)(e), Florida Statutes (1977). I believe the hearing officer's findings are correct as a matter of fact and as a matter of law.

The majority's view will command respect from philosophers who hold that all things palpable are but shadows of some ideal. In a sense every work of art, indeed every wheel and lever, is a design separable from the tangible property in which it is embodied. But as the question is what Southern Bell has purchased—the image in the artist's mind or the one he drew with ink on paper—I cannot believe that the thing acquired is "the artist's idea and the fact that the idea is transmitted on tangible personal property is an inconsequential element of the transaction." If it were true that "the designs created by the artist could be disassociated from the tangible personal property" in which the designs are manifested, a Caruso record would be sold as wax and a Tolstoy novel as wood pulp, inconsequential elements of the artistry which created them, and hence nontaxable.

The hearing officer found as a fact that the end purpose of Southern Bell's transactions with artists is the acquisition of drawings, rough or finished, to show to prospective advertisers or to reproduce in the yellow pages. In my view our inquiry ends when we have found substantial competent evidence to support that finding. See Green v. Sgurovsky, 133 So.2d 663 (Fla. 3d DCA 1961); Federated Dep't Stores, Inc. v. Kosydar, 45 Ohio St.2d 1, 340 N.E.2d 840 (1976). I cannot grasp the majority's distinction between the taxable sale of stock art and the nontaxable sale of speculative or finished art. In either case Southern Bell has characterized the transaction by specifying what is useful to it, and in either case the thing specified is a tangible drawing, valuable in itself, which Southern Bell uses and discards or retains as its own. Thus distinguished are the lawyer's brief and the physician's written prescription, which are but the means by which personal services are provided. Thus distinguished are the court reporter's transcripts and the punch cards and magnetic tapes of a computer service, which have only paper value apart from the information or events they record. See Askew v. Bell, 248 So.2d 501 (Fla. 1st DCA 1971); Commerce Union Bank v. Tidwell, 538 S.W.2d 405 (Tenn.1976); State v. Central Computer Services, Inc., 349 So.2d 1160 (Ala.1977).

A different case might be presented if Southern Bell's artists licensed the use of their skill for particular purposes on particular occasions, as by drawing in chalk upon an advertiser's blackboard, then reclaiming their proprietary images by erasure. Compare Washington Times–Herald, Inc. v. District of Columbia, 94 U.S.App.D.C. 154, 213 F.2d 23 (1964), with District of Columbia v. Norwood Studios, Inc., 118 U.S.App.D.C. 358, 336 F.2d 746 (1964). But in my view this case is no different than if Southern Bell had acquired a Rembrandt to hang in its executive office.

I would affirm.

FEDERATED DEPARTMENT STORES, INC. v. KOSYDAR

Supreme Court of Ohio, 1976
45 Ohio St.2d 1, 340 N.E.2d 840

J.J.P. Corrigan, Justice.

At issue in this case are two categories of tangible personal property claimed by appellant to be excepted from Ohio sales and use taxes, pursuant to R.C. 5739.01(B) and (E)(2). For purposes of this discussion, the tax in issue will be treated as sales tax, pursuant to R.C. 5741.02(C)(2).

I.

The first category of goods assessed by the Tax Commissioner, and at issue herein, consists of advertising materials. These materials consist, in general, of radio and T.V. commercials, and free-lance artists' sketches used in newspaper and magazine compositions. The assessment relating to radio and T.V. commercials consists specifically of tapes and films used to produce the commercials.

Appellant maintains that this property is the end product of an individual's personal or professional skills and is unsuitable for use by anyone other than the appellant. Appellant contends further that the property in question is an inconsequential part of the transaction, and, therefore, the transaction is a personal service, notwithstanding the evidence in the record to the effect that the appellant would not have paid the price but for the transfer of said property. We disagree.

It should be noted at the outset that R.C. Chapter 5739 taxes only tangible personal property. The so-called personal service exception in reality excepts from taxation that tangible personal property transferred as an inconsequential element of a personal service transaction.

This court, in Accountant's Computer Services v. Kosydar (1973), 35 Ohio St.2d 120, 298 N.E.2d 519, states the test for determining whether a "sale" of tangible personal property may be excepted from the sales tax by virtue of R.C. 5739.01(B). The first three paragraphs of the syllabus in Accountant's, supra, state:

"1. In determining whether a 'sale' of tangible personal property may be excepted from the sales tax by the last sentence of R.C. 5739.01(B), the proper test is to determine whether the transaction involves a consequential or inconsequential professional, insurance, or personal service. If the service rendered is inconsequential, the exception is not available and the *entire* transaction is taxable. If a consequential service *is* rendered, then it must be ascertained whether the transfer of the tangible personal property was an inconsequential element of the transaction. If so, then none of the consideration paid is taxable.

"2. In determining whether a mixed transaction constitutes a consequential personal service transaction, a distinction must be made as to the *true object* of the transaction contract; that is, is the real object sought by the buyer the service *per se* or the property produced by the service.

"3. Where a transaction is mixed in such a manner that the tangible personal property transferred and the service rendered are distinct consequential elements having a fixed and ascertainable relationship between the value of the property and the value of the service rendered so that both may be separately stated, there exist two separate transactions, and the one attributable to the sale of the tangible personal property is subject to taxation under R.C. 5739.01(B) while the other is not."

This court, in *Accountant's,* explained that once it has been concluded that a sale of tangible personal property has occurred, then the next step is to determine whether a consequential professional insurance or personal service is involved. The court states at page 132, 298 N.E.2d at page 527:

"To accomplish this, the Tax Commissioner, the Board of Tax Appeals, and this court, as necessary, must examine the *real object sought by the buyer, i.e.,* the service *per se* or the property produced by the service, and determine if it was the buyer's object to obtain an act done personally by an individual as an economic service involving either the intellectual or manual personal effort of an individual, or if it was the buyer's object to obtain only the saleable end product of some individual's skill. Koch v. Kosydar, supra (32 Ohio St.2d 74, 290 N.E.2d 847)."

If the professional, insurance or personal service is inconsequential, then the exception cannot be available and the entire transaction is taxable.

Appellant relies upon Columbus Coated Fabrics v. Porterfield (1972), 30 Ohio St.2d 307, 285 N.E.2d 50, for the proposition that where the item of tangible personal property transferred is an inconsequential element of the transaction, unsuitable for uses other than those intended by the purchaser and prepared at the request of a specific purchaser, the transaction is a personal service, notwithstanding the fact that the purchaser would not have paid the price but for the transfer of the property. We think this reliance is misplaced. This court, in Columbus Coated Fabrics, supra, recognized the fact that there exists no article fabricated by machine or handcrafted that is not the product of the exercise and application of individual ability and skill. The court, in its decision, pointed out that Recording Devices v. Porterfield (1972), 30 Ohio St.2d 208, 382 N.E.2d 626, provided the framework within which that case was to be decided.

Recording Devices, supra, at page 213, 283 N.E.2d at page 629, defined personal service as "an act done personally by a particular individual; it is, in effect, an economic service involving either the intellectual or manual personal effort of an individual, not the saleable product of his skill."

The court, in Columbus Coated Fabrics, supra, did not substitute the criteria relied upon by appellant in the present case for the true object of the transaction, but merely cited the record in that case that the property was suitable for other uses and was neither prepared at the request of, nor for the specific purchaser, as evidence of the purchaser's real object to acquire the property and not the services producing it.

In United States Shoe Corp. v. Kosydar (1975), 41 Ohio St.2d 68, 322 N.E.2d 668, this court held similar expenditures to advertising agencies for T.V. and radio commercials, sales brochures and photographs to be items of tangible personal property subject to taxation. The court based its holding on the finding of the Board of Tax Appeals that the taxpayers' main concern was to acquire possession of the films, commercials, radio tapes, brochures, photographs and annual reports. The court determined that the record established the taxpayers' intention to acquire materials to use in advertising, and that the personal property purchased was the real object sought by the buyers. The court added that the main function of the agencies was not to analyze, interpret, and present information to the taxpayers, but that the taxpayers paid a substantial consideration for their services, and it was unlikely that this would have occurred without receipt of the items in question.

In the present case, the Board of Tax Appeals found that " * * * the appellant was distinctly interested in the television commercials, photographs, radio tapes, advertising compositions and 'layouts.' The real object sought by the appellant in each of the transactions listed * * * was clearly the tangible personal property which it acquired for a consideration."

In appeals from the Board of Tax Appeals, this court's review is limited to a determination from the record as to the reasonableness and lawfulness of the board's decision. Citizens Financial Corp. v. Porterfield (1971), 25 Ohio St.2d 53, 266 N.E.2d 828.

Our examination of the record before the Board of Tax Appeals indicates sufficient probative evidence that the appellant's real object in the transactions in question was to acquire possession of the radio and T.V. tapes and films to use in advertising, rather than the service performed in producing them. In regard to such radio and T.V. tapes and films, the decision of the board is affirmed.

II.

In respect to the free-lance art work, the Board of Tax Appeals found that the transactions were personal service transactions. The board based this finding upon the fact that the appellant requested that the artists produce specific types of art work unusable for other than those purposes intended by the appellant. The payments of predetermined hourly fees to the artists, stated the board, was a payment for both the intellectual and manual skill of the individual artist and not for the art work itself. The board felt that transactions of this nature are not subject to sales and use taxes.

The board's finding that the free-lance artists' sketches were transferred as part of a personal service transaction was apparently based upon the testimony in the record that the sketches were specifically requested by the taxpayer, were unsuitable for uses other than those the taxpayer intended, and that the artists were paid an hourly fee for their services. As pointed out earlier in this decision, in commenting on the appellant's argument based upon Columbus Coated Fabrics, supra (30 Ohio St.2d 307, 285 N.E.2d 50), those facts are evidence tending to show a real object to acquire the services of the artists. The record in this case, however, contains evidence to the effect that appellant usually specifies the type of sketch to be produced and the items to be involved in the sketch.

The testimony also definitely establishes the appellant's real object in hiring the artists is to acquire the sketches, themselves, so that the sketches may be turned over to the advertising department to be used in newspaper or magazine compositions. The record clearly establishes an objective to acquire tangible personal property, and, pursuant to our decision in Accountant's, supra, the personal service rendered is an inconsequential element in the transaction. The decision of the Board of Tax Appeals is against the weight of the evidence and contrary to the standards established by this court in Accountant's, supra. The decision of the board as to the artists' sketches, the issue in the cross-appeal, is, therefore, reversed.

III.

Appellant maintains, in its second proposition of law, that merchandise display fixtures, purchased by a person engaged in the business of making retail sales, are used directly in making such sales and are, therefore, excepted from sales and use taxes, notwithstanding the fact that they may also incidentally partition or separate areas of a mercantile establishment.

The items in question consist of portable partitions extending to ceiling height and the cornices, light fixtures and interior signs variously attached to them. The partitions, the record indicates, were constructed of lumber and plywood and served to separate various departments in the store. The partitions were frequently decorated with elaborate wallpaper, paneling, cornices, and signs. The shelving attached to these panels and used to display merchandise was not taxed. The record, including photographs of the panels or partitions, indicates the basic difference between discount stores and department stores. Both types of stores involve the same basic construction. Both types of stores are architecturally similar in that they are large square or rectangular shaped empty buildings. In the discount store, few, if any, walls are constructed in addition to the four basic walls. The interior is separated by low display shelves or racks. The department store, however, derives its name from the fact that merchandise display areas are divided and separated from each other by decorative ceiling height walls, panels or partitions. These divided areas are designated by decorative signs and separated for the convenience of customers. These panels, the record indicates, frequently function as walls for dressing rooms and stock rooms. The panels are portable and can be used again in remodeling or changing a merchandise display. The appellant's witnesses stated that the primary purpose of these panels was to attractively display the appellant's merchandise. Appellant contends that these panels and associated cornices, light fixtures and signs constitute display systems or fixtures used primarily in making retail sales and are excepted from the definition of "retail sale," pursuant to R.C. 5739.01(E).

R.C. 5739.01(E) provides, in pertinent part:

"'Retail sale' and 'sales at retail' include all sales except those in which the purpose of the consumer is:

"＊　＊　＊

"(2) ＊　＊　＊ to use or consume the thing transferred ＊　＊　＊ directly in making retail sales ＊　＊　＊."

R.C. 5739.01(P) provided during the audit period that " '[m]aking retail sales' " did not include " ＊　＊　＊ the preliminary acts of promoting or soliciting the retail sales."

At the time of the audit in question, Rule TX–15–11, Rules of the Tax Commissioner, read as follows:

"Tangible personal property which is to be used or consumed directly in making retail sales may, when purchased by a person engaged in making retail sales, be purchased under a claim of exemption. Articles subject to such claim include show cases, equipment and shelves used to display merchandise for sale; store furniture and fixtures; supplies and equipment used in consummating retail sales; and equipment for use or consumption in storing or preserving goods and merchandise in the sales area.

"This exemption does not apply to equipment used for general heating of the sales area, to fuels for such equipment, to any other supplies not used directly in making retail sales or not specifically used in storing or preserving goods and merchandise in the sales area, to delivery equipment, nor to items used to promote or solicit retail sales. Examples of items to which the exemption would not apply include lumber, wall board and similar items used as partitions whether in the retail rooms, display windows or elsewhere; janitor and cleaning supplies, fans, decorative items, items used in offices, stock or delivery rooms, outside signs, trucks or equipment used to deliver merchandise sold at retail, and advertising materials.

" 'Sales area' means any area in which retail sales are customarily made."

A reading of the applicable statutes and an interpretation of the Tax Commissioner's rules establish the importance of appellant's use of the property in question. In this case, however, the panels and associated cornices, light fixtures and signs serve to both partition and identify departments, a non-excepted use, and to display merchandise, an excepted use. In such a case, it is the primary use which is determinative of taxability, and incidental uses are not controlling. Mead Corp. v. Glander (1950), 153 Ohio St. 539, 93 N.E.2d 19; Jewel Companies v. Porterfield (1970), 21 Ohio St.2d 97, 255 N.E.2d 630.

" ＊　＊　＊ 'Primary use' connotes primacy in utility or essentiality, in quality as well as quantity." Ace Steel Baling v. Porterfield (1969), 19 Ohio St.2d 137, 140, 249 N.E.2d 892, 895.

In the present case, the Board of Tax Appeals found that paneling and associated fixtures were indirectly facilitative to making retail sales but not used directly in making retail sales. An examination of the record supports a finding that the paneling was used primarily in separating various departments in appellant's stores in conformity with their designation as "department stores." Moreover, the burden was upon the appellant to affirmatively establish its right to an exception. National Tube Co. v. Glander (1952), 157 Ohio St. 407, 105 N.E.2d 648.

Since the record in this case with regard to the appeal contains sufficient probative evidence to support the Board of Tax Appeals' decision, the decision is reasonable and lawful and must be affirmed.

Decision affirmed as to appeal and reversed as to cross-appeal.

C. WILLIAM O'NEILL, C.J., and HERBERT, STERN, CELEBREZZE, WILLIAM B. BROWN and PAUL W. BROWN, JJ., concur.

Notes and Problems

A. The "true object" test suffers from the inherent weakness that whether dealing with art work, records, tapes, or other articles, both the article, and the services embodied in the article, are essential to the purchaser. What objective or other basis is there for determining the purchaser's "true object"? Does it depend on the court's "gut reaction"? If the true object test is unacceptable, what alternative test would you propose to a court for determining the personal service—tangible personal property issue? For an alternative approach, see J. Hellerstein, "Significant Developments During the Past Half Century," 39 Vand.L.Rev. 962, 972 (1986).

(2) Computer Software

COMPTROLLER OF THE TREASURY v. EQUITABLE TRUST COMPANY

Court of Appeals of Maryland, 1983.
296 Md. 459, 464 A.2d 248.

RODOWSKY, JUDGE.*

This is a sales tax case. It involves computer programs in the business data processing field. At issue is how the computer program license transactions presented here are to be conceptualized under the statute which reaches sales of "any tangible personal property." Md. Code (1957, 1980 Repl.Vol.), Art. 81, § 324(f). Did the taxpayer, a computer user, acquire from the proprietors of canned, transactional computer programs

 1. intangible personal property, namely, the right to use the programs, with copies of the programs transferred by the medium of magnetic tapes; or

 2. intangible personal property, namely, "knowledge" or "information," which was transferred to the taxpayer by the temporary medium of magnetic tape; or

 3. tangible personal property, namely, magnetic tapes which had been enhanced in value by the copies of the programs coded thereon?

---

* [Some of the court's footnotes have been omitted.]

Alternatives 1 and 2 result in no tax. An *amicus,* Data Processing Management Association, has raised the first alternative. The taxpayer, Equitable Trust Company (Equitable), emphasizes the second analysis. The Comptroller urges the third position, which we adopt.

As of September 16, 1974, Equitable entered into a written contract, delineated "License Agreement," with Auxton Computer Enterprises, Incorporated (AUXCO). AUXCO granted Equitable a nontransferable and nonexclusive right to use a program, the "AUXCO Project Management System," at a one-time price of $20,000. There was no termination date. Equitable covenanted not to publish or disclose to any third person any information concerning the program and not to copy the program tapes or documentation except for internal use. Paragraph 10 of the agreement in part provided that "[l]egal title to the System shall remain with AUXCO, and [Equitable] agrees that AUXCO may repossess the System" upon breach by Equitable of its obligations. This program was acquired for use by Equitable's systems and programming people in tracking project performance.

By a "License Agreement" of December 13, 1974 with PACE Applied Technology, Inc. (PACE), Equitable acquired the right to use two PACE programs in perpetuity. One was the "KOMAND Data Acquisition System" for the price of $10,800. The other was the "KOMAND Resource Billing System" for a price of $4,365. The agreement placed restrictions on Equitable's disclosing PACE's proprietary information. The PACE programs were described in testimony as an accounting system which would allow Equitable to know exactly how much its computer and peripheral equipment were used for running specific applications, such as the main deposit program or the time deposit program.

During an audit in 1975, the Comptroller assessed sales tax against Equitable based upon the prices paid pursuant to the foregoing agreements. That assessment was affirmed by a hearing officer in the Sales Tax Division whose decision was affirmed by the Maryland Tax Court. On appeal to the Baltimore City Court (now the Circuit Court for Baltimore City), the assessment was abated. That court concluded as a matter of law that the dominant purpose or essence of the transactions was the programs and that computer programs are intangible. The Comptroller appealed to the Court of Special Appeals. We issued the writ of certiorari on our own motion prior to consideration of the matter by the intermediate appellate court.

1

Before the legal contentions can be considered, some fundamentals should be stated. A computer is a machine. It does not think. It is designed to execute predetermined instructions. Ultimately a "program" is a set of such instructions. An "applicational program," as we shall use the term, is a set of instructions that will cause the machine to perform a specific task. An example from the banking field would be a program which listed certain information with respect to each installment loan account for which any payment was delinquent. Unless otherwise specified, "program" as used in this opinion will mean an applicational program.[2]

Development of a program requires knowledge, time and effort. A program may be said to exist in different levels of language and in different physical forms. Theoretically, a program could exist in the mind of the programmer, but, as a practical matter, programs as obviously complex as those involved here must be recorded somewhere in some physical representation. In human readable form on paper, this representation might be in a procedure oriented language, e.g., COBOL or FORTRAN, in a symbolic language, or in machine language. "Machine language * * * is a series of numbers, letters of the alphabet, or special characters that are used to represent bit [(binary digit)] patterns which can be recognized by the computer and cause specific operations to take place." W. Fuori, *Introduction to the Computer,* at 270 (2d ed. 1977). Symbolic language is "very closely related to machine language in that, in general, one symbolic instruction will translate into one-machine language instruction." Id. at 273. The representations might also be in machine readable form as a code on tape, disc or punched cards. The code might directly represent procedure oriented language or symbolic language which may be converted into machine instructions by operational programs called compliers or assemblers. The machine readable representation might also be in machine instructions, the binary code which the machine executes. See generally Gemignani, Product Liability and Software, 8 Rutgers J. Computers, Tech. & L. 173, 181–183 n. 27 (1981).

The programs involved here are stipulated to be existing, prepackaged programs of general application, called "canned" programs. The stipulation further states:

2. Applicational programs are sometimes distinguished from operational programs. A description of operational programs, considered as a whole, may be found in J. Vles, *Computer Fundamentals for Nonspecialists,* at 33 (1981).

Every computer has a "background" program running at all times. This background program, called by many names but usually referred to as "monitor," "operating system," or "executive system," does exactly what its name says it should do: it monitors and directs everything that is going on in the computer. It allocates space for data on disk (and it remembers where it put it), it tells the memory to get data from the disk, and it decides where there is room in memory for these data; it mingles in everything from getting the user "signed on" to getting him '"signed off" the computer; it is the universal "policeman" of the system. Everything that goes on inside the computer, at any time, is guided by the monitor. Needless to say, the monitor is usually the largest and most complicated program that is running; it is certainly the most important, for without it even the most sophisticated computer is only a bunch of wires, transistors, and metal that is totally inadequate to solve any problems.

Operational software

includes compilers, which translate input symbolic codes into machine [instructions] and can replace certain items of input with series of instructions called subroutines; sorts, which place items of data in order; and utility routines, which perform tasks useful for the efficient operation of the machine, such as copying one magnetic tape from another.

Note, *Sales and Use Tax of Computer Software—Is Software Tangible Personal Property?,* 27 Wayne L.Rev. 1503, 1508 (1981) (the Wayne Note). (Footnote omitted).

The programs assessed were not developed exclusively for use by Equitable but were developed to be sold to many different purchasers. None of the assessment for computer software relates to programs specially designed and developed exclusively for Equitable [, i.e., a custom program].

The advantage to a computer user of a canned program is that the user need not start from the beginning in developing the particular program. Reinventing the wheel is avoided. However, because the developer or proprietor is marketing a program for use by many different organizations of the same general type, and possibly for use on machines of various manufacture, there will ordinarily be a need for a particular user to make some adaptations in a canned program to meet the specifics of that user's situation. Equitable made some adaptations, but they are not described in evidence.

Each program received by Equitable was delivered to it on magnetic tape. This means that the proprietor of the program made a copy of it, directly or indirectly, from a master which was in some physical form. The physical form of the program copies, as delivered, was a coded series of magnetic impulses. Each code was readable by Equitable's computer and seems to have been in machine instructions. Equitable loaded the program copy tape into computer memory and started the process of adaptation. At that point, Equitable had no further need for the particular copy delivered from the standpoint of instructing its computer. That copy, however, was retained by Equitable.

In order for a program to instruct computer execution, the magnetic tape copy of the program is loaded into memory. "In loading a program, nothing is taken from the storage media and nothing is added to the memory; rather, the user's computer reads the storage media and *rearranges its memory* to create a corresponding pattern of magnetic impulses." Note, *Software and Sales Taxes: The Illusory Intangible,* 63 B.U.L.Rev. 181, 189 (1983) (the B.U. Note) (Emphasis in original. Footnote omitted.). See also Note, *Software Taxation: A Critical Reevaluation of the Notion of Intangibility,* 1980 B.Y.U.L.Rev. 859, 871–72. The process of making changes to a program also takes place while the program is in memory. Equitable did not store the reproductions of the subject programs, or any adaptations thereof, in memory when they were not in use. They were stored peripherally. On any day when adaptations were made to a program, Equitable represents that it produced at least two tapes of the program, as changed. One was for storage on the computer premises, and the other was for storage off premises.

2

The Comptroller's position is that Equitable acquired tapes containing program copies. Magnetic tapes are tangible personal property. Acquisition of such tapes under the license agreements is a sale, because Art. 81, § 324(d) provides that "sale" means "any transaction whereby title or possession, or both, of tangible personal property is or is to be transferred by any means whatsoever for a consideration including rental, lease, or license to use * * *."

Amicus says that the transaction is a license to use the program, and that such a license is a form of intangible property. Equitable contends that the predominant purpose or essence of the transaction governs classification of the sale as involving either tangible or intangible property. In the transfer of computer programs via magnetic tape, the purpose is to obtain the program, an intangible, and not the tangible tape. In taking this position, Equitable is supported by the overwhelming numerical majority of reported cases applying tax statutes restricted to tangible personal property.

* * *

4

Equitable's principal argument is that this Court should conceptually sever the program copy contained on the magnetic tape from the tangible tape itself. The argument is that the transaction should be viewed as operating on two levels, one the transfer of intangible knowledge or information and the other the delivery of a tangible tape. To have a scalpel for this legal surgery, it would be necessary for us to adopt as part of Maryland sales tax law a principle that the buyer's predominant purpose for a transaction controls the classification of the acquisition as either tangible or intangible.

Quotron Systems v. Comptroller, 287 Md. 178, 411 A.2d 439 (1980) recognized a predominant purpose test as one of several factors in determining use tax applicability to the type of transaction presented there. That taxpayer undertook concurrently to render two types of interrelated performances. One was to maintain and continuously to update a computerized data bank of economic information, such as the selling prices of securities, which its customers could randomly access through remote terminals. The other was to install Quotron-owned hardware, including the remote terminals, on customers' premises for their use in requesting and receiving electronic transmissions of the economic data. We held that the first analytical step was to characterize the performances as a single, overall function, either rental of equipment or the provision of services. Id. at 186, 411 A.2d at 443. The dominant purpose was to obtain services and not to rent hardware. Based on that factor, on the taxpayer's retention of control over the hardware, and on the fact that Quotron's hardware could not be obtained without subscribing to the service, we concluded that the transaction was the provision of services. Id. at 188, 411 A.2d at 444. This approach is quite similar to that which we have used to determine whether a contract of sale is one for goods or for services under Art. 2 of the Uniform Commercial Code, where the performance involves both. See Anthony Pools v. Sheehan, 295 Md. 285, 455 A.2d 434 (1983); Burton v. Artery Company, 279 Md. 94, 367 A.2d 935 (1977). *Quotron* did not say that the dominant purpose of obtaining data made the subject of the contract intangible because information is intangible.

The rule of *Quotron* has been implicitly applied in the case at bar on an aspect which is not disputed by Equitable. In addition to providing program copies on tape, each proprietor agreed to furnish certain installation services. AUXCO also contracted to furnish a limited amount of training within the fixed contract price. Equitable does not argue, however, that these services predominate. Any intellectual effort rendered in the past in developing the programs is now embodied in the products for sale, the copies of the programs. That effort is reflected in the price for the copies just as engineering costs of a model of a television receiver are part of the selling price of a particular unit of that model.

We have no doubt that the dominant purpose of the subject transactions was to obtain a copy of the programs. But there are problems in adopting a dominant purpose test in order conceptually to sever information or data from the physical medium employed to deliver a copy of the information, and next to declare that the information predominates, so as thereby to classify the transaction as a sale of intangible property. One factor used in determining the dominant purpose is the admittedly insignificant value of a blank magnetic tape when compared to the price paid for a program copy on tape. But § 324(i) defines "price" to mean

the aggregate value in money * * * promised to be paid or delivered by a purchaser to a vendor in the consummation and complete performance of a retail sale without any deduction therefrom on account of the cost of the property sold, cost of materials used, labor or service cost, or any other expense whatsoever.

While Equitable points out that the question of price is not reached unless it is first determined that property sold is tangible, the legislative policy embraced in the definition of price runs contrary to the conceptual severing of the insignificant blank tape from the valuable program copy superimposed thereon as magnetic impulses.

A second concern is the precedent established for apparently comparable transactions. If the dominant purpose is to obtain knowledge, information or data which thereby results in severing the dominant purpose object from the physical medium of transfer, the analogy to books, motion picture films, video display discs, phonorecords and music tapes immediately comes to mind. In sales of the latter, the purchaser's dominant purpose ordinarily is to obtain the knowledge, information or data thereby conveyed. While the book is in human readable form, the other media are machine readable. A purchase of any of these information conveying media is within the imposition of the sales tax as tangible personal property. Such transactions escape taxation only if there is an applicable statutory exclusion or exemption. These analogies, however, have been argued to other courts which have held that tape copies of programs are intangible. We turn now to a consideration of the rationale of those opinions.

5

The earliest decision, which set the tone for the later cases, is District of Columbia v. Universal Computer Associates, Inc., 465 F.2d 615 (D.C.Cir.1972). It involved a property tax on hardware which was assessed based on the cost of a bundled IBM data processing installation. Two programs were included, one the usual standard program and the other a custom tax program. Both programs were on punched cards. The court stated the legal issue to be "whether the two sets of punched cards (the software) represent tangible personal property * * * or whether they represent intangible values which are not subject to tax." Id. at 617. The custom program was said to be basically a service. However, the canned program was said to represent "an investment of IBM in an intellectual property, which it licenses users like Universal to employ in the computers IBM sells." Id. at 618. Another factor of significance to the court was that

> [t]he punched cards themselves are placed in the machine and then taken out, and in fact could be returned to IBM. It is the information derived by the machine from the cards which stays in the computer, and which is employed repeatedly by the machine when it is used by [the taxpayer]. What rests in the machine, then, is an intangible— "knowledge"—which can hardly be thought to be subject to a personal property tax. The only visible evidence of that knowledge, the punched pasteboard, could be stacked in a warehouse, returned to IBM, or destroyed, without interfering with the efficiency of the computer machine to perform its designed function. [Id.]

Here the court is talking about memory in the computer. What rests in a programmed memory is not "knowledge" in any true sense of the word, but machine instructions. Further, the taxability of a sale of a canned program copy should not turn on whether the buyer stores the program in memory. A tax system cannot be administered dependent upon whether or not, at the time of the transaction, the buyer's intent is to store the program continuously in memory. Nor should taxability turn on the capacity of memory of the buyer's machine; otherwise, program copies bought for large storage machines would not be taxed, but those for small storage machines would be taxed.

The District of Columbia Circuit also concluded that both programs were to be likened to cartoon mats which had been involved in Washington Times–Herald v. District of Columbia, 213 F.2d 23 (D.C.Cir.1954). Cartoon mats are the medium by which a cartoonist's drawings are transferred for reproduction in newspapers. *Washington Times–Herald* held that the sale of one time use of the mats was a sale of professional and personal services, because the price was paid for the work of the artist and not for the mats which had inconsequential value. Professor Jerome R. Hellerstein in his article, *The Scope of the Taxable Sale Under Sales and Use Tax Acts: Sales As Distinguished From Services*, 11 Tax L.Rev. 261, 275 (1956) has criticized the holding in *Washington Times–*

Herald, saying that "[t]his rationale and holding undercut much established sales tax law." (Footnote omitted.)

An assessment of sales tax on the transfer of custom and canned, applicational programs, and of two operational programs, was abated in Commerce Union Bank v. Tidwell, 538 S.W.2d 405 (Tenn.1976). The Tennessee court adopted all of the reasons advanced in Universal Computer, supra, including the characterization of a programmed memory as intangible knowledge, and added some additional reasons, the first of which may be called the alternative methods approach. A computer might be programmed without purchasing a copy of a program on any tangible medium. With appropriate equipment at both termini, a program could be reproduced in memory from electronic impulses conveyed over telephone lines; or the proprietor, working from a human readable copy which is not transferred to the customer, could manually type the program into the computer for compilation into machine instructions. Whether these alternatives are ways in which the business of selling programs is actually conducted need not presently concern us. Of significance is that the alternative methods approach does not determine taxability on the basis of a transaction's actual facts.

The tax collector argued the phonorecord analogy in *Commerce Union Bank.* In distinguishing, the Tennessee court said that the buyer has no viable method of bringing the particular music into his living room other than by the record, whereas the above-described alternative methods are available for acquiring programs. Secondly the court stated flatly that the tape containing the program copy "is not retained in the possession of the user." Id. at 408. This latter point is contrary to Equitable's representation of the facts in the instant matter. More importantly, intangibility should not be determined by the extent of use. After all, a book that is read only once is and remains tangible personal property. The court also said that the phonorecord is complete and ready for use at the time of purchase, while a program copy on tape "must be translated into a language understood by the computer." Id. We are at a loss to understand this distinction. A computer user purchases a canned program copy on tape because it is considered to be sufficiently compatible with the user's machine to be read by it and, either directly or after having been compiled, executed by it.

* * *

[The court's treatment of the decisions in other States that adopt the view of the *Commerce Union Bank* case has been omitted.]

A case departing from the analytical mold of the preceding authorities is Maccabees Mutual Life Insurance Company v. State, Department of Treasury, 122 Mich.App. 660, 332 N.W.2d 561 (1983) (per curiam). It is a use tax case involving trade-named programs acquired from software proprietors. Consequently, adaptations had been made for the taxpayer's particular installation. The tangibility issue was presented on summary judgment with a concession by the tax collector that the programs, as adapted, were customized. It was held:

> The depositional evidence presented by plaintiffs illustrates that the software programs in question present a personalized service, customized to fit plaintiffs' particular computer configurations. . . .

> Customized computer software programs should be distinguished from canned software programs, *e.g.,* TV games, albums, and cassette tapes, because the latter are all end products in themselves. The focus of the instant transaction is on the personalized service of the software vendors, an intangibles transaction. [Id. at 683, 332 N.W.2d at 563–64.]

Here the parties have stipulated that the programs are "canned," by which they mean a program other than one originally developed exclusively for the buyer. While the record shows that adaptations were made to the programs acquired by Equitable, Equitable does not contend that services rendered to Equitable by the proprietors were of sufficient magnitude to classify either subject transaction as a purchase of services under the rule of Quotron, supra.

6

The tangible-intangible debate with respect to computer software can arise in contexts other than that of state and local sales, use and property taxes. The problem arises under the federal income tax as to eligibility for investment credit and accelerated depreciation. When the hardware manufacturers' segment of the industry unbundled their installation contracts and began separately to state prices for software, it was necessary for the Internal Revenue Service to adopt a position. Basically, bundled software is treated as part of the hardware, while unbundled software is treated as an intangible. See Rev.Proc. 69–21, 1969–2 C.B. 303; Rev.Rul. 71–177, 1971–1 C.B. 5; Bigelow, The Computer And The Tax Collector, 30 Emory L.J. 357, 362, 365 (1981).

* * *

The severability argument is not a new one in sales tax cases. It has been rejected in a line of cases where those who rent motion picture films from producers have argued that the intellectual property or the right to use the copy transmitted for commercial exhibition should be severed from the tangible copy of the film. See, e.g., Boswell v. Paramount Television Sales, Inc., 291 Ala. 490, 282 So.2d 892 (1973); Columbia Pictures Industries, Inc. v. Tax Commissioner, 176 Conn. 604, 410 A.2d 457 (1979); Florida Association of Broadcasters v. Kirk, 264 So.2d 437 (Fla.Dist.Ct.App.1972); United Artists Corp. v. Taylor, 273 N.Y. 334, 7 N.E.2d 254 (1937); Crescent Amusement Co. v. Carson, 187 Tenn. 112, 213 S.W.2d 27 (1948). In the latter case the court reasoned that

> [t]here is scarcely to be found any article susceptible to sale or rent that is not the result of an idea, genius, skill and labor applied to a physical substance. A loaf of bread is the result of the skill and labor of the cook who mixed the physical ingredients and applied heat at the temperature and consistency her judgment dictated. A radio is the

result of the thought of a genius, or of several such persons, combined with the skill and labor of trained technicians applied to a tangible mass of substance. An automobile is the result of all these elements, and of patents, etc.; and so on, ad infinitum. If these elements should be separated from the finished product and the sales tax applied only to the cost of the raw material, the sales tax act would, for all practical purposes, be entirely destroyed. The material used in the making of a phonograph record probably costs only a few cents. The voice of a Caruso recorded thereon makes it sell for perhaps a dollar. To measure the sales tax only by the value of the physical material in this phonograph record is to apply an impossible formula. [Id. at 116–17, 213 S.E.2d at 29.[9]]

The movie film cases have been applied to reject the severability argument in the leasing of video tapes for television broadcasting. See Turner Communications Corp. v. Chilivis, 239 Ga. 91, 236 S.E.2d 251 (1977). A transfer of film negatives and master recordings used for making audio-visual aids for the training of medical personnel was held subject to sales tax, despite the purchaser's argument that its primary interest was not in the physical objects but in the right to exploit the intellectual products they embodied. Simplicity Pattern Company, Inc. v. State Board of Equalization, 27 Cal.3d 900, 167 Cal.Rptr. 366, 615 P.2d 555 (1980).

At the administrative level, taxing authorities in at least 36 states, as of 1981, reportedly imposed a sales tax on software transfers. See White and Venecek, Taxpayer Beware! The Current State of Computer Software Taxation, 60 Taxes 373 (1982). According to the Wayne Note, supra, at 1531–36, as of 1977, 24 states taxed the sale of both canned and custom software, and 10 other states taxed canned software only.

7

From the standpoint of Maryland law, we conclude that the program copy acquisitions by Equitable are subject to sales tax for the following reasons.

We have indicated in parts (1) and (5) of this opinion both certain misconceptions in the technological underpinnings of the decisions holding taped copies to be intangible and our concerns with the apparent departures in reasoning from that usually applied in sales tax cases. Secondly, there is a substantial question whether the decision that set the course for the line of program cases, Universal Computer, supra, is consistent with existing Maryland law. That decision rested largely on *Washington Times–Herald* which held the acquisition of cartoon mats to be the purchase of personal services. Md.Code, Art. 81, § 326(dd) exempts, inter alia, the sale of mats under circumstances therein set forth. The exemption was added by Chapter 530 of the Acts

---

9. *Crescent Amusement* was distinguished by the Supreme Court of Tennessee in Commerce Union Bank v. Tidwell, supra, involving computer programs, because the latter were said to involve no product but only information, with the tangible tape as an incidental.

of 1973. At a minimum, enactment of the exemption indicates a legislative recognition that the sales tax statute could be applied to purchases of mats. Similarly, § 326(k) exempts rentals of motion picture films to persons whose gross receipts are subject to amusement tax. The indication is that, absent the exemption, neither the artistic content nor the right to exhibit the film copy would be severed from the tangible medium and thereby placed beyond the reach of the sales tax act.

Additionally, this Court's discussion of computer software in the context of a bundled installation in the *Greyhound* case leads to the classification of the subject programs as tangible.[10] [Greyhound Computer v. St. Dept., 271 Md. 674, 320 A.2d 52 (1974).] * * *

* * * [A]t page 679 of 271 Md., 55–56 of 320 A.2d, this Court said:

However, it cannot be ascertained from the record before us that portion of the purchase price attributable to such of the software as is tangible, or that portion attributable to that which is intangible.

The difference between the two categories can best be delineated by a simple illustration. A privately commissioned recording, with no restriction on use, of a symphony played by a noted orchestra, has a value far in excess of that of the plastic disc or tape on which it is recorded, and would be subject to assessment for tax purposes at its full cash value. A privately commissioned performance of the same symphony by the same orchestra, however, although it might entail the same expenditure, would produce nothing tangible that could be reached by a tax on personal property.

Two concepts are involved in this passage, tangibility and cost. While the passage may be dicta, it was nevertheless expressed for the guidance of the agency on remand. Our analogy to a phonorecord recognized both its tangibility and its valuation based on cost, including the entire cost of the privately commissioned performance assumed in the illustration. Similarly, in the property tax context, a newly acquired phonorecord owned by a commercial radio station would be taxed as tangible personal property. The assessment would not be based simply on the value of its tangible material; rather, original cost less depreciation or its market value would be used.

The same is true in the instant matter. A tape containing a copy of a canned program does not lose its tangible character, because its

---

10. Other courts have read *Greyhound* in different ways. Compare State v. Central Computer Services, supra, 349 So.2d at 1160 ("Other jurisdictions have distinguished between computer software and tangible personal property [citing *Greyhound*]."); Honeywell Information Systems, Inc. v. Maricopa County, supra, 118 Ariz. 171, 575 P.2d at 803 ("There is little doubt that computer software is intangible property * * * every jurisdiction which has considered the issue agrees [citing *Greyhound*]."); University Microfilms v. Scio Township, Washtenaw County, 76 Mich.App. 616, 619, 257 N.W.2d 265, 267 (1977) (plaintiff directs court to *Greyhound* which holds that computer software, i.e., cards, tapes, discs, are intangible); with First National Bank of Springfield v. Department of Revenue, supra, 85 Ill.2d at 92, 51 Ill.Dec. at 671, 421 N.E.2d at 179 (*Greyhound* seen as "holding that only so much of software as consists of services is intangible and not taxable").

content is a reproduction of the product of intellectual effort, just as the phonorecord does not become intangible, because it is a reproduction of the product of artistic effort. The price paid for a copy of a canned program reflects the cost of developing the program which the proprietor hopes to recover, with profit, by spreading the cost among its customers. Simply because the canned program on tape is much more expensive than the typical phonorecord, the program tape is not any less tangible.

The phonorecord analogy is directly addressed by Equitable. It says that in the case of the recording "*the intangible information has no value without the tangible record * * *.*" (Emphasis in original.) The same is true of the program copies Equitable acquired in the transactions being taxed. The millions of magnetic impulses which in their precise order have meaning were conveyed to the computer, in the transactions as carried out, by tapes. A meaningful sequence of magnetic impulses cannot float in space. Equitable's argument has merit, if the direct input by keyboard, without documentation, alternative (a service transaction) or the electronic transmission, without documentation, alternative (no tangible carrier) is the form of transaction under consideration. But, because a taxable transaction might have been structured in a nontaxable form, it does not thereby become nontaxable.

It is said each tape is used only once. But a dress pattern purchased at retail and used to make only one dress (or, even if never used) is taxable.

Equitable points to the provisions of the contract under which a delivery copy of a program, if lost or destroyed, will be replaced by the proprietor at minimal or no additional cost. On the other hand, the purchaser of a phonorecord which is lost or destroyed would have to replace it by paying the current price for another copy. This economic fact simply reflects that the proprietors of canned programs are better able to obtain thousands of dollars for a program copy by eliminating the customer's risk of accidental loss. It would be overreaching to attempt to charge a second retail price when a replacement copy is reproduceable at minor cost.

Finally, Equitable argues that a purchased program "can be and was in fact *severed and exists apart* from the tangible transfer medium * * *." (Emphasis in original.) As shown above, the copy delivered to Equitable does not become severed in any physical sense from the tape when the tape is used to structure computer memory.

We do not discern any legally significant difference for sales tax purposes between the canned computer program on magnetic tape and music on a phonograph record. As stated in the *National Commission on New Technological Uses of Copyrighted Works, Final Report* at 10 (1978): "Both recorded music and computer programs are sets of information in a form which, when passed over a magnetized head, cause minute currents to flow in such a way that desired physical work is accomplished." In the case of the phonograph record, the sales tax statute in Maryland has never been viewed as conceptually severing the copy of the performance from the tangible carrier. We conclude that the statute does not sever copies of computer programs from the tangible carriers employed in the subject sales.

JUDGMENT OF THE CIRCUIT COURT FOR BALTIMORE CITY REVERSED.

Notes and Problems

A. As the cases and authorities cited in the principal case suggest, the taxation of computer software has been the focus of considerable judicial and scholarly interest. In recent years, many States have dealt specifically with the taxability of computer software, through legislation or administrative regulations, in an effort to resolve the questions raised by cases like *Equitable Trust.* See Fenchel & Koeppel, "Computer Software and Sales Taxation," 3 J.State Tax. 165 (1984) (summarizing the position of each State with citation to the relevant legislative, administrative, or case authority). The trend has been to tax canned but not custom-made software. As of 1987, 28 of 46 jurisdictions (45 States and the District of Columbia) followed that practice. CCH All States Guide, p. 6022 (Chart). Sixteen States taxed both canned and custom-made programs. Id. And only one State—Illinois—exempted both all software from sales taxation. Id.

B. *Canned as Compared to Custom-made Software.* The practice of taxing canned but not custom-made software collides with the widely applied sales tax view that there is no justification for exempting custom-made articles from tax, so long as the same article, when bought off-the-peg, is taxable. If custom-made articles were not taxed, a dress bought in a department store would be taxed, but not a specially designed gown made by a fashionable couturier. Exempting custom-made computer software programs, while taxing canned programs, tends to favor larger businesses at the expense of smaller ones. Moreover, there is an element of delusion in categorizing as "canned" any except the simplest and most standardized types of software. In many of the decided cases, including those holding the software taxable, some modification in the programs was required to adapt them to the customer's needs. Consequently, a persuasive case can be made for treating both canned and custom-made software alike. Revenue needs point to the wisdom of subjecting both types of programs to tax, as some legislatures have done.

As the senior author of this casebook has written:

> There are * * * persuasive reasons for taxing both custom-made and canned computer software programs. First, as a matter of tax equality, if canned programs are taxed, customized programs should not be tax free. Second, there is no good reason for taxing phonographic records and music tapes and dramatic and other presentations, while not taxing records, tapes, and punch cards that embody computer software programs. Finally, there is the overriding wisdom of the view of tax economists that, so long as the states tax sales of tangible

personal property generally, services likewise should be taxed, except for special areas such as medical and health services.

J. Hellerstein, "Significant Sales and Use Tax Developments During the Past Half–Century," 39 Vand.L.Rev. 961, 973 (1986). For other references dealing with the taxation of computer software, see Tunick & Schechter, "State Taxation of Computer Programs: Tangible or Intangible," 63 Taxes 54 (1985); Hanlon, "Computer Software and Sales Taxes: New Cases Take an Old Direction," 25 J.State Tax. 315 (1984); Raabe, "Property, Sales, and Use Taxation of Custom and 'Canned' Computer Software: Emerging Judicial Guidelines," 36 Tax Exec. 227 (1984); Comment, "Software and Sales Taxes: The Illusory Intangible," 63 B.U.L.Rev. 181 (1983); Politi, Barbiarz & Ferrente, "Sales Taxation of Computer Software and Hardware: A Massachusetts Perspective," 1 J.State Tax. 329 (1983); Fenchel & Koeppel, "Computer Software and Sales Taxation," 3 J.State Tax. 165 (1984). For a case dealing with the rental of computer time, see p. 701 infra.

C. *"Operational" versus "Applications" Programs.* The Kansas Supreme Court distinguished between "operational" and "applications" programs in ruling on the taxability of computer software under the State's ad valorem property tax. In Matter of Protest of Strayer, 239 Kan. 136, 716 P.2d 588 (1986), the court held that operational programs, without which a computer cannot operate, have a value that is to be considered an essential component of the computer hardware and are therefore taxable as tangible personal property in conjunction with the hardware. Application programs, which are particularized instructions adopted for special purposes, are intangible property exempt from the State's tax on tangible personal property. See generally Bryant & Mather, "Property Taxation of Computer Software," 18 N.Y.L.F. 59 (1972); Heinzman, "Computer Software: Should it be Treated as Tangible Property for Ad Valorem Tax?," 37 J.Taxation 184 (1972).

References. Kilpatrick, "Scope of State Sales Transactions," in Reappraisal of Business Taxes, Tax Institute, Inc., 76 (1962); Beckwith, "Application of Sales Tax to Services," 1965 Procs. Nat. Ass'n of Tax Adm'rs. 116; Annot., 172 A.L.R. 1317; Marx, "Sales Taxation in the Service and Information Economy," 7 Hamline L.Rev. 19 (1984); McCloud, "Sales Tax and Use Tax: Historical Developments and Differing Features," 22 Duquesne L.Rev. 823 (1984).

ASSIGNMENT

Analyze the sales and use tax statutes of your State and the rules and regulations bearing on the distinction between sales and services. Classify the treatment of transactions involving (a) professionals, (b) the graphic arts, (c) computer software, and (d) others. What tests are used for distinguishing tangible personal property from services for purposes of your State's sales or use tax?

(b) License to Use Tangible Personal Property as a Sale

HERBERTSON v. CRUSE

Supreme Court of Colorado, 1946
115 Colo. 274, 170 P.2d 531

JACKSON, JUSTICE. This case arose when plaintiff in error, to whom we will hereinafter refer as taxpayer, sought a declaratory judgment defining his rights in respect to application of the Colorado sales and service tax statutes. His complaint was dismissed on motion of defendant, director of revenue, in whose favor judgment was entered for $4,643.67. This assessment covered the period from October 1, 1941 to May 31, 1944. By writ of error, the taxpayer brings the case here for review.

Taxpayer is engaged in the driverless-car business in the City and County of Denver. This involves the purchase of automobiles in wholesale quantities and renting them to the public. The renter's payment includes "(a) a time charge, (b) a mileage charge, (c) a service charge, (d) an oil and gas charge, and (e) a damage charge."

In its judgment, the trial court adopted the director's theory that a sales tax was due on each auto purchased and used by taxpayer in his business, that a service tax was due upon the sums received as a time charge and mileage charge for the use of each car, as well as on the other elements making up the total charge for the use of the rented car. The Colorado service tax was repealed as of February 28, 1945, S.L. '45, chapter 227, but was in force during the time covered by this litigation.

Taxpayer's theory is that he should not be required to pay a sales tax upon automobiles purchased in his business (third specification of points), but that he should collect from his customers and pay to the director a sales tax upon the time charge and mileage charge under section 2(q) of the Sales Tax Act, S.L. '37, chapter 230, page 1075, 1079 (fourth specification of points) * * *

Taxpayer relies especially on section 2(q), supra, of the sales tax law, which reads as follows:

"When right to continuous possession or use of any article of tangible personal property is granted under a lease or contract and such transfer of possession would be taxable if outright sale were made, such lease or contract shall be considered the sale of such article and the tax shall be computed and paid by the vendor upon the rentals paid."

Based upon this section, the director promulgated special rule 12, September 15, 1940, which reads:

"Motor Vehicles—Continuous Possession Leases.—Where a right to continuous possession of a motor vehicle is granted under a lease or contract for which the lessee pays a monthly rental, these transactions are hereby deemed to come within the provisions of Sec. 2(q) of the Sales Tax statute so as to subject the monthly rentals to the two per cent sales tax. The original purchase of the leased equipment by the lessor is therefore held to be a purchase for resale exempt from the sales tax. The purchase of repair parts and supplies which are used on such motor vehicles are also wholesale purchases and exempt from the sales tax. The continuous possession leases hereby made subject to the sales tax will not henceforth be subject to the service tax. This regulation shall be in full force and effect on and after September 1, 1940. All prior rules and regulations in conflict herewith are hereby revoked."

We, like the director and the trial court, are of the opinion that the continuous possession contemplated by both the statute and the rule is not shown in this case. It seems apparent that the most clear cut example of what the law is intended to reach is the case of a calculating machine or multigraph machine installed at the place of lessee's business and supervised by lessor under a rental agreement covering a continuous (and usually a very considerable) period of time. This involves a more permanent type of lessee than the multifarious types, renting driverless cars for their various purposes, where it might well happen that thirty different persons, each on a different day within a month, could have the rental service of the same car. In the former case, the lessee is securing the most permanent title that the nonselling policy of the lessor allows him to acquire. In the latter case, it doubtless never enters the head of the temporary renter-driver that anyone could possibly call him a purchaser or part owner of the car he was driving, especially when he knows that his name has never appeared as the registered owner of the car; nor does he ever appear as the taxpayer, subject to a property tax on the car.

Taxpayer also relies upon the fact that he purchases the cars at wholesale as a reason why he should not be subject to a sales tax on these autos. He contends that he is not the ultimate user contemplated by the statute, but that the renter is the ultimate user; that the automobiles are not entirely consumed by the renters, but that they are resold either to a dealer for resale or to a user—in which event a sales tax is collected and remitted to the revenue department. Taxpayer then argues that in Bedford v. Colorado Fuel & Iron Corp., 102 Colo. 538, 81 P.2d 752, the tax sustained was upon property used and consumed in the manufacturing business to produce articles for sale. Likewise, in Carpenter v. Carman Distributing Co., 111 Colo. 566, 144 P.2d 770, the tax sustained was upon supplies used in a laundry and dry cleaning business. But in the case at bar, taxpayer argues that he neither uses nor consumes the automobiles, nor are they used to produce any commodity.

In Bedford v. Colorado Fuel & Iron Corp., supra [102 Colo. 538, 81 P.2d 754], we said of the sales tax: "The statute was fundamentally intended to impose a tax upon that which is consumed and used and exempts only that which is sold for resale." Taxpayer at no time has contended that he is in the business of selling the cars at retail. The fact that he buys the cars at wholesale rates does not, therefore, of itself exempt him from the tax. His ultimate argument is therefore that he is not the consumer or user, but that the various renters (few or numerous as the case may be) of the cars are the real consumers or users and each should pay the sales tax based on the length of time the car is rented.

Without an express statutory provision, we do not feel there is justification in adopting such a position, which clearly goes beyond the purview of section 2(q) supra. We also believe the position so urged by taxpayer is not consistent with the basic definitions of "wholesale sale" and "retail sale" found in the statute. Section 2(e) and section 2(g), S.L. '35, chapter 189, read as follows:

"2(e). The term 'wholesale sale' means a sale by wholesalers to retail merchants, jobbers, dealers or other wholesalers for resale and does not include a sale by wholesalers to users or consumers, not for resale; and the sales shall be deemed a retail sales, and subject to the provisions of this Act."

"2(g). 'Retail sale' includes all sales made within the state except wholesale sales."

We are of the opinion that under the foregoing provisions the sale of an automobile by the wholesaler to the taxpayer in the instant case was a sale by a wholesaler to a user or consumer not for resale, and was therefore subject to a sales tax as a retail sale; that the user and consumer of an automobile may not only be he who devotes it to his own personal use, but also he who, for hire, lends or leases it to a third person; and that there was no showing of continuous use by the renter sufficient to bring the case within section 2(q), supra, of the statute and special rule 12, supra, promulgated thereunder.

* * *

Notes and Problems

A. *Holdings Under License to Use Provisions.* The statute involved in the principal case did not tax a "license to use" tangible personal property. Many of the statutes use the broader language of license to use, and they cover auto rentals of the character involved in the principal case. See, e.g., N.Y.Tax Law § 1101(b)(5), CCH ¶ 97–353, P–H ¶ 22,510.85; Buckley Funeral Homes, Inc. v. City of New York, 199 Misc. 195, 105 N.Y.S.2d 478 (Sup. Ct., N.Y.Co.1949), affirmed 277 A.D. 1096, 100 N.Y.S.2d 1023 (1st Dept. 1950).

Under broad definitions of sale covering licenses to use, a baby diaper service, Saverio v. Carson, 186 Tenn. 166, 208 S.W.2d 1018 (1948), and a supplier of office coats and towels, Philadelphia Ass'n of Linen Suppliers v. Philadelphia, 139 Pa. 560, 12 A.2d 789 (1940), have been held taxable on receipts from their customers. An ice skating rink has been taxed on its receipts from rentals of skates. Pla Mor, Inc. v. Glander, 149 Ohio St. 301, 78 N.E.2d 725 (1948).

A taxpayer who rented juke boxes and pin ball machines to taverns and storekeepers in Florida was held taxable under the State's sales tax, which covered the "gross proceeds derived from the lease or rental of tangible personal property," but only on his share of the receipts, not the total take of the instruments. Gay v. Supreme Distributors, Inc., 54 So.2d 805 (Fla.1951). In Undercofler v. Whiteway Neon Ad, Inc., 114 Ga.App. 644, 152 S.E.2d 616 (1966), a lessor of specially built illuminated signs, who contended that a large part of the rental payments represented repair and maintenance, was required to collect tax from lessees under a sales tax statute that includes rentals of property. See generally Annot., 2 A.L.R. 4th 859.

B. *Rental of Coin–Operated Facilities.* Is the rental of lockers in railroad stations and other public places a "sale" within the meaning of a license to use provision of a sales tax? The taxpayer owned coin-operated lockers in which baggage and other personal belongings may be checked for a dime or a quarter for no more than 24 hours. The court held that the locker use did not constitute a "license to use" tangible personal property because the New York City statute covers only transactions in which there is a transfer of title or possession in the article; the taxpayer's patrons do not, like the taxpayer who rents a chauffeur-driven car or the motion picture exhibitor who is licensed to show a film, obtain "possession" of the article. Instead, the court analogized the case to the "service" rendered in a railroad station when luggage is hand-checked in the baggage room. American Locker Co., Inc. v. City of New York, 308 N.Y. 264, 125 N.E.2d 421 (1955). But see State Tax Comm'n v. Peck, 106 Ariz. 394, 476 P.2d 849 (1970), in which proceeds from coin-operated laundromats and car-washing machines were held taxable under the definition of sales as including "[l]easing or renting tangible personal property for a consideration." See Ariz.Rev.Stat. § 42–1309, CCH ¶ 93–755, P–H ¶ 22,717–0. Compare with the locker rental cases the taxability of outdoor billboard advertising. Is the owner of the billboard subject to sales tax on the payments it receives for exhibiting its customers' advertisements on its billboards? White Advertising Co. v. Kosydar, Ohio CCH ¶ 60–204.15, P–H ¶ 23,423 (Ohio Board of Tax Appeals 1975).

Is the court in *American Locker* correct in declaring that, in the case involving a chauffeur-driven funeral car (Buckley Funeral Service Home v. City of New York, Note A supra), the licensee rather than the car owner's driver has "possession" of the car? Should the issue as to whether there is a taxable "license to use" the lockers depend on whether there is a transfer of "possession" of the article? The possession concept has its usefulness and its niceties of delineation for various purposes of property law, but query whether it is the key issue in determining sales tax liability. The purpose of the license to use provision is to sweep into the taxable sale rental or leasing substitutes for sales, such as the now widespread leasing of vehicles and office machinery in industrial and commercial businesses; it also encompasses in many States the gradual use of the article by various users, such as rentals of books, tuxedos, and other articles. The economic consumption of the lockers is made by the renter; should that rather than "possession" be the test of taxability? Is the sounder basis for the holding that the court regarded the use of the lockers as essentially a service, closely analogous to hand-checking in railroad stations?

C. *Rental of Computer Time.* The Ohio definition of a sale includes "all transactions by which ＊ ＊ ＊ a license to use or consume tangible personal property is or is to be granted ＊ ＊ ＊ for a consideration in any manner," Ohio Rev.Code § 5739.01(B), CCH ¶ 95–003, P–H ¶ 22,520.4, but exempts "personal service transactions which involve the transfer of tangible personal property as an inconsequential element, for which no separate charges are made." Id. See p. 678 supra. The Ohio Supreme Court has held that the rental of computer time constitutes a taxable license to use tangible personal property under the statute. The court has rejected the view that there was no license to use or consume because users had "no exclusive right to use the computers, no exclusive control of the computers ＊ ＊ ＊ and therefore no license to use or consume." Babcock & Wilcox Co. v. Kosydar, 48 Ohio St.2d 251, 257, 358 N.E.2d 544, 548 (1976). The court has also rejected the view that the "hard copy printouts" that customers sometimes receive in connection with their rentals of computer time constitute an "inconsequential element" in a personal service transaction, on the ground that the true object of the customers was obtaining possession of such printouts. Citizens Financial Corp. v. Kosydar, 43 Ohio St.2d 148, 331 N.E.2d 435 (1975). See also Accountants Computer Services, Inc. v. Kosydar, 35 Ohio St.2d 120, 298 N.E.2d 519 (1973).

D. *Miscellaneous Rentals.* The rental of mailing lists was held to be a taxable rental of tangible personal property in Alan Drey Co., Inc. v. State Tax Comm'n, 67 A.D.2d 1055, 413 N.Y.S.2d 516 (1979). In Fingerhut Products Co. v. Commissioner of Revenue, 258 N.W.2d 606 (Minn.1977) and Spencer Gifts, Inc. v. Taxation Div. Director, 182 N.J.Super. 179, 440 A.2d 104 (1981), however, the courts held that the rental of mailing lists constituted the lease of nontaxable "intangible" information with the use of the tangible mailing lists being "merely incidental to the use of the incorporeal information contained in those lists." Fingerhut Products Co. v. Commissioner of Revenue, supra, 258 N.W.2d at 610.

(c) License to Use Intangibles as Distinguished From a Sale of Tangibles

Notes and Problems

A. Because the retail sales taxes of many States generally apply only to sales of *tangible* personal property, controversy has developed as to the classification of transactions as sales of tangibles, as distinguished from dealings in intangibles. An interesting series of cases arose in New York involving the use of art work and photographs in publications. In Howitt v. Street & Smith Publications, Inc., 276 N.Y. 345, 12 N.E.2d 435 (1938), the court held that no sales tax was payable on a license granted by a painter to reproduce several of the artist's works in a magazine, on the theory that the reproduction rights were intangibles. The physical use of the paintings was limited to taking a photograph for use by the photo-engraver. Subsequently, in Pagano and Andersen v. City of New York, 176 Misc. 896, 30 N.Y.S.2d 302 (Sup.Ct.1939), affirmed 267 A.D. 980, 48 N.Y.S.2d 692, 693 (1st Dep't 1944), affirmed 295 N.Y. 782, 784, 66 N.E.2d 298, 299 (1946), the court dealt with commercial illustrations drawn expressly for advertising or other use in publications, and photographs of models, articles of clothing, automobiles, and so on, taken especially for use in the publications. The court rejected the view that the commercial illustrators and photographers, who claimed title to their drawings and photographs, merely granted the advertiser or publications an intangible right to reproduce their art work and held that the transactions were subject to sales tax as involving licenses to use tangible personalty.

Subsequently, the issue arose again in the case of photographs taken for a publication. The testimony of the photographer was that title to the negative and prints remained in her; that she delivered prints to the publishers for photo-engraving; and that the prints were returned to her after they had been used. The court set aside the tax, distinguishing the *Pagano* and *Andersen* cases on the ground that the City of New York had offered proof in those cases that the publishers assumed dominion over the prints by retouching and correcting them—proof which established "virtually a transfer of title." Frissell v. McGoldrick, 300 N.Y. 370, 91 N.E.2d 305 (1950). In the absence of such evidence, the court found that the publisher's possession of the prints was not such a "transfer of possession" as is taxed, because it was a mere incident to the right to reproduce the print. In 1955 the Appellate Division, in a case closely similar to the *Washington Times–Herald* facts, see p. 669, supra, held taxable the products of commercial artists who did drawing and lettering for a comic strip publisher; the work was done on cardboards or art boards. Hillman Periodicals, Inc. v. Gerosa, 285 App.Div. 441, 137 N.Y.S.2d 863 (1st Dep't 1955), affirmed 308 N.Y. 982, 127 N.E.2d 842 (1955). The Court distinguished the *Frissell* and *Howitt* cases by pointing out that there the artists "assigned all right, title and interest" in the material to the publisher, whereas here "there was an integration of the services rendered into tangible personal properties which were sold irrevocably to petitioner."

Should the key test in these cases be whether the economic usefulness of the article is exhausted when the articles are used by the publisher? Under this test, if a work of art such as a painting, whether specially commissioned or already in existence, is used for advertising or other reproduction purposes and still retains substantial utility as a painting, then the payment to the artist would be classified as consideration for an intangible reproduction right, but where all substantial use of the article, such as comic strip mats or advertising illustrations, is ended on publication, the transaction should be classified as a taxable sale, regardless of where title is lodged.

Compare In the Matter of Cut–Outs, Inc. v. State Tax Comm'n, 85 A.D. 2d 838, 446 N.Y.S.2d 436 (3d Dept.1981), in which, in deciding a sale for resale question, the court adopted as its test whether the primary utility of the property at issue had been exhausted before it was transferred to the customer:

> Petitioner was engaged in die cutting, mounting and finishing work for the graphic arts industry. It purchased the steel rule cutting dies, made to its customers' specifications, from die makers for use in its cutting presses. Upon completion of petitioner's work, the dies became the property of the customers, and were stored by petitioner for a two-year period, after which the dies were either sent

to the customers, if so requested, or discarded. While the prices fixed by petitioner reflected a charge for the cost of the dies, the amount was not shown separately on the invoices. No such charge was made on reorders, or where the customer provided the necessary die. From these facts, the commission concluded that the cutting dies purchased by petitioner were used in its production process prior to any transfer of title or possession to the customer and, accordingly, it denied petitioner the benefit of the "sale for resale" exclusion.

Since the dies were used by petitioner as part of the production process, it is apparent that their primary utility to petitioner and its customers was exhausted prior to any transfer to the customers, except to the extent that the dies might later be used again in the production process for reorders. Unlike containers, which fall within the "sale for resale" exclusion (see, e.g., Matter of Burger King v. State Tax Comm., 51 N.Y.2d 614, 435 N.Y.S.2d 689, 416 N.E.2d 1024), the dies are not "a critical element of the final product sold to customers" (id. p. 623, 435 N.Y.S.2d 689, 416 N.E.2d 1024). Petitioner's purchase of the dies was not for the primary purpose of reselling them to its customers, but rather for petitioner to use in its presses to make the final product, and any resales of the dies were purely incidental (Matter of Laux Adv. v. Tully, 67 A.D.2d 1066, 414 N.Y.S. 2d 53). [446 N.Y.S.2d at 437.]

B. In the *Washington Times–Herald* case, p. 669 supra, Judge Stephens in concurring took the position that the transaction did not involve a sale of tangible personal property but instead merely a license to use an intangible, namely, a right to produce a comic strip, which is non-taxable. The difficulty with this view is that it is not borne out by the findings, for all interest in the mat was in the newspaper and the mat was used in the reproduction process. The entire usefulness of the artist's comic strip is in a series of publications in newspapers and perhaps comic books, carried out through the preparation of mats of the strip. Therefore, the case would seem to fall within the decisions in other jurisdictions holding taxable dress designs, People ex rel. Foremost Studio, Inc. v. Graves, 246 App.Div. 130, 284 N.Y.S. 906 (3rd Dep't 1936), and commercial illustrations and photographs created for reproduction in advertising. In the *Times-Herald* case, although the price paid is essentially for the right to reproduce the work, the work is embodied in the tangible property transferred to the purchaser or user.

C. *Exhibition of Motion Pictures, Television Films, and Video Tapes.* In Matter of United Artists Corporation v. Taylor, 273 N.Y. 334, 7 N.E.2d 254 (1937), a Delaware corporation, with its principal office in New York, obtained licenses from Hollywood motion picture producers to distribute their films as an independent contractor. Motion picture theatre operators paid United Artists a percentage of the box office gross receipts for the right to show the films. The exhibition contracts were made in New York City but the films were exhibited throughout the world. New York City sought to tax all the receipts of United Artists under the license to use clause of its sales tax; the statute defines a sale as:

any transfer of title or possession or both, exchange or barter, license to use or consume, conditional or otherwise, in any manner or by any means whatsoever for a consideration, or any agreement therefor.

The court held that the taxable transaction was the transfer of possession of the positive print to the exhibitor with a license to use the print for a specified time. Under the then-prevailing New York City enabling act, the City's authorization by the State legislature to impose a sales tax precluded "the imposition of a tax on any transaction originating and/or consummated outside of the territorial limits of such city." The court sustained the tax as applied to licenses to exhibit the films within the city's limits, but annulled the levy, in view of the enabling act's restrictions, with respect to licenses to exhibit outside the city.

While this result appears sound, how can it be squared with the language of the taxing act as including "any agreement therefor," inasmuch as the agreement was made within the city? Is the agreement the transaction taxed?

For other cases holding that a license to exhibit motion pictures is a taxable sale or use under substantially similar provisions taxing licenses to use or rentals of tangible personal property and not, as contended by the taxpayers, payment merely for an intangible right of exhibition, see Saenger Realty Corp. v. Grosjean, 194 La. 470, 193 So. 710 (1940), appeal dismissed 310 U.S. 613, 60 S.Ct. 1089 (1940); Crescent Amusement Co. v. Carson, 187 Tenn. 112, 213 S.W.2d 27 (1948); American Television Co. v. Hervey, 253 Ark. 1010, 490 S.W.2d 796 (1973); Boswell v. Paramount Television Sales, Inc., 291 Ala. 490, 282 So.2d 892 (1973); Columbia Pictures Industries, Inc. v. Tax Commissioner, 176 Conn. 604, 410 A.2d 457 (1979); Universal Images, Inc. v. Missouri Dept. of Revenue, 608 S.W.2d 417 (Mo. 1980). See generally, Annot., 10 A.L.R.4th 1209.

The question as to whether a license to use films and video tapes in telecasting constitutes a taxable sale arose in Vermont under a statute defining a "rental, lease, license to use" tangible personal property as a sale. The Vermont Supreme Court sustained a use tax on films and video tapes licensed to television stations, saying:

Although the question presented is one of first impression in Vermont, there is no dearth of analogous case law in other jurisdictions on both sides of the issue. Without engaging in a protracted analysis of the subtle factual and statutory language distinctions which can be found in cases cited by both parties here, it is fair to say that the cases which taxpayer has cited in support of its position generally support the theory that transactions of the type here in question involve "intangible" reproduction rights as opposed to "tangible" property rights. These cases take the view that products such as television films are nothing without the attendant right to broadcast and that they thus cannot be classified as "tangible personal property" for tax purposes. See Washington Times Herald v. District of Columbia, 94 U.S.App.D.C. 154, 213 F.2d 23 (1954); Watson Industries, Inc. v. Shaw, 235 N.C. 203, 69 S.E.2d 505 (1952); Burgess v. Ames, 359 Ill. 427, 194 N.E. 565 (1935).

Cases cited by the Department of Taxes, on the other hand, stand for the proposition that it is a finished product (video tape or film) which is the subject of the transaction and that a license to exhibit or broadcast without the tangible finished product itself would be valueless. See Boswell v. Paramount Television Sales, Inc., 291 Ala. 490, 282 So.2d 892 (1973); Florida Association of Broadcasters v. Kirk, 264 So.2d 437 (Fla.Dist.Ct.App.), cert. denied, 268 So.2d 534 (Fla.1972); Crescent Amusement Co. v. Carson, 187 Tenn. 112, 213 S.W.2d 27 (1948).

To the extent that these cases can be extracted from their singular factual and statutory contexts and reduced to abstract legal holdings, we must recognize the existence of a genuine split of authority on the issue before us. The opposing theories are not difficult to conceptualize; the choices are clear.

We are pursuaded by the reasoning of the more recent decisions in this area which have embraced the theory now advanced by the Department of Taxes. We find particularly germane the point made by the Supreme Court of Arkansas that "the right to use property cannot be separated from the property itself." American Television Co. v. Hervey, 253 Ark. 1010, 1014, 490 S.W.2d 796, 799 (1973). The right of which taxpayer speaks is simply of no value to it without the use of the video tape or film itself. [Mount Mansfield Television, Inc. v. Vermont Commissioner of Taxes, 133 Vt. 284, 336 A.2d 193, 194–195 (1975).]

The owner of the copyright of musical plays granted residents of California licenses to perform the musicals, and furnished the licensees with copies of the music for use in the production. The State Board of Equalization sought to subject the payments by the licensees to the copyright owner to use taxes. See Tams–Witmark Music Library, Inc. v. Municipal Court (unreported opinion, Cal.Ct.App., 9/29/75), certiorari denied [on issue of whether copyright holder was subject to personal jurisdiction in California], 425 U.S. 913, 96 S.Ct. 1511 (1976). Do the music copies perform a lesser function in a dramatic presentation than television and other films, video tapes, and records, so as to justify a holding that Tams–Witmark granted essentially an intangible right to produce the musical, to which the copies of the music were incidental?

D. *Sale–Leaseback Transactions.* In order to finance the purchase of equipment, a purchaser may enter into an arrangement whereby it sells the equipment it has purchased to a third party which immediately leases back the equipment to the original purchaser. In substance, these arrangements amount to little more than a loan transaction, whereby the "lessee" (borrower) amortizes the loan by paying "rent" to the "lessor" over the term of the loan. The question has arisen whether the rental payments made pursuant to a sale-leaseback arrangement are nevertheless taxable under a sales and use tax scheme that generally taxes rentals of tangible personal property. In Cedars-Sinai Medical Center v. State Board of Equalization, 162 Cal.App.3d 1182, 208 Cal.Rptr. 837 (1984), the court held that such rental payments were not taxable for the following reasons:

Plaintiff entered into the agreements with the leasing companies in order to obtain alternative financing of the equipment. That such was the object of the agreements, and the mutual intention of the companies, is shown by reasonable inference (from the undisputed evidence) that the companies, all of which are located outside of California, had no use for the equipment and were not interested in purchasing it from plaintiff. Indeed, following execution of the agreements the equipment remained at plaintiff's facility and was used by plaintiff there, just as it had been used after plaintiff purchased it from the vendors. Under the lease agreements between plaintiff and the companies plaintiff was responsible for payment of all license fees, assessments, and property, sales, use and other taxes imposed by any federal, state or local government or agency upon any of the equipment. Plaintiff assumed all risk of loss and liability in the operation, maintenance and storage of the equipment, and for damages for injury or death to persons or property arising therefrom. Plaintiff was required to keep the equipment insured against all risks of loss or damage "as are customarily insured against by companies owning equipment of similar character and engaged in a business similar to that engaged in" by plaintiff. The foregoing circumstances and provisions are inconsistent with a "sale" of the equipment by plaintiff to the leasing companies and indicate that despite plaintiff's formal transfer of title to the companies, plaintiff remained the owner of the equipment.

* * * As a practical matter plaintiff had no reason to "sell" the equipment to the companies and "rent" it back from them at a total cost to plaintiff of approximately $1,426,400 more than the original cost of the equipment. Viewed in their entirety plaintiff's transactions with the leasing companies were devices by which plaintiff in effect borrowed from them the money necessary to pay the full purchase price of the equipment to the vendors; the leasing companies reimbursed plaintiff for that portion of the purchase price it had paid to the vendors and then paid the balance of the price to the vendors on plaintiff's behalf; plaintiff, in the form of rent, repaid the companies the total amount of the purchase price plus interest. [208 Cal.Rptr. at 840–41.]

In some jurisdictions, however, sale-leasebacks have been determined to be taxable sales. In Midwest Federal Savings & Loan Ass'n v. Commissioner of Revenue, 259 N.W.2d 596 (Minn.1977), the bank sold computer equipment that it owned, and immediately leased it back for a 96–month period, the approximate useful life of the equipment. Monthly lease payments were provided for the equipment, which never left the bank's premises. In affirming a sales tax assessment of the rental payments, the court stated:

[The leasing agreement] provides no option for Midwest Federal to purchase the equipment or for lease payments to build equity in the equipment. The lease also allows Midwest Federal to cancel at any time after 66 months, although a penalty is imposed. Additionally, the lease provides that Midwest Federal is liable for any sales and use taxes levied on the lease. These are among the indicia that the agreement was a lease in fact as well as in form. Having elected to arrange its business in that manner, Midwest Federal is subject to the tax consequences of it. [259 N.W.2d at 599.]

Accord: Petrolane Northwest Gas Service, Inc. v. State Tax Com'n, 79 A.D.2d 1043, 435 N.Y.S.2d 187 (3d Dept.1981).

Similar results have been reached in other States. Bullock v. Citizens National Bank of Waco, 663 S.W.2d 923 (Tex.App.1984); Footpress Corp. v. Strickland, 242 Ga. 686, 251 S.E.2d 278 (1978); Rockwell International Corp. v. Commonwealth of Pennsylvania, 99 Pa.Cmwlth. 130, 512 A.2d 1332 (1986); Matter of Sherwood Diversified Services, Inc., 382 F.Supp. 1359 (S.D.N.Y.1974). Compare a sale-leaseback of medical equipment used by a hospital in which the initial acquisition of the equipment from the manufacturer was sought to be brought within the hospital's sales tax exemption. Continental Illinois Leasing Corp. v. Department of Revenue, 108 Ill.App.3d 583, 64 Ill.Dec. 189, 439 N.E.2d 118 (1982). The court held that the commercial leasing company acquired the equipment from the manufacturer in a sales taxable transaction.

The New York Regulations provide as follows:

A lease which has been entered into merely as a security agreement, but which does not in fact represent a transaction in which there has been a transfer of possession from the lessor to the lessee, is not a "sale" within the meaning of the Tax Law. [Reg. § 526.7(c)(3), CCH ¶ 65–116, P–H ¶ 22,128.]

SECTION 3. RETAIL SALE

(a) Sale for Resale Exemption

FAIRLAWN SHOPPER, INC. v. DIRECTOR, DIVISION OF TAXATION

Supreme Court of New Jersey, 1984.
98 N.J. 64, 484 A.2d 659.

CLIFFORD, J.

In these consolidated tax appeals we address the applicability of the New Jersey Sales and Use Tax Act, N.J.S.A. 54:32B–1 to –29 (Act), to the amounts expended by plaintiffs for certain outside printing costs in the plaintiffs' publication of free-circulation newspapers. The Director of the Division of Taxation (Director) seeks to apply the Act to so much of the printers' bills to plaintiffs as represent printing services, as well as to all materials other than newsprint. Plaintiffs allege two grounds of exemption: (1) that receipts from sales of newspapers are exempt from the tax imposed by the Act, see N.J.S.A. 54:32B–8(e)[1], and (2) that the sale of the newspapers from the printers to plaintiffs are sales for resale, which are exempt from the Act's tax pursuant to N.J.S.A. 54:32B–2(e)(1)(A). Alternatively, plaintiffs allege that the applica-

---

1. N.J.S.A. 54:32B–8(e) was repealed in 1980. L.1980, c. 105, § 46. This provision is now embodied in N.J.S.A. 54:32B–8.5. L.1980, c. 105, § 17.

tion of this tax to sales such as those at issue here is unconstitutional under the first amendment, N.J. Const. art. 1, para. 6, and the equal protection clause, U.S. Const. amend. XIV.

The record is embodied in the two-page "Stipulation of Facts" filed in each of these now-consolidated cases. The essential facts are as follows:

1. Plaintiff Fairlawn Shopper, Inc., owns, publishes, and distributes a newspaper entitled the "Fairlawn Shopper" and plaintiff Shopper Distributors, Inc., owns, publishes, and distributes newspapers entitled the "Hawthorne Shopper" and the "Garfield Shopper."

2. For the purposes of this litigation, the "Fairlawn Shopper," the "Hawthorne Shopper," and the "Garfield Shopper," when ultimately distributed to readers, are "newspapers" within the meaning of the Act.[2]

3. The newspapers are primarily distributed free-of-charge and their revenues are derived almost entirely from advertising.

4. The newspapers are actually produced by independent contract printing firms, which supply the necessary paper, ink, and dyes, printing the paper with their own machinery and employees. Plaintiffs nonetheless supply most of the substantive content of the newspapers.

5. The finished product is delivered by the printers to plaintiffs, who distribute the newspapers to the public on a weekly basis.

6. The amount of the tax in issue represents sales or use tax on the portions of the printers' bills to plaintiffs that represent the cost of printing services as well as materials other than newsprint.

7. The parties do not dispute the amount of tax that was assessed.[3]

On this factual basis the Tax Court found that the exemption afforded by N.J.S.A. 54:32B–8(e) was not intended to exempt newspapers as they pass between printer and publisher. However, Judge Andrew concluded that "the purchases by these plaintiffs of printing services and materials should properly be characterized as sales for the purpose of resale and exempt from sales and use tax. N.J.S.A. 54:32B–2(e)." (Footnote omitted). The Appellate Division, in an unreported decision, reversed the Tax Court judgment "for the reasons expressed in our opinion in Del Val Pennysaver, Inc. v. Director, Division of Taxation, [188 N.J.Super. 108, 456 A.2d 115 (1983)] * * *." In Del Val Pennysaver the court concluded that neither N.J.S.A. 54:32B–8(e) nor

2. The Director's contention before this Court that plaintiffs publish "advertising circulars" or "shoppers' guides" is contrary to the record before the Tax Court.
* * *

3. The tax assessed against plaintiff Fairlawn Shopper, Inc. was $11,760.47 plus penalty and interest. Plaintiff Shopper Distributors, Inc. was assessed $5,198.85 plus penalty and interest. The amounts in issue are secured by irrevocable documentary letters of credit.

N.J.S.A. 54:32B–2(e) was applicable in circumstances such as these. In so deciding, the court, relying on Princeton Community Phone Book, Inc. v. Director, Div. of Taxation, 145 N.J.Super. 589, 368 A.2d 933 (App.Div.1976), certif. den., 73 N.J. 66, 372 A.2d 331 (1977), stated that "what plaintiff's advertisers were buying was advertising space and not the finished shoppers guides per se. * * * It is equally apparent that what the printer sold to plaintiff was neither purchased by plaintiff for resale as such nor converted into a component part of a product produced for resale by plaintiff." Del Val Pennysaver, supra, 188 N.J. Super. at 114, 456 A.2d 115. We granted certification, 94 N.J. 516, 468 A.2d 175 (1983), to determine the impact of the Act on the free-circulation newspaper industry.

I

This appeal poses two entangled issues concerning tax exemptions. On the one hand we must determine what constitutes a "newspaper" for purposes of the Act and thereafter apply that determination to the publications at issue here. On the other hand we must review the "sale for resale" exemption of the Act to discern its effect on free-circulation publication. The resolution of these questions begins with an examination of the pertinent provisions of the Act.

N.J.S.A. 54:32B–8(e) provides that "[r]eceipts from the following shall be exempt from the tax on retail sales imposed under subsection (a) of section 3 and the use tax imposed under section 6: * * * (e) Sales of newspapers, magazines and periodicals * * *." The parties have stipulated that the publications at issue, when ultimately distributed to readers, were "newspapers" within the meaning of the Act. However, disagreement remains as to whether the newspapers in these circumstances should receive the tax exemption afforded by N.J.S.A. 54:32B–8(e).

* * *

[The court held that although the publications may be newspapers, the newspaper exemption was applicable only to an ultimate sale to a reader, not to the printing of the newspaper for the publisher.]

However, the fact that plaintiffs cannot successfully claim an exemption under N.J.S.A. 54:32B–8(e) does not diminish support for plaintiffs' assertion of a "sale for resale" exemption pursuant to N.J. S.A. 54:32B–2(e). In fact N.J.S.A. 54:32B–3(b)(1), while imposing a tax on the printing process, expressly excludes from the tax printing purchased for resale. In addition, the potential applicability of N.J.S.A. 54:32B–2(e) to circumstances such as these was specifically left unaddressed by the court in Jefferson Publishing Corp., supra, 217 Va. at 992 n. *, 234 S.E.2d at 301 n. * ("[W]e do not have the question whether such a transaction between a printer and a publisher-taxpayer may be exempt as a sale for resale."). We now conclude, as did the Tax Court, that the subject transactions constitute sales for resale and that plaintiffs are therefore entitled to an exemption in accordance with N.J.S.A. 54:32B–2 and –3.

N.J.S.A. 54:32B–3(a) imposes a tax on "[t]he receipts from every retail sale of tangible personal property, except as otherwise provided in this act." A "retail sale" is defined as "[a] sale of tangible personal property to any person for any purpose, other than (A) for resale either as such or as converted into or as a component part of a product produced for sale by the purchaser * * *." N.J.S.A. 54:32B–2(e)(1). Moreover, N.J.S.A. 54:32B–3(b) imposes a tax on "[t]he receipts from every sale, except for resale, of the following services: (1) Producing, fabricating, processing, printing or imprinting tangible personal property, performed for a person who directly or indirectly furnishes the tangible personal property, not purchased by him for resale, upon which such services are performed." Thus, the basic thrust of these provisions is that sales for the purpose of resale are to be exempted from the tax imposed by the Act. In other words, if the purchases by plaintiffs of printing services and materials are found to be sales for the purpose of resale, then plaintiffs would be exempt from the Act's tax on those purchases.

Consequently, the consideration that remains is whether the purchases in question satisfy the "sale for resale" exemption provision. While the Act fails to supply a definition of "resale", the fact that the plaintiffs distribute the subject newspapers free-of-charge seems to fly in the face of a conclusion that plaintiffs' purchases of printing services and materials were "sales for resale". However, the Act does provide a definition of "sale, selling or purchase," N.J.S.A. 54:32B–2(f), that supports plaintiffs' assertion of a "sale for resale" exemption.

N.J.S.A. 54:32B–2(f) provides as follows:

> Sale, selling or purchase. Any transfer of title or possession or both, exchange or barter, rental, lease or license to use or consume, conditional or otherwise, in any manner or by any means whatsoever *for a consideration,* or any agreement therefor, including the rendering of any service, taxable under this act, for a consideration or any agreement therefor. [Emphasis added.]

Thus, the Act requires *some* consideration to pass during the transfer of title or possession, although the Act is unclear as to the source of the consideration. Judge Andrew, relying on the decision of the Supreme Court of Ohio in Penton Publishing Co. v. Kosydar, 45 Ohio St.2d 16, 340 N.E.2d 396 (1976), concluded that

> a sale for resale is established under New Jersey law when the consideration for the resale comes from a third party other than the consumer. * * * The only logical conclusion to be drawn from the facts presented is that the contract between advertiser and publisher, in the case of free distribution publications such as these, must reflect not only a purchase of advertising space but the obligation of the publisher to distribute the publications as well.

The decision in Del Val Pennysaver, supra, 188 N.J.Super. 180, 456 A.2d 115, relied on by the Appellate Division here, rejected this determination as one "that defies logic, flies in the face of both the statute and our determination in [Princeton Community Phone Book, supra, 145 N.J.Super. 589, 368 A.2d 933], and mandates a repeal of the Tax Court judgment under review." Del Val Pennysaver, supra, 188 N.J. Super. at 112, 456 A.2d 115.

However, the Appellate Division's conclusion that "*Princeton [Community] Phone Book* is directly in point" is off the mark. That case involved a claim of exemption from sales tax imposed on the sales of paper and of printing and binding services to a publisher of a community telephone directory. In concluding that no exemption was justified, the court summarily stated that the Princeton Community Phone Book "is not produced for resale and therefore is not exempt from the tax under N.J.S.A. 54:32B–2(e)(1)(A)." As the Tax Court below noted with reference to the decision in Princeton Community Phone Book, supra, 145 N.J.Super. 589, 368 A.2d 933,

> [t]he court's brief opinion did not address the question of whether the free distribution of the phone book could constitute a resale on the basis that the consideration provided by the advertisers was not only for advertising but also for distribution to the public of the phone book free of charge. The court merely stated that the book was not produced for resale, based apparently on the fact that it was given away free. [Footnote omitted.]

Like the court in *Princeton Community Phone Book*, the Appellate Division in Del Val Pennysaver, supra, 188 N.J.Super. 108, 456 A.2d 115, merely stated that

> it is obvious that what plaintiff's advertisers were buying was advertising space and not the finished shoppers guides *per se.* These publications were distributed by plaintiff to the public free of charge. It is equally apparent that what the printer sold to plaintiff was neither purchased by plaintiff for resale as such nor converted into a component part of a product produced for sale by plaintiff. The subject transactions were not exempt from the tax under N.J.S.A. 54:32B–2(e) (1)(A). [Id. at 114, 456 A.2d 115.]

We disagree, and concur with the Tax Court's conclusion below that "[i]n effect, the advertisers are subsidizing the readers of these papers to the extent of the price per copy that the publisher would otherwise charge the consumer."

Although we recognize that tax exemptions are to be strictly construed against those seeking exemptions, "that principle does not justify distorting the language or the legislative intent." Paper Mill Playhouse v. Millburn Tp., 95 N.J. 503, 506–07, 472 A.2d 517 (1984) (quoting Boys' Club of Clifton, Inc. v. Jefferson, 72 N.J. 389, 398, 371 A.2d 22 (1977)); see also Millington Quarry, Inc. v. Taxation Div. Director, 5 N.J.Tax 144, 147–48 (1983) ("[T]he rule of strict construction does not require a strained construction or a construction that begrudges."). As this Court noted in Schierstead v. Brigantine, 29 N.J. 220, 148 A.2d 591 (1959), "statutes are to be read sensibly rather than literally and the controlling legislative intent is to be presumed as 'consonant to reason and good discretion.'" Id. at 230, 148 A.2d 591; see also State v. Clark, 29 N.J.Law 96, 99 (1860) ("If a literal construction of the words of a statute be absurd, the act must be so construed as to avoid the absurdity. The court must restrain the words."). In this case, to accept the Director's interpretation—that no consideration passes when the newspapers are distributed to the readers—would generate an unacceptable consequence: the subject newspapers would charge their readers some nominal price for the sole purpose of receiving the "sale for resale" exemption. We cannot accept this potential result.

Rather, we conclude that the consideration necessary to satisfy the Act's definition of a "sale" (and, by inference, a "resale") can be found to have been supplied by third parties—in this case, the advertisers who finance the publications. As Judge Andrew noted, "[i]t makes no logical sense for advertisers to purchase advertising space along with no guarantee that the publications will reach the reading public. This court will not close its eyes to the economic realities of the situation." Accordingly, we concur in the Tax Court's conclusion that plaintiffs' purchases of printing services and materials are "sales for resale" and are exempt, pursuant to N.J.S.A. 54:32B–2(e) from the tax imposed by the Act. Consequently, we need not address plaintiffs' alternative constitutional argument. See Donadio v. Cunningham, 58 N.J. 309, 325–26, 277 A.2d 375 (1971).

The judgment of the Appellate Division is reversed.

For reversal —CHIEF JUSTICE WILENTZ and JUSTICES CLIFFORD, SCHREIBER, HANDLER, POLLOCK, O'HERN and GARIBALDI—7.

For affirmance —None.

Notes and Problems

A. *Scope of Resale Provision.* In Mendoza Fur Dyeing Works, Inc. v. Taylor, 272 N.Y. 275, 5 N.E.2d 818 (1936), the taxpayer was engaged in the business of dying and processing fur skins owned by dealers and manufacturers. The taxpayer contended, and the intermediate appellate court agreed, that the taxpayer's purchases of dyes were excluded from the definition of a retail sale as a sale for resale on the ground that the dyes maintained their chemical character after completion of the dyeing process and that the dyer is therefore not the ultimate consumer of the dye. The Court of Appeals reversed, declaring.

> While double taxation is not to be favored and a statute is to be construed, if possible, to avoid such a result, a taxing statute must be given a practical construction, and where the tax involved is a sales tax upon the sale of tangible personal property to the consumer, it is not always possible to reach a practical determination as to who is the ultimate consumer with entire certainty so as to avoid entirely the possibility of a resultant double taxation to a limited extent. To carry to its logical conclusion the argument that only the sale to the ultimate consumer should be taxed would result in excluding from taxation

many sales of tangible personal property. We think, therefore, that the construction thus far placed upon the law as it applies to the sale of chemicals and dye stuffs to a dyer who does not resell the product as such but consumes it in performance of services upon the property of another, is entirely too narrow. The mere fact that some part of the product so sold to the dyer adheres to the property of another upon which his services are performed and such part is discernible by microscopic examination is insufficient to make the dyer a vendor of the dyes and chemicals purchased by him. [5 N.E.2d at 820.]

An interesting excursion into physics was made in Farrand Coal Co. v. Halpin, 10 Ill.2d 507, 140 N.E.2d 698 (1957). The taxpayer contended that its sales of coal to the City of Springfield were not subject to the Illinois retailers' occupation tax under the provision taxing sales of tangible personal property "for use or consumption and not for resale in any form as tangible personal property." It argued that its sales of coal to the city were merely sales of one form of energy; that the utility transformed the form of energy bought into electrical energy; that since the energy purchased by the utility (the city) was tangible personal property and the same energy was resold "to the customer it is not used or consumed by the utility," but is resold. Extensive testimony was given by professors of physics testifying on behalf of both parties, who disagreed as to "whether or not energy is tangible as a matter of scientific fact." The court paid its respects to the scientists but concluded that the words of the statute must be given their "ordinary and popularly understood meanings." By this test, it concluded that "energy" falls far short of the "tangible" requirement of the statute and held that the coal was consumed by combustion in producing electricity and that no "tangible" personal property was sold when the utility furnished its customers with electricity. Compare Granite City Steel Co. v. Department of Revenue, p. 727 infra, involving the manufacturing and processing exemption of the Illinois statute.

B. *Sales for Resale and the Rendition of Services.* The question as to whether a transaction is a non-taxable sale for resale or a taxable sale for use or consumption is often intimately interconnected with the question as to whether the purchaser is engaged in rendering services or in making sales.[3]

Thus, sales of paper towels, napkins, and cups to hotels and office buildings for use by their tenants have been held to be retail sales for consumption by the purchaser in rendering service to its customers. Hotels and office buildings, it is held, do not resell these articles to their tenants. Theo. B. Robertson Co. Inc. v. Nudelman, 389 Ill. 281, 59 N.E.2d 655 (1944); Atlanta Americana Motor Hotel Corp. v. Undercofler, 222 Ga. 295, 149 S.E.2d 691 (1966); Kentucky Board of Tax Appeals v. Brown Hotel Co., 528 S.W.2d 715 (Ky.1975).

Professionals are generally treated as rendering services; hence, a lawyer is taxable on the paper he purchases for preparing contracts, wills, and other documents, although the legal documents are turned over to the

---

3. The repair and renovation cases present the same kind of problem of distinguishing between purchases for resale and purchases for consumption by the repairmen. See p. 751 infra.

client. Likewise, it has been held that dentists purchase crowns and bridges from the dental laboratory at retail and not for resale to their patients, and thus the transaction between the dentist and the laboratory is a taxable sale. Kilbane v. Director, Department of Revenue, 544 S.W.2d 9 (Mo.1976). But see Department of Revenue v. Milwaukee Refining Corp., 80 Wis.2d 44, 257 N.W.2d 855 (1977) (sales of gold to dentists are not retail sales).

A hospital purchased drugs that were dispensed to its patients, on order or prescription of an attending physician. The charge for the drugs was separately listed on the patient's bill. The charge to the patient was determined by adding to the cost of the drugs to the hospital a portion of (a) the cost of operating the hospital pharmacy, (b) the hospital's general overhead and (c) a return on the equity interest of the owners of the hospital. Sales tax was asserted on the hospital's purchases; the hospital contended that the drugs were purchased for resale to the patients. The court disagreed, saying:

> Hospitals are not in the business of selling drugs or other tangible personal property, but are primarily in the business of *rendering services* to their patients. Drugs and other items are purchased by them for use or consumption in the rendition of these professional services, and any transfer of the drugs by a hospital to its patients is but an incident to the services rendered. Consequently, the sales by Tri–State to Coffee General Hospital are "retail sales," and sales tax is due to be collected by Tri–State as the retail seller. [State v. Tri–State Pharmaceutical, 371 So.2d 910, 914 (Ala.Civ.App.1979) (emphasis by the court).]

C. *Restaurant Meals as Involving Resales.* Restaurant meals are taxable in all States, either as sales of tangible personal property, or by special statutory provision. See Advisory Comm'n on Intergovernmental Relations, "Significant Features of Fiscal Federalism," Table 60, p. 88 (1984). A fast food establishment was taxable on the disposable plastic and paper plates it purchased, Sta–Ru Corp. v. Mahin, 64 Ill.2d 330, 1 Ill.Dec. 67, 356 N.E.2d 67 (1976).

Airlines and other institutions, such as hospitals and schools operating lunch programs that purchase the meals they serve, contend that the meals are purchased for resale. In the airline cases, since the meals are frequently served in the air above States other than those in which the airline purchases the food, if the purchase by the airline is exempt as a resale, no State will collect a tax. The Florida court rejected an airline's resale contention, saying:

> In our view this argument cannot stand because there is in fact no resale. It is uncontroverted that the price of the meal is included in the price of the ticket. It is estimated that the price of the meal is actually about 1% of the cost of the ticket. To subdivide the cost of the ticket into percentages to cover the various services rendered by the airline in order to reach the artificial conclusion that there is a sale is to strain the meaning of the term "resale." When a passenger buys a ticket, he buys many services, including baggage handling, the services of flight attendants, and in appropriate cases, meals. In addition, a

portion of his ticket goes to purchase gasoline and the services of the flight personnel. It is artificial to attempt to divide this package of services into separate sales and say that one of them is the sale of meals furnished to passengers. [Air Jamaica, Ltd. v. State Dept. of Revenue, 374 So.2d 575, 578 (Fla.App., 3d Dist.1979).]

There was, however, a dissent in the case, in which it was stated:

In my judgment, the meals are in fact resold by the carrier to its passenger and the transaction between *those* two parties is properly viewed as a sale of two separate things: transportation and the meal. I have no difficulty, as does the majority, in distinguishing between those various "services" which go into furnishing the transportation, such as gasoline and flight personnel; and the transfer directly *to* the passenger of a discrete item which he himself consumes. I hardly think, for example, that the passenger would be given a cash refund if any of the other "services" were not rendered, as he is if the airline fails to serve the meal. [374 So.2d at 580.]

For decisions in other States, see Commonwealth v. United Airlines, 219 Va. 374, 248 S.E.2d 124 (1978) (meals taxed to airlines); American Airlines, Inc. v. Department of Revenue, 58 Ill.2d 251, 319 N.E.2d 28 (1974) (meals taxed to airlines). *Per contra*: State v. Hertz Skycenter, Inc., 55 Ala.App. 481, 317 So.2d 319 (1975), corrected 294 Ala. 336, 317 So.2d 324 (1975); Undercofler v. Eastern Air Lines, Inc., 221 Ga. 824, 147 S.E.2d 436 (1966). For a case dealing with a school lunch program, see ARA Services, Inc. v. South Carolina Tax Com'n, 271 S.C. 146, 246 S.E.2d 171 (1978), cert. denied 439 U.S. 1048, 99 S.Ct. 725 (1978).

D. *Promotional Items Distributed "Free."* The Milwaukee Brewers Baseball Club purchased bats and jackets outside the State that it distributed to attendants at its home games in connection with their purchase of tickets. The State asserted use tax on the articles. The baseball club contended that the promotional items were free of the tax because they were purchased for resale. The court sustained the assessment on the ground that the baseball club did not resell the bats and jackets because they were given away to the attendants. Wisconsin Dept. of Revenue v. Milwaukee Brewers Baseball Club, 108 Wis. 553, 322 N.W.2d 528 (1982). Is an article received "free" if one obtains it only by buying another article?

A manufacturer purchased outside the State miniature samples of its products and printed advertising materials, which it distributed free to its wholesale and retail customers within the State. Does the sale for resale exemption cover these articles? See United States Gypsum Co. v. Green, 110 So.2d 409 (Fla.1959).

E. *Sale of Art Work With Right of Reproduction as a Sale for Resale.* The Minnesota statute excludes from the term "retail sale" (which is taxed) "a sale for any purpose other than resale in the regular course of business." Standard Packaging Corp. v. Commissioner of Revenue, 288 N.W.2d 234 (Minn.1979). A producer of calendars and other advertising specialties purchased paintings from commercial artists, along with the right to reproduce them in its products. Tax was assessed on the purchases of the paintings, but the court set it aside, saying:

In our opinion, the purchase of the paintings are sales for the purpose of "resale in the regular course of business" to the extent that with exceptions hereafter noted they serve no function or purpose and have no value to [the producer] other than to be part of the process of converting them into decorative art work on playing cards, calendars, and other advertising specialties. [Id. 288 N.W.2d at 238.]

For a further treatment of this case, see p. 732 infra. Is the court in error on the ground that the taxpayer does not resell the art work it purchases, but only the image of the art work, and that does not satisfy the provision? Moreover, is the sale of an image the sale of an intangible? Does the statute require a resale of the tangible property purchased? Compare the cases on transfers of intangibles treated at p. 701 supra.

F. *Wholesalers Distinguished From Retailers.* An issue related to the sale for resale problem arises under statutes that tax both wholesalers and retailers, but at different rates. In Fineberg v. School District of Pittsburgh, 415 Pa. 108, 202 A.2d 26 (1964), mercantile license taxes were levied by the School District and the City of Pittsburgh on wholesalers at one-half mill and on retailers at one mill per dollar of sales. The Pennsylvania courts have ruled that the test "of whether one is a wholesaler or a retailer is whether his customers buy for the purpose of reselling." Fineberg purchased work clothes, which he resold to industrial laundry service companies. His customers, in turn, rented the clothing to their customers, but they also provided laundry pick-up service for the clothing. Fineberg claimed that he was a wholesaler, that his customers bought to "resell," but the court held that since his customers retained title to the work clothes, they made no resales. A dissent by two Justices argued that this was an excessively restrictive construction of "reselling," taking the position that the real issue is whether Fineberg's customers were the "ultimate consumer" of the work clothes. On this basis, they contended that Fineberg was entitled to the wholesaler's tax rate.

G. *Intention to Resell After Use of Article.* Does an article qualify under a resale provision if it is purchased with the intention to use it and then to resell it? In Baltimore Foundry and Machine Corp. v. Comptroller, 211 Md. 316, 127 A.2d 368 (1956), a foundry purchased patterns or molds used by it to make steel castings which it sold to its customers, and after the castings had been made, the foundry sold the patterns to the customer. In all instances the agreement for the resale of the patterns was made at the time the purchase order for castings was given. The State argued that the resale provision is inapplicable unless the only purpose of the use is resale. The court held that the resale provision applies in view of the contemporaneous resale intention.[4]

The Ohio Supreme Court reached a contrary result under essentially the same facts, holding that the patterns and models were not bought by the tool and dye maker, in the words of the Ohio statute, "to resell * * * in the form in which the same is * * * received by" it. This conclusion

---

4. Compare Hawley v. Johnson, 58 Cal. App.2d 232, 136 P.2d 638 (1943), holding that an automobile dealer purchasing cars for use as demonstrators (three percent of the cars on hand were demonstrators) with periodic resale obtained the benefit of the resale exemption.

was bottomed on the fact that "no consideration was paid for the patterns, as such, by the customers and the transfers of possession to the customers were not 'sales'." If, as the court suggests, the taxpayer's customers were purchasing tools and dyes, not patterns and models, it may be argued that the purchases of the latter articles by the taxpayers were exempt under another provision of the Ohio statute that exempts transactions in which "the purpose of the consumer is * * * to use or consume the thing transferred directly in the production of tangible personal property for sale by manufacturing." See Ohio Rev.Code § 5739.01(E)(2). This issue is not discussed by the court, but the provision is considered in United States Steel Corp. v. Bowers, 170 Ohio St. 558, 167 N.E.2d 87 (1960). The Ohio Supreme Court also denied exemption for purchases of shoe samples and related materials that were subsequently sold to retailers for resale, on the ground that the "primary use" to which the property is put is determinative; here it was to promote the company's sales. United States Shoe Corp. v. Kosydar, 41 Ohio St.2d 68, 322 N.E.2d 668 (1975). But see Dresser Industries, Inc. v. Lindley, 12 Ohio St.3d 68, 465 N.E.2d 430 (1984) where the court held that the taxpayer's primary purpose in purchasing material that was used in the design process of projects was nevertheless to resell it as an integral part of a finished product.

The California Court of Appeal held a computer manufacturer liable for use tax on computer components used for testing purposes and then refurbished and sold to its customers. Burroughs Corp. v. State Board of Equalization, 153 Cal.App.3d 1152, 200 Cal.Rptr. 816 (1984). The Georgia Supreme Court has held that cars used as "demonstrators" by auto dealerships are subject to sales tax when purchased by the dealer, even though they are ultimately resold to customers. Law Lincoln Mercury, Inc. v. Strickland, 246 Ga. 237, 271 S.E.2d 152 (1980).

The mixed intention to use and resell arose in Jacobs v. Joseph, 282 A.D. 622, 126 N.Y.S.2d 274 (1st Dep't 1953), a case involving race horses. The taxpayer, "a well-known owner of race horses," purchased two horses, Lady Alice and Fox Ring, in Florida in 1950. The horses were brought to New York and run in "claiming races"—races in which every horse raced is entered at a price at which any owner registered in the race may acquire the animal. Lady Alice was claimed and sold in New York City after running in four claiming races; Fox Ring ran in three claiming races in New York City and was thereafter claimed in a race in California. The court sustained the New York City use tax, saying:

> There can be little doubt that where a horse is purchased outside of the City of New York and is run in a race within the city that this utilization is such an exercise of right or power over tangible personal property as to constitute a "use" within the intent with which this word was employed in the statute. Inquiry then turns to whether the purchase of a horse by a claim or otherwise and its later use in claiming races is a purchase "for any purpose other than for resale."

The converse of this exclusionary statement, i.e., purchases "for resale," sweeps in all ordinary commercial transactions where goods are bought solely for wholesale or retail trade. But the way the language runs makes the legislative purpose reasonably clear to exempt only property then solely used for resale because "any purpose" would include all purposes generally. The words "other than" narrow the exempted purpose down to the singular. It would seem reasonable to think that using the property for resale and some other purpose or purposes would not carry with it the singular exemption created by this statute.

This record suggests to us that there is more to a claiming race than just a resale of horses. There is the desire to win races; to receive prizes and to test training and breeding. There are in such races all of the other dynamic incentives that underlie this dramatic sport. It has been seen that statistically the ratio of claims to entries in this type of race is very small.

A horse owner who has the full right to enter a horse in other than claiming races as well as in claiming races and who has the horse available within the tax area has some additional difficulty in showing the horse is in the tax area solely for resale where the stipulated fact is that about half the races in the area are not claiming races. We think we are not required to say on the record before us that the petitioner utilized these two horses in New York entirely "for" resale.

H. Another case involving horses provided taxpayer's counsel with an opportunity to demonstrate the subtlety of the legal mind. The taxpayer, a breeder of horses, contested the imposition of a sales tax on stud fees paid for having his mares bred. Conceding that the transfer of semen from the stallion to the mare amounted to a transfer of tangible personal property, the taxpayer argued that the transaction was exempted under the "sale for resale" provision which included within its scope "the physical incorporation of personal property as an ingredient or constituent into other personal property which is to be sold in the regular course of business." The court rejected the argument: "A view of the statutory pattern as a whole satisfies us that the lawmakers never intended that biological processes be included within the concept of 'physical incorporation' written into * * * the Act." Commonwealth v. Wetzel, 435 Pa. 468, 472, 257 A.2d 538, 540 (1969).

I. *Purchase of Property for Rental as a Sale for Resale.* The treatment of the rental of tangible personal property, or a license to use the property, as a sale presents the possibility of double taxation, unless the purchase of the property by the lessor is exempted from tax. In some States a purchase of tangible personal property for leasing or licensing is included in the definition of sale for resale, or is explicitly exempted from tax. See N.J.Rev.Stat. § 54:32B(e)–1, CCH ¶ 96–057, P–H ¶ 22,510.18 (defines retail sale as including a sale for resale), and N.J. Rev.Stat. § 54:32B(f), CCH ¶ 96–065, P–H ¶ 22,510.36 (defines retail sale as including rental, lease, or license to use or consume); see Code of Va. § 58.1–608–16, CCH ¶ 91–532, P–H ¶ 22,535.32. In other States a purchaser of property for the purpose of renting or leasing it out is given the option of either paying sales tax on the purchase or collecting tax on the rental or license payments he receives from his lessee. See Cal. Rev. & Tax.Code § 6006(g), CCH ¶ 162–031, P–H ¶ 22,510.35; Mich.Rule 82, "Rentals of tangible personal property," CCH ¶ 60–085, P–H

¶ 21,762. In some States, however, there is no explicit provision in the statute eliminating double tax, with the result that tax has, in some cases, been imposed on both the purchase and lease or license of the property by the lessor.

In Ryder Truck Rental, Inc. v. Bryant, 170 So.2d 822 (Fla.1964), the court sustained a two percent sales tax on the purchase of motor vehicles by a rental agency despite the imposition of a three percent tax on the agency's rentals received from its customers. The decision was based on the court's analyses of the levies. It determined that the sales tax was levied on the vendor for the privilege of selling, and the rental tax on the taxpayer for the privilege of renting the cars. Both taxes are imposed by the Florida sales and use taxes; since both taxes are collected from the customer, is not the court's argument that "there is no 'pyramiding' or duplication of the tax since each is a separate and distinct taxable privilege" true only in the most formalistic sense? Nevertheless, both the legislative history and the language of the statute suggest that the case was properly decided, not for the reason given by the court, but on the ground that the Florida Legislature did in fact impose the complained of pyramiding of taxes. Accord, American Video Corp. v. Lewis, 389 So. 2d 1059 (Fla.App.1980) (provider of cable TV service levied on purchase of equipment used in service installation, even though the provider collected a separate tax on the use of the equipment by customers). See also Lafayette Parish School Board v. Market Leasing Co., Inc., 440 So.2d 81 (La.1983), where the court held the sales tax applicable to rental of cars even though the cars had been subjected to sales tax when purchased by the lessor. In Rent–A–Car Co., Inc. v. Lynch, 298 N.C. 559, 259 S.E.2d 564 (1979), the court held that a car rental company must pay tax on the sale of cars formerly used for rental, even though a sales tax had been paid on the earlier lease of the cars.

Compare with the foregoing decisions the holding in Trimount Coin Machine Co. v. Johnson, 152 Me. 109, 124 A.2d 753 (1956). There the taxpayer bought coin-operated amusement machines outside the State and entered into leases outside the State for their use in Maine and elsewhere. The court held that the taxpayer was not subject to the use tax because it did not use the machines in Maine; rather, its customers did. The lessees were not subject to use tax in Maine because they were not the machines' purchasers. "The person taxable," said the court, "must be both a user and the purchaser at retail sale." It is to be noted that Maine is one of the States whose sales tax covers leases or other rental arrangements "only when such leases are deemed to be in lieu of purchase." Query, does this case go to the other extreme in allowing all parties to escape sales or use tax on the rentals? Recent Maine cases have scrutinized alleged leases quite carefully in determining whether they constitute sales. See e.g., Measurex Systems, Inc. v. State Tax Assessor, 490 A.2d 1192 (Me.1985) (lease renewable at termination of 102 month term evidences a sale, and is therefore taxable under Maine law); Hannaford Bros., Co. v. State Tax Assessor, 487 A.2d 251 (Me.1985) (rental agency's lease of vehicle fleet to taxpayer deemed a sale on ground that title to vehicles was retained for security only).

J. Flowers sent by out-of-state telegraph order to recipients located within the State were held subject to the Illinois Retailers Occupation Tax. The customer who ordered the flowers paid the out-of-state florist for the flowers and the telegram, and the Illinois correspondent-florist delivered flowers to the recipient from its stock within the State. The court held that the transaction did not come within the statutory exemption of a sale for resale by the Illinois florist to his out-of-state correspondent, since the out-of-state customer was regarded by the court as the buyer from the Illinois florist. The out-of-state florist was treated as rendering a service. Since the sale took place in Illinois, the court also held that the tax did not run afoul of the Commerce Clause. O'Brien v. Isaacs, 32 Ill.2d 105, 203 N.E.2d 890 (1965). Which State ought to collect the tax, Illinois or the State of the customer? Would it be feasible to apportion the tax between the two States, as is done, for example, in corporate franchise and net income taxes? Subsequent to the *O'Brien* decision, Illinois changed the result in the case by regulation:

> Where Illinois florists receive telegraphic instructions from other florists located either within or outside Illinois for the delivery of flowers, the receiving florists will not be held liable for tax with respect to any receipts which he may realize from the transaction. In this instance, if the order originated in Illinois, the tax will be due from and payable by the Illinois florist who first received the order and gave telegraphic instructions to the second florist. [Ill. Retailer's Occupation Tax Reg. § 130.1965, CCH ¶ 67–215, P–H ¶ 21,603.]

K. *Limitation of Resale Exemption to Resales Taxable by the State.* A related problem has arisen under the resale provisions. May a State limit its exclusion from tax for sales for resale to cases in which the resale transaction will take place within its boundaries? In Don McCullagh, Inc. v. Department of Revenue, 354 Mich. 413, 93 N.W.2d 252 (1958), appeal dismissed 359 U.S. 343, 79 S.Ct. 897 (1959), a Michigan corporation with offices in Detroit bought cars within the State and leased them to its customers, who used them entirely outside the State. Because rentals from leasing property are taxable under the statute (use tax), a sale of property to a purchaser for the purpose of renting the property to others is exempt from tax as a "retail sale," but only in cases in which "the rental receipts are taxable under the statute." The court rejected the taxpayer's principal contention, that the tax discriminates against interstate commerce, by holding that the State could constitutionally integrate the sales and use taxes and limit this area of sales tax exemption to cases in which a use tax would be payable to the State. It noted that Florida, the State in which the cars would be used by plaintiff's lessee, imposes no sales tax on the rentals so that multiplicity of taxation would not result.

L. *Repossession of Car on Default.* The Alabama statute imposes a tax on persons engaged in the business of selling automotive vehicles which are "bought for the purpose of resale," at the rate of one percent of the gross proceeds on the resale. The taxpayer, an automobile dealer, who sold cars under conditional sales agreements, entered into a contract with General Motors Acceptance Corporation (GMAC), under which the dealer assigned the conditional sales contracts to GMAC and received payment from GMAC; the taxpayer, however, guaranteed the purchase price. On default by the purchaser, GMAC repossessed the cars and transferred them to the taxpayer. The issue in State v. Hayes, 266 Ala. 632, 98 So.2d 422 (1957), was whether on the resale of such repossessed cars by the taxpayer, he became liable for the Alabama tax. The court on rehearing reversed its earlier decision sustaining a tax on the transactions on the ground that, on the repossession, the cars were not "bought" from GMAC. It was conceded that title had passed to GMAC and that on the repossession title was reacquired by the taxpayer, but the court held that such a repossession did not fall within the term "bought." Cf. the sales tax cases dealing with transfers of property in connection with sale-leasebacks discussed at p. 705 supra and in connection with mergers discussed at p. 788 infra. If the taxpayer paid a tax on the original transaction and did not on the default receive a credit or refund for the tax paid, the result would appear sound in order to avoid a double tax on the price ultimately received for the car; but if a credit or refund was allowed, the result appears questionable for then there would be no tax on the sales proceeds. See Ala.Code Ann. § 40–23–1 et seq., CCH ¶ 96–231 et seq., P–H ¶ 22,701–k et seq. and Northrup, "The Measure of Sales Taxes," 9 Vand.L.Rev. 237, 269 (1956) for a summary of the statutory provisions.

(b) Manufacturing, Processing and Fabrication Exemptions

KAISER STEEL CORPORATION v. STATE BOARD OF EQUALIZATION

Supreme Court of California, 1979
24 Cal.3d 188, 154 Cal.Rptr. 914, 593 P.2d 864

Manuel, Justice.*

Plaintiff Kaiser Steel Corporation (Kaiser) appeals from a judgment denying recovery of certain sales and use taxes paid to defendant State Board of Equalization (Board) in the period October 31, 1967, through December 31, 1973. We conclude that Kaiser purchased the materials which are the subject of the disputed taxes for a "purpose other than resale" and that the transactions were "retail sales" within the provisions of Revenue and Taxation Code, section 6007. We therefore affirm the judgment.

The case was tried by the court upon stipulated facts as follows: At its plant in Fontana, Kaiser is engaged in the manufacture and production for sale of steel, pig iron, and other products. Kaiser purchased certain materials to charge its furnaces and to remove impurities from the molten metal, namely, limestone, burnt lime, fluorspar, raw dolomite, burnt dolomite, bentonite, aluminum bar and shot, gravel, and aluminum magnesium alloy (materials). The removal of impurities is accomplished by combining them with the materials to form slag.

Portions of the materials were incorporated in the steel to achieve a specific quality; portions simply remained in the finished steel;

* [Some of the court's footnotes have been omitted.]

portions were dissipated or lost in the manufacturing process; and portions, ranging from 52 percent to 97 percent of various materials, became components of the slag. None of the aluminum magnesium alloy became part of the slag; 80 percent remained in the steel product and 20 percent was dissipated. Forty percent of the aluminum bar and shot was incorporated into the steel, giving it a fine grained quality; the remaining 60 percent ended up in the slag. Only those portions of those materials which became components of the slag are at issue in this litigation.

An independent company removed the slag from Kaiser's premises, paid Kaiser 1 cent for each ton removed, reprocessed the slag, and remitted to Kaiser a 10 percent royalty on the net sales price of the reprocessed slag, which is used in a wide variety of businesses and for a number of differing purposes. Through this arrangement Kaiser recovered 8.7 percent of the cost of the raw materials (including the value of removing the slag).[2]

When it purchased the materials Kaiser either paid the sales tax (§ 6052) or gave the vendors a resale certificate (§ 6091) and later paid a use tax (§ 6094, subd. (a)). Kaiser filed claims for refund with the Board for sales and use taxes paid with respect to the materials that combined to form slag, alleging that the materials had been purchased for the purpose of resale. The company brought the instant action pursuant to section 6934 when the Board failed to take action on the claims.

The Board took the position that Kaiser purchased the materials for a purpose other than resale, namely to aid in the manufacture of steel, and that therefore the purchases were not tax exempt. Kaiser contended that it purchased the materials for the purpose of resale in the form of slag, a by-product in the manufacture of steel. Kaiser asked the court to order an apportionment of the cost of the materials between the exempt and nonexempt uses of the materials.

The trial court construed the pertinent authorities and concluded that Kaiser's "primary purpose" for purchasing the raw materials determines their taxability. It found the Board's conclusion that Kaiser purchased the materials primarily to aid in manufacturing steel was reasonable. The court therefore held that the purchases of raw materials were subject to sales and use tax. We agree.

Section 6051 provides for a tax on all retail sales. Section 6007 defines a retail sale as "a sale for any purpose other than resale in the regular course of business in the form of tangible personal property." Normally, the tax is collected by the retailer from the purchaser. (§ 6052.) If the purchaser pays the tax, then resells the property "prior

---

2. In a typical year, 1971, Kaiser paid approximately $3.8 million for the materials and produced almost 2,500,000 tons of steel which it sold for approximately $255 million; in the same year Kaiser produced almost 1,250,000 tons of slag for which it received approximately $99,000 in royalties. (Kaiser credited the 1 cent per ton purchase price against the royalty). The value to Kaiser in having the slag removed from its premises was $233,000.

to making any use of the property other than retention, demonstration, or display while holding it for sale in the regular course of business," a deduction is allowed. (§ 6012, subd. (a)(1).) On the other hand, if the purchaser gives a resale certificate to the seller (§ 6091) and thereafter makes use of the property before reselling it, a "use" tax is imposed on the original purchase price. (§ 6094, subd. (a).)

A Board regulation generally applicable to manufacturers, producers, and processors provides: "(a) Tax applies to the sale of tangible personal property to persons who purchase it for the purpose of use in manufacturing, producing or processing tangible personal property and not for the purpose of physically incorporating it into the manufactured article to be sold. Examples of such property are machinery, * * * and chemicals used as catalysts or otherwise to produce a chemical or physical reaction such as the production of heat or the removal of impurities.

"(b) Tax does not apply to sales of tangible personal property to persons who purchase it for the purpose of incorporating it into the manufactured article to be sold, as, for example, any raw material becoming an ingredient or component part of the manufactured article." (Reg.1525.)

In determining whether a sale is taxable as a retail sale or exempt as a sale for resale, the California courts have consistently looked to the primary intent of the purchaser or primary purpose of the purchase. (People v. Puritan Ice Co. (1944) 24 Cal.2d 645, 151 P.2d 1; * * *. In *Puritan*, ice was sold to vegetable packers and shippers for use in preserving perishable products. This court held that the sales to packers and shippers were retail sales and taxable despite the fact that the packers and shippers separately charged their customers for the ice. "The essence of the matter is that the purchasers of the ice are acquiring it for purpose other than resale. They are not engaged in the ice selling business. They are selling vegetables and the use of the ice or purported sale thereof to the purchasers of the vegetables is merely an incident of that activity. It is common knowledge that the dominant purpose for the use of ice in shipping perishable produce is to preserve the produce by means of refrigeration * * *" (24 Cal.2d at pp. 651–652, 151 P.2d at p. 4; accord Good Humor Co., supra, 152 Cal. App.2d at p. 877, 313 P.2d 640 [dry ice merely passed on "as an incident" of ice cream product sales activity]; Monterey Ice & Dev. Co., supra, 29 Cal.App.2d at p. 424, 84 P.2d 1069 ["real purpose" of ice purchase was to furnish refrigeration as a "necessary incident" of business of selling lettuce].)

In Kirk v. Johnson, supra, 37 Cal.App.2d 224, 99 P.2d 279, the "primary purpose" test was applied where cows, purchased for milk production, were eventually sold for beef. The original purchase was taxable in full because the primary purpose was dairy use, not resale for beef. In Safeway Stores, supra, 148 Cal.App.2d 299, 306 P.2d 597, the company purchased cartons which were used to ship products from the warehouse to retail stores; 80 percent remained in good condition and were eventually used for crating retail customers' grocery purchases, an exempt use. The court held that the total carton purchase was subject to sales tax because Safeway first used all of them for a nonexempt purpose.

We recognize that none of the cases discussed thus far involve the purchase of materials for manufacturing. We cannot agree with Kaiser, however, that the primary purpose test has no application in the manufacturing industries. In our view, regulation 1525, quoted earlier, *is* a statement of the primary-purpose test. Thus, if property is purchased as an aid in the manufacturing process, it is taxable despite the fact that some portion remains in the finished product or that an incidental waste or by-product results. Conversely, if the property is purchased for incorporation as a component of the finished product, it is not taxable despite the fact that some portion may be lost or otherwise dissipated in the manufacturing process.

Our interpretation of the regulation accords with the interpretation of the Board in its tax counsel rulings. * * *

Significantly, burnt lime, limestone, and aluminum (in several forms) were among the products purchased by Kaiser and either used as an aid to manufacture the steel (all of the lime, limestone and aluminum in alloy form and 60 percent of the aluminum bar and shot) or incorporated into the steel (40 percent of the aluminum bar and shot). As in the prior rulings, the Board here considered the purpose for which the materials were purchased; its conclusion that Kaiser purchased all the materials which eventually ended up in the slag primarily for aid in the manufacture of the steel is eminently reasonable.

Given the economics of steel versus slag production, the resale of the slag is as collateral to the production of steel as the resale of cows in *Kirk* was collateral to dairy farming. It is as incidental to Kaiser's business as the resale of ice in *Puritan* and the sale of carbon dioxide and fusel oil in *American Distilling*. The primary-purpose test of *Puritan* and *Kirk* is applicable to the manufacturing industries.

Kaiser attempts to distinguish *Kirk* and *Puritan* on grounds that the uses there were successive rather than simultaneous. The argument is not persuasive. The Board has made no distinction in its rulings based upon simultaneous as contrasted to successive use. Where there are simultaneous uses but only one or primary purpose for the purchase, the entire unit of material is taxed or not taxed, depending on that purpose: "If the primary purpose of purchasing chromic acid is to supply the chrome which is applied through a plating process to articles to be sold, the chromic acid is purchased for resale, even though the acid contains ingredients which aid in the application of the chrome to the articles." (C.C.H. 60–118.31; Tax Counsel Ruling 6/29/51.) Conversely, use of forged steel balls to grind silica sand to a desired fineness determines the taxability of the purchase of the balls as a retail sale, even though in the course of the grinding the balls wear out and all of the steel from the balls eventually becomes a part of the product. (C.C.H. 60–118.41; Tax Counsel Ruling 5/16/52.)

Similarly, when the entire unit is first utilized as an aid in processing or manufacturing and subsequently incorporated into a manufactured product to be sold, the entire unit is taxable. For example, paper pulp and wood fiber, first used in a filtration process, is later incorporated into cattle feed and sold. The purchases of pulp and fiber are taxable. (C.C.H. 60–118.693; Tax Counsel Ruling 3/25/65.) Also, the sale of sulphuric acid, first used as a dehydrating agent, is a retail sale and subject to tax even though it is subsequently incorporated into other tangible personal property which is sold. (C.C.H. 60–118.121; Tax Counsel Ruling 5/26/55.)

It is evident from the record that Kaiser's dominant motive or purpose in purchasing the materials in question was to use them in removing the impurities from its molten steel, a "purpose other than resale." (§ 6007.) Although Kaiser intended to eventually resell the materials in the form of slag, Kaiser first *used* all of the materials in question in a nonexempt manner, thereby determining their taxability. (§ 6012, subd. (a)(1) and § 6094, subd. (a).)[4]

Kaiser suggests that in the manufacturing field, the courts should, as the Board has done, apportion the tax according to uses made of the materials purchased. Indeed, the Board has apportioned the tax in some circumstances, not here applicable. When the purchaser buys a quantity of materials and has two purposes in mind (within the meaning of § 6007), the Board permits apportionment of the tax if the purchaser can establish what portion he is using for the exempt purpose and what portion for the nonexempt purpose. This is so even though the portions will be utilized at the same time. Thus, in the instant case Kaiser had purchased a quantity of aluminum bar and shot and was able to establish that 60 percent was used as an aid in manufacturing and 40 percent was incorporated into the steel.[5] Tax counsel rulings are in accord: "Where scrap carbon or graphite is added to the charge in addition to the normal coke charge, and is used solely to add carbon to the iron and is not used as a fuel, the sale of the scrap carbon or graphite would be exempt from tax as a sale for resale. If, however, any portion of such scrap carbon or graphite does in fact

4. "Use" is defined in section 6009: "'Use' includes the exercise of any right or power over tangible personal property incident to the ownership of that property, and also includes the possession of, or the exercise of any right or power over, tangible personal property by a lessee under a lease, except that it does not include the sale of that property in the regular course of business."

5. The parties stipulated and the court found that upon auditing Kaiser's tax re-

turns, the Board accepted Kaiser's claim that "a portion of the aluminum bar and shot is purchased to incorporate it into steel according to customer specifications." The customer wanted a special fine grained quality. We are not here concerned with the 40 percent incorporated into the steel. As noted earlier our issue relates only to the taxation of the materials which became slag.

oxidize or burn and, therefore, provide heat which aids the manufacturing process, that proportion would be considered as sold for consumption as is the case of the 55% of the coke considered used by Ruling 17." (C.C.H. 60–118.481; Tax Counsel Ruling 7/19/55.) Tax Ruling 17, referred to in the above quoted ruling, has been adopted as regulation 1530. It applies to foundries in general and determines the taxability of coke in terms of proportions utilized for the dual purposes of aid in manufacture and for resale. The industry has apparently been able to establish to the satisfaction of the Board that any purchase of a quantity of coke in that industry is for dual purposes and utilized thus in the proportions provided by the section. Likewise, the fur dressers and dyers have been able to establish that certain dyestuffs and chemicals used by them are for incorporation into skins and furs which they process. The Board has noted, however, that two of the materials (sodium chloride and hydrogen peroxide) are also commonly used for "fleshing" and "bleaching" respectively, and insofar as the furriers give the vendor resale certificates and then "consume" any portion of the materials for fleshing or bleaching, the entire purchase of the material is taxable unless the furrier keeps accurate records showing the respective amounts used for each purpose. (Reg.1531.)

Apportionment has no place in the instant case because Kaiser did not have dual purposes for the quantities purchased. *All* quantities of the materials which ended up in the slag and are the subject of the instant dispute were purchased for use as an aid in the manufacturing process. It is settled law that the eventual resale of personal property by a person who purchases such property for use will not prevent the original sale of such property from being a retail sale subject to tax. (§§ 6009, 6094, subd. (a).)

Kaiser cites out-of-state cases which support its position. Since the sales tax schemes in states where those cases arise differ from California's, no purpose is served in reviewing them here.

The primary-purpose test, which we reaffirm in this decision, finds support in tax policy. The test assures that the entire amount of materials will be taxed at its highest value. Permitting an exemption when materials are incorporated into the finished product is rational, since the materials enhance the value of the product which will eventually be sold and taxed at its highest value. Kaiser's position would permit use of materials costing millions of dollars in aid of manufacturing a profitable article, while avoiding taxation in the reselling of a relatively worthless waste by-product. In other words, instead of materials being taxed at their highest value, they will be taxed at a tiny fraction of that value. Such a result does not comport with the legislative scheme as indicated by the court decisions and administrative interpretations.[6]

6. Since we hold that the Board has uniformly administered the tax provisions in question and that the Board's treatment of Kaiser is consistent with the treatment of taxpayers similarly situated, we do not reach Kaiser's constitutional claim that the Board has discriminated against it in failing to apportion and exempt from tax

The judgment is affirmed.

BIRD, C.J., and TOBRINER, MOSK, CLARK, RICHARDSON and NEWMAN, JJ., concur.

Notes and Problems

A. *Property Used in Manufacture, Transportation, or Sale.* A retail sales tax which is limited to sales to the final consumer in the lay sense would be more sharply restricted than most retail sales taxes. Thus, it is common under retail sales taxes to impose a levy on sales of machinery to manufacturers of goods. In fact, the machine is consumed at an intermediate point in the economic process. For income tax purposes, it is recognized that a part of the cost of the machine is to be allocated to the goods manufactured each year by allowing a deduction from gross income for depreciation of the machine. By subjecting the machine to sales tax, the ultimate consumer is likely to pay a tax on a tax, since the sales tax paid on the machinery will ordinarily find its way into the price paid by the final consumer. This is multiplied at many points, e.g., cotton picking machinery purchased by the farmer, coal mining equipment, railroad cars and steel rails, stationery, office supplies, and office furniture purchased by manufacturers, wholesalers, and retailers of other products, type purchased by printers, and trucks purchased by wholesalers or retailers. The consequence is that so-called retail sales taxes ordinarily subject to tax a large number of articles never reaching the ultimate consumer in the economic process and have the effect of spiraling into the measure of the tax paid by the final consumer numerous taxes absorbed all along the line from the producer of raw materials to the retailer. Some States sought to limit this pyramiding of the sales tax by provisions such as that involved in the principal case, or by exempting purchases of machinery used in manufacturing or processing, or otherwise. Inevitably, controversy has developed as to the metes and bounds of these exemptions. Other States have adopted broader exemptions for property used or consumed at intermediate stages of the economic process.

B. *Ingredient or Component Part of Manufactured Product: Guiding Principles.* In Granite City Steel Co. v. Department of Revenue, 30 Ill.2d 552, 198 N.E.2d 507 (1964), the court approved the Department's construction of the ingredient-component part exemption as permitting a division of property between an ingredient and a non-ingredient portion. A producer of pig iron and steel used coke for two distinct purposes. The coke was burned and used as heat, and the carbon from the coke was infused into the product. The Department's action in exempting roughly one-third of the coke that was infused as carbon under the ingredient provision was approved. The taxpayer had argued that the entire cost of property is exempt as an ingredient if "any portion * * * however small that portion may be, is intended to and does become a necessary ingredient in a furnished product." [198 N.E.2d at 511.]

those materials that became components of the slag.

A different rule was adopted in Nucor Steel v. Herrington, 212 Neb. 310, 322 N.W.2d 647 (1982). There, the Nebraska court held that if a substantial part of the material becomes an ingredient of the finished product—even though there are other primary uses for the material—and the rest is consumed in the manufacturing process, the material in toto constitutes an exempt ingredient. The court justified its view as follows:

> On the facts in the present record the trial court correctly determined that the graphite electrodes were used in this case for two primary purposes and functions and that a substantial amount of the graphite electrodes entered into and remained an ingredient and component part of the finished steel product. The electrodes involved here were within the specific terms of the statute and we see no reason to read into the statute a requirement that a majority of the substance used must remain in the finished product in order to make the purpose of its use primary. There is no justification for holding that the purpose of using a substance which is an essential and critical ingredient of the finished product is not a primary and important purpose simply because there is also another reason for using the substance which is also important. It is tacitly conceded that if the graphite involved here was used in a form other than an electrode, it would not be subject to tax. The fact that the same substance can serve an additional purpose in the manufacturing process if it is in the form of an electrode does not change the factual reality or the terms of the tax statute.
>
> Where graphite electrodes are used in the manufacture of steel for the dual purpose of providing essential carbon for the steel manufacturing process and for the conduction of electricity which provides heat for the process, and where a substantial part of the graphite electrodes enters into and becomes an essential ingredient or component part of the finished steel and the remainder is consumed in the manufacturing and refining process, the use of such graphite electrodes in the manufacturing and processing of steel for ultimate sale at retail is not subject to taxation under the provisions of §§ 77–2702 and 77–2703. [322 N.W.2d at 651.]

The Illinois court's views, as expressed in the *Granite City Steel* case, were reaffirmed in Mobil Oil Corp. v. Johnson, 93 Ill.2d 126, 66 Ill.Dec. 285, 442 N.E.2d 846 (1982), which held that an oil company was taxable on its use of waste products produced from crude oil it purchased. The tax was based on the difference between the volume of crude oil purchased and the volume of products resold, measured by the purchase price of the crude oil.

The Louisiana Supreme Court has held that coke purchased by a manufacturer of manhole covers was taxable under a statute exempting materials purchased "for further processing into articles of tangible personal property for resale," because the coke was used primarily as a fuel, and the small amount of coke absorbed by the iron was regarded as incidental. Vulcan Foundry, Inc. v. McNamara, 414 So.2d 1193 (La.1981).

The Washington Court of Appeals adopted an even more generous view of the exemption when it ruled that the purchase of coke used in manufacturing iron was exempt from tax on the ground that "[t]he important fact for application of the ingredient exemption is that a necessary ingredient is supplied, not that the quantity is small." Van Dyk v. Department of Revenue, 41 Wash.App. 71, 702 P.2d 472 (1985); see also State v. Alabama Metallurgical Corp., 446 So.2d 41 (Ala.Civ.App.1984).

Skinless Frankfurter Casings. Skinless frankfurters confronted the Nebraska Court with the need to circumscribe that State's exemption for property "which will enter into or become an ingredient part of tangible personal property manufactured, processed or fabricated for ultimate sale at retail." American Stores Packing Co. v. Peters, 203 Neb. 76, 277 N.W.2d 544 (1979). A meat packer bought cellulose casing outside Nebraska for use in making skinless frankfurters and luncheon meats. The casing was stuffed mechanically with the prepared meat product. It was cooked and treated, during which "an undetermined amount of the glycerine with which the casing is impregnated, moves by osmosis from the casing into the meat." Id. 203 N.W.2d at 546. The casing was then split, blown off, and discarded. The taxpayer argued that " 'enough [of the glycerine] goes in [to the product] to make a difference' and this should be the test of whether the casing enters into or becomes an ingredient or component part of the product." Id. at 546. The court reviewed the cases from other jurisdictions and sustained the use tax on the casings, saying:

> The determination of whether or not tangible property enters into or becomes an ingredient or component part of other property does not ordinarily offer any difficulty. The lumber which goes into the manufacture of a piece of furniture obviously becomes a component part of that furniture, i.e., the function of the lumber is that of being a component and it serves no other purpose. In the case before us, the casing served the apparently indispensable function of a mold. In the end, the casing is discarded. It does not become an ingredient or component in any real sense, as it does not reach the ultimate consumer of the meat product. If one judges solely by the physical evidence, i.e., a sample of unused casing and a sample of used casing, the answer seems almost obvious. The casing remains after the manufacture. The principal function of the glycerine and moisture is to enable the casing to serve its function. The transfer of some part of the glycerine into meat which already contains glycerine appears incidental. [Id. at 548.]

Whiskey Barrels for Aging Bourbon. New white oak barrels were purchased by a distiller for use in aging bourbon whiskey. The "function of the barrel," without which bourbon cannot be produced, "is to provide flavor bodies and extracts from the wood," which become parts of the whiskey. American Distilling Co. v. Department of Revenue, 53 Ill.App.3d 42, 10 Ill.Dec. 946, 368 N.E.2d 541, 543 (1977). The whiskey would be harsh and unpalatable without the tannin and other wood extracts that become part of the bourbon. The barrels can be used only once, and thereafter are useless to the distiller. Were the barrels exempt from use tax under the Illinois statutory provision exempting tangible personal property purchased, as "an ingredient or constituent" of other tangible personal property for sale in the regular course of business?

Insecticides. Are insecticides which are used by fruit and vegetable growers exempt from tax as articles which "enter into and become an ingredient or component part of the tangible personal property?" E.C. Olsen Co. v. State Tax Commission, 109 Utah 563, 168 P.2d 324 (1946).

Ingredient of Services. The Kansas statute also excludes from tax articles that become an ingredient of services sold. It excludes from the tax "any article * * * which is actually used in the production * * * and becomes an ingredient of * * * the service" furnished to the purchaser. In Southwestern Bell Tel. Co. v. State Commission of Revenue & Taxation, 168 Kan. 227, 212 P.2d 363 (1950), a telephone company argued that telephone poles, wire, switchboard equipment, and other property purchased outside the State and installed within the State in the company's telephone system fell within this provision. The court rejected this contention, holding that the test of the exemption is whether "the sale in question is for resale or to be finally consumed by the buyer."

C. *Lithographic Plates Used by a Printer as a Component of Printed Matter.* The Georgia sales and use tax statute exempts industrial materials used as a component of the finished product or coated upon or impregnated into the product at any stage of its processing, manufacture or conversion. Chilivis v. Stein, 141 Ga.App. 536, 233 S.E.2d 881 (1977). The question arose as to whether lithographic plates used by a printer were covered by the exemption. Thin aluminum plates were treated with a light sensitive coating. An image of the printing design was achieved by transferring it from a photographic negative to the plates. Ink and water were applied to the image area; the plate then rotated against a cylinder covered with a rubber blanket, which transferred the image to the rubber blanket. From there it was transferred to the printed matter. The court denied the exemption, saying:

> The lithographic plates do not become a component part of the finished product as is the case of the industrial materials found in Blackmon v. Atlantic Steel Co., 130 Ga.App. 492(2), 203 S.E.2d 710. Nor do they become impregnated or are they coated upon the product at any stage of its processing, manufacture or conversion. Only the ink applied to the lithographic plates is transferred from the plate rotating on a cylinder to a rubber blanket, thus transferring the printed image which is thereafter transferred to the final product on paper. [233 S.E.2d at 882–83.]

But see Standard Packaging Corp. v. Commissioner, Note D, p. 732 infra, which held that transparencies of photographs and paintings used in printing various advertising specialties are exempt from sales or use tax, under Minnesota's broad exemption for articles "used or consumed in industrial production".

A juke box operator (Ramco) challenged a use tax on the records it purchased for playing in its juke boxes, under the Iowa fabrication provision. That provision exempts property purchased for processing property that is intended for sale at retail. Processing was defined by the statute as involving becoming "an integral part of other tangible personal property." The court stated the supporting argument as follows:

Ramco's argument is simply this: the records are tangible personal property which by processing "become an integral part of other tangible personal property"; that the phonograph records when placed in the juke box and played produce a musical tune; and that this tune is "other tangible personal property intended to be sold ultimately at retail." [Ramco, Inc. v. Director, Dept. of Revenue, 248 N.W.2d 122, 123 (Iowa 1976).]

Would you give credence to this argument?

D. *Property Used or Consumed in Manufacturing Products for Sale.* Some statutes have fabrication exemptions that are not limited to property that becomes an ingredient or component of the product sold.

The Ohio exemption excludes from its levy articles purchased by the consumer where his purpose is "to use or consume the thing transferred directly in the production of tangible personal property * * * for sale by manufacturing, processing, refining or mining." Ohio Rev.Code § 5739.01(E), CCH ¶ 95–006, P–H ¶ 22,520.14. It has been ruled that fuel used to make steam in producing the taxpayer's products is covered by the exemption, Emery Industries, Inc. v. Kosydar, 43 Ohio St.2d 34, 330 N.E.2d 686 (1975), but that coal purchased to make coke (which is used in the manufacture of pig iron) is not exempt. Interlake, Inc. v. Kosydar, 42 Ohio St.2d 457, 330 N.E.2d 444 (1975). The coal-to-coke process is preliminary to manufacturing.

The Maine use tax exempts purchases of property that is consumed or destroyed in the manufacture of personal property for resale. A corporation engaged in printing purchased metal plates which it used in the printing process. Because the plates were stored and reused in subsequent reprints of the same copy, the court held that the plates were not consumed in the process and, hence, were not covered by the exemption. Bonnar–Vawter, Inc. v. Whuson, 157 Me. 380, 173 A.2d 141 (1961).

The court also rejected the contention that the purchases were nontaxable on the ground that they were bought from a wholly-owned subsidiary at cost. It refused to treat the subsidiary as merely an operating department of the taxpayer. This aspect of the case points up the disparities of treatment that sometimes result in sales taxation between taxpayers engaged in a single step in the economic process and vertically integrated enterprises. Compare Kroger Grocery & Baking Co. v. Glander, p. 747 infra, in which the court was conscious of such differentials in the obverse type of case, i.e., the integrated enterprise is sometimes disadvantaged as compared with the operation of a single horizontal level.

In Midwestern Press, Inc. v. Commissioner, 295 Minn. 59, 203 N.W.2d 344 (1972), the court distinguished the *Bonnar–Vawter* case on the ground that the metal plates there at issue were, unlike the lithographic plates involved in the case at hand, durable. It relied on the tax court's reasoning that

> the term "consumed" as used in our statute does not necessarily mean physical consumption but is broad enough to include economic consumption of the subject property. It is the opinion of this Court that the lithographic plates are "economically consumed" in the printing

process, having only junk value at the end of their run. [295 Minn. at 62–63, 203 N.W.2d at 347.]

The Minnesota statute exempts the receipts from the sale or use of "all materials * * * used or consumed in * * * industrial production of personal property intended to be sold ultimately at retail, whether or not the item so used becomes an integral part of the property produced." See Standard Packaging Corp. v. Commissioner of Revenue, 288 N.W.2d 234, 237 (Minn.1979). In *Standard Packaging,* the taxpayer, which manufactured playing cards, calendars and other advertising specialties, purchased paintings and other art work from artists for reproduction in its products. The art work was photographed and made into color transparencies, which were used in the printing of the products. The court held that the purchases of the paintings and other art work were not taxable. It stated:

> Finally, the commissioner argues that under Minn.Reg.Tax S & U 605(b)(4) (1979) paintings and transparencies are not entitled to exemptions unless they become "physically an ingredient or component of the tangible personal property sold" by B. & B. We do not read the statute so narrowly. Nor do we agree that the right of reproduction is not "used or consumed in industrial production" within the meaning of the statute. The statutory scheme is to devise a unitary tax which exempts intermediate transactions and imposes it only on sales when the finished product is purchased by the ultimate user. The items here for consideration, in our opinion, fall into that category. [288 N.W.2d at 239.]

Could a similar contention be made that the purchase by a printer or publisher of art work and the right of reproduction are exempt under a State's ingredient and component provision, on the ground that the art work becomes a physical ingredient in a component part of the printed article by reproduction?

(c) Machinery or Equipment Used in the Manufacture, Production, or Processing of Tangible Personal Property to Be Sold

In order to encourage the location of manufacturing and processing plants in the State, many States exempt or exclude from sales and use taxation machinery and equipment, and in some States tools and parts, used in the manufacture of tangible personal property that is to be sold. See P–H All States Guide ¶ 254. Some States also extend the provision to farm machinery. Id. Other States allow the exemption only if the machinery or equipment is to be used in new or expanded industries in the State. Id.

A principal limitation on the scope of the exemption or exclusion is that the machinery, equipment, or other article must be used "directly," and in some States, "predominantly" in the manufacture, production, or processing. Id. Consequently, one of the major recurring controversies in construing the provisions lies in drawing the line between operations that precede manufacturing or producing, and the manufacturing or producing process itself, and the activities that take place after the manufacturing or producing has terminated.

COURIER CITIZEN COMPANY v. COMMISSIONER OF CORPORATIONS AND TAXATION et al.[1]

Supreme Judicial Court of Massachusetts, 1971
358 Mass. 563, 266 N.E.2d 284

CUTTER, JUSTICE.

The plaintiff (Courier) sought declaratory relief in the county court concerning its liability for sales tax (G.L. c. 64H) on its purchase of certain machinery, equipment, and supplies, "used directly" by it in its "fully integrated" printing business. The single justice reserved the matter, without decision, for the determination of the full court on the pleadings[2] and statements of agreed facts, which amount to a case stated. The general question presented is whether particular items of materials, machinery, and replacement parts are exempt from sales tax under subsecs. (r) and (s) of c. 64H, § 6 (as amended through St.1968, c. 711, § 1). These provisions are set out in the margin.[3]

Courier manufactures in Massachusetts printed material upon orders from its customers. Its operations include every stage of manufacture from receipt of original "copy" of many types "through the pressrun and binding of * * * finished products." Courier makes in its own plants various types of printing plates. These plates, when treated with ink, are used to transfer to paper (through the operation of printing presses) the image to be printed. Such plates are often referred to as "composition." Courier uses principally two types of composition, viz. (a) photo-offset plates and (b) molded printing plates.

A. The manufacture of a *photo-offset plate* involves (1) photographing the original copy with an offset camera; (2) processing the film to produce a "flat" containing the composite image to be printed, and superimposing that "flat" upon, and affixing it to, a thin plate treated with a light-sensitive emulsion; (3) exposing the plate to a high intensity lamp; and (4) treating the exposed plate with chemicals to make image areas ink receptive and nonimage areas ink repellant, after which the plate is coated to protect it, and mounted on the plate cylinder of a printing press.

B. *Molded printing plates* are used on high speed presses for the production of high volume items such as newspapers and telephone directories. Manufacture of this type of plate involves (1) setting the

1. The other defendant is the State Tax Commission.

2. The defendants' answer admits all allegations of fact in the bill.

3. Section 6 reads in part, "The following sales and the gross receipts therefrom shall be exempt from the tax imposed by this chapter. * * * (r) Sales of materials, tools and fuel, or any substitute therefor, which become an ingredient or component part of tangible personal property to be sold or which are consumed and used directly * * * in an industrial plant in the process of the manufacture of tangible personal property to be sold, including the publishing of a newspaper; * * * (s) Sales of machinery, or replacement parts thereof, used directly * * * in an industrial plant in the manufacture, conversion or processing of tangible personal property to be sold, including the publishing of a newspaper; * * *" See later amendments of other portions of § 6, by St.1970, c. 566, § 7, and c. 597.

original copy in lead type by linotype or monotype; (2) producing from the pages of assembled type a plastic nonflexible relief image molding mat; and (3) making from this molding mat a flexible raised image plate which is installed on the press.[4]

Both photo-offset plates and molded printing plates, with rare exceptions, are scrapped after the pressrun. Once removed from the press, they cannot be reused without adversely affecting the quality of the printed product.

The present controversy arose in the following manner. On May 23, 1968, the Department of Corporations and Taxation notified Courier of its intention to assess a deficiency in sales taxes for a period prior to May, 1968, amounting to $112,129.99, plus interest and penalties. Courier requested a ruling whether "[a] purchases by a printer, and other manufacturers of composition, of machinery and replacement parts therefor, used for the manufacture of composition, and [b] purchases of materials and supplies used and consumed in the manufacture of composition, [are] exempt under the Sales and Use Tax." The Commissioner ruled that the exemptions under § 6(r) and § 6(s), see fn. 3, *supra,* "apply only to materials * * * or machinery * * * 'used directly' in 'the process of the manufacture' or in the 'manufacture' of 'tangible personal property to be sold.' Since the machinery and materials are * * * used [by Courier and other similar concerns] to produce composition for the manufacturer's own use, it is not used directly in the manufacture of any tangible personal property to be sold." [5] The Commissioner proposes to assess to Courier sales taxes with respect to its purchases of machinery and replacement parts used, and of materials and supplies used and consumed, in the manufacture of composition.

Courier contends that machinery used at any stage of an integrated printing process is "used directly * * * in the manufacture * * * of tangible personal property to be sold" within the meaning of c. 64H, § 6(s).[6] See fn. 3, supra. The Commissioner's ruling would deny the statutory exemption to purchases of photo-offset cameras, linotype and

4. The several steps of each process are more fully outlined in Appendix A to this opinion. The appendix describes items of machinery, equipment, or materials used in each step and their ultimate disposition, and refers to the section of the sales tax statute (G.L. c. 64H) under which Courier contends its purchase of each item is exempt from tax.

5. The ruling proceeds, "The property being sold is printing matter. The composition used on the printing presses is used directly in the manufacture of such goods. Therefore, any material which becomes an ingredient or component part of the composition is exempt. However, the machinery used and materials used and consumed in making such composition is indirectly used in manufacturing printing matter and is, thus, not exempt."

6. It is also Courier's contention that materials, tools and fuels so used are within the comparable language of § 6(r). For convenience, we discuss the issues primarily under § 6(s). See Wakefield Ready–Mixed Concrete Co. Inc. v. State Tax Commn., 356 Mass. 8, 9, n. 3, 247 N.E.2d 869. In this discussion, we deal with the fundamental issue whether the transaction was subject to § 6(r) or § 6(s), and see no occasion to discuss mechanics of the imposition of the excise, such as the use of resale and exempt use certificates. See G.L. c. 64H, § 8, inserted by St.1967, c. 757, § 1, especially subsecs. (b) and (d), and also subsecs. (f) to (i), inclusive, inserted by St.

monotype machines, and photo-composing machines (see Appendix A), even though they are used in a continuous production flow of which the end product (printed material) is to be sold.[7]

We reject the suggestion in the Commissioner's ruling (see fn. 6, *supra,* and related text of this opinion) that printing plates and other forms of composition are made for the "manufacturer's own use." The plates are not reusable tools, for they normally are discarded after the pressrun. They have no purpose except in connection with a particular printing job. They are made as the necessary first stage of a long process, culminating in a specifically ordered finished printed product. The Commissioner's ruling thus appears to rest only upon the circumstances that the typesetting, photographic, and other machinery and various materials employed in making the plates are not at any time placed immediately in contact with any material going into the finished product.

Sections 6(r) and 6(s) were recognized early in the history of the sales tax as being difficult of interpretation. See Dane, The New Sales and Use Tax Law, 51 Mass.L.Q. 239, 258,[8] where it was said in 1966, "Massachusetts belongs to the minority of sales tax states which excludes sales of machinery and replacement parts. However, to qualify for such exclusion, the machinery must be used directly in one of the specified activities listed above in connection with the exclusion of materials, tools and fuel. ＊ ＊ ＊ While this exclusion is highly desirable to promote industrial expansion in the state and to prevent the removal of industry to other states granting this exclusion, it is antici-

---

1968, c. 89, § 1. See 1968 House Doc. No. 142, p. 8.

7. Courier refers us to Massachusetts Sales and Use Tax Regulation No. 18, Machinery Exemption (effective December 1, 1968), see 13 Boston Bar J. No. 4, p. 27. This was not incorporated in either statement of agreed facts. See Finlay v. Eastern Racing Ass'n. Inc., 308 Mass. 20, 26–28, 30 N.E.2d 859. Although we need not take judicial notice of the regulation, we may refer to it in view of the defendants' concession that Courier's quotations are accurate. See Commonwealth v. Minicost Car Rental, Inc., 354 Mass. 746, 747, 242 N.E.2d 411. It affords slight assistance, not only because it took effect on December 1, 1968, but also because it is no less ambiguous than the statute. Pertinent portions of Reg. No. 18 read: "(2) Machinery is 'used directly' when it is employed (a) to effect a physical change in tangible personal property during a manufacturing, converting, or processing operation, the finished product of which is to be sold ＊ ＊ ＊. (3) 'Industrial plant' means a business establishment primarily engaged

in a process of manufacturing, converting, or processing of tangible personal property for sale in the regular course of business and generally recognized as such. (4) 'Manufacturing ＊ ＊ ＊' means an operation or series of operations whereby through the application of machines and labor to raw or semi-processed materials, ＊ ＊ ＊ at any stage of becoming finished tangible personal property, the form or composition of the material or materials is significantly changed."

8. The author of this 1966 article (who served, see 51 Mass.L.Q. 239, as special consultant to the Governor in connection with the preparation of sales tax legislation) has joined in filing in the present case an amicus brief in behalf of Associated Industries of Massachusetts and of several large manufacturers who purchase machinery and materials "used to make dies, production fixtures, jigs, patterns, composition or" other objects required in their respective manufacturing processes for purposes analogous to Courier's purpose in its manufacture and use of composition now under discussion.

pated that serious problems will arise in the interpretation of the words 'used directly.' "

The same article points out (p. 255) that a "retail sales tax * * * is a levy on consumer expenditures" and "not a turnover tax imposed at each step of the production and distribution process." This purpose to tax only ultimate sales at retail explains why the term "Sale at retail" is defined in § 1(13) as "a sale of tangible personal property *for any purpose other than resale in the regular course of business* " (emphasis supplied). This definition and the provisions of c. 64H, § 3 (as amended by St.1967, c. 797, § 2; see later revision by St.1970, c. 683), 5, 8, and 23, all indicate the legislative intention to have the sales tax passed on to the final retail consumer, even though the registered vendor must pay the excise in the first instance (see, however, third sentence of fn. 6, supra) and even though the "incidence" of the tax (despite its reimbursement to the registered vendor) has been ruled to be on the registered vendor, at least in situations where Federal immunity from State taxation is not involved. See Supreme Council of Royal Arcanum v. State Tax Commn., Mass.,[a] 260 N.E.2d 822. See also Barrett and Bailey, Taxation (1970 supp.) §§ 1310–1312, 1320, 1339–1340 where (§ 1310) the purpose of excluding sales for resale is said to be "to avoid pyramiding the sales tax upon successive buyers and sellers." See also, Due, Retail Sales Taxation in Theory and Practice, 3 Natl.Tax.J. 314, 317–318, 322.

The effect of the Commissioner's ruling is to impose a sales excise at a pre-retail stage of the production of the ultimate product, viz. the printed material. The amici curiae (fn. 8) point out that a tax so imposed inevitably enters into the cost of the final product to be sold at retail, and that the tax is subject to the normal markup on final resale just as much as any other cost. The cost of such a tax to the consumer is hence greater than the amount of revenue collected by the government.

The amici also argue that, if Courier (instead of producing the plates itself) had bought them from a supplier, the purchase would have been exempt from sales tax under c. 64H, § 6(s), as "replacement parts" for machinery, i.e. the printing presses (to which the plates are attached), "used directly * * * in an industrial plant in the manufacture * * * of tangible personal property to be sold." This, the amici say, results (if the Commissioner's position is correct) in a discrimination against integrated producers, and tends to repel integrated industry (with such industry's employment opportunities) from Massachusetts.

Our own cases do not resolve the present controversy concerning an ambiguous statute. In Wakefield Ready–Mixed Concrete Co. Inc. v. State Tax Commn., 356 Mass. 8, 10–12, 247 N.E.2d 869, 870, we said (a) that the "legislative history affords no assistance in the interpretation of § 6(s)"; and (b) that the "purpose of § 6(r) and § 6(s) is to exclude

a. Mass.Adv.Sh. (1970) 1217, 1218.

entirely certain items from the impact of the sales * * * tax on the basis of the nature of the items." Consequently, we regarded these provisions as not being "the type of exemption concerning which a special burden rests upon a taxpayer, claiming the benefit of the provision, to bring himself within its scope," i.e. there is no requirement that this type of exemption be interpreted narrowly.[9] The present issues did not then arise.

The parties thus rely in large measure on cases in other States. These decisions interpret and apply statutory provisions by no means precisely the same as the Massachusetts statute.

The Commissioner places principal emphasis on cases from Ohio which take a narrow view of the word "directly." Fyr–Fyter Co. v. Tax Commr., 150 Ohio St. 118, 124, 80 N.E.2d 776 (under a statutory exemption of goods used "directly in the production of tangible personal property for sale by * * * mining," fire-protection and safety equipment and certain motor vehicles were held subject to tax). Jackson Iron & Steel Co. v. Tax Commr., 154 Ohio St. 369, 373, 96 N.E.2d 21 (coal produced in a taxpayer's mines for use in the manufacture of pig iron for sale was held not exempt). Youngstown Bldg. Material & Fuel Co. v. Tax Commr., 167 Ohio St. 363, 367–368, 149 N.E.2d 1 (the court declined to recognize as part of an "integrated plant" the machinery used in bringing together the ingredients of mixed concrete and held only machinery used in actual mixing to be subject to exemption under a statute exempting property used or consumed "directly in the production of tangible property for sale by manufacturing, [or] processing").[10]

Other cases point in a somewhat different direction. In United Aircraft Corp. v. Tax Commr., 145 Conn. 176, 183–184, 140 A.2d 486, 490, "jigs, dies, and fixtures," were "not incorporated in the end product" but were "used up in the process of manufacture" and became "practically worthless." These were held within a Connecticut exemption of materials "consumed and used directly * * * in an industrial plant in the * * * manufacture of * * * property to be sold." A similar result was reached (pp. 185–186) with reference to X-ray films

---

9. We went on to say (at p. 12), "The subsections are merely part of the statutory definition of the types of sales and uses of tangible personal property which are to be employed in measuring the excises and of those which are not so to be used. We perceive no legislative intention that there should be any such restrictive interpretation of subsecs. (r) and (s) as that for which the commission contends."

10. See General Motors Corp. v. Tax Commr., 169 Ohio St. 361, 362, 159 N.E.2d 739 (tools purchased for use in producing dies, to be used in stamping automobile parts, held not exempt); Ohio Stove Co. v. Tax Commr., 171 Ohio St. 484, 485, 172 N.E.2d 295 (machines used in producing sand molds, in which metal castings are made, held not exempt). See also Warren Tel. Co. v. Tax Commr., 173 Ohio St. 164, 165, 180 N.E.2d 595. Cases dealing with fuel include State v. Cherokee Brick & Tile Co., 89 Ga.App. 235, 242, 79 S.E.2d 322 (gas used to produce heat which in turn was used to produce brick products held not directly used in processing those products), and Phillips & Buttorff Mfg. Co. v. Carson, 188 Tenn. 132, 140–142, 217 N.E.2d 1 (coal and fuel oil, used to generate steam which in turn was used to operate certain machinery, were not exempt as "industrial materials for * * * conversion into articles * * * for resale" or as "materials * * * used directly in * * * processing such materials").

and chemicals used in testing metal parts before delivery. In Hudson Pulp & Paper Corp. v. State Tax Assessor, 147 Me. 444, 446, 449–450, 88 A.2d 154, 157, the statute exempted property "consumed * * * in the manufacture of * * * property for later sale." The statute was held to refer "to all those things which may be consumed * * * in the process of manufacture, whether or not they be those things which * * * are acted upon therein and thereby." Lubricating oils and felts used on paper machines thus were held exempt. In Androscoggin Foundry Co. v. State Tax Assessor, 147 Me. 452, 456–457, 88 A.2d 158, molding sand, refractories, fire clay, steel shot and grit, and crucibles used in an iron foundry were held exempt. In Bonnar–Vawter, Inc. v. State Tax Assessor, 157 Me. 380, 390, 173 A.2d 141, printing plates, not physically destroyed but stored against further use and orders, were held not within an exemption of property " 'consumed or destroyed' in the manufacturing process." Courier's plates, however, ordinarily cannot be reused.

Perhaps the case which most strongly supports Courier's position is Niagara Mohawk Power Corp. v. Wanamaker, 286 App.Div. (N.Y.) 446, 144 N.Y.S.2d 458, aff'd 2 N.Y.2d 764, 157 N.Y.S.2d 972, 139 N.E.2d 150, where the court interpreted a county sales tax exempting sales of tangible personal property "for use or consumption directly and exclusively in the production of tangible personal property to be produced for sale by manufacturing [or] processing." Tangible personal property was defined as including electricity. The power company in its generating plants used coal and ash handling equipment and various structures to house the machinery. In considering whether this equipment was exempt under the tax resolution, the court said (286 App.Div. [N.Y.] 446, 449, 144 N.Y.S.2d 458, 461), "There is no simple test of what constitutes 'consumption directly and exclusively in the production' of electricity. The basic questions are the following: (1) Is the disputed item necessary to production? (2) How close, physically and causally, is the disputed item to the finished product? (3) Does the disputed item operate harmoniously with the admittedly exempt machinery to make an integrated and synchronized system?" In holding the coal and ash handling equipment to be within the exemption, the opinion said (at p. 449, 144 N.Y.S.2d at p. 461), "That equipment is as essential to production as the generator itself. A serious breakdown in it would quickly stop or impair the output of electricity. We are further impressed with the synchronization and integration of the boiler and coal and ash equipment. The one could not operate without the other. Working together they make up a system which supplies the power from which electricity is produced. A taxing statute should receive a practical construction. * * * That is particularly true here, for the resolutions are designed to achieve a practical, economic result—avoidance of multiple taxation, at least to some extent. It is not practical to divide a generating plant into 'distinct' stages. It was not built that way, and it does not operate that way. The words 'directly and exclusively' *should not be construed to require the division into theoreti-*

cally distinct stages of what is in fact continuous and indivisible" (emphasis supplied [by the court]).[11]

Courier also refers us to various administrative rulings or regulations in other jurisdictions which, on varying language, support a somewhat broader interpretation of statutes generally comparable to the provisions of § 6(s), than has been adopted by the Ohio courts with respect to the Ohio statute.[12]

The authorities from other States do not seem to us conclusive. We think the Ohio cases are too restrictive in their interpretation of the term "directly in the production of tangible personal property for sale." The language quoted above from the Niagara Mohawk Power Corp. case (286 App.Div. [N.Y.] 446, 449, 144 N.Y.S.2d 458, 461) reaches a more realistic result. The integrated process of modern printing cannot reasonably be reduced to fragments or segments. When a lawyer sends a typewritten brief to be printed, the process normally will begin with setting type on a linotype machine. If the brief has illustrations, it may be necessary to prepare engravings or offset plates. Each step is as direct a step in the production process as the actual printing after the insertion of assembled pages of type in a printing press. The linotype and the machinery used in preparing plates we think are directly used in production. Any other interpretation runs counter to the plain statutory purpose to tax only the sale of the end product.[13]

11. With reference to the structures, it was said: "The structures and supports which house and steady the machinery are essential to production. They are physically annexed to the machinery, specially designed therefor, and necessary to the proper functioning thereof. As a whole, the plant is a producing unit. The structures do not play as active a role as, for example, the turbine. But activity is not the test of directness. The walls of the boiler have a 'passive' function in one sense. The important thing is that all parts of the plant contribute continuously and vitally to production, and they are all integrated and harmonized."

12. Kentucky Rev.St. § 139.480(8) exempts certain new machinery. Regulation SU–6–1, and Circular SU–30 under it (1968 C.C.H. State Tax Reporter, Ky., pars. 38–506, 38–863), exempt, for newspaper publishers, photo laboratory activities, the production of engravings, printing composition and its production, plate making. New York has ruled (Op.1968, N.Y.T.B. v. 1, p. 70 (1969 C.C.H. State Tax Reporter, N.Y. par. 99–150) that included in exempt "[m]achinery or equipment for use or consumption directly and exclusively in the production of tangible personal property * * * for sale by manufacturing" are items purchased by newspaper publishers, such as stereotype matrices, unexposed off-

set plates, and unexposed photo-engraving plates. Pennsylvania Stat.Ann. Tit. 72, § 3403–2(c) defines "manufacture" as including processing "for sale or use by the manufacturer," and also the "[p]ublishing of books * * * or other * * * printing." Under Reg. 225 (1969 C.C.H. State Tax Reporter, Pa., par. 63–621), the manufacturing exemption covers purchases of "property * * * predominantly used directly * * * in manufacturing * * * operations." One factor to be considered in "determining whether property is directly used" is the "active causal relationship between the use of the property in question and the production of a product."

13. Our conclusion, consistent with some administrative results elsewhere (fn. 12), may be supported in some degree by the provision (see fn. 3, supra) found both in § 6(r) and § 6(s) expressly placing within the manufacturing exemption "the publishing of a newspaper." It seems unlikely that there was a legislative intention to separate the ultimate printing by rotary presses from the linotype composition and the preparation of the plates placed upon those presses without which the newspaper could not be produced or have any value. Newspaper printing cannot reasonably be viewed as a more integrated process than other forms of commercial printing.

We hold that each of the items listed in Appendix A as one where exemption is claimed under § 6(s) is within the exemption thereby provided. What has been said with respect to machinery and equipment used in producing composition and in "pre-press preparation," by a parity of reasoning applies also under § 6(r) to film, chemicals, emulsion, ingredients of plates, and similar materials used directly in such pre-press preparation.

The case is remanded to the county court for the entry of a decree declaring the rights of the parties in accordance with this opinion.

So ordered.

APPENDIX A

The parties have agreed to the following description of the pertinent procedures employed by Courier in its manufacturing operations.

A. The steps involved in the manufacture of *photo-offset plates* and the items purchased by the plaintiff necessary to the completion of each step and the statutory provisions which the plaintiff contends exempt the purchase from tax are set out in the table below together with a statement of what occurs to each item during each step of the manufacturing process:

Step	Items Purchased	Section of Statute (G.L. c. 64H)	Disposition of Item
1) Taking photograph of original copy	Camera	6(s)	This machine has indefinite reuse
	Film	6(r)	Discarded following step 3 below
2) Processing of film to form a negative or positive "flat" which contains the composite image to be printed	Developing Chemicals	6(r)	Disposed of following completion of this step
3) Negative or positive "flat" containing the composite image to be printed is positioned over a thin plate usually made of zinc, aluminum, steel or in some cases paper or plastic, which is surface treated with a light-sensitive emulsion. The plate is then exposed to an arc lamp of high intensity.	Photo-composing machine	6(s)	Machine has indefinite reuse
	Emulsion	6(r)	Disposed of after this step
	Plate* (Note 1)	6(r) & 6(s)	Discarded after press-run

(Note 1—The Commissioner has ruled that the materials which are an ingredient or component part of a plate are exempt.)

Step	Items Purchased	Section of Statute (G.L. c. 64H)	Disposition of Item
4) Developing of exposed plate by treating it in chemical solution which makes image areas ink receptive and non-image areas ink repellant. Development is accomplished by placing plate in tank containing mechanical agitator.	Chemical solution	6(r)	Discarded after this step
	Development tank and agitator	6(s)	Machine has indefinite reuse

The finished plate is discarded following its removal from the press after the pressrun.

B. The steps involved in the manufacture of a *molded printing plate* and the items purchased by the plaintiff necessary to the completion of each particular step and the statutory provisions which the plaintiff contends exempt the purchase from tax are set out in the table below together with a statement of what occurs to each item during each step of the manufacturing of *molded printing plates:*

Step	Items Purchased	Section of Statute (G.L. c. 64H)	Disposition of Item
1) Original copy is set in lead type by use of a linotype or monotype machine. These machines produce raised impression characters out of molten lead which are then assembled into lines and page size forms.	Linotype or monotype machines	6(s)	Machine has indefinite reuse
	Lead ingots	No exemption claimed	Has physical life of 176 years and is subject to constant reuse through remelting and refining
2) The standing lead forms are covered with a heating setting plastic which is applied with pressure resulting in the production of a nonflexible relief image molding mat.	Heat pressure molding machine	6(s)	Machine has indefinite reuse
	Plastic compound	6(r)	Discarded after step 3 below
3) The relief image mat is then covered with a liquid plastic compound such as daxene. Pressure and heat are then applied which produces a raised image plate which is the final print medium installed on the press.	Heat pressure molding machine	6(s)	Machine has indefinite reuse
	Daxene	6(r)	Discarded in the form of the plate following completion of pressrun

Molded printed plates are discarded after removal from the press following the completion of the pressrun.

Notes and Problems

A. *Scope of Manufacturing.* Processing scrap metal has been held to be "manufacturing"; thus machines and processing equipment used in the scrap processor's operation are exempt from sales and use taxes. H. Samuels Co. v. Department of Revenue, 70 Wis.2d 1076, 236 N.W.2d 250 (1975). The same is true of water softening machines used by manufacturers. Kress v. Department of Revenue, 322 Mich. 590, 34 N.W.2d 501 (1948). But commercial fishermen who buy fish nets to use in sorting marketable from unmarketable fish are not engaged in "processing"; this activity, said one court, is merely "sorting." Huron Fish Co. v. Glander, 146 Ohio St. 631, 67 N.E.2d 546 (1946). And the business of quarrying and crushing stone is generally held not to constitute manufacturing because the raw material is not sufficiently transformed. Tilcon–Warren Quarries Inc. v. Commissioner of Revenue, 392 Mass. 670, 467 N.E.2d 472 (1984) (reviewing cases).

An Arkansas statute imposes a use tax on purchases made out of the State, but exempts "property used by manufacturers or processors * * * for further processing, compounding or manufacturing." A commercial hatchery purchased out-of-state incubators for hatching eggs and contended that it fell within the exemption. In Peterson Produce Co. v. Cheney, 237 Ark. 600, 374 S.W.2d 809 (1964), the court denied the exemption, declaring:

> We agree with the learned Chancellor, who delivered an excellent opinion at the conclusion of the case, to the effect that one does not "manufacture" a baby chick, and the use of incubators is not a "processing" step therein. As he stated,
>
> "Thus, by plaintiff's [appellant's] view, if he chose to hatch his eggs in the old-fashioned way, by having brooder hens sit on them, his purchase of hens from out of state would be exempt from use tax, because such hens were 'processing' the eggs into chicks. An incubator merely aids and abets the natural course of hatching, and is not a process in itself." [374 S.W.2d at p. 810.]

Accord: Heath v. Westark Poultry Processing Corp., 259 Ark. 141, 531 S.W.2d 953 (1976) (poultry packager not entitled to exemption); State Tax Com'r v. Flow Research Animals, Inc., 221 Va. 817, 273 S.E.2d 811 (1981) (company in the business of raising and breeding laboratory animals engaged neither in manufacturing nor processing). *Per contra:* Master Hatcheries, Inc. v. Coble, 286 N.C. 518, 212 S.E.2d 150 (1975); see also Wilson & Co. v. Department of Revenue, 531 S.W.2d 752 (Mo.1976) in which the court held that hog butchering constitutes "manufacturing" for purposes of sales/use tax exemption for machinery and equipment used in manufacturing; Hawthorn Mellody, Inc. v. Lindley, 65 Ohio St.2d 47, 417 N.E.2d 1257 (1981), in which the court held that milk processing constitutes manufacturing.

Publishing a newspaper has been held to constitute "manufacturing" or "processing"; hence machinery and parts of a newspaper printing plant were exempt from tax, State v. Advertiser Co., Inc., 257 Ala. 423, 59 So.2d 576 (1952); Hearst v. Department of Assessments and Taxation, 269 Md.

625, 308 A.2d 679 (1972), as were flashbulbs, film, and tapes purchased in connection with newsgathering. McClure Newspapers, Inc. v. Department of Taxes, 132 Vt. 169, 315 A.2d 452 (1974). But see Western Paper Co. v. Qualls, 272 Ark. 466, 615 S.W.2d 369 (1981) ("[i]n the ordinary use of the term we do not think of printing, photography, and binding as manufacturing"); Colorcraft Corp. v. Department of Revenue, 112 Ill.2d 473, 98 Ill.Dec. 45, 493 N.E.2d 1066 (1986) (photofinishing does not constitute manufacturing).

The Washington National Arena, located in Maryland, provides large scale entertainment. The arena purchased computer terminals and printing machines that it placed in various locations at which tickets to the arena are sold. They were all linked to a central computer. It was contended that the equipment was exempt from the Maryland sales tax under the exemption for "manufacturing machinery and equipment * * * used in manufacturing processing or refining products for sale". Washington National Arena v. Comptroller of the Treasury, Md.Tax Ct., May 1, 1984, P–H ¶ 23,150, affirmed 66 Md.App. 416, 504 A.2d 666 (1986). The court disagreed holding that "the sale of a ticket to an entertainment event does not constitute a sale of tangible personal property". Id. at p. 23,077. Instead "a ticket represents * * * a license or right [that] is a sale of intangible property", which does not qualify the machines for the exemption. Id. at p. 23,078.

The definition of "manufacturing" also arises under the ingredient or component provision. The issue in Zook v. Perkins, 118 Colo. 464, 195 P.2d 962 (1948) under the Colorado provision exempting articles which become an ingredient or component of a manufactured article was whether the recapping of automobile tires constituted "manufacture," so as to exempt purchases by the recapper of gum, cord, and other materials used in the process. The court held that the term "manufacture," as used in the statute, means the creation of a new article and that since the recapper always works with old tires, he is not a manufacturer. Instead, it was held that the recapper "renders a service by repairing and restoring an article theretofore manufactured." Had a contrary conclusion been reached, would the recapper be considered a vendor of the recapped tires and be required to collect a tax on the "sale" of such tires to the customer-tire owner?

B. *"Used" or "Directly Used" in Manufacturing, Producing, or Processing*. Equipment used in the handling, storage, and transportation of raw materials is not used directly in manufacturing. Southwestern Portland Cement Co. v. Lindley, 67 Ohio St.2d 417, 424 N.E.2d 304 (1981). The Alabama statute exempts from use tax "machines used in mining * * * processing, and manufacturing of personal property." Platform trucks used in transporting articles from one point in a factory to another were held not to be used in "processing," and hence their use was taxed. Alabama–Georgia Syrup Co. v. State, 253 Ala. 49, 42 So.2d 796 (1949); cf. W.E. Anderson & Sons Co. v. Glander, 154 Ohio St. 561, 97 N.E.2d 29 (1951), where a truck chassis onto which a concrete mixer was loaded was held taxable under a somewhat similar Ohio statute.

In another Alabama case, the issue was whether casing, tubing, and other equipment used in producing oil wells fell within the exemption for a "machine used in * * * processing tangible personal property." An extensive analysis of the oil production process was made in the case to determine whether "the equipment below the surface actually 'processes' the crude oil," as the taxpayer contended, or whether, as the State contended, "the equipment involved merely conveys or transports the crude oil to the surface where processing actually begins." Based on expert testimony that the "process of separating" gas and the water and the oil and the sand "begins at the bottom of the well," the court held the casing and related equipment within the statutory exemption. State v. Four States Drilling Co., 278 Ala. 273, 177 So.2d 828 (1965). Just how fine the line was that the court struggled with is indicated by the earlier case of Southern Natural Gas Co. v. State, 261 Ala. 222, 73 So.2d 731 (1953), in which the extraction of moisture and distillate was held to be "merely incidental to the transportation of the gas," with the result that the compressors that forced the gas along the pipe lines were not exempt from the use tax.

The Georgia Court of Appeals has ruled that equipment which controls the flow of electric current in the process of refining scrap copper is not "used directly" in manufacturing. Southwire Co. v. Chivilis, 139 Ga.App. 329, 228 S.E.2d 295 (1976).

The New York State Tax Commission has construed that State's exemption for "[m]achinery or equipment [purchased] for use or consumption directly and predominantly in the production of tangible personal property" as applying to a whole series of articles used in the graphic arts industry. See N.Y.Tax Law § 1115(12), CCH ¶ 97–464, P–H ¶ 22,550.61. The articles exempted extend, inter alia, to photoengraving plates, lithographic film, color separations, photographs, art work, and illustrations. See N.Y. Technical Services Bureau M–79(71)S, CCH ¶ 66,077a; and Matter of Petition of Cosmos Communications, Dec. 2, 1985. The photographs and art work are reproduced in the final product.

The printing and advertising industries are of great economic importance to New York City. They have at times threatened to move out of the State if the types of articles enumerated above were not exempted from sales and use taxes. What argument would you make in support of the treatment of art work that is purchased for reproduction in a department store's Christmas catalog as "machinery or equipment" purchased "for use or consumption directly and predominantly in the production" of the catalogs? Is the construction given the statute by the State Tax Commission within the proper province of the tax administrator?

Are the results reached in the cases discussed in this section, with the inevitable refinements industry by industry, growing out of the choice of standards employed by legislatures in drawing the line between exempt and non-exempt purchases, adequately adapted to determining how the States' sales and use tax burden ought to be distributed? How would you draw an exemption provision better adapted (and if possible with fewer niceties and refinements) to accomplish what you regard as the fiscal and economic objectives of the provisions being considered?

References. The trend of the cases in construing the manufacturing machinery exemption has been to adopt the "integrated plant" rule articulated by the Massachusetts and New York courts. See the *Courier Citizen* case, supra, and Neff, "Judicial and Administrative Circumscription of the Sales and Use Tax Manufacturing Exemption," 1983 N.Y.U. Institute on State and Local Taxation 149 (1983). See generally Annot., 3 A.L.R.4th 1129; Note, "Ohio Sales Tax Exemptions for Personal Property Used Directly in the Production of Other Personal Property for Resale," 23 U.Cin.L.Rev. (1954); Cline, "Sales Tax Exemption of Producer Goods," 1952 Nat. Tax Ass'n Procs. 618; Note, "The Manufacturer's Exemption in the Pennsylvania Sales and Use Tax," 58 Dick.L.Rev. 152 (1953).

(d) Containers

A. *Exemption of Containers Under Resale Provisions.* Some States have no explicit statutory provision dealing with the taxability of containers or packaging. The taxability of containers in such States is usually decided under the resale exemption. The New York courts struggled with the treatment of containers and packaging materials under the New York City sales tax and ruled that purchases of large metal drums and burlap sacks by producers of molasses and sugar for use in delivering their products to wholesalers and retailers were made for resale, not for consumption, and hence were exempt from sales tax. Sterling Bag Co., Inc. v. City of New York, 256 App.Div. 645, 11 N.Y.S.2d 297 (1st Dep't), affirmed 281 N.Y. 269, 22 N.E.2d 369 (1939); The American Molasses Co. v. McGoldrick, 256 App.Div. 649, 11 N.Y.S.2d 289 (1st Dep't), affirmed 281 N.Y. 269, 22 N.E.2d 369 (1939). See also Wood Packing Box Co. v. McGoldrick, 262 App.Div. 720, 28 N.Y.S.2d 719 (1st Dep't), affirmed 286 N.Y. 665, 36 N.E.2d 698 (1941). Thereafter, in Matter of Colgate–Palmolive–Peet Co. v. Joseph, 283 App.Div. 55, 126 N.Y.S.2d 9 (1st Dep't 1953), the question arose as to whether the sale of paper cartons used by a manufacturer to deliver soap, dental, and other products to retailers constituted taxable sales or, as claimed by the taxpayer, were sales for resale. The case did not involve the individual packages that go to the druggist's customer, such as the small cardboard boxes in which toothpaste is sold, which were concededly purchased for resale, but the cartons in which such articles were delivered to Colgate's customers.

The Appellate Division rejected the notion that a seller of soap and toilet goods is engaged in selling cartons and held that Colgate consumed the cartons in delivering the goods to its customers. Reuse and resale of the cartons were regarded as insubstantial and incidental. 283 A.D. at 58, 126 N.Y.S.2d at 12. The earlier cases were distinguished on the ground that large containers for which there were regular resale markets were there involved, and in addition prices varied depending on the type of container used.

That decision was, however, reversed by the Court of Appeals in Matter of Colgate–Palmolive–Peet Co. v. Joseph, 308 N.Y. 333, 125 N.E. 2d 857 (1955), which held that Colgate buys the cartons for purpose of resale and, therefore, is not taxable on the purchases, but may be liable for tax as a vendor. If that liability had been enforced, it would have created a nuisance of administrative and compliance complications for small amounts of tax. Fortunately, the matter was resolved by the N͏ New York State sales tax law (which for most purposes applies to the current New York City tax), by the inclusion of an explicit exemption from sales and use taxes for cartons, containers, and wrapping and packaging materials and supplies. N.Y.Tax Law § 1115(a)(19), CCH ¶ 94–471, P–H ¶ 22,550.64–E. See Servomation Corp. v. State Tax Com'n, 51 N.Y.2d 608, 435 N.Y.S.2d 686, 416 N.E.2d 1022 (1980).

B. *Reusable Bottles and Cases.* The Court of Appeals for the District of Columbia has passed on the issue as to whether a bottler of soft drinks is subject to use tax on bottles and cases purchased by him and used for filling and delivery of soft drinks. The bottler argued that he purchased the bottles and cases for resale. The court rejected this position, basically on the grounds that the bottles and cases were normally returned for credit; that the cost of the bottles and cases far exceeded the credits allowed and, indeed, the price received for filled bottles and cases; and that the taxpayer could not remain in business unless the bottles and cases were reused many times. District of Columbia v. Seven–Up Washington, Inc., 214 F.2d 197 (D.C.Cir.), cert. denied 347 U.S. 989, 74 S.Ct. 851 (1954). The court conceded that the bottles and cases may in fact be sold by the bottler to his customer, but it was unwilling to dispose of the issue on that ground. It declared:

> We conclude that respondents' dominant purpose in acquiring the bottles and cases was not to resell them but to secure their availability for recurring use in marketing their products and accordingly that the assessments for the use of the bottles and cases were valid. [214 F.2d at 201.]

Accord: Arkansas Beverage Co. v. Heath, 257 Ark. 991, 521 S.W.2d 835 (1975); Pepsi Cola Bottling Co. v. Peters, 189 Neb. 271, 202 N.W.2d 582 (1972).

Other courts, however, have held that reusable soft drink bottles are purchased for resale by the bottlers. See, e.g., Coca–Cola Bottling Works Co. v. Kentucky Department of Revenue, 517 S.W.2d 746 (1974); Nehi Bottling Co. v. Gallman, 39 A.D.2d 256, 333 N.Y.S.2d 824 (3d Dept. 1972), affirmed 34 N.Y.2d 808, 359 N.Y.S.2d 44, 316 N.E.2d 331 (1974). These courts usually stress the fact that title to the bottle passes to the purchaser, who is free to do with the bottles whatever he pleases. The cases are collected in Annot., 97 A.L.R.3d 1205.

C. *Statutory Exemption of Containers and Packaging Materials.* Containers and packaging materials are exempted from sales and use taxes by the statutes of many States. See P–H All States Guide (Chart of Sales and Use Taxes—Part III) ¶ 255. Florida, for example, excludes from the definition of a retail sale "materials, containers, labels, sacks, or bags intended to be used one time only for packaging tangible personal property for sale." Fla.Stat. § 212.02(19)(c), CCH ¶ 94.032, P–

H ¶ 22,002.25. See also State Dept. of Revenue v. Adolph Coors Co., 724 P.2d 1341 (Colo.1986) (construing Colorado's container exemption provision to embrace beer kegs).

The Ohio statute was interpreted in a case involving the Kroger Grocery chain, which purchased packing and wrapping materials, cartons, crating, containers, and other packaging materials for two purposes: (1) to wrap and package groceries and other articles, which were delivered to customers; (2) to package and ship the groceries and other items from its warehouses to its stores. Kroger manufactured or processed in its own plants some of the foods it sold in its stores.

The Ohio statute goes further than most State laws in excluding from sales tax intermediate transactions between production of tangible personal property and its ultimate sale to the consumer. Such statutes commonly exempt articles purchased "for use directly in manufacturing or processing products for sale." The Ohio statute so provides, but it also goes further and exempts articles purchased for use "directly in making retail sales." [5]

The Commissioner's rules exempted the wrapping papers, cartons and packaging that were delivered to the stores' customers, but sought to tax those used within the Kroger chain itself in handling and shipping the goods. The court rejected this construction of the statute. Kroger Grocery & Baking Co. v. Glander, 149 Ohio St. 120, 77 N.E.2d 921 (1948). In holding "that the containers at issue were used and consumed in connection with the processing and manufacture of Kroger's goods ultimately sold to the consumer, or in protecting or conserving such property and making it ready for transportation to Kroger's retail stores," the court was influenced by its concern that any other construction would discriminate against a vertically integrated enterprise, as compared with a manufacturer or processor of goods sold to independent dealers and retailers.

> The language of the rule in question is broad and unambiguous and may well be interpreted to cover all sales of packing and wrapping materials, cartons and containers whether sold with the article subject to a retail sale or used in the preparation and shipment of property so sold at retail. Such an interpretation should also be given it as would avoid any discrimination against Kroger as between it and an independent manufacturer of merchandise for sale to whom cartons and wrapping materials are likewise sold. Kroger claims that, under the resale theory of the Tax Commissioner, a tax could be levied against Kroger when it purchases such wrapping materials and containers because it does not resell them to any one; but that no tax is assessable against an independent manufacturer of merchandise when he purchases such wrapping materials and containers for the distribution of his merchandise because he purchases them to resell with his merchandise to an independent retailer. [77 N.E.2d at 925.]

---

5. The applicable provisions, which have not been materially changed, now appear at Ohio Rev.Code §§ 5739.01(E), 5741.01(C), and 5741.02(C)(2), CCH ¶¶ 95–006, 95–404 and 95–412b, P–H ¶¶ 22,520.10, 22,750.15, and 22,755.20.

D. *Paper and Plastic Cups, Containers, Napkins, and the Like Purchased by Fast Food Restaurants and Hotels.* The courts differ as to whether fast food restaurants, cafeterias, and hotels are taxable on their purchases of paper and plastic containers, wrapping materials, paper napkins, and the like. The Illinois court held, without benefit of an explicit statutory provision dealing with containers, that Dairy Queen was the consumer of such articles. "No thought of 'transfer or resale' of such articles to the customer is indulged." Sta–Ru Corp. v. Mahin, 64 Ill.2d 330, 1 Ill.Dec. 67, 356 N.E.2d 67 (1976), quoting from Theodore B. Robertson Products Co. v. Nudelman, 389 Ill. 281, 59 N.E.2d 655 (1945).

A contrary result was reached in the case involving the fast food restaurant chain Burger King, which challenged the sales tax on its purchases of paper and plastic wrappers for hamburgers, cups for beverages, and sleeves for french fries. This decision was reached without the benefit of an explicit statutory provision dealing with the articles. Judge Fuchsberg delivered a colorful comment on the fast food industry:

> [The fast food industry's] universal proliferation on our national scene has made it common knowledge that such restaurants, for better or worse, are designed to mass-produce uniform, popular-priced food and drink products for consumption on ready demand on a conveyor-like, assembly-line basis. The amount of service it incorporates in its operation may be different from that of other types of restaurants, but, if anything, may be more significant. For its method of doing business requires that the food and drink it serves be in a form available for delivery whenever the unheralded patron chooses to arrive. The goal is streamlined movement of bagged food in sanitary form from restaurant to customer, who takes it in its ready-to-eat state without pause to wherever, on or off the premises, she or he wishes to consume it. Key to imparting these vaunted service features—of speed, sanitation and portability—is the use of paper or plastic goods in its preparation, storage and delivery (see, generally, Levitt, Production Line Approach to Service, Harv Bus Rev, Sept–Oct 1972). [Burger King v. State Tax Commission, 51 N.Y.2d 614, 435 N.Y.S.2d 689, 692, 416 N.E.2d 1024 (1980).]

New York did have a statutory exemption for container and other packaging material, see Note A, p. 746 supra, but the provision was held inapplicable to meals.

The court decided the case by following its earlier decision in *American Molasses* (see Note A, p. 745 supra), and held that Burger King bought the wrappers, cups, and sleeves for resale, and was therefore not taxable on the purchases. Quoting from *American Molasses* that the "cartons, although '*not-inseparable*' from the contents were * * * being resold 'as containers,'" the court declared:

> All the more is this so in the case of Burger King, whose packaging, as we have seen, is such a critical element of the final product sold to customers. So regarded, the packaging material is as much a part

of the final price as is the food or drink item itself. It would be exalting form over substance, therefore, to hold that a resale of these paper products does not take place merely because Burger King does not list a separate price. [435 N.Y.S.2d at 693.]

References. Redlich, "Sales Taxes and the Resale Exemption in the Manufacture and/or Distribution of Personal Property," 9 Tax.L.Rev. 435 (1954); Northrup, "The Measure of Sales Taxes," 9 Vand.L.Rev. 237 (1956). The cases dealing with containers are collected in Annot., 4 A.L.R. 4th 581.

SECTION 4. TAXATION OF SERVICES

INTRODUCTORY NOTE *

The general sales tax began in this country essentially as a tax on sales of tangible personal property. Real property already was regarded as heavily overburdened by taxes. When the general sales tax began to take hold, a new source of revenue was sought.[6] Intangibles, such as securities, copyrights, patents, and the like, were excluded from the levy, and in general, services were not taxed, except for utilities and amusement admissions.[7] Utility services, particularly gas and electricity, always have been a ready target for taxation, despite the fact that they are regressive.[8] That is, of course, because the poor spend a greater proportion of their incomes on gas and electricity for their homes than do the rich.

Tax economists long have deplored the exclusion of consumer services other than health and, in some cases, utility services from sales taxation.

> Most advisory groups and most scholars who have examined the desirability of including services in the sales-tax base have been in favor of doing so. The reasons most frequently cited are (1) service inclusion alleviates regressivity and improves neutrality; (2) inclusion makes the sales tax more income elastic; (3) service inclusion can raise much revenue; and (4) inclusion is administratively feasible.[9]

Professor John Due of the University of Illinois, a leading economic authority on sales taxation, has written:

> There has been a tendency to confine sales taxes, especially of the single stage character, to sales of commodities, that is of tangible personal property, thus excluding the rendering of services. Most of the American state sales taxes do not apply to any services or to only a

---

* This Note is taken from the author Jerome R. Hellerstein's, "Significant Sales and Use Tax Developments During the Past Half-Century," 39 Vand.L.Rev. 961, 964–65 (1986). Used with the consent of the Vanderbilt Law Review.

6. See Chapter 1, p. 4 supra.

7. J. Due, Sales Taxation 297 (1957).

8. J. Due & J. Mikesell, Sales Taxation 83 (1983).

9. D. Morgan, Retail Sales Tax 127 (1963) (footnotes omitted).

few categories. * * * From an economic standpoint, the distinction between a service and a commodity is not a very significant one, since both satisfy personal wants. A haircut, an opera concert, or a plane ride satisfy persons' desires in the same manner as a loaf of bread, a piano, or an automobile. Obviously services rendered to business firms, whether by employees or commercial service establishments, are not suitable bases for a sales tax, since they are essentially producers' goods, and do not in themselves satisfy personal wants. But the failure to include services rendered to consumers gives rise to the same objectionable results as the exemption of specific commodities. Persons making relatively high expenditures for services are favored compared to those concentrating their purchases on tangible goods, resource allocation may be distorted, and in some cases administrative complications are created. This is particularly true when services are rendered by establishments also selling commodities; the line of distinction between service and commodity is by no means a sharp one, and the two may be provided jointly, particularly in the case of repair and fabrication service. Any sale, of course, involves the rendering of some services (that of the merchant, for example, with a retail tax); when services, as such, are not taxed, the line of demarkation is not actually made between commodity sale and the rendering of service, but between the type of service regarded as typical merchandising activity and another type, which is not so regarded. The drawing of this line of distinction is highly arbitrary, and gives rise to a number of administrative problems. Especially with the retail sales tax, in which the problems are most acute, so-called service establishments encounter greater difficulty with the application of the tax than any other type of business. The service industries require the greatest number of special regulations and rulings, and the greatest care in inspection.[10]

During the half century between the 1930's and the 1980's, taxation of services under the sales tax laws has broadened greatly. By 1985 there were thirty-two States taxing gas and electricity;[11] admissions to movie theaters and other places of amusement were taxed by twenty-seven States and the District of Columbia.[12] Hotels, motels, and other transient accommodations currently are taxed by every sales tax State except California and Nevada, and in those States local governments tax transient accommodations.[13] In fourteen States the taxation

10. J. Due, supra note 7, at 374–75. This material is used with the consent of the copyright owner, Routledge and Kegan Paul, Ltd. See also D. Morgan, supra note 9, at 126–27.

11. See Advisory Commission on Intergovernmental Relations, "Significant Features of Fiscal Federalism: 1984 Edition," Table 60, at 88 [hereinafter cited as ACIR]. The figures are as of January 1985. There were a variety of exemptions and exclusions from the utility taxes in the various States. Id. In some States telephone, telegraph, transportation, water, and other utilities were taxed. For a detailed state-

ment of the scope of taxation of sales by utilities, see J. Due & J. Mikesell, supra note 8, at 83. In some States sales by utilities are taxed under special statutes other than the general sales tax law. Id.

12. A few States tax country club dues, Nevada has a cabaret tax, and Rhode Island applies its admissions tax to racing events with pari-mutuel betting. See ACIR, supra note 11, Table 60 at 88.

13. J. Due & J. Mikesell, supra note 8, at 85–86. As is true with respect to some other services, the taxes on transient accommodations in some States are imposed

of services was further broadened to the extent that there was what the Advisory Commission on Intergovernmental Relations (ACIR) categorized as "substantial taxation of services," which included, in one or more States, repairs, laundry, dry cleaning, cable television, parking, landscaping, bookkeeping, and collection services.[14] In three States the ACIR found "broad taxation of services" under laws imposing sales taxes on the services of investment counselors, bank service charges, beauty parlors, barber shops, carpenters, and interior decorators.[15] In three other States—Hawaii, New Mexico, and South Dakota—general taxation of services obtained, including legal, accounting, and other professional services, except for health services.[16]

There has been strong resistance by professional organizations to the extension of the sales tax to cover their services. The movement to tax professional services has not met with much success,[17] particularly since lawyers, who dominate State legislatures, have consistently opposed taxation of legal or other professional services.

Restricting the scope of State and local sales taxes to specified services, while taxing sales of tangible personal property other than specifically excluded sales, has given rise to a great deal of litigation.

(a) Repair and Renovation of Personal Property

WESTERN LEATHER & FINDING CO. v. STATE TAX COMMISSION

Supreme Court of Utah, 1935
87 Utah 227, 48 P.2d 526

ELIAS HANSEN, CHIEF JUSTICE. This cause is before us for review on a statement of facts agreed to by the parties litigant. The facts so agreed to which we deem material to the questions presented are: The plaintiff is, and at the time of this controversy was, a Utah corporation engaged in the sale of leather and shoe findings either for resale in the same form or for use in the repair of old or used shoes. Between May 31, 1933, and May 31, 1934, plaintiff company sold within this State to shoe repairers operating in the State leather and shoe findings of the value and agreed price of $58,360.94. Plaintiff paid a sales tax on sales made by it to shoe shiners and hat cleaners, but denied liability for the payment of the sales tax on the materials sold to shoe repairers. Contrary to plaintiff's contention, the defendant Tax Commission found that plaintiff was liable for the payment of a sales tax upon such

by statutes other than the State's general sales tax. Id.

14. See ACIR, supra note 11, at 81–89. The term "substantial taxation of services" is used by the ACIR.

15. Id.

16. Id.

17. Id. For an unsuccessful attempt to extend sales taxes to professional services, other than medical services, see the recommendation of the N.J. Tax Policy Committee. 5 N.J.Tax Policy Committee Report, 68–69 (1972). The proposal was not adopted by the state legislature. Similarly, for a discussion of the defeat of similar efforts in Connecticut, see N.Y. Times, May 5, 1983, § B at 10. For a summary statement of Florida's abortive effort to impose a broad-based sales tax on services, see Section 5 infra.

leather and shoe findings as were sold to shoe repairers and accordingly assessed plaintiff with a sales tax thereon. According to the stipulated facts, it is a custom with shoe repairers within the State not to make a separate charge for materials used and the labor performed in the repairing of shoes. In the average repair job the cost of materials used is about 30 per cent and the labor 70 per cent of the total charge.

The act here brought in question * * * provided [for]:

(a) A tax upon every retail sale of tangible personal property made within the state of Utah equivalent to 2% of the purchase price paid or charged.

* * * 2. * * * (c) The term "wholesaler" means a person doing a regularly organized wholesale or jobbing business, and known to the trade as such and selling to retail merchants, jobbers, dealers or other wholesalers, for the purpose of resale;

(d) The term "wholesale sale" means a sale of tangible personal property by wholesalers to retail merchants, jobbers, dealers or other wholesalers for resale and does not include a sale by wholesalers to users or consumers, not for resale;

(e) The term "retailer" means a person doing a regularly organized retail business in tangible personal property, known to the trade and public as such and selling only to the user or consumer and not for resale. "Retail sale" includes all sales made within the state of tangible personal property except wholesale sales.

(f) Each purchase of tangible personal property or product made by a person engaged in the business of manufacturing, compounding for sale, profit or use, any article, substance or commodity which enters into and becomes an ingredient or component part of the tangible personal property or product which he manufactures or compounds or the container, label, or the shipping case thereof shall be deemed a wholesale sale and shall be exempt from taxation under this act.

* * *

Plaintiff is engaged in the wholesale business. The sales here involved are wholesale sales unless it may be said that shoe repairers are consumers of the materials which are used in the mending and repairing of shoes. If the charge made for repairing shoes constitutes a sale by the shoe repairer to the owner of the shoes of the materials used in the repair jobs, then and in such case under the express provisions of the act the plaintiff is not liable for the payment of the tax here sought to be imposed upon it. The word "consume" is thus defined in Webster's New International Dictionary, Second Edition: "1. To destroy the substance of, esp. by fire;—formerly and still figuratively used of any destructive or wasting process, as evaporation, decomposition, and disease. 2. To spend wastefully; hence, to use up; expend; waste. 3. To use up (time) whether wastefully or usefully; as, hours consumed in reading. 4. To eat or drink up (food); devour. 5. To waste or burn away; to perish. Syn.—Absorb, spend, squander, dissipate."

A person who places soles, heels, and patches on old worn shoes does not consume material so used within the definitions above quoted or within the meaning of the statute. The consumer is the person who wears the shoes after they are repaired. If there were any doubt about the legislative intention as to whose duty it is to pay the sales tax, such doubt is removed by the provisions of subsection (f) of section 2 of the act above quoted. Under the provisions of such subsection it is clear that a sale of leather or other material to be used in the manufacture of new shoes is not subject to the tax. The mere fact that the leather and other materials here in question were used to make only a part of a shoe does not change the nature of the transaction. A "sale of goods" is defined as "an agreement whereby the seller transfers the property in goods to the buyer for a consideration called the price." R.S.Utah 1933, 81–1–1. A sale is in effect so defined in the act here involved. When a shoe repairer delivers the repaired shoes to the owner thereof and receives payment therefor the title to the materials used in the repair job passes to the owner. The amount paid includes the price of the materials used. Such a transaction possesses all of the elements of a sale of the materials used in the repair job.

It is urged on behalf of the commission that shoe repairers should not be requested to pay a sales tax on the materials used to repair shoes because there is a custom among them not to make separate charges for services rendered and for materials furnished in repairing shoes. The act does not make such fact, nor the fact, if it be a fact, that it is difficult for shoe repairers to make separate charges for labor performed and materials furnished in repairing shoes, the basis for shifting the duty of collecting and paying the sales tax on to others. Much is said in the briefs of counsel as to the orders made by the commission affecting who shall pay the tax in other transactions somewhat analogous to the case in hand. The rulings made by the commission as to who shall pay the tax in the transactions mentioned are not of controlling importance in the instant case. Such rulings may, or may not, be open to the objections urged against the ruling here brought in question. Our duty is to give effect to the legislative intention as expressed in the language used in the act.

The order complained of should be, and accordingly is reversed. This cause is remanded to the State Tax Commission of the State of Utah, with directions to vacate the order here reviewed and for such other and further proceedings not inconsistent with the views here expressed as may be deemed proper. Costs to plaintiff.

FOLLAND, EPHRAIM HANSON, and MOFFAT, JJ., concur.

WOLFE, JUSTICE (concurring especially).

Whether the sales described in the prevailing opinion were sales by wholesale, or whether sales to the consumer, as meant by the act, is the real question at issue in this case.

*   *   *

The problems can be best approached by assuming extreme cases on both ends of the gamut. When a barber shaves a person, the lather and soap and soothing lotion which go upon the customer are mere incidentals as compared to the service performed. It is likewise true of shoe shiners. These illustrate cases on one end of the gamut. Where a merchant sells ready-made clothing and in connection therewith does alterations and perhaps furnishes materials, such as a small piece of cloth or thread, we have a case in which the services are merely incidental to the sale. Other cases lie in between. The automobile repair shop furnishes parts as well as services. The parts may at times amount to more than the services and other times vice versa. Some trades have long customarily separated their charges for services and parts. The automobile repair trade is an example. There it is quite easy to make the separation because the parts are usually very definite. In the shoe repairing industry, on the other hand, the practice has been just the opposite. A gross charge is made without separation. Indeed, it might be difficult to make the separation in this trade because of the difficulty of determining just how much leather cut from a larger piece goes into each job.

The Commission is entitled to promulgate rules and regulations for the practical and proper administration of the act. Such cannot be against the teeth of the law. They can serve to fill up the details as long as they do not run counter to the express will of the Legislature. If the ruling requiring the leather and findings companies to collect the tax from the repairman is contrary to the method of assessment and collection of the sales tax laid down by the Legislature, such regulation is invalid. If, on the other hand, there is a reasonable question about it or it is certain that it is harmonious with the provisions laid down by the Legislature, then it should be upheld. Considerations of practicality may be taken into account. Where two constructions of an act giving administrative powers to a commission are permissible, that construction which comports more practically with the actual execution and administration of the law by the commission should be adopted. The Commission has the duty of executing and administering the law. The practical difficulties in accomplishing that should be recognized by the courts. The court, sitting purely in an atmosphere of abstract argument and reasoning without recognizing the realities of the situation under which the Commission works, might adhere to a strictly logical construction of the provisions of an act which would make it entirely unworkable. From the examples on either end of the gamut given above we can see that certain practical concessions must be made by the Commission in the construction of law. It could not possibly require a separation of materials used in connection with services of barbers, shoe shiners, or shoe repairmen where they, for instance, used only shaving soap and lotion (although these are really consumed), a piece of thread to sew up a shoe, or polish to shine the shoes (also really consumed). Likewise, it is the same with tailors repairing clothes. Also with some materials furnished by cleaners and dyers (perhaps also consumed). Theoretically and perhaps logically those service industries may effect a sale to the patron of tangible articles which they use in connection with their services. If so, the value of the articles sold and contributed in connection with the services are so incidental and so proportionately small as compared to the value of the services that for practical reasons they cannot be considered as a sale. On the other hand, when an article is sold and the servicing of the same incidental to the sale is such a small part of the price of the whole, such value of the services cannot be subtracted from the sale price. Where to draw the line is questionable, but unless this court is convinced that the Commission erred in drawing the line where it did, this court should not interfere with or upset its rulings.

It is stipulated that the value of the property which is applied to the repair of the shoes amounts to about 30 per cent of the entire price. I concur with the prevailing opinion on the ground that the amount of goods which goes into a shoe repair job as compared with the value of the whole job is apparently not a mere incidental of the repair job. It appears to be a very substantial part of the cost of the whole job. If the repairing industry would come under the category of the clothing repairer or others where the amount of goods used in repair was a mere trifle compared to the labor, under the maxim de minimis non curat lex, the Commission would be justified in treating the shoe repairer as the end purchaser in the course of the trade. Under the evidence it cannot do this. All along the line from the production of raw materials to the finished product, the fabrication of goods entails the working in of materials which cannot be said to be used or consumed until they reach the person who is actually using, consuming, or wearing the totally assembled article. The sales tax applies to the sale of the end product; not only to the sale of the end product, but to the sale of the end product at retail.

In the case of shoe repairers, Illinois, Iowa, Missouri, New York, Oklahoma, and Washington seem to have taken the view that our own Tax Commission has taken. On the other hand, California, Colorado, Michigan, Idaho, and Ohio seem to have taken the view contended for by the plaintiff.

For reasons stated herein, I concur with the results of the prevailing opinion.

Notes and Problems

A. In W.J. Sandberg Co. v. State Board of Assessment & Review, 225 Iowa 103, 278 N.W. 643 (1938), modified in 225 Iowa 103, 281 N.W. 197 (1938), the court reached a conclusion contrary to the holding of the principal case. The taxpayer, who was engaged in selling leather and shoe findings to shoe repairmen, was held to be making sales to the "consumer or user." The tax there at issue defined "sale at retail" as "the sale to a consumer or to any person for any purpose, other than for processing or for resale."

B. *The Position of the Repairman Under Retail Sales Taxes.* In those States in which the sales tax covers both the rendition of repair or renovation services and sales of goods, the repairer or renovator usually presents no special difficulties. Where, however, such services are not subject to tax, troublesome problems are presented by the repairer and renovator.

If an upholsterer manufactures a new couch for a consumer, furnishing his own materials, he is treated as making a taxable sale. In fact, of course, he is not only utilizing materials, but is also rendering services. However, we experience no great difficulty in regarding the services and use of materials as preliminary to a sale of a couch. (See the discussion of the separation of the purchase of materials and the rendition of services in cases involving the manufacture of new articles, Section 2(a) supra.) More difficult problems arise, however, where an existing article owned by the consumer is repaired or renovated. Suppose the customer sends his old couch to the upholsterer to be renovated by him. If the upholsterer provides the materials, is he making a sale? When does title to the new covering materials pass, and is that question relevant to the sales tax issue? If the cost of the goods is stated separately, will the measure of the tax exclude the value of the services?

Now, turn to a repairman or renovator who may be in a different position from the upholsterer. Consider the case of a cabinet-maker who renovates a table. He uses paint remover, paint, glue, nails, and so forth. Or consider the case of a watchmaker who repairs a watch, using chemicals for cleaning, a main spring, and a stem. The materials in these cases tend to comprise a comparatively small part of the value of the entire job, although the more substantial parts can be separated out in billing. We are accustomed to regarding the furniture refinisher and the watchmaker as essentially engaged in rendering services. Would it be proper to treat such craftsmen as solely rendering services, while treating the upholsterer as entirely engaged in selling goods? Or, should the price be split up in all these instances between taxable sales of goods and non-taxable services if the parties by their billing have made a separation? Should the measure of the tax be affected by the choice of the parties, made through the method of billing employed? See A.H. Benoit & Co. v. Johnson, 160 Me. 201, 202 A.2d 1 (1964); Craig–Tourial Leather Co. v. Reynolds, 87 Ga.App. 360, 73 S.E.2d 749 (1952), shoe repairs; Leakas Furriers v. Bowers, 98 Ohio App. 337, 129 N.E.2d 478 (1954), fur garments; The May Co. v. Lindley, 1 Ohio St.3d 6, 437 N.E.2d 295 (1982); Jewelers Muench v. Glander (BTA) 42 Ohio Ops. 142, 57 Ohio L.Abs. 371, 93 N.E.2d 606 (1949), watch and clock parts.

C. *Fabrication, Producing, or Processing Distinguished From Repair.* In some States, receipts from repair services, as well as fabricating, producing, or processing personal property furnished by others (and not held for resale), are taxed. See N.Y.Tax Law § 1105(c)(2) and (3), CCH ¶¶ 97–398— 97,399, P–H ¶¶ 22,525.30–.35. However, in other States in which repairs are not taxed, it has been necessary to draw lines between taxable fabricating, producing, and processing services and repairs, which are not taxable. That is the case in California, where the regulations provide:

Producing, fabricating, and processing include any operation which results in the creation or production of tangible personal property or which is a step in a process or series of operations resulting in the creation or production of tangible personal property. The terms do not include operations which do not result in the creation or production of tangible personal property or which do not constitute a step in a process or series of operations resulting in the creation or production of tangible personal property but which constitute merely the repair or reconditioning of tangible personal property to refit it for the use for which it was originally produced.

See Cal.Reg. 1526, CCH ¶ 65–065, P–H ¶ 21,629. Similar rules obtain in other States. See R.I.Reg. 87–88 "Production, fabricating, and processing property furnished by consumer," CCH ¶ 63–975, P–H ¶ 21,634.

The California regulation was sustained and applied in taxing a tailor on his receipts from altering new clothing. Dennis L. Duffy v. State Board of Equalization, 152 Cal.App.3d 1156, 199 Cal.Rptr. 886 (3d Dist.1984). The tailor's services were found to constitute a step in the fabrication of new clothing. The alteration of a used garment would not be taxable. Moreover, the court held that the new clothes being altered need not be bought from the tailor for his alteration services to fall within the fabrication provision.

D. *Alteration Services.* In some States whose statutes do not tax fabrication, producing, or processing services, the "alteration" of tangible personal property is taxed; and that provision has been used to tax services that are taxed as "processing" in other States. Thus the Kansas tax is imposed on the "service of repairing, servicing altering * * * tangible personal property" not held for resale. Kan.Stat.Ann. § 79–3603(q), CCH ¶ 94–717q, P–H ¶ 22.025.82. A welder who produced drilling rigs also constructed a pipeline. In so doing he welded sections of pipe to create a "continuous conduit." He attacked the sales tax on his services on the ground that he created a new product—a pipeline—but the court disagreed, holding that he merely altered the pipes. The court defined "altering" as meaning:

> To make a change in; to modify; to vary in some degree; to change some of the elements or ingredients or details without substituting an entirely new thing or destroying the identity of the thing affected. To change partially. To change on one or more respects, but without destruction of existence or identity of the thing changed; to increase or diminish. [Appeal of Black, 9 Kan.App.2d 666, 684 P.2d 1036, 1039 (1984) (quoting Black's Law Dictionary).]

In sustaining the tax, the court said:

> In constructing drilling rigs from angle iron, appellant has made no qualitative change in the angle iron itself; all he has done is take a quantity of angle iron and rearrange its spatial arrangement. Despite being put to use as a component part of a completed product, each piece of angle iron retains its identity as angle iron. Thus, appellant has merely altered the angle iron.

The same reasoning holds true for the welding of individual sections of pipe into a continuous and unbroken pipeline. The inherent nature of each segment of pipe is not changed by the simple act of connecting the segments into a continuous conduit; both before and after interconnection, the pipe remains pipe. [Id.]

References. For a collection of cases on repairmen and renovators under retail sales taxes, see Annot., 11 A.L.R.2d 926.

ASSIGNMENT

Analyze the sales and use tax laws and regulations of your State and prepare a report as to how the following transactions would be treated:

(1) A has new rubber heels and soles put on his shoes. He receives a bill of $1 for heels and the leather used in his soles and $3 for labor and miscellaneous materials, such as glue and thread. What is the base, if any, of the tax?

(2) B has her fur coat relined and is billed $20 for the lining and $10 for labor, thread, and miscellaneous materials. What is the base, if any, of the tax?

(3) C's car is smashed in an accident; he receives a bill as follows:

(a) new front fender—materials $15, labor $20;

(b) new radiator—materials $50, labor $10;

(c) straightening back fender and doors—labor $75, bolts, hinges, etc. $9;

(d) repainting—paint $25, labor $90.

What is the base, if any, of the tax?

SECTION 5. FLORIDA'S ABORTIVE BROADENING OF THE SALES TAX ON SERVICES *

Notes and Problems

A. In 1987, Florida enacted a sales and use tax on a broad range of services consumed in the State. Fla.Laws Ch. 87–6, as amended by Fla. Laws Ch. 87–101. Legal, accounting, and other professional services were included in the tax base. Id. Medical, educational, social, and other specified services were excluded. Two features of the tax attracted particular attention. First, the tax systematically sought to tax services that were performed outside the State but used in Florida. Second, the tax sought to tax advertising—including national advertising—if the advertising was used in the State. As a result of these and other aspects of the tax, the levy triggered an enormous storm of protest, with opponents attacking it as unfair, unwise, and unconstitutional. In December 1987, less than six

---

* The material in this section is taken largely from W. Hellerstein, "Florida's Sales Tax on Services," 41 Nat'l Tax J. 1 (1988), and is used with the permission of the National Tax Journal.

months after the tax took effect, the Florida Legislature responded to the widespread opposition to the tax by repealing it. Fla.Laws, Ch. 87–548.

B. *Taxation of Services Performed Outside the State But Used in Florida.* To determine the extent to which a service that was performed outside the State was used or consumed and was taxable in Florida, the statute established a series of rules. One set of rules was applicable to individual, nonbusiness purchasers; another set of rules was applicable to business purchasers.

If the purchaser was an individual and the purchased service related directly to real property, the benefit of the service was presumed to be enjoyed where the real property was located. If the purchased service did not relate directly to real property, the benefit of the service was presumed to be enjoyed where the purchaser received tangible personal property representing the service.

The rules regarding the place of enjoyment of services purchased by business were more complicated. A series of presumptions for the attribution of the use or enjoyment of services was used:

(a) If the service related directly to real property, it was attributed to the location of the property.

(b) If the service related directly to tangible personal property, it was attributed to the business situs of the property if it had acquired a situs.

(c) If (a) and (b) were inapplicable and the service was related to the purchaser's local market, it was attributed to that market.

(d) If none of the foregoing presumptions applied, the service was attributed to Florida to the extent that the purchaser was doing business in the State. That determination was made by reference to the taxpayer's Florida apportionment percentage. If the taxpayer was part of the affiliated group of corporations as defined for Federal income tax purposes (with some qualifications), the service was attributed to the State of Florida to the extent of the entire affiliated group's apportionment percentage.

If the purchaser could demonstrate to the satisfaction of the Department of Revenue that the benefit of the service was enjoyed outside the State, despite the foregoing presumptive attribution rules, the service would not be taxable.

C. *Attribution of Advertising Services Rendered by Newspapers, Magazines, and Broadcast Media.* Advertising in newspapers, magazines, and by radio and television presented their own distinctive problems that required special treatment. Florida adopted essentially the market coverage principle that is widely used by the States in attributing receipts from publications and the media for corporate franchise and income tax purposes. See J. Hellerstein, State Taxation I, Corporate Income and Franchise Taxes ¶¶ 10.3, 10.4 (1983). The Florida statute, accordingly, provided that receipts from advertising services were to be apportioned to the State based on the proportion of the Florida market coverage to the total market coverage of the service provider. This applied, inter alia, to national advertising that reached the State.

D. *Legal Challenges to the Tax.* From its inception, Florida's sales tax on services was embroiled in both legal controversy and a political struggle between the Republican Governor and the Democratic Legislature. See N.Y. Times, Dec. 11, 1987. The lawsuits brought to challenge the constitutionality of the statute were never brought to a head because of its repeal. In the interim, the Florida Supreme Court rendered an advisory opinion that sustained the tax. In re Advisory Opinion to the Governor, 509 So.2d 292 (Fla.1987).[18] In addition, newspapers, magazines, and radio-television stations attacked the tax on advertising services as violative of the First Amendment; the organized bar claimed that a tax on legal services violated its clients' constitutional right to assistance of counsel. The basic concept that services performed outside the State may be taxed by the State of use was challenged. See Statement of the Tax Executives Institute, Sept. 17, 1987, published in Tax Highlights, Sept. 25, 1987; Wall Street Journal, April 27, 1987, p. 4 (quoting Henry King, Esq., Davis, Polk & Wardwell). The constitutionality of the attribution of such services rendered to a corporation, on the basis of its Florida apportionment percentage for income tax purposes, and particularly the use of the apportionment fraction of the entire affiliated group, were challenged. The attribution rules were also severely criticized as creating formidable and unnecessary compliance and administration difficulties.

E. *References.* See the articles by W. Hellerstein, who was a drafter of the Florida statute, "A Primer on Florida's Sales Tax on Services," Tax Notes, June 22, 1987, p. 1218, and "Florida's Sales Tax on Services," 41 Nat'l Tax J. 1 (1988), and by Vicki Weber, who was also a drafter of the Florida statute, "Florida's Fleeting Sales Tax on Services," 15 Fla.St.U.L.Rev. 613 (1987); see also Mundstock, "Florida Services: You Only Tax Twice?," Tax Notes, June 15, 1987, p. 1137; Landers, "Taxing Business Services," Cong.Q.Editorial Res.Rep., Vol. 2, No. 8 (Aug. 27, 1987).

SECTION 6. REAL ESTATE CONSTRUCTION AND REPAIR

G.S. LYON & SONS LUMBER AND MANUFACTURING COMPANY v. DEPARTMENT OF REVENUE

Supreme Court of Illinois, 1961
23 Ill.2d 180, 177 N.E.2d 316

KLINGBIEL, JUSTICE. The Department of Revenue assessed taxes under the Retailers' Occupation Tax Act and related statutes against G.S. Lyon & Sons Lumber and Manufacturing Company, measured by its sales of building materials to real-estate developers or speculative builders. Contending that such sales are not within the statute, the company filed a complaint in the circuit court of Macon County for

---

18. Advisory opinions under Florida practice "are merely legal opinions of the individual justices, offered for the Governor's guidance in the performance of his or her constitutional duties." In re Advisory Opinion to the Governor, supra, 509 So.2d at 302. The opinions do not constitute decisions of the Florida Supreme Court and therefore do not finally decide the issues in any case or bind future judicial determinations.

review under the Administrative Review Act. The circuit court agreed with the company, holding that it was entitled to a credit against the assessment for the amount representing the tax on such sales. The Department appeals directly to this court, the public revenue being involved.

The facts are not in dispute. The company is engaged in the business of selling building materials in Decatur, Illinois. During the period involved here, it sold materials to real-estate developers or speculative builders who incorporated them into structures on land they owned themselves. Such builders construct houses or other improvements on land they own, and later sell the improved properties to prospective home owners and other buyers. In some of the instances the builders, prior to beginning construction or purchasing any materials, had made an oral agreement to sell the home to be built.

The trial court determined that the applicability of the act depends upon the intent or purpose of the sale and purchase, and held that since the builder intends to sell the home to be built, his purchase of materials is for the purpose of resale. The Department contends that because the materials are not resold as "tangible personal property" but as real estate, the sales made by the company to the builders were sales at retail for use and consumption, as contemplated by the act.

The retailers' occupation tax is imposed upon "persons engaged in the business of selling tangible personal property at retail." (Ill.Rev. Stat.1959, chap. 120, par. 441.) The statute defines a sale at retail as "any transfer of the ownership of, or title to, tangible personal property to a purchaser, for use or consumption and not for resale in any form as tangible personal property, for a valuable consideration." (Ill.Rev.Stat. 1959, chap. 120, par. 440.) To justify the assessment of a tax, therefore, two tests or conditions must be met: (1) the transfer must be for use or consumption, and (2) it must not be for resale in any form as tangible personal property. Beatrice Foods Co. v. Lyons, 12 Ill.2d 274, 146 N.E. 2d 68; Material Service Corp. v. Hollingsworth, 415 Ill. 284, 112 N.E.2d 703; Burrows Co. v. Hollingsworth, 415 Ill. 202, 112 N.E.2d 706.

We think it is clear, as the Department points out, that where the material is used in constructing a house on land owned by the builder, the one who sells materials to him incurs the tax even though the builder intends to sell the house after it is completed. To take the initial sale out of the category of retail sales within the meaning of the act it is necessary that the contemplated resale be a sale of the property in its form "as tangible personal property." It is obvious that building materials, after they have been used in the construction of a house, constitute real estate rather than personal property, and that they are not transferred to the homeowner in any form as tangible personal property when the house is subsequently sold. The sale of materials to the builder, therefore, is not for resale in any form as tangible personal property and the second condition of taxability is accordingly satisfied.

As to whether the sales of materials to the real-estate developers are "for use or consumption," the Department argues that the sales take the articles off the retail market, and that although the house or other structure is thereafter the subject of a sale, the materials themselves are not resold for a direct and specific consideration. We think the test relied upon by the Department, and announced by this court in Modern Dairy Co. v. Department of Revenue, 413 Ill. 55, 108 N.E.2d 8, is based upon the proper construction of the act. We observed in the Modern Dairy case, 413 Ill. at page 67, 108 N.E.2d at page 15, that "The title to this act describes sales 'to purchasers for use or consumption.' It is noted that the terms are in the disjunctive rather than the conjunctive, indicating that the legislature intended 'use' to mean one thing and 'consumption' something else. Considering the purpose of the Retailers' Occupation Tax Act, it is reasonable to assume the legislature intended the term 'use' to include any employment of a thing which took it off the retail market so that it was no longer the object of a tax on the privilege of selling it at retail."

The process or employment engaged in by a builder results in destroying the identity of the material as personal property and converting it into real estate. Using them for purposes of construction obviously takes the materials as such off the retail market, and since the act has no application to sales of real estate, the materials of which improvements are constructed can no longer be an object of the tax. It seems clear, in view of the purpose and intent of the act, that who uses the structure, which, in turn, has been built or created by a use of the materials, is irrelevant. The personal property has been transformed by the process of building, and in every sense contemplated by the act it is used or consumed in the process of construction or fabrication. The sale to the builder is the last transfer of the materials as personal property, and is a sale for use or consumption within the meaning of the act.

The company argues that the builders are not the users or consumers because "each of the purchasers in this case was engaged in the business of building homes, not for use, but for resale." Such reasoning, like that which this court reconsidered and rejected in the Modern Dairy case, ignores the fact that the tax is not concerned with sales of "homes" but with sales of materials or other kinds of tangible personal property. Whether the builder uses the improved real estate as a home, or sells it to someone else, is immaterial. It is the building *material*—the tangible personal property—the use of which is in question, and it is plain that the one who uses it, in the sense of that term as construed in the Modern Dairy case, is the one who erects out of it the house or other structure.

* * *

When construed in the light of its purpose, the act contemplates that use or consumption of personal property which takes it off the retail market so that it is no longer an object of the tax. Under this test it is clear that a builder uses or consumes lumber and the like. He has no intention of reselling the lumber or the other items of construction material which he buys. He is not in the business of selling materials. He is in the business of using them to build houses: the business of contracting, or of selling houses. It is evident that the materials he buys are taken off the retail market and are no longer objects of the tax. It follows that their sale to him is a measure of the tax.

In our opinion this conclusion applies whether or not the builder has entered into a contract for sale of the real estate, either oral or written. The controlling factor in determining taxability is the purpose for which the material is bought, and in ascertaining this purpose the mere matter of who owns the land is of little significance. Whether the builder is a speculative real-estate developer intending to sell the improved real estate at a profit, or whether he is a contractor having undertaken to improve another person's property, his purpose in purchasing lumber and other materials is to use them, not to resell them. In either case the material, in the process of use, loses its identity as personal property, becomes real estate by accession and is no longer the object of a tax on the privilege of selling it at retail. The builder buys his material to use, and not to resell as personal property, whether the real estate belongs to him or to a third party at the time he is engaged in improving it.

We recognize that the result reached here is not in harmony with that arrived in Material Service Corp. v. Hollingsworth, 415 Ill. 284, 112 N.E.2d 703, upon which the lumber company relies. In that case the argument was made, as here, that the materials become real estate upon incorporation into the building, and are not transferred as tangible personal property. We rejected the argument because no reasons were advanced in support of it, and because it had apparently been rejected in earlier cases, decided prior to the Modern Dairy case.

Upon reconsideration of the question we think that in this respect the decision in Material Service Corp. v. Hollingsworth, 415 Ill. 284, 112 N.E.2d 703, is not supported by sound reasons and can no longer be followed. The legislature must be presumed to have been aware of the well-recognized distinction between real estate and personal property, and it has clearly expressed its intention to exclude only where the contemplated resale is a resale of the property as personal property. In this case the lumber or other material, if it can be considered as having been bought for resale at all, was obviously bought for resale as real estate. It follows that the circuit court erred in reversing that part of the deficiency assessment measured by receipts on the sales in question here.

* * *

Reversed and remanded, with directions.

SCHAEFER, JUSTICE (dissenting).

In this case a very limited issue was submitted for decision. The opinion adopted by the court has gone far beyond that limited issue, and has said that the tax falls upon transactions which the Department of Revenue in its brief in this case conceded are not subject to the tax, and which the legislature has clearly indicated are not subject to the tax. The Department of Revenue has amended its regulations to reflect the views expressed in the opinion of the court. The net result is a tax imposed by this court rather than by the General Assembly, and Mr. Justice House and I therefore dissent.

The extent to which the court's opinion deviates from the existing law, as well as the extent to which it goes beyond the question submitted for decision, can most readily be shown by quotations from the Department's brief in this case [quoted as follows]:

* * *

"For all purposes relevant to a decision in this case, sales by materialmen and purveyors of building supplies for the construction of homes and buildings may be divided into four distinct classes:

"In the *first* class, the materials and supplies are sold to and paid for by a contractor who amalgamates them into a home or building upon the land of an owner who is not the contractor but who has employed the contractor to build the home or other building. In this class of cases, not involved in this case, this Court has held that the materialmen and supply houses do not incur the tax because the contractor 'transfers' the materials and supplies and therefore 'resells' them to the owner of the land *as tangible personal property*. They do not become real estate until they are incorporated into the home by incorporating them into a building that is constructed on the land. The Department does not attempt to impose any tax measured by such sales. Material Service Corp. v. McKibbin (1942), 380 Ill. 226 [43 N.E.2d 939].

"In the *second* class of these transactions, the builder has sold or has at least entered into a definitive and enforcible written contract for the sale of a home (or super market or filling station or other edifice) with the purchaser. Such a contract transfers equitable title to the vendee, subject only to the vendor's right of forfeiture or right of foreclosure of a vendor's lien from any defaults in the payment of the purchase price. The contractor then builds the home for the purchaser or prospective vendee under a written contract with that purchaser. The Department concedes that such sales are to the builders as a contractor and that the gross receipts from those sales do not measure the Illinois Retailers' Occupation Tax. This type of transaction is not involved in this case." (Italics as in Department's brief.)

The third class of cases described in the Department's brief are those in which the builder builds a home, upon land that he owns, at a time when he has no arrangement whatever for its resale. The fourth class is like the third, but includes those cases in which the builder has only an oral agreement, characterized by the Department as unenforceable, with the prospective purchaser. The contention of the Department as stated in its brief, is "that sales of building materials of these latter two classes result in the incidence of the Retailers' Occupation Tax."

The opinion of the court, however, has held that all four classes of transactions described by the Department are taxable, despite the Department's repeated concessions that the first two of them are not.

* * *

The court's opinion proceeds upon two grounds. One of them is that "In this case the lumber or other material, if it can be considered as having been bought for resale at all, was obviously bought for resale as real estate." As to the first two classes of transactions it seems impossible to say that the building contractor transfers anything as real estate. By hypothesis he owns neither the land on which the building is built, nor the building that he builds. His statutory lien is a far cry from ownership. Real property is transferred by deed, and the contractor cannot, and of course in fact does not, convey by deed the title to real property that he does not own. I would have no quarrel with the proposition announced in the opinion if it were limited to the third and fourth classes, which were all that were before the court. But the opinion is not so limited, and the Department has not so interpreted it.

The other ground upon which the opinion is based is that the building contractor "uses or consumes" the materials that go into the building. Back in 1941 the General Assembly did enact such a definition of "use or consumption," applicable not only to building contractors but to all service occupations. But this definition was repealed in 1945 (Laws of 1945, p. 1278), and it has never been re-enacted. The text of this repealed provision, together with its history, which includes this court's decision holding it unconstitutional (Stolze Lumber Co. v. Stratton, 386 Ill. 334, 54 N.E.2d 554) is set forth in Burrows Co. v. Hollingsworth, 415 Ill. 202, at page 210, 112 N.E.2d 706.

The only other relevant legislative changes since 1945 show an approach that contradicts the position taken in the opinion.

In 1955 the General Assembly amended section 1 of the act by adding a provision "that any person who is engaged in a business which is not subject to the tax imposed by this Act because of involving * * * a construction contract to improve real estate, but who, in the course of conducting such business, transfers tangible personal property to users or consumers in the finished form in which it was purchased, and which does not become real estate, under any provision of a construction contract * * * shall be considered to be engaged in the business of selling tangible personal property at retail to the extent of the value of the tangible personal property so transferred." (Ill.Rev. Stat.1959, chap. 120, par. 440.) This provision is still in effect. As the Department's Regulations state, it refers to "gas or electric stoves, refrigerators, washing machines, portable ventilating units and other portable equipment of this kind." Part of its significance here is that it shows that the General Assembly has considered the problem, and has singled out for taxability only transfers of portable equipment of the kind described. As to the many other kinds of materials and fixtures that are used in constructing a building, it made no change in the existing law, and the inference that no change was intended seems inescapable.

But more important than any inferences, however clear, is the fact that by this provision the General Assembly has stated explicitly that the "users or consumers" are not the construction contractors, but the persons for whom the buildings are built and to whom the materials are transferred by the contractors in the course of performing their contract. The opinion of the court imposes the tax upon those who supply materials to construction contractors, in the first two classes of cases described by the Department, on the ground that the construction contractors are the users or consumers of the building materials. It does not mention the fact that this position flatly contradicts the position that the legislature has taken on this point.

The final item of legislation that contradicts the court's opinion was enacted in 1961. Construction contractors have often been described, both by the General Assembly and by this court, as persons engaged in a "service occupation." The seventy-second General Assembly has enacted a "Service Occupation Tax Act" which seems clearly designed to reach the first two classes of transactions described by the Department. It imposes a tax "at the rate of 3% of the cost price of all tangible personal property transferred by said servicemen either in the form of tangible personal property *or in the form of real estate* as an incident to a 'sale of services' under any contract ＊ ＊ ＊." (72nd General Assembly, S.B. 558, sec. 3. Italics supplied.) The legislature, however, has imposed its tax upon the construction contractor, while the tax imposed by the court in this case falls upon the supplier.

HOUSE, J., concurs in this dissent.*

Notes and Problems

A. In State ex rel. Otis Elevator Co. v. Smith, 357 Mo. 1055, 212 S.W.2d 580 (1948), the court held that a corporation constructing and installing elevators was engaged in selling tangible personal property at retail and, therefore, was required to collect sales tax. The decision largely depended on provisions in the contracts retaining in the taxpayer title to the elevators and other apparatus until final payment was made. To buttress this security, the contracts provided that the apparatus "can be removed without material damage to the freehold." In the light of these clauses of the contracts, the court concluded that there is not an "inseparable commingling of labor and material that produced the finished product," but instead a taxable sale of tangible personal property. The recitals in

* [For later Illinois decisions following the principal case, see Material Service Corp. v. Isaacs, 25 Ill.2d 137, 183 N.E.2d 164 (1962); Spurgeon v. State, Department of Revenue, 52 Ill.App.3d 29, 6 Ill.Dec. 450, 362 N.E.2d 1370 (1977).]

the contract as to the removability of the elevators and apparatus were obviously inserted to secure payment to the vendor. Should they have any bearing on the disposition of the tax problem? In a later case, the court held that charges made for the construction and installation of wooden cabinets in homes did not constitute receipts from sales of tangible personal property; the installation, said the court, was an integral part of the contract, and the transfer was consummated when the cabinets were affixed to the real estate; there was therefore no transfer of tangible personalty. Marsh v. Spradling, 537 S.W.2d 402 (Mo.1976). *Otis Elevator* was distinguished on the ground that the general principle—"that upon the installation of personal property into real estate as a part of a general construction contract the article becomes a part of the real estate," 537 S.W.2d at 406—was inapplicable due to the agreement in the *Otis* case by which title was retained in the annex or after installation. Cf. with the principal case, Duhame v. State Tax Comm'n, 65 Ariz. 268, 179 P.2d 252, 171 A.L.R. 684 (1947); American Sign & Indicator Corp. v. City of Lake Charles, 320 So.2d 234 (La.App.1975).

B. In some States there are specific provisions dealing with the taxability of building contractors. Thus, Alabama has a provision that the "use within this State of tangible personal property by the manufacturer thereof, as building materials in the performance of a construction contract shall * * * be considered as a retail sale * * * by the manufacturers." The tax is measured by the "reasonable and fair market value [of the articles] used or consumed" by the taxpayer. In State v. Air Conditioning Engineers, Inc., 277 Ala. 675, 174 So.2d 315 (1965), the taxpayer fabricated component parts of air conditioners, using sheet metal in constructing air conditioning duct systems. It bent, crimped, and partially shaped the sheet metal as component parts of the finished duct system. These partially finished parts were then taken to job sites where they were further shaped, bent, fitted, and connected into the finished duct system, which was then affixed to the building. The court rejected the State's contention that the taxpayer was a "manufacturer," and held that it was not taxable on the articles used because it does not "manufacture a finished product," but is merely a contractor using building materials to carry out a construction contract. Consequently, it was taxable on its purchases of sheet metal but not on the putative sale of the ducts. The court relied on the regulations to support the line it drew; metal awnings and metal car parts when prefabricated were listed as within the manufacturer's tax provision by the regulations, but siding, roofing, flooring, and inside trim were, in circumstances similar to the principal case, excluded from that levy.

In California, regulations have been adopted governing the taxation of construction contractors under its sales and use tax statutes. Such contractors are deemed to be consumers of the "materials" they furnish and install in the performance of construction contracts, but they are retailers of the "fixtures" they so furnish and install. Rule 11, which appears in 18 Cal.Admin.Code § 1521, CCH ¶ 65–040, P–H ¶ 21,614, specifies what constitutes "materials," as distinguished from "fixtures." In an extensive opinion, the Superior Court for the County of Los Angeles struck down the regulations on the grounds that they were "unreasonable, arbitrary, ambiguous, discriminatory and * * * in excess of the statutory rule making powers of the Board [of Equalization]," Honeywell, Inc. v. State Board of Equalization, CCH ¶ 204–952, P–H ¶ 23,790–Q (1973), but the Court of Appeal reversed, holding that Rule 11 was valid, and noting:

> The trial court found fault with rule 11 because it is sometimes difficult to draw a line of demarcation between fixtures and materials which are taxed to the contractor as a consumer. Unquestionably it is sometimes difficult to draw that line. But that difficulty stems not from rule 11 but from problems inherent in the basic legal concept of fixtures. The law has frequently encountered problems in drawing a precise line between fixtures and materials in areas outside of the sales tax law. * * * There are admittedly many gray areas. But that very uncertainty justifies a process of initial administrative determination subject to judicial review, since it is far better to resolve the gray areas, no matter how laborious the effort, than that retail sellers of fixtures be permitted to escape their fair share of the tax. [Honeywell, Inc. v. State Bd. of Equalization, 48 Cal.App.3d 907, 915, 122 Cal.Rptr. 243, 248 (1975).]

Like California, Florida has detailed regulations governing sales taxation of construction contractors. Department of Revenue Rule 12A–1.051, CCH ¶ 60–137, P–H ¶ 21,611. Construction contractors are generally regarded as the consumers of the materials, supplies, and equipment that they use in performing construction services. They are not viewed as reselling such tangible personal property to their customers. Contractors therefore pay a sales tax to their suppliers on the materials they purchase. There is an exception to the rule for contracts in which the contractor agrees to sell specifically described and itemized materials at a specified price and to complete the work for an additional agreed price or on the basis of time consumed. In this case, the contractor is viewed as a reseller of the property he purchases, and he must collect a tax on its resale from the purchaser.

C. *Sales of Prefabricated Homes.* Are sales of prefabricated homes sales of tangible personal property under a retail sales tax? In State Tax Comm'n v. Boise Cascade Corp., 97 Idaho 312, 543 P.2d 865 (1975), landowners entered into contracts with the Boise Cascade Corporation for the construction of prefabricated buildings. Boise Cascade proceeded to construct the building in its factories. When its work was completed, Boise Cascade transported the building to the owner's site, where it placed the building on the foundation and performed various related tasks. Title to the building did not pass to the landowner until Boise Cascade placed the building on his site and attached the building to its foundation. After a detailed consideration of the legislative history of the Idaho Sales Tax Act, the court concluded that Boise Cascade was engaged in improving real property and not in making retail sales of personalty. The court said:

> The only distinction between Boise Cascade's method of construction and that of the traditional on-site contractor is that Boise Cascade does a majority of its construction at their plant while a majority of the traditional contractor's work is done at the homeowner's lot. The legislature considered the process of construction to be a service and enacted I.C. § 63–3609(a) to tax the contractor for the materials con-

sumed in the building process. The fact that Boise Cascade's method of construction involves hauling the nearly completed home to the buyer's lot does not change the end result, that is, the landowner having a home on his previously unimproved lot. [97 Idaho at 315, 543 P.2d at 868 (footnote omitted).]

The consequence was that a tax was payable on sales to Boise Cascade of materials used in its operations, but not on the transaction between Boise and the owner of the site. See also Department of Revenue v. Smith Harvestore Products, Inc., 72 Wis.2d 60, 240 N.W.2d 357 (1976) (tax imposed upon sale by manufacturer to dealer of components for silo-like structure); Adrian Housing Corp. v. Collins, 253 Ga. 263, 319 S.E.2d 852 (1984) (sales of modular homes taxable).

In Sterling Custom Homes Corp. v. Commissioner of Revenue, 391 N.W.2d 523 (Minn.1986), the court held that a company that prepares plans for custom-designed homes, then constructs components of those homes and delivers them to the construction site of the home, unloads the components and oversees the erection of the component, but which does not assume responsibility for construction, is a supplier of building materials. It is not a construction contractor; it, therefore, is taxable on the sale of its homes and not on the purchase of the materials. But see Wisconsin Dept. of Revenue v. Sterling Custom Homes Corp., 91 Wis.2d 675, 283 N.W.2d 573 (1979), in which the same company was held to be a construction contractor. The Wisconsin statutes recognize that construction contractors can act either as retailers or consumer, and that activities including alteration, repair, or improvement of real property represent consumption on the part of such contractors. Wis.Stat. §§ 77.51(4), 77.52(2)(a), CCH ¶¶ 92–845(c), 846d(5), P–H ¶¶ 22,005.20, 22,201.60. Minnesota, on the other hand, classifies the sale of building materials used for alteration, repair, or improvement of real property as retailing by a contractor, regardless of any intent to resell. Minn.Stat. § 297A.01 (subd. 4), CCH ¶ 95–439, P–H ¶ 21–218.

D. *References.* See Annots., 163 A.L.R. 276, 171 A.L.R. 697; Spencer, "The Slippery Path of Contractor Sales Tax Compliance," 52 Taxes 555 (1974); Note, "Ohio Use Tax—Construction Contractor's Dilemma," 42 U.Cin.L.Rev. 319 (1973).

ASSIGNMENT

Analyze the provisions of your State's sales and use tax laws and regulations, and consider the taxability of the building supplier and contractor under: (a) a lump sum contract, and (b) a contract requiring the contractor to sell the materials and supplies at the usual retail price and to render services for an additional consideration. In this connection, consider the function and purpose of the exemption of sales for resale, or the limitation of the tax to retail sales, sales at retail, and the like.

Assuming that you represent the following persons in the negotiation of the building contracts enumerated below, what provisions would you recommend as to price, billings, and so forth, of materials and services?

Client	**Type of Contract**
(a) Supplier of contractor (b) Contractor (c) Church	Contract to build a church for religious organization.
(a) Supplier of contractor (b) Contractor (c) Realty corporation	Contract to build apartment house for private realty corporation.

C. USE TAXES

Much of the material considered in this chapter under the title "Retail Sales Taxes" is applicable to the use tax. The materials here set forth deal with special problems particularly arising under use tax acts.

INTRODUCTORY NOTE

Use taxes were developed as an ingenious instrument to meet two weaknesses in sales taxes. First, local merchants lost business through purchases made by their customers of goods delivered to them in adjoining non-sales tax areas to escape paying the tax. Second, many purchases of goods shipped into the State were regarded as immune from the tax because of the Commerce Clause. See, e.g., Matter of Nat. Cash Register Co. v. Taylor, 276 N.Y. 208, 11 N.E.2d 881 (1937), certiorari denied, 303 U.S. 656, 58 S.Ct. 759 (1938).

Use taxes are functionally equivalent to sales taxes. They are typically levied upon the use, storage, or other consumption in the State of tangible personal property that has not been subjected to a sales tax. The use tax imposes an exaction equal in amount to the sales tax that would have been imposed on the sale of the property in question if the sale had occurred within the State's taxing jurisdiction. The State overcomes the constitutional hurdle of taxing an out-of-state or interstate sale by imposing the tax on a subject within its taxing power—the use, storage, or consumption of property within the State.

The Supreme Court of Tennessee has described the use tax as follows:

> The use tax is a compensating tax, designed to prevent the avoidance of sales taxes and ensure that Tennessee manufacturers and merchants remain on equal competitive footing with nonresidents who enter this state to do business. Broadacre Dairies, Inc. v. Evans, 193 Tenn. 441, 246 S.W.2d 78 (1952). Taken together, the sales and use taxes provide a uniform scheme of taxation on goods (tangible personal property) purchased within the state and goods purchased outside the state for "storage, use, or consumption" within the state. Broadacre

Dairies, supra. See also, Henneford v. Silas Mason Co., Inc., 300 U.S. 577, 57 S.Ct. 524, 81 L.Ed. 814 (1936).

Broadly speaking, the use tax is a tax "on the enjoyment of that which was purchased, after a sale has spent its interstate character." McLeod v. Dilworth, 322 U.S. 327, 64 S.Ct. 1023, 88 L.Ed. 1304 (1943). More specifically, the use tax is a tax on the "privilege of using, consuming, distributing or storing tangible personal property after it is brought into this State from without this State." Broadacre Dairies, 193 Tenn. at 444–45, 246 S.W.2d at 79. This definition is fairly uniform throughout the states. See 68 Am.Jur. Sales and Use Taxes § 171 (1953). Thus, it was the legislative intent, as manifested in Section 67–3005, T.C.A., to impose a use tax on all tangible personal property imported from other states and used and consumed in this state, provided a similar tax, equal to or greater, has not been paid in the exporting state. Young Sales Corp. v. Benson, 224 Tenn. 88, 450 S.W.2d 574 (1970). [Woods v. Kelley, 592 S.W.2d 567, 570 (Tenn.1980).]

MODERN MERCHANDISING, INC.
v. DEPARTMENT OF REVENUE

Supreme Court of South Dakota, 1986.
397 N.W.2d 470.

FOSHEIM, JUSTICE.

This is an appeal from a circuit court judgment affirming a Department of Revenue (Department) order assessing use tax and interest against LaBelle's. We reverse.

LaBelle's is a Minnesota corporation and a subsidiary of Modern Merchandising. It retails consumer goods by mail order and through stores located in Minnesota, North Dakota, and South Dakota. Department assessed use taxes and interest against LaBelle's from April 1, 1982 through February 29, 1984, on catalogs and flyers mailed to South Dakota residents. Following a hearing, Department issued an order approving the assessment and denying LaBelle's request for a refund.

From the stipulated facts it appears companies related to LaBelle's contracted with printers located in Minnesota to print the catalogs and flyers. These printers either mailed the literature from Minnesota directly to the South Dakota residents or turned the materials over to common carriers who delivered them to post offices located in South Dakota for mailing to the South Dakota residents. LaBelle's furnished the printers with the names of those to whom the literature was to be delivered. The catalogs were delivered free of charge to the residents who were free to use or discard them as they wished. Catalogs not delivered in South Dakota were returned directly to the Minnesota printers.

The tax was levied pursuant to SDCL 10–46–2 which, in pertinent part, provides:

An excise tax is hereby imposed on the privilege of the use, storage, and consumption in this state of tangible personal property purchased on or after July 1, 1939, for use in this state at the same rate [as the state sales tax].

It is Department's position that since LaBelle's paid the printers for the catalogs and flyers and those items were mailed to the South Dakota residents as determined by LaBelle's customer list, LaBelle's exercised "right or power" over the catalogs and, therefore, "use[d] the flyers and catalogs to generate sales in South Dakota and to operate its catalog business in South Dakota within the definition of 'use' in SDCL 10–46–1(2)", which in pertinent part reads:

"Use" means and includes the exercise of right or power over tangible personal property incidental to the ownership of that property.

*   *   *

*   *   *

The issue on appeal is whether LaBelle's had sufficient "right or power * * * incidental to the ownership" of the catalogs and flyers once in South Dakota to qualify as a "use * * * in this state" under SDCL 10–46–1(2) and 2.

Department relies heavily upon our K–Mart Corp. v. Dept. of Revenue, 345 N.W.2d 55 (S.D.1984), decision. The retailer in *K–Mart* contracted with local newspapers to have its advertisements inserted in its publications for distribution in South Dakota. The supplements were printed and sent to a publisher outside of South Dakota. The publisher received a distribution list from K–Mart setting forth the South Dakota newspapers to which it sent the supplements. Essentially, K–Mart made the same arguments we find here. We held that because K–Mart owned the supplements and retained the power to control the date of distribution and the numbers of copies to be distributed after the copies entered South Dakota, K–Mart "use[d]" the supplements within the meaning of SDCL 10–46–2.

Although the facts of *K–Mart* are similar to those in this case, we distinguish advertisements delivered in the *K–Mart* fashion from the direct mailings in this case. Unlike K–Mart, LaBelle's had no in-state contract and no similar in-state power. All control over the present literature within our state belonged to either the post office or the advertisement recipients. Even if the literature could not be delivered, it again would be handled by the post office until outside of South Dakota. By concluding the catalogs and flyers were taxable, Department concentrated more on the material's generation of in-state sales for LaBelle's than on whether LaBelle's activities fit the language of the tax statutes. In contrast, *K–Mart* focuses and turns upon the statutory language; not merely upon whether the newspaper supplements generated in-state sales for K–Mart.

Department cites Northwestern National Bank of Sioux Falls v. Gillis, 82 S.D. 457, 148 N.W.2d 293 (1967), as demonstrating a legislative intent behind SDCL 10–46–2 and 1(2) to tax LaBelle's for its activities in question here. *Gillis* states that the purpose of the use tax is not only to raise money but also to "help the retailers in this state, who are subject to the sales tax, compete on an equal footing with out-of-state competitors." 82 S.D. at 467, 148 N.W.2d at 298. Department also points out that the use tax is designed to prevent avoidance of our state sales tax. E.g., Woods v. M.J. Kelley Co., 592 S.W.2d 567 (Tenn. 1980). Since a local printer selling flyers or catalogs (or its purchaser) would be liable for the sales tax, LaBelle's should pay a use tax on the literature, according to Department. Department also argues that if LaBelle's does not pay tax on the catalogs local retailers are put at a competitive disadvantage contrary to legislative intent. While we agree with Department's interpretation of our legislature's intent, we cannot apply the statute to activity which is plainly alien to its language. See Famous Brands, supra. We must honor the rule that statutes imposing a tax are to be construed liberally in favor of the taxpayer. Nash Finch, supra.

Department argues it is illogical to subject advertisements delivered in the *K–Mart* fashion to the use tax, but not those delivered as in this case. However, we find support for this dichotomy in J.C. Penney, supra, relied upon in *K–Mart*. In *J.C. Penney,* the Wisconsin Supreme Court considered both the *K–Mart* situation and the one before us now,[1] and reached the same contrasting conclusions as this court. Similarly, that Court was also confronted with the argument that reaching such contrasting results was irrational. We agree with its observation that "[t]his contention is more appropriately directed to the legislature." J.C. Penney, 323 N.W.2d at 170.[2]

The circuit court's judgment is reversed and taxpayer's refund request of $42,673 shall be honored.

WUEST, C.J., and MORGAN and HENDERSON, JJ., concur.

SABERS, J., dissents.

SABERS, JUSTICE (dissenting).

I dissent for all of the following reasons.

LaBelle's argues that it had insufficient "right or power * * * incidental to the ownership" of the catalog and flyer shipments once in South Dakota to qualify as a "use" under SDCL §§ 10–46–1(2) and –2. For LaBelle's to succeed on this theory, it must distinguish K–Mart Corp. v. Dept. of Revenue, 345 N.W.2d 55 (S.D.1984). The retailer in *K–Mart* published advertisements to be distributed as part of South Dakota newspapers. The supplements were printed in Michigan and sent to a publisher also located outside of South Dakota. The publisher received a distribution list from K–Mart setting forth the South Dakota newspapers to which the publisher then sent the supplements. K–Mart made basically the same arguments that LaBelle's does here, contend-

---

1. In holding the directly mailed material untaxable, *J.C. Penney* employs a rationale differing from that relied upon here. See id., 323 N.W.2d at 170.

2. Counsel for LaBelle's concede that the Wisconsin Legislature amended their statute after the *J.C. Penney* decision to make the advertising procedures LaBelle's utilized here subject to the Wisconsin Use Tax. *See* Wisc.Stat. § 77.51(15)(b).

ing that SDCL §§ 10–46–1(2) and –2 were not met because K–Mart did not use the advertisements within South Dakota and that K–Mart exercised no "right or power" over the newspaper supplements from the time the supplements were printed out of state. This court disagreed. Instead, we adopted

> * * * Department's position that K–Mart uses the supplements within the state within the meaning of SDCL 10–46–2 by virtue of its ownership of the supplements and its power to determine the date of distribution and the numbers of copies to be distributed.

345 N.W.2d at 58, citing Wisconsin Dept. of Revenue v. J.C. Penney Co., 108 Wis.2d 662, 323 N.W.2d 168 (1982).

Unlike the retailer in *K–Mart,* LaBelle's contends that it did not own nor have control over the catalogs and flyers once in South Dakota. It cites no authority for this proposition. LaBelle's contrasts its situation with *K–Mart* where the retailer owned the supplements after they were received by the South Dakota newspapers. LaBelle's argues that once delivered, the catalogs and flyers belonged to the residents. LaBelle's further argues that K–Mart had more power over its advertisements than did LaBelle's because K–Mart had the power to " 'determine the date of distribution and the number of copies to be distributed,' *after the [K–Mart] supplements were delivered in South Dakota."* Id., (emphasis added).

Department claims the cases are essentially identical except that LaBelle's catalogs were shipped directly to the in-state residents instead of to newspapers. Department argues that K–Mart had less in-state control than does LaBelle's because the newspapers in *K–Mart* had the power to edit the advertisements, and their personnel handled the supplements.

Both sides cite considerable authority for their respective positions. Apart from J.C. Penney, supra, which this court relied on in *K–Mart,* these cases are not extremely helpful. The *J.C. Penney* case ruled on the taxability of both (1) catalogs sent directly to consumers from out of state (this case), and (2) out-of-state shipments of advertisements to in-state newspapers for insertion (*K–Mart*). The case holds per *K–Mart* that shipments to newspapers fall within the use tax. However, *J.C. Penney* also holds that mailings directly to the consumers are not taxable.

In *J.C. Penney,* the court held that catalogs printed in Indiana and mailed to Wisconsin were not taxable in Wisconsin, but that newspaper supplements printed out-of-state, but delivered by local newspapers, were subject to tax. 323 N.W.2d at 171–172. The court determined that J.C. Penney "used" the newspaper supplements, but did not "use" the catalogs. This appears illogical and honors form over substance. A catalog is similar to a newspaper supplement. They both contain pictures of items for sale with prices and descriptions. In actual practice, J.C. Penney got more use out of the *catalogs* than they did the *supplements.* A supplement is only an advertisement. If a sale is made to a person who uses a supplement, J.C. Penney must still use its local store to make the sale. Although some customers use the catalog in the same manner, many customers use the catalog to order merchandise. In addition to pictures and descriptions, the catalog contains order blanks and ordering and shipping instructions. The supplements are an inducement to buy. The catalogs are used not only to induce sales, but to make sales. If the supplements are used in the state of receipt, so are the catalogs.

The use tax is not a property tax or a tax on consumption of property. In Inter–State Nurseries, Inc. v. Iowa Department of Revenue, 164 N.W.2d 858 (Iowa 1969), the court held that an Iowa nursery company was "using" its catalogs " * * * as a means of advertising and promoting the sale of its products * * * " even though they were received, read, or discarded by others. Id. at 863.

Under cases such as Philco Corporation v. Department of Revenue, 40 Ill.2d 312, 239 N.E.2d 805 (1968), physical manipulation of property is not a necessary incident to use of the property for use tax purposes. In construing a definition of "use" similar to South Dakota's, the court quotes with approval from Keesling, *Conflicting Conceptions of Ownership in Taxation,* 44 Cal.L.Rev. 886, 867 (1956): "When a person buys property in one state for the purpose of leasing it and transporting it to a person in another state where a use tax law is in effect, the lessor is considered as using the property in the second state for the production of income and hence is subject to such state's use tax even though he personally makes no physical use of the property in such state." One of the appellants in Philco, supra, Rental Equipment Company, Inc., signed its leases in Missouri, the lessees picked up the equipment in Missouri, and the lessor never had representatives in Illinois, but the court nevertheless upheld Illinois' assessment of use tax on the rental equipment even though one of the items was in Illinois for only nine days. Id. at 809. Although renting equipment may seem different from mailing catalogs at first glance, all of the important elements are the same. In both cases, tangible personal property is brought into the state by an unrelated third party and use tax liability arises even though the taxpayer is not the person who physically possesses the property within the taxing state.

LaBelle's asserts that tax liability should be avoided because it did not use the catalogs in South Dakota. However, LaBelle's has stores in South Dakota, the catalogs are in South Dakota, and the recipients of the catalogs are in South Dakota. LaBelle's furnishes and controls the mailing list for the catalogs and also pays for them. The reason the catalogs are in this state is to generate sales for LaBelle's. This constitutes the same use that K–Mart made of its advertising supplements. The method of delivery should be irrelevant.

This court's decision in Northwestern National Bank of Sioux Falls v. Gillis, 82 S.D. 457, 148 N.W.2d 293 (1967), is helpful in discerning the legislative intent behind SDCL §§ 10–46–1(2) and –2. This case states that the purpose of the use tax is not only to raise money but also to help "the retailers in this state, who are subject to the sales tax, compete on an equal footing with out-of-state competitors." 82 S.D. at 467, 148 N.W.2d at 298. It seems plain that the use tax is designed to prevent avoidance of the sales tax. See, e.g., Woods v. M.J. Kelley Co., 592 S.W.2d 567, 570 (Tenn.1980). Department reasons that since a local printer selling flyers or catalogs (or its purchaser) would be liable for the sales tax, LaBelle's should pay a use tax on the literature. Department further reasons that local retailers are put at a competitive disadvantage if LaBelle's does not pay tax on the catalogs. LaBelle's does not argue that our legislature did not intend to impose a tax on LaBelle's for these activities. It merely repeats its argument that the language of the statutes clearly excludes this activity.

In my view, LaBelle's arguments simply miss the controlling point. LaBelle's used the catalogs in South Dakota. They even stored those catalogs not delivered until returned. It is not necessary that LaBelle's employees physically ride on the mail truck—the use of the catalogs by South Dakota residents was LaBelle's use under the statute. LaBelle's exercised power and control through its agents in South Dakota even though its own employees may not have physically entered the state. The evidence shows that LaBelle's exercised power and control over the catalogs through the printing, the number of catalogs distributed, the timing of the delivery of the catalogs in South Dakota, and even the return of undelivered catalogs, all to the same or greater extent than in the *K–Mart* case. As stated by the trial court, "LaBelle's has raised a number of distinctions between (*K–Mart*) and this case, however, I am of the opinion that they are distinctions without difference." So am I. This court should discern substance over form and affirm the use tax.

Notes and Problems

A. The dissenting opinion in the *Modern Merchandising* case declares that "LaBelle exercised power and control through its agents in South Dakota." May the United States post office be regarded as LaBelle's agent for delivering the catalogs and flyers? If so, would delivery by the United States post office to the prospective customers in the State constitute a taxable use? Can such a result be accommodated to *National Bellas Hess* (p. 812 infra) in which catalogs, flyers, and merchandise ordered were delivered to the customers in Illinois, but unlike *Modern Merchandising* which had stores in South Dakota, had no "presence" in Illinois? The view of the dissent in *Modern Merchandising* finds some support in the widespread attribution of sales, for apportionment purposes, to the customer's State under the sales destination test. See p. 477 supra. See McNamara v. D.H. Holmes Co., 505 So.2d 102 (La.App.1987), probable juris. noted, ___ U.S. ___, 108 S.Ct. 283 (1987), which sustained the application of Louisiana's use tax on facts essentially the same as *Modern Merchandising* and held that the assessment did not violate the Commerce Clause. The case is pending before the Supreme Court as this work goes to press.

A Rhode Island decision reached the same result as the South Dakota case. The taxpayer, which did business in Rhode Island, ordered advertising circulars printed in Massachusetts. They were addressed and deposited in the United States mail in New Hampshire, for delivery to potential customers in Rhode Island. The statute taxed "storing, using, or otherwise consuming in this State tangible personal property." It was agreed that the taxpayer had neither "used" nor "stored" the circulars in the State; the dispute focused on the question whether it had "otherwise consumed" them. The court declared:

> We agree with the trial justice's statement that the following situations would constitute consumption, namely, "the receipt and reading," "the receipt and discarding" and "the receipt and tearing up or destruction of the circulars by the ultimate occupant." In each of these instances receipt of the materials, that is, physical possession, is an integral part of the consumption. While all of these definitions may apply to the ultimate recipient, the question remains whether they apply to petitioner here. In other words, even if we assume there was a consumption in Rhode Island, the question remains whether there was a consumption in this state by petitioner who never "received," "tore up," "destroyed," "discarded" or "wore away the advertising circulars." Since petitioner never received the circulars in this state, we fail to see how petitioner could be a "person * * * otherwise consuming in this state." [Mart Realty, Inc. v. Norberg, 111 R.I. 402, 407–08, 303 A.2d 361, 364–65 (1973).]

The court also rejected the taxing authority's argument that "the bringing about" of consumption within the State was sufficient to subject the taxpayer to liability, in light of the statutory language which mentions only consumption. Accord: Hoffman–LaRoche, Inc. v. Porterfield, 16 Ohio St.2d 158, 243 N.E.2d 72 (1968).

Compare, however, K–Mart Corp. v. Idaho State Tax Comm'n, 111 Idaho 719, 727 P.2d 1147 (1986), appeal dismissed, ___ U.S. ___, 107 S.Ct. 1597 (1987), which involved advertising supplements printed out-of-state that were delivered to in-state newspapers. The supplements were inserted in the newspapers sold to customers in the State. Presumably, K–Mart had stores in Idaho. The court held that the advertising inserts were "used" in the State by K–Mart and were, therefore, subject to use tax.

B. *Construction of "Purchased for Use" Provisions.* The use tax laws of some States are imposed only on "property purchased for use in this state." Iowa Code Ann. § 432.2, CCH ¶ 93–015, P–H ¶ 22,512. That provision was passed on in the case of a corporation engaged in large construction jobs, with its principal place of business in Idaho. The corporation brought heavy construction equipment into Iowa in May, 1945, to work on the Rock Island Railroad; it completed the job in about a year. Much of the equipment had been bought during a period of eight years prior to the commencement of the Iowa job, some in Washington, Oregon, and Idaho, and other pieces in New York and North Carolina; and this equipment had been used, some for long periods of time, in States other than Iowa. However, 22 of the 105 pieces of equipment at issue were purchased in May, 1945, and were first used in the Iowa job. The taxpayer conceded Iowa use tax liability for such equipment, but contested liability for the other equipment as not having been "purchased for use" in Iowa. The tax had been assessed on the original purchase price of all the equipment. The Iowa statute allows a credit against its use tax for sales or use tax paid to any other State. The court held that the statute does not "impose a tax upon personal property first used in this State for a limited period long after its purchase and use in other States, without prior intent to use it here." Morrison–Knudsen Co., Inc. v. State Tax Commission, 242 Iowa 33, 44 N.W.2d 449 (1950).

Four of the nine Justices dissented in an opinion, which declared in part:

> * * * The tax is imposed on "the use in this state of tangible personal property purchased * * * for use in this state." The difference between the two constructions centers around the words "for use in this state," the majority holding that the primary intent must be "to use in the state of Iowa." The theory of this dissent being that in the case of a general contractor who had work in more than one state the original intent in purchase of the property would be to use the property where such property is actually taken and used. * * *
>
> * * *
>
> There is no question but that the property within the definition was used by the plaintiff in the state of Iowa. Defendants argue that the tax in question is on the privilege of that use within the state of Iowa, and we do not have to speculate about the plaintiff's intent because it is presumed to have intended the natural consequences of its act, namely, the use of the property in Iowa.
>
> * * *
>
> The equipment or a large part of the property in question was purchased for use where the business of the plaintiff required it to be used, and it was used here. I am satisfied that to carry out the purpose of the law and at the same time to equalize the burden upon the local taxpayer, that when equipment is purchased for the general purpose of use wherever needed the commission is within its rights in assessing a tax in such amount as will equalize it with the burden of tax assumed by retailers in Iowa.
>
> The statute under consideration seeks to equalize, since it may be offset if another use or sales tax has been paid on the same thing. The purpose of the use tax is that retailers in the state of Iowa shall not be subjected to an unfair advantage taken by one who purchases at retail in another state where no sales tax is exacted.[19] [44 N.W.2d at 457.]

C. *Use Tax on Building Material Shipped Into the State by Out-of-State Contractor for Use by Subcontractors in the State.* M.J. Kelley Co., an Ohio building contractor, was under contract to construct the mechanical

---

19. The *Morrison–Knudsen* case was followed in Rowan Drilling Co., Inc. v. Bureau of Revenue, 60 N.M. 123, 288 P.2d 671 (1955). A similar result was reached in Comptroller v. James Julian, Inc., 215 Md. 406, 137 A.2d 674 (1958), where the court found that the statute established a presumption of intention to use equipment within the State at the time it was purchased outside the State, a presumption which was rebutted on the facts. See Annot., 41 A.L.R.2d 535.

facilities for a non-governmental building being erected in Memphis, Tennessee. Kelley's portion of the job consisted of the plumbing, heating, air conditioning, and sprinkler work of the building. It engaged local subcontractors to do the work, but Kelley maintained the project manager, a secretary, and sometimes an assistant at the job to oversee and coordinate the work of the sub-contractors and handle the paperwork.

The materials used on the contract were purchased primarily from out-of-state vendors. In some cases the material was shipped directly to Kelley in Cleveland and reshipped to Memphis. No sales or use tax was paid on such materials. On the materials shipped directly to Tennessee, if the vendor was registered, the Tennessee tax was paid, but not if the vendor was not registered. A use tax was assessed by Tennessee on all the articles on which no tax had been paid to that State. The court sustained the assessment, describing the use tax in the terms quoted in the Introductory Note to this Subdivision (p. 770 supra). Woods v. M.J. Kelley Co., 592 S.W. 2d 567, 570–71 (Tenn.1980).

Citing in its support a similar Ohio building contractor's use tax case (Plowden & Roberts, Inc. v. Porterfield, 21 Ohio St.2d 276, 257 N.E.2d 350 [1970]), the court concluded:

> Use is just one of the many rights contained in the bundle of rights known as ownership. Henneford, supra. This scheme of taxation is meant to encompass much more than simple title to and possession of the tangible personal property. The state has the power to tax storage of goods ultimately used in Tennessee. Beecham Laboratories v. Woods, 569 S.W.2d 456 (Tenn.1978). * * *

> The concept of use has not been confined to physical manipulation of the property. The taxable privilege of use extends to the "utilization of property for profit-making purposes." See, e.g., Union Oil Co. of California v. State Bd. of Equalization, 34 Cal.Rptr. 872, 386 P.2d 496 (1963). Also taxable is the "power to allow property one owns to be used for one's benefit," for this is an "exercise" of "'an incident of ownership' under the Act." Miller Brewing Co. v. Korshak, 35 Ill.2d 86, 219 N.E.2d 494, App.Dismd. 386 U.S. 684, 87 S.Ct. 1325, 18 L.Ed.2d 405 (1966).

* * *

> Kelley had fabricated and delivered to the Memphis construction site the materials needed by [its subcontractor] to complete its subcontracts with Kelley. The materials were delivered, and came to rest within the state. They were unloaded and installed pursuant to Kelley's contracts with [the subcontractor]. Thus, this tangible personal property, brought into this state for use in construction, became part of "the mass of property in this state." Section 67–30007, T.C.A. [Id. at 570–72.]

D. *Temporary Use Within the State.* The attempts of States to impose their use taxes on property temporarily located within their jurisdiction raise problems not only under the Commerce Clause, see 226–28 supra, but also under the language of State use tax statutes. In Skelton v. Federal Express Corp., 531 S.W.2d 941 (Ark.1976), the taxpayer transported 18 of its jet aircraft into Arkansas, where they remained for approximately 50 days for modifications, prior to being used in the taxpayer's air carrier operations. They had not been placed in service in the State. Over the objection that the use tax statute was inapplicable since it did not apply to "any article of tangible personal property purchased, produced or manufactured outside this State until the transportation of such article has finally come to rest within this State," the court declared:

> The extensive modification of the jets in Arkansas was "incidental" to the transportation of the aircraft * * * but it was for the purposes of the owner. So here the aircraft left the stream of commerce and "finally came to rest" in Arkansas and consequently were subject to taxation at this point. [531 S.W.2d at 944.]

The Arkansas legislature subsequently amended the statute to exempt from use tax aircraft brought into the State for repairs for less than 60 days. Ark.Stat. § 84–3105(a), CCH ¶ 94–916, P–H ¶ 22,620.17. See also Airlift International, Inc. v. State Tax Comm'n, 52 A.D.2d 688, 382 N.Y.S.2d 572 (1976); but see Realco Services, Inc. v. Halperin, 355 A.2d 743 (Me.1976), in which the court held that trailers leased to railroads for temporary use within the State were not subject to the State's use tax.

The Washington Supreme Court has held that an airplane used principally to transport the executives and customers of an Oregon company between Oregon and the company's Washington facilities was not used in the State under a statute similar to the Arkansas statute at issue in the *Federal Express* case. Pope & Talbot, Inc. v. State, Department of Revenue, 90 Wash.2d 191, 580 P.2d 262 (1978).

Other courts, however, have upheld use taxes on executive airplanes under factual patterns more or less similar to that of the Washington case. In a New Jersey case, the company planes had been hangared and serviced at the outset outside the State. They were later transferred to a hangar at Teterboro, New Jersey, where they were serviced. The planes were used in interstate and foreign flights. The use tax was upheld on the ground "when the aircraft were between interstate flights and were stored at the Teterboro Airport, they became part of a mass of property in New Jersey upon which property rights could be taxed". First National City Bank v. Taxation Div. Director, 5 N.J.Tax. 310 (1983), CCH ¶ 201–075, P–H ¶ 23,738. See also Sundstrand Corp. v. Department of Revenue, 34 Ill.App.3d 694, 339 N.E.2d 351 (1975); In re Woods Corp., 531 P.2d 1381 (Okl.1975).

E. In Matter of Atlantic Gulf & Pacific Co. v. Gerosa, 16 N.Y.2d 1, 261 N.Y.S.2d 32, 209 N.E.2d 86 (1965), appeal dismissed 382 U.S. 368, 86 S.Ct. 553 (1966), the court upheld the application of New York City's use tax to dredging equipment purchased and used outside the state for eight years and brought into the city for dredging contracts in the city's harbor waters, which took about six weeks, after which the equipment was again moved outside the State. The court noted the broad language of the use tax statute, which embraced within its scope the "exercise of any right or power over tangible personal property by the purchaser thereof and includes but is not limited to the receipt, storage or any keeping or retention *for any length of time.*" The court rejected the taxpayer's argument that the sole purpose of the statute was to eliminate sales tax avoidance by imposing a use tax identical with the sales tax only on property purchased outside the city and brought into the city within a reasonable period after the purchase. It is not insignificant, perhaps, that the court observed that "[i]t appears that no sales or use tax (on these items) was paid to any other jurisdiction." 209 N.E.2d at 87 n. 1. On facts similar to those at issue in the *Atlantic Gulf* case, the Rhode Island Supreme Court reached a similar conclusion. Great Lakes Dredge & Dock Co. v. Norberg, 117 R.I. 600, 369 A.2d 1101 (1977).

F. *Promotional and Other Materials Distributed "Free" With Purchases.* When articles are purchased outside the State and distributed "free" in connection with the purchase of items inside the State, is a use tax due on the "cost price" of the "free" item? See Wisconsin Dept. of Revenue v. Milwaukee Brewers Baseball Club, 111 Wis.2d 571, 331 N.W.2d 383 (1983), discussed in Section 3(a), Note D supra in connection with the sale for resale provisions, which sustained the application of a use tax to baseball bats, helmets, and jackets distributed without charge to home game fans who purchased tickets to attend the game. Use tax controversies over items distributed "free" have also arisen in connection with matches distributed by vending machines to cigarette purchasers, Terminal Vending Co. v. Director, Division of Taxation, N.J. Div. of Tax Appeals, Dec. 7, 1978, CCH ¶ 200–801, P–H ¶ 23,648, and racks distributed by a wholesale novelty dealer to retail stores for display of the novelties purchased. Wallace Berrie & Co. v. State Board of Equalization, 157 Cal.App. 3d 117, 203 Cal.Rptr. 662 (1984), modified on denial of petition for rehearing 157 Cal.App.3d 122 (1984), affirmed 40 Cal.3d 60, 219 Cal.Rptr. 142, 707 P.2d 204 (1985).

G. *Legislative Relief From Multiple Sales and Use Taxes.* From a policy point of view, there is no warrant for a double sales or use tax, merely because articles are bought in one jurisdiction and used in another, or are used in more than one State. The Congressional Subcommittee on State Taxation of Interstate Commerce (see p. 419, supra) recommended that the conflicting claims be resolved as follows:

(1) Only the State of "destination" of the sale of goods subject to tax would be empowered to impose a *sales* tax on interstate sales. The State of destination of the sale was defined as the State where the property is delivered to the purchaser, regardless of f.o.b. point or other conditions of sale.

(2) The State and local governments would be prohibited from imposing a *use* tax, unless the taxpayer has a "business location" in the State, or a dwelling place there.

(3) A compulsory tax credit provision was proposed, so that if a sales or use tax had previously been paid, credit must be given for the prior tax against the tax now being imposed.

(4) Where individuals had acquired personal effects, household goods or automobiles at least 30 days before establishing a residence in a new State, the Committee proposed that no sales or use tax could be levied by the State into which they moved. This was held to be needed, because, unlike in the case of business purchases, the crediting device would not be adequate, since individuals would be unlikely to keep the requisite records to substantiate the tax payment.

See Note, "State Sales and Use Taxation in Interstate Commerce: Congress Makes Some Suggestions," 1966 Duke L.J. 599.

The adoption of the Multistate Tax Compact by many States enacted most of these changes into law. Under the Compact, a credit is granted for sales or use taxes paid to other States. An exemption is provided for household goods brought into the taxing jurisdiction acquired and used at least 180 days before establishing "an abode" within the State (Art. V, §§ 1 and 2). As of 1987, the laws of 43 States and the District of Columbia allowed a use tax credit for sales or use taxes paid in other States. See P–H All States Guide ¶ 256. Many non-Compact States also provide exemptions for automobiles, household goods, or personal effects bought and used outside the State for stated periods. See Note B supra.

H. *Credit for Sales or Use Taxes Paid Other States.* In State v. Sinclair Pipeline Co., 605 P.2d 377 (Wyo.1980), the taxpayer purchased pipe for delivery in Canada that it stored temporarily in Colorado, where the pipe was covered with a protective coating. The pipe was then shipped to Wyoming for use in the pipeline. After the taxpayer had paid use tax to Wyoming, Colorado issued a notice of deficiency claiming use taxes were due based on the use of the pipe in Colorado. The taxpayer paid the Colorado tax and sought a refund of the Wyoming tax, apparently conceding that Colorado was correct in its assertion of use tax liability. The court, construing the Multistate Tax Compact's credit provision, nevertheless denied the refund. It declared:

> The statute says that a taxpayer who has "*paid*" his tax to one state will receive a credit upon any tax which may be due another state on that same property. In the instant matter, Sinclair had *paid,* the Wyoming tax before Colorado ever assessed the taxpayer. *   *   *
>
>   *   *   *
>
> We need not look to any general rules of use taxation to read this statute. Paid means paid. Nothing could be more clear. It is the past tense of pay. It means that payment has occurred. Under Article V [of the Multistate Tax Compact], when a proper use-tax payment has occurred in one state, another taxing entity seeking to impose a use tax on the same property must give credit to the taxpayer for the first-paid tax. That is what the statute says and we are not allowed to give it another meaning. [605 P.2d at 379–80.]

Is this a sensible rule? If not, how should the issue be decided as to which State is entitled to the tax?

For a useful survey of the current practice with regard to credits for sales or use taxes paid to other States, see McCray, "Commerce Clause Sanctions Against Taxation on Mail Order Sales: A Reevaluation," 17 Urb. Law. 529, 529–36 (1985).

I. *Border State Problems.* Every State imposing sales and use taxes encounters difficulties with its communities that border on neighboring tax-free States or those with substantially lower rates. Local merchants in the former States complain that they lose trade as a result of the levies because their customers go across State lines to purchase goods. While the customers are typically subject to the State's use tax when they bring the goods back into their home State there is, as a practical matter, ordinarily no ready means of checking most sales, and people are not usually given to reporting such purchases voluntarily. Where a customer goes to a store in one State and there buys goods which are delivered to him in his State of residence, that State cannot ordinarily impose a duty on the out-of-state vendor to collect the use tax. See Miller Bros. Co. v. Maryland, 347 U.S. 340, 74 S.Ct. 535 (1954). However, there are some articles—automobiles being the most important item—which will ordinarily be registered in the State of the buyer's residence. State laws frequently forbid registration of the car until proof of payment of the tax is produced; in other States the taxing authorities regularly check motor vehicle registrations and enforce collection of the use tax.

J. *Discrimination Against Out-of-State Purchases.* The Willis Committee found that many sales tax statutes favor local transactions over interstate transactions. Some States allow the value of trade-ins to be deducted from the measure of the tax only on local transactions. Others allow deductions for bad debts under the sales tax, but not under the use tax. Still others impose no sales tax if certain products are purchased locally, but impose a use tax if the same products are imported from outside the State. Willis Comm. Rep., Vol. 4, at 45. As a result, the Committee recommended the enactment by Congress of a general prohibition of discrimination against transactions wholly or partly out-of-state that would apply to all States imposing sales or use taxes. Id. at 46.

The constitutionality of taxes discriminating against out-of-state purchases of motor vehicles with respect to the trade-in allowance has been universally condemned by the courts that have considered the matter. The Commerce Clause has been held to forbid the States from denying a trade-in allowance in computing the use tax on motor vehicles purchased out-of-State while granting the allowance under the sales tax on motor vehicles purchased in-state. Matthews v. State, Department of Revenue, 193 Colo. 44, 562 P.2d 415 (1977); Robert Emmet & Son Oil & Supply Co. v. Sullivan, 158 Conn. 234, 259 A.2d 636 (1969); Nuckols v. Athey, 149 W.Va. 40, 138 S.E.2d 344 (1964). See generally, Note, "The Trade–In Deduction: Discrimination Under Sales and Use Taxes," 37 N.Y.U.L.Rev. 306. The trade-in rules are summarized on a State-by-State basis in CCH Sales Tax Rptr. ¶ 4–200. There is a wide variation in the sales tax laws and regulations concerning such transactions.

Levies discriminating against interstate commerce are considered generally in Chapter 6, subd. B, § 8 supra; see, in particular, Halliburton Oil Well Cementing Co. v. Reily, 373 U.S. 64, 83 S.Ct. 1201 (1963), id. at pp. 281–88 supra, dealing with the application of the Louisiana use tax to goods brought in from out of State; see also J. Hellerstein, "State Tax Discrimination Against Out-of-Staters," 30 Nat.Tax J. 113 (1977). Compare, however, Public Utility Dist. No. 2 of Grant County v. State, 82 Wash.2d 232, 510 P.2d 206 (1973), in which the court upheld the constitutionality of the limitation of the "sale for resale" provision to "resale as such within the state," as applied to a utility selling power for resale to both in-state and out-of-state customers.

K. *Differences in Treatment Under Sales and Use Tax.* In Colonial Pipeline Co. v. Clayton, 275 N.C. 215, 166 S.E.2d 671, (1969), transportation charges paid by a purchaser for transporting property from an out-of-state point of purchase for use within the taxing State were held to be includible in the *use* tax base. The taxpayer alleged that because "transportation charges are not included in the *sales* tax base when a sales tax is imposed on in-state sales with title passing at point of origin * * * this results in an unconstitutional discrimination against interstate commerce." The court responded:

> [T]he taxable event for assessment of the sales tax occurs at the time of sale and purchase within the state. G.S. § 105–164.4(1). No transportation charges have been incurred by the *purchaser* at that moment. The retail price upon which the sales tax is paid by the purchaser necessarily takes into account the transportation charges that have been paid on the goods to bring them to the retail outlet in North Carolina where the sale takes place. * * * Thus, the net effect of including interstate transportation charges in the use tax base and excluding intrastate transportation charges in the sales tax base is to equalize the burden of the tax on property sold locally and property purchased out of state. [275 N.C. at 224, 166 S.E.2d at 677.]

A Colorado regulation that subjected to use tax labor and overhead added to the cost of materials purchased was invalidated as drawing an impermissible distinction between the sales and use tax. International Business Machines Corp. v. Charnes, 198 Colo. 374, 601 P.2d 622 (1979). (The case did not involve a Commerce Clause issue.) The regulation provided as follows:

> [t]angible personal property that was purchased tax free for resale or an ingredient of a manufactured or compounded product and is subsequently withdrawn from stock and/or modified prior to use shall be taxed at the full finished goods cost of all materials, labor and other charges usually included in a work in process inventory. [Dep't of Rev. Reg. 138–5–34(3), quoted at 601 P.2d at 623 n. 1.]

The States commonly follow the Colorado practice of exempting purchases from sales tax if they are purchased for resale or for use as an ingredient of goods to be manufactured for sale, but taxing them if they are subsequently diverted to other uses. IBM used some of the materials purchased that had been exempted from sales tax as an ingredient of goods to be manufactured for sale. It thereupon paid the use tax on the purchase price of the materials. The Department of Revenue assessed IBM on the "full finished goods" cost or "capitalized cost," which the taxpayer challenged. The court set aside the assessment, stating:

> Given the supplementary nature and equalizing function of the use tax, the burden on the taxpayer should be no greater than necessary to compensate for the sales tax originally avoided on the purchases.
>
> The state, by asserting the use tax against the enhanced finished or "capitalized" value of IBM's inventory withdrawals, rather than against the initial cost of materials and components, has attempted to extend the use tax beyond its intended function. A levy upon the "full finished goods cost" or "capitalized cost" inevitably would have the

effect of taxing the company's labor and overhead. In effect, it would amount to a value added tax.

In arguing that an actual retail purchase is not even a necessary antecedent for the use tax, and that an inventory withdrawal should suffice to trigger use tax liability, the state asks us to extend statutory language which the legislature has left unattenuated. A use tax is imposed upon the storage, use or consumption of "tangible personal property purchased at retail." Section 39–26–202, C.R.S. 1973 (emphasis added). Since "tax statutes are construed strictly against the taxing authority," we cannot conclude, absent circumstances clearly demonstrating a contrary legislative intent, that the term "retail purchase" means—in these circumstances—anything other than an actual retail purchase. [601 P.2d at 624–25.]

In Spatt v. City of New York, 14 A.D.2d 30, 218 N.Y.S.2d 409 (2d Dep't 1961), affirmed 13 N.Y.2d 618, 191 N.E.2d 91 (1963), noted in 36 N.Y.U.L. Rev. 1465 (1961) and 37 N.Y.U.L.Rev. 307 (1962), a resident of the City of New York purchased an automobile outside the city, but within the State. When he brought it into the city, he paid a use tax, but only on the net balance after deducting the trade-in allowance on his old car that he had received on the purchase. He was assessed a use tax by the city on the amount of the trade-in.

Under the New York City regulations a purchaser of an automobile in the city was not taxable on the trade-in value, but a resident who purchased the automobile outside the city and used it in the city was taxed on the trade-in value. Spatt challenged the rule under the New York and United States constitutional Equal Protection Clauses, citing the broad equal protection doctrine that any "state of facts reasonably justifying" a classification that "can be conceived" satisfies the constitutional requirement. In sustaining the tax, the court stated:

> The distinction between the sales and use taxes of the city is justifiable here on the conceivable grounds, *inter alia,* of: (1) encouragement of sales within the city (Allied Stores of Ohio, supra; Williams v. Fears, supra); (2) greater cost of enforcing the use tax, which involves a check on automobile registrations in all the counties of the State; and (3) probability of resale of the used trade-in automobile within the city as opposed to probability of its resale without the city (Madden v. Kentucky, supra). [218 N.Y.S.2d at 412.]

The *Spatt* case is no longer law in New York. Under the current New York statute, the trade-in allowance granted by a dealer is deducted from the sales price for both sales and use tax purposes. N.Y.Tax Law § 1110, CCH ¶ 97–445, P–H ¶ 22,1535.

L. *References.* Beck, "Application of Use Taxes to Restoration of Worn–Out Equipment," 17 Ala.L.Rev. 347 (1965); Greener, "The Use Tax: Its Relationship to the Sales Tax," 9 Vand.L.Rev. 349 (1956); Burke, "Place of Compensatory Use Taxes in The American Economy," 1941 Nat.Tax Ass'n Procs. 415. There is an extensive annotation on use tax problems in 153 A.L.R. 609; see also, Annot., 146 A.L.R. 1011. There is an illuminating discussion of the interrelation of sales and use taxes in In re Los Angeles

Lumber Products Co., 45 F.Supp. 77 (S.D.Cal.1942); see also T.L. Herbert & Sons v. Woods, 539 S.W.2d 28 (Tenn.1976).

ASSIGNMENT

An automobile is purchased outside your State by a resident of a neighboring State, who drives it to his business within the taxing State daily but uses the car in that State only for his personal commuting. Is the use within the State subject to your State's use tax? Suppose that after the car has been used for several months in the manner indicated, the owner now begins to use it within your State to make deliveries of goods sold by the retail store he operates within your State. Is the use taxable; and, if so, how is the tax measured, by the original purchase price or by its value when first used in the business? See Fontenot v. S.E.W. Oil Corp., 232 La. 1011, 95 So.2d 638 (1957).

D. EXEMPTIONS AND MISCELLANEOUS EXCLUSIONS FROM SALES AND USE TAXES

Notes and Problems

A. *Exemptions and Exclusions in General.* All States provide for exemptions and exclusions from the retail sales and use tax base. Exemptions and exclusions built into the structure of the retail sales tax, including provisions dealing with sale for resale, manufacturing, processing, and fabrication, containers, and the like are treated above. In addition, however, the States provide exemptions for other tax policy reasons, such as tax equity or the encouragement of industrial location in the State. Charitable, religious, and educational organizations are exempt from tax on their purchases; and in many States casual sales are exempt. A good many States also exempt the sale of food, some exempt clothing, and virtually all States exempt prescription drugs. See generally J. Due & J. Mikesell, Sales Taxation 50–82 (1983); Annot., 15 A.L.R.4th 269.

B. *Casual, Occasional, or Isolated Sales.* A majority of State statutes exempt "casual," "occasional," or "isolated" sales. See P–H All States Guide ¶ 253. In Arizona Dep't of Revenue v. Mountain States Tel. & Tel. Co., 113 Ariz. 467, 556 P.2d 1129 (1976), the court held that the casual sale provision exempted from tax the sale by a telephone company of a telephone communications system to the United States Department of the Army. "The facts submitted by the parties clearly support the conclusion that Mountain Bell made an unanticipated and isolated sale of its equipment to the United States Government. We cannot say that Mountain Bell is in the business of selling telephone communications equipment on the basis of one sale." 113 Ariz. at 469.

Washington's gross receipts tax does not apply to an isolated or casual sale, which is defined as "a sale made by a person who is not engaged in the business of selling the type of property involved." RCW 82.04.040, CCH ¶ 92–505, P–H ¶ 22,435.10. A rent-a-car agency contended that its resale of rental vehicles to the original dealer after 10,000 to 20,000 miles of use constituted casual sales and were therefore not taxable. The court rejected this argument, noting that it was irrelevant for purposes of the statute whether the taxpayer realized a profit on the transactions and that the sale of late-model used cars was a regular part of the taxpayer's business. Budget Rent–A–Car of Washington–Oregon, Inc. v. Department of Revenue, 81 Wash.2d 171, 500 P.2d 764 (1972). Compare the treatment of motor vehicles, rented by a car rental agency and thereafter sold, as a capital asset under § 1231 of the Internal Revenue Code, on the ground that the vehicles did not constitute "property held by the taxpayer primarily for sales to customers in the ordinary course of his trade or business." Philber Equipment Corp. v. Commissioner, 237 F.2d 129 (3d Cir.1956); Rev.Rul. 54–229, 1954–1 C.B. 124.

The California statute exempts from tax "occasional sales" and defines "occasional sales" as including:

> (a) A sale of property not held or used by the seller in the course of activities for which he is required to hold a seller's permit * * * provided such sale is not one of a series of sales sufficient in number, scope and character to constitute an activity for which he is required to hold a seller's permit * * *;

> (b) Any transfer of all or substantially all the property held or used by a person in the course of such activities when after such transfer the real or ultimate ownership of such property is substantially similar to that which existed before such transfer. For the purposes of this section, stockholders, bondholders, partners, or other persons holding an ownership interest in a corporation or other entity are regarded as having the "real or ultimate ownership" of the property of such corporation or other entity. [Cal.Rev. & Tax Code § 6006.5, CCH ¶ 162–052, P–H ¶ 22,511.]

The California Supreme Court held that, under this statute, the sale by a paper mill and wire mill of all of their assets failed to qualify for the exemption, because the capital assets in question were "held or used" in the course of business for which the mills were required to hold sellers' permits. Davis Wire Corp. v. State Bd. of Equalization, 17 Cal.3d 761, 132 Cal.Rptr. 133, 553 P.2d 229 (1976). Accord, Ramrod, Inc. v. Department of Revenue, 64 Wis.2d 499, 219 N.W.2d 604 (1974). Is such a construction consistent with the underlying purpose of such provisions? Compare the case of a conglomerate which periodically sells businesses it has acquired and has been operating. Should the sale of the entire assets of a business by such an enterprise qualify for the occasional sale exemption? See ACF Industries, Inc. v. Comptroller, 257 Md. 513, 263 A.2d 574 (1970); cf. also Husky Oil Co. v. State Tax Comm'n, 556 P.2d 1268 (Utah 1976). See generally Goodhue, "Taxation—Application of Sales Tax to Occasional and Isolated Sales," 12 Drake L.Rev. 81 (1962).

In Ontario Community Foundation, Inc. v. State Board of Equalization, 35 Cal.3d 811, 201 Cal.Rptr. 165, 678 P.2d 378 (1984), a hospital, which held a seller's permit for operation of a food service facility, a pharmacy, and the sale of miscellaneous items, sold all its assets. It conceded the taxability of its kitchen and dietary equipment, presumably on the strength of the *Davis Wire* case, but contended that the sale of its other assets, for which no seller's permit was held, was nontaxable. The SBE argued that the sales were taxable, relying on its regulation denying exemption for an otherwise tax-exempt occasional sale if the seller is a "unitary business" also engaged in other sales which are not tax exempt. The court held the regulation was inconsistent with the statute, and it sustained the exemption.

C. *Exemption for Articles Not Readily Obtainable in the State.* Some States have exempted from use tax articles the sale of which is subject to sales tax, if they are "not readily obtainable in the state." See the Iowa, South Dakota, and Wyoming statutes. In Dain Manufacturing Co. v. Iowa State Tax Commission, 237 Iowa 531, 22 N.W.2d 786 (1946), the court considered the use tax exemption for "industrial materials and equipment which are not readily obtainable in Iowa." It determined that articles are "readily obtainable" in the State if "kept in Iowa for sale or manufactured in Iowa for sale, as distinguished from being obtainable by giving an order to an agent in Iowa for delivery of the same from some point outside the State." The articles are "not readily obtainable" unless they can be procured in substantially the required quantity and quality in the State; a saving in price by purchase outside the State is insufficient to qualify under the exemption.

D. *Exemption for Newspapers.* Many sales and use taxes exempt from tax the sale of newspapers or periodicals. In Green v. Home News Publishing Co., 90 So.2d 295 (Fla.1956), the question was presented as to whether the Shopping Advertiser, which was distributed free to the public, fell within the State's exemption for "newspapers." The publication varied in size—some issues were 12 pages and others 16 pages; and while some local governmental news was carried, as well as recipes, household hints, and advice to parents, the entire publication, except for a page or two, was devoted to advertising. Holding that to qualify as a newspaper a publication must have as its "principal purpose" the dissemination of news and not advertising, the court denied the exemption. Accord: Shoppers Guide Publishing Co. v. Woods, 547 S.W.2d 561 (Tenn.1977). Contrast Sears, Roebuck & Co. v. State Tax Comm'n, 370 Mass. 127, 345 N.E.2d 893 (1976), in which the court held that advertising supplements inserted in newspapers were within the sales/use tax exemption, noting, inter alia, that a "tax on the advertising revenue of newspapers could have a devastating effect on First Amendment freedoms." 345 N.E.2d at 896. Cf. Minneapolis Star & Tribune Co. v. Minnesota Com'r of Revenue, 460 U.S. 575, 103 S.Ct. 1365 (1983) and Arkansas Writers' Project, Inc. v. Ragland, __ U.S. __, 107 S.Ct. 1722 (1987), in which the Supreme Court struck down State taxes on First Amendment grounds because they discriminated against the press; Texas Monthly, Inc. v. Bullock, 731 S.W.2d 160 (Tex.App.1987), probable juris. noted, __ U.S. __, 108 S.Ct. 1217 (1988), in which the court sustained an exemption from sales tax for religious publications over the objection of a general interest magazine that the exemption illegally discriminated on the basis of the magazine's content in violation of the First Amendment.

E. *Mergers, Reorganizations, and Liquidations.* A manufacturing company owns all the capital stock of its selling subsidiary. Suppose the selling company is merged into the parent company. Included in the assets acquired by the parent are furniture, fixtures, and office supplies. Is a sales tax payable on the transaction? Cf. Superior Coal Co. v. Dept. of Finance, 377 Ill. 282, 36 N.E.2d 354 (1941). In holding that where a parent corporation acquires motor vehicles through the merger of a wholly-owned subsidiary, the transaction is not subject to Missouri sales and use tax, National Dairy Products Corp. v. Carpenter, 326 S.W.2d 87 (Mo.1959), the court declared that the term "purchase price," used in defining the measure of the tax, implies a contract of sale or exchange; where corporations merge, the transfer is by operation of law, not by contract for sale or exchange. The case is noted in Weathers, "Taxation in Missouri," 25 Mo.L. Rev. 398 (1960). Per contra, in a case involving a transfer of trucks on the incorporation of an individual business. Frank Amodio Moving & Storage Co., Inc. v. Connelly, 144 Conn. 569, 135 A.2d 737 (1957). In George Wohrley, Inc. v. Commonwealth, 495 S.W.2d 173 (Ky.1973), the court refused to construe the term "retail sale" so as to exclude from the scope of the sales tax statute a cigarette retailer's liquidation sale of office equipment, vehicles and vending machines.

F. *References.* Brabson, "Analysis of Sales and Use Tax Exemptions," 9 Vand.L.Rev. 294 (1956); Sato, "The Sales Tax and Capital Transactions," 45 Calif.L.Rev. 450 (1957). For an extensive collection of cases dealing with specific exemptions from sales taxes, see Annot., 157 A.L.R. 804.

E. MEASURE OF THE SALES AND USE TAX

A. *Discounts, Coupons, and Rebates.* A cash discount given by the seller at the time of the sale, and not dependent on time of payment, volume of purchases, or the like, is usually excluded from the sales tax base, on the ground that the discount is not part of the price. Chart of Sales–Use Taxes—Basis or Measure of Tax—Part I, P–H All States Guide ¶ 256. In some States, the statute explicitly excludes discounts or "cash discounts" from the tax base. Kan.Stat.Ann. § 79–3602(g), CCH ¶ 94–708, P–H ¶ 22,002.35; Va.Code Ann. § 58.1–602.17, CCH ¶ 91–490, P–H ¶ 22,515.85, Sales, Receipts and Use Tax Reg. § 630–10–95.2, CCH ¶ 64–401, P–H ¶ 21,754; Mich.Sales & Use Tax Reg. 22, CCH ¶ 60–307, P–H ¶ 21,556.

A good many States distinguish early payment discounts from cash discounts and disallow discounts given for prompt payment of the purchase price. The New Jersey statute, for example, disallows "any deduction for * * * early payment discounts". N.J.Rev.Stat. § 54:32B–2(d), CCH ¶ 96–056, P–H ¶ 22,510.16; see also Vt.Stat.Ann., tit. 32, § 9701(4), CCH ¶ 94–605, P–H ¶ 22,800.20. Is such a distinction warranted under the statute of your State?

Discount coupons issued by a retailer to the purchaser usually have the effect of reducing the sales tax base. See Fla.Rule 12A–1.18, CCH ¶ 60–308, P–H ¶ 21,544; Md.Reg. 14(d), CCH ¶ 63–813, P–H ¶ 21,635.85; Ohio Rule 5703–9–36, CCH ¶ 60–325, P–H ¶ 21,643; Tex. 34TAC § 3.301, CCH ¶ 66–097, P–H ¶ 21,532. Wis.Rule Tax § 11.28, ¶ 60–115a, P–H ¶ 21,628. In a good many States, however, manufacturers' coupons, although honored by retailers, do not reduce the sales tax base.

See Fla.Rule 12A–1.18 supra, Kan.Reg. 92–19–16, CCH ¶ 60–102a, P–H ¶ 21,616; N.J. P–H ¶ 21,316.10. Can you justify such a distinction under your statute? Would such a distinction be sound tax policy?

Similar rules obtain with respect to cash rebates. If they are granted by the retailer, they reduce the sales price and hence the tax base, but if they are given by the manufacturer, they do not reduce the tax base. See Md.Reg. .14, CCH ¶ 63–813, P–H ¶ 21,635.60; Ohio CCH ¶ 60–326.0276, P–H ¶ 21,146.24. For a decision denying a reduction in the sales tax measure for a manufacturer's rebate paid to an automobile purchaser, see Keystone Chevrolet Co. v. Kirk, 69 Ill.2d 483, 14 Ill. Dec. 455, 372 N.E.2d 651 (1978).

B. *Taxes.* The determination of whether the tax is imposed on the consumer is an important factor in deciding whether another tax is to be included in the measure of a retail sales tax. Thus, if the levy is imposed on the consumer, as is the case in the Federal tax on transportation of persons (I.R.C. § 4261), there is no warrant for including the amount of such a tax in the vendor's sales price, for he is merely a collector of the Federal tax. On the other hand, where the tax is imposed on the vendor, e.g., the Federal excise tax on certain tires (I.R.C. § 4071 et seq.), a stronger case can be made for regarding the entire purchase price, including the tax, as within the measure of the sales tax.

In Gurley v. Rhoden, 421 U.S. 200, 95 S.Ct. 1605 (1975), the Supreme Court held that the Federal excise tax on gasoline and lubricating oils (I.R.C. §§ 4081 et seq.) was imposed on statutory producers (which included gasoline vendors who purchased gasoline tax-free from other producers) and not on the purchaser-consumer, even though the latter may have borne the economic burden of the tax. It thus upheld the application of Mississippi's retail sales tax, whose legal incidence is on the vendor, to the receipts of a producer-vendor which included an amount corresponding to the Federal excise tax. The taxpayer had unsuccessfully argued that he was merely a tax collector. Compare American Oil Co. v. Mahin, 49 Ill.2d 199, 273 N.E.2d 818 (1971), in which the Illinois Supreme Court found the legal incidence of the Illinois Motor Fuel Tax to be on the consumer and therefore not includible in the measure of the State's sales and use tax that was imposed on persons engaged in the business of selling tangible personal property at retail. Accord: ITT Canteen Corp. v. Spradling, 526 S.W.2d 11 (Mo.1975) (Missouri cigarette tax). Note, however, that the Illinois court later held that the legal incidence of the *Federal* excise tax on gasoline fell on the producer-distributor and was therefore includible in the measure of the Illinois sales and use tax base. Martin Oil Service, Inc. v. Department of Revenue, 49 Ill.2d 260, 273 N.E.2d 823 (1971).[20]

---

20. Contra: Ken Holt Co. v. State Tax Comm'n, 29 Utah 2d 467, 511 P.2d 736 (1973). In Socony–Vacuum Oil Co. v. City of New York, 247 A.D. 163, 287 N.Y.S. 888 (1st Dep't 1936), aff'd 272 N.Y. 668, 5 N.E.2d 385 (1936), the court held that State gasoline taxes should not be included in a city sales tax. There is likewise a holding that other taxes included in the sales price may not be deducted from the measure of

The Supreme Court of the United States in the *Gurley* case relied heavily on the Illinois court's opinion in *Martin Oil*.

C. *Trade–Ins.* Trade-ins present interesting questions under the sales tax statutes. Where A goes to a dealer and trades in his old car for a new one, receiving an allowance of $1,000 on a $10,000 new car, are there two taxable sales? Is the sales tax on the new car measured by $10,000 or $9,000? And is the dealer required to collect a tax when he resells the car received in the trade-in? These issues have produced extensive litigation. See Bedford v. Hartman Bros., Inc., 104 Colo. 190, 89 P.2d 584 (1939); State ex rel. Sioux Falls Motor Co. v. Welsh, 65 S.D. 68, 270 N.W. 852 (1936); Philadelphia v. Heinel Motors, Inc., 142 Pa. Super. 493, 16 A.2d 761 (1940); Davis v. Bowers, 81 Ohio L.Abs. 505, 162 N.E.2d 868 (1958); Annot., 4 A.L.R.2d 1059 (1949); McCoy Ford, Inc. v. Department of Revenue, 60 Ill.App.3d 429, 17 Ill.Dec. 754, 376 N.E.2d 1083 (1978).

A number of State statutes deal specifically with these issues. Thus the New York sales and use tax excludes from its measure "any credit for tangible personal property accepted in part payment and intended for resale." N.Y.Tax Law §§ 1101(b)(3), 1110, CCH ¶ 97–345, 97–445, P–H 22,510.25, 22,535. For the statutes and cases dealing with the discrimination as to trade-in allowances against out-of-state purchasers under the use tax as compared to the sales tax, see Subd. C, Note J, p. 783 supra.

The post-World War II shortages of automobiles and the high prices of second hand cars produced an interesting controversy in Michigan over trade-in values for sales tax purposes. Under the Michigan law, the "gross proceeds" by which the sales tax is measured include the value of "property received in trade-ins." In Howard Pore, Inc. v. Nims, 322 Mich. 49, 33 N.W.2d 657 (1948), the facts showed a consistent practice among automobile dealers to allow customers a much smaller trade-in credit than the market values of the cars, as a device for increasing the actual price received. The Commissioner of Revenue disregarded the allowances actually made as arbitrary and as not reflecting the value of the property received and taxed the vendors on the cash and the market value of the cars received in exchange. The court sustained this action. This decision is in line with the principle generally followed in tax cases of disregarding arbitrary prices fixed in non-arm's-length bargaining. Cf. Int.Rev.Code § 482.

D. *Trading Stamps.* When a customer redeems trading stamps he received on the purchase of goods, has a taxable sale taken place? Typically sales tax statutes embrace exchanges as well as sales, so

the tax in a case arising under the Indiana gross receipts tax, which is not a retail sales tax but a turnover tax at each stage in the economic process. Sun Oil Co. v. Gross Income Tax Division, 238 Ind. 111, 149 N.E.2d 115 (1958). For a case holding that State admissions and boxing taxes should be included in the measure of a gross receipts tax applied to admissions at boxing exhibitions, see Leader v. Glander, 149 Ohio St. 1, 77 N.E.2d 69, 174 A.L.R. 1258 (1948).

that taxing authorities have contended that the redemption of the trading stamp is a taxable sale. In State Tax Commission v. Consumers Market, Inc., 87 Ariz. 376, 351 P.2d 654 (1960), an opinion which contains acute observations on the trading stamp practice, the Arizona Supreme Court rejected a levy on trading stamp redemptions. It declared (doubtless to the consternation of the plaintiff's public relations department) that the cost to the plaintiff of the premium "given" to customers "was reflected in higher prices which its customers were * * * required to pay" in making their purchases; that the original transaction in which groceries were purchased and the trading stamps were given out was not closed at that time, although its full purchase price was paid by the customer; that "the transaction of exchanging trading stamps for articles of merchandise is nothing more and nothing less than a system of advanced spending and deferred enjoyment of the fruits thereof by the plaintiff's customers"; and that the imposition of the levy would result in double taxation of the purchase price paid by the customer. Contrast Colonial Stores, Inc. v. State Tax Comm'n, 253 S.C. 14, 168 S.E.2d 774 (1969), in which the court held the vendor liable for a use tax on goods purchased for transfer in connection with trading stamp redemptions; it rejected the argument that the goods were in effect resold to the customer (and thus within the "sale for resale" exemption), on the ground that no identifiable tangible personal property was exchanged at the time the alleged consideration was paid. See also State Tax Comm'n v. Ryan–Evan Drug Stores, 89 Ariz. 18, 357 P.2d 607 (1960). Accord: Colonial Stores, Inc. v. Undercofler, 223 Ga. 105, 153 S.E.2d 549 (1967).

Some States treat trading stamps as in substance a cash discount and accordingly reduce the measure of the tax by the value of the trading stamps. See Eisenberg's White House, Inc. v. State Bd. of Equalization, 72 Cal.App.2d 18, 164 P.2d 57 (1945). When the stamps are redeemed, a sales tax becomes payable on the value of the articles transferred. See opinions of California Sales Tax Counsel Regulations, P–H ¶ 21,318.500 et seq.; Botney v. Sperry & Hutchinson Co., 55 Cal.App.3d 49, 127 Cal.Rptr. 263 (2d Dist.1976).

This method produces unnecessarily complicated administrative problems, for an estimate must be made of the value of the stamps when given and the measure of the tax reduced thereby; and when the stamps are redeemed, the value of the articles delivered must likewise be estimated. Moreover, as a matter of business practice, customers are probably nettled at the necessity of paying sales tax when redeeming trading stamps. Overall, the California rule is a good example of literal-minded statutory construction and tax administration, which produce inconvenience and annoyance, but have little or no effect on the revenues. See Annots., 80 A.L.R.2d 1221, 90 A.L.R.2d 338.

E. *Shipping and Storage Charge.* Are shipping and storage charges includible in the measure of sales or use taxes? Is a distinction to be drawn between freight-in, i.e., the retail vendor's expense in bringing the goods from his supplier to his warehouse, and freight-out, the charges for delivery by the retailer to his customer? See Gee Coal Co. v. Department of Finance, 361 Ill. 293, 197 N.E. 871 (1935); U.S. Gypsum Co. v. Green, 110 So.2d 409 (Fla.1959); State v. Natco Corp., 265 Ala. 184, 90 So.2d 385 (1956); Schemmer v. Iowa State Tax Comm'n, 254 Iowa 315, 117 N.W.2d 420 (1962); Gifford–Hill & Co. v. State, 442 S.W.2d 320 (Tex.1969); Belvedere Sand & Gravel Co. v. Heath, 259 Ark. 767, 536 S.W.2d 312 (1976); In re Puna Sugar Co., Ltd., 56 Haw. 621, 547 P.2d 2 (1976). The New York statute excludes from the measure of sales and use taxes "the cost of transportation of tangible personal property * * * where such cost is separately stated in the written contract, if any, and on the bill rendered to the purchaser." N.Y.Tax Law §§ 1101(b)(3), 1110, CCH ¶¶ 97–345, 97–445, P–H ¶¶ 22,510.25, 22,535. For a consideration of the treatment of freight-in under use taxes, see Ford J. Twaits Co. v. Utah State Tax Commission, 106 Utah 343, 148 P.2d 343 (1944); Dain Manufacturing Co. v. Iowa State Tax Commission, 237 Iowa 531, 22 N.W.2d 786 (1946).

The Willis Committee found that in some States freight is included in the measure of sales or use taxes only in the case of interstate sales. The Committee recommended that Congress enact a uniform rule providing that if interstate freight charges are separately stated, the States would not be permitted to include the freight charges in the measure of a sales or use tax. Willis Comm.Rep., Vol. 4, at 46. See generally P–H All States Guide ¶ 256 (Chart: Sales–Use Taxes—Basis or Measure of Tax, Part I).

F. *Installment Sales and Bad Debts.* At what point is the tax to be collected in an installment or conditional sale—when the goods are delivered, or as the price is paid, or at the time the final payment is made? Suppose the purchaser defaults and the balance of payments is not made, does the seller bear the tax loss? See Ohio Sales Tax, Rule 5703–9–17, CCH ¶ 60–336, P–H ¶ 21,536. There is an "amazing variety" of sales and use tax provisions dealing with credit sales. In some States the tax is payable only as collections are made, but in others this may be done only with the taxing authority's approval. P–H All States Guide ¶ 253 (Chart: Sales–Use Taxes—Taxability of Specific Transactions, Part I).

In the absence of an explicit statutory provision dealing with credit sales, it has been held that the entire tax is payable when the sales agreement is made, Gardner–White Co. v. State Board of Tax Administration, 296 Mich. 225, 295 N.W. 624 (1941) and De Ville Photography, Inc. v. Bowers, 169 Ohio St. 267, 159 N.E.2d 443 (1959), and that no refund or credit is allowable on default and repossession under a conditional sale. Rudolph Wurlitzer Co. v. State Board of Tax Administration, 281 Mich. 558, 275 N.W. 248 (1937). Many States, however, explicitly authorize refund or credit on default and repossession. P–H All States Guide ¶ 257 (Chart: Sales Taxes—Basis or Measure of Tax, Part II).

G. *Tips and Service Charges.* Are tips and service charges includible in the measure of a retail sales tax? Some cases turn on the question whether the employer derives any benefit from the tips or charges at issue. Thus, in Anders v. State Bd. of Equalization, 82 Cal. App.2d 88, 185 P.2d 883 (1947), it was held that tips to waitresses were includible in the measure of the tax to the extent that they were credited against the minimum wages due and payable to the waitresses; but the excess was not within the sales tax measure. See also St. Paul Hilton Hotel v. Commissioner, 298 Minn. 202, 214 N.W.2d 351 (1974), in which the court held that service charges added to customers' bills and apportioned among hotel employees, no part of which went to the hotel as operating revenue, were not subject to State sales tax. Other cases turn on the question whether the tips or service charges are mandatory or voluntary. In Cohen v. Playboy Clubs Int'l, Inc., 19 Ill.App.3d 215, 311 N.E.2d 336 (1974), a mandatory fifteen percent service charge was held includible within the measure of the tax. Contra: Big Foot Country Club v. Department of Revenue, 70 Wis.2d 871, 235 N.W.2d 696 (1975), in which the court relied on the absence of benefit to the club. Where the only compulsion on the club members to observe the club's tipping schedule was social, the Tennessee Supreme Court held that the tips were voluntary and therefore not part of the "sale price" of the services. Memphis Country Club v. Tidwell, 503 S.W.2d 919 (Tenn.1973). In Lakeview Inn and Country Club, Inc. v. Rose, 338 S.E.2d 166 (W.Va.1985), the court followed the mandatory/voluntary test in holding tips nontaxable, but added that the business must neither retain any part of the amounts collected nor guarantee an amount other than that collected to its employees. See generally Annot., 73 A.L.R.3d 1226.

F. COLLECTION OF THE TAX BY THE VENDOR

A. *Vendor's Duty to Verify Customer's Purchase as Being for Resale.* How far must a vendor go in verifying his customer's assertion that he is purchasing goods for resale? In Merriwether v. State of Alabama, 252 Ala. 590, 42 So.2d 465 (1949), a wholesaler-dealer in automobile parts and repair supplies made sales to retailers, who in turn resold the supplies to the trade, but also used some of the supplies in reconditioning their own used cars preparatory to resale. Such use by the retailers of the supplies on their own cars was a consumption of the supplies and, hence, not an exempt purchase for resale. Nevertheless, in making the purchases the retailers represented that all were purchased for resale. The taxpayer was held liable for sales tax on the ground that reliance on the purchasers' representation was insufficient. The taxpayer was "bound at his peril" to have sufficient knowledge of the nature of his customers' business in order to ascertain whether the goods were delivered to an establishment engaged in resale only, or to suffer the consequences of failure to collect the tax, if in fact the goods were finally consumed by the retailer. See General Electric Co. v. Butler, 211 Tenn. 196, 364 S.W.2d 361 (1963), for a holding that the receipt of a resale certificate from the customer and the vendor's honest mistake as to the purchaser's use of the goods sold did not relieve the vendor of the duty to collect the tax; the court went to the extreme of upholding a penalty for the "honest" failure to collect.

On the other hand, in some factual circumstances, a vendor's assertion that it acted in good faith in accepting a resale certificate must be viewed with skepticism. See Department of Revenue v. Warren Chemical & Janitor Supply Co., 562 S.W.2d 644 (Ky.App.1977) ("It is ludicrous that the appellee could have received in good faith the resale certificates from a funeral home which purchased a weed killer, or from the Kentucky State Police in the purchase of toilet bowl cleaner").

Other courts have held that the vendor has only the duty of making a reasonable and prudent inquiry to determine whether a resale certificate received from the vendee applied to the latter's intended use of the articles purchased. Long Manufacturing Co. v. Johnson, 264 N.C. 12, 140 S.E.2d 744 (1965).

A still different view was taken by the New York Court of Appeals in Matter of American Cyanamid and Chemical Corp. v. Joseph, 308 N.Y. 259, 125 N.E.2d 247 (1955):

> This petitioner sells, in New York City, various acids and chemicals, to numerous customers engaged in a variety of businesses. The proceeding is brought to review sales tax assessments made against petitioner on findings that, over a period of years, it failed to collect the tax on numerous sales transactions. The record sufficiently shows these facts: that in every such instance petitioner had a resale certificate covering the sale, from its vendee, who was registered with the city as authorized to issue certificates; that, however, none of the sales were in fact for resale; that petitioner had reason for suspicion or belief that the sales were taxable but in no case did petitioner or any of its responsible officers have any actual knowledge of that fact; that petitioner at all times acted in good, not bad, faith in taking the resale certificates and in failing to collect the tax. Petitioner was informed by its own chemist that some of the products it sold were not such as ordinarily became identifiable ingredients or components of other products later to be resold. As to other sales, petitioner was put on notice, by its customers' corporate names or otherwise, that those customers were in dyeing, cleaning, stamping or coating businesses, etc., and were, presumably, consuming in processes of their own the goods bought from petitioner. The fact remains, however, that petitioner did not know the exact uses, did not know that the resale certificates were inaccurate, and made no further investigation. The question of law is: did petitioner's possession of such notice or informa-

tion make it liable for the tax, despite its receipt, in good faith of resale certificates? Our answer is in the negative.

To this question of statutory interpretation, i.e., legislative intent, there is no direct answer in the statute itself, or, indeed, in the comptroller's regulations. We assume that there would be no protection for a vendor, who, knowing that there was to be no resale, nevertheless took and acted on such a resale certificate, fraudulently or in bad faith. But this law, which goes very far in burdening the vendor by making him an unpaid tax collector for the city, does not, expressedly or impliedly, put on him a duty of investigating or policing his own customers. The problem, of taxability or no, is sometimes a difficult one as to items which are not resold as such but which may or may not be considered as becoming components of another article which is to be resold, see Mendoza Fur Dyeing Works v. Taylor, 272 N.Y. 275, 5 N.E.2d 818; Mounting & Finishing Co. v. McGoldrick, 294 N.Y. 104, 108, 60 N.E.2d 825; Redlich on Sales Taxes and the Resale Exemption in the Manufacture and/or Distribution of Personal Property, 9 Tax L.Rev., p. 435. We do not think the statute forces a vendor to debate such questions with his customer. [125 N.E.2d at 248–49.]

See the subsequently enacted New York State provision cited after the next paragraph infra.

The imposition of tax and penalties on the interstate vendor holding a resale certificate has proved to be a vexatious problem. From the point of view of tax compliance, whether dealing with an out-of-state or in-state vendor, both the "prudent man" standard and the absolute liability rule are onerous burdens to impose on sellers. This ought to be the job of the tax collector, and so long as the vendor receives a resale certificate in proper form, his collection obligation ought to cease. This was the view taken by the Subcommittee on State Taxation of Interstate Commerce; its legislative proposal called for exculpating the vendor on receipt of a resale certificate in authorized form. (H.R. 2158, § 304 [89th Cong.2d Sess.]). The Multistate Tax Compact imposes a "good faith" standard:

> Whenever a vendor receives and accepts in good faith from a purchaser a resale or other exemption certificate or other written evidence of exemption authorized by the appropriate State or subdivision taxing authority, the vendor shall be relieved of liability for a sales or use tax with respect to the transaction. [Art. V, § 3.]

Some States have enacted provisions that exonerate a vendor from any duty to collect tax from a purchaser, if the vendor has received from the purchaser a resale certificate, containing the purchaser's registration number with the States and otherwise in proper form, or an exemption certificate in proper form. See N.Y.Tax Law § 1132, CCH ¶ 97–562, P–H ¶ 22,595.

The good faith standard could result in onerous burdens and unwarranted tax impositions on sellers. Realistically, some employees of busy organizations will be careless and not satisfy standards of "good faith"; yet, it is hard to see why the seller should be obliged to pay the tax to the State so long as he has a resale certificate from a local retailer.

B. *Theft of Sales Tax Collections From Vendor.* The precise role of the vendor in making sales tax collections was severely tested in a case which raised the interesting question of who suffers the loss when sales tax collections are stolen from the vendor. In Spencer v. Mero, 52 So.2d 679 (Fla.1951), a vendor alleged in a suit to enjoin the collection of sales taxes from his customers that he had kept the taxes so collected separate from his other funds; that his place of business had been broken into on three separate occasions; and that the taxes, as well as cash of his own, had been stolen. The Florida levy requires collection of the tax from the customer as a separately stated charge. The lower court dismissed the bill in equity but the Florida Supreme Court reversed. The court was confronted by cases holding that a public officer is liable for public funds stolen from him, but distinguished those cases as involving "voluntary trustees." Here, said the court, the vendor is an involuntary trustee, and such trustees are not liable for theft if prudence and care are exercised. While the court admonished that "clear and convincing proof of the loss by theft will be required," it sustained the bill.[21] See also Butler & Kennamer Wholesale Co. v. State, 293 Ala. 216, 301 So.2d 178 (1974), in which it was held that a wholesale grocer was not liable for a tobacco tax on stolen cigarettes.

A contrary result was reached by the Georgia Supreme Court in Williams v. Bear's Den, Inc., 214 Ga. 240, 104 S.E.2d 230 (1958), on the theory that the vendor is the taxpayer. This theory is open to question under the Georgia statute. While the statute imposes "a privilege or license tax upon every person who engages in the business of selling tangible personal property at retail in this state," the statute goes on to declare that:

> The privilege tax herein levied * * * shall be collected by the dealer from the purchaser or consumer. Notwithstanding any other provision, it is the purpose and intent of this Act that the tax imposed hereunder is, in fact, a levy on the purchaser or consumer of the tangible personal property or services described in this Act, and the levy on dealers as specified is merely as agent of the State for collection of said tax.

Moreover, as an economic matter, the real test of "who is the taxpayer" under the sales tax ought to be the person who is intended to bear the incidence of the tax; while incidence cannot be controlled by law and is affected by many marketplace pressures, nevertheless, the legislative purpose is to fasten the burden of the tax onto the consumer insofar as possible, and presumably to a great extent this result is normally accomplished.

21. The holding in the *Spencer* case that the tax is imposed on the vendee was overruled in Green v. Panama City Housing Authority, 115 So.2d 560 (Fla.1959); although the later case involved a different problem, presumably the Florida courts would now deny relief to a vendor whose sales tax collections were stolen.

Despite the court's reasoning, the result reached in the Georgia case seems sound. To follow the Florida rule is likely to result in abuses; the logic of the holding would presumably likewise cover accidental loss and destruction of paper money by fire. A reasonably prudent businessman would be protected against such loss by insurance and probably would bank his receipts promptly. Since the States typically impose the costs of collection and accounting for retail sales and use tax collections on the vendor (although some States allow a percentage of the tax collections to be retained by the vendor in view of the costs to him), it seems not unreasonable to require absolute liability for collections, which in practice will in most cases mean merely a slight added expenditure for insurance coverage.

The Rhode Island Supreme Court reached a result similar to that reached by the Georgia court in holding a cigarette distributor liable for tax on stolen cigarettes intended for sale in the State. Daniels Tobacco Co., Inc. v. Norberg, 114 R.I. 502, 335 A.2d 636 (1975); accord, Allied Grocers Co-op, Inc. v. Tax Com'r, 36 Conn.Supp. 59, 411 A.2d 313 (1979).

C. *Collection of Tax From Vendor and Vendee.* In Matter of Fifth Avenue Bldg. Co. v. Joseph, 297 N.Y. 278, 79 N.E.2d 22 (1948), the issue was raised as to whether the taxing authority, having collected a sales tax from the vendor, which had failed to collect the tax from the purchaser, could pursue the purchaser and seek a double tax. The City of New York argued that unless it could require the purchaser to pay the tax, vendors could in effect avoid the statutory requirement of collecting the tax from the purchaser and thereby obtain an advantage over their competitors. Should the double tax collection be permitted?

D. *Liability of Officers of Corporate Vendor for Sales Tax.* Are officers of a vendor corporation personally liable for failure of the corporation to collect sales tax, or, having collected the tax, for failure to maintain the tax collections as trust funds? This problem arises in connection with the insolvency of a vendor. See two cases dealing with this problem decided by New York courts of original jurisdiction. City of New York v. Bernstein, 193 Misc. 224, 84 N.Y.S.2d 139 (Sup.Ct., N.Y. Cty.1948); City of New York v. Bernstein, 90 N.Y.S.2d 759 (Sup.Ct., N.Y.Cty.1949). See also State v. Equinox House, Inc., 134 Vt. 59, 350 A.2d 357 (1975), in which the court held that a corporate president was personally liable for collecting sales and use taxes in the event of the corporation's failure to do so; State v. Longstreet, 536 S.W.2d 185 (Mo. App.1976), in which the court held corporate officers criminally liable for failure to make timely payment of sales taxes collected; Matter of Jonas, 70 N.C.App. 116, 318 S.E.2d 869 (1984), in which the court held a corporate president personally liable for sales tax after the corporation went out of business; Chapter 16, § 2(b) infra.

In one case the court pierced the corporate veil to hold the shareholders personally liable for a corporation's delinquent sales and use taxes. People v. Clauson, 231 Cal.App.2d 374, 41 Cal.Rptr. 691

(1964). The shareholders, who owned substantially all of the stock of the corporation, exercised complete control over the business of the corporation; they were its "alter ego."

E. *Breakage in Collections Brackets.* Vendors sometimes face the problem that the collection brackets establish schedules which make it difficult, as a business matter, to collect as much tax as they are required to pay. This tends to happen where there is a large number of sales of low cost items. The problem was illustrated by a Wyoming case involving the Walgreen drug chain. The Wyoming statute imposed a two percent tax on sales of 25 cents or more, to be paid by the customer, and a one percent tax on sales of 24 cents or less. If the seller failed to segregate in his records the under–24 cents sales, he was required to pay a tax of two percent on all his sales. The statute also provided that if the seller collected taxes in excess of two percent of his sales, he was required, nevertheless, to pay the State the full amount collected.

The Walgreen drug chain sought to offset its under-collections against its over-collections, but the court refused to accept this procedure. Its theory was that the statute imposed two distinct taxes, and that sellers could not utilize excess monies collected by them under the tax on purchasers in order to satisfy their own tax liabilities arising from the one percent tax. Walgreen Co. v. State Board of Equalization, 62 Wyo. 288, 166 P.2d 960 (1946); for a comment on this case see 1 Wyo. L.J. 89 (1947).

The holding in the *Walgreen* case that the vendor could not offset against the tax on its under-first-bracket sales his collections in excess of two percent produced by the bracket schedule has been rejected by some courts. H.L. Green Co., Inc. v. Joseph, 297 N.Y. 588, 74 N.E.2d 832 (1947), a case (without opinion) involving the New York City sales tax. Since the breakage problems grow essentially out of administrative difficulties in sales tax collecting procedures, what justification is there for failing to allow the merchant to offset the tax on under-schedule sales by over-collections, provided he has not actually collected tax on the lower price sales? Moreover, the sales tax, as an economic matter, is regarded as a consumer's tax, to be passed on so far as possible; why, then, should the tax be payable at all on low bracket sales as to which the administrative problems have prevented the establishment of bracket schedules? As a matter of business practice, the merchant cannot collect, *qua* tax, amounts not covered by the schedules.

In W.F. Jensen Candy Co. v. State Tax Commission, 90 Utah 359, 61 P.2d 629 (1936), the court dealt with retail candy sales, most of which fell under 50 cents, below which no sales tax collection was required. The court rejected the taxpayer's contention that no tax was payable on under–50 cents sales and met the taxpayer's statutory and constitutional objections to the levy by holding that, under the statute, the vendor is required to collect taxes on sales of 50 cents or more and that he may, but is not compelled to, collect the tax on sales under 50 cents; he is liable for the tax, nevertheless.

The problem is exacerbated in the case of vending machines, as to which it is often difficult to add the tax to the purchase price. A number of cases have, nevertheless, required the vendor in such cases to pay the tax. New York Automatic Canteen Co. v. Joseph, 8 N.Y.2d 853, 203 N.Y.S.2d 905, 168 N.E.2d 709 (1960); Stevens Enterprises, Inc. v. State Commission of Revenue and Taxation, 179 Kan. 696, 298 P.2d 326 (1956); White v. State of Washington, 49 Wash.2d 716, 306 P.2d 230 (1957), appeal dismissed, 355 U.S. 10, 78 S.Ct. 23 (1957). See 91 Annot., A.L.R.2d 1127.

F. Does the customer have a legitimate complaint when, under a stated three percent sales tax, the vendor collects one cent on a 15 cent sale, even though under the rule such as that obtaining in New York the vendor pays to the taxing authority only 4½ mills? See De Aryan v. Akers, 12 Cal.2d 781, 87 P.2d 695, cert. denied 308 U.S. 581, 60 S.Ct. 101 (1939).

G. *The Duty to Account for Over–Collections.* If a vendor in fact collects more than the statutory percentage tax of two percent, four percent or five percent, as the case may be, because of the operation of the bracket schedule (after taking into account in some States non-collections on sales below the first bracket), he must pay over the excess to the taxing authority. The practical difficulties that this rule presents to retailers selling a large number of small items is illustrated by Matter of W.T. Grant Co. v. Joseph, 2 N.Y.2d 196, 159 N.Y.S.2d 150, 140 N.E.2d 244 (1957), cert. denied 355 U.S. 869, 78 S.Ct. 119 (1957). Before its financial collapse, the Grant chain was a modern day counterpart of the old 5 and 10 cent store and no tape or other records were kept of individual sales; the sale was rung up in the cash register and the sales tax collected was expected to be deposited in a little tin box attached to the register. Grant reported as tax the total amount shown in the daily records of its stores as having been collected, or the then statutory two percent of sales, whichever was larger. The New York City sales tax regulations required the keeping of "such records as are necessary or required to determine * * * tax liability." Being dissatisfied with the payments, the city caused a test check of the company's sales to be made and as a result assessed a deficiency of $66,000 for a period of 3¼ years. The check was made by Grant's own employees for a stated period in stores selected by Grant. The results of individual actual sales, broken down by price for an entire week, were thus obtained and a sales tax deficiency was projected on the basis of this test. The court sustained the use of the test check and the resulting deficiency, since it grew out of Grant's failure to keep ade-quate records and since the method was largely determined by the taxpayer itself.

H. *Disposition of Improper Collections From Customers.* Suppose a gasoline station or a mail order house collects taxes under a sales or use tax regulation which it regards as improper and it eventually prevails. The vendor has thousands of customers, most of whom will never seek a refund of the improperly collected tax. If the names of the customers were known, the cost of refunding the tax would often exceed the amount of the tax itself. In several such cases the issue has arisen: who keeps the windfall, the vendor or the taxing authority? In Kesbec, Inc. v. McGoldrick, 278 N.Y. 293, 16 N.E.2d 288 (1938) and Cook v. Sears–Roebuck & Co., 212 Ark. 308, 206 S.W.2d 20 (1947), the courts held that the funds must be turned over to the taxing authority on whose behalf the vendor acted in collecting the tax. See Annots., 93 A.L.R. 1485 and 119 A.L.R. 542 for collections of cases dealing with this issue.

There have been a number of cases that have raised this issue recently in connection with taxes that have been held to violate the Commerce Clause. See, e.g., Bacchus Imports, Ltd. v. Dias, 468 U.S. 263, 104 S.Ct. 3049 (1984) (remanding to State court case involving discriminatory liquor excise tax imposed on wholesalers so that State court could consider whether wholesalers were entitled to refund of tax in light of allegation that they passed burden of tax on to their customers).

I. *Class Action by Customers.* In Cohon v. Oscar L. Paris Co., 17 Ill.App.2d 21, 149 N.E.2d 472 (1958), a class action was brought by a customer of a vendor and installer of carpets to recover a retailers occupation tax which had been collected by the vendor; the tax had been paid over to the State, but had subsequently been refunded to the defendant, following a holding in a prior case that the defendant was not subject to the levy. The defendant had charged the tax separately to its customers, a practice not required by Illinois law, and the levy had been held to constitute a tax on the retailer, not the consumer. People's Drug Shop, Inc. v. Moysey, 384 Ill. 283, 51 N.E.2d 144 (1943). Curiously, the defendant had continued to collect the tax as a separate charge from its customers after the Illinois Supreme Court's decision holding that the tax was not applicable to the transaction. The court held that the class action would lie for monies collected both before and after the decision, that the amount collected as a separate tax charge belonged, in equity and good conscience, to the customers, and that a constructive trust of the fund was created, recoverable in the class action.

G. THE TAXATION OF INTERSTATE SALES AND THE VENDOR'S DUTY TO COLLECT SALES AND USE TAXES

McLEOD v. J.E. DILWORTH CO.

Supreme Court of the United States, 1944
322 U.S. 327, 64 S.Ct. 1023

GENERAL TRADING CO. v. STATE TAX COMMISSION

Supreme Court of the United States, 1944
322 U.S. 335, 64 S.Ct. 1028

INTERNATIONAL HARVESTER CO. v. DEPARTMENT OF TREASURY

Supreme Court of the United States, 1944
322 U.S. 340, 64 S.Ct. 1019

[MR. JUSTICE RUTLEDGE wrote the following highly realistic opinion covering the *Dilworth, General Trading,* and *International Harvester* cases. It shed a new, fresh light on the interrelation of the Commerce and Due Process Clauses. The essential facts and the majority's disposition of each of the three cases are set out in MR. JUSTICE RUTLEDGE's opinion.]

MR. JUSTICE RUTLEDGE, concurring in No. 355 (this case) and No. 441, ante, p. 335, and dissenting in No. 311, ante, p. 327:

These three cases present in various applications the question of the power of a state to tax transactions having a close connection with interstate commerce.

In No. 311, McLeod v. J.E. Dilworth Co., ante, p. 327, Arkansas has construed its tax to be a sales tax, but has held this cannot be applied where a Tennessee corporation, having its home office and place of business in Memphis, solicits orders in Arkansas, by mail, telephone or sending solicitors regularly from Tennessee, accepts the orders in Memphis, and delivers the goods there to the carrier for shipment to the purchaser in Arkansas. This Court holds the tax invalid, because "the sale—the transfer of ownership—was made in Tennessee. For Arkansas to impose a tax on such transaction would be to project its powers beyond its boundaries and to tax an interstate transaction." Though an Arkansas "use tax" might be sustained in the same situation, "we are not dealing with matters of nomenclature even though they be matters of nicety." And the case is thought to be different from the Berwind–White case, 309 U.S. 33, where New York City levied the tax, because, in the Arkansas court's language, "the corporation maintained its sales office in New York City, took its contracts in New York City and made actual delivery in New York City. * * *"

On the other hand, in No. 441, General Trading Co. v. State Tax Commission, ante, p. 335, Iowa applies its "use tax" to a transaction in which a Minnesota corporation ships goods from Minnesota, its only place of business, to Iowa purchasers on orders solicited in Iowa by salesmen sent there regularly from Minnesota for that purpose, the orders being accepted in Minnesota. This tax the Court sustains. While "no State can tax the privilege of doing interstate business, * * * the mere fact that property is used for interstate commerce or has come into an owner's possession as a result of interstate commerce does not diminish the protection which it may draw from a State to the upkeep of which it may be asked to bear its fair share. But a fair share precludes legislation obviously hostile or practically discriminatory toward interstate commerce. * * * None of these infirmities affects the tax in this case. * * *" And the foreign or nonresident seller who does no more than solicit orders in Iowa, as the Tennessee seller does in Arkansas, may be made the state's tax collector.

In No. 355, International Harvester Co. v. Dept. of Treasury, ante, p. 340, the state applies its gross income tax, among other situations to one (Class D) where a foreign corporation authorized to do and doing business in Indiana sells and delivers its product in Indiana to out-of-state customers who come into the state for the transaction. The Court sustains the tax as applied.

I

For constitutional purposes, I see no difference but one of words and possibly one of the scope of coverage between the Arkansas tax in No. 311 and the Iowa tax in No. 441. This is true whether the issue is one of due process or one of undue burden on interstate commerce. Each tax is imposed by the consuming state. On the records here, each has a due process connection with the transaction in that fact and in the regular, continuous solicitation there. Neither lays a greater burden on the interstate business involved than it does on wholly intrastate business of the same sort. Neither segregates the interstate transaction for separate or special treatment. In each instance therefore interstate and intrastate business reach these markets on identical terms, so far as the effects of the state taxes are concerned.

And in my opinion they do so under identical material circumstances. In both cases the sellers are "nonresidents" of the taxing state, foreign corporations. Neither seller maintains an office or a place of business there. Each has these facilities solely in the state of origin. In both cases the orders are taken by solicitors sent regularly to the taxing state for that purpose. In both the orders are accepted at the home office in the state of origin. And in both the goods are shipped by delivery to the carrier or the post in the state of origin for carriage across the state line and delivery by it to the purchaser in his taxing state.

In the face of such identities in connections and effects, it is hard to see how one tax can be upheld and the other voided. Surely the state's power to tax is not to turn on the technical legal effect, relevant for other purposes but not for this, that "title passes" on delivery to the carrier in Memphis and may or may not so pass, so far as the record shows, when the Minnesota shipment is made to Iowa. In the absence of other and more substantial difference, that irrelevant technical consideration should not control. However it may be determined for locating the incidence of loss in transit or other questions arising among buyer, seller and carrier, for purposes of taxation that factor alone is a will-o'-the-wisp, insufficient to crux a due process connection from selling to consuming state and incapable of increasing or reducing any burden the tax may place upon the interstate transaction.

The only other difference is in the terms used by Iowa and Arkansas, respectively, to describe their taxes. For reasons of her own Arkansas describes her tax as a "sales tax." Iowa calls hers a "use tax." This court now is committed to the validity of "use" taxes. * * * Similarly, "sales taxes" on "interstate sales" have been sustained. In McGoldrick v. Berwind–White Coal Mining Co., 309 U.S. 33, 60 S.Ct. 388, such a tax applied by the state of the market was upheld. * * * Other things being the same, constitutionality should not turn on whether one name or the other is applied by the state. Wisconsin v. J.C. Penney Co., 311 U.S. 435, 61 S.Ct. 246. * * *

II

The Court's different treatment of the two taxes does not result from any substantial difference in the facts under which they are levied or the effects they may have on interstate trade. It arises rather from applying different constitutional provisions to the substantially identical taxes, in the one case to invalidate that of Arkansas, in the other to sustain that of Iowa. Due process destroys the former. Absence of undue burden upon interstate commerce sustains the latter.

It would seem obvious that neither tax of its own force can impose a greater burden upon the interstate transaction to which it applies than it places upon the wholly local trade of the same character with which that transaction competes. By paying the Arkansas tax the Tennessee seller will pay no more than an Arkansas seller of the same goods to the same Arkansas buyer; and the latter will pay no more to the Tennessee seller than to an Arkansas vendor, on account of the tax, in absorbing its burden. The same thing is true of the Iowa tax in its incidence upon the sale by the Minnesota vendor. The cases are not different in the burden the two taxes place upon the interstate transactions. Nor in my opinion are they different in the existence of due process to sustain the taxes.

"Due process" and "commerce clause" conceptions are not always sharply separable in dealing with these problems. Cf. e.g., Western Union Telegraph Co. v. Kansas, 216 U.S. 1, 30 S.Ct. 190. To some extent they overlap. If there is a want of due process to sustain the tax, by that fact alone any burden the tax imposes on the commerce among the states becomes "undue." But, though overlapping, the two conceptions are not identical. There may be more than sufficient factual connections, with economic and legal effects, between the transaction and the taxing state to sustain the tax as against due process objections. Yet it may fall because of its burdening effect upon the commerce. And, although the two notions cannot always be separated, clarity of consideration and of decision would be promoted if the two issues are approached, where they are presented, at least tentatively as if they were separate and distinct, not intermingled ones.

Thus, in the case from Arkansas no more than in that from Iowa should there be difficulty in finding due process connections with the taxing state sufficient to sustain the tax. As in the Iowa case, the goods are sold and shipped to Arkansas buyers. Arkansas is the consuming state, the market these goods seek and find. They find it by virtue of a continuous course of solicitation there by the Tennessee seller. The old notion that "mere solicitation" is not "doing business" when it is regular, continuous and persistent is fast losing its force. In the General Trading case it loses force altogether, for the Iowa statute defines this process in terms as "a retailer maintaining a place of business in this State." * The Iowa Supreme Court sustains the definition and this Court gives effect to its decision in upholding the tax. Fiction the definition may be; but it is fiction with substance because, for every relevant constitutional consideration affecting taxation of transactions, regular, continuous, persistent solicitation has the same economic, and should have the same legal, consequences as does maintaining an office for soliciting and even contracting purposes or maintaining a place of business, where the goods actually are shipped into the state from without for delivery to the particular buyer. There is no difference between the Iowa and the Arkansas situations in this respect. Both involve continuous, regular, and not intermittent or casual courses of solicitation. Both involve the shipment of goods from without to a buyer within the state. Both involve taxation by the state of the market. And if these substantial connections are sufficient to underpin the tax with due process in the one case, they are also in the other.

That is true, if labels are not to control, unless something which happens or may happen outside the taxing state operates in the one case to defeat the jurisdiction, but does not defeat it in the other.

As I read the Court's opinion, though it does not explicitly so state, the Arkansas tax falls because Tennessee could tax the transaction and, as between the two states, has exclusive power to do so. This is because "the sale—the transfer of ownership—was made in Tennessee." Arkansas' relation to the transaction is constitutionally different from that of New York in the Berwind–White case, though both are the state of the market, because the Berwind–White Company "maintained its sales office in New York City, took its contracts in New York City and made actual delivery in New York City." This "constituted a sale in

_____
* [Some footnotes have been omitted.]

New York and accordingly we sustained a retail sales tax by New York." So here the company's "offices are maintained in Tennessee, the sale is made in Tennessee, and the delivery is consummated either in Tennessee or in interstate commerce. * * *" The inevitable conclusion, it seems to me, is that the Court is deciding not only that Arkansas cannot tax the transaction but that Tennessee can tax it and is the only state which can do so. To put the matter shortly, Arkansas cannot levy the tax because Tennessee can levy it. Hence "for Arkansas to impose a tax on such transaction would be to project its powers beyond its boundaries and to tax an interstate transaction."

This statement of the matter appears to be a composite of due process and commerce clause ideas. If so, it is hard to see why the same considerations do not nullify Iowa's power to levy her tax in the identical circumstances and vest exclusive jurisdiction in Minnesota to tax these transactions. For in the Iowa case the selling corporation maintains its office and place of business in Minnesota, accepts the orders there, and the delivery, which is to carrier or post, is consummated, so far as the record shows, exactly in the manner it is made in the Tennessee–Arkansas transaction. If these facts nullify Arkansas' power to tax the transaction by vesting exclusive jurisdiction in Tennessee, it would seem *a fortiori* they would nullify Iowa's power and give Minnesota exclusive jurisdiction to tax the transactions there involved. Unless the sheer difference in the terms "sale" and "use," and whatever difference these might make as a matter of legislative selection of the transactions which are to bear the tax, are to control upon the existence of the power to tax, the result should be the same in both cases.

Merely as a matter of due process, it is hard to see why any of the four states cannot tax the transactions these cases involve. Each has substantial relations and connections with the transaction, the state of market not less in either case than the state of origin. It "sounds better" for the state of origin to call its tax a "sales tax" and the state of market to name its tax a "use tax." But in the Berwind–White case the latter's "sales tax" was sustained, where it is true more of the incidents of sale conjoined with the location of the place of market than do in either No. 311 or No. 441. If this is the distinguishing factor, as it might be for selecting one of the two connected jurisdictions for exclusive taxing power, it is not one which applies to either of these transactions. The identity is not between the Dilworth case and Berwind–White. It is rather between Dilworth and General Trading, with Berwind–White differing from both. And, so far as due process alone is concerned, it should make no difference whether the tax in the one case is laid by Arkansas or Tennessee and in the other by Iowa or Minnesota. Each state has a sufficiently substantial and close connection with the transaction, whether by virtue of tax benefits conferred in general police protection and otherwise or on account of ideas of territorial sovereignty concerning occurrence of "taxable incidents" within its borders, to furnish the due process foundation necessary to sustain the exercise of its taxing power. Whether it exerts this by selecting for "impingement" of the tax some feature or incident of the transaction which it denominates "sale" or "use" is both illusory and unimportant in any bearing upon its constitutional authority as a matter of due process. If this has any substantive effect, it is merely one of legislative intent in selecting the transactions to bear the tax and thus fixing the scope of its coverage, not one of constitutional power. "Use" may cover more transactions with which a state has due process connections than "sale." But whenever sale occurs and is taxed the tax bears equally, in final incidence of burden, upon the use which follows immediately upon it.

The great difficulty in allocating taxing power as a matter of due process between the state of origin and the state of market arises from the fact that each state, considered without reference to the other, always has a sufficiently substantial relation in fact and in tax benefit conferred to the interstate transaction to sustain an exertion of its taxing power, a fact not always recognized. And from this failure, as well as from the terms in which statutes not directed specifically to reaching these transactions are cast, comes the search for some "taxable incident taking place within the state's boundaries" as a hook for hanging constitutionality under due process ideas. "Taxable incident" there must be. But to take what is in essence and totality an interstate transaction between a state of origin and one of market and hang the taxing power of either state upon some segmented incident of the whole and declare that this does or does not "tax an interstate transaction" is to do two things. It is first to ignore that any tax hung on such an incident is levied on an interstate transaction. For the part cannot be separated from the whole. It is also to ignore the fact that each state, whether of origin or of market, has by that one fact alone a relation to the whole transaction so substantial as to nullify any due process prohibition. Whether the tax is levied on the "sale" or on the "use," by the one state or by the other, it is in fact and effect a tax levied on an interstate transaction. Nothing in due process requirements prohibits either state to levy either sort of tax on such transactions. That Tennessee therefore may tax this transaction by a sales tax does not, in any proper conception of due process, deprive Arkansas of the same power.

III

When, however, the issue is turned from due process to the prohibitive effect of the commerce clause, more substantial considerations arise from the fact that both the state of origin and that of market exert or may exert their taxing powers upon the interstate transaction. The long history of this problem boils down in general statement to the formula that the states, by virtue of the force of the commerce clause, may not unduly burden interstate commerce. This resolves itself into various corollary formulations. One is that a state may not single out interstate commerce for special tax burden. McGoldrick v. Berwind–

White Coal Mining Co., 309 U.S. 33, 55–56, 60 S.Ct. 388, 397, 398. Nor may it discriminate against interstate commerce and in favor of its local trade. Welton v. Missouri, 91 U.S. at 275; Guy v. Baltimore, 100 U.S. 434; Voight v. Wright, 141 U.S. 62, 11 S.Ct. 855. Again, the state may not impose cumulative burdens upon interstate trade or commerce. Gwin, White & Prince v. Henneford, 305 U.S. 434, 59 S.Ct. 325; Adams Mfg. Co. v. Storen, 304 U.S. 307, 58 S.Ct. 913. Thus, the state may not impose certain taxes on interstate commerce, its incidents or instrumentalities, which are no more in amount or burden than it places on its local business, not because this of itself is discriminatory, cumulative or special or would violate due process, but because other states also may have the right constitutionally, apart from the commerce clause, to tax the same thing and either the actuality or the risk of their doing so makes the total burden cumulative, discriminatory or special.[2]

In these interstate transactions cases involving taxation by the state of origin or that of market, the trouble arises, under the commerce clause, not from any danger that either tax taken alone, whether characterized as "sales" or "use" tax, will put interstate trade at a disadvantage which will burden unduly its competition with the local trade. So long as only one tax is applied and at the same rate as to wholly local transactions, no unduly discriminatory clog actually attaches to the interstate transaction of business.

The real danger arises most obviously when both states levy the tax. Thus, if in the instant cases it were shown that, on the one hand, Arkansas and Iowa actually were applying a "use" tax and Tennessee and Minnesota a "sales" tax, so that in each case the interstate transaction were taxed at both ends, the heavier cumulative burden thus borne by the interstate business in comparison with the local trade in either state would be obvious. If in each case the state of origin were shown to impose a sales tax of three per cent and the state of market a use tax of the same amount, interstate transactions between the two obviously would bear double the local tax burden borne by local trade in each state. This is a difference of substance, not merely one of names, relevant to the problem created by the commerce clause, though not to that of "jurisdiction" under due process conceptions. And the difference would be no less substantial if the taxes levied by both the state of origin and that of market were called "sales" taxes or if, indeed, both were called "use" taxes.

The Iowa tax in No. 441 avoids this problem by allowing credit for any sales tax shown to be levied upon the transaction whether in Iowa or elsewhere. Clearly therefore that tax cannot in fact put the interstate transaction at a tax disadvantage with local trade done in Iowa or elsewhere.

2. Cf. the opinion of the Chief Justice in
Northwest Airlines v. Minnesota, 322 U.S.
292, 64 S.Ct. 950.

However, the Arkansas tax in No. 311 provides for no such credit. But in that case there is no showing that Tennessee actually imposes any tax upon the transaction. If there is a burden or clog on commerce, therefore, it arises from the fact that Tennessee has power constitutionally to impose a tax, may exercise it, and when this occurs the cumulative effect of both taxes will be discriminatorily burdensome, though neither tax singles out the transaction or bears upon it more heavily than upon the local trade to which it applies. In short, the risk of multiple taxation creates the unconstitutional burden which actual taxation by both states would impose in fact.

In my opinion this is the real question and the only one presented in No. 311. And in my judgment it is determined the wrong way, not on commerce clause grounds but upon an unsustainable application of the due process prohibition.

Where the cumulative effect of two taxes, by whatever name called, one imposed by the state of origin, the other by the state of market, actually bears in practical effect upon such an interstate transaction, there is no escape under the doctrine of undue burden from one of two possible alternatives. Either one tax must fall or, what is the same thing, be required to give way to the other by allowing credit as the Iowa tax does, or there must be apportionment. Either solution presents an awkward alternative. But one or the other must be accepted unless that doctrine is to be discarded and one of two extreme positions taken, namely, that neither state can tax the interstate transaction or that both may do so until Congress intervenes to give its solution for the problem. It is too late to accept the former extreme, too early even if it were clearly desirable or permissible to follow the latter.

As between apportionment and requiring one tax to fall or allow credit, the latter perhaps would be the preferable solution. And in my opinion it is the one which the Court in effect, though not in specific statement, adopts. That the decision is cast more largely in terms of due process than in those of the commerce clause does not nullify that effect.

If in this case it were necessary to choose between the state of origin and that of market for the exercise of exclusive power to tax, or for requiring allowance of credit in order to avoid the cumulative burden, in my opinion the choice should lie in favor of the state of market rather than the state of origin. The former is the state where the goods must come in competition with those sold locally. It is the one where the burden of the tax necessarily will fall equally on both classes of trade. To choose the tax of the state of origin presents at least some possibilities that the burden it imposes on its local trade, with which the interstate traffic does not compete, at any rate directly, will be heavier than that placed by the consuming state on its local business of the same character. If therefore choice has to be made, whether as a matter of exclusive power to tax or as one of allowing credit, it should be in favor of the state of market or consumption as the one most certain to place the same tax load on both the interstate and competing local business. Hence, if the risk of taxation by both states may be said to have the same constitutional consequences, under the commerce clause, as taxation in actuality by both, the Arkansas tax, rather than the power of Tennessee to tax, should stand.

It may be that the mere risk of double taxation would not have the same consequences, given always of course a sufficient due process connection with the taxing states, that actual double taxation has, or may have, for application of the commerce clause prohibition. Risk of course is not irrelevant to burden or to the clogging effect the rule against undue burden is intended to prevent. But in these situations it may be doubted, on entirely practical grounds, that the mere risk Tennessee may apply its taxing power to these transactions will have any substantial effect in restraining the commerce such as the actual application of that power would have. In any event, whether or not the choice must be made now or, as I think, has been made, it should go in favor of Arkansas, not Tennessee.

For all practical purposes Indiana's gross income tax in No. 355 may be regarded as either a sales tax or a use tax laid in the state of market, comparable in all respects (except in words) to the Arkansas tax laid in No. 311 and to the Iowa tax imposed in No. 441, except that here the seller as well as the buyer does business and concludes the transaction in Indiana, the state of the market. This is clearly true of Classes C and E. It is true also of Class D, in my opinion, although the buyer there resided in Illinois but went to Indiana to enter into the transaction and take delivery of the goods. That he at once removed them on completion of the transaction there, to Illinois, intended to do this from the beginning and this fact may have been known to the seller, does not take from the transaction its character as one entered into and completed in Indiana. Whether or not Illinois, in these circumstances, could impose a use tax or some other as a property tax is not presented and need not be determined. If the Arkansas and Iowa taxes stand, as either does, *a fortiori* the Indiana tax stands in these applications.

Accordingly, I concur in the decisions in Nos. 441 and 355, but dissent from the decision in No. 311.

Notes and Problems

A. In Norton Co. v. Department of Revenue, 340 U.S. 534, 71 S.Ct. 377 (1951), the Supreme Court considered an Illinois tax imposed "upon persons engaged in the business of selling tangible personal property at retail" and measured by the gross receipts of the business.* The taxpayer was a

---

* The discussion in this Note draws heavily from W. Hellerstein, "State Taxation of Interstate Business and the Supreme Court, 1974 Term: *Standard Pressed Steel* and *Colonial Pipeline,*" 62 Va.L.Rev. 149, 161–76 (1976), and the material is used with the consent of the copyright owner, the Virginia Law Review.

Massachusetts manufacturer and vendor of abrasive machines and supplies with a branch office and warehouse in Chicago from which it made local sales. Illinois assessed its levy upon the gross receipts of *all* of Norton's sales to Illinois customers, which included sales resulting from

(1) Direct over-the-counter purchases at the Chicago office;

(2) Orders filled in Massachusetts but received by and/or shipped via the Chicago office; and

(3) Orders sent directly to Massachusetts and filled by direct shipment to Illinois customers.

The Court initially noted that "[u]nless some local incident occurs sufficient to bring the transaction within its taxing power, the vendor is not taxable." 340 U.S. at 537. Since Norton had satisfied this test by having "gone into the State to do local business," id., the Court next confronted the question whether Norton's local activity was sufficiently related to the assertion of State tax power to justify the exaction. First, it laid down the basic evidentiary rule that all the sales at issue were presumed to be related to the local activity; "only by showing that particular transactions are dissociated from the local business and interstate in nature" (id.) can a taxpayer rebut this presumption and avoid taxation on such transactions. Turning to the facts, the Court held that the Illinois court's judgment "attributing to the Chicago branch income from all sales that utilized it either in receiving orders or distributing the goods was * * * permissible," id. at 539, since the taxpayer—and here the Court fleshed out its "dissociation" test—had "not established that the services rendered by the Chicago office were not decisive factors in establishing and holding this market" and "no other source of customer relationship [had been] shown." Id. Hence sales in categories (1) and (2) above gave rise to taxable receipts. As to category (3), however, the Court declared that these sales were "so clearly interstate in character that the State could not reasonably attribute their proceeds to the local business," id. at 539, and they were therefore nontaxable.

B. *Over-the-Counter Sales: Due Process of Law and the Duty to Collect Use Tax of State of Residence From Out-of-State Customers.* A Wilmington, Delaware department store made sales of merchandise to customers residing in nearby Maryland, who came to the store to make their purchases. Some of the customers received delivery of the merchandise at the store; in other cases, the goods were delivered to them in Maryland by common carrier or the store's trucks. The facts showed that about $12,000 worth of merchandise was sold over a 4½ year period to Maryland purchasers for use in Maryland. About two-thirds of this merchandise was delivered into Maryland by the store's trucks. Maryland sought to require the department store to collect its use tax on all sales to its residents, no matter how delivery was made. On the department store's refusal to comply, Maryland seized one of the store's trucks while in the State to make deliveries. The Supreme Court held that the Maryland action violated the Due Process Clause and noted that it need not consider the Commerce Clause issue. Miller Bros. Co. v. Maryland, 347 U.S. 340, 74 S.Ct. 535 (1954). Admittedly, no sales tax could be imposed by Maryland when the sale was made in Delaware.

Mr. Justice Jackson, writing for the majority, declared that:

> little constructive discussion can be found in responsible commentary as to the grounds on which to rest a state's power to reach extraterritorial transactions on non-residents with tax liabilities. * * * But the course of decisions does reflect at least consistent adherence to one time-honored concept: that due process requires some definite link, some minimum connection between a state and the person, property or transaction it seeks to tax. [347 U.S. at 344–45, 74 S.Ct. at 538–39.]

After referring to the holding in McLeod v. Dilworth, supra, and concluding from that case that "Maryland could not have reached this Delaware vendor with a sales tax on these sales," the Court asked whether the same Delaware sale can be made

> a basis for imposing on the vendor liability for use taxes due from her own inhabitants? It would be strange law that would make appellant more vulnerable to liability for another's tax than to a tax on itself. [347 U.S. at 346, 74 S.Ct. at 539.]

Did not the *General Trading Co.* case establish the precise result, which Justice Jackson refers to as "strange law," by imposing a tax-collecting duty on a vendor in circumstances where the vendor could not have been made the taxpayer?

Mr. Justice Douglas dissented in an opinion concurred in by Chief Justice Warren and Justices Black and Clark. The dissent found

> no constitutional difficulty in making appellant a tax collector for Maryland under the general principles announced in General Trading Co. v. Tax Commission * * *.
>
> This is not a case of minimal contact between a vendor and the collecting State. Appellant did not sell cash-and-carry without knowledge of the destination of the goods; and its delivery truck was not in Maryland upon a casual, nonrecurring visit. Rather there has been a course of conduct in which the appellant has regularly injected advertising into media reaching Maryland consumers and regularly effected deliveries within Maryland by its own delivery trucks and by common carriers. [347 U.S. at 357–358, 74 S.Ct. at 547.] *

NATIONAL BELLAS HESS, INC. v. DEPARTMENT OF REVENUE

Supreme Court of the United States, 1967
386 U.S. 753, 87 S.Ct. 1389

MR. JUSTICE STEWART delivered the opinion of the Court.

The appellant, National Bellas Hess, is a mail order house with its principal place of business in North Kansas City, Missouri. It is licensed to do business in only that State and in Delaware, where it is incorporated. Although the company has neither outlets nor sales representatives in Illinois, the appellee Department of Revenue obtained a judgment from the Illinois Supreme Court that National is

---

* [The case is noted in 53 Mich.L.Rev. 133 (1954); 68 Harv.L.Rev. 129 (1954); 2   U.C.L.A.L.Rev. 134 (1954); 8 Vand.L.Rev. 126 (1954).]

required to collect and pay to the State the use taxes imposed by Ill. Rev.Stats. (1965), c. 120, § 439.3.[1] Since National's constitutional objections to the imposition of this liability present a substantial federal question, we noted probable jurisdiction of its appeal.[2]

The facts bearing upon National's relationship with Illinois are accurately set forth in the opinion of the State Supreme Court:

"[National] does not maintain in Illinois any office, distribution house, sales house, warehouse or any other place of business; it does not have in Illinois any agent, salesman, canvasser, solicitor or other type of representative to sell or take orders, to deliver merchandise, to accept payments, or to service merchandise it sells; it does not own any tangible property, real or personal, in Illinois; it has no telephone listing in Illinois and it has not advertised its merchandise for sale in newspapers, on billboards, or by radio or television in Illinois." [3]

All of the contacts which National does have with the State are via the United States mail or common carrier. Twice a year catalogues are mailed to the company's active or recent customers throughout the Nation, including Illinois. This mailing is supplemented by advertising "flyers" which are occasionally mailed to past and potential customers. Orders for merchandise are mailed by the customers to National and are accepted at its Missouri plant. The ordered goods are then sent to the customers either by mail or by common carrier.

This manner of doing business is sufficient under the Illinois statute to classify National as a "[r]etailer maintaining a place of business in this State," since that term includes any retailer:

"Engaging in soliciting orders within this State from users by means of catalogues or other advertising, whether such orders are received or accepted within or without this State." Ill.Rev.Stats. (1965), c. 120, § 439.2.

Accordingly, the statute requires National to collect and pay to the appellee Department the tax imposed by Illinois upon consumers who purchase the company's goods for use within the State.[4] When collecting this tax, National must give the Illinois purchaser "a receipt therefor in the manner and form prescribed by the [appellee]," if one is demanded.[5] It must also "keep such records, receipts, invoices and other pertinent books, documents, memoranda and papers as the [appellee] shall require, in such form as the [appellee] shall require," and must submit to such investigations, hearings, and examinations as are needed by the appellee to administer and enforce the use tax law.[6] Failure to keep such records or to give required receipts is punishable by a fine of up to $5,000 and imprisonment of up to six months.[7] Finally, to allow service of process on an out-of-state company like

---

1. 34 Ill.2d 164, 214 N.E.2d 755.

2. 385 U.S. 809, 87 S.Ct. 58, 17 L.Ed.2d 50.

3. 34 Ill.2d, at 166–167, 214 N.E.2d, at 757.

4. Ill.Rev.Stats. (1965), c. 120, § 439.3.

5. Id., § 439.5.

6. Id., § 439.11.

7. Id., § 439.14.

National, the statute designates the Illinois Secretary of State as National's appointed agent, and jurisdiction in tax collection suits attaches when process is served on him and the company is notified by registered mail.[8]

National argues that the liabilities which Illinois has thus imposed violate the Due Process Clause of the Fourteenth Amendment and create an unconstitutional burden upon interstate commerce. These two claims are closely related. For the test whether a particular State exaction is such as to invade the exclusive authority of Congress to regulate trade between the States, and the test for a State's compliance with the requirements of due process in this area are similar. See Central R. Co. of Pa. v. Commonwealth of Pennsylvania, 370 U.S. 607, 621–622, 82 S.Ct. 1297, 1306–1307, 8 L.Ed.2d 720 (concurring opinion of Mr. Justice Black). As to the former the Court has held that "State taxation falling on interstate commerce * * * can only be justified as designed to make such commerce bear a fair share of the cost of the local government whose protection it enjoys." Freeman v. Hewit, 329 U.S. 249, 253, 67 S.Ct. 274, 277, 91 L.Ed. 265. * * * And in determining whether a State tax falls within the confines of the Due Process Clause, the Court has said that the "simple but controlling question is whether the State has given anything for which it can ask return." Wisconsin v. J.C. Penney Co., 311 U.S. 435, 444, 61 S.Ct. 246, 250, 85 L.Ed. 267. * * * The same principles have been held applicable in determining the power of a State to impose the burdens of collecting use taxes upon interstate sales. Here, too, the Constitution requires "some definite link, some minimum connection, between a State and the person, property or transaction it seeks to tax." Miller Bros. Co. v. State of Maryland, 347 U.S. 340, 344–345, 74 S.Ct. 535, 539, 98 L.Ed. 744; Scripto, Inc. v. Carson, 362 U.S. 207, 210–211, 80 S.Ct. 619, 621–622, 4 L.Ed.2d 660.[9] See also American Oil Co. v. Neill, 380 U.S. 451, 458, 85 S.Ct. 1130, 1134, 14 L.Ed.2d 1.

In applying these principles the Court has upheld the power of a State to impose liability upon an out-of-state seller to collect a local use tax in a variety of circumstances. Where the sales were arranged by local agents in the taxing State, we have upheld such power. Felt & Tarrant Mfg. Co. v. Gallagher, 306 U.S. 62, 59 S.Ct. 376, 83 L.Ed. 488; General Trading Co. v. State Tax Comm'n, 322 U.S. 335, 64 S.Ct. 1028, 88 L.Ed. 1309. We have reached the same result where the mail order seller maintained local retail stores. Nelson v. Sears, Roebuck & Co., 312 U.S. 359, 61 S.Ct. 58, 85 L.Ed. 888; Nelson v. Montgomery Ward &

8. Id., § 439.12a.

9. Strictly speaking, there is no question of the connection or link between the State and "the person * * * it seeks to tax." For that person in Miller Bros. Co. v. State of Maryland, 347 U.S. 340, 74 S.Ct. 535, 98 L.Ed. 744, in Scripto, Inc. v. Carson, 362 U.S. 207, 80 S.Ct. 619, 4 L.Ed.2d 660, and in the present case is the user of the goods to whom the out-of-state retailer sells. National is not the person being directly taxed, but rather it is asked to collect the tax from the user. It is, however, made directly liable for the payment of the tax whether collected or not. Ill.Rev. Stats. (1965), c. 120, § 439.8.

Co., 312 U.S. 373, 61 S.Ct. 593, 85 L.Ed. 897.[10] In those situations the out-of-state seller was plainly accorded the protection and services of the taxing State. The case in this Court which represents the furthest constitutional reach to date of a State's power to deputize an out-of-state retailer as its collection agent for a use tax is Scripto, Inc. v. Carson, 362 U.S. 207, 80 S.Ct. 619, 4 L.Ed.2d 660. There we held that Florida could constitutionally impose upon a Georgia seller the duty of collecting a state use tax upon the sale of goods shipped to customers in Florida. In that case the seller had "10 wholesalers, jobbers, or 'salesmen' conducting continuous local solicitation in Florida and forwarding the resulting orders from that State to Atlanta for shipment of the ordered goods." 362 U.S., at 211, 80 S.Ct., at 621.

But the Court has never held that a State may impose the duty of use tax collection and payment upon a seller whose only connection with customers in the State is by common carrier or the United States mail. Indeed, in the *Sears, Roebuck* case the Court sharply differentiated such a situation from one where the seller had local retail outlets, pointing out that "those other concerns * * * are not receiving benefits from Iowa for which it has the power to exact a price." 312 U.S., at 365, 61 S.Ct., at 589. And in Miller Bros. Co. v. State of Maryland, 347 U.S. 340, 74 S.Ct. 535, 98 L.Ed. 744, the Court held that a State could not constitutionally impose a use tax obligation upon a Delaware seller who had no retail outlets or sales solicitors in Maryland. There the seller advertised its wares to Maryland residents through newspaper and radio advertising, in addition to mailing circulars four times a year. As a result, it made substantial sales to Maryland customers, and made deliveries to them by its own trucks and drivers.

In order to uphold the power of Illinois to impose use tax burdens on National in this case, we would have to repudiate totally the sharp distinction which these and other decisions have drawn between mail order sellers with retail outlets, solicitors, or property within a State, and those who do no more than communicate with customers in the State by mail or common carrier as part of a general interstate business. But this basic distinction, which until now has been generally recognized by the state taxing authorities,[11] is a valid one, and we decline to obliterate it.

10. National acknowledges its obligation to collect a use tax in Alabama, Kansas, and Mississippi, since it has retail outlets in those States.

11. As of 1965, 11 States besides Illinois had use tax statutes which required a seller like National to participate in the tax collection system. However, state taxing administrators appear to have generally considered an advertising nexus insufficient. For they have testified that doubts as to the constitutionality of such statutes underlay their failure to take full advantage of their statutory authority. Report of the Special Subcommittee on State Taxation of Interstate Commerce of the Committee on the Judiciary, House of Representatives, H.R.Rep. No. 565, 89th Cong., 1st Sess., 631–635 (1965). These doubts were substantiated by the only other State Supreme Court that has considered the issue now before us. The Alabama Supreme Court, dealing with a situation very much like the present one, found that this application of the use tax statute would be invalid under the Federal Constitution.

We need not rest on the broad foundation of all that was said in the *Miller Bros.* opinion, for here there was neither local advertising nor local household deliveries, upon which the dissenters in *Miller Bros.* so largely relied. 347 U.S., at 358, 74 S.Ct., at 547. Indeed, it is difficult to conceive of commercial transactions more exclusively interstate in character than the mail order transactions here involved. And if the power of Illinois to impose use tax burdens upon National were upheld, the resulting impediments upon the free conduct of its interstate business would be neither imaginary nor remote. For if Illinois can impose such burdens, so can every other State, and so, indeed, can every municipality, every school district, and every other political subdivision throughout the Nation with power to impose sales and use taxes.[12] The many variations in rates of tax,[13] in allowable exemptions, and in administrative and record-keeping requirements [14] could entangle National's interstate business in a virtual welter of complicated obligations to local jurisdictions with no legitimate claim to impose "a fair share of the cost of local government."

The very purpose of the Commerce Clause was to ensure a national economy free from such unjustifiable local entanglements. Under the Constitution, this is a domain where Congress alone has the power of regulation and control.[15]

The judgment is reversed.

Reversed.

MR. JUSTICE FORTAS, with whom MR. JUSTICE BLACK and MR. JUSTICE DOUGLAS join, dissenting.

In my opinion, this Court's decision in Scripto, Inc. v. Carson, 362 U.S. 207, 80 S.Ct. 619, 4 L.Ed.2d 660 (1960), as well as a realistic approach to the facts of appellant's business, dictates affirmance of the judgment of the Supreme Court of Illinois.

State v. Lane Bryant, Inc., 277 Ala. 385, 171 So.2d 91.

12. "Local sales taxes are imposed today [1965] by over 2,300 localities. * * * In most States, the local sales tax is complemented by a use tax." H.R.Rep. No. 565, supra, at 872.

13. In 1964 there were seven different rates of sales and use taxes: 2, 2¼, 2½, 3, 3½, 4, and 5%. H.R.Rep. No. 565, supra, at 611–613, 607–608. The State of Washington has recently added an eighth, 4.2%. Wash.Rev.Code Ann. § 82.12.020 (Supp. 1966).

14. "The prevailing system requires [the seller] to administer rules which differ from one State to another and whose application—especially for the industrial retailer—turns on facts which are often too remote and uncertain for the level of accuracy demanded by the prescribed system." H.R.Rep. No. 565, supra, at 673.

"Given the broad spread of sales of even small and moderate sized companies, it is clear that if just the localities which now impose the tax were to realize anything like their potential of out-of-State registrants the recordkeeping task of multistate sellers would be clearly intolerable." Id., at 882.

15. Congress has in fact recently evidenced an active interest in this area. See Tit. II, Pub.L. 86–272, 73 Stat. 556, as amended by P.L. 87–17, 75 Stat. 41, which authorized the detailed congressional study of state taxation of interstate commerce that resulted in H.R.Rep. No. 565, supra. See also H.R.Rep. No. 2013, 89th Cong., 2d Sess. (1966).

National Bellas Hess is a large retail establishment specializing in wearing apparel. Directly and through subsidiaries, it operates a national retail mail order business with headquarters in Kansas City, Missouri, and its wholly owned subsidiaries operate a large number of retail stores in various States. In 1961, appellant's net sales were in the neighborhood of $60,000,000, and its accounts receivable amounted to about $15,500,000.[1]

Its sales in Illinois amounted to $2,174,744 for the approximately 15 months for which the taxes in issue in this case were assessed. This substantial volume is obtained by twice-a-year catalogue mailings, supplemented by "intermediate smaller 'sales books' or 'flyers,' " as the court below styled them. The catalogue contains about 4,000 items of merchandise. The company's mailing list includes over 5,000,000 names. The "flyers" are sent to an even larger list than the catalogues and are occasionally mailed in bulk addressed to "occupant."

A substantial part of Bellas Hess' sales is on credit. Its catalogue features "NBH Budget Aid Credit"—which requires no money down but requires the purchaser to make monthly payments which include a service fee or interest charge, and which also incorporates an agreement, unless expressly rejected by the purchaser, for "Budget Aid Family Insurance." The company also offers "charge account" services—payable monthly including a "service charge" if the account is not fully paid within 30 days. The form to be filled in for credit purchases contains the usual type of information, including place of employment, name of bank, marital status, home ownership or rental. Merchandise can also be bought c.o.d. or by sending check or money order with the order for goods.[*]

There should be no doubt that this large-scale, systematic, continuous solicitation and exploitation of the Illinois consumer market is a sufficient "nexus" to require Bellas Hess to collect from Illinois customers and to remit the use tax, especially when coupled with the use of the credit resources of residents of Illinois, dependent as that mechanism is upon the State's banking and credit institutions. Bellas Hess is not simply using the facilities of interstate commerce to serve customers in Illinois. It is regularly and continuously engaged in "exploitation of the consumer market" of Illinois (Miller Bros. Co. v. State of Maryland, 347 U.S. 340, 347, 74 S.Ct. 535, 540, 98 L.Ed. 744 (1954)) by soliciting residents of Illinois who live and work there and have homes and banking connections there, and who, absent the solicitation of Bellas Hess, might buy locally and pay the sales tax to support their State. Bellas Hess could not carry on its business in Illinois, and particularly its substantial credit business, without utilizing Illinois banking and credit facilities. Since the case was tried on affidavits, we are not informed as to the details of the company's credit operations in Illinois. We do not know whether it utilizes credit information or collection agencies, or similar institutions. The company states that it

---

1. Moody's Industrials (1962).   * [Some footnotes have been omitted].

has "brought no suits in the State of Illinois." Accepting this as true, it would nevertheless be unreasonable to assume that the company does not either sell or assign its accounts or otherwise take measures to collect its delinquent accounts, or that collection does not include local activities by the company or its assignees or representatives.

Bellas Hess enjoys the benefits of, and profits from the facilities nurtured by, the State of Illinois as fully as if it were a retail store or maintained salesmen therein. Indeed, if it did either, the benefit that it received from the State of Illinois would be no more than it now has—the ability to make sales of its merchandise, to utilize credit facilities, and to realize a profit; and, at the same time, it would be required to pay additional taxes. Under the present arrangement, it conducts its substantial, regular, and systematic business in Illinois and the State demands only that it collect from its customer-users—and remit to the State—the use tax which is merely equal to the sales tax which resident merchants must collect and remit. To excuse Bellas Hess from this obligation is to burden and penalize retailers located in Illinois who must collect the sales tax from their customers. In Illinois the rate is 3½%, and when it is realized that in some communities the sales tax requires, in effect, that as much as 5% be added to the amount that customers of local, tax-paying stores must pay, the importance of the competitive discrimination becomes apparent. While this advantage to out-of-state sellers is tolerable and a necessary constitutional consequence where the sales are occasional, minor and sporadic and not the result of a calculated, systematic exploitation of the market, it certainly should not be extended to instances where the out-of-state company is engaged in exploiting the local market on a regular, systematic, large-scale basis. In such cases, the difference between the nature of the business conducted by the mail order house and by the local enterprise is not entitled to constitutional significance. The national mail order business amounts to over $2,400,000,000 a year.[4] Some of this is undoubtedly subject to the full range of taxes because of the location of stores in the various States,[5] and some of it is and should be exempt from state use tax because of its sporadic or minor nature. See Report of the Special Subcommittee of the House Judiciary Committee, on State Taxation of Interstate Commerce, H.R.Rep. No. 565, 89th Cong., 1st Sess., Vol. 3 (1965), pp. 770–777. But the volume which, under the present decision, will be placed in a favored position and exempted from bearing its fair burden of the collection of state taxes certainly will be substantial, and as state sales taxes increase, this haven of immunity may well increase in size and importance.

In *Scripto*, supra, this Court applied a sensible, practical conception of the Commerce Clause. The interstate seller who, in that case,

4. U.S. Bureau of the Census, 1963 Census of Business, Retail Trade Area Statistics, pt. 1, table 2, p. 1–8 (1966).

5. See Nelson v. Sears, Roebuck & Co., 312 U.S. 359, 61 S.Ct. 586, 85 L.Ed. 888 (1941); Nelson v. Montgomery Ward & Co., 312 U.S. 373, 61 S.Ct. 593, 85 L.Ed 897 (1941).

claimed constitutional immunity from the collection of the Florida use tax had, like appellant here, no office or place of business in the State, and had no property or employees there. It solicited orders in Florida through local "independent contractors" or brokers paid on a commission basis. These brokers were furnished catalogues and samples, and forwarded orders to Scripto, out of state. The Court noted that the seller was "charged with no tax—save when * * * he fails or refuses to collect it" (362 U.S., at 211, 80 S.Ct., at 621)[6] and that the State "reimburs[ed the seller] * * * for its service[s]" as tax collector (362 U.S., at 212, 80 S.Ct., at 622). The same is true in the present case.[7] I do not see how *Scripto* is meaningfully distinguishable from this case. In fact, *Scripto* involved the sale of a single article of commerce. The "exploitation" of the State's market was by no means as pervasive or comprehensive as is here involved, nor was there any reference to the company's use of the State's credit institutions.

The present case is, of course, not at all controlled by Miller Bros. Co. v. State of Maryland, 347 U.S. 340, 74 S.Ct. 535, 98 L.Ed. 744 (1954). In that case, as this Court said, the company sold its merchandise at its store in Delaware; there was "no solicitation other than the incidental effects of general advertising * * * no invasion or exploitation of the consumer market * * *." 347 U.S., at 347, 74 S.Ct., at 540. As the Court noted in *Scripto*, supra, *Miller Bros.* was a case in which there was "no regular, systematic displaying of its products by catalogs, samples or the like." 362 U.S., at 212, 80 S.Ct., at 622. On the contrary, in the present case, appellant regularly sends not only its catalogue, but even bulk mailings soliciting business addressed to "occupant," and it offers and extends credit to residents of Illinois based on their local financial references.

As the Court says, the test whether an out-of-state business must comply with a state levy is variously formulated: "whether the State has given anything for which it can ask return"; whether the out-of-state business enjoys the protection or benefits of the State; whether there is a sufficient nexus: "some definite link, some minimum connection, between a state and the person, property or transaction it seeks to tax." However this is formulated, it seems to me entirely clear that a mail order house engaged in the business of regularly, systematically,

6. Our observation in Nelson v. Sears, Roebuck & Co., 312 U.S. 359, 365–366, 61 S.Ct. 586, 589, 85 L.Ed. 888 (1941), is an apt response to appellant's claim that it will not be able to collect all of the tax from its purchasers: "[S]o far as assumed losses on tax collections are concerned, respondent is in no position to found a constitutional right on the practical opportunities for tax avoidance which its method of doing business affords Iowa residents, or to claim a constitutional immunity because it may elect to deliver the goods before the tax is paid." Actually, it appears that appel-

lant's method of doing business is such as to minimize the noncollection of the tax.

7. The Illinois statute provides for a "discount of 2% or $5 per calendar year, whichever is greater * * * to reimburse the retailer for expenses incurred in collecting the tax, keeping records, preparing and filing returns, remitting the tax and supplying data * * *." Ill.Rev.Stat. (1963), c. 120, § 439.9. Appellant does not claim that this amount is inadequate to reimburse it for its expenses in collecting the tax for the State.

and on a large scale offering merchandise for sale in a State in competition with local retailers, and soliciting deferred payment-credit accounts from the State's residents, is not excused from compliance with the State's use tax obligations by the Commerce Clause or the Due Process Clause of the Constitution.

It is hardly worth remarking that appellant's expressions of consternation and alarm at the burden which the mechanics of compliance with use tax obligations would place upon it and others similarly situated should not give us pause. The burden is no greater than that placed upon local retailers by comparable sales tax obligations; and the Court's response that these administrative and record keeping requirements could "entangle" appellant's interstate business in a welter of complicated obligations vastly underestimates the skill of contemporary man and his machines. There is no doubt that the collection of taxes from consumers is a burden; but it is no more of a burden on a mail order house such as appellant located in another State than on an enterprise in the same State which accepts orders by mail; and it is, indeed, hardly more of a burden than it is on any ordinary retail store in the taxing State.

I would affirm.

Notes and Problems

A. The National Geographic Society, a District of Columbia corporation, made substantial mail-order sales of maps, atlases, globes, and books to California residents who responded to its magazine and direct mail solicitations. The Society also maintained two offices in California which solicited advertising for its magazine, but no activities relating to the Society's operation of its mail-order business were conducted at those offices. California assessed a use tax against the Society on its mail-order sales to California customers. The California Supreme Court sustained the Board's position, reasoning that the "slightest presence" of the seller within the State established a sufficient nexus to require the seller to collect use tax. Although the United States Supreme Court affirmed, it disavowed the State court's "slightest presence" test, stating:

> Our affirmance of the California Supreme Court is not to be understood as implying agreement with that court's "slightest presence" standard of constitutional nexus. Appellant's maintenance of two offices in the State and solicitation by employees assigned to those offices of advertising copy in the range of one million dollars annually, Tr. of Oral Arg., at 6, establish a much more substantial presence than the expression "slightest presence" connotes. Our affirmance thus rests upon our conclusion that appellant's maintenance of the two offices in California and activities there adequately establish a relationship or "nexus" between the Society and the State that renders constitutional the obligations imposed upon appellant * * * [National Geographic Society v. State Bd. of Equalization, 430 U.S. 551, 97 S.Ct. 1386, 1390 (1977).]

In response to the Society's contention that the case was controlled by *National Bellas Hess,* the Court said that its opinion in that case had:

> carefully underscored * * *, the "sharp distinction * * * between mail order sellers with retail outlets, solicitors, or property within [the taxing] State, and those [like Bellas Hess] who do no more than communicate with customers in the State by mail or common carrier as part of a general interstate business." Appellant Society clearly falls into the former category. [430 U.S. at 559, 97 S.Ct. at 1392 (citation omitted).]

The Court also rejected the Society's argument that the two California offices should be disregarded for purposes of determining whether the requisite nexus existed because such offices played no role with respect to the mail-order sales at issue:

> The Society argues in other words that there must exist a nexus or relationship not only between the seller and the taxing State, but also between the activity of the seller sought to be taxed and the seller's activity within the State. We disagree. However fatal to a direct tax a "showing that particular transactions are dissociated from the local business * * *," Norton Co. v. Department of Revenue, supra, 340 U.S. 537, 71 S.Ct. 380, * * * such dissociation does not bar the imposition of the use tax collection duty. * * * [T]he relevant constitutional test to establish the requisite nexus for requiring an out-of-state seller to collect and pay the use tax is not whether the duty to collect the use tax relates to the seller's activities carried on within the State, but simply whether the facts demonstrate "some definite link, some minimum connection, between [the State and] the *person* * * * it seeks to tax." Miller Bros. v. Maryland, supra, 347 U.S., at 344–345, 74 S.Ct., at 539. (Emphasis added.) Here the Society's two offices, without regard to the nature of their activities, had the advantage of the same municipal services—fire and police protection, and the like— as they would have had if their activities * * * included assistance to the mail order operations that generated the use taxes. [430 U.S. at 560–61, 97 S.Ct. at 1392–93 (footnote omitted).]

B. In State v. MacFadden–Bartell Corp., 280 Ala. 386, 194 So.2d 543 (1967), the court held that an out-of-state magazine publisher was not required to collect the Alabama use tax on magazines delivered to residents of the State, where the subscriptions were obtained by mail advertising through an independent Alabama corporation, which solicited magazine subscriptions for several publishers. The Alabama corporation did not, in form at least, receive "commissions" on the subscriptions. Instead, it paid the publisher an agreed amount for each subscription sold. The court accepted this formal contractual arrangement as making the Alabama corporation not an agent of the publisher, but a wholesaler buying and reselling. On this premise, the court held that the publisher did not have sufficient nexus with Alabama to require collection of the use tax. Query, whether such a contractual arrangement should enable the parties to bring themselves within rule of *National Bellas Hess?* On these facts, should *Scripto,* rather than *National Bellas Hess,* govern?

In contrast to the *MacFadden–Bartell* case, see Ex Parte Newbern, 286 Ala. 348, 239 So.2d 792 (1970), which held that *Scripto* rather than *MacFadden–Bartell* was controlling in a case involving direct interstate shipment to in-state purchasers after local solicitation. The court deemed it immaterial whether local "salesmen" were called salesmen, drummers, dealers, solicitors, representatives, or brokers. See also Reader's Digest Ass'n v. Mahin, 44 Ill.2d 354, 255 N.E.2d 458, appeal dismissed 399 U.S. 919, 90 S.Ct. 2237 (1970), in which the Illinois Supreme Court sustained use tax collection liability with respect to mail-order sales by an out-of-state corporation on the basis of the activities of the corporation's in-state subsidiaries.

C. *Local Incidents of Interstate Transactions.* The drawing of the line at which local incidents may be cut off from interstate commerce and be subjected to State tax continues to be one of the most troublesome problems in this field. In American Oil Co. v. Neill, 380 U.S. 451, 85 S.Ct. 1130 (1965), the taxpayer sold gasoline for use of the Atomic Energy Commission in Idaho. Delivery of the gasoline was made in Utah, and it was transported by common carriers selected and paid by the AEC. The taxpayer was authorized to do business in Idaho as a licensed dealer, and submitted to the tax collector monthly reports of gasoline shipped into the State. Idaho levied a tax of six cents per gallon on the sales of gasoline shipped into the State under the AEC contract. The State court sustained the tax on the ground that the incidence of the levy fell exclusively on the dealer as a privilege tax, but the United States Supreme Court held that it violated the Due Process Clause. The fact that taxpayer was licensed to do business in the taxing State did not provide the requisite territorial nexus to the sales taxed, since the invitation for the bids for the contract had been sent from Washington, the taxpayer had submitted its bid from Utah, and the contract called for delivery of the gasoline in Utah, where title passed.

May a seller of fuel oil to towboats traveling on the Mississippi River be taxed by Illinois when, during the fueling process, "the towboat captains for navigational and safety purposes try to stay in the center of the channel of the Mississippi River which is the boundary of Missouri and Illinois"? See Sinclair Refining Co. v. Department of Revenue, 50 Ill.2d 201, 277 N.E.2d 858 (1971); cf. Central Greyhound Lines, Inc. v. Mealey, 334 U.S. 653, 68 S.Ct. 1260 (1948).

D. *Use Taxes as Applied to Articles Shipped Into the State Across State Lines.* If the taxpayer purchases goods outside the State, which are delivered to him across State lines, ordinarily no successful Commerce Clause objection can be made to the imposition of a use tax by the taxpayer's State in which the goods are used. The articles have come to rest, interstate commerce has ended, so that the use taxed is a local, intrastate event. Where the goods thus brought into the State are there used by an interstate railroad or telephone company in the interstate operations, taxpayers have urged that the use tax violates the Commerce Clause. The Supreme Court has rejected this contention, holding that a taxable event occurred between the time the article was brought into the State and the time it was consumed in interstate operations. During this interval, the use, storage, and exercise of other powers over railroad equipment and supplies and telephone equipment and apparatus were locally taxable events. Southern Pacific Co. v. Gallagher, 306 U.S. 167, 59 S.Ct. 389 (1939); Pacific Telephone & Telegraph Co. v. Gallagher, 306 U.S. 182, 59 S.Ct. 396 (1939). These cases are discussed in Hartman, "Sales Taxation in Interstate Commerce," 9 Vand.L.Rev. 138 (1956). A use tax has been disallowed, however, where the alleged "use" within the State consisted solely of the purported control exercised by a merchandiser over printed material produced outside the State and delivered directly by common carrier to post offices located in the State for shipment to the merchandiser's customers. Service Merchandise Co. v. Tidwell, 529 S.W.2d 215 (Tenn.1975). But see McNamara v. D.H. Holmes Co., 505 So.2d 102 (La.App.1987), probable juris noted, __ U.S. __, 108 S.Ct. 823 (1987), where the court held that the Commerce Clause was no bar to the application of a use tax on facts essentially the same as those in the *Service Merchandise* case. As this work goes to press, the case is pending before the United States Supreme Court.

In cases involving gasoline storage and withdrawal taxes, which are a special form of use tax, the taxes have been upheld as applied to goods brought into the taxing State from another State, stored for a brief period and withdrawn for consumption in interstate transportation. Nashville, C. & St. L. Ry. v. Wallace, 288 U.S. 249, 53 S.Ct. 345 (1933); Edelman v. Boeing Air Transport, 289 U.S. 249, 53 S.Ct. 591 (1933); United Airlines, Inc. v. Mahin, 410 U.S. 623, 93 S.Ct. 1186 (1973).

E. *Evasion of Use Taxes on Out-of-State Purchases.* The practical problems of preventing use tax evasion in cases of goods bought in other States have proved extremely difficult. See R. Haig & C. Shoup, The Sales Tax in the American States (1934); Due, Sales Taxation (1957); J. Due & J. Mikesell, Sales Taxation (1983). Out-of-state automobile purchases are commonly ferreted out through check-up on registrations. An important step in assisting States in enforcing use taxes was taken when Congress in 1949 passed an act designed to eliminate avoidance of cigarette sales and use taxes through mail order purchases in non-sales tax States. 63 Stat. 884, Pub.L. No. 363, 1949, 81st Cong., 1st Sess. (1949), codified at 15 U.S.C. § 375. Under this act persons selling cigarettes in interstate commerce shipped to persons, other than a distributor licensed by or located in a State taxing the sale or use of cigarettes, are required to report all such sales to the taxing authority of the State into which the goods are shipped. The validity of this act was upheld in Consumer Mail Order Ass'n of America v. United States, 94 F.Supp. 705 (D.D.C.1950), aff'd, 340 U.S. 925, 71 S.Ct. 500 (1951).

The most significant problem of evasion of use taxes is the States' inability to collect taxes on out-of-state mail order sales. Mail-order sales are estimated to be running at $44.9 billion dollars per year and the States are estimated to be losing more than a billion dollars a year in unpaid use taxes on out-of-state mail order purchases. ACIR, "State and Local Taxtion of Out-of-State Mail Order Sales," A–105 (1986). The States' inability to force the out-of-state vendor to collect taxes on mail order sales, regardless of the volume of business conducted in the State by mail order seller, stems from the limits imposed on State tax jurisdiction by National Bellas Hess v.

Department of Revenue, supra. Some observers share the view of Professor Paul Hartman, that *National Bellas Hess* is ripe for reconsideration in light both of the dramatic changes in marketing techniques since *National Bellas Hess* was decided and of the evolution of Supreme Court doctrine:

> *Bellas Hess* is the judicial barricade to the collection of the use taxes when the out-of-state seller has *no physical presence* in the taxing state. * * * At the time of *Bellas Hess,* the mail-order industry was ringing up only about thirteen billion dollars in annual sales. Since that time, consumers have gone on a mail-order shopping binge, buying everything from expensive home computers and telephone equipment to a vast array of clothing, household furnishings, and other items sold by companies like American Express, Sharper Image, Brookstone, and Lillian Vernon. No doubt this mail-order buying binge from out-of-state sellers has been triggered, in part, by the tax immunity afforded by *Bellas Hess.*

> Marketing techniques have dramatically changed since *Bellas Hess* was decided in 1967. Out-of-state mail-order sellers have used sophisticated technological advances, such as toll-free (800) telephone numbers and an array of computer hookups that facilitate mail-order sellers in the invasion of the taxing states' consumer markets for the capture of profits. The entire pursuit of business has taken on an entirely new meaning.

> * * *

> An unrealistic facet of the *Bellas Hess* doctrine is that the Court presumably thought that a few "warm bodies" in the taxing state—either operating from an office, or traipsing around hawking their wares without any in-state office—constitute a more satisfactory nexus with a state, for constitutional purposes, than other more substantial and meaningful connections. Benefits from the taxing state that are unrelated to physical contact with the state may be of vastly greater significance than those derived from the presence of a whole swarm of the out-of-state seller's agents soliciting business. Practically speaking, some form of physical presence within the state in furtherance of a business purpose is not essential to the existence of a meaningful nexus with the state. As noted earlier, in *Burger King* [v. Rudzewicz, 471 U.S. 462, 105 S.Ct. 2174 (1985)] the Supreme Court recognized the realities of the situation. The Court there declared that "it is an inescapable fact of modern commercial life that a substantial amount of business is transacted solely by mail and wire communication across state lines, thus obviating the need for physical presence within a state in which the business is conducted." * * *

> For use tax collection purposes, the connection or nexus between the taxing state and out-of-state mail-order sellers should be an economic, rather than physical, relationship. When an out-of-state mail-order seller, for the purpose of realizing a profit, takes advantage of the taxing state's economic climate and milieu through systematic, continuous, and large-scale solicitation of that state's consumer market, that activity should constitute a connection or nexus sufficient to require the out-of-state seller to collect the use tax. When the state provides a

substantial economic benefit to the production of income for the out-of-state seller, the taxing state should be able to demand a tithe from the seller. [Hartman, "Collection of the Use Tax on Out-of-State Mail–Order Sales," 39 Vand.L.Rev. 993 (1986) (footnotes omitted).*]

In light of the existing barrier to requiring out-of-state sellers to collect use taxes on mail order sales and the uncertainty of future evolution of judicial doctrine in the field, the States have been pressing for Federal legislation to relieve them of the restrictions imposed by *National Bellas Hess.* The ACIR has developed and endorsed proposed Federal legislation authorizing the States to require out-of-state vendors to collect use taxes on mail order sales. See ACIR, supra; State Taxation of Interstate Commerce: Hearing on S. 1510 Before the Subcomm. on Taxation and Debt Management of the Senate Comm. on Finance, 99th Cong., 1st Sess. (1985). Under the proposal, there would be an exemption for vendors with sales below a certain threshold amount. In addition, sellers who operate in States where there are also local use taxes, would be given an election to collect taxes at a State rate only or at a single combined State and local rate. The broad objectives of the ACIR recommendations have been embodied in proposed legislation. See H.R. 1242, 100th Cong., 1st Sess. (1987) (the Dorgan bill); H.R. 1891, 100th Cong., 1st Sess. (1987) and H.R. 3521, 100th Cong., 1st Sess. (1987) (the Brooks bills.). The Brooks bills would authorize the States to require any person who engages in "regular or systematic soliciting of sales in such State" to collect "sales tax" on sales having a destination in the State. They apply only to vendors whose gross receipts from all sales of tangible personal property in the United States exceed $12,500,000 during the preceding year, or $500,000 in the State. The Dorgan bill would empower the States to require collection of State and local sales or use tax only from a "retailer engaged in business in that State * * * on the sale or use of tangible personal property shipped or delivered into that State and political subdivision." The term "retailer engaged in business" is defined so as to include a broad variety of in-state types of solicitation, including advertising broadcast from, printed at or distributed from the State, intended for local consumers and "substantial and recurring" solicitation if the retailer benefits from banking, financing, debt collection, telecommunications, or marketing activities in the State, or from authorized installation, servicing, or repair facilities in the State. In addition, a retailer is deemed to be engaged in business in the State if it is owned or controlled by the same interests that own or control any retailer engaged in the same or a similar line of business in the State, or if it has a franchisee or licensee operating under its trade name which is required to collect the tax. The threshold requirement under the Dorgan bill for the application of the duty to collect tax is minimal nationwide gross sales of tangible personal property in excess of $5,000,000.

Constitutional objections have been raised to the proposed Federal legislation on the grounds that the restrictions on State power to impose use tax collection responsibility are rooted in the Due Process Clause under *National Bellas Hess* and that even though Congress has power to lift

* [This material is reprinted with the consent of the Vanderbilt Law Review.]

judicially-imposed Commerce Clause restraints on State taxation it lacks the power to lift judicially-imposed Due Process restraints on such power. For the view that *National Bellas Hess* is based essentially on the Commerce Clause and that, even if based on the Due Process Clause, Congress is empowered to lift the restraints imposed by *National Bellas Hess* on State jurisdiction to require collection of use taxes, see J. Hellerstein, "Significant Sales and Use Tax Developments During the Past Half Century," 39 Vand.L.Rev. 961, 982–92 (1986).

F. *References.* In addition to the articles cited in Note G supra, see McCray, "Overturning *Bellas Hess:* Due Process Considerations," 1985 B.Y. U.L.Rev. 265; McCray, "Commerce Clause Sanctions Against Taxation on Mail Order Sales: A Re–Evaluation," 17 Urb.Law. 529 (1985); Simet, "The Concept of 'Nexus' and State Use and Unapportioned Gross Receipts Taxes," 73 Nw.L.Rev. 112 (1978); Powell, "Sales and Use Taxes; Collection from Absentee Vendors," 57 Harv.L.Rev. 1086 (1944); Small, "The Constitutionality of Legislative Relief from the Scripto Decision," 12 Tax Exec. 330 (1960); Stetson, "When Can Collection of Use Taxes Be Required of Nonresident Vendor?," 19 J.Taxation 376 (1963).

ASSIGNMENT

A foreign corporation not authorized to do business in your State maintains in the State full-time salesmen who solicit orders for sales of hosiery. It maintains no office or place of business in the State. A down payment on each order is taken by the salesmen. The orders are forwarded to the main office of the corporation, located in State X, for acceptance. The goods are shipped from State X by parcel post C.O.D. to the customer. The order slips recite that title to the goods will pass to the customer upon delivery by the taxpayer to the post office in State X. The corporation advertises its product in local publications, radio, and television.

Analyze the statutes, regulations, and decisions under the sales and use tax laws of your State, and prepare a report setting forth your views as to whether the corporation is required to collect your State's sales or use tax on the sales of goods shipped to customers in your State.

Part 6

DUE PROCESS CLAUSE RESTRICTIONS ON STATE TAXATION

Chapter 11

DUE PROCESS CLAUSE RESTRICTIONS ON STATE PROPERTY, DEATH, AND PERSONAL INCOME TAXES

SECTION 1. INTRODUCTORY NOTE

* * * nor shall any State deprive any person of life, liberty, or property, without due process of law * * * [U.S.Const., Amend. XIV, § 1.]

For a decade beginning in 1930, the prevailing doctrine [1] was that the Due Process Clause forbade "double taxation" of intangibles.[2] The Court acted as arbiter of the competing claims of the States by fixing a single and exclusive *locus* for the taxation of each type of intangible— whether the State of the creditor, the debtor, incorporation, or commercial domicile.

The current doctrine of the majority is that the Due Process Clause does not bar "double taxation." [3] It sets up as the test of validity that the taxing State must furnish protection to or exercise control over the persons whose relationships give rise to intangible property rights. It

1. The ensuing discussion is adapted from J. Hellerstein & Hennefeld, "State Taxation in a National Economy," 54 Harv.L.Rev. 949 (1941). It is used with the consent of the copyright owner, Harvard Law Review Association, copyright 1940, 1941.

2. Farmers Loan & Trust Co. v. Minnesota, 280 U.S. 204, 50 S.Ct. 98 (1930); see A. Harding, Double Taxation of Property and Income (1933); Brown, "Multiple Taxation by the States," 48 Harv.L.Rev. 407 (1935); Lowndes, "Spurious Conceptions of the Constitutional Law of Taxation," 47 Harv.L.Rev. 628 (1934).

3. Graves v. Elliott, 307 U.S. 383, 59 S.Ct. 913 (1939); Curry v. McCanless, 307

U.S. 357, 59 S.Ct. 900 (1939). Chief Justice Hughes and Justices McReynolds and Roberts dissented from both decisions. See also Wisconsin v. J.C. Penney Co., 311 U.S. 435, 61 S.Ct. 246 (1940), and concurring opinion of Justice Frankfurter joined by Justices Stone, Black, and Douglas, in Newark Fire Ins. Co. v. State Board of Tax Appeals, 307 U.S. 313, 59 S.Ct. 918 (1939); cf. Pearson v. McGraw, 308 U.S. 313, 60 S.Ct. 211 (1939). For a discussion of the *McCanless* case, see Tweed & Sargent, "Death and Taxes Are Certain—But What of Domicile," 53 Harv.L.Rev. 68 (1939); Note, 53 Harv.L.Rev. 1013 (1940).

asserts that sufficient protection and control may be afforded not only by the State of domicile but also by other States to which a person extends activities resulting in the creation of intangibles.[4] It holds that the State of the creditor's domicile,[5] the State of the debtor's domicile,[6] and as to trusts, the State in which the trust is administered [7]—at least these—exercise sufficient protection and control over intangibles [8] to impose inheritance or estate taxes concurrently upon their devolution. Presumably, the States of the debtor's and creditor's domicile may both similarly levy property taxes on intangibles.[9] Net income may be taxed not only by the State in which it is earned or in which the income-

4. See Curry v. McCanless, 307 U.S. 357, 367–68, 59 S.Ct. 900, 906 (1939); cf. Wisconsin v. J.C. Penney Co., 311 U.S. 435, 61 S.Ct. 246 (1940).

5. Curry v. McCanless, 307 U.S. 357, 59 S.Ct. 900 (1939); Graves v. Elliott, 307 U.S. 383, 59 S.Ct. 913 (1939); Citizens' National Bank v. Durr, 257 U.S. 99, 42 S.Ct. 15 (1921); Virginia v. Imperial Coal Co., 293 U.S. 15, 55 S.Ct. 12 (1934); Blodgett v. Silberman, 277 U.S. 1, 48 S.Ct. 410 (1928). Domicile may be a highly elusive and troublesome legal fact to determine. Cf. Texas v. Florida, 306 U.S. 398, 59 S.Ct. 563 (1939); In re Dorrance, 115 N.J.Eq. 268, 170 A. 601 (1934); Dorrance v. Thayer–Martin, 116 N.J.L. 362, 184 A. 743 (1936), cert. denied 298 U.S. 678, 56 S.Ct. 949 (1936); Dorrance's Estate, 309 Pa. 151, 163 A. 303 (1932), cert. denied 287 U.S. 660, 53 S.Ct. 222 (1932), 288 U.S. 617, 53 S.Ct. 507 (1933); see Federa, "Inheritance Taxation After the *Green* Case," 17 Taxes 267 (1939); Tweed & Sargent, "Death and Taxes Are Certain—But What of Domicile," 53 Harv. L.Rev. 68 (1939).

6. Blackstone v. Miller, 188 U.S. 189, 23 S.Ct. 277 (1903); see cases cited supra note 3. But cf. Beidler v. South Carolina Tax Comm., 282 U.S. 1, 51 S.Ct. 54 (1930).

7. Curry v. McCanless, 307 U.S. 357, 59 S.Ct. 900 (1939); Safe Deposit & Trust Co. v. Virginia, 280 U.S. 83, 50 S.Ct. 59 (1929).

8. Gift taxes, which are excises, present similar problems of multiple taxation. Cf. Pearson v. McGraw, 308 U.S. 313, 60 S.Ct. 211 (1939); Van Dyke v. Wisconsin Tax Commission, 235 Wis. 128, 292 N.W. 313 (1940), affirmed per curiam, 311 U.S. 605, 61 S.Ct. 36 (1940). The State in which the gift is made, the domicile of the donor or donee, the State in which the property taxed is located, or has a "situs," or is otherwise protected by the State or subjected to the State's control—all may lay claim to tax. The inheritance and sales tax decisions have been variously suggested as affording the governing principles for State gift tax jurisdiction. See Cahn, "State Gift Tax Jurisdiction," 87 U.Pa.L.Rev. 390, 395 (1939); 54 Harv.L.Rev. 151 (1940).

9. The rationale of the death and personal property tax decisions has been essentially the same. When the situs fiction was used by the Court as the basis for invalidating State taxes, the death and property tax decisions were often cited and relied upon interchangeably. See, e.g., Mr. Justice Hughes' citation of the death tax case of Blackstone v. Miller, 188 U.S. 189, 23 S.Ct. 277 (1903), in the property tax case of Liverpool & L. & G. Ins. Co. v. New Orleans, 221 U.S. 346, 354, 31 S.Ct. 550, 553 (1911), and Mr. Justice McReynolds' citation in the death tax case of Farmers Loan & Trust Co. v. Minnesota, 280 U.S. 204, 208, 50 S.Ct. 98, 99 (1930), of the property tax case of State Tax on Foreign–Held Bonds, 15 Wall. 300, 21 L.Ed. 179 (1872). While Mr. Justice Stone, dissenting in the *Farmers Loan & Trust Co.* case, contended that the property tax cases were inapplicable to an excise tax, the rationale and language used by him in Curry v. McCanless, 307 U.S. 357, 59 S.Ct. 900 (1939), are equally applicable to a property tax case. Moreover, as pointed out by Mr. Justice Holmes in *Blackstone v. Miller*, the value of a debt depends in a large measure upon the creditor's ability to sue and collect from the debtor in the courts of the debtor's State or domicile. Accordingly, it seems likely that Curry v. McCanless, supra, and Graves v. Elliott, 307 U.S. 383, 59 S.Ct. 913 (1939), foreshadow judicial sanction of property taxation of intangibles by the debtor's as well as the creditor's State of domicile.

Taxes on intangibles may also be levied by the State of "commercial domicile" of a corporation, or of "business situs" of the intangibles. First Bank Stock Corp. v. Minnesota, 301 U.S. 234, 57 S.Ct. 677 (1937); Wheeling Steel Corp. v. Fox, 298 U.S. 193, 56 S.Ct. 773 (1936); see Powell, "Business Situs of Tax Credits," 28 W.Va. L.Q. 89 (1922).

producing property is located, but in addition in the State of the recipient's domicile.[10]

However, the Court is apparently unanimous in holding that real property and tangible personal property are taxable under property and under death tax laws only by the States in which they are located.[11]

The view of the present majority, that double taxation is not proscribed by the Fourteenth Amendment but that taxes which may be termed extraterritorial are forbidden, completes a cycle of constitutional history. In 1854, fourteen years *before* the Fourteenth Amendment had been adopted, the Court for the first time invalidated a tax on the ground that the taxing State had no "jurisdiction" of the property taxed.[12] Subsequent decisions, even after the Fourteenth Amendment was adopted in 1868, based similar results upon natural-law conceptions of "jurisdiction" and "situs." [13] It was not until 1903 that the Court announced that the prohibition of extraterritorial taxation was grounded upon the Due Process Clause.[14] Nearly three decades more elapsed before the Court's discovery that double taxation was also prohibited.[15] Now that it has been determined that the Due Process Clause does not forbid double taxation, the Court is largely back where it was in 1854, except that extraterritoriality as a basis for invalidation has now been woven into the Fourteenth Amendment.[16]

10. Shaffer v. Carter, 252 U.S. 37, 40 S.Ct. 221 (1920); Travis v. Yale & Towne Mfg. Co., 252 U.S. 60, 40 S.Ct. 228 (1920); Lawrence v. State Tax Comm., 286 U.S. 276, 52 S.Ct. 556 (1932). Compare Guaranty Trust Co. v. Virginia, 305 U.S. 19, 59 S.Ct. 1 (1938), with the dissent in New York ex rel. Cohn v. Graves, 300 U.S. 308, 317, 57 S.Ct. 466, 469 (1937); cf. Maguire v. Trefry, 253 U.S. 12, 40 S.Ct. 417 (1920).

11. See Frick v. Pennsylvania, 268 U.S. 473, 45 S.Ct. 603 (1924); Treichler v. Wisconsin, 338 U.S. 251, 70 S.Ct. 1 (1949) and Professor Bittker's penetrating discussion of "The Taxation of Out-of-State Tangible Property," 56 Yale L.J. 640 (1947).

12. Hays v. Pacific Mail Steamship Co., 17 How. 596, 15 L.Ed. 254 (1854); accord: Morgan v. Parham, 16 Wall. 471, 21 L.Ed. 303 (1872).

13. Railroad Company v. Jackson, 7 Wall. 262, 19 L.Ed. 88 (1868); St. Louis v. The Ferry Co., 11 Wall. 423, 20 L.Ed. 192 (1870); State Tax on Foreign-Held Bonds, 15 Wall. 300, 21 L.Ed. 179 (1872) (extraterritoriality question intertwined with obligations of contracts question); cf. Delaware Railroad Tax, 18 Wall. 206, 21 L.Ed. 888 (1873); Tappan v. Merchants' National Bank, 19 Wall. 490, 22 L.Ed. 189 (1873). These cases all came into the Federal courts not by the avenue of a Federal con-

stitutional question, but through diversity of citizenship.

14. Louisville & J. Ferry Co. v. Kentucky, 188 U.S. 385, 23 S.Ct. 463 (1903); cf. Union Refrigerator Transit Co. v. Kentucky, 199 U.S. 194, 26 S.Ct. 36 (1905); Goodnow, "Congressional Regulation of State Taxation," 28 Pol.Sci.Q. 405 (1913); Lowndes, "Spurious Conceptions of the Constitutional Law of Taxation," 47 Harv. L.Rev. 628 (1934).

15. Farmers Loan & Trust Co. v. Minnesota, 280 U.S. 204, 50 S.Ct. 98 (1930). For an earlier intimation that double taxation might be a ground of invalidity, see Frick v. Pennsylvania, 268 U.S. 473, 489–90, 45 S.Ct. 603, 604 (1925).

16. It is interesting to note the similarity of the conception of extraterritoriality as the basis for invalidating taxes under the Due Process Clause and the requirement of apportionment as the prerequisite of validation under the Commerce Clause. Both simmer down to essentially the same result, namely, that a State can tax only what is "justly attributable" to it. Under both clauses, the judgment of what is "justly attributable" to a State is made by the Court. Cf. Wisconsin v. J.C. Penney Co., 311 U.S. 435, 61 S.Ct. 246 (1940).

In the course of this cycle of judicial history, the original concepts of "jurisdiction" and "situs," as the basis for the power to tax, have been refined by the introduction of notions of "protection" and "control." Although these new notions have had a liberalizing effect on the States' power of taxation, they are vague and fluid conceptions which necessarily leave room for ad hoc judgments as to the social desirability of particular exercises of the taxing power.[17] There seems, however, quite as much difficulty in finding warrant in the Constitution for the present due process restrictions on State taxation as there was for the now rejected prohibition of double taxation.

The competing claims of two or more States to tax the same economic interest may require some mediating agency adequate to resolve the conflict or alleviate the burden of cumulative taxes. There are adequate constitutional resources which can be utilized to cope with the problem, without reading into the Due Process Clause a restriction on the State taxing power which the provision does not justify.[18]

SECTION 2.   TAXATION OF TANGIBLE PROPERTY

Notes and Problems

A. *The Line Between Tangibles and Intangibles.* In Blodgett v. Silberman, 277 U.S. 1, 48 S.Ct. 410 (1928), the Court considered a Connecticut inheritance tax on a resident decedent's property consisting of:

(1) An interest in a New York partnership. The Court held this to be intangible personalty subject to the Connecticut inheritance tax, even though part of the partnership assets consisted of land located in New York.

(2) United States coupon bonds and Treasury certificates deposited in New York. These were held taxable as intangibles.

(3) A savings bank account in New York. This was held to be intangible personalty taxable by Connecticut.

(4) Paper money and silver coin in a safe deposit box in New York.

The paper money and coin were held to be tangible personal property and not subject to inheritance tax by the State of domicile. Chief Justice Taft said:

But we think that money, so definitely fixed and separated in its actual situs from the person of the owner as this was, is tangible property and cannot be distinguished from the paintings and furniture held in the *Frick* case to be taxable only in the jurisdiction where they were. [277 U.S. at 18.]

17. Only a judgment as to social desirability can underlie the view that the State which provides sufficient protection and control to justify taxing its residents on all their *intangibles*, wherever located and employed, does not provide sufficient protection and control to justify taxing them on all their *tangibles* wherever situated. See

A. Harding, Double Taxation of Property and Income 35 et seq. (1933).

18. See J. Hellerstein & Hennefeld, note 1 supra, for a discussion of the use by Congress of its taxing and spending powers along with the commerce power, to deal with these problems.

But cf. Pearson v. McGraw, 308 U.S. 313, 60 S.Ct. 211 (1939) as to paper money. The *Blodgett* case was followed in Thomas v. Virginia, 364 U.S. 443, 81 S.Ct. 229 (1960), where the Court in a brief per curiam decision, with Black, J., dissenting, held that Virginia could not subject to its death tax money owned by a resident decedent but kept in a safe deposit box in the District of Columbia. This case is noted in 46 Minn.L.Rev. 393 (1961).

Are warehouse receipts for personal property tangibles or intangibles? See Selliger v. Kentucky, 213 U.S. 200, 29 S.Ct. 449 (1909). And how are negotiable instruments and stock certificates classified? Compare New Orleans v. Stempel, 175 U.S. 309, 20 S.Ct. 110 (1899), with Greenough v. Tax Assessors of City of Newport, p. 861, infra.

B. *Degree of Permanence of Location of Personal Property in the State.* A New York statute taxes as real property trailers or mobile homes located within a local taxing district for 60 days or more. N.Y. Real Prop. Tax Law § 102.12(g), CCH ¶ 91–933, P–H ¶ 32,101.60. In New York State Trailer Coach Ass'n v. Steckel, 208 Misc. 308, 144 N.Y.S.2d 82 (Monroe Co.1955), a trial court held the provision unconstitutional on the ground that the 60–day provision does not establish the requisite permanence of location to permit taxation by the State. The decision was reversed but on procedural grounds. 3 A.D.2d 643, 158 N.Y.S.2d 179 (1956). Accord: Barnes v. Gorham, 12 Misc.2d 285, 175 N.Y.S.2d 376 (Onondaga Co.1957). For cases upholding the validity of the statute, see Mobile Homes Ass'n v. Steckel, 12 Misc.2d 761, 176 N.Y.S.2d 482 (Monroe Co.1958) and cases there cited, modified on procedural grounds, 11 A.D.2d 751, 201 N.Y.S.2d 595 (1960). See also Chapter 5, § 1 supra.

C. Are land trust certificates, which entitle the holder to participate in rents and in the proceeds in case of sale, interests in real property or intangibles for property tax purposes? In Senior v. Braden, 295 U.S. 422, 55 S.Ct. 800 (1935), the Court held, with Justices Stone, Brandeis, and Cardozo dissenting, that such certificates represented interests in real property and hence were not taxable to a resident under an ad valorem tax where the land was located outside the State. In Security Trust Co. v. Department of Revenue, 263 S.W.2d 130 (Ky.1953), it was held that such interests constitute intangible personalty and are subject to both property and death taxes when held by a person domiciled in the State, even though the underlying property is located outside the State. The court declared that:

> the holders of the certificates are clothed with none of the legal incidents of ownership. The rights which they hold are in personam, enforceable against the trustee, rather than in rem against the trust property. As pointed out in the dissenting opinion of Mr. Justice Stone in Senior v. Braden, supra, the holder of the certificate in every practical aspect stands in the same relationship to the land as the stockholder of a land-owning corporation. [263 S.W.2d at 132.]

Where a beneficiary of a trust in Illinois land possesses all the attributes of the owner of a fee, except the power to sign instruments of conveyance, but has the power to direct conveyance of the fee by the trustee, his interest was in the out-of-state land and not subject to Michigan inheritance tax. In re Stahl's Estate, 334 Mich. 380, 54 N.W.2d 691 (1952).

D. *Equitable Conversion.* Does the doctrine of equitable conversion of real property affect the power of the States to impose death taxes? Suppose a resident of Pennsylvania devises his out-of-state realty to his executor with instructions to sell. Is this an equitable conversion by will which gives Pennsylvania the power to tax? See Matter of Estate of Swift, 137 N.Y. 77, 32 N.E. 1096 (1893). Or suppose T, before his death, had entered into a contract to sell the out-of-state land. Could Pennsylvania tax? See Paul's Estate, 303 Pa. 330, 154 A. 503 (1931), certiorari denied 284 U.S. 630, 52 S.Ct. 13 (1931); Ryan's Estate, 102 N.W.2d 9 (N.D.1960), discussed in Note, "Effect of Equitable Conversion on Inheritance Taxation," 36 N.D.L.Rev. 185 (1960); Matter of Estate of Plasterer, 149 Wash. 333, 301 P.2d 539 (1956), discussed in 32 Wash.L.Rev. 127 (1957).

E. *References.* See Bittker, "The Taxation of Out–of–State Tangible Property," 56 Yale L.J. 640 (1947), for a highly provocative piece of skepticism as to the justification for the well-entrenched view that tangibles and real estate are taxable only by the State in which they are more or less permanently located. See also Guterman, "Revitalization of Multiple State Death Taxation," 42 Col.L.Rev. 1249 (1942); Note, "Jurisdiction to Tax Tangible Personal Property," 44 Iowa L.Rev. 412 (1959).

SECTION 3. THE TAXATION OF INTANGIBLES

(a) The Doctrines of "Commercial Domicile" and "Business Situs"

WHEELING STEEL CORPORATION v. FOX

Supreme Court of the United States, 1936.
298 U.S. 193, 56 S.Ct. 773.

MR. CHIEF JUSTICE HUGHES delivered the opinion of the Court.*

This appeal presents the question of the validity of an ad valorem property tax laid by West Virginia upon accounts receivable and bank deposits of appellant, Wheeling Steel Corporation, organized under the laws of Delaware.

* * *

The case was submitted upon agreed statements which disclosed the following facts: The Corporation maintains its principal office in Delaware through the Corporation Service Company, as permitted by the laws of that State. It keeps there a duplicate stock ledger and records of all transactions with respect to its capital stock, the originals of such ledger and records being kept in New York City. It files reports and pays franchise taxes as required by Delaware.

The general business offices of the Corporation are located in Wheeling, Ohio County, West Virginia. There, the general books and accounting records are kept. The chairman of the board, president, treasurer, secretary and chief counsel reside at Wheeling. There, its stockholders' and directors' meetings, as permitted by the laws of Delaware, are held. Dividends, when declared, are ordered to be paid

---

* [Some footnotes have been omitted.]

and distributed at meetings held at Wheeling, although the checks are drawn and distributed by the dividend disbursing agent located in New York City and are paid with funds there deposited.

The Corporation maintains sales offices in various cities of the United States. Sales contracts are negotiated and orders are taken by these offices subject to acceptance or rejection at Wheeling.

The principal manufacturing plants of the Corporation are located in the State of Ohio. The plant offices maintain original detailed accounting records showing materials received, railroad cars received and shipped, detailed labor costs, production and shipments, and detailed stocks of goods and payrolls. Employment offices are maintained at each plant. The Portsmouth, Ohio, plant makes up and mails out invoices for all products shipped from that plant, together with bills of lading and shipping notices. The other plants prepare complete invoices with exception of information relating to the price of materials described. The latter invoices are then forwarded to Wheeling where they are completed and mailed to the customer. Bills of lading and shipping notices are, however, mailed to customers from the individual plants. All invoices are payable in Wheeling. The majority of commercial accounts are paid by check issued at Wheeling. Payrolls are made up and payroll checks are prepared and signed at the various plants and are there distributed to the employees. Such checks are paid with funds on deposit in banks in the localities where the plants are situated.

The Corporation owns vessels operating on the Allegheny, Ohio and Mississippi Rivers, transporting coal and steel. These vessels are registered at the port of Pittsburgh.

The total assessed value of the real estate and tangible personal property owned by the Corporation on January 1, 1933, was $31,977,600. The assessed value of its real estate and tangible personal property in West Virginia was $8,673,205, or 27.10 per cent of the total.

At least 80 per cent of the sums spent by the Corporation in the conduct of its business, including the purchase of materials, maintenance and repairs of plants, building of improvements, property additions, payrolls and other operating expenses were made in connection with the operation of its plants and business outside the State of West Virginia and all such payments, aside from moneys borrowed, were made from the proceeds of sales of its products. The moneys thus expended in the conduct of its business in Ohio and States other than West Virginia are expended by executive action taken at Wheeling, and by the drawing of checks or drafts at that place, except in connection with the payment of payrolls at its Portsmouth, Ohio, and Steubenville, Ohio, plants, where payroll checks or orders are drawn against moneys sent to banks at those points for the express purpose of meeting the payrolls and for incidental items as they arise. All moneys are controlled and the expenditures directed by the Wheeling office, and if the immediate expenditure be made elsewhere, it is made only under specific or general direction and control of that office.

On January 1, 1933, the Corporation had on deposit to its credit in various banks the sum of $2,307,773.61, of which $849,161.99 was on deposit in West Virginia. Of the last mentioned amount the Corporation had received $121,684.91 from sales of goods manufactured in West Virginia and the remainder from sales of goods manufactured in, and shipped from, points outside that State. The money on deposit in banks outside West Virginia on January 1, 1933, had been deposited by the Corporation by sending from its Wheeling office the original checks or drafts received from its customers. The deposits outside West Virginia are not segregated for the purpose of keeping separately the receipts from sales of products manufactured in, and shipped from, West Virginia plants. Ordinarily not more than 20 per cent of the total amounts on deposit at any time within and without West Virginia have been derived from sales of products manufactured in that State.

The total amount of the Corporation's accounts and notes receivable on January 1, 1933, was $2,234,743.11. Of this amount, $374,410.42 were receivables for goods sold and manufactured in, and shipped from, West Virginia to resident and non-resident purchasers. It appeared that the Corporation had been assessed in Ohio, as of January 1, 1933, on accounts and notes receivable amounting to $250,133.42.

The Supreme Court of Appeals of West Virginia held that there had been "such a localization of the corporation's business at Wheeling" that there was imparted "to its entire intangible property a prima facie situs for taxation at that place." But the court thought that the "statutory limitation of the assessment of property 'liable to taxation'" indicated that the legislature "did not propose to tax intangibles which were primarily subject to taxation in another jurisdiction." And referring to the above mentioned taxation in Ohio, the Supreme Court of Appeals said: "For the purposes of this opinion, we assume that the claim of our sister state is well founded, and should be deducted from the assessment as corrected by the Tax Commissioner." And in remanding the cause to the Circuit Court, the Supreme Court of Appeals gave opportunity to have it determined "whether or not further deductions should be made in deference to the legal demands of other states." In the further proceeding in the Circuit Court, it was stipulated that "no states other than Ohio and West Virginia have assessed taxpayer upon any of its intangibles for the year 1933."

First.—The tax is not a privilege or occupation tax. It is not a tax on net income. See Hans Rees' Sons v. North Carolina, 283 U.S. 123, 133, 51 S.Ct. 385. It is an ad valorem property tax. We have held that it is essential to the validity of such a tax, under the due process clause, that the property shall be within the territorial jurisdiction of the taxing State. This rule receives its most familiar illustration in the case of land. The rule has been extended to tangible personal property which is thus subject to taxation exclusively in the State where it is permanently located, regardless of the domicile of the owner. Union Refrigerator Transit Co. v. Kentucky, 199 U.S. 194, 204, 206, 26 S.Ct. 36; Frick v. Pennsylvania, 268 U.S. 473, 489, 45 S.Ct. 603. We have said that the application to the States of the rule of due process arises from the fact "that their spheres of activity are enforced and protected by the Constitution and therefore it is impossible for one State to reach out and tax property in another without violating the Constitution." United States v. Bennett, 232 U.S. 299, 306, 34 S.Ct. 433. Compare Burnet v. Brooks, 288 U.S. 378, 401, 53 S.Ct. 457. When we deal with intangible property such as credits and choses in action generally, we encounter the difficulty that by reason of the absence of physical characteristics they have no situs in the physical sense, but have the situs attributable to them in legal conception. Accordingly we have held that a State may properly apply the rule mobilia sequuntur personam and treat them as localized at the owner's domicile for purposes of taxation. Farmers Loan & Trust Co. v. Minnesota, 280 U.S. 204, 211, 50 S.Ct. 98. And having thus determined "that in general intangibles may be properly taxed at the domicile of their owner," we have found "no sufficient reason for saying that they are not entitled to enjoy an immunity against taxation at more than one place similar to that accorded to tangibles." Id., p. 212. The principle thus announced in Farmers Loan & Trust Co. v. Minnesota has had progressive application. Baldwin v. Missouri, 280 U.S. 586, 50 S.Ct. 436; Beidler v. South Carolina Tax Commission, 282 U.S. 1, 51 S.Ct. 54; First National Bank v. Maine, 284 U.S. 312, 328, 329, 52 S.Ct. 174. But despite the wide application of the principle, an important exception has been recognized.

In the case of tangible property, the ancient maxim, which had its origin when personal property consisted in the main of articles appertaining to the person of the owner, yielded in modern times to the "law of the place where the property is kept and used." First National Bank v. Maine, supra. It was in view "of the enormous increase of such property since the introduction of railways and the growth of manufacturers" that it came to be regarded as "having a situs of its own for the purpose of taxation, and correlatively to exempt at the domicile of its owner." Union Transit Refrigerator Co. v. Kentucky, supra, p. 207. There has been an analogous development in connection with intangible property by reason of the creation of choses in action in the conduct by an owner of his business in a State different from that of his domicile. New Orleans v. Stempel, 175 U.S. 309, 20 S.Ct. 110; Bristol v. Washington County, 177 U.S. 133, 20 S.Ct. 585; Board of Assessors v. Comptoir National, 191 U.S. 388, 24 S.Ct. 109; Metropolitan Life Insurance Co. v. New Orleans, 205 U.S. 395, 27 S.Ct. 499; Liverpool & L. & G. Insurance Co. v. New Orleans, 221 U.S. 346, 31 S.Ct. 550.

These cases, we said in Farmers Loan & Trust Co. v. Minnesota, supra, p. 213, "recognize the principle that choses in action may acquire a situs for taxation other than at the domicile of their owner if they have become integral parts of some local business." We adverted to this reservation in Beidler v. South Carolina Tax Commission, supra, p. 8, and in First National Bank v. Maine, supra, p. 331.

In the instant case, both parties recognize the principle and the exception. It is appellant's contention that the State creating a corporation has the sole right to tax its intangible property "unless such intangible property has acquired a 'business situs' elsewhere." Counsel for the State agrees with appellant on this point and in fact asserts "that, generally, the taxable situs of accounts receivable and of money in bank is at the domicile of the owner." But the State insists that the accounts receivable and bank deposits of the Wheeling Steel Corporation had acquired a taxable situs in West Virginia and that they have no taxable situs in Delaware, where the Corporation was chartered.

Second.—The Corporation complied with the laws of the State of its creation in designating its "principal" office in that State. It is manifest that this designation, while presumably sufficient for the purpose, was a technical one and that the office is not a principal office so far as the actual conduct of business is concerned. While a duplicate stock ledger and records of transactions with respect to capital stock are maintained in Delaware, the business operations of the Corporation are conducted outside that State. The office in Delaware is maintained through the service of an agency organized to furnish this convenience to corporations of that description. To attribute to Delaware, merely as the chartering State, the credits arising in the course of the business established in another State, and to deny to the latter the power to tax such credits upon the ground that it violates due process to treat the credits as within its jurisdiction, is to make a legal fiction dominate realities in a fashion quite as extreme as that which would attribute to the chartering State all the tangible possessions of the Corporation without regard to their actual location.

The constitutional authority of West Virginia to tax the accounts receivable and bank deposits in question cannot be denied upon the ground that they are taxable solely in Delaware. The question is whether they should be deemed to be localized in West Virginia.

Third.—The Corporation established in West Virginia what has aptly been termed a "commercial domicile." It maintains its general business offices at Wheeling and there it keeps its books and accounting records. There its directors hold their meetings and its officers conduct the affairs of the Corporation. There, as appellant's counsel well says, "the management functioned." The Corporation has manufacturing plants and sales offices in other States. But what is done at those plants and offices is determined and controlled from the center of authority at Wheeling. The Corporation has made that the actual seat of its corporate government.

The question here is not of the taxation of the plants in other States. The real estate, equipment and all tangible property there located is taxable by those States respectively. The accounts receivable with which we are now concerned are the proceeds of contracts of sale.

While these contracts are negotiated and orders are taken at the various sales offices throughout the country, they are subject to acceptance or rejection at the Wheeling office. All invoices are payable at Wheeling. Thus the contracts of sale become effective by the action taken at the Wheeling office and there the accounts are kept and the required payments are made. In the face of these facts, it cannot properly be said that the credits arise either where the goods are manufactured or at the sales offices where the orders are taken. The tax is not on the manufacturing or on the privilege of maintaining sales offices. The tax is not on the net profits of a unitary enterprise demanding a method, not intrinsically arbitrary, of making an apportionment among different jurisdictions with respect to the processes by which the profits are earned. Underwood Typewriter Company v. Chamberlain, 254 U.S. 113, 120, 121, 41 S.Ct. 45; Bass, Ratcliff & Gretton, Ltd. v. State Tax Commission, 266 U.S. 271, 282, 283, 45 S.Ct. 82; Hans Rees' Sons v. North Carolina, supra. Such a tax on net gains is distinct from an ad valorem property tax on the various items of property owned by the Corporation and laid according to the location of the property within the respective tax jurisdictions. Here, the tax is a property tax on the accounts receivable, as separate items of property, and these are not to be regarded as parts of the manufacturing plants where the goods sold are produced.

Hence we cannot agree with appellant's counsel that the only fair rule in such a case is one "which allocates intangibles on the basis of tangible property owned and used in production of material for sale." This is to confuse two distinct subjects of ad valorem property taxation, the accounts receivable which arise from sales and the manufacturing plants. The accounts are not necessarily localized in whole or in part where the goods are made but are attributable as choses in action to the place where they arise in the course of the business of making contracts of sale. We said, in Virginia v. Imperial Coal Sales Co., 293 U.S. 15, 20, 55 S.Ct. 12, that we were not able to perceive "any sound reason for holding that the owner must have real estate or tangible property within the State in order to subject its intangible property within the State to taxation."

The tax is laid both on accounts receivable and on the amount of deposits in banks. It appears that the Corporation has deposit accounts in several States. The deposits outside West Virginia were made by sending from the Wheeling office to the various banks the original checks or drafts received by the Corporation from its customers. From these deposit accounts the Corporation, by executive action at Wheeling, pays the amounts required for payrolls, materials, equipment, maintenance and operating expenses as these amounts become payable in the course of its operations in Ohio and other States. Checks and drafts on these bank accounts are drawn at Wheeling, except in connection with the payment of payrolls at certain manufacturing plants where payroll checks or orders are drawn against moneys sent to banks at such points for that express purpose and for meeting incidental items. The agreed statement shows that "All moneys are controlled and the expenditures directed by the Wheeling office, and if the immediate expenditure be made elsewhere, such immediate expenditure is made only under specific or general direction and control of the Wheeling office." The so-called "money in bank" is not cash or physical property of the Corporation but is an indebtedness owing by the bank to the Corporation by virtue of the deposit account. From the Wheeling office proceed the items deposited and there the withdrawals are directed and controlled. In the light of this course of business as shown by the agreed statement of fact, we find no sufficient basis for concluding that the bank accounts thus maintained and controlled were properly attributable to the Corporation at any place other than at its general office at Wheeling. If there were any special circumstances by which any of these deposits could be deemed to have been localized elsewhere, they do not appear upon the present record.

*   *   *

Our conclusion is that appellant has failed to show that West Virginia in laying the tax has transcended the limits of its jurisdiction and thus deprived appellant of its property without due process of law.

*   *   *

The judgment of the state court is affirmed.

Affirmed.*

Notes and Problems

A. *Power of State of Corporate Domicile to Tax Intangibles That Have Acquired "Business Situs" Elsewhere.* ** The principal case implies, though it does not hold, that Delaware could not have taxed the intangibles in controversy. Standard Oil Co. v. Commonwealth of Kentucky, 311 S.W.2d 372 (Ky.1958), deals with a similar issue under an ad valorem property tax. The taxpayer, a Kentucky corporation, had its home office in Louisville and was engaged in marketing petroleum products in Kentucky and four neighboring States. It engaged in no refining or production; it bought from producers outside Kentucky oil and other products, which were shipped directly to the market States by the supplier; only the products to be sold in Kentucky came into that State. The business in each State was managed by a division manager and a local staff; collections were made in each State and deposits made in local banks. All local expenses were paid out of local collections, but at periodic intervals unneeded balances were sent by the division manager to the home office in Louisville by check drawn on the local banks. The issue in the case was whether Kentucky could levy a property tax on the bank deposits in the out-of-state banks and on notes and accounts receivable derived from the out-of-state business.

* [Noted in 21 St. Louis L.Rev. 356 (1936); 85 U.Pa.L.Rev. 121 (1936); 21 Minn.L.Rev. 114 (1936); 15 Texas L.Rev. 130 (1936); and 35 Mich.L.Rev. 1032 (1937).]

** [For a consideration of the constitutional aspects of the apportionment and allocation of income from intangibles, see Chapter 9, § 11 supra.]

It was apparently conceded—and held by the court—that "the taxpayer's accounts receivable and notes have a commercial, legal and taxable situs" in each of the four out-of-Kentucky States. Two of the States—Florida and Georgia—had actually taxed the intangibles there held; the other two—Alabama and Mississippi—do not tax such intangibles. The Kentucky court interpreted the *Wheeling Steel* case as holding that the Due Process Clause prevented Kentucky, the State of incorporation and here the seat of the corporate executive offices, from taxing intangibles which had acquired a taxable "situs" elsewhere and, accordingly, set aside the levy. The case is noted in 44 Iowa L.Rev. 443 (1959).

Does the *Wheeling Steel* case justify this holding? While there is an intimation in that case that the taxing powers of the State of corporate domicile are divested and acquired by the State of commercial domicile where there is only a statutory office in the State of incorporation, would a similar result follow where the State of corporate domicile is the active executive seat of the corporation? Is the court confusing "commercial domicile" with "business situs"? Here the intangibles acquired a "business situs" outside Kentucky, but the executive and corporate seat remained in Kentucky. Is the court in effect seeking to reestablish the doctrine repudiated by the Supreme Court that double taxation is prohibited by the Due Process Clause? If the Due Process issue depends upon connection with the taxing State, the benefits derived by the taxpayer, and the taxing State's powers over them, does not Kentucky have adequate basis for taxation?

In a subsequent decision, the Kentucky court reiterated the view that "Kentucky could not levy a direct ad valorem tax on intangible property of a Kentucky corporation doing business in Kentucky and other states when the intangibles had a foreign business situs," Kentucky Department of Revenue v. Bomar, 486 S.W.2d 532, 533 n. 4 (Ky.1972), but it also observed that taxation by another State would not, in and of itself, prevent Kentucky from taxing the intangible property in question. Id. at 533 n. 1. In the *Bomar* case, the court held that the intangible property at issue—a trust corpus managed in Georgia for the benefit of a Kentucky resident—had never acquired a foreign business situs because "control of the intangibles was never ' * * * localized in some independent business or investment away from the owner's domicile so that its substantial use and value primarily attached to and (became) an asset of the outside business.' " Id. at 536 (quoting Grieves v. State, 168 Okl. 642, 35 P.2d 454 (1934)). Accord Humpage v. Robards, 229 Kan. 461, 625 P.2d 469 (1981).

Compare the Kentucky court's decision in Standard Oil Co. v. Commonwealth of Kentucky, supra, with Cream of Wheat Co. v. Grand Forks, 253 U.S. 325, 40 S.Ct. 558 (1920). In *Cream of Wheat,* the Supreme Court upheld North Dakota's right to tax all of the intangible property of a corporation domiciled in the State, and observed that "[t]he view we take of the matter renders it unnecessary to consider the question whether or not the law under discussion imposed a franchise tax or a property tax." 253 U.S. at 328. The court in *Standard Oil* misunderstood the Court's holding in *Cream of Wheat,* characterizing the Supreme Court's decision as having distinguished a corporate franchise tax measured by intangibles from a direct property tax on the intangibles. Standard Oil Co. v. Commonwealth of Kentucky, supra, 311 S.W.2d at 376. See also Chicago, Duluth & Georgian Bay Transit Co. v. Michigan Corp. & Sec. Com'n, 319 Mich. 14, 29 N.W.2d 303 (1947). Is the distinction between a corporate privilege tax measured by intangibles outside the State and a direct property tax on such intangibles a sound one?

In Florida Steel Corp. v. Dickinson, 308 So.2d 623 (Fla.App.1975), the court sustained a property tax on accounts receivable of a domestic corporation, arising from sales of the taxpayer's products which had been manufactured at, and shipped from, its plants outside Florida, saying:

> The final question now remaining is: Does this taxation by Florida of accounts receivable owned by its domiciled corporations, which have been taxed by other states, result in an unlawful burden on interstate commerce so as to violate Article I, Section 8, of the Florida Constitution and the Fourteenth Amendment of the Constitution of the United States? Intangibles have always been considered valuable property rights which, through a fiction of the law, were taxed to the domicile of the owner. * * * As corporations passed from frailing infants to sprawling multistate and multinational giants which affected business life and drew economic wealth from states and nations other than their legal home, legislatures and courts recognized that to allow only the state of incorporation to tax the intangibles of the corporation was an anachronism of the economic life of America.[5] Legislatures and courts began to look to the realities of today's economic life, and states in which corporations had acquired what is termed a "business situs" other than the domiciliary state were allowed to place a tax on the corporations' intangibles. The idea being that these foreign corporations were participating in the benefits and protection of the sovereign's power, and thus should contribute their fair share to the cost of government.[6] The taxation of accounts receivable by a state in which a corporation has acquired a business situs does not preclude the corporation domiciliary state from also levying an intangible tax on accounts receivable, as a corporation must pay its share of the cost of government to the sovereign from which it derives its very existence.[7] The situation is to be distinguished from tangibles which are only taxable at the site of their locality, as only one sovereign may control them and they may derive benefits and protections from only one sovereign.[8]

Before concluding, we feel compelled to comment as to the arguments of the parties directed to "business situs".

5. United Gas Corp. v. Fontenot, 241 La. 488, 129 So.2d 748 (1961).

6. Curry v. McCanless, 307 U.S. 357, 59 S.Ct. 900, 83 L.Ed. 1339 (1939); and Utah v. Aldrich, 316 U.S. 174, 62 S.Ct. 1008, 86 L.Ed. 1358 (1942).

7. Even though Curry v. McCanless, supra, leaves some doubt as to whether two states may levy a tax on the same intangibles, our reading and understanding of the later case of Utah v. Aldrich, supra, is that such taxing is permissible if both sovereigns provide some benefits and protections.

8. Curry v. McCanless, supra, and Utah v. Aldrich, supra.

As pointed out above, whether Florida Steel has acquired a business situs in North Carolina and Georgia makes no difference as to the outcome of this cause. [308 So.2d at 626, original footnotes and footnote numbering retained.]

The decision was affirmed by the Florida Supreme Court. 328 So.2d 418 (Fla.1976). Accord: National Linen Service Corp. v. Thompson, 103 Ga. App. 786, 120 S.E.2d 779 (1961).

In Newark Fire Insurance Co. v. State Board of Appeals, 307 U.S. 313, 59 S.Ct. 918 (1939), New Jersey assessed a capital stock tax on a domestic corporation, including in its assessment intangible values. The taxpayer contended that the corporation had established a "commercial domicile" in New York and that its intangibles had a "business situs" there. Because they found that such a New York domicile and situs had not been proved, four of the Justices found it unnecessary to consider the problem. Mr. Justice Frankfurter, however, wrote an opinion, concurred in by Justices Stone, Black, and Douglas, which took the position that the State of incorporation may tax since its "taxing power over a corporation of its own creation ＊ ＊ ＊ has neither been restricted nor impaired" by the authorities. Mr. Justice McReynolds, by dissenting, apparently indicated his view that the State of incorporation was without power to tax the intangibles. The case is noted in 8 Geo.Wash.L.Rev. 240 (1939) and 12 Temp.L.Q. 264 (1939).

In Pennsylvania v. Universal Trades, Inc., 392 Pa. 323, 141 A.2d 204 (1958), the court held that Pennsylvania could impose a capital stock tax on a domestic corporation based in part on intangible assets located outside the State which had acquired a "commercial or business situs in Florida," without violating the Due Process Clause.

B. *Accounts Receivable Growing Out of Sales to Local Customers and Other Intangibles.* A foreign corporation maintained a sales office in Atlanta in the charge of a divisional sales manager, through which its soap business was conducted with wholesalers, national chains, and 600–700 retail dealers in Georgia. Orders received in Georgia were forwarded to an Indiana office for approval and acceptance. While orders were ordinarily filled from out-of-state plants, an emergency warehouse and stock of goods were maintained in Atlanta from which some orders were filled. In Colgate–Palmolive–Peet v. Davis, 196 Ga. 681, 27 S.E.2d 326 (1943), the issue was whether accounts receivable arising out of the sales to Georgia customers were subject to the State's property tax on intangibles. The court held that because the intangibles were "connected substantially with some business transacted in Georgia by the non-resident owner," they have a "tax situs" in the State and are, therefore, taxable. In an earlier case, the same court stated that "a debt of a citizen of this State owned by a non-resident and held at his domicile outside of this State is taxable in this State if it accrues out of or is an incident to property owned or a business conducted by the non-resident or his agent in this State." Suttles v. Owen–Illinois Glass Co., 206 Ga. 849, 59 S.E.2d 392, 394 (1950).

A property tax on intangibles of a Virginia corporation operating a pipe line, which transported petroleum in Virginia and other States, was sustained in Colonial Pipe Line Co. v. Commonwealth, 206 Va. 517, 145

S.E.2d 227 (1966), appeal dismissed 384 U.S. 268, 86 S.Ct. 1476 (1966), over the taxpayer's objection that the intangibles were subject to tax only in Georgia, where the corporation had its commercial domicile. The tax as assessed was limited to intangibles allocated to Virginia.

In Allis–Chalmers Credit Corp. v. Department of Revenue, 456 So.2d 899 (Fla.App.1984), petition for review dismissed, 458 So.2d 271 (1984), Florida's power to apply its intangibles tax to loans made to Florida customers by a foreign corporation was upheld. The court found that the loans had acquired a business situs in Florida. The same court had previously sustained the application of Florida's intangibles tax to the accounts receivable of a domestic corporation arising from out-of-State sales. See Florida Steel Corp. v. Dickinson, Note A supra.

In Boise Cascade Corp. v. State, Dept. of Treasury, 88 Mich.App. 626, 278 N.W.2d 699 (1979), an intangible tax imposed on property owned by a non-resident corporation was set aside on the ground that a taxable situs of the intangibles was not established by the fact that income from the intangibles is sent to Michigan for the use in the taxpayer's Michigan operations. See Saxe, "Taxation of Intangibles in Interstate Commerce," 1960 Nat. Tax Ass'n Procs. 177.

C. *Taxation of Bonds Held by a Non–Resident Creditor and Secured by Property in the State.* A Delaware corporation having its principal place of business and owning real property in Florida issued to a New York corporation bonds secured by the Florida realty. The loan was negotiated and the bonds were delivered outside Florida. The bonds were not held or used in any business in Florida by the creditor, which did, however, conduct an insurance business in that State. The Florida statute imposes an annual tax on intangibles. A three mill rate was applicable to indebtedness secured by realty in the State. In practice, no effort was made by the Florida tax collector to collect the tax on mortgaged indebtedness, except at the time the mortgage is recorded.

In earlier decisions the Florida Supreme Court had held that the tax was not an excise on the recording of a mortgage, but instead an ad valorem tax on intangibles, and that it could not be applied to non-residents because intangibles are taxable only at the owner's domicile. State ex rel. Seaboard Airline Railroad v. Gay, 160 Fla. 445, 35 So.2d 403 (1948); State ex rel. Tampa Electric Co. v. Gay, 40 So.2d 225 (Fla.1949). In State ex rel. U.S. Sugar Corp. v. Gay, 46 So.2d 165 (Fla.1950), noted in 3 U. of Fla.L.Rev. 250 (1950), this position was reversed and the court held that the State is within its constitutional powers in taxing a note secured by Florida real estate because of the benefits and protection afforded the obligation through the lien safeguard resulting from the recording of the mortgage in Florida. See also Kelly v. Bastedo, 70 Ariz. 371, 220 P.2d 1069 (1950).

The Mississippi statute provides that "[b]usiness income derived from intangible property of any kind or nature shall be treated as income from sources within this state if the evidence of ownership of such property has acquired a business, commercial, or actual situs in this state." Miss.Code Ann. § 27–7–23, CCH ¶ 92–532, P–H ¶ 12,254–K.24. The State Tax Commission interpreted the forerunner of this provision as meaning that "promissory notes secured by real property in this state when transferred to a non-resident owner had the effect of transmitting the source of income to the non-resident's state," unless the owner maintained a "business situs in the state." Such a business situs "required a degree of permanence evidenced by offices, agents, bank accounts or some such symbol." Brady v. John Hancock Mutual Life Ins. Co., 342 So.2d 295, 301–02 (Miss.1977). The Mississippi Supreme Court rejected this construction in a case involving a foreign insurance company which engaged in a substantial insurance business in Mississippi and made to local residents substantial loans secured by mortgages on real property in the State. The loans were handled through an unaffiliated local company. Although all the notes, deeds of trust or mortgages were held by the insurer at its home office in Massachusetts, the court concluded that the "evidence of ownership" of the interest-bearing obligations had "acquired a business situs within the state," because the mortgages and deeds of trust were recorded in the State and grew out of the commercial operations carried on by the insurer in the State. Id. at 304.

Whatever may be said of this tortured construction of the archaic Mississippi provision, which appeared to make the taxation of interest turn on the place where the taxpayer chose to keep its notes, mortgages, and the like and constituted an open invitation to tax avoidance by sending the documents outside the State, the result appears sound.

As an economic matter, a non-resident who invests in bonds of a business in the State or makes mortgage loans secured by property in the State has a stake in that State's wealth, laws, courts, and government. Should not traditional notions of "situs" yield to the increasing displacement of locally owned and locally financed proprietorships and small corporations by large corporations owned throughout the land and financed by widely scattered investors in bonds? If the economic owners of modern businesses are to bear their fair share of the local tax burden, should not the States in which the businesses and property are located and the income is earned be allowed to impose levies on corporate securities held by non-resident owners? The Georgia courts appear to be sympathetic to this general view, although some "minimum connection" of the non-resident, in addition to loans to residents and the recording of security, has been found to exist in the cases in which the tax has been sustained. See Columbia Bank for Cooperatives v. Blackmon, 232 Ga. 344, 206 S.E.2d 424 (1974), and Note B supra.

D. *"Business Situs" of Capital Stock.* In First Bank Stock Corp. v. Minnesota, 301 U.S. 234, 57 S.Ct. 677, 113 A.L.R. 228 (1937), noted in 22 Minn.L.Rev. 121 (1937), a Delaware corporation owning stocks in Montana and North Dakota banks and authorized to do business in Minnesota maintained in that State a domestic subsidiary corporation. The subsidiary maintained an accounting and general banking advisory service for the banks controlled by the taxpayer, for which it was paid by the banks. The Court upheld a Minnesota property tax on the taxpayer's Montana and North Dakota bank shares on the theory that the taxpayer "maintains within the state an integrated business of protecting its investment in bank shares, and enhancing their value, by the active exercise of its power of control through stock ownership of its subsidiary banks." The Court found that the taxpayer had a Minnesota "commercial domicile" and that its Montana and North Dakota shares had a "business situs" in Minnesota. The question as to whether Montana and North Dakota could tax the shares of stock was left open.

E. A Missouri corporation dealing in grains for farmer-owned cooperative elevators, with terminals in Nebraska and Missouri, owned certificates of indebtedness which were taxed under the Nebraska ad valorem tax on intangibles. In setting aside the assessment, in Equity Union Grain Co. v. Board of Equalization, 182 Neb. 182, 153 N.W.2d 741 (1967), the court said:

> In the present instance, plaintiff maintains and operates a separate business at the place of its incorporation in Missouri, and another in Denver, Colorado, as well as one in Lancaster County, Nebraska. The Kansas City Terminal Elevator Co., which issued the certificates of indebtedness in question, was purchased and is owned by plaintiff and its associate, Missouri Farmers Association, is located in Kansas City, Missouri, and is operated in connection with the business of the plaintiff at its Missouri office completely independent of the Lincoln office. The certificates of indebtedness, which are used as evidence of ownership, are subject to taxation in Missouri, are clearly an adjunct of the Missouri branch of plaintiff's business, having no situs for any purpose in Nebraska, and are not subject to taxation therein. [153 N.W.2d at 743.]

F. A Boston member of the New York Stock Exchange, not doing business in New York, sold a "right" to one fourth of a new seat on the Exchange. Did this right have a "business situs" in New York, warranting a tax by that State on the proceeds of the sale? See New York ex rel. Whitney v. Graves, 299 U.S. 366, 57 S.Ct. 237 (1937), discussed in 50 Harv. L.Rev. 704 (1937).

G. *Utilization of Business Situs Doctrine in Capital Stock Allocation.* A Michigan corporate franchise tax, which was a capital stock tax allocated on the basis of the property located, used, or owned in the State, provided that "in determining the amount or value of intangible property, including capital investments, owned or used in this state by either a domestic or foreign corporation, such property shall be considered to be located, owned or used in this state for the purposes hereof, if used in or acquired from the conduct of its business in this state, irrespective of the domicile of the corporation." In Udylite Corporation v. Corporation and Securities Commission, 319 Mich. 1, 29 N.W.2d 132 (1947), a Delaware corporation maintained its manufacturing facilities and its principal office in Michigan. Offices and warehouses were also maintained in other States to facilitate the conduct of its national business. The issue was whether the corporation's intangibles, consisting of United States Treasury notes, shares of stock in a foreign subsidiary, and a post-war refund of excess profits taxes, were includible in the measure of the tax as property "located, used or owned" in Michigan. The court concluded that this statute embodied both the "commercial domicile" and "business situs" rules, that the corporation had its commercial domicile in Michigan, and that the intangibles in dispute had a business situs in the State. It quoted the distinction offered by counsel between the two doctrines as follows:

> a commercial domicile may be established in a State other than the State of incorporation if the corporation makes its chief place of business in such other State. * * * a business situs as to a corporation's intangibles in a State other than the State of incorporation arises only if such intangibles are acquired from or used in the business of the corporation in such other State. [319 Mich. at 9–10, 29 N.W.2d at 136.]

References. Glander & Dewey, "Taxation of Accounts Receivable in Ohio: Impact of Constitutional Limitations," 11 Ohio St.L.J. 173 (1950); J. Hellerstein, "Federal Constitutional Limitations on State Taxation of Multistate Banks," Report of Study under P.L. 91–156, "State and Local Taxation of Banks," App. 11, prepared by Board of Governors, Federal Reserve System, Senate Committee on Banking, Housing & Urban Affairs (92nd Cong. 1st Sess., 1971).

(b) Death Taxes on Intangibles Under the Due Process Clause

CURRY v. McCANLESS

Supreme Court of the United States, 1939.
307 U.S. 357, 59 S.Ct. 900, 123 A.L.R. 162.

MR. JUSTICE STONE delivered the opinion of the Court.*

The questions for decision are whether the States of Alabama and Tennessee may each constitutionally impose death taxes upon the transfer of an interest in intangibles held in trust by an Alabama trustee but passing under the will of a beneficiary decedent domiciled in Tennessee; and which of the two states may tax in the event that it is determined that only one state may constitutionally impose the tax.

Decedent, a domiciled resident of Tennessee, by trust indenture transferred certain stocks and bonds upon specified trusts to Title Guarantee Loan & Trust Company, an Alabama corporation doing business in that state. So far as now material, the indenture provided that the net income of the trust property should be paid over to decedent during her lifetime. She reserved the power to remove the trustee and substitute another, which was never done; the power to direct the sale of the trust property and the investment of the proceeds; and the power to dispose of the trust estate by her last will and testament, in which event it was to be "handled and disposed of as directed" in her will. The indenture provided further that in default of disposition by will the property was to be held in trust for the benefit of her husband, son, and daughter. Until decedent's death the trust was administered by the trust company in Alabama and the paper evidences of the intangibles held by the trustee were at all times located in Alabama.

* [Some of the Court's footnotes have been omitted.]

By her last will and testament decedent bequeathed the trust property to the trust company in trust for the benefit of her husband, son, and daughter, in different amounts and by different estates from those provided for by the trust indenture, with remainder interests over to the children of the son and the daughter respectively, and to his wife and her husband. By her will testatrix appointed a Tennessee trust company executor "as to all property which I may own in the State of Tennessee at the time of my death," and an Alabama trust company executor "as to all property which I may own in the State of Alabama and also as to all property which I may have the right to dispose of by last will and testament in said state." The will has been probated in Tennessee and in Alabama, and letters testamentary have issued to the two trust companies named as executors in the will.

[Suit for a declaratory judgment was brought by the executors of the estate in the Tennessee Chancery Court against both the Alabama and Tennessee taxing authorities, who appeared in the proceeding. Alabama had assessed an inheritance tax on the trust property. Tennessee had not yet assessed but it asserted the right to levy a transfer tax.]

The doctrine, of recent origin, that the Fourteenth Amendment precludes the taxation of any interest in the same intangible in more than one state has received support to the limited extent that it was applied in Farmers Loan & Trust Co. v. Minnesota, 280 U.S. 204, 50 S.Ct. 98; Baldwin v. Missouri, 281 U.S. 586, 50 S.Ct. 436; First National Bank v. Maine, 284 U.S. 312, 52 S.Ct. 174. Still more recently this Court has declined to give it completely logical application.[1] It has never been pressed to the extreme now urged upon us, and we think that neither reason nor authority requires its acceptance in the circumstances of the present case.

That rights in tangibles—land and chattels—are to be regarded in many respects as localized at the place where the tangible itself is located for purposes of the jurisdiction of a court to make disposition of putative rights in them, for purposes of conflict of laws, and for purposes of taxation, is a doctrine generally accepted both in the common law and other legal systems before the adoption of the Fourteenth Amendment and since. Originating, it has been thought, in the tendency of the mind to identify rights with their physical subjects, see Salmond, Jurisprudence (2nd ed.) 398, its survival and the consequent cleavage between the rules of law applicable to tangibles and those relating to intangibles are attributable to the exclusive dominion exerted over the tangibles themselves by the government within whose

1. See, in the case of income taxation, Lawrence v. State Tax Comm'n, 286 U.S. 276, 52 S.Ct. 556; New York ex rel. Cohn v. Graves, 300 U.S. 308, 57 S.Ct. 466; Guaranty Trust Co. v. Virginia, 305 U.S. 19, 59 S.Ct. 1; cf. Senior v. Braden, 295 U.S. 422, 431–432, 55 S.Ct. 800. And in the case of taxation of shares of stock, see Corry v. Baltimore, 196 U.S. 466, 25 S.Ct. 297; First Bank Stock Corp. v. Minnesota, 301 U.S. 234, 239–240, 57 S.Ct. 677; Schuylkill Trust Co. v. Pennsylvania, 302 U.S. 506, 514–516, 58 S.Ct. 295.

territorial limits they are found. * * * The power of government and its agencies to possess and to exclude others from possessing tangibles, and thus to exclude them from enjoying rights in tangibles located within its territory, affords adequate basis for an exclusive taxing jurisdiction. When we speak of the jurisdiction to tax land or chattels as being exclusively in the state where they are physically located, we mean no more than that the benefit and protection of laws enabling the owner to enjoy the fruits of his ownership and the power to reach effectively the interests protected, for the purpose of subjecting them to payment of a tax, are so narrowly restricted to the state in whose territory the physical property is located as to set practical limits to taxation by others. Other states have been said to be without jurisdiction and so without constitutional power to tax tangibles if, because of their location elsewhere, those states can afford no substantial protection to the rights taxed and cannot effectively lay hold of any interest in the property in order to compel payment of the tax. See Union Transit Co. v. Kentucky, 199 U.S. 194, 202, 26 S.Ct. 36; Frick v. Pennsylvania, 268 U.S. 473, 489 et seq., 45 S.Ct. 603.[3]

Very different considerations, both theoretical and practical, apply to the taxation of intangibles, that is, rights which are not related to physical things. Such rights are but relationships between persons, natural or corporate, which the law recognizes by attaching to them certain sanctions enforceable in courts. The power of government over them and the protection which it gives them cannot be exerted through control of a physical thing. They can be made effective only through control over and protection afforded to those persons whose relationships are the origin of the rights. * * * Obviously, as sources of actual or potential wealth—which is an appropriate measure of any tax imposed on ownership or its exercise—they cannot be dissociated from the persons from whose relationships they are derived. These are not in any sense fictions. They are indisputable realities.

3. But there are many legal interests other than conventional ownership which may be created with respect to land of such a character that they may be constitutionally subjected to taxation in states other than that where the land is situated. No one has doubted the constitutional power of a state to tax its domiciled residents on their shares of stock in a foreign corporation whose only property is real estate located elsewhere. Darnell v. Indiana, 226 U.S. 390, 33 S.Ct. 120; Hawley v. Malden, 232 U.S. 1, 34 S.Ct. 201 * * * or to tax a valuable contract for the purchase of land or chattels located in another state, see Citizens National Bank v. Durr, 257 U.S. 99, 108, 42 S.Ct. 15 * * * or to tax a mortgage of real estate located without the state, even though the land affords the only source of payment, see Kirkland v. Hotchkiss, 100 U.S. 491 * * *. Each of these legal interests finds its only economic source in the value of the land, and the rights which are elsewhere subjected to the tax can be brought to their ultimate fruition only through some means of control of the land itself. But the means of control may be subjected to taxation in the state of its owner whether it be a share of stock or a contract or a mortgage. There is no want of jurisdiction to tax these interests where they are owned in the sense that the state lacks power to appropriate them to the payment of the tax. No court has condemned such action as so capricious, arbitrary or oppressive as to bring it within the prohibition of the Fourteenth Amendment, for it is universally recognized that these interests are of themselves in some measure clothed with the legal incidents of property enjoyed by their owner, in the state where he resides, through the benefit and protection of its laws.

The power to tax "is an incident of sovereignty, and is co-extensive with that to which it is an incident. All subjects over which the sovereign power of a State extends, are objects of taxation; but those over which it does not extend are, upon the soundest principles, exempt from taxation." McCulloch v. Maryland, 4 Wheat. 316, 429. But this does not mean that the sovereign power of the state does not extend over intangibles of a domiciled resident because they have no physical location within its territory, or that its power to tax is lost because we may choose to say they are located elsewhere. A jurisdiction which does not depend on physical presence within the state is not lost by declaring that it is absent. From the beginning of our constitutional system control over the person at the place of his domicile and his duty there, common to all citizens, to contribute to the support of government have been deemed to afford an adequate constitutional basis for imposing on him a tax on the use and enjoyment of rights in intangibles measured by their value. Until this moment that jurisdiction has not been thought to depend on any factor other than the domicile of the owner within the taxing state, or to compel the attribution of intangibles of a physical presence within its territory, as though they were chattels, in order to support the tax. * * *

In cases where the owner of intangibles confines his activity to the place of his domicile it has been found convenient to substitute a rule for a reason, cf. New York ex rel. Cohn v. Graves, 300 U.S. 308, 313, 57 S.Ct. 466; First Bank Stock Corp. v. Minnesota, 301 U.S. 234, 241, 57 S.Ct. 677, by saying that his intangibles are taxed at their situs and not elsewhere, or perhaps less artificially, by invoking the maxim *mobilia sequuntur personam*. Blodgett v. Silverman, supra; Baldwin v. Missouri, supra, which means only that it is the identity or association of intangibles with the person of their owner at his domicile which gives jurisdiction to tax. But when the taxpayer extends his activities with respect to his intangibles, so as to avail himself of the protection and benefit of the laws of another state, in such a way as to bring his person or property within the reach of the tax gatherer there, the reason for a single place of taxation no longer obtains, and the rule is not even a workable substitute for the reasons which may exist in any particular case to support the constitutional power of each state concerned to tax. Whether we regard the right of a state to tax as founded on power over the object taxed, as declared by Chief Justice Marshall in McCulloch v. Maryland, supra, through dominion over tangibles or over persons whose relationships are the source of intangible rights; or on the benefit and protection conferred by the taxing sovereignty, or both, it is undeniable that the state of domicile is not deprived, by the taxpayer's activities elsewhere, of its constitutional jurisdiction to tax, and consequently that there are many circumstances in which more than one state may have jurisdiction to impose a tax and measure it by some or all of the taxpayer's intangibles. Shares of corporate stock may be taxed at the domicile of the shareholder and also at that of the corporation which the taxing state has created and controls; and income may be taxed both by the state where it is earned and by the state of the recipient's domicile. Protection, benefit, and power over the subject matter are not confined to either state. The taxpayer who is domiciled in one state but carries on business in another is subject to a tax there measured by the value of the intangibles used in his business. * * * But taxation of a corporation by a state where it does business, measured by the value of the intangibles used in its business there, does not preclude the state of incorporation from imposing a tax measured by all its intangibles. Cream of Wheat Co. v. County of Grand Forks, supra, 329; see Fidelity & Columbia Trust Co. v. Louisville, 245 U.S. 54, 38 S.Ct. 40.

The practical obstacles and unwarranted curtailments of state power which may be involved in attempting to prevent the taxation of diverse legal interests in intangibles in more than a single place, through first ascribing to them a fictitious situs and then invoking the prohibition of the Fourteenth Amendment against their taxation elsewhere, are exemplified by the circumstances of the present case. Here, for reasons of her own, the testatrix, although domiciled in Tennessee and enjoying the benefits of its laws, found it advantageous to create a trust of intangibles in Alabama by vesting legal title to the intangibles and limited powers of control over them in an Alabama trustee. But she also provided that by resort to her power to dispose of property by will, conferred upon her by the law of the domicile, the trust could be terminated and the property pass under the will. She thus created two sets of legal relationships resulting in distinct intangible rights, the one embodied in the legal ownership by the Alabama trustee of the intangibles, the other embodied in the equitable right of the decedent to control the action of the trustee with respect to the trust property and to compel it to pay over to her the income during her life, and in her power to dispose of the property at death.

Even if we could rightly regard these various and distinct legal interests, springing from distinct relationships, as a composite unitary interest and ascribe to it a single location in space, it is difficult to see how it could be said to be more in one state than in the other and upon what articulate principle the Fourteenth Amendment could be thought to have withdrawn from either state the taxing jurisdiction which it undoubtedly possessed before the adoption of the Amendment by conferring on one state at the expense of the other, exclusive jurisdiction to tax. See Paddell v. City of New York, 211 U.S. 446, 448, 29 S.Ct. 139. If the "due process" of the Fifth Amendment does not require us to fix a single exclusive place of taxation of intangibles for the benefit of their foreign owner, who is entitled to its protection, Burnet v. Brooks, 288 U.S. 378, 53 S.Ct. 457; cf. Russian Volunteer Fleet v. United States, 282 U.S. 481, 489, 51 S.Ct. 229, the Fourteenth can hardly be thought to make us do so here, for the due process clause of each amendment is directed at the protection of the individual and he is entitled to its immunity as much against the state as against the national government.

If taxation is but a means of distributing the cost of government among those who are subject to its control and who enjoy the protection of its laws, see New York ex rel. Cohn v. Graves, supra, 313; First Bank Stock Corp. v. Minnesota, supra, 241, legal ownership of the intangibles in Alabama by the Alabama trustee would seem to afford adequate basis for imposing on him a tax measured by their value. We can find no more ground for saying that the Fourteenth Amendment relieves it, or the property which it holds and administers in Alabama, from bearing that burden, than for saying that they are constitutionally immune from paying any other expense which normally attaches to the administration of a trust in that state. The Court has never denied the constitutional power of the trustee's domicile to subject them to property taxation. Safe Deposit & Trust Co. v. Virginia, 280 U.S. 83, 50 S.Ct. 59; see cases collected in 30 Columbia Law Rev. 530; 2 Cooley, Taxation (8th ed.) § 602. And since Alabama may lawfully tax the property in the trustee's hands, we perceive no ground for saying that the Fourteenth Amendment forbids the state to tax the transfer of it or an interest in it to another merely because the transfer was effected by decedent's testamentary act in another state.

No more plausible ground is assigned for depriving Tennessee of the power to tax in the circumstances of this case. The decedent's power to dispose of the intangibles was a potential source of wealth which was property in her hands from which she was under the highest obligation, in common with her fellow citizens of Tennessee to contribute to the support of the government whose protection she enjoyed. Exercise of that power, which was in her complete and exclusive control in Tennessee, was made a taxable event by the statutes of the state. Taxation of it must be taken to be as much within the jurisdiction of the state as taxation of the transfer of a mortgage on land located in another state and there subject to taxation at its full value. See Kirtland v. Hotchkiss, supra; cf. Paddell v. City of New York, supra.

For purposes of taxation, a general power of appointment, of which the testatrix here was both donor and donee, has hitherto been regarded by this Court as equivalent to ownership of the property subject to the power. * * * Whether the appointee derives title from the donor, under the common law theory, or from the donee by virtue of the exercise of the power, is here immaterial. In either event the trustee's title under the will was derived from decedent, domiciled in Tennessee. Cf. Wachovia Trust Co. v. Doughton, 272 U.S. 567, 47 S.Ct. 202. There is no conflict here between the laws of the two states affecting the transmission of the trust property. The title of the trustee under the original Alabama trust came to an end upon the exercise of the testatrix's power of appointment; and although the trustee after her death still had title to the securities, it was in by a new title as legatee under her will, and a new beneficial interest was created, both derived through the exercise of her power of disposition. The resulting situation was no different from what it would have been if she had bequeathed the intangibles upon a new trust to a new and different trustee, either within or without the state of Alabama. So far as the power of Tennessee to tax the exercise of the power of appointment is concerned, there is no substantial difference between the present case and any other case in which at the moment of death the evidences of intangibles passing under the will of a decedent domiciled in one state are physically present in another. See Blodgett v. Silberman, supra; Baldwin v. Missouri, supra.

It has hitherto been the accepted law of this Court that the state of domicile may constitutionally tax the exercise or non-exercise at death of a general power of appointment, by one who is both donor and donee of the power, relating to securities held in trust in another state. Bullen v. Wisconsin, supra. If it be thought that it is identity of the intangibles with the person of the owner at the place of his domicile which gives power over them and hence "jurisdiction to tax," and this is the reason underlying the maxim *mobilia sequuntur personam,* it is certain here that the intangibles for some purposes are identified with the trustee, their legal owner, at the place of its domicile and that in another and different relationship and for a different purpose—the exercise of the power of disposition at death, which is the equivalent of ownership—they are identified with the place of domicile of the testatrix, Tennessee. In effecting her purposes, the testatrix brought some of the legal interests which she created within the control of one state by selecting a trustee there and others within the control of the other state by making her domicile there. She necessarily invoked the aid of the law of both states, and her legatees, before they can secure and enjoy the benefits of succession, must invoke the law of both.

We can find nothing in the history of the Fourteenth Amendment and no support in reason, principle, or authority for saying that it prohibits either state, in the circumstances of this case, from laying the tax. On the contrary this Court, in sustaining the tax at the place of domicile in a case like the present, has declared that both the decedent's domicile and that of the trustee are free to tax. * * * That has remained the law of this Court until the present moment, and we see no reason for discarding it now. We find it impossible to say that taxation of intangibles can be reduced in every case to the mere mechanical operation of locating at a single place, and there taxing, every legal interest growing out of all the complex legal relationships which may be entered into between persons. This is the case because in point of actuality those interests may be too diverse in their relationships to various taxing jurisdictions to admit of unitary treatment without discarding modes of taxation long accepted and applied before the Fourteenth Amendment was adopted, and still recognized by this Court as valid. See Paddell v. New York, supra, 448. The Fourteenth Amendment cannot be carried out with such mechanical nicety without infringing powers which we think have not yet been withdrawn from the states. We have recently declined to press to a logical extreme the doctrine that the Fourteenth Amendment may be invoked to compel the taxation of intangibles by only a single state by attributing to them a situs within that state.[7] We think it cannot be pressed so far here.

If we enjoyed the freedom of the framers it is possible that we might, in the light of experience, devise a more equitable system of taxation than that which they gave us. But we are convinced that that end cannot be attained by the device of ascribing to intangibles in every case a locus for taxation in a single state despite the multiple legal interests to which they may give rise and despite the control over them or their transmission by any other state and its legitimate interest in taxing the one or the other. While fictions are sometimes invented in order to realize the judicial conception of justice, we cannot define the constitutional guaranty in terms of a fiction so unrelated to reality without creating as many tax injustices as we would avoid and without exercising a power to remake constitutional provisions which the Constitution has not given to the courts. * * *

So far as the decree of the Supreme Court of Tennessee denies the power of Alabama to tax, it is reversed.

MR. JUSTICE REED concurs in this opinion except as to the statement that "taxation of a corporation by a state where it does business measured by the value of the intangibles used in its business there, does not preclude the state of incorporation from imposing a tax measured by all its intangibles." Upon this point he reserves his conclusion.

MR. JUSTICE BUTLER, dissenting.

* * *

Rightly the parties agreed and the state courts assumed that, consistently with the due process clause of the Fourteenth Amendment, both States may not impose transfer taxes in respect of the same property. * * *

The parties agree that, upon execution of the indenture, title, possession, and control passed completely to the trustee and so continued until the death of Mrs. Scales. There being no provision authorizing revocation, the grant was irrevocable. * * * Unquestionably it presently vested full legal and equitable title in the trustee and beneficiaries, subject to be divested only by the exertion by Mrs. Scales of her power of appointment by will. * * * That power did not amount to an estate or interest in the trust property. * * * All doubt as to that is precluded by the clause of the indenture which provides that in the absence of disposition by her will the property shall continue to be held in trust for purposes there specified.

The reserved authority to direct investment contemplates action as trustee and not control as owner. Reinecke v. Trust Co., 278 U.S. 339, 346–347, 49 S.Ct. 123. The authority to remove the trustee and to appoint a successor detracts nothing from the plenary grant of title. See Bowditch v. Banuelos, 1 Gray 220, 230. When read as it must be in connection with the provisions of the Alabama statute above referred

---

7. See Footnote 1, ante.

to, that provision of the indenture does not reserve power to remove the trust securities from the State of Alabama.

As the death of Mrs. Scales and taking effect of her will were coincident, the legal title remained in the trustee. The purposes Mrs. Scales intended to effect by the trusts defined by her will are like those she intended to serve by the trusts created by the indenture which, in absence of will, were to continue after death. Stripped of mere legalism, and taken according to substance, the will operated to amend and continue the trusts created by the indenture. Questions of power to tax are governed by the substance of things rather than by technical rules, concerning title. Tyler v. United States, 281 U.S. 497, 503, 50 S.Ct. 356.

It follows that, save her right to income, Mrs. Scales, after her relinquishment, January 11, 1929, and at the time of her death, had no estate or interest in the securities held by the trustee. There is no basis for application of the fiction *mobilia sequuntur personam.* * * * Tennessee may not impose the inheritance tax claimed in this suit by its Commissioner of Finance and Taxation.

Moreover, if contrary to the indenture as above construed, it should be held that at the time of her death Mrs. Scales in addition to having power of appointment by will owned an interest in the trust property, Tennessee would nevertheless be without power to impose a tax on the transfer of that interest because the intangibles in question had no situs in that State.

Intangibles, like tangibles, may be so held and used outside the State of the domicile of the owner as to become taxable in the State where kept. * * * The general rule of *mobilia sequuntur personam* must yield to the established fact of legal ownership, actual presence and control in a State other than that of the domicile of the owner. The phrase "business situs" as used to support jurisdiction of a State other than that of the domicile of the owner to impose taxes on intangible personal property is a metaphorical expression of vague signification; its meaning is not limited to investment or actual use as an integral part of a business or activity, but may extend to the execution of trusts such as those created by the indenture and imposed on the trustee in this case. * * *

The stock certificates, bonds or other documents evidencing the intangibles constituting the trust property were never held in Tennessee. Neither their issue or validity nor the enforcement or transfer, inter vivos or from the dead to the living, of any right attested or supported by them was at all dependent on the laws of that State. From the beginning, the trust estate has been under the protection of, and necessarily the trusts have been and are being executed under, the laws of Alabama unaffected by those of any other State. * * *

At least since 1917, Mrs. Scales had no power to remove the trust or any of the trust property from Alabama. Exertion of any right or power reserved to her by the indenture was dependent on the laws of Alabama and not upon or subject to those of Tennessee, where she happened to have her domicil. Wachovia Trust Co. v. Doughton, ubi supra. Subject to the laws of Alabama, all transactions in which the trust properties were capable of being used were identified with that State. The securities, held there not only for safekeeping but as well for collection of income and principal, and subject to sale and reinvestment of proceeds, could not be more completely localized anywhere. DeGanay v. Lederer, ubi supra.

The judgment of the Supreme Court of Tennessee should be reversed and the case remanded to that court for further proceedings in accordance with this opinion.

MR. CHIEF JUSTICE HUGHES, MR. JUSTICE MCREYNOLDS and MR. JUSTICE ROBERTS join in this opinion.*

Notes and Problems

A. *Transfers Intended to Take Effect in Possession or Enjoyment at or After Death.* Many States, like the Federal Government, impose death taxes on gifts intended to take effect in possession or enjoyment at or after death. Suppose a resident of State A sets up an irrevocable *inter vivos* trust of stocks and bonds with a bank in State B, retaining the income for life and giving the remainder to his children residing in State B. The settlor of the trust dies several years after he had created the trust, still a resident of State A. The trust is at all times administered in State B. If State A seeks to impose the tax, may the decedent's estate successfully argue that the taxable event was the decedent's death and that at that date decedent owned no property located in State A which was subject to its taxing power? This issue arose in Central Hanover Bank and Trust Co. v. Kelly, 319 U.S. 94, 63 S.Ct. 945 (1943). Similar problems were presented in connection with the taxation of gifts in contemplation of death. Cf. the possible effects on the results of the classification of the tax as an inheritance tax as distinguished from an estate tax. See Chapter 12, § 1, infra.

B. *Relinquishment of Power of Revocation.* A resident of Colorado, during his lifetime, transferred certain securities to a Denver bank in trust, reserving the power of revocation. At his death, he was a resident of New York. Colorado assessed a tax on the transmission at death of the trust funds. In Graves v. Elliott, 307 U.S. 383, 59 S.Ct. 913 (1939), a companion case of *Curry v. McCanless,* the Court upheld the power of New York to tax the relinquishment at death of the power to revoke the trust.

C. *Powers of Appointment.* In Graves v. Schmidlapp, 315 U.S. 657, 62 S.Ct. 870 (1942), a decedent resident and domiciled in New York exercised by will a general power of appointment granted to him under the will of his father. The decedent's father had been a resident of Massachusetts, where his will had been probated and the trust estate, which was the subject of the power, had been created and administered. The Court upheld a New York estate tax on the property passing by this exercise of the power of appointment, on the ground that decedent's "complete and exclusive power

---

* [This case has been the subject of extensive law review comment. See Saunders, "Multi–State Taxation of Intangible Property: Background and Recent Developments," 1 Wash. & Lee L.Rev. 75 (1939).]

to dispose of the intangibles at death was property in his hands in New York, where he was domiciled." This case is commented on in 42 Cal.L. Rev. 1064 (1942), 40 Mich.L.Rev. 1233 (1942), and 90 U.Pa.L.Rev. 975 (1942); see In re Newton's Estate, 35 Cal.2d 830, 221 P.2d 952 (1950). See Annot., 19 A.L.R.2d 1415 for a note on cases dealing with State death taxation of disposition of property under a power of appointment.

Is the result otherwise when the decedent possesses a special power of appointment but fails to exercise it? That issue arose in People of the State of Colorado v. Cooke, 150 Colo. 52, 370 P.2d 896 (1962), in which a resident of Colorado died in 1957, without exercising a power of appointment over an inter vivos trust of intangibles that her mother had established. The trust had been set up in 1931 by the decedent's mother, when the latter resided in Connecticut. A New York bank was named trustee, and the assets of the trust were held and administered by the bank in New York. Decedent had been the income beneficiary of the trust during her lifetime. The power had originally been a general power, but during her lifetime, while a resident of New Jersey, the decedent had, by a proper instrument, reduced the power to a special power limited to her descendants and certain other relatives. By her will, she explicitly set forth her intention not to exercise her power of appointment over the remainder of the trust. A Colorado inheritance tax on the value of the trust remainder was upheld. Citing both Graves v. Schmidlapp and Graves v. Elliott, supra, the court declared:

> It is abundantly clear from the authorities above cited that a general power of appointment, exercised or non-exercised, is a proper foundation upon which to impose a succession tax, even though the intangible assets are located in a state other than that where the person possessing the power of appointment is domiciled. It is also clear that a special power of appointment exercised, is subject to tax under the same circumstances. But the Executor contends that, where a special power of appointment is *not* exercised by a decedent, an attempt to tax the intangibles received by the beneficiaries under the terms of the trust instrument is unconstitutional.
>
> *   *   *
>
> We fail to perceive a distinction between the situation which arises from the non-exercise of a general power and that which arises from the non-exercise of a special power. In either case, beneficiaries named in the trust receive their bounty by the inaction of the decedent. The failure to act affects the course of succession just as fully as if the power had been exercised, and until the failure is complete the succession is not fully determined. Where the donee of the power of appointment holds the power, he is in control of the succession. He can allow it to go to the persons named in the trust or he can appoint others within the limits of the power of appointment—limits which, by the way, the donee in this case imposed upon herself.
>
> We conclude that the statute is not unconstitutional as applied to the facts of this case and that the Commissioner properly included the entire corpus of the New York trust in his report. [370 P.2d at 899–900.]

D. *Death Taxation of Shares of Stock by State of Incorporation.* In State Tax Commission v. Aldrich, 316 U.S. 174, 62 S.Ct. 1008 (1942), the Court upheld the power of the State of incorporation to impose a death tax on the transfer of stocks held by a non-resident decedent, overruling First National Bank v. Maine, 284 U.S. 312, 52 S.Ct. 174 (1932). In that case, Edward Harkness, a New York resident, held stock in Union Pacific Railroad, a Utah corporation. Harkness had no other connection with the State of Utah. The stock certificates were not kept there, and the railroad's stock transfer agent was located in New York. In upholding Utah's power to tax, the Court said:

> The corporation owes its existence to Utah. Utah law defines the nature and extent of the interest of the shareholders in the corporation. Utah law affords protection for those rights. Utah has power over the transfer by the corporation of its shares of stock. Certainly that protection, benefit, and power over the shares would have satisfied the test of Blackstone v. Miller and Curry v. McCanless. [316 U.S. at 180.]

Mr. Justice Jackson delivered a dissenting opinion as follows: *

State taxation of transfer by death of intangible property is in something of a jurisdictional snarl, to the solution of which this Court owes all that it has of wisdom and power. The theoretical basis of some decisions in the very practical matter of taxation is not particularly satisfying. But a switch of abstract concepts is hardly to be expected without at least careful consideration of its impact on the very practical and concrete problems of states and taxpayers. Weighing the highly doctrinaire reasons advanced for this decision against its practical effects on our economy and upon our whole constitutional law of state taxation, I can see nothing in the Court's decision more useful than the proverbial leap from the frying pan into the fire.

I.

This is little persuasion and certainly no compulsion in the authorities mustered by the Court's present opinion, which are either admittedly overruled cases, such as Blackstone v. Miller, 188 U.S. 189, 23 S.Ct. 277, or admittedly distinguishable ones, such as Curry v. McCanless, 307 U.S. 357, 59 S.Ct. 900; Graves v. Elliott, 307 U.S. 383, 59 S.Ct. 913; Wisconsin v. J.C. Penney Co., 311 U.S. 435, 61 S.Ct. 246. Such authorities are not impressive in vindication of such a judgment. Without discussion of the academic merits of the decision that is being overruled I am willing to proceed on the estimate of it made at the time of its pronouncement by the present Chief Justice, who said in his dissent: "Situs of an intangible, for taxing purposes, as the decisions of this Court, including the present one, abundantly demonstrate, is not a dominating reality, but a convenient fiction which may be judicially employed or discarded, according to the result desired." First National Bank v. Maine, 284 U.S. 312, 332, 52 S.Ct. 174. The Court now discards this fiction in favor of one calling for a different result.

* [Footnotes have been omitted.]

This older rule ascribed a fictional consequence to the domicile of a natural person; it is overruled by ascribing a fictional consequence to the domicile of an artificial corporation. The older rule emphasized dominance by the individual over his intangible property, the tax situs of which followed the domicile of its owner. Today's new rule emphasizes the dominance of the corporation, a creature of the legal imagination. To this fictional personality it ascribes a hypothetical "domicile" in a place where it has but a fraction of its property and conducts only its formal corporate activities; and on the union of these two fictions it permits the chartering state to tax the estates of persons who never lived or did business therein. The reasoning back of the holding is this: Because Utah issued a charter to a corporation, which issued stock to a nonresident, which changed hands at his death, which required a transfer on the corporation's books, which transfer was permitted by Utah law, Utah got jurisdiction to tax succession to the stock. It is really as remote as that.

No one questions that a state which charters a corporation, even though it amounts to no more than giving "to airy nothing a local habitation and a name," has the right to exact a charter fee, an incorporation tax, or a franchise tax from the artificial entity it has created. But that such chartering enables the taxing arm of the state to reach the estate of every stockholder, wherever he lives, and to tax the entire value of the stock because of "opportunities which it has given," "protection which it has afforded," or "benefits which it has conferred" is quite another matter. Utah is permitted to tax the full value of each share of Union Pacific stock passing by death. Any conceivable "opportunity," "protection," or "benefit" derived by the Union Pacific stockholders from Utah is negligible in proportion to the values Utah is authorized to tax.

It would be hard to select a case that would better demonstrate the fictional basis of the Court's doctrine of benefits and protection than this case of Utah and the Union Pacific Railroad.

* * *

If it had only the "opportunities" and "benefits" conferred by Utah and only the properties protected by her laws, the Union Pacific would cut little figure either in transportation or finance. It holds its stockholders' meetings in that State. But it maintains no executive office or stock transfer office in Utah. Its executive and stock transfer offices are in New York City. Its stocks are listed on the New York, Boston, London and Amsterdam stock exchanges. Over 200,000 shares of its stock were traded on the New York Stock Exchange in 1939. Its western operating office is not in Utah, but in Omaha, Nebraska. It is stipulated that less than 9% of its 9877 miles of trackage are in Utah and that during 1939, the railway operating revenue from Utah intrastate business plus the Utah proportion on a mileage basis of its interstate business was 8.97% of the entire gross operating revenues of the company.

What gives the Union Pacific stock its value, all of which is appropriated by this decision to Utah's taxing power, is its operation in interstate commerce, a privilege which comes from the United States and one which Utah does not give or protect and could not deny. The Union Pacific system itself is in interstate operation, embracing thirteen states and drawing its business from the whole country. Approximately 37% of its total tonnage was received from connecting lines. If the values derived from privileges extended by the National Government and from rendering national transportation were to be allocated to any single State for tax purposes, a realistic basis would entitle the five States of Idaho, Kansas, Nebraska, Oregon, and Washington to some consideration, for each embraces, authorizes, and protects by its laws more miles of trackage than does Utah.

These facts leave nothing of Utah's claim to tax the full value of Union Pacific shares when transferred by death of a nonresident stockholder, and no basis for the Court's decision that it may do so, except the metaphysics of the corporate charter.

II.

The theories on which this case is decided contrast sharply with certain hard facts which measure the decision's practical wisdom or lack of it.

1. The effect of the Court's decision is to intensify the already unwholesome conflict and friction between the States of the Union in competitive exploitation of intangible property as a source of death duties.

The practical issue underlying this case is not whether the Harkness estate shall pay or avoid a transfer tax. The issue is whether Utah or New York will collect this tax. It is admitted that if this Court breathes constitutionality into this Utah tax, all that Utah gets will be credited to the Harkness estate on its tax payable in New York as the state of domicile. The right of a state to tax succession to corporate stock by death of one domiciled therein, while not abrogated, is now subjected to an interfering and overlapping right of the State which chartered the corporation to tax the same stock transfer on a different and inconsistent principle. Since the chartering state has apparently been empowered to exact its tax as a condition of permitting the transfer, the taxing power of the state of the stockholder's domicile is really subordinated and deferred to the taxing power of the chartering state. By laying its tax on the gross value transferred, irrespective of the net value of the decedent's estate, the chartering state may give its tax an effective priority of payment over the taxes laid by the domiciliary state and may collect what amounts to an inheritance tax, even when there is no net estate to transfer. Thus, through the corporate charter fiction the chartering State may thrust its own tax with extraterritorial effect between the taxing power of the State of domicile and tax resources to which that State has had, and I think should have, first and under ordinary circumstances exclusive resort.

2. To subject intangible property to many more sources of taxation than other wealth prejudices its relation to other investments and other wealth by a discrimination which has no basis in the function that intangibles perform for our present society. * * * Whether for good or ill, the stubborn fact is that in our present system the corporation carries on the bulk of production and transportation, is the chief employer of both labor and capital, pays a large part of our taxes, and is an economic institution of such magnitude and importance that there is no present substitute for it except the state itself. Except for the easy circulation and

ready acceptability of pieces of paper characterized as stocks or bonds, this existing system could not function. It is these intangible symbols or tokens which give liquidity and mobility to otherwise fixed underlying plant assets, which give ready negotiability to fractional interests therein that would otherwise transfer with difficulty, and which divide among many both benefits and risks from aggregation of properties whose successful functioning for society requires unified management of the bulk. * * * When this Court determines that the effect of owning this type of circulating medium is to subject the estate of the owner to an inheritance tax from every State that chartered one of the companies in which he has invested, it imposes a handicap on such ownership that is substantial and influential upon our economy.

*   *   *

3. A large majority of the states by experience prior to the First National Bank v. Maine decision found the system of taxation which this Court imposes on all States today to be unworkable and to constitute a threat to the death tax on intangibles as a State source of revenue. Competitive use by the States of death taxation and immunities invited federal invasion of the field, one phase of which was the enactment by Congress of § 301, Revenue Act of 1926, sustained by this Court in Florida v. Mellon, 273 U.S. 12, 47 S.Ct. 265. There the Federal Government had laid an estate tax but retained only 20% of the revenue and used an 80% credit provision to equalize the demands of the states. There was an uneasy premonition among the states that overlapping, capricious, and multiple taxation would lead to federal occupation of the field. * * *

Farsighted states saw that the total revenue sources practically available to the states was not increased by overlapping their taxation and invading each other's domiciliary sources of taxation. Many felt that justice required credits to their own domiciled decedents' estates for taxes exacted elsewhere, and the credits granted offset largely the revenue derived from the tax. The multiple taxation added substantially to the cost of administration and to the annoyance of taxpayers. Because of these considerations, at the time of argument of First National Bank v. Maine, thirty-seven States had enacted reciprocity statutes which voluntarily renounced revenues from this type of taxation. The Court was urged to stay the hand of sister States which would not cooperate. The restraint laid by this Court in response to those appeals is now withdrawn at the behest of a state which has at no time enacted a reciprocity statute or given a credit for such taxes paid by its domiciled decedents elsewhere. We have not heard the views of any other state nor considered their concern about retaining the sources of taxation opened to them. I do not doubt that today's decision will give a new impetus to federal absorption of this revenue source and to federal incorporation of large enterprises.

*   *   *

III.

The Court casts aside former limitations on state power to tax nonresidents in such terms as to leave doubt whether any legal limitations are hereafter to be recognized or applied.

*   *   *

Certain it is that while only corporate stock is expressly mentioned in the opinion or involved in the judgment today, the fiction of benefits and protection is capable of as ready adaptability to other intangible property. Our tomorrows will witness an extension of the taxing power of the chartering or issuing State to corporate bonds and bonds of States and municipalities (by overruling Farmers Loan & Trust Co. v. Minnesota, 280 U.S. 204, 50 S.Ct. 98), to bank credits for cash deposited (by overruling Baldwin v. Missouri, 281 U.S. 586, 50 S.Ct. 436) and to choses in action (by overruling Beidler v. South Carolina, 282 U.S. 1, 51 S.Ct. 54.) And while today the Court sustains only a death transfer tax, its theories are equally serviceable to sustain an income or excise tax on dividends from such stock or interest on bonds or a sales tax, or a gift tax. Whether each chartering or issuing state will be permitted to calculate its tax on some formula that will consider the total property owned by the decedent, I do not know, but in the present trend of decision there is little restraint on such formulas. I therefore take today's decision to mean that any State may lay substantially any tax on any transfer of intangible property toward which it can spell out a conceivable legal relationship.

And since the Due Process Clause speaks with no more clarity as to tangible than as to intangible property, the question is opened whether our decisions as to taxation of tangible property are not due to be overhauled. And if the State of Utah is not denied jurisdiction over the transfer of this stock owned by a New York resident it is difficult to see where the Court could find a basis for denying it jurisdiction to prescribe the rule of succession to it.

The Court, it seems to me, will be obliged to draw the line at which State power to reach nonresidents' estates and extraterritorial transactions comes to an end. I find little difficulty in concluding that exaction of a tax by a State which has no jurisdiction or lawful authority to impose it is a taking of property without due process of law. The difficulty is that the concept of jurisdiction is not defined by the Constitution. Any decision which accepts or rejects any one of the many grounds advanced as jurisdictional for state taxing purposes will read into the Constitution an inclusion or an exclusion that is not found in its text. To read into the Constitution the Court's present concept of jurisdiction through charter granting, and to hold that it follows that the Constitution does not prohibit this tax, is to make new law quite as certainly as to adhere to the concept of jurisdiction according to the decedent's domicile and to hold that the Constitution therefore does prohibit it.

I am content with existing constitutional law unless it appears more plainly that it is unsound or until it works badly in our present day and society.

Mr. Justice Roberts concurs in this opinion.

(c) Taxation of Intangibles of Out–of–State Testamentary Trust by State of Trustee's Domicile

A. In Greenough v. Tax Assessors of the City of Newport, 331 U.S. 486, 67 S.Ct. 1400 (1947), the Court considered a local personal property tax assessed against a resident trustee of a testamentary trust, created under the will of a non-resident decedent, where the assets consisted of shares of stock maintained outside the State. George H. Warren died a resident of New York, where his estate was probated and administered; one of his trustees was a resident of Newport, Rhode Island and the other a resident of New York. No letters of trusteeship were ever issued in Rhode Island. The City of Newport assessed against the Rhode Island trustee a personal property tax on one-half the value of the stock held by the estate; the statute calls for a proportionate assessment where there is more than one trustee. The trustees assailed the assessment as violative of the Due Process Clause, but the Court upheld the levy on the basis of the local domicile of the trustee, in accordance with the traditional power of the States to tax their domiciliaries on their intangibles wherever located. The Court pointed out that Rhode Island provided the beneficiaries of the trust with the benefits of a local forum through which to enforce their claims against the resident trustee. Justices Jackson, Murphy, Rutledge, and Chief Justice Vinson dissented, holding that the State's power to tax its residents on their intangibles does not extend to trustees of a trust created by a non-resident decedent and administered outside the State. The *Greenough* case is discussed in 33 Corn.L.Q. 305 (1947); 27 Neb.L. Rev. 98 (1947); 33 Iowa L.Rev. 423 (1948); 21 So.Cal.L.Rev. 190 (1948).

In Florida National Bank v. Simpson, 59 So.2d 751 (Fla.1952), an intangible property tax was assessed on shares of stock owned by testamentary trustees. One of the four trustees was a non-resident, but the court refused to reduce the taxed stock by one-fourth. In the case, the custody and control of the trust res were in Florida.

B. *Taxation of Beneficiary of Trust.* A property tax on an equitable life interest of a resident of Pennsylvania in a trust fund created by a resident of New York, with trustees who are residents of that State, where the trust corpus, consisting of stocks and bonds, are held and administered, does not violate the Due Process Clause. Commonwealth v. Stewart, 338 Pa. 9, 12 A.2d 444 (1940), affirmed per curiam 312 U.S. 649, 61 S.Ct. 445 (1941). Cf. Safe Deposit and Trust Co. of Baltimore v. Virginia, 280 U.S. 83, 50 S.Ct. 59 (1929).

In 1945 the Michigan Supreme Court held that the State's intangible personal property tax did not extend to the interest of a resident of Michigan in a trust created and administered outside the State. Tyler v. State Department of Revenue, 311 Mich. 698, 18 N.W.2d 257 (1945). Thereafter, the State legislature amended the statute so as to tax such a beneficiary. A case arose in which a resident of Michigan had a life estate in a part of the income of a trust of securities created and administered outside the State. The statute provides for a tax on income-producing property of three percent of the income, but in any event no less than one-tenth of one percent of the face, par, or contributed value of corporate securities held by the trust, and in case of non-income producing intangibles, one-tenth of one percent of the face, par, or contributed value. The taxpayer conceded her liability for tax on the income producing property, but contested the tax on the non-income producing property. Did such an income beneficiary possess any "ownership" in the intangibles which could be taxed? See Goodenough v. State, 328 Mich. 56, 43 N.W.2d 235 (1950), modified 328 Mich. 502, 44 N.W.2d 161 (1950).

C. Prior to the *Greenough* case, some State courts had held that a property tax on intangibles is assessable only by the State in which the trust is administered. Hutchins v. Commissioner of Corporations and Taxation, 272 Mass. 422, 172 N.E. 605 (1930); In re Dorrance, 333 Pa. 162, 3 A.2d 682 (1939). Others had held that where there are trustees domiciled in several States, each State may levy a property tax on an aliquot share of a trust of intangibles. Mackay v. City and County of San Francisco, 128 Cal. 678, 61 P. 382 (1900); People ex rel. Van Norden Trust Co. v. Wells, 118 App.Div. 881, 103 N.Y.Supp. 874, affirmed without opinion 192 N.Y. 552, 85 N.E. 114 (1908).

D. *Death Tax Reciprocity Provisions.* The movement to alleviate double death taxation of intangibles has resulted in statutory provisions limiting estate or inheritance taxes on non-resident estates to tangible property located in the State. In some States, the provision is dependent on the existence of a similar provision on the statute books of the non-resident's State of domicile. See 1 P–H State Inheritance Taxes ¶ 851. A perplexing problem arising under these statutes is that of delineating the scope of the intangibles exempted from the levy.

Some States, e.g., West Virginia (W.Va.Code Ann. § 11–11–8, 3 CCH Inh., Est. & Gift Tax Rptr. ¶ 1118, 5 P–H State Inh. Taxes ¶ 31), have incorporated in their reciprocal exemption provisions the following definition of intangibles proposed by the National Tax Association in its "Model Inheritance Tax Reciprocal Exemption Provision," 1928 Nat. Tax Ass'n Proc. 486:

> Intangible personal property means incorporeal property, including money, deposits in banks, mortgages, debts, receivables, shares of stock, bonds, notes, credits, evidences of an interest in property and evidences of debt.

E. *References.* Note, "Due Process Limits on State Estate Taxation: An Analogy to the State Corporate Income Tax," 94 Yale L.J. 1229 (1985); Morton & Cotton, "Limitations on State Jurisdiction to Levy Death Taxes," 5 Miami L.Q. 449 (1951); Thomas, "How Far Will Multi–State Death Taxation Go? *Curry v. McCanless* Revisited," 1 Vand.L.Rev. 93 (1947); Faught, "Reciprocity in State Taxation as the Next Step in Empirical Legislation," 92 U.Pa.L.Rev. 258, 271 (1944), in which Congressional action is urged to alleviate multiple taxation of intangibles. See "Reciprocity in Nondomiciliary Inheritance Taxation of Intangibles," 26 Iowa L.Rev. 694 (1940); Orr, "Reciprocal Exemption from Inheritance Taxation," 18 B.U.L.Rev. 39 (1938).

SECTION 4. INCOME TAXATION UNDER THE DUE PROCESS CLAUSE

(a) Income Taxation of a Resident

Residence in a State provides a sufficient basis under the Due Process Clause to permit a State to tax all the resident's income from whatever source derived, including rentals from out-of-state real estate. In New York ex rel. Cohn v. Graves, 300 U.S. 308, 57 S.Ct. 466 (1937), which upheld such a levy, the Court said (300 U.S. at 312–315, 57 S.Ct. at 467–469):

> That the receipt of income by a resident of the territory of a taxing sovereignty is a taxable event is universally recognized. Domicile itself affords a basis for such taxation. Enjoyment of the privileges of residence in the state and the attendant right to invoke the protection of its laws are inseparable from responsibility for sharing the costs of government. "Taxes are what we pay for civilized society * * *," see Compania Gen. de Tobacos v. Collector, 275 U.S. 87, 100, 48 S.Ct. 100. A tax measured by the net income of residents is an equitable method of distributing the burdens of government among those who are privileged to enjoy its benefits. The tax, which is apportioned to the ability of the taxpayer to pay it, is founded upon the protection afforded by the state to the recipient of the income in his person, in his right to receive the income and in his enjoyment of it when received. These are rights and privileges which attach to domicile within the state. To them and to the equitable distribution of the tax burden, the economic advantage realized by the receipt of income and represented by the power to control it, bears a direct relationship. See Lawrence v. State Tax Comm., 286 U.S. 276, 52 S.Ct. 556; Maguire v. Trefry, 253 U.S. 12, 14, 40 S.Ct. 417; Virginia v. Imperial Sales Coal Co., 293 U.S. 15, 19, 55 S.Ct. 12; compare Shaffer v. Carter, 252 U.S. 37, 50, 40 S.Ct. 221.

> Neither the privilege nor the burden is affected by the character of the source from which the income is derived. For that reason income is not necessarily clothed with the tax immunity enjoyed by its source. A state may tax its residents upon net income from a business whose physical assets, located wholly without the state, are beyond its taxing power. Lawrence v. State Tax Comm., supra; see Shaffer v. Carter, supra, at 50. It may tax net income from bonds held in trust and administered in another state, Maguire v. Trefry, supra, although the taxpayer's equitable interest may not be subjected to the tax, Safe Deposit & Trust Co. v. Virginia, supra. It may tax net income from operations in interstate commerce, although a tax on the commerce is forbidden, United States Glue Co. v. Town of Oak Creek, 247 U.S. 321, 38 S.Ct. 499; Shaffer v. Carter, supra. Congress may lay a tax on net income derived from the business of exporting merchandise in foreign commerce, although a tax upon articles exported is prohibited by constitutional provision (Art. I, § 9, Cl. 5). Peck & Co. v. Lowe, 247 U.S. 165, 38 S.Ct. 432; Barclay & Co. v. Edwards, 267 U.S. 442, 447, 45 S.Ct. 348.

Neither analysis of the two types of taxes, nor consideration of the bases upon which the power to impose them rests, supports the contention that a tax on income is a tax on the land which produces it. The incidence of a tax on income differs from that of a tax on property. Neither tax is dependent upon the possession by the taxpayer of the subject of the other. His income may be taxed, although he owns no property, and his property may be taxed, although it produces no income. The two taxes are measured by different standards, the one by the amount of income received over a period of time, the other by the value of the property at a particular date. Income is taxed but once; the same property may be taxed recurrently. The tax on each is predicated upon different governmental benefits; the protection offered to the property in one state does not extend to the receipt and enjoyment of income from it in another.

It would be pressing the protection which the due process clause throws around the taxpayer too far to say that because a state is prohibited from taxing land which it neither protects nor controls, it is likewise prohibited from taxing the receipt and command of income from the land by its resident, who is subject to its control and enjoys the benefits of its laws. The imposition of these different taxes, by the same or different states, upon these distinct and separable taxable interests, is not subject to the objection of double taxation, which has been successfully urged in those cases where two or more states have laid the same tax upon the same property interest in intangibles or upon its transfer at death. * * * These considerations lead to the conclusion that income derived from real estate may be taxed to the recipient at the place of his domicile, irrespective of the location of the land, and that the state court rightly upheld the tax.

Nothing which was said or decided in Pollock v. Farmers Loan & Trust Co., 157 U.S. 429, 15 S.Ct. 673, calls for a different conclusion. There the question for decision was whether a federal tax on income derived from rents of land is a direct tax requiring apportionment under Art. I, § 2, Cl. 3, of the Constitution. In holding that the tax was "direct," the Court did not rest its decision upon the ground that the tax was a tax on the land, or that it was subject to every limitation which the Constitution imposes on property taxes. It determined only that for purposes of apportionment there were similarities in the operation of the two kinds of tax which made it appropriate to classify both as direct, and with the constitutional command.*

An individual's income derived from services rendered outside the State is likewise subject to tax by the State of his residence. Lawrence v. State Tax Commission, 286 U.S. 276, 52 S.Ct. 556 (1932), noted in 42 Yale L.J. 283 (1932), and 32 Col.L.Rev. 1078 (1932).

In Guaranty Trust Co. v. Virginia, 305 U.S. 19, 59 S.Ct. 1 (1938), a Virginia resident received income from a testamentary trust created by her husband, who had died a resident of New York. The trust was

* [This case is noted in 85 U. of Pa.L.Rev. 645 (1937); 9 Rocky Mt.L.Rev. 287 (1937).]

administered in New York by trustees located in that State. In rejecting a Due Process Clause attack on the Virginia income tax, Mr. Justice McReynolds said for a unanimous bench:

> The insistence is that the challenged assessment was upon the identical income already rightly taxed by New York; that under numerous decisions by us two or more states may not tax the same subject; this would amount to double taxation and infringe the Due Process clause. [cited by the taxpayer.]

> Those cases go upon the theory that the taxing power of a state is restricted to her confines and may not be exercised in respect of subjects beyond them. Here, the thing taxed was receipt of income, within Virginia by a citizen residing there. The mere fact that another state lawfully taxed funds from which the payments were made did not necessarily destroy Virginia's right to tax something done within her borders. After much discussion the applicable doctrine was expounded and applied in Lawrence v. State Tax Commission, 286 U.S. 276, 52 S.Ct. 556, and New York ex rel. Cohn v. Graves, 300 U.S. 308, 57 S.Ct. 466. The attempt to draw a controlling distinction between them and the present cause, we think has not been successful.

Notes and Problems

A. Land situated in State A is mortgaged. The interest on the mortgage is paid to the taxpayer-mortgagee in State B, where he resides and makes his mortgage-loans. Is the interest on the mortgage taxable by State A or State B or both? Suppose that the mortgagee-taxpayer conducts an active mortgage loan business in State C, negotiating the loans there and receiving interest there. May State C tax the mortgage interest?

B. *References.* Rottschaefer, "State Jurisdiction to Impose Taxes," 42 Yale L.J. 305, 323 (1933); A. Harding, Double Taxation of Property and Income 218 (1933); Brown, "Multiple Taxation by the States," 48 Harv.L. Rev. 407 (1935).

(b) Income Taxation of a Non–Resident

The seminal cases setting forth the Due Process limitations on the States' power to tax the income of non-residents are discussed in Chapter 8, pp. 358–61 supra.

Notes and Problems

A. *Profit Derived by Non–Resident From Sale of a "Right" to Seat on Stock Exchange Located in the State.* T, a broker residing in Massachusetts, owned a seat on the New York Stock Exchange. His firm used the seat to enable it to effect sales on the Exchange at reduced commission rates for members. Neither T nor his firm had a New York office, and they carried on no business in New York, except for the operations through the Stock Exchange. When the number of Exchange seats was increased in 1929, each member obtained a "right" to one fourth of a new seat. T sold his "right." New York imposed an income tax on the sale, which was sustained against attack under the Due Process Clause. The Court held that the "dominant feature" of the seat was the "privilege of conducting the business of buying and selling securities on the floor of the Exchange," which "localizes it at the Exchange." New York ex rel. Whitney v. Graves, 299 U.S. 360, 57 S.Ct. 237 (1937).

B. *Wisconsin Dividend Tax.* In Wisconsin v. J.C. Penney & Co., 311 U.S. 435, 61 S.Ct. 246 (1940), the Court considered a tax on "the privilege of declaring and receiving dividends out of income derived from property located and business transacted" in Wisconsin. An apportionment formula is used to determine the portion of the income derived from Wisconsin, where business is done in other States. The taxpayer, a Delaware corporation with its principal office in New York, declared dividends at a meeting in New York and paid the dividends from that State. The Wisconsin court had construed the tax as a levy on "the privilege of declaring dividends," not "a supplementary income tax," and had held that it violated the Due Process Clause. In sustaining the tax, in a 5 to 4 decision, Mr. Justice Frankfurter stated (311 U.S. at 444, 61 S.Ct. at 249):

> The substantial privilege of carrying on business in Wisconsin, which has here been given, clearly supports the tax, and the state has not given the less merely because it has conditioned the demand of the exaction upon happenings outside its own borders. The fact that a tax is contingent upon events brought to pass without a state does not destroy the nexus between such a tax and transactions within a state for which the tax is an exaction.*

Relying on the *J.C. Penney* case, the Oregon Supreme Court in a thoughtful opinion by Judge Linde upheld the State's power to impose personal income taxes on non-residents' shares of the distributed and undistributed income of a Subchapter S Corporation. Kulick v. Department of Revenue, 290 Or. 507, 624 P.2d 93 (1981), appeal dismissed 454 U.S. 803, 102 S.Ct. 76 (1981). Under the Subchapter S provisions of the Internal Revenue Code, I.R.C. §§ 1371–1378 as incorporated by the State of Oregon, once a corporation and its shareholders have elected Subchapter S treatment, the distributed and undistributed taxable income of the corporation "derived from or connected with sources in this state" is taxed as income of the individual shareholders. In sustaining the application of Oregon's personal income tax to the non-resident shareholders, over Due Process objections, the court declared:

> The practical effect of the tax imposed here is identical as if it were imposed on the shareholder's gains in the hands of the corporation, as plaintiffs concede it could be under Wisconsin v. J.C. Penney Co., supra, or by one of the "jurisdictional" devices employed by other states. The "fiscal relation" to the opportunities and benefits available in Oregon as an "orderly, civilized society," in the language of *J.C. Penney Co.,* is exactly the same. [624 P.2d at 99.]

---

* [This case is noted in 8 U.Chi.L.Rev. 605 (1941); 18 N.Y.U.L.Rev. 589 (1941); 50 Yale L.J. 900 (1941). Other excerpts from the Court's opinion are set forth in Chapter 8, p. 360 supra. For further consideration of the nature of the tax in the Wisconsin case, see International Harvester Co. v. Wisconsin Department of Taxation, 322 U.S. 435, 64 S.Ct. 1060 (1944) and Wisconsin Gas & Electric Co. v. United States, 322 U.S. 526, 64 S.Ct. 1106 (1944).]

D. *References.* W. Hellerstein, "Some Reflections on the State Taxation of a Nonresident's Personal Income," 72 Mich.L.Rev. 1309 (1974).

(c) Income Taxation of Trusts

The income taxation of trusts, which raises questions under both the Due Process Clause and under State income tax statutes, is treated in Chapter 13, § 5 infra.

SECTION 5.   RETROACTIVITY UNDER THE DUE PROCESS CLAUSE

The Supreme Court has held that the Federal estate tax on gifts intended to take effect in possession at or after death, which came into the law in 1918, cannot be applied to inter vivos gifts made in 1907 and 1917 by a decedent who died in 1921.   Such a retroactive tax violates the Due Process Clause of the Fifth Amendment:

> [The inclusion] in the gross estate [of] the value of property transferred by a decedent prior to its passage merely because the conveyance was intended to take effect in possession or enjoyment at or after his death, is arbitrary, capricious and amounts to confiscation. [Nichols v. Coolidge, 274 U.S. 531, 543, 47 S.Ct. 710, 714 (1927).]

Likewise, the Due Process Clause prevents the imposition of a gift tax on a gift made before Congress adopted the first gift tax, Blodgett v. Holden, 275 U.S. 142, 48 S.Ct. 105 (1927); Untermeyer v. Anderson, 276 U.S. 440, 48 S.Ct. 353 (1928), even as applied to a gift made while the bill designed to tax gifts was pending before Congress.[19]   But see Pabst v. Commissioner of Taxes, 136 Vt. 126, 388 A.2d 1181 (1978), appeal dismissed 439 U.S. 922, 99 S.Ct. 303 (1978) (upholding over due process objections gift tax whose rates depended on gifts made prior to effective date of statute).

In the income tax area, as distinguished from excises such as estate and gift taxes, the Court has tolerated "limited retroactivity."   As the Court said in sustaining a Wisconsin income tax, adopted in 1935 as an emergency levy for unemployment relief purposes which was measured by 1933 and 1934 income:

> Assuming that a tax may attempt to reach events so far in the past as to render that objection [unconstitutional retroactivity] valid, we think that no such case is presented here.   For more than seventy-five years it has been the familiar legislative practice of Congress in the enactment of revenue laws to tax retroactively income or profits received during the year of the session in which the taxing statute is enacted, and in some instances during the year of the preceding session.   [Welch v. Henry, 305 U.S. 134, 148, 59 S.Ct. 121, 126 (1938).] [20]

19. In Untermeyer v. Anderson, supra, the gift at issue had been made just two days before Congress enacted the gift tax and while the House–Senate conference report was pending.

20. See also MacLauglin v. Alliance Ins. Co., 286 U.S. 244, 52 S.Ct. 538 (1932).

The estate and gift tax cases were distinguished as involving voluntary actions by the taxpayer at a time when the tax was not in force and the taxpayer might have chosen to "give or not to give" in the light of the tax. 305 U.S. at 147. See also United States v. Darusmont, 449 U.S. 292, 101 S.Ct. 549 (1981) (change in the "minimum tax" provisions pertaining to the sale of property could be retroactively applied to the transaction made within the year prior to the amendment of the Internal Revenue Code without violating due process).

Taxpayers have also attacked under the Due Process Clause the taxation of appreciation in the value of property which took place before the State imposed an income tax, or before its income tax included capital appreciation in the measure of the levy. A number of State courts have held that such cases do not involve retroactive taxation because the State is justified in treating the capital gain as income only when the property is sold or exchanged or a similar taxation event occurs.[21]

This retroactivity issue arose in Florida, which adopted its first corporate income tax in 1971. The issue was exacerbated by the fact that for decades Florida has sought to attract migrants from other States, not only by its warm climate but also by its constitutional prohibition against the imposition of income taxes. However, the State's revenue needs led to the amendment of the Florida Constitution effective November 2, 1971, so as to authorize the legislature to impose income taxes on taxpayers other than natural persons. A corporation which sold Florida real estate, after a corporation income tax was enacted pursuant to the constitutional amendment, challenged the constitutionality of the application of the tax to the pre–November 2, 1971 appreciation in the property. The Florida Supreme Court, in Department of Revenue v. Leadership Housing, Inc., 343 So.2d 611 (Fla. 1977), appeal dismissed and certiorari denied, 434 U.S. 805, 98 S.Ct. 35 (1977), rejected the taxpayer's argument that

> the appreciation became immunized from income taxation as it accrued by the Florida constitutional prohibition

by saying:

> * * * appreciation becomes income only upon the sale, exchange, or other disposition of the capital asset together with the accretions

---

21. Fullerton Oil Co. v. Johnson, 2 Cal. 2d 162, 39 P.2d 796 (1934); Kellems v. Brown, 163 Conn. 478, 313 A.2d 53 (1972), appeal dismissed 409 U.S. 1099, 93 S.Ct. 911 (1973); Chope v. Collins, 48 Ohio St.2d 297, 358 N.E.2d 573 (1976). For other cases rejecting constitutional challenges to the taxation of earlier years' capital appreciation on various grounds, see Norman v. Bradley, 173 Ga. 482, 160 S.E. 413 (1931), appeal dismissed 285 U.S. 526, 52 S.Ct. 404 (1932); City National Bank of Clinton v. Iowa State Tax Commission, 251 Iowa 603, 102 N.W.2d 381 (1960); Shangri–La, Inc. v. State, 113 N.H. 440, 309 A.2d 285 (1973); Tiedemann v. Johnson, 316 A.2d 359 (Me. 1974). An Illinois case set aside an income tax on appreciation occurring before the effective date of the statute on the basis of its construction of the statute as not covering such appreciation, but the opinion reflects the court's doubt as to whether such a tax, if embraced by the statute, would have been constitutional. Thorpe v. Mahin, 43 Ill.2d 36, 250 N.E.2d 633 (1969).

thereto, and * * * such realized gain is income in the year of disposition regardless of when it accrued. [343 So.2d at 615.] [22]

Prior to November 2, 1971, Florida's Constitution had provided that "[n]o tax upon inheritances or upon the income of residents or citizens of this State shall be levied by the State of Florida," and this prohibition had been construed as applicable to corporations. The taxpayer in *Leadership Housing* contended that this provision, fairly interpreted, embraced within its prohibition taxation *at any time* of pre-amendment appreciation. Does the court's holding in *Leadership Housing* that appreciation is not income until realized by a taxable event meet the taxpayer's objection? [23]

In Klebanow v. Glaser, 80 N.J. 367, 403 A.2d 897 (1979), the court upheld the application of New Jersey's tax on capital gains, enacted in August 1975, to a gains realized on or after January 1, 1975—in this instance a transaction that occurred on January 8, 1975. But see Holly S. Clarendon Trust v. State Tax Commission, 43 N.Y.2d 933, 403 N.Y.S.2d 891, 374 N.E.2d 1242 (1978), cert. denied 439 U.S. 831, 99 S.Ct. 108 (1978) (due process denied by application of 1973 tax law amendment to 1972 capital gain). In State ex rel. Van Emmerick v. Janklow, 304 N.W.2d 700 (S.D.1981), appeal dismissed 454 U.S. 1131, 102 S.Ct. 986 (1982), the State Supreme Court had held in 1980 that excessive sales taxes on utilities had been collected since 1969. In 1981, legislation was enacted providing a retroactive sales tax increase on utility services since 1969, thus ratifying the prior unauthorized collections. Despite the eleven and one-half year period of retroactivity, the statute was upheld. The court noted that there were no precise guidelines for determining when retroactivity violates due process strictures, and that "it is necessary to consider the nature of the tax and the circumstances in which it is laid before it can be said to be so harsh and oppressive as to transgress the constitutional limitation." 304 N.W.2d at 705 (quoting Welch v. Henry, supra, 305 U.S. at 147, 59 S.Ct. at 125). In concluding that the taxpayer had not been deprived of due process, the court declared that "[t]he tax at issue * * * could not have been avoided through an altered course of conduct in the same manner that income taxes or estate taxes might be avoided through alternative methods of financial and estate planning." 304 N.W.2d at 706.

---

22. The United States Supreme Court dismissed the taxpayer's appeal for want of jurisdiction and, treating the appeal papers as a petition for a writ of certiorari, the Court denied the writ, 434 U.S. 805, 98 S.Ct. 35 (1977).

23. Some State constitutions contain explicit provisions declaring that the legislature "shall have no power to pass retroactive laws." For a holding that an increase in corporate franchise tax liability for an accounting year already closed at the time of the enactment violated such provision in the Ohio Constitution, see Lakengren, Inc. v. Kosydar, 44 Ohio St.2d 199, 339 N.E.2d 814 (1975). This constitutional provision did not, however, prevent income taxation of appreciation in capital prior to the enactment of the statute. See Chope v. Collins, note 21 supra.

References. Slawson, "Constitutional and Legislative Considerations in Retroactive Lawmaking," 48 Cal.L.Rev. 216 (1960); Hochman, "The Supreme Court and the Constitutionality of Retroactive Legislation," 73 Harv.L.Rev. 692 (1960); Note, "Setting Effective Dates for Tax Legislation: A Rule of Prospectivity," 84 Harv.L.Rev. 436 (1970); Graetz, "Legal Transitions: The Case of Retroactivity in Tax Revision," 126 U.Pa.L.Rev. 47 (1977).

*

Part 7

DEATH, GIFT, AND PERSONAL INCOME TAXES

Chapter 12

DEATH AND GIFT TAXES

No attempt is made in this chapter to treat generally the problems of gross estate, deductions, and the like, which are ordinarily dealt with in a study of the Federal estate tax. The materials presented are limited essentially to problems peculiar to State taxation. The student should study the statutes and regulations of his or her State dealing with gross estate, net estate, and so forth, and compare them with the Federal estate tax. The same should be done with respect to the State and Federal gift taxes.

A. DEATH TAXES

INTRODUCTORY NOTE

1. The Development of American State Death Taxes. Inheritance and estate taxes are among the oldest levies used by the American States. Pennsylvania in 1826 was the first State to levy a tax on inheritances. This inheritance tax was not, however, without precedent. Death duties had long been in vogue in Great Britain, and the American colonies collected probate fees. The Federal Government had enacted a legacy duty in 1797, but this levy fell victim to the Jeffersonian assault on the excise tax system. Although 11 States in addition to Pennsylvania enacted inheritance or estate taxes prior to 1885, most of them were failures as revenue producers. Poor administration and hostile courts contributed considerably to their failure; some of the levies were declared unconstitutional. See Curry v. Spencer, 61 N.H. 624 (1882); State v. Gorman, 40 Minn. 232, 41 N.W. 948 (1889).

"The turning point in the development of state death duties appears to have been the enactment of the New York collateral tax of 1885. The success of this measure precipitated a wave of legislation that had by no means run its course when the federal estate tax was enacted in 1916. The intervening period is notable not only for the large increase in the number of states using this form of taxation and the rapid growth of the total revenues which state death duties produced, but also for the evolution of what came to be the traditional American state death duty—a progressive inheritance tax on both direct and collateral heirs." Oakes, "Development of American State Death Taxes," Symposium on State Inheritance and Estate Taxation, 26 Iowa L.Rev. 451, 457 (1941). By 1916, when the Federal Government came into the estate tax field to remain, 42 States were taxing inheritances and one State was taxing estates.

The use of progressive rates, adapted to various classes of beneficiaries, was introduced with the inheritance tax laws of North Carolina in 1901 and Wisconsin in 1903. Until 1916 many States patterned their inheritance tax laws on the Wisconsin tax of 1903. Following the Wisconsin example, States frequently used progressive rates and rates graduated according to the relationship of beneficiaries and heirs to the decedent. At present every State except Nevada levies either an inheritance tax, an estate tax, or some combination of the two taxes.

OAKES, "DEVELOPMENT OF AMERICAN STATE DEATH TAXES"

Symposium on State Inheritance and Estate Taxation
26 Iowa L.Rev. 451, 460 (1941).*

The motives prompting death tax legislation are undoubtedly mixed and in the present state of our knowledge difficult to evaluate or to disentangle. However, it does seem permissible to begin with the assumption that the major forces behind this legislation can be lumped into two categories: the need for revenue and the desire for "equity" or to put it more directly, the desire to use taxation as an instrument for "social reform." Our task then is reduced to an appraisal of the relative strength of these two factors.

Fiscal pressure was an important factor in most States. The strain on State and local tax systems had been increasing ever since the Civil War, and the result had been increased pressure on the property tax. The administration of the latter was known to be crumbling under the impact of the resulting high rates, and many States were seeking other methods of raising money. As soon as a few had demonstrated that substantial income could be obtained from death duties and that the latter were administratively feasible, there was every reason to expect the general adoption of the death duty as an instrument for the relief of the property tax.

"Social reform" was also an important factor. Discrimination against particular groups by means of a State death duty had ample precedent in early legislation, and the period now in question was characterized by a major general reform movement. The latter manifested itself in the Populist revolt, the Granger movement, anti-trust

* [This material is used with the consent of the Iowa Law Review. Footnotes have been omitted.]

legislation, and federal income taxation and led to a presidential proposal to levy a federal inheritance tax for the express purpose of destroying large fortunes. In addition economists had evolved certain ideas of "equity" in terms of psychological pain-cost which were being disseminated and which fitted neatly into the logic of a reform movement of this character. These ideas were applied to the special problem of inheritance taxation in Dr. West's famous monograph which was widely cited as an authority in the reports of the special tax commissions of this period. In view of all this, one might well anticipate a distinct element of reform in the State death tax legislation of the years under review.

In a few cases such as the Oklahoma tax of 1907 the motive of social reform appears to have been predominant. It was probably a major factor in the development of the progressive inheritance tax by the State of Wisconsin and an important cause of the spread of this form of taxation especially in the Western States.

But the major taxes in the East were less affected by this motive, more heavily influenced by the need for revenue and by the policy of developing replacement taxes for the relief of the levy on property. For example, the appearance of the leading tax for its period, the most important in the nation from the point of view of revenue, the New York law of 1885, can be explained exclusively in terms of the need for funds. This tax was in fact part of a general revision of the New York system recommended in the interests of relief for the property taxpayer ever since the reports of the famous Wells Commission of 1872 and 1873. The collateral tax itself was first recommended as a replacement tax by another special commission reporting in 1880, and its final adoption in 1885 is explainable in these same terms. There is little doubt that the New York legislature was responding to the pressure for more revenue on the one hand and the substantial income which the neighboring State of Pennsylvania was obtaining from its collateral tax on the other.

The extension of the New York levy to the passage of personalty to direct heirs in 1891 can also be explained in terms of what was happening to the property tax. The basic problem of relief for real estate still remained, since revenues from new taxes had not prevented an increase in the State levy on property from $4,559,000 in 1885 to $7,642,000 in 1891; and the restriction of the new tax on direct heirs to personal property reflects a second fiscal motive behind this law, the desire to tax personalty which by now was almost completely beyond the practical scope of the tax on general property.

The appearance during the next few years of proposals to extend the 1891 law to real estate and to use progressive rates reflects social reform motivation. This factor is also undoubtedly responsible for the very determined effort to set up a progressive tax in 1897. However, the movement for progressive taxation seems to have receded during the period which followed. The extension of the direct tax (first applied to personalty in 1891) to real estate in 1903 was accomplished with no fanfare, and there is nothing to cast doubt on the idea that this was a purely revenue measure.

Another special commission reporting in 1907 urged the adoption of a tax with progressive rates. Since New York was by this time operating under a system of separation of sources and by no means embarrassed by lack of funds, the motives behind this recommendation must have been almost entirely considerations of "equity" or "social reform." The arguments used in support of the progressive rate schedule in fact had nothing to do with the need for revenue, but stressed the State partnership and State protection arguments so frequently used in support of heavy death taxes, and cited the now familiar utterances of Andrew Carnegie on the subject of the social production of large fortunes. The imprint of this report is clearly discernible in the legislation of 1910 which introduced to the New York taxpayer a progressive inheritance tax. There was a violent reaction to this measure, and a reduction in rates followed shortly. While the progressive rate schedule survived the assault, it is fairly clear that revenue rather than equity was the predominant consideration prompting this later legislation. It is clear from this story that the revenue motive dominated death tax policy in New York during most of the interval between 1885 and 1916. Ideas of social reform were strong in the middle nineties and between 1907 and 1910, but towards the end of the period policy was again based primarily on considerations of revenue.

The experience of Massachusetts was similar. The original act of 1891 was the direct result of an agitation begun by a group of Boston merchants who wanted to establish a tax which would make possible the exemption of personalty from the local levy on property. The element of reform does not seem to enter the picture until 1894 when this factor appears in the report of a special committee on taxation. No results were achieved by this document nor by the 1897 report of another select commission of which Professor Taussig was chairman. It is noteworthy that the argument of social reform is not stressed in the latter, the recommendations relating to the inheritance tax being based squarely upon considerations of fiscal expediency. Nor was the reform motive present to any marked degree in the legislation of 1907 which set up the progressive inheritance tax in Massachusetts. Hence it appears that this factor which was clearly dominant in some States and played a substantial role in New York had a distinctly minor influence on the Massachusetts legislation.

In the present state of our knowledge any conclusion on the relative importance of these two motives for the country as a whole must be tentative, and the only one which may safely be suggested is that advanced above. One of these motives, social reform, was probably dominant in a few cases, but in most instances revenue was also a major consideration, and in some the need for new taxes completely overshadowed the desire for social reform. [End of excerpt from Oakes, supra.]

2. *The Existing State Death Tax Structure.* Most of the States have designed their existing death tax structures to insure full absorption of the credit allowed under the Federal estate tax for State death taxes. See p. 921 infra. A number of States have insured full absorption of the Federal credit by basing their death taxes entirely on the Federal levy, but in most States a differential estate tax is levied in addition to an inheritance tax in order to absorb the full Federal credit. A few States rely on inheritance or independent estate taxes, or combinations of the two taxes, without special provisions to insure full utilization of the Federal credit.[1] Some States impose death taxes which are designed to absorb only the Federal estate tax credit and no more. See, e.g., Alabama, Alaska, Arkansas, Florida, Georgia, New Mexico, North Dakota, and Utah. A summary chart of the death tax levies in force in the various States is set forth in CCH Inh., Est. & Gift Tax Rep. (State Compilation) ¶ 1100.

Graduated inheritance taxes have been attacked under equality and uniformity clauses of State constitutions. The New Hampshire Supreme Court declared such a levy unconstitutional. Foster v. Farrand, 81 N.H. 448, 128 A. 683 (1925); Williams v. State, 81 N.H. 341, 125 A. 661 (1924), overruled on a different issue in Amoskeag Trust Co. v. Trustees of Dartmouth College, 89 N.H. 471, 200 A. 786 (1938). Other courts, however, have sustained graduated inheritance taxes on the ground that they are not property but excise taxes, not covered by the uniformity requirements. See, e.g., In re Fulham's Estate, 96 Vt. 308, 119 A. 433 (1923).

In 1963, the New York estate tax was revised so as to conform the applicable provisions to the Federal estate tax. Simplification and ease of administration and compliance were the motivating forces behind the revision. In carrying out this objective, the term "New York gross estate" was defined as "Federal gross estate," with specific adjustments to deal with such matters as out-of-state, non-taxed assets. N.Y.Tax Law §§ 951–63. The deductions allowed for Federal estate tax purposes are, generally speaking, limited to expenses and allowances attributable to property comprising the New York gross estate. See Miller, "An Introduction to New York's Federally–Based Estate Tax Statute," 34 N.Y.State Bar J. 267 (1962). In the State income tax field, similar conformity to the Federal law has been developing rapidly in recent years (see p. 933 infra), but no comparable movement in this direction has taken place in the death tax field, although in many aspects, such as the definition of "gross estate" and other terms, the State death tax statutes are, in fact, closely modeled after the Federal law.

1. See Sen.Doc. No. 69, 78th Cong., 1st Sess. "Federal, State and Local Government Fiscal Relations," 473 et seq (rev. ed. 1949).

(a) Impact on the States of Federal Estate Tax Changes in the 1970's and 1980's

The Tax Reform Act of 1976 drastically changed the Federal estate tax. That act eliminated the prior $60,000 specific exemption and replaced it with a unified credit against estate and gift taxes. Subsequently, the credit was enlarged so as to eliminate by 1987 the tax otherwise payable on an estate of as much as $600,000. See Stephens, Maxfield & Lind, Federal Estate and Gift Taxation ¶ 3.01 (5th ed. 1983) for this history.

In 1981 in the Economic Recovery Tax Act, Congress took another major step by broadening the previous marital deduction that was limited to approximately 50 percent of the spouse's estate so as to make interspousal gifts entirely tax free. Id. ¶ 5.06. These drastic changes in the Federal estate tax, which have had the practical effect of repealing Federal death taxation for all except wealthy estates, have also had repercussions in State inheritance and estate taxation. Some States—California, New Mexico, and Oregon are among them—have joined Florida in making their States in effect State death tax-free havens. Those States have limited their death taxes so as merely to sop up the maximum credit allowable under the Federal estate tax for State death taxes. See e.g., Cal.Rev. & Tax. Code, Division 2, Part 8, P–H Inheritance, Estate & Gift Tax Rptr.Cal. ¶ 1000; Ore.Rev.Stat., § 118.100, id. Ore. ¶ 1110.[2]

Other States, however, have followed the Federal rule by making interspousal gifts completely free of the death tax. See. Conn.Gen. Stat., § 12–344(b), ¶ 1105 CCH Inheritance, Estate & Gift Tax Rptr.; N.J.Rev.Stat. 54:34–2, id. N.J. ¶ 1114; N.Y. Tax Law § 249–s(3), id. N.Y. ¶ 1107; and N.C.Gen.Stat., § 105–3(10), id. N.C. ¶ 1112.

Not all States, however, have gone so far in reducing death taxes. Colorado is such a State. Spouses are Class A beneficiaries, along with children and parents. They are taxed at rates beginning at 3 percent and graduating to 9 percent of the value of the property transferred to the beneficiary in excess of exemptions. Colo.Rev.Stat. § 39–23–112(a), CCH Inheritance, Estate & Gift Tax Rptr. ¶ 1114. Exemptions of $75,000 are allowed in the case of transfers to a spouse, $37,500 on a transfer to a child under 18 years of age, and $10,000 to other Class A beneficiaries. Colo.Rev.Stat. § 39–23–113(2)(a), CCH Inheritance, Estate & Gift Tax Rptr. ¶ 1115.

---

2. In computing the Federal estate tax liability, the basic estate tax and the additional estate tax are no longer computed separately, as was required under the earlier Federal statutes. Both taxes have been integrated into a single rate schedule. The credit for State death taxes, which is applied to the taxable estate in excess of $40,000, is applied to the integrated tax, § 2001 IRC. For a table of the maximum credit allowable for State death taxes, see P–H Federal Estate and Gift Taxes, ¶ 120,111; see also Stephens, Maxfield & Lind, supra, at ¶ 3.03.

SECTION 1. THE NATURE OF THE TAX: DEATH TAX OR INHERITANCE TAX

Notes and Problems

A. In In re Kohrs' Estate, 122 Mont. 145, 199 P.2d 856 (1948), the settlor in 1915 transferred stock to a trust for the benefit of her husband for his life and upon his death to the settlor. On the settlor's death, the income was to be paid to her two daughters for their lifetimes and on the death of the survivor, the trust was to terminate and the assets distributed to the settlor's grandchildren. The transfer was determined to be taxable as a transfer intended to take effect in possession or enjoyment at or after death. The settlor died in 1945. The issue was whether the inheritance tax rate in force in 1915 or in 1945 was applicable. For all practical purposes, the relevant portions of the statute in force in 1915 were the same as those in effect in 1945, except for the rates. In holding that the 1945 rate applied, the court declared:

> From the beginning this court has declared the tax imposed by the statute to be an inheritance tax, i.e., a tax not on the property of decedent but upon the right and privilege of receiving property by will or succession or by any *inter vivos* transfer operating as substitutes for testamentary dispositions. * * *

> Such a tax must be distinguished from an "estate tax" which has been defined as a tax imposed "upon the privilege of transfer at death." 28 Am.Jur., "Inheritance, Estate & Gift Taxes," section 10, p. 12. The federal government and some of the states impose estate taxes. A majority of the states impose inheritance taxes.

>   * * *

> A transfer intended to take effect in possession or enjoyment at or after death is [made] when the legal title is transferred by way of a trust, reservation of life estate or some other such device whereby the grantor attempts to retain the beneficial interest until his death or after.

> A transfer to a trust projects the effect of the transfer into the future and splits the ownership of the property so that under some circumstances less than a complete transfer takes place and actual possession and enjoyment of the fruits of the property by the transferee is postponed.

> This division of the attributes of ownership has led to two lines of decisions. Some courts have looked to the vesting in interest of the property as the determinative time for the imposition of the transfer tax and the fixing of the rate of tax. [Other courts have looked to the vesting in possession as the determinative time for the imposition of the transfer tax and the fixing of the rate of tax.]

>   * * *

> The distinction has been well stated by the Minnesota court in the Rising case, supra [In re Estate of Rising, 186 Minn. 56, 242 N.W. 459 (1932)]. "Our Legislature, without impugning the common-law concept of the *vesting in interest* of the remainder, which is effected by a gift with reservation of life estate or use to the donor, has simply

recognized that death, although not the 'generating source' of interest, is yet the operative event which causes 'the *vesting in possession*,' and the coming into enjoyment, and so perfects title in the remainderman. That operation is plainly, and in any view, a succession of such real and substantial sort, with such vital and enlarging effect on property rights as to make it the proper subject of an excise."

When we consider that our inheritance tax is an excise upon the right to receive and that the tax upon transfers intended to take effect in possession or enjoyment at or after death is a tax upon such a transfer when it is used as a substitute for testamentary disposition, the logic of making the moment of death the time at which the transfer is made becomes apparent. [199 P.2d at 859–60.]

See 5 A.L.R.2d 1046 for an annotation on the problem presented by the *Kohrs' Estate* case; cf. Chase v. Commissioner of Taxation, 226 Minn. 521, 33 N.W.2d 706 (1948).

B. In Thurston's Estate, 36 Cal.2d 207, 223 P.2d 12 (1950), the decedent in 1941 conveyed realty to his children and reserved a life estate to himself. A gift tax was paid on this transfer. In 1942, the decedent relinquished his life estate to his children, who paid him $10,000 therefor, which the State Controller agreed constituted fair and adequate consideration. The Controller sought to impose an inheritance tax on the 1941 transfer, measured by the market value of the property at the date of the decedent's death (less the $10,000 paid for the relinquishment of the life estate). The court rejected the contention that there was a taxable gift to take effect in possession or enjoyment at or after death. A tax attached when the 1941 transfer was made because of the decedent's life estate, but the court held that it was avoided by the subsequent relinquishment of that estate. It took the position that there can be no inheritance tax on the transfer intended to take effect in possession at or after death if nothing passes at or after death. Compare Estate of Crowell v. Cory, 56 Cal.App.3d 564, 128 Cal.Rptr. 613 (2d Dist.1976), where the California court held that an *inter vivos* transfer to an irrevocable trust was subject to California's inheritance tax as a transfer intended to take effect in possession and enjoyment after death.

C. *Rate Applicable to Revocable Trust.* Is the death tax rate in force at the date of the creation of a revocable trust, which is includible in the gross estate, applicable where the rate has been modified by the date of the settlor's death? See Commissioner of Corporations and Taxation v. Ayer, 323 Mass. 579, 83 N.E.2d 260 (1949).

D. A non-resident of New Jersey created an *inter vivos* trust of stock in a corporation reserving the dividends on the stock to himself for life and on his death, to his wife. The trust agreement was executed in New Jersey, where the trustees resided. Thereafter, the settlor took up residence in New Jersey, which was his domicile at the date of his death. New Jersey sought to tax the value of the trust corpus as a transfer intended to take effect in possession at or after death. The court set aside the assessment on the ground that the New Jersey statutes did not tax a completed transfer that took place while the decedent was domiciled outside the State and that here the execution of the irrevocable trust effected such a transfer. Hooton v. Neeld, 12 N.J. 396, 97 A.2d 153 (1953). One Judge dissented on the ground that the reservation of the dividends postponed beneficial enjoyment of the property until the decedent's death; the coming into possession of the dividends was the event taxed by statute.

In Estate of Perry, 35 Wis.2d 412, 151 N.W.2d 58 (1967), the decedent had created a revocable *inter vivos* trust in Illinois while he was a resident of that State. Both the trust assets and the trustee were located in Illinois. Subsequently, the decedent moved to Wisconsin. The Wisconsin inheritance tax statute does not tax transfers effected by non-residents when the property transferred is not physically located within the State. The court nevertheless held that the assets in the trust were subject to the Wisconsin inheritance tax on the ground that the transfer which the statute was designed to tax—the shifting of the economic use and benefit to the donee—took place at the time of the decedent's death.

E. *References*. Rottschaefer, "Taxation of Transfers Taking Effect in Possession at Grantor's Death," 26 Iowa L.Rev. 514 (1941); Brown & Sherman, "Premium Payments as Transfers in Contemplation of Death," 37 Cal.St.Bar J. 418 (1962); Moore, "Transfers Intended To Take Effect in Possession or Enjoyment at or after Death," 40 Taxes 876 (1962); Note, "Taxation—Gross, Estate—Intervivos Transfers—Retention of Possession and Enjoyment," 44 N.C.L.Rev. 230 (1965); Page, "Maryland Death Taxes," 25 Md.L.Rev. 89 (1965); Tournier, "Steps the Estate Planner Can Take to Minimize Taxes Where Estates Will Hold Out-of-State Property," 2 Estate Planning 66 (1975); Annot., 19 A.L.R.2d 1415; Keeler, "The California Inheritance Tax Scheme: 1981 Version," 8 West.St.U.L.Rev. 21 (1980); Taylor, "The 1978 Kansas Inheritance Tax Act," 27 Kans.L.Rev. 593 (1979).

SECTION 2. THE MEASURE OF THE TAX

(a) Delineation of Real and Personal Property

IN THE MATTER OF THE ESTATE OF HAVEMEYER

Court of Appeals of New York, 1966.
17 N.Y.2d 216, 270 N.Y.S.2d 197, 217 N.E.2d 26.

VAN VOORHIS, JUDGE. The State Tax Commission appeals from an order excluding from the gross estate certain real property located in Connecticut owned by the decedent and his son which has been taxed in Connecticut. Perhaps an error was made in imposing an inheritance or succession tax on this real estate in Connecticut which was not reviewed in the Connecticut courts. With that we are not, however, concerned on this appeal.

Decedent and his son were partners. The partnership agreement was made in New York State, between residents of New York, subject, necessarily, to the New York State Partnership Law, Consol. Laws, c. 39, which enacted the Uniform Partnership Law in this State. It is a fundamental principle that "All contracts are made subject to any law prescribing their effect, or the conditions to be observed in their performance; and hence the statute is as much a part of the contract in question as if it had been actually written into it, or made a part of the stipulations." (Strauss v. Union Cent. Life Ins. Co., 170 N.Y. 349, 356, 63 N.E. 347, 349.) Sections 12 and 51–52 of the New York Partnership Law, in force when this partnership agreement was executed, became a part of the agreement. Section 12 provides that all property originally brought into the partnership or subsequently acquired is partnership property. Section 51 states that a partner is co-owner with his partners of specific partnership property holding as a tenant in partnership, and that the incidents of this tenancy are such that "(d) On the death of a partner his right in specific partnership property vests in the surviving partner or partners, except where the deceased was the last surviving partner, when his right in such property vests in his legal representative. Such surviving partner or partners, or the legal representative of the last surviving partner, has no right to possess the partnership property for any but a partnership purpose."

Section 249–r of the Tax Law, Consol. Laws, c. 60, of course, exempts from the New York Estate Tax "real property situated and tangible personal property having an actual situs outside this state" to the extent "of the interest therein of the decedent at the time of his death".

Whatever may have been the law in New York prior to adoption of the Uniform Partnership Act, under the terms of the act specific partnership real estate is converted into personal property and, on the death of a partner, passes to the other partner under the partnership agreement (Matter of Finkelstein, 40 Misc.2d 910, 245 N.Y.S.2d 225). Prior to adoption of this statute, what became of partnership real property on the death of a partner was sometimes debatable. If the business of the partnership had been trading in real estate, it was regarded as having been converted into personalty for the purposes of the partnership by mutual agreement of the partners, and on the death of one of them passed to his next of kin instead of to his heirs at law (Buckley v. Doig, 188 N.Y. 238, 80 N.E. 913). In Darrow v. Calkins (154 N.Y. 503, 49 N.E. 61, 48 L.R.A. 299) it was said that in the absence of any agreement, express or implied, between the partners to the contrary, partnership real estate retains its character as realty, with all the incidents of that species of property, between the partners themselves and also between a surviving partner and the real and personal representatives of a deceased partner, except that each share is impressed with a trust implied by law in favor of the other partner that so far as is necessary it shall be first applied to the adjustment of partnership obligations and the payment of any balance found to be due from the one partner to the other on winding up the partnership affairs. Nevertheless it was held in the *Darrow* case, prior to the adoption of the Uniform Partnership Law, that an intention was there manifested in the agreement between the partners that the partnership lands should be treated and administered as personalty for all purposes. And effect was given thereto.

The New York State common law was thus to the effect that in the absence of a contrary intent, implied from circumstances or expressed in the partnership agreement, lands descended to the heirs at law of a deceased partner subject to payment of the partnership debts and adjustments of existing equities as between the partners. That, as was held below, may be assumed to be the law of Connecticut where the Uniform Partnership Law has not, as yet, been adopted (Morgan v. Sigal, 114 Conn. 39, 157 A. 412). Although as pointed out in Matter of Finkelstein, the legal concept of a partnership as an entity has gained force, we recognize that the Connecticut law should govern inasmuch as this real property is located in Connecticut. The common law of Connecticut is, quite evidently, similar to what was the common law of New York before the enactment of the Partnership Law. In Connecticut, it was said in Steinmetz v. Steinmetz (125 Conn. 663, 666–667, 7 A.2d 915, 917): "While the fact that a partnership exists between parties in whose names the title to real estate stands will not of itself prevent them from being regarded as tenants in common therein (Sigourney v. Munn, 7 Conn. 11, 18), much depends upon their understanding and intention; circumstances such as purchase with partnership funds and the course of their conduct and dealings, such as the carrying of income or expenses in the partnership accounts, are significant and may be determinative of status as a partnership asset. McKinnon v. McKinnon, 8 Cir., 56 F. 409, 413; Johnson v. Hogan, 158 Mich. 635, 651, 123 N.W. 891, 37 L.R.A., N.S., 889; Fairchild v. Fairchild, 64 N.Y. 471, 477; City of Providence v. Bullock, 14 R.I. 353; 47 C.J. 760; 1 Rowley, Modern Law of Partnership, §§ 282, 283."

This renders clear that intention is the touchstone of the Connecticut common law, as it was of the New York State common law before being superseded by statute. The brief for the respondents recognizes "that a case might be taken out of the general rule of Darrow v. Calkins" and an equitable conversion into personal property for all purposes of the partnership "by proof that it was the intention of the partners that on dissolution the property should be converted 'out and out' into personalty." As to intention the Surrogate said, as respondents' brief points out, that this partnership agreement "is wholly silent as to any accountability of the surviving partner to the representative of the deceased partner for the value of the Connecticut real estate."

That touches the heart of the issue. Unfortunately for respondents, this agreement was made in New York State subject to the New York State Partnership Law which, as we have seen, contains express provisions converting partnership real estate into personalty and providing that on death it shall pass to the surviving partner or partners as tenants in partnership. That is read into the contract as though it had been expressly stated therein. The traditional rule has been that matters bearing upon the execution, the interpretation and the validity of contracts are governed by the law of the State where the contract was made (Swift & Co. v. Bankers Trust Co., 280 N.Y. 135, 141, 19

N.E.2d 992, 995; Union Nat. Bank v. Chapman, 169 N.Y. 538, 543, 62 N.E. 672, 57 L.R.A. 513; Employers' Liab. Assur. Corp. v. Aresty, 11 A.D.2d 331, 205 N.Y.S.2d 711). That rule, no longer to be slavishly followed, nevertheless still signifies that the place where a contract is made is a significant contact in applying the center of gravity rule of Auten v. Auten, 308 N.Y. 155, 124 N.E.2d 99, 50 A.L.R.2d 246. Not only was this contract made in New York, but also it was between New York State residents, one of whom has died and his estate is being administered in Suffolk County. Under the grouping of contacts criteria of the *Auten* case, the significant contacts here are with New York State. The devolution of the property of this New York State testator would normally be governed by the law of this State, and the partnership agreement would normally be interpreted in accordance with the law of the State where it was made.

Intention is, of course, the dominant factor, as was explained in detail in the opinion by Chief Justice Taft for the United States Supreme Court in Blodgett v. Silberman (277 U.S. 1, 11–12, 48 S.Ct. 410, 414, 72 L.Ed. 749), quoting from Darrow v. Calkins, 154 N.Y. 503, 515–516, 49 N.E. 61, 64, 48 L.R.A. 299, supra, as follows: " 'It is, however, generally conceded that the question whether partnership real estate shall be deemed absolutely converted into personalty for all purposes, or only converted *pro tanto* for the purpose of partnership equities, may be controlled by the express or implied agreement of the partners themselves, and that where by such agreement it appears that it was the intention of the partners that the lands should be treated and administered as personalty for all purposes, effect will be given thereto. In respect to real estate purchased for partnership purposes with partnership funds and used in the prosecution of the partnership business, the English rule of "out and out" conversion may be regarded as properly applied on the ground of intention, even in jurisdictions which have not adopted that rule as applied to partnership real estate acquired under different circumstances and where no specific intention appeared. The investment of partnership funds in lands and chattels for the purpose of a partnership business, the fact that the two species of property are in most cases of this kind, so commingled that they cannot be separated without impairing the value of each, has been deemed to justify the inference that under such circumstances the lands as well as the chattels were intended by the partners to constitute a part of the partnership stock and that both together should take the character of personalty for all purposes, and Judge Denio in Collumb v. Read [24 N.Y. 505], expressed the opinion that to this extent the English rule of conversion prevailed here. That paramount consideration should be given to the intention of the partners when ascertained, is conceded by most of the cases.' "

In Blodgett v. Silberman, Connecticut was allowed to tax as intangible personal property a decedent's interest in a partnership which held real estate and also personal property having a situs in New York State.

The Court regarded it as immaterial whether succession to the property there involved was also taxable in another jurisdiction saying (277 U.S. p. 10, 48 S.Ct. p. 414): "As to that we need not inquire. It is not the issue in this case. For present purposes it suffices that intangible personalty has such a *situs* at the domicile of its owner that its transfer on his death may be taxed there."

In Matter of Finkelstein (supra) it was said, 40 Misc.2d at page 915, 245 N.Y.S.2d at page 229: "Petitioner makes the point that the Ohio real estate has already been taxed there. This is hard to understand, since Ohio has adopted the Uniform Partnership Law and New York would not do the same in the reverse situation. Allen v. Pfaltz & Bauer Realty Co., 227 App.Div. 666, 236 N.Y.S. 210. However, it is not the issue here. Blodgett v. Silberman, supra, at 277 U.S. page 10, 48 S.Ct. pages 413, 414, 75 A.L.R. 980. And double taxation is not necessarily to be avoided by the courts. State Tax Commission v. Aldrich, 316 U.S. 174, 181, 62 S.Ct. 1008, 1011, 1012, 86 L.Ed. 1358, 1370."

If the partnership property is held to be taxable in New York State, the question becomes academic whether partnership liabilities for the maintenance of the Connecticut real estate are deductible. If the value of the real property is included in the valuation of the partnership assets, manifestly these items are deductible.

If this real estate had been owned by decedent individually, it would of course have been exempt from the New York estate tax (Tax Law, § 249–r; Matter of Swift, 137 N.Y. 77, 32 N.E. 1096, 18 L.R.A. 709). Instead, it was expressly deeded to the partnership, and the partners were careful to see that it was purchased with partnership capital.

* * *

The order appealed from should be reversed and the value of the Connecticut real estate included in the evaluation of the partnership.

KEATING, JUDGE (concurring).

We like to think of courts as established to do justice. In this case we are forced by our decision to do an injustice. There just seems to be no way to wriggle out of the manifestly inequitable result.

I concur in the decision of the court only because the mandate of sections 12, 51 and 52 of the Partnership Law is clear and binding (cf. Tax Law, § 249–r).

Although taxation by both New York and Connecticut is not unconstitutional in the present circumstances (Blodgett v. Silberman, 277 U.S. 1, 48 S.Ct. 410, 72 L.Ed. 749) the fact remains that land representing a single economic value is being taxed as realty in Connecticut and as personalty in New York. In all probability, the Connecticut tax would not have been imposed if the facts as they clearly exist had been brought to that jurisdiction's attention (Steinmetz v. Steinmetz, 125 Conn. 663, 7 A.2d 915). That question, however, cannot be resolved in New York. It is to be hoped that the estate is not precluded from reopening the proceedings in Connecticut and that the Connecticut court will recognize the injustice which it alone would have the power to rectify.

DESMOND, C.J., and FULD, BURKE, SCILEPPI and BERGAN, JJ., concur with VAN VOORHIS, J.

Notes and Problems

A. Decedent, domiciled in California at the time of his death, owned the beneficial interest in land trusts in Illinois. The executor argued that California had no jurisdiction to tax such interest because it represented real property outside the State. Relying on Illinois law which "is definitely settled to the effect that the interest of a beneficiary in the customary Illinois Land Trust is personal property," the court held the decedent's interest was taxable by California. In re Tutules' Estate, 204 Cal.App.2d 481, 22 Cal.Rptr. 427 (1962); cf. Security Trust Co. v. Department of Revenue, 263 S.W.2d 130 (Ky.1953).

B. *Land Subject to Contract for Sale.* When a decedent dies holding a seller's interest in a contract for the sale of land, many State courts hold that the sales contract converts the realty into intangible personalty under the doctrine of equitable conversion. See, e.g., Department of Revenue v. Baxter, 486 P.2d 360 (Alaska 1971). The property is therefore taxable by the decedent's domicile rather than by the State where the property is located. In In re Estate of Highberger, 468 Pa. 120, 360 A.2d 580 (1976), however, the court held that the doctrine did not apply to land located in Pennsylvania and characterized a non-resident vendor's interest as taxable realty. See generally Note, "Problematic Definitions of Property in Multi-state Death Taxation," 90 Harv.L.Rev. 1656 (1977).

(b) Jointly Held Property

Notes and Problems

A. In State Bd. of Equalization v. Cole, 122 Mont. 9, 195 P.2d 989 (1948), the decedent had caused several of her checking and savings accounts to be transferred to joint bank accounts. The court held that the full value of the joint bank accounts was subject to inheritance tax. One-half the value was taxable under the statutory provision explicitly treating the disposition of joint property upon death of a joint owner as the transfer of one-half the value by the decedent to the survivor. The other half of the value was taxable as a gift in contemplation of death, because the joint bank account was created less than three years before the decedent's death. The court also held that United States Savings bonds purchased by the decedent and payable to her or in the alternative to a person named on the face of the bond were subject to inheritance tax upon their full fair market value. It declared:

> The bonds in question are not held in the joint names of two or more persons. So long as the bonds remained in the possession of Mrs. Perier they were hers. The contract with the government provided that in the event of her death the value of the bonds would be paid to

the person therein designated but so long as Mrs. Perier was alive and retained possession of the bonds, they were hers solely. ＊ ＊ ＊ They constituted a transfer of personal property without consideration intended to take effect in possession or enjoyment of the named donees at or after the death of Mrs. Perier and were therefore taxable ＊ ＊ ＊ [195 P.2d at 997.]

The case is discussed in Note, "Inheritance Tax on Jointly Owned Property," 10 Mont.L.Rev. 100 (1949). *Caveat:* In many cases jointly held or joint-survivorship bank accounts are held by husband and wife. Interspousal transfers are no longer subject to death tax in many States. See Introductory Note 2(a) supra.

B. United States Savings Bonds have become an increasingly important asset in the portfolios of decedents' estates of modest size. These, together with joint-survivorship savings accounts, offer a tempting avenue for death tax exemption without the relinquishment of control over the property. The decedent retains full control of the property through possession of the savings bond certificates or the savings bank pass book. If there is a completed *inter vivos* gift for death tax purposes, the estate has achieved a result much desired by tax-minded persons. For Federal estate tax purposes, the scheme does not work. The statute generally provides that the entire value of the bonds or the savings account is deemed to pass to the co-owner on the decedent's death if the co-owner paid no part of the consideration. I.R.C. § 2040. The *Cole* case, Note A supra, reflects the tendency of the State courts to reach similar results, despite the absence in some cases of specific statutory provisions. See Mitchell v. Carson, 186 Tenn. 228, 209 S.W.2d 20 (1948); Connelly v. Kellogg, 136 Conn. 33, 68 A.2d 170 (1949); In re Estate of Le Duc, 5 Mich.App. 390, 146 N.W.2d 711 (1966); State v. Parmelee, 115 Vt. 429, 63 A.2d 203 (1949); In re Estate of Hughes, 74 Misc.2d 1041, 347 N.Y.S.2d 227 (Surr.Ct.1973); In re Estate of Abernathy, 211 Tenn. 168, 364 S.W.2d 350 (1963). Contra: In re Schroeder's Estate, 144 N.E.2d 512 (Ohio Probate Ct.1957) (savings accounts); In re Gerling's Estate, 303 S.W.2d 915 (Mo.1957) (joint tenancy property not subject to inheritance tax). See also Estate of Sabol, 272 Cal.App.2d 798, 77 Cal.Rptr. 725 (1969), which considers these issues in the context of community property. See generally Annot., 39 A.L.R.2d 698.

Some States have explicitly dealt with the problem by statute. Thus, in Pennsylvania the statute provides that where property is held in the joint names of two or more persons, including bank accounts in joint names, in a manner so that in the event of death the survivor has a right to immediate ownership, "the accrual of such right upon the death of one of them shall be deemed a transfer, subject to tax under this act of a fractional portion of such property to be determined by dividing the value of the whole property by the number of joint tenants in existence immediately preceding the death of the deceased joint tenant." Pa.P.L. 521, as amended by P.L. 44, 72 P.S. § 2301, Act of June 15, 1961, P.L. 373, § 241, 72 P.S. 2485-241. This provision is inapplicable to property held by a husband and wife. See In re Kleinschmidt's Estate, 362 Pa. 353, 67 A.2d 117 (1949); In re Myers' Estate, 359 Pa. 577, 60 A.2d 50 (1948). Under the statute it has been held that because the decedent was the sole party with access to the safe deposit box in which the savings bonds were kept, the full value of United States savings bonds were included in the decedent's estate, even though the bonds were registered in the name of the decedent and another. In re Estate of Beggy, 446 Pa. 166, 285 A.2d 89 (1971); cf. In re Estate of Monheim, 451 Pa. 489, 304 A.2d 115 (1973). When the joint tenant in a savings account acted as a trustee rather than as a co-owner with right of survivorship and distributed the proceeds of the account to beneficiaries designated by the decedent upon her death, the West Virginia court held that the inheritance tax was due upon the separate shares of the beneficiaries rather than upon the surviving joint tenant's technical right to the proceeds of the account. Estate of Hobbs v. Hardesty, 167 W.Va. 239, 282 S.E.2d 21 (1981). *Caveat*: See Introductory Note 2(a) supra for States that follow the 1981 amendment to the Federal estate tax exempting in full interspousal gifts.

C. Joint survivorship bank accounts present additional complications under State succession taxes where the funds are on deposit in out-of-state banks. In Eastman v. Johnson, 161 Me. 387, 213 A.2d 305 (1965), the decedent, a resident of Maine, had held bank accounts in Massachusetts banks, naming the plaintiff as joint-survivor owner. The plaintiff had contributed no funds to the accounts; the Maine death tax called for inclusion of such assets within the decedent's estate. The plaintiff contended that Massachusetts law alone permitted her to succeed to deposits in banks in that State, and that as a result, only Massachusetts could tax their disposition on the depositor's death. Applying the doctrine of *mobilia sequuntur personam*, and dryly observing that "Massachusetts has displayed no intention to impose the tax," the court held that the decedent's domicile in Maine provided ample authority for the levy.

D. Compare with the foregoing cases, Estate of Hounsel v. Department of Taxation, 252 Wis. 138, 31 N.W.2d 203 (1948), cert. denied, 335 U.S. 844, 69 S.Ct. 66 (1948), in which *H* and *W* jointly held certain real estate, mortgages and bank accounts. *H* had contributed all the funds with which these joint tenancies were created from his business and investments. *H* reported the income in his income tax returns. *W* contributed no funds, nor did she use the above bank accounts except at *H's* request. At *W's* death, the court held that one-half of the jointly owned property transferred was subject to an inheritance tax, against *H's* contention that the property was actually already his. The court construed the statute as bottoming taxability on transfers of title to the property. Had *H* died first, what portion of the property would be includible in his gross estate?

E. *Inheritance Taxation of Dower and Statutory Shares.* In some States a widow's dower rights are treated as her own property interest not deriving from her husband's estate and hence not subject to inheritance taxation. In re Estate of Sanford, 91 Neb. 752, 137 N.W. 864 (1912); see Note, "Inheritance Taxation of Dower and other Marital Interests," 99 U.Pa.L.Rev. 979 (1951), which contains a survey of State materials on the subject. Will the result be the same where the widow takes her statutory share in lieu of dower? In Estate of Strahan, 93 Neb. 828, 142 N.W. 678 (1913), the court excluded the statutory share from the measure of an inheritance tax on the theory that the statutory share, like dower, is the widow's inchoate right.   Accord: In re Rogers' Estate, 50 S.W. 576 (Mo. 1923); Estate of Castles, 23 Utah 2d 4, 455 P.2d 628 (1963).   The result of such a holding is to produce an inequity as between the widow who takes under the will (and is taxable) and the widow who takes against the will; this factor has influenced some courts to uphold taxation of the widow's statutory share where an election is made.   Stovall v. Dep't of Revenue, 165 Mont. 180, 527 P.2d 62 (1974); State ex rel. Petit v. Probate Court, 137 Minn. 238, 163 N.W. 285 (1917); see In re Estate of Sharon, 121 Vt. 322, 157 A.2d 475 (1960), which is commented on in 40 Boston U.L.Rev. 456 (1960).   Taxation of dower and statutory rights has been eliminated in States that have adopted the 1981 Federal estate tax amendment making interspousal gifts totally tax-free.   See Introductory Note 2(a) supra.

F.   *Jointly Held Property Acquired by Gift of Third Party.*   H and W desired to purchase a plantation.   W's father gave W $100,000 to be used for the purchase.   The deed ran to both H and W.   H made no contribution toward the purchase price, taxes, or upkeep of the plantation.   W made all payments.   On H's death, is any part of the property to be includible in his gross estate for inheritance tax purposes?   For an affirmative answer, see Legendre v. Tax Commission, 215 S.C. 514, 56 S.E.2d 336 (1949).   There, the inclusion of H's name in the deed was construed by the court as a gift by W to H of one-half interest in the property as a "token of affection."

G.   For a case dealing with the "community exemption" in a community property State, see Kuchel v. Miller, 31 Cal.2d 191, 187 P.2d 722 (1947); cf. Estate of Allen, 108 Cal.App.3d 614, 166 Cal.Rptr. 653 (1980).   The allowance of a marital deduction for property transferred at death between spouses, embodied in the Revenue Act of 1948, has been followed by some noncommunity property States.   California, a community property State, has also adopted such a provision.   See Cal.Rev. & Tax Code § 13805.   Under the conformity of the New York estate tax to the Federal definition of taxable estate, the marital deduction is allowed.   See N.Y.Tax Law § 953.   For analysis of the Federal provision, see Surrey, "Federal Taxation of the Family—The Revenue Act of 1948," 61 Harv.L.Rev. 1097 (1948). Current Federal law provides for the reduction of the value of the taxable estate by an amount equal to the value of any interest in property passed to the surviving spouse.   I.R.C. § 2056(a).

H.   *References.*   The statutory materials and cases in Illinois, Michigan, and Ohio dealing with jointly held property are treated in Comment, "Inheritance Taxation—Selected Provisions of Michigan, Illinois and Ohio—A Study in Application and Justification," 57 Mich.L.Rev. 864 (1959). See also Note, "Gift and Inheritance Taxation of Community Property by Common Law States," 34 N.C.L.Rev. 564 (1956); Rollison, "Co–Ownership of Property in Estate Planning," 37 Notre Dame Lawyer 608 (1962); Poore, "Montana Inheritance Tax," 26 Mont.L.Rev. 173 (1965); Note, 8 Houston L.Rev. 808 (1971).

(c) Mortgaged Property

IN RE BILLINGS' ESTATE

Surrogate's Court of New York, New York County, 1947.
70 N.Y.S.2d 191.

COLLINS, SURROGATE. Appeal is taken by the executors of the estate of a non-resident decedent from a pro forma order fixing estate tax on the appraiser's report, Tax Law, § 249–x, presenting a question, apparently not heretofore decided in the state, of the valuation in such an estate of New York real property subject to a mortgage the indebtedness for which the estate is not liable.

The facts are not in dispute. Decedent, a resident of Vermont, died in 1944 leaving property in the state of her domicile. She also left certain real property situated and tangible personal property having an actual situs in this state. Our estate tax is imposed upon the transfer of so much of the net estate of a non-resident decedent as consists of such property. Tax Law, § 249–p. One of the parcels of real property, No. 274–276 Madison Avenue, New York City, was subject at decedent's death to an open mortgage of $447,450, securing the bond of decedent's grantor. Decedent had not assumed the indebtedness so that her estate is not liable therefor. The appraiser valued this parcel at $447,450 for determination of the gross estate, and allowed a deduction in the same amount for valuation of the net estate.

In reading the first paragraph of Section 249–p of the Tax Law, we would hardly expect our estate tax to be imposed on this parcel of realty the net value of which is zero. That portion of the statute clearly says the tax is imposed upon the transfer of so much of the net estate of a non-resident decedent as consists of real property situated within this state. The second paragraph of Section 249–p creates the problem. It directs: "Ascertain the amount of tax which would be payable under this article if the decedent had died a resident of this state with all his property (except real property situated and tangible personal property having an actual situs outside this state) situated or located within this state, and multiply the net tax so ascertained by a fraction the denominator of which shall be the value of the gross estate as ascertained for the purpose of computing such tax and the numerator of which shall be the said gross estate value of the real property situated and the tangible personal property having an actual situs in this state. The product shall be the amount of tax payable to this state. No credit shall be allowed against the tax so determined."

Following the above-quoted formula, the appraiser reported the gross estate at $1,434,470.83 with deductions of $775,131.58, and an exemption of $5,000, resulting in a net taxable estate of $654,339.25, upon which the tax would be $21,416.96 if decedent had been a resident. The appraiser further reported the total valuation of real property situated and tangible personal property having an actual situs within this state at $515,848. The resulting fraction, transposed into percentage, is .35960857, producing a tax upon this non-resident's estate of $7,701.72. But, if the parcel of realty with which we are here concerned had been valued at zero in determining the gross as well as the net estate, the resulting fraction, transposed into percentage, would be .06901446, producing a tax of $1,478.08.

Accordingly, the inclusion of the appraised value of the Madison Avenue property, undiminished by the mortgage, in computing the gross estate, has the effect of subjecting the transfer of this parcel of realty to an estate tax under Article 10–C which would not have been imposed thereon by such article had decedent died a resident of this state. The executors contend that this is violative of the Fourteenth Amendment of the Constitution of the United States and Article I, Section 11, of the Constitution of the State of New York. But we are not confronted with the question of constitutionality unless the statutory burden imposed by Article 10–C of the Tax Law for the privilege of transmitting real and tangible personal property within this state at death is, when judicially construed, clearly more onerous on the estates of non-resident decedents than upon the estates of deceased citizens of this state.

We have already observed that Tax Law, Section 249–p, which imposes the estate tax with regard to estates of non-resident decedents, speaks of both "net estate" and "gross estate." For definition of these terms Section 249–m refers to Sections 249–r and 249–s. Section 249–r directs that the gross estate shall be determined by including the value, "1. *To the extent of the interest therein* of the decedent at the time of his death." (Emphasis supplied.) Section 249–s directs that "the value of the net estate shall be determined by deducting from the value of the gross estate: 1. Such amounts * * * (d) for unpaid mortgages upon, or any indebtedness in respect to, *property where the value of decedent's interest therein, undiminished by such mortgage or indebtedness, is included in the value of the gross estate.*" (Emphasis supplied.)

Reading the language of both sections together, Sections 249–r and 249–s express as clearly as language permits the legislative intent to measure the tax only by the decedent's equity in mortgaged property. There is no statutory requirement that the value for determining the gross estate be undiminished by the mortgage thereon, and Section 249–r expressly permits the deduction for such purpose; where the mortgage is deducted in arriving at the gross estate a duplicate deduction may not be taken under Section 249–s. These sections, so read, provide a practical answer where the decedent was obligated on the bond and the mortgage exceeds the appraised value of the property—in such a situation the deduction for the mortgage can be taken under Section 249–s so as to accurately value the net estate.

No regulations have been issued by the Tax Commission under our estate tax statutes. However, the form of Return and Schedules (form TT 143) prescribed by the Commission contains the instruction, with regard to Schedule A–Real Estate, that "The full valuation of the property and not the equity must be given. The mortgage should be deducted under Schedule J." The State Tax Commission insists that the quoted instruction validly requires the result reached by the appraiser in this proceeding. While instructions issued by the Commission are in the nature of regulations and are accorded the same effect, the power of the Commission is expressly limited by statute to the making of rules and regulations "not inconsistent with law." Tax Law, § 171, Third. While considerable weight should be accorded the Commission's rulings, they are not controlling. An administrative practice contrary to or inconsistent with the statute is without legal effect and will be disregarded by the courts. Morrill v. Jones, 106 U.S. 466, 1 S.Ct. 423, 27 L.Ed. 267; Robinson v. Lundrigan, 227 U.S. 173, 33 S.Ct. 255, 57 L.Ed. 468. And it is well settled that in case of doubt taxing statutes should be construed in favor of the taxpayer. Matter of Vanderbilt, 281 N.Y. 297, 313, 22 N.E.2d 379, 389.

"An estate tax measured by the size of the estate *transmitted* to others upon the owner's death might, however, produce unjust inequality if the law arbitrarily includes for such purpose any property which is in no real sense a part of the estate in which it is taxed." Matter of Vanderbilt, supra, 281 N.Y. 311, 22 N.E.2d 388. Nothing in Tax Law, § 249–p, suggests a legislative intent to tax the property in this state of a non-resident decedent at a higher valuation than we would place upon it if the owner had been one of our own citizens. And it would require more than a suggestion to ascribe such an intent to our legislature or to find a legislative intent to permit such inequality of taxation to be imposed by an administrative regulation of the State Tax Commission. "A statute must be construed, if fairly possible, so as to avoid not only the conclusion that it is unconstitutional, but also grave doubts upon that score." United States v. Jin Fuey Moy, 241 U.S. 394, 401, 36 S.Ct. 658, 659, 60 L.Ed. 1061; Ann.Cas. 1917D, 854; Matter of Vanderbilt, 281 N.Y. 297, 313, 22 N.E.2d 379, 389.

As construed here, Section 249–r and 249–s are in harmony with the regulations issued by the Commissioner of Internal Revenue with regard to the Federal estate tax. Regulations 105, Secs. 81.38, 81.49. "It is the established legislative policy of the State to conform the estate tax law to the provisions of the Federal estate tax law, and in determining the effect of provisions of the New York Tax Law similar to those of the Federal estate tax law we give great weight to the construction of corresponding provisions adopted in the Federal courts 'for the purpose of maintaining uniformity of administration of the Tax Law * * * which the Legislature has sought to achieve.' Matter of Cregan, 275 N.Y. 337, 341, 9 N.E.2d 953, 954, 112 A.L.R. 260."

The pro forma order here fixes a tax upon a fictitious premise of value where, in fact, there is no value. The Tax Commission's argument emphasizes the nature of our estate tax, as a privilege tax upon the right to transmit property at death, rather than a tax on the property itself. But it does not follow that our legislature intended to impose a greater measure of tax upon the privilege in the estates of non-residents than in the estates of residents—the language employed in Article 10–C of the Tax Law, hereinabove quoted, is persuasively to the contrary. Nor does it follow that the Tax Commission possesses the power, by administrative fiat, to create such inequality. It is unnecessary to decide whether the imposition of such an unequal tax burden would be constitutional if the legislature had so directed.

(d) Pensions and Annuities

IN THE MATTER OF THE ESTATE OF BANNON

Court of Appeals of Indiana, First District, 1976.
171 Ind.App. 610, 358 N.E.2d 215.

LYBROOK, JUDGE.*

The Inheritance Tax Division of the Department of Revenue (State) appeals the judgment of the Marion Probate Court that Violet F. Bannon was not required to pay any state inheritance tax on money she received following the death of her husband. We affirm.

The payment in question arose from a contract of employment, executed on June 26, 1969, between decedent Luther M. Bannon and Ra Dis Co., Inc. The provision which provided for the payment to Bannon's widow reads in part as follows:

* * *

"Bannon accepts employment with the Corporation for a period of ten (10) years, at a salary of Twenty Thousand Dollars ($20,000.00) per annum for five (5) years, beginning June 1, 1969, and for a salary of Ten Thousand Dollars ($10,000.00) per annum for a period of five (5) years beginning June 1, 1974. If Bannon should die before the end of the ten (10) year period described above, then if his wife should survive him, Corporation agrees to pay to her Five Thousand Dollars ($5,000.00) per annum for the years remaining in said ten (10) year term but in no event to continue beyond her death."

Until his death on June 25, 1972, Bannon remained with the corporation in an advisory capacity. Pursuant to the terms of the agreement, an annuity totalling $34,600 thus became payable to his widow for the remainder of the ten year period.

The probate court ruled on the attendant tax consequences in response to the State's Petition for Rehearing, Reappraisement and Redetermination of Inheritance and Transfer Tax and the estate's Motion for Partial Summary Judgment. The court concluded in part:

* * *

"1. The annuity from Ra–Dis–Co., Inc. in the amount of Thirty-four Thousand Six Hundred Dollars ($34,600) is non-taxable for the reason that there was no transfer of a property interest from decedent on payment or the obligation of payment of said annuity from Ra–Dis–Co., Inc. to decedent's widow."

* [Some of the court's footnotes have been omitted.]

*   *   *

From this judgment, the State appeals.

The inheritance tax statute in effect at the time of decedent's death, IC 1971, 6–4–1–1 (Burns Code Ed.), reads in pertinent part as follows:

> "A tax is hereby imposed, under the conditions and subject to the exemptions and limitations hereinafter described, upon all transfers, in trust or otherwise, of the following property, or any interest therein or income therefrom:

> "When the transfer is from a resident of this state, of real property situated in this state, or of any tangible personal property except such as has an actual situs without this state, or of any and all intangible personal property wherever situated.

*   *   *

> "All transfers enumerated in this section shall be taxable *   *   * if made by gift or grant intended to take effect in possession or enjoyment at or after the death of the transferor *   *   * "

"Transfer" is defined by IC 1971, 6–4–1–32 (Burns Code Ed.) to include "the passing of property or any interest therein in possession or enjoyment, present or future by inheritance, descent, devise, bequest, grant, bargain, sale or gift, in the manner herein described or the exercise of the right of survivorship in cases of joint ownership."

In determining whether the present transfer is taxable under this statute, we are guided by a number of cases from other jurisdictions which have dealt with related problems. The cases are divided according to two distinct theories of taxation.[3] Under the "receipt" or "succession" theory, the taxable event is an enlargement of the beneficiary's interest at the transferor's death, regardless of whether the transferor retained an interest in the property during his lifetime. In contrast, under the "ownership" or "divestment" theory, property passing to a transferee at decedent's death will escape taxation if the decedent had no interest in it at his death.

The estate urges us to align our statute with the "ownership" theory and to require, as prerequisites to taxation, (1) a transfer from decedent (2) of an interest in property which the decedent owned at death. As authority for its contention that this transfer fails to meet either requirement, the estate cites cases from "ownership" jurisdictions.[4] The State, on the other hand, relies upon cases from "receipt" jurisdictions to support the imposition of tax.[5]

---

3. See D.R. Brink, Minnesota Inheritance Tax: Some Problems and Solutions, 43 Minn.L.Rev. 443 (1959); R. Meisenholder, Taxation of Annuity Contracts Under Estate and Inheritance Taxes, 39 Mich.L. Rev. 856 (1941).

4. In re Estate of Shade (Probate Ct. Ohio, 1966), 38 Ohio Ops.2d 357, 9 Ohio Misc. 199, 224 N.E.2d 401; In re Estate of

Kramer (Probate Ct.Ohio, 1964), 30 Ohio Ops.2d 370, 1 Ohio Misc. 76, 203 N.E.2d 271; In re Estate of Dolbeer (1962), 117 Ohio App. 517, 193 N.E.2d 174; Enbody and Burke Estates (1953), 85 Pa.Dist. & Co. R. 49.

5. Narva v. Commissioner of Corporations and Taxation (1971), 358 Mass. 648, 266 N.E.2d 638; National Shawmut Bank

We are of the opinion that our statute, on the whole, utilizes the "ownership" theory. In each of the transfers specifically enumerated by the statute the decedent retained some control over the property. See State Department of Revenue, Inheritance Tax Division v. Estate of Powell (1975), Ind.App., 333 N.E.2d 92. Furthermore, the "ownership" test reflects a basic distinction which underlies our inheritance tax system. The inheritance tax is directed toward transfers of property by will, by intestate succession, and by other such transfers that substitute for testamentary depositions. The death tax is not intended to apply to absolute *inter vivos* gifts. Armstrong v. State ex rel. Klaus (1919), 72 Ind.App. 303, 120 N.E. 717. The only meaningful distinction between an *inter vivos* gift and a testamentary gift is that in the latter the transferor enjoys the property throughout his life. See Note, "The 'Transfer Intended' Clause in Indiana Inheritance Tax," 35 Ind.L.J. 519 (1960).

The decisive question, then, is *whether the decedent had an interest in the property which passed to the beneficiary upon his death.* In the case at bar the salary payable to decedent for his services must be distinguished from the annuity payable to his widow upon his death. The right to receive salary payments while alive during the ten year period was the only property right which decedent possessed under the agreement and that right ceased with his death. The decedent had no interest in the annuity which was payable to his widow. The payment was not a transfer from decedent, rather, it came directly from the corporation in response to a contract for valuable consideration. See In re Estate of Dolbeer (1962), 117 Ohio App. 517, 193 N.E.2d 174; In re Estate of Kramer (Probate Ct.Ohio 1964), 30 Ohio Ops.2d 370, 1 Ohio Misc. 76, 203 N.E.2d 271.

Even if we accept the State's characterization of this arrangement as one involving deferred compensation, we are not persuaded that this fact, standing alone, qualifies as a sufficient property interest under the "ownership" test. The only reported case from an "ownership" state to consider this question is *Cameron Estate* (1958), 15 Pa.Dist. & Co.R.2d 557. The corporation there entered into a contract with its employee to pay a deferred compensation of $50,000 over a period of ten years beginning upon his retirement; the payments were to be made to his widow if he died before that amount was exhausted. A majority concluded that the payments were subject to taxation, since the widow's rights under the contract could have been assigned by the employee prior to his death.

Our view of the contract rights in the case at bar, however, leads us to a contrary result. The employment agreement here, contra to *Cameron, did not give decedent the power to change the beneficiary.* Under general contract law, any change in the agreement could only be

of Boston v. Commissioner of Corporations and Taxation (1968), 354 Mass. 350, 237 N.E.2d 290; Gould v. Johnson (1960), 156 Me. 446, 166 A.2d 481; Dolak v. Sullivan (1958), 145 Conn. 497, 144 A.2d 312; Borchard v. Connelly (1953), 140 Conn. 491, 101 A.2d 497; Cruthers v. Neeld (1954), 14 N.J. 497, 103 A.2d 153.

made with the consent of the other signatory to it. Moreover, there is the question of whether the widow was a third party donee-beneficiary of the agreement whose rights were vested and who could not have been prejudiced by the parties to the agreement without her consent. Decedent thus relinquished his interest in the amount payable to his widow once he entered into the agreement because he could not thereafter take any unilateral action to affect her rights.

The judgment is therefore

Affirmed.

ROBERTSON, C.J., and LOWDERMILK, J., concur.

Notes and Problems

A. *Death Taxation of Employee Pension Plan Benefits.* Under most State death tax statutes joint survivorship annuities purchased by a decedent who retains the right to designate and change the beneficiary of the sums payable at his death are taxable. See the cases collected in Annot., 73 A.L.R.2d 157, 183. The decedent's death is treated as completing a transfer intended to take effect in possession or enjoyment at or after death. Employee pension plans present somewhat different problems; the plan may be non-contributory so that the employee, unlike the purchaser of a commercial annuity, made no payment for the annuity, or where it is contributory, he has paid for only a part of the benefits. It is customary to permit employees a number of options, including an annuity during his own lifetime or a smaller annuity during his lifetime and that of his beneficiary; normally, the employee is given full freedom to select and to change the beneficiaries.

Compare with *Estate of Bannon* In re Stone's Estate, 10 Wis.2d 467, 103 N.W.2d 663 (1960), in which an employee elected a joint survivorship annuity under an employer's retirement plan. As a result, his widow received a monthly benefit of some $600 during her lifetime. The decedent's estate argued that the decedent had transferred nothing to his wife, that he had no property interest in the pension that he could transfer, and that her rights had accrued directly under the employer's pension plan. The court, however, held that by making the election to take the joint-survivorship annuity, the decedent had made a "transfer of property * * * intended to take effect at or after the death of the * * * donor," and hence had made a taxable disposition under the statute. Accord: Estate of Stevens, 74 Wis.2d 1, 245 N.W.2d 673 (1976). *Caveat*: See the exemption in toto for interspousal gifts enacted by some States following the 1981 amendments to the Federal estate tax. Introductory Note 2(a) supra.

In some States, the employee's power to designate or change the beneficiary has been used as a basis for bringing employees' annuities within death tax statutes. See State v. Schallerer, 12 Ill.2d 240, 145 N.E.2d 585, 146 N.E.2d 193 (1957); In re Endemann's Estate, 307 N.Y. 100, 120 N.E.2d 514 (1954); In re Dorsey's Estate, 366 Pa. 557, 79 A.2d 259 (1951); In re Daniel's Estate, 93 Ohio App. 123, 112 N.E.2d 56 (1952), affirmed 159 Ohio St. 109, 111 N.E.2d 252 (1953), noted in 32 Chi.–Kent L.Rev. 256

(1954). Yet, some courts have ignored the decedent's ability to change beneficiaries if that power was the decedent's only interest in the fund. See Valley Fidelity Bank & Trust Co. v. Benson, 223 Tenn. 503, 448 S.W.2d 394 (1969). As indicated by the principal case, an inability to change beneficiaries has led courts to conclude that an annuity should not be included in the decedent's estate.

A variation of the problem is presented where the employer or a committee selected under an employees' pension plan designates the secondary beneficiary. Actually, it is customary under such provisions for the committee in most cases to make the designation requested by the employee. In Cruthers v. Neeld, 14 N.J. 497, 103 A.2d 153 (1954), the court sustained the inheritance tax on the annuity on the ground that the enjoyment of the annuity could take effect in beneficial enjoyment and possession only at or after the decedent's death.

Under some civil service pension plans, the statute itself designates the beneficiary and the employees cannot change the designation. Under such a statute the pension payable to a civil servant's widow has been held nontaxable. In re Estate of Sweet, 270 Wis. 256, 70 N.W.2d 645 (1955); accord, 34 Op.Atty.Gen.N.C. 173. The Wisconsin Supreme Court reaffirmed this view in In re Estate of Peter King, 28 Wis.2d 431, 137 N.W.2d 122 (1965), a case involving a pension to a Federal employee, which arose after *In re Stone's Estate* had been decided. The holding was grounded on the fact that under the Federal retirement system, only the decedent's wife may receive the pension on the employee's death. See also People v. Hollingsworth, 164 Colo. 461, 436 P.2d 114 (1968).

Do these cases draw a line that can be justified in death tax policy? Is there a sound social reason for preferring pension plans in which an employee has no election as to his survivor-beneficiary? Do the statutes lend themselves to a construction which would treat all death benefits under employee pension plans alike? For a comprehensive annotation dealing with these problems, see Annots., 73 A.L.R.2d 150; 59 A.L.R.3d 969.

B. *Application of Insurance Exemption to Annuities.* Employee annuities or pensions may be purchased by the employer from an insurance company, or may be handled through a trustee, usually a bank, which administers the funds paid by the employer to the pension trust. The question has arisen as to whether the value at death of an insured annuity is covered by death tax exemptions for life insurance, or by general provisions treating life insurance as property of the beneficiary not coming through the estate. A Montana case excluded such an annuity from the gross estate as insurance covered by the State's insurance exemption. In re Estate of Hammerstrom, 133 Mont. 536, 326 P.2d 699 (1958). Accord: Department of Revenue v. Estate of Powell, 165 Ind.App. 482, 333 N.E.2d 92 (1975). Contrary holdings are to be found in In re Estate of Clark, 10 Utah 2d 427, 354 P.2d 112 (1960); In re Simpson's Estate, 43 Cal.2d 594, 275 P.2d 467 (1954); Borchard v. Connelly, 140 Conn. 491, 101 A.2d 497 (1953). The essential question in these cases, according to the Massachusetts Supreme Court, is whether the pension or annuity at issue has "the characteristics of life insurance." Roberts v. Commissioner of Revenue, 380 Mass. 428, 403 N.E.2d 418 (1980) (holding a statutory pension in favor of a judge's widow exempt, but distinguishing other cases involving interests "too remote from the concept of life insurance to be treated as life insurance").

C. *Provisions Protecting Pensions From Attachment and Other Legal Process as Affecting Death Taxation.* The Washington statute provides that no annuity or pension payments shall be "subject to any tax, garnishment, attachment or other legal process." The State Tax Commission contended that this provision, which is not a part of the inheritance tax statute, is inapplicable to the inheritance tax. The State Attorney General, however, has ruled otherwise and has held that the exemption provision applies to the inheritance tax. Op.Atty.Gen.Wash. to State Tax Commissioner, Dec. 22, 1958.

As a matter of death tax policy, the treatment of pension payments to be made after an employee's death, whether under a trusteed or an insured plan, requires reexamination, in view of the tremendous growth of employee pension plans and their key importance in the lives and the financial planning for death of the bread-winner in a great many families. The death benefits under pension plans, many of which are contributory, serve essentially the same function as life insurance, and it may be that the comparative importance of life insurance in the savings of many families has declined, in view of the existence of pensions carrying over to the pensioner's major beneficiary. Economically, the survivor annuity or pension and life insurance serve essentially the same functions; should not the death taxation or exemption of both, therefore, be placed on the same footing?

D. To the extent that the pension is attributable to the employee's own contributions, a different set of problems may be presented. In the cases cited in Notes A and B supra. the courts did not focus on the question whether the pensions were contributory or non-contributory in reaching the results indicated, but the question is sometimes important. Thus, in People v. Estate of Schilling, 41 Ill.App.3d 73, 354 N.E.2d 88 (1976), the court relied in part on the fact that the employer had funded the pension plan in holding that benefits receivable thereunder were not includible in the decedent's estate. What if the pension plan is based on profit-sharing and the employee-decedent had the power to withdraw funds and designate his survivorship beneficiary? In Commerce Union Bank v. Benson, 495 S.W.2d 537 (Tenn.1973), the decedent contributed a percentage of his salary to the fund and the company contributed a percentage of its earnings. The court held that the amount paid to the decedent's designated beneficiary was not subject to the State inheritance tax. Should the rule be different depending on whether the employer or the employee funded the pension plan? Is there any real distinction between an employee-funded pension plan and individually purchased insurance?

E. *Bonus to Widow.* A Wisconsin case held that a $9,000 bonus declared by the decedent's employer after his death and paid to his widow was not subject to inheritance tax. In re Stevens' Estate, 266 Wis. 331, 63 N.W.2d 732 (1954). Although the employer was under no obligation to pay the bonus, bonuses had been declared for several years at the year end. The court held that since the decedent had no claim to a bonus at his death, no property could be passed by him to his widow that was within the measure of the tax. Accord: Shaughnessy v. Commissioner, 3 Mass.App. 249, 326 N.E.2d 912 (1975); cf. Introductory Note 2(a) supra.

F. *References.* There is a useful summary and analysis of many of the cases in Annot., 73 A.L.R.2d 157, 167, and in Annot., 59 A.L.R.3d 969. See also 29 Wash.L.Rev. 166 (1954); Sager & Weinberg, "State Taxation of Employee Retirement and Death Benefits," 31 Ford.L.Rev. 413 (1963); Parks, "State Inheritance Taxation of Employee Death Benefits," 45 Den. L.J. 719 (1968).

SECTION 3. DEDUCTIONS, APPORTIONMENT OF TAXES AND OTHER ISSUES

Notes and Problems

A. *Deduction of Federal Estate or Gift Tax.* States need not allow a deduction for Federal estate taxes. Frick v. Pennsylvania, 268 U.S. 473, 45 S.Ct. 603 (1925). Some States, however, allow a deduction for Federal estate taxes in determining the State tax. In Clarke v. Welden, 204 Md. 26, 102 A.2d 560 (1954), the issue arose as to whether the entire Federal estate tax was deductible from a resident's inheritance tax, where a part of the estate consisted of real estate located in the District of Columbia, which is not taxable by Maryland. Indeed, the District had already allowed a deduction in computing its death tax for a proportionate part of the Federal levy. The Maryland court, nevertheless, held that under the statute the entire Federal tax was deductible in the case of a resident. See also Estate of Aul v. Haden, 154 W.Va. 484, 177 S.E.2d 142 (1970). In many States the Federal tax is not deductible in any circumstances. For a case so holding, see Succession of Henderson, 211 La. 707, 30 So.2d 809 (1947), criticized but followed in Kahn v. Inheritance Tax Collector, 286 So.2d 428 (La.App.1974). Accord: In re Estate of Heidner, 7 Wash.App. 488, 500 P.2d 1284 (1972); Camden v. People, 184 Colo. 131, 518 P.2d 1172 (1974). Compare Estate of Miller, 467 Pa. 193, 355 A.2d 577 (1976), in which the taxpayer successfully argued that the State inheritance tax on a remainder interest in a trust should not be computed by "adding back" the amount of Federal tax paid at the time of formation of the trust.

In a Washington case, the sole legatee contended that the Federal estate tax must be deducted in determining the amount of the State's inheritance tax on the bequests made to him. His theory was that the State's levy is "an excise tax on the receipt by the legatee or devisee of the property of a deceased person and not a tax on the deceased person's right to transmit property." The statute taxes all "property within the jurisdiction of this State * * * which shall pass" to the legatee. He argued that only the net estate, after Federal taxes, passed to him; and that he would be denied due process of law by a tax on more property than he inherited. The Washington inheritance tax did, at one time, allow a deduction for the Federal estate tax as "a claim or indebtedness against the estate," but this allowance had been repealed in 1961. Holding that the statute levies both "an inheritance tax and an estate tax," the court, in a five to three decision, denied the deduction for the Federal estate tax. In re Carlson's

Estate, 61 Wash.2d 359, 378 P.2d 435 (1963), reaffirmed in Estate of Toomey, 75 Wash.2d 915, 454 P.2d 420 (1969).

With regard to the deductibility of the Federal gift tax on *inter vivos* transfers on which no tax was paid during the life of the decedent, the courts have universally denied a deduction for such payment in computing the State inheritance tax. Annot., 56 A.L.R.3d 1322. In denying such a deduction, a California court observed that to permit the deduction of a gift tax as a claim against the estate or as an expense of administration, when the gift tax is in substance a down payment on the Federal estate tax, "would be to sanction the circumvention of the law which does not permit the deduction of the federal estate tax." In re Giolitti's Estate, 26 Cal.App. 3d 327, 103 Cal.Rptr. 38 (5th Dist.1972).

B. *Optional Valuation Date.* Some States followed the lead of the Federal estate tax (I.R.C. § 2032) in allowing the estate the option of valuing the estate as of one year (later changed to six months) after the date of the decedent's death. See the Vermont provision in In re Clark's Estate, 100 Vt. 217, 136 A. 389 (1927). Utah has a nine-month-after-death optional valuation proviso. Utah Code, Title 80, § 80–12–3. These provisions set up methods of handling sales and distributions where the optional valuation date is used. For the statutory provisions of the various States, see 1 P–H Inh. & Trans.Tax Serv. ¶ 702.

C. *Apportionment of Death Taxes Among Legatees.* Traditionally, the burden of estate taxes fell on the residuary legatee unless the will directed otherwise. 4 Page, Wills 1770 (3d ed.1941). See, e.g., National Newark and Essex Bank v. Hart, 309 A.2d 512 (Me.1973) (exhaustive opinion reviewing leading cases). This at times imposed on the testator's principal beneficiaries a tax burden far beyond anything intended. For that reason statutes have been enacted creating a contrary presumption, namely, that estate taxes are to be apportioned pro rata unless the will provides otherwise. Such a statute was sustained as to the apportionment of the Federal estate tax in Riggs v. Del Drago, 317 U.S. 95, 63 S.Ct. 109 (1942), noted in 41 Mich.L.Rev. 1209 (1943). Ordinarily, similar difficulties are not encountered under inheritance taxes, since each legacy is normally reduced by the amount of the tax allocable thereto, unless the will contains contrary directions. For a case dealing with apportionment of death taxes where some property passed under the will and the balance outside the will, see National State Bank of Newark v. Nadeau, 57 N.J.Super. 53, 153 A.2d 854 (1959). See Annot., 67 A.L.R.3d 199; Annot., 67 A.L.R.3d 273; Annot., 68 A.L.R.3d 714; Annot., 70 A.L.R.3d 691; Annot., 69 A.L.R.3d 122.

D. *Will Settlements.* In Estate of Abraham Burtman, 95 N.H. 383, 63 A.2d 798, certiorari denied 338 U.S. 820, 70 S.Ct. 64 (1949), a widow claimed her statutory distributive share of her husband's estate. The legatees under the will contested the widow's right to a statutory share, in view of her antenuptial agreement to accept a bequest of $50,000 in lieu of her statutory rights. The case was compromised by the parties, with the approval of the Probate Court, by the allowance of $100,000 to the widow in addition to the $50,000 bequest by the will. The State assessed an inheritance tax on the residuary estate by reducing it only by the $50,000 allowed to the widow by the will. The executors contended that the residuary estate should be further reduced by the additional $100,000 allowed in the compromise agreement. Under the New Hampshire statute the amount left to the widow was exempt from tax. The court upheld the tax, following what it declared to be "the great weight of authority" that successions in compromise cases "shall be taxed only in the manner as provided by the will, and not in accordance with an agreement subsequently entered into among the heirs or beneficiaries." Branch, C.J., dissented, relying in part on Caskey v. State, 93 N.H. 438, 43 A.2d 768 (1945). For the Federal rule, see Lyeth v. Hoey, 305 U.S. 188, 59 S.Ct. 155 (1938); I.R.C. Reg. § 20.2056(e)–2(d). For other cases dealing with the will compromise issue, see Note, 36 N.C.L.Rev. 236 (1958).

E. *References.* Neuhoff, "Deductions, Exemptions and Credits in State Inheritance and Estate Taxation," 26 Iowa L.Rev. 593 (1941). For a discussion of problems of apportionment, see Schiaroli, "Apportionment of Federal and State Estate Taxes in Connecticut," 20 Conn.B.J. 198 (1946), 24 Taxes 1086 (1946); Karch, "The Apportionment of Death Taxes," 54 Harv. L.Rev. 10 (1940). There is an extensive Note on "Inheritance and Estate Tax Law in New England" in 40 B.U.L.Rev. 413 (1960); see also Note, "A Comparison of Estate Taxes in the Southeast," 5 U.Fla.L.Rev. 35 (1952); 37 A.L.R.2d 170, 68 A.L.R.3d 714, 71 A.L.R.3d 247.

SECTION 4. EXEMPTIONS AND REDUCED RATES FOR GIFTS TO PREFERRED BENEFICIARIES

A. *Illegitimate and Adopted Children.* Most State death taxes allow a special exemption for property transferred to the decedent's children. In some States the rates applicable to children and other preferred beneficiaries are lower than the rates generally applicable. These provisions have produced an inordinate amount of litigation as to the meaning of "child" or "children," particularly with regard to illegitimate and adopted children. Such issues cannot be addressed today without considering their constitutional implications. The Supreme Court has handed down a number of decisions limiting the power of the States to distinguish between illegitimate and legitimate children. In Trimble v. Gordon, 430 U.S. 762, 97 S.Ct. 1459 (1977), the Court held that the Illinois inheritance statute which precluded illegitimate children from inheriting by intestate succession from their father while allowing legitimate children to do so violated the Equal Protection Clause of the Constitution. Query whether decisions holding that the word "child" in a transfer tax act excludes illegitimate children (thus denying them exemptions or lowered rates), e.g., Bank of Montclair v. McCutcheon, 107 N.J.Eq. 564, 152 A. 379 (1930), can be squared with the Supreme Court's decision in *Trimble v. Gordon.* The increasing community recognition that an illegitimate child should not suffer because of his parents' violation of accepted mores has resulted in more enlightened judicial decisions affecting the inheritance rights of illegitimate children and the tax position of their inheritances. See, e.g., Whorff v. Johnson, 143 Me. 198, 58 A.2d 553 (1948).

McLaughlin v. People, 403 Ill. 493, 87 N.E.2d 637 (1949), noted in 28 Chi.–Kent L.Rev. 174 (1950), dealt with the adoption of an adult. The Illinois law does not allow the adoption of adults, whereas the Connecticut law does. Decedent, a resident of Connecticut, exercised a power of appointment over certain Illinois real property in favor of X, whom decedent had adopted when X was 48 years of age. The Illinois taxing authority refused to allow X, the legatee, the lower rates of tax and exemptions, provided by the inheritance tax statute for adopted children. The court held that X should be classified as an "adopted child" on the theory that a legally adopted person should be entitled to whatever benefits the statutes provide for natural children. In Estate of Bauer, 111 Cal.App.3d 554, 168 Cal.Rptr. 743 (1980), the court rejected the proposition that the decedent's nephew, though raised and treated like their son, was "equitably adopted" for State inheritance tax purposes and entitled to preferential rates for children.

Does a bequest to a partnership composed of the decedent's two sons constitute a gift to one's "children" under an inheritance tax statute? See Commonwealth v. Gregory, 193 Va. 721, 71 S.E.2d 80 (1952).

The cases on the subject are collected in Annot., 3 A.L.R.2d 160 and Annot., 79 A.L.R.2d 1230.

B. A Texas inheritance tax statute taxes at the lowest rates bequests to a husband or wife, or to "any direct lineal descendant" of a husband or wife. Does the term "lineal descendant" of a husband or wife include the descendants of a predeceased wife? Does it include the adopted daughter of the testator's predeceased wife? See Decker v. Williams, 215 S.W.2d 679 (Tex.Civ.App.1948). Should a common-law wife be taxed as a widow or a person unrelated to the decedent? See Matter of Estate of Miller, 243 N.W.2d 788 (S.D.1976). Do grandchildren obtain the benefits granted by an inheritance tax to "children" of the deceased? Walker Bank & Trust Co. v. State Tax Comm'n, 18 Utah 2d 300, 422 P.2d 201 (1967). How should stepchildren be treated? In Ingram v. Johnson, 260 N.C. 697, 133 S.E.2d 662 (1963), the Court held that stepgrandchildren should be treated like grandchildren under North Carolina's inheritance tax statute. Other State statutes have been read to require the opposite conclusion. See, e.g., In re Plaisted Estate, 109 N.H. 350, 253 A.2d 48 (1969). Does *Trimble v. Gordon*, discussed in Note A supra, have any bearing on the issues raised in these cases?

C. Many States impose a lower rate of tax on lineal descendants than on other beneficiaries. If decedent's children have been adopted by decedent's ex-wife's second husband, should the children still take as lineal descendants under their natural parent's will? Although the adoption completely terminated all the decedent's rights and obligations towards the children, in People v. Estate of Murphy, 29 Colo.App. 195, 481 P.2d 420 (1971), the court ruled that the children should be taxed as "lineal descendants." The Oregon court, however, has held that adoption leaves the legal relationship between a natural parent and a child as though the child had not been born to the natural parent. Thus an adopted child was viewed as a stranger to the natural parent's estate and not entitled to a preferential rate for inheritance tax purposes. Department of Revenue v. Martin, 3 Or.App. 594, 474 P.2d 355 (1970).

D. *The Taxation of Contingent Interests under Inheritance Tax Laws.* In States in which an inheritance tax is imposed, it is common to impose a tax only when an interest in the decedent's property vests in the beneficiary. If a decedent leaves a will with a life estate to *A* and the remainder to *B*, if *B* survives *A*, otherwise the remainder to *C*, a serious administrative problem is presented. In some States such contingent interests are not taxed at the decedent's death. The collection of the inheritance tax on the remainder is deferred until the termination of the precedent estate. See, e.g., Indiana, Oregon, and Wyoming. In this way, the amount of exemption and the applicability of preferential rates to the beneficiary will be determined by reference to the actual facts as they eventually occur. Or if the actual remainderman turns out to be an exempt charitable or educational institution, no tax will be imposed on the inheritance of the remainder.

Other States tax the entire property at the decedent's death, assessing contingent interests at the highest rate and amount which would be applicable under any contingency. When the contingency ends and the estate becomes vested, the tax is recomputed and, if necessary, a refund is allowed. See, e.g., Connecticut, Colorado, and South Carolina.

A few States, however, reverse the order and impose a tax in the first instance at the lowest possible rate and amount applicable under the alternative contingencies, postponing collection of the balance of the tax, if any, until the contingency has been eliminated. See, e.g., Rhode Island and Wisconsin.

And some States initially impose the tax on the basis of the most probable happening of the contingencies, with provision for refund when the final event occurs. See, e.g., Kentucky.

Typically, there is a provision in the statute for finally compromising the issue with the taxing authority without awaiting the occurrence of the final contingencies; and in some statutes which require the payment of the highest tax in the first instance, the lowest tax may be paid, provided a bond is filed to secure payment of the additional amount which may finally become due. See, e.g., California and Ohio; In re Estate of Kruse, 36 Cal.App.3d 909, 112 Cal.Rptr. 50 (1974).

E. *Exemption for the State's Bonds.* State and municipal bonds are often exempted from various types of State and local taxes, in addition to the exemption from Federal income taxation of the interest on such bonds. I.R.C. § 103. In Estate of Pittman, 7 Ohio Misc. 21, 215 N.E.2d 737 (1965), the court held such bonds subject to the State inheritance tax notwithstanding the provision in the Ohio Constitution that "such bonds, and the interest thereon as income, shall be exempt from all taxes levied by the State of Ohio." The court's decision turned essentially on the distinction between the subject and the measure of the tax: "[t]he Ohio inheritance or succession tax is not a tax upon the property itself, but upon the right to succeed to the property." Id. at 740. Cf. the distinction between the subject and the measure of the tax that is critical for purposes of 31 U.S.C. § 3124, which exempts Federal obligations and the interest thereon from every form of State taxation except "a nondiscriminatory franchise tax or another nonproperty tax instead of a franchise tax, imposed on a corporation; and * * * an estate or inheritance tax." The provision is considered in more detail in Chapter 15, p. 1004 infra.

F. *References.* The provisions of the various States dealing with the taxation of contingent interests are collected in P–H State Inh. Tax Serv. ¶ 132 of each State; see "Illinois Inheritance Taxation of Contingent Interests and Powers of Appointment," 59 Nw.U.L.Rev. 59 (1964). For a consideration of State death tax exemptions, see Neuhoff, "Deductions, Exemptions and Credits in State Inheritance and Estate Taxation," 26 Iowa L.Rev. 593 (1941); Note, 1970 Utah L.Rev. 42. See also Annot., 47 A.L.R.2d 999.

SECTION 5. RECIPROCAL DEATH TAX PROVISIONS
Notes and Problems

A. In Indiana Department of Revenue v. Griffith's Estate, 129 Ind. App. 278, 156 N.E.2d 395 (1959), the question was whether shares of stock in an Indiana corporation, owned by a Georgia resident and located in Georgia, were exempt from Indiana's inheritance tax reciprocity provision which provided:

> Nonresidents' estates—Reciprocity.—The tax imposed by the provisions of this act (* * *) in respect of personal property, except tangible personal property having an actual situs in this state, shall not be payable if the transferor at the time was a resident of a state or territory of the United States, or of any foreign country, which at said time of his death, by the laws of such state, territory or country of residence of the transferor contained a reciprocal exemption provision under which non-residents were exempted from transfer taxes or death taxes of every character in respect of personal property, except tangible personal property having an actual situs therein: Provided, that the state, territory or country of residence of such non-residents allowed a similar exemption to residents of the State, territory, or country of residence of such transferor.

Although Georgia did not have a formal reciprocity provision, the taxpayers alleged that the (now repealed) Georgia inheritance tax law would not apply to the value of shares in Georgia corporations owned by non-resident decedents—a proposition that was supported by a letter from the Georgia Attorney General. They further contended that omission to tax by Georgia is equivalent to a reciprocal exemption provision as required by the Indiana inheritance tax law. The court disagreed:

As the consideration for authorizing the exemption of transfers of shares of stock in Indiana corporations owned by a resident of another State, the Indiana law requires the certainty and stability of "laws" containing "a reciprocal exemption provision" assuring Indiana residents of the exemption of transfers of shares of stock owned by them under similar circumstances. The requirement of the Indiana statute is not satisfied by the opinion of the Attorney General of Georgia, unsupported by such a law, which opinion (as in this case) is subject to reversal by successors in office or by case law of the Courts of Authority in Georgia without a corresponding change in the law.

* * *

We are of the opinion that it is not the intent of our Legislature that our Indiana Department of State Revenue shall be obligated to look further than the statutes or rulings of Courts of Authority of the state of domicile of a non-resident of Indiana whose estate is being subjected to tax in order to ascertain whether or not the laws of such state grant the reciprocity necessary for application of the aforementioned reciprocity section of the Indiana Inheritance Tax Law. [156 N.E.2d at 400.]

B. *Classification of Property as Tangible Personal Property Under Reciprocal Provision.* As the reciprocal provision set out in Note A discloses, "tangible personal property having an actual situs" within the taxing State is not subject to the exemption or exclusion of the statute. The application of the provision, therefore, presents problems as to the distinction between tangibles and intangibles and between personal property and real property. See Chapter 11, § 2 supra. In Denver Nat. Bank v. State Comm'n of Revenue and Taxation, 176 Kan. 617, 272 P.2d 1070 (1954), a resident of Colorado owned a "working interest" in oil and gas leases on Kansas property. Declaring that it is well settled that a "working interest," which includes the right to develop the leased property and to retain a percentage of the proceeds of oil or gas produced, conveys not "interest in land but is merely a license to explore and is personal property, an incorporeal hereditament—a profit *a prendre*" (176 Kan. 617, 272 P.2d 1070 at 1073), the court held that the estate was not subject to inheritance taxation under the reciprocal statute. Colorado, the decedent's State of residence, is a reciprocal State.

In In re Perry's Estate, 121 Mont. 280, 192 P.2d 532 (1948), discussed in 34 Iowa L.Rev. 129 (1948), the decedent, a resident of California, was a partner in a Montana mining enterprise. Montana sought to collect inheritance taxes on the succession to his partnership interest. The Montana reciprocal exemption statute, which is typical of the reciprocity provisions of many States, exempted from death taxation the personal property of a non-resident decedent, except tangible personal property having an actual situs within the State, provided the State of decedent's residence allows such an exemption, reciprocal or absolute. Mont.Rev.Code § 72–16–801, 2 CCH Inh., Est. & Gift Tax Rep. ¶ 1122, 4 P–H Est.Plan.Serv., State Inh. Taxes ¶ 99.37. The court sustained the Montana tax, holding that although the partnership interest itself was intangible, the actual property passing to the heirs at death was tangible and therefore taxable by Montana. There was a vigorous dissenting opinion.

C. *Contributions to Out-of-State Charities.* In many States deductions or exemption from inheritance or estate tax for contributions to religious, charitable, educational and similar organizations were formerly limited to charities organized or located within the taxing State. This rule has widely yielded to a reciprocal exemption provision, allowing a deduction for bequests or devises by a resident estate to the prescribed exempt organizations of other States, provided the latter State has a reciprocal provision. The statutes are summarized in 1 P–H State Inh.Tax Serv. ¶ 854.

In Angevine v. Commissioner, 361 Mass. 611, 281 N.E.2d 583 (1972), the decedent, a Massachusetts domiciliary, made bequests to charitable institutions in Florida, which has no inheritance tax, although it has a pick-up tax. See pp. 921–22 infra. Massachusetts has a reciprocal tax provision which exempts from death taxation bequests to charities in other States, provided the other State exempts bequests to Massachusetts' charitable institutions. The court ruled that the absence of a tax statute was equivalent to an exemption from taxation, and the Massachusetts exemption was allowed.

In McLaughlin v. Poucher, 127 Conn. 441, 17 A.2d 767 (1944), a person domiciled in Connecticut made testamentary gifts to charities located in New Jersey. The Connecticut statute allowed exemption from its succession tax for gifts to charities organized in other States "whose laws provide a similar exemption of transfers to any similar Connecticut" charities. The New Jersey statute allowed such exemption but only to the extent of $5,000. The court denied the exemption on the ground that a statute which limits the allowance to foreign charities to $5,000 is not a "similar exemption" to that granted by Connecticut. The court refused to follow the lower court's allowance of exemption up to the New Jersey $5,000 ceiling.

C. A resident of Wisconsin died leaving the residue of his estate to Dr. Theodore Heuss, President of the Federal Republic of Germany, or his successor in office, in trust to relieve the suffering and hardship of persons who have been driven or displaced from East Germany. The Wisconsin inheritance tax exempts charitable transfers to trustees located in other States if the law of that State contains a reciprocal exemption for such transfers made by residents of that State to Wisconsin trustees. The court denied the exemption on the ground that the reciprocal exemption provision relates to States only within the Union, not to foreign countries. State v. First Wisconsin Trust Co., 5 Wis.2d 363, 92 N.W.2d 849 (1958). The court rejected the contention that a contrary holding was required by existing treaties with Germany.

In Estate of Fegestad, 124 Cal.App.3d 208, 178 Cal.Rptr. 202 (1981), an exemption for a charitable bequest to a Norwegian hospital was upheld by reason of the California reciprocity provision, which included charitable organizations organized under the laws of foreign countries. Although Norway's exemption provisions were not identical to California's, the court declared that "[i]n testing the reciprocity provision of the foreign sovereign, we do not look for identical guarantees under the foreign laws ∗ ∗ ∗ but rather to *parity in the treatment* accorded Californians under the foreign law." 178 Cal.Rptr. at 204 (emphasis in original).

D. *References.* Faught, "Reciprocity in State Taxation as the Next Step in Empirical Legislation," 92 U.Pa.L.Rev. 258 (1944); Note, "Reciprocity in Nondomiciliary Inheritance Taxation of Intangibles," 26 Iowa L.Rev. 694 (1940).

SECTION 6. THE DECEDENT'S DOMICILE

TEXAS v. FLORIDA

Supreme Court of the United States, 1938.
306 U.S. 398, 59 S.Ct. 563, 121 A.L.R. 1179.

MR. JUSTICE STONE delivered the opinion of the Court.*

This original suit, in the nature of a bill of interpleader, brought to determine the true domicile of decedent as the basis of rival claims of four states for death taxes upon his estate, raises two principal questions: Whether this Court has jurisdiction of the cause and, if so, whether the report of the Special Master, finding that decedent at the time of his death was domiciled in Massachusetts, should be confirmed.

On March 15, 1937, this Court granted the motion of the State of Texas for leave to file its bill of complaint against the States of Florida and New York and the Commonwealth of Massachusetts, and against decedent's wife, Mabel Harlow Green, and his sister, Hetty Sylvia Ann Howland Green Wilks, both alleged to be residents of New York. The bill of complaint alleges that Edward H.R. Green died at Lake Placid, New York, on June 8, 1936, leaving surviving him his wife and sister as his only heirs and next of kin; that he left a gross estate of approximately $44,348,500, and a net estate valued at $42,348,500, comprising real estate and tangible personal property located in Texas, New York, Florida and Massachusetts, of an aggregate value of approximately $6,500,000, and intangible personal property consisting principally of stocks, bonds and securities, the paper evidences of most of which were located in New York.

The bill of complaint alleges that decedent, at the time of his death, was domiciled in Texas, but that Florida, New York, and Massachusetts each asserts, through its taxing officials, that decedent was at the time of his death domiciled within it. It alleges in detail that Texas and each of the defendant states maintains and enforces a system of taxation upon the inheritance or succession of the estates of decedents domiciled within the state at death, under which laws real estate and tangible personal property located within the state and all intangibles, regardless of their situs, are subjected to the tax; that each of the four states asserts and proposes to exercise the right to tax the estate of decedent on the assumption that decedent was domiciled within it at the time of his death; and that certain judicial proceedings have been instituted in each of the four states for the administration of decedent's

---

* [Some of the Court's footnotes have been omitted.]

estate or some parts of it. It is further alleged that none of the four states and no officer or representative of any state, except as already noted, has become a party to any of those proceedings, and that no state or its officer or representative will appear or become a party to any such proceedings instituted in any other state to fix or assess death taxes on decedent's estate, and that no judgment in any such proceeding will be binding on any state not a party to it; that each of the four states claims a lien for taxes and the right to collect a tax, based on decedent's alleged domicile within it, upon the tangibles located in the state and upon all decedent's intangibles wherever located, the total of such claims amounting to a sum far greater than the net value of the estate; that the amount of decedent's property located in Texas is negligible in amount and insufficient to pay its tax, and in the event that the states should obtain adjudications in their own or other courts in pending proceedings, or others instituted for the purpose of collecting the tax on the ground that decedent was domiciled elsewhere than in Texas, Texas would be deprived of its lawful tax. The bill prays that the Court determine whether decedent's domicile, for purposes of taxation, was in either of the defendant states and that particularly it determine and adjudicate that his domicile was in Texas and that it alone has the right to assess and collect death taxes on decedent's intangibles.

The several defendant states, answering, admit that decedent's estate is insufficient to satisfy the total amount of the taxes claimed. All deny that Green was domiciled in Texas, and by way of counterclaim and cross-bill against the other defendants, each asserts that he was domiciled in it and that it is entitled to collect death taxes upon all of decedent's intangible property and upon all his tangibles within the state. The answer of decedent's wife admitted that he was domiciled in Texas and asserted that by Texas law she owned, as community property, one-half of substantially all of decedent's estate acquired by him after their marriage, free and clear of all death taxes. Pursuant to stipulation showing that she had released all interest in decedent's estate, the suit was dismissed as to her by order of the Court on January 17, 1938. 302 U.S. 662, 58 S.Ct. 478. The answer of defendant Wilks, decedent's sister, denies that Green was domiciled in Texas and asks the Court to determine in which of the defendant states he was domiciled for purposes of taxation.

On June 1, 1937, this Court appointed a Special Master, 301 U.S. 671, 57 S.Ct. 935, to take evidence, to make findings of fact and state conclusions of law, and to submit them to this Court, together with his recommendations for a decree. The Special Master has reported his findings, with certain evidentiary facts, and his finding that decedent at the time of his death was domiciled in the Commonwealth of Massachusetts, this latter conclusion being supported by elaborate subsidiary findings. The case is now before us on exceptions to the Special

Master's conclusions of fact and subsidiary findings that decedent's domicile was in Massachusetts at the time of his death.

JURISDICTION

While the exceptions do not challenge the jurisdiction of the Court, the novel character of the questions presented and the duty which rests upon this Court to see to it that the exercise of its powers be confined within the limits prescribed by the Constitution make it incumbent upon us to inquire of our own motion whether the case is one within its jurisdiction. Minnesota v. Hitchcock, 185 U.S. 373, 382, 22 S.Ct. 650. By the Judiciary Article of the Constitution, the judicial power extends to controversies between states, and this Court is given original jurisdiction of cases in which a state shall be a party. Art. III, § 2. The present suit is between states, and the other jurisdictional requirements being satisfied, the individual parties whose presence is necessary or proper for the determination of the case or controversy between the states are properly made parties defendant. Cf. United States v. West Virginia, 295 U.S. 463, 470, 55 S.Ct. 789. So that our constitutional authority to hear the case and grant relief turns on the question whether the issue framed by the pleadings constitutes a justiciable "case" or "controversy" within the meaning of the Constitutional provision, and whether the facts alleged and found afford an adequate basis for relief according to accepted doctrines of the common law or equity systems of jurisprudence, which are guides to decision of cases within the original jurisdiction of this Court. * * *

Before the Constitution was adopted a familiar basis for the exercise of the extraordinary powers of courts of equity was the avoidance of the risk of loss ensuing from the demands in separate suits of rival claimants to the same debt or legal duty. * * * Since, without the interposition of equity, each claimant in pursuing his remedy in an independent suit might succeed and thus subject the debtor or the fund pursued to multiple liability, equity gave a remedy by way of bill of interpleader, upon the prosecution of which it required the rival claimants to litigate in a single suit their ownership of the asserted claim. A plaintiff need not await actual institution of independent suits; it is enough if he shows that conflicting claims are asserted and that the consequent risk of loss is substantial. * * *

The peculiarity of the strict bill of interpleader was that the plaintiff asserted no interest in the debt or fund, the amount of which he placed at the disposal of the court and asked that the rival claimants be required to settle in the equity suit the ownership of the claim among themselves. But as the sole ground for equitable relief is the danger of injury because of the risk of multiple suits when the liability is single * * * and as plaintiffs who are not mere stakeholders may be exposed to that risk, equity extended its jurisdiction to such cases by the bill in the nature of interpleader. The essential of the bill in the

nature of interpleader is that it calls upon the court to exercise its jurisdiction to guard against the risks of loss from the prosecution in independent suits of rival claims where the plaintiff himself claims an interest in the property or fund which is subjected to the risk. The object and ground of the jurisdiction are to guard against the consequent depletion of the fund at the expense of the plaintiff's interest in it and to protect him and the other parties to the suit from the jeopardy resulting from the prosecution of numerous demands, to only one of which the fund is subject. While in point of law or fact only one party is entitled to succeed, there is danger that recovery may be allowed in more than one suit. Equity avoids the danger by requiring the rival claimants to litigate before it the decisive issue, and will not withhold its aid where the plaintiff's interest is either not denied or he does not assert any claim adverse to that of the other parties, other than the single claim, determination of which is decisive of the rights of all.
* * *

When, by appropriate procedure, a court possessing equity powers is in such circumstances asked to prevent the loss which might otherwise result from the independent prosecution of rival but mutually exclusive claims, a justiciable issue is presented for adjudication which, because it is a recognized subject of the equity procedure which we have inherited from England, is a "case" or "controversy," within the meaning of the Constitutional provision; and when the case is one prosecuted between states, which are the rival claimants, and the risk of loss is shown to be real and substantial, the case is within the original jurisdiction of this Court conferred by the Judiciary Article. See Nashville, C. & St.L.Ry. v. Wallace, 288 U.S. 249, 261 et seq., 53 S.Ct. 345, and cases cited.

Here it is conceded by the pleadings and upon brief argument that the sole legal basis asserted by the four states for the imposition of death taxes on decedent's intangibles is his domicile at death in the taxing state. There is no question presented of a situs of decedent's intangibles differing, for tax purposes, from the place of his domicile. * * * And no determination made here as to domicile can hereafter foreclose the determination of such questions by any court of competent jurisdiction in which they may arise. By the law of each state a decedent can have only a single domicile for purposes of death taxes, and determination of the place of domicile of decedent will determine which of the four states is entitled to impose the tax on intangibles so far as they have no situs different from the place of domicile. No relief is sought to restrain collection of the tax or to interfere with the determination of its amount by appropriate state procedure.

The Special Master has found that each of the four states in good faith asserts that the decedent was domiciled within it at his death; that prior to the commencement of these proceedings each state in good faith was preparing to enforce a lien on decedent's intangibles wherever located and would now be taking appropriate action but for these proceedings; and that the net estate is not sufficient to pay the aggregate amount of the taxes claimed by them and by the federal government.[2] He has also found, as averred in the pleadings, that none of the four states has become or will consent to become a party to any proceedings for determining the right to collect the tax in any other state; that the right of Texas to assert its tax lien and to prosecute its claim for taxes with success is in jeopardy and that it is without adequate remedy save in this Court.

The risk that decedent's estate might constitutionally be subjected to conflicting tax assessments in excess of its total value and that the right of complainant or some other state to collect the tax might thus be defeated was a real one, due both to the jurisdictional peculiarities of our dual federal and state judicial systems and to the special circumstances of this case. That two or more states may each constitutionally assess death taxes on a decedent's intangibles upon a judicial determination that the decedent was domiciled within it in proceedings binding upon the representatives of the estate, but to which the other states are not parties, is an established principle of our federal jurisprudence. Thormann v. Frame, 176 U.S. 350, 20 S.Ct. 446; Overby v. Gordon, 177 U.S. 214, 20 S.Ct. 603; Burbank v. Ernst, 232 U.S. 162, 34 S.Ct. 299; Baker v. Baker, Eccles & Co., 242 U.S. 394, 37 S.Ct. 152; Iowa v. Slimmer, 248 U.S. 115, 120, 121, 39 S.Ct. 33; Worcester County Trust Co. v. Riley, 302 U.S. 292, 299, 58 S.Ct. 185. And a judgment thus obtained is binding on the parties to it and constitutionally entitled to full faith and credit in the courts of every other state. Milwaukee County v. White Co., 296 U.S. 268, 56 S.Ct. 229. The equity jurisdiction being founded on avoidance of the risk of loss resulting from the threatened prosecution of multiple claims, the risk must be appraised

---

2. The Special Master has found as follows: The net estate, after payment of debts and administration expenses other than death taxes, will amount to $36,137,335; and the tangible property taxable in the state of its situs is as follows:

Texas	$ 2,220.00
Florida	222,276.00
New York	1,583,221.00
Massachusetts	2,498,707.00

Decedent's intangibles at the time of his death had a value of $35,831,303. The paper evidences of decedent's intangibles were located outside of the states of Texas, Florida, and Massachusetts. "The aggregate value of the shares of stock in and obligations of corporations and associations organized or having a principal place of business in Texas, Massachusetts and Florida, respectively, and of the obligations of persons residing in said States and of the obligations of said States and political subdivisions thereof, together with the value of the real estate and tangible property in Texas, Massachusetts and Florida, respectively, is less than the amount of the tax claimed by each of said States and the amount of such tax claimed by Texas, Massachusetts, and Florida, respectively, greatly exceeds the value of the property subject to the jurisdiction of their respective Courts and from which the tax might be collected in any proceeding in said Courts." The Special Master found that the death taxes due to the United States, and due to each state, if its contentions be sustained, are as follows:

United States	$17,520,987
Texas	4,685,057
Florida	4,663,857
New York	5,910,301
Massachusetts	4,947,008
Total	$37,727,213

This exceeds the total net estate by the sum of $1,589,877. In addition the State of New York asserts a claim for unpaid personal income taxes of $920,827.

in the light of the circumstances as they are in good faith alleged and shown to exist at the time when the suit was brought. Cf. Clark v. Wooster, 119 U.S. 322, 7 S.Ct. 217; Rice & Adams v. Lathrop, 278 U.S. 509, 49 S.Ct. 220; Maclennan [Law of Interpleader], supra, 132 et seq. In this case, as will presently be noted, the relations of decedent to each of the demanding states was such as to afford substantial basis for the claim that he was domiciled within it, with fair probability that the claim would be accepted and favorably acted upon if there were no participation by the other states in the litigation. See New Jersey v. Pennsylvania, 287 U.S. 580, 53 S.Ct. 313; Hill v. Martin, 296 U.S. 393, 56 S.Ct. 278; Dorrance's Estate, 309 Pa. 151, 163 A. 303, certiorari denied 287 U.S. 660, 53 S.Ct. 222; 288 U.S. 617, 53 S.Ct. 507; In re Dorrance, 115 N.J.Eq. 268, 170 A. 601; Dorrance v. Martin, 116 N.J.L. 362, 184 A. 743, certiorari denied 298 U.S. 678, 56 S.Ct. 949. Cf. Matter of Trowbridge, 266 N.Y. 283. In addition the facts most essential to establishing that attitude and relationship of person to place which constitute domicile were in this case obscured by numerous self-serving statements of decedent as to his domicile, which, because made for the purpose of avoiding liability for state income and personal property taxes levied on the basis of domicile, tended to conceal rather than reveal the true relationship in this case. Taken as a whole the case is exceptional in its circumstances and in the principles of law applicable to them, all uniting to impose a risk of loss upon the state lawfully entitled to collect the tax.

We think that the Special Master's findings of jeopardy is sustained; that a justiciable "case" between the states is presented; and that a cause of action cognizable in equity is alleged and proved.

* * *

DOMICILE

The Special Master took voluminous testimony in each of the four states, recording every available fact having any bearing on the issue of decedent's domicile. After an exhaustive study of the evidence the Special Master has prepared elaborate subsidiary findings in which he has stated what he considers to be the essential facts of decedent's life which, taken together, were the controlling factors in his arriving at the conclusion that decedent, at the time of his death, was domiciled in the Commonwealth of Massachusetts.

* * *

[The Court's discussion of the domicile issue has been omitted.]

The report of the Special Master is confirmed.

Opinion of MR. JUSTICE FRANKFURTER.

The authority which the Constitution has committed to this Court over "Controversies between two or more States," serves important ends in the working of our federalism. But there are practical limits to the efficacy of the adjudicatory process in the adjustment of interstate controversies. The limitations of litigation—its episodic character, its necessarily restricted scope of inquiry, its confined regard for considerations of policy, its dependence on the contingencies of a particular record, and other circumscribing factors—often denature and even mutilate the actualities of a problem and thereby render the litigious process unsuited for its solution. Considerations such as these have from time to time led this Court or some of its most distinguished members either to deprecate resort to this Court by States for settlement of their controversies (see New York v. New Jersey, 256 U.S. 296, 313, 41 S.Ct. 492), or to oppose assumption of jurisdiction. * * *

The presupposition of jurisdiction in this case is the common law doctrine of a single domiciliary status. That for purposes of legal rights and liabilities a person must have one domicile, and can have only one, is an historic rule of the common law and justified by much good sense. Nevertheless, it often represents a fiction. Certainly in many situations the determination of a man's domicile is by no means the establishment of an event or a fact that exists in nature. Even assuming that there is general agreement as to the elements which in combination constitute domicile, a slight shift of emphasis in applying the formula produces contradictory results. But, on the whole, the doctrine of domicile has adequately served as a practical working rule in the simpler societies out of which it arose. More particularly, its difficulties of application were circumscribed when wealth predominantly consisted of realty and tangibles, and when restricted modes of transportation and communication conditioned fixity of residence. In view of the enormous extent to which intangibles now constitute wealth, and the increasing mobility of men, particularly men of substance, the necessity of a single headquarters for all legal purposes, particularly for purposes of taxation, tends to be a less and less useful fiction. In the setting of modern circumstances, the inflexible doctrine of domicile—one man, one home—is in danger of becoming a social anachronism. Recent applications and modifications of this rule to satisfy the vague contours of the due process clause have hardly mitigated its inadequacies for our day. E.g., Frick v. Pennsylvania, 268 U.S. 473, 45 S.Ct. 603; Blodgett v. Silberman, 277 U.S. 1, 48 S.Ct. 410; Farmers Loan & Trust Co. v. Minnesota, 280 U.S. 204, 50 S.Ct. 98; First National Bank v. Maine, 284 U.S. 312, 52 S.Ct. 174.

The facts in this case doubtless present a bizarre story. But in Green's peregrinations from State to State, in the multiplicity of his residences, and in the conflicting appeals which various States made upon his interests from time to time, the case is hardly unique nor are analogues to it unlikely to appear in the future. As a result, this Court is asked to determine the conflicting claims of different States of the Union to a share of the estate of individuals who, as a matter of hard fact, at different periods and contemporaneously invoked and enjoyed such benefits as the existence of State governments confer. It is asked to do so by applying an old doctrine of limited validity to modern circumstances whereby, through the elusive search for an often nonexistent fact called domicile, only one State to the exclusion of all others would be allowed to levy a tax. The inherent difficulties of this problem have been widely recognized. The old formulas are simply inadequate to the new situation. On the other hand, it is not for this Court in these cases of multiple residences to evolve new taxing policies based on more equitable considerations than the all-or-nothing consequence of the old domiciliary rule.

I am not unaware of the dilemma presented by such a situation as the Dorrance litigation. The circumstances attending the Green estate do not preclude like possibilities. But merely because no other means than litigation have as yet been evolved to adjust the conflicting claims of several States in a single estate is not sufficient reason for utilizing as a basis of our jurisdiction oversimplified formulas of the past that have largely lost their relevance in the contemporary context.

The controlling assumption in taking jurisdiction in this case is that the ascertainment of a single domicile for Green is merely the determination of a fact. The auxiliary assumption is the existence of solid danger that the highest courts of four States will ascertain this fact in four different ways. Texas has no standing here except on the basis that three State courts will despoil her of her rights by leaving no assets in the estate out of which to satisfy her claim. But the fact that the political officers of four States make claims to an estate so as to safeguard any possible interest, is hardly a substantial reason for assuming that their judiciaries will sanction the claims.

It is not to be assumed that the State courts will make findings dictated solely by fiscal advantages to their States. The contrary assumption must be made—and the assumption rests on adjudicated experience, e.g., Matter of Trowbridge, 266 N.Y. 283, 194 N.E. 756. To the extent that there is danger that out of the same events four State courts will spell four different domiciles, it is inherent in the search for a domiciliary status. The result is arrived at not through ascertainment of an external fact but by attributions made as a matter of law to satisfy the supposed abstract legal requirement of a single domicile no matter what the actualities of human behavior may be. Even a small change of portions in the admixture of factors which in combination yield the legal concept of domicile, may place the domicile in one State rather than another and, thereby, give estate duties to this State rather than that. But the State treasuries are not alone under powerful motives to exploit the doctrine of domicile. The tax systems of different States have varying degrees of attraction for those in control of an estate, and it is to their natural interest to seek a single, inclusive disposition of the elusive issue of domicile by having the original jurisdiction of this Court invoked.

It is hardly an answer that this Court can protect itself against feigned controversies. The difficulty is that in these modern multiple residence situations the issue of domicile is too often an inherently feigned issue. Two State courts can very legitimately find two different domiciles, in that two equally competent tribunals utilizing the same outward facts in the alembic of the same common law concept of domicile may easily distill contradictory conclusions. Merely to avoid such a conflict is not enough to give jurisdiction. The variant that this case presents is the allegation that if the claims of all four States prevail the estate would be more than eaten up and Texas would lose her potential right. This added requirement—the absorption of the entire estate by having numerous States stake out claims—is too readily supplied.

To extend the neat procedural device of interpleader to such a situation is another illustration of transferring a remedy from one legal environment to circumstances qualitatively different. To settle the interests of different claimants to a single *res* where these interests turn on narrow and relatively few facts and where conflicting claims cannot have equal validity in experience, is one thing; it is a wholly different thing to bring into court in a single suit States which even remotely might assert domiciliary claims against a decedent and where one State court might with as much reason as another find domicile within its State. Certainly when the claim of the moving State is so obviously without basis as this Court has now found in the case of Texas, the linchpin of jurisdiction is gone and the other State should be remitted to appropriate remedies outside this Court. Such a disposition would be a real safeguard against the construction of a suit to give this Court jurisdiction over matters which as such, this Court has already held, are not within our province. To find that the decedent could not, on self-serving grounds, elect to make his home in Texas "where he in fact had no residence" and yet to retain the bill and dispose of it on its merits amounts, in effect, to a declaration of rights on behalf of the estate which could not be adjudicated otherwise than through the screen of a controversy between States.

In this case we do not even have substantial translation into effective legal action of the assertions by the four States of their domiciliary claims. To be sure, the Master has found, as summarized in the Court's opinion, "that each of the four States in good faith asserts that the decedent was domiciled within it at his death." This is a natural attitude of prudence on the part of law officers of States in the case of decedents who had scattered their lives as well as their holdings. But to give this Court the extraordinary jurisdiction which is invoked, there ought to be more than these caveats. There should be manifestation of that hard determination to press a State's claim which is implied in setting the tax-collecting machinery of a State in motion. Allegation, affirmative proof, and finding of such attempts by the various States are lacking. And New York denies without contradiction that its procedure for tax levy and collection has been set in operation. These circumstances are, therefore, not comparable to the issues in a conventional interpleader suit brought to forestall conflicting actions. Initiation of litigation is, of course, not a prerequisite to an ordinary interpleader. This only serves to emphasize the inappropriateness of utilizing a remedy invented to settle private controversies of limited scope to the resolution of conflicting governmental interests.

Jurisdictional doubts inevitably lose force once leave has been given to file a bill, a master has been appointed, long hearings have been held, and a weighty report has been submitted. And so, were this the last as well as the first assumption of jurisdiction by this Court of a controversy like the present, even serious doubts about it might well go unexpressed. But if experience is any guide, the present decision will give momentum to kindred litigation and reliance upon it beyond the scope of the special facts of this case. To be sure, the Court's opinion endeavors to circumscribe carefully the bounds of jurisdiction now exercised. But legal doctrines have, in an odd kind of way, the faculty of self-generating extension. Therefore, in picking out the lines of future development of what is new doctrine, the importance of these issues may make it not inappropriate to indicate difficulties which I have not been able to overcome and potential abuses to which the doctrine is not unlikely to give rise.

I am authorized to say that MR. JUSTICE BLACK concurs in these views and in the conclusion that the bill should be dismissed.*

Notes and Problems

A. In a later case, Massachusetts sought leave to file a complaint to institute an original action against Missouri and certain of its citizens, in which it alleged that *D*, domiciled in Massachusetts, had died after creating revocable trusts of securities comprising the bulk of her property, which she had transferred to Missouri trustees. The securities were held in Missouri, where the trusts were administered. Both Massachusetts and Missouri had inheritance taxes; and both exempted from tax intangibles of non-residents (in one case only if the other State does not tax non-residents on such property). Federal taxes and administration costs had exhausted the Massachusetts estate other than the trusts. Both States claimed the exclusive right to tax the inheritance of the trust property. There were, however, sufficient assets in the estate including the trusts to meet Federal, Missouri, and Massachusetts taxes. Should the filing bill of complaint have been allowed by the Court? See Massachusetts v. Missouri, 308 U.S. 1, 60 S.Ct. 39 (1939), noted in 24 Minn.L.Rev. 573 (1940); 28 Geo.L.J. 372 (1939).

B. In Worcester County Trust Co. v. Riley, 302 U.S. 292, 58 S.Ct. 185 (1937), Massachusetts and California each claimed a tax on intangibles on the ground that the decedent was domiciled in the State. The Massachusetts executor sought to bring the taxing officials of both States into the Federal district court of Massachusetts under the Federal Interpleader Act. The Massachusetts officials raised no objection, but the California officials denied jurisdiction, contending that this was a suit against the State of California in violation of the Eleventh Amendment. The Supreme Court

---

* [This case was widely discussed in the law reviews. See 19 B.U.L.Rev. 480 (1939); 39 Colum.L.Rev. 1017 (1939); 16 N.Y. U.L.Q.Rev. 651 (1939); 12 So.Cal.L.Rev. 469 (1939).]

unanimously held that the district court had no jurisdiction. Justice Stone declared that "[n]either the Fourteenth Amendment nor the full faith and credit clause requires uniformity of different States as to the place of domicile, where the exertion of State power is dependent upon domicile within its boundaries." 302 U.S. at 299.

C. In a series of three cases connected with the estate of the wealthy recluse Howard Hughes, the Court was presented with a fact pattern identical to that in *Texas v. Florida*. In the course of litigation, the Court was asked to overrule *Texas v. Florida* and *Worcester County Trust Co. v. Riley*, Note B supra. The Court declined to overrule either precedent. California v. Texas, 437 U.S. 601, 98 S.Ct. 3107 (1978) (denying leave to file complaint, with concurring opinion suggesting use of interpleader); Cory v. White, 457 U.S. 85, 102 S.Ct. 2325 (1982) (denying use of interpleader on authority of *Worcester County Trust Co. v. Riley*); California v. Texas, 457 U.S. 164, 102 S.Ct. 2335 (1982) (granting leave to file complaint in view of unavailability of other forum under *Cory v. White* and allegations, as in *Texas v. Florida,* that the combined tax plus interest would exceed 100 percent of the value of the estate). In his dissent from *Cory v. White*, Justice Powell, speaking also for Justices Marshall and Stevens, voiced the following due process concerns about the Court's decision:

> The Court today continues to reason from the premise, accepted by *Worcester County,* that multiple taxation on the basis of domicile does not offend the Constitution—even in a case in which both of the taxing States concede that a person may have but one domicile.* In my view this premise is wrong. As an alternative to the approach that I embraced in *California v. Texas,* I now would be prepared to overrule *Worcester County* on this point and to hold that multiple taxation on the basis of domicile—at least insofar as "domicile" is treated as indivisible, so that a person can be the domiciliary of but one State—is incompatible with the structure of our federal system.

> * * *

> Our decisions consistently have recognized that state taxation must be rationally related to " 'values connected with the taxing state.' " Moorman Mfg. Co. v. Bair, 437 U.S. 267, 273 (1978), quoting Norfolk & Western R. Co. v. Missouri State Tax Comm'n, 390 U.S. 317, 325 (1968). * * * Under these principles tangible property generally may be taxed only by the State where it is located. Curry v. McCanless, 307 U.S. 357, 364 (1939). Physical presence also is required to justify a state succession tax on the transfer of real property occasioned by the death of the owner. Treichler v. Wisconsin, 338 U.S. 251 (1949); Frick v. Pennsylvania, 268 U.S. 473, 492 (1925).

> In contrast with real property, intangible personal property is not physically located in any particular place, at least in any simple sense. Moreover, there may be more than one State that has a significant connection with intangible property—for example, the State in which a trust's assets are administered and the State in which the trustee is domiciled. See Curry v. McCanless, supra. Recognizing these differences, this Court has upheld the multiple taxation of intangible proper-

---

* [Footnotes have been omitted].

ty. The decisions in which the Court has done so have not, however, undermined the fundamental principle that a State's levy of a tax must be connected rationally with the values on which the tax is imposed or with protections that the State has afforded.

In this case both California and Texas—as most States—recognize that a person can have but one domicile. And it would appear settled that domicile provides the only adequate basis for taxation of intangible property in a decedent's estate, not located in the State or otherwise dependent on the protection of its laws. See Curry v. McCanless, supra, at 365–366; cf. Complete Auto Transit, Inc. v. Brady, 430 U.S. 274, 286–288 (1977) (defining Commerce Clause limits on state taxation in terms of connections to and benefits conferred by the taxing State). Here neither State alleges an entitlement to tax the Hughes estate on any other basis. From these premises it follows that multiple taxation based solely on conflicting determinations of domicile not only is unfair, but that taxation on this basis by at least one of the States must lack the only predicate asserted to justify its levy under the Due Process Clause.

It is, of course, true that in 1937 Worcester County Trust Co. v. Riley, 302 U.S. 292, held that this admitted unfairness did not offend the Constitution. But *Worcester County's* holding on this point already has been undermined, not only by intervening decisions reiterating due process limits on state taxation of intangible property, see Norfolk & Western R. Co. v. Missouri State Tax Comm'n, supra, at 323–326, and of income, see, e.g., Mobil Oil Corp. v. Commissioner of Taxes, 445 U.S. 425, 436–442 (1980), but also by cases in which this Court has recognized a fundamental right to travel. See, e.g., Dunn v. Blumstein, 405 U.S. 330 (1972); Shapiro v. Thompson, 394 U.S. 618 (1969). * * *

By holding that multiple taxation based on domicile is prohibited by the Due Process Clause, the Court could lay the basis for resolution of disputes such as this one under the interpleader jurisdiction of the federal district courts. By alleging that state taxing officials threatened the estate with multiple liability, an administrator would state a colorable claim that the relevant state officers were acting outside of constitutional limits and thus that they were acting in their individual capacities under Ex parte Young, 209 U.S. 123 (1908). The Eleventh Amendment thus would not bar the suit under *Ex parte Young* and *Edelman v. Jordan,* and the interpleader requirement of competing claimants would be satisfied.

Professor Zechariah Chafee, the father of the federal interpleader statute, argued: "It is our federal system which creates the possibility of double taxation. Somewhere within that federal system we should be able to find remedies for the frictions which that system creates." Federal Interpleader Since the Act of 1936, 49 Yale L.J. 377, 388 (1940).

In my view the Due Process Clause provides the *right* to be free of multiple taxation of intangibles based on domicile. The Federal Interpleader Act provides the remedy. [457 U.S. at 97–101.]

See generally Note, "Due Process Limits on State Estate Taxation: An Analogy to the State Corporate Income Tax," 94 Yale L.J. 1229 (1985).

D. *The Dorrance Case.* The celebrated Dorrance Estate saga arose out of the claims by both New Jersey and Pennsylvania that Dr. John Dorrance, of Campbell Soup Company fame, died domiciled within its borders. He owned homes in both New Jersey and Pennsylvania, and he and his family divided their time between the two States. Dorrance had claimed that he was a resident of New Jersey, where his executors filed his will for probate. In the meantime the Pennsylvania taxing authorities proceeded to assess a tax on his entire estate, which consisted principally of intangibles, on the theory that Dorrance resided in that State. The State's contention was upheld. Dorrance's Estate, 309 Pa. 151, 163 A. 303 (1932), noted in 81 U.Pa.L.Rev. 177 (1932). The Supreme Court denied certiorari to review this decision. 287 U.S. 660, 53 S.Ct. 122 (1932). New Jersey's motion to intervene in these proceedings was denied. Thereafter, New Jersey unsuccessfully sought to bring an original proceeding against Pennsylvania in the Supreme Court. New Jersey v. Pennsylvania, 287 U.S. 580, 53 S.Ct. 313 (1933). Subsequently, an original bill which Pennsylvania had brought against New Jersey was dismissed. Pennsylvania v. New Jersey, 288 U.S. 618, 53 S.Ct. 385 (1933). The New Jersey courts, however, decided that the Pennsylvania decision was erroneous, and refused to give it effect. In re Dorrance's Estate, 115 N.J.Eq. 268, 170 A. 601 (1934), affirmed 116 N.J.L. 362, 184 A. 743 (1936), certiorari denied 298 U.S. 678, 56 S.Ct. 949 (1936), rehearing denied 298 U.S. 692, 56 S.Ct. 957 (1936). A suit by the executors in the Federal courts to enjoin the New Jersey officials from collecting the inheritance tax was rejected. Dorrance v. Martin, 12 F.Supp. 746 (D.C.N.J.1935), affirmed in Hill v. Martin, 296 U.S. 393, 56 S.Ct. 278 (1935). As was pointed out by one commentator:

> The New Jersey courts added insult to injury by refusing to allow the executors to deduct the Pennsylvania inheritance and personal property taxes from the value of the taxable estate in New Jersey, although the New Jersey statute specifically provided that inheritance taxes levied in other States were so deductible. This paradoxical result was based upon the conclusion that the Pennsylvania taxes were invalid and that the New Jersey statute permitted only deductions of valid inheritance taxes paid in other States. [Note, 37 Mich.L.Rev. 1279, 1281 (1939).]

E. *Cooperation Between the States to Deal With Conflicting Claims of the Decedent's Domicile.* In some cases the voluntary intervention by one State in the proceedings of another State has been successfully employed. In Matter of Trowbridge, 266 N.Y. 283, 194 N.E. 756, 759 (1935), a petition for intervention was filed by the State of Connecticut in a New York estate tax proceeding. The petition was granted in connection with a determination of the domicile. After the facts were heard, the court found that the decedent was domiciled at his death in Connecticut.

A more promising development in interstate cooperation to cut through the Gordian knot of double domicile has been the adoption by the States of legislation for the compromise or arbitration of domiciliary disputes. California and New York have pioneered in the field and a number of other States have adopted compromise and arbitration statutes. As of 1987, the Uniform Interstate Arbitration of Death Taxes Act had been adopted by 14 States.[2] For a discussion of the statutes, see Note, "Interstate Arbitration of Death Taxes," 30 B.U.L.Rev. 396 (1950); Culp, "Selected Problems in Multistate Taxation," 44 Iowa L.Rev. 280 (1959); the statutes are listed in CCH Inh., Est. & Gift Tax Rep. (State Compilation) ¶ 12,035 and 1 P–H State Inh. Tax Serv. ¶ 853.

Use of the arbitration method to resolve a double domicile controversy occurred in the Estate of Isabel Anderson, 1 P–H State Inh. Tax Serv. ¶ 853, in which Massachusetts and New Hampshire each claimed that the decedent was domiciled in its territory. A Board of Arbitration was appointed under Chapter 65B of the General Laws of Massachusetts and Chapter 89A of the Revised Laws of New Hampshire. Hearings were held and a majority of the Board found for Massachusetts. In addition to the Arbitration Act, 16 States[3] have enacted the Uniform Interstate Compromise of Death Taxes Act, which allows the tax commissioners of the several States which claim the decedent as a domiciliary to reach a binding compromise with the executor of the estate as to the tax payable to each State.

F. *References.* Lentz, "Problems in Determining Domicile," 15 N.Y.U.Inst. on Fed.Tax. 945 (1957); Chrystie, "Where Is or Was or Will Be Your Client's Domicile," 1 Prac.Law. 13 (1955); Reese, "Does Domicile Bear a Single Meaning?," 55 Colum.L.Rev. 589 (1955); Tweed & Sargent, "Death and Taxes Are Certain—But What of Domicile," 53 Harv.L.Rev. 68 (1939); Federa, "Multiple Domicile in Inheritance Taxation," 17 Taxes 142 (1939); Chrystie, "The Legal Monstrosity of Double Domicil," 1937 Nat'l Tax Ass'n Procs. 467; Note, "Extraterritorial Enforcement of State Revenue Claims by Original Bill in the Supreme Court," 34 Ill.L.Rev. 610 (1940); Note, "Interstate Arbitration and Compromise of Death Taxes," 37 Calif.L.Rev. 664 (1949); Restatement of the Law of Conflict of Laws, "Domicil," ch. 2 (1934); Barry, "Inheritance Tax Consequences—Change of Domicile," 1963 Proc. Nat'l Ass'n of Tax Adm'rs. 51; Morrill, "Multistate Estates: Domicile, Jurisdiction, and Administrative Problems," 103 Trusts and Estates 734 (1964).

SECTION 7. THE FEDERAL ESTATE TAX CREDIT

Congress has exercised its taxing power in a manner designed to force the States to enact death taxes. In 1924, Congress first allowed a credit against Federal estate tax liability for State death taxes. The credit was limited to 25 percent of Federal estate tax liability. Two years later, it increased the credit for State death taxes (and those of the District of Columbia and the territories and possessions) up to 80 percent of the estate tax imposed by the Revenue Act of 1926 (the so-called "basic estate tax"). This credit did not apply to the "additional tax." See I.R.C. of 1939, § 813(b). The effect of the statute was to

---

2. California, Colorado, Connecticut, Maine, Maryland, Massachusetts, Michigan, Minnesota, Nebraska, Pennsylvania, Tennessee, Vermont, West Virginia, and Wisconsin.

3. All the States listed in footnote 2 supra except Wisconsin and, in addition, New Jersey, and New Hampshire, and New York.

reduce the advantages, from a death tax point of view, of residing in such death-tax-free "havens" as Florida, a factor that had undoubtedly influenced some wealthy persons to move into that State. As a result of the Federal tax credit, Florida, which levied no death tax, adopted such a levy in order to absorb the credit. Fla.Laws 1931, c. 14739. The same procedure was followed by Alabama and Georgia. These States impose a death tax measured solely by the Federal credit.

In one way or another most of the States modified their death statutes so as to get the full benefit of the Federal credit. A method commonly employed was to add onto the existing levy, typically an inheritance tax, a new estate tax, whose purpose was to increase the State tax to the full 80 percent Federal credit. This accounts for the existence of two death taxes in many States. The Louisiana provision, for example, specifically recites that the statute "shall be liberally construed" in order to effectuate its purpose "to obtain for this state the benefit of the credit" allowed by the Federal Government. See La.Rev. Stat.Ann. § 47:2434, discussed in Succession of Edenborn v. Flournoy, 209 La. 174, 24 So.2d 368 (1945). In Cook v. Taylor, 210 Ark. 803, 197 S.W.2d 738 (1946), the court made the following comment as to the credit:

> The method of levying a tax by reference to a credit allowed under a federal statute, is—to say the least of it—an awkward and anomolous method of taxation by a sovereign State. In receiving the benefit of the federal credit, the State has surrendered a modicum, at least, of its right of free determination. But until clear unconstitutionality is shown in such surrender of sovereignty, then this method of levying taxes is for the Legislative Department of government, rather than for the Judicial. [197 S.W.2d at 741.]

In revising the Internal Revenue Code in 1954, Congress integrated the two Federal estate taxes—the basic 1926 Act tax and the additional tax imposed by later enactments. This two-tier tax system had been perpetuated solely because of the State tax credit, which had always been tied in with the 1926 tax. This cumbersome system was eliminated, so that the 1954 Code established a single rate schedule. The State tax credit is fitted into the new schedule by a provision which is designed to produce the same amount of credit as was allowable under the old two-tier rate system. I.R.C. § 2011; Report of the House Ways and Means Committee to Accompany H.R. 8300 (H.R. No. 1337, 83rd Cong., 2d Sess.1954) p. A. 308 et seq. The same scheme has been continued in the current Internal Revenue Code. See I.R.C. § 2011 as of 1988.

Notes and Problems

A. In Luman v. Resor, 406 P.2d 527 (Wyo.1965), the court considered two issues arising from the application to a non-resident's estate of Wyoming's "additional tax" designed to absorb the Federal estate tax credit. The decedent, a Connecticut resident, died owning an estate located partly in Connecticut and partly in Wyoming. Wyoming's "additional tax" statute provided that "the total federal and state inheritance and estate taxes upon any estate, shall not be increased under this act above the total amount which would be due without reference hereto." Wyo.Stat. § 39–341. The taxpayer argued that the additional tax should not apply because the total of the death taxes paid to the States of Wyoming and Connecticut, without reference to Wyoming's "additional tax," exceeded the maximum Federal estate tax credit. The court rejected the argument on the ground that Wyoming intended the reference to "state" inheritance and estate taxes to refer only to Wyoming taxes and not to all State death taxes by whatever State imposed. Since the Wyoming inheritance tax did not exceed the Federal credit, the "additional tax" was applicable.

The court then turned to the question of how to apportion the credit, which was the measure of the "additional tax," to Wyoming. The Inheritance Tax Commissioner took the position that the appropriate approach was to take a percentage of the total Federal estate tax credit available to the estate—the percentage being determined by the value of the gross estate in Wyoming divided by the total value of the gross estate. The taxpayer contended that only that portion of the decedent's estate that was actually located in Wyoming should be considered in determining the Wyoming share of the credit, and hence the tax. Since the Federal estate tax is imposed at progressive rates, the Tax Commissioner's approach resulted in a higher tax because it assigned to Wyoming a portion of the credit based on the average tax rate applicable to the entire estate. The taxpayer's approach, on the other hand, determined the credit based on the lower marginal rates applicable to that portion of the estate located in Wyoming. The court concluded that the legislature intended to do no more than have only that portion of a taxable estate located in Wyoming considered in determining the Federal credit. It indicated, however, that the legislature possessed the constitutional power to measure the Wyoming share of the Federal estate tax credit by reference to out-of-state values. See Maxwell v. Bugbee, 250 U.S. 525, 40 S.Ct. 2 (1919), discussed in Chapter 2, subd. C supra, and the reference to the common practice among the States of determining their progressive death tax rates in terms of a nonresident's entire estate wherever situated. For a thoughtful opinion considering the analogous question in the context of a proration of exemptions in proportion to the fraction of the estate located within the State, see Tharalson v. State, 281 Or. 9, 573 P.2d 298 (1978) (Linde, J.).

B. The Florida Constitution denies to the Legislature the power to levy any death tax which exceeds the allowable Federal estate tax credit. Fla. Const., Art. IX, Sec. 11. In several cases involving residents of Florida who died leaving property situated in both Florida and other States, controversies arose as to the proper apportionment of the Federal credit among the States. The Attorney General of Florida claimed that other States had absorbed an excessive amount of the credit, that Florida was not bound by these determinations, and that the credit should be apportioned by reference to the proportionate values determined for Federal estate tax purposes of the properties located in the various States. Else, Florida would, in effect, be allowing a credit for "taxes levied by other states with funds due, or of, the State of Florida."

The Supreme Court of Florida rejected this contention. Green v. State, 166 So.2d 585 (Fla.1964). It read the Florida Constitution and the statute as imposing only a Florida tax which is allowable as a credit on Federal taxes after allowing the estate to claim credits against the Federal tax for all estate taxes paid to other States. 166 So.2d at 589. The court reaffirmed its holding in Green in Department of Revenue v. Golder, 326 So.2d 409 (Fla.1976).

C. State "pick-up" statutes are also considered in Estate of Fasken, 19 Cal.3d 412, 138 Cal.Rptr. 276, 563 P.2d 832 (1977), cert. denied 434 U.S. 877, 98 S.Ct. 230 (1977); Estate of Amar, 255 Cal.App.2d 404, 63 Cal.Rptr. 444 (1967); State v. Purdue Nat. Bank, 171 Ind.App. 76, 355 N.E.2d 414 (1976).

D. *References.* For a consideration of the history and operation of the credit, see Perkins, "State Action Under the Federal Estate Tax Credit Clause," 13 N.C.L.Rev. 270 (1935); Oakes, "Development of American State Death Taxes," 26 Iowa L.Rev. 451 (1941); Graves, Gulick & Newcomer, "Federal, State, and Local Government Fiscal Relations," Doc. No. 69, 78th Cong., 1st Sess. 476–496 (1943); Cogburn, "The Credit Allowable against the Basic Federal Estate Tax for Death Taxes Paid Under Statutes Enacted to Take Advantage Thereof," 30 N.C.L.Rev. 123 (1952).

ASSIGNMENT

John Barrister, a lawyer, was a resident of and domiciled in State A at his death on March 15 of last year. By his will Barrister left one-half his estate (including his life insurance as part of his estate) to his widow, who was 45 years of age at his death, and one-fourth to each of his two children. Barrister practiced law in State B as a member of a law partnership. The firm's offices were located in State B. Barrister's estate consisted of the following assets, after deducting debts (other than the mortgage debt noted below), administration expenses, and so forth (but not exemptions):

Property	Value
1. Bank accounts	
(a) Personal accounts with banks located in State A	$ 30,000
(b) Personal accounts with banks located in State B	20,000
(c) Cash in the form of U.S. Federal Reserve notes in a bank safe deposit box in State B	5,000
Note: The bank accounts were all joint survivorship accounts with Barrister's wife. The funds in the accounts were derived entirely from Barrister's earnings. The bank books were kept in Mrs. Barrister's separate safe deposit box.	
2. Interest in law firm; value of the decedent's pro-rata interest in	
(a) office furniture, fixtures, and supplies	$ 5,000
(b) accounts receivable from clients and anticipated billings for work done but not yet billed for clients located in	
(1) State B	50,000
(2) State A	20,000 $ 75,000

Property		**Value**
3. Stocks and bonds		

The corporations whose stock Barrister had owned were organized and engaged in business exclusively in

(a) State A $100,000		
(b) State X 150,000		$250,000
4. Real Estate.. $150,000		

The property was located in State B and was subject to a mortgage of $25,000 assumed by the decedent. The valuation figure is given before deducting the mortgage.

5. Life Insurance payable to the estate	$ 40,000

In addition, the decedent left $50,000 in life insurance payable to his wife and $1,000 payable to each of his children. He had paid all premiums.

A. Assume that State A is your State. Prepare: (1) a State A death tax return for the estate and compute the tax; (2) a memorandum explaining your treatment of the various items on the return.

B. Assume that State B is your State. Without preparing a return, set forth in a brief memorandum the property of the estate which would be taxed by State B's death tax, making appropriate references to the statute or regulations in support of your conclusions.

B. GIFT TAXES

The first Federal gift tax was enacted in 1924. It was repealed in 1926, and the present Federal gift tax was adopted in 1932. See I.R.C. c. 12. Oregon in 1933 was the first State to enact a gift tax, although Oregon's inheritance and gift taxes were repealed after 1986. See CCH All States Guide ¶ 89–200 et seq., P–H All States Guide ¶ 210. As of 1987, gift taxes were in force in Delaware, Louisiana, New York, North Carolina, South Carolina, Tennessee, and Wisconsin. Id. Like the Federal gift tax, the State gift taxes are designed to supplement the death tax by reaching *inter vivos* gifts which might otherwise escape transfer taxation.

Some States follow the Federal statute by generally taxing all gifts in the same manner regardless of the donee and by taking into account gifts made in prior years in order to apply graduated rates to the cumulative gifts. Del.Code tit. 30, § 1401 et seq., P–H State Inh.Tax Serv. ¶ 4001 et seq. Other States follow the pattern of their inheritance tax statutes by taxing separately gifts to each donee, with a separate graduation of rates in each case. See Wis.Stat. § 72.75 et seq., CCH ¶ 91–899 et seq., P–H ¶ 4001 et seq. (repealed in 1987 for transfers after Jan. 1, 1992). The Wisconsin statute ignores the prior years' gifts to the donee; but in other States the graduated rates aggregate the prior years' gifts made to the donee. See N.C.Gen.Stat. § 105–188, P–H St. Inh.Tax Serv ¶ 4005. Typically, the donor is primarily liable for the tax but the tax is a lien on the property and a levy may be made on the donee.

Notes and Problems

A. State gift tax litigation has not been extensive, with only a comparatively small number of States imposing the levy. See CCH Inh. Est. & Gift Tax Rep. (State Compilation) ¶ 1075. A major problem has been the extent to which the tax can be avoided by making gifts in non-gift tax States. Here the opportunity for tax avoidance is considerably greater than in the death tax field because of the control over *inter vivos* transactions that the parties can exercise. Thus, in Van Dyke v. Wisconsin Tax Commission, 235 Wis. 128, 292 N.W. 313, affirmed without opinion 311 U.S. 605, 61 S.Ct. 36 (1940), a resident of Milwaukee held $270,000 in United States bonds, which he had intended to transfer to a trust he was about to create. Before the trust was created, the bonds were called. Having found that he could collect the proceeds of the bonds in silver dollars, the settlor on November 25th appointed a Chicago bank his agent to receive 270,000 silver dollars in payment of the bonds. On December 3rd the Federal Reserve Bank in Chicago placed the dollars in a private vault maintained at the Federal Reserve by the Chicago bank, designated as the settlor's agent. Three days later the settlor and the trustees, a Wisconsin bank and the settlor's two sons, executed the trust agreement in Chicago, making the silver dollars the corpus of the trust. On instructions from the Wisconsin bank trustee, the Chicago bank invested the silver dollars in various securities; the investment program was completed in a few months.

In contesting a Wisconsin gift tax on the transaction, the donor argued that he had made a gift outside the State of tangible personal property there located; that the Wisconsin gift tax act excluded gifts of tangible property located outside the State; and that the Due Process Clause precluded the tax. Relying on Blodgett v. Silberman, 277 U.S. 1, 48 S.Ct. 410 (1928), p. 831 supra, the Court looked at the entire transaction as a series of integrated steps, with the intermediate holding of "seven and one-half tons" of silver dollars "as a device which possessed no utility in the making of the transfer." Compare in this connection the "step transaction" and the "business purpose" doctrines in Federal income taxation. See B. Bittker, Fundamentals of Federal Income Taxation ¶ 1.3 at 1–24 to 1–25 (Student Ed.1983). Here the taxpayer intended to transfer his government bonds or their proceeds for conversion into intangible property to be held by the trust. Moreover, the court held that the statutory provision exempting transfers by residents of tangibles located outside the State "refers to situs and not to mere physical presence"; chattels are taxable at the donor's domicile unless they are more or less permanently located elsewhere.

A later Wisconsin gift tax case dealt with a transfer in trust by a *non-resident* of securities and cash. Wuesthoff v. Wisconsin Department of Taxation, 261 Wis. 98, 52 N.W.2d 131 (1952). The securities had been kept in Milwaukee for years and the cash was withdrawn from a Milwaukee bank account of long standing. The donor executed the trust instrument in Switzerland, where she resided, and sent it to her attorney in Milwaukee. About a week later, the securities and cash were taken to Chicago and turned over to a Chicago bank, which executed the trust agreement as trustee. The Wisconsin gift tax statute imposes tax:

> When the transfer is by gift of property within the state or within its jurisdiction and the donor was a non-resident of the state at the date of such gift.

The State sought to tax on the theory that the cash and securities had for many years had a "situs" in Milwaukee, relying on the *Van Dyke* case, supra. The court set aside the tax, distinguishing the earlier case as dealing with a resident. A non-resident may be taxed on intangibles having a situs in the State, said the court, but "there must be a transfer by gift completed within the state in order to subject such transfer to taxation in Wisconsin." 261 Wis. at 105, 52 N.W.2d at 134. While this may be sound State policy and may be the import of the Wisconsin statute, does the court's statement correctly define the State's power of gift taxation? Suppose the balance in the bank account, not the cash itself, had been transferred to the trustee in Chicago; could Wisconsin have taxed?

B. In Hassemer v. Wisconsin Dept. of Taxation, 4 CCH Inh., Est. and Gift Tax Rep. ¶ 19–980 (1966), the State Board of Tax Appeals held that a taxable gift took place when a husband transferred to his wife a half interest in two farms owned by him, in exchange for her relinquishment of her dower rights. The value of the dower rights—"at best a contingent future interest"—was inadequate consideration for the $25,000 sales proceeds she received.

C. In Keck v. Cranston, 236 Cal.App.2d 39, 45 Cal.Rptr. 634 (1965), the court held that no California gift tax was payable on the creation of an irrevocable trust, where the beneficiary, the settlor's son, had a testamentary power of appointment to his issue, but the settlor had reserved to himself the right to direct payment of all or a part of the corpus to the beneficiary. When the settlor executed a "Statement of Clarification and Renunciation" of the latter power, gift tax liability arose. The court followed the view of the Supreme Court in interpreting the Federal gift tax as enunciated in Sanford's Estate v. Commissioner of Internal Revenue, 308 U.S. 39, 60 S.Ct. 51 (1939). The court followed the rule frequently applied by State courts under statutes modelled after Federal taxing acts:

> In short, we adopt a construction of the California Gift Tax Act which makes our law operate in a manner consistent with the federal law on the same transfers, and which is the construction adopted by the officer charged with the administration of that law contemporaneously with its coming into effect and which has been the uniform and unquestioned construction of the statute for twenty-five years. [45 Cal. Rptr. at 642.]

See also Estate of Moore, 29 Cal.App.3d 481, 105 Cal.Rptr. 568 (1973). California's gift tax was repealed in 1982.

Chapter 13

PERSONAL INCOME TAXES

This chapter is not designed to deal with problems of gross income, deductions, exemptions, and so on, which are normally dealt with in Federal income tax courses. It is limited to income tax problems peculiar to State taxation.

INTRODUCTORY NOTE

The personal income tax has roots deep in colonial America. The colonial "faculty taxes" combined property and income as the tax base. And the income element of the faculty tax persisted after 1776 in several States. The panic of 1837 resulted in the adoption of income taxes in a number of States. Thus, Pennsylvania in 1840 levied a tax of one percent on salaries and a one-tenth of one percent tax on other incomes. During the Civil War all the Confederate States and several Union States enacted income taxes. Without exception, however, the nineteenth century income taxes were administrative failures, and their revenue yields trifling.

In 1911, Wisconsin opened a new chapter in American fiscal history with an income tax administered by a State tax commission. See W.E. Brownlee, Progressivism and Economic Growth: The Wisconsin Income Tax 1911–1929 (1974). The rate schedule of this tax was progressive, beginning at one percent over a moderate exemption and rising to six percent on the excess over $12,000. The success of the Wisconsin income tax was immediately apparent, and several other States were induced to enact income tax laws. Federal and Wisconsin experience with income taxes demonstrated that a centrally administered income tax could be a practicable source of revenue. Scholars had long pointed to the income tax as a highly desirable form of taxation because of its close conformity to the principle of taxation according to ability to pay.

At the beginning of the 1920's, there were many who thought that personal income taxes would soon become a universal form of State taxation. But the movement which began with New York and North

Dakota taxes in 1919 soon waned. However, another wave of State income tax enactments began in 1929. Tennessee imposed a special income tax on income derived from stocks and bonds, and Arkansas, Georgia, and Oregon enacted general income tax laws. During the next decade, 13 more States instituted personal income taxes. In 1987, 41 States and the District of Columbia levied broad-based personal income taxes. The total yield of personal income taxes in the fiscal year 1986 was $67.5 billion which represented 29.6 percent of total State tax collections.[1]

Local governments collected $6.5 billion in personal income taxes in the fiscal year 1985.[2] See Chapter 1, § 6 supra, for a description of the growth of local income taxes.

SECTION 1. CONFORMITY OF STATE INCOME TAXES TO THE FEDERAL INCOME TAX

ALASKA STEAMSHIP CO. v. MULLANEY

United States Court of Appeals, Ninth Circuit, 1950.
12 Alaska 594, 180 F.2d 805.

POPE, CIRCUIT JUDGE. The appellant operates a line of vessels for the transportation of freight and passengers between Seattle, Washington, and ports of Alaska. At the time to which this controversy relates, its 12 vessels were manned by 706 seamen all of whom were non-residents of Alaska. It also had 19 resident Alaska shore employees and some Seattle resident shore employees who made extended trips for the Company to Alaska.

* * *

[The Alaska net income tax law of 1949 imposed a tax of a flat ten percent of the amount of a taxpayer's Federal income tax "as now in effect or hereafter amended," but non-residents were, at their option, permitted to pay a tax equal to ten percent of what the Federal tax would be, as applied only to income from sources attributable to the then Territory of Alaska. In the case of Alaska personnel of vessels engaged in Alaska trade, the tax was applicable only to the portion of the voyage pay earned in the waters of Alaska.

The taxpayer was required to withhold the Alaska tax from the wages of its employees. The employee members of the Sailors Union of the Pacific obtained an injunction from the U.S. District Court for the Western District of Washington, Northern Division, against the plaintiff, Alaska Steamship Company, which enjoined it from paying over to the Territory the wages withheld, and required that the withholdings be kept in a special fund pending further court action.

Faced with the demand of the Commissioner of Taxation of Alaska for payment of the withholdings, the steamship company brought the present suit seeking to have the income tax act, and its withholding

---

1. U.S. Bureau of the Census, "State Government Tax Collections in 1986," Table 1 (GF 85 No. 1, March 1987).

2. U.S. Bureau of the Census, "Governmental Finances in 1984–85," Table 2 (GF 85 No. 5, Dec. 1986).

provisions as applied to the plaintiff, declared invalid. The portions of the opinion dealing with the attack on the withholding provisions have been omitted.]

3. The attack upon the Alaska Act "in its entirety."

Appellant says that since we must necessarily consider the question of the validity of the withholding requirements, that while we are at it we should have a look at the entire Act; that when we do we shall find it so shot through with invalid and unconstitutional requirements that we shall see that the Act is invalid "in its entirety," and therefore necessarily invalid as to seamen.

The Steamship Company then proceeds to list numerous respects in which it claims that the Act either violates constitutional restrictions, or contravenes the limitations of the Organic Act.* First objection enumerated is that the Alaska Act, in adopting "the Internal Revenue Code of the United States (53 Stat. 1 [26 U.S.C.A. § 1 et seq.]) as now in effect *or hereafter amended,*" attempts to delegate legislative functions to Congress, which it is not permitted to do. Appellee suggests that even if the words we have italicized, "or hereafter amended," must be held to have attempted such an invalid delegation, yet that under Section 15 of the Act, which is the "separability" clause of the Act,[8] the objectionable phrase may be ignored, as invalid, without its affecting the validity of the remainder of the Act. It is pointed out that no amendments have been made in the Internal Revenue Code since the adoption of the Alaska Act, and hence, it is said, the present application of the Act involves no necessity of incorporating any subsequently adopted amendments.

* * *

So far as this appellant is concerned, it is not now required to conform to any requirements resulting from Congressional amendments of the Internal Revenue Code adopted after the Alaska Act was enacted. * * * What appellant faces, therefore, are these rules stated in the often quoted words of Mr. Justice Brandeis in the Ashwander case, supra, as follows: "The Court will not 'anticipate a question of constitutional law in advance of the necessity of deciding it,' " and "The Court will not pass upon the validity of a statute upon complaint of one who fails to show that he is injured by its operation." As Mr. Justice Cardozo put it, "The plaintiffs are not the champions of any rights except their own." [10]

* [Some of the court's footnotes have been omitted.]

8. Section 15. "Severability. If any provision of this Act, or the application thereof to any person or circumstance is held invalid, the remainder of the Act and such application to other persons or circumstances shall not be affected thereby."

Such a clause creates no more than a presumption of separability. Williams v. Standard Oil Co., 278 U.S. 235, 49 S.Ct. 115, 73 L.Ed. 287, 60 A.L.R. 596. Even in the absence of such a clause, the Supreme Court has been inclined to find separability in state tax laws. Stern, "Separability and Separability Clauses in the Supreme Court," 51 Harvard L.R. 76, at p. 90.

10. Henneford v. Silas Mason Co., 300 U.S. 577, 583, 57 S.Ct. 524, 527, 81 L.Ed. 814.

We therefore proceed to consider the various arguments addressed to us, and urged as reasons why the Alaska Act must be held invalid, having constantly in mind the important bearing of both the presumption created by the separability clause and the rules of self-restraint to which we have just referred.

4. As to the claim of invalidity due to delegation of legislative powers.

What has been said sufficiently indicates the basis for our opinion that even if we were to hold the attempted incorporation by reference of amendments to the Internal Revenue Code to be adopted in the future were an invalid delegation, yet as of this day and hour appellant is not affected by any such amendments, for there have been none. The right to incorporate by reference provisions of the federal law "now in effect," cannot be questioned. Franklin v. United States, 216 U.S. 559, 568, 30 S.Ct. 434, 54 L.Ed. 615; Santee Mills v. Query, 122 S.C. 158, 115 S.E. 202; Featherstone v. Norman, 170 Ga. 370, 395, 153 S.E. 58, 70 A.L.R. 449; In re Burke, 190 Cal. 326, 212 Pac. 193.

We do not overlook the fact that if the words "or hereafter amended" were dropped from the Act, what remains would, in the long run, be unworkable under the legislative scheme here devised, for if the federal income tax requirements were changed substantially by future amendments, it would be impossible, administratively, to calculate the Alaska income tax merely by dividing the tax shown on the federal return by 10. That is a hypothetical question which conceivably may never arise. Commonwealth v. Alderman, 275 Pa. 483, 487, 119 A. 551, 553.

We think it is far from clear that any invalid delegation is attempted. There are of course many cases which have held attempts by a legislative body to incorporate provisions into its enactments, by reference to future acts or amendments by other legislatures, to be invalid. But where it can be said that the attempt to make the local law conform to future changes elsewhere it is [sic] not a mere labor-saving device for the legislators, but is undertaken in order to attain a uniformity which is in itself an important object of the proposed legislative scheme, there are a number of precedents for an approval of this sort of thing. Reciprocal and retaliatory legislation falls in this category.[11] People v. Fire Ass'n of Philadelphia, 92 N.Y. 311, 44 Am. Rep. 380.[12]

---

11. See Joseph R. Starr, "Reciprocal and Retaliatory Legislation in the American States," 21 Minn.L.R. 371.

12. "Possibly we may get nearer the ultimate point of the objection urged. That would seem to be that, while the legislature might, by a series of separate acts, each passed because of a then existing foreign law, follow its changes, yet it cannot do so by one act which adopted and enacts such future and contingent muta-

tions. This doctrine requires us to hold that a law, so framed as to follow and recognize the changes of foreign legislation, and thereby incorporate such changes into its own operation, is a delegation of the legislative power and therefore inadmissible. We have found no authority for such a broad and general proposition." For a case contra, see Clark & Murrell v Port of Mobile, 67 Ala. 217.

Similarly the efforts of the states to take advantage, in their inheritance tax laws, of the 80 percent credit provision in the federal laws relating to Estate Tax, 44 Stat. 70, now 26 U.S.C.A. 813(b), have been carried out by simple reference to the federal estate tax law.[13] Brown v. State, 323 Mo. 138, 19 S.W.2d 12. Perhaps the best-known instance of action by Congress encompassing within its regulation the laws of states, then or thereafter enacted, was the Conformity Act, 17 Stat. 196, 197, referred to by Mr. Justice Holmes, dissenting, in Knickerbocker Ice Co. v. Stewart, supra, 253 U.S. at page 169, 40 S.Ct. at page 443, 64 L.Ed. 834, 11 A.L.R. 1145. There, also, making the procedure in common law actions conform to that prevailing in the states was a prime object of the legislation.

The effort of the Alaska legislature to make its territorial income tax machinery conform to the federal act, and to preserve and continue such conformity, makes sense. It makes for convenience to the taxpayer and for simplicity of administration. Cf. Underwood Typewriter Co. v. Chamberlin, 94 Conn. 47, 65, 108 A. 154, 160. A similar coordination has been recommended by students of income tax problems for adoption by the states generally.[14] Since the attainment of this uniformity was in itself a major objective of the Alaska legislature, in enacting that the local law must conform, the Alaska legislature, which alone could make this decision, was itself acting, and was not abdicating its functions, nor, in our opinion, making an invalid delegation to Congress.[15]

There are two other ways in which, it is asserted, an invalid delegation is made. One is the provision that "rules and regulations promulgated by the United States Commissioner of Internal Revenue * * * shall be regarded as regulations promulgated by the Tax Commissioner under * * * this Act." We think what we have said concerning incorporation of the Internal Revenue Code sufficiently disposes of this question. If the one is valid, the other is also.

* * *

We are of the opinion that the judgment of the Court below must be affirmed.

It is so ordered.*

---

13. Thus, Sec. 13442, California Revenue and Taxation Code, provides in certain cases for a "tax equal to the maximum State tax credit allowed by the Federal estate tax law."

14. Kassell, "No Uniformity in State Income Taxes—Why?", 87 Journal of Accountancy, 293, 296 (April, 1949); "Federal, State and Local Government Fiscal Relations," S.Doc. 69, 78 Const. 1st Sess. pp. 417, 418–9, 452. Cf. Mermain, "Cooperative Federalism," 57 Yale L.J. 1, 18 (Nov. 1947).

15. It would appear that the intended administrative simplicity of the Act is somewhat impaired by the inclusion of the words "as computed without the benefit of the deduction of the tax payable hereunder to the Territory," in Section 5A(1) and (2). Since the federal law would permit such deductions, it would seem that the federal returns would have to be recomputed in each case to meet this requirement before the 10 percent could be applied.

* [The concurring opinion of Chief Judge Denman has been omitted. For a case construing the Alaska conformity provision with respect to the limitation period on deficiency assessments, see Hickel v. Stevenson, 416 P.2d 236 (Alaska 1966). After revising its income tax scheme in 1975 to one based on Federal income tax defini-

Notes and Problems

A. *Federally Based State Income Taxes.* As the Federal income tax has grown more complicated with increasing refinements and frequent changes—most recently illustrated by the dramatic changes in the personal income tax base made by the Tax Reform Act of 1986—the differences between Federal and State taxable income have increased. In some States efforts have been made to incorporate Federal changes into State law, but this has often encountered obstacles and delays and has consumed substantial time of State legislatures. Moreover, a number of States have had their own local variations which have made the differences between Federal and State income taxes more marked.

The burden on taxpayers of preparing and filing two tax returns, involving sharply varying provisions and complicated differences in computation, has caused widespread annoyance, considerable expense, and much grumbling. Moreover the difficulties of audit and enforcement have mounted with these disparities. The consequence has been a strong movement among the States to conform their income taxes to the Federal income tax.

The statute involved in the principal case reflects the most complete type of Federalization of the State income tax. The constitutional objections raised in the case, namely, the alleged impropriety of incorporation of another statute by reference and the claimed illegality of the delegation by a State legislature of its powers to Congress, have impeded the growth of conformity. In a good many States, incorporation of other statutes by reference has had a long history of statutory or judicial acceptance, but the problem often remains. Serious doubt as to the propriety of the legislative delegation has persisted; as a result limited types of conformance to the Federal tax have been utilized in some States. In Featherstone v. Norman, 170 Ga. 370, 153 S.E. 58 (1931), the court considered an income tax statute which, generally speaking, adopted by reference the Federal definition of net income and imposed tax at rates set forth in the Georgia statute. After noting that incorporation by reference in a legislative act was a well established method, the court considered the contention that the act was invalid because it constituted an unconstitutional delegation of the legislative power of the Georgia legislature to Congress. The court met this claim by holding that the act merely adopts the then current Federal income tax, which would not be affected by future changes in the Federal statute. A similar statute was sustained in Santee Mills v. Query, 122 S.C. 158, 115 S.E. 202 (1922). See also Wallace v. Commissioner, 289 Minn. 220, 184 N.W.2d 588 (1971).

In 1954 when Iowa sought to conform its income tax to the Federal statute, the constitutional doubts produced a similar limitation. The Iowa conformance is limited to the Internal Revenue Code of 1954, and as changes are made in the Federal statute, the Iowa legislature acts to conform its statute to the Federal Code as thus amended. This static

tions, rather than one based on a percentage of the Federal tax, Alaska repealed its personal income tax in 1979.]

Federal base has been adopted in a number of States. It is interesting to note that the Iowa death tax in effect incorporates the provisions of the Federal estate tax, including future amendments that may be adopted.

More recently, as the principal case shows, full-blown Federalization of a State income tax, including amendments to be adopted in the future, has been enacted. In 1955 Montana adopted by reference the Federal definition of gross income and Federal deductions as "defined in * * * the Internal Revenue Code of 1954 as that * * * code shall be * * * amended." In 1960 New York, acting on the basis of a constitutional amendment, adopted a conformity statute which authorizes the inclusion of future Federal amendments. A number of other States now use this moving Federal base.

Nebraska was one of the States that resorted to a constitutional amendment to achieve full income tax conformity, an amendment whose effectiveness was, nevertheless, challenged. In Anderson v. Tiemann, 182 Neb. 393, 155 N.W.2d 322 (1967), appeal dismissed 390 U.S. 714, 88 S.Ct. 1418 (1968), the State's highest court upheld the validity of the 1967 Nebraska income tax act, adopted pursuant to the constitutional amendment. That act calls for conformity not only to the Federal statute, as it may be amended in the future, but also to "the rules and regulations issued under such laws, as the same may become effective from time to time * * *."

The risk that the delegation of powers under a moving Federal base may be held unconstitutional is one, as indicated above, that some States have been unwilling to take, for the invalidation of an entire year's income tax could prove disastrous. There are cases that suggest that the risk is substantial, at least in some States. Thus, in Cheney v. St. Louis Southwestern Ry. Co., 239 Ark. 870, 394 S.W.2d 731 (1965), there was at issue an Arkansas income tax statute, applicable to railroads and other utilities, which employs the Interstate Commerce Commission standard classification of accounts in computing taxable income. This standard classification of accounts is a system promulgated by the Interstate Commerce Commission for use by interstate carriers to assure uniformity in reporting for ratemaking purposes. The Interstate Commerce Act grants the Commission discretionary authority to prescribe the accounts. The court held that the taxing statute violated the Arkansas Constitution, because it surrendered to a Federal agency the responsibility of determining the taxable net income of the taxpayer, and based Arkansas tax liability on a formula subject to prospective Federal legislation or administrative rules. Such a delegation, of course, goes far beyond the long accepted practice among the States of delegating broad authority to a taxing official to prescribe apportionment and allocation methods, in order to determine the income attributable to a State from the operation of a multistate business. See Columbia Gulf Transmission Co. v. Barr, 194 So.2d 890 (Miss.1967), in which such a delegation was sustained against constitutional attack. As is typical, in that case broad standards for determining the income attributable to the State were set up by the statute, but it vested in the taxing authority wide scope in promulgating methods to be used.

Most of the State statutes, despite general conformity to the Federal base and the incorporation of the key Federal income tax terms, provide for special adjustments adapted either to local needs or to the idiosyncrasies of (or political pressures on) State legislatures. Thus see the deduction for amounts paid for insulation of residences and installation of alternative energy devices permitted under the Idaho income tax, but not under the Federal income tax. Idaho Code § 63–3022B, CCH ¶ 94–132f P–H ¶ 12–609–B. The State conformity provisions are summarized in P–H All States Guide ¶ 221.

B. The adoption of the simplest Federalization program, namely, using a percentage of Federal tax, presents fundamental policy decisions. Thus, Federal exemptions may be inadequate, the Federal graduation schedule may be unacceptable, the treatment of capital gains may be unacceptable, and so forth. Moreover, the taxation of non-residents, whose income is limited to sources within the State, frequently with restrictions on deductions and exemptions, requires special treatment. See pp. 941–60 infra. Many of these policies can be left for independent determination by the State legislature by adopting the overall Federal definition of gross income and Federal deductions, but keeping exemptions and rates (including the rates to be applied to capital gains) for separate State determination, without losing the major simplification benefits. At the same time where departure from the Federal definition of gross income or the scope of allowable deductions is regarded as important, these can be retained. Thus, the New York statute, although generally adopting the Federal levy, taxes interest on bonds issued by other States and excludes from gross income pensions to employees of the State and its subdivisions. See N.Y. Tax Law §§ 612(b)(1), 612(c)(3) CCH ¶¶ 95–214, 95–233, P–H ¶¶ 59,080.15, 59,080.75.

Controversies have arisen over the relationship between the State personal income tax laws and the Federal personal income tax provisions upon which they rely. In Burpulis v. Director of Revenue, 498 A.2d 1082 (Del.1985), the taxpayers had filed a joint Federal income tax return taking advantage of the deduction for two-earner married couples permitted by former I.R.C. § 221. In filing separate State returns, the taxpayers allocated their joint Federal adjusted gross income between their separate Delaware returns, with the wife receiving a $913 two-earner married couple deduction. The Tax Appeal Board sustained this position and held that when the legislature chose "Federal adjusted gross income" as the basis upon which to compute State tax liability, it intended to incorporate all the adjustments to adjusted gross income permitted under Federal law, including the two-earner married couple deduction. On appeal the superior court reversed, and the Delaware Supreme Court affirmed the reversal. The court held that the purpose underlying the deduction—to offset the "marriage penalty" precipitated by the use of different tax rate schedules based on the taxpayer's filing status—would not be served by granting it to married taxpayers filing separately, because Delaware applies the same tax rate schedule to all individuals regardless of the status in which they file their returns. Hence the court sustained the administrative regulation forbidding the deduction for two-earner married couples who file separate State returns. "Indeed, to permit the two-earner married couple deduction in Delaware would be to introduce inequities in the tax system where none existed before." 498 A.2d at 1087.

In Calhoun v. Franchise Tax Bd., 20 Cal.3d 881, 143 Cal.Rptr. 692, 574 P.2d 763 (1978), it was held that the taxpayers were estopped from relitigating in the State court the amount of their gross income for the years in question, which had been determined in a prior Federal tax case.

The conformance of State income taxes to Federal income tax definition has not only eased reporting complications but it has also simplified auditing and, with increasing Federal–State cooperation, improved and tightened up State income tax enforcement.

C. *The Federal–State Tax Collection Act of "1972."* The incentives for States to conform their personal income taxes to the Federal model were increased with the enactment of the Federal–State Tax Collection Act of 1972, which is codified at 26 U.S.C. §§ 6361–65. In substance, the Act provides that a State with a "qualified State individual income tax," i.e., a tax closely conforming to the Federal model, see 26 U.S.C. § 6362, may enter into an agreement with the United States to have its individual income taxes collected and administered by the Federal Government. 26 U.S.C. § 6363. Among other requirements, the qualifying State income tax law must adopt the regulations "as in effect from time to time" under the Federal statute. Id. § 6362(f)(2). The arguments both for and against participation in the Federal collection program are set out in a report prepared by the National Association of Tax Administrators which is reprinted in part in O. Oldman & F. Schoettle, State and Local Taxes and Finance 665–84 (1974).

The principal objection to State participation is loss in control over the taxing power that would result from the conformity requirements. Not only would the loss of State autonomy be reflected in an automatic acceptance of Congressional determinations regarding the definition of tax base and taxable income—that is, decisions regarding such matters as deductions, credits, depreciation, capital gains, and the like—but it might also expose State tax systems to significant changes in their revenues as a result of changes at the Federal level. Consider, for example, the impact of the drastic reduction in Federal corporate income taxes in the early 1980's under the first Reagan Administration and the potential "windfall" to the States resulting from broadening of the personal income tax base in the Tax Reform Act of 1986, discussed in Note D infra.

As originally enacted, the Act provided that it would not be effective until at least two States with more than five percent of the Federal tax returns had entered into an agreement under the statute; that requirement was eased by the 1976 Tax Reform Act to provide that the Act shall be effective on the first January 1 which is more than one year after at least one State enters into such an agreement. P.L. 94–455 § 2116, 90 Stat. 1520 (1976). As of this writing, no State has in fact entered into such an agreement. The 1976 Tax Reform Act also makes it clear that the Federal collection plan is to be without added costs to the States—a provision that was adopted in response to suggestions that the States would or might be charged for the services provided by the Federal Government. See Stolz & Purdy, "Federal Collection of State Individual Income Taxes," 1977 Duke

L.J. 59, 92; Angelini & Horvitz, "Federal–State Tax Policy Differentials: Why Piggybacking Will Never Work," 4 J.St.Tax. 125 (1985).

D. *Federal–State Conformity and the Tax Reform Act of 1986.* The Federal Tax Reform Act of 1986 broadened the Federal personal income tax base while lowering rates. Some deductions were eliminated (e.g., the deduction for State sales taxes and for two-earner married couples, see Note B supra); other deductions were substantially limited (e.g., the deductions for contributions to Individual Retirement Accounts and for consumer interest); and the treatment of other items was altered (e.g., the treatment of long-term capital gains and the deductibility of employee business expenses). For the majority of States whose tax bases are tied to the Federal personal income tax base but whose tax *rates* are independent of the Federal rate structure, the broadening of the Federal tax base offered the prospect of substantial increases in tax revenues if the States did not lower their own rates, as the Federal Government had done. See Tax Notes, Dec. 15, 1986, p. 983. Only the States whose personal income taxes were a percentage of the Federal personal income tax—Nebraska, North Dakota, Rhode Island, and Vermont—were predicted to suffer substantial losses as a result of changes at the Federal level. Id. For the 34 States that were expected to experience a revenue "windfall," the questions were whether to pass the revenue gains back to taxpayers, or to retain them for governmental purposes. Some argued that the States "should use the added revenues to ease the tax load on overburdened middle- and lower-income families or to improve the services that benefit everyone." Wilhelm, "Tax Revision at the State Level," N.Y. Times, Business Section, Feb. 22, 1987, p. 2. Others argued that the States should follow the Federal principle of "revenue neutrality" and return the windfall to the taxpayers. Weinstein & Gross, "States Should Follow the Federal Cue," N.Y. Times, Business Section, Feb. 22, 1987, p. 2.

E. *References.* Miller, "The New Iowa Income Tax Law," 41 Iowa L.Rev. 85 (1955); Kamins, "Federally Based State Income Taxes," 9 Nat. Tax J. 46 (1956); "Simplification of Income Tax Returns for New York State Taxpayers—Report to Senate Committee on Finance and Assembly Committee on Ways and Means," 15 Tax L.Rev. 367 (1960), a report dealing with the recommendation to adopt a Federally based New York income tax; Note, "Constitutionality of North Dakota's Federalized State Income Tax," 35 N.D.L.Rev. 151 (1959); Zubrow, "Recent Trends Toward Uniformity in State Personal Income Taxation," 19 Nat.Tax J. 86 (1966); Dane, "Problems in Conforming State Income Taxes with the Federal Model," 47 Taxes 94 (1969); Whiteside & Moss, "Conformity of Kentucky Personal Income Tax with the Federal Model," 61 Ky.L.J. 462 (1972–73); Traigle, "The Louisiana Approach to the Simplification of a State's Income Tax Laws," 43 J.Tax. 177 (1975). For a panel discussion on income tax conformity, see Cohen, "Knotty Problems in the Branches of the Federal Tree," 13th Ann. Tax Conf., College of William and Mary 51 (1968); Rogers, "The Case for Greater Uniformity of Federal and State Law with Respect to Individual Income Taxpayers," id. at 71; Harris, "Coordination of Federal and State Tax Laws: Effect on Virginia Corporations and Their Shareholders", id. at 77; Annots., 166 A.L.R. 516, 42 A.L.R.2d 797; Pomp, "Restructuring a State Income Tax in Response to the Tax Reform Act of 1986," Tax Notes,

Sept. 21, 1987 p. 1195; Tannenwald, "State Response in New England to Federal Tax Reform," Tax Notes, Nov. 2, 1987, p. 537.

SECTION 2. THE TAXATION OF INCOME OF RESIDENTS

Notes and Problems

A. Minnesota does not seek to tax the income of a resident derived from a business conducted outside the State, unless it consists principally of the performance of services. Minn.Stat. § 290.17(1)(a), CCH ¶ 94–063, P–H ¶ 12,110.10. In Bechert v. Commissioner of Taxation, 221 Minn. 65, 21 N.W.2d 101 (1945), the question was whether a Minneapolis-based partner of a national accounting firm was taxable only on his distributive share of income produced by partnership activities carried on in Minnesota State or, in addition, to his distributive share of income produced by activities carried on in other States. The court held that the statutory language, assigning to the State "[t]he entire income of all resident or domestic taxpayers * * * from a business consisting of the performance of personal or professional services," clearly required the assignment of all of the taxpayer's income to Minnesota.

> [The taxpayer's] distributable share was a distribution of income to him from a business consisting principally of the performance of personal or professional services. Net income is determined only by treating the partnership as an entity, and the tax is based upon the partner's distributable share of the partnership's net income. [21 N.W.2d at 103.]

Compare Tax Review Board of Philadelphia v. D.H. Shapiro, Co., 409 Pa. 253, 185 A.2d 529 (1962), in which the court set aside an attempt to tax all the receipts of a Philadelphia firm of accountants from accounting services performed within and without the city, where some of the partners did not reside in Philadelphia. Although the firm had its offices only in Philadelphia, the residence of the partners was decisive; the entity conception of a partnership, as the basis for finding a Philadelphia domicile for the firm, was rejected. See, also, Fennell v. So. Car. Tax Commission, 233 S.C. 43, 103 S.E.2d 424 (1958).

In Bolier v. Commissioner of Taxation, 233 Minn. 72, 45 N.W.2d 802 (1951), the issue was whether a fee received by a resident road contractor for a job done outside the State was taxable. The job was done for the Federal Government under a cost plus fixed fee contract and all the work was performed outside the State. The taxpayer provided heavy road building equipment and crews of men, including foremen and supervisors, who did the work; the taxpayer himself knew little about construction work and had little to do with the actual road building. The State's contention that the taxpayer derived his income from construction work, which constituted personal services, was rejected. Instead, the taxpayer was held to have derived the income from the operation of a business not consisting principally of the performance of services. Just as the income from a non-service business conducted outside Minnesota is exempt from personal income taxation, so the losses associated with such a business are not deductible for Minnesota personal income tax purposes. Friedell v. Commissioner of Taxation, 270 N.W.2d 763 (Minn.1978) (rejecting argument that losses incurred by resident partners in out-of-state cattle breeding partnership were losses from ownership of intangible property—partnership interests—and therefore assignable to the taxpayers' domicile).

B. *Constitutionality of Disallowance of Deductions.* The Arkansas income tax act allowed a deduction of one-half the amount of Federal income tax paid or accrued. In Sims v. Ahrens, 167 Ark. 557, 271 S.W. 720 (1925), the Arkansas Supreme Court declared unconstitutional a gross income tax on the ground that it was arbitrary and discriminatory. In a later case, a taxpayer contended that the disallowance of a full deduction for Federal income tax in effect resulted in a levy on gross income. The court sustained the tax, holding that there is an area of legislative discretion in determining the particular deductions to be granted under a net income tax. Cook v. Walters Dry Goods Co., 212 Ark. 485, 206 S.W.2d 742 (1947), noted in 2 Ark.L.Rev. 459 (1948). The court, however, stated its agreement with counsel "that the ordinary and necessary expenses of doing business, including salaries, rentals, interest, losses, bad debts, etc., as set out in Section 13 of Act 118 of 1929, must be deducted in order to determine net income, and that the legislature could not exclude such items as deductions from gross income." 206 S.W.2d at 744. In 1949 the Arkansas statute was amended so as to eliminate all deductions for Federal income tax; this provision was upheld in Morley v. Remmell, 215 Ark. 434, 221 S.W.2d 51 (1949). For a collection of cases dealing with the deduction of Federal income taxes under State levies, see CCH All States Guide ¶ 10–602, P–H All States Guide ¶ 3187.

C. In Matter of Young v. Bragalini, 3 N.Y.2d 602, 170 N.Y.S.2d 805, 148 N.E.2d 143 (1948), the issue arose under the New York unincorporated business tax (which has many of the characteristics of an income tax) as to whether a New York insurance brokerage partnership was doing business outside the State so as to warrant an apportionment of its income. Admittedly, the firm was part of an insurance business being conducted in Texas and Brazil, but because of local law requirements, separate firms were set up in each jurisdiction. Some of the partners in the Texas and Brazilian firms were also members of the New York firm; although the New York firm had a considerable investment in the other firms, the latter had their own dealings with the local clients in their own names. The court sustained the Tax Commission in denying any out-of-state apportionment to the New York partnership for its out-of-state income, including its income from the Texas and Brazil partnerships, on the ground that the New York partnership had no place of business outside the State. The foreign partnerships were separate legal entities conducting their own separate businesses. Three judges dissented, holding that the foreign partnerships were agents of the New York firm.

D. *Taxation of Oil Royalties From Out–of–State Properties.* An individual residing in Idaho owned oil producing land in Wyoming and received royalties from a large oil company on account of oil removed from the property. The Idaho statute exempted from tax income derived from a trade or business carried on outside the State. The court denied the claimed exemption from tax of the royalties on the ground that they were not derived from the conduct by the taxpayer of a business outside the

State. Kopp v. Baird, 79 Idaho 152, 313 P.2d 319 (1957). Moreover, the court determined that the right to royalties was a chose in action, not an interest in land, and that only when "such personal property has acquired a 'locus, situs' foreign to the owner's domicil, by becoming an integral part of a business of the owner there carried on, does it assume a taxable situs in the foreign jurisdiction." Idaho now taxes its residents essentially on the basis of their Federal taxable income. Idaho Code §§ 63–3022, –24, CCH ¶¶ 94–122, –134, P–H ¶¶ 12,605, 12,615.

Colorado taxes non-residents on income attributable to the "ownership of any interest in real or tangible personal property in Colorado." C.R.S. § 39–22–115(2)(a), CCH ¶ 94–409, P–H ¶ 12,090.5. Two Wyoming residents who derived income from a retained royalty interest in Colorado oil leases assigned to third parties challenged the application of the statute to them on the ground that their leases were obtained under the Federal Mineral Leasing Act, 30 U.S.C. §§ 181–263, whose provisions suggested that no interest in real or tangible personal property could have been reserved by the assignors so as to create a taxable incident under the Colorado taxing statute. The court rejected the taxpayers' contention on the ground that Colorado law considered their royalty interest as an "interest in real * * * property" and that without a more explicit showing that the Federal "provisions and regulations promulgated thereunder were meant to *exclusively* define property interests *for all purposes*," the court would not presume that Congress intended to preempt Colorado law on this issue. Hagood v. Heckers, 182 Colo. 337, 513 P.2d 208 (1973).

E. *Income Earned During Portion of Year Taxpayer Was a Non-Resident.* Is a taxpayer who resides in a State during only part of the taxable year taxable on the entire net income for the full year by the State of his new residence? In District of Columbia v. Davis, 371 F.2d 964 (D.C. Cir.), certiorari denied 386 U.S. 1034, 87 S.Ct. 1487 (1967), the Tax Court had held that the statute's effort to reach the full year's income, where the taxpayer resided in the District for nine months of the year, violated the Due Process Clause. The United States Court of Appeals exercised the judicial prerogative of avoiding the constitutional point by holding that the taxing statute did not, by its terms, subject the income to taxation. Compare Petersen v. Department of Revenue, 301 Or. 144, 719 P.2d 869 (1986), where the court held that a taxpayer who contributed amounts to a tax-deferred annuity through a salary reduction agreement while working in California was taxable by Oregon when he withdrew his contributions as a retired resident of that State. The court relied on the doctrine that payments of compensation are income to a cash basis taxpayer in the year of receipt, unless the income has been constructively received. The issues that arise in connection with the taxation of appreciation occurring before the taxpayer became a resident of the taxing State are considered in Chapter 10, § 5 supra.

F. *References.* G. Altman & F. Keesling, Allocation of Income in State Taxation, ch. 3 (2d ed. 1950); Kressbach, "Local Income Taxation: Comparative Analysis," 37 Mich.Mun.Rev. 161 (1964); Advisory Commission on Intergovernmental Relations, "Federal–State Coordination of Personal Income Taxes" (1965).

ASSIGNMENT

A. Compare the provisions of your State's income tax law, as applied to residents, with the Federal income tax. Consider, *inter alia,* the following:

1. The taxation of capital gains and the extent of the deductibility of capital losses.

2. Does the State income tax law allow deductions for non-trade or non-business expenses? Cf. I.R.C. § 212.

3. Under the State law, are net operating loss deductions and capital loss carryovers allowed? Cf. I.R.C. §§ 172 and 1212.

4. Compare Federal and State personal exemptions and credits for dependents.

5. Has the State adopted a split income provision for husbands and wives filing joint returns? Cf. I.R.C. § 1. If your State is a community property State, analyze the effect of the community property system on the income tax of husbands and wives.

B. Examine the personal income tax law of your State and be prepared to discuss the extent to which the State has refrained from exercising its full constitutional power to tax the income of residents.

SECTION 3. THE TAXATION OF INCOME OF NON–RESIDENTS

MATTER OF SPENO v. GALLMAN

Court of Appeals of New York, 1974.
35 N.Y.2d 256, 360 N.Y.S.2d 855, 319 N.E.2d 180.

WACHTLER, JUDGE.

Frank Speno, Jr. and his wife Peggie B. Speno, residents of Summit, New Jersey, filed joint New York State non-resident income tax returns for the years 1960 and 1961. During these years Mr. Speno was the president of the Frank Speno Railroad Ballast Cleaning Co., Inc., which had its principal office in Ithaca, N.Y. with additional offices in Syracuse, N.Y. and Geneva, Switzerland. Although he was the corporate president his duties were not executive in nature but rather entailed public relations, entertainment and attendance at railroad meetings in order to promote the services of the company. As such, Mr. Speno was required to do a great deal of traveling through the United States and Europe.

In their 1960 New York State income tax return, the appellants claimed 236 days of work outside New York (106 of which were days worked at the Speno home in New Jersey) and computed their tax liability on the basis of 60 days worked in New York. The 1961 return showed 252 days worked outside New York, 174 of which were days worked at the Speno home in New Jersey.

In contrast to the numerous meetings and promotional activities Mr. Speno engaged in while in the other States and Europe, the work performed at home in New Jersey consisted essentially of making phone calls. No business calls were received on the unlisted Jersey number, and Mr. Speno entertained no business contacts in New Jersey. Accordingly, the Department of Taxation and Finance rejected the appellants' allocation and recomputed their taxes by deeming the days worked in New Jersey as nonworking days in the 1960 return, and by including them within the time worked in New York in the 1961 return.

The Spenos protested and a formal hearing was held before the State Tax Commission which found that his duties did not necessitate his residing in Summit, New Jersey. As Mr. Speno stated, "I could live in Hong Kong and do what I am doing."

Applying the "convenience of employer" test which is embodied in New York Income Tax Regulation (§ 131.16; 20 NYCRR 131.16), the commission reassessed the Speno tax liability to include the days worked in New Jersey. This determination was confirmed by the Appellate Division. Two of the Justices of that court dissented on the ground that the "convenience of the employer" test should be applied "[o]nly in cases where the employee is based or is required to work in New York, and works outside during a tax year."

The appellants challenge both the validity and the application of the "convenience of the employer" test.

The New York State Tax Law, Consol.Laws, c. 60, (§ 359, subd. 3; § 632, subd. [b]) provides in substance that non-residents must pay taxes on gross income from "sources within the state." The meaning of the phrase "sources within the state" is the focal point in this case. Apparently, the first interpretation was made in 1919 by the Attorney–General who stated that the source of income relates to "the work done, rather than the person paying for it" (1919 Report of Atty.Gen. 301). This resulted in the place of performance doctrine, i.e., that personal services performed outside the State would not be taxable.

In view of the large number of non-residents who avail themselves of employment within New York State, the place of performance doctrine was refined by virtue of the "convenience of the employer" test. Under this refinement, a non-resident who performs services in New York or has an office in New York is allowed to avoid New York State tax liability for services performed outside the State only if they are performed of necessity in the service of the employer. Where the out-of-State services are performed for the employee's convenience they generate New York State tax liability.

This refinement has been consistently applied by our courts (Matter of Burke v. Bragalini, 10 A.D.2d 654, 196 N.Y.S.2d 391 [where the additional tax was assessed despite the claim that the work was done at home to be free from interruptions and to utilize the research materials kept there]; Matter of Morehouse v. Murphy, 10 A.D.2d 764, 197

N.Y.S.2d 763, app. dsmd., 8 N.Y.2d 932, 204 N.Y.S.2d 170, 168 N.E.2d 840 [where a claim that the work done at home increased efficiency was rejected]; Matter of Churchill v. Gallman, 38 A.D.2d 631, 326 N.Y.S.2d 917 [where the additional tax was assessed despite the claim that work was done for personal health reasons].) In conjunction with the long-standing judicial application, the "convenience of the employer" test has been utilized by the State Tax Commission and has been incorporated into the New York Income Tax Regulations: "However, any allowance claimed for days worked outside of the State must be based upon the performance of services which of necessity—as distinguished from convenience—obligate the employee to out-of-State duties in the service of his employer" (20 NYCRR 131.16). The policy justification for the "convenience of the employer" test lies in the fact that since a New York State resident would not be entitled to special tax benefits for work done at home, neither should a non-resident who performs services or maintains an office in New York State. Consequently, the appellants' attack on the test's validity is without merit.

Turning to the application of the test in this case, the appellants rely heavily on two cases cited by the dissenters in the Appellate Division (Matter of Oxnard v. Murphy, 19 A.D.2d 138, 241 N.Y.S.2d 333, affd. 15 N.Y.2d 593, 255 N.Y.S.2d 260, 203 N.E.2d 648; Matter of Linsley v. Gallman, 38 A.D.2d 367, 329 N.Y.S.2d 486, affd. 33 N.Y.2d 863, 352 N.Y.S.2d 199, 307 N.E.2d 257). However, their reliance is misplaced.

In *Oxnard* (supra) the place of performance doctrine was properly applied. The "convenience" test was not appropriate since the Arizona executor performed no personal services whatsoever in New York, nor did he maintain an office here.

The approach used in *Linsley* (supra) is also inapplicable. There, ill health forced the petitioner to retire from a New York investment banking corporation and to move to Connecticut. The petitioner and the corporation entered into a consultation agreement whereby he would perform advisory services via telephone. He maintained no office in New York, nor was he required to come here. Accordingly, the place of performance doctrine was applied and the petitioner was absolved of New York State tax liability.

Neither of these cases is controlling in the instant case for the reason that Mr. Speno performed services within New York State for his employer. The record shows that he allocated 60 days in New York in 1960 and 43 days in 1961, which in each year was more than any other location except New Jersey. As a non-resident employee who performs services both within and without the State, the "convenience" test was properly applied.

The order of the Appellate Division confirming the determination of the State Tax Commission should be affirmed.

BREITEL, C.J., and GABRIELLI, JONES, SAMUEL RABIN, STEVENS and WITMER, JJ., concur.

Order affirmed, with costs.

Notes and Problems

A. *The Personal Convenience Test and Services of a Non–Resident Employee Performed Outside the State.* Under the statutory test of taxing a non-resident only on "gross income from sources within the state," what bearing do the taxpayer's reasons for working at home instead of at his office have on the "source" of the income? Would the New York income tax of two non-resident corporate executives vary because Employee A, who happens to live in the same community in New Jersey as his employer, at the latter's request, confers with him about business matters at the employer's home, while Employee B works evenings at his own home in New Jersey on his employer's business? Compare with the principal case Fischer v. State Tax Comm'n, 107 A.D.2d 918, 484 N.Y.S.2d 345 (3d Dept. 1985), in which the court held that a licensed engineer, a principal in a structural engineering firm that maintained an office in New York City and in the engineer's New Jersey home, could allocate his income based on the days spent partly at construction sites in New Jersey and partly at his home, but not based on the days spent entirely at his office in his home. A dissenting judge would have allowed the taxpayer to allocate his income based on all of the days spent in New Jersey, on the ground that he "had to be physically present not only for on site work, but readily available for the myriad consultations attendant on such work." 484 N.Y.S.2d at 348.

B. *Place of Business Test as Applied to Non–Resident Professional.* In Matter of Carpenter v. Chapman, 276 A.D. 634, 97 N.Y.S.2d 311 (3d Dept. 1950), the court did not use the personal convenience test applied in the principal case. Carpenter was not an employee but a self-employed lawyer who resided outside New York. His income from work done at home in New Jersey and at his summer retreat in Vermont—presumably work on briefs and opinions and reading advance sheets and so forth, the whole gamut of work which a lawyer can readily do at home—was taxed by New York on the theory that he was licensed to practice law only in that State. Therefore, in the court's view, the out-of-state services must be deemed to be a part of the taxpayer's New York law practice. Does this result necessarily follow? Should the result have been any different if the taxpayer had been licensed to practice in Vermont or New Jersey, but had no offices or clients in those States? And is there any sound basis for distinguishing between licensed professions or businesses, such as law and medicine, and unlicensed occupations, such as advertising or unlicensed accounting?

A lawyer who lived in Connecticut was admitted to the New York and District of Columbia bars but not to the Connecticut bar. His practice was devoted exclusively to matters relating to patent and trademark law before the United States Patent and Trademark Office and in matters before the Federal courts. The lawyer had an office in New York, which handled all his typing, billing, and secretarial work, and an office in his Connecticut home. He represented clients in both New York and Connecticut. In computing his New York income, the taxpayer allocated his income between New York and Connecticut based on the hours he spent in each location. The New York State Tax Commission contended that since the taxpayer did not maintain an office in the District of Columbia, the only local bar other than New York to which he was admitted to practice, all of his income was derived from or connected with his New York practice, regardless of where he performed the work. The taxpayer argued that by virtue of his registration with the Patent Office, his right to practice patent law is a right he holds independent of his admission to any State bar, and that he could lawfully practice law both in New York and Connecticut, and allocate to New York only so much of his total income as was attributable to New York sources. The court sustained the taxpayer's contention. Johnston v. State Tax Comm'n, 115 A.D.2d 196, 495 N.Y.S.2d 265 (3d Dept. 1985).

C. *State of Performance of Services as Test of Taxability of Non-Resident.* Most of the States tax personal income to a non-resident only when derived from "sources within the State." And many States, including New York, have construed the term "sources within the State," in the case of personal service income, to mean income from services there rendered. See Solomon, "Non-Resident Personal Income Tax: A Comparative Study in Eight States," 29 Fordham L.Rev. 105 (1960). Nevertheless, the principal case (and the precedents it cites), as well as the cases discussed in Notes A and B supra, appear to be cutting into that rule by taxing non-residents on income derived from services actually rendered in part in other States.

Does the Due Process Clause prevent the States from taxing a non-resident on income from personal services rendered outside the State? The principal case and *Matter of Carpenter v. Chapman* tie in the work done outside the State with the taxpayer's business or the employer's office in the taxing State. Could the States provide, for example, that a non-resident employee's income from his employer will be taxed *in toto* if his only office is located at the employer's place of business in the State? Thus, a non-resident traveling salesman attached to a New York office, or a non-resident corporate officer whose office is at the company's place of business in New York but who spends time at the company's plants in other States, in Washington, and at industry conventions outside the State, would be taxed by New York on his entire salary. This is contrary to the present prevailing practice.

There are authorities dealing with persons carrying on their own service businesses (in addition to the *Carpenter* case)—not as employers but as entrepreneurs—which suggest that such taxation would be within the taxing powers of the States. In People ex rel. Lummis v. Graves, 251 App. Div. 591, 297 N.Y.S. 967 (3rd Dep't 1937), a resident of New Jersey was "employed on a commission basis as eastern sales agent" for an Ohio corporation; his territory included New York and some other eastern States. His only office was in New York, where he maintained a sales force and "employed three salesmen on commission." The taxpayer and the other salesmen solicited orders, subject to confirmation by the employer. The taxpayer contended that he was subject to New York income tax only on commissions received for orders for goods sold and delivered in New York. The court held that the entire income was derived from "carrying on a business within the State of New York and not elsewhere," although admittedly the solicitation and the commissions involved activities carried on outside the State.[3] See also People ex rel. Stafford v. Travis, 231 N.Y. 339, 132 N.E. 109 (1921). In effect, therefore, a non-resident was here taxed on income derived from work actually performed outside the State.

Similarly, in Stocke v. Department of Taxation, 249 Wis. 408, 25 N.W. 2d 65 (1946), a non-resident employed in Wisconsin as a personal representative of a construction contractor was entitled to the higher of a monthly salary of $350 or 15 percent of the profits derived from the construction contracts. He also assumed 15 percent of any losses. He remained in Wisconsin for six months supervising the jobs, and received his share of the profits. The court held that the income was taxable as being derived from business transacted in Wisconsin, not personal services, because his "liability to replace capital loss is equivalent to furnishing it".[4]

The opinions in these cases proceed on the premise that the taxpayers were "engaged in business" in the State and, therefore, taxable there. But is that a *sine qua non* to their taxation? Suppose in the *Lummis* case the taxpayer had clearly been an employee of the out-of-state corporation, with no office of his own, working out of his employer's New York sales office. Would his income to any lesser degree be derived from sources within the State on that account? Is there any reason why the non-resident employee's income may not be allocated to the employer's place of business out of which he works, in the same way as allocation is made to a non-resident entrepreneur's place of business where his sole office is within the taxing State?

In some States the statutes clearly preclude such a result, for they explicitly exclude income from services rendered outside the State. Others, such as the New York statute, are susceptible of a broadening of the notion of income from sources within the State, as the principal case discloses, to include income from some services actually rendered outside the State. However, in the light of the long history of administrative and judicial construction so as to omit from tax income from services of the salesman or corporate executive of the type suggested in our hypothetical cases, statutory change may be desirable and perhaps necessary to tax such income. As a constitutional matter, the business service cases suggest that the States may have the power to tax the entire income from his employment in the case of a non-resident employee, whose only office is at the employer's place

---

3. The language of the opinion treats the taxpayer as an "employee," but there is a question on the facts as to whether he was actually an employee or an independent contractor. The actual holding that the taxpayer was carrying on a "business" seems inconsistent with the categorization of his relationship as that of an employee.

4. In Wiik v. Department of Taxation, 249 Wis. 325, 24 N.W.2d 685 (1946), the court held that a non-resident receiving a percentage of profits on a construction project in the State, with a minimum guaranty per month until the project was completed, was not deriving income from "business transacted" in Wisconsin but instead "income from personal services within the state." Are the varying results in the two cases warranted? The Wisconsin cases are discussed in Teschner & Sorden, "A Review of Wisconsin Income Tax Case Law Since 1946," 1955 Wis.L.Rev. 254.

of business in the taxing State, even though the employee actually does some work on his employer's business in other States at other plants or offices of the employer, or the places of business of customers, and so forth. The issue would be whether, as a matter of due process of law, there is sufficient connection between the non-resident employee and his employer's business in the taxing State—the employee's only office—to warrant taxation of his entire income from his employment, even though part of his services are rendered elsewhere. See Chapter 11 supra. Compare the corporate franchise and business taxes which deny any out-of-state apportionment to businesses (including foreign corporations) that have no out-of-state place of business. See, e.g., Montag Bros. v. State Revenue Commission of Georgia, 50 Ga. 660, 179 S.E. 563 (1935).

There are serious policy questions which such broader taxation of non-residents, if adopted by the States, would pose. If the non-resident employee is taxable in the other States in which he renders the services for his employer, hardship will result unless there is a deduction or a credit allowed by the State of his residence to avoid a duplication of tax. This problem can perhaps be most equitably dealt with through an extension and refinement of crediting provisions or exemption of income in cases of duplication of tax, but such a solution is likely to produce heated controversies between neighboring States.

WHEELER v. STATE OF VERMONT

Supreme Court of Vermont, 1969.
127 Vt. 361, 249 A.2d 887, appeal dismissed 396 U.S. 4, 90 S.Ct. 24.

BARNEY, JUSTICE.

The plaintiff is a Vermont taxpayer and a New Hampshire resident. He is seeking reduction of tax levies against his Vermont-earned income on the grounds that they are so formulated as to be unconstitutionally discriminatory. The tax commissioner and then the lower court denied relief and he has appealed.

The facts are not in dispute. The plaintiff lives in Enfield, New Hampshire, and is employed as a salesman by Ward Foods, Inc., of White River Junction, Vermont. He solicits orders from retail food outlets in both Vermont and New Hampshire, and receives commissions based on his sales. These commissions were his only income during 1966, the year involved in this litigation, and totaled $7,714.47. This income was the "adjusted gross income" for the plaintiff for 1966, under the definition in 32 V.S.A. sec. 5811(1), as it appears in No. 61 of the Public Acts of the Special Session of 1966. Of this total income, $1,928.62 represented compensation earned in Vermont, and is his "Vermont derived income" under 32 V.S.A. sec. 5811(17). It amounts to 25% of his total compensation of $7,714.47.

Under Vermont taxing procedure for the year 1966, all individual taxpayers commenced the computation of their income taxes in the same way. Starting with "adjusted gross income," which is defined in 32 V.S.A. sec. 5811(1) as the adjusted gross income determined under the laws of the United States, except for capital gains and losses and certain exempt income not applicable here, the "Vermont taxable income" is arrived at. 32 V.S.A. sec. 5811(19). This is the taxable income of the taxpayer under the laws of the United States, but again excluding any consideration of capital gains or losses or exempt income. In other words, it is the adjusted gross income less all deductions available to the taxpayer on his federal return, without distinguishing their Vermont, New Hampshire or other derivation. 32 V.S.A. sec. 5811(13). From this is also deducted the appropriate personal exemptions allowed by Vermont law. 32 V.S.A. sec. 5826. With Vermont taxable income arrived at, every individual taxpayer, resident or non-resident, * * * [computed his 1966 tax at graduated rates beginning at 2% of the first $1,000 of Vermont taxable income and reaching 7.5% on such income in excess of $5,000.]

For the Vermont resident, this final figure is the tax he pays. For the non-resident, this tax figure is further reduced by the application of 32 V.S.A. sec. 5823, which provides:

> The tax imposed upon the income of a non-resident under section 5822 of this title is reduced by a percentage equal to the percentage of his adjusted gross income for the taxable year which is not Vermont derived income.

For the further protection of the non-resident taxpayer, 32 V.S.A. sec. 5827 allows a credit to avoid double taxation of income by the income tax law of another state, provided that state accords a reciprocal credit. Since New Hampshire assesses no general income tax based on ordinary earned income, this credit is not involved in this case. This leaves as the plaintiff's tax, the amount arrived at by applying the percentage relationship between his Vermont income and his total income to the tax figure based on his full income.

* * *

The plaintiff * * * argues that a New Hampshire taxpayer with some New Hampshire income pays a higher tax on his Vermont-earned portion than a Vermont taxpayer whose total income is the same as the Vermont income of the New Hampshire taxpayer. Reference to two of his examples may make his argument clearer:

	Vt. Taxpayer	N.H. Taxpayer	
Adjusted gross income	$4000.	$6000.	($4000. Vt. earned)
Two exemptions	1000.	1000.	
10% standard deduction	400.		600.
Vermont taxable income	$2600.		$4400.
Vermont tax	$ 84.		$ 184.
⅔ ration Vt./N.H. earnings			67%
Adjusted Vermont tax			$ 122.28

It is his contention that the true comparison lies, not between taxpayers with the same adjusted gross income, but between taxpayers having identical Vermont income. He further complains that an increase in the New Hampshire taxpayer's income from New Hampshire sources will increase the amount of tax he pays on his Vermont earnings, if it moves him up another tax bracket.

This last is, of course, true. In fact an increase in adjusted gross income from any taxable source might do the same thing. It is conceivable that this New Hampshire resident with Vermont earnings could be in the same predicament if he had no New Hampshire income at all, but did have income from someplace outside of Vermont that put his adjusted gross income at the level in question, and was not of a sort to be eligible for any reciprocal income tax credit.

It is the argument of the plaintiff that, since the addition of New Hampshire income increases the tax, it must be New Hampshire income that is being taxed. However, in reality what is happening is that Vermont income is being taxed at an increased rate, and nothing more.

If the contention of the plaintiff is sound, at some point as progressive tax rates advanced, the measure of the tax payable would begin to go beyond the total Vermont income earned and require resort to money earned in New Hampshire. This certainly would be true if progressive rates in Vermont began to reach the highest levels applicable in federal income taxation.

This is made abundantly clear if, in any of these situations, we assume a totally confiscatory tax rate on Vermont income of 100%. As, we have said, if New Hampshire income were in fact being taxed, the application of such a rate would necessarily, at some point, create a tax liability larger than the total Vermont income. But this cannot occur, because even with no deductions and that confiscatory rate, the provisions of 32 V.S.A. sec. 5823 will impose a limit measured by the Vermont derived income. This illustrates that the contention that the Vermont procedure taxes property beyond its jurisdiction cannot be supported. With it falls the argument that the Due Process Clause has been violated. McCutchan v. Oklahoma Tax Commission, 191 Okl. 578, 579, 132 P.2d 337.

It is also arithmetically obvious that the plaintiff would have no cause to complain if the Vermont income tax was a flat rate rather than progressive, since the variations in the size of his adjusted gross income would not affect the tax on his Vermont earnings. An evaluation of all of his contentions makes it clear that it is the progressive nature of the tax rate which is truly under attack.

Progressive tax rates on income, widespread among the United States and firmly imbedded in the federal tax structure, are intended to make more equitable the tax burden as it falls upon citizens of various states of affluence. It is their purpose to take into account variations in ability to pay. As such they found early and complete constitutional acceptance in Brushaber v. Union Pacific, 240 U.S. 1, 25, 36 S.Ct. 236, 60 L.Ed. 493, dealing with the 1913 federal income tax, and the question has remained at rest in that area. Shaffer v. Carter, 252 U.S. 37, 51, 40 S.Ct. 221, 64 L.Ed. 445, in 1920 indicated that it is within the taxing power of state governments to levy income taxes with progressive rates. We view this aspect of the matter as constitutionally settled.

We must then determine whether the application of these tax rates, applied to the plaintiff as a non-resident, is a transgression of constitutional bounds. His arguments are framed in terms of discriminatory treatment which he claims violates his privileges and immunities under Article 4, Section 2 of the United States Constitution, and also his right to equal protection of the laws under the Fourteenth Amendment. He contends that since he, as a non-resident, is taxed at a higher rate on his Vermont derived income than a Vermont resident whose total income is of Vermont derivation, he has been treated with such unfair diversity as to violate these constitutional prohibitions. To show such a violation, it is his burden to demonstrate discrimination to the extent that it is arbitrary and unreasonable. Underwood Typewriter Co. v. Chamberlain, 254 U.S. 113, 121, 41 S.Ct. 45, 47, 65 L.Ed. 165, 169.

If the principle of ability to pay is accepted, his contention is misleading, for he limits his comparison to a taxpayer of lower income than his. Going back to the examples already set out, if, in any of them relating to a combination of Vermont and New Hampshire income, the taxpayer were a Vermont resident, he would pay the full assessed tax on his combined Vermont and New Hampshire incomes, with no percentage reduction. To show discrimination, the plaintiff must first demonstrate that he is disadvantaged compared to another in an equivalent position. He has made no such showing. There is no place where his burden is increased over that of a resident in an equivalent income position. Even if it were, the taxpayer would still be confronted with the burden of showing such discrimination, nonexistent here, to be such an invidious inequality as to be arbitrary, for it to be condemned as unconstitutional. Maxwell v. Bugbee, 250 U.S. 525, 543, 40 S.Ct. 2, 63 L.Ed. 1124.

But, again, his real objection is the operation of the taxing progression. He objects to the importation of his total income for rate determination purposes. Yet this principle, too, has already been approved as constitutional. Maxwell v. Bugbee, supra, 250 U.S. 525, 539, 40 S.Ct. 2; Great Atlantic & Pacific Tea Co. v. Grosjean, 301 U.S. 412, 425, 57 S.Ct. 772, 81 L.Ed. 1193. A similar principle was recognized and accepted in our own case of Gulf Oil Corp. v. Morrison, 120 Vt. 324, 330, 141 A.2d 671, which states the necessity of establishing by appropriate evidence any claim that extraterritorial values are being taxed.

It was for the plaintiff to show that the Vermont taxing system was arbitrary and unreasonable in its classification to sustain a violation of the Equal Protection Clause. Maxwell v. Bugbee, supra, 250 U.S. 525, 543, 40 S.Ct. 2. It was for the plaintiff to demonstrate diversity of treatment without reasonable basis to sustain an abridgment of his constitutional privileges and immunities. Travis v. Yale and Towne Mfg. Co., 252 U.S. 60, 79, 40 S.Ct. 228, 64 L.Ed. 460. He has not done so.

Judgment affirmed.

Notes and Problems

A. In Landgraf v. Commissioner, 130 Vt. 589, 298 A.2d 551 (1972), the court considered the provision of the statute that a taxpayer's net "Vermont income tax" should not under any circumstances exceed "4½ percent of the total income of the taxpayer for that taxable year." In calculating the 4.5 percent ceiling, a non-resident was required to look to his "total income" *wherever earned;* but in determining whether the ceiling limited his Vermont tax bill, the non-resident was required to look to his actual "net" Vermont tax liability, which had been reduced to reflect only income *earned in Vermont.* As a result, the non-resident would in some circumstances be deprived of the benefit of the 4.5 percent limitation even though a resident with the same "total income" who paid Vermont tax on all such income would benefit by it. The provision, which has since been repealed, was sustained on the ground that the non-resident "taxpayer would never pay any greater tax than his Vermont counterpart." 130 Vt. at 597, 298 A.2d at 556. Query whether the ceiling destroys the premise on which the approval of the Vermont method of taxation was predicated, namely, that the resident and non-resident taxpayer with the same ability to pay ought to pay to Vermont the same percentage of their income taxable by Vermont.

The Vermont cases are considered in W. Hellerstein, "Some Reflections on the State Taxation of a Nonresident's Personal Income," 74 Mich.L.Rev. 1309 (1974). See also pp. 111–12 supra, for a discussion of Maxwell v. Bugbee, 250 U.S. 525, 40 S.Ct. 2 (1919), cited in the principal case, which raised essentially the same problem under a State inheritance tax; and United States v. Kansas, 810 F.2d 935 (10th Cir.1987), which sustained the consideration of income exempt from taxation under the Soldiers and Sailors Relief Act (see Chapter 15, p. 1012 infra) in determining the rate at which non-resident military personnel pay tax on their income taxable by Kansas.

B. *Privileges and Immunities Clause and Income Taxation of Non-Residents.* In Travis v. Yale and Towne Mfg. Co., 252 U.S. 60, 40 S.Ct. 228 (1920), one of the early key decisions dealing with State income taxes, the Supreme Court invalidated a provision of the New York law which granted personal exemptions and dependency allowances to residents but not to non-residents (who were taxed only on income derived from sources within the State). In setting aside the tax under Article IV, Section 2 of the Constitution, the Court declared that the Privileges and Immunities Clause "secures and protects the right of a citizen of one state * * * to be exempt from any higher taxes or excises than are imposed by the state upon its own citizens." The case was applied in State ex rel. McCulloch v. Ashby, 73 N.M. 267, 387 P.2d 588 (1963).

Corporations are not citizens and therefore are not protected by the Privileges and Immunities Clause. See Western Turf Ass'n v. Greenberg, 204 U.S. 359, 27 S.Ct. 384 (1907); Chapter 3 supra.

C. *Deductions and Exemptions for Non–Residents.* The automobile and the commuter train have blurred State lines, but have brought in their wake a whole host of tax problems, exacerbated by the strong feelings generated when taxpayers believe they are discriminated against. The problem has been dramatized in New York City, into which many thousands of commuters from certain areas in New Jersey and Connecticut travel each day to run their businesses or professions or to work as employees. For many years, following the decision in the *Yale & Towne* case, the State of New York allowed non-residents full personal exemptions and, since its adoption, the State's optional standard deduction and other expenses connected with their income which is taxed by New York. It had not, however, allowed non-residents deductions not connected with income earned, or business carried on, or property held, in New York and hence not taxed by the State. This denial of deductions included real estate taxes on the non-resident's home, interest on the mortgage on his home or other loans not connected with his New York employment or business or property, medical expenses, and life insurance premiums. See Art. 22, N.Y.Tax Law §§ 601 et seq. pre–1961. Such limitation of non-residents to deductions connected with income taxed by the State was upheld against attack under the Privileges and Immunities Clause in Goodwin v. State Tax Comm'n, 286 A.D. 694, 146 N.Y.S.2d 172 (1st Dep't 1955), aff'd mem., 1 N.Y.2d 680, 150 N.Y.S.2d 203, 133 N.E.2d 711, appeal dismissed 352 U.S. 805, 77 S.Ct. 47 (1956). Accord, Berry v. State Tax Comm'n, 241 Or. 580, 397 P.2d 780 (1964), appeal dismissed 382 U.S. 16, 86 S.Ct. 57 (1965); Davis v. Franchise Tax Bd., 71 Cal.App.3d 998, 139 Cal.Rptr. 797 (1977), appeal dismissed 434 U.S. 1055, 98 S.Ct. 1222 (1978) (denial of income averaging); Barney v. State Tax Assessor, 490 A.2d 223 (Me.1985), cert. denied 474 U.S. 828, 106 S.Ct. 90 (1985). But see Golden v. Tully, 88 A.D.2d 1058, 452 N.Y.S.2d 748 (3d Dep't 1982), affirmed 58 N.Y.2d 1047, 462 N.Y.S.2d 626, 449 N.E.2d 406 (1983) (denial of moving expense deduction to non-residents violates Privileges and Immunities Clause; Goodwin v. State Tax Comm'n, supra, distinguished on ground that personal exemptions and deductions there at issue were "peculiarly related to the factor of residence within the State"); Spencer v. South Carolina Tax Comm'n, 281 S.C. 492, 316 S.E.2d 386 (1984), affirmed by an equally divided Court on issue of recovery of attorneys fees, 471 U.S. 82, 105 S.Ct. 1859 (1985) (denial of proration of personal deductions to non-residents unless non-residents' State of residence allows reciprocal proration of such deductions to non-residents violates Privileges and Immunities Clause).

While New York at one time allowed a credit to non-residents on account of income taxes paid to other States, where a reciprocal provision existed (former N.Y.Tax Law § 640), the difficulties were heightened by the fact that New York's neighbors, New Jersey and Connecticut, imposed no income taxes.[5] Consequently, an employee or professional residing in East

5. New Jersey enacted a limited, largely proportional income tax in 1976.

Orange, New Jersey or Westport, Connecticut and deriving all his income from his work in New York City, found himself paying a higher income tax than his fellow employee or his partner living in Baldwin, L.I. or Scarsdale, New York, who had the same amount and type of income, due to the disallowance of personal deductions to the non-resident.

In 1958 and 1959 the tax relations among the three States resulted in meetings of representatives of the Governors of the three States. The New York representatives submitted a report recommending a pro-rating of both exemptions and the disputed personal deductions by reference to the non-resident's proportion of income taxed by New York.[6] The New Jersey and Connecticut representatives pressed for full exemptions as well as the pro-rated deductions.[7] New York State Tax Commissioner Joseph H. Murphy estimated that the full pro-rating proposal would reduce the State's revenues by about $3,000,000, whereas the Connecticut–New Jersey proposals would cut the yield by $5,300,000.[8]

In the meantime another issue crept into the negotiations—the escape from tax of income derived by New York residents from New Jersey or Connecticut, a substantial amount of which is believed to go unreported. New York sought the co-operation of Connecticut and New Jersey in collecting income tax from such persons through information returns and possibly withholding provisions. New York eventually yielded to the Connecticut and New Jersey requests for full exemptions and a pro-rating of deductions, conditional, however, on the enactment of legislation by the other States providing for the desired co-operation in the collection of New York taxes on income derived by its residents from the other States.[9] Legislation embodying these results was enacted in New York in 1961.[10] Thereafter, in 1962, New York modified its statute so as to provide that only residents are allowed credits for out-of-state taxes paid; no credit is allowed a non-resident. N.Y. Tax Law § 620, CCH ¶ 95–840, P–H ¶ 59,096. The issues arising in connection with deductions, exemptions, and credits for non-residents are discussed in W. Hellerstein, Note A supra, and J. Hellerstein, "State Tax Discrimination Against Out-of-Staters," 30 Nat.Tax J. 113 (1977).

D. *Discriminatory Taxation of Commuters.** In 1971 New Hampshire, one of the few States which levies no general personal income tax, followed

6. Nonresident Tax Study Committee, "Report on Taxation of Non-residents by New York State" (1959). The recommendations are summarized in Solomon, "Nonresident Personal Income Tax: A Comparative Study of Eight States," 29 Fordham L.Rev. 105, 122 (1960).

7. See N.Y. Times, Dec. 27 and 30, 1959. A report by their advisors made to the Governors of Connecticut and New Jersey is summarized in the New York Times, Dec. 30, 1959.

8. See N.Y. Times, Dec. 30, 1959.

9. See N.Y. Times, Jan. 27, 1960.

10. Chapter 68 of the New York Laws of 1961 granted the deductions indicated to

non-residents; such broadened deductions were not, however, to be allowed to persons residing in States in which at least 5,000 residents of New York are employed, unless such State has provided for the withholding of New York income tax from compensation paid to the non-residents, or has entered into an agreement with the New York State Tax Commission for furnishing, without cost to New York, information relating to income earned in such States by residents of New York. See N.Y. Tax Law § 635, CCH ¶ 95–896, P–H ¶ 59,108, repealed for tax years beginning in 1987.

* [The ensuing discussion is drawn from J. Hellerstein, "State Tax Discrimination Against Out-of-Staters," 30 Nat.Tax J. 113

the ingenious, albeit offensive, lead as a matter of fiscal policy, taken ten years earlier by New Jersey by adopting a Commuters Income Tax. The tax was imposed on the income of non-residents earned in New Hampshire, which was reduced to any lower amount of tax that would have been imposed by the State of the taxpayer's residence, if the income had been earned in that State. In one of the strangest provisions of any tax law in the country, the statute also levied a tax on the income of New Hampshire residents on income earned outside the State, but immediately nullified its effect by another provision that exempts such income from tax. This piece of lawyers' legerdemain did not blind the Supreme Court of the United States to the realities, for when the tax came before that tribunal on a challenge to its constitutionality, the Court stated: "The effect of these imposition and exemption features is that no resident of New Hampshire is taxed on his foreign income," and that "the State taxes only the income of non-residents working in New Hampshire." [11]

The New Hampshire Supreme Court had sustained the tax in a class action for a declaratory judgment brought by residents of Maine working in New Hampshire.[12] It was that decision which was reversed by the Supreme Court of the United States, on the ground that the tax violated the Interstate Privileges and Immunities Clause.[13] Analyzing the case, the Court concluded that the "overwhelming fact, as the State concedes, is that the tax falls exclusively on the income of non-residents; and it is not offset even approximately by other taxes upon residents alone."

The Court took note of the oft-applied principle that although "in taxation, even more than in other fields, legislatures possess the greatest freedom in classification," a different principle comes into play when a "tax measure is challenged as an undue burden on an activity granted special constitutional recognition." [14] Then, the State's power of taxation must be weighed against the need to protect "the competing constitutional value from erosion." The Court equated the "maintenance of our constitutional

---

(1977); it is used with the consent of the copyright owner, The National Tax Association—Tax Institute of America.]

11. Austin v. State of New Hampshire, 420 U.S. 656, 95 S.Ct. 1191 (1975), dissent by Blackmun J. The 1961 New Jersey statute was euphemistically labeled "Emergency Transportation Tax Act." N.J.Laws of 1961, Chapters 32 and 129 and Laws of 1962, Chapter 70; N.J.Rev.Stat. Tit. 54:8–A; CCH ¶¶ 93–930 et seq. It was a tax on net income derived from New Jersey by residents of New York, and on New Jersey residents with respect to income derived from "a critical area State" outside New Jersey. This inventive term, "critical area State," in fact refers essentially to the bordering States of New York and Pennsylvania. Residents of those States are allowed a credit against the New Jersey tax for taxes paid to their home States, whereas residents of other States are allowed no credit for taxes paid to their home States.

12. 114 N.H. 137, 316 A.2d 165 (1974).

13. The Court relegated to a footnote its response to the State's contention that the taxpayers lacked "standing to maintain this action on the theory that their economic position was unchanged * * * because they received an offsetting credit under the tax laws of Maine * * * It held that the taxpayers were affected by the requirements that they file New Hampshire tax returns and by their employer's tax withholding of 4 percent of their incomes. "These effects may not be substantial, but they establish appellants' status as parties 'adversely affected by the State's tax laws,' giving them 'a direct stake in the outcome of this litigation.' Sierra Club v. Morton, 405 U.S. 727, 740 (1972)," 420 U.S. at 659, note 4.

14. 420 U.S. at 662.

federalism" with the now familiar special protection given by the Constitution to the protection of individual liberties. Because the Privileges and Immunities Clause contributes to maintaining the "structural balance essential to the concept of federalism," non-residence is an inappropriate basis for "a special burden." [15]

Mr. Justice Blackmun dissented on the ground that the real mischief in the case arises because of Maine's grant to its residents of a credit against the income taxes they pay other States, and that Maine "has the cure within its grasp" by repealing the credit provision.[16] The majority rejected that position by saying, "we do not think the possibility that Maine could shield its residents from New Hampshire's tax cures the constitutional defect of the discrimination in that tax * * * Nor * * * can the constitutionality of one State's statutes affecting non-residents depend upon the present configuration of the statutes of another State." [17]

Fourteen years after New Jersey enacted its commuter's tax in 1961, but only after decision in the *Austin* case, the officials of New York and Pennsylvania filed motions with the Supreme Court, for permission to bring original suits against New Jersey to recover taxes illegally siphoned off from their treasuries—in New York's case that amounted to an asserted $225 million. See CCH State Tax Rev., Vol. 37, No. 18, p. 7 (May 4, 1976). The New Jersey tax had all the essential discriminatory characteristics of the New Hampshire tax. Massachusetts, Maine, and Vermont filed similar motions for permission to sue New Hampshire in the Supreme Court. The Supreme Court denied the motions of all the States on several grounds: (a) no injury was done the States by the New Jersey or New Hampshire taxes; the "injuries to the plaintiffs' fiscs were self-inflicted," as Justice Blackmun had shown in *Austin*, because of their action in granting their residents credits against the income taxes of other States; (b) both the Privileges and Immunities Clause, on which *Austin* was decided, and the Equal Protection Clause "protects people, not States"; and (c) Pennsylvania's assertion of its standing to act in *parens patriae* on behalf of its citizens was rejected, because a State may "sue only when its sovereign or quasi-sovereign interests are implicated and it is not merely litigating as a volunteer the personal claims of its citizens." Pennsylvania v. New Jersey, Maine v. New Hampshire, 426 U.S. 660, 96 S.Ct. 2333, 2336 (1976). Justices White and Brennan dissented; Justices Powell and Stevens did not sit; and Justice Blackmun concurred, with obvious relish, by quoting his dissent in the *Austin* case. New York's petition was dismissed in reliance on the other cases. New York v. New Jersey, 429 U.S. 810, 97 S.Ct. 48 (1976).

Three New York residents, who commuted from their homes in New York to work in New Jersey, subsequently brought an action challenging the constitutionality of the New Jersey commuter's tax. In

---

15. Id.

16. As Justice Blackmun also stated:

One wonders whether this is just a lawyers' lawsuit. Certainly, the appellants, upon prevailing today, have no direct or apparent financial gain * * * If there is an element of injury, it is Maine-imposed. [420 U.S. at 669.]

He concluded:

For me, this is a noncase. I would dismiss the appeal for want of a substantial federal question. We have far more urgent demands upon our limited time than this kind of litigation. [Id. at 667.]

17. 420 U.S. at 665.

Salorio v. Glaser, 93 N.J. 447, 461 A.2d 1100 (1983), cert. denied 464 U.S. 993, 104 S.Ct. 486 (1983), the court held that the tax violated the Privileges and Immunities Clause. Since there was no question that the tax discriminated against the New York resident, the critical issue was whether the discrimination could be justified because it was "linked to some evil or problem caused by the non-resident and, if linked, the revenue derived from the tax should bear a substantial relationship to the cost of amelioration of the evil or the solution of the problem." 461 A.2d at 1104. The State's justification for the differential imposed on the non-resident is that his commuting has created a need for additional facilities to meet the commuting crunch between New York and New Jersey during peak hours in the morning and afternoon. The court concluded, however, that even if non-resident commuters impose increased costs on New Jersey, the tax could not be justified because the costs were less than half the revenues collected under the tax over two decades, and that such a relationship was "too disparate to withstand constitutional challenge." 461 A.2d at 1108. The tax was invalidated, but on a prospective basis only.[18]

In Clark v. Lee, 273 Ind. 572, 406 N.E.2d 646 (1980), the court held that Indiana's local income tax violated the Privileges and Immunities Clause because a credit against local income tax liability was provided in the State income tax. The tax therefore fell exclusively on non-residents because State income tax liability always exceeded local income tax liability, which effectively insulated residents from the tax, and non-residents never had any Indiana State income tax liability to absorb the credit due to reciprocal non-resident income tax exemption agreements between Indiana and neighboring States.

E. Some unusual income tax problems were presented in State of Alaska v. Petronia, 69 Wash.2d 460, 418 P.2d 755 (1966), appeal dismissed 389 U.S. 7, 88 S.Ct. 36 (1967), in a suit brought by the Attorney General of Alaska under the Washington reciprocal tax collection act to collect income taxes claimed by Alaska.[19] The suit was brought against several seamen, residents of Washington and Oregon, who signed on and shipped out on vessels from Seattle, but spent 17 percent to 26 percent (and in one case a larger percentage) of their time aboard the vessels in Alaskan waters. The Alaskan tax, imposed at the rate of 16 percent of the Federal income tax for the year, was in these cases reduced to the percentage of time worked in Alaskan waters. The court summarily rejected the seamen's contention that the imposition of the levy deprived them of due process of law, because, as non-residents, they did not obtain from Alaska the same kinds of benefits and protection as are provided to persons working on the State's land. A Commerce Clause contention was made that Congress has so completely occupied the field of regulation of maritime matters that a State

18. In Salorio v. Glaser, 82 N.J. 482, 414 A.2d 943 (1980), cert. denied and appeal dismissed 449 U.S. 804, 101 S.Ct. 49 (1980), it was held that the tax did not violate the Equal Protection Clause of the Fourteenth Amendment. However, the court remanded the case for further factfinding to enable the trial court to consider whether the tax violated the Privileges and Immunities Clause, which led to the opinion discussed in the text supra.

19. See p. 1044 infra, for a consideration of this type of statute.

income tax on seamen plying United States coastal and interstate waters is unconstitutional. The court likewise rejected this contention, citing the landmark decision of Cooley v. Board of Wardens, 12 How. (U.S.) 299, 13 L.Ed. 996 (1851), in which the Supreme Court had found no interference with the Federal control of maritime affairs by a State statute requiring the licensing of harbor pilots. Nor was a levy on a seaman's earnings an interference with Federal regulation of shipping. The court also observed that, after Alaska had enacted its income tax, requiring seamen's wages to be withheld by the employer, a provision that had been sustained in Alaska Steamship Co. v. Mullaney, p. 929 supra, Congress prohibited such withholding in the case of seamen working on vessels engaged in foreign or coastal trade, but that Congress had not disturbed the power of the States to levy a tax on the wages. See 46 U.S.C.A. § 601. Accord: Stephan v. State Tax Comm'r, 245 A.2d 552 (Del.1968), appeal dismissed 394 U.S. 573, 89 S.Ct. 1299 (1969).

F. *Allocation of Income.* Provision is made in personal income tax laws for allocating a portion of the non-resident's income to the taxing State, where the income is derived from services rendered, or business done, both within and without the State. Thus, if an employee works within and without the State, an allocation is typically made by reference to the number of days' work performed in the State, as compared with the total number of days worked during the year. Should the rule be any different for a non-resident professional football player who may be present in the taxing State on only one or two days during the year when he actually participates in a game, but who plays in only a limited number of such games during the year? The California State Board of Equalization agreed with the Franchise Tax Board that it should be, and sustained the "games-played" formula used to apportion the non-resident professional football players' income to California. Appeal of Partee, Cal.S.B.E., Oct. 6, 1976, P–H ¶ 55.521.60. The Board of Equalization sustained the application of the "games played" formula to a "playing bonus" received by a non-resident athlete, but indicated that the result might be different for a "signing bonus." Appeal of Foster, Cal.S.B.E., Nov. 11, 1984, CCH ¶ 400–991, P–H ¶ 63,987. The Franchise Tax Board's guidelines provide that bonuses paid for signing a sports contract are not to be apportioned but are taxable on the basis of the taxpayer's residence. FTB AR 125.1, Sept. 1977, cited in id. CCH ¶ 400–991 at 23,503. This reflects the view that a signing bonus is consideration for a player's covenant not to compete rather than consideration for services and should be assigned to the residence of the player as owner of an intangible property right. Where businesses are involved, more comprehensive formulas or separate accounting methods are used. See G. Altman & F. Keesling, Allocation of Income in State Taxation, ch. 3 (2d ed. 1950), and see generally Chapter 9 supra.

G. *References.* Solomon, "Nonresident Personal Income Tax: A Comparative Study in Eight States," 29 Fordham L.Rev. 105 (1960). This study deals with four Eastern states—New York, Delaware, Vermont, and Massachusetts; three Midwestern States—Iowa, Wisconsin, and Minnesota; and one far Western State—California. See Annots., 156 A.L.R. 1370, 87 A.L.R. 380, and 143 A.L.R. 147.

SECTION 4. TAXATION OF NON–RESIDENT PARTNER OF PARTNERSHIP DOING BUSINESS IN THE TAXING STATE

MATTER OF THOMAS M. DEBEVOISE v. STATE TAX COMM.

Supreme Court of New York, Appellate Division, Third Department, 1976.
52 A.D.2d 1023, 383 N.Y.S.2d 698.

MEMORANDUM DECISION.

Proceeding pursuant to CPLR article 78 (transferred to this court by order of the Supreme Court at Special Term, entered in Albany County) to review a determination of the State Tax Commission which denied petitioners' application for redetermination of New York personal income tax for the year 1967.

Petitioners resided in Washington, D.C. during 1967 and filed a joint non-resident income tax return for that year with the respondent New York State Tax Commission. This proceeding was commenced following their receipt of a notice of deficiency in the amount of taxes paid and respondent's subsequent denial, after a hearing, of their application for a redetermination of that deficiency. It raises for our review the propriety of respondent's method for determining the amount of income petitioner Thomas Debevoise received which was derived from or connected with New York sources as a partner in a New York law firm.

Petitioners sought to apportion income from that law firm according to the number of days Thomas Debevoise was actually present and engaged in legal work within this jurisdiction, whereas the respondent attributed this same income to New York sources on the same basis utilized by the law partnership in allocating the distributive share of each partner according to the proportion that partnership net income from sources outside New York bore to partnership net income from all sources. Petitioners complain that respondent's determination failed adequately to consider the appropriateness and equity of their alternate allocation and suggest that the result constitutes an unconstitutional double taxation. We disagree.

Petitioners do not attack the apportionment rules contained in section 637 of the Tax Law and they recognize the validity of that statute insofar as it generally prohibits any attribution of a partner's income to foreign sources beyond the formula adopted here by the law firm and respondent (Tax Law, § 637, subd. [b], par. [2]).* Instead,

---

* [The relevant provisions of the New York Tax Law are as follows:

§ 632. New York adjusted gross income of a non-resident individual

(a) General. The New York adjusted gross income of a non-resident individual shall be the sum of the following:

(1) The net amount of items of income, gain, loss and deduction entering into his federal adjusted gross income, as defined in the laws of the United States for the taxable year, derived from or connected with New York sources, including:

(A) his distributive share of partnership income, gain, loss and deduction,

they argue that respondent acted arbitrarily in not accepting the method they employed, as it had the discretionary power to do (Tax Law, § 637, subd. [d]), given the undisputed facts that Thomas Debevoise undertook most of his efforts in Washington, D.C., and generated more partnership income from clients in that locale than his ultimate distributive share of partnership income reflected. Petitioner's arguments merely present a ground for dispute over the division of law firm profits; they have no impact on the taxability of the distributive share of income from that partnership. Their method of allocation predicated on time spent within this jurisdiction might conceivably have some support if Thomas Debevoise had simply been a Washington practitioner servicing clients here, but it was properly rejected by the respondent for two reasons. There was an insufficient showing that the percentage of time Thomas Debevoise spent in New York had any relation to the distributive share of partnership income he received during the tax year in question. Secondly, it is the portion of that distributive share attributable to New York sources, not the value of his personal services here, which is properly subject to taxation by this jurisdiction (Tax Law, § 632, subd. [a], par. [1], cl. [A]). Having failed to demonstrate that their formula was more appropriate or equitable, or that respondent's method taxed extraterritorial values, petitioners' application for a redetermination was properly denied.

Determination confirmed, and petition dismissed, without costs.

Notes and Problems

A. In another case involving the taxation of a non-resident partner of a New York law firm, the State Tax Commission held that the partner was entitled to allocate his share of the partnership income between New York and New Jersey because the New York partnership carried on business in New Jersey. However, the Commission rejected the non-resident partner's method of allocation, which was based on the time spent in New Jersey, and instead insisted that the allocation be made on the basis of the ratio of gross receipts from New Jersey clients to the firm's gross receipts. Petition of Howard Carter, Jr., N.Y. CCH ¶ 199–990 (N.Y. State Tax Comm'n 1976).

determined under section six hundred thirty-seven, and

* * *

(c) Income and deductions partly from New York sources. If a business, trade, profession or occupation is carried on partly within and partly without this state, as determined under regulations of the tax commission, the items of income, gain, loss and deduction derived from or connected with New York sources shall be determined by apportionment and allocation under such regulations.

* * *

§ 637. **Nonresident partners**

(a) Portion derived from New York sources.

(1) In determining New York adjusted gross income of a non-resident partner of any partnership, there shall be included only the portion derived from or connected with New York sources of such partner's distributive share of items of partnership income, gain, loss and deduction entering into his federal adjusted gross income, as such portion shall be determined under regulations of the tax commission consistent with the applicable rules of section six hundred thirty-two.]

A non-resident partner of a New York law firm sought to exclude from his distributive share of partnership income amounts received for nonlegal services performed outside of New York for foreign corporations which neither maintained offices nor did any business in New York. These services could not have been performed satisfactorily in New York, but the fees they generated were paid directly to the New York law firm. The court held that the taxpayer was not entitled to reduce his New York taxable income by the amounts in question, because the New York law firm was retained to serve the foreign clients and, in rendering the services at issue, the taxpayer acted as an agent of the firm and not in his individual capacity. Knapp v. State Tax Com'n, 67 A.D.2d 1024, 413 N.Y.S.2d 237 (3d Dept.1979). See also Jablin v. State Tax Com'n, 65 A.D.2d 891, 410 N.Y.S.2d 414 (3d Dept.1978), in which the court rejected a non-resident partner's contention that amounts he received from the partnership were commission income not derived from or connected with New York sources rather than a share of partnership profits.

B. *Limited Partnerships.* The treatment of income and losses incurred by non-resident partners in limited partnerships turns on the question whether the partnership is carrying on its business within the State. Compare Ausbrooks v. Chu, 66 N.Y.2d 281, 496 N.Y.S.2d 969, 487 N.E.2d 879 (1985) (non-resident filing New York personal income tax return could not deduct losses as limited partner in non–New York partnership engaged in out-of-state real estate development) with Vogt v. Tully, 53 N.Y.2d 580, 444 N.Y.S.2d 441, 428 N.E.2d 847 (1981) (non-resident filing New York personal income tax return could deduct losses as limited partner in New York partnership engaged in leasing of railroad cars).

C. *References.* Hayes, "Interstate Partnerships—Some State Income Tax Considerations," 5 J. State Tax. 141 (1986).

SECTION 5. TAXATION OF INCOME OF ESTATES AND TRUSTS

MERCANTILE–SAFE DEPOSIT AND TRUST COMPANY v. MURPHY

Supreme Court of New York, Appellate Division, Third Department, 1963.
19 A.D.2d 765, 242 N.Y.S.2d 26.

Before BERGAN, P.J., and GIBSON, HERLIHY, REYNOLDS and TAYLOR, JJ.

MEMORANDUM DECISION.

This controversy is submitted upon agreed facts pursuant to sections 546–548 of the Civil Practice Act. The question to be determined is whether upon such facts a non-resident trustee of an *inter vivos* trust created in Maryland by a resident of New York is subject to taxation upon income accumulated thereunder after the death of the donor.

The donor, a domiciled resident of this State, by a trust agreement dated June 1, 1953 transferred and delivered to plaintiff, as sole trustee, 3500 shares of the capital stock of a certain corporation and provided that the net income of the trust property should be distributed to him during his lifetime. While living he received such income from the trustee and paid the New York State income taxes imposed thereon. He reserved to himself power of revocation but without exercising it died in 1956. By his will which was admitted to probate in this State he bequeathed cash and securities to an amount exceeding $1,000,000 to the trustee for the uses and purposes of the trust pursuant to a reserved right to add to its *res* by testamentary disposition. So far as now material the trust indenture provided further that upon the death of the donor if his wife should survive him, the net income of the intangible assets held in trust should be paid to her during her life subject to the power of the trustee in its absolute discretion to withhold and accumulate all or any part of the trust income otherwise payable to her and to merge it with the principal of the fund from which it was derived; upon the death of the widow the trustee, subject to certain consents, was empowered to accumulate the income or to distribute it among his descendants per stirpes.

The donor was survived by his widow who is and has been for many years a resident of this State. Since his death the trustee has exercised the granted power to accumulate the trust income, has filed no State income tax returns reporting its receipt for the succeeding taxable periods and has paid no income tax thereon. It is conceded that the trustee is domiciled in the State of Maryland, that the trust is administered there and that the intangibles constituting its corpus have been at all times in its exclusive possession and control in that State.

Although this trust must be deemed a resident trust by statutory definition (Tax Law, § 350, subd. 7; § 605, subd. [c], par. [3]) the related statutes which impose a tax upon its accrued income (Tax Law, §§ 351, 365, subd. [1], par. [c]) undertake in the circumstances disclosed here to extend the taxing power of the State to property wholly beyond its jurisdiction and thus conflict with the due process clause of the Fourteenth Amendment of the Federal Constitution. (Safe Deposit & Trust Co. of Baltimore, Md. v. Commonwealth of Virginia, 280 U.S. 83, 50 S.Ct. 59, 74 L.Ed. 180.) We find no merit either in the continuing jurisdiction theory advanced by defendants or in their thesis that since the resident beneficiaries of the trust could be taxed on income distributed the non-resident trustee can be taxed on income accumulated.

Judgment in favor of plaintiff granted, without costs.

In affirming this decision the Court of Appeals said, in a memorandum opinion (15 N.Y.2d 582, 255 N.Y.S.2d 579 [1964]):

Safe Deposit & Trust Co. of Baltimore, Md. v. Virginia, 280 U.S. 83, 50 S.Ct. 59, 74 L.Ed. 180, does not appear to have been overruled by Guaranty Trust Co. of New York v. Virginia, 305 U.S. 19, 59 S.Ct. 1, 83 L.Ed. 16, nor by Graves v. Elliott, 307 U.S. 383, 59 S.Ct. 913, 83 L.Ed. 1356, in both of which property was taxed which was within or which was being distributed into the taxing State. The lack of power of New York State to tax in this instance stems not from the possibility of double taxation but from the inability of a State to levy taxes beyond its border. Instead of overruling *Safe Deposit & Trust Co. of Baltimore, Md. v. Virginia, Guaranty Trust Co. of New York v. Virginia* recognized its authority by citing it and stating (305 U.S., p. 23, 59 S.Ct., p. 3) that it went "upon the theory that the taxing power of a state is restricted to her confines and may not be exercised in respect of subjects beyond them." This confirmed rather than refuted the determination in *Safe Deposit & Trust Co. of Baltimore, Md.* that the imposition of a tax in the State in which the beneficiaries of a trust reside, on securities in the possession of the trustee in another State, to the control or possession of which the beneficiaries have no present right, is in violation of the Fourteenth Amendment.

Notes and Problems

A. On virtually identical facts, the Supreme Court of Vermont, in First National Bank of Boston v. Harvey, 111 Vt. 281, 16 A.2d 184 (1940), held the trustee taxable on undistributed income. The court stated:

We approve the reasoning in Harrison v. Commissioner of Corporations and Taxation, 272 Mass. 422, 172 N.E. 605, 71 A.L.R. 677, to the effect that a state has the power to establish a situs for purposes of taxation over testamentary trust funds, created by its deceased residents in intangible personal property being administered by appointees of its own court, under its own laws, and thus to continue for practical purposes within its jurisdiction all control over the trusts, and especially control for purposes of taxation; and hold that under our statutes the Legislature has established such a situs here for the purpose of taxing such trust funds, and whether the trustee is named in the will or appointed by the court makes no difference in this respect. This conclusion attributes no extra-territorial effect to P.L. 874.

As shown in an annotation in 67 A.L.R. 393, there is considerable diversity in the statutes and decisions of the various jurisdictions relative to the situs for taxation of personal property, or interests therein, held by trustees, executors or administrators. Generally an executor, administrator, or trustee is regarded as the owner, for purposes of property taxation, of the personal property which he holds by virtue of his office, and is taxable in the state in which he is domiciled. There are certain trends depending upon the location of the property, whether in the state of the decedent's domicile or that of the fiduciary, and whether the fiduciary and deceased were domiciled in the same or different states. Some jurisdictions treat executors and administrators differently from testamentary trustees, and some differentiate between testamentary trustees and trustees appointed by a court. A few jurisdictions adopt the theory of an official, as distinguished from a personal, residence, and seem to arrive at the same ultimate conclusion that we do, but we do not consider it necessary to adopt that theory in support of our holding. See also "The Taxation of Trust Property" by Professor Robert C. Brown, 23 Kentucky Law Journal, 403.

It is very evident that some jurisdictions are troubled by the possibility of double taxation, but regardless of the desirability of avoiding double taxation, it is apparent from the holdings in Curry v. McCanless, 307 U.S. 357, 59 S.Ct. 900, 83 L.Ed. 1339; New York ex rel. Cohn v. Graves, 300 U.S. 308, 57 S.Ct. 466, 81 L.Ed. 666, 108 A.L.R. 721, and other United States Supreme Court cases, that the tax in question raises no constitutional objection on that ground. [16 A.2d at 190, 191.]

Recent cases that have considered the conflict between the principal case and First National Bank of Boston v. Harvey, supra, over the power of a State to tax the income of a trust created by a resident decedent but administered in other States where the trust assets are located have followed the principal case. See In re Swift, 727 S.W.2d 880 (Mo.1987); Pennoyer v. Taxation Division Director, 5 N.J.Tax 386 (1983); Potter v. Taxation Division Director, 5 N.J. Tax 399 (1983); Taylor v. State Tax Comm'n, 85 A.D.2d 821, 445 N.Y.S.2d 648 (3d Dept.1981).

Many States follow the Federal rule of treating the trustee as a conduit for income tax purposes, with the result that the trustee is not taxable with respect to trust income required to be distributed under discretionary powers. I.R.C. § 641 et seq. The real problem arises, however, with respect to income accumulated by the trustee under discretionary provisions. For Federal income tax purposes, the trustee ordinarily pays the tax, and when the distribution of accumulated income is made, no tax is incurred by the beneficiary. Id.

As suggested by the principal case, the accumulations problem is complicated in the State tax field by the State jurisdictional limitations, where the trustee and beneficiaries are located in different States. In addition, the State in which the trust was set up *inter vivos* or by will may claim jurisdiction to tax as is indicated by the cases considered in Chapter 11, § 4(b) supra. The income tax laws of some States distinguish between resident and non-resident trusts (and estates), and in some States define a resident trust or estate as one created *inter vivos* by a person then residing within the taxing State or under the will of a resident of the State. See, e.g., N.Y.Tax Law § 605(c) CCH ¶ 95–155, P–H ¶ 59,070.15. The residence of the fiduciary and the place of administration are irrelevant. Under such statutes, undistributed income of the trust accumulated under a discretionary power of the trustee may be declared subject to tax, although they can raise problems of the type considered in the principal case.

As a matter of State tax policy, the result reached by the principal case has much to commend it, for the State of domicile of the donor or the decedent has, at best, only a historical connection with the trust (even if its courts have jurisdiction of accountings by the trustee in the case of a testamentary trust), and the trustee's activities and the trust assets now have a locus outside the State. The problem is somewhat different, however, where the underlying assets consist of real estate or tangible personal property, or a business located in the State of domicile of the donor or of the decedent. There, New York would have adequate constitutional basis, by reason of the benefits and protection it affords the trust assets, to impose an income tax on the income accumulated by the trustee, for in such cases, if the income had been distributed to the non-resident beneficiaries, they would be taxable by New York. Such a tax ought to be imposed for the further reason that its absence might encourage the manipulation of discretionary powers so as to avoid State income taxes.

B. A resident of New York created a testamentary trust of intangibles, which was administered in New York under the supervision of the New York courts. Some of the trustees resided in Massachusetts. The accretions to the corpus of the trust were being accumulated for the benefit of unascertained contingent remainder beneficiaries. Gains were realized from the sales of securities held in the trust. Could New York or Massachusetts or both tax these gains? See Hutchins v. Long, 272 Mass. 422, 172 N.E. 605, 71 A.L.R. 677 (1930).

C. *The Taxation of Revocable Trusts.* Section 676(a) of the Internal Revenue Code of 1986 provides that "[t]he grantor shall be treated as the owner of any portion of a trust * * * where at any time the power to revest in the grantor title to such portion is exercisable by the grantor or a nonadverse party, or both." In Bruner v. State Dept. of Revenue, 57 Wis. 2d 70, 203 N.W.2d 663 (1973), the court held that a resident grantor of a revocable trust administered out-of-state was not taxable on capital gains that were accumulated by the trustee. The Wisconsin court refused to follow the Federal rule and held that the trustee was the legal recipient of the income, despite the fact that under the laws of many States the result would be to allow the income to go untaxed. It was not clear whether Illinois, the State where the trust was administered, would tax the trustee under these circumstances.

D. *Income Taxation of Beneficiaries of a Trust.* A resident beneficiary of a trust is taxable by the State of his residence on income distributed to him by the trustee, although the trust was created by a non-resident, and its assets are held by a non-resident trustee, who administers the trust outside the State. Guaranty Trust Co. of New York v. Commonwealth of Virginia, 305 U.S. 19, 59 S.Ct. 1 (1948). This holding is an application of the familiar principle, established by Lawrence v. State Tax Comm'n, 286 U.S. 276, 52 S.Ct. 556, 87 A.L.R. 374 (1932), that the State of domicile may tax an individual on all income, from whatever source derived. But see State Tax Comm'n v. Fine, 356 Mass. 51, 247 N.E.2d 701 (1969), in which a resident holder of shares in an out-of-state real estate trust was held exempt from Massachusetts income tax. Since the Massachusetts income tax had been construed as a tax on the underlying property, see p. 65 supra, the application of the tax on income from out-of-state realty was deemed to violate principles of extraterritorial taxation.

The rule generally obtains that non-residents are taxed only on income from sources within the State. P–H All States Guide ¶ 3043. Hence, the non-resident beneficiary is typically not taxed on distributions made by a resident trustee of income from a securities portfolio, managed within the State. He is, however, typically taxed, for example, on income from real property in the State held by the trust. In short, the usual underlying source rules normally govern taxability to the non-resident beneficiary of income from a resident trust. See Matter of McCormac, 64 Hawaii 258, 640 P.2d 282 (1982), in which the court held that non-resident beneficiaries of a trust consisting entirely of intangible property were nevertheless taxable on the income from the trust, because the property generating the income had acquired a "business situs" in Hawaii.

E. *References.* Freeman, "State Power to Tax Trust Income on Basis of Settlor's or Grantor's Residence," 53 Taxes 237 (1975); Ferrell, "State Taxation of Income Accumulated in Trusts," 51 A.B.A.J. 566 (1965); Comment, "Trusts: Tax on Trust Income by State of Beneficiary's Residence Held Constitutional," 113 U.Pa.L.Rev. 621 (1962); Annot., 5 A.L.R.3d 606.

SECTION 6. RESIDENCE, DOMICILE, AND PLACE OF ABODE

Notes and Problems

A. *The Definition of Resident Under State Income Tax Laws.* Most of the States levying income taxes subject residents to tax on income from all sources, although there are a number of States which limit the measure of the tax on residents to income from particular sources outside the State. Residence, therefore, is a crucial factor in determining the extent of the taxpayer's liability in virtually every income tax State. Altman and Keesling classify the definitions of "residence" used by the States as including one or more of five concepts:

(1) Domicile;

(2) Presence in the State for other than a temporary or transitory purpose;

(3) Presence in the State for a specified period of time—either six, seven or nine months;

(4) Maintenance of a permanent place of abode or a place of abode for a specified period of time; and

(5) A combination of (3) and (4), i.e., presence in the State for a specified period of time accompanied by the maintenance of a permanent place of abode. [G. Altman & F. Keesling, Allocation of Income in State Taxation 43 (2d ed. 1950).*]

The definition of resident includes "domicile" in most States; however, California, Delaware, and New York exclude from "resident" persons domiciled in the State provided they meet other qualifications. See, e.g., Ryan v. Chapman, 276 A.D. 99, 76 N.Y.S.2d 341 (3d Dep. 1948) (construing New York's definition of resident, former N.Y. Tax Law 350, now N.Y. Tax Law § 605, CCH ¶ 95–153, P–H ¶ 59,070, which generally includes domiciliaries, except those who (1) retain no permanent abode in the State (2) retain a permanent abode elsewhere, and (3) spend 30 days or less in the State). The court held in the case that a commissioned army officer who was domiciled in New York but was stationed in California was not a "resident" by reason of the following provision of the New York statute:

> Notwithstanding the provisions of subdivision seven, the term "resident" shall not include a person in the armed forces of the United States who is not domiciled in the State, notwithstanding the fact that he maintains a permanent place of abode within the State and spends

* Quoted by permission of Commerce Clearing House, Inc.

in the aggregate more than seven months of the taxable year within the State. [Sec. 350, subd. 7–a, N.Y. Tax Law.]

A few States seek to tax as residents persons temporarily residing in the State on all income derived from whatever source; this result appears questionable as to income derived from sources outside the State. A number of States, with a much more solid constitutional and economic justification for their action, tax the entire income of persons who maintain a permanent place of abode in the State for a prescribed period, even though not domiciled in the State. Other States add to the requirement of a permanent place of abode in the State, physical presence within the jurisdiction for a stated period if the taxpayer is to be subjected to income tax on his income from sources outside the State.

A series of decisions has been handed down by the California State Board of Equalization dealing with the meaning of the term "resident" under the State's statute defining resident as including every individual in the State for other than a temporary or transitory purpose. Calif.Rev. and Tax.Code § 17014, CCH ¶ 191–556, P–H ¶ 58,027. Appeal of Fox, CCH ¶ 401–291, P–H ¶ 64,166 (1986); Appeal of Gordy, CCH ¶ 401–283, P–H ¶ 64,154 (1986); Appeal of Gabrik, CCH 401–247, P–H ¶ 64,127 (1986).

B. *Constitutionality of Taxation of Entire Income of Resident Who Is Not Domiciled in the State.* A person who was a resident of New York under the statutory definition of the term (i.e., he maintained a permanent place of abode in the State and spent in the aggregate more than seven months of the taxable year within the State), but claiming to be domiciled in Montana, contested the taxation by New York of his entire net income. He contended that a State may not tax income from sources outside the State to a taxpayer who is not domiciled in the State. The Court of Appeals rejected the contention, holding that "in personal income taxes domicile plays no necessary part [in determining the State's power to tax income from intangibles]. Residence at a fixed date has determined the liability for tax." People ex rel. Ryan v. Lynch, 262 N.Y. 1, 186 N.E. 28 (1933). Quoting from Shaffer v. Carter, p. 358 supra, the court said, "as to residents it [the State] may, and does, exert its taxing power over their income from all sources, whether within or without the State." Id.

In Texas v. Florida, 306 U.S. 398, 59 S.Ct. 563 (1938), pp. 908–17 supra, the Court noted: "[t]hat two or more States may each constitutionally assess death taxes on a decedent's intangibles upon a judicial determination that the decedent was domiciled within it in proceedings binding upon the representatives of the estate * * * is an established principle of our federal jurisprudence." 306 U.S. at 410. The result of such a doctrine as applied to income and death taxes can be harsh and oppressive. The situation is further exacerbated by the fact that residence in addition to domicile may provide a basis for taxing all of a taxpayer's income or intangibles, and the definition of residence may vary from State to State. A more equitable result would obtain if the Court were to hold that the extraordinary power of taxing all of a taxpayer's income and all intangibles held by the estate were limited to one State under the Due Process Clause. The issue of "domicile" or "residence," whichever test were used, ought then become a constitutional question, and only one State would be able to tax all a taxpayer's intangibles at death, or all his income wherever earned. This was the position espoused by Justice Powell in his dissenting opinion in Cory v. White, 457 U.S. 85, 97–102, 102 S.Ct. 2325, 2332–35 (1982), in which Justices Marshall and Stevens joined. See Chapter 12, pp. 918–19 supra, where Justice Powell's views are set forth.

C. *Change of Residence.* Suppose a taxpayer changes his residence during the taxable year, how is he taxed? In some States, he is taxed as a non-resident for the period of non-residence and as a resident for the period of residence. Other States have adopted the rule that the taxpayer is subject to a levy based on the proportion of his total income for the year that the period of residence bears to the entire year. This method of prorating may be significant in view of graduated surtax rates. It was upheld in McCarty v. Tax Commission, 215 Wis. 645, 255 N.W. 913 (1934). However, the same court rejected an attempt to apply this method in a case where the taxpayer was able to segregate his income and establish the amount earned before becoming a resident. Greene v. Tax Commission, 221 Wis. 531, 266 N.W. 270 (1936).

Although a Kentucky statute levies a tax on the "entire net income" of a resident and defines resident as including every person domiciled in the State on the last day of the year, the statute was construed as treating the taxpayer as a resident only from the date of domicile within the State. Martin v. Gage, 281 Ky. 95, 134 S.W.2d 966 (1939). To hold otherwise would raise serious constitutional questions. Id. The case is annotated in 126 A.L.R. 455; the annotation deals with "Computation of income as affected by fact that taxpayer was domiciled within State for only part of taxable year." See also McLaughlin v. New York State Tax Comm'n, 87 A.D.2d 712, 448 N.Y.S.2d 891 (3d Dept.1982), in which the taxpayer, who was a non-resident alien for eleven of twelve months of the taxable year, reported one-twelfth of her distributive share of partnership income from a foreign partnership for State tax purposes. The taxing authority took the position that all of the partnership income should have been included as income on the State tax return because the taxpayer was a resident on the last day of the year. The court rejected this "extraordinary" contention, and upheld the trial court's judgment annulling the deficiency assessment.

Cf. Evans v. Comptroller, 273 Md. 172, 328 A.2d 272 (1974), in which the taxpayer received income in his new State of residence, which he had earned outside the State before he became a resident. Evans reported his income on a cash basis. The holding that Evans was taxable by Maryland is consistent with the cases noted above, since the taxpayer reported on a cash basis. If Evans had reported on an accrual basis, those cases point to the opposite result. Accord: Rogers v. Chilivis, 141 Ga.App. 407, 233 S.E.2d 451 (1977), cert. denied 434 U.S. 891, 98 S.Ct. 266 (1977); Hardy v. State Tax Comm'r, 258 N.W.2d 249 (N.D.1977).

After President Nixon's Chief of Staff H.R. Haldeman returned to California in 1973, he earned income from writing and making television appearances relating to this role as Chief of Staff and his involvement in the Watergate scandal. He reported these amounts as California income during the 1974–76 tax years. Haldeman deducted substantial expenses for attorneys fees and other defense costs in connection with the Watergate trials, the Senate Watergate Hearings, and related matters. The California personal income tax statute disallows a deduction for "[a]ny amount * * * allocable to * * * income wholly exempt from the taxes imposed by this part." See former Cal.Rev. & Tax Code § 17280, which now appears in substantially the same form as Cal.Rev. & Tax Code § 17280, CCH ¶ 195–000, P–H ¶ 58,683. Relying on this provision, the court sustained the Franchise Tax Board's disallowance of the deductions in question because the expenses were related to income which was earned prior to the time that Haldeman became a California resident. Haldeman v. Franchise Tax Board, 141 Cal.App.3d 373, 190 Cal.Rptr. 155 (2d Dist.1983). As a non-resident of California, the income Haldeman earned from Federal employment during that period was not taxable by California.

D. *Place of Abode of Congressman.* A Congressman from Arkansas showed unusual temerity in attacking his State's income tax levy on him on the ground that his "place of abode" was not among his constituents, but instead in Washington, D.C. He conceded that Arkansas was his domicile but not his "place of abode," which is the statutory test. The court, with its eye on the uncertainties of Congressional tenure, concluded that the term "place of abode" implies "a degree of permanence that did not attach to appellant's stay in Washington." Cravens v. Cook, 212 Ark. 71, 204 S.W.2d 909 (1947). Federal legislation now provides that Members of Congress may not, for purposes of State income tax laws, be treated as residents of any State other than the State from which they are elected. P.L. 95–67, (1977). The measure, which is retroactive, applies only to income taxes and not to other types of State levies. The apparent purpose of the legislation is to prevent Maryland, Virginia, and the District of Columbia from treating Congressmen as residents under their income tax laws. See United States v. Maryland, 488 F.Supp. 347 (D.Md.1980), affirmed per curiam 636 F.2d 73 (4th Cir.1980), cert. denied 451 U.S. 1017, 101 S.Ct. 3005 (1981) (sustaining constitutionality of statute).

E. The domicile of employees of the Federal Government working in Washington, but typically voting "back home" and some day expecting to return, has given rise to litigation in the income tax field. The opinion by Justice Jackson in District of Columbia v. Murphy, 314 U.S. 441, 62 S.Ct. 303 (1941), deals with this problem, and details the factors to be considered in deciding the domicile issue. See also Beckham v. District of Columbia, 163 F.2d 701 (D.C.Cir.1947), certiorari denied 332 U.S. 825, 68 S.Ct. 166 (1947) and Collier v. District of Columbia, 161 F.2d 649 (D.C.Cir.1947).

F. *References.* There is an excellent discussion of the definition of resident in G. Altman & F. Keesling, Allocation of Income in State Taxation, ch. 3 (2d ed. 1950), on which the foregoing notes are based. See also Reese & Green, "That Elusive Word 'Residence,'" 6 Vand.L.Rev. 561 (1953); Note, "Multi–State Taxation of Personal Income," 111 U.Pa.La.Rev. 974 (1963); Annot., 82 A.L.R.3d 1274.

SECTION 7. CREDIT OR ALLOWANCE FOR TAXES PAID TO OTHER STATES

All States with broad-based personal income taxes have adopted provisions granting credits against their income taxes for income taxes paid to other States whose income tax laws include similar crediting provisions. Every such State allows a credit to residents for taxes paid in foreign States, thereby reverting the final tax to the State which is the source of the income taxed. Some States also allow non-residents credits for taxes paid to the States of their residence on income derived from sources in the State of non-residence, provided there is a reciprocal credit granted the non-resident's State. However, the effects of the denial of credits cannot be considered without a study of the income actually taxed, for some States exempt some types of income from tax instead of granting credits for taxes paid. The crediting provisions that are on the statute books are circumscribed by ceilings and provisions limiting income actually taxed by other States. The conflicting crediting devices and the wide variation in their scope have produced inequitable results; greater uniformity among the States would produce greater equity among taxpayers.

Notes and Problems

A. *Income Derived From Sources Outside the State.* The issue has arisen under the California provision allowing residents an income tax credit for taxes paid in other States as to whether the credit applies to dividends and profits on stocks of a corporation doing all its business outside the State. In Miller v. McColgan, 17 Cal.2d 432, 110 P.2d 419, 134 A.L.R. 1424 (1941), a California resident claimed an income tax credit for taxes paid on dividends on stock in a Philippine Islands mining corporation and on capital gain derived from the sale of a part of the stock in the Philippine Islands. Income taxes were paid to the Philippine government on the dividends and the profit. The California statute limits the credit to residents to foreign taxes paid on "income derived from sources outside this State." The court denied the credit on the ground that the source of the income was the stock in the corporation and that its "taxable situs" was the domicile of the owner of the stock—here California. The same principle was held to apply to the profit on the sale of the stock even though the transaction took place outside the State.

In Henley v. Franchise Tax Board, 122 Cal.App.2d 790, 264 P.2d 179 (1953), the court refused to follow the *Miller* case on the ground that later Supreme Court decisions, such as State Tax Comm'n v. Aldrich, 316 U.S. 174, 62 S.Ct. 1008 (1952), had undermined the foundation of the *Miller* case in its reliance on the doctrine of *mobilia sequuntur personam.* But see the more recent decision in Christman v. Franchise Tax Bd., 64 Cal.App.3d 751, 134 Cal.Rptr. 725 (1976), which reaffirms the *Miller* case in this context; see also Appeal of Baker, Cal. State Bd. of Equaliz., Oct. 9, 1985, P–H ¶ 64,077 (Nebraska tax on interest income earned in connection with sale of Nebraska property by California resident not creditable against California tax because not derived from source outside California).

B. *Limitations on Amount of Credit.* In an Alabama case a State tax credit issue arose out of the disparity between the Alabama corporate income tax rate of three percent and the Mississippi corporate graduated rate of one to five percent. Alabama grants residents and Alabama corporations a credit on account of taxes paid on income derived from and taxed in other States. In State v. Robinson Land and Lumber Co. of Alabama, 262 Ala. 146, 77 So.2d 641 (1954), the Department of Revenue construed the statute as limiting the credit to such ratio of the total Alabama tax as gross income derived from the foreign State bears to total gross income from all sources. The court, however, found that the Alabama credit is not so limited, distinguishing a California case so holding, Miller v. McColgan, 17 Cal.2d 432, 110 P.2d 419, 134 A.L.R. 1424 (1941), as being based on an explicit statutory provision. The Alabama statute does, however, contain limitations which restrict the credit paid to the effective Alabama rate applied to the same net income taxed.

C. *Credits for Taxes Paid by Trusts and Trust Beneficiaries on the Same Income.* A trust administered in Massachusetts paid income taxes on amounts earned by the trust and subsequently distributed to a New York beneficiary. The beneficiary paid New York income tax on the amounts distributed by the trust and sought to take a credit against her New York tax liability for the taxes paid by the trust. The State Tax Commission took the position that she was not entitled to the credit on the ground that, since Massachusetts had imposed the tax upon the trust, the taxpayer had not paid any income tax to Massachusetts. The court reversed:

> respondent required petitioner to include the taxes which were paid by the trust in her New York adjusted gross income. The resultant effect of this is that Mrs. Smith has borne the burden of paying the Massachusetts taxes. Having so borne the burden of the income taxes paid to Massachusetts, petitioners have constructively paid "income tax imposed for the taxable year by another state" and are thus entitled to a credit under Tax Law § 620(a). [Smith v. State Tax Com'n, 120 A.D.2d 907, 503 N.Y.S.2d 169, 170–71 (3d Dept.1986).]

However, in an earlier case, the Massachusetts Supreme Court refused to treat a trust and its beneficiary as essentially a single taxpayer when the question arose whether the trust was entitled to a credit against Massachusetts income taxes paid on income distributed to a Massachusetts beneficiary who had paid personal income tax to California on amounts distributed to him. Whiteside v. Commissioner of Revenue, 394 Mass. 206, 474 N.E.2d 1128 (1985). For tax credit purposes, the trust and the beneficiary were treated as separate taxable entities under the statute.

D. *Nature of the Foreign Tax Affecting the Credit.* The Maryland income tax statute allows residents a credit for an "income tax" paid to "another State upon such part of his net income * * * as is properly subject to taxation in such State." In Gardalla v. Comptroller of the State of Maryland, 213 Md. 1, 130 A.2d 752 (1957), credit was denied for the District of Columbia tax on unincorporated business, levied at the rate of five percent of taxable income, on the privilege of carrying on trade or business in the District. The court held that the levy was a privilege or franchise tax and not an income tax, and hence not subject to the crediting provision. For a similar holding under the Tennessee franchise tax measured by net income, see Algernon Blair, Inc. v. State, 285 Ala. 44, 228 So. 2d 803 (1969).

In Keyes v. Chambers, 209 Or. 640, 307 P.2d 498 (1957), an Oregon resident sought a credit against his income tax for a Canadian tax paid on dividends received from a Canadian corporation; the dividends were taxed by Oregon. Because the Canadian tax of fifteen percent was withheld at the source, without allowance of exemptions or deduction, the court held that the crediting provision did not apply; credit is allowed only for "net income" taxes, and the Canadian tax on dividends was held to be a "gross income" tax. Moreover, the tax did not qualify for the credit for the further reason that the levy was limited to non-residents of Canada, and the crediting provision applies only to levies that are imposed "irrespective of the residence or domicil of the recipient."

E. *Credit for Tax Paid to Foreign Countries and Municipalities.* Under State statutory provisions providing a credit for taxes paid to other "States," the courts have held that the term does not embrace taxes paid to other countries. See Ludka v. Department of Treasury, 155 Mich.App. 250, 399 N.W.2d 490 (1986); Elsola v. Commissioner of Revenue, Minn.Tax.Ct., April 9, 1984, CCH ¶ 10–337.40, P–H ¶ 13,428; cf. Shulevitz v. Department of Treasury, 78 Mich.App. 655, 261 N.W.2d 31 (1977) (denying credit for tax paid to Puerto Rico). The Virginia Supreme Court has likewise held that the credit for an "income tax [paid] to the state where [the non-resident] resides" does not include local Maryland income taxes. Department of Taxation v. Smith, 232 Va. 407, 350 S.E.2d 645 (1986).

F. *References.* See Annot., 12 A.L.R.2d 359.

SECTION 8. MUNICIPAL INCOME TAXES

A. *Double Taxation by Municipalities of a Single State.* An individual residing in the City of Loveland, Ohio, and working in the City of Cincinnati, found himself in the unenviable position of paying taxes on his wages to both cities, and yet failed in a declaratory judgment suit brought to prevent the double taxation. The Ohio Constitution contains a broad grant of authority to municipalities to "levy taxes for local purposes," subject, however, to the power of the General Assembly to "restrict their power of taxation * * * so as to prevent the abuse of such power." Art. XIII, Sec. 6. The General Assembly in 1957 exercised its authority by limiting income taxes of municipalities to a one percent rate, unless a higher rate is authorized by the local voters. Ohio R.C. § 718.01.

Loveland adopted a two percent tax, which applied to the income of residents of the city, but granted no deduction or credit for income taxes paid to other cities. Cincinnati adopted a one percent tax, but in the case of its residents, allowed a credit for taxes paid on income earned in other cities and there taxed. The plaintiff, taxable on his wages by both cities without deduction or credit, contended that the City of Loveland could not tax him on his income earned and taxed in Cincinnati.

The Ohio Supreme Court reversed a judgment of the trial court that had upheld the taxpayer's contentions. Thompson v. City of Cincinnati, 2 Ohio St.2d 292, 208 N.E.2d 747 (1965). It rejected his contention that the State law required the allowance of a deduction to a resident for income earned and taxed by another municipality in the State, by referring to the refusal of the General Assembly to adopt a proposed provision "that would have obligated all municipalities to allow a tax deduction for income tax paid by a resident of a municipality on wages earned outside a municipality," although income from businesses and professions is taxable in a municipality only to the extent derived from sources within its boundaries. See the provision for allocating and apportioning such income. Ohio R.C. § 718.02. See also Glander, "The Uniform Municipal Income Tax Act," 18 Ohio St. L.J. 489, 498 (1958).

The taxpayer's anguished plea that he was being discriminated against, in that people who work and reside in the same city pay only one tax on their wages, while he is subjected to double taxation, was met by the court's citation of authorities holding that the Due Process Clause does not prevent either the State of residence, or the State where income is earned, or both, from taxing wages without allowance of deduction or credit.

The court's reading of the cases is unimpeachable, but there is little that can be said in support of the result, from the point of view of fiscal policy. The primary responsibility for this result lies, however, with the Ohio General Assembly and the City of Loveland. The action of the General Assembly, in particular, in prohibiting double taxation by Ohio municipalities of business and professional income, while acquiescing in such taxation of the income of wage earners, may reflect the varying attitudes of Ohio legislators toward the tax burdens of individuals, as contrasted with their attitudes toward businesses and the professions; or perhaps the result may be a response to political pressures.

B. *References.* Dewey, "Municipal Income Taxation in Ohio— Limitation Due to State Preemption," 7 U.Toledo L.Rev. 501 (1976); Note, "Municipal Income Tax—State Preemption in California," 11 Santa Clara L.Rev. 343 (1971); Note, "The Limits of Municipal Income Taxation: The Response in Ohio," 7 Harv.J.Legis. 271 (1970); Munhnick, "A Municipal Income Tax for Boston: Discourse in Possibilities," 5 Suffolk U.L.Rev. 127 (1970); Note, 22 Vand.L.Rev. 1314 (1969); Sato, "Municipal Occupation Taxes in California: The Authority to Levy Taxes and the Burden on Intrastate Commerce," 53 Cal.L.Rev. 801 (1965).

Part 8

EXEMPTIONS FROM TAXATION

INTRODUCTORY NOTE

In a broad sense, any article or person or transaction not included within the reach of a tax is exempt from the levy. Thus, real property might be regarded as exempt from a personal property tax. However, the term "exemption" is usually given a narrower meaning, as covering all exclusions from the scope of the subject matter of a tax, i.e., property, persons, transactions, and so forth, which are logically within the tax base.[1] Thus, the personal exemption of $2,000 under the Federal income tax for taxable years beginning after December 31, 1988, the exemption of sales of food under sales tax acts, and the exemption from death tax of gifts to charitable and educational organizations, are illustrative of the term exemption as commonly employed.

Exemptions have been classified into four categories:[2]

(1) *Exemption to protect the minimum of subsistence.* Income taxes, personal property taxes, and death taxes typically exempt minimum amounts of income or property in order to avoid undue burdens. Exemptions of small amounts of income and property are also important from an administrative point of view.

(2) *Exemption of public property, income and activities.* The broad basis for the exemption of public property, income, and activities is that in substance the government would be paying itself a tax. This problem in practice is complicated by the numerous governmental units within a State, i.e., county, city, town, village, water district, school district, and so forth. Thus, a State university or hospital established for the benefit of the entire State obtains fire and police protection and other governmental services from the locality in which it operates. Typically, however, the university or hospital is exempt from local levies as well as State taxes. In the area of taxation by the States of Federal properties and activities, and vice versa, the constitutional doctrine of immunity from tax of intergovernmental instrumentalities comes into play.

1. This definition of exemption is based on Martin, "General Theory of Tax Exemption," Tax Exemptions 3 (Tax Policy League 1939).

2. This classification and the ensuing discussion are based on Martin, note 1 supra.

(3) *Exemption of private agencies performing public functions.* The limitations and scope of exemption for charitable, educational, and public welfare organizations, and a host of other specific quasi-public institutions, varying State by State and tax by tax, account for a substantial amount of litigation in the tax field year in and year out. The revenue losses to States and their subdivisions attributable to this area of exemption, particularly in real property taxes, have caused deep concern to students of State and local finance and have resulted in searching questioning as to the validity and scope of the exemptions. In many States, exemption provisions are written into the constitution so that in approaching the issues in exemption cases, the courts are frequently confronted with constitutional as well as statutory problems.

(4) *Exemptions as a subsidy of desirable enterprise or activity.* Tax exemption has been widely used in this country as a form of subsidy to encourage activities as widely varied as the location of businesses in an area, slum clearance housing projects, home ownership (through the homestead exemption), and the carrying on of religious activities by churches. Currently in an effort to reduce dependence on traditional energy sources, State tax exemption is being employed as an incentive to the use of solar energy for home heating purposes. The use of tax exemption as a form of indirect subsidy has been criticized as a crude instrument for encouraging activities, since the amount of the subsidy is ordinarily not completely controlled by the State and there is no check on the relationship between the amount of indirect subsidy and the benefits conferred on the community by the exempt activities or property.

Chapter 14

EXEMPTION OF EDUCATIONAL, PHILANTHROPIC AND RELIGIOUS ORGANIZATIONS

KILLOUGH, "EXEMPTIONS TO EDUCATIONAL, PHILANTHROPIC AND RELIGIOUS ORGANIZATIONS"

Tax Exemptions 23 (Tax Policy League, 1939).*

" * * * Let us consider first the reasons for exempting from taxation private organizations which are supplying services which the State would be called upon to supply if it were not for the private organizations. If private schools, colleges, and charitable institutions were taxed, their services and benefactions would be cut down by the amount of their taxes. Then if the State were to take over some of the functions which these institutions have had to give up because of taxation, there would be no net gain to the community. Money would simply have been put into one pocket and taken out of another. There would even be a net loss to the community if it is true, as tax exemption proponents frequently argue, that private institutions are more efficiently managed than public ones.

"So far the argument has assumed that taxation would cut down the amount of service rendered by educational and charitable institutions and that, if taxed, they would continue to function but on a somewhat lesser scale. It is frequently implied, however, that private benefactions would cease if it were not for tax exemptions of contributions to and of the property of these private organizations. Tax exemption is cited as a necessary incentive to private giving, and taxation called a menace to philanthropy. For those who believe that taxation would mark the beginning of the end of privately supported education and charity the justification of exemption is complete. If taxation were to make it necessary for government to supply not only those services formerly rendered with funds not collected in taxes, but also to supply many services formerly rendered through private gifts,

---

* [This material is reprinted with the consent of the Tax Institute of America, which was formerly known as the Tax Policy League.]

governmental costs would increase by an amount materially greater than the new tax collections. It follows from this line of reasoning that the community receives a net profit from tax exemption which is the difference between the total value of the services of the tax-exempt organizations and the cost, in foregone taxes, of the exemption.[1]

"The second category of exemptions includes those to religious and other organizations which perform services not likely to be thought of as state functions, although commonly held to be socially desirable. The reasons usually given for these exemptions are more general in nature and somewhat less concerned with dollars and cents. Tax exemption of church property is defended on the ground that religious organizations promote morality and thus further the welfare of the state. It is said that without the influence of religion 'the whole framework of our civilization would be severely threatened,'[2] and that 'religion and morality are essential * * * to the very existence of the organic state.'[3]

"The aspect of the present method which is most in need of modification concerns the problem of control. If an institution falls within a category generally accepted as educational, benevolent, literary, charitable, or whatever fits into a particular legally accepted vocabulary, it is automatically exempted from taxation by constitutional or legislative requirement. There is no way of effectively considering the question as to whether the community or the tax-exempt organization would make best use of the money not paid in taxes at a particular time. The mildest reform would provide for periodic evaluations of the status of even the most deserving recipients of exemption. Similarly no additions should be made to the tax-exempt list without careful evaluation, if, in fact, they should be made at all. These minor changes would require constitutional amendment in many States and the repealing of existing and enactment of new legislation by others and by the federal government. Educational institutions can scarcely uphold their status as bulwarks of democracy if they are unwilling to subject their efforts to this small measure of democratic control.

* * *

"This is probably too half-hearted a measure. It might be better if all individuals and institutions paid taxes without exemptions for any contribution to, or expenditure for, however charitable or educational a purpose. When the indirect subsidies had been disposed of in this way the question of direct grants should be considered. In response to a plea for exemptions from a group of hospitals the special California Tax Commission of 1929 stated:

1. For an analysis on these lines see Tobin, Charles J., Hannan, William E., and Tolman, Leland L., The Exemption from Taxation of Privately Owned Real Property Used for Religious, Charitable and Educational Purposes in New York State, 100 State Street, Albany, 1934, Part III.

2. Tobin, et al., op. cit., [note 1] p. 21.

3. Brown, T. Edwin, Some Reasons for the Exemption of Church Property from Taxation, pamphlet, Scranton, Wetmore and Co., Rochester, 1881, p. 12.

It is the feeling of the Commission that the exemptions should be curtailed, rather than extended, but it also realizes the extreme difficulty of bringing about such a contraction. With respect to the plea of the hospitals, to which it has given sympathetic study, it has concluded that, while it cannot recommend any expansion of the exemption list, it does desire to record its conviction that recognition should be given to the public importance of the work of certain of these institutions through more liberal public grants and payments where activities of these institutions clearly have the effect of caring for cases which otherwise would be a charge on the public funds.[4]

"This recommendation might well be heeded by other States and applied not only to hospitals but also to other organizations.

"There are a number of advantages in direct grants. They provide for continuous evaluation of the merits of particular projects. They might be made by more appropriate jurisdictions than frequently happens at present with many communities granting enormous indirect subsidies to institutions largely used by people from other regions. Direct grants would make evident the real financial relationship between the institutions and the community. Direct grants might be a simpler way of distinguishing between functions entitled to public support and those not so entitled than an attempt partially to tax and partially to exempt institutions performing such mixed functions. It seems to the writer that these advantages outweigh the disadvantages many of which have been suggested in the foregoing pages.

"There is little reason to believe that any such great change in present practice is probable in the near future. The difficulties involved are emotional as well as legal and financial. The first step should be the prevention of increases in the exemptions, to be followed as far as possible by their gradual elimination."

"THE LIMITS OF PROPERTY TAX PHILANTHROPY"

Report of Advisory Commission on Intergovernmental Relations *

"In the admirably succinct words of one perturbed civil organization, 'The clamor for tax exemption unfolds somewhat like a contagious disease. One specific exemption in itself may appear quite harmless. However, going back to the turn of the century, one exemption leads to another until today, including intangibles, more property has been taken from the tax base than now remains.'[5]

"This expression of concern over the decreasing generalness of the general property tax is well justified by the erosion of the property tax base that has occurred over the past half century or more and continues to occur. Total figures for tax exempt property are available only in a limited number of States, and these figures admittedly are only

4. Final Report of the California Tax Commission, Sacramento, 1929, p. 90.

* [ACIR, 1 The Role of the States in Strengthening the Property Tax 76 (1963).]

5. League of Wisconsin Municipalities, Readings on the Wisconsin Assessment Process, vol. 1, 1961, p. 4.

approximations; but quite obviously there is an enormous difference between the total value of all property in the United States and the value of property that actually is taxed. With a total assessed value of taxable property of less than $2,000 per capita, and an assessed value of taxable personal property of only $315 per capita, in 1961, the tax base for local general property taxation bears little resemblance to the Nation's affluence in property values. As compared with an estimated national wealth of $1,682.1 billion in 1958 (a figure that does not include intangibles), the aggregate of locally taxable assessed valuation was $355.7 billion in 1961 (inclusive of intangibles).[6] Because of fractional assessment, the contrast is less extreme than these figures appear to indicate, but still great." [End of excerpt from ACIR Report.]

The ACIR report discusses the various types of property tax exemptions now in force. The homestead exemption, categorized as one "of the durable by-products of the 1930's depression," was a "benevolent device," designed to prevent the loss of dwellings and farms during the emergency; it has now grown to large proportions long after the economic conditions that gave birth to the exemption have passed.[7] As of 1984, all but a handful of States granted some type of homestead exemption, although in many States the exemption was limited to particular categories of homesteaders (e.g., the elderly, the poor, the disabled).[8] More than 20 States granted exemptions to all homesteaders. In dollar amounts, the exemptions ranged from $1,000 to total exemption. The importance of the exemption is further indicated by the fact that in 1984 revenue losses from the program ran into hundreds of millions of dollars in States such as California, Louisiana, Minnesota, and New Jersey.

Property tax exemption for veterans is provided by constitution or statute in about 32 States.[9] Typically, they cover the life of the veteran, his widow and minor children, and in ten States ceilings ranging from $3,600 to $8,000 are imposed. While complete data are unavailable, fifteen States reported exempt veterans property totalling $2.6 billion in 1961, a figure which appears to be growing. As suggested by the ACIR, property tax exemption is a poor way to provide soldiers' bonuses, for they benefit only veterans who are property owners.[10]

The ACIR Report notes that about one-third of the States, mainly in the South and New England, grant property tax exemption to new industries or new plants, usually for a five- or ten-year period. An

---

6. Estimate of national wealth by National Bureau of Economic Research; data for taxable assessed valuations from U.S. Bureau of Census, Property Tax Assessments in the United States, op. cit.

7. ACIR, 1 The Role of the States in Strengthening the Property Tax 78 (1963) [hereinafter cited as ACIR Report].

8. See ACIR, "Significant Features of Fiscal Federalism 1984 Edition," Table 72,

pp. 116–21 (1985) on which the discussion in the balance of this paragraph relies.

9. ACIR Report, note 7 supra, at 81–83.

10. Id. There is also beginning to crop up the extension of tax exemption for the aged. Id. at 85 et seq. This movement has been given impetus by the double personal exemption allowed for Federal income tax purposes to persons who are age 65 or over. I.R.C. § 151(c).

intensive investigation of industrial tax exemption in Louisiana concluded that:

> (1) tax exemption as a device for inducing new industrial expansion which would not otherwise occur has produced meager results in Louisiana; (2) the cost of the program in terms of lost revenue is out of proportion to the direct results obtained; (3) the 10–year industrial tax exemption program for new industry in Louisiana should be reevaluated. [Ross, "Tax Concessions and Their Effect," 1957 Nat.Tax Ass'n Procs. 221.]

The ACIR concludes that the grant of industrial tax exemptions is an "unsound policy," because such exemptions "harm competitors, place a burden on the taxpayers who have to carry the tax * * * and promote interstate tax warfare that endangers the development of fair and adequate tax systems generally." [11] See Pinsky, "State Constitutional Limitations on Public Industrial Financing: An Historical and Economic Approach," 111 U.Pa.L.Rev. 265 (1963).

The institutional exemptions granted to non-profit religious, charitable, and educational institutions make a very deep cut in the property tax base but are nevertheless, "almost impervious to question." [12] Published data to measure the magnitude of this erosion of the tax base are largely unavailable; in California, which publishes the data, the assessed value of property of exempt institutions in 1961 was two percent of the assessed value of taxable property. [13] In New Jersey the 1961 figure was eight percent. A study by the Connecticut State Tax Department estimated that $1.7 billion of property was exempt from tax in 1961, representing an annual loss to the municipalities of $62.5 million, or nearly $25 per capita; and about thirty percent of these exemptions and revenue losses were due to institutional exemptions. [14] The ACIR Report summed up its conclusions as to institutional exemptions as follows:

"There is little opposition to government aid for private, nonprofit institutions clearly affected with a public interest, but there has long been a strong feeling that institutional tax exemption has been carried beyond its basic purpose and has been abused, and also some feeling that tax exemption is an undesirable method of providing such aid. The method may be questioned for three reasons. The exemptions must be absorbed not by a statewide tax base but by individual local tax bases. The impact tends to be very unequal and in some instances a community must bear the exemption for an institution that serves a much wider area. Second, the State legislature may feel unduly benevolent when it can make a generous contribution to some worthy private cause without any obvious cost to the State. The legislators might be more discriminating if the gift had to appear in the budget. Third, the legislature actually is imposing forced contributions on the taxpayers of the State's communities without their consent and outside

11. ACIR Report, note 7 supra, at 81.
12. Id. at 83.
13. Id. at 84.
14. Id.

local budgetary processes. As a joint committee of the New York State Legislature expressed it some years ago: [15]

> "Tax exemption does give a subsidy, but the trouble is that it is a blind subsidy, controlled by accident. And it is, moreover, a compulsory subsidy which cannot be reviewed and fixed by those who pay it as sound finance demands.

"Outright government grants, as an alternative to waivers of property taxes, have often been urged for institutions whose services clearly are of a public nature, together with abolition of exemptions for organizations for which grants could not be justified. This policy would avoid the inequity imposed on some local communities by the present system and would replace hidden subsidies by accountable public appropriations. Opponents of this change, however, argue that a system of grants would subject some institutions to governmental regulation and pressure from which they should be free. Prof. M. Slade Kendrick, in a cogent exposition of this point of view, said: [16]

> " * * * exemption from taxation is the only way that the government can help the institutions concerned without making them lose their independence of action. A subsidy of a university or church would be a matter of public record, for an expenditure would have been made. On the other hand, the value of an exemption is concealed. But for the purposes thereby served, the very merit of an exemption lies in its hidden nature. No money is paid out of the treasury, no loss of revenue is computed, and no competition between institutions is engendered in the State legislature or the city council. The government simply refrains from taxation. As a result, each institution is helped, is on the same footing as the others, and is under no pressure to change its operations.

"Although the use of grants may be undesirable in some instances, there is no good reason why the validity of each type of institutional exemption should not be subject to the test of whether it would justify a continuing grant—in other words, would it be a wise permanent expenditure. State legislatures and the public, however, are unlikely to consider seriously so strict a criterion unless they have far more carefully analyzed data regarding the magnitude and effect of this creeping tax base erosion than are now available to them in the great majority of States.

"A forthright solution of the institutional tax exemption problem— and one that has been proposed in more than one State constitutional convention—would be to do away with such exemptions entirely. This proposal has had limited support thus far; but, as one apprehensive commentator has warned, if the States are unable to control the exemption flood "the only alternatives we will have open to us are either to abolish the tax or eliminate exemptions, and I rather think we

---

15. Quoted in New York State Constitutional Convention Committee, 1938, Problems Relating to Taxation and Finance, Albany, 1938, p. 225.

16. M. Slade Kendrick, ["Property Tax Exemptions and Exemption Policies," 1958 Nat.Tax Ass'n Procs. 84, 88.]

will have to do the latter.[17] "   [ACIR, 1 The Role of the States in Strengthening the Property Tax 84–85 (1963).]

For a strong criticism of real property tax exemptions, see A. Balk, The Free List (1971).

THE EROSION OF THE AD VALOREM REAL PROPERTY TAX BASE BY TAX EXEMPTIONS

There has been in recent years increasing alarm among tax officials and students of public finance over the erosion of the real property tax base as a result of the proliferation of exemptions. A 1972 report by the Property Taxation Committee of the National Tax Association—Tax Institute of America estimated that real property tax exemptions had risen from 11.7 percent of the 1922 assessed value of all real property in this country to 32.6 percent in 1968.[18] Although a substantial part of the exemption is attributable to property owned by Federal, State, and local governments and their agencies, in many States exempt privately owned property accounts for large amounts and percentages of the total base. Thus, (based on figures for 1964 in some States and 1963 in others) the value of exempt non-governmental property amounted to approximately 22 percent of the assessed value of all taxable property in Illinois, 19 percent in California, 36 percent in Florida, and 75 percent in Louisiana. The percentages were considerably lower in other States, but still loomed large, amounting to 3 percent in Colorado, 10 percent in Connecticut, 16 percent in Indiana and Oklahoma, 15 percent in Massachusetts, 7 percent in New York, and 10 percent in Pennsylvania.[19]

Despite some legislative and administrative efforts to curb exemption,[20] the erosion of the property tax base continues in no small degree because of the knee-jerk reaction of many legislators who, upon every new economic or social crisis, enact tax incentives, which have the political advantage of not standing out in the budget in the same way as direct cash subsidies.[21] Property tax exemption to encourage the

---

17. William O. Winter, "Tax Exemption of Institutional Property," in Municipal Finance, February 1960, p. 146.

18. "The Erosion of the Tax Base," 1972 Nat.Tax Ass'n Procs. 3.

19. Id., Table II, at 5.

20. See the 1971 revision in the New York statute, (Ch. 414, L. of 1971, amending § 420 [now § 421] of the Real Property Tax Law), which resulted in the restoration to the tax rolls of property owned and used by Bar Associations, Matter of the Association of the Bar of the City of New York v. Lewisohn, 34 N.Y.2d 143, 356 N.Y.S.2d 555, 313 N.E.2d 30 (1974), a bible publishing organization, American Bible Society v. Lewisohn, 40 N.Y.2d 78, 386 N.Y.S.2d 49, 351 N.E.2d 697 (1976), and the

Explorers Club, Matter of the Explorers Club v. Lewisohn, decided in the same opinion as Matter of the Association of the Bar, supra. For the view that the "overall effect of the 1971 statute has been minor," see Ginsberg, "Realty Tax Exemptions—Policy or Politics?," N.Y.Law J., Dec. 1, 1976. See also the efforts in Florida to restrict the free and easy property tax exemptions granted to "hundreds of havens around the state—including homes, resorts and posh hotels * * * whether they are church connected, whether they are non-profit and whether they utilize public land or facilities." Wall Street J., Oct. 17, 1971.

21. For a critical view of the use of tax exemption and other tax incentives to achieve economic and social goals, see Sur-

installation of solar energy equipment and devices to reduce air and water pollution is the most recent case in point.[22] And, particularly in economically depressed areas, we have witnessed a rash of exemptions as an incentive to new businesses and building and construction renovation. Thus, acting under 1976 enabling State legislation, the City of New York granted exemptions for new construction of industrial or commercial properties for a ten-year period, beginning at 50 percent of the new construction and reduced by 5 percent each year.[23] In the case of reconstruction of such properties, the exemption continued for 19 years and was reduced at the rate of 5 percent a year.[24] The American Broadcasting Company was granted exemption under this provision for the renovation, at an estimated cost of $3 million, of an armory which houses new ABC studios.[25] In more affluent Westchester County, however, the local legislature refused to adopt the permissive legislation, in part because of the concern that "the abatement program would be automatic for all qualifying businesses" and "would apply to two of the county's biggest taxpayers and frequent developers—Consolidated Edison and the New York Telephone Company." [26]

REVOLT IN THE CATSKILLS AGAINST PROPERTY TAX EXEMPTIONS

The Town of Hardenburgh, in the farming and logging area of the Catskill Mountains of New York, became the center of a large scale taxpayer's revolt against the proliferation of property tax exemption for religious, educational, and other organizations. About $5.1 million of the $11 million of assessed value of the town's property was held by Zen Buddhists, the Tibetan Monks, and the Boy Scouts. N.Y. Times, Jan. 16, 1977.

One of the supervisors of the town reported that, as a result of tax exemption, the taxes on his 120 acre plot (rose) in five years from $800 to $4,000. Id., Jan. 30, 1977. In the Livingston Manor School District in the area, the Transcendental Meditation organization, which obtained exemption as an educational institution, owned a 536–acre tract, on which were situated a former 400–room resort hotel and a 75–acre private lake. Fifty percent of all property in the school district was said to be off the taxable rolls.

rey, "Tax Reform," Panel Discussion, House Ways and Means Committee 19 et seq. (94th Cong., 1st Sess.1975).

22. During the year 1976, legislation was enacted in Connecticut, Georgia, Hawaii, Idaho, Kansas, Maryland, Massachusetts, and Michigan providing for property or sales tax exemption, income tax credits or deductions, or, in some cases, accelerated depreciation for the installation of solar or wind-powered heat devices. See the review of 1976 State tax legislation in 38 CCH State Tax Rev., No. 2 (Jan. 11, 1977).

For a summary of existing solar energy tax exemptions, see P–H All States Guide ¶ 299. See also McNulty, "State Tax Incentives to Fight Pollution," 56 A.B.A.J. 747 (1970).

23. N.Y.Real Property Tax Law title 2–C, § 489aaa et seq., CCH ¶ 92–377; N.Y. City Administrative Code §§ 1301–07.

24. Id.

25. See N.Y.Times, April 16, 1977.

26. Id., Feb. 8, 1977.

To dramatize their plight and obtain legislative relief, more than 200 of the Town's 236 residents became "ministers" of the Universal Life Church and claimed exemption by filing covenants with the Town Assessor asserting that they use their homes, farms and other buildings as church property. Id., April 16 and July 3, 1977. The new "ministers" were ordained en masse by a former local plumber; doctorates of divinity were obtainable by mail from the California-based Universal Life Church for a fee of $20. Id., Jan. 16, 1977. Under New York law, in addition to the exemption for property owned and used exclusively for religious purposes, a minister's home used for religious purposes is exempt up to $1,500 of assessed value. N.Y. Real Property Tax Law, §§ 421, 460, CCH ¶¶ 90–900, 90–939, P–H ¶¶ 32,118–D, 32,139. In addition, under the New York law in effect in 1977, real property "held by any officer of a religious denomination" was entitled to "the same exemption from taxation * * * as property owned by a religious corporation." Former N.Y. Real Property Tax Law § 436.

The State Board of Equalization issued an opinion determining that there is no basis for either partial or complete exemption of the "ministers'" property (the opinion was advisory and is not binding on the assessor), but the assessor accommodated his neighbors by announcing that he would grant exemption, apparently without any serious effort to verify the representations in the covenants. N.Y. Times, Jan. 16, 1977. The Board's suit to enjoin the assessor from filing the assessment roll allowing the exemptions was rejected by the local court, on the ground that the Board had no standing in the matter. Id., July 3, 1977.

The Hardenburgh movement spread to other parts of the Catskills and to Long Island. The "First Cardinal of New York" of the Universal Life Church (the former plumber) has asserted that by the end of 1976, he had ordained more than 5,000 new "ministers." Id., December 5, 1976.

In response to the Hardenburgh movement, the New York legislature amended § 436 of the Real Property Tax Law (quoted above) to provide that "[r]eal property held *in trust* by a clergyman or minister of a religious denomination *for the benefit of the members of his * * * church*" shall be entitled to exemption. 1978 N.Y. Laws ch. 738, codified at N.Y. Real Property Tax Law § 436, CCH ¶ 92–083, P–H ¶ 32,127 (emphasis supplied). The effect of the amendment was to deny exemptions to the Hardenburgh "ministers." The Town of Hardenburgh and some of its residents challenged the amended statute on the ground that it violated the First Amendment by interfering with the free exercise of their religion, but the courts dismissed the attack. Town of Hardenburgh v. State, 99 Misc.2d 1036, 418 N.Y.S.2d 503 (Sup. Ct., Spec. Term, Ulster Cty.1979), modified and, as so modified affirmed 72 A.D.2d 192, 424 N.Y.S.2d 531 (3d Dept.1980), appeal dismissed as to town and town officials and affirmed as modified as to individual plaintiffs 52 N.Y.2d 536, 439 N.Y.S.2d 303, 421 N.E.2d 795 (1981), appeal dismissed 454 U.S. 958, 102 S.Ct. 496 (1981).

Despite the ultimate disallowance of the exemptions, the Catskills protest poses a larger and more threatening challenge to the property tax structure, namely, the growing indignation that the taxpayers who make up the solid base of the taxpaying public feel toward the burden exemption is putting on them. To be sure, the widespread willingness of property owners to resort to the ordination tax avoidance device is probably due in part to their distaste for the tenets and practices of the off-beat religious and other organizations which are buying up property in their areas. Nevertheless, the developments in the Catskills reflect a deep-seated resentment among taxpayers.

CIRCUIT BREAKERS

Circuit breakers are designed to cut off or reduce a qualified taxpayer's tax load when the property tax reaches too high a proportion of the family's household income.

A *circuit-breaker* is a property-tax credit, the value of which depends on a household's property-tax bill and its income. Circuit-breakers are generally divided into two types: threshold and sliding scale. A threshold program provides a credit for taxes exceeding a certain proportion of income (that is, the threshold percentage). For example, Connecticut's circuit-breaker for senior citizens is equal to taxes exceeding 5 percent of income, with the maximum credit being $400. A sliding-scale circuit-breaker provides a credit for a certain percentage of property taxes, with the percentage decreasing as income rises. Iowa's circuit-breaker, for example, covers the entire property-tax bill for elderly households with an income under $2,000, 95 percent of the tax bill for those with an income between $2,000 and $3,000, and diminishing percentages to the $9,000 to $10,000 income level, at which it pays 20 percent of the tax. As in all circuit-breakers, the state limits the largest credit that can be received. A circuit-breaker may be administered either as an income-tax credit or as a free-standing program for which an application must be filed. [Gold, "Circuit-breakers and Other Relief Measures," C.L. Harriss, ed., The Property Tax and Local Finance 148, 149 (1983).*]

The development of circuit-breaker legislation in this country is treated in Chapter 4, § 3, Note H, p. 149 supra. See generally Gold, "Circuit-breakers and Other Relief Measures," supra.

* Reprinted with the permission of the Academy of Political Science.

Chapter 15

IMMUNITY OF FEDERAL INSTRUMENTALITIES FROM STATE TAXATION

SECTION 1. HISTORICAL OVERVIEW

The origins of the doctrine that the Federal Government and its instrumentalities are immune from State taxation lie in the seminal case of McCulloch v. Maryland, 17 U.S. (4 Wheat.) 316 (1819). In *McCulloch*, the Court confronted a Maryland tax levied on notes issued by any bank not chartered by the State. No equivalent levy was imposed on Maryland banks. The only bank in Maryland actually fitting the statutory description was the Bank of the United States, created and incorporated by an act of Congress. In Chief Justice Marshall's landmark opinion, the Court held that Congress had constitutional authority to create the Bank and that Maryland's levy upon it was invalid under the Supremacy Clause:

> The question is, in truth, a question of supremacy; and if the right of the States to tax the means employed by the general government be conceded, the declaration that the constitution, and the laws made in pursuance thereof, shall be the supreme law of the land, is empty and unmeaning declamation. [17 U.S. (4 Wheat.) at 320–21.]

McCulloch involved a tax that discriminated against the the operations of the Federal Government, and Chief Justice Marshall was careful to point out that the implied prohibition against State taxation of the Federal Government would

> not extend to a tax paid by the real property of the bank, in common with other real property within the state, nor to a tax imposed on the interest which citizens of Maryland may hold in this institution in common with other property of the same description throughout the state. [17 U.S. (4 Wheat.) at 436.]

Nevertheless, decisions following *McCulloch* broadened the scope of the immunity into a prohibition against State taxes upon the Federal Government and its instrumentalities, and, for a period, even to the invalidation of taxes on the receipts or income of persons who contracted with or worked for the Federal Government. Chief Justice Marshall's celebrated dictum in *McCulloch* —"the power to tax involves the power to destroy," 17 U.S. (4 Wheat.) at 431—was also invoked by the Court to invalidate gross receipts taxes on Federal contractors, see, e.g., Panhandle Oil Co. v. Mississippi ex rel. Knox, 277 U.S. 218, 48 S.Ct. 451 (1928), and income taxes on the wages of Federal employees, see, e.g., Dobbins v. Commissioners of Erie County, 41 U.S. (16 Pet.) 435 (1842). Taxes on the profits derived from exploitation of oil and gas leases on Indian lands, see, e.g., Gillespie v. Oklahoma, 257 U.S. 501, 42 S.Ct. 171 (1922), and license taxes on the business of a telegraph company performing Postal Office work, see Leloup v. Port of Mobile, 127 U.S. 640, 8 S.Ct. 1380 (1888), were held unconstitutional.

The pressure on the Court to narrow Chief Justice Marshall's "rhetorical absolute"[1] intensified as the Federal Government's commercial role increased and with it the volume of activity exempt from State taxation. Beginning in the 1930's, the Court reformulated the doctrine of Federal immunity from State taxation and dramatically cut back on its scope, especially with regard to the derivative immunity that the Court had accorded to the private sector in its dealing with the Federal Government and its agencies. Thus in James v. Dravo Contracting Co., 302 U.S. 134, 58 S.Ct. 208 (1937), the Court repudiated the rule that a State tax is invalid if it increases the cost of the Federal Government's operations in upholding a gross receipts tax imposed on receipts from the construction of dams and locks for the Federal Government. The Court declared that even if "the gross receipts tax may increase the cost to the government, that fact would not invalidate the tax." 302 U.S. at 160, 58 S.Ct. at 221. It relied instead on a "practical criterion" that would sustain the application of State taxation "to those subjects which fall within the general application of nondiscriminatory laws, and where no direct burden is laid upon the governmental instrumentality." 302 U.S. at 150, 58 S.Ct. at 216. Shortly thereafter, the Court upheld a New York income tax on an employee of the Federal Home Owners' Loan Association, saying:

> So much of the burden of a non-discriminatory general tax upon the incomes of employees of a government, state or national, as may be passed on economically to that government, through the effect of the tax on the price level of labor or materials, is but the normal incident of the organization within the same territory of two governments, each possessing the taxing power. The burden, so far as it can be said to exist or to affect the government in any indirect or incidental way, is one which the Constitution presupposes, and hence it cannot rightly be deemed to be within an implied restriction upon the taxing power of the national and state governments which the Constitution has expressly granted to one and has confirmed to the other. The immunity is not one to be implied from the Constitution, because if allowed it

1. New York v. United States, 326 U.S. 572, 576, 66 S.Ct. 310 (1946) (Frankfurter, J., concurring).

would impose to an inadmissible extent a restriction on the taxing power which the Constitution has reserved to the state governments. [Graves v. New York ex rel. O'Keefe, 306 U.S. 466, 487, 59 S.Ct. 595, 601 (1939).]

The process of delineating the precise bounds of the Federal Government's immunity from State taxation continues with every term of the Court. Broadly speaking, however, modern case law has narrowed the immunity to a proscription against taxes whose legal incidence falls on the United States and its instrumentalities and to levies that discriminate against the Federal Government. See Washington v. United States, 460 U.S. 536, 540, 103 S.Ct. 1344 (1983); United States v. New Mexico, 455 U.S. 720, 102 S.Ct. 1373 (1982); United States v. County of Fresno, 429 U.S. 452, 457–64, 97 S.Ct. 699 (1977); W. Hellerstein, "State Taxation and the Supreme Court: Toward a More Unified Approach to Constitutional Adjudication," 75 Mich.L.Rev. 1426, 1434–41, 1446–54 (1977).

SECTION 2. THE IMMUNITY OF STATE INSTRUMENTALITIES FROM FEDERAL TAXATION

Collector v. Day, 78 U.S. (11 Wall.) 113 (1870), was the first case invalidating a Federal tax on a State instrumentality. For the next 67 years the doctrine was applied equally to Federal and State instrumentalities, except for the development of the rule that a State or locality is not protected by the immunity doctrine when it engages in business of a private, non-governmental character. South Carolina v. United States, 199 U.S. 437, 26 S.Ct. 110 (1905); Ohio v. Helvering, 292 U.S. 360, 54 S.Ct. 725 (1934). This "doctrine of functions" has never been applied to the Federal government. In Helvering v. Gerhardt, 304 U.S. 405, 58 S.Ct. 969 (1938), in sustaining a Federal income tax on salaries of State employees, the Court reiterated the distinction drawn by Chief Justice Marshall in McCulloch v. Maryland, 17 U.S. (4 Wheat.) 316 (1819), between the position of the national government, representative of the entire country (and acting with powers of supremacy under the Constitution), and the States, which are not subject to a similar restraint. See also State of New York v. United States, 326 U.S. 572, 66 S.Ct. 310 (1946); Massachusetts v. United States, 435 U.S. 444, 98 S.Ct. 1153 (1978) (upholding the application of a Federal excise tax on civil aircraft to a State police helicopter); State of South Carolina v. Baker, ___ U.S. ___, 108 S.Ct. 1355 (1988) (sustaining constitutionality of denial of Federal tax exemption for interest from unregistered State and local bonds and declaring that doctrine of intergovernmental tax immunity did not bar Federal income taxation of State and local bond interest).

In an exhaustive review of the intergovernmental immunities doctrine, one commentator has concluded that "since the beginning of 1938, it is apparent that the Court has rejected the reciprocal rule of immunity, returned to the basis of earlier decisions and reaffirmed Chief Justice Marshall's understanding that the immunity doctrine protected the Federal Government against taxation by the States but did not equally shield the States against the exercise of the delegated and supreme taxing power of the Federal Government." Rakestraw, "The Reciprocal Rule of Governmental Tax Immunity—A Legal Myth," 11 Feb.B.J. 3, 27 (1950), quoted with the consent of the Federal Bar Association.

Some States tax the interest on bonds issued by other States and their political subdivisions, while refraining from taxing the interest on their own bonds (and, of course, on the bonds of the Federal Government). Is there any constitutional objection to this practice? If so, what would be the basis for the constitutional argument? See Dominion Nat. Bank v. Olsen, 771 F.2d 108 (6th Cir.1985).

SECTION 3. THE IMMUNITY OF INTEREST ON STATE AND LOCAL BONDS FROM FEDERAL INCOME TAXATION

Whatever there remains of the *constitutional* immunity of State instrumentalities from Federal taxation, see Section 2 supra, Congress has by statute exempted the interest on State and local bonds from Federal income taxation. I.R.C. § 103. In 1968, Congress limited the extent to which "industrial development bonds" could qualify for the exemption by imposing restrictions on the size of the issue ($1 million or, in some cases, $5 million), unless the proceeds therefrom were used for specified exempt activities. I.R.C. § 103(c). Such bonds have been widely used by cities, counties, and taxing districts to buy land and/or construct buildings for new industry in order to attract such industry to the locality. See N.Y. Times, Business Section, October 17, 1971. The limitations imposed by I.R.C. § 103(c) were the "result of voluminous attacks on the concept of subsidization of industry by state and local governments utilizing tax-exempt bonding." O. Oldman & F. Schoettle, State and Local Taxes and Finance 810 (1974).

In 1984 and 1986, Congress imposed substantial additional limitations on the use of tax-exempt financing for private purposes. See I.R.C. §§ 103, 141–50. The limitations are based on the purpose for which the proceeds of the financing are used. Id. Although interest from bonds used to finance traditional governmental functions such as schools, roads, and sewers remains exempt, all other bonds are denominated "private activity bonds" and the income therefrom is exempt only if the bonds meet specific criteria for exemption. See I.R.C. §§ 141–50. The most important category of "private-activity bonds" that still qualifies for tax exemption is the "exempt facility bond," I.R.C. § 142 which includes bonds, 95 percent or more of the net proceeds of which are used to provide airports, docks and wharves, and water, heating, cooling, waste disposal, mass commuting, and similar facilities. See generally "Recent Trends in the Use of Tax–Exempt Bonds for Private Purposes, Hearings on the Administration's Fiscal Year 1983 Budget Proposal before the Senate Comm. on Finance, 97th Cong., 2d Sess. (1982).

SECTION 4. SALES, USE, GROSS RECEIPTS, AND OTHER EXCISE TAXES

In the companion cases of Alabama v. King & Boozer, 314 U.S. 1, 62 S.Ct. 43 (1941) and Curry v. United States, 314 U.S. 14, 62 S.Ct. 48 (1941), the Court considered the application of State sales and use taxes to contractors employed by the Federal Government. In both cases, the sales and use taxes were applied to purchases by the contractors who were performing under cost-plus contracts for the Federal Government. In both cases, the Court sustained the taxes. Chief Justice Stone, reaffirming the analysis he had articulated in Graves v. New York ex rel. O'Keefe, supra, observed that the fact that the economic burden of the tax was passed on to the United States was not a grounds for invalidating it under the immunity doctrine.

> So far as such a nondiscriminatory state tax upon the contractor enters into the cost of the materials to the Government, that is but a normal incident of the organization within the same territory of two independent taxing sovereignties. The asserted right of the one to be free of taxation by the other does not spell immunity from paying the added costs, attributable to the taxation of those who furnish supplies to the Government and who have been granted no tax immunity. [314 U.S. at 8–9, 62 S.Ct. at 45.]

Moreover,

> [t]he added circumstance that [the federal contractors] were bound by their contract to furnish the purchased material to the Government and entitled to be reimbursed by it for the cost, including the tax, no more results in an infringement of the Government immunity than did the tax laid upon the contractor's gross receipts from the Government in James v. Dravo Contracting Co. [supra]. [314 U.S. at 14, 62 S.Ct. at 47.]

In light of the Court's explicit rejection of the "economic burden" test as a criterion for determining the constitutional immunity of the Federal Government from State taxation, the critical constitutional issue—apart from any question of discrimination—became whether the "legal incidence" of the tax fell on the Federal Government or its instrumentalities. In Kern–Limerick, Inc. v. Scurlock, 347 U.S. 110, 74 S.Ct. 403 (1954), the Court struck down the application of a sales tax to a Federal Government contractor. Even though the substance of the underlying transaction in *Kern–Limerick* was in all essential respects identical to the transaction in *King & Boozer,* the Court struck down the tax because the contractor was deemed, under the applicable contract, to be a "purchasing agent" for the Federal Government. Hence the "legal incidence" of the tax fell on the Federal Government as purchaser rather than on the contractor. The Court acknowledged that the contract in *Kern–Limerick* "differs in form but not in economic substance" from the contract in *King & Boozer* and that "the form of contracts, when governmental immunity is not waived by Congress, may determine the effect of state taxation on federal agencies, for decisions consistently prohibit taxes levied on the property or purchases of the Government itself." 347 U.S. at 122–23, 74 S.Ct. at 410–411.

In Mississippi v. State Tax Comm'n, 421 U.S. 599, 95 S.Ct. 1872 (1975), the Court found that a Mississippi regulation requiring out-of-state liquor distillers and suppliers to collect a wholesale markup on liquor sold to military installations amounted to an unconstitutional State tax on Federal instrumentalities. The Court perceived no difference between the markup and a sales tax, and it found that the legal incidence of the tax was intended to rest and did rest upon the Federal purchasers. In response to the State's contention that the wholesalers and not the Federal installations were liable for the tax, the Court noted that it had "squarely rejected the proposition that the legal incidence of a tax falls always upon the person legally liable for its payment." 421 U.S. at 607, 95 S.Ct. at 1877. Where, as in the case before it, "a state requires that its sales tax be passed on to the purchaser and be collected by the vendor from him, this establishes as a matter of law that the legal incidence of the tax falls upon the purchaser." Id. at 608, 95 S.Ct. at 1878.

The Court has also considered the question as to whether the government contractors are so inextricably involved with the Federal Government that they should be regarded as separate from the Government for purposes of the immunity doctrine. In United States v. New Mexico, 455 U.S. 720, 102 S.Ct. 1373 (1982), the United States conceded that the legal incidence of the sales and gross receipts taxes at issue fell on the government contractors, but argued that the contractors could not realistically be considered as entities independent of the United States. The Government's contention was rejected, but the Court acknowledged that its precedents in this area had been "confusing" (455 U.S. at 733, 102 S.Ct. at 1382). It reviewed the prior cases and said:

> What the Court's cases leave room for, then, is the conclusion that tax immunity is appropriate in only one circumstance: when the levy falls on the United States itself, or on an agency or instrumentality so closely connected to the Government that the two cannot realistically be viewed as separate entities, at least insofar as the activity being taxed is concerned. This view, we believe, comports with the principal purpose of the immunity doctrine, that of forestalling "clashing sovereignty," McCulloch v. Maryland, 4 Wheat., at 430, by preventing the States from laying demands directly on the Federal Government. See City of Detroit v. Murray Corp., 355 U.S., at 504–505 (opinion of Frankfurter, J.). As the federal structure—along with the workings of the tax immunity doctrine [11]—has evolved, this command has taken on

11. With the abandonment of the notion that the economic—as opposed to the legal—incidence of the tax is relevant, it becomes difficult to maintain that federal tax immunity is designed to insulate federal operations from the effects of state taxation. It remains true, of course, that state taxes on contractors are constitutionally invalid if they discriminate against the Federal Government, or substantially interfere with its activities. See United States v. County of Fresno, 429 U.S. 452, 463, n. 11, 464 (1977); Moses Lake Homes, Inc. v. Grant County, 365 U.S. 744 (1961);

essentially symbolic importance, as the visible "consequence of that [federal] supremacy which the constitution has declared." McCulloch v. Maryland, 4 Wheat., at 436. At the same time, a narrow approach to governmental tax immunity accords with competing constitutional imperatives, by giving full range to each sovereign's taxing authority. See Graves v. New York ex rel. O'Keefe, 306 U.S., at 483.

Thus, a finding of constitutional tax immunity requires something more than the invocation of traditional agency notions: to resist the State's taxing power, a private taxpayer must actually "stand in the Government's shoes." City of Detroit v. Murray Corp., 355 U.S., at 503 (opinion of Frankfurter, J.). That conclusion is compelled by the Court's principal decisions exploring the nature of the Constitution's immunity guarantee. Chief Justice Hughes' opinion for the Court in *James*, which set the doctrine on its modern course, suggested that a state tax is impermissible when the taxed entity is "so intimately connected with the exercise of a power or the performance of a duty" by the Government that taxation of it would be " 'a direct interference with the functions of government itself.' " 302 U.S., at 157, quoting Metcalf & Eddy v. Mitchell, 269 U.S. 514, 524 (1926). And the point is settled by [United States v. Boyd, 378 U.S. 39, 84 S.Ct. 1518 (1964), treated in Note A infra], the Court's most recent decision in the field. There, the Government argued that its contractors were tax-exempt because they were federal agents. Without any discussion of traditional agency rules the Court rejected that suggestion out-of-hand, declaring that "we cannot believe that [the contractors are] 'so assimilated by the Government as to become one of its constituent parts.' " 378 U.S., at 47, quoting United States v. Township of Muskegon, 355 U.S., at 486. And the Court continued:

> "Should the [Atomic Energy] Commission intend to build or operate the plant with its own servants and employees, it is well aware that it may do so and familiar with the ways of doing it. It chose not to do so here. We cannot conclude that [the contractors], both cost-plus contractors for profit, have been so incorporated into the government structure as to become instrumentalities of the United States and thus enjoy governmental immunity." 378 U.S., at 48.

The Court's other cases describing the nature of a federal instrumentality have used similar language: "virtually * * * an arm of the Government," Department of Employment v. United States, 385 U.S., at 359–360; "integral parts of [a governmental department]," and "arms of the Government deemed by it essential for the performance of governmental functions," Standard Oil Co. v. Johnson, 316 U.S. 481, 485 (1942).

Granting tax immunity only to entities that have been "incorporated into the government structure" can forestall, at least to a degree, some of the manipulation and wooden formalism that occasionally have marked tax litigation—and that have no proper place in deter-

City of Detroit v. Murray Corp., 355 U.S. 489, 495 (1958). New Mexico, however, is not discriminating here. [Footnote by the Court.—Eds.]

mining the allocation of power between co-existing sovereignties.
* * *

If the immunity of federal contractors is to be expanded beyond its narrow constitutional limits, it is Congress that must take responsibility for the decision, by so expressly providing as respects contracts in a particular form, or contracts under particular programs. James v. Dravo Contracting Co., 302 U.S., at 161; Carson v. Roane–Anderson Co., 342 U.S. 232, 234 (1952). And this allocation of responsibility is wholly appropriate, for the political process is "uniquely adapted to accommodating the competing demands" in this area. Massachusetts v. United States, 435 U.S. 444, 456 (1978) (plurality opinion). See United States v. City of Detroit, 355 U.S., at 474. But absent congressional action, we have emphasized that the States' power to tax can be denied only under "the clearest constitutional mandate." Michelin Tire Corp. v. Wages, 423 U.S. 276, 293 (1976). [455 U.S. at 735–38, 102 S.Ct. at 1383–1385.]

Notes and Problems

A. In Carson v. Roane–Anderson Co., 342 U.S. 232, 72 S.Ct. 257 (1952), the Atomic Energy Act was held to immunize from State sales tax purchases made by contractors with the Atomic Energy Commission, on the theory that the contractors were "agencies" of the Commission whose activities were covered by the explicit exemption provision of the Federal statute. The immunity provision on which the case was decided was repealed in 1953 as a result of the protest of the States in which the Atomic Energy Commission maintained large installations and operations. 60 Stat. 765 (1946), as amended by 67 Stat. 575, 42 U.S.C.A. § 1809(b).

In 1955 Tennessee, which had suffered the adverse decision in the *Roane–Anderson* case, amended its sales tax statute by adding a contractor's use tax, which was imposed on contractors using property in the performance of their contracts, regardless of the ownership of the property by persons exempt from sales tax (other than churches and property used for church construction). Again, contractors with the Atomic Energy Commission, Union Carbide Corp. and H.K. Ferguson Co., operating the Oak Ridge Atomic Energy complex, sought immunity, this time from the Tennessee sales and contractor's use taxes. The Court sustained the validity of the levies, rejecting the contention that "under the present contracts Carbide's and Ferguson's use of government property is not used by them for their own commercial advantage which the State may tax but a use exclusively for the benefit of the United States." United States v. Boyd, 378 U.S. 39, 84 S.Ct. 1518 (1964), noted in 17 Vand.L.Rev. 1543 (1964). Compare the technique used by Tennessee of levying a contractor's use tax with the method employed, also successfully, by Michigan in the property tax area of levying tax on lessees of property owned by the United States. See Section 5 infra.

B. *Mortgage Recording Tax.* A contractor who built a group of houses at the Plattsburgh Air Force Base on land leased from the United States borrowed money from a commercial bank to finance the project. The loans, secured by mortgages on the leased property, were insured by the

Federal Housing Administration. The contractor contested the validity of the mortgage recording tax enacted by the State of New York. The contractor contended that it was an instrumentality of the United States and that the levy violated the provision of the Housing Act of 1956 (12 U.S.C. §§ 1748–1748h). In sustaining the tax the court held that the tax was imposed, not on a leasehold or other Federal property covered by the Housing Act, but on the privilege of recording the mortgage, which was not reached by the statute. Matter of Silberblatt, Inc. v. State Tax Commission, 5 N.Y.2d 635, 159 N.E.2d 195 (1959), cert. denied 361 U.S. 912, 80 S.Ct. 253 (1959).

C. *Tax on Net Worth or Capital and Surplus, Including Federal Bonds.* New Jersey levied a tax against the intangible personal property of a domestic title insurance corporation, in the amount of 15 percent of its paid up capital and surplus. The value of United States Government bonds held by the taxpayer was not deducted in making the assessment. The taxing statute imposed, in the case of certain types of insurance companies, a tax "upon the full amount or value of its [intangible] property," but allowed a deduction for debts, reserves, and Federal obligations. However, it also provided that "the assessment against the intangible property * * * shall in no event be less than fifteen percentum of the sum of the paid-up capital and the surplus in excess of * * * all liabilities."

In sustaining a tax measured by the 15 percent minimum of net worth, inclusive of Federal bonds held, the New Jersey Supreme Court held that the "tax levied is not an ad valorem tax or property tax but rather is a * * * tax upon the net worth of the company," which was not within the protection of the intergovernmental immunity. The Supreme Court reversed (New Jersey Realty Title Insurance Co. v. Division of Tax Appeals, 338 U.S. 665, 70 S.Ct. 413 [1950]), declaring:

> It matters not whether the tax is, as appellee contends, an indirect or excise levy on net worth measured by corporate capital and surplus or is, as appellant urges, a tax on personal property based on a valuation gauged by capital and surplus. Our inquiry is narrowed to whether in practical operation and effect the tax is in part a tax upon federal bonds. We can only conclude that the tax authorized by § 54:4–22, whether levied against capital and surplus less liabilities or against entire net worth, is imposed on such securities regardless of the accounting label employed in describing it.

> * * *

> If the assessment is considered to be 15 per cent of capital and surplus less liabilities or of entire net worth, we agree with the court below that the tax levied under § 54:4–22 does not impose a discriminatory burden on federal issues as did the tax statute against which § 3701 was invoked in Missouri Ins. Co. v. Gehner, 281 U.S. 313, 50 S.Ct. 326 (1930). But since the decision in Bank of Commerce v. New York City, supra, it has been understood that a tax on corporate capital measured by federal securities may be invalid even though imposed without discrimination against federal obligations.

> If, however, the assessment of $75,700 is viewed as if it were levied exclusively upon appellant's net worth remaining after deduction of

government bonds and interest, the assessment would be discriminatory since it would be levied at the rate of over 79 per cent of appellant's assessable valuation of $94,936.87 rather than at the rate of 15 per cent prescribed by § 54:4–22. Such increased rate of assessment would result solely from appellant's ownership of federal issues. In the *Gehner* case, supra, this Court held that § 3701 was offended by a computation which allowed deduction of the full amount of the taxpayer's federal bonds yet at the same time pared down the net value of other allowable exemptions, to the taxpayer's disadvantage, solely because of such ownership of federal bonds. Consistently with the *Gehner* decision, we can only hold that § 3701 is violated by an automatic increase in the rate of assessment applied to appellant's valuation after deduction of federal bonds. [338 U.S. at 673–75.]

Mr. Justice Black dissented, taking the position that the levy was in essence a franchise tax, and as such ought to have been sustained. When treated as a property tax, the Justice contended that actual property taxed—some $75,000 in value on the 15 percent net worth basis—did not embrace Federal bonds, since the corporation had more than $75,000 in nonexempt intangibles. On the facts, he denied the existence of discrimination against corporations owning government bonds. The New Jersey case is discussed in Note, "The Supreme Court, 1949 Term," 64 Harv.L.Rev. 114, 134 (1950). Cf. Idaho Compensation Co. v. Hubbard, 70 Idaho 59, 211 P.2d 413 (1949), in which a lower rate of gross premiums tax was applied to insurers at least 50 percent of whose assets were invested in securities issued by the State or in taxable property. The statute was unsuccessfully attacked by an insurance company, the bulk of whose assets were invested in exempt Federal securities.

D. *Franchise Tax Measured by Net Income, Including Interest on Federal Securities.* State tax commissioners viewed with alarm the possible impact of the New Jersey case on the long-established practice of including in the measure of franchise taxes securities issued by the Federal Government and its instrumentalities and the interest on such securities. An Ohio decision gave credence to these fears by holding the New Jersey case applicable to the State's franchise tax. Wren Paper Co. v. Glander, 156 Ohio St. 583, 103 N.E.2d 756 (1952). The Supreme Court, however, held to the contrary in Werner Machine Co. v. Division of Taxation, 350 U.S. 492, 76 S.Ct. 534 (1956), determining that the New Jersey case did not preclude the inclusion of Federal bonds in the measure of a franchise tax.

E. *Nature of Tax and Immunity.* The key importance of the nature of the tax and the determination of who is the taxpayer in the intergovernmental immunities field was re-emphasized by the decision in Society for Savings in City of Cleveland v. Bowers, 349 U.S. 143, 75 S.Ct. 607 (1955). Two mutual savings banks, having no capital or shareholders, protested the inclusion in the measure of a tax assessed against them of the value of United States bonds. They contended that the levy was a property tax on the book value of "capital employed or the property representing it at the aggregate amount of the capital, the surplus or reserve fund, and the undivided profits" (Ohio Gen.Code, §§ 5408 and 5412). The State court upheld the levy imposed at the rate of two mills on the dollar as a tax on the depositors, not the banks. It concluded that the tax was imposed on the "intangible property interests of the depositors," who are the owners of the mutual savings bank, measured by the capital, surplus, and undivided profits. It relied on the cases holding that the States may impose a tax on stockholders' interests in State banks, even though the value of such interests takes into account the Federal bonds owned by the bank. Cleveland Trust Co. v. Lander, 184 U.S. 111, 22 S.Ct. 394 (1902). And the State may require the bank to act as a collecting agent for the tax. Corry v. Mayor and Council of Baltimore, 196 U.S. 466, 25 S.Ct. 297 (1905).

The Supreme Court, however, unanimously reversed the Ohio court (Mr. Justice Burton did not participate) and held that the levy was imposed on the banks, not the depositors. It did so on the grounds that: (1) the language of the statute contains no hint that it is imposed on the depositors; (2) the banks are given no right to recover the tax from the depositors, which the Court thought would be the case if the banks were merely tax collectors; and (3) there is no provision in case the banks should be unable to pay the tax for the State to move directly against the depositors. The Court rejected the State's argument that these provisions were unnecessary, since the assets out of which the tax was paid were the depositor's assets. In reaching its conclusion, the Court said:

> The Ohio court, however, has held that this tax is imposed on the depositors. But that does not end the matter for us. We must judge the true nature of this tax in terms of the rights and liabilities which the statute, as construed, creates. In assessing the validity of the tax under federal law we are not bound by the State's conclusion that the tax is imposed on the depositors, even though we would be bound by the State court's decision as to what rights and liabilities this statute establishes under State law. The court's mere conclusion that the tax is imposed on the depositors is no more than a characterization of the tax. "Where a federal right is concerned we are not bound by the characterization given to a State tax by State courts or Legislatures, or relieved by it from the duty of considering the real nature of the tax and its effect upon the federal right asserted." Carpenter v. Shaw, 1930, 280 U.S. 363, 367, 50 S.Ct. 121, 123, 74 L.Ed. 478. * * * "Neither ingenuity in calculation nor form of words in State enactments can deprive the owner of the tax exemption established for the benefit of the United States." Missouri ex rel. Missouri Ins. Co. v. Gehner, 1930, 281 U.S. 313, 321, 50 S.Ct. 326, 328, 74 L.Ed. 870. [349 U.S. at 151, 75 S.Ct. at 612.]

SECTION 5. PROPERTY TAXES

In three companion cases, the imposition of property taxes on interests of contractors in property owned by the Federal Government was considered. United States v. City of Detroit, 355 U.S. 466, 78 S.Ct. 474 (1958) (*Detroit*); United States v. Township of Muskegon, 355 U.S. 484, 78 S.Ct. 483 (1958) (*Muskegon*); City of Detroit v. Murray Corp., 355 U.S. 489, 78 S.Ct. 458 (1958) (*Murray*). *Detroit* and *Muskegon* presented essentially the same question under a Michigan statute providing that tax-exempt property used by a private party in a business conducted for profit "shall be subject to taxation in the same amount and to the same extent as though the lessee or user were the owner of such property." The contractor in *Detroit* leased property from the Federal Government for use in his private business. The contractor in *Muskegon* used the Federal Government's property under a permit in the performance of his contracts with the Government. In both cases, the tax was imposed on the contractor and measured by the value of the tax-exempt property.

Both taxes were sustained. In *Detroit,* the Court rejected the Government's argument "that since the tax is measured by the value of the property used it should be treated as nothing but a contrivance to lay a tax on the property." 355 U.S. at 470, 78 S.Ct. at 476. The Court observed that "it may be permissible for a state to measure a tax imposed on a valid subject of state taxation by taking into account Government property which is itself tax exempt." 355 U.S. at 471, 78 S.Ct. at 477. On this ground, the Court distinguished its earlier decision in United States v. Allegheny County, 322 U.S. 174, 64 S.Ct. 908 (1944), in which it had invalidated an ad valorem property tax on Government property used by contractors with the Government. A dissenting opinion, relying on *Allegheny,* accused the Court of elevating form over substance, declaring that it was "crystal clear" that the tax is a "direct imposition upon the Government's property interests." 355 U.S. at 478, 78 S.Ct. at 480.

In upholding the levy in *Muskegon,* the Court held that it was controlled by the principles articulated in *Detroit.* There were only two factual differences between *Detroit* and *Muskegon:* the taxpayer in *Muskegon* was not using the Federal property under a formal lease, as was the case in *Detroit,* but under a "permit"; and the taxpayer, unlike the situation in *Detroit,* was using the property in performance of its contracts with the Federal Government. With regard to the lease versus permit issue, the Court declared that "[c]onstitutional immunity from state taxation does not rest on such insubstantial formalities as whether the party using government property is formally designated a 'lessee,'" 355 U.S. at 486, 78 S.Ct. at 485, because immunity could then be conferred "by a simple stroke of a draftsman's pen." Id. What was critical was that the taxpayer was using the property in connection with its own commercial activities. With regard to the fact that the taxpayer was using the property in the performance of Government contracts, the Court also found the distinction immaterial. The taxpayer "was not so assimilated by the Government to become one of its constituent parts," id., and although "[i]n a certain loose way it might be called an 'instrumentality' of the United States," it would be "no more so than any other private party supplying goods for his own gain to the Government." 355 U.S. at 486–87, 78 S.Ct. at 485.

Murray presented a slightly different issue. The case again involved a Government contractor that used Federally-owned property in performing its contracts, but the statute provided that "[t]he owners or persons in possession of any personal property shall pay all taxes assessed thereon." See 355 U.S. at 489, 78 S.Ct. at 458. The Court again rejected the argument that this amounted to a direct tax on the Federal Government's property, finding the case indistinguishable in substance from *Detroit* and *Muskegon:* "We see no essential difference so far as constitutional tax immunity is concerned between taxing a person for using property he possesses and taxing him for possessing property he uses when in both instances he uses the property for his own private ends." 355 U.S. at 493, 78 S.Ct. at 461.

In United States v. County of Fresno, 429 U.S. 452, 97 S.Ct. 699 (1977), the principles of the *Detroit–Muskegon–Murray* trilogy were invoked in sustaining the constitutionality of a local tax on possessory interests in houses owned by the United States Government that were rented to Federal employees. The Taxpayers, who were employees of the United States Forest service, and worked in national forests, were required to live in Government houses in the forests. The Forest Service deducted from salaries of the employees the fair rental value of the housing. The Court found that the legal incidence of the tax fell on the employees, not on the Federal Government, and that the *Detroit–Muskegon–Murray* cases are equally applicable to Federal property used for personal purposes, as to property used in a business.

Notes and Problems

A. *The Magnitude of Tax Immune Federal Property.*

PAYMENTS IN LIEU OF TAXES ON FEDERAL REAL PROPERTY

Report of the Advisory Commission on Intergovernmental Relations
(Report A–90, 1981), pp. 1–18

The federal government is the single largest owner of real property in the United States. It currently owns 775.3 million acres, more than one-third of the country's entire land area. In addition, it owns 23,988 installations, 2,598 million square feet of floor area, and various other buildings and structures and facilities. In 1978, the total value of U.S. real property was valued at approximately $279 billion, 23% in land, 53% in buildings, and 24% in structures and facilities.

These holdings include forest reserves, office buildings, harbors, housing projects, grazing lands, waterways, airports, cemeteries, hospitals, defense bases, parks, power lines, utility systems, museums, industrial facilities, communications systems, railroads, navigation and traffic aids, monuments and memorials, and even islands used for military target practice. Moreover, the magnitude of these holdings can be expected to grow. * * *

The incidence of federally owned properties varies widely across the 50 states. They are located in both rural and urban areas, and are industrial and nonindustrial, residential and commercial, permanent and semipermanent. Some of them provide largely local services, while others are regionally or nationally oriented. Some profoundly affect the fiscal and economic base of their communities, while others have only the most minor of impacts.

The one generalization that can best be made regarding the array of federally owned property is that there is no guiding principle regarding the extent to which the federal government as a property owner should contribute to the financial support of state and local governments. Some local governments share in the revenues generated by federal establishments operating within their borders, primarily from mineral leasing or from the sale of grazing, farming, and forestry rights to private interests. On other properties, Congress has recognized a responsibility for a partial or full payment in lieu of taxes (PILOT) to state and local governments as compensation for property taxes foregone. For some of its instrumentalities, such as its various banking and credit institutions, the federal government has authorized the full range of direct state/local taxation. Most commonly, however, the Congress has declared the U.S. government exempt from both direct state/local taxation as well as from any in lieu of tax responsibility. This is true despite the fact that, over the years, its own committees and study groups have recommended enactment of some form of uniform payment system to compensate all states and localities for the effect of the federal presence on property tax revenues. Indeed, in 1969, the Joint Economic Committee of the U.S. Congress, arguing "only basic equity," urged that Congress make payments in lieu of real property taxes on property owned by both the U.S. government and foreign governments (embassies, consulates, missions) in the U.S.

* * *

Major Conclusions

A number of major conclusions have been drawn by the Commission staff based on the research findings associated with the broad scope of this study. These conclusions are:

A. The federal government lacks any procedure that permits it to know the current value of its real property holdings in the U.S. Except for the estimates for 1978 made in this report, there is no inventory of the total value of tax immune federal property. In order to receive useful information for policy regarding the federal government's property wealth, Congress must require that the General Services Administration make major adjustments in its methods of collecting information.

* * *

B. The Nature of the Legal Framework for Property Tax Immunity Has Changed Over Time.

* * *

C. Federal tax exemptions erode a large part of state and local tax bases.

Several arguments can be marshaled both for and against any type of institutional exemption from a comprehensive tax base. The justification given for exemptions range from the "need" to provide locational incentives to some private firms, to the simple fact that the exemption is mandated by a higher level of government and therefore is beyond local control. The arguments against exemptions usually center on the concerns for taxpayer equity and economic efficiency, and the erosion of the local tax base. Each of these topics has been examined in this report as it relates specifically to the immunity of the federal government from state and local taxation.

From an overall local policy perspective, perhaps the most important of these issues centers on the local government revenue loss from real property tax exemption. In the context of the federal immunity issue, this loss is, indeed, quite large. In 1978, the current dollar value of all federally owned property in the U.S. that was exempt from real property taxation amounted to $279 billion. If one excludes "open space" lands (as is proposed in Chapter 3 of this study), the total erosion amounts to $210 billion. To put this in perspective, if this $210 billion were fully taxable, and no other adjustments were made in current property tax rates or federal payment programs, $3.65 billion would have been added to state and, primarily, local treasuries (96%). This is equivalent to an increase in total local property collections of almost 6%.

If local governments could make up for this revenue loss by simply using nonproperty tax sources more extensively, the policy concern regarding this erosion of the revenue base might not be so important. However, the "open economy" * characteristic of subnational government virtually dictates that local governments must employ taxes on immovable property as the mainstay of their own-source revenues. Moreover, in the present fiscal environment, which provides for a growing local dependency upon outside—state and federal—aid to local governments, the maintenance of own-source revenues to meet both traditional and recently mandated costs at the local level has become more important.

Stated otherwise, if an accepted goal of U.S. federalism is to have a financially strong and independent local government sector that is able to carry out peculiarly local functions—such as the provisions of police, fire, and judicial protection, public education, and low to moderate income housing services—then a closer look at the policy of federal real property tax immunity is clearly warranted.

D. The federal immunity from state and local taxes violates major equity principles of public finance.

Because the federal government is exempt from paying state and local taxes on most of its activities and properties, a basic equity principle of public finance is violated: that "taxpayers" (herein, institutions) in similar circumstances should be treated similarly. This equity violation arises both when the direct property taxpaying status of private institutions is juxtaposed with that of federal government agencies and instrumentalities and when the indirect taxable status of

---

* An open economy is characterized by a high degree of mobility of goods and factor movements across jurisdictional borders— activities which a local government cannot constrain.

federal leasehold activity is contrasted with the exempt nature of federal property ownership.

* * *

E. Although Congress has recognized a responsibility to some local governments for making some form of in lieu of tax payment to "compensate" for the federal presence, the result has been a patchwork of uncoordinated and ad hoc federal payment programs that has developed over the years.

* * *

F. In general, existing federal grant programs are not designed to compensate subnational governments for revenue losses which result from the federal government tax immunity.

* * *

G. Authorization for either full real property taxation of the federal government or a full tax equivalency system of payments in lieu of real property taxes is an appropriate policy response to the status quo.

* * *

H. Real property taxation of the federal government or a full tax equivalency system of payments in lieu of real property taxes is a workable policy response to the status quo. [End of excerpt from ACIR report.]

In addition to the report excerpted above, see Advisory Commission on Intergovernmental Relations, The Adequacy of Federal Compensation to Local Governments for Tax Exempt Lands, Report A–68 (1978); Report of the Property Taxation Committee to the 65th Annual Conference of the National Tax Association (1972), reprinted in 40 Tax Policy 1 (1972); Rasmuseen, "Payments to State and Local Governments on Account of Federal Real Property," 1956 Nat.Tax Ass'n Procs. 284. In the Brief for the United States in Petition for Rehearing in the City of Detroit v. Murray Corp., supra, it was estimated that the Michigan cases would, if followed by all the States and local governments, subject the Defense Department to annual taxes of $452 million and the Atomic Energy Commission to annual taxes of $166 million. See Van Cleve, "States' Rights and Federal Solvency: A Recent Study of Supreme Court Decisions Permitting Local Taxation of the Possession of Federal Property," 1959 Wisc.L.Rev. 190, 207. See also Federal Ownership of Real Estate and its Bearing on State and Local Taxation, H.R.Doc. No. 111, 76th Cong., 1st Sess. (1939); Interim Report on Taxation of Public Property, H.R.Rep. No. 1884, 78th Cong., 2d Sess. (1944); Hearings on S.R. 2473 and H.R. 5605, Subcommittee on Legislative Program, Committee on Government Operations (83rd Cong., 2d Sess., June 2–3, 1954); Advisory Commission on Intergovernmental Relations, "Report to the President for Transmittal to the Congress" (the "Kestenbaum Report") and "A Study Committee Report on Payments in Lieu of Taxes and Shared Revenues" (1955).

B. *Relief From Immunity of Federal Property by Congressional Action.* Three principal methods are used by Congress in relieving Federal property from tax immunity:

(1) Payments to States and localities by the Federal instrumentality of a specified percentage of revenues from Federal operations. This method is used with respect to national forests, grazing and mineral lands, and other large tracts from which the Federal Government derives revenues from its own operations or from leasings, etc. The Tennessee Valley Authority pays to the local taxing authorities a percentage of its gross revenues from power sales, with a guaranteed minimum equal to the former property taxes paid on the acquired property.

(2) Payment by the Federal instrumentality of a tax equivalent out of revenue receipts or appropriations. Federal housing projects are the outstanding area in which that method is used.

(3) The waiver of Federal tax immunity by act of Congress. Real property acquired by the Reconstruction Finance Corporation on foreclosure and many war plants acquired during or after World War II are subject to local property tax as a result of Congressional action. See 47 Stat. 5, 9 (1932), 15 U.S.C. § 608, 55 Stat. 248, 15 U.S.C.A. § 610. In a Pennsylvania case, it was held that the effect of Congress' consent to local real property taxes is to authorize the imposition of a lien for the unpaid taxes so authorized. Borough of Homestead v. Defense Plant Corp., 356 Pa. 500, 52 A.2d 581 (1947). Generally speaking, however, no provision has been made for payments to or taxation by the States or localities for office buildings, court houses, post offices, and other property used for general governmental administration, hospitals, prisons, military and naval installations, and radio and meterological facilities.

It is not surprising to find that many State and local taxing officials, particularly in the Western States where Federal land holdings are most extensive, do not believe that the Federal Government has gone far enough in relieving its property from tax immunity. N.Y. Times, March 13, 1977. And it may well be, as a result of pressure from Western Congressmen, that Congress will move to increase the Federal Government's payments in this area. Representative Frank Evans of Colorado, where the Federal Government owns 24.1 million acres of land, introduced legislation to increase Federal payments in lieu of taxes; despite White House opposition on the ground that the measure would cost $100 million annually, preelection pressure from Western Republicans induced then President Ford to sign it. Id. Additional legislation was enacted by Congress in 1976 to give the States a larger share of the fees or rents collected by the Federal Government for use of Federal lands. Id.

C. *Vendee in Possession Under Contract of Purchase From Federal Agency.* When the Federal Government has entered into a contract for the sale of realty and the purchaser has taken possession but has not yet completed the payment of the purchase price, a condition which must be met before he receives the deed to the property, is the property subject to local ad valorem taxation? See S.R.A. Inc. v. State of Minnesota, 327 U.S. 558, 66 S.Ct. 749 (1946). May the purchaser's interest in such property be subjected to a tax lien? See 22 Ind.L.J. 192 (1947); 19 Rocky Mt.L.Rev. 407 (1947); 20 So.Calif.L.Rev. 212 (1947); 46 Col.L.Rev. 660 (1946).

D. *Taxation of Open Account Claim Against the United States.* The taxpayers, who had engaged in construction work for the United States, had a claim against the Government in the amount of approximately $30,000. The balance owing "was in the nature of an open account and represented an account receivable." A Georgia personal property tax assessed on this open account was assailed by the taxpayers as a levy on a Federal instrumentality. The Court rejected the contention, holding that an open account claim against the United States "does not represent a credit instrumentality of the Federal Government within the meaning of this constitutional immunity." Smith v. Davis, 323 U.S. 111, 113, 65 S.Ct. 157 (1944). It held that the obligations of the United States which are subject to the rule had been limited to interest bearing indebtedness issued to public creditors pursuant to act of Congress. The Court also pointed out that the taxation of the open account claim can in no sense embarrass the credit of the United States or its ability to secure aid from independent contractors for military and civilian construction projects. See Annot., 9 A.L.R.2d 515.

In an Illinois case, Ford Motor Company was held immune from a personal property tax on machinery, materials, and goods in process, purchased to manufacture airplane parts for the United States Air Force. While Ford bore the risk of loss until acceptance of the finished product by the government and had power of disposition and scrap rights in machinery and tools, the court, nevertheless, held that the government had title throughout, and that the company's rights were merely "possessory interests" that the Illinois statute, unlike the statutes involved in the Michigan cases, did not tax. Ford Motor Co. v. Korzen, 30 Ill.2d 314, 196 N.E.2d 656 (1964), cert. denied 379 U.S. 837, 85 S.Ct. 73 (1964), noted in 14 DePaul L.Rev. 217 (1964); 1964 U. of Ill.L.F. 680.

SECTION 6. STATE TAXES DISCRIMINATING AGAINST THE FEDERAL GOVERNMENT

From the very beginning of our constitutional history it has been clear that the States may not impose taxes discriminating against the Federal Government. See Section 1 supra. The narrowing of the Federal Government's immunity in cases involving nondiscriminatory taxes has not undermined this fundamental principle. For example, in Phillips Chemical Co. v. Dumas Independent School District, 361 U.S. 376, 80 S.Ct. 474 (1960), the Court held that a tax assessed against a private lessee of Federally-owned property was unconstitutional because no tax was assessed against private lessees of property owned by the State of Texas or its political subdivisions. See also Thiokol Chemical Corp. v. Morns County, 76 N.J.Super. 232, 184 A.2d 75 (1962), which held that Federal contractors occupying premises rent-free could not be taxed on their possessory interest, so long as contractors with similar interests in State-owned property were not taxed. The Court reached a similar conclusion in striking down a Tennessee tax on the net earnings of banks that included interest received on Federal but not on Tennessee obligations. Memphis Bank & Trust Co. v. Garner, 459 U.S. 392, 103 S.Ct. 692 (1983).[2]

In United States v. County of Fresno, discussed in Section 5 supra, the Court also addressed the claim that the possessory interest tax on the interests of the United States Forest Service employees in their Federally-owned residences violated the Supremacy Clause, because it discriminated against Federal employees. The Court found the levy nondiscriminatory, because it did not tax Federal employees living in Federally-owned houses differently from State employees living in State-owned houses. Justice Stevens dissented from this conclusion, because, in his view, the possessory interest tax applied only to publicly-owned realty, not to all tax-exempt property.

In Washington v. United States, 460 U.S. 536, 103 S.Ct. 1344 (1983), the Court considered a claim of discrimination against the Federal Government in the context of the State of Washington's sales and use tax as applied to Federal contractors. Washington generally places the legal incidence of its sales and use tax on the landowner who purchases construction work from the contractor. The tax is measured by the full cost of the construction contract, including markups. When construction work is performed for the United States on its property, however, the Supremacy Clause precludes the State from applying the tax to the United States as landowner. To prevent the Federal Government construction industry from escaping the State's sales tax, Washington provided that construction contractors who work for the Federal Government ("Federal contractors") should pay a sales tax on their purchases of materials.

The United States attacked this levy claiming that it discriminated against the Federal Government and those who deal with it by imposing a sales tax on purchases made by Federal contractors but not on purchases made by other contractors. The Court, while acknowledging the surface plausibility of the argument, responded:

> Washington does, however, impose a sales tax on all purchases from contractors who do not deal with the Federal Government. The tax is imposed on every construction transaction, and the tax rate is the same for everyone. The only deviation from equality between the Federal Government and federal contractors on the one hand, and every other taxpayer on the other, is that the former are taxed on a smaller percentage of the value of the project than the latter. * * * This hardly seems * * * to be the mistreatment of the Federal Government against which the Supremacy Clause protects. [460 U.S. at 541–42 (footnote omitted).]

In upholding the levy, the Court refused to focus solely on the tax that the contractor is required to pay, as the United States had urged,

---

2. Although the issue technically involved the question whether the tax violated the statutory prohibition against State taxation of Federal obligations, 31 U.S.C. § 742 (now 31 U.S.C. 3124), see Section 5 infra, the Court noted that "[o]ur decisions have treated 742 as principally a restatement of the constitutional rule." 459 U.S. at 397, 103 S.Ct. at 695.

because it viewed the critical question to be "whether a contractor who is considering working for the Federal Governement is faced with a cost he would not have to bear if he were to do the same thing for a private party." 460 U.S. at 541 n. 4, 103 S.Ct. at n. 4. This required the Court to consider the economic burden on the contractor and the owner together. Citing the *Detroit–Muskegon–Murray* trilogy and *County of Fresno,* the Court declared that the "important consideration ∗ ∗ ∗ is not whether the State differentiates in determining what entity shall bear the legal incidence of the tax, but whether the tax is discriminatory with regard to the economic burdens that result." 460 U.S. at 544, 103 S.Ct. at 1349. The Court further observed that Washington, rather than discriminating against the Federal Government, was "merely accommodat[ing] for the fact that it may not impose a tax directly on the United States as project owner." 460 U.S. at 546, 103 S.Ct. at 1350. See generally W. Hellerstein, "Complementary Taxes as a Defense to Unconstitutional State Tax Discrimination," 39 Tax Law. 405 (1986).

SECTION 7. FEDERAL STATUTORY RULES GOVERNING FEDERAL IMMUNITY FROM STATE TAXATION

The preceding discussion has dealt primarily with the implied *constitutional* immunity that the Federal Government and its instrumentalities enjoy from State taxation without regard to congressional legislation. Congress has the power to expand, modify, or waive that immunity by specific legislation. Indeed, it has generally been regarded as settled that Congress has full power to define the scope of immunity from State taxation for its agencies and instrumentalities employed in carrying out its powers under the Constitution. See Federal Land Bank of St. Paul v. Bismarck Lumber Co., 314 U.S. 95, 62 S.Ct. 1 (1941), in which the Court held that Congress has the power under the Necessary and Proper Clause of Article 1, Section 8 of the Federal Constitution, in furtherance of its lending functions, to immunize Federal Land Banks from State sales taxes.

The most important Congressional legislation providing immunity for the Federal Government and its instrumentalities from State taxation is directed at State taxation of Federal obligations and State taxation of national banks.

(a) State Taxation of Federal Obligations

The statutory immunity of Federal obligations from State taxation is rooted in the constitutional doctrine that the obligations of the United States are immune from State taxation. See Weston v. City of Charleston, 27 U.S. (2 Pet.) 449 (1829) (invalidating on constitutional grounds local property tax on Federal securities in the hands of the owner). In 1862, in order to assure the immunity of the increasing amount of Federal obligations that were issued in connection with the Civil War, Congress enacted a statute embodying the rule of *Weston.*

The statute, as amended in 1864, appeared for many years as Revised Statutes § 3701, 31 U.S.C. § 742, and provided:

> all stocks, bonds, Treasury notes, and other obligations of the United States, shall be exempt from taxation by or under State or municipal or local authority.

In construing this statute, the Supreme Court consistently held that the language prohibited State taxes imposed *on* Federal obligations as part of a tax on the taxpayer's property or assets. See, e.g., Society for Savings v. Bowers, 349 U.S. 143, 75 S.Ct. 607 (1955) (tax on total assets of a corporation is a tax on Federal obligations it owns), discussed in Section 4, Note E, p. 994 supra. At the same time, however, the Court held that Revised Statutes § 3701 did not prevent the States from imposing nondiscriminatory taxes on discrete property interests, such as corporate shares, or corporate or other franchises, even though the value of the interest was measured in part by United States obligations. As a consequence, corporate franchise taxes have long been measured by net income that includes income from United States Government obligations that may not be taxed directly. See, e.g., Reuben L. Anderson–Cherne, Inc. v. Commissioner, 303 Minn. 124, 226 N.W.2d 611 (1975), appeal dismissed 423 U.S. 886, 96 S.Ct. 181 (1975). The same is true of corporate franchise taxes measured by capital stock; United States Government obligations are includable in the tax measure. See, e.g., Home Ins. Co. v. New York, 134 U.S. 594, 10 S.Ct. 593 (1890). Similarly, the Court interpreted the statute as permitting taxes imposed on the right to take property by inheritance, even though the value of the inheritance was measured by the value of the Federal obligation transferred. Plummer v. Coler, 178 U.S. 115, 20 S.Ct. 829 (1900) (inheritance tax measured by value of the property passing). These cases depend on the formal distinction between the subject and the measure of the taxes involved. Income from United States obligations and the obligations themselves may not be made the subject of a tax, but they may be included in the tax measure. In 1956, the Court declared that this formal but economically meaningless distinction between taxes on Federal obligations and taxes on separate interests was "firmly embedded in the law." Society for Savings v. Bowers, supra, 349 U.S. at 148, 75 S.Ct. at 610.

Despite the Supreme Court's recognition that Revised Statutes § 3701 precluded direct taxation of the interest on Federal obligations as well as taxation of the underlying obligations themselves, see New Jersey Realty Title Ins. Co. v. Division of Tax Appeals, 338 U.S. 665, 675–76, 70 S.Ct. 413, 418–19 (1950), discussed in Section 4, Note C, p. 993 supra, the State of Idaho had taken the position that it could avoid the import of this holding by imposing a tax on individuals measured by such interest rather than imposing a tax on the interest itself. See American Bank and Trust Co. v. Dallas County, 463 U.S. 855, 866, 103 S.Ct. 3369, 3376 (1983) (discussing legislative history of Revised Statute § 3701). In response to this potential frustration of the purposes of

Revised Statute § 3701, Congress added the following language to the statute in 1959:

> This exemption extends to every form of taxation that would require that either the obligations or the interest thereon or both, be considered, directly or indirectly, in the computation of the tax, except nondiscriminatory franchise or other nonproperty taxes in lieu thereof imposed on corporations and except estate or inheritance taxes.[3]

In American Bank & Trust Co. v. Dallas County, supra, the Court considered the impact of the 1959 amendment on a State property tax on bank shares computed on the basis of the bank's net assets without any deduction for tax-exempt United States obligations held by the bank. The Court observed that the exemption for Federal obligations under the amended statute is "sweeping," extending to " '*every form* ' of taxation that would require that either the obligations or the interest thereon, or both, *be considered, directly or indirectly, in the computation of the tax.*" 463 U.S. at 862, 103 S.Ct. at 3374 (emphasis by the Court). Under this reading of the statute, the bank shares statute could not stand because Federal obligations were considered in computing the bank shares tax at issue. The tax was computed by the use of an "equity capital formula," which involved determining the amount of the bank's capital assets (including Federal obligations), subtracting from that figure the bank's liabilities and the assessed value of the bank's real estate, and then dividing the result by the number of shares.

In holding that Revised Statutes § 3701, as amended, barred a bank shares tax measured by Federal obligations, the Court left open the question whether a State must permit a bank to deduct from its net worth the full value of Federal obligations it holds or whether the State may limit the deduction to the portion of Federal obligations attributable to assets rather than liabilities. In Missouri ex rel. Missouri Insurance Co. v. Gehner, 281 U.S. 313, 50 S.Ct. 326 (1930), discussed in Section 4, Note C, p. 993 supra, the Court had held that Revised Statutes § 3701 prohibited a State from increasing an insurance company's personal property tax base by the liabilities proportionate to the amount of its tax-exempt Federal obligations, which had been subtracted from its taxable assets. The Court reasoned that the pro rata deduction violated § 3701 because it made ownership of United States bonds the basis for denying a full deduction of liabilities, and thereby increased the tax burden of the taxpayer.

---

3. In 1982, Revised Statutes § 3701, 31 U.S.C. § 742, was "reformulated without substantive change," see American Bank & Trust Co. v. Dallas County, supra, 463 U.S. at 859 n. 1, 103 S.Ct. at 3374 n. 3, as 31 U.S.C. § 3124. The statute now reads:

Stocks and obligations of the United States Government are exempt from taxation by a state or political subdivision of a state. The exemption applies to each form of taxation that would require the obligation, the interest on the obligation, or both, to be considered in computing a tax except—

(1) a nondiscriminatory franchise tax or another nonproperty tax instead of a franchise tax, imposed on a corporation; and

(2) an estate or inheritance tax.

In First National Bank of Atlanta v. Bartow County Board of Tax Assessors, 470 U.S. 583, 105 S.Ct. 1516 (1985), the Court revisited this question in connection with a Georgia bank shares tax. As construed prior to the *American Bank* case, Georgia's bank shares tax, which was measured by the fair market value of a bank's shares, included the value of United States obligations held by the bank. The Georgia Supreme Court sought to save the statute by construing it to allow a bank to deduct from its net worth the percentage of assets attributable to Federal obligations. The court rejected the banks' argument that the total value of the Federal obligations had to be subtracted from net worth under Revised Statutes § 3701, observing that such a deduction would not merely insulate Federal obligations from the tax but would go beyond the requirements of § 3701 by sheltering the bank's taxable assets from tax.

The Supreme Court agreed with the Georgia court and sustained the proportionate deduction. The Court recognized that if *Gehner* were controlling, the banks' argument would prevail because *Gehner* held that anything less than a full deduction for Federal obligations failed to satisfy the requirements of § 3701. 470 U.S. at 590–91, 105 S.Ct. at 1520–21. After reexamining *Gehner,* however, the Court concluded that its reasoning had been undermined by cases raising analogous problems. See United States v. Atlas Life Ins. Co., 381 U.S. 233, 85 S.Ct. 1379 (1965) (insurance company required to apportion tax-exempt interest between its gross income and policy holders' income). The Court therefore upheld the proportionate deduction of Federal obligations from the bank shares tax base declaring that Revised Statutes § 3701, as amended, requires only that " 'a State may not subject one to a greater tax burden upon his property because he owns tax-exempt government securities,' " 470 U.S. at 590, 105 S.Ct. at 1520 (quoting National Life Ins. Co. v. United States, 277 U.S. 508, 48 S.Ct. 591 (1928)).

(b) State Taxation of National Banks

The immunity of national banks from State taxation, like the immunity of Federal obligations, has constitutional roots that go back to McCulloch v. Maryland, 17 U.S. (4 Wheat.) 316 (1819). See Section 1 supra. Shortly after enacting the National Banking Act in 1863, Congress provided that the States could tax national banks only on their real estate and shares. 13 Stat. 111 (1864). This statute, which became known as Revised Statutes § 5219 (codified at 12 U.S.C. § 548), was amended in 1926 to provide that the States could tax national banks in four ways: (1) by taxing bank shares, (2) by including bank share dividends in the taxable income of a shareholder, (3) by taxing national banks on their net income, and (4) by levying a franchise tax on national banks measured by their net income. 44 Stat. 223 (1926).

In 1968, the Supreme Court held that 12 U.S.C. § 548 forbade the States from imposing sales and use taxes on a national bank's purchase of waste paper baskets, office supplies, and the like. First Agricultural National Bank of Berkshire County v. State Tax Commission, 392 U.S. 339, 88 S.Ct. 2173 (1968). The Supreme Court recognized the force of the contention that national banks, under present day conditions, were essentially indistinguishable from State banks and should not enjoy immunity from taxation as a Federal instrumentality. It nevertheless felt that the legislative history of 12 U.S.C. § 548 was clear in prescribing the only way in which the States may tax national banks and that "if a change is to be made in state taxation of national banks it must come from the Congress." 392 U.S. at 346, 88 S.Ct. at 2177. Justice Marshall vigorously dissented from the Court's opinion on the ground that national banks should no longer be considered as tax-immune Federal instrumentalities and that 12 U.S.C. § 548 should be construed only as limiting the types of taxes specifically mentioned in the statute. See also Dickinson v. First National Bank of Homestead, 393 U.S. 409, 89 S.Ct. 685 (1969) (invalidating Florida's mortgage recording and documentary stamp taxes on a national bank).

These cases jolted Congress into reexamining the existing immunities of national banks from State taxation.* In 1969, legislation was enacted directing the Federal Reserve Board to make a study of State and local taxation and to report to Congress its recommendations as to what, if any, further legislation "may be needed to reconcile the promotion of the economic efficiency of the banking systems of the nation with the achievement of effectiveness and local autonomy in meeting the fiscal needs of the States and their political subdivisions." [4] For the interim period, Congress enacted a temporary amendment to 12 U.S.C. § 548, which authorized the States and local governments to impose on national banks sales and use, real and tangible personal property, and documentary stamp taxes, and excises or other fees or taxes on the ownership or use of tangible personal property located within the jurisdiction, provided they are imposed generally throughout the jurisdiction on a nondiscriminatory basis.[5] The temporary amendment also empowered the States to apply to national banks having their principal offices in the State whatever taxes (other than taxes on intangible personal property) they levied generally, on a nondiscriminatory basis throughout the State or local government, to the same extent as they tax their own domestic State banks.[6] At the same time, a permanent amendment to the statute was adopted, which terminated, as of January 1, 1972, all Congressionally granted immunity of national banks from State taxation.[7] The effectiveness of the permanent

---

* The ensuing discussion in this Section is based on co-author J. Hellerstein's "Current Issues in Multistate Taxation of Banks," 30 Tax L.Rev. 155, 156–58 (1975), and is used with the consent of the copyright owner, New York University School of Law.

4. P.L. 91–156, 83 Stat. 434 (1969).

5. Id. at § 1.

6. Id.

7. Id. at § 2. For purposes of the permanent amendment, 12 U.S.C. § 548 was also amended to provide that a national bank is to be treated as a bank organized under the laws of the State or other jurisdiction in which its principal office is located.

amendment was postponed until September 12, 1976 because of the sharp conflicts between and among the commercial banks, savings banks, and savings and loan associations, and the States as to how far the States should be permitted by Congress to tax out-of-state domiciled depository institutions.[8] As of this writing, legislation further to restrict the power of the States to tax national banks has not been enacted. See generally McCray, "State Taxation of Interstate Banking," 21 Ga.L.Rev. 283, 290–94 (1986).

Apparently dissatisfied with the Federal Reserve Board's recommendations made in the report of its study in 1971 [9]—its most controversial proposal was that the power of the States and local governments to subject out-of-state depository institutions, Federal and State, to net income, gross receipts, capital stock or other doing business taxes should be limited and the rules for such taxation prescribed by Federal legislation—Congress in 1973 directed the Advisory Commission on Intergovernmental Relations (ACIR) to make a new study and report its own recommendations.[10] In 1975 the ACIR filed its voluminous report (more than 1000 pages), which reflects the continuing disagreements among the parties in interest over the key issues, i.e., the extent of State jurisdiction to tax, the methods of dividing the tax bases, and the taxation of foreign source income [11]—a déjà vu of the State taxation of nondepository multistate and multinational businesses. At this writing, Congress has not acted on the ACIR recommendations.

(c) Other Congressional Statutes Delineating Federal Immunity from State Taxation

Notes and Problems

A. *Occupational License Tax as Applied to Naval Ordnance Employees Working on Federal Land.* Employees at a Federal ordnance plant located on land owned by the United States challenged the validity of a tax imposed by the City of Louisville, within whose borders the plant was located, levied on persons engaged in any trade, occupation or profession within the city. An annual "license or privilege fee for the privilege of engaging in such activities," measured by one percent of salaries, wages and the net profits of trades, businesses or professions, was imposed. The taxpayers argued that the State and localities are not authorized to tax the privilege of working on Federal land although located within a State. Here, Congress had modified that jurisdiction by the enactment of the Buck Act, which declares that no "person shall be relieved from liability for any income tax levied by any State, or by any duly constituted taxing authority therein" by reason of the Federal nature of the area; the issue was

---

8. See P.L. 92–213, 85 Stat. 775 (1971); P.L. 93–100, 87 Stat. 342 (1973); P.L. 94–222, 90 Stat. 197 (1976).

9. See "State and Local Taxation," Report of Study Prepared by the Board of Governors, Federal Reserve System, Senate Banking, Housing and Urban Affairs Committee (92d Cong., 1st Sess.1971).

10. P.L. 93–100, note 8 supra.

11. "State and Local 'Doing Business' Taxes on Out-of-State Financial Depositories," Report of Study by ACIR, Senate Banking, Housing and Urban Affairs Committee (94th Cong., 1st Sess.1975).

whether the term "income tax," which Congress had defined for this purpose to mean "any tax levied on, with respect to, or measured by, net income, gross income, or gross receipts," embraced the Louisville license tax. 61 Stat. 641 (1947), 4 U.S.C. §§ 105–10. The majority of the Court, in an opinion by Mr. Justice Minton, held the tax to be an "income tax" within the meaning of the Buck Act since it was measured by gross receipts, despite the holding of the Kentucky court that the levy was not an income tax within the meaning of the Kentucky Constitution. Howard v. Commissioners of Sinking Fund of Louisville, 344 U.S. 624, 73 S.Ct. 465 (1953). Justices Douglas and Black dissented on the ground that the levy was, as the Kentucky court had held, a "license fee" levied on the privilege of engaging in stated activities, whose measure was narrowly confined to salaries, wages, commissions and the net profits of businesses, professions and occupations, with dividends, interest and capital gains excluded, and hence not the type of levy consented to by Congress. In reaching its conclusion, the dissent, by declaring that "the Congress has not yet granted local authorities the right to tax the privilege of working for or doing business with the United States," appeared to ignore the sweeping grant of authority to the States to apply to Federal employees and land any levy measured by gross or net income.

The Colorado Supreme Court reached a different conclusion from that reached in the *Louisville* case with respect to the Denver Employee Occupational Privilege Tax, a "head tax" imposed at the rate of $2.00 per month on every natural person who performs sufficient services in Denver to be paid $250.00 per month. The court agreed with the plaintiffs, Federal employees working at the Air Force Finance Center, a Federal enclave located entirely within Denver, that the "head tax" was neither an income tax nor a sales or use tax within the meaning of the Buck Act. Johnson v. City and County of Denver, 186 Colo. 398, 527 P.2d 883 (1974). As a result, the Federal employees were held not to be subject to the levy.

B. *Other Cases Construing Waiver of Immunity Provisions.* Many controversies have arisen as to how far Congress has waived immunity under the Buck Act, which relates to Federal military and other reservations. 4 U.S.C. § 105 et seq. That Act provides that a person shall not be relieved of liability for any income tax levied by a State, because he resides in a Federal area or receives income from transactions occurring, or services performed in such an area. See also Note A supra. The Alaska business license act, measured by gross receipts, was held to be an income tax, and hence was properly applied to a contractor for the United States which performed work exclusively on a United States military reservation. Alaska v. Baker, 64 Wash.2d 207, 390 P.2d 1009 (1964), appeal dismissed 380 U.S. 260, 85 S.Ct. 952 (1965). In Burns v. State Bureau of Revenue, 79 N.M. 53, 439 P.2d 702, cert. denied, 393 U.S. 841, 89 S.Ct. 119 (1968), the State court applied the Buck Act to deny immunity from New Mexico's income tax, as applied to residents of Texas who worked as civilian employees of the Federal Government at the White Sands Missile Range in New Mexico. The State had ceded jurisdiction over the area to the United States in 1941, and had not reserved taxing jurisdiction in the grant. The court held that neither the failure to reserve such jurisdiction nor the fact that the grant to the Federal Government was made after the passage of the Buck Act in 1940 prevented taxation by New Mexico, in view of the provisions of that Act.

The Supreme Court of Texas reached a dubious result in construing the Texas franchise tax, which is measured essentially by capital stock, as an "income tax" within the meaning of the Buck Act. The court reasoned that "the granting of the privilege to transact business in the State of Texas represents the realization of gross income" and that the franchise tax was "measured by * * * gross receipts," since the apportionment formula included a receipts factor. General Dynamics Corp. v. Bullock, 547 S.W.2d 255, 259 (Tex.1976). The taxpayer sought review in Supreme Court, but the Court, after inviting the Solicitor General to file a brief in the case expressing the views of the United States, 434 U.S. 811, 98 S.Ct. 48 (1977), denied the taxpayer's petition for certiorari. 434 U.S. 1009, 98 S.Ct. 717 (1978). See also Humble Oil & Refining Co. v. Calvert, 478 S.W.2d 926 (Tex.1972), in which the court held that occupation taxes measured by the value of oil and gas produced constituted "income taxes" for purposes of the Buck Act.

For a case invalidating a property tax on pipe lines and equipment owned by an oil company and used by it on a military reservation on land leased from the Federal Government, see Humble Pipe Line Co. v. Waggoner, 376 U.S. 369, 84 S.Ct. 857 (1964). As a result of this decision, the Court of Appeals for the Fifth Circuit overruled its earlier holding in Mississippi River Fuel Corp. v. Fontenot, 234 F.2d 898 (5th Cir.1956), which had sustained a Louisiana severance tax on oil and gas produced under a mineral lease on property in a Federal enclave. Mississippi River Fuel Corp. v. Cocreham, 382 F.2d 929 (5th Cir.1967).

A Federal Land Bank in Kansas was organized under the Federal Farm Loan Act, which exempts such banks from all taxes, except taxes on real estate. The bank acquired farm land through a mortgage foreclosure and thereafter sold it, retaining a half interest in the mineral properties. As a result, the bank received royalties from a lease of the oil and gas rights in the land. Under the Kansas statute, such mineral interests constitute "personal property." The Supreme Court held that the ad valorem tax on the mineral interest as personal property was in conflict with the Federal Farm Loan Act. Federal Land Bank v. Kiowa County, 368 U.S. 146, 82 S.Ct. 282 (1961).

In C.R. Fedrick, Inc. v. State Bd. of Equalization, 37 Cal.App.3d 564, 112 Cal.Rptr. 598 (1974), the court upheld a State sales tax on sales to a contractor of the United States Corps of Engineers, which occurred in a Federal enclave. Although the court's opinion is not a model of clarity, it seemed to rely on the Buck Act as constituting, in part, a waiver of the Federal Government's own immunity from State taxation. Such a construction of the Buck Act cannot be reconciled with the Supreme Court's more recent statement in United States v. State Tax Comm'n, 421 U.S. 599, 95 S.Ct. 1872 (1975):

> Section 107(a) of the Buck Act * * * provides that § 105(a) "shall not be deemed to authorize the levy or collection of any tax on or from the United States or any instrumentality thereof * * *" * * * That section can only be read as an explicit congressional preservation of

federal immunity from state sales taxes unconstitutional under the immunity doctrine announced by Mr. Chief Justice Marshall in McCulloch v. Maryland * * * [421 U.S. at 611–12.]

C. *Power of Congress to Extend Immunity.* It has generally been regarded as settled that Congress has full power to define the scope of immunity from State taxation for its agencies and instrumentalities employed in carrying out its powers under the Constitution. Thus, in Federal Land Bank of St. Paul v. Bismarck Lumber Co., 314 U.S. 95, 62 S.Ct. 1 (1941), the Court held that Congress has the power under the Necessary and Proper Clause of Art. 1, § 8 of the Federal Constitution, in furtherance of its lending functions, to immunize Federal Land Banks from State taxation. The case involved a sales tax on land bank purchases of lumber to be used in the repair of foreclosed premises. Promissory notes issued to the Federal Home Loan Bank by a Federal savings and loan association for advances may not be subjected to a State stamp tax, in view of the provisions of the Home Owners' Loan Act of 1933. Laurens Federal Savings & Loan Ass'n v. State of South Carolina, 365 U.S. 517, 81 S.Ct. 719 (1961). Various types of Federal payments to veterans or their beneficiaries have also been exempted from State taxation.

D. *Soldiers and Sailors Relief Act.* Congress has enacted legislation to prevent State taxation in areas in which the States would be free to tax in the absence of such action. Thus the Soldiers and Sailors Relief Act of 1940, as amended, prohibits, among other things, State taxation of personal property, not owned in a trade or business, owned by military personnel who are in the State (other than the State of domicile) on military orders. 50 U.S.C. § 574. See Dameron v. Brodhead, 345 U.S. 322, 73 S.Ct. 721 (1953) (invalidating Denver personal property tax on household furnishings of officer located in rented apartment near airfield where he was stationed). In Sullivan v. United States, 395 U.S. 169, 89 S.Ct. 1648 (1969), the Supreme Court held that the Soldiers and Sailors Relief Act did not bar a State from imposing sales and use taxes on tangible personal property purchased by non-resident servicemen present in a State under military orders. The Court found that the statutory language limiting "taxation in respect of the personal property" of non-resident servicemen did not include or exclude sales taxes. The Court relied instead on the statute's legislative history which reflected a congressional purpose to relieve non-resident servicemen of the risk of double taxation from annually recurring property taxes but not to shield them from sales or use taxes of the host State.

E. *State Taxation of Indians.* "State laws generally are not applicable to tribal Indians on an Indian reservation except where Congress has expressly provided that State laws shall apply. It follows that Indians and Indian property on an Indian reservation are not subject to State taxation except by virtue of express authority conferred upon the State by act of Congress." U.S. Dep't of the Interior, Federal Indian Law 845 (1958), quoted with approval in McClanahan v. Arizona State Tax Comm'n, 411 U.S. 164, 171, 93 S.Ct. 1257, 1261 (1973). In *McClanahan,* the Court, after examining the relevant treaties and statutes, held that the State of Arizona had no power to impose a tax on the income of Navajo Indians on the

Navajo Reservation when the income was wholly derived from reservation sources. In another case decided on the same day, the Court, construing the applicable provision of the Indian Reorganization Act, 25 U.S.C.A. § 465, held that the State of New Mexico could impose a nondiscriminatory gross receipts tax on a ski resort operated by an Indian Tribe on non-reservation land leased from the Federal Government; but it denied the State power to impose a use tax on personalty installed in the construction of ski lifts. Mescalero Apache Tribe v. Jones, 411 U.S. 145, 93 S.Ct. 1267 (1973). The Supreme Court has also held that the applicable statutes forbid the State of Montana from imposing a property tax on personal property located within a reservation; a vendor license fee applied to reservation Indians conducting a cigarette business for the Tribe on the reservation; and a sales tax on cigarette sales on the reservation to Indians by Indians. But the Court held that the State could require the Indian seller to collect a tax validly imposed on non-Indians. Moe v. Confederated Salish & Kootenai Tribes of the Flathead Reservation, 425 U.S. 463, 96 S.Ct. 1634 (1976). See also Bryan v. Itasca County, 426 U.S. 373, 96 S.Ct. 2102 (1976).

In Warren Trading Post Co. v. Arizona Tax Comm'r, 380 U.S. 685, 85 S.Ct. 1242 (1965), a Federally licensed retailer was held immune from Arizona sales taxes on sales made on a Navajo Indian reservation. A member of the Onondaga Nation, one of the six Indian Tribes comprising the Iroquois Confederacy, who operated a gift shop on an Indian reservation located in New York and traded in Indian artifacts, could not be subjected to the State's sales and use tax. Pierce v. State Tax Comm., 29 A.D.2d 124, 286 N.Y.S.2d 162 (4th Dep't 1968). The Onondaga Reservation had been reserved to the Onondagas by a treaty with the State of New York, executed in 1788. The Indians' right of self-government within their reservation has been recognized by the courts. "The Onondaga Nation is a quasi foreign nation and its reservation is quasi-extraterritorial." 286 N.Y.S.2d at 164. Congress, under its constitutional power to regulate Indian affairs (U.S. Const., Art. I, Sec. 8, Clause 3), has not authorized the States to tax sales of artifacts made on the Reservation. Indeed, "such a tax would frustrate the evident congressional purpose that no burden shall be imposed on the development of Indian arts and crafts * * *." Id. at 165.

During the 1980's, the Court handed down a number of cases concerning the State's power to tax Indians and Indian-related activity. The resolution of these cases turned largely on the Court's reading of the complex web of specific treaties, laws, and administrative rulings governing the relationship between the States and the Indian Tribes. Thus in Montana v. Blackfeet Tribe of Indians, 471 U.S. 759, 105 S.Ct. 2399 (1985), the Court held that a State could not levy taxes on a tribe's royalty interests in oil and gas produced under leases issued by the tribe. The critical question was whether the provision of a 1924 Federal statute, that authorized State taxation of such royalty payments, was implicitly repealed by the Indian Mineral Leasing Act of 1938, 25 U.S.C. § 396a et seq., which was silent on the question. In rejecting the State's argument that repeal by implication is not favored, the Court noted that ordinary principles of statutory construction did not have their usual force in Indian cases, and that "[t]he canons of construction applicable * * * are rooted in the unique trust relationship between the United States and the Indians." 471 U.S. at 766, 105 S.Ct. at 2403. Because the States may tax Indians only when explicit Congressional authorization exists, and such authorization was not granted by the 1938 Act, the Court denied Montana the power to tax the royalty payments. See also Ramah Navajo School Board, Inc. v. Bureau of Revenue, 458 U.S. 832, 102 S.Ct. 3394 (1982) (Federal statutes encouraging the development of Indian-controlled institutions, and detailed Federal regulations governing school construction on reservation, preempt State tax on gross receipts received by non-Indian construction company from tribal school board for constructing school on Indian reservation); White Mountain Apache Tribe v. Bracker, 448 U.S. 136, 100 S.Ct. 2578 (1980) (pervasive Federal regulation of commercial timber activity on tribal lands preempts State tax on non-Indian enterprise harvesting timber on Indian reservation); Washington v. Confederated Tribes of the Colville Indian Reservation, 447 U.S. 134, 100 S.Ct. 2069 (1980) (Washington may impose sales tax on purchases of cigarettes made on Indian reservations by nonmembers of the tribe).

SECTION 8. REFERENCES

The most comprehensive treatment of Federal immunity from State and local taxation is to be found in the excellent work of Professor Paul Hartman, Federal Limitations on State and Local Taxation ch. 6 (1981). The classic treatments of the doctrine remain Powell, "The Waning of Intergovernmental Tax Immunities," 58 Harv.L.Rev. 663 (1945) and Powell, "The Remnant of Intergovernmental Immunities," 58 Harv.L.Rev. 757 (1945). For more recent discussions of Federal immunity, see Cavin, "Federal Immunity of Government Contractors from State and Local Taxation," 61 Denver L.Rev. 797 (1984); Note, "Federal Immunity from State Taxation: A Reassessment," 45 U.Chi.L. Rev. 695 (1978); and Tribe, "Intergovernmental Immunities in Litigation, Taxation, and Regulation: Separation of Powers Issues in Controversies About Federalism," 89 Harv.L.Rev. 682 (1976).

There is a thoughtful discussion of the problems presented by the *Kern–Limerick* case, discussed in Section 4, in Miller, "State Power Over the Federal Contractor: A Problem in Federalism," 11 Vand.L. Rev. 175 (1957); see also Rollman, "Recent Developments in Sovereign Immunity of the Federal Government from State and Local Taxes," 38 N.Dak.L.Rev. 26 (1962); Comment, "Power of State to Tax Where the Incidence Falls Upon the Federal Government," 12 De Paul L.Rev. 240 (1963); Wolf, "A Questionable Source of Revenue—Indirect Taxation of the Federal Government," 1963 Nat.Tax. Ass'n Procs. 299; Annotation, "State Sales or Use Tax as Violating Immunity of United States— Supreme Court Cases," 44 L.Ed.2d 692; "Standards for Determining the Legal Incidence of State Taxes," 29 Tax Law. 372 (1976).

The Michigan property tax cases discussed in Section 5 were the subject of extensive comment. For a discussion of Michigan's experience under the decisions, see Purnell, "Business Use of Exempt Properties," The Property Tax: Problems and Potentials 307 (Tax Inst. of America, Symposium 1966). See also Gaberman, "Paths Through Jungle of State and Local Taxation of Defense Contractors," 23 Fed. Bar J. 61 (1963); Roberts, "Property Taxation: Taxable Status of Property Rented to Government," 35 So.Calif.L.Rev. 361 (1962). Useful critical analyses of the cases, with varying views as to the proper solution to the conflicts presented, are to be found in Pierce, "Tax Immunity Should Not Mean Tax Inequity," 1959 Wisc.L.Rev. 173; Van Cleve, "States' Rights and Federal Solvency: A Study of Recent Supreme Court Decisions Permitting Local Taxation of the Possession of Federal Property," id. at 190; and Whelan, "Government Contract Privileges: A Fertile Ground for State Taxation," 44 Va.L.Rev. 1099 (1958). For economic studies, see the Congressional reports referred to above and Rasmussen, "Payments to State and Local Governments on Account of Federal Real Property," 1956 Nat'l Tax Ass'n Procs. 284; Heller, "The Taxation of Federally Owned Real Estate," 1945 Nat'l Tax Ass'n Procs. 139; Shere, "Developments in the Tax Treatment of Federal Real Property," 1948 Nat'l Tax Ass'n Procs. 273.

For references dealing with State taxation of Indians, see R. Strickland, ed., Felix S. Cohen's Handbook of Federal Indian Law 405–31 (1982); Ball, "Constitution, Court, Indian Tribes," 1987 Am.Bar Found. Res.J. 1, 100–110; Dockins, "Limitations on State Power to Tax Natural Resource Development on Indian Reservations," 43 Mont.L.Rev. 217 (1982); Laurence, "The Indian Commerce Clause," 23 Ariz.L.Rev. 203 (1981); Note, "State Taxation on Sales to Reservation Indians," 49 N.Dak.L.Rev. 343 (1973); Note, "Recent Developments—State Taxation of Indians," 49 Wash.L.Rev. 191 (1973); Davies, "State Taxation of Indian Reservations," 1966 Utah L.Rev. 132.

Other references include Cohen, "Federal Immunity from State Taxation," 68 Dickinson L.Rev. 469 (1964); Flick, "State Tax Liability of Servicemen and their Dependents," 21 Wash and Lee L.Rev. 22 (1964); Franck, "State and Municipal Taxation of United States Government Securities," 25 Munic.Sec. 111 (1963); Bartlett, "State Taxation Power in Federal Areas," 1 Washburn L.J. 551 (1962); Lent, "The Origin and Survival of Tax–Exempt Securities," 12 Nat.Tax J. 305 (1953); "Taxation of Government Bondholders and Employees, The Immunity Rule and the Sixteenth Amendment," prepared by the Attorney General of the United States (1938); Annot., 32 A.L.R.2d 618.

*

Part 9

TAX PROCEDURES

INTRODUCTORY NOTE

Legal procedure is not merely a bread and butter study designed to avoid the pitfalls of suing in the wrong court, bringing the wrong type of proceeding, or defaulting in the time of filing a pleading. The adjective law field is far more fertile and yields richer rewards. Thus, probably the best introduction to our substantive law generally is a tracing of the growth of the common law forms of actions. So, in the tax field, adjective and substantive law are integrated and interdependent.

The history of State and local tax procedures illuminates the development of the levies themselves. Moreover, it reflects, *inter alia,* the early development in this country of administrative taxing agencies, vested with summary powers of distraint of property, in order to protect the fisc from the slow moving machinery of the courts; the tugging and pulling between the demand for home rule and the need for State centralization; the emergence of new obligations of the citizen as tax collector and withholding agent as new types of levies were enacted; and the impact on the States of the gargantuan growth of Federal taxation and the establishment of an elaborate Federal system of reviewing tax returns. Inevitably, tax collection and review procedures vary markedly, depending on the nature of the tax, the existing State and local governmental patterns, and other factors.

Chapter 16

THE ASSESSMENT AND COLLECTION OF TAXES AND THE TAXPAYER'S JUDICIAL REMEDIES

SECTION 1. THE ASSESSMENT OF TAXES

The variety of taxing procedures is reflected in the marked differences in assessment methods utilized in the various taxes levied in virtually any single State. Thus, in real property taxes, assessment—the listing and valuation of the properties subject to tax—is made in the first instance by the assessor. The taxing authority thus initiates the process. In personal property tax assessments, on the other hand, the taxpayer initiates the process by filing a sworn report of his taxable property. Assessment of property is almost entirely a function of local assessors—village, town, school district, or city officials in some States; county officials in most States; and a combination of county and subdistrict officials in still others. Often administrative review of assessments is provided in the first instance before a village, town, or school district board of review, with a right of appeal to a county board of review. In large cities, independent boards of review, with wider experience and expertise than the boards of smaller units, are frequently found. In many States, the findings of the county board of review may be appealed to the State board of equalization or the State tax commission. Some businesses, typically public utilities with properties scattered over the State and often presenting difficult problems of valuing intangible rights or franchises to maintain railroads or pipes or wires in or along public property, are assessed in the first instance directly by a State authority.

A now classic statement of the procedure for assessing and collecting taxes was made by Mr. Justice Roberts in Bull v. United States, 295 U.S. 247, 259–260, 55 S.Ct. 695, 699–670 (1935):

> A tax is an exaction by the sovereign, and necessarily the sovereign has an enforceable claim against every one within the taxable

class for the amount lawfully due from him. The statute prescribes the rule of taxation. Some machinery must be provided for applying the rule to the facts in each taxpayer's case, in order to ascertain the amount due. The chosen instrumentality for the purpose is an administrative agency whose action is called an assessment. The assessment may be a valuation of property subject to taxation, which valuation is to be multiplied by the statutory rate to ascertain the amount of tax. Or it may include the calculation and fix the amount of tax payable, and assessments of federal estate and income taxes are of this type. Once the tax is assessed, the taxpayer will owe the sovereign the amount when the date fixed by law for payment arrives. Default in meeting the obligation calls for some procedure whereby payment can be enforced. The statute might remit the Government to an action at law wherein the taxpayer could offer such defense as he had. A judgment against him might be collected by the levy of an execution. But taxes are the lifeblood of government, and their prompt and certain availability an imperious need. Time out of mind, therefore, the sovereign has resorted to more drastic means of collection. The assessment is given the force of a judgment, and if the amount assessed is not paid when due, administrative officials may seize the debtor's property to satisfy the debt.

In recognition of the fact that erroneous determinations and assessments will inevitably occur, the statutes, in a spirit of fairness, invariably afford the taxpayer an opportunity at some stage to have mistakes rectified. Often an administrative hearing is afforded before the assessment becomes final; or administrative machinery is provided whereby an erroneous collection may be refunded; in some instances both administrative relief and redress by an action against the sovereign in one of its courts are permitted methods of restitution of excessive or illegal exaction. Thus the usual procedure for the recovery of debts is reversed in the field of taxation. Payment precedes defense, and the burden of proof, normally on the claimant, is shifted to the taxpayer. The assessment supersedes the pleading, proof, and judgment necessary in an action at law, and has the force of such a judgment. The ordinary defendant stands in judgment only after a hearing. The taxpayer often is afforded his hearing after judgment and after payment, and his only redress for unjust administrative action is the right to claim restitution. But these reversals of the normal process of collecting a claim cannot obscure the fact that after all what is being accomplished is the recovery of a just debt owed the sovereign. If that which the sovereign retains was unjustly taken in violation of its own statute, the withholding is wrongful. Restitution is owed the taxpayer. Nevertheless he may be without a remedy.

Because taxation involves an involuntary taking of property, the adjective requirements of due process of law must be observed. Consequently, a determination of tax liability will violate the Due Process Clause of the Federal and State Constitutions unless the taxpayer is given adequate notice and an opportunity for a hearing. Turner v. Wade, 254 U.S. 64, 41 S.Ct. 27 (1920); Londoner v. Denver, 210 U.S.

373, 28 S.Ct. 708 (1908). The rule, as stated in McGregor v. Hogan, 263 U.S. 234 at 237, 44 S.Ct. 50 at 51 (1923) is:

> It is not essential to due process of law that the taxpayer be given notice and hearing before the value of his property is originally assessed; it being sufficient if he is granted the right to be heard on the assessment before the valuation is finally determined. Pittsburgh Railway v. Backus, 154 U.S. 421, 426, 14 S.Ct. 1114, 38 L.Ed. 1031. * * * The requirement of due process is that after such notice as may be appropriate the taxpayer have opportunity to be heard as to the amount of the tax by giving him the right to appear for that purpose at some stage of the proceedings before the tax becomes irrevocably fixed.

Much litigation has revolved about issues as to the character of notice and hearing required. It is clear that the carefully safeguarded type of notice required to commence judicial proceedings is not required in making tax assessments. Personal service of process or notice is not essential. Typically, in property tax assessments, notice by publication or posting in some public place is sufficient warning to all property owners of the assessment proceedings; or the taxing statute itself may prescribe the time and place when the assessors will meet to make assessments and the period of protest and hearing. Such statutory notice satisfies the due process requirements.

If the tax statute itself contains no provision for notice or hearing, the due process requirements will, nevertheless, be satisfied if the taxpayer has the right to contest the tax in an action for its collection or an injunction proceeding. Nickey v. Mississippi, 292 U.S. 393, 54 S.Ct. 743 (1934); McGregor v. Hogan, supra. "In short, so long as the taxpayer can present his suit as a matter of right, before the court, whether by the tax statutes, a separate statute, or by holdings of the court, he has been afforded due process even though he had no notice and hearing before the tax authorities." Note, 29 N.C.L.Rev. 169, 170 (1951).

Notes and Problems

A. *Designation and Description of Property and Owners on Assessment Books.* In property tax assessments, the usual method of giving notice of the assessed value of property is the preparation of assessment books or rolls describing the property, its owner, and the valuation proposed to be assessed. Typically, assessment rolls or books are open for a brief period prescribed by statute and thereafter—also within a stated statutory period—taxpayers may make their complaints and have their hearings before the assessing or reviewing board. Material misdescriptions of the property or material errors in designating the owner's name may invalidate the assessment. The extent to which erroneous or inaccurate listing will invalidate a tax depends in part on the applicable statute. See, e.g., Stout v. Mastin, 139 U.S. 151, 11 S.Ct. 519 (1891), involving error or ambiguity as to the location of the real estate; People v. Commonwealth Edison Co., 367 Ill. 260, 11 N.E.2d 408 (1937), in which different classes of property were not separately listed; Smith v. Russell, 172 App.Div. 793, 159 N.Y.S. 169 (1916), where there was error in the name of the owner of the property; and State ex rel. Oklahoma Tax Com'n v. Estate of Hewett, 621 P.2d 542 (Okl.1980), where there was insufficient notice of potential personal liability. See 71 Am.Jur.2d § 731 et seq. for cases dealing with problems relating to the description of property and the owner.

B. *The Type of Hearing Required.* The right to a hearing is not satisfied if the taxpayer may merely file written objections to the levy. An adequate tax hearing "demands that he who is entitled to it shall have the right to support his allegations by argument however brief, and, if need be, by proof, however informal." Londoner v. Denver, 210 U.S. 373, 386, 28 S.Ct. 708 (1908). A single opportunity to be heard before an impartial tribunal prior to the conclusive determination of tax liability is sufficient. McGregor v. Hogan, supra; Dietman v. Hunter, 5 Ill.2d 486, 126 N.E.2d 22 (1955).

C. *Increase of Assessment Without Notice.* May a taxpayer's assessment be increased by a board of equalization without notice to him? In Lander v. Mercantile Bank, 186 U.S. 458, 22 S.Ct. 908 (1902), the taxpayer made its return to the county auditor, who fixed the value of the property and transmitted a statement of his action to the State board of equalization. The State board met on the date prescribed by statute and adjourned three times, finally to meet at the call of its president. Subsequently, the board met, without notice to the taxpayer, and increased the assessed value of the property. The Court upheld the assessment, despite the lack of further notice.

A more modern view was expressed in Northwestern Bell Telephone Co. v. State Board of Equalization, 119 Neb. 138, 227 N.W. 452 (1929), where the court said:

> The great weight of authority, as disclosed by text-writers and adjudicated cases, clearly holds to the proposition that an assessed valuation of property cannot be increased without due notice to the owner of such property, and this to the end that he may first be heard. Where an increase in the assessed valuation of any class or classes of property, as returned by any county or counties, is made by the state board of equalization and assessment without notice to such county or counties, and without affording sufficient opportunity to be heard, such increase is in violation of section 5901, Comp.St.1922, and amounts to confiscation of property without due process and is therefore a void increase of assessment. [119 Neb. at 141–142, 227 N.W. at 454.]

See generally 72 Am.Jur.2d § 822 et seq.

If the assessment of the whole district is raised, the prevailing rule is that notice to individual property owners affected by a general increase in assessments is not required. Bi–Metallic Inv. Co. v. State Bd. of Equalization, 239 U.S. 441, 36 S.Ct. 141 (1915). Professor Kenneth Culp Davis distinguishes the *Bi–Metallic* case from the cases cited above on the basis of the distinction between legislative and adjudicative facts: a party has a right to be heard when official action is based on individual grounds (an adjudicative fact), but not when official action is based on general grounds (a legislative fact). See K.C. Davis, Administrative Law Treatise § 12:3, at 414 (2d ed. 1979).

D. *Judicial Review.* The due process requirements of notice and review at some stage of the taxing proceedings are satisfied by a proceeding before an administrative agency. Judicial review of assessments is not an essential ingredient of due process of law. See Hodge v. Muscatine County, 196 U.S. 276, 25 S.Ct. 237 (1905), in which the Court said:

> * * * If a taxpayer be given an opportunity to test the validity of the tax at any time before it is made final, whether the proceedings for review take place before a board having a quasi-judicial character, or before a tribunal provided by the state for the purpose of determining such questions, due process of law is not denied. [196 U.S. at 281, 25 S.Ct. at 240.]

Most States, however, now provide for judicial review of property tax assessments. See, e.g., Mass.Gen.Laws Ann. ch. 58A § 13, CCH ¶ 90–389, P–H ¶ 66,175; N.Y.Real Prop.Tax Law § 700, CCH ¶ 91–120, P–H ¶ 32,210; Ohio Rev.Code Ann. §§ 5717.04, –.05, CCH ¶¶ 93–011, 93–021, P–H ¶¶ 66,550, 66,555. See Note, "The Road to Uniformity in Real Estate Taxation: Valuation and Appeal," 124 U.Pa.L.Rev. 1418 (1976).

E. The notice and hearing requirements discussed do not apply to all types of taxes. Thus, where a statute provided for an assessment of $300 per annum against every person selling cigarettes, the Court said that "no notice of the assessment or levy of the tax is necessary. If the person carries on the business, the imposition of the tax follows as a matter of course. There is no discretion as to the amount." See Hodge v. Muscatine County, 196 U.S. 276, 280, 25 S.Ct. 237 (1905). The same rule applies to poll taxes and other levies which are essentially self-assessing and do not require a determination of the value of property, or the amount of net income or gross income or other flexible measure. In such cases, since notice and hearing perform no useful purpose, they are not required before the assessment becomes final. See Hagar v. Reclamation District, 111 U.S. 701, 4 S.Ct. 663 (1884).

F. *Irregularities in Assessment Procedures.* Assessments have often been attacked because of formal irregularities in the assessment proceeding. Thus, in Security Trust & Savings Bank v. Mitts, 220 Iowa 271, 261 N.W. 625 (1935), the plaintiffs sought to enjoin a capital stock tax assessment on the ground, *inter alia,* that the assessment was invalid because the assessor had not signed or sworn to the assessment. The banks made their returns and the assessors failed to sign the statement at the bottom of the forms certifying to the taxable value of the property. The assessors turned these reports over to the local board of review and did not otherwise place the banks' names or assessments on the assessment rolls. The court recognized that the assessments were "irregular" but nevertheless held them valid on the basis of the assessors' testimony that they had adopted the banks' valuations. In so doing, the court distinguished Smith v. McQuistion, 108 Iowa 363, 79 N.W. 130 (1899), in which a clerical error in entering an assessment on the rolls invalidated the assessment.

The vicissitudes produced by the casual procedures that frequently obtain in personal property tax assessments are illustrated by St. Joe Paper

Co. v. Ray, 172 So.2d 646 (Fla.1965). The Florida statute provides that where a taxpayer has tangible personal property in more than one county within the State, a separate return must be filed in each county, listing the property; and that where tangible property is moved from one county to another after January 1—presumably before April 1—the property is taxable in the county where it was located on January 1. The taxpayer notified the Assessor of Calhoun County that it owned no tangible personal property in his county at any time between Dec. 3, 1961 and April 1, 1962. The Assessor, nevertheless, assessed the taxpayer $10,000 on certain fire fighting equipment that the company had maintained in the county for several prior years. Although the Assessor deposed in an affidavit that he had seen the property on Jan. 1 in the county, nevertheless, he had not, as required by law, filed a schedule of the taxable items, but had merely used the 1959 rolls in making the assessment. The taxpayer alleged that the property at issue had been moved to Gulf County in 1961, that it was there reported, and the tax there paid.

The Assessor seized a caterpillar tractor and advertised it for sale for non-payment of the tax, and the taxpayer sued to enjoin the sale. In response to the taxpayer's contention that the assessment was void for failure to file the schedule listing the items taxed, the court declared:

> Unless specifically declared otherwise, all the provisions of law relating to the assessment and collection of revenue are directory only, designed for the orderly arrangement of records and procedure of officers in enforcing the revenue laws. Therefore, the primary duty to ascertain and pay the tax is upon the property owner. As stated in Hackney v. McKenney [2] in this state *liability* for ad valorem taxes does not depend upon a proper assessment of particular property or of all taxable property.
>
> A number of cases [3] involving void assessments have held that a valid assessment is the first prerequisite to a valid tax and its enforcement. An assessment is void where it was not authorized by law [4] where the property is not subject to the tax assessed, or where the levy is authorized but the tax roll is illegal due to some affirmative wrongdoing by the taxing official.[5] None of these conditions exist here.

* * *

> Though we do not condone the negligence of the Tax Assessor in ignoring the directive statutory requisites by waiting two years to file the required schedule, such delay could not render void a voidable assessment. Not only does Section 200.02 authorize the correcting of such omissions at any time, but complete failure to assess tangible personal property can be corrected by including in any current assessment that property which has escaped taxation for any or all of the three previous years.[7] [172 So.2d at 648–49.]

2. Hackney v. McKenney, 113 Fla. 176, 151 So. 524 (1933).

3. State v. Beardsley, 84 Fla. 109, 94 So. 660 (1932) and Lewis State Bank v. Bridges, 115 Fla. 784, 156 So. 144 (1934).

4. State v. Beardsley, supra.

5. Hackney v. McKenney, supra.

7. § 200.16, Florida Statutes, 1961, F.S.A.

Since the assessment was merely "voidable" and not "void," the taxpayer was presumably now barred from contesting it, in view of the 60–day statute of limitations.*

If the tax assessment is void per se suit may be filed at any time when the right to redress has not been waived or otherwise lost, but where it is voidable the taxpayer must seek appropriate relief within the time limitations of the * * * statute. [172 So.2d at 650].

G. *References.* Note, "The Michigan Property Tax: Assessment, Equalization, and Taxpayer Appeals," 17 Wayne L.Rev. 1397 (1971); Ehrman, "Administrative Appeal and Judicial Review of Property Tax Assessments in California—the New Look," 22 Hastings L.J. 1 (1970); Hartman, Henry & Foster, "State Tax Collection Problems," 9 Vand.L.Rev. 316 (1956); Young, "Taxpayers' Remedies," in Symposium on Illinois Property Tax Problems, 1952 U.Ill.L.F. 248, 251 et seq. There is an excellent review of administrative procedures in Culp, "Administrative Remedies in the Assessment and Enforcement of State Taxes," 17 N.C.L.Rev. 118 (1939). See also Annots., 24 A.L.R. 331, 84 A.L.R. 197.

SECTION 2. THE COLLECTION OF TAXES

(a) Summary Proceedings and Distraint

Notes and Problems

A. *Distraint and Sale in Property Tax Enforcement.* The traditional method of enforcement of property taxes in the American States is by recourse to the property taxed, through the satisfaction of tax liens. In view of the crucial importance of property taxation, especially the real property tax, to local revenues, widespread delinquency in property tax payments may become a major problem to local governments. During the 1930's, as stated by one commentator, "delinquencies have mounted in many communities to so high a proportion of the tax levy as to jeopardize the payment of governmental obligations and the maintenance of essential services which have been dependent on this tax." Cavers, in Foreword, "The Collection of Property Taxes," 3 Law & Contemp.Probs. 335 (1936). Typically, taxes levied on property are made a lien against the property and collection is authorized by warrant. The power to collect taxes by distraint and sale is "almost as old as the common law." Springer v. United States, 102 U.S. 586, 593 (1880).

As is noted below, in many States resident owners of property are personally liable for property taxes. And in some States, including most of the New England States, Connecticut, Maine, Massachusetts, New Hampshire, and Vermont, imprisonment is provided by statute for nonpayment of taxes. However, in City of Cincinnati v. DeGolyer, 25 Ohio St.2d 101, 267 N.E.2d 282 (1971), it was held that imprisonment for nonwillful failure to pay taxes violated the State constitutional ban on imprisonment for debt. For an illuminating discussion of property tax delinquency problems, see Allen, "Collection of Delinquent Taxes by Recourse to the Taxed Property,"

---

* Actually, the case was remanded for further hearing, because it arose on motion and there were controversial factual issues.

3 Law & Contemp.Probs. 397 (1936); Brandis, "Sales and Foreclosures under the Model Tax Collection Law," id. at 406.

B. *The Constitutionality of Summary Proceedings.* In Bomher v. Reagan, 522 F.2d 1201 (9th Cir.1975), California's summary tax collection procedure was sustained over the objection that it violated the taxpayer's due process rights. The Franchise Tax Board had sent the taxpayer several requests for payment of delinquent taxes, and, after failing to receive a satisfactory response, issued a warrant for the collection of amounts due. The warrant was executed by levy upon and sale of the taxpayer's automobile. The taxpayer claimed the procedure deprived him of due process because he was given no prior notice or hearing in which the tax debt would have to be proved before his property could be seized. The court held, however, that the taxpayer's right to subsequent judicial review and a tax refund, if necessary, satisfied due process requirements. See also Phillips v. Commissioner, 283 U.S. 589, 51 S.Ct. 608 (1931). See generally Comment, "Procedural Due Process in Tax Collection: An Opportunity for a Prompt Postdeprivation Hearing," 44 U.Chi.L.Rev. 594 (1977).

C. May the tax collector distrain exempt personal property in order to collect delinquent personal property taxes assessed against the owner? In Ryder v. Livingston, 145 Neb. 862, 18 N.W.2d 507 (1945), the court upheld the right of a county treasurer to issue a distress warrant and sell household goods of a taxpayer which were themselves exempt from the levy to satisfy the owner's unpaid personal property tax. The court said, "The personal property of the taxpayer is the primary fund out of which all his taxes are to be collected, and for this purpose almost every variety of personal property is subject to compulsory process * * * and he [the collector] is not restricted to those particular articles on which the particular assessment was laid or on which particular tax lien rests." 18 N.W.2d 507, 509.

D. *Distraint of Mortgaged Property.* The effects of tax liens on personal property which is sold or mortgaged is the cause of much litigation. Thus, in Owens v. Oregon Livestock Loan Co., 151 Or. 63, 47 P.2d 963 (1935), on April 22, 1930, the owner of several thousand sheep granted to a loan company a chattel mortgage on the sheep. After the mortgage had been recorded, the county sheriff seized the sheep for unpaid personal property taxes of the owner for the years 1927 to 1930. The sheep owner argued that the only sheep which the sheriff could distrain for any year's taxes were the sheep on which the assessments had been levied for a particular year. The court upheld this contention, as between the rights of the chattel mortgagee and the sheriff, saying, after a review of the cases:

> It will be observed from the above decisions that only the property assessed is liable for payment of the tax unless the collector distrains other property. But his distraint is ineffective unless the property he seizes belongs to the tax debtor at the time of the distraint. The fact that it belonged to the tax debtor at the time the tax was levied is immaterial if it now belongs to someone else. [47 P.2d at 967.]

E. *Requirements of Notice to Mortgagee of Proceeding to Sell Mortgaged Property for Nonpayment of Taxes.* In Mennonite Board of Missions v. Adams, 462 U.S. 791, 103 S.Ct. 2706 (1983), the Supreme Court addressed the question whether notice by publication and posting provided a mortgagee of real property with adequate notice under the Due Process Clause of a proceeding to sell the mortgaged property for nonpayment of taxes. Like many States, Indiana provided for the sale of real property on which payments of property taxes have been delinquent for a specified period. Prior to sale, the county auditor had to post notice in the county courthouse and publish notice once each week for three consecutive weeks. The owner of the property was entitled to notice by certified mail to his last known address. Under the law then in effect, however, Indiana law did not provide for notice by mail or personal service to mortgagees of property that was to be sold for nonpayment of taxes.

In Mennonite Board of Missions, the purchaser of property at a tax sale brought an action to quiet title to the property. The mortgagee of the property opposed the action on the ground that it had not received constitutionally adequate notice of the pending sale or of the opportunity to redeem the property following the tax sale. The Court, relying on Mullane v. Central Hanover Bank & Trust Co., 339 U.S. 306, 70 S.Ct. 652 (1950) sustained the mortgagee's claim. In *Mullane,* the Court had declared that prior to an action that will affect an interest in life, liberty, or property protected by the Due Process Clause, a State must provide "notice reasonably calculated, under all the circumstances, to apprise interested parties of the pendency of the action and afford them an opportunity to present their objections." 339 U.S. at 314, 70 S.Ct. at 657. Under this standard, the Court held that published notice of an action to settle the accounts of a common trust fund was not sufficient to inform beneficiaries of a trust whose names and addresses were known.

> This case is controlled by the analysis in *Mullane.* To begin with a mortgagee possesses a substantial property interest that is significantly affected by a tax sale. Under Indiana law, a mortgagee acquires a lien on the owner's property * * * A mortgagee's security interest generally has priority over subsequent claims or liens * * * [T]he tax sale may result in the complete nullification of the mortgagee's interest, since the purchaser acquires title free of all liens and other encumbrances at the conclusion of the redemption period.

> Since a mortgagee has a legally protected property interest, he is entitled to notice reasonably calculated to apprise him of a pending tax sale. * * * When the mortgagee is identified in a mortgage that is publicly recorded, constructive notice by publication must be supplemented by notice mailed to the mortgagee's last known available address or by personal service. But unless the mortgagee is not reasonably identifiable, constructive notice alone does not satisfy the mandate of *Mullane.* [462 U.S. at 798.]

F. *References.* See "The General Property Tax in Wyoming—A Symposium," 4 Wyo.L.J. 226 (1950); Eldridge, "Property Tax Collection Procedure in Washington," 17 Wash.L.R. 123 (1942).

(b) Personal Liability of the Taxpayer

Notes and Problems

A. *Personal Liability for Property Taxes.* Personal liability for property taxes has a long history in the American law. As noted in an excellent discussion by Rubin in "Collection of Delinquent Real Property Taxes by Action *in Personam*," 3 Law & Contemp. Probs. 416 (1936), a Massachusetts statute enacted in 1789 permitted a tax collector to bring an action for debt for taxes in some cases, 1 Mass. Laws 465 (1801); and in Mayor v. McKee, 10 Tenn. 150 (1826), a tax on town lots was held a debt of the taxpayer which could be recovered by an action in the name of the town. Generally, however, the rule developed that in the absence of an explicit statutory provision, no personal action will lie to recover property taxes. These holdings are grounded on the theory that taxes are not debts, or in the view that since the statute provides only for proceedings *in rem*, personal liability is not imposed.

Many States have enacted statutes drawn in the light of Dewey v. Des Moines, 173 U.S. 193, 19 S.Ct. 379 (1899), in which the Court held that a non-resident owner of real property located in Des Moines could not be subjected to personal liability for a special assessment for street paving. Because the State had no personal jurisdiction over the non-resident, its remedy was limited to collecting the tax out of the value of the property. Such statutes impose personal liability for property taxes only on owners who are residents of the State. See Rubin, supra, at note 4, for a listing of States having such provisions; for cases arising under these provisions, see Collector of Taxes v. Revere Building, Inc., 276 Mass. 576, 177 N.E. 577 (1931); Village of Massapequa Park v. Massapequa Park Villa Sites, Inc., 278 N.Y. 28, 15 N.E.2d 177 (1938); Pennsylvania Co., Trustee v. Bergson, 307 Pa. 44, 159 A. 32 (1932).

Is the holding in *Dewey v. Des Moines,* which was enunciated in 1899, consistent with more recent due process conceptions? Modern long-arm statutes usually deem ownership of property to be a submission to the jurisdiction of the courts of the State. See, e.g., Illinois Civil Practice Act § 17, Ill.Rev.Stat. ch. 110, ¶ 17, which has provided a model for the long-arm statutes of many States. Consider also the Supreme Court's decision in Shaffer v. Heitner, 433 U.S. 186, 97 S.Ct. 2569 (1977), which held that the constitutional limitations on State court jurisdiction are to be governed by a single standard of "minimum contacts," even when the jurisdiction is predicated on the presence of property within the State.

Furthermore, as the cases discussed in Section 7 infra show, a foreign corporation which does business in a State may be required to consent to summary proceedings for fixing tax liabilities without service of process in the State; and presumably such liability can be imposed on a corporation doing business in the State which failed, although it was required, to consent to such procedure. Suppose a State statute provides that any person or corporation, resident or non-resident or domestic or foreign, which acquires title to property in the State is thereby deemed to have consented to service of process on the Secretary of State in any proceeding brought to establish personal liability for taxes on the property, coupled with a provision establishing personal liability on the owner for ad valorem taxes. Would a judgment obtained by serving the Secretary of State, with no appearance in the proceeding by the non-resident owner of property on which taxes due for periods of his ownership had not been paid, be valid? There is an extensive discussion of *Dewey v. Des Moines* in Strecker, "Can a

State Make a Non–Resident Personally Liable for Taxes," 23 U.Cin.L.Rev. 135 (1954); see also Note, "Personal Liability for Real Estate Taxes in Pennsylvania as Affected by a Tax Sale," 12 U. of Pitt.L.Rev. 408 (1951); Annot., 41 A.L.R. 187.

B. *Attachment Proceeding Against Other Property of a Non–Resident.* Under a Mississippi statute, every lawful tax was declared to be a debt on which an action may be brought in the State courts. A non-resident of the State owned land in Mississippi on which he failed to pay ad valorem taxes. The State attached other property owned by him in the State, on which taxes had been paid, and sued for recovery of the delinquent tax. To obtain a release of the attachment, the owner filed a surety bond which exceeded the amount of the tax. The Supreme Court of the United States upheld a judgment for the State. Nickey v. Mississippi, 292 U.S. 393, 54 S.Ct. 743 (1934).

C. The taxpayer is personally liable for the payment of most levies other than ad valorem taxes. Thus, the taxpayer is typically liable for income, sales, gross receipts, franchise, and other State and local taxes. Under sales taxes, ordinarily both the vendor and the vendee are liable for the tax, although the vendor's function is primarily that of a tax collector. Under death taxes, the executor or administrator is usually obliged to see to the payment of the levies and he may be held personally liable for distributing the property without payment of the tax; and the taxing authority may independently pursue the property into the hands of the legatees in order to satisfy its claims.

Most jurisdictions recognize personal liability of corporate officers who fail to collect and pay sales taxes. In the Matter of Jonas, 70 N.C.App. 116, 318 S.E.2d 869 (1984). Generally, the officer must possess some control over making the returns and paying over taxes to be subject to liability. See, e.g., Pantaleo v. Michigan Dept. of Treasury, Mich.Tax Trib., Nov. 26, 1986, CCH ¶ 201–309.

In State of Missouri v. Longstreet, 536 S.W.2d 185 (Mo.App.1976), a corporate officer charged with the duty of collecting sales taxes and filing the required returns with the State was found criminally liable after collecting the taxes and failing to file the returns. The court reasoned that to insulate such officers from liability would defeat the intent of the statute, and that liability need only rest on the fact that the officer "received the payment or consideration involved in the transaction." Id. at 189.

Civil liability may exist even where mere negligence of a responsible corporate officer results in non-payment of sales tax. Willis v. Lindley, 61 Ohio St.2d 356, 402 N.E.2d 1185 (1980). In *Willis,* the defendant secured a small business loan with an account into which collected sales taxes were deposited. The Small Business Administration called the loan and subsequently closed defendant's business, resulting in a tax deficiency owed the State. In reversing the Board of Tax Appeals, the court held that because the defendant supervised the filing of returns and payment of taxes, liability existed and the loan arrangement in no way altered this liability. Id. at 1186.

For an attempt to impose personal liability on an officer of a corporate vendor for the failure of the corporation to collect or pay sales taxes to the City of New York, see p. 798 supra; see also State v. The Equinox House, Inc., 134 Vt. 59, 350 A.2d 357 (1975), in which the court indicated that the corporate president-treasurer was personally liable for collecting employee withholding taxes, sales and use taxes, and rooms and meals taxes, in the event the corporation fails to collect such taxes.

For a compilation of State laws and decisions concerning officer liability, see 1 CCH All States Sales Tax Rptr. ¶ 2–075.

(c) Civil Arrest

The archaic practice of civil arrest in tax cases still prevails in some jurisdictions, at least as to tax penalties. In Non–Resident Taxpayers Ass'n of Pennsylvania and New Jersey v. Murray, 347 F.Supp. 399 (E.D.Pa.1972), a group of taxpayers brought an action challenging the constitutionality of the Pennsylvania statute authorizing civil arrest for recovery of tax penalties; they alleged that the statute violated the Equal Protection Clause of the Fourteenth Amendment, since certain classes of persons were excluded from the scope of the statute, and that it violated the Eighth Amendment's proscription against excessive bail. The court rejected these contentions and upheld the constitutionality of the statute. The Supreme Court of the United States affirmed. 410 U.S. 919, 93 S.Ct. 1356 (1973).

SECTION 3. SUITS TO RECOVER TAXES

Notes and Problems

A. *The Rule Preventing Recovery of Taxes "Voluntarily" Paid.* The rule at common law, which still prevails in some States, is that taxes, even though illegally exacted, may not be recovered where they have been "voluntarily" paid. See, e.g., Goldstein Oil Co. v. Cook County, 156 Ill.App. 3d 180, 108 Ill.Dec. 842, 509 N.E.2d 538 (1987). The "voluntary payment" rule stems from Lord Ellenborough's holding in Bilbie v. Lumley, 2 East 469, 102 Eng.Rep. 448 (K.B.1802) that payments made under a mistake of law may not be recovered. See Field, "The Recovery of Illegal and Unconstitutional Taxes," 45 Harv.L.Rev. 501 (1932).

A well engrained exception to the common law rule against recovery of taxes exists for taxes paid under duress. See Restatement of Restitution 75 (1937); G. Palmer, The Law of Restitution 9.16, 14.20 (1978). Thus courts have frequently held that one who pays a tax to avoid the loss of its right to do business has paid the tax under duress and is entitled to a refund if the tax is found to be invalid. See, e.g., Atchison, T. & S.F.Ry. Co. v. O'Connor, 223 U.S. 280, 32 S.Ct. 216 (1912). As one court explained:

> The early common law doctrine of duress has been expanded and many courts have adopted the modern doctrine of "business compulsion" under which "it is established that where by reason of the particular facts a reasonably prudent man finds that in order to preserve his property or protect his business interest it is necessary to make payment of money which he does not owe and which in equity and good

conscience the receiver should not retain, the payment may be recovered." 40 Am.Jur., p. 831. [Crow v. City of Corpus Christi, 146 Tex. 558, 562, 209 S.W.2d 922, 924 (1948).]

In Illinois Institute of Technology v. Rosewell, 137 Ill.App.3d 222, 92 Ill.Dec. 106, 484 N.E.2d 837 (1985), it was held that the voluntariness bar to recovery of taxes was inapplicable unless it is shown that the taxpayer had knowledge of the facts upon which to frame a protest. See 64 A.L.R. 9, 84 A.L.R. 294, and 72 Am.Jur.2d §§ 1080–84 for annotations on the circumstances in which a tax will be regarded as having been paid involuntarily.

Does the rule which denies recovery for taxes "voluntarily" paid operate unfairly against the average taxpayer, who cannot afford to have a legal adviser at hand when he pays his taxes? Should this rule be perpetuated in our times? See Pannam, "The Recovery of Unconstitutional Taxes in Australia and the United States," 42 Tex.L.Rev. 777 (1964).

B. *Payment of Taxes Under Protest.* Most States have replaced the common law rules regarding recovery of taxes with specific refund provisions. See Note C infra. These statutes frequently provide that taxes must be paid "under protest" as a condition to recovery. The payment "under protest" puts the taxing jurisdiction on notice that the tax will be contested, and, if the statutory refund procedures are followed, it renders irrelevant the question whether the taxes have been "voluntarily" paid.

C. *Suits to Recover Non–Property Taxes.* Many non-property taxes, particularly those developed in comparatively recent times, have been accompanied by more liberal statutory provisions allowing recovery of taxes paid and a greater latitude of judicial review than are permitted in many States in the case of property taxes. This is generally true under franchise, income, and sales taxes and other levies. It is important to observe that, unlike property tax assessments, many current State taxes typically do not involve principally problems of valuation (although there are sometimes valuation issues presented), as to which the taxing authorities are presumably expert. They involve a great variety of problems which the courts regard as properly within their own province of expertise—e.g., the scope of the term "sale" in a sales tax statute, the nature of a "business" expense in an income tax statute, the existence of an independent contractor or an agency relationship in a gross receipts tax case. These issues are much more akin, in the property tax field, to problems as to the exemption from taxation of a particular piece of property. The courts generally feel free to review the assessor's decision as to exemption issues. On the other hand, capital stock taxes often involve valuation questions; and death and gift tax cases typically present those issues. The determination of the proper scope and extent of judicial review in tax litigation is one aspect of the fundamental problem of administrative law generally as to the relations between the courts and administrative agencies. Each taxing statute must be examined carefully for its particular review provisions, whether set forth *in haec verba* or by judicial interpolation.*

---

* For a consideration of the taxpayer's right to judicial review in property tax cases, see Chapter 4 supra.

C. *Class Actions.* A device sought to be used with increasing frequency by taxpayers, particularly when small amounts are involved for the individual, is the class action. Courts in some jurisdictions have been receptive to such suits. Thus in Javor v. State Bd. of Equalization, 12 Cal. 3d 790, 117 Cal.Rptr. 305, 527 P.2d 1153 (1974), the plaintiff, individually and purportedly on behalf of some 500,000 purchasers of motor vehicles, sued the retailers and the State Board of Equalization seeking a refund of State sales taxes, to the extent they had been measured by the Federal excise tax that had been retroactively repealed by Congress. In holding that the plaintiff had stated a proper cause of action, the California Supreme Court observed:

> It would require a suit by each member of plaintiff class individually to compel defendant retailers to file a claim with defendant Board for a refund of the erroneously collected tax. Such demands would result in a multiplicity of actions. The amount due each member of the class is relatively small and when compared with the costs of suit, would discourage individual legal action. Unless this class action is permitted defendant Board and defendant retailers will be unjustly enriched at the expense of plaintiff class. [12 Cal.3d at 795.]

Courts in other jurisdictions, however, have been less hospitable to taxpayer class actions. Thus in Hagerty v. General Motors Corp., 59 Ill.2d 52, 319 N.E.2d 5 (1974), the Illinois Supreme Court rejected the class action allegations of plaintiff's complaint for a refund of sales taxes paid in connection with automobile repairs. The substance of the complaint was that the repairs involved the sale of services with an incidental transfer of personal property rather than the sale of tangible personal property at retail; the sales taxes would be substantially higher in the latter case than in the former. The court said:

> In order to determine which tax should have been imposed in a particular transaction, the facts of that transaction must be known. Consequently, a decision in this case sustaining the plaintiff's contention as to her transaction with GM would not establish a right of recovery in any other customer of GM who had work performed on his automobile and replacement parts installed therein. The required common interest of the purported class members in the questions involved is therefore lacking in this case, and the circuit court was correct in striking the class action allegations of the plaintiff's complaint. [59 Ill.2d at 59.]

See generally Annot., 10 A.L.R.4th 655.

D. *Interest on Overpayments of Tax.* Because of the immunity of the sovereign from suit, in the absence of a waiver of immunity, the taxpayer cannot recover interest on an unconstitutional levy unless the statute provides for interest. In Public Service Co. of New Hampshire v. State, 102 N.H. 54, 149 A.2d 874 (1959), the taxpayer sought the recovery of interest on a franchise tax paid under protest, which had been held unconstitutional in a prior proceeding. The State had refunded the tax without interest. Repeating its traditional view of sovereign immunity, from which it concluded that "the plaintiff can recover interest only if the Legislature has provided for it by statute," the New Hampshire court found no basis for the contention that by implication the State statutes authorize a refund of interest. Accord: Marsh v. Brown, 31 Conn.Supp. 134, 325 A.2d 466 (1974); State ex rel. Cleveland Concession Co. v. Peck, 161 Ohio St. 31, 117 N.E.2d 429 (1954). For cases adopting a contrary view, in some instances based on the fact that suit was brought against the tax collector who it was held could not claim sovereign immunity, see the annotations on "Right to interest on tax refunds" in 57 A.L.R. 357, 76 A.L.R. 1012, 112 A.L.R. 1183, 88 A.L.R.2d 823; 72 Am.Jur.2d § 1068.

People v. Union Oil Co. of California, 48 Cal.2d 476, 310 P.2d 409 (1957), considered the taxpayer's contention that a statutory provision allowing interest on tax refunds could not be modified retroactively. At the time the taxpayer paid its franchise tax, six percent interest on overpayments was authorized by the statute if the "overpayment was not made because of an error or mistake on the part of the taxpayer." Subsequently the statute was amended so as to allow six percent interest on refunds if the "overpayment was made because of an error or mistake on the part of the commissioner." The taxpayer's refund grew out of its election to amortize emergency war facilities at an accelerated rate; the election was made, as permitted by law, subsequent to the filing of the return and the payment of the tax, a part of which was refunded, but without interest. The court held that no unconstitutional action was involved in the change in the statute, pointing out that it is "the settled law of this state that illegal taxes voluntarily paid may not be recovered in the absence of a statute permitting a refund thereof." 48 Cal.2d at 481, 310 P.2d at 412. Since there was no "vested right to the refund of the taxes, but rather such action is a matter of legislative grace, it necessarily follows that the right to payment of interest on such refunds is not vested and the Legislature may enact a statute cutting off such rights theretofore accorded the taxpayer." Id.

SECTION 4. INJUNCTION TO RESTRAIN ENFORCEMENT OR COLLECTION OF TAXES AND OTHER EQUITABLE REMEDIES

Notes and Problems

A. In Andersen v. King County, 18 Wash.2d 176, 138 P.2d 872 (1943), the court discussed the effect of a statute restricting the use of injunctions in tax matters:

> Under our statute, the court has no jurisdiction to grant injunctions restraining the collection of taxes except in cases "where the law under which the tax so imposed is void"; and "where the property upon which the tax is imposed is exempt from taxation". * * * But the statute has substituted what is universally held to be an adequate remedy; payment of the tax under protest with the right of an action to recoup. [138 P.2d at 873.]

In a later case a taxpayer sought to enjoin a county treasurer from distraining personal property to enforce the payment of taxes which the plaintiff alleged had already been paid. If the taxpayer were now to pay the taxes a second time under protest and sue for refund, he could not recover because, under the statute, such a proceeding may not be commenced "after the 30th day of the next succeeding June following the year in which said tax became payable." That period had long since passed. May the court grant an injunction despite the fact that the taxing statute was valid and the property was not exempt from tax under the statute? See O'Brien v. Johnson, 32 Wash.2d 404, 202 P.2d 248 (1949). For discussions of statutes restricting the use of the injunction in State tax proceedings and substituting a tax recovery procedure, see Casco Co. v. Thurston County, 163 Wash. 666, 2 P.2d 677 (1931); 72 Am.Jur.2d § 1115 et seq.; 65 A.L.R.2d 550.

B. *General Requirements for Equitable Relief.* Resort to the injunction proceeding imposes on the taxpayer the burden of meeting the normal prerequisites for relief from a court of equity. Thus, the availability of an adequate remedy through a refund procedure will ordinarily result in a denial of equitable relief. In Proprietors of the Cemetery of Mount Auburn v. Massachusetts Unemployment Compensation Commission, 301 Mass. 211, 16 N.E.2d 666 (1938), the taxpayer sued to enjoin the defendants from collecting contributions and enforcing penalties under the unemployment insurance act. The injunction was denied on the ground that the remedy at law was adequate. In Shanks v. Winkler, 210 Ala. 101, 97 So. 142 (1923), where the statute did not restrict the court's jurisdiction to enjoin or suspend tax assessments, equitable relief was granted, in spite of the general availability of another remedy, in order to prevent multiplicity of actions at law. See also Lee v. Bickel, 292 U.S. 415, 54 S.Ct. 727 (1934). The necessity of showing irreparable injury is also at times met in tax cases by the penalties to which the taxpayer will be subjected if he takes the risk, unaided by a judicial determination, of his own construction of the statute or his view of its validity. Wallace v. Hines, 253 U.S. 66, 40 S.Ct. 435 (1919). Likewise, injunction proceedings may be maintained to remove a tax cloud on real property. Id.

C. *Injunction in the Federal Courts to Restrain State Tax Proceedings.* The Johnson Act, which provides that "[t]he district courts shall not enjoin, suspend or restrain the assessment, levy or collection of any tax under State law where a plain, speedy and efficient remedy may be had in the courts of such State" (28 U.S.C. § 1341), was brought into play in a case involving New York sales taxes sought to be imposed on a Vermont furniture store operating six miles from the New York border. Tully v. Griffin, 429 U.S. 68, 97 S.Ct. 219 (1976). Griffin advertised on radio and television and in newspapers that served the Albany–Schenectady–Troy area of New York and made substantial sales at its place of business to customers from that State. It regularly delivered furniture to the New York buyers in its own trucks, and its employees also entered New York on occasion to repair furniture it had sold.

The New York State Tax Commission determined that Griffin was "doing business" in New York and was thus required to collect that State's sales tax from its New York customers. When the Commission sought to audit its books, Griffin filed suit in Federal court contending that the State tax, if imposed on it, would violate the Commerce, Due Process and Equal Protection Clauses. It argued that it had no "plain, speedy and efficient remedy," since it would be required to prepay the tax or post bond in seeking relief from any assessment, and that it is unfair to compel a taxpayer to litigate in an unfamiliar forum, when its contacts with the forum State are so minimal. The Commission responded by making an estimated assessment of some $218,000. Griffin was thereupon granted a preliminary injunction by a three-judge Federal district court.

The Supreme Court reversed, without expressly dealing with the issue whether the necessity of prepaying the tax or the unavailability of preliminary relief made the remedy inadequate. The Court found that the taxpayer had means of contesting the levy and obtaining preliminary relief without the prepayment or bond. It declared:

> A federal district court is under an equitable duty to refrain from interfering with a State's collection of its revenue except in cases where an asserted federal right might otherwise be lost. * * * This policy of restraint has long been reflected and confirmed in the congressional command of 28 U.S.C. § 1341 that no injunction may issue against the collection of a state tax where state law provides a "plain, speedy and efficient remedy." As the Court has frequently had occasion to note, the statute has its roots in equity practice, in principles of federalism, and in recognition of the imperative need of a State to administer its own fiscal operations. * * *

> These principles do not lose their force, and a State's remedy does not become "inefficient," merely because a taxpayer must travel across a state line in order to resist or challenge the taxes sought to be imposed. If New York provides an otherwise adequate remedy, the mere fact that Griffin must go to New York to invoke it does not jeopardize its ability to assert its rights. To accept the District Court's holding that it would be "unfair" to make Griffin litigate in New York would undermine much of the force of 28 U.S.C. § 1341. [429 U.S. at 73–74, 97 S.Ct. at 222.]

In Ammex–Champlain Corp. v. Gallman, [unreported in F.Supp.] N.Y. P–H ¶ 23,370 (N.D.N.Y.), affirmed sub nomine Ammex Warehouse Co. v. Gallman, 414 U.S. 802, 94 S.Ct. 163 (1973), the Supreme Court had summarily affirmed a district court determination that New York offered a taxpayer a "plain, speedy and efficient" remedy for challenging the constitutionality of a State tax. In Tully v. Griffin, supra, the Court declared that "having now had a full opportunity to consider the issue after briefing and argument, we adhere to our judgment in the *Ammex* case." 429 U.S. at 75, 97 S.Ct. at 223. For a determination that the Rhode Island scheme for contesting tax assessments provides the taxpayer with a "plain, speedy and efficient" remedy, see Sterling Shoe Co. v. Norberg, 411 F.Supp. 128 (D.R.I.1976).

In Garrett v. Bamford, 538 F.2d 63 (3rd Cir.), certiorari denied 429 U.S. 977, 97 S.Ct. 485 (1976), residents of a predominantly black area brought a class action in Federal district court alleging that their properties were assessed at values higher than those established for similar properties in white areas of the county. Alleging that the assessors had engaged in systematic and intentional racial discrimination in making the assessments in question, the plaintiffs sought an injunction requiring the immediate reassessment of all residential property on a nondiscriminatory basis and annual assessments thereafter. The court held that a Federal district court had jurisdiction over such a suit when the State procedures provided for neither continuing injunctive relief nor class actions. The case is considered in "Racial Discrimination and the Tax Injunction Act: *Garrett v. Bamford*," 90 Harv.L.Rev. 616 (1977).

In Georgia Railroad & Banking Co. v. Redwine, 342 U.S. 299, 72 S.Ct. 321 (1952), the taxpayer sued to enjoin the Georgia Revenue Commissioner from assessing ad valorem taxes against its property. The Court held that since the plaintiff could resort neither to an injunction nor to an appeal from an assessment to test out the validity of the tax, and no other adequate remedy was available, the requirement for injunctive relief in the Federal courts that no "plain, speedy and efficient" remedy be available in the State court had been met. The Court rejected the contention that this was a suit against the State and thereby contravened the Eleventh Amendment, citing Ex Parte Young, 209 U.S. 123, 28 S.Ct. 441 (1908) and a long line of cases holding that "a suit to restrain unconstitutional action threatened by an individual who is a state officer is not a suit against the state," 342 U.S. at 304, 72 S.Ct. at 324, and sustained the jurisdiction of the district court.

The broad jurisdictional barrier prohibiting Federal court injunctions against State tax proceedings has been held inapplicable to suits brought by the United States "to protect itself and its instrumentalities from unconstitutional state exactions." Department of Employment v. United States, 385 U.S. 355, 358, 87 S.Ct. 464, 467 (1966); cf. Moe v. Confederated Salish & Kootenai Tribes of the Flathead Reservation, 425 U.S. 463, 96 S.Ct. 1634 (1976), in which the Court held that an Indian Tribe was not barred by 28 U.S.C. § 1341 from seeking to enjoin enforcement of a State tax statute. See also United States and Western Electric Co. v. Dorgan, 413 F.Supp. 173 (D.N.D.1976), in which the court, in ordering a stay of State tax proceedings, stated that "where the federal government has a pecuniary interest in enjoining state collection proceedings * * * as where it is obligated by contract to reimburse its contractor for state taxes, * * * that interest weighs heavily in favor of staying state proceedings seeking to impose taxes upon the contractor. Here the United States has alleged such an interest." Id. at 175.

In Rosewell v. LaSalle National Bank, 450 U.S. 503, 101 S.Ct. 1221 (1981), the Supreme Court addressed the question whether an Illinois remedy which requires property owners contesting their property taxes to pay under protest and, if successful, to obtain a refund *without interest* is a "plain, speedy and efficient remedy" within the meaning of the Johnson Act when the customary delay from the time of payment until receipt of refund upon successful protest is two years. The taxpayer claimed that the two-year delay between payment and refund was neither "speedy" nor "efficient" and that the failure to provide interest made the State remedy inadequate. Emphasizing that the Johnson Act requires only that State remedies meet "certain minimal *procedural* criteria," 450 U.S. at 512, 101 S.Ct. at 1228 (emphasis in original), the Court held that Illinois' refund procedure satisfied the statute. It observed that the Illinois State-court refund procedure provided that taxpayer with a full hearing and judicial determination at which she could raise all constitutional objections to the tax, and that her only claim of procedural defects in the Illinois remedy was delay. Reviewing the lengthy delays that have become commonplace in judicial proceedings throughout the nation, the Court concluded that

> respondent's 2–year wait, regrettably, is not unusual. Nowhere in the Tax Injunction Act did Congress suggest that the remedy must be the speediest. The payment of interest might make the weight more tolerable, but it would not affect the amount of time necessary to adjudicate respondent's federal claims. Limiting ourselves to the circumstances of the instant case, we cannot say that respondent's 2–year delay falls outside the boundary of "speedy remedy." [450 U.S. at 520–21.]

With regard to the nonpayment of interest on the refund as an independent ground for the alleged inadequacy of the State court remedy, the Court declared:

> When it passed the [Johnson] Act, Congress knew that state tax systems commonly provided for payment of taxes under protest with subsequent refund as their exclusive remedy. * * *

> It is only common sense to presume that Congress was also aware that some of these same States did not pay interest on their refunds to taxpayers, following the then-familiar rule that interest in refund actions was recoverable only when expressly allowed by statute. * * * It would be wholly unreasonable, therefore, to construe a statute passed to limit federal-court interference in state tax matters to mean that Congress nevertheless wanted taxpayers from States not paying interest on refunds to have unimpaired access to the federal courts. If Congress meant to carve out such an expansive exception, one would expect to find some mention of it. The statute's broad prophylactic language is incompatible with such an interpretation. [450 U.S. at 523–24.]

D. *The Relationship Between the Johnson Act and the Civil Rights Act (42 U.S.C. § 1983).* In Fair Assessment in Real Estate Association, Inc. v. McNary, 454 U.S. 100, 102 S.Ct. 177 (1981), the Court affirmed a decision of a Federal district court and of the Court of Appeals for the Eighth Circuit (the latter by an equally divided court) holding that an action for damages may not be brought in federal court under 42 U.S.C. § 1983 to redress the allegedly unconstitutional administration of a State's tax system. The Justices of the Supreme Court were unanimous in affirming the holding below, but the case takes on importance because of the sharp differences among the Justices as to the rationale for the holding.

Justice Rehnquist, writing for himself, and four other Justices, held that the action was barred despite the breadth of § 1983, by principles of comity.

The facts of the case were summarized by Justice Rehnquist:

> Petitioner Fair Assessment in Real Estate is a non-profit corporation formed by taxpayers in St. Louis County ("County") to promote equitable enforcement of property tax laws in Missouri. Petitioners J. David and Lynn F. Cassilly own real property with recent improve-

ments in the County. Petitioners filed suit under § 1983 alleging that respondents, the County's Tax Assessors, Supervisors, and Director of Revenue, and three members of the Missouri State Tax Commission, had deprived them of equal protection and due process of law by unequal taxation of real property.

The complaint focuses on two specific practices by respondents. First, petitioners allege that County properties with new improvements are assessed at approximately 33⅓% of their current market value, while properties without new improvements are assessed at approximately 22% of their current market value. This disparity allegedly results from the respondents' failure to reassess old property on a regular basis, the last general reassessment having occurred in 1960. Second, petitioners allege that property owners who successfully appeal their property assessments, as did the Cassillys in 1977, are specifically targeted for reassessment the next year.

Petitioners have previously sought some relief from respondents' assessments in state proceedings. In 1975, petitioner David Cassilly and others brought an action in which the state circuit court ordered respondent Antonio to reassess all real property in the County. On direct appeal, however, the Missouri Supreme Court reversed on the ground that the State Tax Commission, not the circuit court, should supervise the reassessment process. State ex rel. Cassilly v. Riney, 576 S.W.2d 325 (Mo.1979) (en banc). In 1977, the Cassillys appealed the tax assessed on their home to the County Board of Equalization and received a reduction in assessed value from 33⅓% to 29%. When their home was again assessed at 33⅓% in 1978, the Cassillys once more appealed to the Board of Equalization. That appeal was pending at the commencement of this litigation.

The Cassillys brought this § 1983 action in federal court seeking actual damages in the amount of overassessments from 1975 to 1979, and punitive damages of $75,000.00 from each respondent. Petitioner Fair Assessment sought actual damages in the amount of expenses incurred in efforts to obtain equitable property assessments for its members. As in all other § 1983 actions, the award of such damages would first require a federal court declaration that respondents, in administering the state tax, violated petitioners' constitutional rights. [454 U.S. at 105–07.]

Section 1983, enacted in 1871, provides:

Every person who, under color of any statute, ordinance, regulation, custom, or usage, of any State or Territory, subjects, or causes to be subjected, any citizen of the United States or other person within the jurisdiction thereof to the deprivation of any rights, privileges, or immunities secured by the Constitution and laws, shall be liable to the party injured in an action at law, suit in equity, or other proper proceeding for redress.

In considering the application of Section 1983 to taxation, Justice Rehnquist wrote in part:

This Court, even before the enactment of § 1983, recognized the important and sensitive nature of state tax systems and the need for federal court restraint when deciding cases that affect such systems. As Justice Field wrote for the Court only a year before the enactment of § 1983:

"It is upon taxation that the several States chiefly rely to obtain the means to carry on their respective governments, and it is of the utmost importance to all of them that the modes adopted to enforce the taxes levied should be interfered with as little as possible. Any delay in the proceedings of the officers, upon whom the duty is devolved of collecting the taxes, may derange the operations of the government, and thereby cause serious detriment to the public." Dows v. City of Chicago, 11 Wall. 108, 110 (1870).

After this Court conclusively decided that federal courts *may* enjoin state officers from enforcing an unconstitutional state law, Ex Parte Young, 209 U.S. 123 (1908), Congress also recognized that the autonomy and fiscal stability of the States survive best when state tax systems are not subject to scrutiny in federal courts. Thus, in 1937 Congress provided:

"The district courts shall not enjoin, suspend or restrain the assessment, levy or collection of any tax under State law where a plain, speedy and efficient remedy may be had in the courts of such State." 28 U.S.C. § 1341 (hereinafter "§ 1341" or "the Act").

This legislation, and the decisions of this Court which preceded it, reflect the fundamental principle of comity between federal courts and state governments that is essential to "Our Federalism," particularly in the area of state taxation. See, e.g., Matthews v. Rodgers, 284 U.S. 521 (1932); Singer Sewing Machine Co. v. Benedict, 229 U.S. 481 (1913); Boise Artesian Water Co. v. Boise City, 213 U.S. 276 (1909). Even after enactment of § 1341 it was upon this comity that we relied in holding that federal courts, in exercising the discretion that attends requests for equitable relief, may not even render declaratory judgments as to the constitutionality of state tax laws. Great Lakes Dredge & Dock Co. v. Huffman, 319 U.S. 293 (1943).

Contrasted with this statute and line of cases are our holdings with respect to 42 U.S.C. § 1983.

Obviously § 1983 cut a broad swath. By its terms it gave a federal cause of action to prisoners, taxpayers, or anyone else who was able to prove that his constitutional or federal rights had been denied by any State. In addition, the statute made no mention of any requirement that state remedies be exhausted before resort to the federal courts could be had under 28 U.S.C. § 1343. The combined effect of this newly created federal cause of action and the absence of an express exhaustion requirement was not immediately realized. It was not until our decision in Monroe v. Pape, 365 U.S. 167 (1961), that § 1983 was held to authorize immediate resort to federal court whenever state actions allegedly infringed constitutional rights:

"Although the legislation was enacted because of the conditions that existed in the South at that time, it is cast in general language and is as applicable to Illinois as it is to the States whose names were mentioned over and again in the debates. It is no answer that the State has a law which if enforced would give relief. The federal remedy is supplementary to the state remedy, and the latter need not be first sought and refused before the federal one is invoked." 365 U.S., at 183.

The immediacy of federal relief under § 1983 was reemphasized in McNeese v. Board of Education, 373 U.S. 668 (1963), where the Court stated that "[i]t is immaterial whether [the state official's] conduct is legal or illegal as a matter of state law. Such claims are entitled to be adjudicated in the federal courts." Id., at 674 (citation and footnote omitted). And in the unargued Per Curiam opinion of Wilwording v. Swenson, 404 U.S. 249 (1971), the Court concluded that "[p]etitioners were * * * entitled to have their actions treated as claims for relief under the Civil Rights Acts, not subject * * * to exhaustion requirements." Id., at 251. See also Damico v. California, 389 U.S. 416 (1967); Houghton v. Shafer, 392 U.S. 639, 640 (1968); Steffel v. Thompson, 415 U.S. 452, 472–473 (1974).

Thus, we have two divergent lines of authority respecting access to federal courts for adjudication of the constitutionality of state laws. Both cannot govern this case. On one hand, the Tax Injunction Act, 28 U.S.C. § 1341, with its antecedent basis in the comity principle of Matthews v. Rodgers, supra, and Boise Artesian Water Co. v. Boise City, supra, bars at least federal injunctive challenges to state tax laws. Added to this authority is our decision in Great Lakes Dredge & Dock Co. v. Huffman, supra, holding that declaratory judgments are barred on the basis of comity. On the other hand is the doctrine originating in Monroe v. Pape, supra, that comity does not apply where § 1983 is involved, and that a litigant challenging the constitutionality of any state action may proceed directly to federal court. With this divergence of views in mind, we turn now to the facts of this case, a § 1983 challenge to the administration of state tax laws which implicates both lines of authority. We hold that at least as to such actions, which is all we need decide here, the principle of comity controls. [454 U.S. at 102–05.]

It was that conclusion that "sets the 'principle of comity' against the strong policies of 42 U.S.C. § 1983 favoring a federal forum to vindicate deprivation of federal rights, and resolves the issue in favor of comity," that Justice Brennan protested in an opinion, joined in by Justices Marshall, Stevens and O'Connor. Instead, the concurring Justices reached the same decision as the majority, that the petition should be dismissed, but rested their case on the Tax Anti–Injunction Act, 28 U.S.C. § 1341. It is worth noting that the availability of State remedies was not at issue in the case. The Court pointed out that the Missouri Supreme Court had expressly held that plaintiffs such as petitioners may assert a § 1983 claim in state court.

For the construction and application of 28 U.S.C. § 1341, see Williams, "Tax Injunction Act and Judicial Restraint: Property Tax Litigation in

Federal Courts," 12 Rutgers L.J. 653 (1981); Note, "The Tax Injunction Act and Suits for Monetary Relief" 46 U.Chi.L.Rev. 736 (1979); Pratt, "How to Use Federal Courts to Enjoin Collection of State and Local Taxes," 46 J.Tax. 178 (1977); Note "Federal Court Interference with the Assessment and Collection of State Taxes," 59 Harv.L.Rev. 780 (1946).

E. *Mandamus.* In a proper case, mandamus may be used to force tax officials to act. Like the injunction, mandamus is an extraordinary remedy and will not be granted where other adequate remedies are available. Mandamus is ordinarily restricted to acts that are ministerial in character, requiring no acts of a discretionary or judicial nature. Selig v. Price, 167 Miss. 612, 142 So. 504 (1932); Debevoise v. Back, 359 A.2d 279 (D.C.1976). Thus, if a refund is due the taxpayer and the amount of the refund is not in dispute, mandamus may be used to compel the remittance. People ex rel. Blome v. Nudelman, 373 Ill. 220, 25 N.E.2d 811 (1940). In some States, however, mandamus plays a broader role. The Kansas court has declared that "where the desideratum of the litigation is merely to obtain an authoritative determination of some purely legal question for the guidance of public officers mandamus has become the familiar vehicle to accomplish that objective." Kittredge v. Boyd, 136 Kan. 691, 693–694, 18 P.2d 563, 564 (1933). On this principle the court allowed a mandamus proceeding as a vehicle for the recovery of inheritance taxes paid under protest on shares of stock in a Kansas corporation owned by a non-resident decedent, saying: *

> * * * Having exacted this illegal demand from plaintiff, having accepted payment thereof under protest, having refrained from turning the money into the general revenue fund where it ought to have gone if it had been lawfully due and lawfully exacted, so far as this case turns on a mere question of procedure we must hold that mandamus is a proper remedy. [18 P.2d at 564.]

The Rhode Island Supreme Court, taking a broad view of the power of a court to issue a writ of mandamus, held a writ of mandamus was appropriate to order an assessor to assess a shopping center complex in the same manner in which he has assessed other property in the town. Rosen v. Restrepo, 119 R.I. 398, 380 A.2d 960 (1977).

F. Under the Alabama sales tax, a taxpayer may file a bill in equity in the circuit court for a cancellation of an assessment, provided he files a notice of appeal from the Department of Revenue's assessment within 30 days after the assessment is made and files a bond for the tax, interest and costs. Merriwether v. State, 252 Ala. 590, 42 So.2d 465, 11 A.L.R.2d 918 (1949).

G. *References.* Perkins, "Tax Injunctions and Suits to Recover Taxes," 12 N.C.L.Rev. 20 (1934); Ela, "Some Aspects of Colorado Taxpayers' Remedies," 23 Rocky Mt.L.Rev. 145 (1950); Garner, Sloan & Haley, "Taxpayers' Suits to Prevent Illegal Exactions in Arkansas," 8 Ark.L.Rev. 129 (1954); 1 Pomeroy, Equity Jurisprudence, § 293(f) (5th ed. 1941). See Annots., 93 A.L.R. 585, 115 A.L.R. 20, 159 A.L.R. 634, 65 A.L.R.2d 550; see also 72 Am.Jur.2d § 1120 et seq.

---

* First National Bank v. Maine, 284 U.S. 312, 52 S.Ct. 174 (1932), was decided after the tax had been paid. Under that decision, the tax was concededly collected illegally. See Chapter 11 supra.

SECTION 5. DECLARATORY JUDGMENT

Notes and Problems

A. *The Scope of Declaratory Relief.* The requirement in some States that taxes be paid before the taxpayer may seek an adjudication of his liability under the usual statutory procedure has been an important factor in the popularity of the declaratory judgment proceeding in tax litigation. The declaratory judgment has been used in a great variety of situations. Thus, it has been used to test the constitutionality of a tax, as applied to the plaintiff. Spector Motor Service Inc. v. O'Connor, p. 221 supra; Curry v. McCanless, p. 713 supra; George v. Bernheim Distilling Co., 300 Ky. 179, 188 S.W.2d 321 (1945). See Hillsborough Township v. Cromwell, 326 U.S. 620, 66 S.Ct. 445 (1946), in which the use of the declaratory judgment in the Federal courts to test the validity of a State levy under attack as violating the Federal Constitution is discussed. The remedy may be employed to determine the operative date of a levy, Berndson v. Graystone Materials Co., 34 Wash.2d 530, 209 P.2d 326 (1949), or whether a particular person is subject to tax, Tirrell v. Johnston, 86 N.H. 530, 171 A. 641 (1934). And the proceeding has been used to determine whether a particular type of transaction is taxable as a wholesale or a retail sale under a gross income tax. Department of Treasury v. J.P. Michael Co., 105 Ind.App. 255, 11 N.E.2d 512 (1937). As stated by the New York Court of Appeals, the remedy is "applicable in cases where a constitutional question is involved or the legality or meaning of a statute is in question and no question of fact is involved." Dun & Bradstreet, Inc. v. City of New York, 276 N.Y. 198, 206, 11 N.E.2d 728 (1937).

Declaratory judgment may be denied for a variety of reasons. If the decree will not terminate the controversy, declaratory relief may be denied. City of Pensacola v. Johnson, 159 Fla. 566, 28 So.2d 905 (1947). When the issues of fact are complicated and subject to conflicting inferences which will have to be resolved by the administrative agency, the court will deny a declaratory judgment. Rahoutis v. Unemployment Compensation Commission, 171 Or. 93, 136 P.2d 426 (1943). Nor may the remedy be resorted to as a device to recover a tax already paid, where the limitations period on refunds has expired. Associated Petroleum Transport, Ltd. v. Shepard, 53 N.M. 52, 201 P.2d 772 (1949). The limitations imposed by 28 U.S.C. § 1341 regarding the power of Federal courts to enjoin State tax proceedings, see Section 4, Note C supra, have been held to impose comparable limits upon Federal courts to grant declaratory relief to taxpayers challenging the propriety of State taxes. Great Lakes Dredge & Dock Co. v. Huffman, 319 U.S. 293, 299, 63 S.Ct. 1070, 1073 (1943); Illinois Central R.R. v. Howlett, 525 F.2d 178 (7th Cir.1975).

B. *References.* E. Borchard, Declaratory Judgments 825–857 (2d ed. 1941); McCarthy, "Declaratory Judgments," 3 Miami L.Q. 365 (1949); Note, "Testing the Validity of a Wisconsin Income Tax Rule through a Declaratory Judgment Action," 41 Marq.L.Rev. 446 (1958). There are extensive annotations on tax questions as a proper subject of an action for a declaratory judgment in 132 A.L.R. 1108 and 11 A.L.R.2d 359.

SECTION 6. EXHAUSTION OF ADMINISTRATIVE REMEDIES

Notes and Problems

A. Where the statute provides a mode of review of the action of a taxing authority, courts typically hold that remedy to be exclusive; failure to exhaust the administrative remedy precludes judicial review. Gager v. Kasdon, 234 Md. 7, 197 A.2d 837 (1964); V–1 Oil Co. v. County of Bannock, 97 Idaho 807, 554 P.2d 1304 (1976); Columbia Developers, Inc. v. Elliott, 269 S.C. 486, 238 S.E.2d 169 (1977). However, in Ballard County v. Citizen's State Bank of Wickliffe, 261 S.W.2d 420 (Ky.1953), the court permitted a suit to enjoin the action of the Commission in raising the valuation of its shares of stock as assessed by the local assessor and approved by the County Board of Supervisors, where the increase was made by the State Commission on its own volition, and without notice. The court distinguished earlier cases such as Reeves v. Fries, 292 Ky. 450, 166 S.W.2d 985 (1942), in which a deficiency in income tax was assessed by the Department of Revenue and the taxpayer failed to take his statutory appeal for a *de novo* determination by the State Tax Commission; there the "action is final unless relief is sought in the manner prescribed by statute." 261 S.W.2d at 423. Here, however, where:

> the Kentucky Tax Commission had not "substantially followed the law" in raising the assessment for ad valorem taxes, its action was not merely an error in valuation or in the exercise of discretionary power. It was void. The taxpayer, then, was not required to appeal from the order which the administrative body had no jurisdiction or power to make, but could by its separate action in court enjoin and restrain its enforcement. [Id.]

B. The doctrine that judicial review will be denied to a taxpayer who has not exhausted his administrative remedies is, of course, merely a specific application to the tax field of a recognized principle of administrative law. See, e.g., People ex rel. Korzen v. Fulton Market Cold Storage Co., 62 Ill.2d 443, 343 N.E.2d 450, certiorari denied 429 U.S. 833, 97 S.Ct. 97 (1976); Fentress County Bank v. Holt, 535 S.W.2d 854 (Tenn.1976). See also Stason, "Judicial Review of Tax Errors—Effect of Failure to Resort to Administrative Remedies," 28 Mich.L.Rev. 637 (1930); and see generally on the subject of exhaustion of administrative remedy, K.C. Davis, Administrative Law Treatise, ch. 26 (2d ed. 1979) and 72 Am.Jur.2d § 811.

C. *References.* For notes and comments dealing with various aspects of administrative and judicial review in particular States, see 55 West Va. L.Rev. 161 (1952), mandamus to obtain refund; 2 Mercer L.Rev. 442 (1951), correction of income tax assessments; 17 La.L.Rev. 646 (1957), mistake of fact as a basis for refund; 25 Wash.L.Rev. 198 (1950), injunctive procedure; "Extent of Judicial Review of Administrative Tax Determinations in West Virginia," 50 W.Va.L.Q. 75 (1946); Fruits, "Contesting Income Tax Assessments in Wisconsin," 1951 Wisc.L.Rev. 485. See Annots., 131 A.L.R. 822; 46 A.L.R.2d 1350; and 71 A.L.R.2d 529.

SECTION 7.   EXTRA–STATE ENFORCEMENT OF TAX CLAIMS

A.   There is a long standing tradition that the courts of one State will not entertain a suit by another State to enforce a tax claim which has not been reduced to judgment. Colorado v. Harbeck, 232 N.Y. 71, 133 N.E. 357 (1921); City of Detroit v. Proctor, 44 Del. 193, 61 A.2d 412 (1948), which is criticized in Comment, 47 Mich.L.Rev. 796 (1949); State of Minnesota v. Karp, 84 Ohio App. 51, 84 N.E.2d 76 (1948); Wayne County v. American Steel Export Co., 277 App.Div. 585, 101 N.Y.S.2d 522 (1st Dep't 1950). See 39 Ky.L.J. 472 (1951); 97 U.Pa.L.Rev. 435 (1949); 10 U. of Pitt.L.Rev. 205 (1948).

In an extensive opinion in State ex rel. Oklahoma Tax Commission v. Rodgers, 238 Mo.App. 1115, 193 S.W.2d 919 (1946), Judge Anderson traced the historical origins for this view to the English cases that produced Lord Mansfield's oft-repeated dictum, that "[o]ne nation does not take notice of the revenue laws of another." Planche v. Fletcher, 1 Doug. 251, 99 Eng.Repr. 164 (1779). Many of the early English and American cases involved the effects of revenue violations on the validity of contracts and property ownership; others had to do with the admissibility in evidence of unstamped documents. See, e.g., Ludlow, Trustee for Creditors of Randall v. Van Renssealaer, 1 Johns (N.Y.) 94 (1806). Moreover, the early cases reflected a long since outmoded judicial hostility towards taxation that treated tax claims like penal laws, which are not enforceable in other States. Judge Anderson rejected such an approach to taxation, and analyzed and rejected the more modern argument against judicial enforcement of out-of-state tax claims, namely, the difficult problems faced by a court in interpreting the tax laws of another State, with which it is likely to have little familiarity.

In the later Missouri case of State of California ex rel. Houser v. St. Louis Union Trust Co., 260 S.W.2d 821 (Mo.App.1953), the court refused to permit California to collect an inheritance tax from Missouri residents where the assets of the decedent, a California resident, were located principally in Missouri, the residence of the decedent's beneficiaries. The court explicitly stated that it regarded the holding in the *Rodgers* case as sound, but it refused to apply it to the California inheritance tax, because of the statutory remedy prescribed by the California statutes for collecting the tax. It found that the California statute requires that a procedure to collect inheritance tax must be brought in a single superior court of that State vested with jurisdiction in probate matters.

The courts have followed the *Rodgers* decision: State of Ohio ex rel. Duffy v. Arnett, 314 Ky. 403, 234 S.W.2d 722 (1950); Oklahoma v. Neely, 225 Ark. 230, 282 S.W.2d 150 (1955); City of Detroit v. Gould, 12 Ill.2d 279, 146 N.E.2d 61 (1957). In the Kentucky case, the court said: "We take our stand with the modern trend as enunciated by the Missouri court in the well reasoned opinion in the Rodgers case." 314 Ky. at 410, 234 S.W.2d at p. 726. For the most recent cases following this trend, see Nelson v. Minnesota Income Tax Div., 429 P.2d 324 (Wyo.1967); Buckley v. Huston, 60 N.J. 472, 291 A.2d 129 (1972); and State Tax Comm'n v. Cord, 81 Nev. 403, 404 P.2d 422 (1965), in which the court said:

> Time, history and review have virtually erased the contentions that taxes are penal in nature and that one State need not enforce the taxes of a sister State because full faith and credit did not apply to criminal or revenue matters. [404 P.2d at 425.]

B. *Legislative Sanction of Reciprocal Extra–State Enforcement of Tax Claims.* The mobility of business and wealth has posed an increasingly difficult problem as to how to collect taxes from taxpayers without property in the State.

Because the courts were slow to overrule the doctrine that the revenue laws of another State will not be enforced by State courts, and out-of-staters were escaping taxes, the legislatures moved into the void. The result is that most of the States now permit collection of out-of-state taxes. By 1987, in some 44 States there existed legislation authorizing such proceedings, where reciprocal provision exists in the taxing State. See P–H All States Guide ¶ 281, which lists the States that have adopted the legislation. Typical of the statutes is the Minnesota act, which provides:

> The courts of this state shall recognize and enforce the liability for taxes lawfully imposed by the laws of any other state which extends like comity in respect of the liability for taxes lawfully imposed by the laws of this state. The officials of such other states are authorized to bring action in the courts of this state for the collection of such taxes. [Minn.Stat. § 272.58, CCH ¶ 91–663 P–H ¶ 66,072–J.]

Typically it is unnecessary to obtain a judgment in the taxing State before filing suit in any of the foreign jurisdictions. In three States (Connecticut, New Jersey, and Texas), the right to sue is limited to specific taxes; a number of States have explicitly extended the statute to taxes imposed by political subdivisions of a State.

C. *Enforcement in a Foreign State of Judgment Obtained Under Summary Administrative Procedure in Taxing State.* The case of State of Ohio v. Kleitch Bros., Inc., 357 Mich. 504, 98 N.W.2d 636 (1959), raises a somewhat different problem from that presented by the Rodgers case and others following that decision, for in the *Kleitch Bros.* case judgment was obtained in Ohio under a summary administrative procedure and Ohio sought enforcement of the judgment in Michigan. The taxpayer, a Michigan corporation, applied for and received a license to operate its trucks over Ohio highways. Under the Ohio statute the grant of such a license makes the Secretary of State the licensee's agent for "service of process or notice in any assessment, action or proceeding instituted in this state." Ohio Rev.Code § 5728.12, CCH ¶ 93–847, P–H ¶ 42,522. The taxpayer filed its Ohio highway use tax returns, based on the axle mileage of its trucks in the State, but paid no tax. The State assessed the use tax, based on the taxpayer's reported figures plus penalty, and served notices of assessment through service on the Secretary of State and by registered mail to the taxpayer at its Michigan business address. The statute provides that the assessment becomes final unless a petition for reassessment is filed within 30 days, accompanied by a surety bond for the amount assessed. No petition for reassessment was filed, except with respect to one of the three reports and assessments, and, as to that assessment, no bond was filed; the petition was accordingly dismissed. In accordance with the Ohio statute, summary judgments were thereupon entered in the Ohio county court, without the service of a summons or any further notice to the taxpayer. Such summary procedure, following an administrative determination on notice, is utilized in many States for excise and income taxes. See People v. Skinner, 18 Cal.2d 349, 115 P.2d 488 (1941). Ohio then brought suit in Michigan to enforce the Ohio judgments.

The validity of the highway use tax, as applied to an interstate trucker, was sustained in Alger v. Bowers, 166 Ohio St. 427, 143 N.E.2d 835 (1957), appeal dismissed 358 U.S. 43, 79 S.Ct. 21 (1958), as a reasonable levy for the use of the State's highways. The taxpayer's major claim was that the Due Process Clause was violated because a judgment was obtained against it in the Ohio courts, without service of process on or notice to the taxpayer. In rejecting this contention the court observed that:

> Ohio had jurisdiction of this taxpayer. The taxpayer submitted to the terms of the statute, including its summary judgment provisions by applying for a license and using the highways.
>
>   *   *   *
>
> The court struggled with the taxpayer's contention that the entry of the judgment * * * was not really a judicial proceeding in the ordinary sense of the term. The statute required the clerk of the court to enter the judgment as a matter of course. There was no hearing. The court exercised no discretion—made no determination. [357 Mich. at 513, 98 N.W.2d at 641.]

Nevertheless, the court distinguished the usual judicial judgment from the statutory judgment authorized in tax cases, following an administrative proceeding, relying on the *Skinner* case, supra; it declared that such tax judgments are not governed by the usual requirements of service of process or notice, hearing and a judicial determination. It concluded (357 Mich. at 516, 98 N.W.2d at 643):

> The United States Constitution, art. 4, § 1, requires Michigan to give "Full Faith and Credit" to "the public Acts, Records and judicial Proceedings of every other State." We deal here with an Ohio tax statute and Ohio assessments, and judgments entered thereunder in an Ohio court.
>
> Even if we do not conceive of the Ohio "judgments" as "judicial proceedings," they plainly represent "records" of that State entered in compliance with one of its "public acts" and should be given full faith

and credit. Michigan certainly has no public policy against collection of taxes which should be weighed against the unifying principle of the full faith and credit clause. See Hughes v. Fetter, 341 U.S. 609, 71 S.Ct. 980, 95 L.Ed. 1212.

It is to be noted that Kleitch Bros. had applied for and obtained a license to use the highways and thereby, as the State contended, voluntarily submitted itself to the Ohio statutes, including the service designation provision and the administrative judgment procedure. Suppose a statute provides that "every foreign corporation" doing business in a State, and therefore subject to corporation franchise tax, "shall file * * * a certificate" designating the Secretary of State as its agent for service of process, and that if such a designation is not filed, the corporation shall be deemed to have designated the Secretary of State as its "agent" for service of process. See N.Y.Tax Law § 216, CCH ¶ 94–016, P–H ¶ 12,050.55. If a foreign corporation is doing business in the State and fails to file the designation, would the procedure followed in the *Kleitch Bros.* case result in a New York judgment or liability for tax that should or must be recognized by another State? Would the same result obtain in an attempt to enforce a judgment for corporate net income tax liability, under a statute providing that all corporations subject to the tax shall be deemed to have designated the Secretary of State as their agent for service of process, where the only activities of the foreign corporation in the State are the solicitation of sales orders, which are accepted outside the state and filled by shipping goods into the state by common carrier from out-of-state sources? Compare the *Northwestern States Portland Cement* and *Stockham Valves* cases, p. 229 supra, and Public Law 86–272, p. 387 supra. In connection with the overall problem, see McGee v. International Life Ins. Co., 355 U.S. 220, 78 S.Ct. 199 (1957).

Compare State Tax Commission of Utah v. Cord, 81 Nev. 403, 404 P.2d 422 (1965), wherein a docketed income tax warrant in Utah was held not entitled to full faith and credit as an enforceable judgment in Nevada. The court distinguished *Kleitch* on the basis of Utah's failure to provide for statutory jurisdiction over the taxpayer, since the taxpayer was not subject to Utah's jurisdiction under ordinary minimum contacts analysis.

D. *Full Faith and Credit Requirements.* In Magnolia Petroleum Co. v. Hunt, 320 U.S. 430, 439, 64 S.Ct. 208, 213 (1944), the Court said: "The constitutional command [of the Full Faith and Credit Clause] requires a state to enforce a judgment of a sister state for its taxes. Milwaukee County v. M.E. White Co. * * *."

In 1948 Congress amended the Federal statutes so as to require full faith and credit to be granted to acts of the legislature, as well as to the judgments of a sister State. 28 U.S.C. § 1738. See Hughes v. Fetter, 341 U.S. 609, 71 S.Ct. 980 (1951), in which the Court adverted to this amendment. In that case, a Wisconsin court refused to entertain a wrongful death action, arising out of an automobile accident that occurred in Illinois, under whose laws a cause of action arose. The Wisconsin wrongful death act applies only to deaths caused within the State, which the State court concluded established a local policy against suits for wrongful deaths occurring in other States. Mr. Justice Black, writing the opinion reversing the Wisconsin Supreme Court, repeated the established rule that:

> full faith and credit does not automatically compel a forum State to subordinate its own statutory policy to a conflicting public act of another State; rather, it is for this Court to choose in each case between the competing public policies involved. [341 U.S. at 611.]

Here, the Supreme Court found no "conflict between the policies" of the two States. It referred to the "strong uniform principle embodied in the Full Faith and Credit Clause looking toward maximum enforcement in each State of the obligations or rights created or recognized by the statutes of sister States," and concluded that "Wisconsin's policy must give way." In the circumstances, can the decisions cited in Note A refusing to enforce out-of-state tax claims stand?

A State is not required to give full faith and credit to a sister State's judgment unless there was jurisdiction to enter such a judgment. Thus in State Tax Commission v. Cord, 81 Nev. 403, 404 P.2d 422 (1965), the Supreme Court of Nevada, which, as indicated in Note A supra, was one of the courts to adopt the approach taken in the *Rodgers* decision, nevertheless refused to give full faith and credit to a Utah tax warrant which had been docketed as a judgment in Utah. The Utah income tax liability on which the warrant was based arose from a single isolated installment sale of uranium in Utah by two Nevada residents. The court concluded that "the tax herein imposed being a personal tax requiring in personam jurisdiction, the single business engagement of the [taxpayers] was not a continuous course of conduct needed to satisfy the Utah [jurisdictional] requirements and is not entitled to full faith and credit as a judgment or public record." Id. at 425.

In City of Philadelphia v. Stadler, 164 N.J.Super. 281, 395 A.2d 1300 (Cty.Dist.Ct.1978), affirmed 173 N.J.Super. 235, 413 A.2d 996 (App. Div.1980), certification denied 85 N.J. 465, 427 A.2d 563 (1980), cert. denied 450 U.S. 997, 101 S.Ct. 1702 (1981), Philadelphia sought to enforce judgments obtained against New Jersey residents for nonpayment of the city's wage tax. The judgments were obtained in a Pennsylvania court under the Pennsylvania long-arm statute by serving the Secretary of the Commonwealth and the taxpayers at their last know addresses by certified mail. When the defendants failed to appear, a default judgment was entered in favor of the city. The taxpayers contended that the Pennsylvania judgments were not entitled to full faith and credit because the Pennsylvania judgments were entered without due process and, in any event, New Jersey public policy precluded entry of the judgments. The court rejected the first contention on the ground that the taxpayers received ample notice of the tax bills and that they had the requisite "minimum contacts" with

Pennsylvania to justify the exercise of the Pennsylvania court's jurisdiction. The "public policy" arguments were also rejected. The court stated that "[a]lthough full faith and credit may on rare occasions give way to the policy of [the] enforcing state, Restatement, Conflicts 2d, § 103 (1969), such an exception has an extremely narrow application." 395 A.2d at 1305. The court acknowledged that New Jersey had evinced "an earnest dislike for the imposition [by Philadelphia] of the wage tax upon all New Jersey residents working in the city," but concluded that "to base a denial of full faith and credit on such an expression would be to revive the status of the several states as 'independent sovereignties, each free to ignore obligations * * * of the others.'" 395 A.2d at 1306 (quoting Milwaukee County v. M.E. White Co., 296 U.S. 268, 276, 56 S.Ct. 229 (1935)).

E. *References.* McElroy, "The Enforcement of Foreign Tax Claims," 38 U.Detroit L.J. 11 (1960), discusses the *Kleitch* Bros. case; Goldstein, "Interstate Enforcement of the Tax Laws of Sister States," 30 Taxes 247 (1952); Note, "International Enforcement of Tax Claims," 50 Col.L.Rev. 490 (1950); Note, "Extrastate Enforcement of State Income Tax Claims," 45 Ill.L.Rev. 99 (1950); Daum, "Interstate Comity and Governmental Claims," 33 Ill.L.Rev. 249 (1938); Goodrich, Conflict of Laws, 163 (3d ed. 1949); "Tax Comity," 25 Corp.J. 99 (1967); Note, "Extraterritorial Enforcement of Tax Claims," 12 Wm. & Mary L.Rev. 111 (1970); Leflar, "Out-of-State Collection of State and Local Taxes," 29 Vand.L.Rev. 443 (1976).

Index

References are to Pages

†